Text, Cases and Materials on Contract Law

Written by leading authors in the field, this clear and highly accessible volume provides full coverage of the topics commonly found in the contract law syllabus, alongside up-to-date illustrative case examples and stimulating commentary.

Composed of approximately one-quarter authors' commentaries and three-quarters cases and materials, including academics' articles and extracts from books and Law Commission papers, this book takes account of a variety of theoretical perspectives, including economic, relational and empirical conceptions of the law.

This book facilitates the development of personal study skills and encourages readers to engage with the leading academic commentaries in the area. Features to support your learning include:

- **chapter introductions** to highlight the salient features under discussion and signpost topics to guide readers through this comprehensive text;
- **additional reading** listed at the end of each chapter to assist further study and independent research;
- **clear and attractive text design** that differentiates between the authors' commentaries and the materials;
- **a companion website** that provides skills materials and self-assessment tasks to help further your learning.

The range of material covered, straightforward style and targeted updates to this fifth edition make *Text, Cases and Materials on Contract Law* a comprehensive and invaluable resource for all undergraduate and postgraduate students of contract law.

Richard Stone, LL.B. (Soton), LL.M. (Hull) is Emeritus Professor of Law and Human Rights at the University of Lincoln, UK. He was called to the Bar (Gray's Inn) in 1998. Over a 40-year career in higher education he has worked at a variety of institutions in the East Midlands and London, including the University of Leicester, Nottingham Trent University, the Inns of Court School of Law and most recently the University of Lincoln.

James Devenney is Head of School and Professor of Transnational Commercial Law at the School of Law, University of Reading, UK and Visiting Full Professor at University College Dublin, Ireland.

"Lucid, comprehensive and authoritative; a truly exceptional exposition of the modern law of contract. Stone and Devenney illuminate the theory and practice of modern contract law and unpack the future challenges faced in this area with style, poise and assurance."

Mel Kenny (Dr. iur.), *Pro-Rector, Riga Graduate School of Law*

"...provides an excellent balance between explanatory text and extracts from key cases, which enables students to master the depths of contract law. Additionally, extracts from academic writings encourage critical reflection on the current state of the law. It is clearly written and has a structure that allows students to develop their knowledge and critical understanding of contract law."

Christian Twigg-Flesner, *Professor of International Commercial Law, University of Warwick*

"Highly popular with lecturers and students of contract law for over a decade, Stone and Devenney combine primary and second materials with substantial commentary enabling students to engage deeply with the principles and practices of modern contract law."

Fidelma White, *Senior Lecturer, University College Cork (UCC)*

"There are many good contract law textbooks, but undergraduate module leaders should seriously consider adopting this one. The book opens with an ambitious and clear setting out of some of the main themes in contract theory and the clarity continues throughout."

Anthony Rogers, *Senior Lecturer, City, University of London*

Text, Cases and Materials on Contract Law

FIFTH EDITION

Richard Stone and James Devenney

Routledge
Taylor & Francis Group
LONDON AND NEW YORK

Cover Image: © Getty Images / gradyreese

Fifth edition published 2023
by Routledge
4 Park Square, Milton Park, Abingdon, Oxon OX14 4RN

and by Routledge
605 Third Avenue, New York, NY 10158

Routledge is an imprint of the Taylor & Francis Group, an informa business

First edition published by Routledge-Cavendish 2007.
Fourth edition published by Routledge 2019.

British Library Cataloguing-in-Publication Data
A catalogue record for this book is available from the British Library

Library of Congress Cataloging-in-Publication Data
A catalog record has been requested for this book

ISBN: 978-0-367-22283-3 (hbk)
ISBN: 978-0-367-22295-6 (pbk)
ISBN: 978-1-003-12407-8 (ebk)

Typeset in Joanna
by Deanta Global Publishing Services, Chennai, India

Visit the companion website: www.routledge.com/cw/stone

Outline contents

Detailed contents

Preface

Contract law often elicits a mixed response from students. Some find it boring; others struggle with its complexity; still others find it challenging and rewarding. The intention behind this book is to enable our readers to experience the satisfaction of falling into the final category.

The book has two main aims. First, and foremost, the book seeks to provide a clear, accessible, and yet detailed exposition of contract law in England and Wales. Complex ideas are explained and hard cases are unpacked. Second, it aims to encourage readers to adopt a critical approach to understanding the law. The book contains numerous academic articles, extracts from books and law reform papers. It is hoped that these will challenge the more discerning readers to question the current conceptions of the law and to develop new ideas and lines of argument for themselves. Key statutory developments since the last edition include the European Union (Withdrawal) Act 2018 and the European Union (Withdrawal Agreement) Act 2020. Indeed, the UK's future relationship with the European Union continues to be uncertain, as is the continuing impact and legacy of European law on the law of contract in England and Wales and the text has been amended in appropriate places to reflect this. In terms of case law, significant new decisions added to this edition include: *Bates v Post Office Ltd (No.3: Common Issues)* [2019] EWHC 606 (QB) (relational contracts); *Four Seasons Holdings Incorporated v Brownlie* [2017] UKSC 80 (formation); *MWB Business Exchange Centres Ltd v Rock Advertising Ltd* [2018] UKSC 24 (alteration of contracts); *Volumatic Ltd v Ideas for Life Ltd* [2019] EWHC 2273 (intention to create legal relations); *Lowick Rose LLP (in liquidation) v Swynson Ltd* [2017] UKSC 32 (third party loss); *Amey Birmingham Highways Ltd v Birmingham City Council* [2018] EWCA Civ 264 (relational contracts); *Goodlife Foods Ltd v Hall Fire Protection Ltd* [2018] EWCA Civ 1371 (incorporation); *Cargill International Trading Pte Ltd v Uttam Galva Steels Ltd* [2019] EWHC 476 (incorporation); *Wood v Capita Insurance Services Ltd* [2017] UKSC 24 (interpretation); *The Federal Republic of Nigeria v JP Morgan Chase Bank, N.A. Andrews* [2019] EWHC 347 (interpretation); *African Export-Import Bank v Shebah Exploration and Production Co Ltd* [2017] EWCA Civ 845 (UCTA 1977); *R & S Pilling (trading as Phoenix Engineering) v UK Insurance Ltd* [2019] UKSC 16 (interpretation); *BV Nederlandse Industrie Van Eiprodukten v Rembrandt Enterprises, Inc.* [2019] EWCA Civ 596 (misrepresentation); *Hughes-Holland v BPE Solicitors* [2017] UKSC 21 (duty of care); *First Tower Trustees Ltd, Intertrust Trustees Ltd v CDS (Superstores International) Ltd* [2018] EWCA Civ 1396 (exclusion of liability for misrepresentation); *FSHC Group Holdings Ltd v GLAS Trust Corp Ltd* [2019] EWCA Civ 1361 (rectification); *Elston v King* [2020] EWHC 55 (compromise agreements); *Times Travel (UK) Ltd v Pakistan International Airlines Corp* [2019] EWCA Civ 828 (lawful act duress); *Canary Wharf (BP4) T1 Ltd v European Medicines Agency* [2019] EWHC 335 (Ch) (frustration); *Singularis Holdings Ltd (In Official Liquidation) (A Company Incorporated in the Cayman Islands) v Daiwa Capital Markets Europe Ltd* [2019] UKSC 50 (illegality); *Okedina v Chilake* [2019] IRLR 905 (illegality); *Egon Zehnder Ltd v Tillman* [2019] UKSC 32 (severance); *Ark Shipping Co LLC v Silverburn Shipping (IoM) Ltd (The Arctic)* [2019] EWCA Civ 1161 (terms); *Classic Maritime Inc v Limbungan Makmur SDN BHD, Lion Diversified Holdings BHD* [2019] EWCA Civ 1102 (damages); *Morris-Garner v One Step (Support) Ltd* [2018] UKSC 20 (negotiating damages); *Fulton Shipping Inc of Panama v Globalia Business Travel S.A.U.* [2017] UKSC 43 (mitigation); *Priyanka Shipping Ltd v Glory Bulk Carriers Pte Ltd* [2019] EWHC 2804 (Comm) (negotiating damages).

The book is composed of approximately one-quarter authors' commentaries and three-quarters cases and materials. The commentary is sufficiently detailed to enable the reader to dip in and out of the cases and materials. It is hoped that the integration of these primary and secondary sources will help to deepen the reader's understanding of the law. We have aimed to keep the extracts from judgments as short as possible. On occasion, however, large extracts have been included in the belief that these provide the best exposition of the current law. The book is suitable for use alongside *The Modern Law of Contract*, 14th edn, 2022. Structurally the books are quite similar, being designed to supplement one another, although either book can be used independently.

Although Richard, who is enjoying his retirement, was not involved in the production of this edition, his work is still, of course, deeply embedded in this book. I would like to take this opportunity to again acknowledge the wide and lasting contribution which Richard made to this area of law and which has inspired so much of my own work. I would also like to thank Richard on behalf of the countless students who he helped develop over the years.

We would also like to thank everyone who assisted with the preparation of this text. In particular, a huge debt of gratitude is owed to our friend Ralph Cunnington whose work is still very much evident in this book. We are also indebted to our students at the University of Reading, University College Dublin and the University of Lincoln who have provided us with numerous opportunities to further develop our understanding of, and ability to explain, the complexities of contract law. Your thoughtful questions and puzzled looks were not in vain. As usual, our thanks go to Routledge for all their patience, encouragement and assistance in the preparation of this book. Special thanks also go to Mary Catherine Lucey of UCD, Ireland for all of her support over the last few years. Finally, we would like to thank James' wife, Claire, for her unfailing support during the writing process.

The law is stated, as far as possible, as it stood on 1 January 2020 (although the publication of this book was delayed by unforeseen circumstances, we were able to take account of some later developments).

James Devenney
Devon
April 2020

Acknowledgements

Grateful acknowledgement is made to all the authors and publishers of copyright material which appears in this book, and in particular to the following for permission to reprint material from the sources indicated:

Cambridge University Press for extracts from Collins, H, *Law of Contract*, 4th edn, (2003) pp 4, 8–9, 104–105, 171–173, 240; Harris, D, Campbell, D, Halson, R, *Remedies in Contract and Tort*, 2nd edn, (2002) pp 131, 139–142; for extracts from *The Cambridge Law Journal*, Hepple, B, 'Intention to create legal relations' (1970) CLJ 122 at 127–129, 130, 133–134; Hamson, CJ, 'Illegal contracts and limited interests' (1949) 10 CLJ 249, 258–259; Stewart, A, and Carter, JW, 'Frustrated contracts and statutory adjustment: the case for a reappraisal' (1992) CLJ 66, 109–110; and for extracts from *Legal Studies*, Buckley, RA, 'Illegal transactions: chaos or discretion?' (2000) 20 LS 155, 179–180; Luther, P, 'Campbell, Espinasse and the sailors: text and comment in the common law' (1999) 19 LS 525, 525–528, 550–551.

DSP Publishing for extracts from *Commercial Law Cases*, *AEG (UK) Ltd v Logic Resource Ltd* [1996] CLC 265, *Commercial Law Cases*, *Bowerman v Association of British Travel Agents* [1996] CLC 451, *Commercial Law Cases*, *O'Brien v MGN Ltd* [2002] CLC 33.

The *Web Journal of Current Legal Issues* for extracts from Hedley, S, '"Very much the wrong people": the House of Lords and publication of spy memoirs' (2000) *Web JCLI*.

Hart Publishing, an imprint of Bloomsbury Publishing Plc, for extracts from Burrows, A, *Understanding the Law of Obligations*, (1998) pp 3–5; and MacDonald, E, *Exemption Clauses and Unfair Terms*, 2nd edn, (2006) pp 105–108.

Informa for extracts from *Building Law Reports*, *Philips Hong Kong Ltd v Attorney General of Hong Kong* [1993] 61 BLR 41; for extracts from *Lloyd's Law Reports*, *Ashmore v Corporation of Lloyd's (No 2)* [1992] 2 Lloyd's Rep 620, *Ecay v Godfrey* [1947] 80 Lloyd's Rep 286, *Hollingworth v Southern Ferries Ltd (The 'Eagle')* [1977] 2 Lloyd's Rep 70, *J Lauritzen AS v Wijsmuller BV (The Super Servant Two)* [1990] 1 Lloyd's Rep 1, *Motis Exports Ltd v Dampskibsselskabet AF 1912 Aktieselskab* [2000] 1 Lloyd's Rep 211, *Ocean Chemical Transport Inc v Exnor Craggs Ltd* [2000] 1 Lloyd's Rep 446, *Overseas Medical Supplies Ltd v Orient Transport Services Ltd* [1999] 2 Lloyd's Rep 273, *Schenkers Ltd v Overland Shoes Ltd* [1998] 1 Lloyd's Rep 498, *Osman v J Ralph Moss Ltd* [1970] 1 Lloyd's Rep 313, *The Post Chaser* [1981] 2 Lloyd's Rep 695 (HC), *Vantage Navigation Corporation v Suhail and Saud Bahwan Building Materials LLC, The 'Alev'* [1989] 1 Lloyd's Rep 138; and for extracts from *Lloyd's Maritime and Commercial Law Quarterly*, Halson, R, 'The offensive limits of promissory estoppel' (1999) LMCLQ 256, 258–261.

John Wiley & Sons, Inc. for extracts from *The Modern Law Review*, Miller, CJ, '*Felthouse v Bindley* revisited' (1972) 35 MLR 489; Waddams, S, 'Unconscionability in contracts' (1976) 39 MLR 369, 390–393; Ogus, A, 'Damages for pre-contract expenditure' (1972) 35 MLR 423 at 424.

The Law Commission for extracts from Unfair Terms in Consumer Contracts: Advice to the Department for Business, Innovation and Skills pp. vii–xiii; Second Report on Exemption Clauses in Contracts, Law Com No 69 (1975); The Law of Contract: The Parol Evidence Rule, Law Com No 154 (1986); Contributory Negligence as a Defence in Contract, Law Com No 219 (1993); Privity of Contract: Contracts for the Benefit of Third Parties, Law Com No 242 (1996);Illegal Transactions: The Effect of Illegality on Contracts and Trusts, Consultation Paper No 154 (1999); The Illegality Defence, Law Com No 320 (2010); Electronic Execution of Documents, Law Com No 386 (2019).

Northwestern University School of Law for extracts from Northwestern University Law Review, Macneil, IR, 'Contracts: adjustments of long-term economic relations under classical, neo-classical and relational contract law' (1978) 72 Northwestern UL Rev 854–860.

Oxford University Press for extracts from Atiyah, PS, Essays on Contract, (1986) pp 39–40, 182–183, 191–192, 226–228, 238–240, 342-344; Birks, P, and Chin, NY, 'On the nature of undue influence, in Beatson, J, and Friedmann, D (eds), Good Faith and Fault in Contract Law, (1995) pp 63–64, p 95; Brownsword, R, Contract Law: Themes for the 21st Century, 2nd edn, (2006) pp 14–15, 18–21, 49–57; Burrows, A, The Law of Restitution, 3rd edn, (2011) p 370; Cheshire, Fifoot and Furmston's Law of Contract, 17th edn, (2017) p 660; Denning, A, The Discipline of Law, (1979) pp 200–205; Smith, S, Atiyah's Introduction to the Law of Contract, (2006) pp 348–350; for extracts from The Oxford Journal of Legal Studies, Gardner, S, 'Trashing with Trollope: a deconstruction of the postal rules' (1992) OJLS 170, 178–184.

Pluto Press for extracts from Wightman, J, Contract: A Critical Commentary, (1996) pp 48–51.

Reed Elsevier (UK) Ltd trading as LexisNexis for extracts from All England Reports, Bigos v Bousted [1951] 1 All ER 92, CTN Cash and Carry v Gallaher [1994] 4 All ER 714, Cutter v Powell [1795] 6 Term Rep 320; [1775–1802] All ER Rep 159, Doyle v Olby (Ironmongers) Ltd [1969] 2 All ER 119, Dunbar Bank plc v Nadeem [1998] 3 All ER 876, Esso Petroleum v Mardon [1976] 2 All ER 5, Hartog v Colin & Shields [1939] 3 All ER 566, Hayes v James and Charles Dodd (a firm) [1990] 2 All ER 815, Hutton v Warren (1836) 1 M & W 466; All ER Rep 151, JEB Fasteners Ltd v Marks, Bloom & Co [1983] 1 All ER 583, Lee (John) & Son (Grantham) Ltd v Railway Executive [1949] 2 All ER 581, TSB Bank plc v Camfield [1995] 1 All ER 951, Watford Electronics Ltd v Sanderson CFL Ltd [2001] 1 All ER (Comm) 696; and extracts from Industrial Relations Law Reports, Bliss v South East Thames RHA [1985] IRLR 308.

Sweet and Maxwell for extracts from Adams, J, and Brownsword, R, Understanding Contract Law, (2007); Beale, H (ed), Chitty on Contracts, 33rd edn, (2018) para 23–018; Coote, B, Exception Clauses, (1964) pp 10–11, 17–18; Enonchong, N, Duress, Undue Influence and Unconscionable Dealing, 2nd edn, (2012); Yates, D, Exclusion Clauses in Contracts, 2nd edn, (1982); Peel, E, Treitel on the Law of Contract, 14th edn, (2015) paras 3–008 and 3–009, pp 987–988 and p 1091; Treitel, G, Frustration and Force Majeure, 2nd edn, (2004); for extracts from Entertainment and Media Law Reports, Experience Hendrix LLC v PPX Enterprises Inc, Edward Chalpin [2003] EMLR 25, Spice Girls Ltd v Aprilia World Services BV [2002] EMLR 27, Timeload Ltd v British Telecommunications plc [1995] EMLR 459; extracts from the Law Quarterly Review, Bridge, M, 'Mitigation of damages in contract and the meaning of avoidable loss' (1989) 105 LQR 398-99, 413–414, Buckley, RA, 'Illegality in the Supreme Court' (2015) 131 LQR 341, 341–343, Ferguson, P, 'Partial rescission for misrepresentation rejected' (1995) 111 LQR 555, 556–558, Hooley, R, 'Damages and the Misrepresentation Act 1967' (1991) 107 LQR 547, Howarth, W, 'The meaning of objectivity in contract' (1984) 100 LQR 265, Lord Steyn, 'Contract law: fulfilling the reasonable expectations of honest men' (1997) 113 LQR 433, MacMillan, C, 'How temptation led to mistake: an explanation of Bell v Lever

Bros Ltd' (2003) 119 *LQR* 625, Peel, EM, 'Remoteness re-visited' (2009) 125 *LQR* 6, Reynolds, FMB, 'Discharge of contract by breach' (1981) 97 *LQR* 541, 548, Treitel, G, '"Conditions" and "Conditions Precedent"' (1990) 106 *LQR* 185; and extracts from *Scots Law Times*, *Irons v Partick Thistle Football Club Ltd* (1997) *SLT* 983.

Sydney Law Review for extracts from Bryan, M, and Ellinghaus, F, 'Fault lines in the law of obligations: *Roxborough v Rothmans of Pall Mall Australia Ltd*' (2000) 22 *Syd LR* 636, 645 and 647.

Taylor & Francis for extracts from Enonchong, N, *Illegal Transactions*, (1998) pp 15–17 and McKendrick, E, 'The common law at work: the saga of *Alfred McAlpine Construction Ltd v Panatown Ltd*' (2003) *OUCLJ* 145, 167–168.

University of Chicago Press for extracts from *The Journal of Legal Studies*, Danzig, R, '*Hadley v Baxendale*: a study in the industrialization of the law' (1975) 4 *J Legal Stud* 249, 279–280; Posner, E, 'Contract law in the welfare state: a defence of the unconscionability doctrine, usury laws, and related limitations on the freedom to contract' (1995) 24 *J Legal Stud* 283, 285–287; Simpson, AWB, 'Quackery and contract law: the case of the Carbolic Smoke Ball' (1985) 14 *J Leg St* 345 375–379.

The *Journal of Obligations and Remedies* for Cunnington, R, 'Rock, restitution and disgorgement' (2004) *JO & R* 46.

Wolters Kluwer Law & Business for extracts from Kronman, A, and Posner, R, *The Economics of Contract Law*, (1979) pp 1–3.

Yale Law Journal for extracts from Fuller, L, and Purdue Jr, W, 'The reliance interest in contract damages' (1936) 46 *YLJ* 52, 52–62.

Every effort has been made to trace and contact copyright holders prior to publication. If notified, the publisher will undertake to rectify any errors or omissions at the earliest opportunity.

Table of cases

C

D

E

F

G

H

I

J

K

L

M

N

O

P

R

S

X

Y

Table of UK and international legislation

UK

A

B

C

D

M

O

P

R

S

T

U

W

Australia

G

I

Canada

F

New Zealand

C

Table of statutory instruments

Table of decisions, directives, regulations, treaties and conventions

Directives

D

Treaties and conventions

H

U

Chapter 1

Introduction

Chapter contents

1.1 Introduction

This chapter considers issues relating to the nature and scope of the law of contract in England and Wales. It discusses the 'classical' law of contract – the origins of which are to be found in the nineteenth century. In broad terms 'classical' contract law is anchored to the concept of freedom of contract and the idea that the typical contract involves a 'one-off' exchange of promises between two parties. This leads to consideration of the subject matter of contract law: for example, whether contracts are in fact about enforcing promises, or regulating markets, or facilitating exchanges, and the implications of each analysis. As a contrast to the 'classical' analysis of contract law, an alternative approach based on the distinction between 'discrete' and 'relational' contracts is discussed. This challenges the idea that all contracts are a one-off discrete event, and considers the extent to which contracts involve continuing relationships between the parties. We will then explore different techniques for analysing contracts, examining the extent to which a 'doctrinal' analysis can be supplemented or replaced by analyses based on economics or sociology. Finally, we shall explore the influence of European law in this area and the impact of Brexit, which is still marked with considerable uncertainty as the U.K. negotiates a new relationship with the E.U.

1.2 The classical law of contract

It is generally agreed that during the latter part of the nineteenth century various writers about contract law, in particular textbook writers such as Anson (whose *Law of Contract*, written for students, was first published in 1879), produced analyses and rationalisations of the case law that have become to be termed the 'classical law of contract'. The process is described by Wightman.

Wightman, J, *Contract: A Critical Commentary*, 1996, London: Pluto Press, pp 48–51

The invention of classical contract

Until the 1970s, the study of contract was divided between those concerned with the modern law and a relatively small group of scholars interested in the evolution of the early precursors of contract before the industrial revolution. Where contract law of the eighteenth and nineteenth centuries was addressed it was usually ahistorically as a part of the modern law which happened to reach further back.

This changed in the 1970s principally as a result of the work of Horwitz, Simpson and Atiyah. They treated the eighteenth and nineteenth centuries as a period of rapid change rather than as the repository of case law the main function of which was to be fitted where possible into modern expository accounts of the law. The switch from regarding the nineteenth century as present to regarding it as history relaxed the presumption of determinacy embodied in the expository tradition and that period of contract history was looked at afresh. In the process, a kind of received wisdom emerged about the flourishing of a particular conception of contract law – classical contract law – by the middle of the nineteenth century, albeit neighboured by controversy over what preceded it and what followed; some scholars saw transformation more easily than others. Classical contract was therefore invented in two senses: it was the nineteenth-century intellectual product of the judges and treatise writers, but it was only identified as such by the invention of the construct of the 'classical law' in the 1970s. As we shall see, the emergence of the modern construct was a vehicle both for the criticism of the model of contractual obligation it embodied, and for the attribution to it of greater intellectual coherence than before.

The first step in unravelling the history of contract is to look more closely at the idea of classical contract law which has so dominated modern perceptions of the history: we will consider the broad contours of this dominant view before turning to probe the story in more depth.

The idea of a classical law of contract

A number of modern writers on contract have made the transformation of contract law in the nineteenth century the linchpin of their account. The version of contract dubbed the classical law or classical model is seen as the mature form which emerged out of the less structured pre-classical clutter of cases infused by a conception of substantive fairness, and which was followed by fragmentation at the hands of the regulatory state of the twentieth century. Although I will be strongly disputing its meaning and importance, there can be no denying the influence of the classical law in shaping broad perceptions of the development of the law of contract. We will examine the idea of the classical law in more detail by focusing on three dimensions: its content, the values on which it was based, and the type of transactions where its normative appeal was most plausible.

The leading feature which distinguished the classical law from what went before was the generality of the scope of its rules. By the third quarter of the nineteenth century the law of contract was regarded as consisting of rules which were not only general in form but also applied to most actual contracts. Before the emergence of the classical law there was no sense that the multifarious relations which became analysed as contracts were instances within the general category of contract: rules were more situation-specific with little attempt to develop an overall theory of liability.

It was a necessary property of the generality of the rules that they were abstract. They were addressed to individuals in general (offeror, seller, etc.) rather than to individuals standing in specific social relationships to others. As Lawrence Friedman (1967) put it:

> 'Pure contract doctrine is blind to details of subject matter and person. It does not ask who buys and sells, and what is bought and sold ... [c]ontract law is an abstraction – what is left when all particularities of person and subject matter are removed'.
>
> (p 7)

Generality and abstractness were ushered in by the spread of the governing idea that both the terms of the contract and its quality of being legally binding were grounded in an exercise of the parties' wills – the 'will theory' of contract. Although the subjectivity of the will theory in its pure form was fairly soon attenuated by emphasising the appearance rather than the reality of consent, its legacy endured in the idea that a contract was formed by the agreement of the parties. A bare agreement – conceptualised as an exchange of promises – came to be seen as a sufficient basis of enforceability, without the necessity for any payment, performance or acts in reliance. This model of contract came to be seen as typical, with the result that all manner of situations were standardly analysed as bilateral executory contracts: bilateral because both parties were bound at once, and executory because the obligations arose before anything was done.

The second dimension of the classical law was the broad moral and political values on which it drew for its justification. At the root was the idea that the only legal obligations imposed on individuals were those not to harm others, which chiefly meant, as far as the civil law was concerned, duties not to interfere with another's property or person. Beyond this, legal obligation could only be incurred by the individual's act of will in agreeing or consenting to be bound. Thus the will theory not only provided the content of contract doctrine with a justification, but also connected it with prevailing ideological conceptions of relationships between individuals within a society increasingly penetrated by market relations.

A corollary of the individualistic basis of the classical law was freedom of contract, so that parties were free not only to decide whether to incur consensual obligations at all, but also to determine the extent and content of such obligations. The role of the court was that of neutral referee or umpire, responsible only for enforcing the parties' agreement and not imposing duties which were not agreed nor removing those which had been agreed.

Where it was necessary to go beyond the parties' wills and derive the content of obligation from norms of behaviour, then the norms adopted tended to assume a robust attitude to a person's ability to look after their own interests and would permit advantage to be taken of poor business sense. This was particularly evident in relation to the development of the objective theory of agreement which attended to the appearance of agreement where subjective agreement was not total. The values which underpinned the classical law were at their most persuasive when applied to something like the following idealised picture of the making of a contract:

- the parties are dealing at arm's length (that is, on a commercial basis without any other connection);
- they are of equal bargaining power (that is, they have similar wealth, knowledge and negotiating skill);
- they negotiate each term of the contract so that the terms are all the product of their deliberation;
- the contract terms provide clearly for all eventualities;
- the parties only come together for one contract (there is no continuing relationship).

Although the classical law could be most plausibly applied to these circumstances, its importance lay in the way it reached out beyond these circumstances and became the default body of rules to apply across a wide range of social relations which came to be regarded as more or less contractual.

The characteristics of the classical contract law model identified by Wightman above apply most obviously to a straightforward commercial contract – for example, a one-off sale of goods contract – and do not necessarily apply easily to more complex transactions. This limitation is considered further later in this chapter, at Section 1.4. At this stage it is appropriate to explore in more detail the concept of freedom of contract, which is central to the classical analysis. As Brownsword has pointed out, freedom of contract has several aspects:

Brownsword, R, *Contract Law: Themes for the 21st Century*, 2nd edn, 2006, Oxford: OUP, 49–57

As we move on to look more carefully at 'freedom of contract' as a distinctive idea within the institution of contract law, it is as well to observe that there is also a background or non-institutional sense in which transactional freedom may be recognised. In this latter sense, we simply mean that it is permissible for agents freely to enter into agreements with one another or to make exchanges and that, concomitantly, agents have a right that others do not interfere with such permissible activity. Whilst, in principle, such transactions can take place in the absence of (or prior to) the development of an institution of contract law, in practice, modern societies develop just such a legal institution, with a whole array of rules relating to what constitutes a contract as well as to who can contract, and with a set of sanctions (remedies) available in the event of non-performance. Once such an institution of contract law is in place, 'freedom of contract' comes to be associated with three key principles, each of which seeks to influence the specific design of contract law. These three principles are: (1) that the law should respect the freedom of contracting parties to pursue their own purposes and to set their own terms (i.e. to make their own bargains) (we can call this 'term freedom'); (2) that the law should respect the freedom of eligible contractors to choose their own partners (that is, the freedom not to contract) (we can call this 'party or partner freedom'); and (3) that where agreements have been freely made, the parties should be held to their bargains (usually expressed as 'sanctity of contract'). Unless we indicate otherwise, 'freedom of contract' should now be understood in its institutional sense; in this sense, and read broadly, 'freedom of contract' signifies 'term freedom', 'partner freedom', and 'sanctity of contract'; and, in a narrow sense, 'freedom of contract' focuses on term freedom, advocating that the law should recognise the importance of respecting the parties' own choices and preferences as expressed in the kinds of transactions they enter upon and the particular terms to which they agree. It follows that freedom of contract in the narrow sense argues for a minimalist (i.e. a light regulatory) approach both to the categories of transaction that are treated as illegal and to the kinds of terms that are blacklisted as void and unenforceable.

Freedom of contract

According to Lord Devlin, it is axiomatic within the classical view that free dealing is fair dealing. Thus, in *Printing and Numerical Registering Co v Sampson*, Sir George Jessel MR famously said:

> '[I]f there is one thing which more than another public policy requires it is that men of full age and competent understanding shall have the utmost liberty of contracting, and that their contracts when entered into freely and voluntarily shall be held sacred and shall be enforced by Courts of justice. Therefore, you have this paramount public policy to consider – that you are not lightly to interfere with this freedom of contract.'

Sir George's remarks suggest that respect for freedom of contract involves two related forms of legislative and judicial restraint. First, freedom of contract enjoins that the parties shall have 'the utmost liberty of contracting', in the sense that they are left free to set their own terms. It follows that legislatures and courts should be slow to limit the kinds of transactions, or the kinds of terms, that the parties can agree upon within the domain of contract. An over-restrictive approach disallows options that should be available to the parties and, to this extent, illegitimately trims the parties' autonomy. Secondly, freedom of contract enjoins that the parties' freely made agreements shall be enforced by the courts. Courts might be tempted to release parties from hard bargains, but where agreements have been freely made such a temptation must be resisted: even well-meaning paternalism betrays a lack of respect for a person's autonomy. To mark these two aspects of freedom of contract (in the broad sense), we can call the first form of restraint the ideal of 'term freedom' (that is, freedom of contract in the narrow sense) and the second the ideal of 'sanctity of contract'.

Term freedom

Absolute term freedom implies a licence to write contracts with any content, that is, an absence of legal restriction upon the kinds of bargains, or the types of contractual provision that the parties can agree upon. A legal system guided by the ideal of term freedom will limit such a licence only where it has good reason. Of course, what constitutes 'a good reason' will depend upon the background philosophy of the particular legal order. Thus, if a legal system is guided by utilitarian (or by wealth maximising) thinking, countervailing good reasons will involve disutilities (or wealth losses) occasioned by term freedom; whereas, in a legal system that is guided by an individual rights-led morality, the right of freedom of contract will be abridged only where more important rights are at stake ...

Sanctity of contract

Closely related to the ideal of term freedom is the ideal of sanctity of contract. Whereas term freedom sets up a presumption against unnecessary restrictions on the kinds of agreements that parties can make, sanctity of contract emphasises that parties are to be held to the agreements that they have freely made. This general idea can be deployed in more than one context. Most obviously, it applies in the context of hard cases and improvident contracts. In a legal system that subscribes to the principle of sanctity of contract, there will be no jurisdiction to grant paternalistic relief where a party is simply trying to avoid the consequences of a bargain that is now regretted. Accordingly, in *Printing and Numerical Registering Co v Sampson*, if the court had felt that the company had contracted for a greater protection than it really needed, and if the contract had subsequently worked a significant hardship upon the vendor-inventor, then sanctity of contract would treat such considerations as irrelevant – contracts, as Sir George said, are sacred, and the justification for their enforcement originates in free agreement, not in some calculus of sympathy and antipathy in relation to the parties. In addition to this obvious application, sanctity of contract can have a bearing on the renegotiation or variation of contracts. In this context, sanctity of contract does not preclude a party waiving the right to hold a fellow contractor to the agreed terms of the bargain, but it does encourage courts to take a hard look at renegotiated agreements apparently showing benefit to just one side – particularly a hard look at whether the renegotiation was free and fully consensual ...

Party freedom

The third element of freedom of contract (in the broad sense), it will be recalled, is party freedom. This is the right to choose one's contracting partners which, in practice, means the right to refuse to deal with a particular person. It is, of course, axiomatic within the general idea of freedom of contract that there is a threshold freedom to decline an offer (even an offer that, in practice, no rational person would refuse). However, party freedom constitutes a licence to discriminate against a particular person or particular types of person by excluding such persons from one's contracting activities for whatever reason or whim one likes. This is not to say that those who actually make offers may then pick and choose amongst acceptors who are eligible relative to the scope of the offer: if the offer is open to everyone, anyone may accept; if the offer is open to any member of a particular class, anyone within that class may accept; if the offer is open to all save for a particular restriction, anyone not excluded by that restriction may accept, and so on. However, what party freedom does mean is that offerors may restrict their offers in the first place (by specifying who is and who is not eligible to accept); that offerees may decline to accept offers because they do not want to deal with particular offerors; and that, in both cases, the grounds that offerors and offerees have for so doing are not subject to legal regulation or judicial scrutiny.

Does the paradigm of a contract which is discrete, based on promises and in relation to which the obligations of the parties are determined by free negotiation, fit with the reality of modern contract law? The answer is that it probably does for a limited range of contracts, but there are many that will not fall within this model. It is often the case, for example, that there is no equality of bargaining power between the parties, so that the idea of a freely negotiated agreement is, to some extent at least, unrealistic. This may most obviously be the case where one party is a consumer and the other a large corporation. Indeed, similar imbalances can occur between large and small companies. In the commercial world, moreover, the totally discrete contractual exchange is by no means typical. Many contracts will be made between businesses that are in a continuing commercial relationship and planning to trade with each other for some time. The classical theory cannot easily deal with such situations. In addition, there is increasing statutory intervention into the area of contract law, some of which, pre-Brexit, originated from the European Union (E.U.) (discussed further at Section 1.6). Such regulation will often take a different approach to that which would have been expected under the common law.

It is nevertheless the case that the courts in England and Wales, as will be seen from many of the extracts in later chapters, have tended to rely in many cases on the language of classical contract law when analysing contractual situations (although see some recent developments at Section 1.4, below). This can be the case even where that approach does not fit comfortably with the facts before the court. There is, therefore, a tension arising from the fact that the courts may be using a nineteenth-century analysis (which even at the time may well have been artificial), to deal with problems that arise in a twenty-first-century context. The following chapters will use the classical doctrine as a framework for exploring the case law, but will draw attention, as appropriate, to the difficulties that this can cause, and to alternative analyses that have been proposed.

1.3 The subject matter of contract law

There are differing views as to the purpose of contract law. For some, as is shown by the extract from Burrows below, 'promises' are at the centre of contract. Contract law is primarily concerned with identifying promises that parties have made to each other, and providing a mechanism for their enforcement.

Burrows, A, *Understanding the Law of Obligations*, 1998, Oxford: Hart Publishing, pp 3–5

2. Contract

The law of contract is concerned with binding promises. It looks at what constitutes a binding promise and how such a promise is made; at the remedies for breach of such a promise; and at who is entitled to those remedies.

It has been a traditionally accepted feature of English law that only bargain promises – that is, promises supported by consideration – are binding. Gratuitous promises, apart from promises made by deed and those enforceable through proprietary or promissory estoppel, are not binding. But even if a bargain promise has been made and accepted, it may still not be binding for various reasons. For example, it may not be sufficiently certain; or it may be a social or domestic promise where it is presumed that the promisor does not intend to create legal relations; or it may have been induced by the promisee's misrepresentation or duress or undue influence; or the promisor may have made a mistake; or there may have been such a change of events subsequent to the making of the promise that the notion of 'frustration' is brought into play; or the plaintiff may have broken his own promise in such a serious way as to make the defendant's promise, performance of which was conditional upon performance of the plaintiff's own promise, no longer binding. A number of these factors which render a promise that would otherwise be binding non-binding, can be coherently linked by saying that a promise is not binding if it is unfair to the promisor to hold him or her to it. Using this notion of fairness, the expansion of invalidating factors that has taken place during the twentieth century, such as the widening of the doctrines of mistake and duress, and the passing of statutes such as the Unfair Contract Terms Act 1977, is readily explicable as reflecting the different view of fairness that holds sway today than in the past. That is, the laissez-faire/freedom of contract view of fairness is today tempered by a paternalistic/protection of the weak view of fairness ...

It is important to add that the notion of 'promise' that is being used, when one refers to the law of contract being concerned with binding promises, is a wide one. One can define a promise, in a wide sense, as 'a statement or action by which the speaker or actor appears to accept an obligation to another (or others) to do or not to do something.' So a promise may be made by an oral statement, by writing, or by conduct. Conduct constituting a promise will be context-specific, but it may include, for example, a handshake, or a nod-of-the-head, or the delivery of requested goods (where, by delivery, one may be taken to have accepted an obligation to provide a certain quality or quantity of goods), or conduct encouraging another to perform services (where, by the encouragement, one may be taken to have accepted an obligation to pay for the services).

Although many would agree with Burrows that promises are central to the idea of 'contract', there are some difficulties with this view, as was pointed out by Brownsword:

Brownsword, R, *Contract Law: Themes for the 21st Century*, 2nd edn, 2006, Oxford: OUP, pp 18–21

Promise as a necessary condition

What is the problem with viewing the giving of a promise as a necessary condition for the existence of a contract? Surely there cannot be a contract without the giving of a promise. Is it not precisely non-performance or defective performance of a promise that the innocent party will cite in an action for breach?

To see how one kind of reservation unfolds, we can consider any typical marketplace transaction, any contract for the sale or supply of goods or services. Without doubt, many transactions of this kind exemplify not only contract as promise, but also agreement and exchange. In a large-scale construction contract, for example, there is an agreement (however understood) that certain building work will be carried out for a certain price; there is an exchange (no-one is making a gift); and the client's promise to pay is reciprocated by the contractor's promise to carry out the work. Alongside such tailored transactions, however, there is a myriad of routine transactions where commerce is conducted on a taken-for-granted basis. Suppose, for example, that the aforementioned construction contract is for a garage and self-service petrol station. When the garage has been built and is functioning, agreements to carry out repair work for customers may well resemble the tailored transacting of the construction project itself. However, motorists who call in at the garage simply to fill up their petrol tanks may well participate in a transaction that is so routine that nothing is actually said between the parties. Similarly, customers who purchase items from the garage self-service shop may complete the transaction by tendering the appropriate money – and, again, neither party to the transaction will necessarily give an express promise; the exchange will simply be made. In other words, in routine everyday transactions, an exchange will often take place in a setting where promising is implicit rather than explicit.

If the only reservation about the necessity of a promise (in a promise-based definition) were that promises are sometimes implicit rather than explicit – that, for example, in routine consumer transactions the purchaser implicitly promises to pay for the goods and services at the advertised prices – this would give rise to no real difficulty. However, the legal backcloth presupposed by routine consumer transactions gives such a reservation a fresh twist. To a large extent, the law supplies the content for standard everyday transactions by writing in various types of implied terms, some of which are strictly non-negotiable. Although these implied terms do take the form of a promise, it would be a distortion to treat them as implicit promises in the sense that we have been using that term thus far. Rather, given widespread ignorance amongst contractors about the details of these implied term regimes, it would be more accurate to say that promises of this kind are attributed (or imputed) to the parties. Nevertheless, so long as a promise-based definition allows for attributed (or imputed) promises, it can cover this difficulty.

A further obstacle to treating promise as a necessary condition for contract might be thought to arise where the law shifts into a remedial gear, constructing contracts *ex post facto* in order to facilitate some form of relief or redress. For example, in cases such as *The Eurymedon* where, in the context of the carriage of goods by sea, a contract was constructed between the owners of the goods (who contracted with the carriers) and the stevedores (who were sub-contracted by the carriers), the parties did not realise that they were entering into a transaction with one another, let alone that they were issuing promises to one another. To be sure, we might defend a promise-based definition by insisting that even such *ex post facto* rationalisation eventually returns to the idea of a promise. In other words, whether we reason forwards from promise to contract to remedy, or backwards from remedy to contract to promise, contract is essentially, and necessarily, about enforceable promises. Such a robust defence, however, might be thought to miss an opportunity to draw out the sophisticated way in which contract law is used to protect the expectations of those who are involved in transactions.

For instance, in *Blackpool and Fylde Aero Club Ltd v Blackpool Borough Council*, the defendants, who owned and managed Blackpool Airport, raised revenue by granting concessions to operators to use it. The plaintiff club was granted the concession in 1975, 1978 and 1980. Shortly before the plaintiff's last (1980) concession was due to expire, the council sent an invitation to the plaintiff to tender for the new concession to the club. The council also sent invitations to six other parties. The invitations stated *inter alia* that tenders received after 12 noon on 17 March 1983 would not be considered. The plaintiff's tender was put in the Town Hall letter box at 11 am on 17 March, but the box was not emptied as it was supposed to be. As a result, the plaintiff's letter was incorrectly recorded as having been received late, and it was not considered when the relevant committee met to award the concession. The plaintiff sued, alleging a breach of warranty on the part of the defendants to the effect that, if the tender were received by the deadline, it would be considered along with the others. The Court of Appeal unanimously upheld the decision of the court at first instance that the defendants were liable for a breach of contract.

Amongst the arguments presented on behalf of the defendants, it was contended that a contract should not be implied merely because it was reasonable to do so; and that there was a distinction between reasonable expectation and contractual obligation. Responding to these arguments, Bingham L.J. observed:

> '[W]hat if, in a situation such as the present, the council had opened and thereupon accepted the first tender received, even though the deadline had not expired and other invitees had not responded? Or if the council had considered and accepted a tender admittedly received well after the deadline? Counsel answered that although by so acting the council might breach its own standing orders, and might fairly be accused of discreditable conduct, it would not be in breach of any legal obligation because at that stage there would be none to breach. This is a conclusion I cannot accept, and if it were accepted there would in my view be an unacceptable discrepancy between the law of contract and the confident assumptions of commercial parties ... [W]here, as here, tenders are solicited from selected parties, all of them known to the invitor, and where a local authority's invitation prescribes a clear, orderly and familiar procedure ... the invitee is in my judgment protected at least to this extent: if he submits a conforming tender before the deadline he is entitled, *not as a matter of mere expectation but of contractual right*, to be sure that his tender will after the deadline be opened and considered in conjunction with all other conforming tenders or at least that his tender will be considered if others are.'

These remarks might seem to gloss over a number of potentially important distinctions, in particular between intentional and unintentional violation of the principles of good tendering practice, and between holding the council contractually bound to consider all conforming tenders, as opposed to holding the council so bound *only if any tenders were considered*. However, for Bingham L.J.'s purposes, such nice points were largely immaterial: the critical question was simply whether tenderers reasonably assumed that the council would observe certain ground rules in dealing with the tenders; if they did, then an appropriate contractual relationship would be implied in line with their expectations.

Taking stock of these remarks, we cannot define a contract in a way that presupposes the giving of an express promise. If a contract is to be defined in terms of promises, we must allow for express, implicit and imputed promises. We must also allow, however, for promises constructed *ex post facto*; and the thought prompted by cases such as *Blackpool* and *The Eurymedon* is that, if a promise is necessary to give form to a contract, reasonable expectation is perhaps the key to contractual substance.

As Brownsword explains, we can only explain contract law in England and Wales in terms of 'promises' if we are prepared to use a broad concept of a promise and, indeed, to find that parties were in effect 'promising' things to one another although they were not aware of it at the time. An alternative approach is suggested by Collins:

Collins, H, *Law of Contract*, 4th edn, 2003, London: Lexis-Nexis, pp 8–9

We need to construct a new conception of the law of contract. It should provide a system of thought that illuminates present concerns of government, and that helps to analyse issues within an intellectual framework which has a place for all the relevant rules and doctrines. It should also provide a key for an interpretation of law's past, which simultaneously reconstructs the law and enables further transformations to take place.

The place to start no doubt, as did the Victorians before us, is with a desire to understand the market order. We still require legal systems of thought for interpreting, analysing and guiding events and relations in the marketplace. The difference between our enterprise and theirs springs not from the site of the inquiry, but rather from the alteration in both the market order itself, and the nature of political and moral justifications for its legal regulation.

During the twentieth century, the state intervened to devise new principles to govern the operation and outcomes of the market. With respect to outcomes, the evidence is incontrovertible. Instead of permitting the distribution of wealth to be determined by voluntary choices to enter market transactions, the social security system which relieves poverty and all the other dimensions of the Welfare State, funded largely through progressive taxation, clearly affect the eventual outcomes of the distribution of wealth. What seems to be less generally perceived is that at the same time similar ideals of social justice have justified the channelling and regulation of market transactions. The purpose of these limits upon the exercise of voluntary choices lies in the realisation of a compatible scheme of social justice. The persistence of traditional descriptions of the law of contract no doubt contributes to this failure to perceive how the ground rules for the establishment of obligations in economic relations have been substantially altered in order that they may fit better with contemporary ideals of social justice.

How, therefore, should we conceive the law of contract today? It comprises those rules, standards and doctrines which serve to channel, control and regulate the social practices which we can loosely describe as market transactions. This branch of the law certainly facilitates the growth of the social practice of making economic transactions, especially those transactions where performance is not instantaneous; but it also sets limits to the exercise of voluntary choice. By emphasising how modern ideals of social justice channel market transactions into approved patterns, this conception of contract removes the assumption that the law provides an open-ended facility for making binding commitments. Although some flexibility persists, especially with regard to the price, this freedom should be regarded as a privilege granted on stringent conditions, rather than a general licence to enter contractual obligations of one's choice.

For Collins, then, contract law is concerned with mechanisms for controlling market transactions. 'Contract' is a device that can be used by those who want to clothe an exchange with legal enforceability. By constructing their transaction in a way that the courts will recognise as 'contractual', they ensure that if anything goes wrong, legal remedies will be available. The agreement will also have the effect of allocating risks between the parties – deciding who is to bear the loss in the event of problems.

There are, however, some difficulties with this analysis. For example, it does not explain how the transfer of property by 'deed', which the courts treat as akin to contract, does not need to involve an exchange in order to be enforceable. Brownsword suggests that it may not be feasible to find one single definition which will work:

Brownsword, R, *Contract Law: Themes for the 21st Century*, 2nd edn, 2006, Oxford: OUP, pp 14–15

Definition

A contract, it seems, is one of those phenomena that is relatively easy to recognise but difficult to define. On the one hand, to state some truisms, one of the functions of the law of contract is to discriminate between those transactions that are enforceable as contracts and those that are not. Doctrine lays down the constituents of a contract (agreement, consideration, certainty, intention and, in exceptional cases, written formality) as well as stipulating the conditions of enforceability (the absence of fraud, coercion, illegal purpose and so on). There will be cases where, for one reason or another, doctrine is uncertain in its application. However, for the most part, lawyers will expect to recognise a 'contract', as specified by the law of contract, when they see one. On the other hand, whilst we might hope to construct a definition of a 'contract' around the shared idea of an enforceable transaction, there is little agreement about how this is best articulated. Some definitions might centre on the idea of an enforceable agreement; others might be anchored to the concept of an enforceable promise (or set of promises); and others might emphasise that contracts are essentially exchanges, or perhaps bargained-for exchanges. Which definition, if any, is correct?

As with any question of definition, it is important to be clear about what kind of defining statement is at issue. Broadly speaking, definitions are either stipulative, prescriptive or reportive. Whereas a stipulative definition specifies (in the definer's own lexicon) a particular meaning for a word (or a concept), and a prescriptive definition purports to lay down for others such a meaning, a reportive definition (as we might expect to find in a dictionary) purports to describe usage (in a particular place at a particular time by a particular group) of a particular word (or concept). When we ask for a general definition of a 'contract' we are not asking for a stipulation; we are not interested in a particular definer's idiosyncratic usage of the term. Nor are we asking for a prescription as to the usage of this term; in a sense, the law of contract already so prescribes. Rather, we are asking for an account that captures the employment of the idea within the law of contract and, thus, the exercise is akin to that of reportive definition. It follows that any proffered general definition will be deficient if it does not fit the various transactions that the law of contract picks out as 'contracts'.

A report that aspires to capture usage of a particular term (such as the term 'contract' as used in the law) might attempt to do so in the form of an essential definition (in which one or more elements are identified as the necessary and sufficient conditions for correct usage) or in the form of a cluster concept (in which several elements are identified with the usage, but where no single set of these elements can be combined to represent the necessary and sufficient conditions for correct usage). Insofar as the puzzle about defining a contract is approached as an exercise in essential (reportive) definition, a proffered definition will fail if the given condition, or conditions (agreement, exchange, promise or whatever) is or are not strictly necessary (i.e. if a contract can exist without meeting such conditions); and, equally, it will fail if the given condition, or conditions, is/are not sufficient (i.e. if, despite meeting such conditions, a transaction fails to be recognised as a contract). Insofar as the puzzle is approached as an exercise in non-essential cluster concept definition, the challenge is less demanding.

As Brownsword suggests, it is probably more satisfactory to look for a 'cluster' definition, indicating common characteristics of a contract, rather than an 'essential' definition, indicating elements that must exist in all situations. That approach is adopted in this book. One such suggested common characteristic is that the transaction is 'voluntary', and that is considered in the next section.

1.3.1 Voluntary transactions

It appears to be a characteristic of a contractual exchange that it is at some level 'voluntary'. Although in practice there may be little choice as to whether to make certain contracts (for example, to buy the necessities of life), or the terms on which contracts are made, some element of freedom must exist. On the other hand, it has been held that if a transaction is entirely regulated by statute, then it cannot be regarded as contractual in nature.

***Norweb plc v Dixon* [1995] 1 WLR 636 (CA)**

Facts: D claimed to have been harassed as a debtor by Norweb plc – an offence under the Administration of Justice Act 1970. The magistrates convicted Norweb, and it appealed.

Held: The particular relationship between Norweb and D was not contractual, as it was entirely regulated by statute.

Dyson J:

... *Conclusion on the contract point*

I deal first with the general question whether an agreement for the supply of electricity between a tariff customer and a public electricity supplier (i.e. not a special agreement within the meaning of section 22) is a contract. There are many examples of cases where the law to some extent restricts the freedom of parties to enter into a relationship, but where the relationship that results is a contract. Mrs. Cover gave some good examples, although I do not consider that her point about section 65 of the Housing Act 1985 is apt. A further good example is that it is unlawful to refuse a person employment 'because he is, or is not, a member of a trade union': section 1(1)(a) of the Employment Act 1990. In all these cases, a relationship which results from some degree of legal compulsion is nevertheless regarded as contractual, because the parties still have considerable freedom to regulate its incidents.

But there are other cases in which a relationship created by legal compulsion is clearly not contractual. Thus a person whose property is compulsorily acquired against his will does not make a contract with the acquiring authority, even though he receives compensation: see *Sovmots Investments Ltd v Secretary of State for the Environment* [1977] Q.B. 411, 443. In *Pfizer Corporation v Ministry of Health* [1965] A.C. 512 the House of Lords held that a patient to whom medicines are supplied under the National Health Service does not make a contract to buy them either from the chemist or the Minister of Health even if he pays a subscription charge ...

The issue in this case is: which side of the line does the relationship between a tariff customer and a public electricity supplier fall? In my judgment, the legal compulsion as to both the creation of the relationship and the fixing of its terms is inconsistent with the existence of a contract. As regards the creation of the relationship, the supplier is obliged by section 16(1) of the Act of 1989 to supply if requested to do so. The exceptions from the duty to supply provided in section 17 are very limited in scope. Mrs. Cover submits that section 17(2)(c) gives the supplier what she calls a 'discretion' not to supply. That is not so. A supplier is excused from supplying if (the burden being on him) it is not reasonable in all the circumstances for him to be required to do so. What is reasonable is a question of fact to be established objectively. Discretion does not come into play. Thus, save in certain narrowly defined circumstances, if a consumer requests the supply of electricity, the supplier is obliged to supply.

As for the terms of the supply, Mrs. Cover submits that there is scope for what she calls 'bargaining'. I cannot agree. The tariff is fixed by the supplier: section 18. The supplier can require the consumer to defray any expenses reasonably incurred in supplying any electric line or plant (section 19), and to give reasonable security: section 20(1). The supplier can also impose additional terms of supply: section 21. The consumer has no bargaining power in relation to these matters. It seems to me that the principal terms are imposed on the consumer by the supplier not as a result of any bargaining, but by the supplier exercising the power conferred on it by the Act of 1989 ...

It must follow that there was no contract between the appellants and the respondent, nor was the debt claimed under a contract. That is because, in the absence of any findings to support a special agreement, the relationship between the appellants and the respondent (both actual and claimed) could only be that of public electricity supplier/tariff customer. For the reasons already given, in my view such a relationship is not founded in contract.

A similar view was taken in a subsequent case concerned with the relationship between foster parents and the local authority from whom they agreed to accept children for fostering (see also *National Union of Professional Foster Carers (NUPFC) v Certification Officer* [2019] IRLR 860).

***W v Essex County Council* [1999] Fam 90 (CA) (reversed in part on other grounds [2000] 2 WLR 601)**

Facts: The plaintiffs signed an agreement with the council, the first defendants, to become foster parents, after receiving assurances that no sexual abuser would be placed with them. A 15-year-old boy (G) was placed with them following a false representation by the council's social worker that the boy was not a sexual abuser. A month after the placement the plaintiffs discovered that G had during that period sexually abused their children, then aged between 7 and 12 years. The plaintiffs sued the council for, *inter alia*, breach of contract and the mental distress thereby caused. The judge struck out the contractual claim. The parents appealed.

Held: The relationship between the plaintiffs and the council was not contractual.

Stuart-Smith LJ:

... *The claim in contract*

47. On 15 October 1992 the parents signed a written document entitled 'Specialist Foster Carer Agreement Supplementary to Form DSS 91 and the Code of Practice' ('the Specialist Foster Carer Agreement'). This document is expressed to be 'between the council and ....' There then follows a blank space, which is obviously intended to include the parents named. No-one has been able to identify Form DSS 91. The plaintiffs alleged in the statement of claim that this agreement, together with a number of other documents, including an unsigned 'Adolescent Foster Carer Agreement', which on its first page has the names and address of the parents, and a 'Specialist Foster Carer Agreement Code of Practice', constitute a legally binding contract between the parents and the council. The Code of Practice begins with the statement that it:

> 'is not legally binding or enforceable in law. It is designated [sic] to act as a guideline for both staff and carers with a view to ensuring the professional discretion is clearly defined and correctly exercised'.

There is a further reference in paragraph 9.1 of the Code of Practice, in which attention is drawn to the need to observe certain statutory requirements, to the fact that it is not legally binding.

48. Paragraph 3 of the Specialist Foster Carer Agreement provides that the parents had the 'right to decline any placement of a child or young person, provided such rejection was not made unreasonably'. Paragraph 6.4 of the Code of Practice provides that 'the social worker will ensure the foster carer will be fully informed about the child's background of any problem relating to that background legal, developmental or practical in writing'. The plaintiffs allege that this paragraph constituted an express term of the contract and that the council were in breach of it. Alternatively they allege that there was an implied term of the contract that the defendants would inform the plaintiffs of any knowledge or suspicion of the child being a sexual abuser, and in support of the implied term they rely on the conversation and assurances to the effect that the foster child would not be a sexual abuser.

49. The judge held that the Code of Practice was not intended to be legally enforceable. He held that the Specialist Foster Carer Agreement was a legally enforceable agreement but that the alleged term was not to be implied. The plaintiffs appeal against the judge's conclusion as to the express or implied term. The defendants cross-appeal against his conclusion that the Specialist Foster Care Agreement was a legally binding agreement.

50. There are, in my judgment, a number of reasons why the plaintiffs' claim in contract must fail. First, although the Specialist Foster Carer Agreement had a number of features which one would expect to find in a contract, such as the payment of an allowance and expenses, provisions as to national insurance, termination and restriction on receiving a legacy or engaging in other gainful employment and other matters to which the judge referred [1997] 2 FLR 535, 565e-f, I do not accept that this makes the agreement a contract in the circumstances of this case. A contract is essentially an agreement that is freely entered into on terms that are freely negotiated. If there is a statutory obligation to enter into a form of agreement the terms of which are laid down, at any rate in their most important respects, there is no contract: see *Norweb plc v Dixon* [1995] 1 WLR 636, 643f.

51. In *S v Walsall Metropolitan Borough Council* [1985] 1 WLR 1150 the question was whether foster parents were the agents of the defendant council who had placed the child in care. Oliver L.J., with whose judgment Balcombe L.J. agreed, reviewed the statutory provisions which are similar to those relevant in this case. He said, at p 1154f, that the statute and the regulations 'provide a statutory code and they underline the fact that the whole of this area is covered by a complicated and detailed statutory scheme' and later he said, at p 1155e, that the 'relationship between the child and the local authority, and indeed between the child and the foster parents, is one which is regulated ... simply and solely by the provisions of the statutory scheme'. It is true that he does not include the relationship between the foster parents and the council as being so regulated; but it must, in my judgment, follow. The contents of the agreement are strictly laid down in the regulations and cannot be varied. The remuneration is set by the statutory scheme and cannot be freely negotiated.

52. Furthermore, I am very doubtful whether the judge was right to consider the Specialist Foster Carer Agreement separate from the Code of Practice, which specifically stated that it is not to be legally binding. The plaintiffs had pleaded that this document formed part of the agreement, and if that is correct it shows that the agreement, whatever it was, was not to be regarded as a legally binding contract.

Arrangements which have some of the appearance of contracts but are in fact entirely regulated by statute, are thus not to be treated as contractual.

1.4 Discrete and relational transactions

As we have seen, the classical law of contract tends to assume that contracts are 'one-off' events – in other words, a 'discrete' transaction. This has been challenged by a number of commentators, the most prominent of whom was Professor Ian Macneil. His view was that contracts are 'relational' – by which he meant: (a) that contracts always exist in a social and economic context; and (b) that many contracts are not isolated transactions between the parties, but part of a continuing relationship. In relation to (b) many contracts are expected to last for a period of time during which the relationship between the parties, or the surrounding circumstances, may change. The classical law of contract has difficulty dealing with such changes because it assumes that all aspects of the contract had been agreed when it was first formed. Under the classical law of contract all that the courts need to do is to discover what the parties intended at the point the contract as concluded, and this will then answer all questions that may in future arise in relation to their agreement. This process is what Macneil calls 'presentiation'. However, such an approach is arguably artificial in that parties may not have considered at the time of formation many of the issues which might subsequently arise. It also has difficulty dealing with, for example, attempts to modify the contract while it is in progress, either because of a changed relationship between the parties or because of changed external circumstances. A relational approach to contracts can cope with such issues much more flexibly. The following extract from one of Macneil's many articles on this topic gives an idea of his approach.

Macneil, IR, 'Contracts: adjustments of long-term economic relations under classical, neo-classical and relational contract law' (1978) 72 *Northwestern UL Rev* 854

Discrete transactions: classical contract law

The nature of discrete transactions

A *truly* discrete exchange transaction would be entirely separate not only from all other present relations but from all past and future relations as well. In short, it could occur, if at all, only between total strangers, brought together by chance (not by any common social structure, since that link constitutes at least the rudiments of a relation outside the transaction). Moreover, each party would have to be completely sure of never again seeing or having anything else to do with the other. Such an event could involve only a barter of goods, since even money available to one and acceptable to the other postulates some kind of common social structure. Moreover, everything must happen quickly lest the parties should develop some kind of a relation impacting on the transaction so as to deprive it of discreteness. For example, bargaining about quantities or other aspects of the transaction can erode discreteness, as certainly does any effort to project the transaction into the future through promises.

The characteristics of entirely discrete transactions, if they could occur at all, deprive them of any utility as social tools of production and distribution of scarce goods and services. That fact by no means, however, renders the construct useless as a tool of economic or legal analysis, because some discreteness is present in all exchange transactions and relations. One must simply not forget that great modification is required before the model can represent a reasonably accurate picture of actual economic life. (Unfortunately, this kind of forgetfulness is an endemic problem in both economics and law.) When so modified, the construct will no longer represent an entirely discrete transaction, but will retain substantial discreteness while nevertheless remaining relatively realistic.

We do find in real life many quite discrete transactions: little personal involvement of the parties, communications largely or entirely linguistic and limited to the subject matter of transaction, the subjects of exchange consisting of an easily monetised commodity and money, little or no social (Blau, 1964) or secondary exchange (Parsons and Smelser, 1956) and no significant past relations nor likely future relations. For example, a cash purchase of gasoline at a station on the New Jersey Turnpike by someone rarely travelling the road is such a quite discrete transaction. Such quite discrete transactions are no rarity in modern technological societies. They have been and continue to be an extremely productive economic technique both to achieve distribution of goods and to encourage their production.

Thus far we have dealt only with present exchanges of existing goods. Such exchanges can, however, play but a limited role in advanced economies. Advanced economies require greater specialisation of effort and more planning than can be efficiently achieved by present exchanges through discrete transactions; they require the projection of exchange into the future through planning of various kinds, that is, planning, permitting and fostering the necessary degree of specialisation of effort. The introduction of this key factor of futurity gives rise to the question: what happens to discreteness when exchanges are projected into the future?

The answer is that a massive erosion of discreteness occurs. This is obvious when projection of exchange into the future occurs within structures such as the family, corporations, collective bargaining and employment, structures obviously relational in nature. Similarly obvious are various relational ways of organising and controlling markets, for example, the guilds of the feudal era or the planning described by Professor Galbraith in *The New Industrial State* (1985, Ch. 3). But this erosion of discreteness occurs even when the projection is by direct and fairly simple promise and where the subject of exchange, if transferred immediately, would permit high levels of discreteness.

Discreteness is lost even in the simple promise situation, because a basis for trust must exist if the promise is to be of any value. Trust in turn presupposes some kind of a relation between the parties. Whether it is that created by a shared morality, by prior experience, by the availability of legal sanction, or whatever, trust depends upon some kind of mutual relation into which the transaction is integrated. And integration into a relation is the antithesis of discreteness (Lowry, 1976).

In spite of the great leap away from pure discreteness occurring when exchange is projected into the future, promises themselves inherently create or maintain at least a certain minimum of discreteness. A promise presupposes that the promisor's individual will can affect the future at least partially free of the communal will, thus separating the individual from the rest of his society. Such separation is an element of discreteness. Promise also stresses the separateness of the promisor and the promisee, another element of discreteness. Moreover, some specificity and measured reciprocity is essential to an exchange of promises – no-one in his right mind promises the world. This, again, results in an irreducible level of discreteness.

The foregoing can be seen in the following definition of contract promise: present communication of a commitment to future engagement in a specified reciprocal measured exchange. Thus, the partially discrete nature of promise permits the retention of a great deal of discreteness in transactions where promise projects exchange into the future. Where no massive relational elements counterbalance this discreteness (as they do, for example, in the case of collective bargaining), sense is served by speaking of the contract as discrete, even though the contract is inevitably less discrete than would be an equivalent present exchange.

The combination of exchange with promise has been one of the most powerful social tools ever developed for the production of goods and services. Moreover, discreteness in transactions so projected has its own special virtues. Just as a system of discrete transactions for exchanging present goods may be an effective way to conduct business free of all sorts of extraneous social baggage, so too may discrete transaction contracts serve this function ...

Classical contract law and discrete transactions

Any contract law system necessarily must implement certain norms. It must permit and encourage participation in exchange, promote reciprocity, reinforce role patterns appropriate to particular kinds of exchange relations, provide limited freedom for exercise of choice, effectuate planning and harmonise the internal and external matrixes of particular contracts. A contract law system reinforcing discrete contract transactions, however, must add two further goals: enhancing discreteness and enhancing presentiation.

Presentiation is a way of looking at things in which a person perceives the effect of the future on the present. It is a recognition that the course of the future is so unalterably bound by present conditions that the future has been brought effectively into the present so that it may be dealt with just as if it were in fact the present. Thus, the presentiation of a transaction involves restricting its expected future effects to those defined in the present, i.e. at the inception of the transaction. No eternal distinctions prevent treating the contract norm of enhancing presentiation as simply an aspect of the norm of enhancing discreteness. It is, however, such an important aspect of the projection of exchange into the future in discrete contracts – to say nothing of microeconomic theory – that separate treatment aids analysis significantly.

A classical contract law system implements these two norms in a number of ways. To implement discreteness, classical law initially treats as irrelevant the identity of the parties to the transaction. Secondly, it transactionises or commodifies as much as possible the subject matter of contracts, e.g. it turns employment into a short-term commodity by interpreting employment contracts without express terms of duration as terminable at will. Thirdly, it limits strictly the sources to be considered in establishing the substantive content of the transaction. For example, formal communication (e.g. writings) controls informal communication (e.g. oral statements); linguistic communication controls nonlinguistic communication; and communicated circumstances (to the limited extent that any circumstances outside of 'agreements' are taken into account at all) control non-communicated circumstances (e.g. status). Fourthly, only limited contract remedies are available, so that should the initial presentation fail to materialise because of non-performance, the consequences are relatively predictable from the beginning and are not open-ended, as they would be, for example, if damages for unforeseeable or psychic losses were allowed. Fifthly, classical contract law draws clear lines between being in and not being in a transaction; e.g. rigorous and precise rules of offer and acceptance prevail with no half-way houses where only some contract interests are protected or where losses are shared. Finally, the introduction of third parties into the relation is discouraged since multiple poles of interest tend to create discreteness-destroying relations.

Since discreteness enhances the possibility and likelihood of presentiation, all of the foregoing implementations of discreteness by the classical law also tend to enhance presentiation. Other classical law techniques, however, are even more precisely focused on presentiation (Macneil 1975b,

592–594). The first of these is the equation of the legal effect of a transaction with the promises creating it. This characteristic of classical contract law is commonly explained in terms of freedom of contract, providing maximum scope to the exercise of choice. Nevertheless, a vital consequence of the use of the technique is presentation of the transaction. Closely related to the first technique is the second: supplying a precise, predictable body of law to deal with all aspects of the transaction not encompassed by the promises. In theory, if not practice, this enables the parties to know exactly what the future holds, no matter what happens to disrupt performance. Finally, stress on expectation remedies, whether specific performance or damages measured by the value of performance, tends to bring the future into the present, since all risks, including market risks, are thereby transferred at the time the 'deal is made'.

In summary, classical contract law very closely parallels the discrete transactional patterns described in the preceding section. Such a legal system, superimposed on economic patterns of such a nature, constitutes the stereotype of interfirm (or firm and consumer or firm and employee) contracting of the laissez faire era.

Macneil's writing has been influential in academic discussions of contract law. It is very useful in understanding why the classical law has difficulty in dealing with certain types of situation – particularly the variation of ongoing contracts – and in suggesting better ways in which these could be approached. The idea of relational contracting has also begun to have more of an impact on the development of contract law in England and Wales. For example, in both *Yam Seng PTE Ltd v International Trade Corporation Ltd* [2013] EWHC 111 and *Bristol Groundschool Ltd v Intelligent Data Capture Ltd* [2014] EWHC 2145, the High Court used it to help explain its decision in those cases. More recently in *Bates v Post Office Ltd (No.3: Common Issues)* [2019] EWHC 606 (QB) at [705] Fraser J. stated: 'the concept of relational contracts is an established one in English law'. Fraser J. ultimately concluded (at [1113]) that:

> the contracts formed between the Post Office and SPMs are relational contracts, which means that there is an implied duty of good faith in the agreement. This means that the Post Office is not entitled to act in a way that would be considered commercially unacceptable by reasonable and honest people.

In reaching this conclusion Fraser J. noted (at [709]):

> Academic learning, and the views of academics and legal authors, do have persuasive effect in our system of law. At [180] and [181] in *SRCL Ltd v NHS England* [2018] EWHC 1985 (TCC) I considered the modern position of academics in legal argument before the courts, by reference to the text of a lecture given by Lord Neuberger in July 2012 at the Max Planck Institute when he was Master of the Rolls. The title was 'Judges and Professors – Ships passing in the night?' and Lord Neuberger made clear what I believe to be non-controversial, that the historic hostility of judges to the views of academics is long gone, and academic opinion is of very great assistance.

In terms of identifying a relational contract Fraser J. stated (at [725]):

> I consider the following characteristics are relevant as to whether a contract is a relational one or not:
>
> 1. There must be no specific express terms in the contract that prevent a duty of good faith being implied into the contract.
> 2. The contract will be a long-term one, with the mutual intention of the parties being that there will be a long-term relationship.

3. The parties must intend that their respective roles be performed with integrity, and with fidelity to their bargain.
4. The parties will be committed to collaborating with one another in the performance of the contract.
5. The spirits and objectives of their venture may not be capable of being expressed exhaustively in a written contract.
6. They will each repose trust and confidence in one another, but of a different kind to that involved in fiduciary relationships.
7. The contract in question will involve a high degree of communication, co-operation and predictable performance based on mutual trust and confidence and expectations of loyalty.
8. There may be a degree of significant investment by one party (or both) in the venture. This significant investment may be, in some cases, more accurately described as substantial financial commitment.
9. Exclusivity of the relationship may also be present.

Subsequently in *TAQA Bratani Ltd v Rockrose UKCS8 LLC* [2020] EWHC 58 (Comm) at [56] H.H.J. Pelling Q.C. stated:

> It is unnecessary for me to attempt to define further what constitutes a 'relational' contract. I am content to treat the J.O.A.s as being at least arguably such contracts. However, that does not lead to the conclusion that it is necessary to imply a good faith obligation into the exercise of the power on which the claimants rely. That is so because: (a) on its true construction that power is an absolute and unqualified power for the reasons explained earlier; in consequence; (b) it is impermissible to imply a term that qualifies what the parties have agreed between them; and (c) it follows that the parties have legislated in the sense referred to by Leggatt J. and it is not necessary, indeed it would be wrong, to imply such a term to qualify the power on which the claimants rely because it is not necessary in order to make the contract the parties have chosen work as it is to be presumed they intended it to work, or, to the extent there is any difference, to give effect to their presumed common intention.

A similar approach had been taken in *UTB LLC v Sheffield United Ltd* [2019] EWHC 2322 (Ch) by Fancourt J.:

> 199. The dichotomy is illustrated by a later judgment of Leggatt L.J. (sitting at first instance), *Sheikh Tahnoon bin Saeed bin Shakhboot Al Nehayan v Kent* [2018] EWHC 333 (Comm). In that case, an oral joint venture had been agreed relating to the acquisition and operation of hotels, and part of the business was later demerged under a rudimentary framework agreement. The express terms were very limited, and yet the joint venture had been intended as a long-term collaboration requiring the co-operation and commitment of both parties. It was based on a strong personal friendship between them.
>
> [*Sheikh Tahnoon bin Saeed bin Shakhboot Al Nehayan v Kent* [2018] EWHC 333 (Comm) is a case which shall be discussed in Chapter 10].
>
> 200. Leggatt L.J. held that implication of an obligation to act in good faith was essential to give effect to the reasonable expectations of the parties, i.e. the term was implied in fact on the conventional approach. The contract was of course a 'relational' contract, and Leggatt L.J. held that the term would also have been implied as a matter of law, given the nature of the contract. Two paragraphs of the Judge's judgment are particularly apposite:
>
>> '[167] It does not follow from the conclusion that he did not owe any fiduciary duties to Mr Kent that the Sheikh's entitlement to pursue his own self-interest was untrammelled. I have previously suggested in [*Yam Seng*], at para. 142, that it is a mistake to draw a simple dichotomy between relationships which give rise to fiduciary duties and other

> contractual relationships and to treat the latter as all alike. In particular, I drew attention to a category of contract in which the parties are committed to collaborating with each other, typically on a long-term basis, in ways which respect the spirit and objectives of their venture which they have not tried to specify, and which it may be impossible to specify, exhaustively, in a written contract. Such 'relational' contracts involve trust and confidence, but of a different kind from that involved in fiduciary relationships. The trust is not in the loyal subordination by one party of its own interests to those of another. It is trust that the other party will act with integrity and in a spirit of cooperation. The legitimate expectations which the law should protect in relationships of this kind are embodied in the normative standard of good faith.
>
> ...
>
> [174] In the circumstances the contract made between these parties seems to me to be a classic instance of a relational contract. In my view, the implication of a duty of good faith in the contract is essential to give effect to the parties' reasonable expectations and satisfies the business necessity test which Lord Neuberger in [*Marks and Spencer*] at paras 16 to 31 reiterated as the relevant standard for the implication of a term into a contract. I would also reach the same conclusion by applying the test adumbrated by Lord Wilberforce in *Liverpool City Council v Irwin* [1976] AC 239 at 254 for the implication of a term in law, on the basis that the nature of the contract as a relational contract implicitly requires (in the absence of a contrary indication) treating it as involving an obligation of good faith.'

In my judgment, it is clear that Leggatt L.J. is there explaining that a particular type of contract, which may be called a 'relational' contract, is one that will as a matter of law include an obligation of good faith. But the type of contract in issue is not any contract that involves a long-term relationship between the parties; it is a contract that requires the parties to collaborate in future in ways that respect the spirit and objectives of their joint venture but which they have not specified or have been unable to specify in detail, and which involves trust and confidence that each party will act with integrity and cooperatively. The contract in that case was exactly as described above and, as explained by Leggatt L.J., in fact necessarily required such a term to be implied if it was to work in accordance with the parties' reasonable expectations.

201. The ratio of the decisions in *Yam Seng* and *Sheikh Tahnoon* are ones that any first instance judge must follow unless he or she were satisfied that they were wrong. I shall follow them. In other recent cases, there has been a tendency to substitute for the question whether a reasonable reader of the contract would consider a term to be necessary or obvious the question of whether the contract is a 'relational' contract: see, e.g. the decision of Fraser J. in *Bates v Post Office* [2019] EWHC 606 (QB). At para. 725, Fraser J. asked what the characteristics are that are expected to be present that will determine whether a commercial contract ought to be considered a 'relational contract'. The Judge set out nine relevant factors, of which only the first was determinative, namely that there must be no express term of the contract that prevents a duty of good faith being implied.

202. If by 'relational contract' it is clear that one means a relational contract of the kind described by Leggatt L.J. in *Sheikh Tahnoon* and not all relational contracts in a broader sense, then there is no difficulty and the characteristics identified by Fraser J. may assist to identify such a contract. But there is a danger in using the term 'relational contract' that one is not clear about what exactly is meant by it. There is a great range of different types of contract that involve the parties in long-term relationships of varying types, with different terms and varying degrees of detail and use of language, and to characterise them all as 'relational contracts' may be in one sense accurate and yet in other ways liable to mislead. It is self-evidently not all long-term contracts that involve an enduring but undefined, co-operative relationship between the parties that will, as a matter of law, involve an obligation of good faith. As Beatson L.J. said (obiter) in *Globe Motors, Inc v TRW Lucas Varity Electric Steering Ltd* [2016] EWCA Civ 396 at para [68]:

'... as seen from the *Carewatch Care Services* case, an implication of a duty of good faith will only be possible where the language of the contract, viewed against its context, permits it. It is thus not a reflection of a special rule of interpretation for this category of contract.'

203. Rather than seek to identify and weigh likely indicia of a 'relational contract' in the narrower sense used by Leggatt L.J., it is, I consider, preferable to ask oneself first – as Leggatt L.J. did in the *Sheikh Tahnoon* case – whether a reasonable reader of the contract would consider that an obligation of good faith was obviously meant or whether the obligation is necessary to the proper working of the contract. The overall character of the contract in issue will of course be highly material in answering that question but so will its particular terms, as recognised by the principle that (as restated in the *Marks and Spencer* case) no term may be implied into a contract if it would be inconsistent with an express term.

1.5 Different approaches to analysing contract

Traditionally, the most common approach to the analysis of contract law has been to look at the cases and statutes and to argue about what principles can be derived from those sources, whether those principles are coherent and consistent and whether there are other principles that would serve the purpose better; in other words – a 'doctrinal analysis'. Other approaches (lenses) are, of course, possible and are increasingly used in academic writing about contract law (although only to a more limited extent in judicial consideration of contract problems). These tend to draw on the social sciences as a means of interpreting contracts – in particular economics, sociology and politics.

1.5.1 Economic analysis

Since contracts are often concerned with the exchange of goods and services for money, it is not surprising that attempts have been made to use economic theories as a basis for analysing them. Much of the work in this area has originated in the U.S. and the approach taken by Kronman and Posner indicates the nature of the type of analysis, based on an acceptance of free market economics, which has resulted.

Kronman, A and Posner, R, *The Economics of Contract Law*, 1979, Boston: Little Brown, pp 1–3

The law of contracts regulates, among other kinds of transactions, the purchase and sale of goods (including real estate) and services. Since buying and selling – and related transactions, such as leasing and borrowing, which are also governed by contract law – are quintessentially economic activities, it would seem that economics should have something useful to say to students of contract law. For example, economics may be able to tell us why people make contracts and how contract law can facilitate the operation of markets. And to the extent that contract doctrines reflect judicial efforts, whether deliberate or unconscious, to achieve efficiency, economics may help toward an understanding of the meaning of the doctrines and their appropriate limits ...

The fundamental economic principle with which we begin is that if voluntary exchanges are permitted – if, in other words, a market is allowed to operate – resources will gravitate toward their most valuable uses. If *A* owns a good that is worth only $100 to him but $150 to B, both will be made better off by an exchange of A's good for B's money at any price between $100 and $150; and if they realise this, they will make the exchange. By making both of them better off, the exchange will also increase the wealth of the society (of which they are members), assuming the exchange does not reduce the welfare of nonparties more than it increases A's and B's welfare. Before the exchange – which, let us say, takes place at a price of $125 – A had a good worth $100 to him and B had $125 in cash, a total of $225. After the exchange, A has $125 in cash and B has a good worth $150 to him, a total of $275. The exchange has increased the wealth of society by $50 (ignoring, as we have done, any possible third-party effects).

The principle is the same whether we are speaking of the purchase of a string of pearls, a lawyer's time, a machine for making shoes, or an ingot of aluminium. The existence of a market – a locus of opportunities for mutually advantageous exchanges – facilitates the allocation of the good or service in question to the use in which it is most valuable, thereby maximising the wealth of society.

This conclusion may be questioned on various grounds. For example, it may be argued that since 'value' in this analysis is measured by willingness to pay, which in turn is affected by the distribution of income and wealth (one cannot offer to buy a good without having money or the means to obtain it), the maximisation of value cannot be regarded as an uncontroversially proper goal for society to pursue. An introductory chapter is not the place to explore the philosophical basis of the economist's concept of value. For our purposes it is enough that the reader understands the technical meaning of the concept. The reader (assisted by some of the selections in this book) can then decide whether there is any 'value', in an ultimate social sense, to the *economic* concept of value which the system of free exchanges promotes.

The principle that voluntary exchange should be freely permitted in order to maximise value is frequently summarised in the concept (or slogan) of 'freedom of contract'. This is something of a misnomer, for the concept of *contract* typically plays an insignificant role in elucidations and critiques of the principle of voluntary exchange. Many value-maximising exchanges occur without contracts, or with contracts so rudimentary or transitory as to have little interest for economists studying the phenomenon of voluntary exchange. If A buys the *Chicago Tribune* from B, a news vendor, paying 20c for it on the spot, this is a value-maximising exchange; but it would be pretentious to speak of a contract between A and B, though technically there is one (if a section of the paper is missing, A can probably rescind the contract and get his 20c back). One can talk about the principle or system of voluntary exchange for quite some time before it becomes necessary to consider the role of contracts and contract law in facilitating the process.

In the newspaper example, the exchange is virtually (though not completely) instantaneous; and this provides a clue to the role of contracts in the process of voluntary exchange. It is true that, although money and good cross at the same moment, the actual *use* of the good – the reading of the newspaper – occurs after the exchange and takes some time; so really the process of exchange is not complete until the paper has been opened and inspected. Only then can the buyer be satisfied that he got what he paid for (that no pages are missing or illegible, etc.). Still, the time required to complete the exchange in the newspaper example is quite short. Where the time is long, contracts and contract law become important.

Suppose that A promises to build a house for B, construction to take six months to complete and B to pay either periodically or on completion. With construction so time-consuming, there is a significant likelihood that something will occur to frustrate the exchange – insolvency, changes in the price of inputs, labour troubles, etc. Nor is A's performance complete when construction of the house is finished. A durable good like a house by definition yields services to the purchaser over a period of time, a long one in the case of a house; and it is these services rather than the physical structure itself that the purchaser is hoping to acquire. If the house wears out long before the purchaser reasonably believed it would, the exchange will be effectively thwarted long after nominal completion of performance by the promisor.

Economists have pointed out that the cost of an undertaking tends to be inversely related to the time allowed for completion. Stated differently, it is costly to accelerate completion of a time-consuming task. It would also be costly to make goods less durable in order to compress the period in which the full exchange of the goods could be completed. These observations suggest that a system of contract rights, and not merely one of property rights, may be necessary to minimise the costs of production in a market system.

1.5.2 Sociopolitical analysis

Any analysis of the law of contract will be based on political assumptions. The classical law of contract is underpinned by a belief in the freedom of contract, which is a political viewpoint. Very often these assumptions are implicit. Some writers bring their political standpoint to the forefront of their analysis, whether it be capitalist, Marxist, socialist, etc. One example is the work of Collins, as indicated in the extract reproduced in Section 1.3.

Another interesting approach, which is useful in analysing many specific areas of contract law, is that expounded by Adams and Brownsword. They identify four particular ideologies that may compete or conflict when considering the application of the law to contractual problems. These are formalism, realism, consumer-welfarism and market-individualism. They are explained and described in the following extract.

Adams, J, and Brownsword, R, *Understanding Contract Law*, 5th edn, 2007, London: Sweet & Maxwell, pp 36–39

Judges and the rule-book: an interpretive framework

In this section we introduce a theoretical framework which we will employ in Part II as a tool for analysis of material in the contract rule-book. Our purpose at this point is merely to develop this framework sufficiently for readers to be able to follow our discussion in Part II. As that discussion proceeds, the theoretical framework and its implications should move more clearly into focus. We therefore postpone a more comprehensive analysis until Chapter 8.

Our first step in constructing the theoretical framework is to think about how judges might proceed where they are called upon to interpret and apply the rule-book. In principle, we suggest, judges may approach their task from two different starting points. According to one approach, let us call it the 'formalist' approach, judges will see their role in terms of unpacking the materials in the rule-book. Crucially, the rule-book will be treated as decisive even where the results are for some reason hard on one party. By contrast, according to the alternative approach, which we can call the 'realist' approach, judges will proceed in a result-orientated fashion, irrespective of the dictates of the rule-book.

We can indicate the significance of these rival approaches if we imagine that a second case had arisen out of Esso's World Cup coins promotion, but with the following facts (which, incidentally, are far removed from the actual facts, which we will recall raised an issue of revenue law). Suppose that Alf, having chased half-way across London, found an Esso garage having a coin showing the head of his favourite England player, and suppose that, having purchased the required amount of petrol, Alf was told that he could not have the coin. Now, suppose that Alf sued Esso for breach of contract, arguing that he had a single contract for the sale of the petrol plus the coin. Guided by the *Esso* decision (where it will be recalled the single contract analysis was rejected by the majority of the Law Lords), a judge following the formalist approach would reject Alf's claim – irrespective of the hardship worked on Alf. By contrast, a judge following the realist approach, sensitive to the result of Alf's case, might well reason that Esso should not be able to get away with such sharp practice, and that Alf must win. This being so, Alf would be allowed to succeed either on his single contract analysis or on a collateral contract analysis (this being easy to square with *Esso* itself).

Now, before we continue, we must enter two clarifying reservations against our distinction between the formalist and realist approaches. First, the distinction is exceedingly stark. The implication of our presentation is that any judge who nods in the direction of the rule-book must be categorised as adopting a formalist approach whilst any judge who shows an interest in results must be pigeonholed as following a realist approach. Plainly, however, this suffers from the sort of distortion which we would instantly recognise if we were to describe everyone living in Britain as 'northerners' or 'southerners'. To do justice to the complexity of judicial reasoning, we would have to construct categories lying between the formalist and realist poles (allowing, for example, for a result-orientated approach which holds only where some degree of fit with the rule-book is possible, or a rule-book approach which becomes result-orientated where the materials in the rule-book fail to settle the point *cf.* Adams and Brownsword, 2003). For our purposes, however, which are a matter of roughly getting our bearings, our crude distinction between formalist and realist approaches will suffice.

Secondly, judicial reasoning has been the focus of a wealth of jurisprudential writing (most recently see Dworkin, 1986). The terms 'formalism' and 'realism' enjoy some currency in this literature; indeed, some would argue that they are so overworked that they are no longer useful labels. The point, however, is that they are labels in common employment and it is difficult to think of satisfactory alternatives. The reader must however be aware of the particular way in which we use these labels. When we use 'formalism' and 'realism' (and similarly when, later on in this chapter, we use the labels 'market-individualism', 'consumer-welfarism' and 'ideology') we use these terms *stipulatively*: that is, they mean in this book what we say they mean, not what anyone else says they mean. We use these approaches as *descriptive* models of how judges *do* decide cases, not as *prescriptive* models recommending how judges *ought* to decide cases. To be sure, the models could be used either descriptively or prescriptively, but in this book, at least, they are employed primarily as a descriptive resource ...

The formalist and realist approaches are 'ideal-typical' in the sense that we can conceive of them without either inspecting judicial practice or supposing that they will be fully instantiated therein (*cf.* Chapter 10). If we focus on the realist approach, however, it will be appreciated that we could conceive, in principle, of any number of criteria to serve as the measure of fitness of particular results. In our contention, however, two realist philosophies dominate contractual thinking in practice. These are what we shall term 'market-individualism' and 'consumer-welfarism'.

Market-individualism has two limbs, a market philosophy and an individualistic philosophy. The market philosophy sees the function of the law of contract as the facilitation of competitive exchange. This demands clear contractual ground rules, transactional security and the accommodation of commercial practice. The individualistic side of market-individualism enshrines the landmark principles of 'freedom of contract' and 'sanctity of contract', the essential thrust of which is to give the parties the maximum licence in setting their own terms, and to hold parties to their freely made bargains. One particularly important entailment of market-individualism is that judges should offer no succour to parties who are simply trying to escape from a bad bargain, for the sum total of freely negotiated bargains is the good of society as a whole in that it results in an economically efficient use of resources.

The tenets of consumer-welfarism cannot be stated so crisply. In the most abstract terms, consumer-welfarism stands for reasonableness and fairness in contracting. More concretely, this is reflected in a policy of consumer-protection and a pot-pourri of specific principles. For example, consumer-welfarism holds that contracting parties should not mislead one another, that they should act in good faith, that a stronger party should not exploit the weakness of another's bargaining position, that no party should profit from his own wrong or be unjustly enriched, that remedies should be proportionate to the breach, that contracting parties who are at fault should not be able to dodge their responsibilities and so on. Crucially, consumer-welfarism subscribes to the paternalistic principle that contractors who enter into bad bargains may be relieved from their obligations where justice so requires.

These four categories are useful shorthand, and will be referred to elsewhere in this text – particularly market-individualism and consumer-welfarism.

1.5.3 Empirical research

Another way of analysing contract law is to look at the way in which it works, or does not work, in practice. Do those who make contracts actually use the law to assist them to make 'better' bargains, or to provide solutions when problems arise? This involves empirical research. Relatively little such work appears in the academic commentaries of contract, but one example is given here, drawn from the work of Yates on exclusion clauses.

Yates, D, *Exclusion Clauses in Contracts*, 2nd edn, 1982, London: Sweet & Maxwell, pp 18–33

A relatively small amount of empirical research has been carried out into the attitude of businessmen towards contractual procedures in their conduct of business affairs. In the U.S.A., Professor Macaulay carried out research among 48 companies and six law firms in Wisconsin. He described contract as involving 'two distinct elements: (a) rational planning of the transaction with careful provision for as many future contingencies as can be foreseen, and (b) the existence or use of actual or potential legal sanctions to induce performance of the exchange or to compensate for non-performance'. It is interesting that these two elements approximately correspond with Summers' private arranging and grievance remedial techniques. Macaulay identified four types of issue which might be planned for – description of the primary obligations, contingencies, defective performances and legal sanctions. Exclusion clauses, of course, may be key devices in planning for all of these. Macaulay concluded that while many business exchanges will involve a high degree of planning about each category, equally many at least 'reflect no planning or only a minimal amount of it, especially concerning legal sanctions and the effect of defective performance'. He found very little use was made of 'contractual practices' in the later adjustment of relationships, though there was some evidence of tacit reliance on contractual rights. Very little use was made of formal dispute-settlement procedures available through the courts.

The most important published research on the attitudes of British businessmen to the use of contractual practices is that carried out by Beale and Dugdale in Bristol during 1973 and 1974. Their conclusions were not dissimilar to Macaulay's. Businessmen tended to eschew contractual remedies as being too inflexible, and lawyers as being unsympathetic to the problems of businessmen. There was a similar reluctance to use the law in planning operations generally, save that if the risk justified it, there might be some careful planning, hard bargaining and detailed legal drafting.

The presence of an exclusion clause indicates either the presence of a risk which one party wishes to transfer to the other, or it indicates a very precise attempt to define the obligations the promisor is undertaking. There is a third possibility, in that the clause is intended to have simply a cosmetic effect, i.e. it is inserted by a party who is indifferent to the clause's efficacy at law, but who believes that its presence has a threatening or deterrent effect upon performance. Whenever a clause is used, however, and whatever its function, it indicates a high level of planning at some stage in the drafting process, and a close regard for the private arranging technique, at least in relation to certain parts of the legal framework for agreement.

An attempt has therefore been made, by means of questions directed towards businessmen, to ascertain first, when exclusion clauses will be drafted into agreements and why, and second, the circumstances in which they are relied upon during the grievance remedy procedures. For this purpose, a survey was conducted during the years 1974–1976 among three groups of business operations in the south west and north west regions of England, using Bristol and Manchester as bases. Fifty-one firms cooperated in the survey, 31 being light or heavy mechanical or civil engineering firms, 12 being finance companies and eight being insurance companies or Lloyd's brokers. Fourteen of the firms who were prepared to answer questions about their practices had their own legal departments. There was quite a significant difference in the attitude of non-lawyer businessmen towards lawyers in those firms with legal departments and those without. As one might expect, those firms who had their own 'in-house' lawyers had a far greater trust of a lawyer's ability to understand business problems, although as one executive in the aero-engine industry said: 'We trust our lawyers to get us out of a jam, but we don't trust them not to get us into one.' Curiously, in the engineering industry particularly, lawyers seemed to be consulted at a much earlier stage in discussions on company policy in those firms without their own legal departments than in those with 'in-house' lawyers. For example, one light engineering company, worried about possible patent infringement, consulted outside lawyers with a view to devising distribution contracts that might relieve them of liability in the event of unintentional infringement, even before the product had completed the design stage. An engine manufacturer with its own legal department, on the other hand, stated that they would not seek the advice of their legal colleagues until the engine reached production stage, and not necessarily then unless one of the lawyers raised it. The general and rather innocent view was that designers and engineers who worked for such large companies had to be trusted not to infringe patents.

The explanation of these differing attitudes to 'in-house' or outside law firms is probably as much to do with the nature of the company and its size as anything else. In-house lawyers tend to be fairly senior in the management hierarchy. They are likely to be known personally to managers who make the major executive decisions, they are viewed more as colleagues than as legal advisors, and that is almost certainly the major reason why greater trust is reposed in them as against outside firms. It is unlikely that judgments of legal competence enter very much into the assessment and, in any event, any such judgments are likely to be distorted by feelings of loyalty and attachment to the common employer. On the other hand, only large business enterprises (or insurance companies, who need not necessarily be large ones) can afford to maintain their own legal departments. In large firms the work is much more compartmentalised. Decisions are reached at departmental level and the development of a product tends to pass through several well-defined stages or departments, with little overlap between them. Interestingly, in those large firms that excluded their legal departments until a late stage in the process, marketing departments were also excluded: design, or research and development departments were given a much longer exclusive contact with the product. In smaller firms such departmentalisation tended not to occur. Often the managing director was personally and directly involved from an early stage, and he insisted upon early consultation with professional advisors, both financial and legal.

The types of businesses dealt with by the firms consulted fell into two very distinct groups. First were those businesses who dealt mainly with other businessmen and whose contracts were geared to what one might term 'commercial' operations, and secondly were those, mainly financial institutions, who dealt with the general public and whose operations were in the consumer market. …

3. Conclusions

It seemed to all those enterprises questioned that detailed contract planning (though not necessarily specially negotiated contracts) had an important place in commercial practice. However, in the non-consumer context, such planning is, generally speaking, aimed at producing commercially efficacious and legally enforceable contracts. It is by no means clear that this is the case in the consumer field. There the contract may have been equally carefully planned (at least, the 'original' of the standard form will have been), yet the legal enforceability of many of the terms will be almost irrelevant. The contract will be planned to have the greatest psychological impact on the average borrower, who will generally not be legally represented, will not be highly educated or well-off and will be intimidated by being faced with the contractual document. In this case efficacy is achieved through non-enforcement.

Perhaps because of what many will see as these less than wholly laudable reasons for recourse to planned exclusions and standard forms, those businesses consulted who dealt directly with the general public were less willing to discuss their justifications for adopting particular contractual practices than were those operating wholly in the commercial field. In the case of those large businesses questioned that operated from more than one factory or office, for instance, the use of standard form contracts was readily justified because they achieved a uniformity of dealing with all customers in accordance with a policy decided upon by head office. Certain issues could then be removed from future negotiation and branch managers and sales staff could not make concessions to customers by altering back-of-order terms without first consulting a departmental head. Also, businesses tended to feel that detailed planning and negotiation of contract terms was worth the time and cost in those cases where significant claims were likely to arise if something went wrong. The degree of injury in a case of default was especially significant and this factor, of course, cut both ways. For example, an airline or bus company is subject to claims from the survivors and dependants of those injured in an accident. Therefore, in buying aeroplanes or buses from the airframe manufacturers or coachbuilders, the airlines or bus companies insist upon carefully defined and legally enforceable obligations. But an aircraft or bus will usually be designed to operate with one and only one particular type of engine, so the aero or bus engine manufacturer has a virtual monopoly, at least so far as that particular design of aircraft or vehicle is concerned. What started as a buyers' market, therefore, with the airline or bus company, finishes with a sellers' market with the engine.

Such empirical research as there is tends to support the conclusions arrived at by Yates – that is, that the law of contract is of much less importance to business people than lawyers would like to think. See, for example, Macaulay, 1963, Beale and Dugdale, 1975, Lewis, 1982.

1.6 European contract law

There are certain aspects of contract law that have been the subject of laws emanating from the E.U. Examples included E.U. law dealing with distance selling, electronic contracts and unfair contract terms. The provisions of these instruments are noted at the appropriate point in subsequent chapters. Most of these instruments were incorporated into the law of England and Wales through statutes or statutory instruments. What impact will Brexit have on those statutes or statutory instruments? At an early stage the U.K. Government indicated that:

> the Great Repeal Bill ... [will] remove the European Communities Act 1972 from the statute book and *convert the 'acquis' – the body of existing E.U. law – into domestic law. This means that, wherever practical and appropriate, the same rules and laws will apply on the day after we leave the E.U. as they did before* ... This allows businesses to continue trading in the knowledge that the rules will not change significantly overnight and provides fairness to individuals whose rights and obligations will not be subject to sudden change. It will also be important for business in both the U.K. and the E.U. to have as much certainty as possible as early as possible ... Once we have left the E.U., Parliament (and, where appropriate, the devolved legislatures) will then be able to decide which elements of that law to keep, amend or repeal.
>
> *(HM Government,* The United Kingdom's exit from and new partnership with the European Union *((2017), Cm 9417) at 1.1ff (emphasis added)).*

Thereafter the European Union (Withdrawal) Act 2018, s 2(1) was to provide *inter alia*:

> E.U.-derived domestic legislation, as it has effect in domestic law immediately before exit day, continues to have effect in domestic law on and after exit day.

As is well known, in October 2019 the U.K. and E.U. agreed a revised Withdraw Agreement and Political Declaration (available at www.gov.uk/government/publications/new-withdrawal-agreement-and-political-declaration). This was agreed by Parliament under the European Union (Withdrawal Agreement) Act 2020, the preamble to which states it is: 'An Act to implement, and make other provision in connection with, the agreement between the United Kingdom and the E.U. under Article 50(2) of the Treaty on European Union which sets out the arrangements for the United Kingdom's withdrawal from the E.U.'

The European Union (Withdrawal Agreement) Act 2020 amended a number of aspects of the European Union (Withdrawal) Act 2018, including s 2 which will read:

> E.U.-derived domestic legislation, as it has effect in domestic law immediately before I.P. completion day, continues to have effect in domestic law on and after I.P. completion day [31 December 2020 at 11.00 p.m.].

The revised E.U.–U.K. Withdrawal Agreement (October 2019), European Union (Withdrawal) Act 2018 and the European Union (Withdrawal Agreement) Act 2020 combine to provide that:

- The European Communities Act 1972 is repealed subject to transitional provisions (see the European Union (Withdrawal) Act 2018, ss 1–1A);
- It recognises 'that the Parliament of the United Kingdom is sovereign' (see the European Union (Withdrawal Agreement) Act 2020, s 38);
- For a period of 4 years after the transition period, the U.K. may be brought before the Court of Justice of the European Union for breaches of E.U. law occurring before the end of the transition period (and sometimes for certain breaches occurring thereafter) (see E.U.–U.K. Withdrawal Agreement (October 2019), art 87);
- 'E.U.-derived domestic legislation, as it has effect in domestic law immediately before exit day, continues to have effect in domestic law on and after exit day' subject to certain qualifications (European Union (Withdrawal) Act 2018, s 1B);
- Provides for enhanced Parliamentary scrutiny of E.U. legislation made during the implementation period (European Union (Withdrawal) Act 2018, s 13A);
- '[T]he principle of the supremacy of E.U. law continues to apply on or after I.P. completion day so far as relevant to the interpretation, disapplication or quashing of any enactment or rule of law passed or made before I.P. completion day' (European Union (Withdrawal) Act 2018, s 5(2) as amended by the European Union (Withdrawal Agreement) Act 2020, s 25(4) (not yet fully in force at the time of writing));
- A court or tribunal is not bound by 'any principles laid down, or any decisions made, *on or after I.P. completion day* by the European Court' nor can it refer a matter to the European Court after that date (European Union (Withdrawal) Act 2018, s 6(1) as amended by the European Union (Withdrawal Agreement) Act 2020, s 26(1) (emphasis added));
- Nevertheless a court or tribunal '*may* have regard to anything done on or after I.P. completion day by the European Court, another E.U. entity or the E.U. so far as it is relevant' (European Union (Withdrawal) Act 2018, s 6(2) as amended by the European Union (Withdrawal Agreement) Act 2020, s 26(1) (emphasis added));
- As regards 'retained E.U. law', questions as to 'validity, meaning or effect' are to be decided '(a) in accordance with any retained case law and any retained general principles of E.U. law, and (b) having regard (among other things) to the limits, immediately before I.P. completion day, of E.U. competences' (European Union (Withdrawal) Act 2018, s 6(3) as amended by the European Union (Withdrawal Agreement) Act 2020, s 26(1));
- However the Supreme Court is not bound by 'retained E.U. case law' and in deciding whether or not to depart from such case law, the Supreme Court must apply the same tests as it would apply in deciding whether or not to depart from its own case law (European Union (Withdrawal) Act 2018, s 6(5));
- It is also possible for regulations to be introduced making provision for other courts or tribunals not to be bound by 'retained E.U. case law' (the European Union (Withdrawal Agreement) Act 2020, s 26(1)); and
- 'The principle of the supremacy of E.U. law does not apply to any enactment or rule of law passed or made on or after I.P. completion day' (the European Union (Withdrawal) Act 2018, s 5(1) as amended by the European Union (Withdrawal Agreement) Act 2020, s 25 (not yet fully in force at the time of writing)).

More difficult questions are whether or not the U.K. will (a) choose to retain existing E.U.-derived domestic law in the future, and (b) choose to continue to align with E.U. laws for trade purposes. In relation to (a), it seems unlikely that there would be a major reworking of E.U.-derived domestic law in the current area, especially given, for example, the immense work which went into the Consumer Rights Act 2015 (see Chapters 6 and 7). As regards (b), at one stage it seemed that there would also be a degree of future alignment:

> The U.K. and the E.U. would maintain a *common rulebook for goods including agri-food, with the U.K. making an upfront choice to commit by treaty to ongoing harmonisation with E.U. rules on goods, covering only those necessary to provide for frictionless trade at the border.* This common rulebook would be legislated for by the U.K. Parliament, as set out in detail in chapter 4.
>
> (*HM Government*, THE FUTURE RELATIONSHIP BETWEEN THE UNITED KINGDOM AND THE EUROPEAN UNION, *Cm 9593 (July 2018) at [11] (emphasis added)*)

However, more recently the U.K. Government has moved away from ideas of future alignment, although the extent to which, if at all, this is a negotiating tactic is unclear.

Additional reading

Beale, H. and Dugdale, T., 'Contracts between businessmen' (1975) 2 *Br J Law Soc* 45.
Campbell, C., Collins, H., and Wightman, J. (eds), *Implicit Dimensions of Contract* (Oxford: Hart Publishing, 2003).
Campbell, D. (ed), *The Relational Theory of Contract: Selected Works of Ian Macneil* (London: Sweet & Maxwell, 2001).
Collins, H., *Regulating Contracts* (Oxford: OUP, 1999).
Gilmore, G., *The Death of Contract* (Columbus: Ohio State University Press, 1974).
Ibrahim, S. and Stone, R., 'Harmonisation of European Contract Law Through an Optional Instrument: principles and practical implications' (2015) 24 *Nott LJ* 19.
Lewis, R., 'Contracts between businessmen: reform of the law of firm offers' (1982) 9 *Brit J Law & Society* 153.
Macaulay, S., 'Non-contractual relations in business' (1963) 28 *Am Sociological Rev* 35.
Mulcahy, L. and Wheeler, S., *Feminist Perspectives on Contract Law* (London: Glasshouse Press, 2005).
Robertson, A. (ed), *The Law of Obligations: Connections and Boundaries* (London: UCL Press, 2004).
Smith, S., *Contract Theory* (Oxford: Clarendon Press, 2004).
Smith, S., *Atiyah's Introduction to the Law of Contract* (6th edn, Oxford: Clarendon Press, 2006).

Chapter 2

Forming the agreement

Chapter contents

2.1 Introduction

An agreement is central to the law of contract in England and Wales. In most cases that are adjudicated by the courts, the courts regard themselves as giving effect to an agreement reached between the parties. The question of whether or not there is a sufficient agreement is, therefore, a crucial one. The agreement must also be intended to be legally binding, and this aspect is considered in detail in Chapter 3. The focus in this chapter is on the mechanisms that the courts use to decide whether an agreement has been reached. One issue relates to formalities (e.g. writing): to what extent does English law use formal mechanisms to decide whether an agreement has been reached? Sometimes statutes require formality in relation to a particular type of contract. In many cases, however, formality is not required and the law will look at more informal evidence of agreement. More specifically, courts decide whether an agreement has been reached by taking an 'objective' approach, looking at what the parties have said or done as indicators of their state of mind. The identification of a matching offer and acceptance is the most common way for the courts to find that an agreement has been made. An offer must be distinguished from an invitation to treat, and an acceptance from a counter-offer. The time and place of acceptance can cause particular problems when parties are contracting at a distance. Special rules apply to posted acceptances, as opposed to those communicated by telephone or electronically. The chapter concludes by considering the ways in which an offer is revoked, and when it will lapse if not accepted.

2.2 Forming an agreement

There are a number of possibilities as to the way in which it could be decided if the parties have reached an agreement. The courts could look for formal signs (for example, a signed written document), or particular forms of words, or simply any extrinsic evidence of an intention to make an agreement – in a sense, a 'meeting of the minds'. As will be seen, the law in England and Wales makes use of a variety of approaches. It is important to note from the outset, however, that formality is by no means an essential requirement for most contracts. Many everyday contracts – for example, purchases from a shop – are made purely orally and with no documentation in writing. It is possible for very large contracts, involving substantial sums of money, to be made in such an informal way, though in practice most large organisations will want to contract on the basis of terms that are set out in writing. It is only in a relatively small number of situations that the law of England and Wales actually imposes on the parties a requirement of formality, and will hold the agreement unenforceable unless it follows these requirements.

2.2.1 Formalities

One way of conclusively demonstrating an agreement is to put it into the form of a 'deed'. The requirements for a valid deed are largely set out in the Law of Property (Miscellaneous Provisions) Act 1989:

1. – *Deeds and their execution*

(1) Any rule of law which –
- (a) restricts the substances on which a deed may be written;
- (b) requires a seal for the valid execution of an instrument as a deed by an individual; or
- (c) requires authority by one person to another to deliver an instrument as a deed on his behalf to be given by deed, is abolished.

(2) An instrument shall not be a deed unless –
  (a) it makes it clear on its face that it is intended to be a deed by the person making it or, as the case may be, by the parties to it (whether by describing itself as a deed or expressing itself to be executed or signed as a deed or otherwise); and
  (b) it is validly executed as a deed
    (i) by that person or a person authorised to execute it in the name or on behalf of that person, or
    (ii) by one or more of those parties or a person authorised to execute it in the name or on behalf of one or more of those parties.

(2A) For the purposes of subsection (2)(a) above, an instrument shall not be taken to make it clear on its face that it is intended to be a deed merely because it is executed under seal.

(3) An instrument is validly executed as a deed by an individual if, and only if –
  (a) it is signed –
    (i) by him in the presence of a witness who attests the signature; or
    (ii) at his direction and in his presence and the presence of two witnesses who each attest the signature; and
  (b) it is delivered as a deed.

(4) In subsections (2) and (3) above 'sign', in relation to an instrument, includes
  (a) an individual signing the name of the person or party on whose behalf he executes the instrument; and
  (b) making one's mark on the instrument, and 'signature' is to be construed accordingly.

(4A) Subsection (3) above applies in the case of an instrument executed by an individual in the name or on behalf of another person whether or not that person is also an individual.

Any contract can be put into a deed. However, a deed must be used in a relation to a lease of land for more than three years, as required by ss 52 and 54(2) of the Law of Property Act 1925.

Other contracts dealing with interests in land do not have to be in the form of a deed, but must be in writing, by virtue of s 2(1) of the Law of Property (Miscellaneous Provisions) Act 1989:

s 2 Contracts for sale etc. of land to be made by signed writing

(1) A contract for the sale or other disposition of an interest in land can only be made in writing and only by incorporating all the terms which the parties have expressly agreed in one document or, where contracts are exchanged, in each.

(2) The terms may be incorporated in a document either by being set out in it or by reference to some other document.

(3) The document incorporating the terms or, where contracts are exchanged, one of the documents incorporating them (but not necessarily the same one) must be signed by or on behalf of each party to the contract....

(5) This section does not apply in relation to –
  (a) a contract to grant such a lease as is mentioned in section 54(2) of the Law of Property Act 1925 (short leases);
  (b) a contract made in the course of a public auction; ...

(7) Nothing in this section shall apply in relation to contracts made before this section comes into force.

(8) Section 40 of the Law of Property Act 1925 (which is superseded by this section) shall cease to have effect.

Note that in *Neocleous v Rees* [2019] EWHC 2462 (Ch) the court held that an automatically generated email footer could amount to a signature for the purposes of the Law of Property (Miscellaneous Provisions) Act 1989.

There are also requirements of writing in relation to certain consumer credit agreements, by virtue of the Consumer Credit Act 1974.

CONSUMER CREDIT ACT 1974

s 61 Signing of agreement

(1) A regulated agreement is not properly executed unless –
   (a) a document in the prescribed form itself containing all the prescribed terms and conforming to regulations under section 60(1) is signed in the prescribed manner both by the debtor or hirer and by or on behalf of the creditor or owner, and
   (b) the document embodies all the terms of the agreement, other than implied terms, and
   (c) the document is, when presented or sent to the debtor or hirer for signature, in such a state that all its terms are readily legible.

Finally, one of the oldest statutes still in force in relation to English contract law, the Statute of Frauds 1677, imposes a requirement of writing in relation to an agreement to guarantee a third party's debts:

> no action shall be brought ... whereby to charge the defendant upon any special promise to answer for the debt, default or miscarriages of another person ... unless the agreement upon which such action shall be brought, or some memorandum or note thereof, shall be in writing, and signed by the party to be charged therewith, or some other person thereunto by him lawfully authorised.

The continuing practical importance of this provision was confirmed by the following decision of the House of Lords:

Actionstrength Ltd v International Glass Engineering [2003] UKHL 17; [2003] 2 AC 541

Facts: The claimant had a contract to supply labour with the first defendant. Concerns about late payment led, according to the claimant, to an agreement with the second defendant, as a result of which the claimant continued with the work, in return for the second defendant promising, if necessary, to pay the claimant directly out of money owed by the second defendant to the first defendant. This agreement was oral. The claimant subsequently tried to sue the second defendant on its promise. The second defendant denied that any promise had been made, but argued that in any case, the agreement was a guarantee falling within s 4 of the Statute of Frauds 1677, and was therefore not enforceable, because it was not in writing. The claimant alleged that by persuading the claimant to carry on with the work, the second defendant was estopped from relying on the Statute. The trial judge held, on a preliminary issue, that the claimant might be able to succeed. The Court of Appeal held that the agreement was a guarantee, and that the second defendant could not be estopped from relying on the Statute of Frauds.

Held: The House of Lords confirmed the decision of the Court of Appeal.

Lord Hoffmann: ...

15. This is a fairly common dispute over who said what; in the ordinary way it would have been resolved by a judge hearing the witnesses and deciding which of them he believed. But St-Gobain [the second defendant] says that a hearing is unnecessary because, even if Actionstrength's [the claimant's] version were to be accepted, the promise would be unenforceable by virtue of section 4 of the Statute of Frauds 1677 ...

16. So St-Gobain applied for summary judgment on the ground that the action had no real prospect of success (CPR r 24.2). The application was refused by Mitting J on the ground that it was arguable that St-Gobain's promise was not 'to answer for the debt ... of another person' and therefore outside the statute. But the Court of Appeal held that it plainly was and this finding has not been challenged in your Lordships' House. Instead, Mr McGhee for Actionstrength submits that St-Gobain should not be allowed to rely on the Statute because, on the facts as alleged, and which must for present purposes be assumed to be true, it would be unconscionable for St-Gobain not to keep its promise.

17. This argument received short shrift in the Court of Appeal. Simon Brown LJ said [2002] 1 WLR 566, 576–577 that it was 'quite hopeless' and dismissed it in one paragraph. The other members of the court had nothing to add.

18. If one assumes that a judge would find that Actionstrength's version of events was right, to hold the promise unenforceable would certainly appear unfair. Actionstrength would have supplied Inglen with services which were indirectly for the benefit of St-Gobain, because they enabled Inglen to perform the main contract, in reliance on St-Gobain's promise to pay for them. Morally, there would be no excuse for St-Gobain not keeping its promise. On the other hand, if one assumes that a judge would find that St-Gobain's version was right, the Statute enables it to dispose summarily of proceedings which should never have been brought.

19. In an application for summary judgment such as this, which is in the nature of a demurrer, one has to assume that Actionstrength's version is true. And that naturally inclines one to try to find some way in which the putative injustice can be avoided. It is, however, important to bear in mind that the purpose of the Statute was precisely to avoid the need to decide which side was telling the truth about whether or not an oral promise had been made and exactly what had been promised. Parliament decided that there had been too many cases in which the wrong side had been believed. Hence the title, 'An Act for prevention of frauds and perjuries.' It is quite true, as Mr McGhee said, that the system of civil procedure in 1677 was not very well adapted to discovering the truth. For one thing, the parties to the action were not competent witnesses. But the question of whether the Act should be preserved in its application to guarantees was considered in 1953 by the Law Reform Committee (First Report, Statute of Frauds and Section 4 of the Sale of Goods Act 1893 (Cmd 8809)) and the recommendation of a very strong committee was to keep it.

20. The terms of the Statute therefore show that Parliament, although obviously conscious that it would allow some people to break their promises, thought that this injustice was outweighed by the need to protect people from being held liable on the basis of oral utterances which were ill-considered, ambiguous or completely fictitious. This means that while normally one would approach the construction of a statute on the basis that Parliament was unlikely to have intended to cause injustice by allowing people to break promises which had been relied upon, no such assumption can be made about the Statute. Although the scope of the Statute must be tested on the assumption that the facts alleged by Actionstrength are true, it must not be construed in a way which would undermine its purpose.

21. It its original form, section 4 of the 1677 Act also applied to sales of land ...

22. Very soon after the Statute of 1677, the courts introduced the doctrine of part performance to restrict its application to sales of land. It was held that a contract, initially unenforceable because of the statute, could become enforceable by virtue of acts which the plaintiff did afterwards. The doctrine was justified by a combination of two reasons. The first was a form of estoppel; as Lord Reid said in *Steadman v Steadman* [1976] AC 536, 540:

> 'If one party to an agreement stands by and lets the other party incur expense or prejudice his position on the faith of the agreement being valid he will not then be allowed to turn round and assert that the agreement is unenforceable'.
>
> ...

25. What Mr McGhee submits in this case is that the estoppel principle which partly underpins the doctrine of part performance is wide enough to be applied to contracts of guarantee. On the facts presently alleged, it is also the case that, in Lord Reid's words, St-Gobain stood by and let Actionstrength prejudice its position, by extending credit to Inglen, on the faith of the guarantee being valid. There is authority for saying that estoppel is a principle of broad, not to say protean, application: see, for example *Taylor Fashions Ltd v Liverpool Victoria Trustees Co Ltd (Note)* [1982] QB 133. Although he cited no case in any jurisdiction in which estoppel had been applied to avoid the application of the Statute to a guarantee, Mr McGhee says that there is no argument of principle against it.

26. The difficulty which faces this submission is that while the nature of a sale of land is such that the contract and part performance can co-exist in their respective domains, no such co-existence is possible between the Statute and the estoppel for which Mr McGhee contends. It is in the nature of a contract of guarantee that the party seeking to enforce it will always have performed first. Unless he has advanced credit or forborne from withdrawing credit, there will be no guaranteed debt for which he can sue. It will always be the case that the creditor will have acted to his prejudice on the faith of the guarantor's promise. To admit an estoppel on these grounds would be to repeal the Statute. ...

29. It is not necessary to consider whether circumstances may arise in which a guarantor may be estopped from relying upon the Statute. It is sufficient that in my opinion the estoppel which Actionstrength seeks to rely upon in this case would be inconsistent with the provisions of the Statute. I would therefore dismiss the appeal.

The result is that an agreement to guarantee a third-party's debts remains one of the exceptional situations where a contract needs to be in writing to be enforceable.

In relation to electronic signatures, the Law Commission (*Electronic Execution of Documents* (Law Com No 386 (2019)) recently provided the following statements of the law (at 2–3):

STATEMENT OF THE LAW: EXECUTION WITH AN ELECTRONIC SIGNATURE

(1) An electronic signature is capable in law of being used to execute a document (including a deed) provided that (i) the person signing the document intends to authenticate the document and (ii) any formalities relating to execution of that document are satisfied.

(2) Such formalities may be required under a statute or statutory instrument, or may be laid down in a contract or other private law instrument under which a document is to be executed. The following are examples of formalities that might be required: (i) that the signature be witnessed; or (ii) that the signature be in a specified form (such as being handwritten).

(3) An electronic signature is admissible in evidence in legal proceedings. It is admissible, for example, to prove or disprove the identity of a signatory and/or the signatory's intention to authenticate the document.

(4) Save where the contrary is provided for in relevant legislation or contractual arrangements, or where case law specific to the document in question leads to a contrary conclusion, the common law adopts a pragmatic approach and does not prescribe any particular form or type of signature. In determining whether the method of signature adopted demonstrates an authenticating intention the courts adopt an objective approach considering all of the surrounding circumstances.

(5) The Courts have, for example, held that the following non-electronic forms amount to valid signatures:
   (a) signing with an 'X';
   (b) signing with initials only;
   (c) using a stamp of a handwritten signature;
   (d) printing of a name;
   (e) signing with a mark, even where the party executing the mark can write; and
   (f) a description of the signatory if sufficiently unambiguous, such as 'Your loving mother' or 'Servant to Mr Sperling'.

(6) Electronic equivalents of these non-electronic forms of signature are likely to be recognised by a court as legally valid. There is no reason in principle to think otherwise.

(7) The courts have, for example, held that the following electronic forms amount to valid signatures in the case of statutory obligations to provide a signature where the statute is silent as to whether an electronic signature is acceptable:
   (a) a name typed at the bottom of an email;
   (b) clicking an 'I accept' tick box on a website; and
   (c) the header of a SWIFT message.

(8) Our view is that the requirement under the current law that a deed must be signed 'in the presence of a witness' requires the physical presence of that witness. This is the case even where both the person executing the deed and the witness are executing/attesting the document using an electronic signature.

However, the Law Commission did make suggestions surrounding deeds (at 112):

> A future review of the law of deeds should include:
>
> (1) consideration of whether the witnessing and attestation requirement of deeds executed electronically should be replaced with an approach based on a specific type of technology, such as Public Key Infrastructure;
>
> (2) consideration of the potential for the introduction of a concept of acknowledgement, for both paper and electronic deeds;
>
> (3) an examination of the statutory requirement for delivery, including a consideration of whether it should be amended or removed, for both paper and electronic deeds;
>
> (4) further consideration of whether the implications of Mercury should be codified, for both paper and electronic deeds;
>
> (5) consideration of whether there should be different requirements for deeds executed in a commercial context and those executed by individuals; and
>
> (6) consideration of whether deeds should be abolished or limited to certain types of documents.

2.2.2 The objective approach to agreement

When the courts are determining whether or not an agreement has been reached, they adopt an objective approach (which focuses on what the parties *appeared* to a reasonable person to have intended), rather than a subjective approach (which would focus on what the parties *actually* intended in their mind, regardless of appearances). Of course, on the facts, there may be no difference between the parties' actual (subjective) intention and their apparent (objective) intention, but if there is a difference, the law usually favours the objective intention. One possible justification for the objective approach is a pragmatic one: there are obvious difficulties with ascertaining parties' actual minds. With the objective approach, the court focuses on what was said and done at the time of the alleged agreement as being evidence of what the parties intended. This does not answer all questions, however, since there are different types of 'objectivity'.

Howarth, W, 'The meaning of objectivity in contract' (1984) 100 *LQR* 265, pp 265–266, 279–281

1. Introduction

A 'general if not universal principle of our law of contract' is that English law adopts an objective test of agreement in matters of contract formation. Indeed, given the overwhelming consensus regarding the need for objectivity in judging contract formation it might be thought that a plea for greater precision in this area can only be regarded as quibbling. Objectivity having been given the universal endorsement of academics and practitioners alike, one might be forgiven for thinking that little in the law of contract could be more certain. What is not so clear however, is the precise *meaning* that should be given to the undisputed requirement of objectivity. A closer examination of the concept of objectivity in this paper will attempt to draw out the different senses in which that concept is capable of being understood and highlight the range of crucially difficult issues which appeals to objectivity commonly neglect.

In order to appreciate the difficulties left unsolved by general appeals to objectivity it is necessary to look at the different perspectives on a situation where contract formation is in contention, and to see the differences between viewpoints which may be claimed to be in some sense 'objective'. Consider the following situation. P (the promisee) enters into an apparent agreement with D (the promisor). P believes (subjectively) that the agreement has been concluded on terms A. D believes (subjectively) that the terms of the contract are B (where A and B are materially different in some contentious respect). The reasonable man taking an objective view of the situation from the position of P would conclude that the terms of the contract were C, but placed in the position of D he would conclude that they were E (where, once again, C and E are different in point of substance and different to either A or B). Finally, if the objective observer were to be placed 'above' the parties in a position where he could take an over-view of the proceedings which was independent of either a reasonable P or a reasonable D, he might conclude that the terms of the contract were actually F (again different to the other conclusions). Doubtless actual cases would never raise all of these complications from a single set of facts, but nonetheless the discrepancies of perspective that are illustrated remain logical possibilities, the existence of any two of which may raise problems for objectivity. Although in most situations the first two perspectives postulated (i.e. promisee subjectivity and promisor subjectivity) can be discounted, there remain three 'objective' options: promisor objectivity, promisee objectivity and detached objectivity. Choosing a preferable version of objectivity from amongst these three presents no small problem of evaluation. None can be initially ruled out as a non-starter on ground of logical incoherence since each is equally objective within its own frame of reference. The important preference lies simply in the choice of perspective which is adopted. On this question of perspective … the problem is compounded by the fact that each of the possibilities seems to enjoy an amount at least, of persuasive support.

5. Conclusion

Having outlined the possibilities and seen that none are necessarily wrong or even internally inconsistent, a choice between these mutually incompatible versions of objectivity remains to be made. The final question that must be asked is, on what ground must preference be based? The answer to this type of inquiry must ultimately fall back upon the higher objectives behind a theory of the law of contract, and the balance of competing purposes which that body of law is designed to achieve. Here the existence of disparity amongst legal values according to the social, economic and political systems in which they arise has been convincingly argued. The remaining task is to relate the versions of objectivity which have been outlined to the polarity between liberal-abstentionist and corporate-interventionist models of legal regulation in modern societies.

On the liberal model the function of a law regarding objectivity in contract formation is to give effect to the intention of the parties and enforce *their* agreements, rather than the court imposing agreement upon them 'from above'. Having started from the premise that objectivity is necessary however, the laissez-faire theorist would wish to limit its effect to a minimum, and it is consistent with this position to adopt either promisor objectivity or promisee objectivity. Both of these perspectives provide a rationale for resolving disputes between the subjective views actually held by the parties whilst doing the minimum damage to the ideal of freedom of contract. They place the greatest possible restraint upon judges (to prevent them 'making agreements' for the parties) which is compatible with the use of objectivity to resolve this kind of dispute. The dilemma confronting the abstentionist however is that he has no reason for preference between the two alternatives open to him. The choice between taking the perspective of a reasonable promisor or a reasonable promisee is a choice between equal degrees of abstention, or put the other way around, equally respectful positions regarding the agreement made by the parties. It is perhaps for this reason that the liberal theory and practice of the law of contract in the courts has, it is suggested, never reached a clearly articulated resolution between these two positions.

On the other side of things, detached objectivity appears to provide greater scope to the judiciary to rule against the actual intentions of the parties on the ground that an objective overview may differ from the actual or reasonable perspective that either the promisor or promisee might have of the situation. The position holds greater scope for judicial intervention and the imposition of agreements upon parties contrary to their intentions. Clearly this is a consequence which has ostensibly been resisted by the courts who with some notable exceptions, have often reaffirmed their reluctance to do more than give effect to what the parties themselves have agreed. The principal judicial line is the stricter abstentionist test for contract formation and, rather than venture beyond this, the judicial tendency has been to find extra-contractual remedies for worthy plaintiffs. Nonetheless the position of detached objectivity and concomitant judicial interventionalism is not without academic support. Atiyah, in his *Introduction to the Law of Contract,* includes a chapter entitled 'Contracts made by the Courts', which provides a number of illustrations of cases where courts have imposed agreements upon the parties in circumstances where they regarded it as just to do so. If his contention that, 'the law of contract has nearly always had room for cases of this character', or alternatively, that the law of contract is presently developing in that direction, is correct, then it would seem that detached objectivity is, or may become, the better theoretical perspective to describe the way that judges approach difficult problems of contract formation.

The dilemma is a compound one. If the courts wish to cling to the liberal values which they have so often espoused in the past then they must clarify what rule of law follows from those values and in so doing choose between two equally acceptable (if imperfect) alternatives: the perspective of the reasonable promisor *or* the perspective of the reasonable promisee. Otherwise the admission must be made that objectivity may involve the imposition of contractual relations upon the parties independently of what either might reasonably be understood to have intended. This is arguably a new departure from previously announced practice but, as we have seen, a departure for which there may be both good reasons of principle and a line of authoritative support as rational as any other open to the courts. What is certain however, and it is hoped that this paper has shown, is that an appeal to objectivity without clarification is to place a cloak over a range of crucial problems in contract formation which lurk underneath the plausibly precise term 'objective', and, in a body of law in principle knowable to all, ought to be articulated and resolved rather than concealed from view.

The application of an 'objective' approach, whether from the perspective of a promisor, a promisee or a third party, means that the courts are looking for the external signs of agreement. Where the courts are trying to decide whether the behaviour of the parties, viewed objectively, indicates that they intended to make a contract, they look primarily for evidence of a matching 'offer' and 'acceptance'.

2.2.3 Offer

An 'offer' is an indication of a firm intention to contract on specified terms. It must be distinguished from a mere invitation to enter into negotiations. The difficulty in drawing this distinction is indicated in a number of cases.

***Gibson v Manchester City Council* [1979] 1 WLR 294 (HL)**

Facts: Mr Gibson had been in correspondence with Manchester City Council about the possible purchase of his council house. The Council changed from Conservative to Labour control and the sale of council houses was stopped. Mr Gibson alleged that he already had a binding contract, based on his correspondence with the Council, for the purchase of his house. The trial judge and Court of Appeal held in favour of Mr Gibson. The Council appealed to the House of Lords.

Held: The House of Lords held that the Council had not made a definite offer to sell the house to Mr Gibson – its communications had not got past the stage of the 'invitation to treat'.

Lord Diplock: My Lords, this is an action for specific performance of what is claimed to be a contract for the sale of land. The only question in the appeal is of a kind with which the courts are very familiar. It is whether in the correspondence between the parties there can be found a legally enforceable contract for the sale by the Manchester Corporation to Mr Gibson of the dwelling-house of which he was the occupying tenant at the relevant time in 1971. That question is one that, in my view, can be answered by applying to the particular documents relied on by Mr Gibson as constituting the contract, well settled, indeed elementary, principles of English law ....

The genesis of the relevant negotiations in the instant case is a form filled in by Mr Gibson on 28th November 1970 enquiring what would be the price of buying his council house at 174 Charlestown Road, Blackley, and expressing his interest in obtaining a mortgage from the council. The form was a detachable part of a brochure which had been circulated by the council to tenants who had previously expressed an interest in buying their houses. It contained details of a new scheme for selling council houses that had been recently adopted by the council. The scheme provided for a sale at market value less a discount dependent on the length of time the purchaser had been a council tenant. This, in the case of Mr Gibson, would have amounted to 20%. The scheme also provided for the provision by the council of advances on mortgage which might amount to as much as the whole of the purchase price.

As a result of that enquiry Mr Gibson's house was inspected by the council's valuer and on 10th February 1971 the letter which is relied on by Mr Gibson as the offer by the council to sell the house to him was sent from the city treasurer's department. It was in the following terms:

> Dear Sir,
> Purchase of Council House
> Your Reference Number 82463 03
> I refer to your request for details of the cost of buying your Council house. *The Corporation may be prepared to sell the house to you at the purchase price of £2,725 less 20% = £2,180 (freehold).*

Maximum mortgage the Corporation may grant:	£2,177 repayable over 20 years.
Annual fire insurance premium:	£2.45
Monthly Repayment charge calculated by: –	
(i) flat rate repayment method:	£19.02

> If you wish to pay off some of the purchase price at the start and therefore require a mortgage for less than the amount quoted above, the monthly instalment will change; in these circumstances, I will supply new figures on request. The above repayment figures apply so long as the interest rate charged on

home loans is 8%. The interest rate will be subject to variation by the Corporation after giving not less than three months' written notice, and if it changes, there will be an adjustment to the monthly instalment payable. This letter should not be regarded as firm offer of a mortgage.

If you would like to make formal application to buy your Council house, please complete the enclosed application form and return it to me as soon as possible.
Yours faithfully,
(Sgd) H. R. Page
City Treasurer
Mr Robert Gibson.

My Lords, the words I have italicised seem to me, as they seemed to Geoffrey Lane LJ [in the Court of Appeal], to make it quite impossible to construe this letter as a contractual offer capable of being converted into a legally enforceable open contract for the sale of land by Mr Gibson's written acceptance of it. The words 'may be prepared to sell' are fatal to this; so is the invitation, not, be it noted, to accept the offer, but 'to make formal application to buy' on the enclosed application form. It is, to quote Geoffrey Lane LJ, a letter setting out the financial terms on which it may be the council would be prepared to consider a sale and purchase in due course.

Edmund-Davies, Russell, Fraser and Keith LJJ. concurred.

In effect, Lord Diplock analysed the letter from the Council as simply an invitation to Mr Gibson to make an offer to buy the house – an 'invitation to treat' (though Lord Diplock never uses that phrase). In coming to this decision, Lord Diplock noted that in the Court of Appeal Lord Denning had rejected the need to identify a specific offer and acceptance in favour of looking at the correspondence as a whole and the conduct of the parties in order to decide if they have come to an agreement. Lord Diplock accepted that there may be 'exceptional' contracts which do not easily fit an 'offer and acceptance' analysis, but said that a contract alleged to have been made by an exchange of correspondence was not one of these. He did not specify what the exceptional cases might be but we shall later in this chapter see some examples where the 'offer and acceptance' approach has been stretched or departed from.

2.2.3.1 Shop sales

Does the display of goods on a shelf in a supermarket or a shop window indicate that the goods are being 'offered' for sale? In everyday speech we would generally say so, but the law takes a different view, as is shown in the following:

***Pharmaceutical Society of Great Britain v Boots Cash Chemists* [1953] 1 QB 401**

Facts: This case involved a criminal prosecution of Boots for selling certain medicines without the supervision of a pharmacist, contrary to the Pharmacy and Poisons Act 1933. The drugs were selected by the customer from the shelf and then paid for at a cash desk, where a pharmacist was able to supervise. The question was whether offer and acceptance (and therefore the contract between the customer and the shop) took place when the goods were selected, or when they were paid for at the till. At trial, the Lord Chief Justice held that the latter was the case, so that no offence was committed. The prosecutor appealed.

Held: The Court of Appeal held that the display of goods did not constitute an offer. The contract was made at the cash desk, where there was supervision by a pharmacist, and so met the requirements of the Pharmacy and Poisons Act 1933.

Somervell LJ: This is an appeal from a decision of the Lord Chief Justice on an agreed statement of facts, raising a question under section 18(1)(a)(iii) of the Pharmacy and Poisons Act 1933. The plaintiffs are the Pharmaceutical Society, incorporated by Royal Charter. One of their duties is to take all reasonable steps to enforce the provisions of the Act. The provision in question is contained in section 18. [His Lordship read the section and stated the facts, and continued:] It is not disputed that in a chemist's shop where this self-service system does not prevail a customer may go in and ask a young woman assistant, who will not herself be a registered pharmacist, for one of these articles on the list, and the transaction may be completed and the article paid for, although the registered pharmacist, who will no doubt be on the premises, will not know anything himself of the transaction, unless the assistant serving the customer, or the customer, requires to put a question to him. It is right that I should emphasize, as did the Lord Chief Justice, that these are not dangerous drugs. They are substances which contain very small proportions of poison, and I imagine that many of them are the type of drug which has a warning as to what doses are to be taken. They are drugs which can be obtained, under the law, without a doctor's prescription. The point taken by the plaintiffs is this: it is said that the purchase is complete if and when a customer going round the shelves takes an article and puts it in the receptacle which he or she is carrying, and that therefore, if that is right, when the customer comes to the pay desk, having completed the tour of the premises, the registered pharmacist, if so minded, has no power to say: 'This drug ought not to be sold to this customer'. Whether and in what circumstances he would have that power we need not inquire, but one can, of course, see that there is a difference if supervision can only be exercised at a time when the contract is completed.

I agree with the Lord Chief Justice in everything that he said, but I will put the matter shortly in my own words. Whether the view contended for by the plaintiffs is a right view depends on what are the legal implications of this layout – the invitation to the customer. Is a contract to be regarded as being completed when the article is put into the receptacle, or is this to be regarded as a more organized way of doing what is done already in many types of shops – and a bookseller is perhaps the best example – namely, enabling customers to have free access to what is in the shop, to look at the different articles, and then, ultimately, having got the ones which they wish to buy, to come up to the assistant saying 'I want this'? The assistant in 999 times out of 1,000 says 'That is all right', and the money passes and the transaction is completed. I agree with what the Lord Chief Justice has said, and with the reasons which he has given for his conclusion, that in the case of an ordinary shop, although goods are displayed and it is intended that customers should go and choose what they want, the contract is not completed until the customer having indicated the articles which he needs, the shop-keeper, or someone on his behalf, accepts that offer. Then the contract is completed. I can see no reason at all, that being clearly the normal position, for drawing any different implication as a result of this layout.

The Lord Chief Justice, I think, expressed one of the most formidable difficulties in the way of the plaintiffs' contention when he pointed out that, if the plaintiffs are right, once an article has been placed in the receptacle the customer himself is bound and would have no right, without paying for the first article, to substitute an article which he saw later of a similar kind and which he perhaps preferred. I can see no reason for implying from this self-service arrangement any implication other than that which the Lord Chief Justice found in it, namely, that it is a convenient method of enabling customers to see what there is and choose, and possibly put back and substitute, articles which they wish to have, and then to go up to the cashier and offer to buy what they have so far chosen. On that conclusion the case fails, because it is admitted that there was supervision in the sense required by the Act and at the appropriate moment of time. For these reasons, in my opinion, the appeal should be dismissed.

Birkett and Romer L.JJ. concurred.

In the following extract, Collins analyses various reasons why it may be appropriate to delay the formation of a contract in a self-service shop and also raises the question of why the Pharmaceutical Society was so concerned as to argue against this approach.

Collins, H, *The Law of Contract*, 2003, 4th edn, London: Lexis-Nexis, pp 171–173

Instrumentalism

Even where the traditional rules of offer and acceptance are applied, it is apparent ... that the facts do not conveniently label themselves as 'offers' and 'acceptances'. On the contrary, a hidden element of discretion permits the courts to label the facts with the terminology of offer and acceptance, whenever they believe it is fair and reasonable to impose contractual liability.

Consider, for example, the purchase of goods in a self-service store. At what point is an agreement completed by an acceptance? Does the customer accept the offer when he or she places the goods in the wire basket? Or does acceptance take place when the customers present the goods to the assistant at the cash register? Alternatively, we can even argue that the assistant accepts the offer to buy by ringing up the prices of the goods on the cash register. Or is that merely an offer, accepted by the customer by the presentation of the right amount of money? Since each interpretation is plausible, a court must make a discretionary choice between them, concealing the real grounds for the decision by the formalist reasoning of offer and acceptance. In this brief section we cannot hope to identify all the relevant considerations which a court takes into account. Instead we will illustrate the surprising variety of such considerations in order to reveal the complexity of the issues.

The variety of potentially relevant considerations emerges with a brief review of conflicting decisions from different jurisdictions concerning the moment of formation of a contract of sale in a self-service store. Sometimes the courts desire to make the moment of responsibility as late as possible, in order to avoid making the customer liable to pay for the goods before he or she has had a chance to inspect them and compare the price between different brands. Courts encourage this consumer circumspection by holding that the customer forms the contract by presenting the goods at the cash register. In contrast, in other cases courts insist that the parties enter a contract when the customer places the goods in the wire basket, if for instance this result strengthens the legal position of a customer injured by a bottle exploding as it is placed in the basket. The relative advantage to a customer of being allowed a contractual claim against the shopkeeper for personal injuries depends upon the state of the law of tort governing the liability of owners of premises towards those injured upon them, so courts in different jurisdictions react in the light of the background law applicable to personal injuries.

Another reason for deferring the moment of acceptance emerges in cases involving charges of shoplifting. If the customer completes the contract when he or she removes goods from the shelf, the shoplifter could defend himself or herself against a charge of theft by arguing that he or she had purchased the goods before taking them from the store. Of course, the shoplifter would in these circumstances be liable to pay the price of the goods, and might also be guilty of another criminal offence involving fraud. But the shoplifter would avoid liability for theft if the contract is formed by taking the goods from the shelf, for logically one cannot steal goods which belong to oneself as a result of a contractual purchase. For this reason, the court is likely to defer the moment of formation of the contract until the goods have been paid for.

These conflicting considerations which influence the determination of the moment of contractual responsibility in a simple case of supermarket purchases explain why courts reach such different results. They also illustrate how difficult it is to anticipate all the relevant considerations. Further complications are introduced in the leading English case, which illustrates how special statutory provisions give added legal significance to a particular result. In *Pharmaceutical Society of Great Britain v Boots Cash Chemists*, the self-service store was required to demonstrate that it satisfied a statutory requirement that all sales of certain non-prescription drugs should be made under the supervision of a registered pharmacist. The store argued that it complied with the statute by posting a pharmacist in the vicinity of the cash register, as opposed to stationing one near all the display shelves. The Court of Appeal facilitated the development of self-service pharmacies, and incidentally reduced the need for registered pharmacists whose professional body had commenced the action, by concluding that customers made contracts of sale at the cash register and therefore the store complied with the law. The reason given by the court for its decision was simply one of permitting customers to inspect the goods and change their minds in the shop. But one wonders also how impressed the court was by the desire of the pharmacists to retain their restrictive practices, although this consideration was not explicitly acknowledged.

The *Boots* case deals with the position where the goods are on display inside the shop. What about the display of goods in a shop window? If, for example, goods are displayed at a particular price, is this an offer that a customer can accept simply by going into the shop and asking for the goods? This issue has also been addressed in a number of criminal cases, a good example of which is *Fisher v Bell*.

Fisher v Bell [1961] 1 QB 394 Divisional Court

Facts: A shopkeeper displayed a 'flick-knife' in his shop window. He was charged with offering the knife for sale, contrary to s 1 of the Restriction of Offensive Weapons Act 1959. The justices dismissed the charge and the prosecutor appealed.

Held: The word 'offer' was not defined in the statute and so had to be interpreted in accordance with its meaning in the law of contract. On that basis, the shopkeeper was not making an offer by displaying the knife and so had not committed the offence.

Lord Parker CJ: The sole question is whether the exhibition of that knife in the window with the ticket constituted an offer for sale within the statute. I confess that I think most lay people and, indeed, I myself when I first read the papers, would be inclined to the view that to say that if a knife was displayed in a window like that with a price attached to it was not offering it for sale was just nonsense. In ordinary language it is there inviting people to buy it, and it is for sale; but any statute must of course be looked at in the light of the general law of the country. Parliament in its wisdom in passing an Act must be taken to know the general law. It is perfectly clear that according to the ordinary law of contract the display of an article with a price on it in a shop window is merely an invitation to treat. It is in no sense an offer for sale the acceptance of which constitutes a contract.

That is clearly the general law of the country. Not only is that so, but it is to be observed that in many statutes and orders which prohibit selling and offering for sale of goods it is very common when it is so desired to insert the words 'offering or exposing for sale', 'exposing for sale' being clearly words which would cover the display of goods in a shop window. Not only that, but it appears that under several statutes – we have been referred in particular to the Prices of Goods Act, 1939, and the Goods and Services (Price Control) Act, 1941 – Parliament, when it desires to enlarge the ordinary meaning of those words, includes a definition section enlarging the ordinary meaning of 'offer for sale' to cover other matters including, be it observed, exposure of goods for sale with the price attached.

In those circumstances I am driven to the conclusion, though I confess reluctantly, that no offence was here committed. At first sight it sounds absurd that knives of this sort cannot be manufactured, sold, hired, lent, or given, but apparently they can be displayed in shop windows; but even if this – and I am by no means saying it is – is a casus omissus it is not for this court to supply the omission. I am mindful of the strong words of Lord Simonds in *Magor and St. Mellons Rural District Council v Newport Corporation* [1952] A.C. 189; [1951] 2 All E.R. 839, H.L. In that case one of the Lords Justices in the Court of Appeal had, in effect, said that the court having discovered the supposed intention of Parliament must proceed to fill in the gaps – what the Legislature has not written the court must write – and in answer to that contention Lord Simonds in his speech said: 'It appears to me to be a naked usurpation of the legislative function under the thin disguise of interpretation.'

These cases meant that, as far as the law of contract was concerned, a shopkeeper who displayed goods at a particular price was not bound by that price, but could tell a customer who asked to buy the goods that they were in fact more expensive. That position raised the possibility, for example, of business sellers taking advantage of consumer buyers. Today, however, such a practice may amount to an offence under the Consumer Protection from Unfair Trading Regulations 2008 (SI 2008/1277). These Regulations, and possible private law actions under the Regulations, will be discussed further in Chapter 8.

2.2.3.2 Advertisements

If a person advertises goods for sale in a newspaper or on a noticeboard or on the internet, does that constitute an offer? Can a person who wants to buy the goods accept and form a binding contract simply by replying? This issue was considered in relation to newspaper advertisements in another criminal case, *Partridge v Crittenden*.

***Partridge v Crittenden* [1968] 1 WLR 1204 (QB)**

Facts: The defendant had placed an advertisement in a periodical, 'Cage and Aviary Birds' indicating that he had bramblefinches for sale at 25s each. In no place was there any direct use of the words 'offers for sale'. In answer to the advertisement, T wrote, enclosing a cheque for 25s, and asked that a hen be sent to him. The defendant was convicted of unlawfully offering for sale a bramblefinch, contrary to section 6(1) of the Protection of Birds Act 1954. The defendant appealed.

Held: The appeal was allowed because the advertisement was an invitation to treat not an offer for sale.

Ashworth J: ... the real point of substance in this case arose from the words 'offer for sale', and it is to be noted in s 6 of the Act of 1954 that the operative words are 'any person sells, offers for sale or has in his possession for sale'. For some reason which counsel for the respondent has not been able to explain, those responsible for the prosecution in this case chose, out of the trio of possible offences, the one which could not succeed. There was a sale here, in my view, because Mr Thompson sent his cheque and the bird was sent in reply; and a completed sale. On the evidence there was also a plain case of the appellant having in possession for sale this particular bird; but they chose to prosecute him for offering for sale, and they relied on the advertisement. A similar point arose before this court in 1960 dealing, it is true, with a different statute but with the same words, that is *Fisher v Bell* [1960] 3 All ER 731 ...

The words are the same here 'offer for sale', and in my judgment the law of the country is equally plain as it was in regard to articles in a shop window, namely that the insertion of an advertisement in the form adopted here under the title 'Classified Advertisements' is simply an invitation to treat. That is really sufficient to dispose of this case ....

Lord-Parker CJ: I agree and with less reluctance than in *Fisher v Bell*, to which Ashworth J has referred, and the case of *Mella v Monahan* [1961] Crim LR 175. I say 'with less reluctance' because I think that when one is dealing with advertisements and circulars, unless they indeed come from manufacturers, there is business sense in their being construed as invitations to treat and not offers for sale. In a very different context Lord Herschell in *Grainger & Son v Gough (Surveyor of Taxes)* [1896] AC 325, said this in dealing with a price-list:

> 'The transmission of such a price-list does not amount to an offer to supply an unlimited quantity of the wine described at the price named, so that as soon as an order is given there is a binding contract to supply that quantity. If it were so, the merchant might find himself involved in any number of contractual obligations to supply wine of a particular description which he would be quite unable to carry out, his stock of wine of that description being necessarily limited'.

It seems to me accordingly that not only is that the law, but common sense supports it.

Generally speaking, therefore, advertisements of goods for sale will not constitute offers. This is likely also to be true of many internet advertisements. (Note, however, that some businesses that sell via the internet will respond to customer offers with an acknowledgement of the offer, but with a statement that the offer is not accepted until the goods are dispatched). The position is similar where an auction is advertised, as is shown by *Harris v Nickerson*:

Harris v Nickerson (1872–3) LR 8 QB 286

Facts: An auction was advertised at which certain office furniture was to be sold. The plaintiff travelled to the auction for the express purpose of bidding for the office furniture. This was, however, withdrawn from the sale. The plaintiff sued the auctioneer for breach of contract, claiming his wasted expenses in attending the auction. The trial judge held for the plaintiff. The defendant auctioneer appealed.

Held: The advertisement of the auction did not constitute an offer capable of becoming a contract.

Blackburn J: I am of opinion that the judge was wrong. The facts were that the defendant advertised bona fide that certain things would be sold by auction on the days named, and on the third day a certain class of things, viz., office furniture, without any previous notice of their withdrawal, were not put up. The plaintiff says, inasmuch as I confided in the defendant's advertisement, and came down to the auction to buy the furniture (which it is found as a fact he was commissioned to buy) and have had no opportunity of buying, I am entitled to recover damages from the defendant, on the ground that the advertisement amounted to a contract by the defendant with anybody that should act upon it, that all the things advertised would be actually put up for sale, and that he would have an opportunity of bidding for them and buying. This is certainly a startling proposition, and would be excessively inconvenient if carried out. It amounts to saying that anyone who advertises a sale by publishing an advertisement becomes responsible to everybody who attends the sale for his cab hire or travelling expenses ... [U]nless every declaration of intention to do a thing creates a binding contract with these who act upon it, and in all cases after advertising a sale the auctioneer must give notice of any articles that are withdrawn, or be liable to an action, we cannot hold the defendant liable.

Quain J: I am of the same opinion. To uphold the judge's decision it is necessary to go to the extent of saying that when an auctioneer issues an advertisement of the sale of goods, if he withdraws any part of them without notice, the persons attending may all maintain actions against him. In the present case, it is to be observed that the plaintiff bought some other lots; but it is said he had a commission to buy the furniture, either the whole or in part, and that therefore he has a right of action against the defendant. Such a proposition seems to be destitute of all authority; and it would be introducing an extremely inconvenient rule of law to say that an auctioneer is bound to give notice of the withdrawal or to be held liable to everybody attending the sale.

Archibald J. agreed.

The court noted, however, that the position might be different if the auction was advertised as being 'without reserve'. This is considered further at Section 2.2.5.2. The fact, however, that there are certain limited situations where an advertisement may constitute an offer is illustrated by the famous case of *Carlill v Carbolic Smoke Ball Company*.

Carlill v Carbolic Smoke Ball Co [1893] 1 QB 256 (CA)

Facts: During a flu epidemic, the Carbolic Smoke Ball Company published an advertisement which offered £100 to any person who caught influenza after using its smoke ball. Mrs Carlill used the smoke ball, but caught influenza. She sued for the £100.

Held: The advertisement was an offer 'to the world'. A customer who accepted by using the smoke ball was entitled to recover £100 if he or she then caught influenza.

Lindley LJ: The first observation I will make is that we are not dealing with any inference of fact. We are dealing with an express promise to pay £100 in certain events. Read the advertisement how you will, and twist it about as you will, here is a distinct promise expressed in language which is perfectly unmistakable – '£100 reward will be paid by the Carbolic Smoke Ball Company to any person who contracts the influenza after having used the ball three times daily for two weeks according to the printed directions supplied with each ball'.

We must first consider whether this was intended to be a promise at all, or whether it was a mere puff which meant nothing. Was it a mere puff? My answer to that question is No, and I base my answer upon this passage: '£1000 is deposited with the Alliance Bank, shewing our sincerity in the matter'. Now, for what was that money deposited or that statement made except to negative the suggestion that this was a mere puff and meant nothing at all? The deposit is called in aid by the advertiser as proof of his sincerity in the matter – that is, the sincerity of his promise to pay this £100 in the event which he has specified. I say this for the purpose of giving point to the observation that we are not inferring a promise; there is the promise, as plain as words can make it.

Then it is contended that it is not binding. In the first place, it is said that it is not made with anybody in particular. Now that point is common to the words of this advertisement and to the words of all other advertisements offering rewards. They are offers to anybody who performs the conditions named in the advertisement, and anybody who does perform the condition accepts the offer. In point of law this advertisement is an offer to pay £100 to anybody who will perform these conditions, and the performance of the conditions is the acceptance of the offer. That rests upon a string of authorities, the earliest of which is *Williams v Carwardine* (1833) 4 B & Ad 621, which has been followed by many other decisions upon advertisements offering rewards.

But then it is said, 'Supposing that the performance of the conditions is an acceptance of the offer, that acceptance ought to have been notified.' Unquestionably, as a general proposition, when an offer is made, it is necessary in order to make a binding contract, not only that it should be accepted, but that the acceptance should be notified. But is that so in cases of this kind? I apprehend that they are an exception to that rule, or, if not an exception, they are open to the observation that the notification of the acceptance need not precede the performance. This offer is a continuing offer. It was never revoked, and if notice of acceptance is required – which I doubt very much, for I rather think the true view is that which was expressed and explained by Lord Blackburn in the case of *Brogden v Metropolitan Ry Co* (1877) 2 App Cas 666 – if notice of acceptance is required, the person who makes the offer gets the notice of acceptance contemporaneously with his notice of the performance of the condition. If he gets notice of the acceptance before his offer is revoked, that in principle is all you want. I, however, think that the true view, in a case of this kind, is that the person who makes the offer shews by his language and from the nature of the transaction that he does not expect and does not require notice of the acceptance apart from notice of the performance.

We, therefore, find here all the elements which are necessary to form a binding contract enforceable in point of law ....

The approach taken in *Carlill* may also be taken where what is being advertised is a 'reward' – for example, for the return of lost property or information leading to the conviction of an offender. These 'unilateral' contracts (discussed in Section 2.2.4), which depend on someone choosing to do something in order to 'earn' a payment, are distinguished from straightforward advertisements promoting goods, or indicating the terms on which they are available for purchase, which are likely to be treated as 'invitations to treat'. In relation to *Carlill*'s case itself, Collins has pointed out some features of the case which might mean that we should be surprised that the court treated it as involving a 'contract':

Collins, H, *The Law of Contract*, 4th edn, 2003, London: Lexis-Nexis, p 4

The amusing circumstances of the cases should not obscure the surprising extent to which the court was prepared to conceive social relations in terms of contracts. The parties to the alleged contract had never met or communicated with each other directly. Nor had they exchanged goods, money or services between themselves. The law of contract is used by the court as an instrument for discouraging misleading and extravagant claims in advertising and for deterring the marketing of unproven, and perhaps dangerous, pharmaceuticals. The court protects the gullible and confused consumer by interpreting the events in the form of a contractual relationship giving rise to reciprocal obligations. In so doing it ignores alternative interpretations of these events, such as the idea that the misleading advertisement might constitute a civil wrong in itself, or that consumers who are ignorant of the properties of goods put on the market should be protected from any harmful consequences.

It is likely that the court in *Carlill*'s case saw that a 'wrong' had occurred and simply used the easiest means at its disposal to provide a remedy – that is, finding that there was a contract which had been broken. However, as is shown by the following extract by Simpson, the case should also be looked at it in its historical context as an important decision in the development of contract theory.

Simpson, AWB, 'Quackery and Contract Law: the case of the Carbolic Smoke Ball' (1985) 14 *J Leg St* 345, pp 375–379

The Smoke Ball and contractual theory

For lawyers, and particularly for law students, *Carlill v Carbolic Smoke Ball Co* rapidly achieved the status of a leading case, a status which it has retained perhaps more securely in England than in the United States. Part of its success derived from the comic and slightly mysterious object involved, but there were two reasons of a legal character that suggest that it deserves its place in the firmament. The first, which is not always fully appreciated, is historical; it was the vehicle whereby a new legal doctrine was introduced into the law of contract. The second is that the decision could be used by expositors of the law of contract to illustrate the arcane mysteries surrounding the conception of a unilateral or one-sided contract.

So far as the first point is concerned, the so-called will theory of contract supposed that all contractual obligations were the product of the joint wills of the contracting parties, embodied in their agreement. The function of law courts, according to this theory, was merely that of faithfully carrying into effect the wishes of the parties to the contract. Further reflection on the implications of this theory, which had powerful support in nineteenth-century thought, suggested that it must necessarily follow that a court should not enforce an agreement unless it was the will of the parties that it should be legally enforced. They might indeed have agreed to do something, for example go on a picnic, but be unwilling to have this agreement legally enforced. There must, it was said, be a joint intention to create legal relations before an agreement should have any legal consequences. The principal exponent of this dogma was the German jurist Savigny, and some English contract writers, in particular Sir Frederick Pollock, had incorporated this notion into their accounts of the law without being able to cite any case in which the doctrine had been laid down as law. It could be used to explain certain old cases in which the courts had held there to be no contract, cases in reality decided in sublime ignorance of the theories of Savigny and some long predating his birth. But in legal dogmatics this retrospective reinterpretation is a normal practice, as it is in theological reasoning, which so resembles legal reasoning. But until Mrs. Carlill brought her action there was no case which had clearly recognized the requirement of an intention to create legal relations; her case did. It was indeed explicitly argued in this trial by Asquith that 'the advertisement was a mere representation of what the advertisers intended to do in a certain event. The defendants did not by issuing it mean to impose upon themselves any obligations enforceable by law.' In all probability he took the idea from one of the text writers. This argument was firmly rejected by the trial judge, who relied in particular on the fact that the advertisement had stated that £1,000 had been deposited in the Alliance Bank 'showing our sincerity in the matter'. This, he argued, 'could only have been inserted with the object of leading those who read it to believe that the defendants were serious in their proposal'. In the Court of Appeal the same view was taken. Thus Lord Justice Lindley, early in his opinion said: 'We must first consider whether this was intended to be a promise at all, or whether it was a mere puff which meant nothing. Was it a mere puff? My answer to that question is No, and I base my answer on this passage: '£1000 is deposited with the Alliance Bank, shewing our sincerity in the matter.'

The fact that the judges found it necessary to make this point entailed their acceptance of the idea that without an intention to create legal relations there could be no actionable contract. In fact in the argument before the Court of Appeal little was made of the point, though Mr. Terrell did argue that the promise was too *vague* to be actionable, adding: 'It is like the case in which the man intended to induce a person to marry his daughter', a reference to *Weeks v Tybald* (1605). The 'vagueness' point was picked up by other counsel engaged in the case. But Lindley's opinion was so framed as to enable the case to be used as an authority for the view that Savigny's doctrine was part of English law.

As for the second point, most contracts that concern the courts involve two-sided agreements, two-sided in the sense that the parties enter into reciprocal obligations to each other. A typical example is a sale of goods, where the seller has to deliver the goods and the buyer to pay for them. The doctrines of nineteenth-century contract law were adapted to such bilateral contracts, but the law also somewhat uneasily recognized that there could be contracts in which only one party was ever under any obligation to the other. The standard example was a published promise to pay a reward for information on the recovery of lost property: £10 to anyone who finds and returns my dog. In such a case obviously nobody is obligated to search for the dog, but if they do so successfully, they are entitled to the reward. Such contracts seem odd in another way; there is a promise, but no agreement, for the parties never even meet until the reward is claimed. Promises of rewards, made to the world at large, will not involve an indefinite number of claims – there is only one reward offered – and the courts will uphold the claimant's right to the reward although he has never communicated any acceptance of the promise. Classified as 'unilateral' contracts, such arrangements presented special problems of analysis to contract theorists, whose standard doctrines had not been evolved to fit them. Thus it was by 1892 orthodox to say that all contracts were formed by the exchange of an offer and an acceptance, but it was by no means easy to see how this could be true of unilateral contracts, where there was, to the eyes of common sense, no acceptance needed.

The analytical problems arose in a particularly acute form in the smoke ball case. Thus it seemed very peculiar to say there had been any sort of agreement between Mrs. Carlill and the company, which did not even know of her existence until January 20, when her husband wrote to them to complain. There were indeed earlier cases permitting the recovery of advertised rewards; the leading case here was *Williams v Cawardine*, where a reward of £20 had been promised by handbill for information leading to the conviction of the murderer of Walter Cawardine, and Williams, who gave such information, successfully sued to recover the reward. But this was long before the more modern doctrines had become so firmly embodied in legal thinking, and in any event the case was quite distinguishable. It concerned a reward, whereas Mrs. Carlill was seeking compensation. There could be at most only a few claimants for this, but there is no limit on the number of those who may catch influenza. Furthermore, the Carbolic Smoke Ball Company had had no chance to check the validity of claims, of which there could be an indefinite number; much was made of this point in the argument. But the judges were not impressed with these difficulties, and their attitude was no doubt influenced by the view that the defendants were rogues. They fit their decision into the structure of the law by boldly declaring that the performance of the conditions was the acceptance, thus fictitiously extending the concept of acceptance to cover the facts. And, since 1893, law students have been introduced to the mysteries of the unilateral contract through the vehicle of *Carlill v Carbolic Smoke Ball Co* and taught to repeat, as a sort of magical incantation of contract law, that in the case of unilateral contracts performance of the act specified in the offer constitutes acceptance, and need not be communicated to the offeror.

Modern consumer law, which overlaps but is not coterminous with contract law, adopts more direct approaches to controlling misleading advertising and selling, through legislation such as the Consumer Protection from Unfair Trading Regulations 2008 (SI 2008/1277), which we have already noted in relation to misleading prices (see Section 2.2.3.1). If the facts of *Carlill v Carbolic Smoke Ball Co* were to occur today, it is by no means certain that it would be treated as a case on the law of contract.

2.2.4 Unilateral and bilateral contracts

As noted by Professor Simpson in the extract in the previous section, *Carlill v Carbolic Smoke Ball Co* was an example of the recognition by the courts of a particular type of contract, generally referred to as a 'unilateral contract'. They are also sometimes known as 'if' contracts, in that they can always be expressed in the form of one party (A) saying to the other (B) – 'Although you are not obliged to do so, if you act in a certain way, then I promise to do something for you'; for example, 'If you find my lost dog, I promise I will pay you £100'. In this type of contract, B, the person doing the action, has not made any promise to A. B is under no obligation to find the dog; neither is B under an obligation to attempt to find the dog. If he or she does find the dog, however, A will be bound by his or her promise. That is why the agreement is 'unilateral'. Under a bilateral contract, both parties have obligations as soon as the contract is made (e.g. A and B agree that B will look for the dog in exchange for a fee).

Offers made 'to the world', as in *Carlill*, will often be 'unilateral', but it is quite possible to have a unilateral contract where the offer is made to a particular person, as in, for example, *Daulia v Four Millbank Nominees*.

***Daulia v Four Millbank Nominees* [1978] Ch 231**

Facts: The parties were negotiating over the sale of some properties. The seller promised the buyer that if the buyer produced a signed contract plus a banker's draft by 10 a.m. the next morning, the seller would go through with the contract. When the buyer complied with this requirement, the seller refused to go ahead.

Held: The Court of Appeal held in favour of the seller because of the lack of writing in relation to what was in effect a contract for the sale of land, but indicated that otherwise there would have been a unilateral contract.

Goff LJ: Was there a concluded unilateral contract by the first defendants to enter into a contract for sale on the agreed terms? The concept of a unilateral or 'if contract' is somewhat anomalous, because it is clear that, at all events until the offeree starts to perform the condition, there is no contract at all, but merely an offer which the offeror is free to revoke.

Doubts have been expressed whether the offeror becomes bound so soon as the offeree starts to perform or satisfy the condition, or only when he has fully done so. In my judgment, however, we are not concerned in this case with any such problem, because in my view the plaintiffs had fully performed or satisfied the condition when they presented themselves at the time and place appointed with a banker's draft for the deposit, and their part of the written contract for sale duly engrossed and signed and there tendered the same, which I understand to mean proffered it for exchange. Actual exchange, which never took place, would not in my view have been part of the satisfaction of the condition but something additional which was inherently necessary to be done by the plaintiffs to enable, not to bind the first defendants to perform the unilateral contract. Accordingly in my judgment, the answer to the first question must be in the affirmative.

Buckley and Orr L.JJ. concurred.

2.2.5 Some special situations

2.2.5.1 Tenders

Generally where, for example, a firm 'puts work out to tender', it is inviting interested parties to offer to do the work. The invitation may be made to selected parties or to the world. In either case it will usually constitute an 'invitation to treat' and responses received may be 'offers'. In some situations, however, the invitation itself may result in a subsidiary obligation in the form of a unilateral contract. If, for example, the invitation to tender indicates that the work will go to the lowest bidder, then the responder who puts in the lowest bid may be entitled to remedies if the other party refuses to contract with it. The situation can be compared to that which applies to auctions, as discussed in the next section.

Even where the invitation to tender contains no commitment to accept the lowest bid, there may be other implicit obligations, as shown by *Blackpool and Fylde Aero Club Ltd v Blackpool Borough Council* [1990] 1 WLR 1195.

***Blackpool and Fylde Aero Club Ltd v Blackpool Borough Council* [1990] 1 WLR 1195**

Facts: A council invited tenders for the operation of an airfield for pleasure flights. Tenders had to be submitted in a particular form by a particular date. The plaintiffs submitted their tender in accordance with these instructions, but it was overlooked and not considered with the other tenders.

Held: The Court of Appeal upheld the trial judge's decision that the defendants were in breach of an implicit obligation to give proper consideration to all bids that had been submitted in the correct form.

Bingham LJ: ... The council own and manage Blackpool Airport. For purposes of raising revenue they have made it a practice to grant a concession to an air operator to operate pleasure flights from the airport, no doubt largely for the entertainment of holiday-makers. The club, one of whose directors was and is a Mr. Bateson, tendered for and were granted this concession in 1975 and again in 1978 and again in 1980. In 1983 the most recently granted concession was due to expire. The council accordingly prepared an invitation to tender. This was sent to the club and to six other parties, all of them in one way or another connected with the airport ....

[The document set out the terms for the operation of the concession which was being offered, and required the tenders to be submitted not later than 12 o'clock noon on Thursday 17 March 1983.]

Only three of the selected tenderers responded to the council's invitation. One put in a low bid for the lighter size of aircraft only. The second, Red Rose Helicopters Ltd, submitted a larger bid, also for the lighter size of aircraft. Mr. Bateson for the club filled in the form of tender, submitting a bid substantially larger, on its face, than the others, for the lighter size of aircraft, and also submitting a bid for the heavier size. He put it in the envelope provided by the council, took it to the town hall and posted it in the town hall letter box at about 11 a.m. on Thursday 17 March. This was about an hour before the advertised deadline expired. The town clerk's staff were supposed to empty the letter box each day at 12 o'clock. They failed to do so. The club's tender accordingly remained in the letter box until the next morning, 18 March, when the letter box was next opened. The envelope was then taken out and date-stamped 18 March 1983 by the town clerk's department. At some time thereafter the word 'late' was written on the envelope, because that is what the club's tender was mistakenly thought to be.

On 29 March 1983 the chairman of the council's relevant committee considered which tender to accept. The club's tender had been recorded as being late, and was in accordance with the council's standing orders excluded from consideration when the chairman made his decision. He accordingly made his choice between the two tenders believed to be in time, recommending acceptance of Red Rose Helicopters' tender, no doubt because it was bigger.

An indication that its tender was accepted was given to Red Rose Helicopters. The town clerk wrote to the club to say that their tender was not received until 18 March and was therefore received too late for consideration. …

[Further investigation revealed that the tender had been received before the deadline, and the Aero Club sued for breach of contract.]

The judge resolved the contractual issue in favour of the club, holding that an express request for a tender might in appropriate circumstances give rise to an implied obligation to perform the service of considering that tender. Here, the council's stipulation that tenders received after the deadline would not be admitted for consideration gave rise to a contractual obligation, on acceptance by submission of a timely tender, that such tenders would be admitted for consideration. …

A tendering procedure of this kind is, in many respects, heavily weighted in favour of the invitor. He can invite tenders from as many or as few parties as he chooses. He need not tell any of them who else, or how many others, he has invited. The invitee may often, although not here, be put to considerable labour and expense in preparing a tender, ordinarily without recompense if he is unsuccessful. The invitation to tender may itself, in a complex case, although again not here, involve time and expense to prepare, but the invitor does not commit himself to proceed with the project, whatever it is; he need not accept the highest tender; he need not accept any tender; he need not give reasons to justify his acceptance or rejection of any tender received. The risk to which the tenderer is exposed does not end with the risk that his tender may not be the highest or, as the case may be, lowest. But where, as here, tenders are solicited from selected parties, all of them known to the invitor, and where a local authority's invitation prescribes a clear, orderly and familiar procedure – draft contract conditions available for inspection and plainly not open to negotiation, a prescribed common form of tender, the supply of envelopes designed to preserve the absolute anonymity of tenderers and clearly to identify the tender in question, and an absolute deadline – the invitee is in my judgment protected at least to this extent: if he submits a conforming tender before the deadline he is entitled, not as a matter of mere expectation but of contractual right, to be sure that his tender will after the deadline be opened and considered in conjunction with all other conforming tenders or at least that his tender will be considered if others are. Had the club, before tendering, inquired of the council whether it could rely on any timely and conforming tender being considered along with others, I feel quite sure that the answer would have been 'of course'. The law would, I think, be defective if it did not give effect to that.

It is of course true that the invitation to tender does not explicitly state that the council will consider timely and conforming tenders. That is why one is concerned with implication. But the council do not either say that they do not bind themselves to do so, and in the context a reasonable invitee would understand the invitation to be saying, quite clearly, that if he submitted a timely and conforming tender it would be considered, at least if any other such tender were considered.

I readily accept that contracts are not to be lightly implied. ... In all the circumstances of this case, and I say nothing about any other, I have no doubt that the parties did intend to create contractual relations to the limited extent contended for. Since it has never been the law that a person is only entitled to enforce his contractual rights in a reasonable way (*White and Carter (Councils) Ltd v McGregor* [1962] A.C. 413, 430A, *per* Lord Reid), Mr. Shorrock was in my view right to contend for no more than a contractual duty to consider. I think it plain that the council's invitation to tender was, to this limited extent, an offer, and the club's submission of a timely and conforming tender an acceptance ...

I accordingly agree with the judge's conclusion on the contractual issue, essentially for the reasons which he more briefly gave ...

I would accordingly dismiss the appeal. The practical consequences of deciding the contractual issue on liability in the club's favour must, if necessary, be decided hereafter.

The result was that there was also a unilateral contract between the parties, whereby the council promised that 'if you get your tender in by the deadline, we will give it proper consideration'. This has the effect that, although putting a contract out for tender is only an invitation to treat, it can involve a parallel unilateral offer, which requires the party seeking the tenders to follow any procedure set out in its tender document.

2.2.5.2 Auctions

The general rule at a 'live' auction is that offers are made by the bidders. The acceptance is made by the auctioneer, signalled by the fall of the hammer.

SALE OF GOODS ACT 1979, S 57

(1) Where goods are put up for sale by auction in lots, each lot is prima facie deemed to be the subject of a separate contract of sale.

(2) A sale by auction is complete when the auctioneer announces its completion by the fall of the hammer, or in other customary manner; and until the announcement is made any bidder may retract his bid.

An advertisement that an auction is going to take place, or that specific goods will be included in it, is not in itself to be treated as an offer. This was the result of the decision in *Harris v Nickerson* (1873) LR 8 QB 286. What is the position, however, if the auction of one or more items is advertised as being 'without reserve'? In such situations the auctioneer is indicating that the there is no minimum bid requirement and that the highest bid, however low it may be, will be accepted. This was considered in *Warlow v Harrison* (1859) 1 E & E 309. The court indicated that it considered the auctioneer to be bound by such an indication, but had to decide against the plaintiff because the case had not been pleaded correctly. The situation was reconsidered more recently in *Barry v Heathcote Ball & Co (Commercial Auctions) Ltd* [2000] 1 WLR 1962.

***Barry v Heathcote Ball & Co (Commercial Auctions) Ltd* [2000] 1 WLR 1962**

Facts: An auction was held by the defendant on 25 June 1997. One of the lots for sale consisted of two engine analysers, the list price of which was over £14,000 each. The claimant had seen the machines and had been told that they were to be sold without reserve. At the auction the claimant bid £200 for each machine. The auctioneer refused to accept this bid, and withdrew the machines. The claimant sued and was awarded damages of £27,600 for breach of contract.

Held: The Court of Appeal held that the statement that the auction was to be without reserve constituted a promise that if the claimant made the highest bid it would be accepted. It upheld the trial judge's decision.

Sir Murray Stuart-Smith: ... The claimant runs a car tuning business. He saw the machines being delivered to the auction house on 20 June. He returned on the viewing day and spoke to Mr Cross [the auctioneer] who said that they would be sold at noon on 25 June without reserve. The claimant decided they would be useful in his business and decided to bid for them.

The claimant attended the auction house for a few minutes before noon. When it came to the lots in question Mr Cross said that the machines were to be 'sold that day' on behalf of the VAT office, that each was worth £14,000, 'ready to plug in and away you go'. He tried to obtain a bid of £5,000 to start with; there was no bid; he tried £3,000; still no response. He then asked what bids there were for the machines, and the claimant bid £200 for each. No other bid was made. In fact Mr Cross had received a bid from his son-in-law for £400 each; but he made no mention of this.

Mr Cross then withdrew the machines from the sale. His explanation was:

> 'I could not see how I could sell for as little as this, even though it was without reserve. I think I am justified in not selling at an auction without reserve if I think I could get more in some other way later. I did not take up [the offer of] £400. I thought they were worth more.'

He told those present that he was not prepared to sell the machines for £200. They were sold a few days later for £1,500 (£750 each) after advertisement in a magazine. The claimant claimed damages on the basis that he was the highest bidder. The particulars of the damage claimed was the difference between the value of the machines, said to be £28,000 and the bid of £400.

The judge held that it would be the general and reasonable expectation of persons attending at an auction sale without reserve that the highest bidder would and should be entitled to the lot for which he bids. Such an outcome was in his view fair and logical. As a matter of law he held that there was a collateral contract between the auctioneer and the highest bidder which was accepted when the bid was made. In so doing he followed the view of the majority of the Court of Exchequer Chamber in *Warlow v Harrison* (1859) 1 E & E 309, [1843–60] All ER Rep 620 ...

[In that case t]he sale was of 'the three following horses, the property of a gentleman, without reserve'. The plaintiff bid 60 guineas for one of the horses; another person, who was in fact the owner, immediately bid 61 guineas. The plaintiff, having been informed that the bid was from the owner declined to bid higher, and claimed he was entitled to the horse. He sued the auctioneer; he based his claim on a plea that the auctioneer was his agent to complete the contract on his behalf. On that plea the plaintiff succeeded at first instance; but the verdict was set aside in the Court of Queen's Bench. The plaintiff appealed. Although the Court of Exchequer Chamber upheld the decision on the case as pleaded, all five members of the court held that if the pleadings were appropriately amended, the plaintiff would be entitled to succeed on a retrial. Martin B gave the judgment of the majority consisting of himself, Byles J and Watson B. He said:

> 'Upon the facts of the case, it seems to us that the plaintiff is entitled to recover. In a sale by auction there are three parties, viz. the owner of the property to be sold, the auctioneer, and the portion of the public who attend to bid, which of course includes the highest bidder. In this, as in most cases of sales by auction, the owner's name was not disclosed: he was a concealed principal. The name of the auctioneers, of whom the defendant was one, alone was published; and the sale was announced by them to be 'without reserve'. This, according to all the cases

both at law and equity, means that neither the vendor nor any person on his behalf shall bid at the auction, and that the property shall be sold to the highest bidder, whether the sum bid be equivalent to the real value or not; *Thornett v Haines* ((1846) 15 M & W 367, 153 ER 892). We cannot distinguish the case of an auctioneer putting up property for sale upon such a condition from the case of the loser of property offering a reward, or that of a railway company publishing a time table stating the times when, and the places to which, the trains run. It has been decided that the person giving the information advertised for, or a passenger taking a ticket, may sue as upon a contract with him; *Denton v Great Northern Railway Company* ((1856) 5 E & B 860, 119 ER 701). Upon the same principle, it seems to us that the highest bona fide bidder at an auction may sue the auctioneer who puts the property up for sale upon such a condition pledges himself that the sale shall be without reserve; or, in other words, contracts that it shall be so; and that this contract is made with the highest bona fide bidder; and, in case of a breach of it, that he has a right of action against the auctioneer.'

(See (1859) 1 E&E 309 at 316–17, [1843–60] All ER Rep 620 at 622.)

So far as textbook writers are concerned both *Chitty on Contracts* (28th edn, 1999) para 2–010 and *Benjamin on Sale of Goods* (5th edn, 1997) para 2–005 adopt the view expressed by the majority of the court in *Warlow's* case.

As to consideration, in my judgment there is consideration both in the form of detriment to the bidder, since this bid can be accepted unless and until it is withdrawn, and benefit to the auctioneer as the bidding is driven up. Moreover attendance at the sale is likely to be increased if it is known that there is no reserve.

For these reasons I would uphold the judge's decision on liability.

Pill L.J. concurred.

The result is similar to the position in relation to tenders described in the previous section. Although the putting of goods up for auction is in itself only an invitation to treat, there may be a parallel unilateral contract to accept the highest bid. This will arise where the auction is stated to be 'without reserve'.

Some 'auctions' take place by means of sealed bids. An issue that can arise in this type of sale is whether a bid which refers to others (a 'referential bid') is valid. If one bidder says in a sealed bid: 'I will pay £5 more than the next highest bid', can this be accepted? The situation was considered by the House of Lords in *Harvela Investments v Royal Trust of Canada* [1986] 1 AC 207.

Harvela Investments Ltd v Royal Trust Co of Canada (CI) Ltd [1986] AC 207 (HL)

Facts: The sellers invited H and L to make offers to buy some shares. The offers were to be in the form of sealed bids. The sellers indicated that they would accept the highest bid. H offered C$2,175,000. L offered C$2,100,000 or 'C$101,000 in excess of any other which you may receive ….' When the bids were disclosed, both parties claimed to be entitled to the shares. The trial judge held for H. The Court of Appeal held for L.

Held: The form in which the invitation to bid was expressed ruled out referential bids. This was not an 'auction' in the true sense, where bidders compete with knowledge of the other bidders' bids, but a 'fixed bidding sale', which ruled out referential bids. H was entitled to the shares as the only valid bid submitted by L was for $2,100,000.

Lord Templeman: On 15 September 1981 the invitation [to bid for the shares] was dispatched to Harvela and Sir Leonard [who had both submitted previous offers to buy them]. The full terms of the invitation, as subsequently amended, were as follows:

> 'We have before us two similar offers but subject to differing terms and conditions and value. Accordingly we invite you to submit to the Royal Trust Company of Canada (C.I.) Limited the registered holder of the shares referred to below any revised offer which you may wish to make by sealed tender or confidential telex to be submitted to our London solicitors, Messrs. Bischoff and Co., City Wall House, 79/83 Chiswell Street, London EC1 by 3 p.m. London time Wednesday 16 September 1981. Attention J. Jowitt who has undertaken not to disclose any details of any revised offer to any party before that time ... Tenders are to be submitted on the following terms: – 1. That tenders are a single offer for all shares held by us. 2. That payment of the agreed purchase price shall be within 30 days of 16th September 1981. (The date of actual payment hereafter called the 'closing date'). 3. Payment shall be in full on the closing date without any deduction. 4. The closing shall take place at Messrs Bischoffs' office payment being by banker's draft payable at sight drawn on the head office of a London clearing bank in Canadian dollars. 5. In the event that closing shall not take place within 30 days other than by reason of any delay on our part interest shall be payable by the purchaser on the full purchase price at a rate higher by 4 per cent than the Bank of Montreal prime rate from time to time for Canadian dollar loans. We hereby agree subject to acceptance by us of any offer made by you ... 6. We confirm that if any offer made by you is the highest offer received by us we bind ourselves to accept such offer provided that such offer complies with the terms of this telex ...'.

Before the invitation expired Harvela and Sir Leonard made the offers which resulted in this litigation, namely by Harvela $2,175,000 and by Sir Leonard $2,100,000 'or C$101,000 in excess of any other offer which you may receive which is expressed as a fixed monetary amount, whichever is the higher'.

Where a vendor undertakes to sell to the highest bidder the vendor may conduct the sale by auction or by fixed bidding. In an auction sale each bidder may adjust his bid by reference to rival bids. In an auction sale the purchaser pays more than any other bidder is prepared to pay to secure the property. The purchaser does not necessarily pay as much as the purchaser was prepared to pay to secure the property. In an auction a purchaser who is prepared to pay $2.5m to secure a property will be able to purchase for $2.2m if no other bidder is prepared to offer as much as $2.2m.

In a fixed bidding sale a bidder may not adjust his bid. Each bidder specifies a fixed amount which he hopes will be sufficient, but not more than sufficient, to exceed any other bid. The purchaser in a fixed bidding sale does not necessarily pay as much as the purchaser was prepared to pay to secure the property ...

The first question raised by this appeal, therefore, is whether Harvela and Sir Leonard were invited to participate in a fixed bidding sale, which only invited fixed bids, or were invited to participate in an auction sale, which enabled the bid of each bidder to be adjusted by reference to the other bid. A vendor chooses between a fixed bidding sale and an auction sale. A bidder can only choose to participate in the sale or to abstain from the sale. The ascertainment of the choice of the vendors in the present case between a fixed bidding sale and an auction sale by means of referential bids depends on the presumed intention of the vendors. That presumed intention must be deduced from the terms of the invitation read as a whole. The invitation contains three provisions which are only consistent with the presumed intention to create a fixed bidding sale and which are inconsistent with any presumed intention to create an auction sale by means of referential bids.

By the first significant provision, the vendors undertook to accept the highest offer; this shows that the vendors were anxious to ensure that a sale should result from the invitation. By the second provision, the vendors extended the same invitation to Harvela and Sir Leonard; this shows that the vendors were desirous that each of them, Harvela and Sir Leonard, and nobody else, should be given an equal opportunity to purchase the shares. By the third provision, the vendors insisted that offers must be confidential and must remain confidential until the time specified by the vendors for the submission of offers had elapsed; this shows that the vendors were desirous of provoking from Sir Leonard an offer of the best price he was prepared to pay in ignorance of the bid made by Harvela and equally provoking from Harvela the best price they were prepared to pay in ignorance of the bid made by Sir Leonard.

A fixed bidding sale met all the requirements of the vendors deducible from the terms of the invitation. ...

It would have been possible for the vendors to conduct an auction sale through the medium of confidential referential bids but only by making express provision in the invitation for the purpose. It would not have been sufficient for the invitation expressly to authorise 'referential bids' without more. For such an authorisation would have rendered the result of the sale uncertain and random in view of the illustrations and examples I have already given. It would have been necessary for the invitation to require each bidder who made a referential bid to specify a maximum sum he was prepared to bid. That requirement would ensure that the sale was not abortive and that both bidders had a genuine chance of winning. A maximum bid requirement would ensure a sale at a price in excess of the maximum bid of the unsuccessful bidder, but it would not necessarily procure a sale at the maximum price of the successful bidder. The sale would in effect be an auction sale and produce the consequences of an auction sale because the vendors would have made express provision for bids to be adjusted and finalised by reference to the maximum bid of the unsuccessful bidder. But without such express provisions the invitation is not consistent with an auction sale.

To constitute a fixed bidding sale all that was necessary was that the vendors should invite confidential offers and should undertake to accept the highest offer. Such was the form of the invitation. It follows that the invitation on its true construction created a fixed bidding sale and that Sir Leonard was not entitled to submit and the vendors were not entitled to accept a referential bid. ...

The vendors were bound to accept Harvela's offer.

Fraser, Diplock, Edmund Davies and Templeman LJ.J. concurred.

The decision that referential bids should not be allowed has the effect of creating a level playing field for all potential bidders; this seems to be the fairest solution in relation to a process involving sealed bids.

2.2.6 Acceptance

Once it is clear that an offer has been made, then a contract can be formed simply by the other party indicating its acceptance. The acceptance must match the offer exactly. If it attempts to modify the offer, or introduce new terms, it will not be an 'acceptance' but a 'counter-offer'. Moreover, once a counter-offer is made, this also constitutes a rejection of the original offer, which is no longer available for acceptance. The application of these rules is exemplified by the following case:

Hyde v Wrench (1840) 3 Beav 334 (Rolls Court)

Facts: The defendant offered to sell a farm to the plaintiff for £1,000. The plaintiff offered £950, which was rejected. The plaintiff then purported to accept the offer to sell at £1,000. The defendant refused to go through with the transaction and the plaintiff sued for specific performance of the contract.

Held: The counter-offer of £950 in effect destroyed the original offer to sell at £1,000 and it was no longer open for acceptance.

Lord Langdale MR: Under the circumstances stated in this bill, I think there exists no valid binding contract between the parties for the purchase of the property. The defendant offered to sell it for £1,000, and if that had been at once unconditionally accepted, there would undoubtedly have been a perfect binding contract; instead of that, the plaintiff made an offer of his own, to purchase the property for £950, and he thereby rejected the offer previously made by the defendant. I think that it was not afterwards competent for him to revive the proposal of the defendant, by tendering an acceptance of it; and that, therefore, there exists no obligation of any sort between the parties; the demurrer must be allowed.

A response to an offer may in some circumstances be neither a counter-offer nor an acceptance. The offeree may simply want clarification on a particular point, without intending to accept or reject the offer. Such a 'request for information' will leave the offer open for later acceptance and has no legal significance as far as the formation of the contract is concerned. This is illustrated by the following decision:

Stevenson v McLean (1880) 5 QBD 346 (QB)

Facts: Following negotiations over the sale of a quantity of iron, a firm offer to sell at a particular price was made, with the offer to be held open for a specified period. The offeree inquired about delivery. The seller did not respond, but sold the iron elsewhere. The offeree, not knowing of this, sought to accept the offer to sell, within the original time limit. When the offeree discovered that the iron had been sold elsewhere, he brought an action for breach of contract.

Held: The inquiry about delivery was not a counter-offer, but simply a request for information. The original offer therefore remained open for acceptance.

Lush J: ... The plaintiffs are makers of iron and iron merchants at Middlesbrough. The defendant being possessed of warrants for iron, which he had originally bought off the plaintiffs, wrote on the 24th of September to the plaintiffs from London, where he carries on his business: 'I see that No. 3 has been sold for immediate delivery at 39s., which means a higher price for warrants. Could you get me an offer for the whole or part of my warrants? I have 3,800 tons, and the brands you know.'

[Lush J. then outlines the correspondence between the parties and Fossick (the defendant's broker), which ended with the plaintiffs being in possession of two letters:]. ... the one from Fossick stating that the defendant was not inclined to make a firm offer; and the other from the defendant himself, to the effect that he would sell for 40s., nett cash, and would hold it open all Monday. This it was admitted must have been the meaning of 'open till Monday'.

On the Monday morning, at 9.42, the plaintiffs telegraphed to the defendant: 'Please wire whether you would accept forty for delivery over two months, or if not, longest limit you would give'.

This telegram was received at the office at Moorgate at 10.1 a.m., as an inquiry, expecting an answer for his guidance, and this, I think, is the sense in which the defendant ought to have regarded it.

It is apparent throughout the correspondence, that the plaintiffs did not contemplate buying the iron on speculation, but that their acceptance of the defendant's offer depended on their finding someone to take the warrants off their hands. All parties knew that the market was in an unsettled state, and that no one could predict at the early hour when the telegram was sent how the prices would range during the day. It was reasonable that, under these circumstances, they should desire to know before business began whether they were to be at liberty in case of need to make any and what concession as to the time or times of delivery, which would be the time or times of payment, or whether the defendant was determined to adhere to the terms of his letter; and it was highly unreasonable that the plaintiffs should have intended to close the negotiation while it was uncertain whether they could find a buyer or not, having the whole of the business hours of the day to look for one. Then, again, the form of the telegram is one of inquiry. It is not 'I offer forty for delivery over two months', which would have likened the case to *Hyde v Wrench* (1840) 3 Bear 334, where one party offered his estate for £1000, and the other answered by offering £950. Lord Langdale, in that case, held that after the £950 had been refused, the party offering it could not, by then agreeing to the original proposal, claim the estate, for the negotiation was at an end by the refusal of his counter proposal. Here there is no counter proposal. The words are, 'Please wire whether you would accept forty for delivery over two months, or, if not, the longest limit you would give'. There is nothing specific by way of offer or rejection, but a mere inquiry, which should have been answered and not treated as a rejection of the offer. This ground of objection therefore fails.

2.2.6.1 Battle of the forms

Where two businesses are negotiating over a contract, they may well both have a set of standard terms that they each insist will apply to the contract. Some aspects of these terms may well be in conflict. If this is the case and performance of the agreement begins, the courts may be left with having to decide whether there was ever a contract between the parties and, if so, on what terms. If there was no matching offer and acceptance, the outcome might be that there was no contract; although the courts are reluctant to come to such a conclusion where an 'agreement' has been performed. At times they may be able to find an oral agreement that did not refer to any of the documentation (as in Hertford Foods Ltd v Lidl UK GmbH [2001] EWCA Civ 938); alternatively they may try to find that there was in fact a matching offer and acceptance, despite initial appearances to the contrary. This may well be said to be what happened in the next case.

***Butler Machine Tool Co v Ex-Cell-O Corporation* [1979] 1 WLR 401 (CA)**

Facts: The case concerned an alleged contract for the sale of a machine. The seller's standard terms included a price variation clause; the buyer's standard terms had no such clause. The final relevant communication was from the seller to the buyer. The seller returned a slip acknowledging the buyer's terms, but also included a letter indicating that their own terms should prevail. The trial judge held that the contract was made on the seller's terms.

Held: The acknowledgement slip was the crucial document. This indicated that the contract was made on the buyer's terms.

Lord Denning MR: This case is a 'battle of forms'. The suppliers of a machine, Butler Machine Tool Co. Ltd ('the sellers'), on 23rd May 1969 quoted a price for a machine tool of £75,535. Delivery was to be given in ten months. On the back of the quotation there were terms and conditions. One of them was a price variation clause. It provided for an increase in the price if there was an increase in the costs and so forth. The machine tool was not delivered until November 1970. By that time costs had increased so much that the sellers claimed an additional sum of £2,892 as due to them under the price variation clause.

The buyers, Ex-Cell-O Corpn, rejected the excess charge. They relied on their own terms and conditions. They said: 'We did not accept the sellers' quotation as it was. We gave an order for the self-same machine at the self-same price, but on the back of our order we had our own terms and conditions. Our terms and conditions did not contain any price variation clause'.

> 'The judge held that the price variation clause in the sellers' form continued through the whole dealing and so the sellers were entitled to rely on it'.

On 23rd May 1969 the sellers offered to deliver one 'Butler' double column planomiller for the total price of £75,535, 'Delivery: 10 months (Subject to confirmation at time of ordering) Other terms and conditions are on the reverse of this quotation'. On the back there were 16 conditions in small print starting with this general condition:

> 'All orders are accepted only upon and subject to the terms set out in our quotation and the following conditions. These terms and conditions shall prevail over any terms and conditions in the Buyer's order'.

Clause 3 was the price variation clause. It said:

> 'Prices are based on present day costs of manufacture and design and having regard to the delivery quoted and uncertainty as to the cost of labour, materials etc., during the period of manufacture, we regret that we have no alternative but to make it a condition of acceptance of order that goods will be charged at prices ruling upon date of delivery'.

The buyers, Ex-Cell-O, replied on 27th May 1969 giving an order in these words: 'Please supply on terms and conditions as below and overleaf'. Below there was a list of the goods ordered, but there were differences from the quotation of the sellers in these respects: (i) there was an additional item for the cost of installation, £3,100; (ii) there was a different delivery date; instead of 10 months, it was 10 to 11 months. Overleaf there were different terms as to the cost of carriage, in that it was to be paid to the delivery address of the buyers; whereas the sellers' terms were ex warehouse. There were different terms as to the right to cancel for late delivery. The buyers in their conditions reserved the right to cancel if delivery was not made by the agreed date, whereas the sellers in their conditions said that cancellation of order due to late delivery would not be accepted.

On the foot of the buyers' order there was a tear-off slip:

> 'Acknowledgement: Please sign and return to Ex-Cell-O Corp. (England) Ltd. We accept your order on the Terms and Conditions stated thereon – and undertake to deliver by Date. Signed'.

In that slip the delivery date and signature were left blank ready to be filled in by the sellers.

On 5th June 1969 the sellers wrote this letter to the buyers:

> 'We have pleasure in acknowledging receipt of your official order dated 27th May covering the supply of one "Butler" Double Column Plano-Miller ... This is being entered in accordance with our revised quotation of 23rd May for delivery in 10/11 months, i.e. March/April, 1970. We return herewith, duly completed, your acknowledgement of order form'.

They enclosed the acknowledgment form duly filled in with the delivery date, March/April 1970, and signed by the Butler Machine Tool Co. Ltd.

No doubt a contract was then concluded. But on what terms? The sellers rely on their general conditions and on their last letter which said 'in accordance with our revised quotation of 23rd May' (which had on the back the price variation clause). The buyers rely on the acknowledgment signed by the sellers which accepted the buyers' order 'on the terms and conditions stated thereon' (which did not include a price variation clause).

If those documents are analysed in our traditional method, the result would seem to me to be this: the quotation of 23rd May 1969 was an offer by the sellers to the buyers containing the terms and conditions on the back. The order of 27th May 1969 purported to be an acceptance of that offer in that it was for the same machine at the same price, but it contained such additions as to cost of installation, date of delivery and so forth, that it was in law a rejection of the offer and constituted a counter-offer.

That is clear from *Hyde v Wrench* (1840) 3 Bear 334. As Megaw J said in *Trollope & Colls Ltd v Atomic Power Construction Ltd* [1962] 3 All ER 1035: '... the counter-offer kills the original offer'. The letter of the sellers of 5th June 1969 was an acceptance of that counter-offer, as is shown by the acknowledgment which the sellers signed and returned to the buyers. The reference to the quotation of 23rd May 1969 referred only to the price and identity of the machine ....

In many of these cases our traditional analysis of offer, counter-offer, rejection, acceptance and so forth is out-of-date. This was observed by Lord Wilberforce in *New Zealand Shipping Co Ltd v AM Satterthwaite* [1974] 1 All ER 1015. The better way is to look at all the documents passing between the parties and glean from them, or from the conduct of the parties, whether they have reached agreement on all material points, even though there may be differences between the forms and conditions printed on the back of them. As Lord Cairns LC said in *Brogden v Metropolitan Railway* (1877) 2 App Cas 666:

> '... there may be a *consensus* between the parties far short of a complete mode of expressing it, and that *consensus* may be discovered from letters or from other documents of an imperfect and incomplete description'.

Applying this guide, it will be found that in most cases when there is a 'battle of forms' there is a contract as soon as the last of the forms is sent and received without objection being taken to it. That is well observed in Benjamin on Sale. The difficulty is to decide which form, or which part of which form, is a term or condition of the contract. In some cases the battle is won by the man who fires the last shot. He is the man who puts forward the latest term and conditions: and, if they are not objected to by the other party, he may be taken to have agreed to them. Such was *British Road Services Ltd v Arthur V Crutchley & Co Ltd* [1968] 1 All ER 811, *per* Lord Pearson; and the illustration given by Professor Guest in Anson's *Law of Contract* where he says that 'the terms of the contract consist of the terms of the offer subject to the modifications contained in the acceptance'. That may however go too far. In some cases, however, the battle is won by the man who gets the blow in first. If he offers to sell at a named price on the terms and conditions stated on the back and the buyer orders the goods purporting to accept the offer on an order form with his own different terms and conditions on the back, then, if the difference is so material that it would affect the price, the buyer ought not to be allowed to take advantage of the difference unless he draws it specifically to the attention of the seller. There are yet other cases where the battle depends on the shots fired on both sides. There is a concluded contract but the forms vary. The terms and conditions of both parties are to be construed together. If they can be reconciled so as to give a harmonious result, all well and good. If differences are irreconcilable, so that they are mutually contradictory, then the conflicting terms may have to be scrapped and replaced by a reasonable implication.

In the present case the judge thought that the sellers in their original quotation got their blow in first; especially by the provision that 'These terms and conditions shall prevail over any terms and conditions in the Buyer's order'. It was so emphatic that the price variation clause continued through all the subsequent dealings and that the buyer must be taken to have agreed to it. I can understand that point of view. But I think that the documents have to be considered as a whole. And, as a matter of construction, I think the acknowledgment of 5th June 1969 is the decisive document. It makes it clear that the contract was on the buyers' terms and not the sellers' terms: and the buyers' terms did not include a price variation clause.

I would therefore allow the appeal and enter judgment for the buyers.

Lawton and Bridge L.JJ. concurred.

It may be questioned why the acknowledgement slip was regarded as such a crucial communication – sufficient to override the clear statement in the sellers' letter that they were relying on their previously stated terms. The decision demonstrates some of the difficulties in applying an offer and acceptance analysis: and which communication or action constitutes the acceptance may well be a matter on which there is disagreement.

It has been recognised that the attempt to fit all dealings between parties into the rigid boxes of 'offer' and 'acceptance' can be rather artificial. Lord Wilberforce, in an often-quoted passage from *New Zealand Shipping Co v Satterthwaite, The Eurymedon* [1975] AC 154 (the facts of which can be found in Section 5.4.4) acknowledged this. Discussing the commercial relationship that existed in that case, and whether it had given rise to a contract, he commented (at p 167):

> It is only the precise analysis of this complex of relations into the classical offer and acceptance, with identifiable consideration, that seems to present difficulty, but this same difficulty exists in many situations of daily life, e.g., sales at auction; supermarket purchases; boarding an omnibus; purchasing a train ticket; tenders for the supply of goods; offers of rewards; acceptance by post; warranties of authority by agents; manufacturers' guarantees; gratuitous bailments; bankers' commercial credits. These are all examples which show that English law, having committed itself to a rather technical and schematic doctrine of contract, in application takes a practical approach, often at the cost of forcing the facts to fit uneasily into the marked slots of offer, acceptance and consideration.

On some occasions the courts have been prepared to recognise that a contract can be made without it being possible to identify a clear offer and acceptance. Until recently this has been regarded as exceptional, as indicated by how Lord Diplock put it in *Gibson v Manchester City Council* (Section 2.2.3):

> My Lords, there may be certain types of contract, though I think they are exceptional, which do not fit easily into the normal analysis of a contract as being constituted by offer and acceptance; but a contract alleged to have been made by an exchange of correspondence between the parties in which the successive communications other than the first are in reply to one another is not one of these.

An example of a judge being prepared to find a contract without a clear offer and acceptance is the judgment of Steyn L.J. in *Trentham Ltd v Archital Luxfer* [1993] 1 Lloyd's Rep 25. He expressed the view that in relation to a fully executed agreement it was possible for a contract to come into existence during performance, even if it cannot be precisely analysed in terms of offer and acceptance (at pp 29–30). Such an approach has now been given support by the Supreme Court in the following case.

RTS Flexible Systems Ltd v Molkerei Alois Müller GmbH & Company KG (UK Production) **[2010] UKSC 14; [2010] 1 WLR 753**

Facts: The parties were in negotiation in relation to the supply of equipment and associated work. Work started on the basis of a Letter of Intent, which later expired. It was always intended that there should be a formal written contract, but although there was agreement on many terms, including the price of £1,682,000, no written contract was ever signed. On a preliminary issue the trial judge held that there was a contract, but simply to supply the equipment at the stated price: none of the other negotiated terms applied. The Court of Appeal held that there was no contract at all. The parties appealed to the Supreme Court.

Held: There was a contract between the parties, and it was intended to be governed by the terms agreed during the negotiations.

Lord Clarke

1. This is the judgment of the court. The appeal arises out of a dispute between RTS Flexible Systems Limited ('RTS') and Molkerei Alois Müller GmbH & Co KG ('Müller') in relation to work carried out and equipment supplied by RTS to Müller. The different decisions in the courts below and the arguments in this court demonstrate the perils of beginning work without agreeing the precise basis upon which it is to be done. The moral of the story to is to agree first and to start work later. The claim was brought by RTS for 'money due under a contract, alternatively damages'....

2. The parties had initially intended to enter into a detailed written contract which would set out all the complex terms on which the work was to be carried out and the equipment supplied. However, as often happens, the terms were not finalised before it was agreed that work should begin. It was common ground before the judge that the parties entered into a contract formed by a letter of intent dated 21 February 2005 and a letter from RTS dated 1 March 2005 ('the LOI contract'), the purpose of which was to enable work to begin on agreed terms. The judge held that the LOI contract was treated by the parties as expiring on 27 May 2005. The judge further held that after the lapse of the LOI contract the parties reached full agreement on the work that was to be done for the price that they had already agreed, which was £1,682,000 and had been agreed in the LOI contract. He held that the natural inference from the evidence was that their contract was that RTS would carry out the agreed work for the agreed price. It was not however essential for them to have agreed the terms and conditions and they did not do so. They continued after the expiry of the LOI contract just as they had before, by calling for and carrying out the work without agreement as to the applicable terms. The judge declined to hold that the parties' contract included the final draft version of certain terms known as the MF/1 terms (the 'MF/1 terms').

3. RTS appealed to the Court of Appeal [2009] 2 All ER (Comm) 542 .... The Court of Appeal allowed the appeal and made a declaration that the parties did not enter into any contract after the LOI contract came to an end.

4. The essential issues in this appeal, which is brought by permission given by the House of Lords, are whether the parties made a contract after the expiry of the LOI contract and, if so, on what terms. As to terms, the argument centres on whether the contract was subject to some or all of the MF/1 terms as amended by agreement. Müller submits that the judge was correct to hold both that there was a contract after the expiry of the LOI contract, and that it was not on any of the MF/1 terms, whereas RTS submits that the Court of Appeal was right to hold that there was no contract but that, if there was, it was on all the MF/1 terms as amended in the course of negotiations. ...

The principles

45. The general principles are not in doubt. Whether there is a binding contract between the parties and, if so, upon what terms depends what they have agreed. It depends not upon their subjective state of mind, but upon a consideration of what was communicated between them by words or conduct, and whether that leads objectively to a conclusion that they intended to create legal relations and had agreed upon all the terms which they regarded or the law requires as essential for the formation of legally binding relations. Even if certain terms of economic or other significance to the parties have not been finalised, an objective appraisal of their words and conduct may lead to the conclusion that they did not intend agreement of such terms to be a precondition to a concluded and legally binding agreement.

46. The problems that have arisen in this case are not uncommon, and fall under two heads. Both heads arise out of the parties agreeing that the work should proceed before the formal written contract was executed in accordance with the parties' common understanding. The first concerns the effect of the parties' understanding (here reflected in clause 48 of the draft written contract) that the contract would 'not become effective until each party has executed a counterpart and exchanged it with the other' – which never occurred. Is that fatal to a conclusion that the work done was covered by a contract? The second frequently arises in such circumstances and is this. Leaving aside the implications of the parties' failure to execute and exchange any agreement in written form, were the parties agreed upon all the terms which they objectively regarded or the law required as essential for the formation of legally binding relations? Here, in particular, this relates to the terms on which the work was being carried out. What, if any, price or remuneration was agreed and what were the rights and obligations of the contractor or supplier?

[Having reviewed all the facts, the Court came to the conclusion that there was (para 85) 'unequivocal conduct on the part of both parties which leads to the conclusion that it was agreed that the project would be carried out by RTS for the agreed price on the terms agreed by 5 July [i.e. the MF/1 terms] as varied on 25 August [in relation to the order of the work]'.]

86. The first point remains. Had the parties agreed to be bound by the agreed terms without the necessity of a formal written contract or, put another way, had they agreed to waive that requirement and thus clause 48? We have reached the conclusion that they had. The circumstances point to the fact that there was a binding agreement and that it was not on the limited terms held by the judge. The price had been agreed, a significant amount of work had been carried out, agreement had been reached on 5 July and the subsequent agreement to vary the contract so that RTS agreed to provide line 1 before line 2 was reached without any suggestion that the variation was agreed subject to contract. The clear inference is that the parties had agreed to waive the subject to contract clause, *viz* clause 48. Any other conclusion makes no commercial sense. RTS could surely not have refused to perform the contract as varied pending a formal contract being signed and exchanged. Nobody suggested that it could and, of course, it did not. If one applies the standard of the reasonable, honest businessman suggested by Steyn LJ, we conclude that, whether he was an RTS man or a Müller man, he would have concluded that the parties intended that the work should be carried out for the agreed price on the agreed terms, including the terms as varied by the agreement of 25 August, without the necessity for a formal written agreement, which had been overtaken by events.

It is noticeable that nowhere in this judgment does Lord Clarke make reference to 'offer and acceptance'. In paragraph 45 he refers simply to looking at what was said and done with a view to seeing if this indicates a clear intention to create legal relations. This seems very much like the approach Lord Denning was advocating in *Gibson v Manchester City Council* (Section 2.2.3), but which was decisively rejected by the House of Lords at that time. It seems that the approach is perhaps less exceptional than Lord Diplock there suggested, particularly when the courts are considering fully or partially executed commercial contracts (for a fuller discussion of the implications of this case, see Stone, R, 'Forming contracts without offer and acceptance: Lord Denning and the harmonisation of English contract law' [2012] 4 *Web JCLI*.)

Very often, however, in this type of situation it will in any case be possible for the court to find acceptance through conduct, as indeed the trial judge had in *Trentham*'s case. More recently in *Farrar v Rylatt* [2019] EWCA Civ 1864 Coulson L.J. stated:

67. The only authority on this topic that Ms Lawrenson referred to the judge at trial was *RTS Flexible Systems Limited v Molkerei Alois Muller GmbH and Co KG (UK Production)* [2010] UKSC 14; [2010] I WLR 753. In that case, the draft contract contained words which were similar to the Subject to Contract tag used here. The Supreme Court held that, if matters had rested there, the draft would not have had any contractual force. But, as a result of the parties' subsequent conduct, the objective interpretation of the parties' words and conduct at formation, the fact that substantial works were carried out and paid for, and that thereafter, the basis for the work done was varied, the failure to formalise the contract did not prevent the formation of a binding contract.

68. *RTS Flexible Systems* was properly described by the judge as an exceptional case and one that turned on its own facts. One particular point of fact in that case was that a good deal of money had been paid and a considerable amount of work done so as to make it 'unrealistic' (see Lord Clarke at [58]) to say there had not been a binding contract. Performance can be a critical factor in demonstrating that the parties intended to create legal relations (see the classic statement of Steyn LJ in *G. Percy Trentham v Archital Luxfer* [1993] 1 Lloyd's Rep 25 at 27, to which Lord Clarke referred).

> But the position is very different here. Building work was done on The Barns but that was paid for by JKR, and there is now no dispute about or under the building contract. No element of any profit share was paid to the appellants because their entitlement to any such profit has always been disputed. That is therefore a significant factual difference between this case and *RTS Flexible Systems*.

See also *Astra Asset Management UK Ltd v The Co-Operative Bank Plc* [2019] EWHC 897 (Comm) and *Devani v Wells* [2019] UKSC 4.

2.2.6.2 Acceptance by conduct

It is not necessary for an acceptance to take the form of words – spoken or written – as long as it is communicated to the other party. Acceptance can be through conduct – for example, by starting to perform the contract. This issue was explored in *Brogden v Metropolitan Railway Company* (1876–77) LR 2 App Cas 666.

***Brogden v Metropolitan Railway Company* (1876–77) LR 2 App Cas 666**

Facts: B had supplied coal to M for a number of years. There were negotiations for a new contract. M sent B a draft agreement. B filled in the name of an arbitrator and completed some other details, and then returned the document to M. M's representative put the agreement in a desk drawer, and there were no further communications about it. M then ordered coal from B. In the course of a subsequent dispute, B claimed that there was no contract, because M had never communicated acceptance of the agreement which B had sent.

Held: The House of Lords confirmed the view of the courts below that there was a contract. The act of ordering coal indicated M's acceptance of the offer made by B.

Lord Cairns (Lord Chancellor): My Lords, there are no cases upon which difference of opinion may more readily be entertained, or which are always more embarrassing to dispose of, than cases where the Court has to decide whether or not, having regard to letters and documents which have not assumed the complete and formal shape of executed and solemn agreements, a contract has really been constituted between the parties. But, on the other hand, there is no principle of law better established than this, that even although parties may intend to have their agreement expressed in the most solemn and complete form that conveyancers and solicitors are able to prepare, still there may be a *consensus* between the parties far short of a complete mode of expressing it, and that *consensus* may be discovered from letters or from other documents of an imperfect and incomplete description; I mean imperfect and incomplete as regards form. …

[The] case finds that at that meeting [on 19 December] the representative of the railway company handed over the form of contract or agreement. The date was in blank, the names of the Messrs. Brogden were not filled up, and, in the clause with regard to arbitration, the name of the arbitrator was also left blank; the price was fixed in the way which had been mentioned in the letter at 20s. a ton, and the continuance of the agreement was to be for a twelvemonth, to run on for another twelvemonth if a notice was not given to terminate by the 1st of November, 1872. This draft, or the agreement in this form, was handed over at this meeting to the Messrs. Brogden or to their agent. On the 21st of December, losing therefore no time, and shewing that the parties at this time were clearly bent upon concluding the business, Mr. Hardman, the agent of Messrs. Brogden, returns the draft agreement with this letter:

> 'Herewith I beg to return your draft of proposed agreement, *re* new contract for coal, which Mr. Brogden has approved. I am obliged to leave town for *Bristol* to-night, and shall be up again on

> Monday week. If you have anything farther to communicate letters addressed to Tondu [the Appellants' collieries] will find me'.

The last sentence is important ...

My Lords, it appears to me that it was with regard to the circumstance that there had been the insertion of this name among other matters, that the letter of the 21st of December contained the words to which I have already called your Lordships' attention, 'If you have anything farther to communicate, letters addressed to "Tondu" will find me'. That appears to me to be just what you would have expected ....

My Lords, that draft having been sent in this form to the railway directors, the statement in the case is that 'Mr. Burnett was the proper custodian of contracts for the supply of coke and coal for the Plaintiffs. On receipt of the paper enclosed in Mr. Hardman's letter he put it into his drawer, and it remained there till the 7th of November, 1872, when it was produced to Mr. Alexander Brogden on the occasion hereinafter mentioned'.

Now, my Lords, I will call your Lordships' attention to what was done subsequent to this date; but before I do so, there is at the very outset this remarkable circumstance, which your Lordships will bear in mind: these two parties having been in negotiation up to the 22nd of December, both of them clearly bent upon making a contract which was to provide for a supply of coals in the following year, both of them engaged upon it, and so seriously engaged upon it that they had reduced it into writing with very considerable minuteness of detail; according to the view of the Appellants, this agreement, which they were so bent on forming, is said suddenly and without any kind of explanation to have passed entirely out of view, an incomplete and unfinished transaction, as regarded which there never was any *consensus* between them, and no explanation is given in any shape or form of why it was, according to the view of the Appellants, that there never was any reference afterwards to the contract, nor any proceeding taken to have it brought to a definite point. My Lords, it would be, indeed, a very strange matter if, both parties having shewn such earnestness in the business to which they were addressing themselves, they were from the moment of the 22nd of December to be held to have parted without any impression whatever that anything had been done towards accomplishing the object of that act upon which they were bent.

But, my Lords, what took place afterwards was this: On the 22nd of December Mr. Burnett, getting this draft, putting it where the contracts of the company were placed for custody, writes in return to Messrs. Brogden & Sons. He makes no objection to anything which had been done with regard to that document; he is silent upon that subject, but he says, 'We shall require 250 tons per week of locomotive coal, commencing not later than the 1st of January next' – the very date which was the date mentioned in the contract for the commencement of the supply – 'Reply by wire that you will do this, that we may arrange with other collieries accordingly'. My Lords, the contract had provided, with regard to the amount of the supply, that it should be '220 tons of coal, and any farther quantity of coal not exceeding 350 tons per week, at such times and in such quantity as the company shall by writing under their agent's hands from time to time require, such notice to be given to the contractors or agents of the contractors for the time being'.

Now reference was made to this letter, and some argument was raised upon it to the effect that it was a letter asking Messrs. Brogden to reply by wire whether they would supply the 250 tons, and that it was therefore inconsistent with a right to order that supply. My Lords, it seems to me to be the most natural letter possible for persons who had a contract to have written. They order a supply within the terms of the contract greater than the minimum, which was 220 tons, but within their power as regards the maximum; and it seems to me that, inasmuch as they had to give notice with regard to the times and the mode of any supply over 220 tons, it was only what men in that position would have done, to ask those who had to make that supply whether they might depend and rely upon their affording it at the times and in the quantity which were thus specified.

My Lords, on the 22nd of December Messrs. Brogden & Sons telegraph to the railway directors, 'We have arranged to supply you quantity you name, 250 tons weekly, from 1st January'. And without going through the letters as to the change of supply, I may say that the quantity was afterwards changed to a quantity of 350 tons per week, which also was a quantity not beyond the maximum mentioned, but the actual maximum mentioned by the contract.

My Lords, those are the grounds which lead me to think that, there having been clearly a *consensus* between these parties, arrived at and expressed by the document signed by Mr. Brogden, subject only to approbation, on the part of the company, of the additional term which he had introduced with regard to an arbitrator, that approbation was clearly given when the company commenced a course of dealing which is referable in my mind only to the contract, and when that course of dealing was accepted and acted upon by Messrs. Brogden & Co. in the supply of coals. Therefore, my Lords, I am of opinion that the conclusion at which the Court of Common Pleas arrived was correct, as was also the conclusion at which the majority of the Court of Appeal arrived.

This treatment of conduct as acceptance is significant, particularly in relation to commercial contracts. For a recent example see *Reveille Independent LLC v Anotech International (UK) Ltd* [2016] EWCA Civ 443, where acceptance by conduct (i.e. engaging in performance of the proposed contract) overrode a previously stated requirement that a signature was required for the contract to come into existence. On the facts, treating the conduct as acceptance prejudiced neither party.

2.2.6.3 Acceptance by silence

What is the position if the offeree makes no response to an offeror, who has said that if nothing more happens the assumption will be that a contract has come into existence (for example, the offeror says 'if I do not receive a response from you, I will assume that you are happy with my proposal and that we have a deal'? We have seen that verbal communication is not necessary – acceptance can be by conduct – but can silence be sufficient to indicate acceptance? The most frequently cited authority in this area is the old case of *Felthouse v Bindley*.

Felthouse v Bindley **(1862) 11 CB (NS) 869 (CP)**

Facts: An uncle and nephew had been negotiating over the sale of a horse, which the nephew had put up for auction. The uncle offered to buy it at a particular price and said that he would assume if he heard nothing further that it was his. The nephew instructed the auctioneer to remove the horse from the sale, but did not communicate further with his uncle. The auctioneer, by mistake, sold the horse at the auction. The uncle sued the auctioneer, claiming that the horse was his under his contract with his nephew.

Held: The uncle was unable to impose a contract on his nephew by indicating that silence would be taken as consent. Communication of an acceptance from the offeree to the offeror was necessary in order for a contract to come into existence.

Willes J: ... The horse in question had belonged to the plaintiff's nephew, John Felthouse. In December, 1860, a conversation took place between the plaintiff and his nephew relative to the purchase of the horse by the former. The uncle seems to have thought that he had on that occasion bought the horse for £30, the nephew that he had sold it for 30 guineas, but there was clearly no complete bargain at that time. On the 1st of January, 1861, the nephew writes, – 'I saw my father on Saturday. He told me that you considered you had bought the horse for £30. If so, you are labouring under a mistake, for 30 guineas was the price I put upon him, and you never heard me say less. When you said you would have him, I considered you were aware of the price'. To this the uncle replies on the following day – 'Your price, I admit, – was 30 guineas. I offered £30; never offered more: and you said the horse was mine. However, as there may be a mistake about him, I will split the difference. If I hear no more about him, I consider the horse mine at £30 15s'. It is clear that there was no complete bargain on the 2nd of January; and it is also clear that the uncle had no right to impose upon the nephew a sale of his horse for £30 15s unless he chose to comply with the condition of writing to repudiate the offer. The nephew might, no doubt, have bound his uncle to the bargain by writing to him; the uncle might also have retracted his offer at any time before acceptance. It stood an open offer, and so things remained until the 25th of February, when the nephew was about to sell his farming stock by auction. The horse in question being catalogued with the rest of the stock, the auctioneer (the defendant) was told that it was already sold. It is clear, therefore, that the nephew in his own mind intended his uncle to have the horse at the price which he (the uncle) had named, – £30 15*s*.: but he had not communicated such his intention to his uncle, or done anything to bind himself. Nothing, therefore, had been done to vest the property in the horse in the plaintiff down to the 25th of February, when the horse was sold by the defendant. ...

Keating J: I am of the same opinion. Had the question arisen as between the uncle and the nephew, there would probably have been some difficulty. But, as between the uncle and the auctioneer, the only question we have to consider is whether the horse was the property of the plaintiff at the time of the sale on the 25th of February. It seems to me that nothing had been done at that time to pass the property out of the nephew and vest it in the plaintiff. A proposal had been made, but there had before that day been no acceptance binding the nephew.

The case of *Felthouse v Bindley* has generally been taken to establish that a bilateral contract can never be accepted by silence. Indeed, in *The Leónidas D* [1985] 2 All ER 796; [1985] 1 WLR 925, Robert Goff J. noted that: 'We have all been brought up to believe it to be axiomatic that acceptance of an offer cannot be inferred from silence, save in the most exceptional circumstances' (at 805; 937). On the other hand, others have suggested that it does depend on the circumstances – in *Felthouse v Bindley* itself, Keating J. notes that if the dispute had been between the uncle and nephew 'there would probably have been some difficulty'. The kinds of argument that might be raised in this context are well explored in the following extract from an article by Professor Miller:

Miller CJ, '*Felthouse v Bindley* Re-visited' (1972) 35 *MLR* 489

An interesting and unresolved point which has given rise to a certain amount of academic discussion is that of the extent to which it is open to an offeror effectively to waive the need for any formal communication of acceptance. ... [Professor Miller notes that such waiver is accepted in unilateral contracts (see, for example, *Carlill v Carbolic Smoke Ball Co*) and refers to cases such as *Weatherby v Bonham* (1832) 5 C & P 228 and *Taylor v Allan* [1965] 1 All ER 557, which he suggests indicate that waiver may be possible in bilateral contracts, The difficulty is *Felthouse v Bindley*.]

The leading English case of *Felthouse v Bindley* (1862) 11 CB (NS) 869 might, however, be thought to point conclusively in the opposite direction [i.e., against the possibility of waiving the communication of acceptance in a bilateral contract]. In this case the plaintiff and his nephew had been negotiating about the sale of a horse and had failed to reach agreement over the price. The plaintiff thereupon wrote to the nephew saying, 'If I hear no more about him, I consider the horse is mine at £30 15s'. The nephew did not reply, but he resolved to accept the offer and informed the defendant auctioneer, who was selling off his farming stock, that the horse in question was not to be disposed of as it had already been sold. The auctioneer mistakenly sold the horse and he was sued by the plaintiff in conversion. The Common Pleas held for the auctioneer on the ground that the plaintiff had no title to sue since at the date of the auction the nephew had not effectively accepted the offer. Given that he had admittedly told the auctioneer that the horse was reserved for his uncle and that the latter had equally assumed that this was so, it is not clear why anything further should have been regarded as essential to the formation of a contract. On balance it is submitted that the approach of the Common Pleas was wrong in principle and that the actual result of the case can only be supported because there had been no delivery, part payment or memorandum in writing to satisfy the then requirements of the Statute of Frauds. This was the alternative reason given by the Common Pleas and it was the reason which appears to have been emphasised by the Exchequer Chamber when affirming the decision on appeal.

If one is prepared to concede that positive conduct falling short of communication is sufficient to conclude a bilateral contract, this still leaves open the question of whether silence coupled with mental assent would be equally sufficient where the offeror has purported to waive the need for notification. The additional difficulty here is, of course, that the lack of any outward expression of assent would effectively enable the offeree to deny or assert the fact of acceptance to suit his own convenience. Lord Denning clearly appreciated the point in *Robophone Facilities v Blank* [1966] 3 All ER 128 when he discussed the effect of a clause providing that, 'This agreement shall become binding on the [plaintiffs] only upon acceptance thereof by signature ... on their behalf'. His Lordship was clear that notwithstanding this terminology,

> 'Signing without notification is not enough. It would be deplorable if it were. The plaintiffs would be able to keep the form in their office unsigned, and then play fast and loose as they pleased. The defendant would not know whether or not there was a contract binding them to supply or him to take. Just as mental acceptance is not enough, nor is internal acceptance within the plaintiff's office'.

This statement accords with the views expressed in the House of Lords in the old case of *Brogden v Metropolitan Railway* (1876) 2 App Cas 666, and it may well be productive of justice where, as in the *Robophone* case itself, the offer is submitted on a standard form agreement drawn up by the offeree. It is not, however, difficult to envisage other situations where insistence on the need for such notification might well work substantial injustice. Thus suppose that A writes to B offering to buy his car for £100 and adding, 'There is no need to reply. If I do not hear from you within the week, I shall assume you accept.' If B wishes to take up the offer and remains silent it would hardly be satisfactory to permit A to deny the existence of a contract on the ground that acceptance had not been notified when he himself had expressly stated that it was unnecessary. Again it would have been equally unsatisfactory if the uncle in *Felthouse v Bindley* could have pointed to the lack of notification if it had been he who was being sued by the nephew for damages for non-acceptance. Presumably if A and the uncle are to be regarded as having entered a contract to purchase then B and the nephew must be regarded as having entered a contract to sell. Notwithstanding the admitted difficulties involved, it is tentatively submitted that in such cases there may be an effective waiver of the need for communication of acceptance, and, moreover, a contract may be concluded without the need for any external manifestation of assent. A similar view is expressed in section 72(1)(b) of the American Restatement on Contracts which reads:

Where an offeree fails to reply to an offer, his silence and inaction operate as an acceptance ... where the offeror has stated or given the offeree reason to understand that assent may be made by silence and the offeree intends to accept.

Despite the arguments put forward in this article it is difficult to see that there is much wrong with the rule that in bilateral contracts some behaviour indicating acceptance is required.

2.2.6.4 Acceptance by post

The standard position, as we have seen, is that acceptance must be communicated to be effective. However, this does not answer all questions which might arise when parties start to contract at a distance through means that may involve delay between one party sending an acceptance and the other receiving it. This issue, for example, arises in connection with contracts made via the postal service. Application of the standard rule would mean that a posted acceptance has no effect until the person to whom it is addressed reads it. But is this the best way of dealing with the situation? Is it right that the acceptor should have to wait for confirmation that his or her letter has been read to know whether or not a contract has been made? The first reported case in which the question was considered dates from before the introduction of the 'penny post'.

Adams v Lindsell (1818) 1 B & Ald 681; 106 ER 250

Facts: The owners of a quantity of wool sent a letter offering it to the plaintiffs. The letter was misdirected and arrived later than would have been expected. The plaintiffs immediately replied by letter accepting the offer. The sellers, however, had sold the wool elsewhere before the letter of acceptance was delivered (though after it had been posted).

Held: The acceptance was effective on posting, and there was a binding contract for the sale of the wool to the plaintiffs at that point.

Action for non-delivery of wool according to agreement. At the trial at the last Lent Assizes for the county of Worcester, before Burrough J it appeared that the defendants, who were dealers in wool, at St. Ives, in the county of Huntingdon, had, on Tuesday the 2nd of September 1817, written the following letter to the plaintiffs, who were woollen manufacturers residing in Bromsgrove, Worcestershire. 'We now offer you eight hundred tods of wether fleeces, of a good fair quality of our country wool, at 35*s*.6*d*. per tod, to be delivered at Leicester, and to be paid for by two months' bill in two months, and to be weighed up by your agent within fourteen days, receiving your answer in course of post.'

This letter was misdirected by the defendants, to Bromsgrove, Leicestershire, in consequence of which it was not received by the plaintiffs in Worcestershire till 7p.m. on Friday, September 5th. On that evening the plaintiffs wrote an answer, agreeing to accept the wool on the terms proposed. The course of the post between St. Ives and Bromsgrove is through London, and consequently this answer was not received by the defendants till Tuesday, September 9th. On the Monday September 8th, the defendants not having, as they expected, received an answer on Sunday September 7th (which in case their letter had not been mis-directed, would have been in the usual course of the post), sold the wool in question to another person. Under these circumstances, the learned judge held, that the delay having been occasioned by the neglect of the defendants, the jury must take it, that the answer did come back in due course of post; and that then the defendants were liable for the loss that had been sustained: and the plaintiffs accordingly recovered a verdict.

Jervis having in Easter term obtained a rule nisi for a new trial, on the ground that there was no binding contract between the parties, Dauncey, Puller, and Richardson, shewed cause. They contended, that at the moment of the acceptance of the offer of the defendants by the plaintiffs, the former became bound. And that was on the Friday evening, when there had been no change of circumstances. They were then stopped by the Court, who called upon Jervis and Campbell in support of the rule. They relied on *Payne v Cave* (1789) 3 Term Rep 148, and more particularly on *Cooke v Oxley* (1790) 3 Term Rep 653. In that case, Oxley who had proposed to sell goods to Cooke, and given him a certain time at his request, to determine whether he would buy them or not, was held not liable to the performance of the contract, even though Cooke, within the specified time, had determined to buy them, and given Oxley notice to that effect. So here the defendants who have proposed by letter to sell this wool, are not to be held liable, even though it be now admitted that the answer did come back in due course of post. Till the plaintiffs' answer was actually received, there could be no binding contract between the parties; and before then, the defendants had retracted their offer, by selling the wool to other persons.

But the court said, that if that were so, no contract could ever be completed by the post. For if the defendants were not bound by their offer when accepted by the plaintiffs till the answer was received, then the plaintiffs ought not to be bound till after they had received the notification that the defendants had received their answer and assented to it. And so it might go on ad infinitum. The defendants must be considered in law as making, during every instant of the time their letter was travelling, the same identical offer to the plaintiffs; and then the contract is completed by the acceptance of it by the latter. Then as to the delay in notifying the acceptance, that arises entirely from the mistake of the defendants, and it therefore must be taken as against them, that the plaintiffs' answer was received in course of post.

Was the court right to suggest that a contract could never be concluded by the post if an acceptance was not effective until read by the offeror? Surely, once the accepting company had received confirmation of its letter's arrival, then both parties could proceed on the basis that there was a binding contract? The argument has even less force in modern times, when it is easy to check on the arrival of a letter by means of a phone call, text message or email. Nevertheless, the view taken in *Adams v Lindsell*, that the most business efficient solution was to treat an acceptance as effective on posting, was adopted by later cases in the nineteenth century (e.g. *Dunlop v Higgins* (1848) 1 HLC 384, *Henthorn v Fraser* [1892] 2 Ch 27), and still represents the position on the issue at the start of the twenty-first century.

Gardner has suggested that there may have been reasons other than simple business efficiency, which contributed to the court's enthusiasm for the postal rule.

Gardner, S, 'Trashing with *Trollope:* a deconstruction of the postal rules' (1992) *OJLS* 170, pp 178–184

The 1840s decisions and postal reform

1840 was the year in which the uniform penny post was introduced, and the circumstances surrounding this event may have much significance for appreciating the decisions of that decade.

The uniform penny post had been proposed in 1837, in a pamphlet entitled *Post Office Reform: Its Importance and Practicability*, published by Rowland Hill. The idea was that there should be a uniform rate of letter postage of 1d across the whole country. Hill's argument was taken up by Robert Wallace MP, who since 1833 had himself been crusading for the reform of the nation's postal arrangements. In 1835 his efforts had procured the appointment of a Commission of Inquiry, which over the next three years produced ten reports, recommending various improvements, many of which were put into effect during the late 1830s. Wallace now obtained the appointment of a Select Committee of the House of Commons to consider Hill's arguments. In fact, the Committee's report, in 1838, found some of Hill's calculations about revenue rather naïve, and as a result did not altogether support his scheme. Nevertheless, in 1839–40 it was enacted and brought into effect.

It is important to understand that the introduction of the penny post was not a random event. It was – and was contemporarily regarded and supported as – an element in the general programme of liberal reform of the age. Robert Wallace was the new MP for Greenock, a town newly enfranchised under the Reform Act, and Wallace was a free-trader, concerned for the economic development of his constituency. Given its remote location, he felt, an efficient system of postage was essential to providing its traders with what is nowadays called 'a level playing-field'; or perhaps, more positively, to their being able to contribute fully to the prosperity of the nation. Hill too was a liberal, though more of the ideological kind: his designs for the postal service seem to have sprung from his concern for the education and general civilization of the people; he regarded the post as a means of disseminating knowledge, and free trade principles as a means of improving its effectiveness. And it was the huge public support for Hill's scheme, especially from amongst the then Whig government's liberal supporters, which in 1838–9 persuaded the government – somewhat against, as we have seen, the Select Committee's advice – that it should be enacted.

This popular support for Hill's scheme may be an important part of the explanation for the rule which the courts were to adopt by their decisions in the 1840s. The general perception seems to have been that the scheme provided something of a panacea, by which the postal service would become in every way thoroughly wonderful.

Examination shows that Hill's ideas – and especially his handling of Post Office affairs when he was appointed to administer it – left much to be desired, but that is not to detract from the reality of the contemporary enthusiasm for them. And it is quite clear that very substantial improvements in postal efficiency were indeed occurring at this time, partly from the recommendations of the 1835 Commission, but above all from the fact that from 1830 the mail began to be carried on the new railways, which by 1846 had entirely superseded the slower and less reliable coach system on routes to and from London.

This contemporary perception may have played a substantial part in the decisions in which the courts established the acceptance rule in the 1840s. In these terms, the basis of the rule might have been not a preference for posting over delivery as the dispositive act. It might have been an idea that delivery was self-evidently important, but that in the newly prevailing conditions posting and delivery were little different: that once posted, a letter was as good as delivered. But there is a certain weakness about this. Despite the great improvements in efficiency to which reference has been made, equating posting with delivery on purely empirical grounds would have been a little foolish: indeed, the reason why these cases came to court at all was because the equation had failed.

However, some of Hill's other innovations added a further dimension to this constructive identification of posting with delivery. One was a dramatic shift towards prepayment of postage. In March 1839, only 14 per cent of letters sent by the London General Post were prepaid, leaving 86 per cent for which payment had to be collected from the addressee. By February 1840 these figures had been precisely reversed. Prepayment was endorsed by none other than Queen Victoria herself, abandoning the privilege of free use of the mail. A year later still, the unpaid element had fallen further to 8 per cent. A second was the further facilitation of prepayment by the introduction in 1840 of the self-adhesive postage stamp: another measure which entranced the public. Of the February 1841 prepaid total of 92 per cent, 45 per cent comprised letters for which the payment was by this means. A third important innovation was the cutting of letter-boxes in front doors of houses, so that letters no longer needed to be handed to their addressee; this too captured the public imagination.

Taken together, these measures may have great significance. Until 1840, the delivery of a letter typically required that the addressee should manually receive it and pay for it. This was not, of course, a significant practical hurdle, but it sat in symbolic contrast with the new position, whereby the sender had only to affix his stamp and post the letter, and it would go through to its destination *without further subvention from outside the system.* So these three innovations of 1840 may be seen as predicating a radically new perception of the nature of the post: the notional equation of the posting of a letter with its delivery. They may thus have been a very powerful influence towards the courts affirming the acceptance rule in the way that they did in that decade. (The empirical efficiency of the system still matters to some extent, in that the argument would not work unless the system was perceived as at least adequately efficient; but we have seen that in the 1840s this was the case.)

This identification of posting with delivery is to be seen in an episode from Anthony Trollope's novel of 1873, *The Eustace Diamonds.* In a conversation, Frank Greystock has told Lucy Morris of his love for her, but has not proposed marriage to her. After some agonizing, he now decides to do so. He puts his proposal into a letter, which, after further agonizing, he decides to post. 'He walked out of the Temple with it in his hand, and dropped it into a pillar letter-box just outside the gate. As the envelope slipped through his fingers, he felt that he had now bound himself to his fate'. The scene then moves to a conversation between Lucy and Lady Fawn, her employer and mentor. Lucy tells Lady Fawn of her inconclusive conversation with Frank. Lady Fawn takes it to mean that Frank is trifling with Lucy's affections, and advises Lucy to think of him no more.

But Lucy shares Frank's feelings, and is discomfited by this advice. The narrator comments: 'If Lucy could only have known of the letter, which was already her own property though lying in the pillar letter-box in Fleet Street, and which had not already been sent down and delivered simply because it was Sunday morning! ... It was so hard on her that she should be so interrogated while that letter was lying in the iron box!'

This material is explicitly along the lines that a letter takes effect on posting, and as such may illuminate the legal rule. To appreciate this, however, we need to explore it in its turn.

Trollope was an employee of the Post Office, and took considerable pride both in his own work there and in the Post Office's service to the public. In *The Eustace Diamonds* (explaining that Lucy's letter was indeed delivered on the Monday morning) he refers to 'that accuracy in the performance of its duties for which it is conspicuous among all offices'. He took pride perhaps above all in having personally secured the introduction of pillar-boxes to this country, in 1852.

Trollope saw pillar-boxes as partnering postage stamps in permitting more convenient use of the postal service: given these two facilities, one no longer needed to go to a post office to mail a letter, either to pay for its postage or, now, to hand it in. (At the same time, he anticipated the fear that letters posted in such boxes might be at risk, and was concerned to rebut it.) These ideas translate very naturally into the notion that, once Frank has put his letter to Lucy into the pillar-box, it is as good as delivered. Even the detail that Frank's letter was held up because it was Sunday is to the same effect. In 1850 the Government had extended Sunday observance to the Post Office, against the latter's wishes. Trollope's presentation of the resulting delay to the letter – and the consequent travail to Lucy's feelings – as the product of an artificial, almost gratuitous inefficiency further emphasizes the underlying identification of posting with delivery. We have already seen how the new postal arrangements captured the public's imagination, so we can surely take it that these ideas would not have been lost on Trollope's readers. If so, the emergent reading of this material in *The Eustace Diamonds* seems to support the view that the 1840s decisions may reflect a common social perception, animated by the contrast with previous arrangements, of a sender having only to post a letter for it automatically to go through to its destination.

Another possible reading of the material in *The Eustace Diamonds* is that it was actually based on the legal rule. Indeed, it comes complete with legal imagery: 'bound', 'property'. Certainly, Trollope was not a legal innocent. In *The Eustace Diamonds* itself he explicitly handles substantive law, having his character Thomas Dove, of the Chancery bar, produce a learned opinion on the subject of heirlooms. This was written for Trollope by a barrister, Charles Merewether, so in itself it by no means indicates that he is likely to have known of the postal rules in contract, but it is not an isolated passage: his novels are full of legal material. Moreover, it was during the 1840s, the period of the seminal decisions on the postal acceptance rule, that (as a postal surveyor in Ireland) his hitherto lackadaisical attitude to his Post Office work changed to one of interest and enthusiasm. It seems plausible that he might well have assimilated the contemporary judicial pronouncements on the subject. The fact that this period also saw the start of his writing may mean that he also began to register their possible symbolic potentialities. So when he was writing *The Eustace Diamonds* in 1870 he may have been drawing on the postal acceptance rule as it had been articulated in the decisions of the 1840s, and conceivably in the obiter dictum in *Hebb's Case* of 1867 (the other cases of this group begin in 1871). However, even if he was drawing on the legal rule here, it seems improbable that Trollope, the great realist, would have used it in this way – not merely as a mode of expression, but as a component of the story itself – unless he judged that it would at least strike a chord with his readers, rather than trying gratuitously to ram a legal curiosity down their throats. Which again returns us to the idea that the judges' rule that a letter takes effect on mailing correlated with a general public consciousness about the post.

The thesis, then, is that the decisions of the 1840s were influenced not so much by internal considerations about offer and acceptance in contract as by a way of regarding the phenomenon of posting as such. It may thus be significant that the first decision of this group – *Stocken v Collin*, which formed the basis of the House of Lords' declaration of the acceptance rule in *Dunlop v Higgins* – was not about the formation of a contract at all, but about notice of the dishonour of a bill of exchange.

2.2.6.5 Limitations on the postal rule

In *Henthorn v Fraser* [1892] 2 Ch 27 it was held that the postal rule would apply wherever it was reasonable to use the post for the acceptance. In that case the offer had been made face to face but the acceptance was by letter. Lord Herschell stated the position in this way (at 33):

> Where the circumstances are such that it must have been within the contemplation of the parties that, according to the ordinary usages of mankind, the post might be used as a means of communicating the acceptance of an offer, the acceptance is complete as soon as it is posted.

This envisages a broad scope for the use of the postal rule, and in *Bruner v Moore* [1904] 1 Ch 305 it was extended to apply to telegrams. Moreover, the rule was taken to its logical conclusion in *Household Fire and Carriage Accident Insurance v Grant* (1879) 4 Ex D 216, where it was held that it would apply even if the letter of acceptance was lost in the post and never received by the offeror. Subsequent case law, however, has tended to limit the application of the rule, rather than extend it. In particular, it seems that in relation to the more modern forms of business communication developed in the twentieth century – telex, fax, email, etc. – the postal rule should not apply, and communication should be required. The starting point is the case of *Entores v Miles Far East Corporation*, where telex was held to be analogous to contracting face to face or over the telephone.

Entores v Miles Far East Corporation [1955] 2 QB 327 (CA)

Facts: A contract was alleged to have been made by exchange of telex between firms operating in England and the Netherlands. The question was whether the contract was made in England or the Netherlands, as this would affect which law governed the transaction.

Held: Where a contract was made by telex, it was formed at the location at which the acceptance was received, not the location from which it was sent.

Denning LJ: ... The plaintiffs are an English company. The defendants are an American corporation with agents all over the world, including a Dutch company in Amsterdam. The plaintiffs say that the contract was made by Telex between the Dutch company in Amsterdam and the English company in London. Communications by Telex are comparatively new. Each company has a teleprinter machine in its office; and each has a Telex number like a telephone number. When one company wishes to send a message to the other, it gets the Post Office to connect up the machines. Then a clerk at one end taps the message on to his machine just as if it were a typewriter, and it is instantaneously passed to the machine at the other end, which automatically types the message onto paper at that end.

The relevant Telex messages in this case were as follows: September 8, 1954: Dutch company: 'Offer for account our associates Miles Far East Corporation Tokyo up to 400 tons Japanese cathodes sterling 240 longton c.i.f. shipment Mitsui Line September 28 or October 10 payment by letter of credit. Your reply Telex Amsterdam 12174 or phone 81490 before 4 p.m. invited'. English company: 'Accept 100 longtons cathodes Japanese shipment latest October 10 sterling £239 10*s*. longton c.i.f. London/Rotterdam payment letter of credit stop please confirm latest tomorrow'. Dutch company: 'We received O.K. Thank you'. September 9, 1954: English company: 'Regarding our telephone conversation a few minutes ago we note that there is a query on the acceptance of our bid for 100 tons payment in sterling and you are ascertaining that your Tokyo office will confirm the price to be longton we therefore await to hear from you further'. September 10, 1954: English company: 'Is the price for the sterling cathodes understood to be for longton by Japan as you were going to find this out yesterday?' Dutch company: 'Yes, price £239 10*s*. for longton'.

At that step there was a completed contract by which the defendants agreed to supply 100 tons of cathodes at a price of £239 10*s*. a ton. The offer was sent by Telex from England offering to pay £239 10*s*.

a ton for 100 tons, and accepted by Telex from Holland. The question for our determination is where was the contract made?

When a contract is made by post it is clear law throughout the common law countries that the acceptance is complete as soon as the letter is put into the post box, and that is the place where the contract is made. But there is no clear rule about contracts made by telephone or by Telex. Communications by these means are virtually instantaneous and stand on a different footing.

The problem can only be solved by going in stages. Let me first consider a case where two people make a contract by word of mouth in the presence of one another. Suppose, for instance, that I shout an offer to a man across a river or a courtyard but I do not hear his reply because it is drowned by an aircraft flying overhead. There is no contract at that moment. If he wishes to make a contract, he must wait till the aircraft is gone and then shout back his acceptance so that I can hear what he says. Not until I have his answer am I bound. I do not agree with the observations of Hill J in *Newcomb v De Roos* (1859) 2 E & E 271.

Now take a case where two people make a contract by telephone. Suppose, for instance, that I make an offer to a man by telephone and, in the middle of his reply, the line goes 'dead' so that I do not hear his words of acceptance. There is no contract at that moment. The other man may not know the precise moment when the line failed. But he will know that the telephone conversation was abruptly broken off because people usually say something to signify the end of the conversation. If he wishes to make a contract, he must therefore get through again so as to make sure that I heard. Suppose next, that the line does not go dead, but it is nevertheless so indistinct that I do not catch what he says and I ask him to repeat it. He then repeats it and I hear his acceptance. The contract is made, not on the first time when I do not hear, but only the second time when I do hear. If he does not repeat it, there is no contract. The contract is only complete when I have his answer accepting the offer.

Lastly, take the Telex. Suppose a clerk in a London office taps out on the teleprinter an offer which is immediately recorded on a teleprinter in a Manchester office, and a clerk at that end taps out an acceptance. If the line goes dead in the middle of the sentence of acceptance, the teleprinter motor will stop. There is then obviously no contract. The clerk at Manchester must get through again and send his complete sentence. But it may happen that the line does not go dead, yet the message does not get through to London. Thus the clerk at Manchester may tap out his message of acceptance and it will not be recorded in London because the ink at the London end fails, or something of that kind. In that case, the Manchester clerk will not know of the failure but the London clerk will know of it and will immediately send back a message 'not receiving'. Then, when the fault is rectified, the Manchester clerk will repeat his message. Only then is there a contract. If he does not repeat it, there is no contract. It is not until his message is received that the contract is complete.

In all the instances I have taken so far, the man who sends the message of acceptance knows that it has not been received or he has reason to know it. So he must repeat it. But, suppose that he does not know that his message did not get home. He thinks it has. This may happen if the listener on the telephone does not catch the words of acceptance, but nevertheless does not trouble to ask for them to be repeated: or the ink on the teleprinter fails at the receiving end, but the clerk does not ask for the message to be repeated: so that the man who sends an acceptance reasonably believes that his message has been received. The offeror in such circumstances is clearly bound, because he will be estopped from saying that he did not receive the message of acceptance. It is his own fault that he did not get it. But if there should be a case where the offeror without any fault on his part does not receive the message of acceptance – yet the sender of it reasonably believes it has got home when it has not – then I think there is no contract.

My conclusion is, that the rule about instantaneous communications between the parties is different from the rule about the post. The contract is only complete when the acceptance is received by the offeror; and the contract is made at the place where the acceptance is received. …

(Birkett and Parker LJJ. concurred).

It is important to note that this case was primarily concerned with *where* the contract was made, not *when* the contract was made. As regards timing, it is clear that the postal rule cannot apply because this would imply that the contract was made at the point it was sent, which is contrary to the decision in *Entores*. Indeed, Lord Denning said (above) that the contract was only complete when the acceptance was 'received' by the offeror. But when does this occur with a communication sent by telex, fax or email? Is it when the message is delivered to the recipient's telex machine, fax machine or email inbox? Or is it when the message is actually read? What if the message is sent out of office hours? Some consideration of these issues in relation to telex occurred in *The Brimnes* [1975] QB 929 and *Brinkibon Ltd v Stahag Stahl* [1983] 2 AC 34. In *The Brimnes* the Court of Appeal held that a telex (in this case a withdrawal notice, rather than an acceptance) received on a telex machine during 'normal office hours' should be regarded as having been effective at that point, whether or not it was actually read. In *Brinkibon v Stahag Stahl*, the House of Lords, while approving *Entores v Miles Far East Corporation*, took a more flexible view.

Brinkibon Ltd v Stahag Stahl GmbH [1983] 2 AC 34 (HL)

Facts: A contract was alleged to have been made by exchange of telexes between London and Vienna, in the form of a counter-offer from Vienna to London (3 May) and an acceptance from London to Vienna (4 May). The Court of Appeal held that the contract was made in Vienna.

Held: Applying the approach taken in *Entores v Miles Far East Corporation*, the contract was made when and where the acceptance was received, in Vienna, but the House of Lords noted the difficulty of applying a general rule to all situations involving telex communications.

Lord Wilberforce: … In the present case it seems that if there was a contract (a question which can only be decided at the trial), it was preceded by and possibly formed by a number of telephone conversations and telexes between London and Vienna, and there are a number of possible combinations upon which reliance can be placed. At this stage we must take the alternatives which provide evidence of a contract in order to see if the test is satisfied. There are two: (i) A telex dated May 3, 1979, from the respondents in Vienna, said to amount to a counter-offer, followed by a telex from the appellants in London to the respondents in Vienna dated May 4, 1979, said to amount to an acceptance. (ii) The above telex dated May 3, 1979, from the respondents followed by action, by way of opening a letter of credit, said to have amounted to an acceptance by conduct.

The first of these alternatives neatly raises the question whether an acceptance by telex sent from London but received in Vienna causes a contract to be made in London, or in Vienna. If the acceptance had been sent by post, or by telegram, then, on existing authorities, it would have been complete when put into the hands of the post office – in London. If on the other hand it had been telephoned, it would have been complete when heard by the offeror – in Vienna. So in which category is a telex communication to be placed? Existing authority of the Court of Appeal decides in favour of the latter category, i.e. a telex is to be assimilated to other methods of instantaneous communication: see *Entores Ltd v Miles Far East Corporation* [1955] 2 QB 327. The appellants ask that this case, which has stood for 30 years, should now be reviewed.

Now such review as is necessary must be made against the background of the law as to the making of contracts. The general rule, it is hardly necessary to state, is that a contract is formed *when* acceptance of an offer is communicated by the offeree to the offeror. And if it is necessary to determine *where* a contract is formed (as to which I have already commented) it appears logical that this should be at the place where acceptance is communicated to the offeror. In the common case of contracts, whether oral or in writing inter praesentes, there is no difficulty; and again logic demands that even where there is not mutual presence at the same place and at the same time, if communication is instantaneous, for example by telephone or radio communication, the same result should follow.

> Then there is the case – very common – of communication at a distance, to meet which the so called 'postal rule' has developed. I need not trace its history: it has firmly been in the law at least since *Adams v Lindsell* (1818) 1 B & Ald 681 …
>
> In this situation, with a general rule covering instantaneous communication inter praesentes, or at a distance, with an exception applying to non-instantaneous communications at a distance, how should communications by telex be categorised? In *Entores Ltd v Miles Far East Corporation* [1955] 2 QB 327 the Court of Appeal classified them with instantaneous communications. Their ruling, which has passed into the textbooks, including *Williston on Contracts*, 3rd edn, 1957, appears not to have caused either adverse comment, or any difficulty to business men. I would accept it as a general rule. Where the condition of simultaneity is met, and where it appears to be within the mutual intention of the parties that contractual exchanges should take place in this way, I think it a sound rule, but not necessarily a universal rule.
>
> Since 1955 the use of telex communication has been greatly expanded, and there are many variants on it. The senders and recipients may not be the principals to the contemplated contract. They may be servants or agents with limited authority. The message may not reach, or be intended to reach, the designated recipient immediately: messages may be sent out of office hours, or at night, with the intention, or upon the assumption, that they will be read at a later time. There may be some error or default at the recipient's end which prevents receipt at the time contemplated and believed in by the sender. The message may have been sent and/or received through machines operated by third persons. And many other variations may occur. No universal rule can cover all such cases: they must be resolved by reference to the intentions of the parties, by sound business practice and in some cases by a judgment where the risks should lie: see *Household Fire and Carriage Accident Insurance Co Ltd v Grant* (1879) 4 Ex D 216, 227 *per* Baggallay LJ and *Henthorn v Fraser* [1892] 2 Ch 27 *per* Lord Herschell.
>
> The present case is, as *Entores Ltd v Miles Far East Corporation* [1955] 2 QB 327 itself, the simple case of instantaneous communication between principals, and, in accordance with the general rule, involves that the contract (if any) was made when and where the acceptance was received. This was on May 4, 1979, in Vienna ….
>
> [Lord Wilberforce went on to reject the alternative analysis put forward and affirmed the decision of the Court of Appeal.]

More recently in *Four Seasons Holdings Incorporated v Brownlie* [2017] UKSC 80 at [16] Lord Sumption (with whom Lord Hughes agreed) stated:

> 'This is the test which has for many years been applied where the contract was made by instantaneous exchanges, e.g. by telephone: see *Entores v Miles Far East Corpn* [1955] 2 QB 327 (CA). It differs from the test applied to contracts made by post, which are complete when and where the letter of acceptance is posted: *Adams v Lindsell* (1818) 1 B & Ald 681, *Dunlop v Higgins* (1848) 1 HLC 381. These rules were adopted for reasons of pragmatic convenience, and provide a perfectly serviceable test for determining whether a contract has been concluded at all. However, their deployment for the purpose of determining when or where a contract was made is not at all satisfactory. It depends on assumptions about the point at which an offer is accepted or deemed to be accepted, which are particularly arbitrary when the mode of communication used is instantaneous (or practically so). It also gives rise to serious practical difficulties. The analysis of an informal conversation in terms of invitation to treat, offer and acceptance will often be impossible without a recording or a total recall of the sequence of exchanges and the exact words used at each stage, in order to establish points which are unlikely to have been of any importance to either party at the time.'

Lady Hale (with whom Lords Wilson and Clarke agreed) stressed that it was not appropriate to reconsider *Entores* in the instance case.

2.2.6.6 Fax and email

It is generally assumed that the approach taken in the telex cases would also be applied to fax and email. Indeed, this has been accepted by the High Court to be the position in relation to email. In *Thomas v BPE Solicitors* [2010] EWHC 306 (Ch), the judge was asked to rule whether an email acceptance sent at 6.00 p.m. should be regarded as effective immediately. He analysed the position as follows:

> **86** The general rule is that the acceptance of an offer is not effective until communicated to the offeror. The 'postal rule' is an anomalous exception to the general rule, which is limited to its particular circumstances. It does not apply to acceptances made by some 'instantaneous' mode of communication ... This was decided in *Entores Ltd v Miles Far East Corporation* [1955] 2 QB 327 as regards communications by telex. At page 334, Denning LJ said that in such a case, 'The contract is only complete when the acceptance is received by the offeror'. Contrary to the claimants' submissions, in my view the same principle applies to communication by email, at least where the parties are conducting the matter by email, as the solicitors were in this case. However, that does not conclude the question, because issues may remain as to when the email in question was received (and also whether it was received). ...
>
> [The judge notes that in *Brinkibon v Stahag Stahal* (above) Lord Wilberforce concluded that 'No universal rule can cover all such cases: they must be resolved by reference to the intentions of the parties, by sound business practice and in some cases by a judgment where the risks should lie' and then continues]:
>
> **88** In *Bernuth Lines Limited v High Seas Shipping Ltd* [2006] 1 Lloyds Rep. 537, it was held that notice of arbitration was validly served by email notwithstanding that it may not have reached the relevant managerial or legal staff in the recipient company. Christopher Clarke J said at pp. 541–42:
>
>> '[29] That is not to say that clicking on the 'send' icon automatically amounts to good service. The e-mail must, of course, be despatched to what is, in fact, the e-mail address of the intended recipient. It must not be rejected by the system. If the sender does not require confirmation of receipt he may not be able to show that receipt has occurred. There may be circumstances where, for instance, there are several e-mail addresses for a number of different divisions of the same company, possibly in different countries, where despatch to a particular e-mail address is not effective service'.
>
> **89** These particular considerations do not apply in the present case. It is not in dispute that the email was received in Mr Cusack's mailbox at or close to 18:00 on 24 August 2007, and was available to be read by him. The question is whether the defendants are correct in their submission that acceptance was not effective from the moment the email was received because it was sent after working hours. In those circumstances, it is submitted, relying on the passage in Lord Wilberforce's judgment that I have quoted, acceptance by the 18.00 email could not in any event have been effective until it came to Mr Cusack's eye on Tuesday morning.
>
> **90** Once one sets aside the 'postal rule' as inapplicable to email communications, the question whether an email acceptance is effective when it arrives, or at the time when the offeror could reasonably be expected to have read it, is not a straightforward one, and does not appear to be settled by authority. On the basis that it must be resolved by reference to the intentions of the parties, by sound business practice and in some cases by a judgment where the risks should lie (*Brinkibon* at page 42), the answer does however appear to me to be clear in the present case. In the context in which the 18:00 email was sent – that is a transaction which (as the earlier emails show) could have been completed that evening – I do not consider that 18:00 was outside working hours. The email was available to be read within working hours, despite the fact that Mr Cusack had in fact gone home. For that reason, I would have held that were the defendants to have accepted the

Rickerbys undertaking by Mr Dew's email, then as a matter of law such acceptance would have been effective upon the receipt of the email at or about 18:00. However, as I have held, they did not do so, nor were they negligent in that regard.

Since the judge found that the email did not constitute an acceptance, his analysis of the issue as to when it was effective is strictly obiter, but nevertheless indicative of the approach of the courts might take. What is clear is that he was of the view that emails should be treated in the same way as telexes. The precise time at which an email acceptance is effective will therefore depend on the surrounding circumstances. In *Greenclose Ltd v NatWest Bank plc* [2014] EWHC 1156 the judge held, again obiter, that the phrase 'giving notice to' implied that the person to whom notice was being given must actually have seen the email – arrival in his inbox would not be sufficient. See also *Kyte v Revenue and Customs Commissioners* [2018] EWHC 1146 (Ch) for a discussion of offer, acceptance, intention to create legal relations and contractual certainty in this context.

2.2.6.7 Websites

Many contracts are currently made through interaction with a website. As far as this type of contract is concerned, the position was affected by a European Directive on Electronic Commerce (2000/31/EC). This was given effect in the U.K. by the Electronic Commerce (EC Directive) Regulations 2002. The relevant paragraphs are to be found in Regulations 11, 12 and 15.

Placing the order

11.–(1) Unless parties who are not consumers have agreed otherwise, where the recipient of the service places his order through technological means, a service provider shall –

(a) acknowledge receipt of the order to the recipient of the service without undue delay and by electronic means; and

(b) make available to the recipient of the service appropriate, effective and accessible technical means allowing him to identify and correct input errors prior to the placing of the order.

(2) For the purposes of paragraph (1)(a) above –

(a) the order and the acknowledgement of receipt will be deemed to be received when the parties to whom they are addressed are able to access them; and

(b) the acknowledgement of receipt may take the form of the provision of the service paid for where that service is an information society service.

(3) The requirements of paragraph (1) above shall not apply to contracts concluded exclusively by exchange of electronic mail or by equivalent individual communications.

Meaning of the term 'order'

12. Except in relation to regulation 9(1)(c) and regulation 11(1)(b) where 'order' shall be the contractual offer, 'order' may be but need not be the contractual offer for the purposes of regulations 9 and 11.

Right to rescind contract

15. Where a person –

(a) has entered into a contract to which these Regulations apply, and

(b) the service provider has not made available means of allowing him to identify and correct input errors in compliance with regulation 11(1)(b), he shall be entitled to rescind the contract unless any court having jurisdiction in relation to the contract in question orders otherwise on the application of the service provider.

The fact that regulation 12 defines 'order' in regulation 11(1)(b) as meaning 'the contractual offer' seems to assume that in this type of transaction it is always the customer who makes the offer and the website operator which accepts it. If so, the power lies with the website operator to decide with whom it wishes to contract and on what terms.

2.2.7 Termination of offers

When does an offer come to an end, so that it can no longer be accepted? We have seen earlier that a rejection by the offeror, or the making of a counter-offer, will have this effect (Section 2.2.6). If the offeror has put a time limit on acceptance, the expiry of this will end the offer; if no time limit is stated, it will lapse after 'a reasonable time', as in *Ramsgate Victoria Hotel Co v Montefiore* (1866) LR 1 Ex 109 (five months was too long for acceptance of an offer to sell shares). The offeror can also, at any time before it has been accepted, revoke an offer, provided this revocation is communicated to the offeree.

***Byrne & Co v Van Tienhoven & Co* (1880) 5 CPD 344 (CP)**

Facts: The defendants wrote from Cardiff on 1 October offering goods for sale to the plaintiffs at New York. The plaintiffs received the offer on 11 October. They accepted it by telegram on the same day and by letter on 15 October. On 8 October the defendants posted to the plaintiffs a letter withdrawing their offer. This letter reached the plaintiffs on 20 October. The plaintiffs sued for breach of contract. The defendants argued that their offer had been withdrawn by the time the plaintiffs purported to accept.

Held: The withdrawal was ineffective. The postal rule did not apply to revocation of acceptance, which had to be communicated.

Lindley J: There is no doubt that an offer can be withdrawn before it is accepted, and it is immaterial whether the offer is expressed to be open for acceptance for a given time or not: *Routledge v Grant* (1828) 4 Bing 653. For the decision of the present case, however, it is necessary to consider two other questions, viz.: 1. Whether a withdrawal of an offer has any effect until it is communicated to the person to whom the offer has been sent? 2. Whether posting a letter of withdrawal is a communication to the person to whom the letter is sent?

It is curious that neither of these questions appears to have actually been decided in this country. As regards the first question, I am aware that Pothier and some other writers of celebrity are of opinion that there can be no contract if an offer is withdrawn before it is accepted, although the withdrawal is not communicated to the person to whom the offer has been made. The reason for this opinion is that there is not in fact any such consent by both parties as is essential to constitute a contact between them. Against this view, however, it has been urged that a state of mind not notified cannot be regarded in dealings between man and man; and that an uncommunicated revocation is for all practical purposes and in point of law no revocation at all. This is the view taken in the United States: see *Tayloe v Merchants Fire Insurance Co* 9 Howard 5 Ct Rep 390 cited in Benjamin on Sales, pp 56–58, and it is adopted by Mr Benjamin. The same view is taken by Mr Pollock in his excellent work on Principles of Contract, ed. ii., p 10, and by Mr Leake in his Digest of the Law of Contracts, p 43. This view, moreover, appears to me much more in accordance with the general principles of English law than the view maintained by Pothier. I pass, therefore, to the next question, viz., whether posting the letter of revocation was a sufficient communication of it to the plaintiff. The offer was posted on the 1st of October, the withdrawal was posted on the 8th, and did not reach the plaintiff until after he had posted his letter of the 11th, accepting the offer. It may be taken as now settled that where an offer is made and accepted by letters sent through the post, the contract is completed the moment the letter accepting the offer is posted: *Harris' Case* (1872) LR 7 Ch App 587;

Dunlop v Higgins (1848) 1 HLC 381, even although it never reaches its destination. When, however, these authorities are looked at, it will be seen that they are based upon the principle that the writer of the offer has expressly or impliedly assented to treat an answer to him by a letter duly posted as a sufficient acceptance and notification to himself, or, in other words, he has made the post office his agent to receive the acceptance and notification of it. But this principle appears to me to be inapplicable to the case of the withdrawal of an offer. In this particular case I can find no evidence of any authority in fact given by the plaintiffs to the defendants to notify a withdrawal of their offer by merely posting a letter; and there is no legal principle or decision which compels me to hold, contrary to the fact, that the letter of the 8th of October is to be treated as communicated to the plaintiff on that day or on any day before the 20th, when the letter reached them. But before that letter had reached the plaintiffs they had accepted the offer, both by telegram and by post; and they had themselves resold the tin plates at a profit.

In my opinion the withdrawal by the defendants on the 8th of October of their offer of the 1st was inoperative; and a complete contract binding on both parties was entered into on the 11th of October, when the plaintiffs accepted the offer of the 1st, which they had no reason to suppose had been withdrawn. Before leaving this part of the case it may be as well to point out the extreme injustice and inconvenience which any other conclusion would produce. If the defendants' contention were to prevail no person who had received an offer by post and had accepted it would know his position until he had waited such a time as to be quite sure that a letter withdrawing the offer had not been posted before his acceptance of it. It appears to me that both legal principles, and practical convenience require that a person who has accepted an offer not known to him to have been revoked, shall be in a position safely to act upon the footing that the offer and acceptance constitute a contract binding on both parties.

It is not essential, however, that the communication of the revocation comes directly from the offeror. As long as the offeree is aware of the fact that the offer has been withdrawn, it seems that that is sufficient. The authority for this is *Dickinson v Dodds*.

***Dickinson v Dodds* (1876) 2 Ch D 463 (CA)**

Facts: On 10 June Dodds offered to sell a property to Dickinson, with the offer to be held open until 12 June. On 11 June, Dickinson learnt from a third party that Dodds was negotiating with Allan. Dickinson made several attempts on the afternoon of 11 June and the morning of 12 June to communicate his acceptance to Dodds but Dodds had already sold to Allan before he was aware of Dickinson's acceptance.

Held: The offer had been withdrawn before Dickinson had effectively accepted.

Mellish LJ: The first question is, whether this document of the 10th of June, 1874, which was signed by Dodds, was an agreement to sell, or only an offer to sell, the property therein mentioned to Dickinson; and I am clearly of opinion that it was only an offer, although it is in the first part of it, independently of the postscript, worded as an agreement ... Well, then, this being only an offer, the law says – and it is a perfectly clear rule of law – that, although it is said that the offer is to be left open until Friday morning at 9 o'clock, that did not bind Dodds. He was not in point of law bound to hold the offer over until 9 o'clock on Friday morning. He was not so bound either in law or in equity. Well, that being so, when on the next day he made an agreement with Allan to sell the property to him, I am not aware of any ground on which it can be said that that contract with Allan was not as good and binding a contract as ever was made. Assuming Allan to have known (there is some dispute about it, and Allan does not admit that he knew of it, but I will assume that he did) that Dodds had made the offer to Dickinson, and had given him till Friday morning at 9 o'clock to accept it, still in point of law that could not prevent Allan from making a more favourable offer than Dickinson, and entering at once into a binding agreement with Dodds.

Then Dickinson is informed by Berry that the property has been sold by Dodds to Allan. Berry does not tell us from whom he heard it, but he says that he did hear it, that he knew it, and that he informed Dickinson of it. Now, stopping there, the question which arises is this – If an offer has been made for the sale of property, and before that offer is accepted, the person who has made the offer enters into a binding agreement to sell the property to somebody else, and the person to whom the offer was first made receives notice in some way that the property has been sold to another person, can he after that make a binding contract by the acceptance of the offer? I am of opinion that he cannot. The law may be right or wrong in saying that a person who has given to another a certain time within which to accept an offer is not bound by his promise to give that time; but, if he is not bound by that promise, and may still sell the property to someone else, and if it be the law that, in order to make a contract, the two minds must be in agreement at some one time, that is, at the time of the acceptance, how is it possible that when the person to whom the offer has been made knows that the person who has made the offer has sold the property to someone else, and that, in fact, he has not remained in the same mind to sell it to him, he can be at liberty to accept the offer and thereby make a binding contract? It seems to me that would be simply absurd. If a man makes an offer to sell a particular horse in his stable, and says, 'I will give you until the day after tomorrow to accept the offer,' and the next day goes and sells the horse to somebody else, and receives the purchase-money from him, can the person to whom the offer was originally made then come and say, 'I accept,' so as to make a binding contract, and so as to be entitled to recover damages for the non-delivery of the horse? If the rule of law is that a mere offer to sell property, which can be withdrawn at any time, and which is made dependent on the acceptance of the person to whom it is made, is a mere *nudum pactum*, how is it possible that the person to whom the offer has been made can by acceptance make a binding contract after he knows that the person who has made the offer has sold the property to someone else? It is admitted law that, if a man who makes an offer dies, the offer cannot be accepted after he is dead, and parting with the property has very much the same effect as the death of the owner, for it makes the performance of the offer impossible. I am clearly of opinion that, just as when a man who has made an offer dies before it is accepted it is impossible that it can then be accepted, so when once the person to whom the offer was made knows that the property has been sold to someone else, it is too late for him to accept the offer, and on that ground I am clearly of opinion that there was no binding contract for the sale of this property by Dodds to Dickinson, and even if there had been, it seems to me that the sale of the property to Allan was first in point of time. However, it is not necessary to consider, if there had been two binding contracts, which of them would be entitled to priority in equity, because there is no binding contract between Dodds and Dickinson.

James L.J. and Bagallay J.A. concurred.

It will be noted that *Dickinson v Dodds* is also authority for the rule that a promise to keep an offer open for a particular time is not generally binding on the offeror (see also *Routledge v Grant* (1828) 4 Bing 653). This is because there is usually no consideration for such a promise – that is, the offeree has not given or promised anything in exchange. The topic of consideration is dealt with fully in the next chapter.

2.2.7.1 Termination of offers in unilateral contracts

A difficulty arises regarding the termination of offers in unilateral contracts. In such a contract, acceptance is generally taken to be the performance of the requested act – for example, returning the lost dog for which a reward has been offered, using a smoke ball in the directed way. We have just seen that an offeror can withdraw an offer at any time before acceptance. Does this mean that an offeror in a unilateral contract can withdraw an offer even though the other party may have started performance, and may even have nearly completed it? This was held to be the case in the early twentieth century U.S. case of *Petterson v Pattberg* (1928) 248 NY 86. More recent authority in England and Wales, however, has suggested that, at least where the offeror is aware that the other party has started performance, the offer may not be unreasonably withdrawn. Two cases need to be noted – *Errington v Errington*, and *Daulia v Four Millbank Nominees*.

Errington v Errington & Woods [1952] 1 KB 290 (CA)

Facts: In 1936 Mr E bought a house for his son and daughter-in-law to live in. He told them that the house would be theirs if they kept up the mortgage payments. They did so for some years. Mr E then died and under his will the house was left to his wife. She sought possession of the house.

Held: The son and daughter-in-law were entitled to remain in the house while they continued to make the mortgage payments, on the basis of a unilateral contract made with Mr E. This could not be terminated while they continued to perform.

Denning LJ: The facts are reasonably clear. In 1936 the father bought the house for his son and daughter-in-law to live in. The father put down £250 in cash and borrowed £500 from a building society on the security of the house, repayable with interest by instalments of 15s. a week. He took the house in his own name and made himself responsible for the instalments. The father told the daughter-in-law that the £250 was a present for them, but he left them to pay the building society instalments of 15s. a week themselves. He handed the building society book to the daughter-in-law and said to her: 'Don't part with this book. The house will be your property when the mortgage is paid.' He said that when he retired he would transfer it into their names. She has, in fact, paid the building society instalments regularly from that day to this with the result that much of the mortgage has been repaid, but there is a good deal yet to be paid .... It is to be noted that the couple never bound themselves to pay the instalments to the building society, and I see no reason why any such obligation should be implied. It is clear law that the court is not to imply a term unless it is necessary, and I do not see that it is necessary here. Ample content is given to the whole arrangement by holding that the father promised that the house should belong to the couple as soon as they had paid off the mortgage. The parties did not discuss what was to happen if the couple failed to pay the instalments to the building society, but I should have thought it clear that, if they did fail to pay the instalments, the father would not be bound to transfer the house to them. The father's promise was a unilateral contract - a promise of the house in return for their act of paying the instalments. It could not be revoked by him once the couple entered on performance of the act, but it would cease to bind him if they left it incomplete and unperformed, which they have not done. If that was the position during the father's lifetime, so it must be after his death. If the daughter-in-law continues to pay all the building society instalments, the couple will be entitled to have the property transferred to them as soon as the mortgage is paid off, but if she does not do so, then the building society will claim the instalments from the father's estate and the estate will have to pay them. I cannot think that in those circumstances the estate would be bound to transfer the house to them, any more than the father himself would have been.

Somervell and Hodson L.JJ. concurred.

Daulia Ltd v Four Millbank Nominees [1978] Ch 231 (CA)

Facts: The parties were negotiating for the sale of some properties. On the afternoon of Tuesday, 21 December the defendants promised that they [the defendants] would enter into a contract for the sale of the properties with the plaintiffs if the plaintiffs procured a banker's draft for the deposit, and attended at the defendants' offices before 10.00 a.m. on Wednesday, 22 December and tendered to the defendants the plaintiffs' part of the contract in the terms already agreed and the banker's draft. When the plaintiffs arrived with the banker's draft at 10.00 a.m. on Wednesday, the defendants refused to go through with the transaction.

Held: There was a unilateral contract, and the defendants could not withdraw their offer until the plaintiffs had a chance to perform, but the contract was in any case unenforceable because it did not comply with the requirements of writing contained in the Law of Property Act 1925 and applying to contracts for the transfer of interests in land.

Goff LJ: ... I therefore turn to the first question. Was there a concluded unilateral contract by the defendants to enter into a contract for sale on the agreed terms?

The concept of a unilateral or 'if' contract is somewhat anomalous, because it is clear that, at all events until the offeree starts to perform the condition, there is no contract at all, but merely an offer which the offeror is free to revoke. Doubts have been expressed whether the offeror becomes bound so soon as the offeree starts to perform or satisfy the condition, or only when he has fully done so. In my judgment, however, we are not concerned in this case with any such problem, because in my view the plaintiffs had fully performed or satisfied the condition when they presented themselves at the time and place appointed with a banker's draft for the deposit and their part of the written contract for sale duly engrossed and signed, and then retendered [sic] the same, which I understand to mean proffered it for exchange. Actual exchange, which never took place, would not in my view have been part of the satisfaction of the condition but something additional which was inherently necessary to be done by the plaintiffs to enable, not to bind, the defendants to perform the unilateral contract.

Accordingly in my judgment, the answer to the first question must be in the affirmative.

Even if my reasoning so far be wrong the conclusion in my view is still the same for the following reasons. Whilst I think the true view of a unilateral contract must in general be that the offeror is entitled to require full performance of the condition which he has imposed and short of that he is not bound, that must be subject to one important qualification, which stems from the fact that there must be an implied obligation on the part of the offeror not to prevent the condition becoming satisfied, which obligation it seems to me must arise as soon as the offeree starts to perform. Until then the offeror can revoke the whole thing, but once the offeree has embarked on performance it is too late for the offeror to revoke his offer.

Because the case was decided on other grounds (that is, the agreement's non-compliance with the formal requirements of the Law of Property Act 1925), Goff L.J.'s statement about the possibility of withdrawing of offers in unilateral contracts is strictly obiter, and so not binding on other courts. Taken with the views expressed by Denning L.J. in *Errington v Errington*, however, it probably does represent the law in this area.

Additional reading

Evans, D.M., 'The Anglo-American Mailing Rule' (1966) 15 *ICLQ* 553.

Goodrich, P., 'The Posthumous Life of the Postal Rule: Requiem and Revival of *Adams v Lindsell*', Ch 4 in Mulcahy, L., and Wheeler, S. (eds), *Feminist Perspectives on Contract Law* (London: Glasshouse Press, 2005).

Hudson, A.H., 'Retraction of Letters of Acceptance' (1966) 82 *LQR* 169.

Macdonald, E., 'Dispatching the Dispatch Rule? The Postal Rule, E-mail, Revocation and Implied Terms' (2013) 19(2) *Web JCLI*.
McClintock, R., 'Objectivity in Contract' (1988–1991) 6 *Auckland UL Rev* 317.
Mitchell, P., and Phillips, J., 'The Contractual Nexus: Is Reliance Essential?' (2002) 22 *OJLS* 115.
Rawlings, R., 'The Battle of the Forms' (1979) 42 *MLR* 715.
Steyn, J., 'Contract Law: Fulfilling the Reasonable Expectations of Honest Men' (1997) 1 13 *LQR* 433.
Stone, R., 'Forming Contracts Without Offer and Acceptance, Lord Denning and the Harmonisation of English Contract Law' (2012) 4 *Web JCLI*.

Chapter 3

Consideration and other tests of enforceability

Chapter contents

3.1 Introduction

Not all agreements will be *legally* enforceable. Contract law in England and Wales uses a number of mechanisms to determine whether or not an agreement is legally enforceable. Generally, an agreement needs to be supported by 'consideration' to be legally enforceable. An exception to this rule is where the agreement is contained in a deed. 'Consideration' is a technical concept that involves finding an element of mutuality, or exchange, in the agreement – each side must bring something to the bargain. If this is present, then an agreement will generally be enforceable. There are also some situations, however, where the law of England and Wales will enforce promises even though there is no deed or consideration; for present purposes the most important of which is through the doctrine of promissory estoppel, which is discussed at the end of this chapter.

There is also an overarching concept of 'intention to create legal relations', which is discussed in Chapter 4.

3.2 Deeds

Traditionally, a 'deed' was a formal document which was signed by the parties *and* had a physical 'seal – made out of wax or paper – attached to it. This explains the origin of the phrase 'signed and sealed'. The modern requirements for the creation of a deed are more relaxed and are set out in s 1 of the Law of Property (Miscellaneous Provisions) Act 1989.

LAW OF PROPERTY (MISCELLANEOUS PROVISIONS) ACT 1989

s 1 Deeds and their execution

(1) Any rule of law which –
  (a) restricts the substances on which a deed may be written;
  (b) requires a seal for the valid execution of an instrument as a deed by an individual; or
  (c) requires authority by one person to another to deliver an instrument as a deed on his behalf to be given by deed, is abolished.

(2) An instrument shall not be a deed unless –
  (a) it makes it clear on its face that it is intended to be a deed by the person making it or, as the case may be, by the parties to it (whether by describing itself as a deed or expressing itself to be executed or signed as a deed or otherwise); and
  (b) it is validly executed as a deed
    (i) by that person or a person authorised to execute it in the name or on behalf of that person, or
    (ii) by one or more of those parties or a person authorised to execute it in the name or on behalf of one or more of those parties.

(2A) For the purposes of subsection (2)(a) above, an instrument shall not be taken to make it clear on its face that it is intended to be a deed merely because it is executed under seal.

(3) An instrument is validly executed as a deed by an individual if, and only if –
  (a) it is signed –
    (i) by him in the presence of a witness who attests the signature; or
    (ii) at his direction and in his presence and the presence of two witnesses who each attest the signature; and
  (b) it is delivered as a deed.

(4) In subsections (2) and (3) above 'sign', in relation to an instrument, includes
  (a) an individual signing the name of the person or party on whose behalf he executes the instrument; and
  (b) making one's mark on the instrument, and 'signature' is to be construed accordingly.

(4A) Subsection (3) above applies in the case of an instrument executed by an individual in the name or on behalf of another person whether or not that person is also an individual.

From this it will be seen that the important questions are whether the parties intended to produce a 'deed', whether it has been signed and whether the signature has been witnessed. There must also be 'delivery', as required by s 1(3)(b).

The position regarding companies incorporated under the Companies Acts is governed by ss 44 and 46 of the Companies Act 2006.

COMPANIES ACT 2006

s 44 Execution of documents

(1) Under the law of England and Wales or Northern Ireland a document is executed by a company –
  (a) by the affixing of its common seal, or
  (b) by signature in accordance with the following provisions.

(2) A document is validly executed by a company if it is signed on behalf of the company –
  (a) by two authorised signatories, or
  (b) by a director of the company in the presence of a witness who attests the signature.

(3) The following are 'authorised signatories' for the purposes of subsection (2) –
  (a) every director of the company, and
  (b) in the case of a private company with a secretary or a public company, the secretary (or any joint secretary) of the company.

(4) A document signed in accordance with subsection (2) and expressed, in whatever words, to be executed by the company has the same effect as if executed under the common seal of the company ...

s 46 Execution of deeds

(1) A document is validly executed by a company as a deed for the purposes of section 1(2)(b) of the Law of Property (Miscellaneous Provisions) Act 1989 (c. 34) and for the purposes of the law of Northern Ireland if, and only if –
  (a) it is duly executed by the company, and
  (b) it is delivered as a deed.

(2) For the purposes of subsection (1)(b), a document is presumed to be delivered upon its being executed, unless a contrary intention is proved.

For companies, therefore, the document must indicate on its face that it is intended to be a deed and must be 'executed' in one of the ways set out in s 44. A seal may be used but it is also permissible for the document to be signed by, for example, directors. It must then be 'delivered as a deed' (s 46). See also *Signature Living Hotel Ltd v Sulyok* [2020] EWHC 257 (Ch) for a case where the document did not comply with the formalities for a deed but the agreement was nevertheless supported by consideration and thus enforceable.

Deeds may be used to create an enforceable obligation that is entirely one-sided – for example, a promise to make a gift at some point in the future. It is also sometimes used in relation to complex construction and engineering projects to give the parties the benefit of a longer period for bringing legal action in the event of breach. For an ordinary contract, the limitation period is normally six years; for a deed, the period is 12 years (Limitation Act 1980, ss 5, 8).

3.3 Consideration

The main method by which agreements are found to be enforceable under the law of England and Wales is through the finding of 'consideration'. This means that both parties must bring something to the bargain (i.e. there must be an exchange). A promise by X to Y for which Y gives nothing in return will not generally be enforceable.

3.3.1 Definition of consideration

What is 'consideration'? In *Currie v Misa* (1874–1875) L.R. 10 Ex. 153, it was suggested that:

> A valuable consideration, in the sense of the law, may consist either in some right, interest, profit or benefit accruing to one party or some forbearance, detriment, loss or responsibility, given, suffered or undertaken by the other.

This is sometimes abbreviated to the idea that consideration must involve some benefit to the promisor or some detriment to the promisee. In many cases it will involve both – as where money is exchanged for goods. The seller has the benefit of the money paid (benefit), but loses ownership of the goods (detriment); for the buyer, the position is reversed.

It is more difficult to see 'benefit and detriment' where a contract is made by the exchange of promises, both of which are to be performed in the future. It is clear that such an exchange will create a binding contract – as is confirmed by Lord Dunedin in the following passage from *Dunlop Pneumatic Tyre Co Ltd v Seliridge & Co Ltd* [1915] AC 847, 855:

> My Lords, I confess that this case is to my mind apt to nip any budding affection which one might have had for the doctrine of consideration. For the effect of that doctrine in the present case is to make it possible for a person to snap his fingers at a bargain deliberately made, a bargain not in itself unfair, and which the person seeking to enforce it has a legitimate interest to enforce. Notwithstanding these considerations I cannot say that I have ever had any doubt that the judgment of the Court of Appeal was right …
>
> My Lords, I am content to adopt from a work of Sir Frederick Pollock, to which I have often been under obligation, the following words as to consideration: 'An act or forbearance of one party, or the promise thereof, is the price for which the promise of the other is bought, and the promise thus given for value is enforceable' (*Pollock on Contracts*, 8th edn, p 175).

Lord Dunedin was clearly of the view, therefore, that, as indicated by Pollock, a 'promise for a promise' results in a binding agreement. As Atiyah has pointed out, however, the acceptance of a 'promise' as valid consideration does not fit easily with the idea of benefit and detriment. In the following passage, when he referred to an 'executory bilateral contract' he meant one which was created by an exchange of promises but where neither side had yet performed any part of the transaction.

Atiyah, PS, *Essays on Contract*, 1986, Oxford: Clarendon Press, pp 191–192

Benefit or detriment is not necessary

... I need hardly stress that many promises are given in order to obtain some reciprocal benefit; and that a detriment incurred by a promisee in reliance on the promise is often a very good reason for enforcing a promise. But it seems incorrect to assert that the presence of benefit or detriment is always a necessary prerequisite for the enforcement of a contract. In the first place, an executory bilateral contract is and has for centuries been enforceable by the courts, although neither benefit nor detriment usually arises until the contract has been at least partly performed. It is of course true that once the law has begun to enforce bilateral executory contracts, the mere giving and receipt of the promises may be said to involve a benefit and detriment because they are legally enforceable. But enforceability comes first, and benefit and detriment afterwards; it is purely circular to assert that the presence of benefit and detriment can be a ground for the enforcement of such contracts. It is also true that if an executory bilateral contract is in due course performed the promisor may receive a benefit and the promisee may incur a detriment. But where the promisee sues for damages for breach of an executory bilateral contract the promisor has in fact received no benefit, and the promisee has not necessarily incurred any detriment.

It is common for lawyers to apply the benefit-detriment analysis even to bilateral executory contracts; the inquiry then takes the form of asking if performance of the promise will be, or would have been beneficial to the promisor or detrimental to the promisee. The fact that the answer may be in the negative may well be a factor which leads the court to decide that there is no reason (or consideration) for enforcing the promise. But the fact that the answer is in the affirmative does not and cannot demonstrate that the promise is being enforced because of a factual benefit or detriment, unless that is, it is possible to argue that a promise may be a benefit or a detriment irrespective of its legal enforceability. In the original essay I assumed perhaps too easily that this could not be so, but Professor Treitel argues cogently that promises can be beneficial or detrimental even if they are not legally enforceable; and if we assume a society in which promises are generally performed, and in which their non-performance carries a certain odium, then I am prepared to admit that this may be the case. Nevertheless, there is an element of unreality in treating bilateral executory contracts in this way. Counter-promises are treated by the courts as beneficial (or detrimental) unless it can be demonstrated that there is or was no possibility of any benefit or detriment being derived from the promise. A counter-promise is thus treated more like a formal reason for the enforcement of a promise than a reason of substance, and in most actions for breach of an executory bilateral contract, there is no possibility of the promisor obtaining any benefit, or the promisee suffering any detriment by the time the case comes for trial.

The truth seems to be that bilateral executory contracts are enforced for other reasons (or considerations) than the existence of benefit or detriment. Quite what those other reasons are, whether they are adequate reasons, and whether they extend to all cases of bilateral executory contracts, are all very difficult questions ... In the original version of the present essay I assumed far too readily (again largely under the influence of Corbin) that bilateral executory contracts are enforced because in modern societies business could scarcely be carried on if they were not enforced. Professor Treitel challenges my reasoning here with some justification; though it is a little ironical that he should do so, given that he has no apparent doubts that bilateral executory contracts *should* be enforced, while I have a great many such doubts.

Treitel, on the other hand, has argued that even an unenforceable promise may constitute a benefit or detriment. Compare *Simantob v Shavleyan* [2019] EWCA Civ 1105.

Peel, E, *Treitel on the Law of Contract*, 14th edn, 2015, London: Sweet & Maxwell, para 3-008

Mutual promises

So far we have discussed performance by one party as consideration for the promise of the other: for example, payment by a buyer as the consideration for the seller's promise to deliver, or delivery by a seller as consideration for the buyer's promise to pay. It is, however, also well settled that mutual promises can be consideration for each other. Hence if a seller promises to deliver goods in six months' time and the buyer to pay for them on delivery, there is an immediately binding contract from which neither party can withdraw, though, of course, performance cannot be claimed till the appointed time. Implied, no less than express, promises can constitute consideration for each other.

Some difficulty has been felt in explaining the rule that mutual promises can be consideration for each other. At first sight, it might seem that the mere giving of a promise was not a detriment nor its receipt a benefit, so as to make the counter-promise binding. It will not do to say that the person making the promise suffers a detriment because he is legally bound to perform it; for if this assumption is made about one of the promises, it must also be made of the other, so that the 'explanation' assumes the very point in issue. Probably the reason for the rule is simpler. A person who makes a commercial promise expects to have to perform it (and is in fact under considerable pressure to do so). Correspondingly, one who receives such a promise expects it to be kept. These expectations, which can exist even where the promise is not legally enforceable, are based on commercial morality, and can properly be called a detriment and a benefit; hence they satisfy the requirement of consideration in the case of mutual promises.

The two options appear to be to downgrade the requirement of 'benefit and detriment', or to accept that a promise to do something which, *in performance*, will constitute a benefit to the other party or a detriment to the party making the promise, can itself be treated as consideration.

3.3.2 Consideration need not be 'adequate' but must be 'sufficient'

The courts are not normally concerned with whether or not a bargain is 'fair' or balanced. In other words, the courts are not concerned with whether what one party provides under the bargain is 'adequate' (equal in financial terms) for what the other party provides under the bargain. However, both parties must provide *something* which the law will *recognise* as consideration under the bargain; in other words each party must provide consideration which is sufficient' (even if unequal).

The point regarding adequacy' as against 'sufficiency' is illustrated by *Thomas v Thomas*.

***Thomas v Thomas* (1842) 2 QB 851**

Facts: Mr Thomas expressed a wish that, following his death, his wife should have his house for the rest of her life. When Mr Thomas died, his executors entered into an agreement to this effect with Mrs Thomas (the plaintiff in the action). The agreement was stated to be 'in consideration' of Mr Thomas's desire but was subject to the proviso that Mrs Thomas paid the executor's £1 a year towards the ground rent and agreed to keep the house in good repair.

Held: Complying with the desire of Mr Thomas could not constitute consideration, but the payment of £1 a year could – so that the agreement was enforceable as a contract.

Patteson J: It would be giving to causa too large a construction if we were to adopt the view urged for the defendant: it would be confounding consideration with motive. Motive is not the same thing with consideration. Consideration means something which is of some value in the eye of the law, moving from the plaintiff: it may be some benefit to the plaintiff or some detriment to the defendant; but at all events it must be moving from the plaintiff. Now that which is suggested as the consideration here, a pious respect for the wishes of the testator, does not in any way move from the plaintiff; it moves from the testator; therefore, legally speaking, it forms no part of the consideration. Then it is said that, if that be so, there is no consideration at all, it is a mere voluntary gift: but when we look at the agreement we find that this is not a mere proviso that the donee shall take the gift with the burthens; but it is an express agreement to pay what seems to be a fresh apportionment of a ground rent, and which is made payable not to a superior Landlord but to the executors. So that this rent is clearly not something incident to the assignment of the house; for in that case, instead of being payable to the executors, it would have been payable to the landlord. Then as to the repairs: these houses may very possibly be held under a lease containing covenants to repair; but we know nothing about it: for anything that appears, the liability to repair is first created by this instrument. The proviso certainly struck me at first as Mr. Williams put it, that the rent and repairs there merely attached to the gift by the donors; and, had the instrument been executed by the donors only, there might have been some ground for that construction; but the fact is not so …

Coleridge J: The concessions made in the course of the argument have, in fact, disposed of the case. It is conceded that mere motive need not be stated: and we are not obliged to look for the legal consideration in any particular part of the instrument, merely because the consideration is usually stated in some particular part: ut res magis valeat, we may look to any part. In this instrument, in the part where it is usual to state the consideration, nothing certainly is expressed but a wish to fulfil the intentions of the testator: but in another part we find an express agreement to pay an annual sum for a particular purpose; and also a distinct agreement to repair. If these had occurred in the first part of the instrument, it could hardly have been argued that the declaration was not well drawn, and supported by the evidence. As to the suggestion of this being a voluntary conveyance, my impression is that this payment of £1 annually is more than a good consideration: it is a valuable consideration: it is clearly a thing newly created, and not part of the old ground rent.

In other words, a desire to comply with the wishes of the testator was not 'sufficient' to amount to consideration (i.e. not something which the law recognises as consideration), but it was irrelevant whether the £1 contribution towards the rent was 'adequate' (or proportionate) to pay for the benefit that Mrs Thomas was receiving.

The decision in *Thomas v Thomas* might be taken to suggest that consideration needs to have some economic value, and that is indeed sometimes suggested as a characteristic. This derives mainly from the old case of *White v Bluett* (1853) 23 LJ Ex 36. In this case, a father promised not to enforce a promissory note against his son, if the son stopped complaining about the distribution of his father's property. It was held that there was no consideration for the father's promise, with Pollock CB commenting (at 37):

> The son had no right to complain, for the father might make what distribution of his property he liked: and the son's abstaining from what he had no right to do can be no consideration.

More recent case law, however, indicates that economic value may not be necessary. For example, in *Ward v Byham* [1956] 2 All ER 318, it was suggested that a promise to ensure that a child was happy could amount to good consideration. Furthermore, in *Chappell v Nestlé*, it was held by the House of Lords that supplying items which were of no intrinsic value to the promisor could nevertheless amount to consideration.

***Chappell & Co v Nestlé & Co* [1960] AC 87**

Facts: Nestlé offered a promotion with their chocolate under which a person who sent in three wrappers, plus a small amount of money, would be sent a record – *Rockin' Shoes*. Chappell claimed that this constituted a breach of copyright which they owned in the song. For the purposes of the law of copyright it was important to determine whether the wrappers constituted part of the consideration for the supply of the record.

Held: The wrappers were part of the consideration, even though they would be thrown away by Nestlé. As a result, Nestlé were in breach of copyright.

Lord Reid: ... I can now turn to what appears to me to be the crucial question in this case: was the 1s. 6d an 'ordinary retail selling price' within the meaning of s. 8? That involves two questions, what was the nature of the contract between the respondents Nestlé and a person who sent 1s. *6d* plus three wrappers in acceptance of their offer, and what is meant by 'ordinary retail selling price' in this context. To determine the nature of the contract, one must find the intention of the parties as shown by what they said and did. The respondents Nestlé's intention can hardly be in any doubt. They were not setting out to trade in gramophone records. They were using these records to increase their sales of chocolate. Their offer was addressed to everyone. It might be accepted by a person who was already a regular buyer of their chocolate; but, much more important to them, it might be accepted by people who might become regular buyers of their chocolate if they could be induced to try it and found they liked it. The inducement was something calculated to look like a bargain, a record at a very cheap price. It is in evidence that the ordinary price for a dance record is 6s *6d*. It is true that the ordinary record gives much longer playing time than Nestlé's records and it may have other advantages. But the reader of the respondents Nestlé's offer was not in a position to know that. It seems to me clear that the main intention of the offer was to induce people interested in this kind of music to buy (or, perhaps, get others to buy) chocolate which otherwise would not have been bought. It is, of course, true that some wrappers might come from chocolate which had already been bought, or from chocolate which would have been bought without the offer, but that does not seem to me to alter the case. Where there is a large number of transactions – the notice mentions 30,000 records – I do not think we should simply consider an isolated case where it would be impossible to say whether there had been a direct benefit from the acquisition of the wrappers or not. The requirement that wrappers should be sent was of great importance to the respondents Nestlé; there would have been no point in their simply offering records for 1s. *6d* each. It seems to me quite unrealistic to divorce the buying of the chocolate from the supplying of the records. It is a perfectly good contract if a person accepts an offer to supply goods if he (a) does something of value to the supplier and (b) pays money; the consideration is both (a) and (b). There may have been cases where the acquisition of the wrappers conferred no direct benefit on the respondents Nestlé but there must have been many cases where it did. I do not see why the possibility that, in some cases, the acquisition of the wrappers did not directly benefit the respondents Nestlé should require us to exclude from consideration the cases where it did; and even where there was no direct benefit from the acquisition of the wrappers there may have been an indirect benefit by way of advertisement.

Lord Tucker and Lord Somervell concurred; Viscount Simonds and Lord Keith dissented.

The decision in *Chappell v Nestlé* suggests that only an indirect economic benefit is required if, indeed, economic benefit is required at all. The overall promotional scheme was to Nestlé's commercial advantage, in that it would encourage increased sales of chocolate, but the supply of the wrappers themselves could not be said to have provided any direct economic benefit, particularly if the chocolate had been bought by someone other than the person who sent them in. More recent discussion of this aspect of consideration is to be found in the Court of Appeal's decision in *Edmonds v Lawson*. The court here also found an indirect, rather than direct, economic benefit to the promisor.

Edmonds v Lawson [2000] QB 501 (CA)

Facts: The claimant was a pupil barrister, arguing that she was entitled to be paid the minimum wage. As part of that argument, it was necessary for the claimant to establish that she was working under a contract of employment.

Held: There was a contract between the pupil and her chambers (though not with her individual pupil master). The consideration was in effect the general benefit to the chambers of having pupils. The contract was not one of employment, however, so the claimant was not entitled to the minimum wage.

Lord Bingham: …

19. The first issue: was there a contract?

20. The claimant contended, and the judge held, that there was a contract between her and all those who were members of Mr. Lawson's chambers on 1 October 1998, made by the chambers' offer of a 12-month pupillage and her acceptance of that offer. Before the judge and on appeal before us the defendants resisted that conclusion. The grounds of resistance were, first, that there was no intent to create legal relations and, secondly, that the pupillage agreement was unsupported by consideration moving from the claimant as promisee and so lacked an essential ingredient of a legally binding contract.

21. Whether the parties intended to enter into legally binding relations is an issue to be determined objectively and not by inquiring into their respective states of mind. … [Lord Bingham then reviewed the procedures relating to the selection of the pupil and the operation of pupillage and concluded, on the issue of intention to create legal arrangements, that] …

[23] this arrangement had all the characteristics of a binding contract. It makes no difference that, if the pupil defaulted, the chambers would be most unlikely to sue; the same is true if an employer engages a junior employee under an employment contract which is undoubtedly binding, and the employee fails to turn up on the appointed day.

24. The defendants' argument on consideration is, we think, much stronger, for while chambers undertake to provide a closely prescribed curriculum of education and training the pupil no longer pays any fee and does not in our view undertake to do anything beyond that which is conducive to his or her education and training. In working on the pupil master's papers (making factual summaries, or drafting chronologies, or writing advices or preparing pleadings) the pupil will be seeking to acquire, under the tutelage of the pupil master, the skills of a professional adviser, pleader and advocate, even though the pupil master will often benefit from the pupil's work and from discussion with him. If the pupil carries out legal research or keeps a note in court, he is again learning and applying professional skills necessary for practice. If the pupil produces any work of real value, whether to the pupil master or any other member of the Bar, the beneficiary is under a professional duty to remunerate the pupil. While any pupil of ordinary common sense would, if asked, carry out mundane tasks (such as photocopying authorities or making a cup of tea) which do not in any way promote his professional development, there is in our view no obligation or duty on the pupil to do anything for the pupil master which is not conducive to his own professional development.

25. This conclusion, if correct, would we think be fatal to any argument that there was a contract between the pupil and the individual pupil master, for the pupil would provide no consideration for the pupil master's educational services. But the claimant does not rely on any contract said to have been made with an individual pupil master and we think a broader view has to be taken of the relationship between chambers and pupil. For reasons on which we have already touched, members of chambers have a strong incentive to attract talented pupils, and their future prospects will to some extent depend on their success in doing so. The funding of awards is not an exercise in pure altruism but reflects an obvious (and wholly unobjectionable) element of self-interest. The agreement of the claimant and other pupils to undertake pupillage at chambers such as the defendants' provides a pool of selected candidates who can be expected to compete with each other for recruitment as tenants. We do not regard this argument as undermined by the fact that some pupils who are accepted as such may be regarded as unlikely candidates for tenancy. The process must be viewed in the round, and not on a pupil by pupil basis, and chambers may well see an advantage in developing close relationships with pupils who plan to practise as employed barristers or to practise overseas. On balance we take the view that pupils such as the claimant provide consideration for the offer made by chambers such as the defendants' by agreeing to enter into the close, important and potentially very productive relationship which pupillage involves.

26. We agree with the judge, although for somewhat different reasons, that the claimant did make a legally binding contract with the defendants.

Once again, the idea of consideration being required to have some economic value is being applied flexibly. This flexibility has led Treitel to refer to the idea of 'invented consideration'.

Peel, E, *Treitel on the Law of Contract*, 14th edn, 2015, London: Sweet & Maxwell, para 3–009

Invented consideration

Normally, a party enters into a contract with a view to obtaining the consideration provided by the other: for example, the buyer wants the goods and the seller the price. In the United States it has been said that this is essential, and that 'Nothing is consideration that is not regarded as such by both parties'. But English courts do not insist on this requirement and often regard an act or forbearance as the consideration for a promise even though it may not have been the object of the promisor to secure it. They may also regard the possibility of some prejudice to the promisee as a detriment without regard to the question whether it has in fact been suffered. These practices may be called 'inventing consideration', and the temptation to adopt one or the other of them is particularly strong when the act or forbearance which was actually bargained for cannot be regarded as consideration for some reason which is thought to be technical and without merit. In such cases the practice of inventing consideration may help to make the operation of the doctrine of consideration more acceptable; but the practice may also be criticised on the ground that it gives the courts a wide discretion to hold promises binding (or not) as they please. Thus the argument that the promisee *might* have suffered prejudice by acting in reliance on a promise is in some cases made a basis of decision, while in others precisely the same argument is rejected. The courts have not been very consistent in the exercise of this discretion and its existence is a source of considerable uncertainty in this branch of the law.

This concept has been roundly rejected by Atiyah, as part of his attack on the orthodox analysis of the doctrine of consideration.

Atiyah, PS, *Essays on Contract*, 1986, Oxford: Clarendon Press, pp 182–183

Professor Treitel's critique of my original essay (and his textbook on the *Law of Contract*) insists that the courts have power to 'invent' consideration, and that this ability is an important phenomenon which I have overlooked and which explains many otherwise puzzling things about the doctrine. I find this a difficult concept to grasp. Is an 'invented' consideration something different from a 'real' consideration or is it the same thing? If it is the same thing, then it is hard to see in what sense it is invented; and if it is not the same thing, then it either violates the rules of law, or it modifies them. Presumably Professor Treitel does not mean to suggest that when judges invent consideration they are defying the law and violating their judicial oaths, but if an invented consideration modifies the rules governing ordinary consideration, then an invented consideration becomes again an ordinary consideration, though the legal significance of the doctrine has now changed. The only other possibility that occurs to me is that the courts might use the concept of 'invented consideration' rather like an equitable or merciful dispensation from the ordinary law, but it is unthinkable that judges should behave in this way. They have no power to invent a consideration in one case and refuse to do so in a relevantly identical case. Thus an invented consideration must in the end be the same thing as an ordinary consideration. I fear that Professor Treitel has himself invented the concept of an invented consideration because he finds it the only way in which he is able to reconcile many decisions with what he takes to be the 'true' or 'real' doctrine. This is, of course, exactly the sort of process against which Corbin warned us, and I give my full allegiance to Corbin on this point.

(Professor Atiyah's views on consideration are discussed further towards the end of this chapter, at 3.4.1).

3.3.3 Past consideration

It is a general rule of contract law in England and Wales that past consideration is not sufficient consideration. This means that if the action that is alleged to provide consideration for a promise was completed before the promise was made, then, in the absence of other factors, the promise will not be supported by consideration and will not be enforceable. The reason is that the action needs to have been done in exchange for and in response to the promise – as a means of 'buying' it; generally, the action cannot perform this role if it preceded the promise. An old example of the basic rule is the case of *Roscorla v Thomas*.

***Roscorla v Thomas* (1842) 3 QB 234**

Facts: The plaintiff bought a horse from the defendant. The defendant then promised that the horse was 'sound and free from vice. This turned out to be untrue, and the plaintiff sued for breach of this promise.

Held: There was no consideration for the promise – the sale had already been completed before it was given.

Lord Denman CJ: It may be taken as a general rule, subject to exceptions not applicable to this case, that the promise must be coextensive with the consideration. In the present case, the only promise that would result from the consideration, as stated, and be coextensive with it, would be to deliver the horse upon request. The precedent sale, without a warranty, though at the request of the defendant, imposes no other duty or obligation upon him. It is clear, therefore, that the consideration stated would not raise an implied promise by the defendant that the horse was sound or free from vice.

But the promise in the present case must be taken to be, as in fact it was, express and the question is, whether that fact will warrant the extension of the promise beyond that which would be implied by law; and whether the consideration, though insufficient to raise an implied promise, will nevertheless support an express one. And we think that it will not.

The cases in which it has been held that, under certain circumstances, a consideration insufficient to raise an implied promise will nevertheless support an express one, will be found collected and reviewed in the note (a) to *Wennall v Adney*, and in the case of *Eastwood v Kenyon*. They are cases of voidable contracts subsequently ratified, of debts barred by operation of law, subsequently revived, and of equitable and moral obligations, which, but for some rule of law, would of themselves have been sufficient to raise an implied promise. All these cases are distinguishable from, and indeed inapplicable to, the present, which appears to us to fall within the general rule, that a consideration past and executed will support no other promise than such as would be implied by law.

The rule for arresting the judgment upon the first count must therefore be made absolute.

So, if an act comes before a promise, it cannot generally be consideration for that promise. A more recent example of the same principle is to be found in *Re McArdle*.

Re McArdle [1951] Ch 669 (CA)

Facts: William McArdle left a house to his children. One of his sons was living in the house, and he and his wife carried out improvements to it. His wife then got each of the siblings to promise to agree to share the costs of this work.

Held: The promise to pay for the work was unenforceable because the doing of the work was 'past consideration' in relation to the promise.

Jenkins LJ: ... The document which is said to operate as an equitable assignment is the document of April 30, 1945, signed by the five children of the testator. That document on the face of it purports to be an agreement for valuable consideration under which when Mrs Marjorie McArdle has carried out certain alterations and improvements to the property known as Gravel Hill Poultry Farm, in consideration of her so doing, the five children agree that she is to be paid a sum of £488, representing the cost of the work, out of the testator's estate when distributed. That is what it purports to be; and I think, notwithstanding the argument to the contrary, that it is really perfectly plain, so far as the construction of the document is concerned, that what it contemplates is the doing by Mrs Marjorie McArdle of work yet to be done; and her doing that work is to form the consideration by virtue of which she is to be entitled to receive £488 out of the estate. That is what the document is, and if the document had correctly represented the facts, for my part I have no doubt that it would have operated as a valid equitable assignment of £488, subject to Mrs Marjorie McArdle's performing her part of the bargain by providing the consideration she had contracted to provide in the form of doing the work. There might have been room for difficulty, and for argument, whether the work had been properly done or not, but those matters could have been resolved one way or the other, if necessary by an action; and ultimately, if Mrs McArdle showed that she had done the work contracted for, her title to the £488 would have been complete and, the agreement being for valuable consideration, it would not have mattered that further steps had to be taken in order to perfect her title.

But the true position was that, as the work had in fact all been done and nothing remained to be done by Mrs Marjorie McArdle at all, the consideration was a wholly past consideration, and, therefore, the beneficiaries' agreement for the repayment to her of the £488 out of the estate was *nudum pactum*, a promise with no consideration to support it. That being so, it is impossible for her to rely upon this document as constituting an equitable assignment for valuable consideration.

Lord Evershed MR and Hodson LJ concurred.

It follows that if Marjorie McArdle had got the siblings to agree to pay for the renovations in advance, she would have been able to recover the costs.

3.3.3.1 Qualifications and exceptions

There are some qualifications and exceptions to the past consideration rule whereby what appears to be past consideration may be sufficient to make a promise enforceable. At common law, the past consideration rule is qualified in some situations where the act alleged to constitute consideration was performed at the *request* of the promisor. This is illustrated by the ancient case of *Lampleigh v Braithwait* (1615) Hob 105; 80 ER 255. The defendant had been convicted of murder and asked the plaintiff to seek a pardon from the king. After the plaintiff had made attempts to do so, the defendant promised him £100 for his efforts. It was held that this promise was enforceable. The situation must, however, be one in which there was an expectation of payment when the action was requested. This point was emphasised in *Re Casey's Patents*.

Re Casey's Patents [1892] 1 Ch 104 (CA)

Facts: The plaintiff had managed certain patents on behalf of the defendants. They then promised him a one-third share in the patents, in return for his efforts.

Held: It was always assumed that the plaintiff would be paid for the work which he was doing. The subsequent promise was simply a formalisation of what that payment should be.

Bowen LJ: ... The document is one by which the signatories agree with Mr Casey to give him 'one-third share of the patents above mentioned, the same to take effect from this date'. It cannot be denied that that is an equitable assignment if it is anything. It is not an agreement to take effect at some future date. It is an agreement to give him the share as from the date of the document, and it immediately passes in Equity the right to the third share.

But then it was said by Mr Daniel, 'But there is no consideration, and this document is not under seal'. We will see if there is consideration. The consideration is stated, such as it is. It is, 'in consideration of your services as the practical manager in working our patents as above for transit by steamer'. Then says Mr Daniel, 'Yes, but that is a future consideration, and a future consideration, if nothing were done under it or nothing was proved to be done, would fail'. The answer to that is that the consideration is not the rendering of the services, as is plain from the fact that the document is to take effect in Equity from the date. The consideration must be something other than rendering services in the future. It is the promise to render them which those words imply, that constitutes the consideration; and the promise to render future services, if an effectual promise, is certainly good consideration. Then, driven from that, Mr Daniel said, 'Oh! but it is past services that it means, and past services are not a consideration for anything'. Well, that raises the old question – or might raise it, if there was not an answer to it – of *Lampleigh v Braithwait* (1615) Hob 105, a subject of great interest to every scientific lawyer, as to whether a past service will support a promise. I do not propose to discuss that question, or, perhaps, I should not have finished this week. I should have to examine the whole state of the law as to, and the history of the subject of, consideration, which, I need hardly say, I do not propose to do. But the answer to Mr Daniel's point is clear. Even if it were true, as some scientific students of law believe, that a past service cannot support a future promise, you must look at the document and see if the promise cannot receive a proper effect in some other way. Now, the fact of a past service raises an implication that at the time it was rendered it was to be paid for, and, if it was a service which was to be paid for, when you get in the subsequent document a promise to pay, that promise may be treated either as an admission which evidences or as a positive bargain which fixes the amount of that reasonable remuneration on the faith of which the service was originally rendered. So that here for past services there is ample justification for the promise to give the third share. Therefore, this is an equitable assignment which cannot be impeached.

Fry LJ and Lindley LJ concurred.

This decision means that this qualification of the rule against past consideration will only operate where, as well as the work having been requested by the promisor, the situation is one where the work would not normally be done without the expectation of some recompense. So, in *Re Casey's Patents*, the work involved in managing the operation of the patents was not something that would normally have been done simply as a matter of 'goodwill' – the manager would be expected to be paid for his work. The issue was considered further by Lord Scarman in *Pao On v Lau Yiu Long* [1980] AC 614, and he summed up the requirements for the situations in which 'past consideration' will be treated at common law as valid in the following passage, at p 629:

> An act done before the giving of a promise to make a payment or to confer some other benefit can sometimes be consideration for the promise. The act must have been done at the promisors' request: the parties must have understood that the act was to be remunerated either by a payment or the conferment of some other benefit: and payment, or the conferment of a benefit, must have been legally enforceable had it been promised in advance.

The first of Lord Scarman's requirements appears clearly in *Lampleigh v Braithwait*, and the second in *Re Casey's Patents*. The third seems simply to require that the consideration, if it had been supplied before the promise, would have been 'sufficient', in the terms discussed above (at 3.3.2). It is important to note that Lord Scarman is indicating that these requirements are not *alternatives* but *cumulative*; in other words, all three must be present before past consideration will be treated as valid.

An example of a statutory exception is to be found in the following provision:

BILLS OF EXCHANGE ACT 1882

s 27 Valuable consideration for a bill [of exchange] may be constituted by (a) any consideration sufficient to support a simple contract, (b) an antecedent debt or liability.

Sub-paragraph (b) shows that a debt that precedes the creation of the bill may be good consideration for it.

3.3.4 Performance of existing duties

To what extent, if at all, can the performance of, or a promise to perform, an act that the person performing, or promising to perform, is already under a duty to perform, constitute sufficient consideration? This topic needs to be considered under three headings: non-contractual duties imposed by law; contractual duties owed to a third party; and contractual duties already owed to the other party.

3.3.4.1 Non-contractual duties imposed by law

The general position here is that, for reasons of public policy, the performance (or promise of performance) of a duty that you owe as a result of some public obligation is not sufficient consideration. A police officer who agreed to make sure that a particular street was free from crime, in return for a promise of payment from a person living there, should not be able to enforce the promise. The potential for corruption is obvious. This applies generally to those who are under public duties. *Collins v Godefroy*, one of the earliest authorities establishing this principle, was concerned with the payment of witnesses in a legal proceeding.

Collins v Godefroy **(1831) 1 B & Ald 950; 120 ER 241**

Facts: Collins (an attorney) was subpoenaed to attend a trial as a witness for Godefroy. Collins did so for six days, but was not called. He claimed he was also promised by the defendant a fee as compensation for his lost time.

Held: Collins had not provided any valid consideration for a promise to pay him.

Lord Tenterden CJ: Assuming that the offer to pay the six guineas without costs was evidence of an express promise by the defendant to pay that sum to the plaintiff as a compensation to him for his loss of time, still, if the defendant was not bound by law to pay that sum, the offer to do so, not having been accepted, will not avail the plaintiff. If it be a duty imposed by law upon a party regularly subpoenaed, to attend from time to time to give his evidence, then a promise to give him any remuneration for loss of time incurred in such attendance is a promise without consideration. We think that such a duty is imposed by law; and on consideration of the Statute of Elizabeth, and of the cases which have been decided on this subject, we are all of opinion that a party cannot maintain an action for compensation for loss of time in attending a trial as a witness.

We are aware of the practice which has prevailed in certain cases, of allowing, as costs between party and party, so much per day for attendance of professional men; but that practice cannot alter the law. What the effect of our decision may be, is not for our consideration. We think, on principle that an action does not lie for a compensation to a witness for loss of time in attendance under a subpoena.

The Statute of Elizabeth referred to – 5 Eliz c 9, s 12 – allowed for the payment of reasonable costs to witnesses – for example, in relation to travel – but not compensation for lost time. Current legislation is less restrictive (see e. g. Senior Courts Act 1981, s 36(4)), and it is accepted that expert witnesses may now have an enforceable claim for lost time (see e.g. *Goulden v Wilson Barca* [2000] 1 WLR 167), but this does not necessarily detract from the general principle that a person performing a public duty should not be able to claim contractual payment for doing so.

Lord Denning, however, suggested in two cases – *Ward v Byham* [1956] 2 All ER 318 and *Williams v Williams* [1957] 1 All ER 305 – that it should be good consideration to perform a duty imposed by law, provided that there was no conflict with the public interest. The duties in question were, respectively, that of a mother to look after her illegitimate child, and of a wife who had left her husband to support herself. The other members of the court in each case managed to reach a decision without using this principle. The question whether such duties can be good consideration remains, to some extent, open. What is clear, however, is that if more is done than is required by the duty imposed by law, this can constitute good consideration. The next case illustrates this point.

***Glasbrook v Glamorgan County Council* [1925] AC 270 (HL)**

Facts: During a miners' strike, the police were obliged to ensure that workers who had the responsibility of keeping the mines safe and in good repair were not prevented from doing so. The police felt that this could be achieved with a mobile force, but the mine owners insisted that officers should be billeted on the premises. They agreed to pay the additional costs of this, but subsequently refused to do so, relying on the fact that the police were doing no more than their public duty. The council succeeded at trial and in the Court of Appeal. The owners appealed to the House of Lords.

Held: By providing the force billeted on the premises, the police had exceeded their public duty and were entitled to recover for the additional costs.

Viscount Cave LC: ... I conclude, therefore, that the practice of lending constables for special duty in consideration of payment is not illegal or against public policy; and I pass to the second question - namely, whether in this particular case the lending of the seventy constables to be billeted in the appellants' colliery was a legitimate application of the principle. In this connection I think it important to bear in mind exactly what it was that the learned trial judge had to decide. It was no part of his duty to say – nor did he purport to say – whether in his judgment the billeting of the seventy men at the colliery was necessary for the prevention of violence or the protection of the mines from criminal injury. The duty of determining such questions is cast by law, not upon the courts after the event, but upon the police authorities at the time when the decision has to be taken; and a court which attempted to review such a decision from the point of view of its wisdom or prudence would (I think) be exceeding its proper functions. The question for the court was whether on July 9, 1921, the police authorities, acting reasonably and in good faith, considered a police garrison at the colliery necessary for the protection of life and property from violence, or, in other words, whether the decision of the chief constable in refusing special protection unless paid for was such a decision as a man in his position and with his duties could reasonably take. If in the judgment of the police authorities, formed reasonably and in good faith, the garrison was necessary for the protection of life and property, then they were not entitled to make a charge for it, for that would be to exact payment for the performance of a duty which they clearly owed to the appellants and their servants; but if they thought the garrison a superfluity and only acceded to Mr James' request with a view to meeting his wishes, then in my opinion they were entitled to treat the garrison duty as a special duty and to charge for it. Now, upon this point the Divisional Superintendent Colonel Smith, who was a highly experienced officer, gave specific and detailed evidence; and the learned judge having seen him in the witness box and heard his examination and cross-examination accepted his evidence upon the point, as the following extract from the judgment shows:

> 'Colonel Smith says that if the matter had been left entirely to him without this requisition, he would have protected this colliery, and he would have protected it amply, but in quite a different way, and I accept his evidence that that is so. He would not have sent his garrison there, and in my judgment, while not desiring for a moment to suggest that it was not the bounden duty of the county council to protect this colliery, and not for one moment suggesting that the performing of a legal duty will support a promise to pay, I have come to the conclusion that when a colliery company or an individual requisitions police protection of a special character for a particular purpose, he must pay for it, and he must pay for it whether he makes a contract to pay or whether he does not – a promise to pay would be implied under those circumstances. In this case, of course, there is an express promise, and in my judgment this promise is not without consideration and must be fulfilled'.

Upon this point Sir John Simon in his powerful argument for the appellants contended that the true inference to be drawn from the evidence was that the police authority, having a discretion to elect between protecting the collieries (which admittedly required protection in some form) by means of the 'mobile body' to which Colonel Smith referred or by means of a garrison, chose the latter alternative in consideration of payment, and that they could not so (as he put it) 'sell their discretion'. Upon the evidence, I do not think that they did anything of the kind. Colonel Smith said clearly that the police garrison was no part of his scheme of protection and did not help him in his scheme at all; that he had an ample force by which to protect the collieries from outside and was well able to cope with the situation. It does not appear that the provision of the garrison, who were brought in from distant parts of the county, relieved the force on the spot from any of their duties, or that the local force was reduced in consequence; and I think that the true inference is that the garrison formed an additional and not a substituted or alternative means of protection.

Viscount Finlay and Lord Shaw concurred; Lord Carson and Lord Blanesburgh dissented.

The position as regards the police is now governed in part by statute:

POLICE ACT 1996

s 25 Provision of special services

(1) The chief officer of police of a police force may provide, at the request of any person, special police services at any premises or in any locality in the police area for which the force is maintained, subject to the payment to local policing body of charges on such scales as may be determined by that body.

This seems to have the effect that a police force can now receive payment for doing no more than fulfilling its public obligation to 'keep the peace' where it is called on to provide a police presence at sporting events or entertainment events. This was confirmed by *Harris v Sheffield Utd FC* [1987] 2 All ER 838 in relation to football matches. The obligation does not extend, however, to policing on land not owned by or under the control of the organiser of the event: *Leeds United FC Ltd v Chief Constable of West Yorkshire* [2013] EWCA Civ 115; [2014] Q.B. 168.

The more general point remains as decided in *Glasbrook v Glamorgan CC*, that it is generally only possible to have an enforceable contract in relation to the performance of public duties where the performance exceeds the obligation imposed by the law.

3.3.4.2 Existing contractual duty owed to a third party

In contrast to the previous situation, here the courts have had no trouble in finding that the performance, or promise to perform, an obligation already owed under a contract with a third party can be sufficient consideration. This is illustrated by *Shadwell v Shadwell*.

***Shadwell v Shadwell* (1860) 9 CB(NS) 159 (Court of Common Bench)**

Facts: The plaintiff's uncle had promised, in consideration of the plaintiff marrying one Ellen Nicholl, to pay him £150 a year, until the plaintiff's annual income exceeded 600 guineas. The plaintiff was, at the time, seeking a career at the Bar, but later abandoned this. Twelve payments were made, and the uncle then died. The plaintiff sought to enforce the uncle's promise against his uncle's estate. The defence argued that the plaintiff had provided no consideration because he was already legally obliged to marry Ellen Nicholl (in that in those days she would have been able to sue him for breach of promise of marriage if he had backed out).

Held: The marriage was sufficient consideration for the uncle's promise, which was therefore enforceable.

Erle CJ: The question raised by the demurrer to the replication to the fourth plea is, whether there is a consideration which will support the action on the promise to pay the annuity of £150 per annum. …

Now, do [the] facts show that the promise was in consideration either of a loss to be sustained by the plaintiff or a benefit to be derived from the plaintiff to the uncle, at his, the uncle's, request? My answer is in the affirmative.

First, do these facts show a loss sustained by the plaintiff at his uncle's request? When I answer this in the affirmative, I am aware that a man's marriage with the woman of his choice is in one sense a boon, and in that sense the reverse of a loss: yet, as between the plaintiff and the party promising to supply an income to support the marriage, it may well be also a loss. The plaintiff may have made a most material change in his position, and induced the object of his affection to do the same, and may have incurred pecuniary liabilities resulting in embarrassments which would be in every sense a loss if the income which had been promised should be withheld; and, if the promise was made in order to induce the parties to marry, the promise so made would be in legal effect a request to marry.

Secondly, do these facts show a benefit derived from the plaintiff to the uncle, at his request? In answering again in the affirmative, I am at liberty to consider the relation in which the parties stood and the interest in the settlement of his nephew which the uncle declares. The marriage primarily affects the parties thereto; but in a secondary degree it may be an object of interest to a near relative, and in that sense a benefit to him. This benefit is also derived from the plaintiff at the uncle's request. If the promise of the annuity was intended as an inducement to the marriage, and the averment that the plaintiff, relying on the promise, married, is an averment that the promise was one inducement to the marriage, this is the consideration averred in the declaration; and it appears to me to be expressed in the letter, construed with the surrounding circumstances.

The second demurrer raises the question whether the plaintiff's continuance at the bar was made a condition precedent to the right of the annuity. I think not. The uncle promises to continue the annuity until the professional income exceeds the sum mentioned. I find no stipulation that the annuity shall cease if professional diligence ceases – no limitation except a defeasance in case of an amount of income from the other source. If the prospect of success at the bar had failed, a continuance to attend the courts might be an unreasonable expense. My judgment on this demurrer is also for the plaintiff.

The above is the judgment of my Brother Keating and myself.

Byles J dissented.

It should be noted that the action for breach of promise of marriage was abolished by the Law Reform (Miscellaneous Provisions) Act 1970, so that the issue discussed in *Shadwell v Shadwell* could not now arise in the same way. The principle it set out has, however, been applied in other contexts, including commercial agreements – as shown by *Scotson v Pegg*.

Scotson v Pegg (1861) 6 H&N 295 (Court of Exchequer)

Facts: The plaintiff was contractually bound *to a third party* to deliver coal to the defendant. The defendant promised to unload it a particular rate, but then failed to do so. The plaintiff sued. The defendant argued that the only alleged consideration for its promise to unload was the plaintiff's delivery of the coal and this could not be valid because it was an obligation already owed to a third party.

Held: The plaintiff's delivery of the coal was good consideration for the defendant's promise.

Martin B: I am of opinion that the plea is bad, both on principle and in law. It is bad in law because the ordinary rule is that any act done whereby the contracting party receives a benefit is a good consideration for a promise by him. Here the benefit is the delivery of the coals to the defendant. It is consistent with the declaration that there may have been some dispute as to the defendant's right to have the coals, or it may be that the plaintiffs detained them for demurrage; in either case there would be good consideration that the plaintiffs, who were in possession of the coals, would allow the defendant to take them out of the ship. Then is it any answer that the plaintiffs had entered into a prior contract with other persons to deliver the coals to their order upon the same terms, and that the defendant was a stranger to that contract? In my opinion it is not. We must deal with this case as if no prior contract had been entered into. Suppose the plaintiffs had no chance of getting their money from the other persons who might perhaps have become bankrupt. The defendant gets a benefit by the delivery of the coals to him, and it is immaterial that the plaintiffs had previously contracted with third parties to deliver to their order.

Wilde B: I am also of opinion that the plaintiffs are entitled to judgment. The plaintiffs say, that in consideration that they would deliver to the defendant a cargo of coals from their ship, the defendant promised to discharge the cargo in a certain way. The defendant, in answer, says 'You made a previous contract with other persons that they should discharge the cargo in the same way, and therefore there is no consideration for my promise'. But why is there no consideration? It is said, because the plaintiffs, in delivering the coals are only performing that which they were already bound to do. But to say that there is no consideration is to say that it is not possible for one man to have an interest in the performance of a contract made by another. But if a person chooses to promise to pay a sum of money in order to induce another to perform that which he has already contracted with a third person to do, I confess I cannot see why such a promise should not be binding. Here the defendant, who was a stranger to the original contract, induced the plaintiffs to part with the cargo, which they might not otherwise have been willing to do, and the delivery of it to the defendant was a benefit to him. I accede to the proposition that if a person contracts with another to do a certain thing, he cannot make the performance of it a consideration for a new promise to the same individual. But there is no authority for the proposition that where there has been a promise to one person to do a certain thing, it is not possible to make a valid promise to another to do the same thing. Therefore, deciding this matter on principle, it is plain to my mind that the delivery of the coals to the defendant was a good consideration for his promise, although the plaintiffs had made a previous contract to deliver them to the order of other persons.

This principle was subsequently applied in *New Zealand Shipping Co Ltd v Satterthwaite (The Eurymedon)* [1975] AC 154, which is discussed in Chapter 5, at 5.4.4. In *Pao On v Lau Yiu Long* [1980] AC 614, the Privy Council suggested that a *promise* to perform an obligation owed to a third party could also be good consideration. This seems to be in line with the general approach to consideration, which recognises promises as sufficient.

3.3.4.3 Existing duty to same promisor

The likely scenario for this issue to arise is that A and B have a contract, and B is having difficulty in performing or in performing on time. What is the situation if A offers B an additional inducement, probably in the form of extra payment, to complete the contract or to complete it on time? Is the promise of the inducement enforceable? Has B provided any consideration for it? The general answer given by the classical law of contract is 'no, there is no consideration, and the promise is not enforceable'. This is generally said to derive from the early nineteenth-century case of *Stilk v Myrick*.

Stilk v Myrick (1809) 2 Camp 317; 170 ER 1168

Facts: The plaintiff had been engaged as part of the crew of a ship, to be paid at £5 a month for a particular voyage. In the course of the voyage, two of the crew deserted, and the captain was unable to replace them. At Cronstadt, he entered into an agreement with the rest of the crew that they should have the wages of the two who had deserted equally divided among them. The ship was worked back to London by the plaintiff and eight more of the original crew, with whom the agreement had been made at Cronstadt. On their return, the ship owners refused to pay the additional wages.

Held: The promise to pay the additional money was not enforceable because there was no consideration for it.

Lord Ellenborough: I think *Harris v Watson* (1791) Peake 102 was rightly decided; but I doubt whether ground of public policy, upon which Lord Kenyon is stated to have proceeded, be the true principle on which the decision is to be supported. Here, I say, the agreement is void for want of consideration. There was no consideration for the ulterior pay promised to the mariners who remained with the ship. Before they sailed from London they had undertaken to do all that they could under all the emergencies of the voyage. They had sold all their services till the voyage should be completed. If they had been at liberty to quit the vessel at Cronstadt, the case would have been quite different; or if the captain had capriciously discharged the two men who were wanting, the others might not have been compellable to take the whole duty on themselves, and their agreeing to do so might have been a sufficient consideration for the promise of an advance of wages. But the desertion of a part of the crew is to be considered an emergency of the voyage as much as their death; and those who remain are bound by the terms of their original contract to exert themselves to the utmost to bring the ship in safety to her destined port. Therefore, without looking to the policy of this agreement, I think it is void for want of consideration, and that the plaintiff can only recover at the rate of £5 a month.

The principle set out by Lord Ellenborough has been widely accepted as stating the correct approach to be applied, but in fact the case is not uncontroversial. The reference to *Harris v Watson* at the start of his judgment is to a case where a similar situation was dealt with on the basis of 'public policy' – more specifically, the risk of a crew in this situation 'blackmailing' the captain. This approach is given much more prominence in the other report of *Stilk v Myrick* by Espinasse (6 Esp 129; 170 ER 851), who was, in fact, one of the counsel for the plaintiff. This difference has led to much academic comment – just two examples are given here. The first is taken from a lengthy examination of the reasons for, and implications of, the difference between the two reports of the case.

Luther, P, Campbell, 'Espinasse and the sailors: text and comment in the common law' (1999) 19 *Legal Studies* 525, pp 525–528, 550–551

1. Introduction

This article scarcely needs any introduction, for it relates to a case which will be familiar to every student of the law of contract: *Stilk v Myrick*. ... Despite the familiarity of the material, it is convenient to quote the two versions of the judgment in full, as this article will include a close examination of each ...

[At this point Luther quotes Campbell's version, which has already been reproduced above. He then goes on to quote the other report]

This is what Espinasse says:

> 'Lord Ellenborough ruled that the plaintiff could not recover this part of his demand. His Lordship said that he recognised the principle of the case of *Harris v Watson* as founded on just and proper policy. When the defendant [sic: it should be "plaintiff"] entered on board the ship, he stipulated to do all the work his situation called upon him to do. Here the voyage was to the Baltick and back, not to Cronstadt only; if the voyage had then terminated, the sailors might have made what terms they pleased. If any part of the crew had died, would not the remainder have been forced to work the ship home? If that accident would have left them liable to do the whole work without any extraordinary remuneration, why should not desertion or casualty equally demand it?'

The orthodox view here is that Espinasse's report is based on considerations of public policy, and that this policy is, in essence, that articulated by Lord Kenyon in *Harris v Watson*: the need to prevent sailors from coercing masters into promising extra pay. Campbell's report, again on the orthodox view, is simply about the doctrine of consideration (and thus capable of general application outside the specific context of sailors' wages). As every law student knows, it is Campbell's version of the judgment – despite frequent criticism of its application – that has, at least until recent times, been generally accepted (even to the extent that his spelling of the master's name, Myrick, has been preferred to Espinasse's Meyrick; the writer has swum with the tide here, though on this point, if no other, one might expect that the opinion of counsel with the papers of the case in front of him would carry more weight than that of an observer). This article looks at some of the questions raised by the case, including the question of how two different reports of a case might come to be written, and the related questions of how one report of a case might come to be preferred, and of how much reliance can be placed upon the words that a reporter has used. Much of the comment on *Stilk v Myrick* has been inclined to be superficial, tending towards statements that 'X is the more reliable reporter', or that 'X's report is right' (and, as noted earlier, for the most part X = Campbell). This article suggests, both in general terms and with specific reference to *Stilk v Myrick*, that the textual problems of reports of the nineteenth century and earlier are more complicated than such comments suggest. It also looks at the policy considerations involving merchant seamen in the eighteenth and nineteenth centuries, and suggests that the avoidance of coercion – while it was undoubtedly a factor when courts considered issues of public policy – was only one strand in an elaborate web of policy considerations surrounding sailors and maritime trade. These issues remain important, despite the fact that *Stilk v Myrick* is almost two centuries old, as can be seen from the reconsideration of the case by the Court of Appeal in *Williams v Roffey Bros & Nicholls*. Although this latter case is itself almost ten years old, the approach taken by the Court to *Stilk* has given rise to difficulties which have yet to be resolved.

5. Conclusion

This article is not intended to be a discussion of the desirability of maintaining the perceived principle of *Stilk v Myrick*. It has merely attempted to show that there are complicating factors, surrounding both the text and context of the case, which modern judges and commentators have tended to ignore. Recent cases – and *Williams v Roffey* is the prime example here – take an over-simplified view of it. As noted earlier, the textual problems (*Espinasse v Campbell*) are altogether ignored in *Williams v Roffey*, though they are addressed in some earlier cases: see the comment of Mocatta J in *North Ocean Shipping Co Ltd v Hyundai Construction Co Ltd (The 'Atlantic Baron')*, that 'Campbell's reports have the better reputation', or the rather fuller analysis of Lord Scarman in *Pao On v Lau Liu Long*. The Court of Appeal in *Williams v Roffey* *does* consider the context of the earlier cases, and *is* prepared to admit that the decisions were driven by public policy, but sees this policy as no more than the need to avoid coercion. This is most obvious in the judgment of Purchas LJ:

> 'The two cases, *Harris v Watson* ... and *Stilk v Myrick* ... involved circumstances of a very special nature, namely the extraordinary conditions existing at the turn of the 18th century under which seamen had to serve their contracts of employment on the high seas. There were strong public policy grounds at that time to protect the master and owners of a ship from being held to ransom by disaffected crews'.

Such an analysis has been enthusiastically adopted by commentators. Adams and Brownsword, for example, state that '[t]he better answer ... must be that *Stilk v Myrick* was a case involving what would nowadays be recognised as economic duress. Halson similarly sees the sailors' cases as 'a rare articulation of the policy consideration underpinning the law in the area of contractual modifications; the non-enforcement of extorted modifications and the enforcement of freely agreed alterations'.

This approach renders the decision in *Williams v Roffey* open to attack. McKendrick points out that there is 'no evidence that Stilk applied any pressure on the master'. Nor, one might add, is there any evidence that the claimant in *Harris v Watson* applied pressure, and nor did Lord Kenyon say that he had. McKendrick also suggests that if the Court of Appeal in *Williams v Roffey* wished to turn *Stilk v Myrick* into a duress case, they could have done so more easily by relying on Espinasse's report and on *Harris v Watson*. This is true, but it would still have been an over-simple view of the case. Espinasse's report of *Stilk v Myrick* was not solely about duress, though this may well be one strand that runs through it, any more than Campbell's was solely about consideration.

As suggested in the fourth section of this article, *Stilk v Myrick* is a case which must be read in the context of the mass of policy concerns which led the courts, throughout the eighteenth century and into the nineteenth century, to treat merchant seamen as in almost every respect different from other workers. It is also a case, as suggested in the second and third sections, in which we need to be aware of the complexity of the issues which surround the very text. It is not enough to look at the two reports and choose one as 'right, or to look at the two reporters and choose one as 'more reliable'. This is true whether or not the view advanced here, that the difference between the texts may be more apparent than real, is accepted. This article may seem like a perverse attempt to muddy the waters at just the time when we had started to see *Stilk v Myrick* more clearly, but it is only by taking a broader view, both of the text of the case and of its context, that the problems it poses will be resolved.

A different analysis of the way in which *Stilk v Myrick*, and in particular the version of the case to be found in the Campbell report, became a leading authority on the common law of contract is to be found in Gilmore, G, *The Death of Contract*, 1974, Ohio State University Press, pp 24–30. Gilmore suggests that the orthodox view of the case can be traced to selective use of the reports and the context by writers of treatises on contract law – in particular, in America, the treatise *Williston on Contracts*, first published in 1920. There is not space to do justice to Gilmore's analysis here, but his review of the cases is worth studying.

Despite these issues relating to the true basis for the decision in *Stilk v Myrick*, until 1991 there was no case in England and Wales which seriously questioned the principle for which it was generally accepted to be authority – that is that a person making a promise to an existing party to the contract was not bound by that promise unless, in exchange, the promisee was required to go beyond his or her existing obligations. The fact that exceeding existing contractual obligations can amount to consideration for a promise of extra payment was confirmed by *Hartley v Ponsonby* (1857) 7 E & B 872 – a case with very similar facts to *Stilk v Myrick*, but where the level of desertion was to a level which rendered the voyage unsafe. In these circumstances, a promise of additional wages for continuing to work the ship was held to be enforceable. As with public duties, therefore, doing more than you are obliged to do may constitute consideration.

In 1991, however, a decision was handed down by the Court of Appeal which involved a more significant reconsideration of the scope of *Stilk v Myrick*.

Williams v Roffey Bros & Nicholls (Contractors) Ltd [1991] 1 QB 1 (CA)

Facts: The defendant building contractors engaged the plaintiff to carry out the carpentry work in the refurbishment of 27 flats at a price of £20,000. When about half the work had been done, it became clear that the plaintiff was in financial difficulties, partly because he had under-quoted for the work. The defendants were concerned that delay would lay them open to a penalty clause in their contract with the developer. They offered the plaintiff extra money at the rate of £575 per completed flat. 8 flats were completed, but the defendant only paid £1,500. The plaintiff then ceased work. The job was completed by other carpenters, and the defendant had to pay a time penalty. The plaintiff sought payment of £575 for each flat completed. The defendant resisted on the basis that there was no consideration for the promise of extra payment.

Held: There was a 'practical benefit' for the defendant in the new arrangement for payment, and this was sufficient to constitute consideration for the promise of additional payment.

Glidewell LJ (giving the first judgment at the invitation of Purchas LJ): This is an appeal against the decision of Mr Rupert Jackson QC sitting as an assistant recorder given on 31 January 1989 in the Kingston-upon-Thames County Court, entering judgment for the plaintiff for £3,500 damages with £1,400 interest and costs and dismissing the defendants' counterclaim.

The facts

The plaintiff is a carpenter. The defendants are building contractors who in September 1985 had entered into a contract with Shepherd's Bush Housing Association Ltd to refurbish a block of flats called Twynholm Mansions, Lillie Road, London SW6. The defendants were the main contractors for the works. There are 28 flats in Twynholm Mansions, but the work of refurbishment was to be carried out in 27 of the flats.

The defendants engaged the plaintiff to carry out the carpentry work in the refurbishment of the 27 flats, including work to the structure of the roof. Originally, the plaintiff was engaged on three separate sub-contracts, but these were all superseded by a sub-contract in writing made on 21 January 1986 by which the plaintiff undertook to provide the labour for the carpentry work to the roof of the block and for the first and second fix carpentry work required in each of the 27 flats for a total price of £20,000. The judge found that, though there was no express term providing for payment to be made in stages, the contract of 21 January 1986 was subject to an implied term that the defendants would make interim payments to the plaintiff, related to the amount of work done, at reasonable intervals.

The plaintiff and his men began work on 10 October 1985. The judge found that by 9 April 1986 the plaintiff had completed the work to the roof, had carried out the first fix to all 27 flats and had substantially completed the second fix to 9 flats. By this date the defendants had made interim payments totaling £16,200.

It is common ground that by the end of March 1986 the plaintiff was in financial difficulty. The judge found that there were two reasons for this, namely: (i) that the agreed price of £20,000 was too low to enable the plaintiff to operate satisfactorily and at a profit. Mr Cottrell, a surveyor employed by the defendants, said in evidence that a reasonable price for the works would have been £23,783; (ii) that the plaintiff failed to supervise his workmen adequately.

The defendants, as they made clear, were concerned lest the plaintiff did not complete the carpentry work on time. The main contract contained a penalty clause. The judge found that on 9 April 1986 the defendants promised to pay the plaintiff the further sum of £10,300, in addition to the £20,000, to be paid at the rate of £575 for each flat in which the carpentry work was completed.

The plaintiff and his men continued work on the flats until the end of May 1986. By that date the defendants, after their promise on 9 April 1986, had made only one further payment of £1,500. At the end of May the plaintiff ceased work on the flats. I will describe later the work which, according to the judge's findings, then remained to be done. Suffice it to say that the defendants engaged other carpenters to complete the work, but in the result incurred one week's time penalty in their contract with the building owners.

The action

The plaintiff commenced this action by specially endorsed writ on 10March 1987…

The judge's conclusions

The judge found that the defendants' promise to pay an additional £10,300, at the rate of £575 per completed flat, was part of an oral agreement made between the plaintiff and the defendants on 9 April 1986, by way of variation to the original contract.

The judge also found that before the plaintiff ceased work at the end of May 1986 the carpentry in 17 flats had been substantially (but not totally) completed. This means that between the making of the agreement on 9 April 1986 and the date when the plaintiff ceased work, eight further flats were substantially completed.

The judge calculated that this entitled the plaintiff to receive £4,600 (8 × £575) 'less some small deduction for defective and incomplete items'. He held that the plaintiff was also entitled to a reasonable proportion of the £2,200 which was outstanding from the original contract sum. (I believe this figure should be £2,300, but this makes no practical difference.) Adding these two amounts, he decided that the plaintiff was entitled to further payments totalling £5,000 against which he had only received £1,500, and that the defendants were therefore in breach of contract, entitling the plaintiff to cease work.

The issues

Before us counsel for the defendants advances two arguments. His principal submission is that the defendants' admitted promise to pay an additional £10,300, at the rate of £575 per completed flat, is unenforceable since there was no consideration for it. This issue was not raised in the defence, but we are told that the argument was advanced at the trial without objection, and that there was equally no objection to it being argued before us. …

Was there consideration for the defendants' promise made on 9 April 1986 to pay an additional price at the rate of £575 per completed flat?

The judge made the following findings of fact which are relevant on this issue. (i) The sub-contract price agreed was too low to enable the plaintiff to operate satisfactorily and at a profit. Mr Cottrell, the defendants' surveyor, agreed that this was so. (ii) Mr Roffey, the managing director of the defendants, was persuaded by Mr Cottrell that the defendants should pay a bonus to the plaintiff. The figure agreed at the meeting on 9 April 1986 was £10,300.

The judge quoted and accepted the evidence of Mr Cottrell to the effect that a main contractor who agrees too low a price with a sub-contractor is acting contrary to his own interests. He will never get the job finished without paying more money. The judge therefore concluded:

> 'In my view where the original sub-contract price is too low, and the parties subsequently agree that the additional moneys shall be paid to the subcontractor, this agreement is in the interests of both parties. This is what happened in the present case, and in my opinion the agreement of 9 April 1986 does not fail for lack of consideration.'

In his address to us counsel for the defendants outlined the benefits to the defendants which arose from their agreement to pay the additional £10,300 as (i) seeking to ensure that the plaintiff continued work and did not stop in breach of the sub-contract, (ii) avoiding the penalty for delay and (iii) avoiding the trouble and expense of engaging other people to complete the carpentry work.

However, counsel submits that, though the defendants may have derived, or hoped to derive, practical benefits from their agreement to pay the 'bonus', they derived no benefit in law, since the plaintiff was promising to do no more than he was already bound to do by his sub-contract, ie continue with the carpentry work and complete it on time. Thus there was no consideration for the agreement.

Counsel for the defendants relies on the principle of law which, traditionally, is based on the decision in *Stilk v Myrick* (1809) 2 Camp 317, 170 ER 1168 …

In *North Ocean Shipping Co Ltd v Hyundai Construction Co Ltd, The Atlantic Baron* [1978] 3 All ER 1170, [1979] QB 705 Mocatta J regarded the general principle of the decision in *Stilk v Myrick* as still being good law …

There is, however, another legal concept of relatively recent development which is relevant, namely that of economic duress. Clearly, if a sub-contractor has agreed to undertake work at a fixed price, and before he has completed the work declines to continue with it unless the contractor agrees to pay an increased price, the subcontractor may be held guilty of securing the contractor's promise by taking unfair advantage of the difficulties he will cause if he does not complete the work. In such a case an agreement to pay an increased price may well be voidable because it was entered into under duress. Thus this concept may provide another answer in law to the question of policy which has troubled the courts since before *Stilk v Myrick* (1809) 2 Camp 317, 170 ER 1168, and no doubt led at the date of that decision to a rigid adherence to the doctrine of consideration ...

Accordingly ... the present state of the law on this subject can be expressed in the following proposition: (i) if A has entered into a contract with B to do work for, or to supply goods or services to, B in return of payment by B and (ii) at some stage before A has completely performed his obligations under the contract B has reason to doubt whether A will, or will be able to, complete his side of the bargain and (iii) B thereupon promises A an additional payment in return for A's promise to perform his contractual obligations on time and (iv) as a result of giving his promise B obtains in practice a benefit, or obviates a disbenefit, and (v) B's promise is not given as a result of economic duress or fraud on the part of A, then (vi) the benefit to B is capable of being consideration for B's promise, so that the promise will be legally binding.

As I have said, counsel for the defendants accepts that in the present case by promising to pay the extra £10,300 the defendants secured benefits. There is no finding, and no suggestion, that in this case the promise was given as a result of fraud or duress.

If it be objected that the propositions above contravene the principle in *Stilk v Myrick*, I answer that in my view they do not: they refine and limit the application of that principle, but they leave the principle unscathed, e.g. where B secures no benefit by his promise. It is not in my view surprising that a principle enunciated in relation to the rigours of seafaring life during the Napoleonic wars should be subjected during the succeeding 180 years to a process of refinement and limitation in its application in the present day.

It is therefore my opinion that on his findings of fact in the present case, the judge was entitled to hold, as he did, that the defendants' promise to pay the extra £10,300 was supported by valuable consideration, and thus constituted an enforceable agreement. ...

Russell LJ and Purchas LJ concurred.

As will be seen, the Court of Appeal was at pains to stress that it was not intending to overrule *Stilk v Myrick*, but at the very least, *Williams v Roffey* requires a reinterpretation of that case. It is arguable that the captain in *Stilk v Myrick* received a practical benefit from the agreement of the crew to continue working. How is this different from the benefit received by the defendant in *Williams v Roffey*? However, *Williams v Roffey* has been applied by the courts in several reported decisions – for example, *Anangel Atlas Companies Naviera SA v Ishikawajima-Harima Heavy Industries Co Ltd (No 2)* [1990] 2 Lloyd's Rep 526; *Simon Container Machinery Ltd v Emba Machinery AB* [1998] 2 Lloyd's Rep 429; and *Lee v GEC Plessey Telecommunications* [1993] IRLR 383. To that extent, it seems to have become an established authority. On the other hand, at least one judge has doubted whether it was good law.

South Caribbean Trading Ltd ('SCT') v Trafigura Beheer BV ('Trafigura')
[2004] EWHC 2676 (Comm)

Colman J: ...

108. But for the fact that *Williams v Roffey Bros Ltd*, supra, was a decision of the Court of Appeal, I would not have followed it. That decision is inconsistent with the long-standing rule that consideration, being the price of the promise sued upon, must move from the promisee. The judgment of Glidewell LJ. was substantially based on *Pao On v Lau Yin Long* [1980] AC 614 in which the Judicial Committee of the Privy Council had held a promise by A to B to perform a contractual obligation owed by A to X could be sufficient consideration as against B. At page 15 Glidewell LJ regarded Lord Scarman's reasoning in relation to such tripartite relationship as applicable in principle to a bipartite relationship. But in the former case by the additional promise to B, consideration has moved from A because he has made himself liable to an additional party, whereas in the latter case he has not undertaken anything that he was not already obliged to do for the benefit of the same party. Glidewell LJ substituted for the established rule as to consideration moving from the promisee a completely different principle – that the promisor must by his promise have conferred a benefit on the other party. Purchas LJ at pages 22–23 clearly saw the non-sequitur but was 'comforted' by observations from Lord Hailsham LC in *Woodhouse AC Israel Cocoa Ltd v Nigerian Product Marketing Co Ltd* [1972] AC 741 at pages 757–758. Investigation of the correspondence referred to in those observations shows that the latter are not authority for the proposition advanced 'with some hesitation' by Purchas LJ.

109. However, seeing that *Williams v Roffey Bros*, supra has not yet been held by the House of Lords to have been wrongly decided, and approaching the validity of consideration on the basis of mutuality of benefit, I would hold that SCT's threat of non-compliance with its delivery obligation under Contract 3053b precluded its reliance on the benefit that its performance by effecting delivery would confer on Trafigura. This threat was analogous to economic duress as contemplated in *Williams v Roffey Bros*, supra because it was not based on any argument that SCT was discharged from its delivery obligation: reliance on clause 7 of Contract 5536 only came later.

Colman J was bound to apply *Williams v Roffey*, since it is a Court of Appeal decision, but was clearly of the view that it might well be overruled by the Supreme Court, although, as we shall see within section 3.3.5.1, the Supreme Court recently declined an opportunity to directly review *Williams v Roffey*.

3.3.5 Consideration and the part payment of debts

A similar issue arises in relation to the part payment of debts. If one party (A) has a contractual obligation to pay the other (B) a sum of money, can that obligation ever be discharged by B agreeing to accept less than the amount due (and to forgive the rest of the debt) and A paying, or promising to pay, the reduced amount? It would seem to follow from the general position on existing obligations – the *Stilk v Myrick* principle – that payment of less than is due would provide no consideration for a promise to take it in satisfaction of the debt (in these cases, there is not even full performance of an existing obligation). The starting point for exploring this issue is the so-called 'rule in *Pinnel's Case*'.

***Pinnel's Case* (1602) 5 Co Rep 117a; 77 ER 237 (Common Pleas)**

Facts: Pinnel brought an action of debt against Cole, for payment of £8 10s due on 11 November 1600. The defendant pleaded that he, at the instance of the plaintiff, had paid £5 2s 9d on the 1 October and that the plaintiff had accepted this in full satisfaction of the debt.

Held: Payment of a less sum on the due date cannot be any satisfaction for the whole. Part payment *before* the day, and acceptance of this, may discharge the whole debt. But, in this case, the plaintiff succeeded because the defendant had not pleaded the defence properly.

Judgment: [I]t was resolved by the whole Court, that payment of a lesser sum on the day in satisfaction of a greater, cannot be any satisfaction for the whole, because it appears to the Judges that by no possibility, a lesser sum can be a satisfaction to the plaintiff for a greater sum: but the gift of a horse, hawk, or robe, etc in satisfaction is good. For it shall be intended that a horse, hawk, or robe, etc might be more beneficial to the plaintiff than the money, in respect of some circumstance, or otherwise the plaintiff would not have accepted of it in satisfaction.

But when the whole sum is due, by no intendment the acceptance of a parcel can be a satisfaction to the Plaintiff: but in the case at Bar it was resolved, that the payment and acceptance of parcel before the day in satisfaction of the whole, would be a good satisfaction in regard of circumstance of time, for peradventure parcel of it before the day would be more beneficial to him than the whole at the day, and the value of the satisfaction is not material: so if I am bound in £20 to pay you £10 at Westminster and you request me to pay you £5 at the day at York, and you will accept it in full satisfaction of the whole, it is a good satisfaction for the whole: for the expenses to pay it at York, is sufficient satisfaction.

Pinnel's Case was not a particularly strong authority, because the plaintiff only succeeded on the basis that the defence had been inadequately pleaded. The principle that part payment of a debt cannot in itself discharge a debt was confirmed, however, by the House of Lords in *Foakes v Beer*.

Foakes v Beer (1884) 9 App Cas 605 (HL)

Facts: Mrs Beer had agreed to accept a judgment debt, owed to her by Dr Foakes, in instalments. When the instalments had been paid, she sued to recover the interest which she alleged had been accrued by the delay in completing payment. Mrs Beer succeeded in the lower courts. Dr Foakes appealed to the House of Lords.

Held: Even if she had promised to take the instalments in full satisfaction, this did not preclude her from recovering the interest. The interest was owed by Dr Foake's and acceptance of part payment could not discharge the whole debt.

Earl of Selborne LC: The question … is nakedly raised by this appeal, whether your Lordships are now prepared, not only to overrule, as contrary to the law, the doctrine stated by Sir Edward Coke to have been laid down by all the judges of the Common Pleas in *Pinnel's Case* in 1602, and repeated in his note to Littleton, s. 344(2), but to treat a prospective agreement, not under seal, for satisfaction of a debt, by a series of payments on account to a total amount less than the whole debt, as binding in law, provided those payments are regularly made; the case not being one of a composition with a common debtor, agreed to, inter se, by several creditors. I prefer so to state the question instead of treating it (as it was put at the Bar) as depending on the authority of the case of *Cumber v Wane* (1721) 1 Stra 426, decided in 1718. It may well be that distinctions, which in later cases have been held sufficient to exclude the application of that doctrine, existed and were improperly disregarded in *Cumber v Wane*; and yet that the doctrine itself may be law, rightly recognised in *Cumber v Wane*, and not really contradicted by any later authorities. And this appears to me to be the true state of the case. The doctrine itself, as laid down by Sir Edward Coke, may have been criticised, as questionable in principle, by some persons whose opinions are entitled to respect, but it has never been judicially overruled; on the contrary I think it has always, since the sixteenth century, been accepted as law. If so, I cannot think that your Lordships would do right, if you were now to reverse, as erroneous, a judgment of the Court of Appeal, proceeding upon a doctrine which has been accepted as part of the law of England for 280 years.

The doctrine, as stated in *Pinnel's Case*, is 'that payment of a lesser sum on the day' (it would of course be the same after the day), 'in satisfaction of a greater, cannot be any satisfaction for the whole, because it appears to the judges, that by no possibility a lesser sum can be a satisfaction to the plaintiff for a greater sum'. As stated in Coke Littleton, 212, it is, 'where the condition is for payment of £20, the obligor or feoffor cannot at the time appointed pay a lesser sum in satisfaction of the whole, because it is apparent that a lesser sum of money cannot be a satisfaction of a greater;' adding (what is beyond controversy), that an acquittance under seal, in full satisfaction of the whole, would (under like circumstances) be valid and binding.

The distinction between the effect of a deed under seal, and that of an agreement by parol, or by writing not under seal, may seem arbitrary, but it is established in our law; nor is it really unreasonable or practically inconvenient that the law should require particular solemnities to give a gratuitous contract the force of a binding obligation. If the question be (as, in the actual state of the law, I think it is), whether consideration is, or is not, given in a case of this kind, by the debtor who pays down part of the debt presently due from him, for a promise by the creditor to relinquish, after certain further payments on account, the residue of the debt, I cannot say that I think consideration is given, in the sense in which I have always understood that word as used in our law. It might be (and indeed I think it would be) an improvement in our law, if a release or acquittance of the whole debt, on payment of any sum which the creditor might be content to receive by way of accord and satisfaction (though less than the whole), were held to be, generally, binding, though not under seal; nor should I be unwilling to see equal force given to a prospective agreement, like the present, in writing though not under seal; but I think it impossible, without refinements which practically alter the sense of the word, to treat such a release or acquittance as supported by any new consideration proceeding from the debtor. All the authorities subsequent to *Cumber v Wane*, which were relied upon by the appellant at your Lordships' Bar (such as *Sibree v Tripp* [1846] 15 M & W 23, *Curlewis v Clark* [1849] 3 Ex 375, and *Goddard v O'Brien* [1882] 9 QBD 37) have proceeded upon the distinction, that, by giving negotiable paper or otherwise, there had been some new consideration for a new agreement, distinct from mere money payments in or towards discharge of the original liability. I think it unnecessary to go through those cases, or to examine the particular grounds on which each of them was decided. There are no such facts in the case now before your Lordships. What is called 'any benefit, or even any legal possibility of benefit,' in Mr Smith's notes to *Cumber v Wane*, is not (as I conceive) that sort of benefit which a creditor may derive from getting payment of part of the money due to him from a debtor who might otherwise keep him at arm's length, or possibly become insolvent, but is some independent benefit, actual or contingent, or a kind which might in law be a good and valuable consideration for any other sort of agreement not under seal.

My conclusion is, that the order appealed from should be affirmed, and the appeal dismissed, with costs, and I so move your Lordships.

The rule set out in *Foakes v Beer* is still good law, and was reaffirmed in *Re Selectmove* [1995] 2 All ER 534 and *Ferguson v Davies* [1997] 1 All ER 315. Compare, however, *Simantob v Shavleyan* [2019] EWCA Civ 1105 at [53], where Simon LJ noted that *Foakes v Beer* might have to be reconsidered in the future. There are, nevertheless, some exceptions to it, both under common law (discussed in the next section, 3.3.5.1) and under the equitable doctrine of promissory estoppel (which is dealt with at 3.3.7).

3.3.5.1 Common-law exceptions to the rule in *Foakes v Beer*

Pinnel's Case itself recognises one exception to the rule applied in *Foakes v Beer*: doing something more than simply paying part of the debt – for example, paying early or at a different place or providing goods as well as (or instead of) money – will be sufficient to make a promise to discharge the debt enforceable. In other words, if there is some consideration other than the payment of the debt, this may make the promise to accept the lesser amount enforceable. An issue that has exercised the courts in several recent cases is whether the existence of a 'practical benefit' to the creditor, as defined in *Williams v Roffey* (above, at 3.3.4.3), could be sufficient to provide such consideration.

The attempt to apply *Williams v Roffey* in this way was first discussed by the Court of Appeal in *Re Selectmove* [1995] 1 WLR 474. The court rejected the suggestion and reaffirmed the strength of *Foakes v Beer*.

Re Selectmove Ltd [1995] 1 WLR 474 (CA)

Facts: In this case, the company was trying to enforce an alleged promise by the Inland Revenue ('the Crown') to accept the payment of a tax debt by instalments. It argued that this would be of 'practical benefit' to the Revenue, following the *Williams v Roffey* principle, in that the firm would be able to stay in business and would be more likely to be able to pay its debts.

Held: Even if the Crown had made the alleged promise, the *Williams v Roffey* approach had no application. On the basis of *Foakes v Beer*, the Crown was entitled to recover.

Peter Gibson LJ: ... Mr Nugee submitted that although Glidewell LJ [in *Williams v Roffey*] in terms confined his remarks to a case where B is to do the work for or supply goods or services to A, the same principle must apply where B's obligation is to pay A, and he referred to an article by Adams and Brownsword 'Contract, Consideration and the Critical Path' (1990) 53 MLR 536 at 539–540 which suggests that *Foakes v Beer* might need reconsideration. I see the force of the argument, but the difficulty that I feel with it is that if the principle of *Williams'* case is to be extended to an obligation to make payment, it would in effect leave the principle in *Foakes v Beer* without any application. When a creditor and a debtor who are at arm's length reach agreement on the payment of the debt by instalments to accommodate the debtor, the creditor will no doubt always see a practical benefit to himself in so doing. In the absence of authority there would be much to be said for the enforceability of such a contract. But that was a matter expressly considered in *Foakes v Beer* yet held not to constitute good consideration in law. *Foakes v Beer* was not even referred to in *Williams'* case, and it is in my judgment impossible, consistently with the doctrine of precedent, for this court to extend the principle of *Williams'* case to any circumstances governed by the principle of *Foakes v Beer*. If that extension is to be made, it must be by the House of Lords or, perhaps even more appropriately, by Parliament after consideration by the Law Commission.

In my judgment, the judge was right to hold that if there was an agreement between the company and the Crown it was unenforceable for want of consideration.

Stuart-Smith and Balcombe LJJ concurred.

This apparently strong rejection of any application of *Williams v Roffey* to the part payment of debts seemed to have settled the issue. However, more recent cases have suggested that there might still be room for the 'practical benefit' concept in such situations. In *Re Sutton* [2014] BPIR 1349, it was suggested that the provision of a 'practical benefit' in form of getting third parties to contribute to the reduced sum that had been agreed with the creditor as settlement for the debt, could be sufficient to make the promise to accept the smaller sum enforceable. Even more recently, the Court of Appeal went somewhat further.

MWB Business Exchange Centres Ltd v Rock Advertising Ltd [2016] EWCA Civ 553 (CA)

Facts: The case concerned a licence for the use of business premises. This was renegotiated to give use of larger premises at a higher fee, with the contract to run for one year from November 2011. By early 2012, it was clear that the defendants were in difficulties as regards meeting the new, higher charge. The claimants subsequently purported to terminate the contract. The defendants argued that an agreement had been made in February 2012, under which the claimants agreed to accept reduced payments for a period, with the balance being made up with larger payments towards the end of the contract. The claimants denied that there was an agreement, but claimed that it would, in any case, be unenforceable for want of consideration on the *Foakes v Beer* principle. The trial judge held that there was an agreement and that there was sufficient consideration to make it enforceable. The claimants appealed.

Held: The Court of Appeal upheld the trial judge's decision. It found that there was sufficient 'practical benefit' to the claimant in the arrangement agreed in February to amount to good consideration for the promise to accept less than was owed.

Kitchin LJ: Having noted the claimant's argument that, on the basis of *Re Selectmove*, there was no room for the *Williams v Roffey* concept of 'practical benefit' in this situation, Kitchin LJ continued –

47. I have to say that I was initially much attracted by these submissions. However, upon reflection, I have come to the conclusion that they fail to take proper account of the full extent of the factual findings of the judge. He was clearly of the view that the oral variation agreement would have a number of beneficial consequences for MWB. First, MWB would recover some of the arrears immediately and would have some hope of recovering them all in due course. But secondly and importantly, Rock would remain a licensee and continue to occupy the property with the result that it would not be left standing empty for some time at further loss to MWB.

48. There has been no suggestion that MWB was at any material time operating under any kind of duress. Rather, acting by Miss Evans, it had for some time been trying to find a way to accommodate Rock's financial difficulties. There was, so it seems to me, a commercial advantage to both MWB and Rock in reaching an agreement if that could be achieved. MWB would receive an immediate payment of £3,500, it would be likely to recover more from Rock than it would by enforcing the terms of the original agreement and it would also retain Rock as a licensee. Rock would remain in occupation of the property, continue its business without interruption and have an opportunity to overcome its cash flow difficulties. Accordingly this is not a case in which the only benefits conferred on MWB by the oral variation agreement were benefits of a kind contemplated by Lord Blackburn in *Foakes v Beer* and by this court in *In re Selectmove*. MWB derived a practical benefit which went beyond the advantage of receiving a prompt payment of a part of the arrears and a promise that it would be paid the balance of the arrears and any deferred licence fees over the course of the forthcoming months. This is therefore a case where, as in *Williams v Roffey*, Rock's immediate payment of £3,500 and its agreement to perform its obligations under the revised payment schedule conferred a practical benefit on MWB which amounted to good consideration, so rendering the oral variation agreement enforceable.

49. I conclude that the judge was right to find that the payment by Rock of the £3,500 and its promise to make further payments in accordance with the revised payment schedule conferred upon MWB a benefit which constituted sufficient consideration to support the oral variation agreement.

Arden and McCombe LJJ concurred.

Although the court argued that its decision is consistent with both *Foakes v Beer* and *Re Selectmove*, it is difficult to see this case as anything other than a significant limiting of the scope of those decisions. The case was subsequently appealed to the Supreme Court ([2018] UKSC 24), but the Supreme Court decided the case on other grounds, with Lord Sumption stating at [18]:

In *Williams v Roffey Bros & Nicholls (Contractors) Ltd* [1991] 1 QB 1, the Court of Appeal held that an expectation of commercial advantage was good consideration. The problem about this was that practical expectation of benefit was the very thing which the House of Lords held not to be adequate consideration in *Foakes v Beer* (1884) ... There are arguable points of distinction, although the arguments are somewhat forced. A differently constituted Court of Appeal made these points in *In re Selectmove Ltd* [1995] 1 WLR 474, and declined to follow *Williams v Roffey*. The reality is that any decision on this point is likely to involve a re-examination of the decision in *Foakes v Beer*. It is probably ripe for re-examination. But if it is to be overruled or its effect substantially modified, it should be before an enlarged panel of the court and in a case where the decision would be more than obiter dictum.

There are two other situations where the common law recognises that a promise to accept less than is owed may be enforceable. The first is where a third party makes the part payment.

Hirachand Punamchand v Temple [1911] 2 KB 330

Facts: The plaintiffs were moneylenders from whom Temple had borrowed money. Temple's father sent them a draft for less than the full amount in settlement of the debt. The plaintiffs cashed the draft, but then sued for the balance. At trial, the plaintiffs succeeded. Temple appealed.

Held: Where part payment was made by a third party and was accepted by the creditor, the creditor could not then sue the debtor for the balance.

Fletcher Moulton LJ: I also think that the plaintiffs' action fails, and that this appeal should be allowed. The facts of this case are such that this result may be arrived at by more than one course of reasoning. I am clearly of opinion that there must be taken to have been an agreement between the plaintiffs and Sir Richard Temple, by which the plaintiffs agreed to accept the money sent by him in satisfaction of the note. No oral testimony was given at the trial, but the facts of the case appear clearly from the correspondence. In the first letter the plaintiffs applied to Sir Richard Temple, the father, in respect of his son's account with them. Then comes a letter from the father's solicitors, in which they offer the plaintiffs a certain sum in settlement of the plaintiffs' two claims against the son, one of which was on a bond and the other on the promissory note. In answer to this letter, two separate letters were written by the plaintiffs, one with regard to the bond, and the other with regard to the note. I need only refer to the latter, as the purport of the two, mutatis mutandis, is the same. The plaintiffs in that letter say 'We shall be glad if you will let us know the amount for which Sir Richard Temple is prepared to settle this debt due from his son.' Therefore it is clear that the plaintiffs realized that the father was proposing to settle the whole claim on the note, and that they accordingly asked what amount he was prepared to give. The father's solicitors wrote in answer one letter dealing with both claims. In the paragraph relating to the promissory note, they say: 'Our instructions are, therefore, to pay you Rs. 500 in respect of the principal and Rs. 150 in respect of the one year's interest, making together Rs. 650. We enclose draft by the National Bank of India on the Bank of Bombay, Poona, in your favour for this amount, and shall be glad to receive the promissory note in exchange.' It is perfectly clear from the previous correspondence that this was an offer made for the full settlement of the claim. The plaintiffs, with knowledge that this was the money of the father, sent to them in full settlement of the claim, took the draft, and cashed it, and kept the money. They must be taken to have known that they could only do this rightly, if they agreed to the terms that it should be in full settlement of the debt. Their action was inconsistent with the duty of an honest man, unless, at the time when they took the money, they accepted the terms on which it was offered. They must have known that they could only possess themselves of this money honestly by accepting those terms, and, knowing that, they possessed themselves of it. That appears to me to be overwhelming evidence of an acceptance by them of the proposal made to them by the father ...

These being the facts, we have to consider how they affect the debt on the note in point of law. I am of opinion that by that transaction between the plaintiffs and Sir Richard Temple the debt on the promissory note became extinct. I agree with the view expressed by Willes J in *Cook v Lister*. The effect of such an agreement between a creditor and a third party with regard to the debt is to render it impossible for the creditor afterwards to sue the debtor for it. The way in which this is worked out in law may be that it would be an abuse of the process of the Court to allow the creditor under such circumstances to sue, or it may be, and I prefer that view, that there is an extinction of the debt; but, whichever way it is put, it comes to the same thing, namely that, after acceptance by the creditor of a sum offered by a third party in settlement of the claim against the debtor, the creditor cannot maintain an action for the balance.

Farwell LJ agreed. Vaughan Williams LJ also held for the defendant, but on different grounds.

The reasoning in this case is, in part, based on the idea that allowing the creditor to recover from the debtor in such circumstances would amount to a fraud on the third party, who has paid the money on the understanding that the debt would be discharged. A similar rationale supports the other common-law exception to *Foakes v Beer*. This arises where a debtor has a number of creditors and they agree between themselves to take only a proportion of the debt owing – for example, 20p for each pound owing. Such an agreement is known as a 'composition agreement'. Once it has been made, none of the creditors will be allowed to sue the debtor for any more than is due under the composition agreement: *Good v Cheeseman* (1831) 2 B & Ald 328.

3.3.6 Consideration and the variation of contracts

The issues considered in the previous two sections are part of the wider issue of how contract law in England and Wales deals with the variation of contractual obligations. It will not infrequently be the case that a contract that lasts for a number of months or years will need to be changed to deal with changed circumstances. The easiest way to achieve this is by what has been described as 'accord and satisfaction'. This effectively means that the parties reach a new agreement, with consideration being provided for any change. So, if one party is seeking to increase the payments, it will have to offer something in exchange for this – for example, more flexibility over delivery. Provided that there is mutuality in the variation, then the variation will be enforceable. The difficulty arises where the change is one sided (e.g. part payment of a debt without any other changes). An approach based on the idea of the 'relational contract' (see Chapter 1, at 1.4) would have little problem coping with this. The classical law of contract in England and Wales, however, with its focus on everything being determined by the initial agreement, struggles with these situations. There are, however, two concepts that have been used to make, at least to some extent, one-sided variations in a contract enforceable. These are 'waiver' and 'promissory estoppel'.

3.3.6.1 Waiver

The concept of waiver involves a party to a contract promising to suspend his or her strict contractual rights. The rights are to be 'waived'. To this extent, it enables the terms of a contract to be varied, though the effect may only be temporary. Thus, a buyer who indicates to the seller that late delivery will be accepted will not subsequently be allowed to reject delivery because it is late: *Hartley v Hymans* [1920] 3 KB 475. An example of the operation of this concept is to be found in *Charles Rickards Ltd v Oppenheim*.

Charles Rickards Ltd v Oppenheim [1950] 1 KB 616 (CA)

Facts: The contract was for a car body to be built on a chassis owned by the defendant. The contract was to be completed in a specified time. When this did not occur, the defendant allowed an extension. Eventually, the defendant indicated that the work must be completed by a particular date. The plaintiffs completed the work after that date and sued for payment.

Held: Although the defendant had waived the original date for delivery, he was entitled subsequently to set a firm deadline, which a failure to meet would constitute a repudiatory breach. The defendant was not obliged to pay for the work.

Denning LJ: Early in 1947 the defendant, Mr Oppenheim, wanted a new Rolls Royce car, and he placed an order in two parts with the plaintiffs Charles Rickards, Ltd, who are motor car traders. He first ordered the chassis, a Rolls Royce Silver Wraith chassis, for estimated delivery in June, 1947, but he also wanted a body built on the chassis, and he particularly wanted to know the time within which that body could be made. The plaintiffs made inquiries of various firms for an estimated time for building a body on to the chassis. In July, 1947, Rolls Royce themselves estimated twenty-one months, and Park Ward at about the same time estimated fifteen months. Those times were too long for the defendant's satisfaction, so the plaintiffs obtained an estimate from Jones Brothers (Coachbuilders) Ltd, who said that they could do it within 'six months or, at the most, seven months.' Thereupon, the plaintiffs gave the same time to the defendant and he gave them the order for the body on that footing. The order was placed in July. The plaintiffs sub-contracted it and put out the work with Jones Brothers (Coachbuilders) Ltd. The actual time from which the six or seven months started is not precisely ascertained. The chassis was actually delivered to the sub-contractors on July 30, 1947, and, if that is taken as the date from which the time ran, the seven months would be up at the end of February, 1948, but the specification for the body work was not finally agreed until August 20, 1947. If that date is taken, the latest time for delivery would be March 20, 1948. Whichever date is taken, though, is immaterial, for the time was plainly exceeded. The body was not built on to the chassis by March 20, nor, indeed, until many months later – not until October 18, 1948, was the car completed.

Meanwhile, however, as from 20 March 1948, at least, onwards, the defendant had been pressing for delivery. During the winter of 1947/8 he went to America, and in the autumn of 1947, before he left, he told the plaintiffs that he hoped the car would be ready by the time he came back. He came back in March, and the car was not ready by 20 March 1948. He could have cancelled the contract there and then, but he did not do so. By pressing for delivery he waived the stipulation as to time …

[Eventually, with no firm delivery date forthcoming, the defendant indicated in August 1948 that he was cancelling the contract and bought another car elsewhere. The plaintiffs sued for breach of contract.]

I agree that that initial time was waived by reason of the requests for delivery which the defendant made after March, 1948, and that, if delivery had been tendered in compliance with those requests, the defendant could not have refused to accept. Supposing, for instance, delivery had been tendered in April, May, or June 1948, the defendant would have had no answer. It would be true that the plaintiffs could not aver and prove that they were ready and willing to deliver in accordance with the original contract. They would have had, in effect, to rely on the waiver almost as a cause of action …If the defendant, as he did, led the plaintiffs to believe that he would not insist on the stipulation as to time, and that, if they carried out the work, he would accept it, and they did it, he could not afterwards set up the stipulation in regard to time against them. Whether it be called waiver or forbearance on his part, or an agreed variation or substituted performance, does not matter. It is a kind of estoppel …

Therefore, if the matter stopped there, the plaintiffs could have said that, notwithstanding that more than seven months had elapsed, the defendant was bound to accept, but the matter does not stop there, because delivery was not given in compliance with the requests of the defendant. Time and time again the defendant pressed for delivery, time and time again he was assured that he would have early delivery, but he never got satisfaction, and eventually at the end of June he gave notice saying that, unless the car was delivered by July 25, he would not accept it. The question thus arises whether he was entitled to give such a notice, making time of the essence, and that is the question which counsel for the plaintiffs has argued before us ...

[I]n my view, it is unnecessary to determine whether it was a contract for the sale of goods or a contract for work and labour, because, whichever it was, the defendant was entitled to give notice bringing the matter to a head. It would be most unreasonable if, having been lenient and having waived the initial expressed time, he should thereby have prevented himself from ever thereafter insisting on reasonably quick delivery. In my judgment, he was entitled to give a reasonable notice making time of the essence of the matter. Adequate protection to the suppliers is given by the requirement that the notice should be reasonable ...

The case, therefore, comes down to this. There was a contract by the plaintiffs to supply and fix a body on the chassis within six or seven months. They did not do it. The defendant waived that stipulation. For three months after the time had expired he pressed them for delivery, asking for it first for Ascot and then for his holiday abroad. But still they did not deliver it. Eventually at the end of June, being tired of waiting any longer, he gave a four weeks' notice and said: 'At all events, if you do not supply it at the end of four weeks I must cancel' and he did cancel. I see no injustice to the plaintiffs in saying that that was a reasonable notice. Having originally stipulated for six to seven months, having waited eleven months, and still not getting delivery, the defendant was entitled to cancel the contract.

Bucknill and Singleton LJJ concurred.

Rickards v Oppenheim illustrates the fact that a 'waiver' of rights may well only be temporary in its effect. The party that has waived its rights may well be able to bring that suspension to an end by giving reasonable notice. In this, it has similarities with the next concept used to vary contracts – promissory estoppel. Indeed, Denning LJ clearly saw *Rickards v Oppenheim* as capable of being regarded as an application of that approach, which he himself had put forward a few years earlier in *Central London Property Trust Ltd v High Trees House Ltd* [1947] KB 130. There are some distinctions, however, as will be explained in the next section.

3.3.7 Promissory estoppel

The doctrine of promissory estoppel can be argued to have largely taken the place of the concept of 'waiver' in the modern law of contract. It was developed, however, to deal with a situation to which waiver had never been applied – the part-payment of debts. As we have seen, the House of Lords in *Foakes v Beer* affirmed the principle that part-payment of a debt by the debtor can never in itself provide consideration to support a promise to forgo the balance. The case that provided the starting point for an exception to this was *Central London Property Trust Ltd v High Trees House Ltd*.

Central London Property Trust Ltd v High Trees House Ltd [1947] KB 130 (HC)

Facts: The contract concerned the lease of a block of flats in London. At the start of the Second World War, the tenants, the defendants, found it difficult to find people to take the flats. The landlords agreed that because of this, the tenants could pay half the rent. After the war, the landlords sought to revert to the original terms of the lease.

Held: The landlords could return to the original terms once the conditions in which the reduction had been granted had ceased to exist. They would not, however, be able to recover in respect of the underpayment during the war years.

Denning J: By a lease under seal made on September 24, 1937, the plaintiffs, Central London Property Trust Ltd, granted to the defendants, High Trees House Ltd, a subsidiary of the plaintiff company, a tenancy of a block of flats for the term of ninety-nine years from September 29, 1937, at a ground rent of £2,500 a year. The block of flats was a new one and had not been fully occupied at the beginning of the war owing to the absence of people from London. With war conditions prevailing, it was apparent to those responsible that the rent reserved under the lease could not be paid out of the profits of the flats and, accordingly, discussions took place between the directors of the two companies concerned, which were closely associated, and an arrangement was made between them which was put into writing. On January 3, 1940, the plaintiffs wrote to the defendants in these terms, 'we confirm the arrangement made between us by which the ground rent should be reduced as from the commencement of the lease to £1,250 per annum', and on April 2, 1940, a confirmatory resolution to the same effect was passed by the plaintiff company. ... The defendants paid the reduced rent from 1941 down to the beginning of 1945 by which time all the flats in the block were fully let, and continued to pay it thereafter. In September, 1945, the then receiver of the plaintiff company looked into the matter of the lease and ascertained that the rent actually reserved by it was £2,500. On September 21, 1945, he wrote to the defendants saying that rent must be paid at the full rate and claiming that arrears amounting to £7,916 were due. Subsequently, he instituted the present friendly proceedings to test the legal position in regard to the rate at which rent was payable. In the action the plaintiffs sought to recover £625, being the amount represented by the difference between rent at the rate of £2,500 and £1,250 per annum for the quarters ending September 29, and December 25, 1945. By their defence the defendants pleaded (I.) that the letter of January 3, 1940, constituted an agreement that the rent reserved should be £1,250 only, and that such agreement related to the whole term of the lease, (2.) they pleaded in the alternative that the plaintiff company were estopped from alleging that the rent exceeded £1,250 per annum and (3.) as a further alternative, that by failing to demand rent in excess of £1,250 before their letter of September 21, 1945 (received by the defendants on September 24), they had waived their rights in respect of any rent, in excess of that at the rate of £1,250 which had accrued up to September 24, 1945.

If I were to consider this matter without regard to recent developments in the law, there is no doubt that had the plaintiffs claimed it, they would have been entitled to recover ground rent at the rate of £2,500 a year from the beginning of the term, since the lease under which it was payable was a lease under seal which, according to the old common law, could not be varied by an agreement by parol (whether in writing or not), but only by deed. Equity, however stepped in, and said that if there has been a variation of a deed by a simple contract (which in the case of a lease required to be in writing would have to be evidenced by writing), the courts may give effect to it as is shown in *Berry v Berry* [1929] 2 KB 316. That equitable doctrine, however, could hardly apply in the present case because the variation here might be said to have been made without consideration. With regard to estoppel, the representation made in relation to reducing the rent, was not a representation of an existing fact. It was a representation, in effect, as to the future, namely, that payment of the rent would not be enforced at the full rate but only at the reduced rate. Such a representation would not give rise to an estoppel, because, as was said in *Jorden v Money* (1854) 5 HL 185, a representation as to the future must be embodied as a contract or be nothing.

But what is the position in view of developments in the law in recent years? The law has not been standing still since *Jorden v Money*: There has been a series of decisions over the last fifty years which, although they are said to be cases of estoppel are not really such. They are cases in which a promise was made which was intended to create legal relations and which, to the knowledge of the person making the promise, was going to be acted on by the person to whom it was made, and which was in fact so acted on. In such cases the courts have said that the promise must be honoured. The cases to which I particularly desire to refer are: *Fenner v Blake* [1900] 1 QB 426, *In re Wickham*, [1917] 34 TLR 158, *Re William Porter & Co Ltd* [1937] 2 All ER 361 and *Buttery v Pickard* [1946] WN 25. As I have said they are not cases of estoppel in the strict sense. They are really promises – promises intended to be binding, intended to be acted on, and in fact acted on. *Jorden v Money* can be distinguished, because there the promisor made it clear that she did not intend to be legally bound, whereas in the cases to which I refer the proper inference was that the promisor did intend to be bound. In each case the court held the promise to be binding on the party making it, even though under the old common law it might be difficult to find any consideration for it. The courts have not gone so far as to give a cause of action in damages for the breach of such a promise, but they have refused to allow the party making it to act inconsistently with it. It is in that sense, and that sense only, that such a promise gives rise to an estoppel. The decisions are a natural result of the fusion of law and equity: for the cases of *Hughes v Metropolitan Ry Co* (1877) 2 App Cas 439 *Birmingham and District Land Co v London & North Western Ry Co* (1888) 40 Ch D 268 and *Salisbury (Marquess) v Gilmore* [1942] 2 KB 38, afford a sufficient basis for saying that a party would not be allowed in equity to go back on such a promise. In my opinion, the time has now come for the validity of such a promise to be recognised. The logical consequence, no doubt is that a promise to accept a smaller sum in discharge of a larger sum, if acted upon, is binding notwithstanding the absence of consideration: and if the fusion of law and equity leads to this result, so much the better. That aspect was not considered in *Foakes v Beer*. At this time of day however, when law and equity have been joined together for over seventy years, principles must be reconsidered in the light of their combined effect. It is to be noticed that in the Sixth Interim Report of the Law Revision Committee, pars. 35, 40, it is recommended that such a promise as that to which I have referred, should be enforceable in law even though no consideration for it has been given by the promisee. It seems to me that, to the extent I have mentioned, that result has now been achieved by the decisions of the courts.

I am satisfied that a promise such as that to which I have referred is binding and the only question remaining for my consideration is the scope of the promise in the present case. I am satisfied on all the evidence that the promise here was that the ground rent should be reduced to £1,250 a year as a temporary expedient while the block of flats was not fully, or substantially fully let, owing to the conditions prevailing. That means that the reduction in the rent applied throughout the years down to the end of 1944, but early in 1945 it is plain that the flats were fully let, and, indeed the rents received from them (many of them not being affected by the Rent Restrictions Acts), were increased beyond the figure at which it was originally contemplated that they would be let. At all events the rent from them must have been very considerable. I find that the conditions prevailing at the time when the reduction in rent was made, had completely passed away by the early months of 1945. I am satisfied that the promise was understood by all parties only to apply under the conditions prevailing at the time when it was made, namely, when the flats were only partially let, and that it did not extend any further than that. When the flats became fully let, early in 1945, the reduction ceased to apply.

In those circumstances, under the law as I hold it, it seems to me that rent is payable at the full rate for the quarters ending September 29 and December 25, 1945.

If the case had been one of estoppel, it might be said that in any event the estoppel would cease when the conditions to which the representation applied came to an end, or it also might be said that it would only come to an end on notice. In either case it is only a way of ascertaining what is the scope of the representation. I prefer to apply the principle that a promise intended to be binding, intended to be acted on and in fact acted on, is binding so far as its terms properly apply. Here it was binding as covering the period down to the early part of 1945, and as from that time full rent is payable.

I therefore give judgment for the plaintiff company for the amount claimed.

Denning J tried, in his judgment, to link his decision to earlier authority. However, none of the earlier authorities he cited were concerned with the part-payment of debt. Moreover, his dismissal of the problem of *Foakes v Beer* on the basis that it simply did not take account of the principles derived from equity appears disingenuous. There is no reason to suppose that the members of the House of Lords in *Foakes v Beer* were unaware, for example, of the decision in *Hughes v Metropolitan Railway* which had been decided only seven years previously. It is fairly clear, therefore, that *Central London Property Trust v High Trees House* was establishing a new principle in the law of contract. What exactly was this principle? Denning J., at the end of his judgment, put it in these terms: 'a promise intended to be binding, intended to be acted on and in fact acted on, is binding so far as its terms properly apply'. In other words, a serious promise which has been relied on is to be legally enforceable. Taken at face value, this is a clear contradiction of the doctrine of consideration which says that such promises are only binding if the promisee has provided something in exchange. Whether Denning J intended such a bold attack at the time is open to question. The following extract from his own account of the case clearly indicates that he felt that the doctrine of consideration was in need of significant reform.

Denning, A, *The Discipline of Law*, 1979, London: Butterworths, pp 200–205

We did a lot of commercial work in No. 4 Brick Court, especially with sale of goods and charterparties of ships. Soon after I started I came upon a pathway which led to the *High Trees*. At that time one dominating factor was that every contract of sale of goods of £10 or more in value had to be in writing. The other dominating factor was that no promise was binding unless there was consideration for it. Those two factors caused injustices of all kinds. We used to resort to many subtleties to get round them. When I was still a pupil we came across a very useful case on the subject. It had just been reported, called *Hartley v Hymans*. I noted it in pencil on my copy of Anson and added 'Suggest Estoppel'. It was a decision of Mr. Justice McCardie in which he had examined many authorities. He was the most diligent collector of cases that has ever been on the Bench. In it he made a passing reference to 'the broad rule of justice stated by Lord Cairns LC in *Hughes v Metropolitan Railway Co* [1877] 2 AC 439'. That case had been overlooked for 50 years. None of the textbooks had noticed it. I made a special note of it: and as it has had so much impact on subsequent developments, I will set it out:

> 'It is the first principle upon which all Courts of Equity proceed, that if parties who have entered into definite and distinct terms involving certain legal results – certain penalties or legal forfeiture – afterwards by their own act or with their own consent enter upon a course of negotiation which has the effect of leading one of the parties to suppose that the strict rights arising under the contract will not be enforced, or will be kept in suspense, or held in abeyance, the person who otherwise might have enforced those rights will not be allowed to enforce them where it would be inequitable having regard to the dealings which have thus taken place between the parties'.

I found also that that principle had been explained by Bowen LJ who said that it was not confined to penalties and forfeitures but extended to all cases of contractual rights. That was in a case in 1888 – *Birmingham and District Land Co v London and NW Railway Co.*

The fences in the way

As I went along the pathway towards the *High Trees*, I found many obstacles had been left in the way. I came across them whilst I was waiting for briefs. They came slowly. It took me seven years before I was making £1,000 a year. During this time Sir Willes Chitty, the Senior Master and one of the most learned of men – coming from a long line of lawyers – asked me to join him as one of the editors of *Smith's Leading Cases*. It took up much of my time until it was published in 1929. Each editor took responsibility for the notes to a particular leading case. I learned more law in those years than I have done before or since. In particular I came across two fences barring the path. They had been put up 70 years before. One was that estopped applies only in respect of representations of fact, and not of statements of intention (*Jorden v*

Money). The other was that a representation, in order to work an estoppel, must be one of fact and not of law. Somehow or other these fences had to be overcome.

In order to leap these fences, I needed a good horse. It turned up. It was the Report of the Law Revision Committee on the Doctrine of Consideration. It came out in 1937 when I was in very busy practice as a junior. So I had no time to read it then. But on a significant day – All Fools' Day – 1 April 1938, I took silk. I had more time then for a year or two. I read the Report. It was made by the leading lawyers of the day. They included Lord Wright MR, Mr. Justice Goddard, Mr. Justice Asquith and Professor Goodhart. Even to this day it has not been implemented by the Legislature. But it was just the horse to get me over the fences. In particular it exposed the injustice of the rule that estoppel only applies to statements of fact, and of the rule that payment of a lesser sum is no consideration for the discharge of a larger sum. The Committee recommended the abolition of both those rules. They made this recommendation. It got me over the fences which obstructed the way to *High Trees*:

> 'We therefore recommend that a promise which the promisor knows, or reasonably should know, will be relied upon by the promisee, shall be enforceable if the promisee has altered his position to his detriment in reliance on the promise'.

Being now on the right path, I pointed it out to the Court of Appeal in my argument as King's Counsel in Salisbury *(Marquess) v Gilmore*. Lord Justice Mackinnon was disposed to follow the path. But he did not feel able to do so. The fences were too high for him. In his usual pungent style, he said that the House of Lords – the 'voices of infallibility' – as they spoke in *Jorden v Money* – were binding on the Court of Appeal. So estoppel was still confined to representations of existing fact.

The *High Trees* case itself – promissory estoppel

At last I came in sight of *High Trees*. It was in July 1946. I had only been a Judge in the King's Bench for some six months. During that time I had been mostly out on circuit where it was all fact and no law. But in my first spell in London there came the *Central London Property Trust Ltd v High Trees House Ltd*. It was argued by Mr. Robert Fortune on the one side – 'Frothy Bob' as we used to call him because of his spluttering – and Mr. Ronald Hopkins on the other, a sound and sensible advocate. They argued it well but they had not the reserves at their command as I had. I delivered judgment straight off the reel – with a tidying up afterwards for the Law Reports ...

There was no appeal. This was probably because the decision could be supported on other grounds. An appeal might have ruined everything.

The principle became known as promissory estoppel.

This seems to indicate that Denning J was making a deliberate attack on the doctrine of consideration as not according with commercial reality. The subsequent development, however, of the doctrine derived from *High Trees* – which has become known as the doctrine of 'promissory estoppel' – means that it has only a limited impact on the doctrine of consideration. There are three clear limiting factors that have been established by subsequent case law:

(a) the need for there to have been an existing legal relationship between the parties with a promise by one party that he/she will not enforce the strict legal rights arising under that relationship;
(b) the fact that the doctrine can only be used 'as a shield, not a sword'; and
(c) the requirement that it must be inequitable for the promisor to go back on the promise.

3.3.7.1 Need for an existing legal relationship and a promise by one party that rights thereunder will not be strictly enforced

The first two constraints are to some extent linked and can both be illustrated by the case of *Combe v Combe*, in which Denning LJ himself was one of the judges.

Combe v Combe [1951] 2 KB 215 (CA)

Facts: H and W divorced. H promised to pay W £100 per annum. He never made any payments. W sued. At trial, it was held that W had given no consideration for H's promise, but could recover on the basis of promissory estoppel.

Held: Promissory estoppel cannot be used as the basis for creating a contractual obligation, but only as a means of varying an existing obligation.

Denning LJ: [The trial judge] held that the [husband's] promise was enforceable on the principle stated in *Central London Property Trust Ltd v High Trees House Ltd* [1947] KB 130 and *Robertson v Minister of Pensions* [1948] 2 All ER 767, because it was an unequivocal acceptance of liability, intended to be binding, intended to be acted on, and, in fact, acted on.

Much as I am inclined to favour the principle of the *High Trees* case, it is important that it should not be stretched too far lest it should be endangered. It does not create new causes of action where none existed before. It only prevents a party from insisting on his strict legal rights when it would be unjust to allow him to do so, having regard to the dealings which have taken place between the parties. That is the way it was put in the case in the House of Lords which first stated the principle – *Hughes v Metropolitan Ry Co* (1877) 2 App Cas 439 – and in the case in the Court of Appeal which enlarged it – *Birmingham and District Land Co v London & North Western Ry Co* (1888) 40 ChD 268. It is also implicit in all the modern cases in which the principle has been developed. Sometimes it is a plaintiff who is not allowed to insist on his strict legal rights.

Seeing that the principle never stands alone as giving a cause of action in itself, it can never do away with the necessity of consideration when that is an essential part of the cause of action. The doctrine of consideration is too firmly fixed to be overthrown by a side-wind. Its ill effects have been largely mitigated of late, but it still remains a cardinal necessity of the formation of a contract, although not of its modification or discharge. I fear that it was my failure to make this clear in *Central London Property Trust Ltd v High Trees House Ltd* which misled Byrne J in the present case. He held that the wife could sue on the husband's promise as a separate and independent cause of action by itself, although, as he held, there was no consideration for it. That is not correct. The wife can only enforce the promise if there was consideration for it. That is, therefore, the real question in the case: Was there sufficient consideration to support the promise?

Denning LJ and Byrne J agreed that Mrs Combe had provided no consideration for her husband's promise.

An existing contract along with a promise not to strictly enforce rights thereunder is clearly one situation in which promissory estoppel might operate. In addition, some later cases have suggested that promissory estoppel may operate in other types of legal relationship where there has been a promise not to insist on strict legal rights. For example, in *Durham Fancy Goods Ltd v Michael Jackson (Fancy Goods) Ltd* [1968] 2 QB 839, at 847, Donaldson J suggested that it was enough that 'there is a pre-existing legal relationship which could in certain circumstances give rise to liabilities and penalties', without this relationship needing to be contractual.

3.3.7.2 'Shield not a sword'

This phrase derives from counsel for the husband in *Combe v Combe* (above). It indicates that the most common use of promissory estoppel will be to defend against an action where a promisor is seeking to enforce a right which he/she had previously promised not to enforce However, it need not be used exclusively by defendants, as indicated by Halson.

Halson, R, 'The Offensive Limits of Promissory Estoppel' (1999) LMCLQ 256, pp 258–261

Promissory estoppel: a new cause of action?

One of the most debated issues in promissory estoppel is whether such an estoppel can itself constitute a cause of action. Cases have undoubtedly foundered when it was realized that one party's cause of action was a 'naked' estoppel. Many commentators and judges have said this cannot be done. So why the debate? Two answers come to mind. First, it seems that here, as elsewhere in estoppel, terminological clarity is lacking. The epithet that is most commonly cited to summarize the traditional wisdom on this subject, the shield/sword distinction which has been described judicially as a 'time-honoured phrase', is unhelpfully ambiguous. In truth, the use that can be made of an estoppel can be represented by a spectrum ranging from a defence to the creation of a new cause of action. Courts appear to use the shield/sword dichotomy to refer to some point on this spectrum ...

A. The estoppel spectrum described

(1) *Estoppel can only be used as a defence*

This is the least ambitious claim that can be made. New legal doctrines often make their first appearance in a truncated and non-threatening guise. Therefore it should occasion no surprise that in both of the seminal cases, *Hughes v Metropolitan Ry* and *Central London Property Trust Co v High Trees House*, estoppel was relied upon as a defence. Indeed, as recently as 1960 this circumscribed role for estoppel was apparently contemplated in *Beesly v Hallwood Estates Ltd* by Buckley, J., who said:

> 'As I understand this part of the law, which has been described as promissory estoppel, it is that ... the doctrine may afford a defence against the enforcement of otherwise enforceable rights. It cannot, in my judgment, be invoked to render enforceable a right which would otherwise be unenforceable'.

(2) *Estoppel can be used by a party seeking to enforce a claim based upon a recognized cause of action to defeat the defence or counter-claim of the other party*

A simple example of this use of promissory estoppel would be provided by a variation of the facts of *High Trees*: the lessor lets directly to an occupying tenant; some time after the representation has been made and reduced rent payments have been accepted, the landlord distrains the tenant's property in order to recover the balance of the rent. Here the tenant could bring an action for conversion; the landlord would reply that he was rightfully distraining, and the tenant could use estoppel to defeat this defence. Academic authority also supports this usage.

A factually more complex example of this use of estoppel occurred in *The Ion*, the relevant facts of which were as follows. The defendant owners chartered their vessel to the plaintiff charterers. The charter incorporated the Hague Rules, which provide in Art III, r 6 that the carrier and the ship shall be discharged from all liability unless an action is brought within one year. There were several cargo claims but proceedings were not instituted within the required period. However, the charterers claimed, *inter alia*, that a letter from the owners' P. & I. club to the charterers' P. & I. club should be construed as amounting to a promissory estoppel to the effect that the owners would not rely on the time bar. The Commercial Court interpreted the letter from the owners' P. & I. club as containing an implied promise not to insist upon the strict time limit, which promise was relied on by the charterers in not making an immediate application under the Arbitration Act 1950, s 27 for an extension of time. In such circumstances the court held that it would be inequitable to allow the owners to enforce their strict legal rights and so the claimed estoppel was established.

Several judicial statements as to the proper limits of the offensive use of promissory estoppel extend further to one of the following two categories.

(3) *Estoppel can be used by a party seeking to enforce a claim to prove one element of a recognized cause of action*

This appears to be the effect the promissory estoppel was stated to have in *Robertson v Minister of Pensions*, where the plaintiff was relieved of the burden of having to prove that his injury was attributable to war service in order to qualify for a disablement pension because the Ministry were estopped from denying this causal connection. The plaintiff's cause of action was a recognized one; in this case statutory or at least *sui generis*. Yet it could not be said that the estoppel relieved the colonel of the obligation to prove all the elements of his cause of action, e.g., that he had served long enough and in a sufficient capacity to qualify for a pension, that the injury was serious enough to so qualify etc. The estoppel related solely to the question of causation; was the injury attributable to military service? This usage may have been what Denning LJ, was thinking of when, in *Combe v Combe*, commenting upon a number of decisions including the *Robertson* case, he said:

> 'In none of these cases was the defendant sued on the promise, assurance or assertion as a cause of action in itself: he was sued for some other cause, for example a pension ... and the promise, assurance or assertion only played a supplementary role – an important role, no doubt, but still a supplementary role'.

(4) *Estoppel can be used by a party seeking to enforce a claim to prove all the elements of a recognized cause of action*

This appears to be the way the promissory estoppel was used in *The Henrik Sif*. The first defendants conducted themselves as if they were a party to a bill of lading, which they were not. This led the plaintiff to allow the limitation period to run out against the second defendant, who was a party to the bill of lading. The judge based his finding for the plaintiff in his action against the first defendants, *inter alia*, upon promissory estoppel. It appears that all the elements (agreement, consideration etc.) of a recognized cause of action (contract) were proved by the estoppel.

The case of *Bruner v Moore*, which, although predating the *High Trees* case, similarly drew upon the *Hughes* principle, may be explained in this way. The plaintiff there was allowed to enforce his option out of time, either because the option had been consensually extended or because an equity arose in his favour as a result of the conduct of the grantor. It would appear that the effect of the equity was to prevent the defendant from denying that the plaintiff had a contractually binding option; the 'equity' provided the plaintiff with all the elements of a recognized cause of action. This decision has been adopted and relied on in Canada. A somewhat more equivocal endorsement has been given by an Australian court. In England the case seems mainly to be cited in connection with the postal rule of acceptance.

As Halson makes clear, promissory estoppel can be used in a variety of situations to prevent a party to a legal action going back on a promise, even though that promise is unsupported by any consideration. It is wrong to categorise it simply as a 'defence', as that suggests too narrow a scope for its use. What it cannot be used for is to create an entirely new contractual obligation, as opposed to enforcing a variation of an existing relationship.

3.3.7.3 Inequitable for the promisor to go back on the promise

Promissory estoppel is a doctrine that has its roots in equity; the courts will not, therefore, allow it to be used unless it is to prevent some inequity arising. A promisee who has not acted fairly is unlikely to be given the benefit of promissory estoppel. This will, for example, be the case where the promisee has taken advantage of the promisor in order to extract the promise in the first place, as occurred in *D & C Builders Ltd v Rees*.

***D & C Builders Ltd v Rees* [1966] 2 QB 617 (CA)**

Facts: The plaintiffs were builders who had done work for the defendant. They were owed about £500. The defendant, who knew that the plaintiffs were in financial difficulties, offered them £300, indicating that they would not get any more. The plaintiffs accepted this in settlement of the debt but later sued for the outstanding balance.

Lord Denning MR: ... In point of law payment of a lesser sum, whether by cash or by cheque, is no discharge of a greater sum.

This doctrine of the common law has come under heavy fire. It was ridiculed by Sir George Jessel in *Couldery v Bartram* (1881) 19 Ch.D. 394, 399. It was said to be mistaken by Lord Blackburn in *Foakes v Beer* 9 App. Cas. 605, 622. It was condemned by the Law Revision Committee (1945 Cmd. 5449), paras. 20 and 21. But a remedy has been found. The harshness of the common law has been relieved. Equity has stretched out a merciful hand to help the debtor. The courts have invoked the broad principle stated by Lord Cairns in *Hughes v Metropolitan Railway Co* (1877) 2 App. Cas. 439, 448:

> 'It is the first principle upon which all courts of equity proceed, that if parties, who have entered into definite and distinct terms involving certain legal results, afterwards by their own act or with their own consent enter upon a course of negotiation which has the effect of leading one of the parties to suppose that the strict rights arising under the contract will not be enforced, or will be kept in suspense, or held in abeyance, the person who otherwise might have enforced those rights will not be allowed to enforce them when it would be inequitable having regard to the dealings which have taken place between the parties'.

It is worth noticing that the principle may be applied, not only so as to suspend strict legal rights, but also so as to preclude the enforcement of them.

This principle has been applied to cases where a creditor agrees to accept a lesser sum in discharge of a greater. So much so that we can now say that, when a creditor and a debtor enter upon a course of negotiation, which leads the debtor to suppose that, on payment of the lesser sum, the creditor will not enforce payment of the balance, and on the faith thereof the debtor pays the lesser sum and the creditor accepts it as satisfaction: then the creditor will not be allowed to enforce payment of the balance when it would be inequitable to do so. This was well illustrated during the last war. Tenants went away to escape the bombs and left their houses unoccupied. The landlords accepted a reduced rent for the time they were empty. It was held that the landlords could not afterwards turn round and sue for the balance, see *Central London Property Trust Ltd v High Trees House Ltd* [1947] 1 K.B. 130; 62 T.L.R. 559; [1956] 1 All E.R. 256. This caused at the time some eyebrows to be raised in high places. But they have been lowered since. The solution was so obviously just that no one could well gainsay it.

In applying this principle, however, we must note the qualification: The creditor is only barred from his legal rights when it would be *inequitable* for him to insist upon them. Where there has been a true *accord*, under which the creditor voluntarily agrees to accept a lesser sum in satisfaction, and the debtor acts upon that accord by paying the lesser sum and the creditor accepts it, then it is inequitable for the creditor afterwards to insist on the balance. But he is not bound unless there has been truly an accord between them.

In the present case, on the facts as found by the judge, it seems to me that there was no true accord. The debtor's wife held the creditor to ransom. The creditor was in need of money to meet his own commitments, and she knew it. When the creditor asked for payment of the £480 due to him, she said to him in effect: 'We cannot pay you the £480. But we will pay you £300 if you will accept it in settlement. If you do not accept it on those terms, you will get nothing. £300 is better than nothing.' She had no right to say any such thing. She could properly have said: 'We cannot pay you more than £300. Please accept it on account'. But she had no right to insist on his taking it in settlement. When she said: 'We will pay you nothing unless you accept £300 in settlement', she was putting undue pressure on the creditor. She was making a threat to break the contract (by paying nothing) and she was doing it so as to compel the creditor to do what he was unwilling to do (to accept £300 in settlement): and she succeeded. He complied with her demand. That was on recent authority a case of intimidation: see *Rookes v Barnard* and *Stratford (J. T.) & Son Ltd v Lindley*. In these circumstances there was no true accord so as to found a defence of accord and satisfaction: see *Day v McLea*. There is also no equity in the defendant to warrant any departure from the due course of law. No person can insist on a settlement procured by intimidation.

Danckwerts and Winn LJJ concurred in the result, but without discussing the doctrine of promissory estoppel.

The behaviour of the defendant in *D & C Builders v Rees* was what, in Lord Denning's view, made it not inequitable to allow the plaintiffs to go back on their promise. However, wrongdoing by the promisee is not a necessary factor of this aspect of the doctrine of promissory estoppel. In *The Post Chaser*, Robert Goff J held that the speed with which the promise had been withdrawn meant that it was not inequitable to allow the promisor to escape from it, even if the promisee had, to some extent, relied on it. In the following passage, where Robert Goff refers to 'equitable estoppel', he means the concept that is referred to in this chapter as 'promissory estoppel'.

The Post Chaser [1981] 2 Lloyd's Rep 695 (HC)

Robert Goff J: [Having found that there was a representation which was sufficient to constitute an estoppel, he continued]: However, there next arises the question whether there was any sufficient reliance by the sellers on this representation to give rise to an equitable estoppel. Here there arose a difference between counsel for the sellers and counsel for the buyers as to the degree of reliance which is required. It is plain, however, from the speech of Lord Cairns LC in *Hughes v Metropolitan Rly Co* (1877) 2 App Cas 439 at 448, [1874–80] All ER Rep 187 at 191 that the representor will not be allowed to enforce his rights 'where it would be inequitable having regard to the dealings which have taken place between the parties'. Accordingly there must be such action, or inaction, by the representee on the faith of the representation as will render it inequitable to permit the representor to enforce his strict legal rights.

On the findings of fact in the award before the court, there is no finding of any reliance by the sellers on the buyers' representation, save the fact that the documents covering the parcel on the Post Chaser were accordingly presented by Kievit (who in this context must be taken to have acted on behalf of the sellers) to Conti. That was done on 20 January; and by 22 January the sellers were informed by the buyers that NOGA had rejected the documents, following which the documents were passed back up the string to the sellers. The question therefore arises whether such action constituted sufficient reliance by the sellers on the buyers' representation to render it inequitable for the buyers thereafter to enforce their right to reject the documents. ...

I approach the matter as follows. The fundamental principle is that stated by Lord Cairns LC, viz that the representor will not be allowed to enforce his rights 'where it would be inequitable having regard to the dealings which have thus taken place between the parties'. To establish such inequity, it is not necessary to show detriment; indeed, the representee may have benefited from the representation, and yet it may be inequitable, at least without reasonable notice, for the representor to enforce his legal rights. Take the facts of *Central London Property Trust Ltd v High Trees House Ltd* (1946) [1956] 1 All ER 256, [1947] KB 130, the case in which Denning J breathed new life into the doctrine of equitable estoppel. The representation was by a lessor to the effect that he would be content to accept a reduced rent. In such a case, although the lessee has benefited from the reduction in rent, it may well be inequitable for the lessor to insist on his legal right to the unpaid rent, because the lessee has conducted his affairs on the basis that he would only have to pay rent at the lower rate; and a court might well think it right to conclude that only after reasonable notice could the lessor return to charging rent at the higher rate specified in the lease. Furthermore it would be open to the court, in any particular case, to infer from the circumstances of the case that the representee must have conducted his affairs in such a way that it would be inequitable for the representor to enforce his rights, or to do so without reasonable notice. But it does not follow that in every case in which the representee has acted, or failed to act, in reliance on the representation, it will be inequitable for the representor to enforce his rights for the nature of the action, or inaction, may be insufficient to give rise to the equity, in which event a necessary requirement stated by Lord Cairns LC for the application of the doctrine would not have been fulfilled.

This, in my judgment, is the principle which I have to apply in the present case. Here, all that happened was that the sellers, through Kievit, presented the documents on the same day as the buyers made their representation; and within two days the documents were rejected. Now on these simple facts, although it is plain that the sellers did actively rely on the buyers' representation, and did conduct their affairs in reliance on it, by presenting the documents, I cannot see anything which would render it inequitable for the buyers thereafter to enforce their legal right to reject the documents. In particular, having regard to the very short time which elapsed between the date of the representation and the date of the presentation of the documents on the one hand and the date of rejection on the other hand, I cannot see that, in the absence of any evidence that the sellers' position had been prejudiced by reason of their action in reliance on the representation, it is possible to infer that they suffered any such prejudice. In these circumstances, a necessary element for the application of the doctrine of equitable estoppel is lacking; and I decide this point in favour of the buyers.

The way in which Robert Goff J dealt with the issue of 'inequitability' in this case shows that it is, at least to some extent, linked to the issue of whether the promisee has 'relied' on the promise. Indeed, the formulation of promissory estoppel by Denning J in *High Trees* included the requirement that the promise had been 'acted upon'. Some judges have suggested that this means that the promisee must have acted to his or her *detriment* in relying on the promise – in other words that 'detrimental reliance' is a requirement of promissory estoppel. Lord Denning himself addressed this issue in *WJ Alan & Co v El Nasr*. Although in the following passage he discusses the case in terms of 'waiver', it is clear that he regards this concept as being part of the doctrine of promissory estoppel, so that the same approach to the issue of 'detrimental reliance' should apply to that doctrine.

WJ Alan & Co v El Nasr [1972] 2 Q.B. 189

Facts: A contract provided for payment to be made in Kenyan shillings. The buyers made payment under a letter of credit for the contract amount in sterling shillings – a lesser sum. The sellers accepted this, but then sued for the difference between the Kenyan and sterling amounts. The trial judge held that the sellers were not bound by their acceptance of the sterling amount, since the buyers had not acted to their detriment on any promise by the sellers to accept the lesser sum.

Held (per Lord Denning): Detrimental reliance was not necessary, where one party had led the other to believe that its strict rights under a contract would not be enforced and the other had acted on this. (The other members of the court decided in favour of the sellers without committing themselves on the issue of 'detriment'.)

Lord Denning: ... There are two cases on this subject. One is *Panoutsos v Raymond Hadley Corporation of New York* [1917] 2 K.B. 473 ... The other is *Enrico Furst & Co v W E Fischer Ltd* [1960] 2 Lloyd's Rep. 340. In each of those cases the letter of credit did not conform to the contract of sale. In each case the non-conformity was in that it was not a confirmed credit. But the sellers took no objection to the letter of credit on that score. On the contrary, they asked for the letter of credit to be extended: and it was extended. In each case the sellers sought afterwards to cancel the contract on the ground that the letter of credit was not in conformity with the contract. In each case the court held that they could not do so.

What is the true basis of those decisions? Is it a variation of the original contract? Or a waiver of the strict rights thereunder? Or a promissory estoppel precluding the seller from insisting on his strict rights? Or what else?

In *Enrico Furst*, Diplock J. said it was a 'classic case of waiver'. I agree with him. It is an instance of the general principle which was first enunciated by Lord Cairns L.C. in *Hughes v Metropolitan Railway Co* (1877) 2 App. Cas 439, and rescued from oblivion by *Central London Property Trust Ltd v High Trees House Ltd* [1947] 1 K.B. 130. The principle is much wider than waiver itself: but waiver is a good instance of its application.

The principle of waiver is simply this: If one party, by his conduct, leads another to believe that the strict rights arising under the contract will not be insisted upon, intending that the other should act on that belief, and he does act on it, then the first party will not afterwards be allowed to insist on the strict legal rights when it would be inequitable for him to do so: see *Plasticmoda Societa per Azioni v Davidsons (Manchester) Ltd* [1952] 1 Lloyd's Rep. 527, 539. There may be no consideration moving from him who benefits by the waiver. There may be no detriment to him by acting on it. There may be nothing in writing. Nevertheless, the one who waives his strict rights cannot afterwards insist on them. His strict rights are at any rate suspended so long as the waiver lasts ...

The judge rejected this doctrine because, he said, 'there is no evidence of the buyers having acted to their detriment'. I know that it has been suggested in some quarters that there must be detriment. But I can find no support for it in the authorities cited by the judge. The nearest approach to it is the statement of Viscount Simonds in the *Tool Metal* case [1955] 1 W.L.R. 761, 764, that the other must have been led 'to alter his position,' which was adopted by Lord Hodson in *Ajayi v R T Briscoe (Nigeria) Ltd* [1964] 1 W.L.R. 1326, 1330. But that only means that he must have been led to act differently from what he otherwise would have done. And if you study the cases in which the doctrine has been applied, you will see that all that is required is that the one should have '*acted* on the belief induced by the other party'. That is how Lord Cohen put it in the *Tool Metal* case [1955] 1 W.L.R. 761, 799, and that is how I would put it myself.

If Lord Denning's analysis is accepted, then the position seems to be that detriment is not a necessary element of reliance, but it may be relevant to the question of whether the court will find it inequitable to allow the promisor to go back on the promise. To some extent, the question is thus not 'Has the promisee suffered detriment as a result of the reliance?' but 'Would it now cause significant detriment to the promisee if the promisor were to be allowed to go back on the promise?'

In *Collier v P & MJ Wright* [2007] EWCA Civ 1329, the facts of which are given below at 3.3.7.4, the Court of Appeal suggested that simply paying the smaller sum that the creditor had asked for constituted sufficient reliance to give rise to promissory estoppel. Provided that there was a true agreement that this was to discharge the debt, then it would also be inequitable to allow the creditor to go back on the promise.

3.3.7.4 Suspensory nature of the doctrine

There is no doubt that in many situations in which it is appropriate for it to be used, the doctrine of promissory estoppel, like waiver, will only be suspensory in its effect. That was the situation in *High Trees* itself – once the circumstances that had led to the promise had disappeared, the landlord was entitled to return to the originally agreed rent. In that case, the change in circumstances led to the ending of the promise. What if there is no change in circumstances? Can the promisor simply decide to withdraw the concession and say that, for the future, the promisee must perform in accordance with the strict terms of the contract? The issue was considered in *Tool Metal Manufacturing Co v Tungsten Electric Co.*

***Tool Metal Manufacturing Co Ltd v Tungsten Electric Co Ltd* [1955] 1 WLR 761 (HL)**

Facts: The defendants were producing metal alloys under a licence from the plaintiffs, who owned the patents in the alloys. The defendants were obliged to pay a royalty of 10% of the value of what was produced, plus a further 30% where production exceeded 50 kilograms a month. When production increased significantly because of the outbreak of the war with Germany in 1939, the plaintiffs did not insist on the 30% payment. After the end of the war, the defendants sued the plaintiffs for fraud and the plaintiffs counter-claimed for payment of the 30%. Both actions were dismissed: the plaintiffs were unsuccessful because they had not given notice of an intention to return to the strict term of the agreement. The plaintiffs then brought a further action to recover the 30%. The trial judge held that the previous counterclaim was sufficient notice of an intention to revert to the strict terms of the agreement. The Court of Appeal disagreed, and the plaintiffs appealed to the House of Lords.

Held: The counterclaim was sufficient notice of the intention to revert to the strict terms of the contract, and so the plaintiffs were now entitled to succeed.

Viscount Simonds: ... My Lords, the decision of the Court of Appeal in the first action was based on nothing else than the principle of equity stated in this House in *Hughes v Metropolitan Ry Co* (1877) 2 App Cas at p 448 and interpreted by Bowen LJ in *Birmingham & District Land Co v London & North Western Ry Co* (1888) 40 ChD at p 286 in these terms:

> 'It seems to me to amount to this, that if persons who have contractual rights against others induce by their conduct those against whom they have such rights to believe that such rights will either not be enforced or will be kept in suspense or abeyance for some particular time, those persons will not be allowed by a court of equity to enforce the rights until such time has elapsed, without at all events placing the parties in the same position as they were before. ...'

The difficulty in the present case lies in the fact that, in the first action, in which it was held that between these parties the principle applies, neither of them in any pleading or other statement between the delivery of the counterclaim in March, 1946 and judgment in April, 1950, took their stand on its existence. TECO asserted a binding agreement for the complete and final abrogation of any compensation: T.M.M.C., though willing to make some concession in regard to the past, denied any agreement in respect of any period at all. The position of neither of them was compatible with the existence of an equitable arrangement by which the right to receive, and the obligation to pay, compensation were suspended for a period which lasted at least until March, 1946, and for a debatable period thereafter.

My Lords, I think that, at this point, the issue is a very narrow one. On the one hand, it is said that a plea resting on the denial of an agreement cannot be a notice determining that agreement. This is the view taken by Romer LJ, in which the other members of the Court of Appeal concurred. On the other hand, it is urged that, since the suspensory period is due to the gratuitous willingness of the one party to forgo their rights, nothing can be a clearer intimation that they propose no longer to forgo them than a claim which, though it may ask too much, can leave the other party in no doubt that they must not expect further indulgence. The problem may, perhaps, be stated in this way: Did equity require that T.M.M.C. should expressly and unequivocably refer to an equitable arrangement which TECO had not pleaded and they did not recognise? Or was it sufficient for them by a reassertion of their legal rights to proclaim that the period of indulgence was over? In favour of the latter view, it is added that such an attitude on the part of T.M.M.C. could not surprise TECO who had not hesitated to bring against them a serious charge of fraud.

... For my part, I have, after some hesitation, formed the opinion that, as soon as the counterclaim was delivered, TECO must be taken to know that the suspensory period was at an end and were bound to put their house in order. The position is a very artificial one, but it was their own ignorance of a suspensory period, or at least their failure to plead it, which created the difficulty, and I do not think that they can take advantage of their own ignorance or default and say that they were entitled to a further period of grace until a further notice was given. Equity demands that all the circumstances of the case should be regarded, and I think that the fair and reasonable view is that TECO could not, after they had received the counterclaim, regard themselves as entitled to further indulgence.

It was, however, urged on behalf of TECO that, even if the counterclaim could otherwise be regarded as a sufficient notice that the equitable arrangement was at an end, yet it was defective in that it did not name a certain future date at which it was to take effect. To this the reply was made that equity did not require a future date to be named in the notice, but that what it did require was that a reasonable time should be allowed to elapse before it was sought to enforce it. Here, too, the Court of Appeal favoured the view of TECO ... And here, too, I am forced to the opposite conclusion. Equity is not held in a strait-jacket. There is no universal rule that an equitable arrangement must always be determined in one way. It may, in some cases, be right and fair that a dated notice should be given. But in this case, what was the position in January, 1947, which I take to be the critical date? Then for nine months TECO must, in my opinion, be taken to have been aware that T.M.M.C. proposed to stand on their legal rights. It is not denied that those nine months gave them ample time to readjust their position. I cannot regard it as a requirement of equity that, in such circumstances, they should have been expressly notified in March, 1946, that they would have nine months and no more to take such steps as the altered circumstances required. ...

Lord Oaksey, Lord Tucker and Lord Cohen concurred.

The position is, therefore, that a party making a promise that varies a continuing contractual obligation, but to which no time limit has been attached, can bring the variation to an end by giving reasonable notice. In this case, the notice was constituted by the issue of the counterclaim, and the plaintiffs had waited a reasonable time before seeking to enforce it.

This clearly applies where the contract being varied involves continuing obligations – such as to pay rent or royalties. It is difficult to see that it could apply if promissory estoppel is used to reduce a single debt – as in *Alan v El Nasr*. It would not seem to make sense to hold, on the one hand, that promissory estoppel prevented the recovery of the full debt but, on the other, that the promisor could withdraw the concession by giving reasonable notice. In this type of situation it is submitted that promissory estoppel would operate to extinguish the debt completely, and would not simply be suspensory in its effect. This was the view of the Court of Appeal in *Collier v P & MJ Wright (Holdings) Ltd*.

***Collier v P & MJ Wright (Holdings) Ltd* [2007] EWCA Civ 1329; [2008] 1 WLR 643**

Facts: A partner claimed that a creditor of a partnership had promised that the partner could discharge his liability by paying off his share (i.e. one-third) of the partnership debts, rather than being liable, as would normally be the case, for the full amount owed by the partnership as whole.

Held: On a preliminary issue, the partner had an arguable claim that the creditor was bound by promissory estoppel. The matter was sent back to be determined at trial.

Arden LJ: ...

42. The facts of this case demonstrate that, if (1) a debtor offers to pay part only of the amount he owes; (2) the creditor voluntarily accepts that offer, and (3) in reliance on the creditor's acceptance the debtor pays that part of the amount he owes in full, the creditor will, by virtue of the doctrine of promissory estoppel, be bound to accept that sum in full and final satisfaction of the whole debt. For him to resile will of itself be inequitable. In addition, in these circumstances, the promissory estoppel has the effect of extinguishing the creditor's right to the balance of the debt. This part of our law originated in the brilliant obiter dictum of Denning J in the *High Trees* case [1947] 1 KB 130. To a significant degree it achieves in practical terms the recommendation of the Law Revision Committee chaired by Lord Wright MR in 1937.

Longmore LJ: ...

45. The first question is: what was the oral promise or representation made by Mr Wright to Mr Collier? Mr Collier says that Mr Wright's promise was that if Mr Collier continued to pay £200 per month the company would look to Mr Broadfoot and Mr Flute for their share and not to Mr Collier. I agree that it is arguable (just) that that constitutes agreement or representation by Mr Wright never to sue Mr Collier for the full judgment sum ...

46. The second question is whether, even if the promise or representation is to be regarded on a permanent surrender of the company's rights, Mr Collier has relied on it in any meaningful way. The judge could find no evidence that he had. The suggested reliance is that, but for the agreement, Mr Collier would (or might) have pursued his co-debtors. But, as the judge pointed out, there is no evidence that had he done so at the time when the promise or representation was being made to him, he would have been in a better position to do so than when the promise was revoked (or, as it might be, when the promise expired). Mr Flute became bankrupt in 2002 and Mr Broadfoot in 2004. The only realistic inference is that if Mr Collier had taken any action against them in 2001, they would only have become bankrupt earlier.

47. Nevertheless, as Arden LJ points out, it seems that on the authority of *D & C Builders Ltd v Rees* [1966] 2 QB 617 it can be a sufficient reliance for the purpose of promissory estoppel if a lesser payment is made as agreed. That does, however, require there to be an accord. No sufficient accord was proved in the *D & C Builders* case itself since the owner had taken advantage of the builder's desperate need for money. For the reasons I have given, I doubt if there was any true accord in this case because the true construction of the promise or representation may well be that there was only an agreement to suspend the exercise of the creditor's rights, not to forgo them permanently.

48. There is then a third question, namely whether it would be inequitable for the company to resile from its promise. That cannot be inquired into on this appeal, but I agree that it is arguable that it would be inequitable. There might, however, be much to be said on the other side. If, as Arden LJ puts it, the 'brilliant obiter dictum' of Denning J in the *High Trees* case [1947] 1 KB 130 did indeed substantially achieve in practical terms the recommendation of the Law Revision Committee chaired by Lord Wright MR in 1937, it is perhaps all the more important that agreements which are said to forgo a creditor's rights on a permanent basis should not be too benevolently construed.

Mummery LJ agreed that there was an arguable case for promissory estoppel on the facts.

Note, however, that this was only a preliminary ruling. Nevertheless, it provides a good indication as to how the courts might decide whether promissory estoppel is applicable to payments of a single debt, as opposed to periodic payments. The approach taken in this case was approved, though not applied, in *MWB Business Exchange Centres Ltd v Rock Advertising Ltd* [2016] EWCA Civ 553 (CA), discussed above at 3.3.5.1.

3.4 Alternative tests of enforceability

Some commentators, most notably Atiyah, have argued that contract law in England and Wales should depart from its insistence on 'consideration' as the hallmark of a contract. One possible alternative approach is noted here – the use of 'reliance' as a test of enforceability.

3.4.1 Reliance

A good starting point for discussion of the possibility of using reliance to enforce what otherwise appears to be a gratuitous promise is the argument to this effect by Professor Atiyah.

Atiyah, PS, *Essays on Contract*, 1986, Oxford: Clarendon Press, pp 226–228, 238–240

The enforcement of gratuitous promises

The frontier between promissory estoppel and unilateral contracts

Orthodox theory draws a firm line between a promise given for consideration, and a promise enforceable on the ground of promissory estoppel. In the case of a promise for an act, the distinction comes down to a very fine point. If the act is stated or specified (or possibly if it is requested) by the promisor, then the promise is enforceable in the ordinary way; the performance of the act is a good consideration. If the act is done by the promisee in reliance on the promise, but it has not been requested or stated or specified by the promisor, then orthodoxy asserts that there is no consideration, though there is a sufficient reason for giving the promise the limited validity recognized by promissory estoppel. It may help to see this distinction in perspective if the following possible fact situations are differentiated:

1. The promisor requests and desires the act, and the act confers a benefit on him, for example A promises commission to an estate agent if the agent introduces a purchaser who buys A's house. This promise is enforceable once the act is done.
2. The promisor requests and desires the act, but it confers no direct benefit on him, though it involves a factual detriment to the promisee, for example A promises to give B the price of a house if B enters into a contract to purchase it from a third party. This promise is enforceable once the act is done.
3. The promisor requests and desires the act though it confers no direct benefit on him and involves no factual detriment to the promisee, for example A promises a reward to the winner of a race. This promise is enforceable by the winner of the race once he has complied with the condition.

4. The promisor states the act to be performed by the promisee, but does not request or desire it; it confers no benefit on him though it might involve a factual detriment to the promisee, for example a father promises to give an allowance to his daughter if she should decide to leave her husband. This promise is, I submit, enforceable if the promisee acts on it.
5. The promisor does not state any act which is to be performed by the promisee but it is reasonably implicit that such an act is requested or desired by him, for example A promises additional payment to his creditor without stating that he asks for more time to pay, but it is reasonably implicit in the circumstances that this is what he wants. This promise is enforceable once some reasonable time has been given. (It would of course be enforceable at the outset if the creditor expressly or impliedly *promised* to give some reasonable time.)
6. The promisor does not state any act which is to be performed by the promisee but the promisee does act in reliance on the promise in a way which was the natural and foreseeable result of the promise. This promise is said to be not enforceable as a contract, but enforceable to the limited extent recognized by promissory estoppel.
7. The promisor states the act to be performed by the promisee, and the promisee performs some other act which is a necessary step towards the performance of the act stated by the promisor, but he does not perform the act stated. The promisee cannot enforce the principal promise but may in some circumstances be able to enforce an implied subsidiary promise.
8. The promisor does not state any act which is to be performed by the promisee, but the promisee acts in reliance on the promise in a way which the promisor had no reason to anticipate.
9. The promisee does not act on the promise at all.

I do not suggest that the above list is an exhaustive statement of the possibilities; indeed, there are plainly other permutations and combinations, but this list will suffice for my purposes. The crucial cases are 6, 7, and 8. Few, I think, would contend that Case 9 is enforceable in the present state of the law, either as a contract or even as a case of promissory estoppel. Certainly *some* factor must be present in this case beyond the bare fact of the promise, if the promise is to be given any recognition, and none is stated in the facts assumed. Case 8 is not a case which has been much discussed. It is, at any rate, clear that orthodoxy would not allow Case 8 to be enforced as a binding contractual promise. The case I wish to concentrate on is Case 6. This is the case of promissory estoppel, but what I want to examine here is not why this case should be enforceable (to a limited extent) as a case of promissory estoppel, but why it should not be enforced as a case of consideration.

[Atiyah then argues, inter alia, that the case of *Jorden v Money* (1854) 5 HL Cas 185, which is generally regarded as deciding that estoppel must be based on a statement of fact, not a promise, was actually decided on the basis that estoppel could not be used to evade the Statute of Frauds 1677, which, at that time, required a promise in consideration of marriage to be proved in writing.]

The true view: an unnecessary frontier

It will be seen, therefore, that virtually all modern academic (and much judicial) discussion of promissory estoppel has been entirely beside the point. This discussion invariably takes as its starting point the assumption that the performance of an act in reliance on a promise, not requested or stated by the promisor, cannot be a good consideration. If this assumption is unfounded then there is not, and never was, any need for promissory estoppel. *Jorden v Money*, far from being (as the new orthodoxy would have it) a difficult obstacle in the way of recognition of promissory estoppel, is a clear indication that promissory estoppel was never necessary at all. The facts of *Jorden v Money* are the clearest possible example of my Case 6 that I have been able to find. The plaintiff undoubtedly married in reliance on the defendant's promise but the defendant never requested the marriage nor did she promise to release the debt if and when the plaintiff married. Her promise was, indeed, originally made before any question of marriage was in contemplation; it was repeated time and again and the plaintiff acted upon it by his marriage. I have myself no doubt that, as the law was then understood, this was a good consideration for the enforcement of the promise which would (apart from the Statute of Frauds) have been enforced by the House of Lords in 1854 …

The present orthodoxy therefore seems to me unnecessarily cumbrous. It would be a great deal simpler if the courts were willing to treat action in reliance which suffices for estoppel as also sufficient to satisfy the requirements of consideration; but it would at the same time be necessary, of course, for the courts to become more sophisticated about when expectation protection is, and when it is not, justified. If American experience is anything to go by, it may well be necessary to retain considerable flexibility as to when to confine contractual redress to the protection of reliance and when to go further; it is unwise to try to draw this line by fastening on the absurdly narrow and unreal distinction between an action in reliance which is requested, and one which is not requested, but merely foreseeable.

The possibility of using reliance on a promise as a test of its enforceability has been recognised much more readily in other common-law jurisdictions. In the U.S.A., for example, even the first American *Restatement of the Law of Contracts* included, at § 90:

> A promise which the promisor should reasonably expect to induce action or forbearance of a definite and substantial character on the part of the promisee and which does induce such action or forbearance is binding if injustice can be avoided only by the enforcement of the promise.

Although the American *Restatement* also recognised consideration as a basis for enforcing promises, reliance has long been part of the law of contract in the United States. There are significant similarities in the above formulation with Denning J's statement of the basis of promissory estoppel in *High Trees*. As we have seen, however, promissory estoppel cannot be used as the basis for creating new contractual obligations, but rather only to modify existing ones. Section 90 of the American Restatement clearly has much broader potential for use as the basis for legal action. The same trend can be seen in other parts of the common-law world, notably Australia. The case of *Waltons Stores (Interstate) Ltd v Maher* is particularly significant in this context.

Waltons Stores (Interstate) Ltd v Maher (1988) 164 CLR 406 (High Court of Australia)

Facts: The owners of a piece of land which was expected to form part of a development project were led to believe that the prospective lessees would proceed with the transaction and that the necessary exchange of contracts would take place. With that expectation, they demolished an existing building on the land in preparation for the construction of a new building to meet the lessees' requirements. In fact, the lessees had already decided not to proceed with the agreement. They failed to communicate this to the owners, even though they knew that the work on demolishing the building had started. The owners sought compensation. They succeeded at trial and in the Australian Court of Appeal. The lessees appealed to the High Court of Australia.

Held: The owners could succeed on the basis of promissory estoppel.

Mason CJ and Wilson J: … The proposition stated in § 90(1) of the *Restatement* seems on its face to reflect a closer connection with the general law of contract than our doctrine of promissory estoppel, with its origins in the equitable concept of unconscionable conduct, might be thought to allow. This is because in the United States promissory estoppel has become an equivalent or substitute for consideration in contract formation, detriment being an element common to both doctrines. None the less the proposition, by making the enforcement of the promise conditional on (a) a reasonable expectation on the part of the promisor that his promise will induce action or forbearance by the promisee and (b) the impossibility of avoiding injustice by other means, makes it clear that the promise is enforced in circumstances where departure from it is unconscionable. Note that the emphasis is on the promisor's reasonable expectation that his promise will induce action or forbearance, not on the fact that he created or encouraged an expectation in the promisee of performance of the promise. …

[Having reviewed various authorities from England, including the Privy Council decision in *Attorney General of Hong Kong v Humphreys Estate Ltd* [1987] 1 AC 114, they continued:]

The foregoing review of the doctrine of promissory estoppel indicates that the doctrine extends to the enforcement of voluntary promises on the footing that a departure from the basic assumptions underlying the transaction between the parties must be unconscionable. As failure to fulfil a promise does not of itself amount to unconscionable conduct, mere reliance on an executory promise to do something, resulting in the promisee changing his position or suffering detriment, does not bring promissory estoppel into play. Something more would be required. *Humphreys Estate* suggests that this may be found, if at all, in the creation or encouragement by the party estopped in the other party of an assumption that a contract will come into existence or a promise will be performed and that the other party relied on that assumption to his detriment to the knowledge of the first party. *Humphreys Estate* referred in terms to an assumption that the plaintiff would not exercise an existing legal right or liberty, the right or liberty to withdraw from the negotiations, but as a matter of substance such an assumption is indistinguishable from an assumption that a binding contract would eventuate. On the other hand the United States experience, distilled in the *Restatement* (2d § 90), suggests that the principle is to be expressed in terms of a reasonable expectation on the part of the promisor that his promise will induce action or forbearance by the promisee, the promise inducing such action or forbearance in circumstances where injustice arising from unconscionable conduct can only be avoided by holding the promisor to his promise.

The application of these principles to the facts of the present case is not without difficulty. The parties were negotiating through their solicitors for an agreement for lease to be concluded by way of customary exchange. *Humphreys Estate* illustrates the difficulty of establishing an estoppel preventing parties from refusing to proceed with a transaction expressed to be 'subject to contract'. And there is the problem … that a voluntary promise will not generally give rise to an estoppel because the promisee may reasonably be expected to appreciate that he cannot safely rely upon it. This problem is magnified in the present case where the parties were represented by their solicitors.

All this may be conceded. But the crucial question remains: was the appellant entitled to stand by in silence when it must have known that the respondents were proceeding on the assumption that they had an agreement and that completion of the exchange was a formality? The mere exercise of its legal right not to exchange contracts could not be said to amount to unconscionable conduct on the part of the appellant. But there were two other factors present in the situation which require to be taken into consideration. The first was the element of urgency that pervaded the negotiation of the terms of the proposed lease. As we have noted, the appellant was bound to give up possession of its existing commercial premises in Nowra in January 1984; the new building was to be available for fitting out by 15 January and completed by 5 February 1984. The respondents' solicitor had said to the appellant's solicitor on 7 November that it would be impossible for Maher to complete the building within the agreed time unless the agreement was concluded 'within the next day or two'. The outstanding details were agreed within a day or two thereafter, and the work of preparing the site commenced almost immediately.

The second factor of importance is that the respondents executed the counterpart deed and it was forwarded to the appellant's solicitor on 11 November. The assumption on which the respondents acted thereafter was that completion of the necessary exchange was a formality. The next their solicitor heard from the appellant was a letter from its solicitors dated 19 January, informing him that the appellant did not intend to proceed with the matter. It had known, at least since 10 December, that costly work was proceeding on the site.

It seems to us, in the light of these considerations, that the appellant was under an obligation to communicate with the respondents within a reasonable time after receiving the executed counterpart deed and certainly when it learnt on 10 December that demolition was proceeding. It had to choose whether to complete the contract or to warn the respondents that it had not yet decided upon the course it would take. It was not entitled simply to retain the counterpart deed executed by the respondents and do nothing ... The appellant's inaction, in all the circumstances, constituted clear encouragement or inducement to the respondents to continue to act on the basis of the assumption which they had made. It was unconscionable for it, knowing that the respondents were exposing themselves to detriment by acting on the basis of a false assumption, to adopt a course of inaction which encouraged them in the course they had adopted. To express the point in the language of promissory estoppel the appellant is estopped in all the circumstances from retreating from its implied promise to complete the contract ...'

Brennan J: '... In my opinion, to establish an equitable estoppel, it is necessary for a plaintiff to prove that (1) the plaintiff assumed or expected that a particular legal relationship then existed between the plaintiff and the defendant or expected that a particular legal relationship would exist between them and, in the latter case, that the defendant would not be free to withdraw from the expected legal relationship; (2) the defendant has induced the plaintiff to adopt that assumption or expectation; (3) the plaintiff acts or abstains from acting in reliance on the assumption or expectation; (4) the defendant knew or intended him to do so; (5) the plaintiff's action or inaction will occasion detriment if the assumption or expectation is not fulfilled; and (6) the defendant has failed to act to avoid that detriment whether by fulfilling the assumption or expectation or otherwise. For the purposes of the second element, a defendant who has not actively induced the plaintiff to adopt an assumption or expectation will nevertheless be held to have done so if the assumption or expectation can be fulfilled only by a transfer of the defendant's property, a diminution of his rights or an increase in his obligations and he, knowing that the plaintiff's reliance on the assumption or expectation may cause detriment to the plaintiff if it is not fulfilled, fails to deny to the plaintiff the correctness of the assumption or expectation on which the plaintiff is conducting his affairs.

This is such a case ...

Deane and Gaudron JJ also held for the owners, but on different grounds.

The court in the above case made reference to *Crabb v Arun District Council* [1975] 3 All ER 865, which was a case concerning a right of access to land. It is often categorised by commentators in England and Wales as falling within a distinct category of estoppel – 'proprietary estoppel' – which the courts of England and Wales have been much more willing to allow to be used as the basis for a cause of action. This distinction between different categories of estoppel was emphasised by the Court of Appeal in *Baird Textile Holdings Ltd v Marks and Spencer plc* when considering the development of the law approved in *Waltons v Maher*.

***Baird Textile Holdings Ltd v Marks and Spencer plc* [2001] EWCA Civ 274**

Sir Andrew Morritt VC

... **34.** Counsel for M&S submits that the judge was wrong. He contends, amongst many and varied arguments, that a conclusion to that effect does not involve the reconciliation of numerous cases but the recognition that this court is, as the judge was, bound by three decisions of the Court of Appeal to conclude that the estoppel claim has no real prospect of success either. The three decisions and the propositions they respectively established are: (1) a common law or promissory estoppel cannot create a cause of action (*Combe v Combe* [1951] 1 All ER 767, [1951] 2 KB 215); (2) an estoppel by convention cannot create a cause of action either (*Amalgamated Investment and Property Co Ltd (in liq) v Texas Commerce International Bank Ltd* [1981] 3 All ER 577, [1982] QB 84); and (3) accepting that a proprietary or equitable estoppel may create a cause of action it is limited to cases involving property rights, whether or not confined to land (*Western Fish Products Ltd v Penwith DC* [1981] 2 All ER 204 at 217).

35. Counsel for Baird did not dispute that those cases established the propositions for which M&S contended. Rather, he submitted, it is wrong to categorise particular types of estoppel and then impose limitations in each category not applicable to one or more of the other categories. He suggested that English law permits some cross-fertilisation between one category and another. He contended that English law should follow where the High Court of Australia has led in *Waltons Stores (Interstate) Ltd v Maher* (1988) 164 CLR 387 and *Commonwealth of Australia v Verwayen* (1990) 170 CLR 394 and permit estoppel to create causes of action in non-proprietary cases. In reply counsel for M&S conceded that if the Australian cases, to the effect that promissory estoppel extends to the enforcement of voluntary promises, represent the law of England then the judge was right and the cross-appeal must fail ...

38. In my view English law, as presently understood, does not enable the creation or recognition by estoppel of an enforceable right of the type and in the circumstances relied on in this case. First, it would be necessary for such an obligation to be sufficiently certain to enable the court to give effect to it. That such certainty is required in the field of estoppels such as is claimed in this case as well as in contract was indicated by the House of Lords in *Woodhouse AC Israel Cocoa Ltd SA v Nigerian Produce Marketing Co Ltd* [1972] 2 All ER 271, [1972] AC 741 and by Ralph Gibson LJ in *Troop v Gibson* [1986] 1 EGLR 1 at 6. For the reasons I have already given I do not think that the alleged obligation is sufficiently certain. Second, in my view, the decisions in the three Court of Appeal decisions on which M&S rely do establish that such an enforceable obligation cannot be established by estoppel in the circumstances relied on in this case. This conclusion does not involve the categorisation of estoppels but is a simple application of the principles established by those cases to the obligation relied on in this. I do not consider that any of the dicta in the line of cases relied on by Baird could entitle this court to decline to apply those principles ...

39. Counsel for M&S was, at one stage, inclined to concede that if we considered that the House of Lords, after the facts had been found at a trial, might adopt the propositions formulated by Mason CJ, Wilson and Brennan JJ in the *Waltons Stores* case, then it might be said that there was a real prospect of succeeding on the estoppel issue so that judgment under CPR 24.2 should not be given at this stage. In reply he submitted that the possibility that the House of Lords might adopt those propositions was an inadequate reason for allowing a trial. I agree. If I am right in believing that English law, as it now stands, does not permit the enforcement of an estoppel in the form alleged in this case then it is the duty of this court to apply it, notwithstanding that it may be developed by the House of Lords, who are not bound by any of the cases relied on, in the future.

Judge and Mance LJJ agreed that the Court of Appeal was bound by decisions which prevented the development of the law, so as to allow promissory estoppel to be used as a cause of action.

It remains the position in the law of England and Wales, therefore, that neither detrimental reliance nor promissory estoppel can be used as the basis of *creating* contractual obligations, as opposed to varying existing obligations.

Additional reading

Adams, J., and Brownsword, R., 'Contract, Consideration and the Critical Path' (1990) 53 MLR 536.
Atiyah, P.S., 'Contracts, Promises and the Law of Obligations' (1978) 94 LQR 340.
Campbell, D., 'The Relational Constitution of the Discrete Contract', Ch 3 in Campbell, D., and Vincent-Jones, P. (eds), *Contract and Economic Organisation* (Aldershot: Dartmouth, 1996).

Fried, C., *Contract as Promise* (Cambridge, MA: Harvard University Press, 1981).
Halson, R., 'Sailors, Sub-contractors and Consideration' (1990) 106 LQR 183.
Hird, N.J., and Blair, A., 'Minding Your Own Business – *Williams v Roffey* Revisited' [1996] JBL 254.
O'Sullivan, J., 'In Defence of *Foakes v Beer*' (1996) 55 CLJ 219.
Thompson, M.P., 'Representation to Expectation: Estoppel as a Cause of Action' (1983) 42 CLJ 257.
Treitel, GH, 'Consideration: A Critical Analysis of Professor Atiyah's Fundamental Restatement' (1976) 50 ALJ 439.

Chapter 4

Intention to create legal relations

Chapter contents

4.1 Introduction

As well as evidence of an agreement, for a contract to be enforceable, the courts need to be sure that it was intended to be legally binding. In most cases where there is offer, acceptance and consideration this is not an issue, but in some cases, a party to an agreement that has all those characteristics may wish to claim that they did not intend to create legal relations. The law of England and Wales deals with such assertions largely by means of presumptions. If the alleged contract is a social or domestic agreement, the courts will presume that it was not intended to be legally binding. If, on the other hand, the alleged contract was a commercial agreement, the courts will presume that it was intended to be legally binding.

In either case, the presumption is rebuttable by appropriate evidence, and much of the case law is concerned with what provides sufficient evidence for this.

Statute also provides that collective agreements between employers and trade unions are not intended to be legally binding unless certain requirements are met – see section 4.5, below.

4.2 Objective approach to intention

As with most areas within the law of contract in England and Wales, the courts purport to use an objective approach to the question of determining what the parties 'intended' at the time they entered into an agreement. It is what the parties have said or done, and how a reasonable person would view that, which is important. This was confirmed by Lord Bingham in Edmonds v Lawson [2000] 2 WLR 1091 at 1099, a case which concerned an alleged contract between a pupil barrister and her chambers:

> Whether the parties intended to enter into legally binding relations is an issue to be determined objectively and not by inquiring into their respective states of mind.

Collins has challenged this analysis:

Collins, H, *Law of Contract*, 4th edn, 2003, London: Lexis-Nexis, pp 104–105

> One of the reasons given in *Balfour v Balfour* for refusing to enforce the agreement was that the parties did not intend to enter a binding contract. In a few instances, the parties may have made it plain that they do not expect to be legally bound. It is a common practice in business, for instance, to issue 'letters of comfort' or 'letters of intent', which contain indications of likely future action and current business strategy, but these are not intended, without more, to create binding obligations, and the courts respect this choice not to enter the market sphere. Similarly, it is normally stated expressly or implied by custom in the UK that the parties to a collective agreement between management and trade unions do not intend to create a legally enforceable agreement. Apart from these clear expressions of intent, however, the libertarian explanation seems to be fatally flawed.
>
> In cases where the issue is litigated, it seems likely that one party intended a legal agreement and the other wanted the agreement to be merely morally binding. This contradiction removes any possibility of justifying the limits on contracts on the basis of the joint intent of the parties. We are forced to the conclusion that the courts must rely upon hidden policy considerations when determining the intent of the parties. The libertarian focus upon the choice of the parties to make contracts in a family context runs the risk of ignoring the obligations imposed by law, which are designed to support the family as a way of life insulated from market considerations. Even if both husband and wife in *Balfour v Balfour* had seriously intended to make a binding contract, the agreement would surely not have been enforceable, because it was likely to subvert the distributive principles of family law, such as depriving the wife of her needs-based right to maintenance.

Although there may well be policy considerations that influence decisions in this area, as in many others in contract law, the attempt to discern what one party could reasonably have believed to be the intentions of the other from their words and conduct is still a central consideration. Such an approach was also adopted, for example, by the European Draft Common Frame of Reference, Art II.–4.102:

> The intention of a party to be legally bound to a contract is to be determined from the party's statements or conduct as they were reasonably to be understood by the other party.

4.3 Domestic or social agreements

The approach to 'domestic' or 'social' agreements is that they are presumed not to involve an intention to create legal relations. The leading case is *Balfour v Balfour*.

Balfour v Balfour [1919] 2 KB 571 (CA)

Facts: Mr Balfour went to work in Ceylon (now Sri Lanka). Mrs Balfour was not well enough to accompany him. Mr Balfour agreed to pay his wife £30 per month while they were apart. The marriage later broke up and Mrs Balfour sued to enforce her husband's promise. Mrs Balfour succeeded at first instance, but Mr Balfour appealed.

Held: The agreement, even if Mrs Balfour had provided consideration, was not intended to be legally binding, and could not be enforced.

Atkin LJ: The defence to this action on the alleged contract is that the defendant, the husband, entered into no contract with his wife, and for the determination of that it is necessary to remember that there are agreements between parties which do not result in contracts within the meaning of that term in our law. The ordinary example is where two parties agree to take a walk together, or where there is an offer and an acceptance of hospitality. Nobody would suggest in ordinary circumstances that those agreements result in what we know as a contract, and one of the most usual forms of agreement which does not constitute a contract appears to me to be the arrangements which are made between husband and wife. It is quite common, and it is the natural and inevitable result of the relationship of husband and wife, that the two spouses should make arrangements between themselves – agreements such as are in dispute in this action – agreements for allowances, by which the husband agrees that he will pay to his wife a certain sum of money, per week, or per month, or per year, to cover either her own expenses or the necessary expenses of the household and of the children of the marriage, and in which the wife promises either expressly or impliedly to apply the allowance for the purpose for which it is given. To my mind those agreements, or many of them, do not result in contracts at all, and they do not result in contracts even though there may be what as between other parties would constitute consideration for the agreement. The consideration, as we know, may consist either in some right, interest, profit or benefit accruing to one party, or some forbearance, detriment, loss or responsibility given, suffered or undertaken by the other. That is a well-known definition, and it constantly happens, I think, that such arrangements made between husband and wife are arrangements in which there are mutual promises, or in which there is consideration in form within the definition that I have mentioned. Nevertheless they are not contracts, and they are not contracts because the parties did not intend that they should be attended by legal consequences. To my mind it would be of the worst possible example to hold that agreements such as this resulted in legal obligations which could be enforced in the courts. It would mean this, that when the husband makes his wife a promise to give her an allowance of 30s. or £2 a week, whatever he can afford to give her, for the maintenance of the household and children, and she promises so to apply it, not only could she sue him for his failure in any week to supply the allowance, but he could sue her for non-performance of the obligation, express or implied, which she had undertaken upon her part. All I can say is that the small courts of this country would have to be multiplied one hundredfold if these arrangements were held to result in legal obligations. They are not sued upon, not because the parties are reluctant to enforce their legal rights when the agreement is broken, but because the parties, in the inception of the arrangement, never intended that they should be sued upon. Agreements such as these are outside the realm of contracts altogether. The common law does not regulate the form of agreements between spouses. Their promises are not sealed with seals and sealing wax. The consideration that really obtains for them is that natural love and affection which counts for so little in these cold courts. The terms may be repudiated, varied or renewed as performance proceeds or as disagreements develop, and the principles of the common law as to exoneration and discharge and accord and satisfaction are such as find no place in the domestic code. The parties themselves are advocates, judges, courts, sheriff's officer and reporter. In respect of these promises each house is a domain into which the King's writ does not seek to run, and to which his officers do not seek to be admitted. The only question in this case is whether or not this promise was of such a class or not. For the reasons given by my brethren it appears to me to be plainly established that the promise here was not intended by either party to be attended by legal consequences. I think the onus was upon the plaintiff, and the plaintiff has not established any contract. The parties were living together, the wife intending to return. The suggestion is that the husband bound himself to pay £30 a month under all circumstances, and she bound herself to be satisfied with that sum under all circumstances, and, although she was in ill-health and alone in the country, that out of that sum she undertook to defray the whole of the medical expenses that might fall upon her, whatever might be the development of her illness, and in whatever expenses it might involve her. To my mind neither party contemplated such a result. I think that the parol evidence upon which the case turns does not establish a contract. I think that the letters do not evidence such a contract, or amplify the oral evidence which was given by the wife, which is not in dispute. For these reasons I think the judgment of the court below was wrong and that this appeal should be allowed.

Duke LJ and Warrington LJ delivered concurring judgments.

The judgments of Duke and Warrington LJJ were based as much on the lack of consideration as the absence of intention to create legal relations. Atkin LJ, however, focused on the 'intention' issue. It is this aspect of the case that has been emphasised subsequently, and *Balfour v Balfour* is thus regarded as a key source of the principle that domestic agreements will be regarded as not intended to be binding, unless there is clear evidence to the contrary.

In terms of agreements between husband and wife, it is clear that in *Balfour v Balfour*, the court regarded as significant the fact that the couple was 'living in amity' at the time of the agreement. One piece of evidence, therefore, that may contribute to overturning the presumption of lack of intention in this context is evidence that the parties were in the process of splitting up when the agreement is made. This was confirmed by *Merritt v Merritt*.

Merritt v Merritt [1970] 1 WLR 1211 (CA)

Facts: H and W were married in 1941. The matrimonial home was subsequently put into joint names. In 1966, H left W. They had a conversation about the future, at the end of which H signed a piece of paper agreeing to transfer the house into W's name if she paid off the mortgage. When she had done so, H refused to make the transfer, claiming that the agreement was not binding. W succeeded at trial, but H appealed.

Held: The agreement was binding. *Balfour* was distinguishable, because in the current case, the agreement was made when the parties were in the process of separating.

Lord Denning MR: Husband and wife married as long ago as 1941. After the war in 1949 they got a building plot and built a house. It was a freehold house, no. 133, Clayton Road, Hook, Chessington. It was in the husband's name, with a considerable sum on mortgage with a building society. There they lived and brought up their three children, two daughters, aged now 20 and 17, and a boy now 14. The wife went out to work and contributed to the household expenses.

Early in 1966 they came to an agreement whereby the house was to be put in joint names. That was done. It reflected the legal position when a house is acquired by a husband and wife by financial contributions of each.

But, unfortunately, about that time the husband formed an attachment for another woman. He left the house and went to live with her. The wife then pressed the husband for some arrangement to be made for the future. On May 25 they talked it over in the husband's car. The husband said that he would make the wife a monthly payment of £40 and told her that out of it she would have to make the outstanding payments to the building society. There was only £180 outstanding. He handed over the building society's mortgage book to his wife. She was herself going out to work, earning net £7 10s. a week. Before she left the car she insisted that he put down in writing a further agreement. It forms the subject of the present action. He wrote these words on a piece of paper:

> 'In consideration of the fact that you will pay all charges in connection with the house at 133 Clayton Road, Chessington, Surrey, until such time as the mortgage repayment has been completed, when the mortgage has been completed, I will agree to transfer the property into your sole ownership.
>
> Signed, John Merritt. May 25, 1966'.

The wife took that paper away with her. She did, in fact, over the ensuing months pay off the balance of the mortgage, partly, maybe, out of the money the husband gave her, £40 a month, and partly out of her own earnings. When the mortgage had been paid off, he reduced the £40 a month down to £25 a month.

The wife asked the husband to transfer the house into her sole ownership. He refused to do so. She brought an action in the Chancery Division for a declaration that the house should belong to her and for an order that he should make the conveyance.

The judge made the order; but the husband now appeals to this court.

The first point taken on his behalf by Mr Thompson is that the agreement was not intended to have legal relations. It was, he says, a family arrangement such as was considered by the court in *Balfour v Balfour* [1919] 2 KB 571 and in *Jones v Padavatton* [1969] 1 WLR 328. So the wife could not sue upon it.

I do not think those cases have any application here. The parties there were living together in amity. In such cases their domestic arrangements are ordinarily not intended to create legal relations. It is altogether different when the parties are not living in amity but are separated, or about to separate. They then bargain keenly. They do not rely on honourable understandings. They want everything cut and dried. It may safely be presumed that they intend to create legal relations.

Mr Thompson then relied on the recent case of *Gould v Gould* [1970] 1 QB 275, when the parties had separated, and the husband agreed to pay the wife £12 a week 'so long as he could manage it'. The majority of the court thought those words introduced such an element of uncertainty that the agreement was not intended to create legal relations. But for that element of uncertainty, I am sure the majority would have held the agreement to be binding. They did not differ from the general proposition which I stated at p 280 that:

> 'when husband and wife, at arm's length, decide to separate, and the husband promises to pay a sum as maintenance to the wife during the separation, the court does, as a rule, impute to them an intention to create legal relations'.

In all these cases the court does not try to discover the intention by looking into the minds of the parties. It looks at the situation in which they were placed and asks itself: Would reasonable people regard the agreement as intended to be binding?

Mr Thompson sought to say that this agreement was uncertain because of the arrangement for £40 a month maintenance. That is obviously untenable. Next he said that there was no consideration for the agreement. That point is no good. The wife paid the outstanding amount to the building society. That was ample consideration. It is true that the husband paid her £40 a month which she may have used to pay the building society. But still her act in paying was good consideration ...

I find myself in entire agreement with the judgment of Stamp J. This appeal should be dismissed.' Widgery and Karminski LJJ concurred.

A presumption of non-enforceability does not just apply to agreements between a husband and a wife. It will also apply as between other family members (as in *Jones v Padavatton*, extracted below) and between friends. The type of agreement is arguably also important. For example, an agreement between a group of students sharing a flat as to who is to perform various domestic chores would be unlikely to be regarded as legally binding; if the agreement related to the payment of bills, however, it would be much more likely to be legally binding.

In *Simpkins v Pays* [1955] 3 All ER 10, an agreement between a group who were not all related concerned the sharing of a prize in a competition that they jointly entered. It was held that there had been an intention to form a legally binding agreement that any winnings would be shared. Sellers J commented:

> It may well be there are many family associations where some sort of rough and ready statement is made which would not, in a proper estimate of the circumstances, establish a contract which was contemplated to have legal consequences, but I do not so find here. I think that in the present case there was a mutuality in the arrangement between the parties. It was not very formal, but certainly it was, in effect, agreed that every week the forecast should go in the name of the defendant, and that if there was success, no matter who won, all should share equally. It seems to be the implication from, or the interpretation of, what was said that this was in the nature of a very informal syndicate so that they should all get the benefit of success.

A further example of the presumption being overturned by the evidence is to be found in *Parker v Clark*.

Parker v Clark [1960] 1 WLR 286

Facts: A niece and her husband agreed to live with her aunt and uncle, who were 20 years older, and help to look after them. They were promised that the house of the aunt and uncle would be left to them. When the arrangement did not work out, and the younger couple were asked to move, they brought an action for damages for breach of contract. The defendants argued that there was no contract, as the agreement was not intended to create legal relations.

Held: There was sufficient evidence to overturn the presumption that a domestic arrangement between family members was not intended to be legally binding. In particular, the fact that the younger couple had sold their house in order to move in with the defendants was an indication of the seriousness of the commitment being undertaken.

Devlin J: ... The contract relied upon by the plaintiffs is said to be contained in the defendants' letter of September 25 and Commander Parker's acceptance thereof. In this part of the case, since Commander Parker and Mr. Clark were the contractual protagonists, it is convenient to refer to them simply as plaintiff and defendant. The defendants' first submission in answer to the claim is that the letters, construed in the light of the surrounding circumstances, show no intention to enter into a legal relationship or to make a binding contract. No doubt a proposal between relatives to share a house, and a promise to make a bequest of it, may very well amount to no more than a family arrangement of the type considered in *Balfour v Balfour*, which the courts will not enforce. But there is equally no doubt that arrangements of this sort, and in particular a proposal to leave property in a will, can be the subject of a binding contract. ...

The question must, of course, depend on the intention of the parties, to be inferred from the language they use and from the circumstances in which they use it. On the plaintiff's side, I accept his evidence that he considered that he was making a binding contract. An important factor in this was that he disposed of his own residence. It does not matter for this purpose whether it was or was not a term of the contract that he should sell 'The Thimble'; the important thing is that the contract required him to give up his occupation of 'The Thimble', and that he was always quite clear, and made it quite clear, that he would not give up occupation unless he also gave up the ownership and parted with the property. He would not have done that, he says – and I believe it – unless he thought that he was securing another permanent home. There is, undoubtedly, in the arrangement a lack of formality, upon which Mr. Park greatly relies. This, I think, is largely explained by the relationship between the parties; it is easier to demand formal documents from a stranger than it is from a relative and friend. It is clear that the plaintiff constantly relied upon the letter as a sort of title to his rights; he kept it and referred to it whenever his rights were called in question. When on October 24, 1957, they were seriously threatened, he went forthwith and consulted a solicitor. He is not, in my judgment, the sort of man who would 'think up' a legal action as an afterthought, when he found he was not getting what he wanted.

The plaintiff is not a moneyed man. On the strength of Mr. Clark's promise he, so to speak, put down £672 10s. That is the figure that is agreed as the expense which he incurred in giving up 'The Thimble', on the assumption that he could repurchase 'The Thimble' or a cottage like it. In addition to that, he tied up £2,000, so that he has never since been in a position to buy another property like 'The Thimble', and has never in fact bought one. The defendant knew this, and had plenty of time to reflect upon it between September 25, 1955, when he wrote his letter, and March 1, 1956, when the plaintiffs arrived. If he had thought that all that his letter involved was an amicable arrangement terminable at will, I cannot believe that he would not have enlightened the plaintiff and, as a cautious man himself, have warned him against the folly of what he was doing. I cannot believe either that the defendant really thought that the law would leave him at liberty, if he so chose, to tell the Parkers when they arrived that he had changed his mind, that they could take their furniture away, and that he was indifferent whether they found anywhere else to live or not. Yet this is what the defence means. The defendant gave several answers which show that this was not really his state of mind. He said that the object of the letter was to induce the Parkers to come to 'Cramond'; and he agreed also that he made the will in fulfilment of the promise. I am satisfied that an arrangement binding in law was intended by both sides.

In some cases, the dividing line between having the requisite intention and a lack of the requisite intention may be hard to discern. In *Jones v Padavatton*, for example, the four judges who considered the case divided equally as to whether there was an intention to create legal relations or not. The majority of the Court of Appeal, however, held that there was no intention to create legal relations, and the plaintiff succeeded in recovering property that was the subject of the agreement. It was probably significant that, since the contract was between a mother and daughter, there was a presumption of unenforceability to be overturned. If the burden had been on the plaintiff to prove that the contract was not intended to be binding, then it is more likely that the defendant would have succeeded.

***Jones v Padavatton* [1969] 1 WLR 328, CA**

Facts: A mother, living in the West Indies, agreed with her daughter, who was living in the United States, that if the daughter went to London to read for the Bar, the mother would support her. Subsequently, the mother bought a house in London in which the daughter lived rent-free, but taking in tenants and using the rent to support herself. After about five years, when the daughter had still not passed her Bar exams, the mother sought to recover the house. At trial, the county court judge dismissed the mother's claim, on the basis that her agreement with her daughter was binding. The mother appealed.

Held (by a majority): The agreement was not intended to be legally binding, so the mother was entitled to recover possession of the house.

Danckwerts LJ: … Of course, there is no difficulty, if they so intend, in members of families entering into legally binding contracts in regard to family affairs. A competent equity draftsman would, if properly instructed, have no difficulty in drafting such a contract. But there is possibly in family affairs a presumption against such an intention (which, of course, can be rebutted). I would refer to Atkin LJ's magnificent exposition of the situation in regard to such arrangements in *Balfour v Balfour* [1919] 2 KB 571, 578–580.

There is no doubt that this case is a most difficult one, but I have reached a conclusion that the present case is one of those family arrangements which depend on the good faith of the promises which are made and are not intended to be rigid, binding agreements. *Balfour v Balfour* was a case of husband and wife, but there is no doubt that the same principles apply to dealings between other relations, such as father and son and daughter and mother …

In the result, of course, on this view, the daughter cannot resist her mother's rights as the owner of the house to the possession of which the mother is entitled.'

Salmon LJ: 'I agree with the conclusion at which my Lord has arrived, but I have reached it by a different route. The first point to be decided is whether or not there was ever a legally binding agreement between the mother and daughter in relation to the daughter's reading for the Bar in England. The daughter alleges that there was such an agreement, and the mother denies it. She says that there was nothing but a loose family arrangement which had no legal effect. The onus is clearly on the daughter. There is no dispute that the parties entered into some sort of arrangement. It really depends upon (a) whether the parties intended it to be legally binding, and (b) if so, whether it was sufficiently certain to be enforceable …

[Salmon LJ noted that the daughter had had a good job in Washington, where she was well-settled, and was reluctant to move to London.]

The daughter was naturally loth to leave Washington, and did not regard her mother's suggestion as feasible. The mother, however, eventually persuaded the daughter to do as she wished by promising her that, if she threw up her excellent position in Washington and came to study for the Bar in England, she would pay her daughter an allowance of $200 a month until she had completed her studies. The mother's attorney in Trinidad wrote to the daughter to confirm this. I cannot think that either intended that if, after the daughter had been in London, say, for six months, the mother dishonoured her promise and left her daughter destitute, the daughter would have no legal redress.

In the very special circumstances of this case, I consider that the true inference must be that neither the mother nor the daughter could have intended that the daughter should have no legal right to receive, and the mother no legal obligation to pay, the allowance of $200 a month. …

Fenton-Atkinson LJ: ... The problem is, in my view, a difficult one, because though one would tend to regard a promise by a parent to pay an allowance to a child during a course of study as no more than a family arrangement, on the facts of this case this particular daughter undoubtedly gave up a great deal on the strength of the mother's promise.

In my judgment it is the subsequent history which gives the best guide to the parties' intention at the material time. There are three matters which seem to me important:

(1) The daughter thought that her mother was promising her 200 United States dollars, or £70 a month, which she regarded as the minimum necessary for her support. The mother promised 200 dollars, but she had in mind 200 British West Indian dollars, £42 a month, and that was what she in fact paid from November 1962 to December 1964. Those payments were accepted by the daughter without any sort of suggestion at any stage that the mother had legally contracted for the larger sum.

(2) When the arrangements for the purchase of No. 181, Highbury Quadrant were being discussed, and the new arrangement was made for maintenance to come out of the rents, many material matters were left open: how much accommodation was the daughter to occupy; how much money was she to have out of the rents; if the rents fell below expectation, was the mother to make up the difference below £42, or £42 less the sum saved by the daughter in rent; for how long was the arrangement to continue, and so on. The whole arrangement was, in my view, far too vague and uncertain to be itself enforceable as a contract; but at no stage did the daughter bring into the discussions her alleged legal right to £42 per month until her studies were completed, and how that right was to be affected by the new arrangement.

(3) It is perhaps not without relevance to look at the daughter's evidence in cross-examination. She was asked about the occasion when her mother visited the house, and she, knowing perfectly well that her mother was there, refused for some hours to open the door. She said: 'I didn't open the door because a normal mother doesn't sue her daughter in court. Anybody with normal feelings would feel upset by what was happening'. Those answers and the daughter's conduct on that occasion provide a strong indication that she had never for a moment contemplated the possibility of her mother or herself going to court to enforce legal obligations, and that she felt it quite intolerable that a purely family arrangement should become the subject of proceedings in a court of law ...

So the Court of Appeal divided 2:1 on the issue of whether the agreement was intended to be legally binding, which indicates how difficult it may be to decide this issue when a contract is between family members. Note that Salmon LJ treated the arrangement in relation to the house as separate from the original contract to provide maintenance, and found it too vague to be legally binding. So all members of the Court of Appeal, in the end, held for the mother against her daughter.

4.4 Commercial agreements

The presumption in relation to commercial agreements is that they are intended to be binding. This can include arrangements that are primarily concerned with education or training, such as those between a pupil barrister and his or her chambers, as held in *Edmonds v Lawson* [2000] 2 WLR 1091.

The presumption is difficult to overturn, as is indicated by *Edwards v Skyways*.

***Edwards v Skyways Ltd* [1964] 1 WLR 349 (QBD)**

Facts: The plaintiff was made the offer of an 'ex gratia' payment as part of a redundancy arrangement. The company subsequently refused to make the payment, denying that it was legally bound to do so.

Held: The use of the phrase 'ex gratia' was not sufficient to overturn the presumption in commercial dealings that parties intend to be legally bound to their agreements.

Megaw, J: ... In the present case, the subject-matter of the agreement is business relations, not social or domestic matters. There was a meeting of minds – an intention to agree. There was, admittedly, consideration for the company's promise. I accept the propositions of counsel for the plaintiff that in a case of this nature the onus is on the party who asserts that no legal effect was intended, and the onus is a heavy one ...

[T]he company says, first, as I understand it, that the mere use of the phrase 'ex gratia' by itself, as a part of the promise to pay, shows that the parties contemplated that the promise, when accepted, should have no binding force in law. It says, secondly, that even if the first proposition is not correct as a general proposition, nevertheless here there was certain background knowledge, present in the minds of everyone, which gave unambiguous significance to 'ex gratia' as excluding legal relationship.

As to the first proposition, the words 'ex gratia', in my judgment, do not carry a necessary, or even a probable, implication that the agreement is to be without legal effect. It is, I think, common experience amongst practitioners of the law that litigation or threatened litigation is frequently compromised on the terms that one party shall make to the other a payment described in express terms as 'ex gratia' or 'without admission of liability'. The two phrases are, I think, synonymous. No one would imagine that a settlement, so made, is unenforceable at law. The words 'ex gratia' or 'without admission of liability' are used simply to indicate – it may be as a matter of amour-propre, or it may be to avoid a precedent in subsequent cases – that the party agreeing to pay does not admit any pre-existing liability on his part; but he is certainly not seeking to preclude the legal enforceability of the settlement itself by describing the contemplated payment as 'ex gratia'. So here. There are obvious reasons why the phrase might have been used by the company in just such a way. It might have desired to avoid conceding that any such payment was due under the employers' contract of service. It might have wished – perhaps ironically in the event – to show, by using the phrase, its generosity in making a payment beyond what was required by the contract of service. I see nothing in the mere use of the words 'ex gratia', unless in the circumstances some very special meaning has to be given to them, to warrant the conclusion that this promise, duly made and accepted, for valid consideration, was not intended by the parties to be enforceable in law.

The company's second proposition seeks to show that in the circumstances here the words 'ex gratia' had a special meaning. What is said is this: when a payment such as this is made by an employer to a dismissed employee the question whether it is subject to income tax in the hands of the recipient is important. It was understood by the company and by the association, and by all their respective representatives at the meeting, that if the company's payment were made as the result of a legally binding obligation, it would be taxable in the hands of the recipient; whereas, if it were to be made without legal obligation on the part of the company, it would not be taxable. It was not argued before me whether this assertion is right or wrong in law. It was said by the company that that is quite immaterial; what is material is that the parties so believed. Thus, it is said, the phrase 'ex gratia' was used, and was understood by all present to be used, deliberately and advisedly as a formula to achieve that there would be no binding legal obligation on the company to pay, and hence to save the recipient from a tax liability. It is said that the offer was accepted by the association with full knowledge and understanding of these matters. Hence, it is said, the agreement by tacit consent, a consent evidenced by the use of the words 'ex gratia' against this background of common understanding, was an agreement from which legal sanction and consequences were excluded.

In my judgment, that submission also fails because the evidence falls far short of showing that this supposed background of avoidance of tax liability was present as an important element in the minds of all,

> or indeed any, of the persons who attended the meeting of February 8; or, if this be something different, in the minds of the company or of the association; or that they all, or any of them, directed their minds to the significance of the words 'ex gratia' which is now suggested on behalf of the company. The question of the liability, and the possible influence thereon of the use of the words 'ex gratia', may indeed have been present in some degree, and as one element, in the minds of some of the persons present at the meeting. That, however, is far from sufficient to establish that the parties – both of them – affirmatively intended not to enter into legal relations in respect of the company's promise to pay.

As Megaw J makes clear at the start of the quoted passage, the burden of proving that there was no intention to create legal relations in an ostensibly commercial contract lies with the party alleging this and this is a heavy burden (the position may be otherwise in relation to collateral warranties [see *New York Laser Clinic Limited v Naturastudios Limited* (2019) EWHC 2892 (QB) at (65)] and in some cases, where the very existence of an agreement is in dispute [e.g. as the parties disagree on whether or not an agreement has been reached by conduct] so that the question of intention to create legal relations merges, to some extent, into whether or not there is an agreement [see *Moorgate Capital (Corporate Finance) Ltd v Sun European Partners LLP* (2020) EWHC 593 at (82)]). A similar approach can be seen in the decision of the majority of the House of Lords in *Esso Petroleum Ltd v Commissioners of Customs and Excise* [1976] 1 All ER 117, where a promotion involving the 'gift' of a World Cup coin to motorists buying petrol was held to involve an intention to create legal relations. One way of attempting to avoid legal effects is to use explicit language, as, for example, was traditionally done by companies running football pools competitions. In that context, in several cases, the use of a phrase such as 'binding in honour only' was held to indicate that the parties did not intend to enter a binding agreement. In *Jones v Vernons Pools* [1938] 2 All ER 626, the following clause was included on the entry coupon:

> It is a basic condition of the sending in and the acceptance of this coupon that it is intended and agreed that the conduct of the pools and everything done in connection therewith and all arrangements relating thereto (whether mentioned in these rules or to be implied) and this coupon and any agreement or transaction entered into or payment made by or under it shall not be attended by or give rise to any legal relationship, rights, duties or consequences whatsoever or be legally enforceable or the subject of litigation, but all such arrangements, agreements and transactions are binding in honour only.

The judge commented on this clause:

> That is a clause which seems to me to express in the fullest and clearest way that everything that follows in these rules is subject to that basic or overriding condition that everything that is promised, every statement made with relation to what a person sending the coupon may expect, or may be entitled to, is governed by that clause.
>
> If it means what I think that they intend it to mean, and what certainly everybody who sent a coupon and who took the trouble to read it would understand, it means that they all trusted to the defendants' honour, and to the care they took, and that they fully understood that there should be no claim possible in respect of the transactions.

Even this type of clause may be given a restrictive interpretation in some circumstances. In *Rose and Frank Co v Crompton Bros*, it was held that an 'honour' clause applied to an overall agency arrangement between the parties, but it did not apply in relation to particular orders placed under it.

***Rose and Frank Co v Crompton Bros* [1925] AC 445**

Facts: The parties enter into an agreement under which the producers of carbonising tissue paper agreed to sell all their output to one company, which agreed in return only to obtain its paper from these producers. The agreement was stated to last for three years, but contained a clause indicating that it was 'binding in honour only'. Orders were placed and honoured, and then a question arose as to the enforceability of the overall agreement. The trial judge held that both the overall agreement and the orders under it were legally binding. The Court of Appeal found that neither was binding. The case was appealed to the House of Lords.

Held: The honour clause indicated that the overall agreement was not intended to be legally binding, but the orders placed under it were binding contracts.

Lord Phillimore: ... The appellants, Rose and Frank Company, carry on business in the United States as dealers in carbonising tissue paper, which they have been in the habit of buying from England, then treating in some manner and selling in the perfected state. Their relations with the respondents, James R. Crompton and Brothers, Ld., began as early as 1905; and there were three arrangements, which for the purposes of this appeal we may assume to have been binding contracts, under which Rose and Frank Company were to be entitled to have the exclusive or nearly exclusive right of selling Crompton and Brothers' carbonising tissues in America, subject to twelve months' notice – notice which was never given.

In 1913, circumstances led to the relations between the parties being reconsidered; and it was then for the first time brought to the notice of Rose and Frank Company that the respondents, Brittains, Ld., had been interested with Cromptons in supplying the carbonising tissue; and thereupon the three parties entered into the arrangement which has given rise to the present litigation. It is dated July 8, 1913, and in the earlier part of it appears to be a binding agreement, under which the English companies agree to confine the sale of all their carbonising tissue in the U.S. and Canada – subject to certain defined exceptions – and Rose and Frank Company agree to confine their purchases of the same stuff exclusively to the two English companies and to do their best to increase their trade. The arrangement was to last for three years subject to six months' notice. The other supplementary provisions need not be stated; but towards the end of the document appears this remarkable clause:

> 'This arrangement is not entered into, nor is this memorandum written, as a formal or legal agreement, and shall not be subject to legal jurisdiction in the Law Courts either of the United States or England, but it is only a definite expression and record of the purpose and intention of the three parties concerned, to which they each honourably pledge themselves with the fullest confidence – based on past business with each other – that it will be carried through by each of the three parties with mutual loyalty and friendly co-operation'.

There is no explanation upon the record, and no suggestion was made by counsel at the Bar of any reason for the introduction of this remarkable clause. During the progress of the hearing it occurred to some of your Lordships that it might have been inserted in order to avoid the operation of some American law discouraging monopolies. But this was a mere surmise. For whatever reason it was introduced the clause is there, and it remains for the Courts to give the proper effect to it.

The terms of this arrangement, whatever may be its force or effect, were continued by correspondence for a second three-yearly period and by arrangement in August, 1918, till March 31, 1920.

During the early part of 1919 differences arose between the parties. The respondents thought that the appellants were not conducting the business as they should, and that their (the respondents') interests were suffering. Accordingly on May 5 they demanded by telegram compliance with certain requirements, threatening, if the requirements were not met, to communicate direct with the consumers.

On the same day the appellants telegraphed back that they refused to consent to terminate the agreement and would hold the respondents accountable for any violation of contract, and they demanded immediate shipment of the parcels they had ordered; but on May 9 and 10, by cable and letter, the respondents definitely refused to allow further deliveries to be made.

During the existence of the arrangement the appellants had been giving to the respondents, Cromptons, from time to time, orders for certain numbers of cases of tissues to be delivered at various dates. The documents took this form: an order from the appellants to Cromptons: 'Please enter our order for the following goods and ship'. Then followed either a specific date – usually the first of the month or, if no specific date, then 'as soon as possible,' and the port to which they were to be shipped, either New York or sometimes Toronto, and the nature of the articles required. In compliance with these orders the respondents used to ship the goods. A few of the orders sent in this way in the early part of 1919 were complied with, but the others had not actually been complied with by the time of the quarrel and were not fulfilled afterwards.

On November 19, 1919, the appellants brought their action, treating the arrangement as a binding contract and claiming damages for the breach, alternatively averring that the three earlier agreements were still in force and claiming damages for their breach, and as a third alternative relying on the several specific orders for parcels of goods in the early part of 1919 as having been accepted by the respondents, Cromptons, and constituting specific contracts and claiming damages for the non-delivery of these goods …

The respondents joined in their defence, and contended that the arrangement was not a binding contract, that the earlier agreements were not binding contracts or had expired by loss of time …

As to the appellants' claim in respect of the specific orders, they denied that these orders gave rise to any contracts, said that the requirements of s 4 of the Sale of Goods Act had not been complied with, and further that these orders and acceptances, if any, were given as part of a specification under the arrangement of 1913, and that if that arrangement did not constitute any legal contract, neither did these orders with provisional acceptances constitute contracts.

They further pleaded misconduct on the part of the appellants justifying them in determining the agreement …

[Lord Phillimore then noted that the decisions of the trial judge and Court of Appeal and continued:]

With regard to the first and most important point, that of the legal force or want of force of the arrangement of 1913, your Lordships are, I conceive, of one mind with the Court of Appeal. I do not propose to repeat their reasoning, with which I venture to concur, but I wish to add one observation. I was for a time impressed by the suggestion that as complete legal rights had been created by the earlier part of the document in question, any subsequent clause nullifying those rights ought to be regarded as repugnant and ought to be rejected. This is what happens for instance in cases where an instrument inter vivos purports to pass the whole property in something either real or personal, and there follows a provision purporting to forbid the new owner from exercising the ordinary rights of ownership. In such cases this restriction is disregarded. But I think the right answer was made by Scrutton L.J. It is true that when the tribunal has before it for construction an instrument which unquestionably creates a legal interest, and the dispute is only as to the quality and extent of that interest, then later repugnant clauses in the instrument cutting down that interest which the earlier part of it has given are to be rejected, but this doctrine does not apply when the question is whether it is intended to create any legal interest at all. Here, I think, the overriding clause in the document is that which provides that it is to be a contract of honour only and unenforceable at law …

Lord Phillimore agreed with the trial judge, however, that the individual orders were intended to create legal relations.

This case shows that even in a commercial agreement, it is possible to rebut the presumption of enforceability by using sufficiently explicit language (compare *MacInnes v Gross* [2017] EWHC 46 (QB) where an 'agreement' over an informal dinner was held not to be intended to create legal relations). See also *Volumatic Ltd v Ideas for Life Ltd* [2019] EWHC 2273 (IPEC), where David Stone J stated:

> 24. Applying an objective test, in my judgment, the parties did not intend the Agreement to be legally binding. It was a document designed to record the consensus reached at the Warwick Meeting – both parties conceded that the Warwick Meeting had no legal effect. Whilst the document is signed, this was done, in my judgment, not to create legal relations, but for the purposes of the parties recording the consensus – the signatures indicate the agreement of both sides that the document accurately expresses what was agreed in Warwick.

However, much of the recent case law has emphasised that it is difficult to rebut the presumption other than by specific language, particularly if lawyers have been involved in the drafting of the relevant document. It should be remembered, though, that the other requirements of a binding agreement (contract) must still be present. In particular, if the agreement leaves important issues undecided so that it is uncertain, or if it amounts to no more than an 'agreement to agree' it will not be enforceable. In *Barbudev v Eurocom Cable Management Bulgaria Eood* [2012] EWCA Civ 548, the main contract concerned the sale of a TV and internet company. There was also a side letter which appeared to give the claimant certain other rights. The trial judge held that this letter was not intended to be legally binding. The Court of Appeal disagreed, but ruled that the letter was no more than an agreement to agree and, in any case, was insufficiently certain to be enforceable. Similarly, in *Dhanani v Crasnianski* [2011] EWHC 926 a signed letter and 'term sheet' relating to the proposed creation of a €50 million private equity fund was held to be unenforceable despite the fact that the parties probably intended it to have legal effect because (as stated at para 101):

> it did not contain the terms which were essential for such an agreement to be enforced. Although many aspects of the fund had been agreed the agreement was an agreement to agree in respect of those matters which remained undefined.

4.5 Collective agreements

In the context of employment law, it is not uncommon for an employer, or group of employers, to come to an agreement with a trade union as to the pay, or other conditions of service, that are to apply to a particular group of employees. Such an agreement will commonly affect the individual contract of employment of each employee and, to that extent, have a binding legal effect. Is it also binding as between the employer and trade union? Since it is an agreement that is clearly 'commercial' rather than 'domestic', the expectation would be that it would be presumed to be binding on the principles outlined in the previous section. In fact, it was held in *Ford Motor Co Ltd v AEF* [1969] 2 QB 303 that the overall context in which industrial relations were conducted in the United Kingdom meant that such agreements should not be regarded as being intended to be legally enforceable. This approach has subsequently been given statutory effect, and the current provision dealing with this is to be found in the Trade Union and Labour Relations (Consolidation) Act 1992.

TRADE UNION AND LABOUR RELATIONS (CONSOLIDATION) ACT 1992

Section 179
Whether agreement intended to be a legally enforceable contract.

(1) A collective agreement shall be conclusively presumed not to have been intended by the parties to be a legally enforceable contract unless the agreement –
  (a) is in writing, and
  (b) contains a provision which (however expressed) states that the parties intend that the agreement shall be a legally enforceable contract.

(2) A collective agreement which does satisfy those conditions shall be conclusively presumed to have been intended by the parties to be a legally enforceable contract.

(3) If a collective agreement is in writing and contains a provision which (however expressed) states that the parties intend that one or more parts of the agreement specified in that provision, but not the whole of the agreement, shall be a legally enforceable contract, then –
  (a) the specified part or parts shall be conclusively presumed to have been intended by the parties to be a legally enforceable contract, and
  (b) the remainder of the agreement shall be conclusively presumed not to have been intended by the parties to be such a contract.

(4) A part of a collective agreement which by virtue of subsection (3)(b) is not a legally enforceable contract may be referred to for the purpose of interpreting a part of the agreement which is such a contract.

As indicated by this provision, collective agreements are not legally binding unless in writing and specifically stated to be intended to be binding.

4.6 Is a requirement of intention necessary?

It has sometimes been argued that the elements of offer, acceptance and consideration should be sufficient to determine the question of whether an agreement is intended to be binding, and that a separate requirement of 'intention' is unnecessary. This approach is exemplified by the arguments put forward by Professor Hepple in the following article.

Hepple, B, 'Intention to create legal relations' (1970) *CLJ* 122, pp 127–129

The requirement of an intention to create legal relations, additional to the test of bargain, has been repeatedly criticised by academic commentators. In essence, the objection raised by the critics is that the whole basis of the common law of contract is the notion of bargain, of which offer, acceptance and consideration are indivisible facets. Every offer may be seen as consisting of a promise and a request to the offeree to do some act (which may be the giving of a promise or the rendering of a performance) in exchange for the promise. From the offeree's side the doing of that act is an acceptance of the offer. From the offeror's angle, the response to his request is consideration. For analytical reasons it has become traditional to separate the element of agreement (usually reduced to an offer and acceptance) from the element of consideration. In determining the existence of agreement the courts have sought to find *consensus ad idem* by objective yardsticks, by strict grammatical rules of construction, and by classifications such as 'invitation to treat', 'puff' and 'offer' which provide *a priori* tests of the respective 'intentions' of the parties. The intervention of equity has made this approach workable by preventing 'hardship amounting to injustice' where appearances are too far removed from reality. Consideration has provided the test of enforceability. This separation of agreement from consideration (in part inspired by a desire to contrast consideration with the civil law *causa*) has resulted in a fundamental point being overlooked. This is that the common law recognised at an early stage that parties usually do not define their intention to enter legal relations. Consequently, the fact that they have cast their arrangement into the form of bargain (offer, acceptance, consideration) provides an extremely practical test of that intention. This test of bargain renders superfluous any *additional* proof of intention.

The difficulties which have arisen in reconciling this approach with the remarks of Atkin L.J. (as he then was) in *Balfour v Balfour* have arisen, as the late Professor Unger showed, only because of Atkin L.J.'s definition of consideration. It will be remembered that his Lordship insisted that 'arrangements made between husband and wife are arrangements in which there are mutual promises, or there is consideration in form within the definition that I have mentioned. Nevertheless they are not contracts. ... because the parties do not intend that they should be attended by legal consequences.' He defined consideration as consisting of a benefit received by one party or a loss suffered by the other, but he failed to add that the benefit or loss must be received or suffered as the price for the other. An agreement between spouses may consist of mutual promises and yet not be a contract precisely because the promise of the one party is not given as the price for the other. The same reasoning can be applied to other domestic agreements. In *Shadwell v Shadwell*, for example, the court was agreed that the question they had to answer was, 'Was the plaintiff's marriage at his uncle's request?' Their Lordships differed only on the construction of the particular promise before them.

The courts, aided by all the standard textbooks, have tended to conceal this simple analysis of every offer into a promise and request by the repeated incantation of Atkin L.J.'s dictum without making the essential qualification about the sense in which he defined consideration.

A recent example is *Jones v Padavatton*. At her mother's request and in return for a promise to provide $200 a month maintenance for her, the plaintiff gave up an 'excellent' job and other advantages of living in Washington in order to come to England in 1962 to read for the Bar. In 1964 the mother bought a house in London for the daughter to live in one or two rooms and let the rest to tenants to cover expenses and provide maintenance. After a quarrel with her daughter in 1967, the mother brought legal proceedings for possession of the house. Danckwerts and Fenton Atkinson L.JJ. agreed that there was good consideration for the mother's promise in 1962 but held that the principle in *Balfour v Balfour* applied and that the presumption against an intention to be bound in family matters had not been rebutted. Accordingly, the mother was entitled to possession. Salmon L.J. reached the same result but by a different route. He held that the presumption had been rebutted in the case of the 1962 agreement, but that the agreement in 1964 regarding possession of the house was unenforceable. A close examination of Salmon L.J.'s judgment (like the well-known inquiry of Scrutton L.J. into the alleged bargain in *Wyatt v Kreglinger and Fernau*) reveals that although he stated the problem in the *language* of intention, the test of that intention was in fact that of bargain. The mother's promise of maintenance (confirmed through her attorney) was the decisive factor which led the daughter to respond to the request to live in London. In regard to the second agreement, however, Salmon L.J. said: 'There is no evidence that the mother bargained away her right to dispose of her home, or to evict her daughter (who was a mere licensee) whenever she wished to do so.' Bargain was once again used as the test of contractual intention.

To require, as Danckwerts and Fenton Atkinson L.JJ. did, some further test of intention is to invite confusion and uncertainty. Indeed, their Lordships were not agreed how that intention should be ascertained. Fenton Atkinson L.J. was influenced by the fact that the daughter had said in cross-examination, 'a normal mother doesn't sue her daughter in court', to which Salmon L.J. responded: 'the fact that a contracting party is in some circumstances unlikely to extract his pound of flesh does not mean that he has no right to it'. Fenton Atkinson L.J. also remarked on the failure of the daughter at any stage prior to the institution of proceedings against her to bring into discussion her right to a particular amount of maintenance.

This surely goes no further than to confirm Professor Unger's view that 'the family circle differs from the market place in that it is not the setting for bargaining but for gratuitous services'.

It has been argued that 'one cannot tell whether mutual promises are a bargain or an 'exchange of gifts' without regard to the intention of the parties'. This attributes unnecessary circularity to the notion of bargain. Once it was conceded that an agreement existed in *Jones v Padavatton*, the only test of intention ought to have been the terms of the promises which were given by mother and daughter. Was there a request to the daughter to come to London in return for the promise of maintenance? Did the daughter respond to that request? This approach would have done much to simplify what Danckwerts L.J. called a 'most difficult' case.

Professor Hepple goes on to argue against the extension of the presumption of lack of intention to collective agreements. As has been noted above, however, such agreements are now dealt with by statute. More generally, it may be questioned whether the requirements of offer, acceptance and consideration can do all the work which Professor Hepple suggests can be placed on them. It would probably require a modification of the approach as to what constitutes valid consideration to achieve this objective, and there is no sign that the courts are interested in exploring this possibility. The traditional approach, exemplified by *Balfour v Balfour* and based on presumptions dependent on whether the agreement is 'domestic' or 'commercial', remains the dominant analysis in this area.

Additional reading

Allen, D., 'The Gentleman's Agreement in Legal Theory and in Modern Practice' (2000) 29 Anglo-American Law Review 204.

Brown, I., 'The Letter of Comfort: Placebo or Promise?' [1990] JBL 281.

Freeman, M., 'Contracting in the Haven: *Balfour v Balfour* Revisited', in Halson, R. (ed), *Exploring the Boundaries of Contract* (London: Dartmouth, 1996).

Hedley, S., 'Keeping Contract in Its Place: *Balfour v Balfour* and the Enforceability of Informal Agreements' (1985) 5 OJLS 391.

Unger, R., *The Critical Legal Studies Movement* (Cambridge, MA: Harvard University Press, 1983), pp 60–6.

Chapter 5

Privity

Chapter contents

5.1 Introduction

The doctrine of privity of contract states that generally only the parties to a contract can have rights and obligations under it. In other words, the parties to a contract generally cannot by their agreement impose obligations on a third party and, more controversially, if they agree to confer a benefit on a third party, the third party cannot sue to recover that benefit. Although privity of contract is often regarded as a cornerstone of contract law in England and Wales, it can operate in ways which unduly restrict the reasonable expectations of both the contracting parties and those whom they may be trying to benefit. As a result, there are a number of exceptions to it including the Contracts (Rights of Third Parties) Act 1999, which allows contracting parties to confer an enforceable benefit on a third party. There are various other ways in which the doctrine may be sidestepped, including:

- Allowing, in some situations, a contracting party to recover damages on behalf of non-parties. There has been significant case law on this in recent years.
- Finding the existence of a trust of a promise. This exception has largely fallen into disuse because of the difficulty of establishing that the parties intended to create an irrevocable trust.
- Finding a collateral contract to create rights or obligations in relation to a person who is not a party to the main contract.
- Various statutory exceptions.
- Creative use of the concept of agency as a means of circumventing privity in order, for example, to give third parties the benefit of an exclusion clause (this is likely to be used less frequently now that the same objective can be achieved through the Contracts (Rights of Third Parties) Act 1999).

There have been far fewer attempts to impose burdens on third parties, but in some circumstances *restrictive covenants* can be used to bind third parties.

The above list of exceptions might suggest that the doctrine of privity of contract no longer has much of a role in contract law in England and Wales. Its resilience, however, is illustrated by the decision in *MacDonald Dickens & Macklin v Costello* [2011] EWCA Civ 930, where the Court of Appeal refused to allow a claim for restitution (ie, that a third party to a contract would otherwise be unjustly enriched) to be used to circumvent the doctrine of privity. Under the doctrine of privity of contract, the third party had no rights or obligations under the contract and the restitution claim should not be used as a means of undermining the distribution of risks as set out in the contract.

5.2 The basic doctrine of privity of contract

The common law doctrine of privity of contract states that generally only a party to a contract can have rights or obligations under it. The basis of the doctrine may be found in *Tweddle v Atkinson*.

Tweddle v Atkinson (1861) 1 B & S 393; 121 ER 762 (QB)

Facts: The fathers of a couple who were about to get married made an agreement with each other under which the father of the bride was to pay £200 and the father of the groom £100 to the bridegroom, William Tweddle. William sued his father-in-law for non-payment.

Held: William Tweddle could not sue on the agreement between the fathers because he was not a party to it, even though he was intended to benefit from it.

Wightman J: Some of the old decisions appear to support the proposition that a stranger to the consideration of a contract may maintain an action upon it, if he stands in such a near relationship to the party from whom the consideration proceeds, that he may be considered a party to the consideration. The strongest of those cases is that cited in *Bourne v Mason* (1 Ventr. 6), in which it was held that the daughter of a physician might maintain assumpsit upon a promise to her father to give her a sum of money if he performed a certain cure. But there is no modern case in which the proposition has been supported. On the contrary, it is now established that no stranger to the consideration can take advantage of a contract, although made for his benefit.

Crompton J: It is admitted that the plaintiff cannot succeed unless this case is an exception to the modern and well established doctrine of the action of assumpsit. At the time when the cases which have been cited were decided the action of assumpsit was treated as an action of trespass upon the case, and therefore in the nature of a tort; and the law was not settled, as is now is, that natural love and affection is not a sufficient consideration for a promise upon which an action may be maintained; nor was it settled that the promisee cannot bring an action unless the consideration for the promise moved from him. The modern cases have, in effect, overruled the old decisions; they show that the consideration must move from the party entitled to sue upon the contract. It would be a monstrous proposition to say that a person was a party to the contract for the purpose of suing upon it for his own advantage, and not a party to it for the purpose of being sued. It is said that the father in the present case was agent for the son in making the contract, but that argument ought also to make the son liable upon it. I am prepared to overrule the old decisions, and to hold that, by reason of the principles which now govern the action of assumpsit, the present action is not maintainable.

Blackburn J concurred.

As these judgments make clear, at the time the doctrine was very much linked to the requirement that consideration must move from the promisee. The later affirmation of *Tweddle v Atkinson* by the House of Lords in *Dunlop v Selfridge* focuses more directly on the principle that generally only a person who is a party to a contract can have rights (or liabilities) under it.

***Dunlop Pneumatic Tyre Co Ltd v Selfridge & Co Ltd* [1915] AC 847**

Facts: Dunlop contracted with D, wholesalers of motor accessories, that D in selling tyres to retailers would require the retailer to observe Dunlop's list price. S entered into such an agreement with D but then sold tyres at below the list price. Dunlop sought an injunction and damages from S.

Held: Dunlop was not in a contractual relationship with S and so could not enforce the terms of the agreement between D and S.

Viscount Haldane, LC: My Lords, in the law of England certain principles are fundamental. One is that only a person who is a party to a contract can sue on it. Our law knows nothing of a *jus quaesitum tertio* arising by way of contract. Such a right may be conferred by way of property, as, for example, under a trust, but it cannot be conferred on a stranger to a contract as a right to enforce the contract in personam. A second principle is that if a person with whom a contract not under seal has been made is to be able to enforce it consideration must have been given by him to the promisor or to some other person at the promisor's request. These two principles are not recognized in the same fashion by the jurisprudence of certain Continental countries or of Scotland, but here they are well established. A third proposition is that a principal not named in the contract may sue upon it if the promisee really contracted as his agent. But again, in order to entitle him so to sue, he must have given consideration either personally or through the promisee, acting as his agent in giving it.

My Lords, in the case before us, I am of opinion that the consideration, the allowance of what was in reality part of the discount to which Messrs. Dew, the promisees, were entitled as between themselves and the appellants, was to be given by Messrs. Dew on their own account, and was not in substance, any more than in form, an allowance made by the appellants. The case for the appellants is that they permitted and enabled Messrs. Dew, with the knowledge and by the desire of the respondents, to sell to the latter on the terms of the contract of January 2, 1912. But it appears to me that even if this is so the answer is conclusive. Messrs. Dew sold to the respondents goods which they had a title to obtain from the appellants independently of this contract. The consideration by way of discount under the contract of January 2 was to come wholly out of Messrs. Dew's pocket, and neither directly nor indirectly out of that of the appellants. If the appellants enabled them to sell to the respondents on the terms they did, this was not done as any part of the terms of the contract sued on.

No doubt it was provided as part of these terms that the appellants should acquire certain rights, but these rights appear on the face of the contract as *jura quaesita tertio*, which the appellants could not enforce. Moreover, even if this difficulty can be got over by regarding the appellants as the principals of Messrs. Dew in stipulating for the rights in question, the only consideration disclosed by the contract is one given by Messrs. Dew, not as their agents, but as principals acting on their own account.

The conclusion to which I have come on the point as to consideration renders it unnecessary to decide the further question as to whether the appellants can claim that a bargain was made in this contract by Messrs. Dew as their agents; a bargain which, apart from the point as to consideration, they could therefore enforce. If it were necessary to express an opinion on this further question, a difficulty as to the position of Messrs. Dew would have to be considered. Two contracts – one by a man on his own account as principal, and another by the same man as agent – may be validly comprised in the same piece of paper. But they must be two contracts, and not one as here. I do not think that a man can treat one and the same contract as made by him in two capacities. He cannot be regarded as contracting for himself and for another *uno flatu*.

My Lords, the form of the contract which we have to interpret leaves the appellants in this dilemma, that, if they say that Messrs. Dew contracted on their behalf, they gave no consideration, and if they say they gave consideration in the shape of a permission to the respondents to buy, they must set up further stipulations, which are neither to be found in the contract sued upon nor are germane to it, but are really inconsistent with its structure. That contract has been reduced to writing, and it is in the writing that we must look for the whole of the terms made between the parties. These terms cannot, in my opinion consistently with the settled principles of English law, be construed as giving to the appellants any enforceable rights as against the respondents.

I think that the judgment of the Court of Appeal was right, and I move that the appeal be dismissed with costs.

Lord Dunedin: My Lords, I confess that this case is to my mind apt to nip any budding affection which one might have had for the doctrine of consideration. For the effect of that doctrine in the present case is to make it possible for a person to snap his fingers at a bargain deliberately made, a bargain not in itself unfair, and which the person seeking to enforce it has a legitimate interest to enforce. Notwithstanding these considerations I cannot say that I have ever had any doubt that the judgment of the Court of Appeal was right.

This was a unanimous decision of a six-person House of Lords and so firmly established the doctrine. The potential unfairness, however, pointed out by Lord Dunedin and the fact that preventing an agreement of this kind from operating may well thwart the intentions of all concerned at the time of contract, meant that the doctrine, at least as far as it prevents the conferment of benefits, was the subject of much criticism throughout the 20th century. The Law Revision Committee, in its Sixth Interim Report (Cmd 5449), recommended legislative reform in 1937. Nevertheless, the House of Lords again confirmed the basic principle in 1968. They were arguably able to do justice in the case despite the doctrine but also rejected one possible route to reducing its impact, advocated by Lord Denning and involving a broad interpretation of the effect of s 56 of the Law of Property Act 1925.

Beswick v Beswick [1968] AC 58 (HL)

Facts: Peter Beswick was a coal merchant. When he retired from the business his nephew, who took over the business, agreed to pay Peter an agreed sum for the rest of Peter's life and a slightly smaller sum to Peter's widow after Peter's death. When Peter died, the nephew refused to make the agreed payments to his widow.

Held: Although the widow was not a party to the contract, in her capacity of administratrix of her husband's estate she could obtain specific performance of the contract.

Lord Reid: My Lords, before 1962 the respondent's deceased husband carried on business as a coal merchant. By agreement of March 14, 1962, he assigned to his nephew, the appellant, the assets of the business and the appellant undertook first to pay to him £6 10s. per week for the remainder of his life and then to pay to the respondent an annuity of £5 per week in the event of her husband's death. The husband died in November, 1963. Thereupon, the appellant made one payment of £5 to the respondent but he refused to make any further payment to her. The respondent now sues for £175 arrears of the annuity and for an order for specific performance of the continuing obligation to pay the annuity. The Vice-Chancellor of the County Palatine of Lancaster decided against the respondent but the Court of Appeal reversed this decision and, besides ordering payment of the arrears, ordered the appellant to pay to the respondent for the remainder of her life an annuity of £5 per week in accordance with the agreement.

It so happens that the respondent is administratrix of the estate of her deceased husband and she sues both in that capacity and in her personal capacity. So it is necessary to consider her rights in each capacity.

For clarity I think it best to begin by considering a simple case where, in consideration of a sale by A to B, B agrees to pay the price of £1,000 to a third party X. Then the first question appears to me to be whether the parties intended that X should receive the money simply as A's nominee so that he would hold the money for behalf of A and be accountable to him for it, or whether the parties intended that X should receive the money for his own behalf and be entitled to keep it. That appears to me to be a question of construction of the agreement read in light of all the circumstances which were known to the parties. There have been several decisions involving this question. I am not sure that any conflicts with the view which I have expressed: but if any does, for example, *In re Engelbach's Estate* [1924] Ch 348, I would not agree with it. I think that *In re Schebsman* [1944] Ch 83 was rightly decided and that the reasoning of Uthwatt J and the Court of Appeal supports what I have just said. In the present case I think it clear that the parties to the agreement intended that the respondent should receive the weekly sums of £5 in her own behalf and should not be accountable to her deceased husband's estate for them. Indeed the contrary was not argued.

Reverting to my simple example the next question appears to me to be: Where the intention was that X should keep the £1,000 as his own, what is the nature of B's obligation and who is entitled to enforce it? It was not argued that the law of England regards B's obligation as a nullity, and I have not observed in any of the authorities any suggestion that it would be a nullity. There may have been a time when the existence of a right depended on whether there was any means of enforcing it, but today the law would be sadly deficient if one found that, although there is a right, the law provides no means for enforcing it. So this obligation of B must be enforceable either by X or by A. I shall leave aside for the moment the question whether section 56(1) of the Law of Property Act, 1925, has any application to such a case, and consider the position at common law.

Lord Denning's view, expressed in this case not for the first time, is that X could enforce this obligation. But the view more commonly held in recent times has been that such a contract confers no right on X and that X could not sue for the £1,000. Leading counsel for the respondent based his case on other grounds, and as I agree that the respondent succeeds on other grounds, this would not be an appropriate case in which to solve this question. It is true that a strong Law Revision Committee recommended so long ago as 1937 (Cmd. 5449):

> 'That where a contract by its express terms purports to confer a benefit directly on a third party it shall be enforceable by the third party in his own name ...' (p 31).

And, if one had to contemplate a further long period of Parliamentary procrastination, this House might find it necessary to deal with this matter. But if legislation is probable at any early date I would not deal with it in a case where that is not essential. So for the purposes of this case I shall proceed on the footing that the commonly accepted view is right.

What then is A's position? I assume that A has not made himself a trustee for X, because it was not argued in this appeal that any trust had been created. So, if X has no right, A can at any time grant a discharge to B or make some new contract with B. If there were a trust the position would be different. X would have an equitable right and A would be entitled and, indeed, bound to recover the money and account for it to X. And A would have no right to grant a discharge to B. If there is no trust and A wishes to enforce the obligation, how does he set about it? He cannot sue B for the £1,000 because under the contract the money is not payable to him, and, if the contract were performed according to its terms, he would never have any right to get the money. So he must seek to make B pay X.

The argument for the appellant is that A's only remedy is to sue B for damages for B's breach of contract in failing to pay the £1,000 to X. Then the appellant says that A can only recover nominal damages of 40s. because the fact that X has not received the money will generally cause no loss to A: he admits that there may be cases where A would suffer damage if X did not receive the money but says that the present is not such a case.

Applying what I have said to the circumstances of the present case, the respondent in her personal capacity has no right to sue, but she has a right as administratrix of her husband's estate to require the appellant to perform his obligation under the agreement. He has refused to do so and he maintains that the respondent's only right is to sue him for damages for breach of his contract. If that were so, I shall assume that he is right in maintaining that the administratrix could then only recover nominal damages because his breach of contract has caused no loss to the estate of her deceased husband.

If that were the only remedy available the result would be grossly unjust. It would mean that the appellant keeps the business which he bought and for which he has only paid a small part of the price which he agreed to pay. He would avoid paying the rest of the price, the annuity to the respondent, by paying a mere 40*s*. damages.

The respondent's first answer is that the common law has been radically altered by section 56(1) of the Law of Property Act, 1925, and that that section entitles her to sue in her personal capacity and recover the benefit provided for her in the agreement although she was not a party to it.'

[Lord Reid then examined the history of s 56 and concluded, contrary to the view advocated by Lord Denning in a number of cases, including this one, that it was not intended to apply outside the area of contracts concerning land, and related rights. As a result it could not be used to assist Mrs Beswick.]

'The respondent's second argument is that she is entitled in her capacity of administratrix of her deceased husband's estate to enforce the provision of the agreement for the benefit of herself in her personal capacity, and that a proper way of enforcing that provision is to order specific performance. That would produce a just result, and, unless there is some technical objection, I am of opinion that specific performance ought to be ordered. For the reasons given by your Lordships I would reject the arguments submitted for the appellant that specific performance is not a possible remedy in this case. I am therefore of opinion that the Court of Appeal reached a correct decision and that this appeal should be dismissed.

Lord Hodson, Lord Guest, Lord Pearce and Lord Upjohn concurred.

This decision confirmed the general principle of privity of contract that a third-party beneficiary of a promise contained in a contract generally has no right to sue the promisor to enforce that benefit. Lord Reid's comments indicate, however, that it was a situation which the House of Lords felt it might need to reconsider if there were to be a 'further long period of Parliamentary procrastination'. In the present case the House was arguably able to do justice for Mrs Beswick without reforming the law on privity and so it left it to Parliament to deal with the issue. In fact it was another 30 years before Parliament got around to introducing a reform giving third parties improved rights. This is dealt with in the next section.

5.3 Reform: Contracts (Rights of Third Parties) Act 1999

There was regular academic criticism of the privity of contract doctrine as confirmed in *Beswick v Beswick*. In 1990, Adams and Brownsword proposed that in relation to many complex commercial contracts an approach based on a 'network' of contracts would come closer to what the contracting parties would expect – see Adams, J and Brownsword, R, 'Privity and the concept of a network contract' (1990) 10 *Legal Studies* 12. The Law Commission, however, went further and proposed that there should be a broad exception to the privity of contract doctrine, applying to virtually all contracts where the parties intended to provide a third party with an enforceable benefit.

Law Commission, Report No 242, *Privity of Contract: Contracts for the Benefit of Third Parties*, 1996, Cmnd 3329

1.1 In 1995 in the Court of Appeal in *Darlington Borough Council v Wiltshier Northern Ltd* Steyn LJ, in criticising the present law, said the following:

> 'The case for recognising a contract for the benefit of a third party is simple and straightforward. The autonomy of the will of the parties should be respected. The law of contract should give effect to the reasonable expectations of contracting parties. Principle certainly requires that a burden should not be imposed on a third party without his consent. But there is no doctrinal, logical, or policy reason why the law should deny effectiveness to a contract for the benefit of a third party where that is the expressed intention of the parties. Moreover, often the parties, and particularly third parties, organise their affairs on the faith of the contract. They rely on the contract. It is therefore unjust to deny effectiveness to such a contract. I will not struggle with the point further since nobody seriously asserts the contrary'.

1.2 In this Report we make recommendations for the reform of that part of the doctrine of privity of contract which lays down that a contract does not confer rights on someone who is not a party to the contract (hereinafter referred to as the 'third party rule'). Our proposals will mean, for example, that subsequent purchasers or tenants of buildings can be given rights to enforce an architect's or building contractor's contractual obligations without the cost, complexity and inconvenience of a large number of separate contracts; that an employer can take out medical expenses insurance for its employees without there being doubts as to whether the employees can enforce the policy against the insurance company; that a life insurance policy taken out for one's stepchild or cohabitee is enforceable (subject to a term to the contrary) by that named beneficiary; and that a contractual clause limiting or excluding one's liability to a third party (for example, the promisee's subsidiary company or sub-contractor or employee) will be straightforwardly enforceable by that third party.

1.3 The Law Commission first became interested in this subject after the Commission's creation in 1965. Item 1 of the First Programme of Law Reform was the codification of the law of contract. Item 3 included the topic of third party rights. A substantial amount of work was done on this topic in conjunction with work on consideration. At that time it was felt that reform of privity could not usefully be undertaken without reform of the doctrine of consideration. The relationship between the doctrines of privity and of consideration is discussed in Part VI below, where we explain why we believe that reform of the third party rule can be profitably undertaken without reassessing the entire doctrine of consideration.

1.4 In 1973 work was suspended on the production of a contract code which, in its draft form, would have provided for the creation of rights in third parties. The Law Commission's strategy since then has been to tackle problems in the law of contract as separate projects. In arriving at the view that a project on privity was justified, we were influenced by, for example, the continued judicial and academic criticism of the doctrine, by the work of Commonwealth law reform bodies, by insights gained from our work on the rights of buyers of goods carried by sea, and by a more cautious judicial approach in the late 1980s and early 1990s to tort liability for pure economic loss. In short we had little doubt that the continued existence of the third party rule represented a pressing problem for the English law of contract.

1.5 In Consultation Paper No 121, we set out the current law on the third party rule, the case for its reform, and the main issues that would need to be dealt with in any reform. In an Appendix, we gave an account of the way in which the problem has been dealt with in other jurisdictions. Our provisional conclusion was that the law ought to be reformed and that the reform should be embodied in a detailed legislative scheme. The principal feature of that scheme (that is, the test of enforceability) would be that a third party should be able to enforce a contract where the parties intended that the third party should receive the benefit of the promised performance and also intended to create a legal obligation enforceable by the third party.

1.6 The Consultation Paper attracted 102 replies. A clear majority accepted the validity of our arguments in favour of reform. Our provisional proposals were particularly welcomed by the legal profession and some other professional bodies, academic lawyers, consumer organisations, and the insurance and banking industries. While it was to be expected that the subject of the Consultation Paper would be of great interest to academic lawyers, the wide range of responses from non-academic lawyers and non-lawyers reflects the degree to which the third party rule still causes significant difficulties in practice.

1.7 The minority who opposed the proposals outlined in the Consultation Paper did so in reliance on four main general arguments. First, that reform was unnecessary because the rule caused few problems in practice given that those who were affected by it could use various devices ... to get round the third party rule. Secondly, that no legislative reform could hope adequately to deal with all the diverse situations where the third party rule is relevant. Thirdly, that the existing legal regime, while complicated, achieved certainty, and that reform would only result in uncertainty and litigation. Fourthly, that the proposals for reform might lead to contracting parties being bound to third parties when this was not their true intention.

1.8 We disagree with the view that the third party rule does not cause significant problems in practice. We cannot ignore those who do not have access to (good) legal advice and, in any event, our proposed reforms will provide a simpler way of affording a third party the right to enforce a contract than the present convoluted techniques. This will not only save the parties costs, it will also save the taxpayer the needless litigation costs caused by the complexity of the present law. Nevertheless the response of the minority who opposed the proposed reform was invaluable in requiring us to reassess whether our proposals were too uncertain and would result in the imposition of unintended liabilities. In certain respects – and especially as regards the test of enforceability – we have modified our provisional recommendations in an attempt to allay those kinds of fears. We should emphasise, at the outset, that our recommendations are not concerned to override the allocation of liability within contracts but rather rest on an underlying policy of effectuating the contracting parties' intentions. At root our recommendations would enable the parties to create enforceable third party rights in contract without the complexities of the devices presently used to circumvent the privity doctrine.

1.9 Our general approach has been to devise moderate reform proposals which can be expected to gain wide support. Some more radical possibilities have been put to one side for fear that the central reform would otherwise be endangered. For example, we do not in this report recommend a special test of enforceability for third parties who are consumers; we do not propose a reform of insurance contracts that goes as far as section 48 of the Australian Insurance Contracts Act 1984; and we do not seek to recast the decision of the House of Lords in *White v Jones* [1995] 2 AC 207 by bringing the claims of disappointed beneficiaries under negligently drafted wills within our proposed Act.

1.10 It has also been important in our thinking that, while we believe that a detailed legislative scheme is the best means of reforming privity, we have no desire to hamper judicial creativity in this area. For example, we have left to the developing common law, what the rights of promisees should be in contracts for the benefit of third parties; and we have left open for the judges to decide what the rights of a joint promisee, who has not provided consideration, should be. In general terms, we see our draft Bill as achieving at a stroke and with certainty and clarity what a progressive House of Lords might well itself have brought about over the course of time. While the draft Bill departs from a long-established common law rule, we hope that it will not be seen as cutting across the underpinning principles of the common law.

The Law Commission's proposals, as outlined in the above report, were given fairly speedy legislative effect, with the consequent Act following very closely the Law Commission's draft Bill.

CONTRACTS (RIGHTS OF THIRD PARTIES) ACT 1999

1. – (1) Subject to the provisions of this Act, a person who is not a party to a contract (a 'third party') may in his own right enforce a term of the contract if –

(a) the contract expressly provides that he may, or

(b) subject to subsection (2), the term purports to confer a benefit on him.

(2) Subsection (1)(b) does not apply if on a proper construction of the contract it appears that the parties did not intend the term to be enforceable by the third party.

(3) The third party must be expressly identified in the contract by name, as a member of a class or as answering a particular description but need not be in existence when the contract is entered into.

(4) This section does not confer a right on a third party to enforce a term of a contract otherwise than subject to and in accordance with any other relevant terms of the contract.

(5) For the purpose of exercising his right to enforce a term of the contract, there shall be available to the third party any remedy that would have been available to him in an action for breach of contract if he had been a party to the contract (and the rules relating to damages, injunctions, specific performance and other relief shall apply accordingly).

(6) Where a term of a contract excludes or limits liability in relation to any matter references in this Act to the third party enforcing the term shall be construed as references to his availing himself of the exclusion or limitation.

(7) In this Act, in relation to a term of a contract which is enforceable by a third party –

'the promisor' means the party to the contract against whom the term is enforceable by the third party, and

'the promisee' means the party to the contract by whom the term is enforceable against the promisor.

2. – (1) Subject to the provisions of this section, where a third party has right under section 1 to enforce a term of the contract, the parties to the contract may not, by agreement, rescind the contract, or vary it in such a way as to extinguish or alter his entitlement under that right, without his consent if –

(a) the third party has communicated his assent to the term to the promisor,

(b) the promisor is aware that the third party has relied on the term, or

(c) the promisor can reasonably be expected to have foreseen that the third party would rely on the term and the third party has in fact relied on it.

(2) The assent referred to in subsection (1)(a) –

(a) may be by words or conduct, and

(b) if sent to the promisor by post or other means, shall not be regarded as communicated to the promisor until received by him.

(3) Subsection (1) is subject to any express term of the contract under which –

(a) the parties to the contract may by agreement rescind or vary the contract without the consent of the third party, or

(b) the consent of the third party is required in circumstances specified in the contract instead of those set out in subsection (1)(a).

3. – (1) Subsections (2) to (5) apply where, in reliance on section 1, proceedings for the enforcement of a term of a contract are brought by a third party.

(2) The promisor shall have available to him by way of defence or set-off any matter that –

(a) arises from or in connection with the contract and is relevant to the term, and

(b) would have been available to him by way of defence or set-off if the proceedings had been brought by the promisee.

(3) The promisor shall also have available to him by way of defence or set-off any matter if –

(a) an express term of the contract provides for it to be available to him in proceedings brought by the third party, and

(b) it would have been available to him by way of defence or set-off if the proceedings had been brought by the promisee.

(4) The promisor shall also have available to him –

(a) by way of defence or set-off any matter, and

(b) by way of counterclaim

any matter not arising from the contract, that would have been available to him by way of defence or set-off or, as the case may be, by way of counterclaim against the third party if the third party had been a party to the contract.

(5) Subsections (2) and (4) are subject to any express term of the contract as to the matters that are not to be available to the promisor by way of defence, set-off or counterclaim.

(6) Where in any proceedings brought against him a third party seeks in reliance on section 1 to enforce a term of a contract (including, in particular, a term purporting to exclude or limit liability), he may not do so if he could not have done so (whether by reason of any particular circumstances relating to him or otherwise) had he been a party to the contract.

4. Section 1 does not affect any right of the promisee to enforce any term of the contract.

5. Where under section 1 a term of a contract is enforceable by a third party, and the promisee has recovered from the promisor a sum in respect of –

(a) the third party's loss in respect of the term, or

(b) the expense to the promisee of making good to the third party the default of the promisor, then, in any proceedings brought in reliance on that section by the third party, the court or arbitral tribunal shall reduce any award to the third party to such extent as it thinks appropriate to take account of the sum recovered by the promisee.

6. – (1) Section 1 confers no rights on a third party in the case of a contract on a bill of exchange, promissory note or other negotiable instrument.

(2) Section 1 confers no rights on a third party in the case of any contract binding on a company and its members under section 33 of the Companies Act 2006 (effect of company's constitution).

(2A) Section 1 confers no rights on a third party in the case of any incorporation document of a limited liability partnership or any agreement (express or implied) between the members of a limited liability partnership, or between a limited liability partnership and its members, that determines the mutual rights and duties of the members and their rights and duties in relation to the limited liability partnership.

(3) Section 1 confers no right on a third party to enforce –

(a) any term of a contract of employment against an employee,

(b) any term of a worker's contract against a worker (including a home worker), or

(c) any term of a relevant contract against an agency worker …

(5) Section 1 confers no rights on a third party in the case of –

(a) a contract for the carriage of goods by sea, or

(b) a contract for the carriage of goods by rail or road, or for the carriage of cargo by air, which is subject to the rules of the appropriate international transport convention, except that a third party may in reliance on that section avail himself of an exclusion or limitation of liability in such a contract.

(6) In subsection (5) '*contract for the carriage of goods by sea*' means a contract of carriage –

(a) contained in or evidenced by a bill of lading, sea waybill or a corresponding electronic transaction, or

(b) under or for the purposes of which there is given an undertaking which is contained in a ship's delivery order or a corresponding electronic transaction …

7. – (1) Section 1 does not affect any right or remedy of a third party that exists or is available apart from this Act.

(2) Section 2(2) of the Unfair Contract Terms Act 1977 (restriction on 1977 c. 50. exclusion etc. of liability for negligence) shall not apply where the negligence consists of the breach of an obligation arising from a term of a contract and the person seeking to enforce it is a third party acting in reliance on section 1 …

8. – (1) Where –

(a) a right under section 1 to enforce a term ('the substantive term') is subject to a term providing for the submission of disputes to arbitration ('the arbitration agreement'), and

(b) the arbitration agreement is an agreement in writing for the purposes of Part I of the Arbitration Act 1996, the third party shall be treated for the purposes of that Act as a party to the arbitration agreement as regards disputes between himself and the promisor relating to the enforcement of the substantive term by the third party.

(2) Where –

(a) a third party has a right under section 1 to enforce a term providing for one or more descriptions of dispute between the third party and the promisor to be submitted to arbitration ('the arbitration agreement'),

(b) the arbitration agreement is an agreement in writing for the purposes of Part I of the Arbitration Act 1996, and

(c) the third party does not fall to be treated under subsection (1) as a party to the arbitration agreement,

the third party shall, if he exercises the right, be treated for the purposes of that Act as a party to the arbitration agreement in relation to the matter with respect to which the right is exercised, and be treated as having been so immediately before the exercise of the right.

It will be seen that s 1 of this Act provides for a third party to have an enforceable right under a contract where that was the intention of the parties. That intention can be express, or it can be presumed from the fact that the contract purports to confer a benefit, unless the court is satisfied that the benefit was not intended to be legally enforceable. The burden of proving this will, presumably, fall on the party arguing against enforceability. This is the implication of the confirmation in *Nisshin Shipping Co Ltd v Cleaves & Co Ltd* [2003] EWHC 2602; [2004] 1 Lloyd's Rep 38 that the Act creates a rebuttable presumption in favour of third-party enforceability.

Nisshin Shipping Co Ltd v Cleaves & Co Ltd [2003] EWHC 2602; [2004] 1 Lloyd's Rep 38

Facts: Charterparties between N and others, negotiated by C as agents for N, contained a provision for commission to be paid to C and for disputes to be referred to arbitration. N withheld commission. C argued that the dispute should go to arbitration on the basis that, applying the 1999 Act, the clauses in the charterparties were for the benefit of C and intended to be enforceable by them.

Held: The clauses were clearly intended to benefit C and there was a rebuttable presumption, as a result of s 1 of the 1999 Act, that this benefit was intended to be legally enforceable. Since the presumption had not been rebutted, the combined effect of ss 1 and 8 of the Act was that C was entitled to insist on arbitration.

Colman J:

21. It is accepted by Miss Philippa Hopkins, on behalf of Cleaves, that the brokers were not parties to the arbitration agreements as a matter of construction of those clauses. Her case is that the effect of s. 8 of the 1999 Act is to impose the arbitration clauses on the owners and the brokers as the means of enforcement of the commission benefit conferred by the commission clause. I shall have to consider this submission more fully when I come to discuss the effect of s. 8. However, for the purposes of the submission in relation to absence of intention to confer a benefit, the wording of the arbitration clauses is, in my judgment, of little or no materiality. First, although the parties to the charterparties clearly expressed their mutual intention that *their* disputes should be arbitrated, that mutual intention is entirely consistent with a mutual intention that the brokers should be obliged to recover their commission by court action rather than by arbitration. Secondly, if, on the proper construction of the 1999 Act, the third party is obliged to enforce the commission benefit by arbitration, even where the agreement does not on its proper construction provide for any participants in an arbitration other than the parties to the main contract, identification of the intention to be imputed to the parties as to enforceability of the third party commission benefit clearly has to take this into account. That is to say, if, as a matter of law, it makes no difference to the broker's ability to enforce his right to commission benefit that no express provision is made for this in the arbitration agreement, the strength of any inference derived from the absence of such express provision could be little more than negligible.

22. Secondly, it is argued by Mr. Ashcroft on behalf of Nisshin that there is no positive indication in the charterparties that the parties did intend the brokers to have enforceable rights. There is no suggestion in those contracts that the owners and charterers were mutually in agreement that the brokers should be entitled to claim against the owners as if they were parties to the contract.

23. It is to be noted that s. 1(2) of the 1999 Act does not provide that sub-s. 1(b) is disapplied unless on a proper construction of the contract it appears that the parties intended that the benefit term should be enforceable by the third party. Rather it provides that sub-s. 1(b) is disapplied if, on a proper construction, it appears that the parties did not intend third party enforcement. In other words, if the contract is neutral on this question, sub-s. (2) does not disapply sub-s. 1(b). Whether the contract does express a mutual intention that the third party should not be entitled to enforce the benefit conferred on him or is merely neutral is a matter of construction having regard to all relevant circumstances. The purpose and background of the Law Commission's recommendations in relation to sub-s. (2) are explained in a paper by Professor Andrew Burrows who, as a member of the Law Commission, made a major contribution to the drafting of the bill as enacted. He wrote at [2000] L.M.C.L.Q. 540 at p 544:

> 'The second test therefore uses a rebuttable presumption of intention. In doing so, it copies the New Zealand Contracts (Privity) Act, 1982, s. 4, which has used the same approach. It is this rebuttable presumption that provides the essential balance between sufficient certainty for contracting parties and the flexibility required for the reform to deal fairly with a huge range of different situations. The presumption is based on the idea that, if you ask yourself, 'When is it that parties are likely to have intended to confer rights on a third party to enforce a term, albeit that they have not expressly conferred that right', the answer will be: 'Where the term purports to confer a benefit on an expressly identified third party'. That then sets up the presumption. But the presumption can be rebutted if, as a matter of ordinary contractual interpretation, there is something else indicating that the parties did not intend such a right to be given'.

24. In the present case, apart from Mr. Ashcroft's third point, the charterparties are indeed neutral in the sense that they do not express any intention contrary to the entitlement of the brokers to enforce the commission term.

> '[Colman J then considered the third argument, which was that the parties had intended to create a trust, with the brokers as beneficiary, but only enforceable by the charterers, and that this indicated an intention that the brokers should not be able to enforce the contract directly.]'

31. This proposition is, in my judgment, entirely unsustainable. The fact that prior to the 1999 Act it would be the mutual intention that the only available facility for enforcement would be deployed by the broker does not lead to the conclusion that, once an additional statutory facility for enforcement had been introduced, the broker would not be entitled to use it, but would instead be confined to the use of the preexisting procedure. Indeed, quite apart from the complete lack of any logical basis for such an inference, the very cumbersome and inconvenient nature of the procedure based on the trustee relationship (described by Lord Wright as a 'cumbrous fiction') would point naturally to the preferred use by the broker of the right to sue directly provided by the 1999 Act. Not only would that original procedure be inconvenient, but it might involve risk that the broker would be prevented from recovering his commission, for example, in a case where the charterer had been dissolved in its place of incorporation or where, in the absence of co-operation by the charterer, proceedings had to be served on it outside the jurisdiction and service could not be effected. There are therefore very strong grounds pointing against any mutual intention to confine the brokers to the old procedure and to deny them the right to rely on the 1999 Act.

32. I therefore reject the third ground relied upon by Nisshin. In so doing I reach the same conclusion as the arbitrators.

33. It follows that Cleaves are entitled to enforce the commission clauses in their own right by reason of s. 1 of the 1999 Act.

The approach taken in the above case was confirmed by the Court of Appeal in *Laemthong International Lines Co Ltd v Artis (The Laemthong Glory) (No 2)* [2005] EWCA Civ 519; [2005] 1 Lloyd's Rep 688. Subsequent cases have tended to rely on the analysis of s 1(1)(b) by Lindsay J in *Prudential Assurance Co Ltd v Ayres* [2007] EWHC 775 (although his decision was overturned by the Court of Appeal on grounds not affecting this analysis) where he stated at [28]:

> It thus seems to me that s.1(1)(b) is satisfied if on a true construction of the term in question its sense has the effect of conferring a benefit on the third party in question. There is within s.1(1)(b) no requirement that the benefit on the third party shall be the predominant purpose or intent behind the term or that it denies the applicability of s.1(1)(b) if a benefit is conferred on someone other than the third party.

In practice, courts have been cautious about finding the existence of an enforceable benefit, as exemplified by the approach of Clarke J in *Dolphin Aviation v Sveriges* [2009] EWHC 716 at [74]:

> **74.** A contract does not purport to confer a benefit on a third party simply because the position of that third party will be improved if the contract is performed. The reference in the section to the term purporting to 'confer' a benefit seems to me to connote that the language used by the parties shows that one of the purposes of their bargain (rather than one of its incidental effects if performed) was to benefit the third party.

The intention to confer a benefit must be clear. The presumption in the section does not relate to the intention to confer a benefit, but only as to whether such a benefit was intended to be legally enforceable.

5.3.1 Changing the agreement

The standard position that parties are entitled, by mutual agreement (supported by consideration etc.), to change their contract, or bring it to an end whenever they wish, is to some extent altered by the Act. The relevant provision is s 2, above. As will be seen, this allows the parties specifically to preserve their right to modify the agreement (s 2(3)). In the absence of a specific preservation of the right to modify, and provided that the conditions set out in s 2(1), involving either 'assent' or 'reliance', are satisfied, the third party's rights will not be capable of rescission or alteration by the parties to the contract.

5.3.2 Defences

Where the third party is taking action, s 3 primarily deals with the defences available to the promisor. Its effect is that in any action by the third party, the promisor can:

- rely on any defence that would have been available as against the promisee (s 3(2));
- if the contracting parties have so agreed, rely on a right of set-off arising from other dealings between them and which would have been available in an action by the promisee (s 3(3));
- rely on any right of defence, set-off, or counterclaim arising from other dealings between the promisor and the third party (s 3(4)); or
- if sued by the third party for negligent performance, rely on an exclusion clause, without its effect being limited by s 2(2) of the Unfair Contract Terms Act 1977 (for which, see Chapter 7, at 7.3.2.1) (s 7(2)).

Section 3(6) also makes it clear that where a third party, who is being sued, seeks to rely on a clause in a contract between two other parties, the third party will only be able to enforce the term if s/he could have done so had s/he been a party to the contract. Section 5 deals with double liability issues.

5.3.3 Exceptions

The types of contract that fall outside the scope of the Act are listed in s 6. Note that although certain types of carriage contract are excluded, this does not apply to third-party reliance on an exclusion clause. The situation which arose in *The Eurymedon* [1975] AC 154 (below, at 5.4.4) might now be dealt with under the Act.

5.4 Common law 'exceptions' to privity of contract

The common law developed a number of ways in which the doctrine of privity of contract could be circumvented (and, although it is commonplace to describe these methods as exceptions to the doctrine of privity of contract, many provide a way to sidestep the doctrine of privity of contract rather than directly challenging it). These are not abolished by the Contract (Rights of Third Parties) Act 1999 Act, nor are they necessarily redundant. As has been noted, the Act does not apply to all contracts. There may also be situations where the Act will not apply on the facts but one of the common law 'exceptions' might be used. These must be considered even if some of them now only justify fairly brief discussion.

5.4.1 Damages on behalf of another

If A and B have contractually agreed with each other that A will provide goods or services that will benefit C and A breaks the contract, can B recover damages that reflect C's loss? If so, is A obliged to hand over any such damages recovered to C? The starting point for answering these questions is *Jackson v Horizon Holidays*.

Jackson v Horizon Holidays [1975] 1 WLR 1468 (CA)

Facts: A father booked a holiday for himself and his family (ie, his wife and three small children), at a cost of about £1,200. The holiday was very unsatisfactory and the father recovered damages for breach of contract. The trial judge refused to award damages for the distress and discomfort of the rest of the family but awarded the father a total of £1,100. The holiday company appealed against the level of damages.

Held: Upholding the judge's award, the damages awarded to the father could take account of the distress and discomfort suffered by the rest of the family.

Lord Denning MR: In *Jarvis v Swans Tours Ltd* [1973] QB 233, it was held by this court that damages for the loss of a holiday may include not only the difference in value between what was promised and what was obtained, but also damages for mental distress, inconvenience, upset, disappointment and frustration caused by the loss of the holiday. The judge directed himself in accordance with the judgments in that case. He eventually awarded a sum of £1,100. Horizon Holidays Ltd appealed. They say it was far too much.

The judge did not divide up the £1,100. Counsel has made suggestions about it. Mr Cheyne for Horizon Holidays suggests that the judge gave £100 for diminution in value and £1,000 for the mental distress. But Mr Davies for Mr Jackson suggested that the judge gave £600 for the diminution in value and £500 for the mental distress. If I were inclined myself to speculate, I think Mr Davies' suggestion may well be right. The judge took the cost of the holiday at £1,200. The family only had about half the value of it. Divide it by two and you get £600. Then add £500 for the mental distress.

On this question a point of law arises. The judge said that he could only consider the mental distress to Mr Jackson himself, and that he could not consider the distress to his wife and children. He said:

> 'The damages are the plaintiff's. ... I cannot consider the effect upon his mind of the wife's discomfort, vexation, and the like, although I cannot award a sum which represents her own vexation'.

Mr Davies, for Mr Jackson, disputes that proposition. He submits that damages can be given not only for the leader of the party – in this case, Mr Jackson's own distress, discomfort and vexation – but also for that of the rest of the party.

We have had an interesting discussion as to the legal position when one person makes a contract for the benefit of a party. In this case it was a husband making a contract for the benefit of himself, his wife and children. Other cases readily come to mind. A host makes a contract with a restaurant for a dinner for himself and his friends. The vicar makes a contract for a coach trip for the choir. In all these cases there is only one person who makes the contract. It is the husband, the host or the vicar, as the case may be. Sometimes he pays the whole price himself. Occasionally he may get a contribution from the others. But in any case it is he who makes the contract. It would be a fiction to say that the contract was made by all the family, or all the guests, or all the choir, and that he was only an agent for them. Take this very case. It would be absurd to say that the twins of three years old were parties to the contract or that the father was making the contract on their behalf as if they were principals. It would equally be a mistake to say that in any of these instances there was a trust. The transaction bears no resemblance to a trust. There was no trust fund and no trust property. No, the real truth is that in each instance, the father, the host or the vicar, was making a contract himself for the benefit of the whole party. In short, a contract by one for the benefit of third persons.

What is the position when such a contract is broken? At present the law says that the only one who can sue is the one who made the contract. None of the rest of the party can sue, even though the contract was made for their benefit. But when that one does sue, what damages can he recover? Is he limited to his own loss? Or can he recover for the others? Suppose the holiday firm puts the family into a hotel which is only half built and the visitors have to sleep on the floor? Or suppose the restaurant is fully booked and the guests have to go away, hungry and angry, having spent so much on fares to get there? Or suppose the coach leaves the choir stranded halfway and they have to hire cars to get home? None of them individually can sue. Only the father, the host or the vicar can sue. He can, of course, recover his own damages. But can he not recover for the others? I think he can. The case comes within the principle stated by Lush LJ in *Lloyd's v Harper* (1880) 16 ChD 290, 321:

> 'I consider it to be an established rule of law that where a contract is made with A for the benefit of B, A can sue on the contract for the benefit of B, and recover all that B could have recovered if the contract had been made with B himself'.

It has been suggested that Lush LJ was thinking of a contract in which A was trustee for B. But I do not think so. He was a common lawyer speaking of common law. His words were quoted with considerable approval by Lord Pearce in *Beswick v Beswick* [1968] AC 58, 88. I have myself often quoted them. I think they should be accepted as correct, at any rate so long as the law forbids the third person themself from suing for damages. It is the only way in which a just result can be achieved. Take the instance I have put. The guests ought to recover from the restaurant their wasted fares. The choir ought to recover the cost of hiring the taxis home. Then is no one to recover from them except the one who made the contract for their benefit? He should be able to recover the expense to which he has been put, and pay it over to them. Once recovered, it will be money had and received to their use. (They might even, if desired, be joined as plaintiffs.) If he can recover for the expense, he should also be able to recover for the discomfort, vexation and upset which the whole party have suffered by reason of the breach of contract, recompensing them accordingly out of what he recovers.

Applying the principles to this case, I think that the figure of £1,100 was about right. It would, I think, have been excessive if it had been awarded only for the damage suffered by Mr Jackson himself. But when extended to his wife and children, I do not think it is excessive. People look forward to a holiday. They expect the promises to be fulfilled. When it fails, they are greatly disappointed and upset. It is difficult to assess in terms of money; but it is the task of the judges to do the best they can. I see no reason to interfere with the total award of £1,100. I would therefore dismiss the appeal.

Orr LJ concurred with Lord Denning's judgment; James LJ came to the same conclusion but on the basis that the father's own loss was increased by the problems suffered by the rest of the family. The view of the majority appeared to open the door to a more general possibility of a claimant being able to claim damages for a third party's loss. In *Woodar v Wimpey* the House of Lords had the opportunity to consider whether this should apply to commercial contracts.

Woodar Investment Development Ltd v Wimpey Construction UK Ltd [1980] 1 WLR 277 (HL)

Facts: In February, the purchasers, W.C. Ltd, entered into a contract to buy certain land from the vendors, W.I.D. Ltd. The purchase price was £850,000 of which £150,000 was to be paid on completion to T.T. Ltd. By a special condition the purchasers reserved the right to rescind if compulsory purchase proceedings were commenced in relation to the land. In March the purchasers sent the vendors a notice purporting to rescind the contract under that condition on the ground that the Secretary of State for the Environment had commenced the procedure for compulsory acquisition of part of the land. At the date of the contract both parties knew that three years previously the minister had given the then owner notice of a draft compulsory purchase order. In November a compulsory purchase order was made. The vendors brought an action against the purchasers for a declaration that the condition gave them no right to rescind. By their defence the purchasers contended that on the true construction of the condition the notice of rescission was valid. In a second action the vendors claimed damages for breach of contract by the purchasers in serving the notice and delivering their defence.

The trial judge and the Court of Appeal held that the purchasers were not entitled to invoke the condition and by doing so had wrongfully repudiated the contract, and that they were, accordingly, liable for damages. The purchasers appealed.

Held: (by a 3 to 2 majority) The purchasers' action did not constitute repudiation and so the issue of damages did not arise. If it had, the vendors would not have been able to recover the sum which was to be paid to the third party, T.T.

Lord Wilberforce: The second issue in this appeal is one of damages. Both courts below have allowed Woodar to recover substantial damages in respect of condition I under which £150,000 was payable by Wimpey to Transworld Trade Ltd on completion. On the view which I take of the repudiation issue, this question does not require decision, but in view of the un-satisfactory state in which the law would be if the Court of Appeal's decision were to stand I must add three observations.

1. The majority of the Court of Appeal followed, in the case of Goff LJ with expressed reluctance, its previous decision in *Jackson v Horizon Holidays Ltd* [1975] 3 All ER 92. I am not prepared to dissent from the

actual decision in that case. It may be supported either as a broad decision on the measure of damages (per James LJ) or possibly as an example of a type of contract, examples of which are persons contracting for family holidays, ordering meals in restaurants for a party, hiring a taxi for a group, calling for special treatment. As I suggested in *New Zealand Shipping Co Ltd v A M Satterthwaite & Co Ltd* [1974] 1 All ER 1015, there are many situations of daily life which do not fit neatly into conceptual analysis, but which require some flexibility in the law of contract. *Jackson's* case may well be one.

I cannot agree with the basis on which Lord Denning MR put his decision in that case. The extract on which he relied from the judgment of Lush LJ in *Lloyd's v Harper* (1880) 16 ChD 290 was part of a passage in which Lush LJ was stating as an 'established rule of law' that an agent (sc an insurance broker) may sue on a contract made by him on behalf of the principal (sc the assured) if the contract gives him such a right, and is no authority for the proposition required in *Jackson's* case, still less for the proposition, required here, that if Woodar made a contract for a sum of money to be paid to Transworld, Woodar can, without showing that it has itself suffered loss or that Woodar was agent or trustee for Transworld, sue for damages for non-payment of that sum. That would certainly not be an established rule of law, nor was it quoted as such authority by Lord Pearce in *Beswick v Beswick* [1967] 2 All ER 1197.

2. Assuming that *Jackson's* case was correctly decided (as above), it does not carry the present case, where the factual situation is quite different. I respectfully think therefore that the Court of Appeal need not, and should not have followed it.

3. Whether in a situation such as the present, viz where it is not shown that Woodar was agent or trustee for Transworld, or that Woodar itself sustained any loss, Woodar can recover any damages at all, or any but nominal damages, against Wimpey, and on what principle, is, in my opinion, a question of great doubt and difficulty, no doubt open in this House, but one on which I prefer to reserve my opinion.'

Lord Russell: 'There is no question on this appeal as to quantum of damage save under the heading of damages for breach of special condition I, under which Wimpey agreed on completion of the sale to pay £150,000 to Transworld, a Hong Kong company. Transworld was in some way connected with Mr Cornwell, who died before action. No evidence connects Transworld with Woodar, the party to the contract. No evidence suggests that Woodar could suffer any damage from a failure by Wimpey to pay £150,000 to Transworld. It is clear on the authority of *Beswick v Beswick* that Woodar on completion could have secured an order for specific performance of the agreement to pay £150,000 to Transworld, which the latter could have enforced. That would not have been an order for payment to Woodar, nor (contrary to the form of order below) to Woodar for the use and benefit of Transworld. There was no suggestion of trust or agency of Woodar for Transworld. If it were necessary to decide the point, which in the light of the views of the majority of your Lordships on the first point it is not, I would have concluded that no more than nominal damages had been established by Woodar as a consequence of the refusal by Wimpey to pay Transworld in the light of the law of England as it now stands. I would not have thought that the reasoning of Oliver J in *Radford v De Froberville* [1978] 1 All ER 33 supported Woodar's case for substantial damages. Nor do I think that on this point the Court of Appeal was correct in thinking it was constrained by *Jackson v Horizon Holidays Ltd* to award substantial damages. I do not criticize the outcome of that case: the plaintiff had bought and paid for a high class family holiday; he did not get it, and therefore he was entitled to substantial damages for the failure to supply *him* with one. It is to be observed that the order of the Court of Appeal as drawn up did not suggest that any part of the damages awarded to him were 'for the use and benefit of' any member of his family. It was a special case quite different from the instant case on the Transworld point.

I would not, my Lords, wish to leave the *Jackson* case without adverting with respectful disapproval to the reliance there placed by Lord Denning MR, not for the first time, on an extract taken from the judgment of Lush LJ in *Lloyd's v Harper* (1880) 16 ChD 290. That case was plainly a case in which a trustee or agent was enforcing the rights of a beneficiary or principal, there being therefore a fiduciary relationship. Lord Denning MR in *Jackson's* case said this:

> 'The case comes within the principle stated by Lush LJ in *Lloyd's v Harper*. ... I consider it to be an established rule of law that where a contract is made with A for the benefit of B, A can sue on the contract for the benefit of B, and recover all that B could have recovered if the contract had been made with B himself. [Lord Denning continued:] It has been suggested that Lush LJ was thinking of a contract in which A was trustee for B. But I do not think so. He was a common lawyer speaking of the common law.'

I have already indicated that in all the other judgments the matter proceeded on a fiduciary relationship between A and B; and Lush LJ in the same passage made it plain that he did also, for he said:

> 'It is true that the person [B] who employed him [the broker A] has a right, if he pleases, to take action himself and sue upon the contract made by the broker for him, for he [B] *is a principal party to the contract*' (Emphasis mine).

To ignore that passage is to divorce the passage quoted by Lord Denning MR from the fiduciary context in which it was uttered, the context of principal and agent, a field with which it may be assumed Lush LJ was familiar. I venture to suggest that the brief quotation should not be used again as support for a proposition which Lush LJ cannot have intended to advance.

As well as disapproving of Lord Denning's use of *Lloyd's v Harper*, this decision appeared to have largely limited the approach taken in *Jackson* to non-commercial situations, where one person, as part of a social or family arrangement, makes a booking on behalf of a group. On that basis, it appeared that there was little general scope in commercial contracts for a contracting party to recover damages on behalf of another. In 1993, however, the House of Lords opened the door again to the possibility of damages being recovered for a third party, even in a commercial situation.

St. Martins Property Corporation Ltd v Sir Robert McAlpine Ltd [1994] 1 AC 85 (HL)

[NB This case involved appeals in two separate actions and is found in the law reports under the name of the other action – *Linden Gardens Ltd v Lenesta Sludge Disposals Ltd*.]

Facts: There was a building contract between a developer, C ('Corporation' in the report of the case), and a construction company, M ('McAlpine'). Before the work was complete, C assigned its interest to I ('Investments'). This assignment did not, however, create any contractual relationship between I and M, since it was done without M's consent. Defective work, carried out after the assignment, cost about £800,000 to repair. C sued but it was argued that it had suffered no loss because at the time of M's breach of contract, C's interests had been assigned to I.

Held: Since it was known from the start that the building would, in the end, be occupied by a third party, rather than C, M could foresee that defective work would cause loss to a third party. In the circumstances, C could recover damages on behalf of I.

Lord Browne-Wilkinson:

(6) What is the measure of damages in the claim by Corporation?

McAlpine accept that, since the attempted assignment by Corporation of its rights under the contract to Investments was ineffective, Corporation has retained those rights and is entitled to judgment against McAlpine for any breach of contract. But, McAlpine submits, Corporation is only entitled to nominal damages. Corporation has suffered no loss: it had parted with its interest in the property (and therefore with the works when completed) before any breach of the building contract; moreover Corporation received full value for that interest on its disposal to Investments. Therefore, it is said, neither of the plaintiffs has any right to substantial damages: Investments has incurred damage (being the cost of rectifying the faulty work) but has no cause of action; Corporation has a cause of action but has suffered no loss. If this is right, in the words of my noble and learned friend, Lord Keith of Kinkel in *GUS Property Management Ltd v Littlewoods Mail Order Stores Ltd*, 1982 S.L.T. 533, 538, 'the claim to damages would disappear ... into some legal black hole, so that the wrongdoer escaped scot-free'.

[Having considered various arguments put forward by counsel for McAlpine, Lord Browne-Wilkinson stated that in his view:] 'the facts of this case bring it within the class of exceptions to the general rule to which Lord Diplock referred in *The Albazero*.

In *The Albazero* Lord Diplock said [1977] A.C. 774,846:

> 'Nevertheless, although it is exceptional at common law that a plaintiff in an action for breach of contract, although he himself has not suffered any loss, should be entitled to recover damages on behalf of some third person who is not a party to the action for a loss which that third person has sustained, the notion that there may be circumstances in which he is entitled to do so was not entirely unfamiliar to the common law and particularly to that part of it which, under the influence of Lord Mansfield and his successors, Lord Ellenborough and Lord Tenterden, had been appropriated from the law merchant. 'I have already mentioned the right of the bailee, which has been recognised from the earliest period of our law, to sue in detinue or trespass for loss or damage to his bailor's goods although he cannot be compelled by his bailor to do so and he is not himself liable to the bailor for the loss or damage: *The Winkfield* [1902] P. 42. Nevertheless, he becomes accountable to his bailor for the proceeds of the judgment in an action by his bailor for money had and received. So too the doctrine of subrogation in the case of insurers, which was adopted from the law merchant by the common law in the eighteenth century, involved the concept of the nominal party to an action at common law suing for a loss which he had not himself sustained and being accountable to his insurer for the proceeds to the extent that he had been indemnified against the loss by the insurer. In this instance of a plaintiff being able to recover as damages for breach of contract for the benefit of a third person a loss which that person had sustained and he had not, the insurer is entitled to compel an assured to whom he has paid a total or partial indemnity to bring the action. A third example, once again in the field of mercantile law, is the right of an assured to recover in an action on a policy of insurance upon goods the full amount of loss or damage to them, on behalf of anyone who may be entitled to an interest in the goods at the time when the loss or damage occurs, provided that it appears from the terms of the policy that he intended to cover their interests'.

In addition, the decision in *The Albazero* itself established a further exception. This House was concerned with the status of a long-established principle based on the decision in *Dunlop v Lambert* (1839) 6 Cl. & F. 600 that a consignor of goods who had parted with the property in the goods before the date of breach could even so recover substantial damages for the failure to deliver the goods. Lord Diplock, identified, at p 847, the rationale of that rule as being:

> 'The only way in which I find it possible to rationalise the rule in *Dunlop v Lambert* so that it may fit into the pattern of the English law is to treat it as an application of the principle, accepted also in relation to policies of insurance upon goods, that in a commercial contract concerning goods where it is in the contemplation of the parties that the proprietary interests in the goods may be transferred from one owner to another after the contract has been entered into and before the breach which causes loss or damage to the goods, an original party to the contract, if such be the intention of them both, is to be treated in law as having entered into the contract for the benefit of all persons who have or may acquire an interest in the goods before they are lost or

damaged, and is entitled to recover by way of damages for breach of contract the actual loss sustained by those for whose benefit the contract is entered into'.

In *The Albazero* it was held that the principle in *Dunlop v Lambert* no longer applied to goods consigned under a bill of lading because both the property in the goods and the cause of action for breach of the contract of carriage passes to the consignee or endorsee by reason of the consignment or endorsement; therefore, since the consignee or endorsee will in any event be entitled to enforce the contract direct there is no ground on which one can impute to the parties an intention that the consignor is entering into the contract for the benefit of others who will acquire the property in the goods but no right of action for breach of contract.

However, this House was careful to limit its decision to cases of carriage by sea under a bill of lading, leaving in force the principle in *Dunlop v Lambert* in relation to other contracts for the carriage of goods where such automatic assignment of the rights of action for breach does not take place. Lord Diplock, after the passage referring to the exceptions which I have already quoted, said, at pp 846–847:

> 'My Lords, in the light of these other exceptions, particularly in the field of mercantile law, to the general rule of English law that apart from nominal damages the plaintiff can only recover in an action for breach of contract the actual loss he has himself sustained, I do not think that the fact that the rule which it is generally accepted was laid down by this House in *Dunlop v Lambert*, 6 Cl. & F. 600 would add one more exception would justify your Lordships in declaring the rule to be no longer law. Nor do I think that the almost complete absence of reliance on the rule by litigants in actions between 1839 and 1962 provides a sufficient reason for abolishing it entirely. The development of the law of negligence since 1839 does not provide a complete substituted remedy for some types of loss caused by breach of a contract of carriage. Late delivery is the most obvious example of these. The Bills of Lading Act 1855 and the subsequent development of the doctrine laid down in *Brandt v Liverpool, Brazil and River Plate Steam Navigation Co Ltd* [1924] 1 K.B. 575, have reduced the scope and utility of the rule in *Dunlop v Lambert* ... where goods are carried under a bill of lading. But the rule extends to all forms of carriage including carriage by sea itself where no bill of lading has been issued, and there may still be occasional cases in which the rule would provide a remedy where no other would be available to a person sustaining loss which under a rational legal system ought to be compensated by the person who has caused it. For my part, I am not persuaded that your Lordships ought to go out of your way to jettison the rule'.

In my judgment the present case falls within the rationale of the exceptions to the general rule that a plaintiff can only recover damages for his own loss. The contract was for a large development of property which, to the knowledge of both Corporation and McAlpine, was going to be occupied, and possibly purchased, by third parties and not by Corporation itself. Therefore it could be foreseen that damage caused by a breach would cause loss to a later owner and not merely to the original contracting party, Corporation. As in contracts for the carriage of goods by land, there would be no automatic vesting in the occupier or owners of the property for the time being who sustained the loss of any right of suit against McAlpine. On the contrary, McAlpine had specifically contracted that the rights of action under the building contract *could* not without McAlpine's consent be transferred to third parties who became owners or occupiers and might suffer loss. In such a case, it seems to me proper, as in the case of the carriage of goods by land, to treat the parties as having entered into the contract on the footing that Corporation would be entitled to enforce contractual rights for the benefit of those who suffered from defective performance but who, under the terms of the contract, could not acquire any right to hold McAlpine liable for breach. It is truly a case in which the rule provides 'a remedy where no other would be available to a person sustaining loss which under a rational legal system ought to be compensated by the person who has caused it'.

Mr. Fernyhough submitted that it would be wrong to distort the law in order to meet what he described as being an exceptional case. He said that this was a one-off or exceptional case since the development was sold before any breach of contract had occurred and there was an express contractual prohibition on assignment. He submitted that to give Corporation a right to substantial damages in this case would produce chaos when applied to other cases where the contractors have entered into direct warranties with the ultimate purchasers of the individual parts of a development. I am not impressed by these submissions. I am far from satisfied that this is a one off or exceptional case. We are concerned with standard forms of building contracts which prohibit the assignment of the benefit of building contracts to the ultimate purchasers. In the prolonged period of recession in the property market which this country has experienced many developments have had to be sold off before completion, thereby producing the risk that the ownership of the property may have become divided from the right to sue on the building contract at a date before any breach occurs. As to the warranties given by contractors to subsequent purchasers, they will not, in my judgment, give rise to difficulty. If, pursuant to the terms of the original building contract, the contractors have undertaken liability to the ultimate purchasers to remedy defects appearing after they acquired the property, it is manifest the case will not fall within the rationale of *Dunlop v Lambert*, 6 Cl. & F. 600. If the ultimate purchaser is given a direct cause of action against the contractor (as is the consignee or endorsee under a bill of lading) the case falls outside the rationale of the rule. The original building owner will not be entitled to recover damages for loss suffered by others who can themselves sue for such loss. I would therefore hold that Corporation is entitled to substantial damages for any breach by McAlpine of the building contract.

The majority of the House of Lords adopted Lord Browne-Wilkinson's analysis. A broader approach was put forward by Lord Griffiths, more directly challenging the assumption that the normal position in this type of situation should be that the promisee can only recover nominal damages. He supported this with the following example (at pp 96–97):

I cannot accept that in a contract of this nature, namely for work, labour and the supply of materials, the recovery of more than nominal damages for breach of contract is dependent upon the plaintiff having a proprietary interest in the subject matter of the contract at the date of breach. In everyday life contracts for work and labour are constantly being placed by those who have no proprietary interest in the subject matter of the contract. To take a common example, the matrimonial home is owned by the wife and the couple's remaining assets are owned by the husband and he is the sole earner. The house requires a new roof and the husband places a contract with a builder to carry out the work. The husband is not acting as agent for his wife; he makes the contract as principal because only he can pay for it. The builder fails to replace the roof properly and the husband has to call in and pay another builder to complete the work. Is it to be said that the husband has suffered no damage because he does not own the property? Such a result would in my view be absurd and the answer is that the husband has suffered loss because he did not receive the bargain for which he had contracted with the first builder and the measure of damages is the cost of securing the performance of that bargain by completing the roof repairs properly by the second builder. To put this simple example closer to the facts of this appeal – at the time the husband employs the builder he owns the house but just after the builder starts work the couple are advised to divide their assets so the husband transfers the house to his wife. This is no concern of the builder whose bargain is with the husband. If the roof turns out to be defective the husband can recover from the builder the cost of putting it right and thus obtain the benefit of the bargain that the builder had promised to deliver. It was suggested in argument that the answer to the example I have given is that the husband could assign the benefit of the contract to the wife. But what if, as in this case, the builder has a clause in the contract forbidding assignment without his consent and refuses to give consent

> as McAlpine has done. It is then said that neither husband nor wife can recover damages; this seems to me to be so unjust a result that the law cannot tolerate it.

Lord Griffiths's approach is more controversial, and arguably runs counter to the prevailing doctrine in relation to contract damages – that is, that contractual damages are awarded for losses actually suffered as the consequence of a breach, not simply for the breach itself. When the matter fell to be considered again by the House of Lords in *Panatown Ltd v Alfred McAlpine Construction Ltd*, a minority of the panel would have been prepared to adopt Lord Griffiths's broader approach but the majority was less enthusiastic about Lord Griffiths's broad ground.

Alfred McAlpine Construction Ltd v Panatown Ltd [2001] AC 518 (HL)

Facts: M, a building contractor, entered into a contract with P to construct an office building and car park on land owned by U, a company within the same group of companies as P. The reason for this arrangement was to avoid (legitimately) the payment of VAT. There was also a 'duty of care deed' (DCD) executed between U and M which gave U a right to sue M for negligence in performance of the building contract. The DCD was assignable to those to whom U might later transfer the property. When problems arose, P initiated arbitration proceedings under its contract with M. M sought to argue as a preliminary point that as P had no proprietary interest in the site, it had suffered no loss. The arbitrator held for P; the trial judge for M; and the Court of Appeal for P. M appealed.

Held: (Lords Goff and Millett dissenting) On the facts, P could not succeed on the contract because the existence of the DCD meant that the case was not one where the claim would otherwise fall into the 'black hole' with no party being able to claim. The majority confirmed the 'narrow ground' identified in the *St Martins* case as a possible basis for recovery on behalf of a third party but was sceptical as to Lord Griffiths's 'broader ground'.

Lord Clyde: The justification for the exception to the general rule that one can only sue for damages for a loss which he has himself suffered was explained by Lord Diplock in *The Albazero* [1977] AC 774, 847. His Lordship noted that the scope and utility of what he referred to as the rule in *Dunlop v Lambert*, 6 Cl & F 600 in its application to carriage by sea under a bill of lading had been much reduced by the passing of the Bills of Lading Act 1855 and the subsequent development of the law, but that the rule extended to all forms of carriage, including carriage by sea where there was no bill of lading:

> 'and there may still be occasional cases in which the rule would provide a remedy where no other would be available to a person sustaining loss which under a rational legal system ought to be compensated by the person who has caused it'.

The justification for *The Albazero* exception is thus the necessity of avoiding the disappearance of a substantial claim into what was described by Lord Stewart in *GUS Property Management Ltd v Littlewoods Mail Order Stores Ltd*, 1982 SC(HL) 157, 166 as a legal black hole, an expression subsequently taken up by Lord Keith of Kinkel in this House, at p 177.

In *The Albazero* [1977] AC 774,847 Lord Diplock sought to 'rationalise the rule in *Dunlop v Lambert*' so that it might fit into the pattern of English law. He did so by treating it:

> 'as an application of the principle, accepted also in relation to policies of insurance upon goods, that in a commercial contract concerning goods where it is in the contemplation of the parties that the proprietary interests in the goods may be transferred from one owner to another after the contract has been entered into and before the breach which causes loss or damage to the goods, an original party to the contract, if such be the intention of them both, is to be treated in

law as having entered into the contract for the benefit of all persons who have or may acquire an interest in the goods before they are lost or damaged, and is entitled to recover by way of damages for breach of contract the actual loss sustained by those for whose benefit the contract is entered into'.

It is particularly this passage in Lord Diplock's speech which has given rise to a question discussed in the present appeal whether *The Albazero* exception is a rule of law or is based upon the intention of the parties. The issue was identified by my noble and learned friend, Lord Goff of Chieveley, in his speech in *White v Jones* [1995] 2 AC 207, 267. The problem arises from two phrases in the speech of Lord Diplock the mutual relationship between which may not be immediately obvious. The two phrases, in the reverse order than that in which they appear, are 'is to be treated in law as having entered into the contract' and 'if such be the intention of the parties'. In my view it is preferable to regard it as a solution imposed by the law and not as arising from the supposed intention of the parties, who may in reality not have applied their minds to the point. On the other hand if they deliberately provided for a remedy for a third party it can readily be concluded that they have intended to exclude the operation of the solution which would otherwise have been imposed by law. The terms and provisions of the contract will then require to be studied to see if the parties have excluded the operation of the exception.

That appears to have been the conclusion adopted in *Linden Gardens Trust Ltd v Lenesta Sludge Disposals Ltd; St Martins Property Corpn Ltd v Sir Robert McAlpine Ltd* [1994] 1 AC 85 (the *St Martins* case).

I have no difficulty in holding in the present case that [The *Albazero*] exception cannot apply. As part of the contractual arrangements entered into between Panatown and McAlpine there was a clear contemplation that separate contracts would be entered into by McAlpine, the contracts of the deed of duty of care and the collateral warranties. The duty of care deed and the collateral warranties were of course not in themselves building contracts. But they did form an integral part of the package of arrangements which the employer and the contractor agreed upon and in that respect should be viewed as reflecting the intentions of all the parties engaged in the arrangements that the third party should have a direct cause of action to the exclusion of any substantial claim by the employer, and accordingly that the exception should not apply. There was some dispute upon the difference in substance between the remedies available under the contract and those available under the duty of care deed. Even if it is accepted that in the circumstances of the present case where the eventual issue may relate particularly to matters of reasonable skill and care, the remedies do not absolutely coincide, the express provision of the direct remedy for the third party is fatal to the application of *The Albazero* exception. On a more general approach the difference between a strict contractual basis of claim and a basis of reasonable care makes the express remedy more clearly a substitution for the operation of the exception. Panatown cannot then in the light of these deeds be treated as having contracted with McAlpine for the benefit of the owner or later owners of the land and the exception is plainly excluded.

I turn accordingly to what was referred to in the argument as the broader ground. But the label requires more careful definition. The approach under *The Albazero* exception has been one of recognising an entitlement to sue by the innocent party to a contract which has been breached, where the innocent party is treated as suing on behalf of or for the benefit of some other person or persons, not parties to the contract, who have sustained loss as a result of the breach. In such a case the innocent party to the contract is bound to account to the person suffering the loss for the damages which the former has recovered for the benefit of the latter. But the so-called broader ground involves a significantly different approach. What it proposes is that the innocent party to the contract should recover damages for himself as a compensation for what is seen to be his own loss. In this context no question of accounting to anyone else arises. This approach however seems to me to have been developed into two formulations.

The first formulation, and the seeds of the second, are found in the speech of Lord Griffiths in the *St Martins* case [1994] 1 AC 85, 96. At the outset his Lordship expressed the opinion that Corporation, faced with a breach by McAlpine of their contractual duty to perform the contract with sound materials and with all reasonable skill and care, would be entitled to recover from McAlpine the cost of remedying the defect in the work as the normal measure of damages. He then dealt with two possible objections. First, it should not matter that the work was not being done on property owned by Corporation. Where a husband instructs repairs to the roof of the matrimonial home it cannot be said that he has not suffered damage because he did not own the property. He suffers the damage measured by the cost of a proper completion of the repair:

> 'In cases such as the present the person who places the contract has suffered financial loss because he has to spend money to give him the benefit of the bargain which the defendant had promised but failed to deliver'.
>
> (See p 97.)

The second objection, that Corporation had in fact been reimbursed for the cost of the repairs was answered by the consideration that the person who actually pays for the repairs is of no concern to the party who broke the contract. But Lord Griffiths added, at p 97:

> 'The court will of course wish to be satisfied that the repairs have been or are likely to be carried out but if they are carried out the cost of doing them must fall upon the defendant who broke his contract'.

In the first formulation this approach can be seen as identifying a loss upon the innocent party who needs to instruct the remedial work. That loss is, or may be measured by, the cost of the repair. The essential for this formulation appears to be that the repair work is to be, or at least is likely to be, carried out. This consideration does not appear to be simply relevant to the reasonableness of allowing the damages to be measured by the cost of repair. It is an essential condition for the application of the approach, so as to establish a loss on the part of the plaintiff. Thus far the approach appears to be consistent with principle, and in particular with the principle of privity. It can cover the case where A contracts with B to pay a sum of money to C and B fails to do so. The loss to A is in the necessity to find other funds to pay to C and provided that he is going to pay C, or indeed has done so, he should be able to recover the sum by way of damages for breach of contract from B. If it was evident that A had no intention to pay C, having perhaps changed his mind, then he would not be able to recover the amount from B because he would have sustained no loss, and his damages would at best be nominal.

But there can also be found in Lord Griffiths's speech the idea that the loss is not just constituted by the failure in performance but indeed consists in that failure. This is the 'second formulation'. In relation to the suggestion that the husband who instructs repair work to the roof of his wife's house and has to pay for another builder to make good the faulty repair work has sustained no damage Lord Griffiths observed, at p 97:

> 'Such a result would in my view be absurd and the answer is that the husband has suffered loss because he did not receive the bargain for which he had contracted with the first builder and the measure of damages is the cost of securing the performance of that bargain by completing the roof repairs properly by the second builder'.

That is to say that the fact that the innocent party did not receive the bargain for which he contracted is itself a loss. As Steyn LJ put it in *Darlington Borough Council v Wiltshier Northern Ltd* [1995] 1 WLR 68, 80: 'He suffers a loss of bargain or of expectation interest'. In this more radical formulation it does not matter whether the repairs are or are not carried out, and indeed in the Darlington case that qualification is seen as unnecessary. In that respect the disposal of the damages is treated as *res inter alios acta*. Nevertheless on this approach the intention to repair may cast light on the reasonableness of the measure of damages adopted. In order to follow through this aspect of the second formulation in Lord Griffiths's speech it would be necessary to understand his references to the carrying out of the repairs to be relevant only to that consideration.

I find some difficulty in adopting the second formulation as a sound way forward. First, if the loss is the disappointment at there not being provided what was contracted for, it seems to me difficult to measure that loss by consideration of the cost of repair. A more apt assessment of the compensation for the loss of what was expected should rather be the difference in value between what was contracted for and what was supplied. Secondly, the loss constituted by the supposed disappointment may well not include all the loss which the breach of contract has caused. It may not be able to embrace consequential losses, or losses falling within the second head of *Hadley v Baxendale* 9 Exch 341. The inability of the wife to let one of the rooms in the house caused by the inadequacy of the repair, does not seem readily to be something for which the husband could claim as his loss. Thirdly, there is no obligation on the successful plaintiff to account to anyone who may have sustained actual loss as a result of the faulty performance. Some further mechanism would then be required for the court to achieve the proper disposal of the monies awarded to avoid a double jeopardy. Alternatively, in order to achieve an effective solution, it would seem to be necessary to add an obligation to account on the part of the person recovering the damages. But once that step is taken the approach begins to approximate to *The Albazero* exception. Fourthly, the 'loss' constituted by a breach of contract has usually been recognised as calling for an award of nominal damages, not substantial damages.

Both of these two formulations seek to remedy the problem of the legal black hole. At the heart of the problem is the doctrine of privity of contract which excludes the ready development of a solution along the lines of a *jus quaesitum tertio*. It might well be thought that such a solution would be more direct and simple. In the context of the domestic and familial situations, such as the husband instructing the repairs to the roof of his wife's house, or the holiday which results in disappointment to all the members of the family, the *jus quaesitum tertio* may provide a satisfactory means of redress, enabling compensation to be paid to the people who have suffered the loss. Such an approach is available in Germany: see W Lorenz, 'Contract Beneficiaries in German Law' in The Gradual Convergence: Foreign Ideas, Foreign Influences, and English Law on the Eve of the 21st Century, edited by Markesinis (1994), pp 65, 78, 79. It may also be available in Scotland (*Carmichael v Carmichael's Executrix*, 1920 SC(HL) 195). But we were not asked to adopt it in the present case and so radical a step cannot easily be achieved without legislative action. Since Parliament has recently made some inroad into the principle of privity but has stopped short of admitting a solution to a situation such as the present, it would plainly be inappropriate to enlarge the statutory provision by judicial innovation. The alternative has to be the adoption of what Lord Diplock in *Swain v The Law Society* [1983] 1 AC 598, 611 described as a juristic subterfuge 'to mitigate the effect of the lacuna resulting from the non-recognition of a *jus quaesitum tertio*'. The solution, achieved by the operation of law, may carry with it some element of artificiality and may not be supportable on any clear or single principle. If the entitlement to sue is not to be permitted to the party who has suffered the loss, the law has to treat the person who is entitled to sue as doing so on behalf of the third party. As Lord Wilberforce observed in *Woodar Investment Development Ltd v Wimpey Construction UK Ltd* [1980] 1 WLR 277, 283, 'there are many situations of daily life which do not fit neatly into conceptual analysis, but which require some flexibility in the law of contract'.

It seems to me that a more realistic and practical solution is to permit the contracting party to recover damages for the loss which he and a third party has suffered, being duly accountable to them in respect of their actual loss, than to construct a theoretical loss in law on the part of the contracting party, for which he may be under no duty to account to anyone since it is to be seen as his own loss. The solution is required where the law will not tolerate a loss caused by a breach of contract to go uncompensated through an absence of privity between the party suffering the loss and the party causing it. In such a case, to avoid the legal black hole, the law will deem the innocent party to be claiming on behalf of himself and any others who have suffered loss. It does not matter that he is not the owner of the property affected, nor that he has not himself suffered any economic loss. He sues for all the loss which has been sustained and is accountable to the others to the extent of their particular losses. While it may be that there is no necessary right in the third party to compel the innocent employer to sue the contractor, in the many cases of the domestic or familial situation that consideration should not be a realistic problem. In the commercial field, in relation to the interests of such persons as remoter future proprietors who are not related to the original employer, it may be that a solution by way of collateral warranty would still be required. If there is an anxiety lest the exception would permit an employer to receive excessive damages, that should be set at rest by the recognition of the basic requirement for reasonableness which underlies the quantification of an award of damages.

The problem which has arisen in the present case is one which is most likely to arise in the context of the domestic affairs of a family group or the commercial affairs of a group of companies. How the members of such a group choose to arrange their own affairs among themselves should not be a matter of necessary concern to a third party who has undertaken to one of their number to perform services in which they all have some interest. It should not be a ground of escaping liability that the party who instructed the work should not be the one who sustained the loss or all of the loss which in whole or part has fallen on another member or members of the group. But the resolution of the problem in any particular case has to be reached in light of its own circumstances. In the present case the decision that Panatown should be the employer under the building contract although another company in the group owned the land was made in order to minimise charges of VAT. No doubt thought was given as to the mechanics to be adopted for the building project in order to achieve the course most advantageous to the group. Where for its own purposes a group of companies decides which of its members is to be the contracting party in a project which is of concern and interest to the whole group I should be reluctant to refuse an entitlement to sue on the contract on the ground simply that the member who entered the contract was not the party who suffered the loss on a breach of the contract. But whether such an entitlement is to be admitted must depend upon the arrangements which the group and its members have decided to make both among themselves and with the other party to the contract. In the present case there was a plain and deliberate course adopted whereby the company with the potential risk of loss was given a distinct entitlement directly to sue the contractor and the professional advisers. In the light of such a clear and deliberate course I do not consider that an exception can be admitted to the general rule that substantial damages can only be claimed by a party who has suffered substantial loss.

I agree that the appeal should be allowed.

The fact that the majority in *Panatown* decided the case on the basis of the existence of the DCD means that the decision was not necessarily decisive on the more general issues. It seemed, however, that it was the narrower ground for recovery, rather than Lord Griffiths's broader ground, which was more favoured, at least at that time. By contrast the broad ground gained some support in *Lowick Rose LLP (in liquidation) v Swynson Ltd* [2017] UKSC 32 at [17] from Lord Sumption (cf. Lord Mance at [53]).

The possibility that parties can now, if they so wish, give a third party a direct right of action under the Contracts (Rights of Third Parties) Act 1999 may well mean that the courts will be reluctant to extend this common law exception much further (although compare *BV Nederlandse Industrie van Eiprodukten v Rembrandt Enterprises Inc* [2019] EWCA Civ 596). Whether the Act would have assisted the parties in the cases discussed above is, however, doubted by Harris, Campbell and Halson:

Harris, D, Campbell, D and Halson, R, *Remedies in Contract and Tort*, 2nd edn, 2002, Cambridge: CUP, pp 80–81

The problem addressed by the courts in the above cases was described as being caused by the fact that the party who has a cause of action for breach of contract is not the same as the person who has most immediately suffered the loss caused by that breach. The courts have shown great ingenuity in their attempt to permit recovery by the party who has the benefit of a direct cause of action. A different approach has been taken by the legislature, which has introduced a general right of action for third parties. In other words the party who has undoubtedly suffered the loss is given a new cause of action. The Contracts (Rights of Third Parties) Act 1999, s 1 provides that a third party to a contract may 'in his own right' enforce a term of a contract if 'the contract expressly provides that he may' or 'purports to confer [such] a benefit on him'. This section creates two distinct categories of third party claimant who can enforce a contract. An illustration of the first would be where X contracts to sell his boat to D in exchange for D's promise to pay C £20k 'who shall enjoy the direct right to enforce D's promise'. Such express provision is likely to be rare particularly in regard to contracts where it is not usual for X to seek legal advice. Therefore the second category of third party claimant is of greater practical importance. The effect of the provision is to create a rebuttable presumption in favour of there being a third party right whenever a contract seeks to confer a benefit on an expressly specified third party. A simple example might be where X contracts to sell his boat as above absent the express conferral on C of a right to sue. The intentions of the original contracting parties, D and X must be ascertained by other means. However, the burden of proof will effectively be borne by D who will have to show that the parties' intention was not to confer an enforceable right on C.

It is unclear whether, if the Act were in force at the time, it would have been of assistance to the third parties in the cases considered above. In *Linden Gardens*, the third party (the new building owner) was not identified in the original contract and so would fall outside s 1. In the *McAlpine* case, it could be convincingly argued that the direct right of action enjoyed by X under the deed would indicate a clear intention that that document should exhaustively define X's rights. However what would be the position where the rights conferred on the third party were more limited? Where third parties do acquire a right under the Act they are entitled to whatever remedy they would be able to exercise if they were a party to the contract. This implies that the limitations (remoteness, mitigation etc) appropriate to an action for damages by a party to the contract will also be applicable to any action by the third party.

5.4.2 The trust of a promise

Before the reform contained in the Contracts (Rights of Third Parties) Act 1999, the courts tried various means to mitigate the effects of the privity of contract doctrine. At one time it appeared that the courts were prepared to use the concept of the 'trust' – where a party who is the legal owner of property has an obligation to use it for the benefit of another – as a means of providing an exception to the privity of contract doctrine. This possibility of holding a promise on trust was approved by the House of Lords in *Les Affréteurs Réunis SA v Leopold Walford (London) Ltd*.

***Les Affréteurs Réunis SA v Leopold Walford (London) Ltd* [1919] AC 801**

Facts: A contract for the hire of a ship included a clause promising a commission to the broker, W, who had arranged the contract. W was not a party to the contract and the parties argued that he could not enforce the promise of commission.

Held: The charterers, to whom the promise had been made, were trustees of this promise, so that it could be enforced by them on behalf of the broker.

Lord Birkenhead LC: My Lords, the issues under debate seem to me to be so plain that they may conveniently be disposed of at once. This is an appeal from a decision of the Court of Appeal delivered on July 9, 1918, reversing a decision of Bailhache J. delivered on April 10, whereby he directed judgment to be entered for the defendants with costs. It follows from what I have said that the defendants are the appellants before your Lordships' House.

The facts are very simple. The charterers' brokers claim commission from the shipowners under a charterparty dated September 28, 1916, which was a continuation of an earlier charterparty dated December 9, 1915, by which the SS *Flore* was demised. The owners were Les Affréteurs Réunis Société Anonyme and the charterers were the Lubricating and Fuel Oils, Ld. The relevant clause in the charterparty is No. 29, and is as follows: 'A commission of three per cent. on the estimated gross amount of hire is due to Leopold Walford (London), Ld., on signing this charter (ship lost or not lost)'.

Your Lordships are not troubled here with any question of amount.

My Lords, the first charterparty, that of December 9, 1915, would have ended on March 5, 1917, but its duration proved longer than the twelve months originally contemplated owing to an interruption with the details of which your Lordships are not concerned. The second charterparty would, if matters had remained normal, have commenced on March 5, but in the month of January the French Government requisitioned the ship. The first charterparty came to an end and the second never became effective. The second charterparty was entered into after an agreement between the owners and the charterers dated September 28, 1916, which contained the following clause: 'The brokers will continue their good services to either party, but their total brokerage fixed for the charterparty at 5 per cent. will be reduced for the extension period to 3 per cent. For all other conditions of detail the brokers of the respective parties will have to fix together the final clauses, it being understood that the question of principle expressed above will be faithfully observed according to the good faith of the parties, and in accordance with the business customs in shipping matters and the spirit of the present agreement'. Clause 34 of the second charterparty incorporated clause 26 of this agreement, and indeed the whole of this agreement, and should, I think, for clearness, be read: 'This charterparty is in extension of that of December 9, 1915, and will take effect at the day and hour at which the earlier charterparty will terminate. Both charterparties are for their due fulfilment subject to the conditions and stipulations contained in the special agreement signed in Paris on September 28, 1916, by the two parties exactly as if these conditions and stipulations were embodied in the present charterparty itself'.

My Lords, under those circumstances, the document must be read, in my judgment, as one whole, containing the clause of the French agreement to which I have directed attention. I do not, therefore, read the agreement in this matter as if your Lordships had to deal with a clause in the charterparty on the one hand, and an independent agreement known as the French agreement on the other. Having regard to the undeniable circumstance that the French agreement is incorporated in the charterparty it is impossible to consider that an independent agreement, in relation to the second charterparty, existed at all. A charterparty is, of course, a contract between owners and charterers, and it is elementary that, so far as the brokers are concerned, it is *res inter alios acta*; but the parties in the present case, by an interlocutory and very sensible arrangement, have agreed that the matter shall be dealt with as if the charterers were co-plaintiffs. The question therefore is, can the charterers succeed in such circumstances as the present in such an action against owners?

My Lords, it was decided nearly seventy years ago in the case of *Robertson v Wait* 8 Ex. 299 that charterers can sue under an agreement of this character as trustees for the broker. I am unable to distinguish between the decision in *Robertson v Wait* 8 Ex. 299 and the conclusion which, in my view, should be reached in the present case. It was conceded by Mr. Wright that unless there was a special and independent agreement in this case he was unable to distinguish the facts in this case from those which were considered in *Robertson v Wait*. In my opinion Mr. Wright has failed to establish the existence of an independent agreement.

My Lords, so far as I am aware, that case has not before engaged the attention of this House, and I think it right to say plainly that I agree with that decision and I agree with the reasoning, shortly as it is expressed, upon which the decision was founded. In this connection I would refer to the well-known case of *In re Empress Engineering Company* 16 Ch. D. 125, 129. In the judgment of Sir George Jessel M.R., the principle is examined which, in my view, underlies and is the explanation of the decision in *Robertson v Wait*. The Master of the Rolls uses this language: 'So, again, it is quite possible that one of the parties to the agreement may be the nominee or trustee of the third person. As Lord Justice James suggested to me in the course of the argument, a married woman may nominate somebody to contract on her behalf, but then the person makes the contract really as trustee for somebody else, and it is because he contracts in that character that the cestui que trust can take the benefit of the contract'.

It appears to me plain that for convenience, and under long-established practice, the broker in such cases, in effect, nominates the charterer to contract on his behalf, influenced probably by the circumstance that there is always a contract between charterer and owner in which this stipulation, which is to enure to the benefit of the broker, may very conveniently be inserted. In these cases the broker, on ultimate analysis, appoints the charterer to contract on his behalf. I agree therefore with the conclusion arrived at by all the learned judges in *Robertson v Wait*, that in such cases charterers can sue as trustees on behalf of the broker.

Although there are other examples in the reported cases of the courts using the trust device as a means of circumventing the privity of contract doctrine, it came to be held that it could only be used where there was a clear intention to create a trust and one that was, moreover, irrevocable. Both of these factors influenced the court in *Re Schebsman*.

Re Schebsman [1944] Ch 83 (CA)

Facts: S's employer agreed on his retirement to pay him £5,500 in instalments over six years. If he died within that period, certain sums were to be payable to his widow. S did die within the six years, shortly after being declared bankrupt. One question was whether or not the payments to Mrs S were made on the basis of a trust. The trial judge rejected this argument and the trustee appealed.

Lord Greene, MR: The first question which arises is whether or not the debtor was a trustee for his wife and daughter of the benefit of the undertaking given by the English company in their favour. An examination of the decided cases does, it is true, show that the courts have on occasions adopted what may be called a liberal view on questions of this character, but in the present case I cannot find in the contract anything to justify the conclusion that a trust was intended. It is not legitimate to import into the contract the idea of a trust when the parties have given no indication that such was their intention. To interpret this contract as creating a trust would, in my judgment, be to disregard the dividing line between the case of a trust and the simple case of a contract made between two persons for the benefit of a third. That dividing line exists, although it may not always be easy to determine where it is to be drawn. In the present case I find no difficulty.

Du Parcq LJ: I may now summarize the position at common law as follows: 1. It is the right, as well as the duty, of the company to make the prescribed payments to Mrs. Schebsman and to no other person. 2. Mrs. Schebsman may dispose of the sums so received as she pleases and is not accountable for them to the personal representatives of the debtor or to anyone claiming to stand in the shoes of the debtor. 3. If anyone standing in the shoes of the debtor were to intercept the sums payable to Mrs. Schebsman and refuse to account to her for them, he would be guilty of a breach of the debtor's contract with the company. 4. The obligation undertaken by the company cannot be varied at the will of the other party to the contract, but may be varied consensually at any time although the debtor is no longer living, as it could have been in his life-time.

It now remains to consider the question whether, and if so to what extent, the principles of equity affect the position of the parties. It was argued by Mr. Denning that one effect of the agreement of September 20, 1940, was that a trust was thereby created, and that the debtor constituted himself trustee for Mrs. Schebsman of the benefit of the covenant under which payments were to be made to her. Uthwatt J. rejected this contention, and the argument has not satisfied me that he was wrong. It is true that, by the use possibly of unguarded language, a person may create a trust, as Monsieur Jourdain talked prose, without knowing it, but unless an intention to create a trust is clearly to be collected from the language used and the circumstances of the case, I think that the court ought not to be astute to discover indications of such an intention. I have little doubt that in the present case both parties (and certainly the debtor) intended to keep alive their common law right to vary consensually the terms of the obligation undertaken by the company, and if circumstances had changed in the debtor's life-time injustice might have been done by holding that a trust had been created and that those terms were accordingly unalterable. On this point, therefore, I agree with Uthwatt J.

There are few recent cases of a trust being successfully used as a means of circumventing the privity of contract doctrine, and it is probably safe to treat this particular exception as effectively obsolete. It seems clear that the majority of judges did not regard it with enthusiasm. The rise and fall of the trust as a means of circumventing privity is summarised in the following extract.

Smith, S, *Atiyah's Introduction to the Law of Contract*, 6th edn, 2006, Oxford: Clarendon Press, pp 348–50

6. Trusts

It has already been mentioned that the law of trusts, being closely associated with the law of property, is not subject to all the restrictions of the privity doctrine. So A and B can create a trust for the benefit of C without the participation of C at all. Indeed, it might happen that C is not even in existence when the trust is created, as frequently used to happen with the classic marriage settlement, where the beneficiaries would include the unborn children of the marriage. Nevertheless, such trusts were enforceable, and the doctrine of privity of contract was, and remains, irrelevant. The trust creates proprietary rights, so that the creation of the trust operates to transfer property rights to C, rather than to create merely personal rights in favour of C. Even if the trust is not completely constituted, so that it has to take effect as a contract, and not as an actual transfer of property (e.g. where the settlor merely covenants to transfer future property to the trustees, rather than making an actual transfer then and there), C will be able to enforce the trust if he is a child of the marriage in question. Despite his being a stranger to the contract and supplying no valuable consideration, he is said to be 'within the marriage consideration. Any other person, however, who attempted to enforce an imperfectly constituted trust would be met by the plea that he was no party to the contract and had supplied no consideration.

Towards the end of the nineteenth century attempts were made to use the device of the trust as a general method to escape the doctrine of privity. Thus it came to be suggested that, whenever a contract purported to confer rights on third parties, the third parties could claim that a trust over such rights (a so-called 'trust of the promise') had been created in their favour; and could enforce their rights by way of trust. This was more or less the process by which assignments first came to be enforceable, for here also the common law at first refused to permit an assignee to sue on the contract because he was no party to it. In equity, the assignor came to be treated as a trustee for the assignee, and, once this result was reached, it became possible for the assignee to enforce the assignment himself. At first this had to be done in the name of the assignor, but after the Judicature Act 1873 even this was usually unnecessary.

For a time it looked as if a third party beneficiary might be treated in a similar way to an assignee. Specifically, there seemed to be a possibility that the third party would be able to enforce a contract by characterizing the promisee as a trustee. But in the twentieth century, the judicial attitude to this method of circumventing privity gradually hardened until it was almost rejected altogether. While it is, of course, still open to a person to enforce a genuine trust of a contractual right without having been a party to its creation, it is no longer possible (unless the circumstances are wholly exceptional) to allege a fictitious trust merely as a device for the enforcement of contractual rights by a third party. Moreover, although it may be possible to find that a genuine trust has been created without the word 'trust' having been used, the cases show that this is an unlikely eventuality.

It is no doubt correct that in most contracts made for the benefit of a third party the contracting parties did not intend to create a trust or (what amounts to the same thing) to create an arrangement with the same legal consequences of a trust. But the validity of the trust in English law shows that English courts are willing to recognize the possibility of individuals obtaining legally enforceable rights by virtue of consensual arrangements to which they were not a party. Indeed, in legal systems that do not recognize trusts, an English trust is generally regarded as a contract for the benefit of a third party.

It should also be noted that there are a number of situations in which the courts are still willing to impose a 'constructive' (or 'fictional') trust on parties who did not intend to make a trust; this is done in order to give the intended beneficiary of the arrangement the same protection she would have had under a genuine trust. For example, where husband and wife make 'mutual wills' under which they agree to leave all their property in an agreed way, it is possible (subject to various limitations) to enforce the arrangements after the death of one of the parties by means of a constructive trust. One reason that courts have refused to take a similar approach in privity cases is that a trust, once constituted, is prima facie irrevocable except with the consent of the beneficiaries; and if some of the beneficiaries are under-age, or still unborn, it may be irrevocable altogether. If a contract between A and B which professes to confer rights on X is treated as creating a trust, it would follow (the courts have reasoned) that the contract was irrevocable as soon as it was made. So, for instance, if a man makes a contract with his employer that the employer will pay the employee's widow a pension if the employee dies in his employment after (say) twenty years' service, the courts have refused to treat the widow's claim to the pension as enforceable by way of trust. The reason given for this is that the employer and the employee might have wanted to vary or rescind the pension arrangements.

Despite the courts' (sensible) concern that implying a trust in these situations would serve to render contractual terms irrevocable, there are at least two ways such a result could have been avoided. First, they could have held that a contract for the benefit of a third party does create a trust, but a revocable trust. The concept of a revocable trust is by no means unknown to the law; and if it is legitimate to 'imply' a trust in order to do justice, there is no greater difficulty in 'implying' a power to revoke the trust for the same purpose. Alternatively, the courts could have held that the promisee holds the right of action to enforce the contract on trust for the third party. It is unnecessary to regard the contract itself as creating a trust in its inception; the need to invoke the concept of a trust only arises when enforcement is sought. At that date the third party could be treated as the beneficiary of a trust.

Thus, it can be seen that here, as so often in the law, results which appear to be dictated by the logic of legal principle are not so dictated at all. Legal rules can often be made to yield up a wide variety of results without any violation of fundamental principles; whether they do so or not depends to a large extent on the willingness of the courts to mould the law to new conditions. Sometimes – as in this area -the courts have taken the easy (one is tempted to say 'lazy') way out and refused to modify the law at all. On other occasions, in different areas of the law, the courts have been much more willing to adapt rules to new situations.

5.4.3 Collateral contracts

One way of avoiding the effect of the privity of contract doctrine is to find that there is, in fact, a collateral contract between one of the main contracting parties and the third party. Since these two parties are now found to be in a contractual relationship, privity becomes irrelevant. The type of situation in which this can be used is illustrated by *Shanklin Pier v Detel Products*, in which the manufacturer of paint was held responsible for defects in it to someone who had specified that it should be used on a particular project.

***Shanklin Pier Ltd v Detel Products Ltd* [1951] 2 KB 854 (KBD)**

Facts: S, the owners of a pier, were promised by D that D's paint, if used to repaint the pier, would last for seven years. S specified to its painters that D's paint was to be used. The paint deteriorated after three months. There appeared to be no contract between S and D, so that S was without a remedy against D. The only contract relating to the paint appeared to be that between D and S's painters.

Held: There was also a collateral contract between S and D. In consideration for D's guarantee that the payment would last, S promised to specify the paint for use on the pier.

McNair J: This case raises an interesting and comparatively novel question whether or not an enforceable warranty can arise as between parties other than parties to the main contract for the sale of the article in respect of which the warranty is alleged to have been given. ...

The defence, stated broadly, is that no warranty such as is alleged in the statement of claim was ever given and that, if given, it would give rise to no cause of action between these parties. Accordingly, the first question which I have to determine is whether any such warranty was ever given. ...

In the result, I am satisfied that, if a direct contract of purchase and sale of the DMU had then been made between the plaintiffs and the defendants, the correct conclusion on the facts would have been that the defendants gave to the plaintiffs the warranties substantially in the form alleged in the statement of claim. In reaching this conclusion, I adopt the principles stated by Holt, C.J., in *Crosse v Gardner* (1688) Comb. 142 and *Medina v Stoughton* (1700) 1 Salkeld 210 that an affirmation at the time of sale is a warranty, provided it appears on evidence to have been so intended.

Counsel for the defendants submitted that in law a warranty could give rise to no enforceable cause of action except between the same parties as the parties to the main contract in relation to which the warranty was given. In principle this submission seems to me to be unsound. If, as is elementary, the consideration for the warranty in the usual case is the entering into of the main contract in relation to which the warranty is given, I see no reason why there may not be an enforceable warranty between A and B supported by the consideration that B should cause C to enter into a contract with A or that B should do some other act for the benefit of A.

Counsel for the defendants, however, relied upon the decision of the Court of Appeal in *Drury v Victor Buckland LD* [1941] 1 All E.R. 269 and particularly upon the judgment of Scott, LJ. In that case the plaintiff, who had been approached by an agent of the defendants, dealers in refrigerating machines, agreed to purchase such a machine, but, being unable or unwilling to pay forthwith the whole of the purchase price, the deal was put through by the defendants' selling the machine to a finance company, who in turn entered into a hire-purchase agreement with the plaintiff, under which she eventually, when the whole of the hire-purchase instalments had been paid, acquired title to the machine. The machine proving unsatisfactory, the plaintiff sued the defendants, claiming damages for breach of the implied warranty or condition under s. 14, sub-s. 1 of the Sale of Goods Act, 1893.

The claim failed, Scott, LJ., saying: 'It was a sale by the Buckland Company [the defendants] to the hire-purchase company. The property passed to them on the terms that they [the defendants] would get paid by the hire-purchase company. Therefore, the claim against them [the defendants] for damages for breach of warranty is a cause of action unsupported by any contract of sale which would carry it'. This judgment can readily be understood in relation to its subject matter, namely, an implied statutory condition or warranty arising out of a contract of sale, and one can well understand it being said that, as there was no contract of sale between the plaintiff and defendants, no such implied warranty or condition could arise between them; but I do not read it as affording any support for the wider proposition for which counsel for the defendants contended.

The same view of the effect of this judgment as I have indicated was, I think, taken by Jones, J., in *Brown v Sheen and Richmond Car Sales LD* [1950] W. N. 316; [1950] 1 All E.R. 1102, a case in which the judge entered judgment against a motor car dealer on an express oral warranty given in relation to the purchase of a car, the transaction, as in Drury's case [1941] 1 All E.R. 269, being carried through with the assistance of a finance company. It was here sought to distinguish Brown's case on the ground that in the statement of facts in the report in All England Law Reports it was stated that 'the plaintiff agreed to buy' the motor car from the defendants, but the pleadings in Brown's case, which I have examined, lend no support for suggesting that in that case there was in any legal sense any agreement to sell between the plaintiff and the defendants. The judgment of Hilbery, J., in *Parker v Oloxo LD* [1937] 3 All E.R. 524, 529 also, I think, negatives the defendants' submission in the present case.

Accordingly, in my judgment the plaintiffs are entitled to recover against the defendants damages for breach of the express warranties alleged.

In the similar case of *Wells Ltd v Buckland Sand and Silica Co Ltd* [1965] 2 QB 170 the same approach was applied, even though there was no specific contract in prospect when the supplier of sand made a promise as to its iron oxide content. It was held that the plaintiff, who later bought a quantity of the defendants' sand from a third party, could sue the defendant on the basis of a collateral contract. It was sufficient that there was a clear understanding that a purchase of the sand was planned for the near future (*animo contrahendi*).

5.4.4 Agency

The law of England and Wales has long recognised the usefulness of the concept of agency, whereby one person (the agent) may be given the authority to make contracts on behalf of another (the principal). This has the effect of bringing the third party, with whom the agent deals, into a *direct* contractual relationship with the principal. In some situations there is no obligation for the agent to disclose to the third party that the contract is in fact being made with the principal. As far as the third party is concerned, the contract is made with the person that s/he has been dealing with. To the extent that the undisclosed principal is given rights and obligations in relation to the contract, this appears to be an exception to the doctrine of privity.

The concept has also been combined with the idea of the collateral contract to enable a third party to take advantage of an exclusion clause in a contract between two other parties.

***New Zealand Shipping Co Ltd v Satterthwaite & Co Ltd, The Eurymedon* [1975] AC 154 (PC)**

Facts: A contract (comprised in a bill of lading) between the consignee of goods and the carrier purported to give stevedores, who had contracted with the carrier to unload the goods, the benefit of a limitation of liability provision. It was argued that the stevedores were not party to the contract between the consignee and the carrier, and so could not benefit from the clause.

Held: The carrier also contracted as agent for the stevedores so as to form a unilateral contract between the consignee and the stevedores, by which the consignee agreed to give the stevedores the benefit of the exclusion clause in exchange for the stevedores unloading the goods.

Lord Wilberforce: The facts of this case are not in dispute. An expensive drilling machine was received on board the ship *Eurymedon* at Liverpool for transhipment to Wellington pursuant to the terms of a bill of lading no. 1262 dated June 5, 1964. The shipper was the maker of the drill, Ajax Machine Tool Co. Ltd ('the consignor'). The bill of lading was issued by agents for the Federal Steam Navigation Co. Ltd ('the carrier'). The consignee was A. M. Satterthwaite & Co. Ltd of Christchurch, New Zealand ('the consignee'). For several years before 1964 the New Zealand Shipping Co. Ltd ('the stevedore') had carried out all stevedoring work in Wellington in respect of the ships owned by the carrier, which was a wholly owned subsidiary of the stevedore. In addition to this stevedoring work the stevedore generally acted as agent for the carrier in New Zealand; and in such capacity as general agent (not in the course of their stevedoring functions) the stevedore received the bill of lading at Wellington on July 31, 1964. Clause 1 of the bill of lading, on the construction of which this case turns, was in the same terms as bills of lading usually issued by the stevedore and its associated companies in respect of ordinary cargo carried by their ships from the United Kingdom to New Zealand. The consignee became the holder of the bill of lading and owner of the drill prior to August 14, 1964. On that day the drill was damaged as a result of the stevedore's negligence during unloading.

At the foot of the first page of the bill of lading the following words were printed in small capitals:

> 'In accepting this bill of lading the shipper, consignee and the owners of the goods, and the holders of this bill of lading agree to be bound by all of its conditions, exceptions and provisions whether written, printed or stamped on the front or back hereof'.

... The incorporation in the bill of lading of the rules scheduled to the Carriage of Goods by Sea Act 1924 meant that the carrier and the ship were discharged from all liability in respect of the damage to the drill unless suit was brought against them within one year after delivery. No action was commenced until April 1967, when the consignee sued the stevedore in negligence, claiming £880 the cost of repairing the damaged drill.

The question in the appeal is whether the stevedore can take the benefit of the time limitation provision. The starting point, in discussion of this question, is provided by the House of Lords decision in *Midland Silicones Ltd v Scruttons Ltd* [1962] A.C. 446. There is no need to question or even to qualify that case in so far as it affirms the general proposition that a contract between two parties cannot be sued on by a third person even though the contract is expressed to be for his benefit. Nor is it necessary to disagree with anything which was said to the same effect in the Australian case of *Wilson v Darling Island Stevedoring and Lighterage Co Ltd* (1956) 95 C.L.R. 43. Each of these cases was dealing with a simple case of a contract the benefit of which was sought to be taken by a third person not a party to it, and the emphatic pronouncements in the speeches and judgments were directed to this situation. But *Midland Silicones* left open the case where one of the parties contracts as agent for the third person: in particular Lord Reid's speech spelt out, in four propositions, the prerequisites for the validity of such an agency contract. There is of course nothing unique to this case in the conception of agency contracts: well known and common instances exist in the field of hire purchase, of bankers' commercial credits and other transactions. Lord Reid said, at p 474:

> 'I can see a possibility of success of the agency argument if (first) the bill of lading makes it clear that the stevedore is intended to be protected by the provisions in it which limit liability, (secondly) the bill of lading makes it clear that the carrier, in addition to contracting for these

provisions on his own behalf, is also contracting as agent for the stevedore that these provisions should apply to the stevedore, (thirdly) the carrier has authority from the stevedore to do that, or perhaps later ratification by the stevedore would suffice, and (fourthly) that any difficulties about consideration moving from the stevedore were overcome and then to affect the consignee it would be necessary to show that the provisions of the Bills of Lading Act 1855 apply'.

The question in this appeal is whether the contract satisfies these propositions. Clause 1 of the bill of lading, whatever the defects in its drafting, is clear in its relevant terms. The carrier, on his own account, stipulates for certain exemptions and immunities: among these is that conferred by article III, rule 6, of the Hague Rules which discharges the carrier from all liability for loss or damage unless suit is brought within one year after delivery. In addition to these stipulations on his own account, the carrier as agent for, *inter alios*, independent contractors stipulates for the same exemptions.

Much was made of the fact that the carrier also contracts as agent for numerous other persons; the relevance of this argument is not apparent. It cannot be disputed that among such independent contractors, for whom, as agent, the carrier contracted, is the appellant company which habitually acts as stevedore in New Zealand by arrangement with the carrier and which is, moreover, the parent company of the carrier. The carrier was, indisputably, authorised by the appellant to contract as its agent for the purposes of clause 1. All of this is quite straightforward and was accepted by all the judges in New Zealand. The only question was, and is, the fourth question presented by Lord Reid, namely that of consideration.

It was on this point that the Court of Appeal differed from Beattie J holding that it had not been shown that any consideration for the shipper's promise as to exemption moved from the promisee, i.e., the appellant company.

If the choice, and the antithesis, is between a gratuitous promise, and a promise for consideration, as it must be in the absence of a *tertium quid*, there can be little doubt which, in commercial reality, this is. The whole contract is of a commercial character, involving service on one side, rates of payment on the other, and qualifying stipulations as to both. The relations of all parties to each other are commercial relations entered into for business reasons of ultimate profit. To describe one set of promises, in this context, as gratuitous, or *nudum pactum*, seems paradoxical and is *prima facie* implausible. It is only the precise analysis of this complex of relations into the classical offer and acceptance, with identifiable consideration, that seems to present difficulty, but this same difficulty exists in many situations of daily life, e.g., sales at auction; supermarket purchases; boarding an omnibus; purchasing a train ticket; tenders for the supply of goods; offers of rewards; acceptance by post; warranties of authority by agents; manufacturers' guarantees; gratuitous bailments; bankers' commercial credits. These are all examples which show that English law, having committed itself to a rather technical and schematic doctrine of contract in application takes a practical approach, often at the cost of forcing the facts to fit uneasily into the marked slots of offer, acceptance and consideration.

In their Lordships' opinion the present contract presents much less difficulty than many of those above referred to. It is one of carriage from Liverpool to Wellington. The carrier assumes an obligation to transport the goods and to discharge at the port of arrival. The goods are to be carried and discharged, so the transaction is inherently contractual. It is contemplated that a part of this contract, viz. discharge, may be performed by independent contractors – viz. the appellant. By clause 1 of the bill of lading the shipper agrees to exempt from liability the carrier, his servants and independent contractors in respect of the performance of this contract of carriage. Thus, if the carriage, including the discharge, is wholly carried out by the carrier, he is exempt. If part is carried out by him and part by his servants, he and they are exempt. If part is carried out by him and part by an independent contractor, he and the independent contractor are exempt. The exemption is designed to cover the whole carriage from loading to discharge, by whomsoever it is performed: the performance attracts the exemption or immunity in favour of whoever the performer turns out to be. There is possibly more than one way of analysing this business transaction into the necessary components; that which their Lordships would accept is to say that the bill of lading brought into existence a bargain initially unilateral but capable of becoming mutual, between the shipper and the appellant, made through the carrier as agent. This became a full contract when the appellant performed services by discharging the goods. The performance of these services for the benefit of the shipper was the consideration for the agreement by the shipper that the appellant should have the benefit of the exemptions and limitations contained in the bill of lading. The conception of a 'unilateral' contract of this kind was recognized in *Great Northern Railway Co v Witham* (1873) LR 9 CP 16 and is well established. This way of regarding the matter is very close to if not identical to that accepted by Beattie J in the Supreme Court: he analysed the transaction as one of an offer open to acceptance by action such as was found in *Carlill v Carbolic Smoke Ball Co* [1893] 1 QB 256. But whether one describes the shippers' promise to exempt as an offer to be accepted by performance or as a promise in exchange for an act seems in the present context to be a matter of semantics. The words of Bowen LJ in *Carlill v Carbolic Smoke Ball Co* [1893] 1 QB 256, 268: 'Why should not an offer be made to all the world which is to ripen into a contract with anybody who comes forward and performs the condition?' seem to bridge both conceptions: he certainly seems to draw no distinction between an offer which matures into a contract when accepted and a promise which matures into a contract after performance, and, though in some special contexts (such as in connection with the right to withdraw) some further refinement may be needed, either analysis may be equally valid. On the main point in the appeal, their Lordships are in substantial agreement with Beattie J.

The following points require mention. 1. In their Lordships' opinion, consideration may quite well be provided by the appellant, as suggested, even though (or if) it was already under an obligation to discharge to the carrier. (There is no direct evidence of the existence or nature of this obligation, but their Lordships are prepared to assume it.) An agreement to do an act which the promisor is under an existing obligation to a third party to do, may quite well amount to valid consideration and does so in the present case: the promisee obtains the benefit of a direct obligation which he can enforce. This proposition is illustrated and supported by *Scotson v Pegg* (1861) 6 H & N 295 which their Lordships consider to be good law.

Viscount Dilhorne and Lord Simon of Glaisdale dissented from the above majority judgment.

The approach taken in the above case was also adopted in *The New York Star* [1981] 1 WLR 138. In *The Mahkutai* [1996] AC 650, while accepting the general principle established in the earlier cases, the Privy Council suggested that it might be time for a more general exception to privity to be adopted, rather than relying on the technical arguments based on agency and consideration set out in *New Zealand Shipping Company v Satterthwaite*.

***The Mahkutai* [1996] AC 650**

Lord Goff of Chievely:

Critique of the Eurymedon principle

In *The New York Star* [1981] 1 W.L.R. 138, 144, Lord Wilberforce discouraged 'a search for fine distinctions which would diminish the general applicability, in the light of established commercial practice, of the principle'. He was there, of course, speaking of the application of the principle in the case of stevedores. It has however to be recognised that, so long as the principle continues to be understood to rest upon an enforceable contract as between the cargo owners and the stevedores entered into through the agency of the shipowner, it is inevitable that technical points of contract and agency law will continue to be invoked by cargo owners seeking to enforce tortious remedies against stevedores and others uninhibited by the exceptions and limitations in the relevant bill of lading contract. Indeed, in the present case their Lordships have seen such an exercise being legitimately undertaken by Mr. Aikens on behalf of the cargo owners. In this connection their Lordships wish to refer to the very helpful consideration of the principle in *Palmer on Bailment*, 2nd edn. (1991), at pp 1610–1625, which reveals many of the problems which may arise, and refers to a number of cases, both in England and in Commonwealth countries, in which the courts have grappled with those problems. In some cases, notably but by no means exclusively in England, courts have felt impelled by the established principles of the law of contract or of agency to reject the application of the principle in the particular case before them. In others, courts have felt free to follow the lead of Lord Wilberforce in *The Eurymedon* [1975] A.C. 154, and of Lord Wilberforce and Barwick C.J. in *The New York Star* [1981] 1 W.L.R. 138; [1979] 1 Lloyd's Rep. 298, and so to discover the existence of a contract (nowadays a bilateral contract of the kind identified by Barwick C.J.) in circumstances in which lawyers of a previous generation would have been unwilling to do so.

Nevertheless, there can be no doubt of the commercial need of some such principle as this, and not only in cases concerned with stevedores; and the bold step taken by the Privy Council in *The Eurymedon* [1975] A.C. 154, and later developed in *The New York Star* [1981] 1 W.L.R. 138, has been widely welcomed. But it is legitimate to wonder whether that development is yet complete. Here their Lordships have in mind not only Lord Wilberforce's discouragement of fine distinctions, but also the fact that the law is now approaching the position where, provided that the bill of lading contract clearly provides that (for example) independent contractors such as stevedores are to have the benefit of exceptions and limitations contained in that contract, they will be able to enjoy the protection of those terms as against the cargo owners. This is because (1) the problem of consideration in these cases is regarded as having been solved on the basis that a bilateral agreement between the stevedores and the cargo owners, entered into through the agency of the shipowners, may, though itself unsupported by consideration, be rendered enforceable by consideration subsequently furnished by the stevedores in the form of performance of their duties as stevedores for the shipowners; (2) the problem of authority from the stevedores to the shipowners to contract on their behalf can, in the majority of cases, be solved by recourse to the principle of ratification; and (3) consignees of the cargo may be held to be bound on the principle in *Brandt v Liverpool, Brazil and River Plate Steam Navigation Co Ltd* [1924] 1 K.B. 575. Though these solutions are now perceived to be generally effective for their purpose, their technical nature is all too apparent; and the time may well come when, in an appropriate case, it will fall to be considered whether the courts should take what may legitimately be perceived to be the final, and perhaps inevitable, step in this development, and recognise in these cases a fully-fledged exception to the doctrine of privity of contract, thus escaping from all the technicalities with which courts are now faced in English law. It is not far from their Lordships' minds that, if the English courts were minded to take that step, they would be following in the footsteps of the Supreme Court of Canada: see *London Drugs Ltd v Kuehne & Nagel International Ltd* (1992) 97 D.L.R. (4th) 261 and, in a different context, the High Court of Australia: see *Trident General Insurance Co Ltd v McNiece Bros Pty Ltd* (1988) 165 C.L.R. 107. Their Lordships have given consideration to the question whether they should face up to this question in the present appeal. However, they have come to the conclusion that it would not be appropriate for them to do so, first, because they have not heard argument specifically directed towards this fundamental question, and second because, as will become clear in due course, they are satisfied that the appeal must in any event be dismissed.

It may well be that the enactment of the statutory exception in the Contracts (Rights of Third Parties) Act 1999, which enables parties to achieve the end result of giving third parties the benefit of an exclusion clause by more direct means, will mean that the courts will be reluctant to take the step suggested by Lord Goff, in the above extract, in creating a more general common law exception to privity.

5.5 Imposition of obligations

The main exception to the aspect of privity which prevents a contract imposing obligations on a third party falls within land law. The seller of a piece of land is able to control the uses to which subsequent purchasers put the land, by means of a 'restrictive covenant' attached to the transfer of ownership. This principle derives from the case of *Tulk v Moxhay* (1848) 2 Ph 774; 41 ER 1143, but its application in the context of land transactions is not discussed further here. In *Taddy v Sterious* an attempt to apply this approach more generally to the law of contract was firmly rejected.

Taddy v Sterious [1904] 1 Ch 354

Facts: The manufacturers of tobacco attached a notice to packets indicating that they were not to be sold below the stipulated price. Acceptance of the goods was deemed to be the acceptance of these conditions and where the goods were bought from a wholesaler, the wholesaler was deemed to be the agent of the manufacturer.

Held: The purchaser of the tobacco from a wholesaler was not bound by the price stipulation clause.

Swinfen Eady J: In this case the plaintiffs are manufacturers of tobacco. There are two defendants – Sterious & Co., who are retail tobacconists at Southend, and James Netten, a wholesale dealer. The plaintiffs submit to have their action dismissed with costs as against Netten; there only remains, therefore, their action against Sterious & Co. The object of the action is to obtain a declaration that these defendants are not entitled to sell any packet tobaccos manufactured by the plaintiffs except at such prices and generally upon terms and conditions of supply as were specified and contained in their invoices, price-lists, and catalogues, and also in labels and notices attached to the boxes in which the tobacco was sold, and an injunction. …

The defendants have dealt in the plaintiffs' tobaccos for some time. It is not suggested that they were ignorant of the terms and conditions issued by the plaintiffs. Complaints were made on several occasions of the defendants selling under the minimum price, and since the writ was issued the defendant Netten has agreed not to sell them any more of this tobacco, and the supply from that source has ceased. But the claim made by Taddy & Co. is not confined to tobacco obtained by Sterious & Co. from Netten, but is quite general. The plaintiffs put their case in two ways. First, they contended that the conditions constituted a contract made by Sterious & Co. with Netten as the plaintiffs' agents, and that they are entitled to restrain Sterious & Co. from acting in breach of that contract. Secondly, they contended that the goods were sold subject to certain conditions, and that even if Netten or any one else had purported to sell them free from the conditions, Sterious & Co., having notice of the conditions, could not sell the goods except according to the conditions, and the plaintiffs were entitled to restrain them from doing so.

With regard to this last contention, there is a short answer. Conditions of this kind do not run with goods, and cannot be imposed upon them. Subsequent purchasers, therefore, do not take subject to any conditions which the Court can enforce. If there was a breach of contract, the plaintiffs could no doubt sue. The question remains, therefore, whether there was any contract. There was no direct contract between Sterious & Co. and Taddy & Co., and the question does not arise as to the effect of a sale by Taddy & Co. direct to a retail trader subject to these terms as to minimum retail price. The part of the conditions now in question is: 'In the case of a purchase by a retail dealer through a wholesale dealer, the latter shall be deemed to be the agent of Taddy & Co'. Now it is quite clear that Taddy & Co. sell to wholesale dealers out and out. The wholesale dealers are not Taddy & Co.'s agents to sell the goods; they buy them out and out, and sell them for their own profit. It was argued that the words in the special condition, 'purchase by a retail dealer through a wholesale dealer', can only refer to cases where the wholesale dealers really are the agents of Taddy & Co., and do not apply to cases where the wholesale dealers first bought and then resold. That seems to be the right construction. If, however, the condition ought to be construed as applying to a purchase from as well as through a wholesale dealer – even then, a wholesale dealer selling for his own profit would not be an agent of Taddy & Co. in the ordinary sense of that term. Nor can it be said that the wholesale dealer was selling the goods for his own profit, and at the same time entered into a collateral contract with the purchaser, as to the subsequent dealing with the goods, as the agent of Taddy & Co. No such collateral contract was in fact entered into. In my opinion, when the wholesale dealer sold the goods for his own profit, he was not in any sense whatever the agent of Taddy & Co., and the mere insertion in the condition of the words that he was to be deemed to be an agent could not make him one. Whatever may be the case as between Taddy & Co. and Netten, there is no contract between Taddy & Co. and Sterious & Co.

Despite this rejection of any general application of a 'restrictive covenant' approach outside the area of land law, in some cases a similar principle was successfully applied in some shipping contracts. In Port Line v Ben Line Ltd, however, Diplock J took the view that these cases were explicable as examples of the tort of wrongful interference with contractual rights, rather than an equitable principle analogous to restrictive covenants.

Port Line Ltd v Ben Line Steamers Ltd [1957 P No 85]; [1958] 2 WLR 551

Diplock J: The plaintiffs' charterparty with Silver Line was a gross time charter, not one by demise. It gave the plaintiffs no right of property in or to possession of the vessel. It was one by which Silver Line agreed with the plaintiffs that for 30 months from March 9, 1955, they would render services by their servants and crew to carry the goods which were put on the vessel by the plaintiffs: see *per* MacKinnon L.J. in *Sea and Land Securities Ltd v William Dickinson & Co Ltd* [1942] 2 K.B. 65, 69; 58 T.L.R. 210; [1942] 1 All E.R. 503. By parting with their property in the vessel on February 8, 1956, and retaining a right to possession and use which terminated on its requisition, Silver Line put it out of their power to continue to perform their contractual services after the vessel was requisitioned. It is true that during the period of requisition (which is the only period with which I am concerned) Silver Line could not have performed their contractual services to the plaintiffs anyway, but the plaintiffs would have been entitled under section 4 (3) of the Compensation (Defence) Act, 1939, to the bareboat element of any compensation received by Silver Line from the Crown, and would have had to pay to Silver Line a rather larger sum by way of hire under the charterparty. It would seem, therefore, that so far as the period of requisition itself is concerned, the plaintiffs would have gained rather than lost by any breach of the contract by Silver Line which relieved the plaintiffs from paying to Silver Line the chartered hire. This, however, is a matter between Silver Line and the plaintiffs with which I am not called upon to deal except in so far (if at all) as it may be relevant to the determination of the plaintiffs' rights against the defendants. There was no privity of contract between the plaintiffs and the defendants. On what ground, therefore, can they assert against the defendants all or any of the contractual rights they had against Silver Line, or any statutory rights which they would have had against Silver Line by virtue of the existence of such contractual rights?

It is contended that the plaintiffs' rights against the defendants stem from the principle laid down by Knight Bruce L.J. in *De Mattos v Gibson* (1858) 4 De G. & J. 276 in 1858 as approved by the Privy Council in the Lord Strathcona case [1926] A.C. 108. …

It may be relevant to note that in the Strathcona case the buyers of the vessel subject to the time charter in favour of the plaintiffs had express notice of the terms of the charter, and had covenanted with the sellers to perform and accept all responsibilities under it. It was, as the Board said, not a mere case of notice of the existence of a covenant affecting the use of the property sold, but a case of acceptance of the property expressly *sub conditione*. The initial emphasis on this, and the reference at a later stage to the possibility that a shipowner might declare himself a trustee of his obligations under a charterparty so as to bind his assignee might suggest as a possible *ratio decidendi* that the Strathcona case was one where either the purchaser used expressions which amounted to a declaration of trust in favour of the charterers, or the vendor himself accepted the benefit of the covenant as trustee for the charterers. But an examination of the Board's opinion as a whole seems to indicate that they accepted the full doctrine of Knight

Bruce L.J. as respects chattels, namely, that mere notice does give rise to the equity, the only qualification that the Board imposed being that 'an interest must remain' (sc. in the person seeking the remedy) 'in the subject matter of the covenant before a right can be conceded to an injunction against the violation by another of the covenant in question'. The only remedy which the Board in terms recognized is a remedy by injunction against the use of the ship by the purchaser inconsistent with the charterparty, but they said, in a passage on which Mr. Roskill for the plaintiffs strongly relies, that the purchaser 'appears to be plainly in the position of a constructive trustee with obligations which a court of equity will not permit him to violate'.

These passages pose several problems: (1) If, as the Board state, the ship is the 'subject-matter' of the covenant of which the violation by another is to be restrained, it is difficult to see in what sense a charterer under a gross time charter has an interest in that subject-matter except in the broad sense that it is to his commercial advantage that his covenantor should continue to use the ship to perform the services which he has covenanted to perform. But the time charter is a contract for services. The time charterer has no proprietary or possessory rights in the ship, and if the covenantee's commercial advantage in the observance of the covenant is sufficient to constitute an 'interest' in the chattel to which the covenant relates, it is difficult to see why the principle does not apply to price fixing cases such as *Dunlop Pneumatic Tyre Co Ltd v Selfridge & Co Ltd*. The Board explain cases like Dunlop's case, which had been cited to them, as cases where the plaintiff had no interest in the subject-matter of the contract. They say that the charterer has and will have during the continuance of the charterparty 'a plain interest' (in the ship) 'so long as she is fit to go to sea'. Plain though it may be, if the expression 'interest' is used colloquially, the Board nowhere explain what the legal nature of that interest is.

(2) Whether the reference to the subsequent purchaser with notice as being, also 'plainly', in the position of a constructive trustee imports that equity provides other remedies against him by his cestui que trust, such as the right to an account, the making of a vesting order or the appointment of a new trustee is nowhere discussed in the Strathcona case; but the whole trend of the opinion, the actual order made and the observation of the Board: 'It is incredible that the owners will lay up the vessel rather than permit its use under the contract' all strongly suggest that the only remedy in the view of the Board that the charterer acquired against the subsequent purchaser was the purely negative remedy, namely, to restrain a user of the vessel inconsistent with the terms of his charter with the former owner, and the obligations of the purchaser which a court of equity will not allow him to violate are the negative obligation not to make such inconsistent user of the vessel. As a 'constructive trustee' the subsequent purchaser seems to be one *sui generis*, and I should hesitate as a common law lawyer to seek to devise other remedies against him which did not apparently occur to the Board

(3) The Board in the Strathcona case, beyond saying that that case was not one of 'mere notice', did not discuss what kind of notice to the purchaser of the charterer's rights gives rise to the equity, namely, whether at the time of his acquisition of his interest in the vessel he must have actual knowledge of the charterer's rights against the seller, the violation of which it is sought to restrain, or whether 'constructive notice' will suffice. 'Reason and justice' – the sole though weighty grounds on which Knight Bruce L.J. based the equity – do not seem to me to prescribe the introduction into commercial matters such as the sale of a ship of the doctrine of constructive notice. I respectfully agree with Lindley L.J.'s observations in *Manchester Trust v Furness* [1895] 2 Q.B. 539, 545. Furthermore, as between vendor and purchaser of real property, where the doctrine has been developed, constructive notice – like estoppel in less esoteric matters – is a shield not a weapon of offence. It protects an already existing equitable interest from being defeated by a purchaser for value without notice. It is not itself the source of an equitable interest.

The Strathcona case, although decided over 30 years ago, has never been followed in the English courts, and has never come up for direct consideration. In *Clore v Theatrical Properties Ltd* [1936] 3 All E.R. 483, 490 Lord Wright M.R. suggested in passing that it might be peculiar to ships, but no such suggestion is to be found in the Strathcona case itself. In *Greenhalgh v Mallard* [1943] 2 All E.R. 234 Lord Greene M.R., in a judgment concurred in by Luxmoore L.J. and Goddard L.J., was clearly of opinion that it was wrongly decided, although it is only fair to add that as recently as 1952, Denning L.J. gave it a not unfriendly passing glance in *Bendall v McWhirter* [1952] 2 Q.B. 466; [1952] 1 T.L.R. 1332; [1952] 1 All E.R. 1307.

It seems, therefore, that it is in this case for the first time after more than 30 years that an English court has to grapple with the problem of what principle was really laid down in the Strathcona case, and whether that case was rightly decided. The difficulty I have found in ascertaining its *ratio decidendi*, the impossibility which I find of reconciling the actual decision with well-established principles of law, the unsolved and, to me, insoluble problems which that decision raises combine to satisfy me that it was wrongly decided. I do not propose to follow it. I naturally express this opinion with great diffidence, but having reached a clear conclusion it is my duty to express it.

If I am wrong in my view that the case was wrongly decided, I am certainly averse from extending it one iota beyond that which, as I understand it, it purported to decide. In particular, I do not think that it purported to decide (1) that anything short of actual knowledge by the subsequent purchaser at the time of the purchase of the charterer's rights, the violation of which it is sought to restrain, is sufficient to give rise to the equity; (2) that the charterer has any remedy against the subsequent purchaser with notice except a right to restrain the use of the vessel by such purchaser in a manner inconsistent with the terms of the charter; (3) that the charterer has any positive right against the subsequent purchaser to have the vessel used in accordance with the terms of his charter. The third proposition follows from the second; *ubi jus ibi remedium*. For failure by the subsequent purchaser to use the vessel in accordance with the terms of the charter entered into by his seller there is no remedy by specific performance as was held in the Strathcona case itself. There is equally no remedy in damages, a consideration which distinguishes the Strathcona case from such cases as *Lumley v Wagner* and *Lumley v Gye*. The charterer's only right is coterminous with his remedy, namely, not to have the ship used by the purchaser in violation of his charter.

The trial judge in *Swiss Bank Corporation v Lloyds Bank Ltd* [1979] Ch 548 held that where there was a specifically enforceable obligation to deal with property in a particular way, this could give the party to whom the obligation was owed an equitable right over the property concerned and that this would bind a third party. The Court of Appeal and House of Lords decided the case on other grounds, and no subsequent case has picked up on it, so it seems that the approach taken in *Port Line v Ben Line* is still likely to represent the general law in this area.

Additional reading

Adams, J., and Brownsword, R., 'Privity and the Concept of a Network Contract' (1990) 10 Legal Studies 12.

Adams, J., Beyleveld, D., and Brownsword, R., 'Privity of Contract – The Benefits and Burdens of Law Reform' (1997) 60 MLR 238.

Burrows, A., 'The Contracts (Rights of Third Parties) Act and Its Implications for Commercial Contracts' [2000] LMCLQ 540.

Davies, Paul S., 'No Leapfrogging of Contract in Unjust Enrichment' (2012) 71 CLJ 37.

Flannigan, R., 'Privity – The End of an Era (Error)' (1987) 103 LQR 564.

Law Commission, Consultation Paper No 121, *Privity of Contract: Contracts for the Benefit of Third Parties*, 1991.

Law Revision Committee, 6th *Interim Report*, 1937, Cmnd 5449.

Smith, S., 'Contracts for the Benefit of Third Parties: In Defence of the Third-Party Rule' (1997) 17 OJLS 643.

Waddams, S., 'Johanna Wagner and the Rival Opera Houses' (2001) 117 LQR 431.

Chapter 6

Contents of the contract

Chapter contents

6.1 Introduction

Once the formation of a contract has been established, the next issue to deal with is the content of the contract. What are the parties' respective rights and obligations under the contract? In practice, this is an extremely important issue for the parties.

Problems may arise in a number of ways. For example, the contract may have been preceded by a lengthy period of negotiation. If so, it will be important for the parties to ascertain which pre-contractual statements have been incorporated into the contract and which have not. The contract may have been oral, written or a combination of both. Even if the contract is written, one of the parties might allege that the written document does not represent their true intentions. In some cases, the job of the court may be to interpret the contract so as to ascertain the legal effect of the language used. In fulfilling this role, the court can take into account evidence of the surrounding factual context – known as the 'factual matrix'. In addition, the court's approach may be influenced by other factors including the relative bargaining power of the parties and, in some situations, statutory regulation (see also the interesting discussion in *Amey Birmingham Highways Ltd v Birmingham City Council* [2018] EWCA Civ 264 where Jackson LJ stated (at [93]): 'Any relational contract of this character [the Court of Appeal was considering a private finance initiative contract with Birmingham City Council] is likely to be of massive length, containing many infelicities and oddities. Both parties should adopt a reasonable approach in accordance with what is obviously the long-term purpose of the contract. They should not be latching onto the infelicities and oddities, in order to disrupt the project and maximise their own gain'). If the contract is entirely verbal the court will have to determine what has been said. The problems that arise here are likely to be evidential and are beyond the scope of this book. Nevertheless, issues of construction may arise here in a similar way to written contracts. Problems may also occur in respect of implied terms. In addition to terms expressly incorporated into the contract, terms may be implied into the contract either by the courts or by statute. In certain situations, terms will be implied by statute, irrespective of the wishes or intentions of the parties. To an extent this is part of a legislative policy to protect the reasonable expectations of vulnerable parties.

The chapter is divided into three parts. First, the distinction between pre-contractual representations and terms will be considered. Second, the approach to express terms and their interpretation will be analysed. Finally, the rules relating to the implication of terms, both at common law and by statute, will be discussed.

6.2 Distinction between representations and terms

It is extremely important to ascertain whether a statement made by one party to the other prior to the formation of the contract has been incorporated into the contract as a term. Essentially, if it has, then a person who fails to comply with the statement will be potentially liable to the full range of contractual remedies as discussed in Chapter 15. If the statement has not been incorporated as a term, then liability cannot be for breach of contract and the claimant will have to pursue a claim, if any, for misrepresentation.

This distinction was once more significant because of the different remedial consequences that attached to a breach of contract and a misrepresentation. Following a breach of contract the claimant will normally be entitled to damages, which will often compensate him for any profits that may have been lost as a result of the broken promise. Following a misrepresentation, the remedies available to a claimant were more restricted: prior to the decision of the House of Lords in *Hedley Byrne & Co Ltd v Heller & Partners* [1964] AC 465 and the enactment of the Misrepresentation Act 1967, damages were only recoverable in English law for fraudulent misrepresentations. This meant that a claimant who wished to claim damages prior to these developments had either to prove fraud (which was notoriously difficult) or prove that the statement had been incorporated into the contract (thus giving rise to a claim for breach of contract). Because of these difficulties, the courts often adopted a generous approach to finding that a statement was a term of the contract in order to award damages to a deserving claimant (see, for example, *De Laselle v Guildford* [1901] 2 KB 215). Now that damages are available for negligent misrepresentation (although such damages adopt the tortious measure), the need to adopt such an approach has diminished.

6.2.1 The basis of the distinction between terms and representations

The basic test as to whether or not a statement has been incorporated into a contract is one of intention. Did the parties intend (objectively assessed) for the statement to be a term? In ascertaining intention the courts take into account a number of factors in determining whether a statement was intended to be a term. Some of these factors have been afforded a greater importance than others, but none of them is decisive of the issue. They are merely aids to establishing the parties' intention.

6.2.1.1 Importance of the statement

The first factor that might be relevant is the importance of the statement. This was seen in the case of *Bannerman v White*.

***Bannerman v White* (1861) 10 CB(NS) 844; 142 ER 685**

Facts: White asked Bannerman if the hops he was selling had been treated with sulphur, stating that if they had been so treated, he would not be willing to purchase them. Bannerman said that they had not been treated with sulphur which he believed to be the case. Later, White discovered that five out of 300 acres had been treated with sulphur.

Held: There had been no fraudulent misrepresentation. However, the statement had become a term of the contract, and Bannerman was in breach of the term.

Erle CJ: [The statement] was a preliminary stipulation; and if it had not been given, the defendants would not have gone on with the treaty which resulted in the sale. In this sense it was the condition upon which the defendants contracted; and it would be contrary to the intention expressed by this stipulation that the contract should remain valid if sulphur had been used. The intention of the parties governs in the making and in the construction of all contracts. If the parties so intend, the sale may be absolute, with a warranty superadded; or the sale may be conditional, to be null if the warranty is broke. And, upon this statement of acts, we think that the intention appears that the contract should be null if sulphur had been used.

It was crucial that the statement was a 'preliminary stipulation'. In the absence of the statement, White would not have been prepared to purchase the hops. Due to the importance of the statement it was construed to be a term of the contract.

6.2.1.2 Requirement of independent verification

It should be noted that, even where the matter is of importance to the recipient, it might not be construed as a term of the contract if the maker of the statement made clear that the truth should be verified independently.

***Ecay v Godfrey* (1947) 80 Lloyd's Law Reports 286**

Facts: Señor José Paniego Ecay, Spanish Vice-consul at Newcastle upon Tyne, agreed to purchase a boat from Mr Godfrey, who stated that the *Tio Pepe* was 'seagoing and capable of going overseas, in excellent condition and with a sound hull'. Prior to the sale, Godfrey recommended that Ecay have the boat surveyed. The boat was neither sea-going nor capable of going overseas, and in view of her condition the plaintiff had to sell the boat at a significantly lower price than that at which he had bought her. The plaintiff brought a claim for breach of contract.

Held: The High Court held that, in light of Godfrey's recommendation that Ecay should have the boat surveyed, Godfrey could not have intended his statement as to the ship's condition to have formed part of the contract.

Lord Goddard CJ: What you have got to think of is: If the parties sat down here and wrote out their contract, would you find in that contract an undertaking by the defendant that so and so existed or so and so was the fact? If we apply that test to the case here, having heard all the evidence, I think it is impossible to come to the conclusion that if these two parties had sat down and written out their contract, intending thereby to put down on paper exactly what they bargained about and all the terms of their bargain, Mr. Godfrey would have said, 'And I promise you ... that the vessel is in good condition'. It would be quite inconsistent, I think, with his statement to the plaintiff at the time, 'Aren't you going to have a survey?' ... because if he was intending to warrant at the time that this boat was in good condition, there would be no point in having a survey.

The same principle may apply where such verification would normally be expected, even if it had not been actively encouraged. For example, this may be the position in relation to the sale of real property, where a purchaser will generally be expected to commission a homebuyer's survey, rather than relying upon the vendor's statements.

6.2.1.3 Contract terms stated in writing

The third factor that might be relevant is the fact that the parties have committed their contract to writing. If the parties have done this, the courts will be very reluctant to incorporate a term into the contract that was not included in the written terms. This was seen in the case of *Routledge v McKay*.

***Routledge v McKay* [1954] 1 WLR 615**

Facts: McKay sold a Douglas motor-cycle to Routledge. Prior to the sale, McKay told Routledge that the motor-cycle was a 1942 model. Routledge prepared a 'written memorandum' at the time of the sale, but this was silent as to the age of the motor-cycle. After the sale, Routledge discovered that the motor-cycle was a 1930 model and he brought a claim for breach of warranty. The county court judge held that there had been a breach of warranty and gave judgment for Routledge.

Held: The Court of Appeal allowed the appeal on the ground that the evidence did not establish a collateral contract by which a warranty was given that the motor-cycle was a 1942 model. It was particularly important to the Court of Appeal that the date of the motor-cycle had not been included in the written memorandum.

Lord Evershed MR: [The written memorandum] represents *prima facie* the record of what the parties intended to agree when the actual transaction took place. Counsel for the defendant has contended that the terms of it necessarily exclude any warranty – that is to say, any collateral bargain, either contemporary or earlier in date. I am not sure that I would go as far ... in that respect. But I think that, as a matter of construction, it would be extremely difficult to say that such an agreement was consistent with a warranty being given at the same time and so as to be intended to form a part of the bargain then made.

The rule is not an absolute one, however, and if a party can show that the term that was not included was of the utmost importance, then the courts may be prepared to incorporate it. This is perhaps more likely where the written contract is in the standard terms of one of the parties.

Evans J & Son (Portsmouth) Ltd v Andrea Merzario Ltd [1976] 1 WLR 1078

Facts: The plaintiffs were English importers of machines from Italy. Since 1959 they had arranged for the carriage of the machines to England under contracts with the defendants. The contracts were in a standard printed form and included conditions allowing for freight to be carried on deck. In 1967 the plaintiffs explained to the defendants that it was of great importance that the machinery should not be carried on deck. The defendants gave an oral assurance that the plaintiff's machinery would be carried below deck. In October 1968 the defendants loaded one of the plaintiffs' machines, valued at nearly £3,000, packed in a container, onto the deck of the ship. Owing to a swell at sea, the container fell overboard and was a total loss. The plaintiffs brought an action claiming damages of £2,720. The forwarding agents denied liability, relying on the exemptions in the printed conditions of carriage. At first instance the judge found for the defendants holding that the oral assurance was not a legally binding warranty such as would override the standard conditions.

Held: The Court of Appeal held that the verbal promise that the machines would be carried below deck took precedence over the written conditions. The defendants were in breach of that promise and were liable to the plaintiffs in damages.

Roskill LJ: [I]t seems to me that the contract was this: 'If we continue to give you our business, you will ensure that those goods in containers are shipped under deck'; and the defendants agreed that this would be so. Thus there was a breach of that contract by the defendants when this container was shipped on deck; and it seems to me to be plain that the damage which the plaintiffs suffered resulted from that breach ... It is suggested that even so these exemption clauses [in the printed written terms] apply. I ventured to ask [counsel for the defendants] what the position would have been if when the defendants' first quotation had come along there had been stamped on the face of that quotation: 'No containers to be shipped on deck': and this container had then been shipped on deck. He bravely said that the exemption clauses would still have applied. With great respect, I think that is an impossible argument. In the words which Devlin J used in *Firestone Tyre and Rubber Co Ltd v Vokins & Co Ltd* [1951] 1 Lloyd's Rep 32, 39, and approved by Lord Denning MR in *Mendelssohn v Normand Ltd* [1970] 1 QB 177, 184, the defendants' promise that the container would be shipped under deck would be wholly illusory ... Interpreting the contract as I find it to have been, I feel driven to the conclusion that none of these exemption clauses can be applied, because one has to treat the promise that no container would be shipped on deck as overriding any question of exempting conditions. Otherwise, as I have already said, the promise would be illusory.

Evans J & Son (Portsmouth) Ltd v Andrea Merzario Ltd [1976] 1 WLR 1078 was more recently considered in *Rock Advertising Ltd v MWB Business Exchange Centres Ltd* [2018] UKSC 24 in the context of an entire agreement clause (essentially a clause stating that the written agreement represents the full agreement between the parties). Lord Sumption stated (at [14]):

In *Brikom Investments Ltd v Carr* [1979] QB 467, 480, Lord Denning MR brushed aside an entire agreement clause, observing that 'the cases are legion in which such a clause is of no effect in the face of an express promise or representation on which the other side has relied.' In fact there were at that time no cases in which the courts had declined to give effect to such clauses, and the one case which Lord Denning cited (*J Evans & Son (Portsmouth) Ltd v Andrea Merzario Ltd* [1976] 1 WLR 1078) was really a case of estoppel and concerned a different sort of clause altogether. In *Ryanair Ltd v SR Technics Ireland Ltd* [2007] EWHC 3089 (QB), at paras 137–143, Gray J treated Lord Denning's *dictum* as a general statement of the law. But in my view it cannot be supported save possibly in relation to estoppel. The true position is that if the collateral agreement is capable of operating as an independent agreement, and is supported by its own consideration, then most standard forms of entire agreement clause will not prevent its enforcement: see *Business Environment Bow Lane Ltd v Deanwater Estates Ltd* [2007] L&TR 26 (CA), at para 43, and *North Eastern Properties Ltd v Coleman* [2010] 1 WLR 2715 at paras 57 (Briggs J), 82 to 83 (Longmore LJ). But if the clause is relied upon as modifying what would otherwise be the effect of the agreement which contains it, the courts will apply it according to its terms and decline to give effect to the collateral agreement. As Longmore LJ observed in the *North Eastern Properties Ltd* case, at para 82:

'if the parties agree that the written contract is to be the entire contract, it is no business of the courts to tell them that they do not mean what they have said.'

Thus in *McGrath v Shah* (1989) 57 P&CR 452, 459, John Chadwick QC (sitting as a Deputy Judge of the Chancery Division) applied an entire agreement clause in a contract for the sale of land, where the clause served the important function of ensuring that the contract was not avoided under section 2 of the Law of Property (Miscellaneous Provisions) Act 1989 on the ground that the terms were not all contained in one document.

See also *JN Hipwell and Son v Szurek* [2018] EWCA Civ 674.

6.2.1.4 Expert knowledge of one of the parties

The relative knowledge of the parties may also be a relevant factor in considering whether a statement is a term or merely a representation. The court may be more inclined to find that a statement is a term if it was made by the person in the best position to have ascertained the truth. The following two cases will illustrate this point.

***Oscar Chess v Williams* [1957] 1 WLR 370**

Facts: Williams, a private individual, sold a Morris car to Oscar Chess, a car dealership. In the pre-contractual negotiations, Williams innocently described the car as a 1948 Morris and produced the registration book for the car. The salesman checked the registration book and it showed that 1948 was the date of the first registration. On this basis he offered Williams a trade-in allowance of £290 against the purchase of a new car. It later turned out that the car was a 1939 model which was only worth £175. The plaintiffs sought to recover from the defendant damages of £115, calculated as the difference in value between £290 and £175. The county court judge held that the assumption that the car was a 1948 model was a fundamental condition of the contract, breach of which entitled the car dealers to damages.

Held: A majority of the Court of Appeal (Morris LJ dissenting) allowed the appeal on the ground that that there was no evidence to support the conclusion that the statement made by the defendant was intended to be a term of the contract; it was a mere innocent misrepresentation.

Denning LJ: It must have been obvious to both that the seller had himself no personal knowledge of the year when the car was made. He only became owner after a great number of changes. He must have been relying on the registration book. It is unlikely that such a person would warrant the year of manufacture. The most he would do would be to state his belief, and then produce the registration book in verification of it. In these circumstances the intelligent bystander would, I suggest, say that the seller did not intend to bind himself so as to warrant that it was a 1948 model. If the seller was asked to pledge himself to it, he would at once have said 'I cannot do that. I have only the log-book to go by, the same as you. ...'

It seems to me clear that the motor-dealers who bought the car relied on the year stated in the log-book. If they had wished to make sure of it, they could have checked it then and there, by taking the engine number and chassis number and writing to the makers. They did not do so at the time, but only eight months later. They are experts, and, not having made that check at the time, I do not think they should now be allowed to recover against the innocent seller who produced to them all the evidence he had, namely, the registration book. I agree that it is hard on the dealers to have paid more than the car is worth: but it would be equally hard on the seller to make him pay the difference.

Denning LJ applied an objective test, referring to the 'intelligent bystander', to determine whether the statement was a term or a representation. The court therefore looked at what the parties said and did rather than what they thought. Of crucial importance was the fact that it was unlikely, in light of his state of knowledge, that the defendant would have guaranteed the age of the car. Furthermore, Denning LJ placed emphasis on the fact that the plaintiffs, as car dealers, could have taken further steps to verify the age of the car. The significance of the knowledge and expertise of the parties is apparent when one compares the facts of *Oscar Chess* with those of *Dick Bentley Productions v Harold Smith (Motors)*.

Dick Bentley Productions Ltd v Harold Smith (Motors) Ltd [1965] 1 WLR 623, CA

Facts: Harold Smith (Motors) sold Dick Bentley Productions a Park Ward drop-head coupé Bentley motor car for the sum of £1,850. The car had recently been fitted with a new engine and gearbox, and in the pre-contractual negotiations, Harold Smith innocently stated that the car had only done 20,000 miles with the new engine and gearbox. In fact, the car had done very near to 100,000 miles. The county court judge held that the statement as to mileage was a warranty. That warranty had been broken and the judge awarded Bentley £400 in damages.

Held: The Court of Appeal dismissed the appeal on the ground that the statement as to mileage was intended and understood as a legally binding promise.

Lord Denning MR: I endeavoured to explain in *Oscar Chess Ltd* [1957] 1 WLR 370, 375, that the question whether a warranty was intended depends on the conduct of the parties, on their words and behaviour, rather than on their thoughts. If an intelligent bystander would reasonably infer that a warranty was intended, that will suffice. ... [I]t seems to me that if a representation is made in the course of dealings for a contract for the very purpose of inducing the other party to act upon it, and actually inducing him to act upon it, by entering into the contract, that is prima facie ground for inferring that it was intended as a warranty. It is not necessary to speak of it as being collateral. Suffice it that it was intended to be acted upon and was in fact acted on. But the maker of the representation can rebut this inference if he can show that it really was an innocent misrepresentation, in that he was in fact innocent of fault in making it, and that it would not be reasonable in the circumstances for him to be bound by it. In the *Oscar Chess* case the inference was rebutted. There a man had bought a second-hand car and received with it a log-book which stated the year of the car, 1948. He afterwards resold the car. When he resold it he simply repeated what was in the logbook and passed it on to the buyer. He honestly believed on reasonable grounds that it was true. He was completely innocent of any fault. There was no warranty by him, but only an innocent misrepresentation. Whereas in the present case it is very different. The inference is not rebutted. Here we have a dealer, Smith, who was in a position to know, or at least to find out, the history of the car. He could get it by writing to the makers. He did not do so. Indeed, it was done later. When the history of this car was examined, his statement turned out to be quite wrong. He ought to have known better. There was no reasonable foundation for it.

It seems that the distinction between *Oscar Chess* and *Dick Bentley* was that, in the former case, the defendant had no knowledge of the age of the car and had made his statement in all innocence. In the latter case, however, the defendant was a car dealer who was in a better position than the purchaser to check the history of the car. Because of this the defendant was prevented from asserting that his statement was a mere representation. The Court of Appeal held that, on the basis of Harold Smith's position as a car dealer, it could be inferred that the parties intended the statement as to mileage to be incorporated into the contract as a term. See also *Brewer v Mann* [2012] EWCA Civ 246.

It should be noted that if the facts of *Dick Bentley* occurred today, it is highly likely that the case could be dealt with as a negligent misrepresentation under s 2(1) of the Misrepresentation Act 1967 (see Chapter 8). That section imposes liability in damages for a misrepresentation where the misrepresentation induces the other party into the contract unless the misrepresentor can prove that he had reasonable grounds to believe – and did believe up to the time the contract was made – that the facts as represented were true. The defendants in *Dick Bentley* would have struggled to prove that they had reasonable grounds for their belief but, at the time, of course, damages for negligent misrepresentation were not available. Therefore, the plaintiff's only recourse was a claim for breach of contract. Even today, a claim for breach of contract may be preferable because it enables the claimant to recover his expectation loss. Damages for misrepresentation essentially compensate the claimant for his reliance loss (*Doyle v Olby* [1969] 2 QB 158, 167).

6.2.2 Incorporation in a collateral contract

As noted above, the courts are reluctant to find that an oral statement has been incorporated as a term in a written contract. Prior to the enactment of the Misrepresentation Act 1967, this could lead to considerable hardship for claimants. For this reason it seems that the courts developed a number of ingenious measures to enable claimants to obtain adequate remedies. One such measure was finding that the oral statement had been incorporated into a collateral contract between the parties. The House of Lords considered the use of such collateral contracts in *Heilbut Symons & Co v Buckleton*.

Heilbut Symons & Co v Buckleton [1913] AC 30

Facts: Heilbut were rubber merchants who underwrote shares in a new rubber company. The manager saw a prospectus claiming that the company had a certain number of rubber trees. On this basis, the manager of Heilbut indicated to Buckleton that the new company was a sound proposition and Buckleton bought 6,000 shares in it. Later on it was discovered that there was a large deficiency in the rubber trees which were said in the prospectus to exist, and the shares fell in value. Buckleton brought a claim against Heilbut for fraudulent misrepresentation, and alternatively for damages for breach of contract. At first instance, it was held that there had been no fraudulent misrepresentation but that the representation had been incorporated into the contract as a term which had been breached.

Held: The House of Lords allowed the appeal on the ground that there had been no fraudulent misrepresentation and that the statement had not been incorporated as a term of the main contract. Their

Lordships considered the possibility that the statement had been incorporated into a collateral agreement between the manager and Buckleton but concluded that it had not.

Lord Moulton: It is evident, both on principle and on authority, that there may be a contract the consideration for which is the making of some other contract ... It is collateral to the main contract, but each has an independent existence, and they do not differ in respect of their possessing to the full the character and status of a contract. But such collateral contracts must from their very nature be rare ... Such collateral contracts, the sole effect of which is to vary or add to the terms of the principal contract, are viewed with suspicion by the law. They must be proved strictly. Not only the terms of such contracts but the existence of an *animus contrahendi* on the part of all the parties to them must be clearly shewn. Any laxity ... would enable parties to escape from the full performance of the obligations of contracts unquestionably entered into by them and more especially would have the effect of lessening the authority of written contracts by making it possible to vary them by suggesting the existence of verbal collateral agreements relating to the same subject-matter. There is in the present case an entire absence of any evidence to support the existence of such a collateral contract.

On the facts of *Heilbut*, the House of Lords was unwilling to find a collateral contract, but in more recent times the courts have sometimes adopted a more flexible approach.

City of Westminster Properties v Mudd [1959] Ch 129

Facts: Mudd became the tenant of an antique shop for a term of three years during which he was allowed by the landlord, City of Westminster Properties, to sleep in an office behind the shop. When the lease came up for renewal, the landlord tried to insert a clause stating that the premises could not be used as a place for lodging, dwelling or sleeping. Mudd objected, but was assured orally that if he signed the lease, he would be allowed to continue to live there. Due to an oversight the new clause was omitted, but a provision requiring the premises only to be used for business activities remained. The landlord subsequently sought to forfeit the lease on the basis that Mudd was still living in the shop in breach of the clause.

Held: The High Court held that the oral statement that Mudd could live in the premises constituted a collateral agreement that overrode the clause in the lease itself.

Harman J: If the defendant's evidence is to be accepted, as I hold it is, it is a case of a promise made to him before the execution of the lease that, if he would execute it in the form put before him, the landlord would not seek to enforce against him personally the covenant about using the property as a shop only. The defendant says that it was in reliance on this promise that he executed the lease and entered on the onerous obligations contained in it. He says, moreover, that but for the promise made he would not have executed the lease, but would have moved to other premises available to him at the time. If these be the facts, there was a clear contract acted upon by the defendant to his detriment and from which the plaintiffs cannot be allowed to resile ... The plea that this was a mere licence retractable at the plaintiffs' will does not bear examination. The promise was that so long as the defendant personally was tenant, so long would the landlords forbear to exercise the rights which they would have if he signed the lease. He did sign the lease on this promise and is therefore entitled to rely on it so long as he is personally in occupation of the shop.

In the following case, Lord Denning MR went even further than Harman J in *Mudd* and recommended the wider scale use of collateral contracts where experts make statements of fact.

***Esso Petroleum v Mardon* [1976] QB 801**

Facts: Mr Mardon was a prospective tenant of a petrol filling station. One of Esso's employees, Mr Leith, who had 40 years' experience in the petrol trade, stated that the estimated throughput of the station was 200,000 gallons per year. This estimate failed to take into account the fact that the local authority had refused to allow the pumps at the station to front on to the main street, thus requiring the station to be built back to front. Mr Mardon was dubious as to the accuracy of the estimate, but accepted it on the basis of the greater experience and expertise of Mr Leith. He entered the lease but the throughput never exceeded 78,000 gallons per year. Mr Mardon brought an action in contract for breach of warranty as to the potential throughput, and alternatively in tort for negligent misrepresentation. At first instance, Lawson J held that the statement as to potential throughput was not a contractual warranty such as to give the defendant a cause of action for breach of contract but that Esso was liable for negligent misrepresentation.

Held: The Court of Appeal allowed the appeal on the ground that Mr Leith's statement was a warranty that Esso had breached. The cross-appeal against Esso's liability for negligent misrepresentation was dismissed.

Lord Denning MR:

Collateral warranty

Ever since *Heilbut, Symons & Co v Buckleton* [1913] AC 30, we have had to contend with the law as laid down by the House of Lords that an innocent misrepresentation gives no right to damages. In order to escape from that rule, the pleader used to allege – I often did it myself – that the misrepresentation was fraudulent, or alternatively a collateral warranty. At the trial we nearly always succeeded on collateral warranty. We had to reckon, of course, with the dictum of Lord Moulton, at p 47, that 'such collateral contracts must from their very nature be rare'. But more often than not the court elevated the innocent misrepresentation into a collateral warranty: and thereby did justice – in advance of the Misrepresentation Act 1967. I remember scores of cases of that kind, especially on the sale of a business. A representation as to the profits that had been made in the past was invariably held to be a warranty. Besides that experience, there have been many cases since I have sat in this court where we have readily held a representation – which induces a person to enter into a contract – to be a warranty sounding in damages. I summarised them in *Dick Bentley Productions v Harold Smith (Motors) Ltd* [1965] 1 WLR 623, 627, when I said:

> 'Looking at the cases once more, as we have done so often, it seems to me that if a representation is made in the course of dealings for a contract for the very purpose of inducing the other party to act upon it, and actually inducing him to act upon it, by entering into the contract, that is prima facie ground for inferring that it was intended as a warranty. It is not necessary to speak of it as being collateral. Suffice it that it was intended to be acted upon and was in fact acted on'.

[Counsel for Esso] retaliated, however, by citing *Bisset v Wilkinson* [1927] AC 177, where the Privy Council said that a statement by a New Zealand farmer that an area of land 'would carry 2,000 sheep' was only an expression of opinion. He submitted that the forecast here of 200,000 gallons was an expression of opinion and not a statement of fact: and that it could not be interpreted as a warranty or promise.

Now I would quite agree with [counsel for the appellant] that it was not a warranty – in this sense – that it did not *guarantee* that the throughput *would* be 200,000 gallons. But, nevertheless, it was a forecast made by a party – Esso – who had special knowledge and skill. It was the yardstick (the estimated annual consumption) by which they measured the worth of a filling station. They knew the facts. They knew the traffic in the town. They knew the throughput of comparable stations. They had much experience and expertise at their disposal. They were in a much better position than Mr Mardon to make a forecast. It seems to me that if such a person makes a forecast, intending that the other should act upon it – and he does act upon it, it can well be interpreted as a warranty that the forecast is sound and reliable in the sense that they made it with reasonable care and skill. It is just as if Esso said to Mr Mardon: 'Our forecast of throughput is 200,000 gallons. You can rely upon it as being a sound forecast of what the service station should do. The rent is calculated on that footing'. If the forecast turned out to be an unsound forecast such as no person of skill or experience should have made, there is a breach of warranty. Just as there is a breach of warranty when a forecast is made – 'expected to load' by a certain date – if the maker has no reasonable grounds for it: see *Samuel Sanday and Co v Keighley, Maxted and Co* (1922) 27 ComCas 296; or bunkers 'expected 600/700 tons': see *Efploia Shipping Corporation Ltd v Canadian Transport Co Ltd (The Pantanassa)* [1958] 2 Lloyd's Rep 449, 455–457 by Diplock J. It is very different from the New Zealand case where the land had never been used as a sheep farm and both parties were equally able to form an opinion as to its carrying capacity: see particularly *Bisset v Wilkinson* [1927] AC 177, 183–184.

In the present case it seems to me that there was a warranty that the forecast was sound, that is, Esso made it with reasonable care and skill. That warranty was broken. Most negligently Esso made a 'fatal error' in the forecast they stated to Mr Mardon, and on which he took the tenancy. For this they are liable in damages. The judge, however, declined to find a warranty. So I must go further.

Negligent misrepresentation

Assuming that there was no warranty, the question arises whether Esso are liable for negligent misstatement under the doctrine of *Hedley Byrne & Co Ltd v Heller & Partners Ltd* [1964] AC 465 ... It seems to me that *Hedley Byrne & Co Ltd v Heller & Partners Ltd* [1964] AC 465, properly understood, covers this particular proposition: if a man, who has or professes to have special knowledge or skill, makes a representation by virtue thereof to another – be it advice, information or opinion – with the intention of inducing him to enter into a contract with him, he is under a duty to use reasonable care to see that the representation is correct, and that the advice, information or opinion is reliable. If he negligently gives unsound advice or misleading information or expresses an erroneous opinion, and thereby induces the other side to enter into a contract with him, he is liable in damages. This proposition is in line with what I said in *Candler v Crane, Christmas & Co* [1951] 2 KB 164, 179–180, which was approved by the majority of the Privy Council in *Mutual Life and Citizens' Assurance Co Ltd v Evatt* [1971] AC 793 ...

Applying this principle, it is plain that Esso professed to have – and did in fact have – special knowledge or skill in estimating the throughput of a filling station. They made the representation – they forecast a throughput of 200,000 gallons – intending to induce Mr Mardon to enter into a tenancy on the faith of it. They made it negligently. It was a 'fatal error' and thereby induced Mr Mardon to enter into a contract of tenancy that was disastrous to him. For this misrepresentation they are liable in damages.

The measure of damages

Mr Mardon is not to be compensated here for 'loss of a bargain'. He was given no bargain that the throughput *would* amount to 200,000 gallons a year. He is only to be compensated for having been induced to enter into a contract which turned out to be disastrous for him. Whether it be called breach of warranty or negligent misrepresentation, its effect was *not* to warrant the throughput, but only to induce him to enter the contract. So the damages in either case are to be measured by the loss he suffered. Just as in *Doyle v Olby (Ironmongers) Ltd* [1969] 2 QB 158, 167 he can say: '... I would not have entered into this contract at all but for your representation. Owing to it, I have lost all the capital I put into it. I also incurred a large overdraft. I have spent four years of my life in wasted endeavour without reward: and it will take me some time to re-establish myself'.

For all such loss he is entitled to recover damages. It is to be measured in a similar way as the loss due to a personal injury. You should look into the future so as to forecast what would have been likely to happen if he had never entered into this contract: and contrast it with his position as it is now as a result of entering into it. The future is necessarily problematical and can only be a rough-and-ready estimate. But it must be done in assessing the loss.

The judgment of the Court of Appeal in *Esso v Mardon* demonstrates the willingness of the courts to manipulate legal concepts in order to achieve their desired result. Esso was found liable to Mr Mardon on two grounds: breach of contractual warranty and negligent misrepresentation. The similarities between the alternative claims are of particular interest to us. Following the decision of the House of Lords in *Hedley Byrne*, Mr Mardon was able to seek damages for non-fraudulent misrepresentation as an alternative to his claim for breach of warranty. Both claims gave rise to a right to recover damages (see *Steel and another v NRAM Limited (formerly NRAM Plc) (Scotland)* [2018] UKSC 13).

What is more noteworthy is that the court held that the same measure of damages was available for both claims. Traditionally, damages for breach of contract protect the innocent party's expectation interest, by placing him in the position he would have occupied had the contract been performed. By contrast, damages for misrepresentation protect the innocent party's reliance interest, by placing him in the position he would have occupied had there been no misrepresentation. However, in *Esso v Mardon*, the Court of Appeal awarded reliance damages for Esso's breach of contractual warranty. This was because, on the facts, the warranty was not a guarantee that the throughput of the station would reach 200,000 gallons per year. Instead, it was a promise that the forecast had been made with reasonable care and skill. Therefore, the measure of damages for breach of the term was not the profit that Mr Mardon expected to make on the projected throughput, but the losses he suffered by relying on Esso's negligent forecast. See also the interesting discussion in *New York Laser Clinic Ltd v Naturastudios Ltd* [2019] EWHC 2892 (QB).

Given that Mr Mardon already had a damages claim for negligent misrepresentation, it is somewhat surprising that the Court of Appeal went to such lengths to find a collateral contract. Indeed, it could be argued that, following the recognition of damages for negligent misrepresentation, the courts should refrain from artificially construing the facts to find a collateral contract (compare *Thinc Group v Armstrong* [2012] EWCA Civ 1227 where, on the facts, Rix LJ thought that any other 'construction [was] … so unreasonable, so uncommercial that it is to my mind impossible'). While the distinction between the claim for breach of contract and the claim for negligent misrepresentation made no difference on the facts of *Esso v Mardon*, the distinction might be more significant in other cases. For example, a claim for misrepresentation provides the claimant with the possibility of rescinding the main contract; a claim for breach of a collateral contract does not. Moreover, the remoteness test applied in actions for breach of contract is more restrictive than the test applied in actions for deceit, or under s 2(1) of the Misrepresentation Act 1967 (see Chapter 8).

6.2.3 Summary

As we have seen, there are a number of actions that may be available in relation to pre-contractual statements. The statement may be incorporated into the main contract, giving rise to a claim for breach of contract. In ascertaining whether this was the intention of the parties the courts will take into account a number of factors including: the importance of the statement, any requirement of independent verification, the written terms of the contract and the relative knowledge of the parties. Alternatively, the statement might be construed to form a collateral contract, giving rise to an action for damages. Nowadays, following the recognition of damages for negligent misrepresentation, it will rarely be necessary for the court to construe the statement as a collateral contract. However, if the statement is not susceptible to construction as a statement of fact, an action for breach of a contractual term may still be the only course open to a claimant.

6.3 Express terms

Having noted the importance of distinguishing between terms of a contract and pre-contractual representations, we turn to examine express terms – clauses that have been put forward by one or other of the parties as a term of the contract. Contracts are normally made up of various express terms, differing in character and importance. The courts are often called upon to decide which terms have been incorporated into a contract, what those terms mean and what the consequences are of breach. In each of these situations the court seeks to determine the parties' intention from an objective perspective. We will look at each of these issues in turn.

6.3.1 Incorporation

The question of whether a term has been incorporated into the contract is an important issue for the parties, particularly when the term in question is an exclusion clause. There are three main ways in which a term can be incorporated into a contract: by signed consent, by notice and by common course of dealings.

6.3.1.1 Signed consent

A signature may operate as a means of incorporating terms into a written contract, whether or not the party signing the contract has read or understood the terms. This can arguably lead to harsh results as seen in *L'Estrange v Graucob*.

L'Estrange v Graucob **[1934] 2 KB 394**

Facts: L'Estrange, a café owner in Llandudno, bought a cigarette vending machine from Graucob. She signed a sales agreement, without reading it, which contained in small print certain special terms one of which was 'any express or implied condition, statement, or warranty, statutory or otherwise not stated herein is hereby excluded'. The machine was delivered to L'Estrange but it did not work satisfactorily, so she brought an action against Graucob in the county court claiming damages for breach of an implied warranty that the machine was fit for the purpose for which it was sold. Graucob argued that the contract expressly excluded all implied warranties.

Held: The Divisional Court reversed the judgment of the county court judge, and held that the exclusion clause was enforceable even though it was written in small print and L'Estrange had not read it.

Scrutton LJ: The main question raised in the present case is whether [the exclusion clause] formed part of the contract. If it did, it clearly excluded any condition or warranty ... When a document containing contractual terms is signed, then, in the absence of fraud, or, I will add, misrepresentation, the party signing it is bound, and it is wholly immaterial whether he has read the document or not.

The plaintiff contended at the trial that she was induced by misrepresentation to sign the contract without knowing its terms, and that on that ground they are not binding upon her. The learned judge in his judgment makes no mention of that contention of the plaintiff, and he pronounces no finding as to the alleged misrepresentation. There is a further difficulty. Fraud is not mentioned in the pleadings, and I strongly object to deal with allegations of fraud where fraud is not expressly pleaded. I have read the evidence with care, and it contains no material upon which fraud could be found. The plaintiff no doubt alleged that the defendants' agent represented to her that the document which was given her to be signed was an order form, but according to the defendants' evidence no such statement was made to her by the agent. Moreover, whether the plaintiff was or was not told that the document was an order form, it was in fact an order form, and an order form is a contractual document. It may be either an acceptance or a proposal which may be accepted, but it always contains some contractual terms. There is no evidence that the plaintiff was induced to sign the contract by misrepresentation.

In this case the plaintiff has signed a document headed 'Sales Agreement', which she admits had to do with an intended purchase, and which contained a clause excluding all conditions and warranties. That being so, the plaintiff, having put her signature to the document and not having been induced to do so by any fraud or misrepresentation, cannot be heard to say that she is not bound by the terms of the document because she has not read them.

Maugham LJ: I regret the decision to which I have come, but I am bound by legal rules and cannot decide the case on other considerations …

I deal with this case on the footing that when the order confirmation was signed by the defendants confirming the order form which had been signed by the plaintiff, there was then a signed contract in writing between the parties. If that is so, then, subject to certain contingencies, there is no doubt that it was wholly immaterial whether the plaintiff read the small print or not …

There are, however, two possibilities to be kept in view. The first is that it might be proved that the document, though signed by the plaintiff, was signed in circumstances which made it not her act. That is known as the case of *Non est factum*. I do not think it is necessary to add anything to what Scrutton LJ has already said about that, the written document admittedly related to the purchase of the machine by the plaintiff. Even if she was told that it was an order form, she could not be heard to say that it did not affect her because she did not know its contents.

Another possibility is that the plaintiff might have been induced to sign the document by misrepresentation. She contended that she was so induced to sign the document inasmuch as (i.) she was assured that it was an order form, (ii.) that at the time when she signed it she knew nothing of the conditions which it contained. The second of these contentions is unavailing by reason of the fact that the document was in writing signed by the plaintiff. As to the first contention it is true that the document was an order form. But further, if the statement that it was an order form could be treated as a representation that it contained no clause expressly excluding all conditions and warranties, the answer would be that there is no evidence to prove that that statement was made by or on behalf of the defendants.

In this case it is, in my view, an irrelevant circumstance that the plaintiff did not read, or hear of, the parts of the sales document which are in small print, and that document should have effect according to its terms. I may add, however, that I could wish that the contract had been in a simpler and more usual form. It is unfortunate that the important clause excluding conditions and warranties is in such small print. I also think that the order confirmation form should have contained an express statement to the effect that it was exclusive of all conditions and warranties.

The rule in *L'Estrange v Graucob* may be considered to operate harshly. However, in *Coys of Kensington Automobiles Ltd v Pugliese* [2011] EWHC 655, Ramsey J stated (at [40]):

> Mr Ticciati, on the other hand referred to the decision of the Court of Appeal in *L'Estrange v Graucob* [1934] 2 KB 394 where Scrutton LJ had said that in the case of an agreement signed by a party 'it is wholly immaterial whether he has read the document or not'. I consider that this is a reflection of the fact that a written agreement has to be construed objectively … Here the background was that the Defendant visiting Monaco completed and signed the Form written in English for an international car auction. Viewed objectively, I do not consider that there is a strong argument that a person who completes a document such as the Form in such circumstances can avoid its consequences by saying that they did not read it or did not understand it. Otherwise, to make the question of consensus, in a case based on a document, depend on the intellectual or linguistic capacity of a party would cause great uncertainty which an objective analysis is intended to overcome.

It should also be noted that there are exceptions to the rule, as recognised by the Court of Appeal. First, the rule is modified where the signature is obtained by fraud or a misrepresentation (see also *Higgins & Co Lawyers Ltd v Evans* [2019] EWHC 507 (Ch) at [75] where HHL Keyser QC stated that it is a: 'well-established principle that a party who signs a document knowing that it is intended to have legal effect will *generally* be treated as being bound by its terms and will be taken to have read them and be on notice of them – at least absent the case being an extreme one where there is cogent evidence of the signature being obtained under pressure or by some other improper conduct.'). This was seen in *Curtis v Chemical Cleaning & Dyeing Co.*

Curtis v Chemical Cleaning & Dyeing Co [1951] 1 KB 805

Facts: Mrs Curtis took a white satin wedding dress trimmed in beads and sequins to the defendant dry cleaners for cleaning. She was asked to sign a 'receipt' by the assistant. When she asked what the significance of the document was, the assistant replied that it excluded liability for the beads and sequins. Mrs Curtis signed the document. The receipt actually contained a general exclusion clause stating that the dress was 'accepted on condition that the company is not liable for any damage howsoever arising'. When the dress was returned to Mrs Curtis it was badly stained. She brought a claim against the dry cleaners and they sought to rely on the general exclusion clause.

Held: The Court of Appeal held that the defendants could not rely on the exclusion clause in light of the innocent misrepresentation made by the shop assistant prior to the plaintiff signing the document.

Denning LJ: This case is of importance because of the many cases nowadays when people sign printed forms without reading them, only to find afterwards that they contain stringent clauses exempting the other side from their common-law liabilities ... If the party ... signs a written document, knowing it to be a contract which governs the relations between them, his signature is irrefragable evidence of his assent to the whole contract, including the exempting clauses, unless the signature is shown to be obtained by fraud or misrepresentation: *L'Estrange v Graucob* [1934] 2 KB 394. But what is a sufficient misrepresentation for this purpose?

In my opinion any behaviour, by words or conduct, is sufficient to be a misrepresentation if it is such as to mislead the other party about the existence or extent of the exemption. If it conveys a false impression, that is enough. If the false impression is created knowingly, it is a fraudulent misrepresentation; if it is created unwittingly, it is an innocent misrepresentation; but either is sufficient to disentitle the creator of it to the benefit of the exemption. In *Rex v Kylsant (Lord)* [1932] 1 KB 443 it was held that a representation might be literally true but practically false, not because of what it said, but because of what it left unsaid; in short, because of what it implied. This is as true of an innocent misrepresentation as it is of a fraudulent misrepresentation. When one party puts forward a printed form for signature, failure by him to draw attention to the existence or extent of the exemption clause may in some circumstances convey the impression that there is no exemption at all, or at any rate not so wide an exemption as that which is in fact contained in the document. The present case is a good illustration. The customer said in evidence: 'When I was asked to sign the document I asked why? The assistant said I was to accept any responsibility for damage to beads and sequins. I did not read it all before I signed it.' In those circumstances, by failing to draw attention to the width of the exemption clause, the assistant created the false impression that the exemption only related to the beads and sequins, and that it did not extend to the material of which the dress was made. It was done perfectly innocently, but nevertheless a false impression was created ... It was a sufficient misrepresentation to disentitle the cleaners from relying on the exemption, except in regard to beads and sequins.

Although Denning LJ appeared to suggest that the exemption clause was incorporated (as he held that it could have been used in relation to the beads and sequins), the other judges (Somervell and Singleton LJJ) held that it was not incorporated (see *Axa Sun Life Services plc v Campbell Martin Ltd* [2011] EWCA Civ 133 at [99]–[103], *per* Rix LJ, *AJ Building & Plastering Ltd* [2013] EWHC 484 and *Athena Capital Fund Sicav-Fis S.C.A. v Crownmark Ltd* [2019] EWHC 1952 (Comm)).

Second, subsequent cases have also shown that the rule in *L'Estrange v Graucob* only operates when the signed document is contractual in effect.

Grogan v Robin Meredith Plant Hire **[1996] 15 Tr LR 371**

Facts: The plaintiff was injured by a machine used to lay pipes in North Wales. The machine and driver had been hired from Meredith Plant Hire by Triact, a firm of civil engineers. Mr Patten, the site agent for Triact, had arranged the hire, and each week he signed the driver's 'time sheet', a form which kept a record of the hours that the driver had worked. The time sheet contained the words 'all hire undertaken under CPA (Contractors Plant Association) conditions. Copies available on request.' Those conditions included an indemnity from Triact to Meredith against liability to third parties incurred in the course of hire. At the time of entering into the contract of hire no terms had been mentioned and there had been no suggestion that the contract was under CPA conditions. At first instance, Pill J held that the clause contained in the time sheet was binding and ordered Triact to indemnify Meredith.

Held: The Court of Appeal allowed the appeal. The verbal contract had not been varied by the site agent's signature of the time sheets and therefore Triact was not obliged to indemnify Meredith.

Auld LJ: The central question ... is whether the time sheet in this case comes within the class of document which the party receiving it knew contained, or which a reasonable man would expect to contain, relevant contractual conditions. Another way of putting it, as Kerr J did in *Bahamas Oil Refining Co v Kris-tiansands Tankrederie A/S (The Polyduke)* [1978] 1 Lloyd's Rep 211 at 215–216, is whether 'the document purport[ed] to have contractual effect' ...

Documents such as a time sheet, an invoice or a statement of account ... do not normally have a contractual effect in the sense of making or varying a contract. The purpose of time sheets is not normally to contain or evidence the terms of a contract, but to record a party's performance of an existing obligation under a contract.

A different result was reached in *Harsco Infrastructure Services Ltd v Bellway Homes Ltd* [2011] EWHC 3519 in relation to an order for scaffolding with HHJ Wilcox stating:

> It was an order. It made clear reference to terms and conditions above the signature block of Mr Hardy, and they were delivered with the document. I remind myself that Mr Hardy was in the position of someone who had access to the commercial department. He had baulked at signing the document originally. He decided later that he would sign it, and did sign it. I ask myself this question. Would a reasonable man looking at it objectively, in the position of Mr Hardy, appreciate and realise that to sign a document such as this would have a contractual effect? I am satisfied that the answer to that question is 'Yes', that to append a signature to a document in those circumstances is to knowingly accept that there would be an incorporation of those terms into the contract. I have no doubt whatsoever that his motive in signing it was primarily to trigger payment, but he must have appreciated that, in so doing, the terms would be incorporated. I have no doubt that, had there not been a fire, nobody would have turned a hair. He would have been paid, the job would have been done, and that would be an end of the matter.

Thirdly (as will be discussed at 6.3.2.3 below), following the decision of the Supreme Court in *Autoclenz v Belcher* [2011] UKSC 41 a more flexible approach may be used in relation to contracts of employment (see also *Qantas Cabin Crew (UK) Ltd v Lopez* [2013] IRLR 4 and A Bogg 41 ILJ 328).

The rule in *L'Estrange v Graucob* is therefore subject to a number of exceptions that seriously limit its scope. Maugham LJ clearly regretted the outcome but felt that he was 'bound by legal rules' to come to the decision. This conclusion has been doubted by several commentators, including J R Spencer, who has argued that the rule was based on a misapplication of the parol evidence rule (see below) and the defence of *non est factum*. He suggests that the claimant should not be bound by the clause where 'he did not mean to consent to the disputed term, and although he appeared to consent to it, the other party either caused or connived at his mistake' (J R Spencer, 'Signature, Consent and the Rule in *L'Es-trange v Graucob*' [1973] CLJ 104, 121).

As J R Spencer noted, the choice to be made was a choice between two evils: either allowing companies to hold ignorant signatories to the letter of sweeping exemption clauses, or allowing liars to evade contractual liabilities freely assumed. The former evil would undermine justice; the latter would undermine the certainty created by a signed contractual document. The English courts have generally decided to accept the former evil in preference to the latter. This may be wise since the Unfair Contract Terms Act 1977 and now the Consumer Rights Act 2015 provide mechanisms for dealing with 'unfair' exemption clauses. However, the 'hands-off' approach adopted by the courts in respect of signed contracts is hard to reconcile with the stricter approach adopted in cases concerned with the incorporation of terms by notice (although cf. *Ocean Chemical Transport Inc v Exnor Craggs Ltd* [2000] 1 Lloyd's Rep 446, at 6.3.1.4 below).

6.3.1.2 Notice of printed terms

Terms can also be incorporated into a contract by notice. A party wishing to incorporate printed terms in this way must take reasonable steps to bring the terms to the other party's attention or knowledge. The burden of showing that the terms have been incorporated is on the party seeking to rely on them. Once again, the courts adopt an objective approach. If it can be shown that the party seeking to rely on the printed terms has taken reasonable steps to bring them to the attention of the other party, the terms will be incorporated into the contract regardless of whether the other party has read or understood the terms.

***Parker v South Eastern Railway* (1877) 2 CPD 416**

Facts: Mr Parker deposited his bag in a station cloakroom. He paid two pence and was given a ticket which said, on the front, 'see back'. On the back of the ticket was an exclusion clause which stated that 'The Company will not be responsible for any package exceeding the value of £10'. His bag was stolen. The trial judge left two questions to the jury: '1. Did the plaintiff read or was he aware of the special condition upon which the article was deposited? 2. Was the plaintiff, under the circumstances, under any obligation, in the exercise of reasonable and proper caution, to read or to make himself aware of the condition?' The jury answered both the questions in the negative, and judgment was directed for the plaintiff. The defendant appealed.

Held: The Court of Appeal ordered a new trial, on the ground that there had been a misdirection by the judge. There was no obligation on the plaintiff to read the condition and the second question left to the jury ought to have been, whether the company did that which was reasonably sufficient to bring the clause to the attention of the plaintiff.

Mellish LJ: I am of opinion ... that the proper direction to leave to the jury in these cases is, that if the person receiving the ticket did not see or know that there was any writing on the ticket, he is not bound by the conditions; that if he knew there was writing, and knew or believed that the writing contained conditions, then he is bound by the conditions; that if he knew there was writing on the ticket, but did not know or believe that the writing contained conditions, nevertheless he would be bound, if the delivering of the ticket to him in such a manner that he could see there was writing upon it, was, in the opinion of the jury, reasonable notice that the writing contained conditions.

I have lastly to consider whether the direction of the learned judge was correct, namely, 'Was the plaintiff, under the circumstances, under any obligation, in the exercise of reasonable and proper caution, to read or to make himself aware of the condition?' I think that this direction was not strictly accurate, and was calculated to mislead the jury. The plaintiff was certainly under no obligation to read the ticket, but was entitled to leave it unread if he pleased, and the question does not appear to me to direct the attention of the jury to the real question, namely, whether the railway company did what was reasonably sufficient to give the plaintiff notice of the condition.

The test to be applied by the court is essentially whether the party seeking to rely upon the term has made a reasonable effort to give the claimant notice of the term. This is an objective test, and in determining whether or not reasonable steps have been taken, the courts have regard to a number of factors including: the location of the notice, the form it takes and the point in time at which it is displayed. The courts have made clear that, in order to be incorporated in this way, terms must have been contained or referred to in a document that was intended to have contractual effect.

Chapelton v Barry UDC [1940] 1 KB 532

Facts: Mr Chapelton wished to hire a deck chair on a beach. The defendant council had placed a notice next to the deck chairs advising members of the public of the cost of the chairs and requesting that they obtain tickets for their chairs from the chair attendants. The notice contained no exclusion clause. Mr Chapelton obtained two chairs from the attendant and received two tickets. He glanced at the tickets and put them in his pocket. On the back of the tickets were the words: 'The council will not be liable for any accident or damage arising from the hire of the chair.' When Mr Chapelton sat on his chair it gave way. He brought an action against the defendants for negligence. The county court found that the accident was due to the defendant's negligence but that they were exempted from liability as the plaintiff had sufficient notice of the exclusion clause printed on the ticket.

Held: The Court of Appeal allowed the appeal on the ground that the ticket was a mere voucher or receipt for the money paid for the hire of the chair. The conditions for hire were to be found on the notice put up next to the pile of chairs and that notice contained no clause excluding the defendant's liability.

Goddard LJ: In this case the appellant paid 2d in order to have the right to sit on a chair on the beach, and he was asked to take a ticket in the form of a receipt for that purpose ... I cannot imagine that anybody paying 2d under those circumstances for the privilege of sitting in a chair on the beach would think for one moment that some conditions were being imposed upon him which would limit his ordinary rights, or that the document he received when paying his 2d was a contractual document in any shape or form. I think the ticket he received was nothing but a receipt for his 2d – a receipt which showed him how long he might use the chair.

It is also necessary for the terms to be brought to the other party's attention prior to the formation of the contract. If communication of the terms comes after the moment in time at which the contract is agreed, the terms will not be effectively incorporated, as seen in *Olley v Marlborough Court Ltd* and *Thornton v Shoe Lane Parking*.

Olley v Marlborough Court Ltd [1949] 1 KB 532

Facts: A man and his wife checked into a hotel, and paid a week's board and residence in advance. They went upstairs to their bedroom where a notice was displayed as follows: 'The proprietors will not hold themselves responsible for articles lost or stolen, unless handed to the manageress for safe custody. Valuables should be deposited for safe custody in a sealed package and a receipt obtained.' The wife's furs were stolen from her room due to the negligence of the hotel's employees who left her key unguarded on the key-board at the reception. The defendant claimed that the notice displayed in the room had effectively excluded their liability for negligence.

Held: The Court of Appeal held that the terms of the notice in the bedroom formed no part of the contract because the contract had been made before the guests could see the notice.

Denning LJ: The first question is whether that notice formed part of the contract. Now people who rely on a contract to exempt themselves from their common law liability must prove that contract strictly. Not only must the terms of the contract be clearly proved, but also the intention to create legal relations – the intention to be legally bound – must also be clearly proved. The best way of proving it is by a written document signed by the party to be bound. Another way is by handing him before or at the time of the contract a written notice specifying its terms and making it clear to him that the contract is on those terms. A prominent public notice which is plain for him to see when he makes the contract or an express oral stipulation would, no doubt, have the same effect. But nothing short of one of these three ways will suffice. It has been held that mere notices put on receipts for money do not make a contract (see *Chapelton v Barry UDC* [1940] 1 KB 532). So, also, in my opinion, notices put up in bedrooms do not of themselves make a contract. As a rule, the guest does not see them until after he has been accepted as a guest. The hotel company no doubt hope that the guest will be held bound by them, but the hope is vain unless they clearly show that he agreed to be bound by them, which is rarely the case.

Thornton v Shoe Lane Parking [1971] 2 QB 163

Facts: Mr Thornton drove his car into a new multi-storey car park which he had not been in before. A notice on the outside gave the charges and stated that all cars were 'parked at owner's risk'. As he drove in a light changed from red to green and a ticket was issued by a machine. He put it in his pocket without fully reading it. The ticket said that it was issued subject to conditions displayed on notices inside the car park. The notices contained a clause excluding all liability for personal injury inside the car park. When Mr Thornton returned to collect his car he was injured in the car park as a result of Shoe Lane's negligence. Thornton claimed damages for the injury but the defendants contended that the ticket incorporated a condition exempting them from liability.

Held: The Court of Appeal held that since Thornton did not know of the exemption clause and Shoe Lane Parking had not done what was reasonably sufficient to bring it to his notice it did not exempt them from liability.

Lord Denning MR: The customer pays his money and gets a ticket. He cannot refuse it. He cannot get his money back. He may protest to the machine, even swear at it. But it will remain unmoved. He is committed beyond recall. He was committed at the very moment when he put his money into the machine. The contract was concluded at that time. It can be translated into offer and acceptance in this way: the offer is made when the proprietor of the machine holds it out as being ready to receive the money. The acceptance takes place when the customer puts his money into the slot. The terms of the offer are contained in the notice placed on or near the machine stating what is offered for the money. The customer is bound by those terms as long as they are sufficiently brought to his notice beforehand, but not otherwise. He is not bound by the terms printed on the ticket if they differ from the notice, because the ticket comes too late. The contract has already been made: see *Olley v Marlborough Court Ltd* [1949] 1 KB 532.

In *Thornton v Shoe Lane Parking*, the exemption clause was not incorporated into the contract because Shoe Lane Parking failed to bring the clause to Mr Thornton's attention prior to the formation of the contract.

Thornton v Shoe Lane Parking was more recently applied by the Irish High Court in the context of websites and so-called 'click-wrap agreements': see *Ryanair v Billiguuege.de Gmbh* [2010] IEHC 47. In that case, which involved the use of Ryanair's website by a price comparison company, Hanna J stated:

> The defendants claim that they never consented to the Terms of Use or entered into any agreement with the plaintiff. The plaintiff says this is not the case and that, at all material times, its Terms of Use governed its relationship with the defendants. As regards whether or not the Terms of Use were binding on the defendant, it is a well established general principle of law that parties to a contract cannot be bound by terms which they have not had an opportunity of reading prior to making the contract. That is not to say that a party will not be bound because they have not read the terms – they will only escape being bound if they can show they were not afforded a reasonable opportunity to read the term in question before entering into the contract. In *Interfoto Picture Library Ltd v Stiletto Visual Programmes Ltd* [1989] QB 433 it was held that where a condition is particularly onerous or unusual, the party seeking to enforce it must show that that condition was fairly brought to the notice of the other party. As per Dillon LJ, at p 439:
>
> > '... if one condition in a set of printed conditions is particularly onerous or unusual, the party seeking to enforce it must show that that particular condition was fairly brought to the attention of the other party.'
>
> Similarly, in *Thornton v Shoe Lane* [1971] 2 WLR 585, a case involving an exclusion of liability clause and a ticket issued by an automatic machine in a car park, Lord Denning MR made the following observations, at p 588:
>
> > 'The customer pays his money and gets a ticket. He cannot refuse it. He cannot get his money back. He may protest to the machine, even swear at it. But it will remain unmoved. He is committed beyond recall. He was committed at the very moment when he put his money into the machine. The contract was concluded at that time. It can be translated into offer and acceptance in this way: the offer is made when the proprietor of the machine holds it out as being ready to receive the money. The acceptance takes place when the customer puts his money into the slot. The terms of the offer are contained in the notice placed on or near the machine stating what is offered for the money. The customer is bound by those terms as long as they are sufficiently brought to his notice before-hand, but not otherwise.'
>
> In *Thornton*, the [Court of Appeal] ... held that the defendant's had not taken sufficient steps to ensure that the notice containing the exclusion of liability clause was brought to the attention of customers of the car-park before they purchased their tickets and in those circumstances that the clause was invalid and of no effect. Here, the exclusive jurisdiction clause was contained in the Terms of Use on the plaintiff's website, highlighted by way of a hyperlink. In such circumstances, the Terms of Use on Ryanair's website were 'fairly brought to the attention of the other party'. It seems that the Terms of Use were clearly accessible by way of a hyperlink which was at all times clearly visible to users of the plaintiff's site. The Terms were not hidden in an awkward part of the screen or in any way concealed or difficult to find. The inclusion by Ryanair of their website terms of use via a hyperlink that the website user is required to view and assent to results in the user entering into what is known as 'a click-wrap agreement' with Ryanair. The plaintiff referred to the US cases of *Caspi v Microsoft Network* 323 NJ Super 118; 732 A 2d 528 (New Jersey Appellate Division, 1999) and *Specht v Netscape & AOL* 306 f 3d 17 in this regard. In addition to claiming that the terms

of use lacked contractual effect, the defendants also argued that regardless of the validity of the terms, they did not 'use' the plaintiff's website, the customer did. In this regard, while the defendants may not be the actual customer or person who will sit on the seat in the plane, they are commercial entities who nonetheless engage with the plaintiff's website for the purpose of gleaning or 'scraping' information from it for onward transmission to their own customers. To claim that that activity is not 'use' of the plaintiff's website by the defendants is an exercise in semantics and an unconvincing argument.

In resolving this issue of the validity of the plaintiff's Terms of Use, the Court has had regard to the traditional contract principles of offer, acceptance and consideration and has asked itself what was the consideration provided in the instant case? The defendants claim there was no consideration, or, for that matter, no acceptance.

Consideration must be provided by the party who seeks to enforce the contract. Here, Ryanair are seeking to enforce their Terms of Use. Ryanair, therefore, must satisfy the Court that they have provided the defendant with consideration. It seems to me that the plaintiff, through their website, offer information for use, subject at all times to their Terms of Use policy, to the users of their website, including the defendants. Although the defendants deny that they use the plaintiff's website and claim that it is the customer or the consumer who does so, it again seems to be that the defendants accept the offer of information made by the plaintiff when they systematically access the Ryanair website though the screen-scraping mechanism. In my view, the provision of information as to flights and prices of flights by Ryanair on their site, subject at all times to their Terms and Conditions, constitutes a sufficient act of consideration for the purposes of making the contract legally binding.

I therefore find for the plaintiffs on the issue of whether or not a legally binding contract exists in this case, being convinced for the reasons set out above that the Terms of Use constitute a contractual document entered into by the parties and in respect of which consideration was provided by the plaintiff in the making available of the information for use by the defendant.

Compare the approach of Charleton J in the same case in the Irish Supreme Court ([2015] IESC 15) which also involved an appeal from *Ryanair Ltd v On the Beach Ltd* [2013] IEHC 124:

18. On this appeal, Ryanair relied on the condition for use of the website term and, peripherally, on the booking consent provision as enabling Ireland to have jurisdiction. Hanna J dealt with the issue of jurisdiction in the Billigfluege litigation by reference to 'traditional contract principles of offer, acceptance and consideration'. Laffoy J, however, in the *On the Beach* case, did not base her judgment on any aspect of the formation of a contract. That emerges as the more correct approach ...

45. In the course of their decisions, Hanna and Laffoy JJ individually reached conclusions that were open to them on the evidence as presented, albeit that their conclusions were reached on different grounds. The conclusion of Laffoy J in the *On the Beach* decision was that the expression of assent to the terms and conditions of the websites of airlines and travel agencies through the clicking or ticking of a box is a practice generally and regularly followed in those commercial sectors. Moreover, she noted, in accordance with that practice, the terms and conditions of use of the website are available throughout such websites by way of hyperlink, with the objective of binding the user of the website to these terms. She held that it was clear that On the Beach were aware of the operation of that practice. Hanna J decided the jurisdiction issue in the *Billigfluege* hearing by reference to traditional contractual analysis. In upholding that decision on this appeal, and in accordance with precedent, no decision is made that a binding contract was entered into, only that a clear choice of jurisdiction has been made by the parties.

It is also possible for terms to be incorporated into a contract by reference to another document (compare also *Hamad M Aldrees & Partners v Rotex Europe Ltd* [2019] EWHC 574 (TCC)).

Hollingworth v Southern Ferries Ltd (The 'Eagle') [1977] 2 Lloyd's Rep 70

Facts: The plaintiff wished to go on holiday to Spain. She asked her friend, who was travelling with her, to make the necessary travel arrangements. He went to a travel agent who gave him a copy of the defendants' brochure, which stated that the conditions of carriage were printed on the inside of the ticket covers. Some time later, the plaintiff's friend purchased a ticket. The ticket contained a general exclusion clause. Midway through the voyage the ship encountered a storm. At the time Mrs Hollingworth was sitting down in the ship's restaurant eating a meal. Her seat toppled over and she fell hitting her head on a hot cupboard. She brought a negligence action against the defendants for the injuries she sustained. The defendants denied liability and relied on the exclusion clause printed on the ticket.

Held: The exclusion clause was not incorporated into the contract.

Deputy Judge Mr Michael Ogden QC: [I]t seems clear … that if the defendants are entitled to rely upon that exclusion clause it is a valid exclusion clause which would result in the plaintiff failing in this action, notwithstanding my finding that the defendants had been negligent … In the present case [Mrs Hollingworth's friend] was not shown the brochure by the defendants at the time when the contract was made, nor just before it was made, so as to make the terms referred to in the brochure part of the contract. Of course, he knew that the defendants had said in the brochure which he collected some time before that they contracted on the basis of conditions of carriage, but in my view that is not enough to make such conditions terms of the contract … I do not consider that merely seeing a statement of this kind in a brochure makes that statement in effect of the same import as would be the case if one were shown that document at the time when one was making the contract; the statement in the brochure merely gives an intending passenger advance notice of the terms which he may expect to find when he enters into the contract.

A notice displaying printed terms is sufficient to incorporate those terms into a contract if, for example, it is presented to the other party at or before the time of contracting. A notice can also have the direct effect of forming a unilateral contract if the notice can be construed as making an offer which the customer accepts. This was seen in *Bowerman v Association of British Travel Agents*.

Bowerman v Association of British Travel Agents [1996] CLC 451

Facts: The plaintiff was planning to go on a school ski trip, but before the trip began the tour operator became insolvent. The tour operator was a member of the Association of British Travel Agents (ABTA) which displayed the following notice in the offices of ABTA members: 'Where holidays or other travel arrangements have not yet commenced at the time of failure [of the tour operator], ABTA arranges for you to be reimbursed the money you would have paid in respect of your holiday arrangements.' The question was whether this notice created a contract between the plaintiff and ABTA.

Held: A majority of the Court of Appeal held that, construed objectively, the notice evinced sufficient intention to create legal relations and constituted an offer that was accepted by the plaintiff.

Hobhouse LJ: [The notice] satisfies the criteria for a unilateral contract and contains promises which are sufficiently clear to be capable of legal enforcement. The principles established in *Carlill* apply.

6.3.1.3 Common course of dealings

It is not always necessary for the terms of the contract to be explicitly stated by the parties. If the parties have dealt with each other on the same terms on a number of previous occasions, it may be reasonable to assume that the parties are aware of the terms of the contract (cf. situations involving an entire agreement clause: see *NHS Commissioning Board (known as NHS England) v Dr Manjul Vasant* [2019] EWCA Civ 1245 at [39]). Thus the terms can be incorporated by a 'common course of dealings'. The leading case on this is *McCutcheon v David MacBrayne Ltd.*

***McCutcheon v David MacBrayne Ltd* [1964] 1 WLR 125**

Facts: Mr McCutcheon asked his brother-in-law, Mr McSporran, to arrange for his car to be shipped to the mainland. Mr McSporran called at the office of David MacBrayne Ltd and booked a place for the car on a ferry. The usual practice of MacBrayne was to ask Mr McSporran to sign a risk note containing various exclusion clauses. On this occasion, MacBrayne forgot and merely gave Mr McSporran a receipt stating that the goods were carried subject to the conditions set out in the notices in MacBrayne's offices. Neither Mr McCutcheon nor Mr McSporran had ever read the words on the receipt or the notices. During the voyage, the ship hit a rock and sank through the negligence of MacBrayne's employees. Mr McSporran brought an action in negligence against MacBrayne, who sought to rely on an exclusion clause contained in their conditions of carriage on the basis that that Mr McSporran had signed risk notes on previous occasions.

Held: The House of Lords held that MacBrayne's terms had not been incorporated into the contract. There was no consistent course of dealings, as on the day in question when the accident occurred, McSporran was offered an oral contract without reference to the conditions usually contained in the risk note.

Lord Reid: Mr McSporran had consigned goods of various kinds on a number of previous occasions. He said that sometimes he had signed a note, sometimes he had not. On one occasion he had sent his own car. A risk note for that consignment was produced signed by him. He had never read the risk notes signed by him. He said: 'I sort of just signed it at the time as a matter of form'. He admitted that he knew he was signing in connection with some conditions but he did not know what they were. In particular, he did not know that he was agreeing to send the goods at owner's risk. [Mr McCutcheon] had consigned goods on four previous occasions. On three of them he was acting on behalf of his employer. On the other occasion he had sent his own car. Each time he had signed a risk note. He also admitted that he knew there were conditions but said that he did not know what they were.

The respondents contend that, by reason of the knowledge thus gained by the appellant and his agent in these previous transactions, the appellant is bound by their conditions. But this case differs essentially from the ticket cases. There, the carrier in making the contract hands over a document containing or referring to conditions which he intends to be part of the contract. So if the consignor or passenger, when accepting the document, knows or ought as a reasonable man to know that that is the carrier's intention, he can hardly deny that the conditions are part of the contract, or claim, in the absence of special circumstances, to be in a better position than he would be if he had read the document. But here, in making the contract neither party referred to, or indeed had in mind, any additional terms, and the contract was complete and fully effective without any additional terms. If it could be said that when making the contract Mr McSporran knew that the respondents always required a risk note to be signed and knew that the purser was simply forgetting to put it before him for signature, then it might be said that neither he nor his principal could take advantage of the error of the other party of which he was aware. But counsel frankly admitted that he could not put his case as high as that.

The only other ground on which it would seem possible to import these conditions is that based on a course of dealing. If two parties have made a series of similar contracts each containing certain conditions, and then they make another without expressly referring to those conditions it may be that those conditions ought to be implied. If the officious bystander had asked them whether they had intended to leave out the conditions this time, both must, as honest men, have said 'of course not'. But again the facts here will not support that ground. According to Mr. McSporran, there had been no constant course of dealing; sometimes he was asked to sign and sometimes not. And, moreover, he did not know what the conditions were. This time he was offered an oral contract without any reference to conditions, and he accepted the offer in good faith.

The respondents also rely on [Mr McCutcheon's] previous knowledge. I doubt whether it is possible to spell out a course of dealing in his case. In all but one of the previous cases he had been acting on behalf of his employer in sending a different kind of goods and he did not know that the respondents always sought to insist on excluding liability for their own negligence. So it cannot be said that when he asked his agent to make a contract for him he knew that this or, indeed, any other special term would be included in it. He left his agent a free hand to contract, and I see nothing to prevent him from taking advantage of the contract which his agent in fact made.

> 'The judicial task is not to discover the actual intentions of each party; it is to decide what each was reasonably entitled to conclude from the attitude of the other (*Gloag on Contract*, 2nd edn, p 7)'.

In this case I do not think that either party was reasonably bound or entitled to conclude from the attitude of the other, as known to him, that these conditions were intended by the other party to be part of this contract. I would therefore allow the appeal and restore the interlocutor of the Lord Ordinary.'

Lord Guest: 'All that the previous dealings in the present case can show is that the appellant and his agent knew that the previous practice of the respondents was to impose special conditions. But knowledge on their part did not and could not by itself import acceptance by them of these conditions, the exact terms of which they were unaware, into a contract which was different in character from those in the previous course of dealing. The practice of the respondents was to insist on a written contract incorporated in the risk note. On the occasion in question a verbal contract was made without reference to the conditions.

The key to establishing a common course of dealings is demonstrating that there has been both a frequency and consistency of dealing between the parties. This is what MacBrayne failed to prove. Although Mr McCutcheon had always been asked to sign a risk note by MacBrayne, Mr McSporran stated in evidence that sometimes he was asked to sign a risk note and sometimes he was not. This appeared to be conclusive for Lord Reid in finding that there was insufficient consistency in dealings between the parties to justify incorporating MacBrayne's conditions into the oral contract. The facts of McCutcheon can be contrasted with those of *British Crane Hire Co Ltd v Ipswich Plant Hire Ltd*.

***British Crane Hire Co Ltd v Ipswich Plant Hire Ltd* [1975] QB 303**

Facts: British Crane Hire (BCH) hired out heavy earth-moving equipment. Ipswich Plant Hire were doing drainage work and hired a dragline crane from BCH over the telephone. Nothing was said on the telephone about the terms and conditions of hire. BCH did send the defendants their standard hire terms and conditions but before they signed them the crane sank into marshy ground. BCH sought to recover from the defendants the cost of recovering the crane on the ground that their written terms and conditions required the defendant to indemnify them against such losses. BCH claimed that the terms and conditions were known to the defendants because they were customarily used in the trade.

Held: The Court of Appeal held that BCH's terms and conditions were incorporated into the contract of hire.

Lord Denning MR: In support of the course of dealing, the plaintiffs relied on two previous transactions in which the defendants had hired cranes from the plaintiffs. One was February 20, 1969; and the other October 6, 1969. Each was on a printed form which set out the hiring of a crane, the price, the site, and so forth; and also setting out the conditions the same as those here. There were thus only two transactions many months before and they were not known to the defendants' manager who ordered this crane. In the circumstances I doubt whether those two would be sufficient to show a course of dealing ...

But here the parties were both in the trade and were of equal bargaining power. Each was a firm of plant hirers who hired out plant. The defendants themselves knew that firms in the plant-hiring trade always imposed conditions in regard to the hiring of plant: and that their conditions were on much the same lines ...

[I]t is clear that both parties knew quite well that conditions were habitually imposed by the supplier of these machines: and both parties knew the substance of those conditions. In particular that if the crane sank in soft ground it was the hirer's job to recover it: and that there was an indemnity clause. In these circumstances, I think the conditions on the form should be regarded as incorporated into the contract. I would not put it so much on the course of dealing, but rather on the common understanding which is to be derived from the conduct of the parties, namely, that the hiring was to be on the terms of the plaintiffs' usual conditions.

As Lord Reid said in *McCutcheon v David MacBrayne Ltd* [1964] 1 WLR 125, 128 quoting from the Scottish textbook, *Gloag on Contract*, 2nd ed. (1929), p 7:

> 'The judicial task is not to discover the actual intentions of each party; it is to decide what each was reasonably entitled to conclude from the attitude of the other'.

It seems to me that, in view of the relationship of the parties, when the defendants requested this crane urgently and it was supplied at once – before the usual form was received – the plaintiffs were entitled to conclude that the defendants were accepting it on the terms of the plaintiffs' own printed conditions -which would follow in a day or two. It is just as if the plaintiffs had said: 'We will supply it on our usual conditions', and the defendants said 'Of course, that is quite understood'.

Two factors influenced the Court of Appeal in coming to its decision. First, it was relevant that Ipswich had previously contracted with BCH on the same terms. This was important but not, in itself, conclusive. Second, there was evidence that it was the normal practice in the trade for liability to be placed on the hirer, rather than the owner. For Lord Denning, it was the combination of these two factors that provided a satisfactory basis for incorporating the terms into the contract.

The issue in such cases is primarily one of fact: Is there evidence of a common course of dealing, either on the basis of past experience or general trade practice, that would lead the parties to reasonably believe that the standard terms had been incorporated into their contract? The answer to this question will depend on the context of the case. A useful summary of the relevant principles was recently given by Edwards-Stuart J in *Transformers & Rectifers Ltd v Needs Ltd* [2015] EWHC 269 (TCC):

The principles

42 From my rather brief review of some of the relevant authorities, I consider that in cases of this sort the following principles apply:

i) Where A makes an offer on its conditions and B accepts that offer on its conditions and, without more, performance follows, the correct analysis, assuming that each party's conditions have been reasonably drawn to the attention of the other, is that there is a contract on B's conditions: see *Tekdata*.

ii) Where there is reliance on a previous course of dealing it does not have to be extensive. Three or four occasions over a relatively short period may suffice: see *Balmoral* at [356] and *Capes (Hatherden)*.

iii) The course of dealing by the party contending that its terms and conditions are incorporated has to be consistent and unequivocal: see *Sterling Hydraulics*.

iv) Where trade or industry standard terms exist for the type of transaction in question, it will usually be easier for a party contending for those conditions to persuade the court that they should be incorporated, provided that reasonable notice of the application of the terms has been given: see *Circle Freight*.

v) A party's standard terms and conditions will not be incorporated unless that party has given the other party reasonable notice of those terms and conditions: see *Circle Freight*.

vi) It is not always necessary for a party's terms and conditions to be included or referred to in the documents forming the contract; it may be sufficient if they are clearly contained in or referred to in invoices sent subsequently: see *Balmoral* at [352], [356].

vii) By contrast, an invoice following a concluded contract effected by a clear offer on standard terms which are accepted, even if only by delivery, will or may be too late: see *Balmoral* at [356].

My analysis

43 It seems to me that one problem facing the Claimant is the fact that it did not place its orders in the same way each time. Whilst I accept that from time to time purchase orders were sent by post, with the result that the Defendant became aware of the existence of the terms and conditions on the back of them, I find that the great majority of purchase orders were sent by fax or e-mail (as was the case with the two orders in question) when the terms and conditions were not sent.

44 In my judgment a buyer who wishes to incorporate his own standard terms and conditions when orders are sent by fax or e-mail must give the seller reasonable notice of the terms and conditions and must do so in circumstances that make it clear to the other party that he intends to rely on them.

45 In the context of this case I consider that this involves doing what the buyers did in *Sterling Hydraulics*, that is to say to fax the terms and conditions on the back of the purchase order as a separate document together with the purchase order or, if being sent by e-mail, to ensure that the pdf attachment includes both the face of the purchase order and the terms and conditions on its back. In my view this is essential if the purchase order does not on its face refer to the terms and conditions on the back.

46 Viewed objectively, therefore, I consider that by not sending its terms and conditions when placing the purchase orders by fax or e-mail, even though they were printed on the reverse of purchase orders which from time to time were sent by post, the Claimant did not make it clear to a reasonable person in the position of the Defendant that it was seeking to rely on them. In my judgment if the Claimant did not follow a consistent practice of enclosing its terms and conditions with every purchase order, particularly in circumstances where the purchase order that was sent did not on its face refer to any terms and conditions, the Defendant was entitled to assume that the Claimant was not intending to rely on them.

It is relatively easy to demonstrate a common course of dealing in the context of a commercial contract but far more difficult when the contract is between a consumer and a business.

***Hollier v Rambler Motors (AMC) Ltd* [1972] 2 QB 71**

Facts: Rambler Motors had repaired Mr Hollier's car on three or four occasions over a period of five years. On at least two of the occasions, Mr Hollier had signed a form containing Rambler's standard terms which included a clause excluding liability for damage caused by fire to customer's cars on the premises. In this instance the parties contracted over the telephone, without any mention of the standard terms. Whilst the car was in the garage it was damaged by fire due to Rambler's negligence. Mr Hollier claimed damages for breach of an implied term that Rambler would take reasonable care of his car. The defendants argued that the term excluding liability for damage caused by fire was incorporated into the oral contract because of the previous course of dealing between the parties. At first instance it was held that the term was incorporated into the contract and excluded the defendants' liability for negligence.

Held: The Court of Appeal allowed the appeal on the ground that the course of dealing on three or four occasions over five years was not sufficient to incorporate the term into the contract.

Salmon LJ: I am bound to say that, for my part, I do not know of any other case in which it has been decided or even argued that a term could be implied into an oral contract on the strength of a course of dealing (if it can be so called) which consisted at the most of three or four transactions over a period of five years ...

It seems to me that if it was impossible to rely on a course of dealing in *McCutcheon v David MacBrayne Ltd*, still less would it be possible to do so in this case, when the so-called course of dealing consisted only of three or four transactions in the course of five years.

6.3.1.4 Onerous or unusual conditions

In determining whether reasonable steps have been taken to bring the term to the attention of the other party the courts will take into account the nature of the term. If the term is particularly onerous or unusual, greater steps will be required to incorporate the term into the contract or to give effect to its provisions. This rule of 'special notice' was suggested by Lord Denning MR in *Thornton v Shoe Lane Parking* [1971] 2 QB 163:

> I do not pause to inquire whether the exempting condition is void for unreasonableness. All I say is that it is so wide and so destructive of rights that the court should not hold any man bound by it unless it is drawn to his attention in the most explicit way. It is an instance of what I had in mind in *J Spurling Ltd v Bradshaw* [1956] 1 WLR 461, 466. In order to give sufficient notice, it would need to be printed in red ink with a red hand pointing to it – or something equally startling.

The requirement of special notice was further considered by the Court of Appeal in *Interfoto v Stiletto Visual Programmes* (although cf. *Photolibrary Group Ltd v Burda Senator Verlag GmbH* [2008] EWHC 1343).

***Interfoto v Stiletto Visual Programmes* [1989] 1 QB 433**

Facts: Stiletto were an advertising agency which needed some photographs of the 1950s for a presentation. They telephoned Interfoto, which had a library of photographs. They had never dealt with Interfoto before. Interfoto sent out some photographs in a bag containing a delivery note upon which were printed a number of conditions in small but visible print. Condition 2 stated that 'a holding fee of £5 plus VAT per day will be charged for each transparency which is retained ... longer than ... 14 days'. The daily rate per transparency was far greater than usual in the market but nothing was done by Interfoto to draw Stiletto's attention particularly to the condition. Stiletto forgot to return the photos on time and were presented with a bill for £3,783.50.

Held: The Court of Appeal held that the clause was not incorporated into the contract because Interfoto had not done what was reasonably necessary to draw the clause to the attention of Stiletto. Interfoto could only recover a holding fee assessed on the basis of a *quantum meruit* which was held to be £3.50 per week per transparency beyond the 14-day period.

Bingham LJ: In many civil law systems, and perhaps in most legal systems outside the common law world, the law of obligations recognises and enforces an overriding principle that in making and carrying out contracts parties should act in good faith. This does not simply mean that they should not deceive each other, a principle which any legal system must recognise; its effect is perhaps most aptly conveyed by such metaphorical colloquialisms as 'playing fair', 'coming clean' or 'putting one's cards face upwards on the table'. It is in essence a principle of fair and open dealing. In such a forum it might, I think, be held on the facts of this case that the plaintiffs were under a duty in all fairness to draw the defendants' attention specifically to the high price payable if the transparencies were not returned in time and, when the 14 days had expired, to point out to the defendants the high cost of continued failure to return them.

English law has, characteristically, committed itself to no such overriding principle but has developed piecemeal solutions in response to demonstrated problems of unfairness. Many examples could be given. Thus equity has intervened to strike down unconscionable bargains. Parliament has stepped in to regulate the imposition of exemption clauses and the form of certain hire-purchase agreements. The common law also has made its contribution, by holding that certain classes of contract require the utmost good faith, by treating as irrecoverable what purport to be agreed estimates of damage but are in truth a disguised penalty for breach, and in many other ways.

The well-known cases on sufficiency of notice are in my view properly to be read in this context. At one level they are concerned with a question of pure contractual analysis, whether one party has done enough to give the other notice of the incorporation of a term in the contract. At another level they are concerned with a somewhat different question, whether it would in all the circumstances be fair (or reasonable) to hold a party bound by any conditions or by a particular condition of an unusual and stringent nature.

[He reviewed the authorities on incorporation of terms.]

These authoritative passages appear to base the law very firmly on consideration of what is fair in all the circumstances.

J Spurling Ltd v Bradshaw [1956] 1 WLR 461 concerned an exemption clause in a warehousing contract. The case is now remembered for the observations of Denning LJ, at p 466:

> 'This brings me to the question whether this clause was part of the contract. Mr Sofer urged us to hold that the warehousemen did not do what was reasonably sufficient to give notice of the conditions within *Parker v South Eastern Railway Co*, 2 CPD 416. I quite agree that the more unreasonable a clause is, the greater the notice which must be given of it. Some clauses which I have seen would need to be printed in red ink on the face of the document with a red hand pointing to it before the notice could be held to be sufficient'.

Here, therefore, is made explicit ... that what would be good notice of one condition would not be notice of another. The reason is that the more outlandish the clause the greater the notice which the other party, if he is to be bound must in all fairness be given ...

The tendency of the English authorities has, I think, been to look at the nature of the transaction in question and the character of the parties to it; to consider what notice the party alleged to be bound was given of the particular condition said to bind him; and to resolve whether in all the circumstances it is fair to hold him bound by the condition in question. This may yield a result not very different from the civil law principle of good faith, at any rate so far as the formation of the contract is concerned.

Turning to the present case, I am satisfied ... that no contract was made on the telephone when the defendants made their initial request. I am equally satisfied that no contract was made on delivery of the transparencies to the defendants before the opening of the jiffy bag in which they were contained. Once

> the jiffy bag was opened and the transparencies taken out with the delivery note, it is in my judgment an inescapable inference that the defendants would have recognised the delivery note as a document of a kind likely to contain contractual terms and would have seen that there were conditions printed in small but visible lettering on the face of the document. To the extent that the conditions so displayed were common form or usual terms regularly encountered in this business, I do not think the defendants could successfully contend that they were not incorporated into the contract.
>
> The crucial question in the case is whether the plaintiffs can be said fairly and reasonably to have brought condition 2 to the notice of the defendants ... In my opinion the plaintiffs did not do so ... The defendants are not to be relieved of that liability because they did not read the condition, although doubtless they did not; but in my judgment they are to be relieved because the plaintiffs did not do what was necessary to draw this unreasonable and extortionate clause fairly to their attention. I would accordingly allow the defendants' appeal and substitute for the judge's award the sum which he assessed upon the alternative basis of *quantum meruit*.

Returning to *Interfoto* Bingham LJ famously stated that English Law does not recognise a general duty of good faith. More recently In *Yam Seng Pte Ltd v International Trade Corporation Ltd* [2013] EWHC 111 at [124] Leggatt J (prior to the referendum on Brexit) stated:

> In refusing, however, if indeed it does refuse, to recognise any such general obligation of good faith, this jurisdiction would appear to be swimming against the tide. As noted by Bingham LJ in the Interfoto case, a general principle of good faith (derived from Roman law) is recognised by most civil law systems – including those of Germany, France and Italy. From that source references to good faith have already entered into English law via EU legislation. For example, the Unfair Terms in Consumer Contracts Regulations 1999, which give effect to a European directive, contain a requirement of good faith. Several other examples of legislation implementing EU directives which use this concept are mentioned in Chitty on Contract Law (31st edn, Vol 1 at para. 1–043). Attempts to harmonise the contract law of EU member states, such as the Principles of European Contract Law proposed by the Lando Commission and the European Commission's proposed Regulation for a Common European Sales Law on which consultation is currently taking place, also embody a general duty to act in accordance with good faith and fair dealing. There can be little doubt that the penetration of this principle into English law and the pressures towards a more unified European law of contract in which the principle plays a significant role will continue to increase.

On this case see further below at 6.4.1.2.4. Returning to *Interfoto* Bingham LJ clearly indicates that the courts adopt a flexible approach in determining whether a term has been incorporated into a contract. The court seeks to do what is fair. This means that the test will vary, depending on the nature of the term: 'What would be good notice of one condition would not be notice of another.' Bingham LJ emphasised that this approach was rooted in well-established authorities. That may be true, but it is surely questionable whether this approach is justified as a matter of principle. The real issue, as Bingham LJ identified, is the principle of fair dealing. It is doubtful whether the doctrine of incorporation of terms is the most appropriate mechanism to deal with unfair bargains. Surely, the courts should tackle the problem at its root by striking out unfair terms on substantive grounds. Indeed, following the enactment of the Unfair Contract Terms Act 1977 and the Consumer Rights Act 2015 (see Chapter 7), there seems to be little need for the special notice rule for incorporation of onerous or unusual terms. This was noted by Hobhouse LJ (dissenting) in *AEG (UK) Ltd v Logic Resource Ltd*. (By contrast in *Goodlife Foods Ltd v Hall Fire Protection Ltd* [2018] EWCA Civ 1371 Coulson LJ stated (at [35]): '... I consider that these two principles (namely incorporation at common law on the one hand, and the reasonableness of any term incorporated pursuant to UCTA, on the other) are separate, and the questions to be decided in respect of each are distinct. There may be some overlap in the matters that fall to be considered under each principle, but that is all.')

AEG (UK) Ltd v Logic Resource Ltd [1996] CLC 265

Hobhouse LJ: It is desirable as a matter of principle to keep what was said in the *Interfoto* case within its proper bounds. A wide range of clauses are commonly incorporated into contracts by general words. If it is to be the policy of English law that in every case those clauses are to be gone through with, in effect, a toothcomb to see whether they were entirely usual and entirely desirable in the particular contract, then one is completely distorting the contractual relationship between the parties and the ordinary mechanisms of making contracts. It will introduce uncertainty into the law of contract.

In the past there may have been a tendency to introduce more strict criteria but this is no longer necessary in view of the Unfair Contract Terms Act. The reasonableness of clauses is the subject matter of the Unfair Contract Terms Act and it is under the provisions of that Act that problems of unreasonable clauses should be addressed and the solution found.

Furthermore in *Thinc Group v Armstrong* [2012] EWCA Civ 1227 at [27] Rix LJ stated that the *Interfoto* doctrine is not aimed at policing commercially unwise agreements. Moreover, the Court of Appeal has cast doubt on the practical application of the 'red-hand rule' to many commercial contracts (although compare *Cargill International Trading Pte Ltd v Uttam Galva Steels Ltd* [2019] EWHC 476 (Comm) at [87]).

Ocean Chemical Transport Inc v Exnor Craggs Ltd [2000] 1 Lloyd's Rep 446

Facts: The claimants owned ships. By an exchange of faxes on 7 February1995, they entered into a contract with the defendants for the supply of bunkers for one of their ships. One of the faxes from the defendants stated that the sale was subject to its general terms and conditions. One of the terms, clause 10, stated: 'All liability whatsoever on our part shall cease unless suit is brought within six months after delivery of the good or the date when the goods should have been delivered.' In July 1996, the claimants discovered that there was a defect in the title to the bunkers and brought an action against the defendants for breach of an implied term to the effect that the seller had a right to sell the goods. The defendants denied liability and alleged that the claim was time barred by clause 10 of their general terms and conditions. The claimants argued that the clause had not been incorporated because the defendants had not taken adequate steps to bring the clause to the claimants' attention.

Held: The Court of Appeal held that the claimants' cause of action was time barred because clause 10 had been incorporated into the contract. The defendants had discharged their duty to bring the existence of the term to the attention of the claimants.

Evans LJ: [Counsel for the claimant] submits that the *Interfoto* test, as he called it, has to be applied, even in a case where the other party has signed an acknowledgement of the terms and conditions and their incorporation. It seems to me that [he] could be right in what might be regarded as an extreme case, where a signature was obtained under pressure of time or other circumstances, and where it was possible to satisfy the *Interfoto* test; that is to say, that the clause was one which was particularly onerous or unusual for incorporation in the contract in question. I would prefer to put the matter more broadly and to say that the question is whether the defendants have discharged the duty which lies upon them of bringing the existence of the clause upon which they rely ... to the notice of the other party in the circumstances of the particular case.

As I have indicated, in some extreme circumstances, even a signature might not be enough. On the other hand, in the present case there was an express acknowledgement. It seems to me that, given the nature of this term and condition and its effect, as relied upon by the respondents, it cannot be said that the respondents failed in their duty to bring the existence of that term to the notice of the buyers ... [Counsel for the claimant] does not hesitate to submit that the clause in question should have had, as he puts it, the red-hand approach. I would doubt very much whether that is practical in the context of a commercial contract such as this. In my view, the respondents did, in this particular case, where there was an express acknowledgement of the existence of the terms, certainly discharge their duty of bringing it sufficiently to the notice of the buyers for the clause to form part of the contract.

Initially in *Sophie Kaye v Nu Skin UK Ltd* [2009] EWHC 3509, Kitchin J stated:

36. Turning to the decision of the judge, he dealt with the argument based upon the *Interfoto* principles from paragraph 8. He expressed the view that the principles were simply not applicable 'by way of factual matrix to the facts of this case' and he then distinguished the Interfoto case on the basis that it was a consumer-type of case. By contrast, he continued, the present dispute concerned a commercial transaction.

37. I agree with the judge that the present case is indeed a commercial transaction, albeit one to which one of the parties was only 23 years old and may have had no prior commercial experience at all. Nevertheless, I consider it is clear that the *Interfoto* principles are as applicable to commercial transactions as to any others, although, plainly, all relevant circumstances must be taken into account. In the case of a commercial transaction, that may have a significant bearing on whether a particular clause is onerous or unusual, and whether it was fairly brought to the attention of the other party.

38. It is against this background that the judge considered whether the clause was one upon which Nu Skin could rely, and, in paragraph 10, he concluded that they could. Moreover, he considered that there was no point in adjourning the application and having further evidence. He took the view that the plain words of the agreement spoke for themselves.

39. In my judgment, the judge fell into error here, too. I believe that further evidence may assist the just determination of this issue. In particular, I have in mind the following. First, I believe that the court would be assisted by evidence of the personal circumstances of Miss Kaye and the circumstances in which she entered into this distributor agreement. Second, I believe the court would also be assisted by evidence as to whether the arbitration clause is onerous or unreasonable and, in particular, whether or not it will in practice mean that Miss Kaye has no real prospect of pursuing her claim. Third, in my judgment it would also be helpful to know how common arbitration clauses of the kind set forth in clause 9.2(v) are in distributor agreements of this kind and, in particular, how common it is to have an arbitration clause which provides for the seat of arbitration in a country far away from the territory where the distributor is living and carrying on business. Finally, it would, in my judgment, be of assistance to have evidence as to the notice which Miss Kaye had of the arbitration clause in this distributor agreement and its effect, her understanding of the avenues open and the procedures available to her to pursue a grievance and how she arrived at that understanding.

However, in further proceedings HHJ Denyer QC ([2012] CTLC 69 at [43]–[59]) stated:

> 'I have to say that I find it slightly difficult to characterise an arbitration clause as being on its face unreasonable and/or extortionate. It is an extremely common clause in many commercial contracts. The real reason why it is suggested it cannot be extortionate but so unreasonable as to be requiring very specific attention drawing can only relate to the fact, not that it is an arbitration, but that it is in Utah ... It seems to me that it comes to this. The provisions of the Utah

arbitration process are remarkably similar to the provisions here in domestic law. Those provisions are clearly set out in the Act to which I have referred. There is no reason to think that those provisions are not adhered to. There is a comity between legal systems that respect each other. I can think of some parts of the world where I would be disinclined to allow another jurisdiction to take control of the proceedings because I would have grave doubts about the fairness of any proceedings in such a country which would extend to, I am afraid, the comity and impartiality of the judge. But there is no basis for making any such finding, any such assumption or any such allegation against the State of Utah … It comes to this. This can only be regarded as in some way unreasonable because it requires that an English claimant has to litigate the matter in Utah. I have already dealt with the fact that it does not seem that any proper enquiries have been made by the claimant as to the availability of help to her in Utah. It does not seem to me to be unreasonable that a multinational corporation, such as the defendants here, based as they are in Utah, but having operatives in many parts of the world, should seek to ensure that mediation matters and arbitration matters are dealt with in one place, to wit, Utah'. (See also [2012] EWCA Civ 1069.)

See also *Higgins & Co Lawyers Ltd v Evans* [2019] EWHC 507 (Ch) at [83] on the limits of *Sophie Kaye v Nu Skin UK Ltd*. See also *Hawksford Trustees Jersey Ltd v Halliwells LLP (In Liquidation)* [2015] EWHC 2996 (Ch) at [63], *per* HHJ Pelling QC. A further issue arises: does the *Interfoto* principle circumscribe the rule in *L'Estrange v Graucob* [1934] 2 KB 394? In *Do-Buy 925 Ltd v National Westminster Bank Plc* [2010] EWHC 2862, Andrew Popplewell QC, sitting as a Deputy Judge, stated:

> [I]t remains an undecided question whether the *Interfoto* principle can ever apply to a signed contract. In that case the Defendant was held not to be bound by a term in a printed set of conditions which had been provided to him in the form of a delivery note, but which he had neither signed nor read. In *Ocean Chemical Transport v Exnor Crags Ltd* [2000] 1 Lloyds 466, Evans LJ, with whom Henry and Waller LLJ agreed, was prepared to assume that the principle might apply to onerous and unusual clauses in a signed contract 'in an extreme case where a signature was obtained under pressure of time or other circumstances'. In *HIH v New Hampshire* [2001] 2 Lloyds 161, Rix LJ doubted whether the principle was properly applicable outside the context of incorporation by notice (see paragraph 209). In *Amiri Flight Authority v BAE Systems Plc* [2004] 1 All ER 385, 392, Mance LJ, with whom Rix and Potter LLJ agreed, noted the doubts of Rix LJ in *HIH v New Hampshire* and stated that it was unnecessary to decide whether the principle could ever apply to signed contracts. He envisaged that it might do so where, for example, a car owner was asked to sign a ticket on entering a car park or a holiday maker asked to sign a long small print document when hiring a car which in either case proved to have a provision of 'an extraneous or wholly unusual nature'; but that such cases might be ones where the application of the provision was precluded by an implied representation as to the nature of the document. He reiterated the normal rule that in the absence of any misrepresentation, the signature of a contractual document must operate as an incorporation and acceptance of all its terms.

See also *One World (GB) Ltd v Elite Mobile Ltd* [2012] EWHC 3706 and *Dawson v Bell* [2016] EWCA Civ 96 at [91]–[92] *per* Tomlinson LJ. More recently in *Cargill International Trading Pte Ltd v Uttam Galva Steels Ltd* [2019] EWHC 476 (Comm) at [88]–[89] Bryan J stated:

> 88. In contrast, in the present case, the APSA Agreement is signed and stamped on every single page and it is not suggested this was done other than by a person having authority. I have already

identified that the normal position is that a written contract signed by a party will be binding on him regardless of whether the other party expressly drew his attention to specific terms.

89. Of course there are exceptional cases in which the signing party was under undue pressure or had no real opportunity to read and consider the contract before signing, such as an individual at an airport presented with a car rental agreement; as to which see *Amiri Flight Authority v BAE Systems Plc* [2003] 2 CLC 662 at 694 to 695, [15] to [16]. But the evidence before me does not begin to support any suggestion that Cargill exerted any undue pressure upon Uttam to sign or that it had no opportunity or time to read the APSA agreements before they were signed. On the contrary, every page was stamped and signed by Uttam. Ultimately it is a matter for Uttam as to whether they read the terms of the agreement that they entered into repeatedly over a number of years.

See also *Higgins & Co Lawyers Ltd v Evans* [2019] EWHC 507 (Ch).

Where the *Interfoto* principle does apply it is not always clear when the courts will find that a term is onerous or unusual, even in a consumer contract. (In *Goodlife Foods Ltd v Hall Fire Protection Ltd* [2018] EWCA Civ 1371 the Court of Appeal noted some of the differences in the language used in the relevant case law (extortionate, Draconian etc.) and also provided a reminder that exclusion clauses are not automatically onerous or unusual.)

O'Brien v MGN Ltd [2002] CLC 33

Facts: The claim concerned a 'scratchcard' game operated by the defendants, Mirror Group Newspapers. The claimant had obtained one of the scratchcards from a newspaper. It was a winning card and he telephoned the 'Mystery Bonus Hotline' number as directed. A recorded message told him that the mystery bonus cash amount for that day was £50,000. Unfortunately for him, a mistake had been made by the defendant. Instead of there being only one winner of the £50,000 prize on that day there were 1,472. Once the mistake was realised, the defendants refused to pay out to all the 'winners' and they relied on Rule 5 of the competition rules which stated that, 'should more prizes be claimed than are available in any prize category for any reason, a separate draw will take place for the prize'. At first instance, the judge held that the defendants had made a contractual offer in the newspaper and that the claimant had accepted the offer by telephoning the defendants to claim the prize. The judge held that the claimant must have seen the rules and that Rule 5 was not sufficiently onerous and unusual as to require special notice.

Held: The Court of Appeal dismissed the appeal. Rule 5 was neither 'onerous' nor 'unusual' and the defendant had taken reasonable steps to bring the term to the attention of the claimant.

Hale LJ: The offer and therefore the contract clearly incorporated the term 'Normal Mirror Group rules apply'. The words were there to be read and it makes no difference whether or not the claimant actually read or paid attention to them.

The question, therefore, is whether those words, in the circumstances, were enough to incorporate the Rules, including Rule 5, into the contract. In the words of Bingham LJ in *Interfoto Library Ltd v Stiletto Ltd* [1989] 1 QB 433, at p 445E, can the defendant 'be said fairly and reasonably to have brought [those rules] to the notice of' the claimant? This is a question of fact ... [W]hat is fair and reasonable notice will depend upon the nature of the transaction and upon the nature of the term ...

In my view, although Rule 5 does turn an apparent winner into a loser, it cannot by any normal use of language be called 'onerous' or 'outlandish'. It does not impose any extra burden upon the claimant, unlike the clause in *Interfoto*. It does not seek to absolve the defendant from liability for personal injuries negligently caused, unlike the clause in *Thornton v Shoe Lane Parking*. It merely deprives the claimant of a windfall for which he has done very little in return. He bought two newspapers, although in fact he could have acquired a card and discovered the hotline number without doing either. He made a call to a premium rate number, which will have cost him some money and gained the newspaper some, but only a matter of pennies, not pounds.

The more difficult question is whether the rule is 'unusual' in this context. The judge found that the claimant knew that there was a limit on the number of prizes and that there were relevant rules. [Evidence was given] that these games and competitions always have rules. Indeed I would accept that this is common knowledge. This is not a situation in which players of the game would assume that the newspaper bore the risk of any mistake of any kind which might lead to more people making a claim than had been intended. Some people might assume that the 'get out' rule would provide for the prize to be shared amongst the claimants. Some might assume that it would provide for the drawing of lots. In the case of a single prize some might think drawing lots more appropriate; but it seems to me impossible to say that either solution would be 'unusual'. There is simply no evidence to that effect. Such evidence as there is was to the effect that such rules are not unusual.

In any event, the words 'onerous or unusual' are not terms of art. They are simply one way of putting the general proposition that reasonable steps must be taken to draw the particular term in question to the notice of those who are to be bound by it and that more is required in relation to certain terms than to others depending on their effect. In the particular context of this particular game, I consider that the defendants did just enough to bring the Rules to the claimant's attention. There was a clear reference to rules on the face of the card he used. There was a clear reference to rules in the paper containing the offer of a telephone prize. There was evidence that those rules could be discovered either from the newspaper offices or from back issues of the paper. The claimant had been able to discover them when the problem arose.

The Court of Appeal had a great deal of sympathy for Mr O'Brien, noting that he was, 'a thoroughly decent young man who must have suffered a cruel disappointment when his hopes were raised only to be dashed'. Nevertheless, the court held that Rule 5 did not require special notice because its effect was merely to disappoint Mr O'Brien's expectations. The term did not impose any extra burden upon Mr O'Brien, nor did it constitute an unreasonable exclusion of liability. It merely deprived Mr O'Brien of a prize for which he had done very little in return. As such, the special notice doctrine had no application.

6.3.2 Interpretation

Having established which terms have been incorporated into the contract the next task for the court is to ascertain the meaning of those terms. The focus is on what the parties intended the terms to mean and, again, the courts adopt an objective approach. This means that, if the contract is put in written form, the written document will be regarded as very strong evidence of what the parties intended.

6.3.2.1 Parol evidence rule

In general terms, the parties to a written contract will not be permitted to 'add to, vary or contradict that writing' (*Henderson v Arthur* [1907] 1 KB 10). This rule is known as the 'parol evidence rule'.

6.3.2.2 Exceptions

Although the purpose of this rule is to promote certainty and to save time and money in the conduct of litigation, it can operate very harshly. Because of this, the rule has been made subject to a number of exceptions. Indeed in *Muneer Hamid (T/A Hamid Properties) v Francis Bradshaw Partnership* [2013]

EWCA Civ 470 at [47] Jackson LJ stated: 'There are a number of exceptions to the parol evidence rule and these have increased in recent years. This may in part be due to the increasing ease and speed with which documents can be created and dispatched. The temptations of the keyboard, the "cut and paste" facility and the mouse cannot always be resisted.'

Accordingly, extrinsic evidence may be admitted to prove that the contract has not yet entered into force because of a condition precedent to the agreement (*Pym v Campbell* (1856) 6 E & B 370). Similarly, a party can lead oral evidence to show that the written agreement was incomplete and that it was the parties' intention to supplement the written agreement with oral terms. A good example of this is the Scottish case of *Irons v Partick Thistle Football Club Ltd*.

Irons v Partick Thistle Football Club Ltd (1997) SLT 983

Facts: David Irons was a professional footballer who signed for Partick Thistle FC and later alleged that certain terms were agreed between himself and the manager, John Lambie, relating to a signing-on fee and a bonus on £20,000 if Partick Thistle were promoted. These statements were not included in the standard form written contract which he signed. In fact, different figures were later inserted into blank spaces in the contract. Partick Thistle alleged that only lower bonuses had been agreed and that these figures were stated in the document.

Held: The Outer House of the Court of Session held that while normally oral evidence was not admissible to contradict the terms of a written contract, as a result of the football club's admission that a bonus of some sort was payable, oral evidence was admissible because both parties had agreed that the written document was incomplete and did not constitute the entire agreement between them.

In this case the court objectively found that the written agreement was incomplete and that it was the parties' intention to supplement the agreement with additional terms. The parties may attempt to avoid such a finding by inserting an 'entire agreement' clause into the written agreement: see *The Inntrepreneur Pub Co (GL) v East Crown Ltd* [2000] 2 Lloyd's Rep 611.

It is clear that the parol evidence rule is subject to a number of wide exceptions. This led the Law Commission to doubt whether it really was a legal rule at all.

Law Commission, _The law of contract: the parol evidence rule_,
Report no 154, Cmnd 9700, 1986 at para 2.7

We have concluded that although a proposition of law can be stated which can be described as the 'parol evidence rule' it is not a rule of law which, correctly applied, could lead to evidence being unjustly excluded. Rather, it is a proposition of law which is no more than a circular statement: *when it is proved or admitted that the parties to a contract intended that all the express terms of their agreement should be as recorded in a particular document or documents, evidence will be inadmissible (because irrelevant) if it is tendered only for the purpose of adding to, varying, subtracting from or contradicting the express terms of the contract.* We have considerable doubts whether such a proposition should be characterised as a 'rule' at all, but several leading textbook writers and judges have referred to it as a 'rule' and we are content to adopt their terminology for the purposes of this report.

This observation about the circularity of the parol evidence rule explains why the Law Commission changed its view on the need for reform. Ten years earlier, in its Working Paper (Law Com WP No 76 (1976)), the Law Commission recommended legislation to abolish the rule stating that it was, 'a technical rule of uncertain ambit which, at least, adds to the complications of litigation without affecting the outcome and, at worst, prevents the courts getting at the truth'. By the time the Law Commission published its report its position had changed. It was of the view that there was no need for legislation since, 'there is no *rule of law* that evidence is rendered inadmissible or is to be ignored solely because a document exists which looks like a complete contract. Whether it is a complete contract depends upon the intention of the parties, objectively judged and not on any rule of law' (at para 2.17).

In summary, the parol evidence rule is merely a presumption that a written document contains all the terms of the contract. That presumption is, of course, capable of rebuttal by evidence of a contrary intention.

6.3.2.3 The move from literal to contextual methods of interpretation

The parol evidence rule was part of a more general literalist approach to contractual interpretation. As Cozens-Hardy MR noted in *Lovell and Christmas Ltd v Wall* (1911) 104 LT 85: '[T]he duty of the court ... [is] to construe the document according to the ordinary grammatical meaning of the words used therein.' The assumption was that contracting parties had an obligation to use correct and appropriate language to convey their objectives. If they used words or phrases that bore alternative meanings, the court would not look behind the words to discover the real intention of the parties.

On the face of it, this was an entirely sensible approach to contractual interpretation, since it enabled the parties to obtain a quick and relatively inexpensive decision on the meaning of a disputed term. However, the approach is ultimately unsatisfactory because it assumes that communication takes place in a vacuum. In reality, the meaning of a communication can only be understood once its context is considered. For example, the utterance 'two fat ladies' has a very different meaning when spoken in a bingo hall than when spoken on the street. In the former situation you are likely to hear a cheer; in the latter you are likely to receive a slap!

The courts have recognised the limitations of the literalist approach and rejected it in favour of a more contextual approach (although note *Wood v Capita Insurance Services Ltd* [2017] UKSC 24, discussed below, on the relevance of textualism). The landmark judgment was that of Lord Wilberforce in *Prenn v Simmonds*.

***Prenn v Simmonds* [1971] 1 WLR 1381**

Facts: Dr Simmonds brought an action against Mr Prenn in which he claimed that, under the terms of an agreement, he was entitled to acquire from Mr Prenn for a price of £6,600 a 4% stake in Radio & Television Trust Ltd ('RTT'). Mr Prenn disputed the claim on the ground that a necessary condition of the agreement had not been satisfied because less than £300,000 profits available for dividend on the ordinary stock of the company had been earned. The central question in the case was whether 'profits' meant: (1) the profits of RTT alone in which case the amount fell short of the £300,000 by less than £10,000; or (b) the consolidated profits of the group consisting of RTT and subsidiaries in which case the amount was largely exceeded.

Held: The House of Lords held that, in construing a written agreement, the court should consider evidence of the factual background known to both parties but not evidence relating to prior negotiations between the parties. Applying this principle of construction, their Lordships found that the word 'profits' meant 'consolidated profits'.

Lord Wilberforce: The time has long passed when agreements, even those under seal, were isolated from the matrix of facts in which they were set and interpreted purely on internal linguistic considerations. There is no need to appeal here to any modern, anti-literal, tendencies, for Lord Blackburn's well-known judgment in *River Wear Commissioners v Adamson* (1877) 2 App Cas 743, 763, provides ample warrant for a liberal approach. We must, as he said, inquire beyond the language and see what the circumstances were with reference to which the words were used, and the object, appearing from those circumstances, which the person using them had in view. Moreover, at any rate since 1859 (*Macdonald v Longbottom*, 1 E & E 977) it has been clear enough that evidence of mutually known facts may be admitted to identify the meaning of a descriptive term.

Lord Wilberforce confirmed this approach in *Reardon Smith Line Ltd v Hansen-Tangen*.

Reardon Smith Line Ltd v Hansen-Tangen [1976] 1 WLR 989

Lord Wilberforce: No contracts are made in a vacuum: there is always a setting in which they have to be placed. The nature of what is legitimate to have regard to is usually described as 'the surrounding circumstances' but this phrase is imprecise: it can be illustrated but hardly defined. In a commercial contract it is certainly right that the Court should know the commercial purpose of the contract and this in turn presupposes knowledge of the genesis of the transaction, the background, the context, the market in which the parties are operating ...

It is often said that, in order to be admissible in aid of construction, these extrinsic facts must be within the knowledge of both parties to the contract, but this requirement should not be stated in too narrow a sense. When one speaks of the intention of the parties to the contract, one is speaking objectively – the parties cannot themselves give direct evidence of what their intention was – and what must be ascertained is what is to be taken as the intention which reasonable people would have had if placed in the situation of the parties. Similarly when one is speaking of aim, or object, or commercial purpose, one is speaking objectively of what reasonable persons would have in mind in the situation of the parties ...

[W]hat the Court must do must be to place itself in thought in the same factual matrix as that in which the parties were. [I]n the search for the relevant background, there may be facts, which form part of the circumstances in which the parties contract in which one, or both, may take no particular interest, their minds being addressed to or concentrated on other facts, so that if asked they would assert that they did not have these facts in the forefront of their mind, but that will not prevent those facts from forming part of an objective setting in which the contract is to be construed.

It is clear that a literal approach to contractual interpretation has been rejected in favour of a purposive approach that takes into account that 'factual matrix' in which the contract was formed (see also *Lloyds TSB Foundation for Scotland v Lloyds Banking Group plc (Scotland)* [2013] UKSC 3 and *Autoclenz Ltd v Belcher* [2011] UKSC 41 at [32]–[35]). The modern approach has now been set out fully by Lord Hoffmann in *Investors Compensation Scheme Ltd v West Bromwich Building Society*.

Investors Compensation Scheme Ltd v West Bromwich Building Society [1998] 1 WLR 896

Lord Hoffmann: I think I should preface my explanation of my reasons with some general remarks about the principles by which contractual documents are nowadays construed. I do not think that the fundamental change which has overtaken this branch of the law, particularly as a result of the speeches of Lord Wilberforce in *Prenn v Simmonds* [1971] 1 WLR 1381, 1384–1386 and *Reardon Smith Line v Hansen-Tangen* [1976] 1 WLR 989, is always sufficiently appreciated. The result has been, subject to one important exception, to assimilate the way in which such documents are interpreted by judges to the common sense principles by which any serious utterance would be interpreted in ordinary life. Almost all the old intellectual baggage of 'legal' interpretation has been discarded. The principles may be summarised as follows.

(1) Interpretation is the ascertainment of the meaning which the document would convey to a reasonable person having all the background knowledge which would reasonably have been available to the parties in the situation in which they were at the time of the contract.

(2) The background was famously referred to by Lord Wilberforce as the 'matrix of fact', but this phrase is, if anything, an understated description of what the background may include. Subject to the requirement that it should have been reasonably available to the parties and to the exception to be mentioned next, it includes absolutely anything which would have affected the way in which the language of the document would have been understood by a reasonable man.

(3) The law excludes from the admissible background the previous negotiations of the parties and their declarations of subjective intent. They are admissible only in an action for rectification. The law makes this distinction for reasons of practical policy and, in this respect only, legal interpretation differs from the way we would interpret utterances in ordinary life. The boundaries of this exception are in some respects unclear. But this is not the occasion on which to explore them.

(4) The meaning which a document (or any other utterance) would convey to a reasonable man is not the same thing as the meaning of its words. The meaning of words is a matter of dictionaries and grammars; the meaning of the document is what the parties using those words against the relevant background would reasonably have been understood to mean. The background may not merely enable the reasonable man to choose between the possible meanings of words which are ambiguous but even (as occasionally happens in ordinary life) to conclude that the parties must, for whatever reason, have used the wrong words or syntax: see *Mannai Investments Co Ltd v Eagle Star Life Assurance Co Ltd* [1997] AC 749.

(5) The 'rule' that words should be given their 'natural and ordinary meaning' reflects the common sense proposition that we do not easily accept that people have made linguistic mistakes, particularly in formal documents. On the other hand, if one would nevertheless conclude from the background that something must have gone wrong with the language, the law does not require judges to attribute to the parties an intention which they plainly could not have had. Lord Diplock made this point more vigorously when he said in *Antaios Compania Naviera SA v Salen Rederierna AB* [1985] AC 191, 201: if detailed semantic and syntactical analysis of words in a commercial contract is going to lead to a conclusion that flouts business commonsense, it must be made to yield to business commonsense.

The factual background that can be taken into account in construing a contract includes 'absolutely everything reasonably available to the parties which would have affected the way in which the language of the document would have been understood by a reasonable man' (see also *Rainy Sky SA v Kookmin Bank* [2011] UKSC 50 at [14], per Lord Clarke). In *Mortgage Express (an unlimited company) v Countrywide Surveyors Ltd* [2015] EWCA Civ 1110 Simon LJ, in interpreting a standstill agreement (the effect of which is to suspend the running of a limitation period) to determine whether or not it covered deceit, stated:

22. Among the background which would reasonably have been available to the parties in the present case was (1) the knowledge that a claim based on fraud and dishonesty is of a different character to a claim based on negligence and breach of contract, see above; and (2) the fact that no specific claim had been intimated prior to Standstill Agreement other than a claim for breach of contract and negligence.

23. On the other hand, as noted above, the Letter of Claim specifically reserved the right to amend and/or raise additional allegations. The words used in Clause 2.1, the operative part of the Standstill Agreement, could hardly be wider: 'for *all* purposes of *any* defence *or argument based limitation* … in connection with the Dispute …' (emphasis added); and the reference to laches was inapposite if the only claims which were subject to the Standstill Agreement were claims in contract and negligence.

24. Furthermore, the definition of 'Dispute' in paragraph 4 of the Background Preamble is itself drafted in very wide terms: 'Dispute means *any claim* or claims *directly or indirectly arising out of* or *in any way connected* with the matters referred to in paragraphs 1, 2 and 3 above', (emphasis added).

25. Paragraph 3 of the Background Preamble referred to allegations which were made of breach of contract and negligence, but in my judgment the wide definition of 'Dispute' plainly extends beyond what had been alleged by the First Claimant at that stage. It would, for example, plainly cover a claim for breach of fiduciary duty based on the payment of a bribe. The difficulty with Mr Lawrence's reading down of the paragraph 4 is that it could have been achieved by a much shorter paragraph 4: 'In this Agreement, 'Dispute' means any claim or claims directly or indirectly referred to in paragraphs 1, 2 and 3', His answer, that the Claimant might have wanted flexibility in relation to particular valuations does not, in my view, give sufficient weight to the words 'in any way connected with'.

26. In my judgment the proper construction of the Standstill Agreement is that if the claims arise 'indirectly' from the matters referred to in paragraphs 1–2 of the Background Preamble, or if they were in some way connected to those matters, they fall within the suspension provisions. The claims based on dishonesty fall within this very broad category of claims since they were at least in some way connected with the factual matters set out in paragraphs 1 and 2 of the Background Preamble and with the specific allegations described in paragraph 3.

Even more recently in *BNY Mellon Corporate Trustee Services Ltd v LBG Capital No 1 Plc* [2016] UKSC 29, Lord Neuberger (with whom Lord Mance and Lord Toulson agreed) stated that background regulatory documents from the Financial Services Authority could be taken into account in interpreting an agreement:

The proper approach to interpretation

29. Much of the argument before us was given over to the question whether, when construing the Trust Deed, and in particular the T&Cs, the Court of Appeal had been entitled to take into account statements in the substantial Exchange Offer Memorandum and in the lengthy letter from the chairman of LBG which accompanied it, and indeed the details of the statements and other documents issued by the FSA in 2008 and 2009.

30. Over the past 20 years or so, the House of Lords and Supreme Court have given considerable (some may think too much) general guidance as to the proper approach to interpreting contracts and indeed other commercial documents, such as the Trust Deed in this case. What, if any, weight is to be given to what was said in other documents, which were available at the time when the contract concerned was made or when the Trust Deed in question took effect, must be highly dependent on the facts of the particular case. However, when construing a contract or Trust Deed which governs the terms upon which a negotiable instrument is held, as in the present case, very considerable circumspection is appropriate before the contents of such other documents are taken into account.

31. In this connection, it is worth repeating the remarks of Lord Collins (with whom Lord Hope and Lord Mance agreed) in *In re Sigma Finance Corp (in administrative receivership)* [2010] 1 All ER 571, paras 36 and 37. Having pointed out that the trust deed in that case concerned 'debt securities' issued to 'a variety of creditors, who hold different instruments, issued at different times, and in different circumstances', Lord Collins, at para 37, said 'consequently this is not the type of case where the background or matrix of fact is or ought to be relevant, except in the most generalised way'. More generally, he said:

'Where a security document secures a number of creditors who have advanced funds over a long period it would be quite wrong to take account of circumstances which are not known to all of them. In this type of case it is the wording of the instrument which is paramount. The instrument must be interpreted as a whole in the light of the commercial intention which may be inferred from the face of the instrument and from the nature of the debtor's business'.

32. As Mr Dicker QC points out on behalf of the Trustee, the same point was made by Lord Macmillan when giving the decision of the Privy Council in *Egyptian Salt and Soda Co Ltd v Port Said Salt Association Ltd* [1931] AC 677, 682. Disapproving the trial judge's reliance on 'surrounding circumstances at the time when the memorandum was framed', Lord Macmillan said that 'the purpose of the memorandum is to enable shareholders, creditors and those who deal with the company to know what is its permitted range of enterprise, and for this information they are entitled to rely on the constituent documents of the company' and that the 'intention of the framers of the memorandum must be gathered from the language in which they have chosen to express it'. (See also the observations of Lord Hoffmann to much the same effect in *Attorney General of Belize v Belize Telecom Ltd* [2009] 1 WLR 1988, para 36, *Homburg Houtimport BV v Agrosin Private* Ltd [2004] 1 AC 715, para 74, and *Chartbrook Ltd v Persimmon Homes Ltd* [2009] AC 1101, para 40).

33. In the present case, the Trust Deed, and in particular those parts of clauses 7, 8 and 19 of the T&Cs which fall to be construed, cannot be understood unless one has some appreciation of the regulatory policy of the FSA at and before the time that the ECNs were issued. That is self-evident from the provisions of clause 19 which are set out in paras 13 and 14 above. Accordingly, I consider that at least the general thrust and effect of the FSA regulatory material published in 2008 and 2009 can be taken into account when interpreting the T&Cs. That would also accord with good sense: while the individual purchasers of the ECNs may not by any means all have been sophisticated investors, it is appropriate to assume that most of them would have had advice from reasonably sophisticated and informed advisers before they purchased such moderately complex financial products. The Exchange Offer Memorandum and the letter from the LBG chairman present more difficulties, and the answer may depend on whether such documents would have been known about or in the minds of subsequent purchasers of the ECNs, a point on which there was no evidence, so far as I am aware.

34. As it is, I do not consider that the terms of the Exchange Offer Memorandum or the letter from the LBG chairman take matters any further in this case. In my view, once one has in mind the general thrust and effect of the FSA regulatory approach in 2009, as summarised in paras 4 to 7 above, coupled with the commercial purpose of the ECNs as summarised in para 15 above, it is simply unhelpful on the facts of this case to cast one's eyes further than the T&Cs when resolving the issues on this appeal. I now turn to those two issues.

Exceptions to the factual background that may be taken into account are evidence relating to previous negotiations of the parties and declarations of their subjective intent. Lord Hoffmann did not give reasons for these restrictions, but Lord Wilberforce in *Prenn v Simmonds* [1971] 1 WLR 1381, said the following:

The reason for not admitting evidence of these exchanges ... is simply that such evidence is unhelpful. By the nature of things, where negotiations are difficult, the parties' positions, with each passing letter, are changing and until the final agreement, though converging, still divergent. It is only the final document which records a consensus ... Far more, and indeed totally, dangerous is it to admit evidence of one party's objective – even if this is known to the other party. However strongly pursued this may be, the other party

> may only be willing to give it partial recognition, and in a world of give and take, men often have to be satisfied with less than they want. So, again, it would be a matter of speculation how far the common intention was that the particular objective should be realised.

Although this can sometimes be a difficult distinction (see the comments of Lord Clarke in *Oceanbulk Shipping & Trading SA v TMT Asia Ltd* [2010] UKSC 44 at [39] and cf. *Merthyr (South Wales) Ltd (FKA Blackstone (South Wales) Ltd) v Merthyr Tydfil County Borough Council* [2019] EWCA Civ 526), in *Chartbrook Ltd v Persimmon Homes Ltd* [2009] UKHL 38, Lord Hoffmann stated:

> **28.** The rule that pre-contractual negotiations are inadmissible was clearly reaffirmed by this House in *Prenn v Simmonds* [1971] 1 WLR 1381, where Lord Wilberforce said (at p. 1384) that earlier authorities 'contain little to encourage, and much to discourage, evidence of negotiation or of the parties' subjective intentions'. It is clear that the rule of inadmissibility has been established for a very long time. In *Inglis v John Buttery & Co* (1878) 3 App Cas 552, 577 Lord Blackburn said that Lord Justice Clerk Moncreiff (at (1877) 4 R 58, 64) had laid down a principle which was nearly accurate but not quite when he said that in all mercantile contracts 'whether they be clear and distinct or the reverse, the Court is entitled to be placed in the position in which the parties stood before they signed'. The only qualification Lord Blackburn made was to reject Lord Moncreiff's view that the Court was entitled to look at the pre-contractual negotiations because unless one did so, one could not be fully in the position in which the parties had been …
>
> **30.** To allow evidence of pre-contractual negotiations to be used in aid of construction would therefore require the House to depart from a long and consistent line of authority, the binding force of which has frequently been acknowledged: see *Bank of Scotland v Dunedin Property Investment Co Ltd* [1998] SC 657, 665 ('well-established and salutary', per Lord President Rodger; *Alexiou v Campbell* [2007] UKPC 11 ('vouched by … compelling authorities', per Lord Bingham of Cornhill.) The House is nevertheless invited to do so, on the ground that the rule is illogical and prevents a court from, as the Lord Justice Clerk in *Inglis v John Buttery & Co* (1878) 3 App Cas 552 said, putting itself in the position of the parties and ascertaining their true intent …
>
> **32.** Critics of the rule, such as Thomas J in New Zealand (*Yoshimoto v Canterbury Golf International Ltd* [2001] 1 NZLR 523, 538–549), Professor David McLauchlan ('Contract Interpretation: What is it About?' (2009) 31:5 Sydney Law Review 5–51) and Lord Nicholls of Birkenhead ('My Kingdom for a Horse: The Meaning of Words' (2005) 121 LQR 577–591) point out that although all this may usually be true, in some cases it will not. Among the dirt of aspirations, proposals and counter-proposals there may gleam the gold of a genuine consensus on some aspect of the transaction expressed in terms which would influence an objective observer in construing the language used by the parties in their final agreement. Why should court deny itself the assistance of this material in deciding what the parties must be taken to have meant? Mr Christopher Nugee QC, who appeared for Persimmon, went so far as to say that in saying that such evidence was unhelpful, Lord Wilberforce was not only providing a justification for the rule but delimiting its extent. It should apply only in cases in which the pre-contractual negotiations are actually irrelevant. If they do assist a court in deciding what an objective observer would have construed the contract to mean, they should be admitted. I cannot accept this submission. It is clear from what Lord Wilberforce said and the authorities upon which he relied that the exclusionary rule is not qualified in this way. There is no need for a special rule to exclude irrelevant evidence.
>
> **33.** I do however accept that it would not be inconsistent with the English objective theory of contractual interpretation to admit evidence of previous communications between the parties as part of the background which may throw light upon what they meant by the language they used. The general rule, as I

said in *Bank of Credit and Commerce International SA v Ali* [2002] 1 AC 251, 269, is that there are no conceptual limits to what can properly be regarded as background. Prima facie, therefore, the negotiations are potentially relevant background. They may be inadmissible simply because they are irrelevant to the question which the court has to decide, namely, what the parties would reasonably be taken to have meant by the language which they finally adopted to express their agreement. For the reasons given by Lord Wilberforce, that will usually be the case. But not always. In exceptional cases, as Lord Nicholls has forcibly argued, a rule that prior negotiations are always inadmissible will prevent the court from giving effect to what a reasonable man in the position of the parties would have taken them to have meant. Of course judges may disagree over whether in a particular case such evidence is helpful or not. In *Yoshimoto v Canterbury Golf International Ltd* [2001] 1 NZLR 523. Thomas J thought he had found gold in the negotiations but the Privy Council said it was only dirt. As I have said, there is nothing unusual or surprising about such differences of opinion. In principle, however, I would accept that previous negotiations may be relevant.

34. It therefore follows that while it is true that, as Lord Wilberforce said, inadmissibility is normally based in irrelevance, there will be cases in which it can be justified only on pragmatic grounds. I must consider these grounds, which have been explored in detail in the literature and on the whole rejected by academic writers but supported by some practitioners.

35. The first is that the admission of pre-contractual negotiations would create greater uncertainty of outcome in disputes over interpretation and add to the cost of advice, litigation or arbitration. Everyone engaged in the exercise would have to read the correspondence and statements would have to be taken from those who took part in oral negotiations. Not only would this be time-consuming and expensive but the scope for disagreement over whether the material affected the construction of the agreement (as in the Yoshimoto case) would be considerably increased. As against this, it is said that when a dispute over construction is litigated, evidence of the pre-contractual negotiations is almost invariably tendered in support of an alternative claim for rectification (as in *Prenn v Simmonds* and in this case) or an argument based on estoppel by convention or some alleged exception to the exclusionary rule. Even if such an alternative claim does not succeed, the judge will have read and possibly been influenced by the evidence. The rule therefore achieves little in saving costs and its abolition would restore some intellectual honesty to the judicial approach to interpretation.

36. There is certainly a view in the profession that the less one has to resort to any form of background in aid of interpretation, the better. The document should so far as possible speak for itself. As Popham CJ said in the *Countess of Rutland's Case* (1604) 5 Co Rep 25b, 26a:

> 'it would be inconvenient, that matters in writing made by advice and on consideration, and which finally import the certain truth of the agreement of the parties should be controlled by averment of the parties to be proved by the uncertain testimony of slippery memory'.

37. I do not think that these opinions can be dismissed as merely based upon the fallacy that words have inherent or 'available' meanings, rather than being used by people to express meanings, although some of the arguments advanced in support might suggest this. It reflects what may be a sound practical intuition that the law of contract is an institution designed to enforce promises with a high degree of predictability and that the more one allows conventional meanings or syntax to be displaced by inferences drawn from background, the less predictable the outcome is likely to be. In this respect, it is interesting to consider the reaction to the statement of principle in *Investors Compensation Scheme Ltd v West Bromwich Building Society* [1998] 1 WLR 896, 912–913, which was viewed with alarm by some distinguished commercial lawyers as having greatly increased the quantity of background material which courts or arbitrators would be invited to consider: see Lord Bingham's recent paper ('A New Thing Under the Sun: The Interpretation of Contract and the ICS Decision' (2008) 12 Edinburgh LR 374–390) and Spigelmann CJ, 'From Text to

Contract: Contemporary Contractual Interpretation' (2007) 81 ALJ 322. As Lord Bingham pointed out, there was little in that statement of principle which could not be found in earlier authorities. The only points it decided that might have been thought in the least controversial were, first, that it was not necessary to find an 'ambiguity' before one could have any regard to background and, secondly, that the meaning which the parties would reasonably be taken to have intended could be given effect despite the fact that it was not, according to conventional usage, an 'available' meaning of the words or syntax which they had actually used.

38. Like Lord Bingham, I rather doubt whether the *ICS* case produced a dramatic increase in the amount of material produced by way of background for the purposes of contractual interpretation. But pre-contractual negotiations seem to me capable of raising practical questions different from those created by other forms of background. Whereas the surrounding circumstances are, by definition, objective facts, which will usually be uncontroversial, statements in the course of pre-contractual negotiations will be drenched in subjectivity and may, if oral, be very much in dispute. It is often not easy to distinguish between those statements which (if they were made at all) merely reflect the aspirations of one or other of the parties and those which embody at least a provisional consensus which may throw light on the meaning of the contract which was eventually concluded. But the imprecision of the line between negotiation and provisional agreement is the very reason why in every case of dispute over interpretation, one or other of the parties is likely to require a court or arbitrator to take the course of negotiations into account. Your Lordships' experience in the analogous case of resort to statements in *Hansard* under the rule in *Pepper v Hart* [1993] AC 593 suggests that such evidence will be produced in any case in which there is the remotest chance that it may be accepted and that even these cases will be only the tip of a mountain of discarded but expensive investigation. *Pepper v Hart* has also encouraged ministers and others to make statements in the hope of influencing the construction which the courts will give to a statute and it is possible that negotiating parties will be encouraged to improve the bundle of correspondence with similar statements.

39. Supporters of the admissibility of pre-contractual negotiations draw attention to the fact that Continental legal systems seem to have little difficulty in taking them into account. Both the Unidroit Principles of International Commercial Contracts (1994 and 2004 revision) and the Principles of European Contract Law (1999) provide that in ascertaining the 'common intention of the parties', regard shall be had to prior negotiations: articles 4.3 and 5.102 respectively. The same is true of the United Nations Convention on Contracts for the International Sale of Goods (1980). But these instruments reflect the French philosophy of contractual interpretation, which is altogether different from that of English law. As Professor Catherine Valcke explains in an illuminating article ('On Comparing French and English Contract Law: Insights from Social Contract Theory') (16 January 2009), French law regards the intentions of the parties as a pure question of subjective fact, their *volonté psychologique*, un-influenced by any rules of law. It follows that any evidence of what they said or did, whether to each other or to third parties, may be relevant to establishing what their intentions actually were. There is in French law a sharp distinction between the ascertainment of their intentions and the application of legal rules which may, in the interests of fairness to other parties or otherwise, limit the extent to which those intentions are given effect. English law, on the other hand, mixes up the ascertainment of intention with the rules of law by depersonalising the contracting parties and asking, not what their intentions actually were, but what a reasonable outside observer would have taken them to be. One cannot in my opinion simply transpose rules based on one philosophy of contractual interpretation to another, or assume that the practical effect of admitting such evidence under the English system of civil procedure will be the same as that under a Continental system.

40. In his judgment in the present case, Briggs J thought that the most powerful argument against admitting evidence of pre-contractual negotiations was that it would be unfair to a third party who took an assignment of the contract or advanced money on its security. Such a person would not have been privy to the negotiations and may have taken the terms of the contract at face value. There is clearly strength in this argument, but it is fair to say that the same point can be made (and has been made, notably by Saville LJ in *National Bank of Sharjah v Dellborg* [1997] EWCA Civ 2070, which is unreported, but the relevant passage is cited in Lord Bingham's paper in the *Edinburgh Law Review*) in respect of the admissibility of any form of background. The law sometimes deals with the problem by restricting the admissible background to that which would be available not merely to the contracting parties but also to others to whom the document is treated as having been addressed. Thus in *Bratton Seymour Service Co Ltd v Oxborough* [1992] BCLC 693 the Court of Appeal decided that in construing the articles of association of the management company of a building divided into flats, background facts which would have been known to all the signatories were inadmissible because the articles should be regarded as addressed to anyone who read the register of companies, including persons who would have known nothing of the facts in question. In *The Starsin* (*Homburg Houtimport BV v Agrosin Private Ltd* [2004] 1 AC 715) the House of Lords construed words which identified the carrier on the front of a bill of lading without reference to what it said on the back, on the ground that the bankers to whom the bill would be tendered could not be expected to read the small print. Ordinarily, however, a contract is treated as addressed to the parties alone and an assignee must either inquire as to any relevant background or take his chance on how that might affect the meaning a court will give to the document. The law has sometimes to compromise between protecting the interests of the contracting parties and those of third parties. But an extension of the admissible background will, at any rate in theory, increase the risk that a third party will find that the contract does not mean what he thought. How often this is likely to be a practical problem is hard to say. In the present case, the construction of the agreement does not involve reliance upon any background which would not have been equally available to any prospective assignee or lender.

41. The conclusion I would reach is that there is no clearly established case for departing from the exclusionary rule. The rule may well mean, as Lord Nicholls has argued, that parties are sometimes held bound by a contract in terms which, upon a full investigation of the course of negotiations, a reasonable observer would not have taken them to have intended. But a system which sometimes allows this to happen may be justified in the more general interest of economy and predictability in obtaining advice and adjudicating disputes. It is, after all, usually possible to avoid surprises by carefully reading the documents before signing them and there are the safety nets of rectification and estoppel by convention. Your Lordships do not have the material on which to form a view. It is possible that empirical study (for example, by the Law Commission) may show that the alleged disadvantages of admissibility are not in practice very significant or that they are outweighed by the advantages of doing more precise justice in exceptional cases or falling into line with international conventions. But the determination of where the balance of advantage lies is not in my opinion suitable for judicial decision. Your Lordships are being asked to depart from a rule which has been in existence for many years and several times affirmed by the House. There is power to do so under the Practice Statement (Judicial Precedent) [1966] 1 WLR 1234. But that power was intended, as Lord Reid said in *R v National Insurance Comrs, Exp Hudson* [1972] AC 944, 966, to be applied only in a small number of cases in which previous decisions of the House were 'thought to be impeding the proper development of the law or to have led to results which were unjust or contrary to public policy'. I do not think that anyone can be confident that this is true of the exclusionary rule.

42. The rule excludes evidence of what was said or done during the course of negotiating the agreement for the purpose of drawing inferences about what the contract meant. It does not exclude the use of such evidence for other purposes: for example, to establish that a fact which may be relevant as background was known to the parties, or to support a claim for rectification or estoppel. These are not exceptions to the rule. They operate outside it.

In *NHS Commissioning Board v Vasant (t/a MK Vasant and Associates)* [2019] EWCA Civ 1245 the Court of Appeal confirmed that extrinsic evidence may be used to explain the meaning of unconventional expressions in a contract. Returning to *Investors Compensation Scheme Ltd v West Bromwich Building Society*, the approach embodied by Lord Hoffmann's five principles is to be welcomed since it advocates a 'common sense' approach to understanding words within their factual context. Undoubtedly, this is preferable to an over-literal approach, which fails to take into account pragmatic inferences drawn from the factual context. Indeed in *Rainy Sky SA v Kookmin Bank* [2011] UKSC 50, Lord Clarke was of the opinion that where a particular term could be interpreted in different ways, a court should choose the interpretation which was in line with business common sense (see also *Pink Floyd Music Ltd v EMI Records Ltd* [2010] EWCA Civ 1429) although in *Arnold v Britton* [2015] UKSC 36 Lord Neuberger (with whom Lord Sumption and Lord Hughes agreed) noted the limits of the use of business common sense:

Interpretation of contractual provisions

14. Over the past 45 years, the House of Lords and Supreme Court have discussed the correct approach to be adopted to the interpretation, or construction, of contracts in a number of cases starting with *Prenn v Simmonds* [1971] 1 WLR 1381 and culminating in *Rainy Sky SA v Kookmin Bank* [2011] UKSC 50; [2011] 1 WLR 2900.

15. When interpreting a written contract, the court is concerned to identify the intention of the parties by reference to 'what a reasonable person having all the background knowledge which would have been available to the parties would have understood them to be using the language in the contract to mean', to quote Lord Hoffmann in *Chartbrook Ltd v Persimmon Homes Ltd* [2009] UKHL 38, [2009] 1 AC 1101, para 14. And it does so by focussing on the meaning of the relevant words, in this case clause 3(2) of each of the 25 leases, in their documentary, factual and commercial context. That meaning has to be assessed in the light of (i) the natural and ordinary meaning of the clause, (ii) any other relevant provisions of the lease, (iii) the overall purpose of the clause and the lease, (iv) the facts and circumstances known or assumed by the parties at the time that the document was executed, and (v) commercial common sense, but (vi) disregarding subjective evidence of any party's intentions. In this connection, see *Prenn* at pp 1384–1386 and *Reardon Smith Line Ltd v Yngvar Hansen-Tangen (trading as HE Hansen-Tangen)* [1976] 1 WLR 989, 995–997, *per* Lord Wilberforce, *Bank of Credit and Commerce International SA (in liquidation) v Ali* [2002] 1 AC 251, para 8, *per* Lord Bingham, and the survey of more recent authorities in *Rainy Sky*, *per* Lord Clarke at paras 21–30.

16. For present purposes, I think it is important to emphasise seven factors.

17. First, the reliance placed in some cases on commercial common sense and surrounding circumstances (eg in *Chartbrook*, paras 16–26) should not be invoked to undervalue the importance of the language of the provision which is to be construed. The exercise of interpreting a provision involves identifying what the parties meant through the eyes of a reasonable reader, and, save perhaps in a very unusual case, that meaning is most obviously to be gleaned from the language of the provision. Unlike commercial common sense and the surrounding circumstances, the parties have control over the language they use in a contract. And, again save perhaps in a very unusual case, the parties must have been specifically focussing on the issue covered by the provision when agreeing the wording of that provision.

18. Secondly, when it comes to considering the centrally relevant words to be interpreted, I accept that the less clear they are, or, to put it another way, the worse their drafting, the more ready the court can properly be to depart from their natural meaning. That is simply the obverse of the sensible proposition that the clearer the natural meaning the more difficult it is to justify departing from it. However, that does not justify the court embarking on an exercise of searching for, let alone constructing, drafting infelicities in order to facilitate a departure from the natural meaning. If there is a specific error in the drafting, it may often have no relevance to the issue of interpretation which the court has to resolve.

19. The third point I should mention is that commercial common sense is not to be invoked retrospectively. The mere fact that a contractual arrangement, if interpreted according to its natural language, has worked out badly, or even disastrously, for one of the parties is not a reason for departing from the natural language. Commercial common sense is only relevant to the extent of how matters would or could have been perceived by the parties, or by reasonable people in the position of the parties, as at the date that the contract was made. Judicial observations such as those of Lord Reid in *Wickman Machine Tools Sales Ltd v L Schuler AG* [1974] AC 235, 251 and Lord Diplock in *Antaios Cia Naviera SA v Salen Rederierna AB (The Antaios)* [1985] AC 191, 201, quoted by Lord Carnwath at para 110, have to be read and applied bearing that important point in mind.

20. Fourthly, while commercial common sense is a very important factor to take into account when interpreting a contract, a court should be very slow to reject the natural meaning of a provision as correct simply because it appears to be a very imprudent term for one of the parties to have agreed, even ignoring the benefit of wisdom of hindsight. The purpose of interpretation is to identify what the parties have agreed, not what the court thinks that they should have agreed. Experience shows that it is by no means unknown for people to enter into arrangements which are ill-advised, even ignoring the benefit of wisdom of hindsight, and it is not the function of a court when interpreting an agreement to relieve a party from the consequences of his imprudence or poor advice. Accordingly, when interpreting a contract a judge should avoid re-writing it in an attempt to assist an unwise party or to penalise an astute party.

21. The fifth point concerns the facts known to the parties. When interpreting a contractual provision, one can only take into account facts or circumstances which existed at the time that the contract was made, and which were known or reasonably available to both parties. Given that a contract is a bilateral, or synallagmatic, arrangement involving both parties, it cannot be right, when interpreting a contractual provision, to take into account a fact or circumstance known only to one of the parties.

22. Sixthly, in some cases, an event subsequently occurs which was plainly not intended or contemplated by the parties, judging from the language of their contract. In such a case, if it is clear what the parties would have intended, the court will give effect to that intention. An example of such a case is *Aberdeen City Council v Stewart Milne Group Ltd* [2011] UKSC 56, 2012 SCLR 114, where the court concluded that 'any … approach' other than that which was adopted 'would defeat the parties' clear objectives', but the conclusion was based on what the parties 'had in mind when they entered into' the contract (see paras 17 and 22).

23. Seventhly, reference was made in argument to service charge clauses being construed 'restrictively'. I am unconvinced by the notion that service charge clauses are to be subject to any special rule of interpretation. Even if (which it is unnecessary to decide) a landlord may have simpler remedies than a tenant to enforce service charge provisions, that is not relevant to the issue of how one interprets the contractual machinery for assessing the tenant's contribution. The origin of the adverb was in a judgment of Rix LJ in *McHale v Earl Cadogan* [2010] EWCA Civ 14, [2010] 1 EGLR 51, para 17. What he was saying, quite correctly, was that the court should not 'bring within the general words of a service charge clause anything which does not clearly belong there'. However, that does not help resolve the sort of issue of interpretation raised in this case.

Subsequently, in *Wood v Capita Insurance Services Ltd* [2017] UKSC 24 Lord Hodge (with whom Lord Neuberger, Lord Mance, Lord Clarke and Lord Sumption agreed) stated that *Arnold v Britton* was not a recalibration of *Rainy Sky*. In Lord Hodge's opinion, interpreting a contract is a unitary exercise where the court has to balance the language used (*Arnold v Britton*) with the implications of rival constructions (*Rainy Sky*). In determining the weight to be given to these factors, a court should consider the quality of the drafting and whether one party has actually just made a bad bargain ([2017] UKSC 24 at [9]–[11]).

More recently, in *Deutsche Trustee Co Ltd v Duchess VI Clo BV* [2019] EWHC 778 at [49], in the context of a financial collateral arrangement, Sir Geoffrey Vos (Chancellor of the High Court) stated: 'This is a case where the language of the Transaction documents is clear in the context of the transaction, applying the iterative approach recommended in *Sigma* and in *Rainy Sky*. Commercial parties buying into such traded instruments expect to be bound by the language of them. They are entitled to the certainty and predictability that the adoption of a proper contextual interpretation of the language produces.'

6.3.3 Categories of terms

There are three types of term: conditions, warranties and innominate terms. The word condition can have a number of meanings, but, in this context, it means a 'promissory condition'. When contrasted with warranties or innominate terms, the label of 'promissory condition' is being used to indicate the legal consequence of a breach, in the sense of whether the injured party has a right to terminate the contract because of the breach. When a party breaches a term that is a condition, the injured party has a right to terminate the contract as well as to claim damages. In contrast, when a party breaches a warranty this only gives rise to the right to claim damages. The consequences of breach of an innominate term will depend upon the seriousness of the breach. If the breach is merely trivial, the injured party will only be entitled to damages. If it is more serious, termination of the contract may be available. The distinction between conditions, warranties and innominate terms was explained by Diplock LJ in *Hong Kong Fir Shipping v Kawasaki Kisen Kaisha*.

***Hong Kong Fir Shipping v Kawasaki Kisen Kaisha* [1962] 2 QB 26**

Diplock LJ: [T]here are many simple contractual undertakings, sometimes express but more often because of their very simplicity ('It goes without saying') to be implied, of which it can be predicated that every breach of such an undertaking must give rise to an event which will deprive the party not in default of substantially the whole benefit which it was intended that he should obtain from the contract; and such a stipulation, unless the parties have agreed that breach of it shall not entitle the non-defaulting party to treat the contract as repudiated, is a 'condition'. So too there may be other simple contractual undertakings of which it can be predicated that no breach can give rise to an event which will deprive the party not in default of substantially the whole benefit which it was intended that he should obtain from the contract; and such a stipulation, unless the parties have agreed that breach of it shall entitle the non-defaulting party to treat the contract as repudiated, is a 'warranty'.

There are, however, many contractual undertakings of a more complex character which cannot be categorised as being 'conditions' or 'warranties' ... Of such undertakings all that can be predicated is that some breaches will and others will not give rise to an event which will deprive the party not in default of substantially the whole benefit which it was intended that he should obtain from the contract; and the legal consequences of a breach of such an undertaking, unless provided for expressly in the contract, depend upon the nature of the event to which the breach gives rise and do not follow automatically from a prior classification of the undertaking as a 'condition' or a 'warranty'.

Whether a term is classified as a condition or a warranty usually depends on the importance of the term. If the parties refer to a term as a 'condition', this may well indicate that the parties intend that breach of the term should entitle the non-defaulting party to treat the contract as discharged. However, use of such labels is not conclusive and the presumption can be rebutted by contrary evidence (see *Schuler AG v Wickman Machine Tools* [1974] AC 235). The distinction between conditions, warranties and innominate terms will be discussed in Chapter 14, which deals with issues of performance and breach. At this point, it is important to note that the parties should have these issues in mind when drafting the contract. They generally can, if they wish, include an express term stating the consequences that will follow from breach of particular obligations. Such a term will provide greater certainty than leaving it to the court to determine the consequences of breach. Note also the Consumer Rights Act 2015, which explicitly specifies some of the consequences of breach of particular statutory rights. The Government's intention was to '[s]et out more clearly the standards that the goods must meet. This will remove references to "conditions", "warranties" and "implied terms" and replace these with less legalistic language' (*Draft Consumer Rights Bill: Government Response to Consultations on Consumer Rights*, June 2013 (BIS/13/916) at p 26).

6.4 Implied terms

It would be unrealistic to expect every term in a contract to be written down or expressed in words. Indeed, if they were, contracts would be absurdly lengthy documents. Therefore, in certain situations a term or terms may be implied into a contract. Parliament has intervened to imply terms into certain types of contract, for example: contracts for the sale and supply of goods, employment contracts and contracts between a landlord and tenant. In the absence of intervention by Parliament, it is left to the courts to imply terms. The relationship between express and implied terms was considered by Lord Diplock in *Photo Production v Securicor Transport* [1980] AC 827:

> A basic principle of the common law of contract ... is that parties to a contract are free to determine for themselves what primary obligations they will accept. They may state these in express words in the contract itself, and, where they do, the statement is determinative; but in practice a commercial contract never states all the primary obligations of the parties in full; many are left to be incorporated by implication of law from the legal nature of the contract into which the parties are entering. But if the parties wish to reject or modify primary obligations which would otherwise be so incorporated, they are fully at liberty to do so by express words.

As we will see there are some terms implied by statute that cannot be excluded because they are necessary for the protection of vulnerable parties, but as Lord Diplock notes, generally all other potential implied terms can be excluded by the express words of the parties. On the relationship between interpretation and the implication of terms see *Trump International Golf Club Scotland Ltd and another v The Scottish Ministers (Scotland)* [2015] UKSC 74 at [35] per Lord Hodge (with whom Lord Neuberger, Lord Mance, Lord Reed and Lord Carnwath agreed):

> Interpretation is not the same as the implication of terms. Interpretation of the words of a document is the precursor of implication. It forms the context in which the law may have to imply terms into a document, where the court concludes from its interpretation of the words used in the document that it must have been intended that the document would have a certain effect, although the words to give it that effect are absent. See the decision of the Privy Council in *Attorney General of Belize v Belize Telecom Ltd* [2009] 1 WLR 1988, per Lord Hoffmann at paras 16 to 24 as explained by this court in *Marks & Spencer plc v BNP Paribas Securities Trust Company (Jersey) Ltd* [2015] UKSC 71, per Lord Neuberger at paras 22 to 30.

We shall return to this point below (at 6.4.1.2.3). For present purposes it should be noted that there are two potential sources of implied terms: the courts and Parliament. We will consider terms implied by the courts first.

6.4.1 Terms implied by the courts

The courts may imply terms into contracts on the ground that they are purporting to realise the presumed intention of the parties. The test is strict. As Lord Bingham said in *Phillips Electronique Grand Public SA v British Sky Broadcasting Ltd* [1995] EMLR 472, 481, 'it is because the implication of terms is so potentially intrusive that the law imposes strict constraints on the exercise of this extraordinary power'. The courts are understandably reluctant to give any encouragement to parties to try to escape from contractual obligations on the basis of some term which was not stated, but which is now alleged to be of great significance. There are certain situations, however, where the courts will be willing to imply terms.

6.4.1.1 Terms implied by custom

The first basis on which the courts will imply terms is where the implication of the term derives from a local trade or custom. Such implications have an important role to play in commercial law. The requirements for implying a term derived from trade or custom were expounded by Ungoed-Thomas J in *Cunliffe-Owen v Teather & Greenwood* [1967] 1 WLR 1421:

> 'Usage' [or custom] may be admitted to explain the language used in a written contract or to add an implied incident to it, provided that if expressed in the written contract it would not make its terms or its tenor insensible or inconsistent ... 'Usage' as a practice which the court will recognise is a mixed question of fact and law. For the practice to amount to such a recognised usage, it must be certain, in the sense that the practice is clearly established; it must be notorious, in the sense that it is so well known, in the market in which it is alleged to exist, that those who conduct business in that market contract with the usage as an implied term; and it must be reasonable.
>
> The burden lies on those alleging 'usage' to establish it ... The practice that has to be established consists of a continuity of acts, and those acts have to be established by persons familiar with them ... Arrangements or compromises to the same effect as the alleged usage do not establish usage; they contradict it. They may be the precursors of usage; but usage presupposes that arrangements and compromises are no longer required ... What is necessary is that for a practice to be a recognised usage it should be established as a practice having binding effect.

To imply a term derived from custom it must be shown that the term is: (1) certain, (2) notorious, (3) reasonable, and (4) recognised as binding. An early example of such a term is seen in the case of *Hutton v Warren*.

Hutton v Warren (1836) 1 M & W 466; All ER Rep 151

Facts: See above.

Parke B: The custom of the country as to cultivation and the term of quitting with respect to allowances for seed and labour, is clearly applicable to a tenancy from year to year and, therefore, if this custom was, by implication, imported into the lease, the plaintiff and defendant were bound by it after the lease expired. We are of opinion that this custom was, by implication, imported into the lease. It has long been settled that, in commercial transactions, extrinsic evidence of custom and usage is admissible to annex incidents to written contracts in matters with respect to which they are silent. The same rule has also been applied to contracts in other transactions of life, in which known usages have been established and prevailed. This has been done on the principle of presumption that, in such transactions, the parties did not mean to express in writing the whole of the contract by which they intended to be bound, but a contract with reference to those known usages.

Such a term may also be implied into an employment contract. For a recent example of which see *CSC Computer Sciences Ltd v McAlinden* (EAT, unreported, 11 December 2012) which was affirmed on appeal ([2013] EWCA Civ 1435) with Underhill LJ stating:

> 11. The correct approach in cases where employees seek to rely on terms to be implied on the basis of 'custom and practice and/or the conduct of the parties' was very recently reviewed by this Court in *Park Cakes Ltd v Shumba* [2013] EWCA Civ 974, [2013] IRLR 800 – see in particular paras. 26–36 (pp. 805–8); and although the term asserted in that case concerned enhanced redundancy benefits the same principles would apply in the present case. Since that decision was handed down after the argument before us we gave the parties the opportunity to submit further written submissions by reference to it. I see no point in reproducing *in extenso* here what was said in *Park Cakes*. But I would draw attention to the fact that the Court, following the lead given by Leveson LJ in *Garratt v Mirror Group Newspapers Ltd* [2011] EWCA Civ 425, [2011] ICR 880, focused less on the language of 'custom and practice' and more on the essential question of what the employees will reasonably have understood from the employer's conduct and words, applying ordinary contractual principles.

However, implication of a term by custom will usually not be possible if the contract contains an express term that is inconsistent with the custom. In that case the express term usually prevails over the implied term.

***Les Affréteurs Réunis SA v Leopold Walford (London) Ltd* [1919] AC 801**

Facts: A clause in a time charterparty provided that 'a commission of three per cent on the estimated gross amount of hire is due to Leopold Walford (London), Limited, on signing this charter (ship lost or not lost)'. The charterers brought an action for payment of the commission. At first instance, Bailhache J found for the ship owners on the ground that no hire had in fact been earned under the charterparty and there was a custom in operation that a broker's commission was payable only in relation to hire which had been earned under the charter.

Held: The House of Lords held that the charterers could enforce the express clause because the ship owners could not lawfully set up a custom which was inconsistent with the express terms of the charterparty.

Lord Birkenhead: The learned judge, in my judgment (and here I think the comments of the learned Lords Justices in the Court of Appeal are perfectly well-founded and in no way exaggerated), has in effect declared that a custom may be given effect to in commercial matters which is entirely inconsistent with the plain words of an agreement into which commercial men, certainly acquainted with so well known a custom, have nevertheless thought proper to enter. Much evidence would be necessary to convince me of the existence of such a custom, and, if it were forthcoming, I should nevertheless hold the custom to be bad on grounds which seem to me to be both notorious and elementary.

6.4.1.2 Terms implied in fact

Terms may be implied into an apparently complete contract from the factual context of the agreement. Terms implied in fact are implied into the contract to give effect to the unexpressed objective intentions of the parties. In other words, the term is implied not as a matter of law, but as a matter of fact to give effect to what the parties had agreed, although the agreement was implicit rather than explicit. Because of this, terms implied in fact will usually be specific to the particular transaction between the parties.

Traditionally the courts have been reluctant to imply a term into a contract as a matter of fact. This is because of concerns about protecting freedom of contract. It is undesirable for the courts to rewrite the contract for the parties. Terms will generally only be implied in fact where it is 'necessary' to do so. Traditionally two tests have emerged:

(i) the business efficacy test; and
(ii) the officious bystander test.

Arguably they are different shades of the same test as to what is 'necessary' to make the contract work.

6.4.1.2.1 The business efficacy test

The Moorcock (1889) LR 14 PD 64

Facts: The defendant agreed to allow the plaintiff's ship to unload cargo at the defendant's Thames wharf. It was well known that ships normally ran aground at low tide on the Thames, but unfortunately the plaintiff's ship was damaged because of the unevenness of the river bed at the defendant's wharf. The contract between the parties contained no express term as to the suitability of the river bed for mooring a ship. The plaintiff brought an action for damages against the defendants. At first instance, Butt J held that the defendants were liable for breach of an implied term to take 'reasonable care to ascertain that the bottom of the river at the jetty was in such a condition as not to endanger the vessel using their premises in the ordinary way'.

Held: The Court of Appeal dismissed the defendant's appeal.

Bowen LJ: The question which arises here is whether when a contract is made to let the use of this jetty to a ship which can only use it, as is known by both parties, by taking the ground, there is any implied warranty on the part of the owners of the jetty, and if so, what is the extent of the warranty. Now, an implied warranty, or, as it is called, a covenant in law, as distinguished from an express contract or express warranty, really is in all cases founded on the presumed intention of the parties, and upon reason. The implication which the law draws from what must obviously have been the intention of the parties, the law draws with the object of giving efficacy to the transaction and preventing such a failure of consideration as cannot have been within the contemplation of either side; and I believe if one were to take all the cases, and they are many, of implied warranties or covenants in law, it will be found that in all of them the law is raising an implication from the presumed intention of the parties with the object of giving to the transaction such efficacy as both parties must have intended that at all events it should have. In business transactions such as this, what the law desires to effect by the implication is to give such business efficacy to the transaction as must have been intended at all events by both parties who are business men; not to impose on one side all the perils of the transaction, or to emancipate one side from all the chances of failure, but to make each party promise in law as much, at all events, as it must have been in the contemplation of both parties that he should be responsible for in respect of those perils or chances.

Now what did each party in a case like this know? For if we are examining into their presumed intention we must examine into their minds as to what the transaction was. Both parties knew that this jetty was let out for hire, and knew that it could only be used under the contract by the ship taking the ground. They must have known that it was by grounding that she used the jetty; in fact, except so far as the transport to the jetty of the cargo in the ship was concerned, they must have known, both of them, that unless the ground was safe the ship would be simply buying an opportunity of danger, and that all consideration would fail unless some care had been taken to see that the ground was safe. In fact the business of the jetty could not be carried on except upon such a basis. The parties also knew that with regard to the safety of the ground outside the jetty the ship-owner could know nothing at all, and the jetty owner might with reasonable care know everything. The owners of the jetty, or their servants, were there at high and low tide, and with little trouble they could satisfy themselves, in case of doubt, as to whether the berth was reasonably safe. The ship's owner, on the other hand, had not the means of verifying the state of the jetty, because the berth itself opposite the jetty might be occupied by another ship at any moment.

Now the question is how much of the peril of the safety of this berth is it necessary to assume that the ship-owner and the jetty owner intended respectively to bear – in order that such a minimum of efficacy should be secured for the transaction, as both parties must have intended it to bear? Assume that the berth outside had been absolutely under the control of the owners of the jetty, that they could have repaired it and made it fit for the purpose of the unloading and the loading. If this had been the case, then the case of *The Mersey Docks Trustees v Gibbs* (1866) LR 1 H L 93 shews that those who owned the jetty, who took money for the use of the jetty, and who had under their control the *locus in quo*, would have been bound to take all reasonable care to prevent danger to those who were using the jetty – either to make the berth outside good, or else not to invite ships to go there – either to make the berth safe, or to advise persons not to go there. But there is a distinction in the present instance. The berth outside the jetty was not under the actual control of the jetty owners. It is in the bed of the river, and it may be said that those who owned the jetty had no duty cast upon them by statute or common law to repair the bed of the river, and that they had no power to interfere with the bed of the river unless under the licence of the Conservators. Now it does make a difference, it seems to me, where the entire control of the *locus in quo* – be it canal, or be it dock, or be it river berth – is not under the control of the persons who are taking toll for accommodation which involves its user, and, to a certain extent, the view must be modified of the necessary implication which the law would make about the duties of the parties receiving the remuneration. This must be done exactly for the reason laid down by Lord Holt in his judgment in *Coggs v Bernard* Ld Raym 909 (918), where he says 'it would be unreasonable to charge persons with a trust further than the nature of the thing puts it in their power to perform'. Applying that modification, which is one of reason, to this case, it may well be said that the law will not imply that the persons who have not the control of the place have taken reasonable care to make it good, but it does not follow that they are relieved from all responsibility. They are on the spot. They must know that the jetty cannot be used unless reasonable care is taken, if not to make it safe, at all events to see whether it is safe. No one can tell whether reasonable safety has been secured except themselves, and I think if they let out their jetty for use they at all events imply that they have taken reasonable care to see whether the berth, which is the essential part of the use of the jetty, is safe, and if it is not safe, and if they have not taken such reasonable care, it is their duty to warn persons with whom they have dealings that they have not done so. This is a business transaction as to which at any moment the parties may make any bargain they please, and either side may by the contract throw upon the other the burden of the unseen and existing danger. The question is what inference is to be drawn where the parties are dealing with each other on the assumption that the negotiations are to have some fruit, and where they say nothing about the burden of this kind of unseen peril, leaving the law to raise such inferences as are reasonable from the very nature of the transaction. So far as I am concerned I do not wish it to be understood that I at all consider this is a case of any duty on the part of the owners of the jetty to see to the access to the jetty being kept clear. The difference between access to the jetty and the actual use of the jetty seems to me, as [counsel for the defendants] says it is, only a question of degree, but when you are dealing with implications which the law directs, you cannot afford to neglect questions of degree, and it is just that difference of degree which brings one case on the line and prevents the other from approaching it. I confess that on the broad view of the case I think that business could not be carried on unless there was an implication to the extent I have laid down, at all events in the case where a jetty like the present is so to be used, and, although the case is a novel one, and the cases which have been cited do not assist us, I feel no difficulty in drawing the inference that this case comes within the line.

According to Bowen LJ, the purpose of implying terms in fact, 'is to give such business efficacy to the transaction as must have been intended at all events by both parties who are business men'. In other words, a term will be implied in fact if, without it, the contract would be rendered unworkable. This is a stringent test. It is based on the presumed intentions of the parties but, on the facts of *The Moorcock*, this was assessed by reference to what was 'necessary' to make the contract work; not by reference to what would be 'reasonably expected'. *The Moorcock* thus establishes a test of 'necessity' in relation to terms implied in fact. The test is not without its difficulties, however, because it rests on the assumption that the parties are agreed as to the objectives of the contract, which is often not true.

Collins, H, *The Law of Contract*, 4th edn, 2003, Cambridge: CUP, p 240

Implied terms are often presented as default rules, ie rules which the parties would agree were the costs of negotiation low or absent. Yet in all probability the parties have not failed to reach agreement on this point because of shortage of time and resources, but have simply not wished to enter into such detailed specification for fear of failure to reach agreement. The attempt to resolve this problem by means of a reification of the purpose of the contract in the business efficacy test only serves to obscure the problem. If the commercial motives of the parties for entering the contract diverge, as they usually will outside the realm of symbiotic contracts such as partnership and joint ventures, the performance of the contract without the implied term might easily satisfy the commercial objective of one party whilst simultaneously frustrating the objective of the other. Although these tests have been hallowed by constant judicial use for over a century, we must doubt whether they always provide a convincing justification for the insertion of additional obligations.

6.4.1.2.2 The 'officious bystander' test

The officious bystander test was put forward by Mackinnon LJ in *Shirlaw v Southern Foundries*.

***Shirlaw v Southern Foundries* [1939] 2 KB 206**

Facts: In 1933 Mr Shirlaw was appointed managing director of Southern Foundries for a term of 10 years. Three years later the beneficial owners of the company removed him from his directorship. The question for the court was whether there existed an implied term that he would not be removed from his directorship.

Held: The Court of Appeal held that such a term would be implied into the contract.

MacKinnon LJ: The question is whether this termination was a breach by the Southern Company of the agreement of December 21, 1933, caused or procured by the Federated Company.

I think that Humphreys J was right in holding that it was, for, as by the contract and the then existing articles, the company had no right to remove Mr Shirlaw from being a director during the ten years, I think it was an implied term that they would not by any alteration of the articles create such a right and exercise it during that period.

I recognise that the right or duty of a Court to find the existence of an implied term or implied terms in a written contract is a matter to be exercised with care; and a Court is too often invited to do so upon vague and uncertain grounds. Too often also such an invitation is backed by the citation of a sentence or two from the judgment of Bowen LJ in *The Moorcock* (1889) 14 PD 64. They are sentences from an extempore judgment as sound and sensible as all the utterances of that great judge; but I fancy that he would have been rather surprised if he could have foreseen that these general remarks of his would come to be a favourite citation of a supposed principle of law, and I even think that he might sympathise with the occasional impatience of his successors when *The Moorcock* (1889) 14 PD 64 is so often flushed for them in that guise.

For my part, I think that there is a test that may be at least as useful as such generalities. If I may quote from an essay which I wrote some years ago, I then said: '*Prima facie* that which in any contract is left to be implied and need not be expressed is something so obvious that it goes without saying; so that, if, while the parties were making their bargain, an officious bystander were to suggest some express provision for it in their agreement, they would testily suppress him with a common 'Oh, of course!'

At least it is true, I think, that, if a term were never implied by a judge unless it could pass that test, he could not be held to be wrong.

Applying that in this case, I ask myself what would have happened if, when this contract had been drafted and was awaiting signature, a third party reading the draft had said: 'Would it not be well to put in a provision that the company shall not exercise or create any right to remove Mr Shirlaw from his directorship, and he have no right to resign his directorship?' I am satisfied that they would both have assented to this as implied already, and agreed to its expression for greater certainty. Mr Shirlaw would certainly have said: 'Of course that is implied. If I am to be bound by this agreement, including the barring of my activities under clauses 11 and 12 when I cease to be managing director, obviously the company must not have, or create, the power to remove me at any moment from the Board and so disqualify me from that post'; and the company, which must be presumed to have been then desirous of binding him to serve them as managing director for ten years, would, I think, with equal alacrity have said: 'Of course that is implied. If you were tempted by some offer elsewhere, it would be monstrous for you to be able to resign your directorship and, by so disqualifying yourself from being managing director, put an end to this agreement'.

The officious bystander test is again a strict one, emphasising that the standard is one of necessity, not reasonableness. This was noted in *Hughes v Greenwich LBC*.

Hughes v Greenwich LBC [1994] 1 AC 170

Lord Lowry: In order that a term may be implied, there has to be a compelling reason for deeming that term to form part of the contract ... I may perhaps illustrate my view by referring to what I said in the Court of Appeal in *JM Reilly Ltd v Belfast Corporation* [1970] NI 68, 83–84, in a passage which has no claim to originality of thought:

> 'It is not enough for the court to conclude, (and I guard myself against doing so), that such a term would have made the contract more reasonable; terms will be implied not in order to make for the parties a contract which the court considers fair, but only to make effective the contract which the parties have made for themselves. The principle is clearly and authoritatively stated in *Luxor (Eastbourne) Ltd v Cooper* [1941] AC 108, and even in *Devonald v Rosser* [1906] 2 KB 728, which may at first sight appear to give a more liberal expression to the doctrine, one finds on analysis a loyal adherence to the rule of *necessary implication* in the passage (at p 743) where Farwell LJ asks: 'What, then, are we to infer would be a reasonable bargain such as the parties, being businessmen, *must have intended* to make?.

6.4.1.2.3 The relationship between the two tests

There is considerable overlap between the two tests. In theory, a term could satisfy the 'officious bystander' test but not the 'business efficacy' test if, without the term, the contract would still have been workable, but both parties, as reasonable persons, would have agreed to the term's inclusion had it been suggested to them. In practice, however, differing commercial objectives will often preclude implication under both tests.

Ashmore v Corporation of Lloyd's (No 2) [1992] 2 Lloyd's Rep 620

Facts: Ashmore, a Lloyd's name, claimed breach of contract against Lloyd's following losses sustained on a number of insurance contracts. Ashmore contended that his contract with Lloyd's contained an implied term that Lloyd's would take reasonable steps to alert names about matters likely to affect their interests.

Held: Gatehouse J dismissed the action. The implied term could not pass the 'business efficacy' test because the Lloyd's names had always operated under the same contractual arrangements as at present and it was impossible to say that the contract would be unworkable without those implied terms. Nor did it pass the 'officious bystander' test because it was impossible to contemplate an officious bystander thinking of such a term.

Gatehouse J: The ... two tests will often overlap and, indeed, have in the past been regarded as a single test embodying both aspects ...

[Regarding] the Moorcock 'business efficacy' ... I am driven to the conclusion that neither of the terms contended for by the plaintiffs comes within measurable distance of passing it. Very many thousands of people over the years have been or are now Names at Lloyd's under the same contractual arrangements and it is obviously impossible to say that without these implied terms the contract will not work.

Turning to the officious bystander test, in my judgment the same result follows. With regard to the alleged 'Duty to alert', I have already remarked on the complexity of the question posed, in its final and alternative form, and the successive versions put forward in the process of reaching it. I sympathise with the plaintiffs' legal advisers, striving to formulate a term which is at the same time sufficiently circumscribed to qualify as both reasonable and necessary, but also sufficiently wide to cover the actual events alleged in the remainder of the points of claim and on which the remedy of damages and indemnity is founded ...

The plain fact is that the more the plaintiffs' advisers strove to bring the implied term within the bounds of reasonableness and necessity, the more divorced from reality the question became. To start with, I find it impossible to contemplate an officious bystander at the Rota Committee being capable of thinking up so complex a question; one which has taken a team of skilled lawyers so long and so many attempts to formulate. Even if he could, the answer of both parties would certainly not be, 'Oh, of course! That is something that is so obvious that it goes without saying'. If Lloyd's had not dismissed the suggestion out of hand, the Rota Committee would at least have required the question to be written down for detailed consideration, no doubt with their lawyers' advice. The eventual answer would, I believe, have been an uncompromising 'No'. At least, I am wholly unpersuaded that it would have been, 'Yes, of course' and certainly such acceptance would not have been given unhesitatingly at the time the question was asked.

More recently, in *Attorney General of Belize v Belize Telecom Ltd* [2009] UKPC 10, Lord Hoffmann noted:

> The court has no power to improve upon the instrument which it is called upon to construe ... It cannot introduce terms to make it fairer or more reasonable. It is concerned only to discover what the instrument means ... It is the meaning which the instrument would convey to a reasonable person having all the background knowledge which would reasonably be available to the audience to whom the instrument is addressed: see *Investors Compensation Scheme Ltd v West Bromwich Building Society* [1998] 1 WLR 896, 912–913. It is this objective meaning which is conventionally called the intention of the parties, or the intention of Parliament, or the intention of whatever person or body was or is deemed to have been the author of the instrument.

Thereafter His Lordship stated (at [19]–[21]):

> The proposition that the implication of a term is an exercise in the construction of the instrument as a whole is not only a matter of logic (since a court has no power to alter what the instrument means) but also well supported by authority ... It follows that in every case in which it is said that some provision ought to be implied in an instrument, the question for the court is whether such a provision would spell out in express words what the instrument, read against the relevant background, would reasonably be understood to mean ... [The] question can be reformulated in various ways which a court may find helpful in providing an answer – the implied term must 'go without saying', it must be 'necessary to give business efficacy to the contract' and so on – but these are not ... to be treated as different or additional tests. There is only one question: is that what the instrument, read as a whole against the relevant background, would reasonably be understood to mean?

See also Low and Loi, 'The Many "Tests" for Terms Implied in Fact: Welcome Clarity' (2009) 125 LQR 561. Cf. also *Cosmetic Warriors Ltd v Gerrie* [2015] EWHC 3718 (Ch) on the factual background which can be taken into account. More recently, however, in *Marks and Spencer plc v BNP Paribas Securities Services Trust Co (Jersey) Ltd* [2015] UKSC 72 Lord Neuberger (with whom Lord Sumption and Lord Hodge agreed) stated that Lord Hoffmann's 'observations [in *Attorney General of Belize v Belize Telecom Ltd* [2009] UKPC 10] should henceforth be treated as a characteristically inspired discussion rather than authoritative guidance on the law of implied terms':

16. There have, of course, been many judicial observations as to the nature of the requirements which have to be satisfied before a term can be implied into a detailed commercial contract. They include three classic statements, which have been frequently quoted in law books and judgments. In *The Moorcock* (1889) 14 PD 64, 68, Bowen LJ observed that in all the cases where a term had been implied, 'it will be found that ... the law is raising an implication from the presumed intention of the parties with the object of giving the transaction such efficacy as both parties must have intended that at all events it should have'. In *Reigate v Union Manufacturing Co (Ramsbottom) Ltd* [1918] 1 KB 592, 605, Scrutton LJ said that '[a] term can only be implied if it is necessary in the business sense to give efficacy to the contract'. He added that a term would only be implied if 'it is such a term that it can confidently be said that if at the time the contract was being negotiated' the parties had been asked what would happen in a certain event, they would both have replied 'Of course, so and so will happen; we did not trouble to say that; it is too clear'. And in *Shirlaw v Southern Foundries (1926) Ltd* [1939] 2 KB 206, 227, MacKinnon LJ observed that, '*[p]rima facie* that which in any contract is left to be implied and need not be expressed is something so obvious that it goes without saying'. Reflecting what Scrutton LJ had said 20 years earlier, MacKinnon LJ also famously added that a term would only be implied 'if, while the parties were making their bargain, an officious bystander were to suggest some express provision for it in their agreement, they would testily suppress him with a common 'Oh, of course!'.

17. Support for the notion that a term will only be implied if it satisfies the test of business necessity is to be found in a number of observations made in the House of Lords. Notable examples included Lord Pearson (with whom Lord Guest and Lord Diplock agreed) in *Trollope & Colls Ltd v North West Metropolitan Regional Hospital Board* [1973] 1 WLR 601, 609, and Lord Wilberforce, Lord Cross, Lord Salmon and Lord Edmund-Davies in *Liverpool City Council v Irwin* [1977] AC 239, 254, 258, 262 and 266 respectively. More recently, the test of 'necessary to give business efficacy' to the contract in issue was mentioned by Lady Hale in *Geys* at para 55 and by Lord Carnwath in *Arnold v Britton* [2015] 2 WLR 1593, para 112.

18. In the Privy Council case of *BP Refinery (Westernport) Pty Ltd v President, Councillors and Ratepayers of the Shire of Hastings* (1977) 52 ALJR 20, 26, Lord Simon (speaking for the majority, which included Viscount Dilhorne and Lord Keith) said that:

'[F]or a term to be implied, the following conditions (which may overlap) must be satisfied: (1) it must be reasonable and equitable; (2) it must be necessary to give business efficacy to the contract, so that no term will be implied if the contract is effective without it; (3) it must be so obvious that "it goes without saying"; (4) it must be capable of clear expression; (5) it must not contradict any express term of the contract'.

19. In *Philips Electronique Grand Public SA v British Sky Broadcasting Ltd* [1995] EMLR 472, 481, Sir Thomas Bingham MR set out Lord Simon's formulation, and described it as a summary which 'distil[led] the essence of much learning on implied terms' but whose 'simplicity could be almost misleading'. Sir Thomas then explained that it was 'difficult to infer with confidence what the parties must have intended when they have entered into a lengthy and carefully-drafted contract but have omitted to make provision for the matter in issue', because it may well be doubtful whether the omission was the result of the parties' oversight or of their deliberate decision, or indeed the parties might suspect that 'they are unlikely to agree on what is to happen in a certain ... eventuality' and 'may well choose to leave the matter uncovered in their contract in the hope that the eventuality will not occur'. Sir Thomas went on to say this at p 482:

'The question of whether a term should be implied, and if so what, almost inevitably arises after a crisis has been reached in the performance of the contract. So the court comes to the task of implication with the benefit of hindsight, and it is tempting for the court then to fashion a term which will reflect the merits of the situation as they then appear. Tempting, but wrong. [He then quoted the observations of Scrutton LJ in Reigate, and continued] [I]t is not enough to show that had the parties foreseen the eventuality which in fact occurred they would have wished to make provision for it, unless it can also be shown either that there was only one contractual solution or that one of several possible solutions would without doubt have been preferred' ...

20. Sir Thomas's approach in *Philips* was consistent with his reasoning, as Bingham LJ in the earlier case *The APJ Priti* [1987] 2 Lloyd's Rep 37, 42, where he rejected the argument that a warranty, to the effect that the port declared was prospectively safe, could be implied into a voyage charter-party. His reasons for rejecting the implication were 'because the omission of an express warranty may well have been deliberate, because such an implied term is not necessary for the business efficacy of the charter and because such an implied term would at best lie uneasily beside the express terms of the charter'.

21. In my judgment, the judicial observations so far considered represent a clear, consistent and principled approach. It could be dangerous to reformulate the principles, but I would add six comments on the summary given by Lord Simon in *BP Refinery* as extended by Sir Thomas Bingham in *Philips* and exemplified in *The APJ Priti*. First, in *Equitable Life Assurance Society v Hyman* [2002] 1 AC 408, 459, Lord Steyn rightly observed that the implication of a term was 'not critically dependent on proof of an actual intention of the parties' when negotiating the contract. If one approaches the question by reference to what the parties would have agreed, one is not strictly concerned with the hypothetical answer of the actual parties, but with that of notional reasonable people in the position of the parties at the time at which they were contracting. Secondly, a term should not be implied into a detailed commercial contract merely because it appears fair or merely because one considers that the parties would have agreed it if it had been suggested to them. Those are necessary but not sufficient grounds for including a term. However, and thirdly, it is questionable whether Lord Simon's first requirement, reasonableness and equitableness, will usually, if ever, add anything: if a term satisfies the other requirements, it is hard to think that it would not be reasonable and equitable. Fourthly, as Lord Hoffmann I think suggested in *Attorney General of Belize v Belize Telecom Ltd* [2009] 1 WLR 1988, para 27, although Lord Simon's requirements are otherwise cumulative, I would accept that business necessity and obviousness, his second and third requirements, can be alternatives in the sense that only one of them needs to be satisfied, although I suspect that in practice it would be a rare case where only one of those two requirements would be satisfied. Fifthly, if one approaches the issue by reference to the officious bystander, it is 'vital to formulate the question to be posed by [him] with the utmost care', to quote from Lewison, *The Interpretation of Contracts* 5th ed (2011), para 6.09. Sixthly, necessity for business efficacy involves a value judgment. It is rightly common ground on this appeal that the test is not one of absolute necessity, not least because the necessity is judged by reference to business efficacy. It may well be that a more helpful way of putting Lord Simon's second requirement is, as suggested by Lord Sumption in argument, that a term can only be implied if, without the term, the contract would lack commercial or practical coherence.

22. Before leaving this issue of general principle, it is appropriate to refer a little further to *Belize Telecom*, where Lord Hoffmann suggested that the process of implying terms into a contract was part of the exercise of the construction, or interpretation, of the contract. In summary, he said at para 21 that '[t]here is only one question: is that what the instrument, read as a whole against the relevant background, would reasonably be understood to mean?'. There are two points to be made about that observation.

23. First, the notion that a term will be implied if a reasonable reader of the contract, knowing all its provisions and the surrounding circumstances, would understand it to be implied is quite acceptable, provided that (i) the reasonable reader is treated as reading the contract at the time it was made and (ii) he would consider the term to be so obvious as to go without saying or to be necessary for business efficacy. (The difference between what the reasonable reader would understand and what the parties, acting reasonably, would agree, appears to me to be a notional distinction without a practical difference.) The first proviso emphasises that the question whether a term is implied is to be judged at the date the contract is made. The second proviso is important because otherwise Lord Hoffmann's formulation may be interpreted as suggesting that reasonableness is a sufficient ground for implying a term. (For the same reason, it would be wrong to treat Lord Steyn's statement in *Equitable Life Assurance Society v Hyman* [2002] 1 AC 408, 459 that a term will be implied if it is 'essential to give effect to the reasonable expectations of the parties' as diluting the test of necessity. That is clear from what Lord Steyn said earlier on the same page, namely that '[t]he legal test for the implication of … a term is … strict necessity', which he described as a 'stringent test'.)

24. It is necessary to emphasise that there has been no dilution of the requirements which have to be satisfied before a term will be implied, because it is apparent that *Belize Telecom* has been interpreted by both academic lawyers and judges as having changed the law. Examples of academic articles include C Peters, 'The implication of terms in fact' [2009] CLJ 513, P Davies, 'Recent developments in the Law of Implied Terms' [2010] LMCLQ 140, J McCaughran, 'Implied terms: the journey of the man on the Clapham Omnibus' [2011] CLJ 607, and JW Carter and W Courtney, 'Belize Telecom: a reply to Professor McLauchlan' [2015] LMCLQ 245). And in *Foo Jong Peng v Phua Kiah Mai* [2012] 4 SLR 1267, paras 34–36, the Singapore Court of Appeal refused to follow the reasoning in Belize at least in so far as 'it suggest[ed] that the traditional 'business efficacy' and 'officious bystander' tests are not central to the implication of terms' (reasoning which was followed in *Sembcorp Marine Ltd v PPL Holdings Pte Ltd* [2013] SGCA 43). The Singapore Court of Appeal were in my view right to hold that the law governing the circumstances in which a term will be implied into a contract remains unchanged following *Belize Telecom*.

25. The second point to be made about what was said in *Belize Telecom* concerns the suggestion that the process of implying a term is part of the exercise of interpretation. Although some support may arguably be found for such a view in Trollope at p 609, the first clear expression of that view to which we were referred was in *Banque Bruxelles Lambert SA v Eagle Star Insurance Co Ltd* [1997] AC 191, 212, where Lord Hoffmann suggested that the issue of whether to imply a term into a contract was 'one of construction of the agreement as a whole in its commercial setting'. Lord Steyn quoted this passage with approval in *Equitable Life* at p 459, and, as just mentioned, Lord Hoffmann took this proposition further in *Belize Telecom*, paras 17–27. Thus, at para 18, he said that 'the implication of the term is not an addition to the instrument. It only spells out what the instrument means'; and at para 23, he referred to 'The danger … in detaching the phrase 'necessary to give business efficacy' from the basic process of construction'. Whether or not one agrees with that approach as a matter of principle must depend on what precisely one understands by the word 'construction'.

26. I accept that both (i) construing the words which the parties have used in their contract and (ii) implying terms into the contract, involve determining the scope and meaning of the contract. However, Lord Hoffmann's analysis in *Belize Telecom* could obscure the fact that construing the words used and implying additional words are different processes governed by different rules.

27. Of course, it is fair to say that the factors to be taken into account on an issue of construction, namely the words used in the contract, the surrounding circumstances known to both parties at the time of the contract, commercial common sense, and the reasonable reader or reasonable parties, are also taken into account on an issue of implication. However, that does not mean that the exercise of implication should be properly classified as part of the exercise of interpretation, let alone that it should be carried out at the same time as interpretation. When one is implying a term or a phrase, one is not construing words, as the words to be implied are *ex hypothesi* not there to be construed; and to speak of construing the contract as a whole, including the implied terms, is not helpful, not least because it begs the question as to what construction actually means in this context.

28. In most, possibly all, disputes about whether a term should be implied into a contract, it is only after the process of construing the express words is complete that the issue of an implied term falls to be considered. Until one has decided what the parties have expressly agreed, it is difficult to see how one can set about deciding whether a term should be implied and if so what term. This appeal is just such a case. Further, given that it is a cardinal rule that no term can be implied into a contract if it contradicts an express term, it would seem logically to follow that, until the express terms of a contract have been construed, it is, at least normally, not sensibly possible to decide whether a further term should be implied. Having said that, I accept Lord Carnwath's point in para 71 to the extent that in some cases it could conceivably be appropriate to reconsider the interpretation of the express terms of a contract once one has decided whether to imply a term, but, even if that is right, it does not alter the fact that the express terms of a contract must be interpreted before one can consider any question of implication.

29. In any event, the process of implication involves a rather different exercise from that of construction. As Sir Thomas Bingham trenchantly explained in *Philips* at p 481:

> 'The courts' usual role in contractual interpretation is, by resolving ambiguities or reconciling apparent inconsistencies, to attribute the true meaning to the language in which the parties themselves have expressed their contract. The implication of contract terms involves a different and altogether more ambitious undertaking: the interpolation of terms to deal with matters for which, *ex hypothesi*, the parties themselves have made no provision. It is because the implication of terms is so potentially intrusive that the law imposes strict constraints on the exercise of this extraordinary power'.

30. It is of some interest to see how implication was dealt with in the recent case in this court of *Aberdeen City Council v Stewart Milne Group Ltd* 2012 SLT 205. At para 20, Lord Hope described the implication of a term into the contract in that case as 'the product of the way I would interpret this contract'. And at para 33, Lord Clarke said that the point at issue should be resolved 'by holding that such a term should be implied rather than by a process of interpretation'. He added that '[t]he result is of course the same'.

31. It is true that *Belize Telecom* was a unanimous decision of the Judicial Committee of the Privy Council and that the judgment was given by Lord Hoffmann, whose contributions in so many areas of law have been outstanding. However, it is apparent that Lord Hoffmann's observations in *Belize Telecom*, paras 17–27 are open to more than one interpretation on the two points identified in paras 23–24 and 25–30 above, and that some of those interpretations are wrong in law. In those circumstances, the right course for us to take is to say that those observations should henceforth be treated as a characteristically inspired discussion rather than authoritative guidance on the law of implied terms.

Cf. the judgment of Lord Carnwath. See also *Trump International Golf Club Scotland Ltd and another v The Scottish Ministers (Scotland)* [2015] UKSC 74 and *Globe Motors, Inc (a corporation incorporated in Delaware, USA), Globe Motors Portugal-Material Electrico Para A Industria Automovel LDA, Safran USA Inc v TRW Lucas Varity Electric Steering Ltd, TRW Ltd* [2016] EWCA Civ 396 at [68] *per* Beatson LJ. It is particularly noteworthy that Lord Neuberger (at [21]) regarded the 'business necessity and obviousness' tests as alternatives.

6.4.1.2.4 Necessity or reasonableness

It is repeatedly emphasised in the cases, whatever test is adopted, that 'the touchstone [for implication] is always *necessity* and not merely *reasonableness*' (*Liverpool City Council v Irwin* [1977] AC 239, 266, *per* Lord Edmund-Davies). However, this distinction may be difficult to maintain in practice because contracts are very rarely unworkable without revision. More often than not, the real problem is that the contract is manifestly unreasonable without the implication of a term.

Equitable Life Assurance Society v Hyman [2000] 3 WLR 529

Facts: Hyman was a representative of approximately 90,000 policyholders who held life assurance policies containing a guaranteed annuity rate (GAR) with Equitable Life Assurance Society. The issue was whether Equitable Life could decide to reduce the level of bonus which certain of its policyholders would receive. This was contrary to past practice and the expectations of the policyholders. The articles of association of the society, however, appeared to permit the directors of the society to take such an action. At first instance the judge held that the directors' policy was in accord with the society's articles of association. The Court of Appeal reversed that decision.

Held: The House of Lords held that, although the society's articles gave the directors a very broad discretion in relation to bonuses, a term should be implied into the articles to the effect that the society would not exercise its discretion under the articles so as to defeat the reasonable expectations of the parties, which included the expectation that the discretion would not be exercised in a way that prejudiced the rights of a particular group of policyholders.

Lord Steyn: [T]he question is whether the implication is strictly necessary. My Lords, as counsel for the GAR policyholders observed, final bonuses are not bounty. They are a significant part of the consideration for the premiums paid. And the directors' discretions as to the amount and distribution of bonuses are conferred for the benefit of policyholders. In this context the self-evident commercial object of the inclusion of guaranteed rates in the policy is to protect the policyholder against a fall in market annuity rates by ensuring that if the fall occurs he will be better off than he would have been with market rates. The choice is given to the GAR policyholder and not to the Society. It cannot be seriously doubted that the provision for guaranteed annuity rates was a good selling point in the marketing by the Society of the GAR policies. It is also obvious that it would have been a significant attraction for purchasers of GAR policies. The Society points out that no special charge was made for the inclusion in the policy of GAR provisions. So be it. This factor does not alter the reasonable expectations of the parties. The supposition of the parties must be presumed to have been that the directors would not exercise their discretion in conflict with contractual rights. These are the circumstances in which the directors of the Society resolved upon a differential policy which was designed to deprive the relevant guarantees of any substantial value. In my judgment an implication precluding the use of the directors' discretion in this way is strictly necessary. The implication is essential to give effect to the reasonable expectations of the parties. The stringent test applicable to the implication of terms is satisfied.

Lord Steyn insisted that the term was implied on the basis of its 'necessity'. But the term was not really necessary to make the contract workable (the business efficacy test) and it was not so necessary that it went without saying (the officious bystander test). Rather, in the words of Lord Steyn, it was 'essential to give effect to the reasonable expectations of the parties'. The touchstone of the implication of the term was arguably the 'reasonable expectations of the parties', not necessity (although cf. *Marks and Spencer plc v BNP Paribas Securities Services Trust Company (Jersey) Ltd* [2015] UKSC 72, particularly at [21] (above)).

***Paragon Finance plc v Nash* [2002] 1 WLR 685**

Facts: Paragon Finance loaned money to Nash under two mortgage agreements which contained variable interest clauses. Nash defaulted on the mortgages and Paragon Finance claimed possession. Nash raised a number of defences, including the claim that the agreements contained an implied term that Paragon Finance was bound to exercise its discretion in varying interest rates fairly, honestly, in good faith, and not arbitrarily, capriciously or unreasonably, having regard to all relevant matters and ignoring the irrelevant.

Held: The Court of Appeal held that the discretion to vary interest rates on the mortgages was not completely unfettered and was subject to the implied term contended for by Nash. However, the fact that Paragon Finance had set interest rates without reference to those of other market lenders did not place Paragon Finance in breach of the implied term and therefore the appeal was dismissed.

Dyson LJ: I would hold that there were terms to be implied in both agreements that the rates of interest would not be set dishonestly, for an improper purpose, capriciously or arbitrarily. I have no doubt that such an implied term is necessary in order to give effect to the reasonable expectations of the parties. I am equally in no doubt that such an implied term is one of which it could be said that 'it goes without saying'. If asked at the time of the making of the agreements whether it accepted that the discretion to fix rates of interest could be exercised dishonestly, for an improper purpose, capriciously or arbitrarily, I have no doubt that the claimant would have said 'of course not'.

In *Paragon Finance*, Dyson LJ stated that the implied term was 'necessary in order to give effect to the reasonable expectations of the parties'. Once again it seems like this is reasonableness paraded in the clothes of necessity. *Paragon Finance* was more recently approved by Lady Hale in *Braganza v BP Shipping Ltd* [2015] UKSC 17:

17. This case raises two inter-linked questions of principle, one general and one particular. The particular issue is the proper approach of a contractual fact-finder who is considering whether a person may have committed suicide. Does the fact-finder have to bear in mind the need for cogent evidence before forming the opinion that a person has committed suicide? The general issue is what it means to say that the decision of a contractual fact-finder must be a reasonable one. There are many statements in the reported cases to the effect that the principles are well-settled and well-understood, but this case illustrates that all is not as clear or as well understood as it might be.

18. Contractual terms in which one party to the contract is given the power to exercise a discretion, or to form an opinion as to relevant facts, are extremely common. It is not for the courts to rewrite the parties' bargain for them, still less to substitute themselves for the contractually agreed decision-maker. Nevertheless, the party who is charged with making decisions which affect the rights of both parties to the contract has a clear conflict of interest. That conflict is heightened where there is a significant imbalance of power between the contracting parties as there often will be in an employment contract. The courts have therefore sought to ensure that such contractual powers are not abused. They have done so by implying a term as to the manner in which such powers may be exercised, a term which may vary according to the terms of the contract and the context in which the decision-making power is given.

19. There is an obvious parallel between cases where a contract assigns a decision-making function to one of the parties and cases where a statute (or the royal prerogative) assigns a decision-making function to a public authority. In neither case is the court the primary decision-maker. The primary decision-maker is the contracting party or the public authority. It is right, therefore, that the standard of review generally adopted by the courts to the decisions of a contracting party should be no more demanding than the standard of review adopted in the judicial review of administrative action. The question is whether it should be any less demanding.

20. The decided cases reveal an understandable reluctance to adopt the fully developed rigour of the principles of judicial review of administrative action in a contractual context. But at the same time they have struggled to articulate precisely what the difference might be. In *Abu Dhabi National Tanker Co v Product Star Shipping Ltd (The 'Product Star') (No 2)* [1993] 1 Lloyd's Rep 397, 404, after contrasting the position in judicial review, Leggatt LJ explained that:

> 'The essential question is always whether the relevant power has been abused. Where A and B contract with each other to confer a discretion upon A, that does not render B subject to A's uninhibited whim. In my judgment, the authorities show that not only must the discretion be exercised honestly and in good faith, but, having regard to the provisions of the contract by which it is conferred, it must not be exercised arbitrarily, capriciously or unreasonably'.

21. That was in the context of a ship-owner's decision as to whether a port to which a vessel was directed was dangerous. In *Paragon Finance plc v Nash* [2001] EWCA Civ 1466, [2002] 1 WLR 685, the court had to consider whether there was any implied term limiting the power of a mortgagee to set interest rates under a variable rate mortgage. Dyson LJ had no difficulty in holding (at paras 32 to 36) that it was necessary, in order to give effect to the reasonable expectations of the parties, to imply a term that the power would not be exercised dishonestly, for an improper purpose, capriciously or arbitrarily. He went on to discuss whether there should also be a term that the power would not be exercised unreasonably. He concluded that there had been a 'somewhat reluctant' extension of the implied term to include 'unreasonableness that is analogous to *Wednesbury* unreasonableness' (paras 37 to 42).

22. These authorities, together with *Ludgate Insurance Co Ltd v Citibank NA* [1998] Lloyd's Rep IR 221, 239–240, and *Gan Insurance Co Ltd v Tai Ping Insurance Co Ltd (No 2)* [2001] EWCA Civ 1047, [2001] 2 All ER (Comm) 299, at paras 64, 67, 73, are helpfully summarised by Rix LJ in *Socimer International Bank Ltd v Standard Bank London Ltd* [2008] EWCA Civ 116, [2008] Bus LR 1304. In his conclusion, at para 66, he substitutes the more modern term 'irrationality' for unreasonableness:

> 'It is plain from these authorities that a decision-maker's discretion will be limited, as a matter of necessary implication, by concepts of honesty, good faith, and genuineness, and the need for the absence of arbitrariness, capriciousness, perversity and irrationality. The concern is that the discretion should not be abused. Reasonableness and unreasonableness are also concepts deployed in this context, but only in a sense analogous to *Wednesbury* unreasonableness, not in

the sense in which that expression is used when speaking of the duty to take reasonable care, or when otherwise deploying entirely objective criteria: as for instance when there might be an implication of a term requiring the fixing of a reasonable price, or a reasonable time. In the latter class of case, the concept of reasonableness is intended to be entirely mutual and thus guided by objective criteria ... Laws LJ in the course of argument put the matter accurately, if I may respectfully agree, when he said that pursuant to the *Wednesbury* rationality test, the decision remains that of the decision-maker, whereas on entirely objective criteria of reasonableness the decision-maker becomes the court itself'.

23. The same point was made (albeit in a completely different context, and so *obiter*) by Lord Sumption in *Hayes v Willoughby* [2013] UKSC 17, [2013] 1 WLR 935, at para 14:

'Rationality is not the same as reasonableness. Reasonableness is an external, objective standard applied to the *outcome* of a person's thoughts or intentions ... A test of rationality, by comparison, applies a minimum objective standard to the relevant person's *mental processes*. It imports a requirement of good faith, a requirement that there should be some logical connection between the evidence and the ostensible reasons for the decision, and (which will usually amount to the same thing) an absence of arbitrariness, of capriciousness or of reasoning so outrageous in its defiance of logic as to be perverse'. (emphasis added)

This is an obvious echo of the classic definition given by Lord Diplock when summarising the grounds of judicial review in *Council of Civil Service Unions v Minister for the Civil Service* [1985] AC 374, 410:

'By "irrationality" I mean what can by now be succinctly referred to as "*Wednesbury* unreasonableness" ... It applies to a decision which is so outrageous in its defiance of logic or of accepted moral standards that no sensible person who had applied his mind to the question to be decided could have arrived at it'.

24. The problem with this formulation, which is highlighted in this case, is that it is not a precise rendition of the test of the reasonableness of an administrative decision which was adopted by Lord Greene MR in *Associated Provincial Pictures Houses Ltd v Wednesbury Corporation* [1948] 1 KB 223, 233–234. His test has two limbs:

'The court is entitled to investigate the action of the local authority with a view to seeing whether they have taken into account matters which they ought not to take into account, or conversely, have refused to take into account or neglected to take into account matters which they ought to take into account. Once that question is answered in favour of the local authority, it may still be possible to say that, although the local authority have kept within the four corners of the matters which they ought to consider, they have nevertheless come to a conclusion so unreasonable that no reasonable authority could ever have come to it'.

The first limb focusses on the decision-making process – whether the right matters have been taken into account in reaching the decision. The second focusses upon its outcome – whether even though the right things have been taken into account, the result is so outrageous that no reasonable decision-maker could have reached it. The latter is often used as a shorthand for the *Wednesbury* principle, but without necessarily excluding the former.

25. The parties in this case disagree as to whether the term to be implied into this contract includes both limbs. Mrs Braganza argues that the employer must 'keep within the four corners of the matters which they ought to consider', while the employer argues that its decision may only be impugned if it is a decision which no reasonable employer could have reached.

26. Mrs Braganza can pray in aid the approach of Mocatta J in *The Vainqueur José*. He held that the common law principles applicable to the exercise of a contractual discretion include fairness, reasonableness, *bona fides* and absence of misdirection in law (p 574). He later quoted (p 575), without reservation, Lord Greene's summary of the public law concept of reasonableness. There is nothing on Mocatta J's judgment to suggest that only the second of those elements is applicable to the exercise of a contractual discretion. He did (at 574) contrast the contractual principles with the principles applicable to the exercise of a statutory discretion by Ministers of the Crown, but on the basis that, in addition, the Minister's decision had to be consistent with the objects and other provisions of the statute in question, citing *Laker Airways Ltd v Department of Trade* [1977] QB 643.

27. On that point, on the other hand, in *Hayes v Willoughby*, just before the passage quoted in para 23 above, Lord Sumption stated that rationality 'has … in recent years played an increasingly significant role in the law relating to contractual discretions, where the law's object is also to limit the decision-maker to some relevant contractual purpose': [2013] 1 WLR 935, para 14. This is consistent with his earlier observations in *British Telecommunications Plc v Telefónica O2 UK Ltd* [2014] UKSC 42, [2014] Bus LR 765, at para 37:

> 'As a general rule, the scope of a contractual discretion will depend on the nature of the discretion and the construction of the language conferring it. But it is well established that in the absence of very clear language to the contrary, a contractual discretion must be exercised in good faith and not arbitrarily or capriciously [citing *Abu Dhabi*, *Gan*, and *Paragon*, above]. This will normally mean that it must be exercised consistently with its contractual purpose [citing *Ludgate Insurance*, above and *Equitable Life Assurance Society v Hyman* [2002] 1 AC 408, 459 (Lord Steyn), 461 (Lord Cooke of Thorndon)]'.

28. There are signs, therefore, that the contractual implied term is drawing closer and closer to the principles applicable in judicial review. The contractual cases do not in terms discuss whether both limbs of the *Wednesbury* test apply. However, in *Gan Insurance*, where the issue was the limits, if any, to the reinsurers' power to withhold approval to the insured's agreement to settle a claim, Mance LJ first commented that 'what was proscribed was unreasonableness in the sense of conduct or a decision to which no reasonable person having the relevant discretion could have subscribed' (para 64); but he concluded that 'any withholding of approval by reinsurers should take place in good faith after consideration of and on the basis of the facts giving rise to the particular claim and not with reference to considerations wholly extraneous to the subject matter of the particular reinsurance …' (para 67).

29. If it is part of a rational decision-making process to exclude extraneous considerations, it is in my view also part of a rational decision-making process to take into account those considerations which are obviously relevant to the decision in question. It is of the essence of '*Wednesbury* reasonableness' (or 'GCHQ rationality') review to consider the rationality of the decision-making process rather than to concentrate upon the outcome. Concentrating on the outcome runs the risk that the court will substitute its own decision for that of the primary decision-maker.

30. It is clear, however, that unless the court can imply a term that the outcome be objectively reasonable -for example, a reasonable price or a reasonable term – the court will only imply a term that the decision-making process be lawful and rational in the public law sense, that the decision is made rationally (as well as in good faith) and consistently with its contractual purpose. For my part, I would include both limbs of the *Wednesbury* formulation in the rationality test. Indeed, I understand Lord Neuberger (at para 103 of his judgment) and I to be agreed as to the nature of the test.

31. But whatever term may be implied will depend upon the terms and the context of the particular contract involved. I would add to that Mocatta J's observation in *The Vainqueur José*, that 'it would be a mistake to expect [of a lay body] the same expert, professional and almost microscopic investigation of the problems, both factual and legal, that is demanded of a suit in a court of law' (577). Nor would 'some slight misdirection' matter, at least if it were clear that, had the legal position been properly appreciated, the decision would have been the same. It may very well be that the same high standards of decision-making ought not to be expected of most contractual decision-makers as are expected of the modern state.

32. However, it is unnecessary to reach a final conclusion on the precise extent to which an implied contractual term may differ from the principles applicable to judicial review of administrative action. Given that the question may arise in so many different contractual contexts, it may well be that no precise answer can be given. The particular context of this case is an employment contract, which, as Lord Hodge explains, is of a different character from an ordinary commercial contract. Any decision-making function entrusted to the employer has to be exercised in accordance with the implied obligation of trust and confidence. This must be borne in mind in considering how the contractual decision-maker should approach the question of whether a person has committed suicide.

On the limits of *Braganza* see *UBS AG v Rose Capital Ventures Ltd* [2018] EWHC 3137 (Ch) (a mortgagee's 'absolute discretion' to require payment within three months was not tapered by such an implied term especially in the light of the duties which existed between a mortgagor and mortgagee in these circumstances) and *TAQA Bratani Ltd v Rockrose UKCS8 LLC* [2020] EWHC 58 (Comm).

In an interesting article, Bryan and Ellinghaus have argued that the true test is one of 'objective necessity'. They contend that the law is rightly moving from the test of the 'officious bystander' to the test of the 'reasonable bystander'.

Bryan, M, and Ellinghaus, F, 'Fault lines in the law of obligations: *Roxborough v Rothmans of Pall Mall Australia Ltd*' (2000) 22 Syd LR, pp 636, 645 and 647

It is important to bear in mind that in asking, via the bystander, what the parties would have decided had they addressed the issue the court is asking a hypothetical question. It is not inquiring into the actual intention of the parties. If it can be shown that the parties actually intended to include a term in their contract there will be no need to imply that term; it is included by virtue of their agreement. If there is a written document from which the term has been omitted, that document will be rectified so as to include it. 'Implication' begins where the ascertainment of intention leaves off. It assumes that the parties did not actually have any agreed intention on the point in issue. So the matter has to be resolved by hypothesis.

Once this is clearly understood, an alternative conception of the bystander suggests itself. It is that of the 'reasonable bystander', or in other words the reasonable person, on whom the law traditionally relies when hypotheses about human conduct are called for. Substituting the 'reasonable bystander' for the 'officious bystander' involves a reversal of the roles of the bystander and the parties. The bystander's role is no longer that of an interrogator who elicits from the parties whether they would have instantaneously agreed on the term sought to be implied by one of them. Rather the bystander replaces the parties as the source of any implied term. The bystander does not ask for a response from the parties, but rather decides what, if anything, reasonable parties would have agreed on in the circumstances …

It is also striking to note that the objective conception of the bystander is applied when the inclusion of an express term of the contract is in issue. For example, whether a statement of the parties is promissory is decided according to the objective judgment of the reasonable (or 'intelligent') bystander. There is no obvious reason why implied terms should be treated differently.

In our view, the time has come to give the 'officious' bystander, conceived of as the interrogator of the contracting parties, 'a decent burial', and to replace him (if he is to be retained at all) with an unequivocally 'reasonable' bystander, conceived of as the objective arbiter of what reasonable parties would have accepted (or would now accept) as appropriate in the circumstances.

Whether the officious bystander will be buried and replaced by the reasonable bystander remains to be seen. What is clear is that the courts are increasingly concerned to satisfy the reasonable expectations of the parties. This has led some to argue that implication in fact is really part of contractual interpretation by pragmatic inference (see *Attorney General of Belize v Belize Telecom Ltd* [2009] UKPC 10 but cf. *Marks and Spencer plc v BNP Paribas Securities Services Trust Co (Jersey) Ltd* [2015] UKSC 72 (above)). More recently in *Yam Seng Pte v International Trade Corporation Ltd* [2013] EWHC 111 at [119] ff Leggatt J explored whether an implied duty of good faith could be found in commercial contracts:

120 The subject of whether English law does or should recognise a general duty to perform contracts in good faith is one on which a large body of academic literature exists. However, I not am aware of any decision of an English court, and none was cited to me, in which the question has been considered in any depth.

121 The general view among commentators appears to be that in English contract law there is no legal principle of good faith of general application: see *Chitty on Contract Law* (31st ed), Vol 1, para 1–039. In this regard the following observations of Bingham LJ (as he then was) in *Interfoto Picture Library Ltd v Stiletto Visual Programmes Ltd* [1989] 1 QB 433 at 439 are often quoted:

> 'In many civil law systems, and perhaps in most legal systems outside the common law world, the law of obligations recognises and enforces an overriding principle that in making and carrying out contracts parties should act in good faith. This does not simply mean that they should not deceive each other, a principle which any legal system must recognise; its effect is perhaps most aptly conveyed by such metaphorical colloquialisms as 'playing fair', 'coming clean' or 'putting one's cards face upwards on the table'. It is in essence a principle of fair open dealing ... English law has, characteristically, committed itself to no such overriding principle but has developed piecemeal solutions in response to demonstrated problems of unfairness'.

122 Another case sometimes cited for the proposition that English contract law does not recognise a duty of good faith is *Walford v Miles* [1992] 2 AC 128, where the House of Lords considered that a duty to negotiate in good faith is 'inherently repugnant to the adversarial position of the parties when involved in negotiations' and 'unworkable in practice' (per Lord Ackner at p. 138). That case was concerned, however, with the position of negotiating parties and not with the duties of parties who have entered into a contract and thereby undertaken obligations to each other.

123 Three main reasons have been given for what Professor McKendrick has called the 'traditional English hostility' towards a doctrine of good faith: see McKendrick, *Contract Law* (9th ed) pp. 221–2. The first is the one referred to by Bingham LJ in the passage quoted above: that the preferred method of English law is to proceed incrementally by fashioning particular solutions in response to particular problems rather than by enforcing broad overarching principles. A second reason is that English law is said to embody an ethos of individualism, whereby the parties are free to pursue their own self-interest not only in negotiating but also in performing contracts provided they do not act in breach of a term of the contract. The third main reason given is a fear that recognising a general requirement of good faith in the performance of contracts would create too much uncertainty. There is concern that the content of the obligation would be vague and subjective and that its adoption would undermine the goal of contractual certainty to which English law has always attached great weight.

124 In refusing, however, if indeed it does refuse, to recognise any such general obligation of good faith, this jurisdiction would appear to be swimming against the tide. As noted by Bingham LJ in the *Interfoto* case, a general principle of good faith (derived from Roman law) is recognised by most civil law systems – including those of Germany, France and Italy. From that source references to good faith have already entered into English law via EU legislation. For example, the Unfair Terms in Consumer Contracts Regulations 1999, which give effect to a European directive, contain a requirement of good faith. Several other examples of legislation implementing EU directives which use this concept are mentioned in *Chitty on Contract Law* (31st ed), Vol 1 at para 1–043. Attempts to harmonise the contract law of EU member states, such as the Principles of European Contract Law proposed by the Lando Commission and the European Commission's proposed Regulation for a Common European Sales Law on which consultation is currently taking place, also embody a general duty to act in accordance with good faith and fair dealing. There can be little doubt that the penetration of this principle into English law and the pressures towards a more unified European law of contract in which the principle plays a significant role will continue to increase.

125 It would be a mistake, moreover, to suppose that willingness to recognise a doctrine of good faith in the performance of contracts reflects a divide between civil law and common law systems or between continental paternalism and Anglo-Saxon individualism. Any such notion is gainsaid by that fact that such a doctrine has long been recognised in the United States. The New York Court of Appeals said in 1918: 'Every contract implies good faith and fair dealing between the parties to it': *Wigand v Bachmann-Bechtel Brewing Co*, 222 NY 272 at 277. The Uniform Commercial Code, first promulgated in 1951 and which has been adopted by many States, provides in section 1–203 that 'every contract or duty within this Act imposes an obligation of good faith in its performance or enforcement'. Similarly, the Restatement (Second) of Contracts states in section 205 that 'every contract imposes upon each party a duty of good faith and fair dealing in its performance and enforcement'.

126 In recent years the concept has been gaining ground in other common law jurisdictions. Canadian courts have proceeded cautiously in recognising duties of good faith in the performance of commercial contracts but have, at least in some situations, been willing to imply such duties with a view to securing the performance and enforcement of the contract or, as it is sometimes put, to ensure that parties do not act in a way that eviscerates or defeats the objectives of the agreement that they have entered into: see e.g. *Transamerica Life Inc v ING Canada Inc* (2003) 68 OR (3d) 457, 468.

127 In Australia the existence of a contractual duty of good faith is now well established, although the limits and precise juridical basis of the doctrine remain unsettled. The springboard for this development has been the decision of the New South Wales Court of Appeal in *Renard Constructions (ME) Pty v Minister for Public Works* (1992) 44 NSWLR 349, where Priestley JA said (at 95) that:

> '... people generally, including judges and other lawyers, from all strands of the community, have grown used to the courts applying standards of fairness to contract which are wholly consistent with the existence in all contracts of a duty upon the parties of good faith and fair dealing in its performance. In my view this is in these days the expected standard, and anything less is contrary to prevailing community expectations'.

128 Although the High Court has not yet considered the question (and declined to do so in *Royal Botanic Gardens and Domain Trust v Sydney City Council* (2002) 186 ALR 289) there has been clear recognition of the duty of good faith in a substantial body of Australian case law, including further significant decisions of the New South Wales Court of Appeal in *Alcatel Australia Ltd v Scarcella* (1998) 44 NSWLR 349, *Burger King Corp v Hungry Jack's Pty Ltd* [2001] NWSCA 187 and *Vodafone Pacific Ltd v Mobile Innovations Ltd* [2004] NSWCA 15.

129 In New Zealand a doctrine of good faith is not yet established law but it has its advocates: see in particular the dissenting judgment of Thomas J in *Bobux Marketing Ltd v Raynor Marketing Ltd* [2002] 1 NZLR 506 at 517.

130 Closer to home, there is strong authority for the view that Scottish law recognises a broad principle of good faith and fair dealing: see the decision of the House of Lords in *Smith v Bank of Scotland*, 1997 SC (HL) 111 esp. at p. 121 (*per* Lord Clyde).

131 Under English law a duty of good faith is implied by law as an incident of certain categories of contract, for example contracts of employment and contracts between partners or others whose relationship is characterised as a fiduciary one. I doubt that English law has reached the stage, however, where it is ready to recognise a requirement of good faith as a duty implied by law, even as a default rule, into all commercial contracts. Nevertheless, there seems to me to be no difficulty, following the established methodology of English law for the implication of terms in fact, in implying such a duty in any ordinary commercial contract based on the presumed intention of the parties.

132 Traditionally, the two principal criteria used to identify terms implied in fact are that the term is so obvious that it goes without saying and that the term is necessary to give business efficacy to the contract. More recently, in *Attorney General for Belize v Belize Telecom Ltd* [2009] 1 WLR 1988 at 1993–5, the process of implication has been analysed as an exercise in the construction of the contract as a whole. In giving the judgment of the Privy Council in that case, Lord Hoffmann characterised the traditional criteria, not as a series of independent tests, but rather as different ways of approaching what is ultimately always a question of construction: what would the contract, read as a whole against the relevant background, reasonably be understood to mean?

133 The modern case law on the construction of contracts has emphasised that contracts, like all human communications, are made against a background of unstated shared understandings which inform their meaning. The breadth of the relevant background and the fact that it has no conceptual limits have also been stressed, particularly in the famous speech of Lord Hoffmann in *Investors Compensation Scheme Ltd v West Bromwich Building Society* [1998] 1 WLR 896 at pp. 912–3, as further explained in *BCCI v Ali* [2002] 1 AC 251 at p. 269.

134 Importantly for present purposes, the relevant background against which contracts are made includes not only matters of fact known to the parties but also shared values and norms of behaviour. Some of these are norms that command general social acceptance; others may be specific to a particular trade or commercial activity; others may be more specific still, arising from features of the particular contractual relationship. Many such norms are naturally taken for granted by the parties when making any contract without being spelt out in the document recording their agreement.

135 A paradigm example of a general norm which underlies almost all contractual relationships is an expectation of honesty. That expectation is essential to commerce, which depends critically on trust. Yet it is seldom, if ever, made the subject of an express contractual obligation. Indeed if a party in negotiating the terms of a contract were to seek to include a provision which expressly required the other party to act honestly, the very fact of doing so might well damage the parties' relationship by the lack of trust which this would signify.

136 The fact that commerce takes place against a background expectation of honesty has been recognised by the House of Lords in *HIH Casualty v Chase Manhattan Bank* [2003] 2 Lloyd's Rep 61. In that case a contract of insurance contained a clause which stated that the insured should have 'no liability of any nature to the insurers for any information provided'. A question arose as to whether these words meant that the insured had no liability even for deceit where the insured's agent had dishonestly provided information known to be false. The House of Lords affirmed the decision of the courts below that, even though the clause read literally would cover liability for deceit, it was not reasonably to be understood as having that meaning. As Lord Bingham put it at [15]:

> 'Parties entering into a commercial contract … will assume the honesty and good faith of the other; absent such an assumption they would not deal'.

To similar effect Lord Hoffmann observed at [68] that parties 'contract with one another in the expectation of honest dealing', and that:

'... in the absence of words which expressly refer to dishonesty, it goes without saying that underlying the contractual arrangements of the parties there will be a common assumption that the persons involved will behave honestly'.

137 As a matter of construction, it is hard to envisage any contract which would not reasonably be understood as requiring honesty in its performance. The same conclusion is reached if the traditional tests for the implication of a term are used. In particular the requirement that parties will behave honestly is so obvious that it goes without saying. Such a requirement is also necessary to give business efficacy to commercial transactions.

138 In addition to honesty, there are other standards of commercial dealing which are so generally accepted that the contracting parties would reasonably be understood to take them as read without explicitly stating them in their contractual document. A key aspect of good faith, as I see it, is the observance of such standards. Put the other way round, not all bad faith conduct would necessarily be described as dishonest. Other epithets which might be used to describe such conduct include 'improper', 'commercially unacceptable' or 'unconscionable'.

139 Another aspect of good faith which overlaps with the first is what may be described as fidelity to the parties' bargain. The central idea here is that contracts can never be complete in the sense of expressly providing for every event that may happen. To apply a contract to circumstances not specifically provided for, the language must accordingly be given a reasonable construction which promotes the values and purposes expressed or implicit in the contract. That principle is well established in the modern English case law on the interpretation of contracts: see e.g. *Rainy Sky SA v Kookmin Bank* [2011] 1 WLR 2900; *Lloyds TSB Foundation for Scotland v Lloyds Banking Group Plc* [2013] UKSC 3 at [23], [45] and [54]. It also underlies and explains, for example, the body of cases in which terms requiring cooperation in the performance of the contract have been implied: see *Mackay v Dick* (1881) 6 App Cas 251, 263; and the cases referred to in *Chitty on Contracts* (31st ed), Vol 1 at paras 13-012–13-014.

140 The two aspects of good faith which I have identified are consistent with the way in which express contractual duties of good faith have been interpreted in several recent cases: see *Berkeley Community Villages Ltd v Pullen* [2007] EWHC 1330 (Ch) at [95]–[97]; *CPC Group Ltd v Qatari Diar Real Estate Investment Co* [2010] EWHC 1535 (Ch) at [246].

141 What good faith requires is sensitive to context. That includes the core value of honesty. In any situation it is dishonest to deceive another person by making a statement of fact intending that other person to rely on it while knowing the statement to be untrue. Frequently, however, the requirements of honesty go further. For example, if A gives information to B knowing that B is likely to rely on the information and A believes the information to be true at the time it is given but afterwards discovers that the information was, or has since become, false, it may be dishonest for A to keep silent and not to disclose the true position to B. Another example of conduct falling short of a lie which may, depending on the context, be dishonest is deliberately avoiding giving an answer, or giving an answer which is evasive, in response to a request for information.

142 In some contractual contexts the relevant background expectations may extend further to an expectation that the parties will share information relevant to the performance of the contract such that a deliberate omission to disclose such information may amount to bad faith. English law has traditionally drawn a sharp distinction between certain relationships – such as partnership, trusteeship and other fiduciary relationships – on the one hand, in which the parties owe onerous obligations of disclosure to each other, and other contractual relationships in which no duty of disclosure is supposed to operate. Arguably at least, that dichotomy is too simplistic. While it seems unlikely that any duty to disclose information in performance of the contract would be implied where the contract involves a simple exchange, many contracts do not fit this model and involve a longer term relationship between the parties which they make a substantial commitment. Such 'relational' contracts, as they are sometimes called, may require a high degree of communication, cooperation and predictable performance based on mutual trust and confidence and involve expectations of loyalty which are not legislated for in the express terms of the contract but are implicit in the parties' understanding and necessary to give business efficacy to the arrangements. Examples of such relational contracts might include some joint venture agreements, franchise agreements and long-term distributorship agreements.

143 The Agreement in this case was a distributorship agreement which required the parties to communicate effectively and cooperate with each other in its performance. In particular, ITC needed to plan production and take account of the expected future demand from Yam Seng for Manchester United products. For its part Yam Seng, which was incurring expense in marketing the products and was trying to obtain orders, was arguably entitled to expect that it would be kept informed of ITC's best estimates of when products would be available to sell and would be told of any material change in this information without having to ask. Yam Seng's case was not advanced in this way, however, and it is therefore unnecessary for me to decide whether the requirements of good faith in this case extended to any such positive obligations of disclosure.

144 Although its requirements are sensitive to context, the test of good faith is objective in the sense that it depends not on either party's perception of whether particular conduct is improper but on whether in the particular context the conduct would be regarded as commercially unacceptable by reasonable and honest people. The standard is thus similar to that described by Lord Nicholls in a different context in his seminal speech in *Royal Brunei Airlines v Tan* [1995] 2 AC 378 at pp. 389–390. This follows from the fact that the content of the duty of good faith is established by a process of construction which in English law is based on an objective principle. The court is concerned not with the subjective intentions of the parties but with their presumed intention, which is ascertained by attributing to them the purposes and values which reasonable people in their situation would have had.

145 Understood in the way I have described, there is in my view nothing novel or foreign to English law in recognising an implied duty of good faith in the performance of contracts. It is consonant with the theme identified by Lord Steyn as running through our law of contract that reasonable expectations must be protected: see *First Energy (UK) Ltd v Hungarian International Bank Ltd* [1993] 2 Lloyd's Rep 194, 196; and (1997) 113 LQR 433. Moreover such a concept is, I believe, already reflected in several lines of authority that are well established. One example is the body of cases already mentioned in which duties of cooperation in the performance of the contract have been implied. Another consists of the authorities which show that a power conferred by a contract on one party to make decisions which affect them both must be exercised honestly and in good faith for the purpose for which it was conferred, and must not be exercised arbitrarily, capriciously or unreasonably (in the sense of irrationally): see e.g. *Abu Dhabi National Tanker Co v Product Star Shipping Ltd (The 'Product Star')* [1993] 1 Lloyd's Rep 397, 404; *Socimer International Bank Ltd v Standard Bank London Ltd* [2008] 1 Lloyd's Rep 558, 575–7. A further example concerns the situation where the consent of one party is needed to an action of the other and a term is implied that such consent is not to be withheld unreasonably (in a similar sense): see e.g. *Gan v Tai Ping (Nos 2& 3)* [2001] Lloyd's Rep IR 667; *Eastleigh BC v Town Quay Developments Ltd* [2010] 2 P&CR 2. Yet another example, I would suggest, is the line of authorities of which the *Interfoto* case is one which hold that an onerous or unusual contract term on which a party seeks to rely must be fairly brought to the notice of the other party if it is to be enforced.

146 There are some further observations that I would make about the reasons I mentioned earlier for the reluctance of English law to recognise an implied duty on contracting parties to deal with each other in good faith.

147 First, because the content of the duty is heavily dependent on context and is established through a process of construction of the contract, its recognition is entirely consistent with the case-by-case approach favoured by the common law. There is therefore no need for common lawyers to abandon their characteristic methods and adopt those of civil law systems in order to accommodate the principle.

148 Second, as the basis of the duty of good faith is the presumed intention of the parties and meaning of their contract, its recognition is not an illegitimate restriction on the freedom of the parties to pursue their own interests. The essence of contracting is that the parties bind themselves in order to co-operate to their mutual benefit. The obligations which they undertake include those which are implicit in their agreement as well as those which they have made explicit.

149 Third, a further consequence of the fact that the duty is based on the parties' presumed intention is that it is open to the parties to modify the scope of the duty by the express terms of their contract and, in principle at least, to exclude it altogether. I say 'in principle at least' because in practice it is hardly conceivable that contracting parties would attempt expressly to exclude the core requirement to act honestly.

150 Fourth, I see no objection, and some advantage, in describing the duty as one of good faith 'and fair dealing'. I see no objection, as the duty does not involve the court in imposing its view of what is substantively fair on the parties. What constitutes fair dealing is defined by the contract and by those standards of conduct to which, objectively, the parties must reasonably have assumed compliance without the need to state them. The advantage of including reference to fair dealing is that it draws attention to the fact that the standard is objective and distinguishes the relevant concept of good faith from other senses in which the expression 'good faith' is used.

151 Fifth, in so far as English law may be less willing than some other legal systems to interpret the duty of good faith as requiring openness of the kind described by Bingham LJ in the *Interfoto* case as 'playing fair' 'coming clean' or 'putting one's cards face upwards on the table', this should be seen as a difference of opinion, which may reflect different cultural norms, about what constitutes good faith and fair dealing in some contractual contexts rather than a refusal to recognise that good faith and fair dealing are required.

152 Sixth, the fear that recognising a duty of good faith would generate excessive uncertainty is unjustified. There is nothing unduly vague or unworkable about the concept. Its application involves no more uncertainty than is inherent in the process of contractual interpretation.

153 In the light of these points, I respectfully suggest that the traditional English hostility towards a doctrine of good faith in the performance of contracts, to the extent that it still persists, is misplaced.

154 I have emphasised in this discussion the extent to which the content of the duty to perform a contract in good faith is dependent on context. It was Mr Salter's submission that the relevant content of the duty in this case was captured by two more specific terms which Yam Seng contends are to be implied into the Agreement. I therefore turn to consider these.

Note, however, a line of subsequent cases which have been keen to stress that the Law of England and Wales does not recognise a general duty of good faith (see, for example, the cases collected in *Monde Petroleum SA v Western Zagros Ltd* [2016] EWHC 1472 (Comm) at [250] ff *per* Richard Salter QC). The relevance of the 'reasonable expectations of the parties' will be returned to at the end of the chapter when we consider the underlying rationale for implying terms into a contract.

6.4.1.3 Terms implied in law

There is a fundamental distinction between terms implied in fact and terms implied in law. Terms implied in fact are designed to supplement the unexpressed but supposed actual intentions of the parties. Terms implied in law, on the other hand, arise where precedent has incorporated such terms into particular types of contract notwithstanding the absence of intention. The distinction was explained by Lord Wright in *Luxor (Eastbourne) Ltd v Cooper* [1941] AC 108:

> The expression 'implied term' is used in different senses. Sometimes it denotes some term which does not depend on the actual intention of the parties but on a rule of law, such as the terms, warranties or conditions which, if not expressly excluded, the law imports, as for instance under the Sale of Goods Act and the Marine Insurance Act ... But a case like the present is different because what it is sought to imply is based on an intention imputed to the parties from their actual circumstances.

The distinction between terms implied in fact and terms implied in law was also considered by the Court of Appeal on the facts of *Shell (UK) Ltd v Lostock Garage Ltd.*

***Shell (UK) Ltd v Lostock Garage Ltd* [1976] 1 WLR 1187**

Facts: Lostock Garage entered into a 'solus agreement' to buy petrol exclusively from Shell. During the petrol price war of 1975 Shell had a temporary support scheme to enable its petrol to be sold at 70p per gallon, and the neighbouring garages were enabled to sell their petrol at that price. Shell, however, insisted on the terms of Lostock Garage's solus agreement, so that Lostock Garage could only reduce their price to 75p. This was having a disastrous effect on their business so Lostock Garage argued that a term should be implied into the solus agreement to the effect that Shell would not discriminate against the garage in the terms on which it supplied the petrol.

Held: The Court of Appeal held that there was no implied term in the contract such as to enable the defendants to terminate the contract.

Lord Denning MR: It was submitted by [counsel for the appellant] that there was to be implied in the solus agreement a term that Shell, as the supplier, should not abnormally discriminate against the buyer and/or should supply petrol to the buyer on terms which did not abnormally discriminate against him. He said that Shell had broken that implied term by giving support to the two Shell garages and refusing it to Lostock: that, on that ground, Shell were in breach of the solus agreement: and that Lostock were entitled to terminate it.

This submission makes it necessary once again to consider the law as to implied terms . . . [T]here are two broad categories of implied terms.

(i) The first category

The first category comprehends all those relationships which are of common occurrence. Such as the relationship of seller and buyer, owner and hirer, master and servant, landlord and tenant, carrier by land or by sea, contractor for building works, and so forth. In all those relationships the courts have imposed obligations on one party or the other, saying they are 'implied terms'. These obligations are not founded on the intention of the parties, actual or presumed, but on more general considerations: see *Luxor (Eastbourne) Ltd v Cooper* [1941] AC 108, 137 by Lord Wright; *Lister v Romford Ice and Cold Storage Co Ltd* [1957] AC 555, 576 by Viscount Simonds, and at p 594 by Lord Tucker (both of whom give interesting illustrations); and *Liverpool City Council v Irwin* [1976] 2 WLR 562, 571 by Lord Cross of Chelsea, and at p 579 by Lord Edmund-Davies. In such relationships the problem is not to be solved by asking what did the parties intend? Or would they have unhesitatingly agreed to it, if asked? It is to be solved by asking: has the law already defined the obligation or the extent of it? If so, let it be followed. If not, look to see what would be reasonable in the general run of such cases ... In these relationships the parties can exclude or modify the obligation by express words; but unless they do so, the obligation is a legal incident of the relationship which is attached by the law itself and not by reason of any implied term ...

(ii) The second category

The second category comprehends those cases which are not within the first category. These are cases -not of common occurrence – in which from the particular circumstances a term is to be implied. In these cases the implication is based on an intention imputed to the parties from their actual circumstances: *Luxor (Eastbourne) Ltd v Cooper* [1941] AC 108, 137 by Lord Wright. Such an imputation is only to be made when it is necessary to imply a term to give efficacy to the contract and make it a workable agreement in such manner as the parties would clearly have done if they had applied their mind to the contingency which has arisen. These are the 'officious bystander' types of case: see *Lister v Romford Ice and Cold Storage Co Ltd* [1957] AC 555, 594, by Lord Tucker. In such cases a term is not to be implied on the ground that it would be reasonable: but only when it is necessary and can be formulated with a sufficient degree of precision. This was the test applied by the majority of this court in *Liverpool City Council v Irwin* [1976] QB 319 and they were emphatically upheld by the House on this point: see [1976] 2 WLR 562, 571D–H by Lord Cross of Chelsea; p 578G–579A by Lord Edmund-Davies ...

Into which of the two categories does the present case come? I am tempted to say that a solus agreement between supplier and buyer is of such common occurrence nowadays that it could be put into the first category: so that the law could imply a term based on general considerations. But I do not think this would be found acceptable. Nor do I think the case can be brought within the second category. If the Shell company had been asked at the beginning: 'Will you agree not to discriminate abnormally against the buyer?' I think they would have declined. It might be a reasonable term, but it is not a necessary term. Nor can it be formulated with sufficient precision.

Lord Denning emphasised that terms implied in law do not necessarily depend on determining the intention of the parties. The term may be imposed on the parties regardless of whether they would have agreed to it or not. Two conditions must be fulfilled, however:

1 The contract has to be of a sufficiently common type, for example, seller/buyer, owner/hirer, master/servant, landlord/tenant;
2 The matter to which the implied term relates must not have been addressed in the contract.

In *Shell v Lostock*, it seems that the garage owner failed on the first test because solus agreements were not sufficiently common that typical terms could be identified. The claimant in *Ashmore v Corporation of Lloyd's (No 2)* (see above) failed for the same reason. He argued, as an alternative claim to implication in fact, that there were so many contracts in identical terms between 'names' and Lloyd's that this constituted a category of contracts and, as such, it was an appropriate situation in which to imply a term in law. Gatehouse J disagreed. Although there were many contracts between names and Lloyd's, running into the thousands, they were all the same and did not form part of a larger category, or genus, of contracts. On the contrary, they were *sui generis*, and for this reason Gatehouse J was not prepared to imply a term in law. It is therefore clear that to fulfil the first condition the claimant must prove that the type of contract is not merely numerous but also part of a broad category or type of relationship.

The second condition mentioned by Lord Denning requires qualification (see also *Haywood v Newcastle upon Tyne Hospitals NHS Foundation Trust* [2018] UKSC 22). As a general rule, it is true that a term will not be implied in law if it relates to a matter that is governed by the contract. The majority of terms implied in law are default rules, which the parties can 'contract out' of. Some implied terms, however, are mandatory and cannot be excluded by the parties' express agreement. In *Johnstone v Bloomsbury Health Authority* [1992] QB 333, a junior hospital doctor's employment contract allowed the defendant health authority to require him to work up to 88 hours per week. The Court of Appeal held that the defendant's power was subject to an implied term that the defendant would exercise reasonable care not to endanger the employee's health and safety. Stuart Smith LJ said that the implied term would prevail over the express term, if necessary, since the express term would amount to an exclusion of liability for personal injury or death, which is void under s 2(1) of the Unfair Contract Terms Act 1977. Other provisions of the Act restrict the parties' ability to 'contract out' of terms implied in law (see Chapter 7).

6.4.1.3.1 The necessity test

Once the two conditions for implication of a term in law have been fulfilled, the court must consider whether a term should be implied and, if so, what the content of that term ought to be.

***Lister v Romford Ice and Cold Storage Co Ltd* [1957] AC 555**

Facts: In 1949 the defendant, a lorry driver employed by the plaintiffs, drove their lorry to a slaughterhouse in order to collect some waste. He took his father with him, and injured him by backing the lorry into him in the slaughterhouse yard. The father recovered damages from the plaintiffs who then obtained indemnity from the defendant on the basis that he had broken an implied term in his contract of employment to drive with reasonable skill and care. The defendant appealed arguing that the contract also contained an implied term that the employers would indemnify the driver if they were insured.

Held: The House of Lords dismissed the appeal and held that no such term could be implied into the contract of employment.

Viscount Simmonds: It was contended ... that a term should not be implied by law of which the social consequences would be harmful. The common law demands that the servant should exercise his proper skill and care in the performance of his duty: the graver the consequences of any dereliction, the more important it is that the sanction which the law imposes should be maintained. That sanction is that he should be liable in damages to his master: other sanctions there may be, dismissal perhaps and loss of character and difficulty of getting fresh employment, but an action for damages, whether for tort or for breach of contract, has, even if rarely used, for centuries been available to the master, and now to grant the servant immunity from such an action would tend to create a feeling of irresponsibility in a class of persons from whom, perhaps more than any other, constant vigilance is owed to the community.

The reasons given for refusing to imply the term proposed by the defendant were partly based on the fact that the implication was not necessary to give business efficacy to the contract, that is, the test for implication in fact. Also weighing heavily on the House of Lords, as the extract above shows, were questions of policy. Viscount Simmonds considered it to be undesirable to allow a driver to recover an indemnity from his employer as he might then drive less carefully. It is now clear that the policy test for whether a term should be implied in law is one of 'necessity'.

***Liverpool City Council v Irwin* [1977] AC 239**

Facts: The case concerned a tenancy agreement for a flat in a council tower block. The agreement contained no express provisions about the common parts of the block and the facilities. The lifts were often broken, the lighting on the stairs did not work, and the rubbish chutes were often blocked. This led to a rent strike. The tenants claimed that a term should be implied into the agreement that the City Council was responsible to keep the common parts of the building in repair.

Held: The House of Lords held that a term would be implied into the tenancy agreement with the effect that the council was responsible to keep the common parts of the building in reasonable repair. However, on the facts, the council was not in breach of that duty.

Lord Wilberforce: The court here is simply concerned to establish what the contract is, the parties not having themselves fully stated the terms. In this sense the court is searching for what must be implied.

What then should this contract be held to be? There must first be implied a letting, that is, a grant of the right of exclusive possession to the tenants. With this there must, I would suppose, be implied a covenant for quiet enjoyment, as a necessary incident of the letting. The difficulty begins when we consider the common parts …

[I]t is necessary to define what test is to be applied, and I do not find this difficult. In my opinion such obligation should be read into the contract as the nature of the contract itself implicitly requires, no more, no less: a test, in other words, of necessity. The relationship accepted by the corporation is that of landlord and tenant: the tenant accepts obligations accordingly, in relation *inter alia* to the stairs, the lifts and the chutes. All these are not just facilities, or conveniences provided at discretion: they are essentials of the tenancy without which life in the dwellings, as a tenant, is not possible. To leave the landlord free of contractual obligation as regards these matters, and subject only to administrative or political pressure, is, in my opinion, inconsistent totally with the nature of this relationship. The subject matter of the lease (high rise blocks) and the relationship created by the tenancy demand, of their nature, some contractual obligation on the landlord.

It remains to define the standard. My Lords, if, as I think, the test of the existence of the term is necessity the standard must surely not exceed what is necessary having regard to the circumstances. To imply an absolute obligation to repair would go beyond what is a necessary legal incident and would indeed be unreasonable. An obligation to take reasonable care to keep in reasonable repair and usability is what fits the requirements of the case. Such a definition involves – and I think rightly – recognition that the tenants themselves have their responsibilities. What it is reasonable to expect of a landlord has a clear relation to what a reasonable set of tenants should do for themselves.

Lord Cross: When it implies a term in a contract the court is sometimes laying down a general rule that in all contracts of a certain type – sale of goods, master and servant, landlord and tenant and so on – some provision is to be implied unless the parties have expressly excluded it. In deciding whether or not to lay down such a *prima facie* rule the court will naturally ask itself whether in the general run of such cases the term in question would be one which it would be reasonable to insert. Sometimes, however, there is no question of laying down any *prima facie* rule applicable to all cases of a defined type but what the court is being in effect asked to do is to rectify a particular – often a very detailed – contract by inserting in it a term which the parties have not expressed. Here it is not enough for the court to say that the suggested term is a reasonable one the presence of which would make the contract a better or fairer one; it must be able to say that the insertion of the term is necessary to give – as it is put – 'business efficacy' to the contract and that if its absence had been pointed out at the time both parties – assuming them to have been reasonable men – would have agreed without hesitation to its insertion. The distinction between the two types of case was pointed out by Viscount Simonds and Lord Tucker in their speeches *Lister v Romford Ice and Cold Storage Ltd* [1957] AC 555, 579, 594, but I think that Lord Denning MR in proceeding – albeit with some trepidation – to 'kill off' MacKinnon LJ's 'officious bystander' … must have overlooked it. Counsel for the appellant did not in fact rely on this passage in the speech of Lord Denning. His main argument was that when a landlord lets a number of flats or offices to a number of different tenants giving all of them rights to use the staircases, corridors and lifts there is to be implied, in the absence of any provision to the contrary, an obligation on the landlord to keep the 'common parts' in repair and the lifts in working order. But, for good measure, he also submitted that he could succeed on the 'officious bystander' test.

I have no hesitation in rejecting this alternative submission. We are not here dealing with an ordinary commercial contract by which a property company is letting one of its flats for profit. The respondent council is a public body charged by law with the duty of providing housing for members of the public selected because of their need for it at rents which are subsidised by the general body of ratepayers. Moreover the officials in the council's housing department would know very well that some of the tenants in any given block might subject the chutes and lifts to rough treatment and that there was an ever present danger of deliberate damage by young 'vandals' – some of whom might in fact be children of the tenants in that or neighbouring blocks. In these circumstances, if at the time when the respondents were granted their tenancy one of them had said to the council's representative: 'I suppose that the council will be under a legal liability to us to keep the chutes and the lifts in working order and the staircases properly lighted', the answer might well have been – indeed I think, as Roskill LJ thought [1976] Q.B. 319, 338, in all probability would have been – 'Certainly not' ...

I turn ... to consider the main argument advanced by the appellants. One starts with the general principle that the law does not impose on a servient owner any liability to keep the servient property in repair for the benefit of the owner of an easement ... But must it follow that the same principle must be applied to the case where a landlord lets off parts of his property to a number of different tenants retaining in his ownership 'common parts' – halls, staircases, corridors and so on – which are used by all the tenants? I think that it would be contrary to common sense to press the general principle so far. In such a case I think that the implication should be the other way and that, instead of the landlord being under no obligation to keep the common parts in repair and such facilities as lifts and chutes in working order unless he has expressly contracted to do so, he should – at all events in the case of ordinary commercial lettings – be under some obligation to keep the common parts in repair and the facilities in working order unless he has expressly excluded any such obligation ... I agree, however, with your Lordships that the obligation to be implied in such cases is not an absolute one but only a duty to use reasonable care to keep the common parts and facilities in a state of reasonable repair and efficiency.

Lord Salmon: I find it difficult to think of any term which it could be more necessary to imply than one without which the whole transaction would become futile, inefficacious and absurd as it would do if in a 15 storey block of flats or maisonettes, such as the present, the landlords were under no legal duty to take reasonable care to keep the lifts in working order and the staircases lit.

Although there was some disagreement on the issue in the Court of Appeal, the House of Lords was in full agreement that the term sought to be implied by the tenants could not be implied in fact because neither the 'officious bystander' test nor the 'business efficacy' test was satisfied (see the speech of Lord Cross, above). The term was implied into the contract in law because the nature of the relationship made it desirable to place some obligation on the landlord to maintain the common parts of the premises. There was some divergence among their Lordships as to what was the appropriate test. Lord Wilberforce was of the view that the test was one of necessity: the term 'should be read into the contract as the nature of the contract itself implicitly requires, no more, no less: a test in other words of necessity'. Lords Salmon, Edmund-Davies and Fraser agreed. Lord Cross, on the other hand, applied a test of reasonableness: 'the court will naturally ask itself whether in the general run of such cases the term in question would be one which it would be reasonable to insert'. In subsequent cases this conflict seems to have been resolved in favour of the test of necessity. It is clear, however, that the test for necessity in the context of terms implied in law involves wider issues and differs from the test applied in relation to terms implied in fact.

***Scally v Southern Health and Social Services Board* [1992] 1 AC 294**

Lord Bridge: A clear distinction is drawn … between the search for an implied term necessary to give business efficacy to a particular contract and the search, based on wider considerations, for a term which the law will imply as a necessary incident of a definable category of contractual relationship.

It seems that the 'necessity' test in this context encompasses issues of justice and public policy. This was seen in *Malik v BCCI*.

***Malik v BCCI* [1998] AC 20**

Facts: Malik had worked for the Bank of Credit and Commerce International which collapsed in 1991. He claimed damages for injury to his reputation and consequent difficulties in finding new employment, which he alleged were caused by BCCI conducting its business in a dishonest and corrupt way.

Held: The House of Lords allowed the appeal, holding that BCCI was under an implied obligation not to conduct a corrupt and dishonest business, being one aspect of a general implied contractual obligation not to engage in conduct likely to undermine the relationship of confidence and trust between employer and employee.

Lord Steyn: [The employees] rely on a standardised term implied by law, that is, on a term which is said to be an incident of all contracts of employment: *Scally v Southern Health and Social Services Board* [1992] 1 AC 294, 307B. Such implied terms operate as default rules. The parties are free to exclude or modify them. But it is common ground that in the present case the particular terms of the contracts of employment of the two applicants could not affect an implied obligation of mutual trust and confidence …

For convenience I will set out the term again. It is expressed to impose an obligation that the employer shall not:

> 'without reasonable and proper cause, conduct itself in a manner calculated and likely to destroy or seriously damage the relationship of confidence and trust between employer and employee'…

A useful anthology of the cases applying this term, or something like it, is given in *Sweet & Maxwell's Encyclopaedia of Employment Law* (looseleaf ed), vol 1, para 1.5107, pp 1467–1470. The evolution of the term is a comparatively recent development. The obligation probably has its origin in the general duty of co-operation between contracting parties: Hepple & O'Higgins, *Employment Law*, 4th ed (1981), pp 134–135, paras 291–292. The reason for this development is part of the history of the development of employment law in this century. The notion of a 'master and servant' relationship became obsolete. Lord Slynn of Hadley recently noted 'the changes which have taken place in the employer-employee relationship, with far greater duties imposed on the employer than in the past, whether by statute or by judicial decision, to care for the physical, financial and even psychological welfare of the employee': *Spring v Guardian Assurance Plc* [1995] 2 AC 296, 335B. A striking illustration of this change is *Scally's Case* [1992] 1 AC 294, to which I have already referred, where the House of Lords implied a term that all employees in a certain category had to be notified by an employer of their entitlement to certain benefits. It was the change in legal culture which made possible the evolution of the implied term of trust and confidence.

There was some debate at the hearing about the possible interaction of the implied obligation of confidence and trust with other more specific terms implied by law. It is true that the implied term adds little to the employee's implied obligations to serve his employer loyally and not to act contrary to his employer's interests. The major importance of the implied duty of trust and confidence lies in its impact on the obligations of the employer: Douglas Brodie, 'Recent cases, Commentary, The Heart of the Matter: Mutual Trust and Confidence' (1996) 25 ILJ 121. And the implied obligation as formulated is apt to cover the great diversity of situations in which a balance has to be struck between an employer's interest in managing his business as he sees fit and the employee's interest in not being unfairly and improperly exploited.

The evolution of the implied term of trust and confidence is a fact. It has not yet been endorsed by your Lordships' House. It has proved a workable principle in practice. It has not been the subject of adverse criticism in any decided cases and it has been welcomed in academic writings. I regard the emergence of the implied obligation of mutual trust and confidence as a sound development.

In light of Lord Steyn's observations in *Malik* it appears that the courts adopt an extremely flexible approach to implying terms in law. Although the courts claim to use a test of necessity, their decisions are based more on considerations of justice and policy. Indeed, it could be contended that this actually amounts to a test of reasonableness since the fair and reasonable person should act in a just manner. The importance of issues of public policy was confirmed by Dyson LJ in the recent case of *Crossley v Faithful & Gould Holdings Ltd* [2004] 4 All ER 447:

> It seems to me that, rather than focus on the elusive concept of necessity, it is better to recognise that, to some extent at least, the existence and scope of standardised implied terms raise questions of reasonableness, fairness and the balancing of competing policy considerations: see Elisabeth Peden, 'Policy Concerns behind Implication of Terms in Law' (2001) 117 LQR 459, 467–475.

This is an approach with which Baroness Hale had sympathy in *Geys v Société London Branch* [2012] UKSC 63 at [56]. See also *James-Bowen v Comissioner of Police of the Metropolis* [2018] UKSC 40.

6.4.2 Terms implied by statute

Terms may be implied into contracts by statute. There are two main reasons why it may be appropriate for Parliament to enact such legislation:

1. **Efficiency.** This reason is based on the presumed intention of the parties. If it is standard practice for certain terms to be used in particular contractual relationships, it is inefficient for the parties to be required to expressly agree to them on every occasion. By means of statute, Parliament can provide a form of words on which the parties can rely as representing their obligations. If this is the reason for the statutory enactment, the parties should be allowed to depart from the statutory wording, if they so wish.
2. **Protection.** This reason is based on the protection of one of the parties. It may be thought that a particular type of contractual relationship is likely to involve inequality of bargaining power. Parliament implies terms into such contracts to provide protection for the weaker party. If this is the reason for the implication, then it may well be that the obligation to include the term should be absolute, with no possibility of exclusion by the parties.

Terms have been implied by Parliament into a broad range of contracts, for example, contracts for the sale of goods, contracts for the supply of services and hire-purchase agreements. In this section, we will focus on contracts for the sale of goods.

SALE OF GOODS ACT (SGA) 1979

Section 12 Implied terms about title, etc

(1) In a contract of sale, other than one to which subsection (3) below applies, there is an implied term on the part of the seller that in the case of a sale he has a right to sell the goods, and in the case of an agreement to sell he will have such a right at the time when the property is to pass.

(2) In a contract of sale, other than one to which subsection (3) below applies, there is also an implied term that –

(a) the goods are free, and will remain free until the time when the property is to pass, from any charge or encumbrance not disclosed or known to the buyer before the contract is made, and

(b) the buyer will enjoy quiet possession of the goods except so far as it may be disturbed by the owner or other person entitled to the benefit of any charge or encumbrance so disclosed or known.

(3) This subsection applies to a contract of sale in the case of which there appears from the contract or is to be inferred from its circumstances an intention that the seller should transfer only such title as he or a third person may have.

(4) In a contract to which subsection (3) above applies there is an implied term that all charges or encumbrances known to the seller and not known to the buyer have been disclosed to the buyer before the contract is made.

(5) In a contract to which subsection (3) above applies there is also an implied term that none of the following will disturb the buyer's quiet possession of the goods, namely –

(a) the seller;

(b) in a case where the parties to the contract intend that the seller should transfer only such title as a third person may have, that person;

(c) anyone claiming through or under the seller or that third person otherwise than under a charge or encumbrance disclosed or known to the buyer before the contract is made.

(5A) As regards England and Wales and Northern Ireland, the term implied by subsection (1) above is a condition and the terms implied by subsections (2), (4) and (5) above are warranties.

...

(7) This section does not apply to a contract to which Chapter 2 of Part 1 of the Consumer Rights Act 2015 applies (but see the provision made about such contracts in section 17 of that Act).

Section 13 Sale by description

(1) Where there is a contract for the sale of goods by description, there is an implied term that the goods will correspond with the description.

(1A) As regards England and Wales and Northern Ireland, the term implied by subsection (1) above is a condition.

(2) If the sale is by sample as well as by description it is not sufficient that the bulk of the goods corresponds with the sample if the goods do not also correspond with the description.

(3) A sale of goods is not prevented from being a sale by description by reason only that, being exposed for sale or hire, they are selected by the buyer.

(5) This section does not apply to a contract to which Chapter 2 of Part 1 of the Consumer Rights Act 2015 applies (but see the provision made about such contracts in section 11 of that Act).

Section 14 Implied terms about quality or fitness

(1) Except as provided by this section and section 15 below and subject to any other enactment, there is no implied term about the quality or fitness for any particular purpose of goods supplied under a contract of sale.

(2) Where the seller sells goods in the course of a business, there is an implied term that the goods supplied under the contract are of satisfactory quality.

(2A) For the purposes of this Act, goods are of satisfactory quality if they meet the standard that a reasonable person would regard as satisfactory, taking account of any description of the goods, the price (if relevant) and all the other relevant circumstances.

(2B) For the purposes of this Act, the quality of goods includes their state and condition and the following (among others) are in appropriate cases aspects of the quality of goods –

(a) fitness for all the purposes for which goods of the kind in question are commonly supplied.

(b) appearance and finish,

(c) freedom from minor defects,

(d) safety, and

(e) durability.

(2C) The term implied by subsection (2) above does not extend to any matter making the quality of goods unsatisfactory –

(a) which is specifically drawn to the buyer's attention before the contract is made,

(b) where the buyer examines the goods before the contract is made, which that examination ought to reveal, or

(c) in the case of a contract for sale by sample, which would have been apparent on a reasonable examination of the sample.

(3) Where the seller sells goods in the course of a business and the buyer, expressly or by implication, makes known –

(a) to the seller, or

(b) where the purchase price or part of it is payable by instalments and the goods were previously sold by a credit-broker to the seller, to that credit-broker, any particular purpose for which the goods are being bought, there is an implied term that the goods supplied under the contract are reasonably fit for that purpose, whether or not that is a purpose for which such goods are commonly supplied, except where the circumstances show that the buyer does not rely, or that it is unreasonable for him to rely, on the skill or judgment of the seller or credit-broker.

(4) An implied term about quality or fitness for a particular purpose may be annexed to a contract of sale by usage.

(5) The preceding provisions of this section apply to a sale by a person who in the course of a business is acting as agent for another as they apply to a sale by a principal in the course of a business, except where that other is not selling in the course of a business and either the buyer knows that fact or reasonable steps are taken to bring it to the notice of the buyer before the contract is made.

(6) As regards England and Wales and Northern Ireland, the terms implied by subsection (2) and (3) above are conditions …

(9) This section does not apply to a contract to which Chapter 2 of Part 1 of the Consumer Rights Act 2015 applies (but see the provision made about such contracts in sections 9, 10 and 18 of that Act).

Section 15 Sale by sample

(1) A contract of sale is a contract for sale by sample where there is an express or implied term to that effect in the contract.

(2) In the case of a contract for sale by sample there is an implied term –

(a) that the bulk will correspond with the sample in quality;

…

(c) that the goods will be free from any defect, making their quality unsatisfactory, which would not be apparent on reasonable examination of the sample.

(3) As regards England and Wales and Northern Ireland, the term implied by subsection (2) above is a condition.

(5) This section does not apply to a contract to which Chapter 2 of Part 1 of the Consumer Rights Act 2015 applies (but see the provision made about such contracts in sections 13 and 18 of that Act).

Following the Consumer Rights Act 2015 (CRA 2015) these provisions of the SGA 1979 no longer apply to sales by traders to consumers (defined in s 2 of the CRA 2015). However, as is hinted at by the revised text of the SGA 1979 (see, for example, s 14(9) of the SGA 1979, above), the CRA 2015 makes similar provision in respect of sales by traders to consumers although, of course, such provisions need to be construed in the consumer context. Indeed, in some situations the CRA 2015 goes beyond the SGA 1979, for example, in giving explicit rights to consumers in relation to the supply of digital content (see ss 33 to 47 of the CRA 2015). Moreover s 12 of the CRA 2015 makes certain pre-contractual information part of the contract:

(1) This section applies to any contract to supply goods.
(2) Where regulation 9, 10 or 13 of the Consumer Contracts (Information, Cancellation and Additional Charges) Regulations 2013 (SI 2013/3134) required the trader to provide information to the consumer before the contract became binding, any of that information that was provided by the trader other than information about the goods and mentioned in paragraph (a) of Schedule 1 or 2 to the Regulations (main characteristics of goods) is to be treated as included as a term of the contract.
(3) A change to any of that information, made before entering into the contract or later, is not effective unless expressly agreed between the consumer and the trader.
(4) See section 2(5) and (6) for the application of this section where goods are sold at public auction.
(5) See section 19 for a consumer's rights if the trader is in breach of a term that this section requires to be treated as included in the contract.

Nevertheless the SGA 1979 continues to be an important piece of legislation because it confers upon non-consumer buyers of goods a number of significant rights. Many of these rights are contained within implied terms, which in general terms have the effect of reversing the presumption of *caveat emptor* (let the buyer beware). Prior to the enactment of the original SGA 1893, it was often necessary for the buyer to obtain a specific undertaking from the seller as to the quality of the goods. Such undertakings are no longer necessary because the implied terms contained in ss 12 to 15 of the SGA 1979 provide buyers with a significant bundle of rights. We will briefly examine the contents of each of these sections.

Section 12(1) of the SGA 1979 is concerned with 'title'. It gives the buyer a remedy against a seller who does not have the right to sell the goods that he has contracted to sell. The implied term is a condition, which means that the buyer has a right to repudiate the contract for breach. This is so even when the buyer has made use of the goods prior to discovery that the seller did not have good title.

Rowland v Divall [1923] 2 KB 500

Facts: The plaintiff car dealer had bought a motor car from the defendant and used it for several months. Unknown to both parties, the car had been stolen. The plaintiff resold the car to a third party, from whom it was reclaimed, some months later, by the true owner's insurance company. The plaintiff had to repay the purchase price to the third party and then sought to recover the purchase price he had paid to the defendant.

Held: The Court of Appeal held that notwithstanding that the plaintiff had had the use of the car for several months the consideration had totally failed, and he was entitled to get the purchase money back. The plaintiff had contracted for the property in and lawful possession of the car, neither of which he had received.

Scrutton LJ: [T]he Sale of Goods Act ... re-enacted that rule ... as a condition, not as a warranty. Section 12 says in express terms that there shall be 'An implied condition on the part of the seller that ... he has a right to sell the goods'. It being now a condition, wherever that condition is broken the contract can be rescinded, and with the rescission the buyer can demand a return of the purchase money.

Section 12 also contains warranties of freedom from encumbrances and quiet possession.

Section 13 concerns the sale of goods by description and implies a condition that the goods will match the description. Section 13(3) makes it clear that the condition will apply even though the buyer has seen the goods and may have even selected the goods himself. The section will only operate, however, if the buyer has entered into the contract in reliance upon the description provided by the seller. In *Harlingdon and Leinster Enterprises v Christopher Hull Fine Art Ltd* [1991] 1 QB 564, the buyer had purchased a painting that turned out not to be by the artist to whom it was attributed in the catalogue. It was found as a matter of fact that the buyer had not relied upon the attribution in the catalogue and, as a result, this was not a sale by description. Not all descriptive words are a description within the meaning of s 13. The words used must identify the subject matter of the contract (*Reardon Smith Line Ltd v Yngvar Hansen-Tangen* [1976] 1 WLR 989).

Section 15 is similar to s 13 and concerns sale by sample. Two conditions are implied. First that the bulk will correspond with the sample in quality and second that the goods will be free from any defect, making their quality unsatisfactory, which would not be apparent on a reasonable examination of the sample. An example of this second condition can be found in the case of *Godley v Perry*.

Godley v Perry [1960] 1 WLR 9

Facts: A six-year-old boy purchased a toy catapult from a shop. It was made of brittle plastic and fractured when the boy fired it, blinding him in one eye. The boy claimed damages against the retailer for breach of s 15 of the SGA.

Held: It was held that the retailer was liable for damages because the defect was not apparent on reasonable examination of the sample.

Edmund Davies J: Counsel ... demonstrated that by squeezing together the two prongs of the catapult in the hand they could be fractured, and further suggested that by holding the toy down with one's foot and then pulling on the elastic its safety could be tested and, as I understand it, its inherent fragility would thereby inevitably be discovered. True, the potential customer might have done any of these things. He might also, I suppose, have tried biting the catapult, or hitting it with a hammer, or applying a lighted match to ensure its non-inflammability, experiments which, with all respect, are but slightly more bizarre than those suggested by counsel. But, looking at the matter realistically, as one must, in my judgment none of those tests are called for by a process of 'reasonable examination', as that phrase would be understood by the common-sense standards of everyday life.

Section 14 implies two different conditions into contracts for the sale of goods. Section 14(2) implies a condition of satisfactory quality. The test of satisfactory quality was substituted for the previous test of 'merchantable quality' by the Sale and Supply of Goods Act 1994. Because of this, the previous case law on s 14(2) is only of limited assistance in the interpretation of the section. Section 14(2B) provides a list of factors that will be relevant in applying the new test.

The second condition is found in s 14(3) and states that the goods must be reasonably fit for their purpose. The seller does not provide a guarantee that the goods will be fit for any purpose. If the buyer intends to use the goods for some unusual purpose then he must make the seller aware of that purpose prior to entering into the contract if he wishes to rely on s 14(3). The condition contained in s 14(3) is merely that the goods will be 'reasonably' fit for their purpose. Therefore, if the goods prove to be unfit for their purpose due to some unexpected occurrence, unknown to the seller, s 14(3) may not operate.

The two conditions contained in s 14 are only implied where a sale of goods contract is made in the course of business. The scope of the phrase 'in the course of business', was considered by the Court of Appeal in *Stevenson v Rogers*.

***Stevenson v Rogers* [1999] QB 1028**

Facts: Mr Rogers, a fisherman, had owned a boat called the 'Jelle' for some time before selling it to Mr Stevenson. Mr Rogers had intended to replace the 'Jelle' with a custom-built boat. However, he changed his mind and bought another boat instead. Mr Stevenson contended that, since Mr Rogers had sold and replaced the very thing without which he could have no fishing business, the sale should have been regarded as being in the course of business for the purposes of s 14(2).

Held: The Court of Appeal allowed the appeal. Their Lordships noted that the original SGA 1893 had limited liability to situations in which the seller dealt 'in goods of that description'. This limitation, however, had been removed by the SGA 1979. The court held that there was no justification for the re-introduction of such a qualification on the apparently wide scope and purpose of s 14. Therefore, on the facts, s 14(2) applied even though the fisherman was not regularly in the business of selling fishing boats. *R and B Customs Brokers v UDT* [1988] 1 WLR 321 and the test applied under UCTA 1977 were distinguished.

Stevenson v Rogers was followed in *MacDonald v Pollock* [2012] CSIH 12.

At the start of this section we noted that there were two main reasons why Parliament enacts legislation to imply terms into contracts: efficiency and protection. What is the basis underlying the terms implied by the SGA 1979? The argument that the terms are implied for the sake of efficiency, to express the parties' presumed intentions, is unconvincing. If that really was the reason then equivalent terms would be implied into contracts for the sale of real property. In actual fact, English law does not imply terms of satisfactory quality or even habitability into contracts for the sale or lease of a house. Furthermore, the efficiency basis is difficult to reconcile with the presumption of *caveat emptor* that operated throughout the 19th century. If the implied terms found in the SGA 1979 really do represent the presumed intentions of the parties, it is inexplicable why the contrary presumption played such a dominant role in the 19th century market.

It seems that the protective function lies behind the terms implied by the SGA 1979. The terms seek to protect the 'reasonable expectations' of buyers of goods and to counter unequal bargaining power. This is confirmed by the fact that Parliament has intervened by enacting the Unfair Contract Terms Act 1977 to make it, generally, impossible for the parties to exclude these terms unless it is shown to be reasonable to do so (see Chapter 7).

6.4.3 The justification for implied terms

As we have seen there are four main categories of implied terms: (1) terms implied by custom, (2) terms implied in fact, (3) terms implied in law, and (4) terms implied by statute. Terms are implied under each of these heads on different bases: necessity, notoriety, reasonableness and protection. It is arguable, however, that the same justification underlies all implied terms: protection of the reasonable expectations of the contracting parties.

Lord Steyn, 'Contract Law: fulfilling the reasonable expectations of honest men' (1997) 113 *LQR* 433, pp 441–442

In systems of law where there is a general duty of good faith in the performance of contracts the need to supplement the written contract by implied terms is less than in the English system. In our system, however, the implication of terms fulfils an important function in promoting the reasonable expectations of parties. Three categories of implied terms can be identified. First, there are terms implied by virtue of the usages of trade and commerce. The assumption is that usages are taken for granted and therefore not spelled out in writing. The recognition of trade usages protects the reasonable expectations of the parties. Secondly, there are terms implied in fact, i.e. from the contextual scene of the particular contract. Such implied terms fulfil the role of ad hoc gap fillers. Often the expectations of the parties would be defeated if a term were not implied, e.g. sometimes a contract simply will not work unless a particular duty to cooperate is implied. The law has evolved practical tests for the permissibility of such an implication, such as the test of whether the term is necessary to give business efficacy to the contract or the less stringent test whether the conventional bystander, when faced with the problem, would immediately say 'yes, it is obvious that there is such an implied term'. The legal test for the implication of a term is the standard of strict necessity. And it is right that it should be so since courts ought not to supplement a contract by an implication unless it is perfectly obvious that it is necessary to give effect to the reasonable expectations of parties. It is, however, a myth to regard such an implied term as based on an inference of the actual intention of the parties. The reasonable expectations of the parties in an objective sense are controlling: they sometimes demand that such terms be imputed to the parties. The third category is terms implied by law. This occurs when incidents are impliedly annexed to particular forms of contracts, e.g. contracts for building work, contracts of sale, hire, etc. Such implied terms operate as default rules. By and large such implied terms have crystallised in statute or case law. But there is scope for further development. In such new cases a broader approach than applied in the case of terms implied in fact must necessarily prevail. The proposed implication must fit the generality of cases. Indeed, despite some confusion in the authorities, it is tolerably clear that the court may take into account considerations of reasonableness in laying down the scope of terms to be implied in contracts of common occurrence. This function of the court is essential in providing a reasonable and fair framework for contracting. After all, there are many incidents of contracts of common occurrence which the parties cannot always be expected to reproduce in writing. This type of supplementation of contracts also fulfils an essential function in promoting the reasonable expectations of the parties.

Additional reading

Goode, R., 'Usage and Its Reception in Transnational Commercial Law' (1997) 46 ICLQ 1.

Havelock, R., 'The "Unitary Exercise" of Contractual Interpretation' (2017) 76 Cambridge Law Journal 486.

Macdonald, E., 'Incorporation of Contract Terms by a "Consistent Course of Dealing"' (1988) 8 LS 48.

McKendrick, E., 'The Interpretation of Contracts: Lord Hoffmann's Re-statement' in S Worthington (ed), *Commercial Law and Commercial Practice* (Oxford: Hart, 2003), p 139.

Mitchell, C., 'Leading a Life of Its Own? The Roles of Reasonable Expectation in Contract Law' (2003) 23 OJLS 639.

Nicholls, D., 'My Kingdom for a Horse: The Meaning of Words' (2005) 121 LQR 577.

Peden, E., 'Policy Concerns Behind Implication of Terms in Law' (2001) 117 LQR 459.

Peden, E., and Carter, J.W., 'Incorporation of Terms by Signature: L'Estrange Rules!' (2005) 21 JCL 96.

Phang, A., 'Implied Terms, Business Efficacy and the Officious Bystander – A Modern History' [1998] JBL 1.

Riley, C., 'Designing Default Rules in Contract Law' (2000) 20 OJLS 367.

Staughton, C., 'How Do the Courts Interpret Commercial Contracts?' (1999) 3 CLJ 03.

Chapter 7

Clauses excluding or limiting liability

Chapter contents

7.1 Introduction

In the previous chapter we considered the contents of contracts and the rules that are applied by the courts in ascertaining what obligations have been assumed by the parties. In this chapter we deal with a particular type of contract term – those that purport to exclude or limit the liability and/or remedies of contracting parties in contract and/or tort. There is nothing inherently objectionable about clauses of this kind. Indeed, they provide an invaluable mechanism for allocating risks within transactions. For example, in contracts for the carriage of goods it may have been agreed that the owner should be responsible for insuring the goods against loss or damage in transit. In such circumstances, it may be entirely reasonable for the carrier to exclude or limit his liability for loss or damage to the goods being carried. Exclusion clauses also perform an important role in high-risk contracts, where the consequential losses might far exceed the contract price. For example, in a contract for the supply of an air-conditioning unit the supplier of a faulty unit to a factory may, for example, incur liability for personal injury to the factory employees, damage to goods stored in the factory and loss of profits caused by closure of the factory. A small business may not be able to bear such extensive loss, so may seek to rely on an exclusion or limitation clause in order to manage their potential liability.

Problems arise when, for example, there is inequality of bargaining power and essentially the clause has been forced upon the weaker party by the strong. In the previous chapter, we saw an example of this in *Parker v South Eastern Railway* (1877) 2 CPD 416, where a railway company incorporated a broad-sweeping exclusion clause into contracts with its passengers. Today, exclusion clauses frequently appear in standard form contracts where the other party has little choice as to whether to accept or reject it. There is often usually no discussion of the contents of the contract and the other party simply has to agree to the terms offered in a 'take it or leave it' fashion. Here, there is a compelling case for control.

Law Commission, Report No 69, *Second Report on Exemption Clauses in Contracts*, 1975, para 11

It is clear that exemption clauses are much used both in dealings with private individuals and in purely commercial transactions. We are in no doubt that in many cases they operate against the public interest and that the prevailing judicial attitude of suspicion, or indeed hostility, to such clauses is well founded. All too often they are introduced in ways which result in the party affected by them remaining ignorant of their presence or import until it is too late. That party, even if he knows of the exemption clause will often be unable to appreciate what he may lose by accepting it. In any case, he may not have sufficient bargaining strength to refuse to accept it. The result is that the risk of carelessness or of failure to achieve satisfactory standards of performance is thrown onto the party who is not responsible for it or who is unable to guard against it. Moreover, by excluding liability for such carelessness or failure the economic pressures to maintain high standards of performance are reduced. There is no doubt that the misuse of these clauses is objectionable. Some are unjustified. Others, however, may operate fairly or unfairly, efficiently or inefficiently depending on the circumstances: for example, the cost and practicability of insurance may be factors in determining how liability should be apportioned between the two contracting parties. The problem of devising methods of controlling the use of these clauses, and indeed of identifying some of them, has proved both difficult and complicated.

The Law Commission recognised that exclusion clauses frequently operate against the public interest, especially in circumstances where they are imposed on parties who do not have sufficient bargaining strength to refuse to accept them. Regulation is necessary but often difficult. This is sometimes due to the difficulty that exists in distinguishing between clauses that exclude/limit liability and those that simply determine the obligations under the contract. To illustrate the point, consider in broad terms a contract for the regular servicing of a motorcar. Michael, the owner of the car, wishes for any spare parts used in the servicing to be manufactured and supplied by Ferrari. The garage, Dodge G Motors, knows that there is no guarantee that such parts will be available when needed. The situation can be dealt with in one of two ways. A clause might be incorporated stating that: 'Dodge G will use parts manufactured and supplied by Ferrari when available, but may substitute equivalent parts if necessary to complete the service within a reasonable time.' Such a clause would define Dodge G's obligations under the contract. Alternatively the clause might be drafted in the following way: 'Dodge G will use parts manufactured and supplied by Ferrari, but in the event that such parts are unavailable, Dodge G will not be liable for any loss arising from the use of equivalent parts.' Such a clause is drafted in the form of a limitation on Dodge G's liability, but in practice it achieves the same purpose as the previous clause. It is generally possible to rewrite any clause that purports to limit/exclude liability for a breach of contract as a clause that defines the parties' obligations under the contract.

Indeed, some commentators go further than that and argue that the true function of all exclusion clauses is to define liability, not to provide a defence to liability.

Coote, B, *Exception Clauses*, 1964, London: Sweet & Maxwell, pp 10–11, 17–18

If we suppose, for example, a promise in general terms, and a series of particular exceptions from that promise, we have a case where an exception clause is directly limiting the substantive contractual content of a promise, or more technically, perhaps, is negativing any primary right to performance of those matters excluded from the promise. Thus, where a horse is sold warranted sound 'except for hunting', a purchaser will have no primary right to call a horse sound for hunting. An exception may have the same effect indirectly, through the operation of the proposition that it is impossible to create valid contractual rights while at the same time agreeing that they shall be at all times unenforceable. A total exclusion, either of sanctioning rights or of procedural rights of enforcement, would have the effect of making the apparent primary right unenforceable. In so far as the 'unenforceable right' would be illusory (that is, would have no existence as a contractual right), exceptions of this type would, accordingly, have the effect on primary rights of preventing their accrual. Thus, if the vendor of a horse should represent that the animal is sound but stipulate that he shall not be required to make compensation if it should prove to be unsound, then unless he is merely contradicting himself, he is indicating thereby that his representation is a 'mere' representation and that he refuses to contract as to the horse's soundness. In other words, by excluding sanctioning rights he is indirectly preventing the purchaser from acquiring any contractual primary right as to soundness ...

[I]t follows that the true juristic function and effect of exception clauses are quite different from those currently ascribed to them, by the courts. Instead of being mere shields to claims based on breach of accrued rights, exception clauses substantively delimit the rights themselves. A large class of them prevent those rights from ever arising in the first place. As it has been put in an American publication: 'the ordinary function of an exception is to take out of the contract that which otherwise would have been in it ...'

People who adopt Professor Coote's position contend that exclusion clauses should be treated in exactly the same way as other clauses of the contract. Such an approach has not been fully embraced in the Law of England and Wales (see, for example, Beatson, J, Burrows, A, and Cartwright, J, (eds), *Anson's Law of Contract*, 30th edn, 2016, Oxford: OUP, p 212). See also *Impact Funding Solutions Ltd v Barrington Support Services Ltd (formerly Lawyers at Work Ltd)* [2016] UKSC 57.

This chapter is divided into three sections. In the first, we will consider the common law rules that have been applied to regulate exclusion/limitation clauses. In the second, we will consider the Unfair Contract Terms Act 1977 (UCTA 1977), and in the third we will examine the Consumer Rights Act 2015 (CRA 2015).

7.2 Common law

Due to the traditional emphasis on freedom of contract, at common law the courts have generally been unable to directly assess exclusion/limitation clauses on their merits. Nevertheless at times they have regulated exclusion/limitation clauses indirectly by, for example, manipulating the rules relating to the determination of the contents of the contract and the scope of the clauses contained in it.

7.2.1 Incorporation

Incorporation was discussed in detail in Chapter 6. Many of the cases discussed in that chapter concerned the incorporation of exclusion clauses. As we saw, the courts have sometimes been reluctant to conclude that an exclusion clause has been incorporated into a contract. One of the devices used for this purpose was the 'redhand rule', which requires 'unusual' or 'onerous' terms to be given special notice (see *Thornton v Shoe Lane Parking* [1971] 2 QB 163; *Interfoto v Stiletto Visual Programmes* [1989] QB 433). Following statutory intervention in this area (now UCTA 1977 and CRA 2015), the importance of the special notice rule has, perhaps, diminished (see *AEG (UK) Ltd v Logic Resource Ltd* [1996] CLC 265). On the other hand, in *Goodlife Foods Ltd v Hall Fire Protection Ltd* [2018] EWCA Civ 1371 Coulson LJ stated (at [35]): 'I consider that these two principles (namely incorporation at common law on the one hand, and the reasonableness of any term incorporated pursuant to UCTA, on the other) are separate, and the questions to be decided in respect of each are distinct. There may be some overlap in the matters that fall to be considered under each principle, but that is all.'

7.2.2 Interpretation

Once the court has concluded that the clause has been incorporated into the contract, it is necessary to determine whether it covers the breach that has occurred. This is a matter of interpretation: does the wording of the clause cover the situation that has arisen? The rules of interpretation, like the rules of incorporation, are of general application and can be used in relation to all clauses within a contract, not just exclusion/limitation clauses. In Chapter 6 we considered the more general issues relating to interpretation. In the context of exclusion clauses, traditionally the courts have generally adopted a stricter approach to interpretation than elsewhere. Here, we will examine the main rules of interpretation that have been applied by the courts and we will consider what impact *Investors Corporation v West Bromwich Building Society* [1998] 1 WLR 896 has had on those rules.

7.2.2.1 Strict interpretation

The first rule of interpretation that was traditionally applied to exclusion/limitation clauses was that plain words would be given no wider meaning than their ambit required. In *Wallis, Son and Wells v Pratt & Havnes* [1911] AC 394, the House of Lords held that a clause stating that the suppliers of seed gave no 'warranty' in relation to its 'growth, description or any other matters' did not protect them from being liable for a breach of condition. The clause was to be given no wider meaning that its ambit required and for that reason it only covered warranties, not conditions. The House of Lords applied this rule in *Beck v Szymanowski*.

Beck v Szymanowski [1924] AC 43

Facts: The defendants agreed to supply the plaintiffs with 2,000 '200 yards reels' of sewing cotton. The contract contained the following exclusion clause: 'The goods delivered shall be deemed to be in all respects in accordance with the contract and the buyers shall be bound to accept and pay for the same accordingly unless the sellers shall within fourteen days after the arrival of the goods at their destination receive from the buyers notice of any matter or thing by reason whereof they may allege that the goods are not in accordance with the contract.' Eighteen months after delivery, the plaintiffs discovered that the length of cotton per reel was only 188 yards and they brought an action against the defendants for breach of contract. The defendants argued that they were protected by the exclusion clause.

Held: The House of Lords held (Lord Buckmaster dissenting) that the exclusion clause applied to quality only and not to quantity. The clause referred to 'goods delivered'. The problem was that the goods had been short delivered and therefore the 14-day notification period did not apply here.

Lord Shaw of Dunfermline: The clause applies to 'the goods delivered', saying that they shall be deemed to be in all respects according to contract.

But one may stop there; for the damages are claimed not in respect of the goods delivered but in respect of goods which were not delivered. And when fourteen days are given for notice of any 'matter or thing of reason whereof they may allege that the goods are not in accordance with the contract' the expression 'the goods' can only mean 'the goods delivered', to which alone the clause applies.

Anything else would mean that the sale was in substance a sale of reels and was not in substance a sale of cotton thread. I think this is to confound make up with substance. And the results would be extraordinary; if a seller innocently sent forward the number of reels with only half the thread that should be upon them, the clause would cover that portion, and the seller would, barring objection within fourteen days, keep the price for the whole thread, although he had only supplied half ...

[I]n my opinion the clause can never be used so as to convert goods undelivered into goods delivered or to warrant an implication to the effect that non-delivery in length or small measure was included in the objections which should, within the time fixed, be made to goods delivered. I am totally unable to make such an implication out of anything in the bargain between these parties – an implication which would seriously affect the security of business dealings.

In *Bominflot Bunkergesellschaft fur Mineraloele mbH & Co KG v Petroplus Marketing AG (The Mercini Lady)* [2010] EWCA Civ 1145 at [58]–[62] the Court of Appeal considered the modern significance of *Wallis*:

58 In a recent case comment on the judge's decision (Of FOB sales, seller's obligations and disclaimers [2009] LMCLQ 417 at 420) Professor Andrew Tettenborn has suggested that *Wallis v Pratt* is now dated and that 'English commercial law would, it is suggested, benefit greatly' if the new trend for the interpretation of exclusion clauses ushered in by *Photo Production v Securicor* were taken to heart. I note that *Benjamin's Sale of Goods*, 8th ed, 2010 refers to the jurisprudence as 'very strict' (at para 13-025).

59 It is not easy to choose between these submissions. On the one hand a principle has been established, on the highest authority, that Sale of Goods Act implied conditions cannot be excluded by reference to guarantees or warranties and require clearer language extending to 'conditions' themselves. Those authorities go beyond the relatively simple clause and stark facts of *Wallis v Pratt* itself, where there was a breach of an express clause as to the product to be supplied, or the case of *Cammell Laird*, where there was no exclusion at all, and extend to *Baldry v Marshall*, where the clause spoke expressly of the exclusion of 'any other guarantee or warranty, *statutory* or otherwise', and above all to *Kendall v Lillico*, where the clause was similar to ours in dealing expressly with the concept of merchantability and went on to refer expressly to 'any *statute* or rule of law to the contrary notwithstanding' (emphasis added).

60 On the other hand, it is extremely difficult to read our exclusion clause as not being intended to cover the exclusion of the statutory implications of satisfactory quality (the new merchantable quality) and fitness for purpose. Mr Edey's reference to the little known or exemplified section 14(4) cannot realistically be considered as the exclusive subject matter of the clause's language about 'merchantability, fitness or suitability of the oil for any particular purpose or otherwise'. Moreover, what other implied terms about quality or fitness for purpose, other than the statutory implications are permitted in the light of section 14(1)? If an implied warranty of quality or fitness of purpose is excluded, why not an implied condition, since only the statute can supply any such term and the statute refers to such terms as conditions? This may be thought to be especially the case in an international sale of goods contract where quality is defined by reference to an express specification and that specification has to be determined once and for all on shipment by a final and binding inspection certificate. The clause 18 exception says 'no guarantees … which extend beyond the description of the oil set forth in this agreement'. What is that 'description'? The word is not used (as far as has been brought to our attention) elsewhere in the contract. Strictly speaking the description may be thought to be found in clause 3, headed 'Product'. However, it is unrealistic and uncommercial to think that for the purpose of this contract 'description' does not also embrace clause 4, albeit it is headed 'Quality', especially since clause 18 refers to merchantability, an aspect of quality.

61 If therefore I were construing this clause untrammelled by past authority, or if such authority was plainly limited, in the way that so many decisions on the construction of individual clauses are limited, by considerations of the precise language and context of those particular clauses, I would feel it open, in the modern world, to give to clause 18 the construction which I believe that it realistically bears: that is to say, that 'guarantees' and 'warranties' are intended to cover all terms, both those which entitle the innocent party in the case of breach to treat the contract as repudiated and those which sound only in damages. As section 11(3) of the 1979 Act itself records, 'a stipulation may be a condition, though called a warranty in the contract': and clause 18 itself demonstrates that buyer's warranties there set out are treated by the contract as conditions. It might be said that what is good enough for Lord Diplock (see at para 55 above) is good enough for commercial traders. However, I am not so free. The jurisprudence extends beyond individual decisions and has become expressive of a principle, and what is more the principle also encompasses clauses very similar to clause 18. I must consider that the parties to this English law contract, foreign as both of them are and quite possibly ignorant of the consequences of their choice of language, intended to contract by reference to what English law had to say about the language which they have adopted. As Lord Diplock said in *Photo Production v Securicor* itself (at 850G/851A):

> 'Since the presumption is that the parties by entering into the contract intended to accept the implied obligations exclusion clauses are to be construed strictly and the degree of strictness appropriate to be applied to their construction may properly depend upon the extent to which they involve departure from the implied obligations. Since the obligations implied by law in a commercial contract are those which, by judicial consensus over the years or by Parliament in passing a statute, have been regarded as obligations which a reasonable businessman would realise that he was accepting when he entered into a contract of a particular kind, the court's view of the reasonableness of any departure from the implied obligations which would be

involved in construing the express words of an exclusion clause in one sense that they are capable of bearing rather than another, is a relevant consideration in deciding what meaning the words were intended by the parties to bear. But this does not entitle the court to reject the exclusion clause, however unreasonable the court itself may think it is, if the words are clear and fairly susceptible of one meaning only'.

62 In the present case, it is not a question of whether the exclusion is unreasonable or not. Either submission of the parties would be perfectly acceptable as long as the position was clear. It is, however, a case where the implied obligations which it is said on behalf of the seller have been excluded are not only fundamental obligations of English law, long enshrined in our Sale of Goods Acts, but there has also been a judicial consensus that such obligations can only be excluded by language which expressly (or perhaps one may add which must necessarily be taken to) refer to conditions: and that such language as has been used in our case falls within that consensus and principle. Lord Diplock was speaking of a judicial consensus which creates implied obligations: but there may also be a judicial consensus which preserves such implied obligations in the face of inadequate exclusions. In such circumstances, there is an importance in the certainty of our commercial law which goes beyond the answer that may be given in a particular case. I cannot say, against the background of the jurisprudence, that the parties' language is fairly susceptible of only one meaning. Whereas I have sympathy for Professor Tettenborn's position, and for the submissions of Mr Jacobs, I do not think that it is open to this court to depart from that long established consensus.

7.2.2.2 *Contra proferentem* rule

The second traditional rule of interpretation was that exclusion/limitation clauses would be interpreted *contra proferentem*. This meant that, if there was ambiguity in the language used, the clause would be construed against the party seeking to rely on it.

***Lee (John) & Son (Grantham) Ltd v Railway Executive* [1949] 2 All ER 581**

Facts: The plaintiffs were the tenants of a warehouse in which they stored certain goods. The goods were damaged by a fire owing to the alleged negligence of the defendant landlords who allowed a spark to be ejected by one of their railway engines. By clause 10 of the tenancy agreement the landlords were released from all liability for damage to property 'however caused ... which but for the tenancy hereby created or anything done pursuant to the provisions hereof would not have arisen'. The defendants claimed that the clause exempted them from liability.

Held: The Court of Appeal applied the *contra proferentem* rule and held that the words 'which but for the tenancy hereby created ... would not have arisen' limited the exclusion to liabilities arising only by reason of the relationship of landlord and tenant created by the lease. The clause was capable of bearing a broader meaning but it had to be construed against the defendant.

Sir Raymond Evershed MR: We are presented with two alternative readings of this document and the reading which one should adopt is to be determined, among other things, by a consideration of the fact that the defendants put forward the document. They have put forward a clause which is by no means free from obscurity and have contended that, on the view for which they argued, it has a remarkably, if not an extravagantly, wide scope, and I think that the rule *contra proferentem* should be applied and that the result is that the present claim is not one which obliges the first plaintiffs to give to the defendants a release and an indemnity.

7.2.2.2.1 Exclusion of negligence liability

The *contra proferentem* rule has often been used in the context of liability for negligence. The presumption is that a party has not excluded liability for his or her own negligence unless express words have been used. The principles to be applied here were set out by the Privy Council in *Canada Steamship Lines Ltd v The King* [1952] AC 192. The court was dealing with Canadian law but it has been confirmed that the principles are equally applicable to English law (see *Shell Chemical v P & O Tankers* [1995] 1 Lloyd's Rep 297). Lord Morton of Henryton said:

> Their Lordships think that the duty of a court in approaching the consideration of such clauses may be summarised as follows:
>
> (1) If the clause contains language which expressly exempts the person in whose favour it is made (hereafter called 'the proferens') from the consequence of the negligence of his own servants, effect must be given to that provision …
> (2) If there is no express reference to negligence, the court must consider whether the words used are wide enough, in their ordinary meaning, to cover negligence on the part of the servants of the proferens …
> (3) If the words used are wide enough for the above purpose, the court must then consider whether 'the head of damage may be based on some ground other than that of negligence' … The 'other ground' must not be so fanciful or remote that the proferens cannot be supposed to have desired protection against it; but subject to this qualification … the existence of a possible head of damage other than that of negligence is fatal to the proferens even if the words used are *prima facie* wide enough to cover negligence on the part of his servants.

The first of these principles is relatively straightforward. If a clause expressly exempts a party from the consequences of his/her negligence then the clause is effective to exclude liability for negligence. The use of the word 'negligence' is obviously sufficient, but synonyms (such as carelessness) may also be enough. In *Monarch Airlines Ltd v London Luton Airport* [1998] 1 Lloyd's Rep 403, Clarke J held that the phrase 'act, omission, neglect or default' was clearly intended to include negligent acts.

Problems arise with the second and third principles because they rest on the assumption that a party does not intend to exclude negligence unless s/he explicitly says so (cf. *Macquarie International Investments Ltd v Glencore (UK) Ltd* [2008] EWHC 1716 (Comm)). This is obviously a dubious assumption since the majority of contract drafters omit to explicitly refer to negligence for fear of putting the other party off of the transaction. Instead they use general words such as 'any loss howsoever caused'. While the natural meaning of such a phrase may be taken to include loss caused by both negligent and non-negligent acts, Lord Morton's third principle dictates that the phrase will be construed to cover only non-negligent sources of liability unless negligently inflicted loss is the only loss likely to be suffered by the claimant. However, in *HIH Casualty & General insurance Ltd v Chase Manhattan Bank* [2003] UKHL 6 at [11] Lord Bingham stated:

> [T]he insurers drew sustenance from the well-known principles propounded by Lord Morton of Henryton giving the judgment of the Board in *Canada Steamship Lines Ltd v The King* [1952] AC 192 at 208. There can be no doubting the general authority of these principles, which have been applied in many cases, and the approach indicated is sound. The courts should not ordinarily infer that a contracting party has given up rights which the law confers upon him to an extent greater than the contract terms indicate he has chosen to do; and if the contract terms can take legal and practical effect without denying him the rights he would ordinarily enjoy if the other party is negligent, they

> will be read as not denying him those rights unless they are so expressed as to make clear that they do. But, as the insurers in argument fully recognised, Lord Morton was giving helpful guidance on the proper approach to interpretation and not laying down a code. The passage does not provide a litmus test which, applied to the terms of the contract, yields a certain and predictable result. The courts' task of ascertaining what the particular parties intended, in their particular commercial context, remains.

See also *Aprile SpA v Elin Maritime Ltd* [2019] EWHC 1001 (Comm) at [68]. Cf. *Greenwich Millennium Village Ltd v Essex Services Group Plc (formerly Essex Electrical Group Ltd)* [2014] EWCA Civ 960.

More recently in *Persimmon Homes Ltd, Taylor Wimpey UK Ltd, BDW Trading Ltd v Ove Arup & Partners Ltd, Ove Arup & Partners International Ltd* [2015] EWHC 3573 (TCC) Stuart-Smith J, after referring to *Canada Steamships*, stated:

> **23.** The Consortium relied upon *Geys v Société Générale* [2013] 1 AC 523 as unqualified endorsement and application of these principles. There, Lord Hope said at [37]:
>
> > 'The approach that ought to be taken to the construction of clauses of this kind is well established. In *Canada Steamship Lines Ltd v The King* [1952] AC 192, 208 Lord Morton of Henryton quoted with approval the principles applicable to clauses which purport to exempt one party to a contract from liability for negligence which were stated by Lord Greene MR in *Alderslade v Hendon Laundry Ltd* [1945] KB 189, 192. In summary, these principles are (1) that if the clause expressly exempts the party in whose favour it is made (the proferens) from liability for negligence, effect must be given to it; (2) if there is no express reference to negligence, the court must consider whether the words used are wide enough to cover it; and (3) if a doubt arises on this point it must be resolved in favour of the other party and against the proferens'.
>
> **24.** It is immediately to be noted that this passage does not include any reference to the third principle as set out by Lord Morton. This omission is unlikely to be accidental. It might be because the claims being brought in *Geys* were not founded in negligence, but that did not prevent the Supreme Court referring to and endorsing the first two of Lord Morton's principles. It is also to be noted that, leaving aside Lord Morton's third principle for the moment, the language used by the Privy Council in Canada Steamship Lines (though not so clearly by the Supreme Court in *Geys*) was consistent with the modern approach to interpretation in requiring the Court to see whether (in the absence of express reference to negligence) 'the words used are wide enough, in their ordinary meaning, to cover negligence'. In *Geys* Lord Hope referred (at [38]) to the statement in *W&S Pollock & Co v McCrae* 1922 SC (HL) 192, 199 that in order to be effective exemption clauses must be 'most clearly and unambiguously expressed'. And he added that 'the more improbable it is that the other party would agree to excluding the liability of the proferens, the more exacting the application of the principle will be'.
>
> **25.** Despite the re-iteration of at least part of Lord Morton's principles in *Geys*, there has been a shift in the approach of the Courts to limitation and exclusion clauses. This shift has come about for two reasons, which are related. The first is the passing of the Unfair Contract Terms Act 1977 ['UCTA']; the second is an increasing recognition that parties to commercial contracts are and should be left free to apportion and allocate risks and obligations as they see fit, particularly where insurance may be available to one or other or both parties to cover the risks being so allocated. The impact of UCTA and, in particular, the fact that Parliament had chosen not to extend its application to commercial contracting parties of equal bargaining status, was recognised by Lord Wilberforce in *Photo Production v Securicor Ltd* [1980] AC 827, 843C–E. Lord Diplock said at 851A–C:

'In commercial contracts negotiated between business-men capable of looking after their own interests and of deciding how risks inherent in the performance of various kinds of contract can be most economically borne (generally by insurance), it is, in my view wrong to place a strained construction upon words in an exclusion clause which are clear and fairly susceptible of one meaning only even after due allowance has been made of the presumption in favour of the implied primary and secondary obligations'.

26. The recognition that parties may choose to allocate risks and liabilities in a way that may at first sight seem unlikely to an outsider has grown in the field of commercial contracts in general and contracts related to construction in particular where the allocation of risk has been a commonplace in standard forms of building contracts for years – see, for example, *Scottish Special Housing Association v Wimpey Construction UK Ltd* [1986] 1 WLR 995.

27. The rationale for this approach was explained (in a slightly different context) by Chadwick LJ in *E A Grimstead & Son Ltd v McGarrigan* (unreported, 27 October 1999, cited in [2001] EWCA Civ 317):

'There are, as it seems to me, at least two good reasons why the courts should not refuse to give effect to an acknowledgement of non-reliance in a commercial contract between experienced parties of equal bargaining power – *a fortiori*, where those parties have the benefit of professional advice. First, it is reasonable to assume that the parties desire commercial certainty. They want to order their affairs on the basis that the bargain between them can be found within the document which they have signed. They want to avoid the uncertainty of litigation based on allegations as to the content of oral discussions at pre-contractual meetings. *Second, it is reasonable to assume that the price to be paid reflects the commercial risk which each party – or, more usually, the purchaser – is willing to accept. The risk is determined, in part at least, by the warranties which the vendor is prepared to give. The tighter the warranties, the less the risk and (in principle, at least) the greater the price the vendor will require and which the purchaser will be prepared to pay. It is legitimate, and commercially desirable, that both parties should be able to measure the risk, and agree the price, on the basis of the warranties which have been given and accepted*'. (Emphasis added.)

28. Moore-Bick LJ summarised the shift that has taken place in *Tradigrain SA and others v Intertek Testing Services (ITS) Canada Ltd and another* [2007] EWCA Civ 154 at [46]:

'It is certainly true that English law has traditionally taken a restrictive approach to the construction of exemption clauses and clauses limiting liability for breaches of contract and other wrongful acts. However, in recent years it has been increasingly willing to recognise that parties to commercial contracts are entitled to apportion the risk of loss as they see fit and that provisions which limit or exclude liability must be construed in the same way as other terms: see, for example, *Photo Production Ltd v Securicor Transport Ltd* [1980] AC 827 …'

29. The requirement for clarity of meaning remains when interpreting limitation and exclusion clauses: see, for example, *Air Transworld Ltd v Bombardier Ltd* [2012] EWHC 243 (Comm) at [26]. I am not convinced that this adds anything material to the normal requirements of contractual interpretation unless it be that, if the normal processes of interpretation do not lead to the conclusion that words have the meaning of an exclusion or limitation clause, they are not to be treated as having that effect.

30. In approaching the limitation and exclusion clauses in this case I bear in mind the authoritative principles I have set out above. I also refer to and gratefully adopt the two following passages.

31. In *HIH Casualty v Chase Manhattan Bank* [2003] 1 All ER (Comm), Lord Bingham said at [11] ... [see above]

> 'There can be no doubting the general authority of [the well-known principles propounded by Lord Morton of Henryton giving the judgment of the Board in *Canada Steamship Lines Ltd v The King* [1952] AC 192 at 208], which have been applied in many cases, and the approach indicated is sound. The courts should not ordinarily infer that a contracting party has given up rights which the law confers upon him to an extent greater than the contract terms indicate he has chosen to do; and if the contract terms can take legal and practical effect without denying him the rights he would ordinarily enjoy if the other party is negligent, they will be read as not denying him those rights unless they are so expressed as to make clear that they do. But, as the insurers in argument fully recognised, Lord Morton was giving helpful guidance on the proper approach to interpretation and not laying down a code. The passage does not provide a litmus test which, applied to the terms of the contract, yields a certain and predictable result. The courts' task of ascertaining what the particular parties intended, in their particular commercial context, remains'.

32. Relying on this and other authority, Popplewell J derived the following principles in *Capita (Banstead 2011) Ltd v RFIB Group* [2014] EWHC 2197 (Comm) at [15]:

'(1) A clear intention must appear from the words used before the Court will reach the conclusion that one party has agreed to exempt the other from the consequences of his own negligence or indemnify him against losses so caused. The underlying rationale is that clear words are needed because it is inherently improbable that one party should agree to assume responsibility for the consequences of the other's negligence: ...

(2) The *Canada Steamship* principles are not to be applied mechanistically and ought to be considered as no more than guidelines; the task is always to ascertain what the parties intended in their particular commercial context in accordance with the established principles of construction: ... They nevertheless form a useful guide to the approach where the commercial context makes it improbable that in the absence of clear words one party would have agreed to assume responsibility for the relevant negligence of the other'.

33. These statements establish that the Court's task is essentially the same when interpreting what is said to be an exclusion or limitation clause as it is when interpreting any other provision of a contract: it is to identify what a reasonable person having all the background knowledge which would reasonably have been available to the parties would have understood the parties to have meant. And in pursuing that task, the commercial and contractual context may make it improbable that one party would have agreed to assume responsibility for the relevant negligence of another, so that clear words are needed. What matters most, to my mind, is not that the words should initially seem clear (though that often makes life much easier – pace *Charter Re*) but that, at the end of the interpretative process their meaning should be clear and established.

On appeal ([2017] EWCA Civ 373) Jackson LJ also stated:

> 56. In recent years, and especially since the enactment of UCTA, the courts have softened their approach to both indemnity clauses and exemption clauses: see *Lictor Anstalt v MIR Steel UK* [2012] EWCA Civ 1397; [2013] 2 All ER (Comm) 54 at [31] to [34]. Although the present judgment is not the place for a general review of the law of contract, my impression is that, at any rate in commercial contracts, the Canada Steamships guidelines (in so far as they survive) are now more relevant to indemnity clauses than to exemption clauses.

Subsequently in *The Federal Republic of Nigeria v JP Morgan Chase Bank, NA* [2019] EWHC 347 (Comm) at [64] Andrew Burrows QC (sitting as a Judge of the High Court) stated:

> Although to be treated as a flexible guide, rather than as a rigid code, the *Canada Steamship* principles indicate that a court should be reluctant to find that a generally worded clause, rather than an explicit reference to negligence, exempts, or indemnifies against, negligence (which would take away a valuable right).

7.2.2.2.2 Exclusion of fraudulent liability

The *contra proferentem* rule has also operated to ensure that a general exclusion clause is not construed to apply to fraud.

Motis Exports Ltd v Dampskibsselskabet AF 1912 Aktieselskab [2000] 1 Lloyd's Rep 211

Facts: The plaintiff was the shipper of various consignments of goods under a number of bills of lading at ports in China and Hong Kong. A clause in the bill of lading stated: 'the Carrier shall have no liability whatsoever for any loss or damage to the goods while in its actual or constructive possession before loading or after discharge over ship's rail, or if applicable, on the ship's ramp, however caused.' The goods were carried to West Africa in ships owned and operated by the defendants. The issue for decision was whether the defendants were liable for the loss of the goods after discharge from their vessels, where the cause of that loss was the use of forged bills of lading to obtain delivery orders in respect of, and thus delivery of, the goods at the discharge port.

Held: The Court of Appeal held that the natural subject matter of the exclusion clause consisted in loss or damage caused to the goods while in the carrier's custody but not deliberate delivery up of the goods against a forged bill of lading.

Stuart-Smith LJ: In my judgment [the clause] is not apt on its natural meaning to cover delivery by the carrier or his agent, albeit the delivery was obtained by fraud. I also agree with the Judge that even if the language was apt to cover such a case, it is not a construction which should be adopted, involving as it does excuse from performing an obligation of such fundamental importance. As a matter of construction the Courts lean against such a result if adequate content can be given to the clause. In my view it can … it is wide enough also to cover loss caused by negligence, provided the loss is of the appropriate kind.

7.2.2.2.3 Strict interpretation should not be strained

Although the *contra proferentem* rule stated that exclusion/limitation clauses would be read strictly against the person seeking to rely upon them, it came to be accepted that the construction applied should not be strained and the words will be given their natural meaning (cf. *George Mitchell (Chesterhall) Ltd v Finney Lock Seeds Ltd* [1983] QB 284 at 297, per Lord Denning MR).

Ailsa Craig Fishing Co Ltd v Malvern Fishing Co Ltd [1983] 1 WLR 964

Facts: Securicor agreed to provide a security service to Ailsa Craig's fishing boats moored in Aberdeen harbour. Due to Securicor's negligent failure to provide the service contracted for, a fishing boat belonging to Ailsa Craig sank, dragging down another boat owned by Malvern Fishing. The contract contained a clause limiting liability to £1,000. Ailsa Craig argued that since Securicor had failed to provide a security service they should not be able to hide behind the clause.

Held: The House of Lords held that the limitation clause was effective because its terms were clear and unambiguous and wide enough to cover the liability of Securicor for their negligence.

Lord Wilberforce: Whether a clause limiting liability is effective or not is a question of construction of that clause in the context of the contract as a whole. If it is to exclude liability for negligence, it must be most clearly and unambiguously expressed, and in such a contract as this, must be construed *contra proferentem*. I do not think that there is any doubt so far. But I venture to add one further qualification, or at least clarification: one must not strive to create ambiguities by strained construction, as I think that the appellants have striven to do. The relevant words must be given, if possible, their natural, plain meaning.

As Lord Wilberforce confirmed, the *contra proferentem* rule did not countenance finding ambiguity where none exists. This was also confirmed by Lord Bridge in *Mitchell (George) (Chesterhall) Ltd v Finney Lock Seeds Ltd* [1983] 2 AC 803, where his Lordship confirmed the need for straightforward interpretation:

> The relevant condition, read as a whole, unambiguously limits the appellants' liability to replacement of the seeds or refund of the price. It is only possible to read an ambiguity into it by the process of strained construction which was deprecated by Lord Diplock in the *Photo Production* case and by Lord Wilberforce in *Ailsa Craig*.

Similarly in *Air Transworld Ltd v Bombardier Inc* [2012] EWHC 243 at [28] Cooke J, after referring to *The Mercini Lady* (above at 7.2.2.) stated:

> No person reading this Article could be in any doubt that every promise implied by law is excluded, in favour of the contractual promises set out in the APA. It is right that there is no term which purports to exclude the buyer's right to reject the goods and recover the price, nor to the specific sections of the Sale of Goods Act, but the words 'all other … obligations … or liabilities express or implied arising by law', which the purchaser expressly waives, necessarily include the conditions implied by the Sale of Goods Act. In my judgment these are apt and precise words which are sufficiently clear to exclude those implied conditions and the Article, by necessary inference does negative the application of those implied conditions. The parties' language is in my judgment fairly susceptible of only one meaning (to employ the expression used by Lord Diplock in *Photo Production* and Lord Justice Rix in the *Mercini Lady*). There is no express reference to the word 'condition' but the language must necessarily be taken to refer to the implied conditions of the Sale of Goods Act, because they are obligations and liabilities 'implied, arising by law'. Moreover, the illustration of the application of this general provision in Article 4.1(B) covers any other obligation or liability devolving on the seller, 'of any nature whatsoever, resulting from the design, manufacture and sale of the aircraft. No buyer could be in any doubt as to the extent of the rights he was getting and the limitation on the seller's obligations. What the buyer was to get was the warranty found in the APA and its Appendix in place of the terms implied by the Sale of Goods Act, whether conditions or warranties.

7.2.2.3 Exclusion and limitation clauses

It has been held that a less rigorous approach should be applied to construing clauses that merely limit liability rather than excluding liability altogether. In *Ailsa Craig Fishing* Lord Wilberforce said:

> Clauses of limitation are not regarded by the courts with the same hostility as clauses of exclusion: this is because they must be related to other contractual terms, in particular to the risks to which the defending party may be exposed, the remuneration which he receives and possibly also the opportunity of the other party to insure.

Lord Fraser of Tulybelton agreed:

> There are ... authorities which lay down very strict principles to be applied when considering the effect of clauses of exclusion or of indemnity ... In my opinion these principles are not applicable in their full rigour when considering the effect of clauses merely limiting liability. Such clauses will of course be read *contra proferentem* and must be clearly expressed, but there is no reason why they should be judged by the specially exacting standards which are applied to exclusion and indemnity clauses. The reason for imposing such standards on these clauses is the inherent improbability that the other party to a contract including such a clause intended to release the *proferens* from a liability that would otherwise fall upon him. But there is no such high degree of improbability that he would agree to a limitation of the liability of the *proferens*, especially when ... the potential losses that might be caused by the negligence of the *proferens* or its servants are so great in proportion to the sums that can reasonably be charged for the services contracted for. It is enough in the present case that the clause must be clear and unambiguous.

The reasons given for distinguishing between exclusion clauses and limitation clauses are unconvincing. In particular, it is unclear why only limitation clauses are 'related to other contractual terms' and to 'the opportunity of the other party to insure'. It is also unclear why a party is any more likely to agree to a limitation clause than to an exclusion clause. In practice, the difference between the two may be non-existent. For example, a clause limiting compensation to one penny is virtually indistinguishable from a total exclusion of liability. In *Atlantic Shipping & Trading Company v Louis Dreyfus & Company* [1922] 2 AC 250, Lord Sumner said: 'There is no difference in principle between words which save [contractors] from having to pay at all and words which save them from paying as much as they would otherwise have had to pay.'

It is submitted that the courts should look to the substance of the clause rather than to the form of words used. A sensible approach was advocated by Evans LJ in *BHP Petroleum Ltd v British Steel plc* [2000] 2 Lloyd's Rep 277: '[T]he more extreme the consequences are, in terms of excluding or modifying the liability which would otherwise arise, then the more stringent the Court's approach should be in requiring that the exclusion or limit should be clearly and unambiguously expressed.'

7.2.2.4 Relaxation of the rules of interpretation

Following the enactment of statutory controls to regulate the use of exclusion/limitation clauses, the courts have increasingly taken the view that there is no longer a need to manipulate the rules of interpretation to provide indirect regulation. Until recently consumer and standard form contracts were, to differing degrees, regulated by UCTA 1977 and the Unfair Terms in Consumer Contracts Regulations 1999 (UTCCR 1999). Following the CRA 2015, which repealed the UTCCR 1999, there is a much clearer separation between consumer and non-consumer contracts: broadly the CRA 2015 regulates consumer contracts and, for present purposes, an amended UCTA 1977 regulates non-consumer contracts. Moreover businesses, to an extent, are expected to be able to look after themselves and it is presumed that if they enter into contracts containing exclusion clauses, they will know what they are doing. In *Photo Production Ltd v Securicor Transport Ltd* [1980] AC 827, Lord Wilberforce commented that:

> [A]fter [UCTA 1977], in commercial matters generally, when the parties are not of unequal bargaining power, and when risks are normally borne by insurance, not only is the case for judicial intervention undemonstrated, but there is everything to be said, and this seems to have been Parliament's intention, for leaving the parties free to apportion the risks as they think fit and for respecting their decisions.

Lord Diplock agreed with Lord Wilberforce, commenting that the need for judicial distortion of the English language has been banished by Parliament's enactment of UCTA 1977:

> In commercial contracts negotiated between businessmen capable of looking after their own interests and of deciding how risks inherent in the performance of various kinds of contract can be most economically borne (generally by insurance), it is, in my view, wrong to place a strained construction upon words in an exclusion clause which are clear and fairly susceptible of one meaning only even after due allowance has been made for the presumption in favour of the implied primary and secondary obligations.

The interpretation of exclusion clauses in commercial contracts should now also take into account the principles set out by Lord Hoffmann in *Investors Compensation Scheme Ltd v West Bromwich Building Society* [1998] 1 WLR 896. There he said that 'almost all the old intellectual baggage of "legal" interpretation has been discarded'. What this meant in the context of the interpretation of exclusion clauses was explained by Lord Hoffmann in his dissenting speech in *BCCI v Ali* [2002] 1 AC 251:

> My Lords, the lesson which I would draw from the development of the rules for construing exemption clauses is that the judicial creativity, bordering on judicial legislation, which the application of that doctrine involved is a desperate remedy, to be invoked only if it is necessary to remedy a widespread injustice. Otherwise there is much to be said for giving effect to what on ordinary principles of construction the parties agreed ...
>
> The disappearance of artificial rules for the construction of exemption clauses seems to me in accordance with the general trend in matters of construction, which has been to try to assimilate judicial techniques of construction to those which would be used by a reasonable speaker of the language in the interpretation of any serious utterance in ordinary life. In *Investors Compensation Scheme Ltd v West Bromwich Building Society* [1998] 1 WLR 896, 912, I said with the concurrence of three other members of the House: 'Almost all the old intellectual baggage of "legal" interpretation has been discarded.' But if [counsel for the claimant's] submissions on the rules of construction are accepted, a substantial piece of baggage will have been retrieved. Lord Keeper Henley's ghost (*Salkeld v Vernon* 1 Eden 64) will have struck back. I think it would be an unfortunate retreat into formalism if the outcome of this case were to require employers using the services of Acas to add verbiage to the form of release in order to attain the comprehensiveness which it is obviously intended to achieve.

The authority of this statement was somewhat difficult to predict. It was clearly *obiter* because the case concerned the interpretation of a release clause, not the interpretation of an exclusion clause. In addition, the statement was made in the context of a dissenting speech. Nevertheless, the comments were of significance because they were made in respect of Lord Hoffmann's majority speech in *Investors Compensation Scheme*. More recently, in *Keele University v Price Waterhouse* [2004] PNLR 43, for example, the Court of Appeal confirmed that exclusion clauses must be interpreted in accordance with the principles of interpretation set out by Lord Hoffmann in *Investors Compensation Scheme* (see also the cases cited above at 7.2.2.2.1). The court's primary purpose is to give effect to the intention of the parties. If the old rules of interpretation are found to be contrary to that purpose they will not be applied (also see *HIH Casualty and General Insurance v Chase Manhattan Bank* [2003] UKHL 6). See further *Transocean Drilling UK Ltd v Providence Resources Plc* [2016] EWCA Civ 372 where Moore-Bick LJ stated:

> **28.** I fully accept that where the language of an exclusion clause leaves room for doubt as to its meaning, the principle applied in these cases may provide a valuable tool for ascertaining its correct meaning and in some cases it may lead to the conclusion that a restricted meaning must be given to the clause in question in order to achieve the parties' common objective. But it does not in my view provide sufficient justification for overriding the parties' intention where that has been clearly expressed. The principle of freedom of contract, which is still fundamental to our commercial law, requires the court to respect and give effect to the parties' agreement. One of the striking features of this contract, to which I have already adverted, is the extent to which the parties have agreed to accept responsibility for losses that might otherwise have been recoverable as damages for breach of contract. If, as a result of incorporating several different provisions of that kind, the parties have effectively agreed to exclude any liability for damages for any breaches, it is difficult to see why the court should not give effect to their agreement.

More recently in *The Federal Republic of Nigeria v JP Morgan Chase Bank, NA Andrews* [2019] EWHC 347 Burrows QC (sitting as a Judge of the High Court) stated:

> 34. When Lord Hoffmann set out the modern approach to contractual interpretation in *Investment Compensation Scheme v West Bromwich*, he said, at 912: 'Almost all the old intellectual baggage of "legal" interpretation has been discarded'. One question that arises, therefore, is whether the traditional rule of interpretation contra proferentem survives and in what form. In the context of exemption clauses that rule was to the effect that an exemption clause should be construed strictly against the person who drew up the exemption clause or was relying on it. But the recent authorities – see, especially, *HIH Casualty and General Insurance Ltd v Chase Manhattan Bank* [2003] UKHL 6, [2003] 2 Lloyd's Rep 61, at [11], [58]–[67], [95], [116]; *Stocznia Gdynia SA v Gearbulk Holdings Ltd* [2009] EWCA Civ 75, [2010] QB 27, at [23]; *Capita (Bamstead 2011) Ltd v FRIB Group Ltd* [2015] EWCA Civ 1310, [2016] QB 835, at [10]; *Nobahar-Cookson v Hut Group Ltd* [2016] EWCA Civ 128, [2016] 1 CLC 573, at [18]–[21] (and see generally *Chitty on Contracts* (ed Beale) (33rd edn, 2018) paras 15-012–15-020) – indicate that the law is as follows:
>
> i. The ambiguity of who is the 'proferens' (is it the person who drew up the exemption or the person relying on it?) means that reference to a *contra proferentem* rule is problematic.
> ii. In any event, the modern objective and contextual approach to the meaning of the words, with business common sense and purpose also being relevant in some cases, renders it unnecessary to regard there as being a separate *contra proferentem* rule.
> iii. Applying the modern approach, the force of what was the contra proferentem rule is embraced by recognising that a party is unlikely to have agreed to give up a valuable right that it would otherwise have had without clear words. And as Moore-Bick LJ put it in the *Stocznia* case, at [23], 'The more valuable the right, the clearer the language will need to be'. So, for example, clear words will generally be needed before a court will conclude that the agreement excludes a party's liability for its own negligence. The well-known principles in *Canada Steamship Lines Ltd v The King* [1952] AC 192 (that general words, not explicitly mentioning negligence, will not exclude or indemnify against negligence unless that is the only possible liability) should be regarded as a flexible guide and not as a rigid code.

> 35. I should add for completeness that the passing of the Unfair Contract Terms Act 1977 (and see now the Consumer Rights Act 2015) adds a further reason for not distorting standard principles of interpretation in the context of exemption clauses (and indemnity clauses in consumer contracts) given the power conferred on the courts by the legislature to strike down such clauses as unreasonable.

Compare *Earl of Plymouth v Rees* [2019] EWHC 1008 (Ch) at [56] where Judge Keyser QC stated:

> This is not a matter of applying a special rule that a certain kind of provision must be construed against a particular party. It is simply a matter of applying the normal approach to construction. Accordingly, if, having regard to all relevant matters, the court finds that the normal approach to construction results in ambiguity, there is nothing irrational in resorting to the *contra proferentem* rule.

See also *Persimmon Homes Ltd v Ove Arup and Partners Ltd* [2017] EWCA Civ 373 and *Hut Group Ltd v Nobahar-Cookson* [2016] EWCA Civ 128.

7.2.3 Fundamental breach

A further rule that the common law sought to introduce to restrict the impact of exclusion clauses was the doctrine of fundamental breach. The rule stated that some breaches of contract are so serious that no exclusion clause can cover them. The idea is rooted in the English tradition that there is a core obligation, the consideration for the contract, which is more fundamental than any condition or warranty and therefore cannot be excluded.

***Harbutt's Plasticine Ltd v Wayne Tank and Pump Co Ltd* [1970] 1 QB 447**

Facts: The defendants agreed to design and install pipe work in the plaintiffs' factory for storing and dispensing a heavy wax. The contract contained printed conditions including a condition 15 which stated that liability would be limited to the contract price of the work. The defendants installed pipe work which was wholly unsuitable for the purpose. This resulted in a fire which destroyed the plaintiffs' factory. The trial judge held that there had been a fundamental breach of contract which disentitled the defendants from relying on the limitation clause.

Held: The Court of Appeal dismissed the appeal.

Lord Denning MR:

Fundamental breach

Assuming that condition 15 does, in terms, purport to limit the liability of the defendants, the next question is whether the defendants were guilty of a fundamental breach of contract which disentitled them from relying on it. I eschew in this context the word 'repudiation' because it is applied so differently in so many different contexts, as Lord Wright explained in *Heyman v Darwins Ltd* [1942] AC 356, 378. There was no repudiation in this case by the defendants – not, at any rate, in its proper sense of denying they are bound by the contract. The defendants have always acknowledged the contract. All that has happened is that they have broken it. If they have broken it in a way that goes to the very root of it, then it is a fundamental breach. If they have broken it in a lesser way, then the breach is not fundamental.

In considering the consequences of a fundamental breach, it is necessary to draw a distinction between a fundamental breach which still leaves the contract open to be performed, and a fundamental breach which itself brings the contract to an end.

(i) The first group

In cases where the contract is still open to be performed, the effect of a fundamental breach is this: it gives the innocent party, when he gets to know of it, an option either to *affirm* the contract or to disaffirm it. If he elects to *affirm* it, then it remains in being *for the future* on both sides. Each has a right to sue for damages for *past or future* breaches. If he elects to disaffirm it (namely, accepts the fundamental breach as determining the contract), then it is at an end from that moment. It does not continue into the future. All that is left is the right to sue for past breaches or for the fundamental breach, but there is no right to sue for *future* breaches.

(ii) The second group

In cases where the fundamental breach itself brings the contract to an end, there is no room for any option in the innocent party. The present case is typical of this group. The fire was so disastrous that it destroyed the mill itself. If the fire had been accidental, it would certainly have meant that the contract was frustrated and brought to an end by a supervening event; just as in the leading case in 1863 when the Surrey Music Hall was burnt down: see *Taylor v Caldwell* (1863) 3 B & S 826 …

All that I have said thus far is so obvious that it needs no authority. But now I come to the great question. When a contract is brought to an end by a fundamental breach by one of the parties, can the guilty party rely on an exclusion or limitation clause so as to avoid or limit his liability for the breach?

I propose to take first the group of cases when the fundamental breach does not automatically bring the contract to an end, but it has to be accepted by the innocent party as doing so. Such a case was *Karsales (Harrow) Ltd v Wallis* [1956] 1 WLR 936, where the hirer, on discovering the fundamental breach, at once rejected the car. In this group it is settled that once he accepts it, the innocent party can sue for the breach and the guilty party cannot rely on the exclusion or limitation clause. That clearly appears from the speeches in the House of Lords in *Suisse Atlantique Société d'Armement Maritime SA v NV Rotterdamsche Kolen Centrale* [1967] 1 AC 361. Lord Reid said, at p 398:

> 'If fundamental breach is established the next question is what effect, if any, that has on the applicability of other terms of the contract. This question has often arisen with regard to clauses excluding liability, in whole or in part, of the party in breach. I do not think there is generally much difficulty where the innocent party has elected to treat the breach as a repudiation, bring the contract to an end and sue for damages. Then the whole contract has ceased to exist including the exclusion clause, and I do not see how that clause can then be used to exclude an action for loss which will be suffered by the innocent party after it has ceased to exist, such as loss of the profit which would have accrued if the contract had run its full term.'

When their Lordships said the contract 'is at an end', they meant, of course, for the future. Such an ending disentitles the guilty party from relying on an exclusion clause in respect of the breach. Such, then, is established as law when there is 'a fundamental breach accepted by the innocent party', that is, when the innocent party has an election to treat the contract as at an end and does so. The position must, I think, be the same when the defendant has been guilty of such a fundamental breach that the contract is *automatically* at an end without the innocent party having an election. The innocent party is entitled to sue for damages for the breach, and the guilty party cannot rely on the exclusion or limitation clause: for the simple reason that he, by his own breach, has brought the contract to an end; with the result that he cannot rely on the clause to exempt or limit his liability for that breach.

> The one question in this case is, therefore: Were the defendants guilty of a fundamental breach which brought the contract to an end? For, if so, they cannot rely on the limitation clause. It was suggested that, in order to determine whether a breach is fundamental or not, you must look at the quality of it, and not at the results. I do not accept this suggestion. It is not the breach itself which counts so much, but the event resulting from it ...
>
> So I come to the question: were the breaches by the defendants and the consequences of them so fundamental as to bring the contract to an end, and thus disentitle the defendants from relying on the limitation clause? The judge thought that they were. I agree with him ...
>
> Before leaving this part of the case, I would just like to say what, in my opinion, is the result of the *Suisse Atlantique* case. It affirms the long line of cases in this court that when one party has been guilty of a fundamental breach of the contract, that is, a breach which goes to the very root of it, and the other side accepts it, so that the contract comes to an end – or if it comes to an end anyway by reason of the breach – then the guilty party cannot rely on an exception or limitation clause to escape from his liability for the breach.
>
> If the innocent party, on getting to know of the breach, does not accept it, but keeps the contract in being (as in *Charterhouse Credit Co Ltd v Tolly* [1963] 2 QB 683), then it is a matter of construction whether the guilty party can rely on the exception or limitation clause, always remembering that it is not to be supposed that the parties intended to give a guilty party a blanket to cover up his own misconduct or indifference, or to enable him to turn a blind eye to his obligations.

Lord Denning's reliance on *Suisse Atlantique* was misplaced and his summary of the decision faulty In *Suisse Atlantique*, the House of Lords actually expressly disapproved of the argument that the doctrine of fundamental breach was a substantive rule of law precluding reliance on an exclusion clause. Viscount Dilhourne said:

> In my view, it is not right to say that the law prohibits and nullifies a clause exempting or limiting liability for a fundamental breach or breach of a fundamental term. Such a rule of law would involve a restriction on freedom of contract and in the older cases I can find no trace of it.

According to the House of Lords, the doctrine of fundamental breach was a rule of construction, not a rule of law. It was relevant to the question of whether the clause covered the breach in question – the more serious the breach the more specific the wording of the clause would need to be. It did not, however, act as a rule of law prohibiting reliance on exemption clauses in cases of fundamental breach.

In *Harbutt's Plasticine*, the Court of Appeal sought to distinguish *Suisse Atlantique* on the ground that the claimant in that case had affirmed the contract following the alleged breach. Lord Denning suggested that the parties following the breach should only follow the approach adopted in *Suisse Atlantique* in cases where there was an affirmation of the contract, and not where the breach itself brought the contract to the end. In cases that fell into this latter category, including *Harbutt's Plasticine*, his Lordship suggested that reliance on an exclusion clause should be prohibited. The problem with Lord Denning's argument is that it ignores the well-established legal principle that a breach of contract never in itself brings a contract to an end. It merely gives rise to an option at the behest of the innocent party, either to accept the breach and terminate the contract or to affirm the contract and claim for damages (see Chapter 14). Contrary to this well-established principle, the Court of Appeal, in *Harbutt's Plasticine*, claimed that this did not apply to certain fundamental breaches, which themselves brought the contract to an end without the need for repudiation by the innocent party. This view, and the fundamental breach doctrine that it supported, was later categorically rejected by the House of Lords in *Photo Production Ltd v Securicor Transport Ltd*.

***Photo Production Ltd v Securicor Transport Ltd* [1980] AC 827**

Facts: Photo Production had a contract with Securicor whereby a security guard visited their factory on a night patrol. Unfortunately, one of the guards employed by Securicor to carry out these duties started a fire at the premises which got out of control and destroyed Photo Production's factory. The loss caused was £615,000. There was an exclusion clause in the contract stating: 'Under no circumstances shall (Securicor) be responsible for any injurious act or default by any employee of the Company unless such act or default could have been foreseen and avoided by the exercise of due diligence on the part of the Company as his employer.' It was clear on the facts that Securicor had not been negligent in employing the guard who started the fire. The question arose as to whether the clause was nullified by a fundamental breach. The Court of Appeal held that it was.

Held: The House of Lords allowed the appeal and held that the exclusion clause applied despite the fact that a fundamental breach had occurred.

Lord Wilberforce: I have no second thoughts as to the main proposition that the question whether, and to what extent, an exclusion clause is to be applied to a fundamental breach, or a breach of a fundamental term, or indeed to any breach of contract, is a matter of construction of the contract. Many difficult questions arise and will continue to arise in the infinitely varied situations in which contracts come to be breached by repudiatory breaches, accepted or not, by anticipatory breaches, by breaches of conditions or of various terms and whether by negligent, or deliberate action or otherwise. But there are ample resources in the normal rules of contract law for dealing with these without the superimposition of a judicially invented rule of law. I am content to leave the matter there with some supplementary observations:

1. The doctrine of 'fundamental breach' in spite of its imperfections and doubtful parentage has served a useful purpose. There was a large number of problems, productive of injustice, in which it was worse than unsatisfactory to leave exception clauses to operate ... But since then Parliament has taken a hand: it has passed the Unfair Contract Terms Act 1977. This Act applies to consumer contracts and those based on standard terms and enables exception clauses to be applied with regard to what is just and reasonable ...

   At the stage of negotiation as to the consequences of a breach, there is everything to be said for allowing the parties to estimate their respective claims according to the contractual provisions they have themselves made, rather than for facing them with a legal complex so uncertain as the doctrine of fundamental breach must be. What, for example, would have been the position of the respondents' factory if instead of being destroyed it had been damaged, slightly or moderately or severely? At what point does the doctrine (with what logical justification I have not understood) decide, *ex post facto*, that the breach was (factually) fundamental before going on to ask whether legally it is to be regarded as fundamental? ...

2. The case of *Harbutt* [1970] 1 QB 447 must clearly be overruled. It would be enough to put that upon its radical inconsistency with the *Suisse Atlantique* case [1967] 1 AC 361. But even if the matter were *res integra* I would find the decision to be based upon unsatisfactory reasoning as to the 'termination' of the contract and the effect of 'termination' on the plaintiffs' claim for damage. I have, indeed, been unable to understand how the doctrine can be reconciled with the well accepted principle of law, stated by the highest modern authority, that when in the context of a breach of contract one speaks

of 'termination', what is meant is no more than that the innocent party or, in some cases, both parties, are excused from further performance. Damages, in such cases, are then claimed under the contract, so what reason in principle can there be for disregarding what the contract itself says about damages – whether it 'liquidates' them, or limits them, or excludes them?

The decision of the House of Lords in *Photo Production* appeared to 'put to bed' the doctrine of fundamental breach (see the comments of Lord Bridge in *Mitchell (George) (Chesterhall) Ltd v Finney Lock Seeds Ltd* [1983] 2 AC 803, 813 and, more recently, Judge Peter Coulson QC in *Decoma UK Limited v Haden Drysys* [2005] EWHC 2948 (TCC), cf. [2006] EWCA Civ 723 (on appeal)). Their Lordships concluded that the doctrine was no longer necessary following the enactment of the UCTA 1977 and *Harbutt's Plasticine* was explicitly overruled. See also *Polypearl Limited v E.on Energy Solutions Ltd* [2014] EWHC 3045 (QB).

Nevertheless, the seriousness of the breach continues to be of relevance to the issue of interpretation and, at times, the courts have come perilously close to reintroducing the fundamental breach doctrine through the back door. It is arguable that this is precisely what Stuart Smith LJ did in *Motis Exports v Dampskibsselsk* [2000] 1 Lloyd's Rep 211. We have already considered the facts of the case. In coming to the conclusion that the exclusion clause did not cover a fraudulent breach of contract, Stuart Smith LJ said:

> I also agree with the Judge [at first instance] that even if the language was apt to cover such a case, it is not a construction which should be adopted, involving as it does excuse from performing an obligation of such fundamental importance. As a matter of construction the Courts lean against such a result if adequate content can be given to the clause.

In practice, there may not be much difference between the substantive doctrine of fundamental breach and the interpretation approach approved by the House of Lords in *Photo Production*.

7.3 Unfair Contract Terms Act 1977

In the previous section we considered the common law techniques used by the courts to regulate exclusion/limitation clauses. To a large extent these have proven to be either flawed or ineffective, and in 1977, Parliament intervened to enact the Unfair Contract Terms Act 1977. The effect of this Act was to render certain exclusion clauses ineffective and to subject others to a test of reasonableness. More recently the Law Commission recommended substantial revision of the 1977 Act. This was largely due to the impact of the Unfair Terms in Consumer Contract Regulations 1994, later repealed and replaced by the Unfair Terms in Consumer Contract Regulations 1999.

***Unfair Terms in Contracts*, 2005, Law Com No 292, Scot Law Com, No 199, Cm 6464 Summary**

1. In 2001, the Department of Trade and Industry asked the Law Commission and Scottish Law Commission to rewrite the law of unfair contract terms as a single regime, in a clearer and more accessible style. At the same time we were asked to consider whether to extend the legislation to protect businesses, particularly small businesses.
2. On 24 February we published a final report setting out our detailed recommendations, together with a draft Bill.

The problem

3. As the law currently stands, there are two major pieces of legislation dealing with unfair contract terms. The Unfair Contract Terms Act 1977 sets out the traditional UK approach, while the Unfair Terms in Consumer Contracts Regulations 1999 implement the 1993 EU Directive. The two laws contain inconsistent and overlapping provisions, using different language and concepts to produce similar but not identical effects. A law that affects ordinary people in their everyday lives had been made unnecessarily complicated and difficult.
4. The 1977 Act is written in a particularly dense style, which even specialist lawyers find difficult to follow. This is made even more complicated by the fact that the Act contains two Parts: one for England, Wales and Northern Ireland, and one for Scotland. The two Parts produce almost the same effect but use different language to do so. Meanwhile the 1999 Regulations use European concepts that are unfamiliar to UK lawyers. The combination of legislation has led to widespread confusion among consumers, businesses and their advisers.
5. The draft Bill rewrites both laws for the whole of the UK in a way that is much clearer and easier to follow. We have also plugged some gaps in protection.

The current law: differences between the act and regulations

6. The 1977 Act extends to a wide range of contracts, including consumer, business, private and employment contracts. However, it only covers a narrow range of terms. It is designed to control exclusion clauses, where one party attempts to exclude or limit their normal liability for negligence or breach of contract, or tries to 'render a contractual performance substantially different from that which was reasonably expected. The 1999 Regulations cover a much wider range of terms, extending to any term other than the main subject matter or the price. However, they only apply to consumer contracts.
7. Under the 1977 Act some terms are automatically ineffective. Under the Regulations, no term is automatically unfair. Instead, they are all subject to a fairness test. However the Regulations permit the Office of Fair Trading (OFT) and other bodies to go to court to prevent unfair terms from being used. These preventive powers have proved to be an important way of regulating the market.
8. The Act and Regulations also differ in their treatment of negotiated clauses; in the way they phrase the fairness test; and in their burden of proof.

Consumer contracts

9. Our aim is to produce a single, unified regime to cover the whole of the UK that preserves the existing level of consumer protection. Where the Act and Regulations differ, we have rounded up rather than rounded down. Thus for consumer contracts, the draft Bill:
   (1) extends to all the terms currently covered by the Regulations (not just exclusion clauses);
   (2) continues to hold that terms which limit liability for death or personal injury, or which exclude basic undertakings about the quality and fitness of goods are ineffective;
   (3) includes negotiated clauses as well as standard clauses (as does the 1977 Act). This closes a current loophole by which some businesses can, for example, demand unreasonable deposits by saying that they are prepared to negotiate the amount from 100% to 75%; and
   (4) states that in claims brought by consumers, the burden of proof lies on the business to show that the term is fair. Again this follows the 1977 Act. The business will generally have far greater resources than the consumer so, where the fairness of a term is in issue, it should be required to justify its position. This is not the case in preventive powers, where it will still be up to the OFT or other body to show that the term is unfair.
10. The OFT and other bodies will gain some additional powers to take action against notices. For example, the OFT would be able to demand that a sign in a store car-park saying 'no liability is accepted for injury' is taken down. Such signs have long been ineffective in legal terms but organisations continue to use them, presumably in an attempt to discourage people from claiming their rights.

Protecting small businesses

11. The report also recommends improved protection for small businesses. At present, where a business contracts on the other party's standard written terms of business, it may challenge unfair exclusion clauses. This means that the court may review the fairness of a term that excludes or limits liability for negligence or breach of contract, or purports to allow the other party to render a contractual performance substantially different from that which was reasonably expected.
12. We were told that small businesses frequently find themselves signing contracts that contain other unfair terms, which the law does not allow to be challenged. This is especially true where a small farmer, manufacturer or builder supplies a much larger business. The small business may be required to indemnify the larger business for losses that are not their fault, or forfeit deposits, or accept variations of price after the contract has been agreed. They may find that the larger business has reserved the right to terminate a contract at will, or for only a minor default, while the small business is bound more rigorously by the contract.
13. We do not wish to interfere with business contracts that are genuinely negotiated between the parties. However, there is a problem when one party imposes its standard terms on a vulnerable small business. The small business may not understand the term or its consequences; and even if it does understand the term it will often lack the bargaining strength to change it.
14. The draft Bill includes special protection for the smallest and most vulnerable businesses, commonly referred to as 'micro businesses'. We define these as businesses with nine or fewer staff.
15. Under our proposals, these very small businesses will be able to challenge any standard term of the contract that has not been altered through negotiation, and is not the main subject matter of the contract or the price.
16. However, we do not wish to interfere where contracts are already sufficiently regulated, or where the business is sufficiently sophisticated to look after its interests. We therefore set out a number of exceptions to the new small business protections. We exclude contracts for financial services, contracts over £500,000 and situations where the apparently small business is associated with other businesses, so that overall the group has more than nine employees. We also recommend that the exemptions currently in the 1977 Act should apply to the new controls on small business contracts. These exclude, for example, contracts for land, intellectual property, or security interests or contracts to form or dissolve contracts. Here people will usually seek legal advice.
17. In an ideal world, a well-resourced organisation would use preventive powers to protect small businesses generally, by challenging those that imposed unfair standard terms on them. However, we have not been able to find an organisation with the resources to take on this task. The draft Bill does not presently include preventive powers to be used on behalf of small businesses. However, if resources could be found, this would provide useful protection. Many small businesses told us about unfair terms that could be challenged under the present law, but which are still used because the small business lacks the ability to bring court action.

Other contracts

18. At present, the 1977 Act includes several other types of contract, such as contracts between larger businesses, employment contracts and private sales. Here our aim is to preserve the effect of the current law, while setting it out in a way that is clearer and easier to understand.
19. We do, however, recommend some small reductions in the way that the 1977 Act regulates negotiated contracts between businesses. At present, the Act allows courts to review any term that limits the effect of the implied undertakings in the Sale of Goods Act 1979, which state that goods should match their description or sample, be of satisfactory quality and fit for their purpose. These controls apply to negotiated terms as well as to standard terms. We think it would be very unlikely for a court to find that a clause is unfair when it had been genuinely negotiated between businesses, and we are not aware that any cases have been brought to challenge negotiated terms under these provisions.

Under our proposals, businesses will generally be allowed to negotiate to limit contractual liability: the controls will only apply to standard terms.

International contracts and choice of law

20. Much criticism has been levelled at how the 1977 Act deals with business contracts involving the cross-border sale of goods. Although the avowed aim of section 26 was to exempt export contracts while protecting UK importers, it was drafted in a way that exempted many import contracts and applied the legislation to some exporters. The Draft Bill rewrites this section to exempt only those contracts under which goods are exported or supplied abroad.

21. For consumer contracts, the Draft Bill prevents businesses from using non-UK law if the consumer was living in the UK when the contract was made and took all the steps necessary to conclude the contract there.

The work of the Law Commissions in this area was influential in shaping the CRA 2015, although not all of their recommendations made it into the CRA 2015 (for example, the recommendations in relation to 'unfair' terms and small businesses). As noted above, prior to the CRA 2015 the UCTA 1977 applied, to varying degrees, to consumer and non-consumer contracts. Following the CRA 2015, which repealed the UTCCR 1999, there is a much clearer separation between consumer and non-consumer contracts: broadly the CRA 2015 regulates consumer contracts and, for present purposes, an amended UCTA 1977 regulates non-consumer contracts.

In most cases concerning an exclusion/limitation clause in a consumer contract, or an exclusion clause in the defendant's written standard terms, it is likely that the relevant statutory provisions will prove to be determinative of the outcome of the case. Indeed, in many cases the statutory provisions will be considered first of all because they are the most significant issue. This is not always the case, however, because if the term has not been incorporated into the contract or does not cover the breach that has occurred then the clause will have no effect at all and the statutory provisions will be irrelevant.

***University of Keele v Price Waterhouse* [2004] PNLR 43**

Facts: Price Waterhouse contracted with the University of Keele to implement a profit related pay scheme. After the scheme had been operated for some three years, it came to light that it did not meet the Inland Revenue's requirements, and it was cancelled. University of Keele brought a claim against Price Waterhouse for the tax it had to pay after cancellation, the savings it would have made had the scheme been valid and the professional fees expended. Price Waterhouse sought to rely on a clause in the contract which stated the following: 'Subject to the preceding paragraph we accept liability to pay damages in respect of loss or damage suffered by you as a direct result of our providing the Services. All other liability is expressly excluded, in particular consequential loss, failure to realise anticipated savings or benefits and a failure to obtain registration of the scheme.' University of Keele contended that the clause did not cover the claimed losses, and that if it did, the clause was ineffective under UCTA 1977.

Held: The Court of Appeal held that on the plain meaning of the clause the relevant loss was not excluded. Therefore the question of whether the clause was ineffective under UCTA 1977 was a moot point and did not need to be discussed.

7.3.1 Scope

Although the UCTA 1977 has had a very significant effect on the law relating to exclusion/ limitation clauses, it must be remembered that it does not apply to all contracts. Indeed, the name of the Act is rather misleading in this respect, as George Applebey has explained (*Contract Law*, 2001, p 283, London: Sweet & Maxwell):

> It only deals with exemption [and limitation] clauses and does not impose a fairness test. It is not restricted to contract law but deals with liability for negligence and other forms of liability, such as that of occupiers of business premises. Although it was created largely as a measure of consumer protection, the 1977 Act, in several important areas, also deals with some exemptions where both parties are in business. A more accurately descriptive title would therefore be the Void and Unreasonable Exemptions Act.

Before discussing the main protective provisions of the Act, it is important to explore its scope.

7.3.1.1 Business liability

Scope of Part I section 1

(3) In the case of both contract and tort, sections 2 to 7 apply (except where the contrary is stated in section 6(4)) only to business liability, that is liability for breach of obligations or duties arising –

(a) from things done or to be done by a person in the course of a business (whether his own business or another's); or

(b) from the occupation of premises used for business purposes of the occupier; and references to liability are to be read accordingly but liability of an occupier of premises for breach of an obligation or duty towards a person obtaining access to the premises for recreational or educational purposes, being liability for loss or damage suffered by reason of the dangerous state of the premises, is not a business liability of the occupier unless granting that person such access for the purposes concerned falls within the business purposes of the occupier.

This section makes it clear that the protective provisions of the Act generally only apply to attempts to exclude or restrict business liability. A non-business contractor is generally free to include exclusion/limitation clauses without fear of their being declared ineffective under the Act. There is no comprehensive definition of business in the Act, although s 14 does provide the following:

Interpretation of Part I section 14

In this Part of this Act –

'business' includes a profession and the activities of any government department or local or public authority.

There is one notable exception to the 'business' requirement of s 1(3): s 6(4). We will consider this in greater detail below.

7.3.1.2 Exclusions

There are certain contracts, listed in Schedule 1, which are not within the scope of the main protective provisions of the UCTA 1977.

Schedule 1

1. Sections 2 and 3 of this Act do not extend to –
   (a) any contract of insurance (including a contract to pay an annuity on human life);
   (b) any contract so far as it relates to the creation or transfer of an interest in land, or to the termination of such an interest, whether by extinction, merger, surrender, forfeiture or otherwise;
   (c) any contract so far as it relates to the creation or transfer of a right or interest in any patent, trade mark, copyright or design right, registered design, technical or commercial information or other intellectual property, or relates to the termination of any such right or interest;
   (d) any contract so far as it relates –
      (i) to the formation or dissolution of a company (which means any body corporate or unincorporated association and includes a partnership), or
      (ii) to its constitution or the rights or obligations of its corporators or members;
   (e) any contract so far as it relates to the creation or transfer of securities or of any right or interest in securities;
   (f) anything that is governed by Article 6 of Regulation (EU) No 181/2011 of the European Parliament and of the Council of 16 February 2011 concerning the rights of passengers in bus and coach transport and amending Regulation (EC) No 2006/2004.
2. Section 2(1) extends to –
   (a) any contract of marine salvage or towage;
   (b) any charterparty of a ship or hovercraft; and
   (c) any contract for the carriage of goods by ship or hovercraft;

   but subject to this sections 2 and 3 and 7 do not extend to any such contract.

   . . .

4. Section 2(1) and (2) do not extend to a contract of employment, except in favour of the employee.

The most significant exclusions contained in Schedule 1 include:

- contracts of insurance;
- contracts relating to the creation, transfer or termination of an interest in land. This includes continuing covenants under a lease: *Electricity Supply Nominees v IAF Group* [1993] 1 WLR 1059; and
- contracts concerning the creation, transfer or termination of intellectual property rights.

It should also be noted that under paragraph 2, the UCTA only has limited application in relation to various types of shipping contract. Under paragraph 4, s 2(1) and (2) (which deal with the exclusion of liability for negligence) do not apply other than in favour of the employee. Finally s 26 states that the Act does not apply to liability arising under an international supply contract (cf. *Trident Turboprop (Dublin) Ltd v First Flight Couriers Ltd* [2009] EWCA Civ 290).

7.3.1.3 Clauses covered

Section 13 of the UCTA adopts a wide definition of an exclusion clause.

Varieties of exemption clause section 13

(1) To the extent that this Part of this Act prevents the exclusion or restriction of any liability it also prevents –
   (a) making the liability or its enforcement subject to restrictive or onerous conditions;

(b) excluding or restricting any right or remedy in respect of the liability, or subjecting a person to any prejudice in consequence of his pursuing any such right or remedy;

(c) excluding or restricting rules of evidence or procedure;

and (to that extent) sections 2, 6 and 7 also prevent excluding or restricting liability by reference to terms and notices which exclude or restrict the relevant obligation or duty.

(2) But an agreement in writing to submit present or future differences to arbitration is not to be treated under this Part of this Act as excluding or restricting any liability.

The operation of s 13 can be seen in *Smith v Eric S Bush*.

Smith v Eric S Bush [1990] 1 AC 831

Facts: The plaintiff applied to a building society for a mortgage to assist her in purchasing a home. The building society instructed the defendants, a firm of surveyors, to prepare a report on the property as to its value and condition. The defendants' valuer, who carried out the inspection, noticed that two chimney breasts had been removed but he negligently failed to check whether the chimneys above had been left adequately supported. The chimneys were not adequately supported and one of them subsequently collapsed causing widespread damage to the rest of the house. The plaintiff claimed damages from the defendants for the loss sustained as a result of the negligent report. The defendants contended that they had excluded liability for negligence by a notice in the contract stating that neither the society nor the surveyor would accept responsibility for the surveyor's report.

Held: The House of Lords held that whilst the surveyor could seek to disclaim liability for negligence by an exclusion notice, such a notice was subject to s 2(2) UCTA. The court said that there could be no difference between a clause that sought to restrict the negligence obligation, and one which sought to exclude negligence liability.

Lord Templeman: In these circumstances it is necessary to consider ... whether the disclaimers of liability are notices which fall within the Unfair Contract Terms Act 1977. In *Harris v Wyre Forest Council* [1988] QB 835, the Court of Appeal (Kerr and Nourse LJJ and Caulfield J) accepted an argument that the Act of 1977 did not apply because the council by their express disclaimer refused to obtain a valuation save on terms that the valuer would not be under any obligation to Mr and Mrs Harris to take reasonable care or exercise reasonable skill. The council did not exclude liability for negligence but excluded negligence so that the valuer and the council never came under a duty of care to Mr and Mrs Harris and could not be guilty of negligence. This construction would not give effect to the manifest intention of the Act but would emasculate the Act. The construction would provide no control over standard form exclusion clauses which individual members of the public are obliged to accept. A party to a contract or a tortfeasor could opt out of the Act of 1977 by declining in the words of Nourse LJ, at p 845, to recognise 'their own answerability to the plaintiff ...'

Section 13(1) of the Act prevents the exclusion of any right or remedy and (to that extent) section 2 also prevents the exclusion of liability:

'by reference to ... notices which exclude ... the relevant obligation or duty'.

... In my opinion both these provisions support the view that the Act of 1977 requires that all exclusion notices which would in common law provide a defence to an action for negligence must satisfy the requirement of reasonableness.

The answer to the second question involved in these appeals is that the disclaimer of liability made by the council on its own behalf in the *Harris* case and by the Abbey National on behalf of the appellants in the *Smith* case, constitute notices which fall within the Unfair Contract Terms Act 1977 and must satisfy the requirement of reasonableness.

It is clear that, under s 13, the test for an exclusion clause is based upon the nature and substance of the clause, not merely upon its form. But this in itself creates problems. Once it is admitted that some obligation-defining clauses fall within the scope of the Act, it is difficult to know where to draw the line (cf. *IFE Fund SA v Goldman Sachs International* [2007] EWCA Civ 811). All contract terms are obligation-defining to a certain extent. What test can be applied to make an appropriate 'form and substance' distinction for the purposes of s 13(1)? Professor MacDonald has suggested the following test as outlined below.

MacDonald, E, *Exemption Clauses and Unfair Terms*, 2nd edn, 2006, Horsham: Tottel Publishing, pp 105–108

Is there some distinction 'in nature' between exclusion clauses and those defining obligations which could provide a form and substance distinction for the purposes of the Act? It can be contended that what must be looked at is the creation, or origin, of the obligations and the relationship of the term (or notice) in question to that creation. In other words, the distinction which must be made is between the exclusion of an obligation purely because of the status of the words in question and its circumstantial displacement. If there is circumstantial displacement, the term or notice in question is 'in nature' part of the definition of the obligation. If the displacement is purely because of the status of the words, then the term or notice -the words in question – is, in nature, an exclusion of liability. In order to consider whether the displacement is 'circumstantial' or merely due to the status of the words as a term, the situation must be viewed absent the artificialities which the law has placed upon it. Artificialities can occur in the very drafting of terms (although less so since *Investors*) and in almost every form of incorporation, and can lead to a situation in which 'the relatively unsophisticated or unwary party will not realise what or how little has been promised' and such artificialities can be recognised even when the situation is viewed objectively, as will normally be required ...

The issue was also considered by Newey J in *Avrora Fine Arts Investment Ltd v Christie, Manson & Woods Ltd* [2012] EWHC 2198 (Ch) at [136]–[146]:

138 It is Avrora's case that, were it not for UCTA, the Conditions would exclude or restrict Christie's' liability for 'negligence' insofar as they negate an assumption of responsibility as well as in other ways. In support of this submission, Mr Legge relied on *Smith v Eric S Bush* [1990] 1 AC 831, where the Court of Appeal had held that UCTA had no application because a disclaimer of liability would at common law have prevented any duty to take reasonable care arising between the parties. The House of Lords decided that UCTA applied. Lord Griffiths said (at 856–857) that the construction of the Act adopted by the Court of Appeal failed to give due weight to sections 11(3) and 13(1). He explained:

> 'I read these provisions as introducing a 'but for' test in relation to the notice excluding liability. They indicate that the existence of the common law duty to take reasonable care, referred to in section 1(1)(b), is to be judged by considering whether it would exist "but for" the notice excluding liability. The result of taking the notice into account when assessing the existence of a duty of care would result in removing all liability for negligent misstatements from the protection

of the Act. It is permissible to have regard to the second report of the Law Commission on Exemption Clauses (1975) (Law Com No. 69) which is the genesis of the Unfair Contract Terms Act 1977 as an aid to the construction of the Act. Paragraph 127 of that report reads:

> 'Our recommendations in this part of the report are intended to apply to exclusions of liability for negligence where the liability is incurred in the course of a person's business. We consider that they should apply even in cases where the person seeking to rely on the exemption clause was under no legal obligation (such as a contractual obligation) to carry out the activity. This means that, for example, conditions attached to a licence to enter on to land, and disclaimers of liability made where information or advice is given, should be subject to control ...
>
> I have no reason to think that Parliament did not intend to follow this advice and the wording of the Act is, in my opinion, apt to give effect to that intention'.

139 Mr Aldridge, however, submitted that UCTA is not in point. There is, he maintained, a fine but important distinction to be drawn between, on the one hand, terms that exclude or restrict the relevant obligation or duty and, on the other, terms that define the basis on which the defendant provides its services and prevent the obligation or duty accruing in the first place. According to Mr Aldridge, paragraphs 2(b), 3(c) and 5 of the Conditions merely defined the scope of the task undertaken by Christie's and so were not caught by UCTA.

140 Mr Aldridge relied in support of his submissions on *IFE Fund SA v Goldman Sachs International* [2006] EWHC 2887 (Comm), [2007] 1 Lloyd's Rep 264 and *Titan Steel Wheels Ltd v Royal Bank of Scotland plc* [2010] EWHC 211 (Comm), [2010] 2 Lloyd's Rep 92. In the former case, one of the claims advanced depended on the defendant having owed a duty to provide information. As to this, Toulson J said (at paragraph 71):

> '[The claimant] relies on the publication of the SIM [i.e. a Syndicate Information Memorandum] to give rise to the alleged duty of care. The relevant paragraphs of the SIM are not in my view to be characterised in substance as a notice excluding or restricting a liability for negligence, but more fundamentally as going to the issue whether there was a relationship between the parties (amounting to or equivalent to that of professional adviser and advisee) such as to make it just and reasonable to impose the alleged duty of care'.

In the *Titan Steel* case, the claimant sought damages from the defendant bank for losses arising from the alleged mis-selling of derivative products. David Steel J accepted a submission on behalf of the bank that contractual terms on which it relied 'merely defined the basis upon which the bank was providing its services' and so fell outside the ambit of UCTA. Of *Smith v Eric S. Bush*, David Steel J said (at paragraph 104):

> 'The focus of course was the issue of liability for poor service rather than the scope of the service to be provided. Further the decision may have been somewhat overtaken by later decisions in regard to the assumption of responsibility and the move away from any 'but for' test in regard to the existence and extent of any duty'.

141 These cases indicate that documents that define the relationship between parties can fall outside UCTA. On the other hand, *Smith v Eric S. Bush* provides authority for the proposition that where, but for a notice excluding liability, a duty of care would exist, UCTA applies. There is surely scope for argument as to what distinguishes the two situations.

142 In the context of the present case, I find the decision of Christopher Clarke J in *Raiffeisen Zentralbank Osterreich AG v The Royal Bank of Scotland plc* [2010] EWHC 1392 (Comm), [2010] 1 Lloyd's Rep 123 helpful.

One of the issues Christopher Clarke J had to consider in that case was whether certain provisions fell within section 3 of the Misrepresentation Act. In the course of so doing, he referred to a passage from the judgment of Gloster J in *JP Morgan Chase Bank v Springwell Navigation Corp* [2008] EWHC 1186 (Comm) in which she had said (at paragraph 602):

> 'terms which simply define the basis upon which services will be rendered and confirm the basis upon which parties are transacting business are not subject to section 2 of UCTA. Otherwise, every contract which contains contractual terms defining the extent of each party's obligations would have to satisfy the requirement of reasonableness'.

In his judgment, Christopher Clarke J said:

> '313 In *Springwell* Gloster J took the view that terms which simply defined the basis upon which the parties were transacting business did not fall within section 2 of UCTA; otherwise, as she said, all contractual terms that did so would have to satisfy the test of reasonableness. It is obviously advantageous that commercial parties of equal bargaining power should be able to agree what responsibility they are taking (or not taking) towards each other without having to satisfy some reasonableness test. At the same time there is a danger that the 'ingenuity of the draftsman' will insert into a myriad of contracts a clause to the effect that the basis upon which the parties are contracting is that no representations have been made, are intended to be relied on or have been relied on, as a means of evading liability which is intended to be impregnable.
>
> 314 In this respect the key question, as it seems to me, is whether the clause attempts to rewrite history or parts company with reality. If sophisticated commercial parties agree, in terms of which they are both aware, to regulate their future relationship by prescribing the basis on which they will be dealing with each other and what representations they are or are not making, a suitably drafted clause may properly be regarded as establishing that no representations (or none other than honest belief) are being made or are intended to be relied on. Such parties are capable of distinguishing between statements which are to be treated as representations on which the recipient is entitled to rely, and statements which do not have that character, and should be allowed to agree among themselves into which category any given statement may fall.
>
> 315 *Per contra*, to tell the man in the street that the car you are selling him is perfect and then agree that the basis of your contract is that no representations have been made or relied on, may be nothing more than an attempt retrospectively to alter the character and effect of what has gone before, and in substance an attempt to exclude or restrict liability'.

143 This part of Christopher Clarke J's judgment was cited when the *Springwell* case reached the Court of Appeal. Aikens LJ, having referred to a provision stating 'no representation or warranty, express or implied, is or will be made ... in or in relation to such documents or information', said:

> 'However, as Christopher Clarke J trenchantly put the point in the *Raiffeisen* case, '... to tell the man in the street that the car you are selling him is perfect and then agree that the basis of your contract is that no representations have been made or relied on, may be nothing more than an attempt retrospectively to alter the character and effect of what has gone before and in substance be an attempt to exclude or restrict liability.' I would therefore be inclined to regard that part of clause 6 ... as falling within section 3 [of the Misrepresentation Act] and therefore subject to the UCTA regime'.

(See *Springwell Navigation Corp v JP Morgan Chase Bank* [2010] EWCA Civ 1221, [2010] 2 CLC 705, at paragraph 181.)

144 Aikens LJ's focus was on section 3 of the Misrepresentation Act rather than section 2 of UCTA and on whether representations had been made rather than on whether there had been an assumption of responsibility. Nonetheless, it seems to me that the passages from his judgment and that of Christopher Clarke J cast light on circumstances in which a provision seeking to deny an assumption of responsibility will come within section 2 of UCTA. Whether or not UCTA applies more widely (as *Smith v Eric S. Bush* suggests), a provision which purports to prevent an assumption of responsibility will, in my judgment, be subject to UCTA if it attempts 'retrospectively to alter the character of what has gone before' or 'to rewrite history or parts company with reality'.

145 In my view, the Conditions do '[part] company with reality' insofar as they negate assumption of responsibility. The reality was that Christie's had taken responsibility for the attribution of 'Odalisque' to Kustodiev. It stated that that was its opinion; it gave Avrora a warranty to that effect; it indicated that its views reflected research (for example, by presenting itself as a centre of excellence and, more specifically, by explaining in the 'Important Notes and Explanation of Cataloguing Practice' that more qualified catalogue entries – e.g. 'Attributed to …' – were 'based upon careful study' and represented 'the opinion of experts', tending to suggest that an unequivocal attribution would be too); and it was intending to charge the buyer a substantial premium. That Christie's may not have wanted to assume tortious liability in respect of the attribution cannot, I think, be determinative. It is noteworthy in this context that in *White v Jones* [1995] 2 AC 207 Lord Browne-Wilkinson said (at 273) that 'the assumption of responsibility referred to is the [defendant's] assumption of responsibility for the task not the assumption of legal liability'.

146 In the circumstances, I consider that UCTA applies.

Section 10 of the UCTA 1977 prevents evasion of the provisions of the Act by means of a secondary contract.

Evasion by means of secondary contract

Section 10
A person is not bound by any contract term prejudicing or taking away rights of his which arise under, or in connection with the performance of, another contract, so far as those rights extend to the enforcement of another's liability which this Part of this Act prevents that other from excluding or restricting.

7.3.2 Protective provisions

Having looked at the scope of the Act, we now need to consider the various forms of liability that it covers.

7.3.2.1 Liability for negligence

Section 2 of the UCTA 1977 is concerned with clauses that purport to exclude or restrict business liability for 'negligence', which is defined in s 1(1) as follows:

Scope of Part I

Section 1

(1) For the purposes of this Part of this Act, 'negligence' means the breach –

(a) of any obligation, arising from the express or implied terms of a contract, to take reasonable care or exercise reasonable skill in the performance of the contract;

(b) of any common law duty to take reasonable care or exercise reasonable skill (but not any stricter duty);

(c) of the common duty of care imposed by the Occupiers' Liability Act 1957 or the Occupiers' Liability Act (Northern Ireland) 1957.

(4) In relation to any breach of duty or obligation, it is immaterial for any purpose of this Part of this Act whether the breach was inadvertent or intentional, or whether liability for it arises directly or vicariously.

This section confirms that the Act encompasses both contractual negligence (that is, liability arising from breach of a contractual duty of care) and tortious negligence (that is, liability arising in the tort of negligence). Section 1(1)(c) recognises liability arising under the statutory duty of care imposed on occupiers towards lawful visitors.

Subsection (4) expands the definition of negligence by confirming that it is immaterial whether the breach was inadvertent or intentional, or whether liability for it arose directly or vicariously.

Negligence liability

Section 2

(1) A person cannot by reference to any contract term or to a notice given to persons generally or to particular persons exclude or restrict his liability for death or personal injury resulting from negligence.

(2) In the case of other loss or damage, a person cannot so exclude or restrict his liability for negligence except in so far as the term or notice satisfies the requirement of reasonableness.

(3) Where a contract term or notice purports to exclude or restrict liability for negligence a person's agreement to or awareness of it is not of itself to be taken as indicating his voluntary acceptance of any risk.

(4) This section does not apply to –

(a) a term in a consumer contract, or

(b) a notice to the extent that it is a consumer notice,

(but see the provision made about such contracts and notices in sections 62 and 65 of the Consumer Rights Act 2015).

Note that, following the CRA 2015, s 2 of UCTA 1977 does not apply to consumer contracts or consumer notices. Where UCTA 1977 does apply, the level of control imposed by s 2 depends on the consequences of the negligent act. Any attempt to exclude/limit liability for death or personal injury resulting from negligence will be totally ineffective (s 2(1)). In respect of other types of loss, a term that purports to exclude/limit liability for negligence will be effective to the extent that it satisfies the 'requirement of reasonableness' (s 2(2)). The test of reasonableness that is to be applied in this context is contained in s 11 and Schedule 2 of the Act. These provisions will be considered in greater detail below. Finally, subs (1) makes it clear that the section only applies to clauses that 'exclude or restrict' liability. This means that the section does not cover clauses that purport to transfer liability from one party to another.

Thompson v T Lohan (Plant Hire) [1987] 1 WLR 649

Facts: The defendants, Lohan, hired an excavator with a driver to a third party called Hurdiss for use in its quarry. Clause 8 of the Contractors Plant Association conditions placed liability for the acts of the driver onto the hirer. The driver drove negligently and killed Mr Thompson. Mrs Thompson, as her husband's personal representative, brought a claim against Lohan and won damages and costs. Lohan then sought an indemnity from Hurdiss pursuant to clause 8. Hurdiss denied liability on the basis that clause 8 was ineffective under s 2(1) of the UCTA 1977.

Held: The Court of Appeal held that s 2(1) had no application to clause 8 because the clause did not purport to restrict or limit liability.

Fox LJ: The plaintiff is not prejudiced in any way by the operation sought to be established of clause 8. All that has happened is that Lohan and the third party have agreed between themselves who is to bear the consequences of Mr Hill's negligent acts. I can see nothing in section 2(1) of the Act of 1977 to prevent that. In my opinion, section 2(1) is concerned with protecting the victim of negligence and, of course, those who claim under him. It is not concerned with arrangements made by the wrongdoer with other persons as to the sharing or bearing of the burden of compensating the victim. In such a case it seems to me there is no exclusion or restriction of the liability at all. The liability has been established by Hodgson J. It is not in dispute and is now unalterable. The circumstance that the defendants have between themselves chosen to bear the liability in a particular way does not affect that liability; it does not exclude it, and it does not restrict it. The liability to the plaintiff is the only relevant liability in the case, as it seems to me, and that liability is still in existence and will continue until discharge by payment to the plaintiff. Nothing is excluded in relation to the liability, and the liability is not restricted in any way whatever. The liability of Lohan to the plaintiff remains intact. The liability of Hamstead to Phillips was sought to be excluded.

In those circumstances it seems to me that, looking at the language of section 2(1), this case does not fall within its prohibition.

For the Court of Appeal it was crucial that clause 8 did not prevent the injured party from making a claim (contrast *Phillips Products Ltd v Hyland* [1987] 1 WLR 659); it merely transferred liability to a third party. This approach is consistent with the claimant-focused emphasis of the Act. The UCTA 1977 was designed to provide 'protection' to claimants, not to inflict 'punishment' on defendants. Therefore, it seems a clause is not caught by the Act so long as the injured party is not prevented from making a claim.

7.3.2.2 Liability in contract

Section 3 covers liability arising in contract.

Liability arising in contract

Section 3

(1) This section applies as between contracting parties where one of them deals on the other's written standard terms of business.

(2) As against that party, the other cannot by reference to any contract term –

(a) when himself in breach of contract, exclude or restrict any liability of his in respect of the breach; or

(b) claim to be entitled –

(i) to render a contractual performance substantially different from that which was reasonably expected of him, or

(ii) in respect of the whole or any part of his contractual obligation, to render no performance at all, except in so far as (in any of the cases mentioned above in this subsection) the contract term satisfies the requirement of reasonableness.

(3) This section does not apply to a term in a consumer contract (but see the provision made about such contracts in section 62 of the Consumer Rights Act 2015).

The section is directed at situations where there may be an inequality of bargaining power. In such situations it is probable that the claimant had no real choice as to whether or not to accept the exclusion/limitation clause. Two types of contract were initially identified in which it assumed that there was an inequality of bargaining power: (1) contracts where the claimant dealt as a consumer (subsequently removed by the CRA 2015); and (2) contracts concluded on the other party's 'written standard terms of business'.

7.3.2.2.1 Written standard terms of business

Section 3(1) states that the section applies where one of the parties deals on the other party's 'written standard terms of business'. The meaning of 'written standard terms of business' is not given in the Act. It is clear, however, that the individual negotiation of some of the terms will not prevent them from being 'standard'. In *St Albans City and District Council v International Computers Ltd* [1996] 4 All ER 481, the Court of Appeal held that a contract to purchase computer software was concluded on the defendant's standard terms of business even though the contract had been preceded by some negotiation in respect of the terms. Nourse LJ said:

> [The judge at first instance] dealt with this question as one of fact, finding that the defendant's general conditions remained effectively untouched in the negotiations and that the plaintiffs accordingly dealt on the defendant's written standard terms for the purposes of s 3(1); see p 706. I respectfully agree with him. The consequence of that finding is that the defendant cannot rely on clause 9(c) except in so far as it satisfies the requirement of reasonableness.

In *African Export-Import Bank v Shebah Exploration and Production Co Ltd* [2017] EWCA Civ 845, the Court of Appeal held that a party could still be said to deal on the 'other's written standard terms of business' if there had been insubstantial amendments to those terms. It has sometimes been suggested that in such cases the exclusion clause itself must remain part of the standard package, although in *African Export-Import Bank v Shebah Exploration and Production Co Ltd* the Court of Appeal stated, in a slightly obscure way, that there was no requirement that there had to be negotiation in relation to the relevant exclusion clauses for s 3 to be inapplicable ([36]).

For the terms to be 'standard' it is not necessary that they are *always* used by the party wishing to rely on them, so long as they are habitually used. In *Chester Grosvenor Hotel Company Ltd v Alfred McAlpine Management Ltd* (1991) 56 Build LR 115, Judge Stannard said:

> I accept that where a party invariably contracts in the same written terms without material variation, those terms will become its 'standard form contract' or 'written standard terms of business'. However, it does not follow that because terms are not employed invariably, or without material variation, they cannot be standard terms. If this were not so the statute would be emasculated, since it could be excluded by showing that, although the same terms had been employed without modification on a multitude of occasions, and were employed on the occasion in question,

> previously on one or more isolated occasions they had been modified or not employed at all. In my judgment the question is one of fact and degree. What are alleged to be standard terms may be used so infrequently in comparison with other terms that they cannot realistically be regarded as standard, or on any particular occasion may be so added to or mutilated that they must be regarded as having lost their essential identity. What is required for terms to be standard is that they should be regarded by the party which advances them as its standard terms and that it should habitually contract in those terms. If it contracts also in other terms, it must be determined in any given case, and as a matter of fact, whether this has occurred so frequently that the terms in question cannot be regarded as standard, and if on any occasion a party has substantially modified its prepared terms, it is a question of fact whether those terms have been so altered that they must be regarded as not having been employed on that occasion.

If the terms used are those of a trade association, which are simply adopted by the mutual consent of the parties, then they can still be treated as standard terms if the claimant can show that the defendant habitually used such terms in its contracts (see *British Fermentation Products v Compair Reavell Ltd* [1999] BLR 352). More recently in *University of Wales v London College of Business Ltd* [2015] EWHC 1280 (QB) at [93], HHJ Keyser QC stated:

> I do not consider that the retention of a stock of forms is necessary; a set of terms may be both written and standard even if it is held on the computer and printed as and when necessary. Negotiation or even minor modification does not necessarily preclude the application of section 3; if it did, the effect of the section could be easily avoided.

Cf. also *Commercial Management (Investments) Ltd v Mitchell Design & Construct Ltd* [2016] EWHC 76 (TCC).

7.3.2.2.2 The effect of s 3

The effect of s 3 is found is subs (2):

Liability arising in contract

Section 3

(2) As against that party, the other cannot by reference to any contract term –
- (a) when himself in breach of contract, exclude or restrict any liability of his in respect of the breach; or
- (b) claim to be entitled –
  - (i) to render a contractual performance substantially different from that which was reasonably expected of him, or
  - (ii) in respect of the whole or any part of his contractual obligation, to render no performance at all,

except in so far as (in any of the cases mentioned above in this subsection) the contract term satisfies the requirement of reasonableness.

Section 3(2)(a) confirms that any attempt to exclude or restrict liability by a party putting forward their own standard terms, will be subject to the requirement of reasonableness. Section 3(2)(b) extends this to any term that seeks to exclude liability indirectly by narrowly defining a party's obligations under the contract. It might apply, for example, if a hotel chain agrees to provide a conference room at a certain hotel, but nevertheless reserves the right, in certain circumstances, to substitute the hotel for another, or to cancel the booking in whole or in part. Such clauses would be permissible, but only to the extent that they satisfy the requirement of reasonableness.

Section 3(2)(b) enables the courts to distinguish between clauses that are a legitimate attempt to define the parties' obligations and those that are, in reality, attempts to evade liability. The scope of s 3(2)(b) was considered by the Court of Appeal in *Timeload Ltd v British Telecommunications plc*.

***Timeload Ltd v British Telecommunications plc* [1995] EMLR 459**

Facts: The plaintiff set up a free telephone inquiry service for people needing particular professional or commercial services. BT sought to disconnect the plaintiff's free phone line and sought to rely on clause 18 of the contract which provided that at any time the contract could be terminated by BT on one month's notice. The plaintiff applied for an interlocutory injunction to restrain BT from terminating the contract. The reason why the plaintiff sought an injunction was that they wished to keep their telephone number (which was included on their publicity) and termination of the contract would have led to the number being withdrawn. The plaintiff argued that by virtue of s 3(2) of the UCTA 1977, BT was not entitled to rely on clause 18 to deliver a performance substantially different from that reasonably expected of it.

Held: The Court of Appeal granted an interlocutory injunction. Although at this stage it was not necessary to finally resolve the issue.

Sir Thomas Bingham MR: Mr Hobbs [counsel for BT] says that section 3(2)(a) is directed to an exemption clause of the classic type exonerating a contractual party in default from the ordinary consequences of the default. I agree, and it seems clear that that subsection has no application here.

The argument accordingly turns on section 3(2)(b) and that I find more difficult. Mr Hobbs submits that the subsection cannot apply where, as here, the clause under consideration defines the service to be provided and does not purport to permit substandard or partial performance. He says that the customer cannot reasonably expect that which the contract does not purport to offer, namely enjoyment of telephone service under a given number for an indefinite period. That may indeed be so, but I find the construction and ambit of this subsection by no means clear. If a customer reasonably expects a service to continue until BT has substantial reason to terminate it, it seems to me at least arguable that a clause purporting to authorise BT to terminate without reason purports to permit partial or different performance from that which the customer expected.

Sir Thomas Bingham MR took a very broad approach to what constitutes 'performance' of the contract. See also *AXA Sun Life Services Plc v Campbell Martin Ltd* [2011] EWCA Civ 133 at [50] where Stanley Burnton LJ stated:

> However, different considerations apply to section 3(2)(b)(i). Quite how that 'paragraph' should operate is not entirely clear, as is demonstrated by the somewhat tentative discussion in *Chitty on Contracts*, 30th edition, at paragraph 14–073. I have no doubt that it is principally aimed at the small print that entitles a party to a contract to provide something other than that defined by the principal terms of the contract, as where a holiday company reserves the right to substitute a hotel or resort for that specified in the main part of the contract. In most cases, as Chitty suggests, the performance reasonably expected of a party is that which is defined by the written contract between the parties. But this 'paragraph' of section 3 refers not to the performance specified in the contract but to the performance 'which was reasonably expected' of that party. It seems to me that in appropriate circumstances a pre-contractual representation or promise may affect the performance that is reasonably expected of a party. It follows that clause 24 may be subject to the reasonableness

> test in UCTA in relation to both collateral warranties and representations. However, section 3(2)(b)(i) will only come into play in the present cases if it is possible to identify both the performance by AXA that was reasonably expected and that defined by the contract. The effect of clause 24, if any, on a representation such as 'We are the largest insurance company in England' will not be within the scope of section 3(2)(b)(i).

See *also Alan Bates and Others v Post Office Ltd* [2019] EWHC 606 (QB). A more cautious approach was taken by the Court of Appeal in *Paragon Finance v Staunton & Another.*

Paragon Finance plc v Staunton & Another [2002] 1 WLR 685

Facts: The claimant made loans to the defendants under a number of mortgage agreements. The agreements contained variable interest clauses which gave the claimant freedom to vary the interest payable at will. The defendant sought to argue that these clauses fell within s 3(2)(b) of the UCTA 1977.

Held: The Court of Appeal held that the fixing of interest rates under the variable interest clauses was not 'contractual performance' within the meaning of s 3(2)(b) since there was no relevant obligation on the claimant to perform a service and therefore nothing that could qualify as 'contractual performance'.

Dyson LJ: It is submitted on behalf of the defendants that they were reasonably entitled to expect that, in performing their side of the bargain, the claimant would not apply rates which were substantially out of line with rates applied by comparable lenders to borrowers in comparable situations to the defendants. It is contended that the setting of interest rates is 'contractual performance' within the meaning of section 3(2)(b)(i) of the 1977 Act, and that the claimant set interest rates that defeated that expectation.

The first question is whether the fixing of rates of interest under a discretion given by the contract was 'contractual performance' within the meaning of section 3(2)(b)(i). [Counsel for the defendants] submits that it is. He relies on two authorities. The first is *Timeload Ltd v British Telecommunications plc* [1995] EMLR 459 ... It was held by the Court of Appeal that it was at least arguable that a clause purporting to authorise BT to terminate without reason purported to permit partial or different performance from that which the plaintiff was entitled to expect, and that section 3(2) of the 1977 Act applied. But the licence agreement imposed clear performance obligations on BT. Thus, clause 1.1 obliged BT to provide the various services there set out. In these circumstances, it is not difficult to see why the court thought that it was at least arguable that a clause authorising termination of the obligation to provide those services for no good reason purported to permit a contractual performance different from that which the customer might reasonably expect.

The second authority is *Zockoll Group Ltd v Mercury Communications Ltd (No 2)* [1999] EMLR 385. This was another telecommunications case. The plaintiff planned to set up a network of franchisees to provide goods and services to the public in response to telephone inquiries. It entered into a contract with Mercury under which it obtained a number of telephone numbers. Mercury wished to withdraw one number from the plaintiff and asserted that it was entitled to do so at its sole discretion. The plaintiff brought proceedings and relied on section 3(2)(b)(i) of the 1977 Act. The court held that the withdrawal of the disputed number did not render the contractual performance substantially different from what was expected. [Counsel for the defendants] points out that it is implicit in the decision of the court that it was accepted that the withdrawal of the disputed number was *capable of being* contractual performance substantially different from that which it was reasonable to expect.

In my judgment, neither of these authorities assists [counsel for the defendants'] submission. In both cases, the defendant telecommunications provider was contractually bound to provide a service. The question was whether the withdrawal of the service in the particular circumstances of the case was such as to render the contract performance (ie the provision of that service) substantially different from that which it was reasonable for the other contracting party to expect. The present cases are quite different. Here, there is no relevant obligation on the claimant, and therefore nothing that can qualify as 'contractual performance' for the purposes of section 3(2)(b)(i). Even if that is wrong, by fixing the rate of interest at a particular level the claimant is not altering the performance of any obligation assumed by it under the contract. Rather, it is altering the performance required of the defendants.

There appears to be no authority in which the application of section 3(2)(b)(i) to a situation similar to that which exists in this case has been considered. The editors of *Chitty on Contracts*, 28th edn (1999) offer this view, at para 14–071:

> 'Nevertheless it seems unlikely that a contract term entitling one party to terminate the contract in the event of a material breach by the other (eg failure to pay by the due date) would fall within paragraph (b), or, if it did so, would be adjudged not to satisfy the requirement of reasonableness. Nor, it is submitted, would that provision extend to a contract term which entitled one party, not to alter the performance expected of himself, but to alter the performance required of the other party (eg a term by which a seller of goods is entitled to increase the price payable by the buyer to the price ruling at the date of delivery, or a term by which a person advancing a loan is entitled to vary the interest payable by the borrower on the loan)'.

In my judgment, this passage accurately states the law. The contract term must be one which has an effect (indeed a substantial effect) on the contractual performance reasonably expected of the party who relies on the term. The key word is 'performance'.

The Court of Appeal distinguished *Timeload* on the basis that it involved a positive obligation to provide something, whereas the clause in *Paragon Finance* enabled the claimant to alter the performance required by the defendant. This distinction has not been maintained, however, and it has been, for example, held that a clause imposing a positive obligation fell outside the scope of s 3(2)(b). *Peninsula Business Services Ltd v Sweeney* [2004] IRLR 49 concerned a term in an employment contract, which stated that 'an employee has no claim whatsoever on any commission payments that would otherwise have been generated and paid, if they are not in employment on the date when they would normally have been paid'. Sweeney resigned his post with the defendants and forfeited substantial commission payments that he otherwise would have been entitled to receive. He argued that the term amounted to an attempt by the defendants to render a performance substantially different from that which was reasonably expected of them. The Employment Appeal Tribunal rejected this argument. Rimer J said:

> All that the paying party has done is to operate the contract in accordance with the terms to which the receiving party agreed at the outset. In this case, [the term] simply defined the limits of Mr Sweeney's rights, and there is no basis on which he could ever have reasonably expected any rights greater than those that section B gave him. This is not a case in which Peninsula has endeavoured to cut down or restrict his rights in any way.

This reasoning is wholly unsatisfactory because the majority of terms that fall under s 3(2)(b) are likely to define the limits of the party's rights. Indeed, this is precisely what the clause in Timeload did. The real point of distinction between this case and *Timeload* is that the tribunal did not believe that Sweeney could have reasonably expected to receive greater rights than those conferred under the contract. How are we to identify the situations in which the party has reasonable expectations other than those created by the contract? On the one hand, it is arguable that the parties' expectations are only ever *reasonable* to the extent that they correspond to the enforceable rights contained in the contract. On the other hand, it is clear that reasonable expectations must extend beyond those contained in the contract, otherwise s 3(2)(b) would be rendered meaningless. Until the source of these extra-contractual expectations is identified there will continue to be confusion and uncertainty as to the scope of s 3(2)(b).

7.3.2.3 Liability arising from contracts for the supply of goods

Sale and hire purchase

Section 6

(1) Liability for breach of the obligations arising from –
  (a) section 12 of the Sale of Goods Act 1979 (seller's implied undertakings as to title, etc.);
  (b) section 8 of the Supply of Goods (Implied Terms) Act 1973 (the corresponding thing in relation to hire-purchase), cannot be excluded or restricted by reference to any contract term.

(1A) Liability for breach of the obligations arising from –
  (a) section 13, 14 or 15 of the 1979 Act (seller's implied undertakings as to conformity of goods with description or sample, or as to their quality or fitness for a particular purpose);
  (b) section 9, 10 or 11 of the 1973 Act (the corresponding things in relation to hire purchase), cannot be excluded or restricted by reference to a contract term except in so far as the term satisfies the requirement of reasonableness.

(4) The liabilities referred to in this section are not only the business liabilities defined by section 1(3), but include those arising under any contract of sale of goods or hire-purchase agreement.

(5) This section does not apply to a consumer contract (but see the provision made about such contracts in section 31 of the Consumer Rights Act 2015).

Section 6 deals with clauses that purport to exclude or limit liability for breach of implied terms arising in contracts for the sale of goods and contracts of hire purchase. Following the CRA 2015, this section no longer applies in relation to consumer contracts. The effect of s 6 of UCTA 1977 is that attempts to exclude/restrict terms implied by ss 13–15 of the Sale of Goods Act 1979 or ss 9–11 of the Supply of Goods (Implied Terms) Act 1973 will be subject to the requirement of reasonableness. Moreover, s 6(1) states that liability arising under s 12 of the Sale of Goods Act 1979 and s 8 of the Supply of Goods (Implied Terms) Act 1973, which both concern the seller's implied undertaking as to title, cannot be excluded in any contract to which s 6 applies. Section 6(4) extends the scope of the section to include attempts to exclude or limit non-business liability.

Miscellaneous contracts under which goods pass

Section 7

(1) Where the possession or ownership of goods passes under or in pursuance of a contract not governed by the law of sale of goods or hire-purchase, subsections (2) to (4) below apply as regards the effect (if any) to be given to contract terms excluding or restricting liability for breach of obligation arising by implication of law from the nature of the contract.

(1A) Liability in respect of the goods' correspondence with description or sample, or their quality or fitness for any particular purpose, cannot be excluded or restricted by reference to such a term except in so far as the term satisfies the requirement of reasonableness.

(3A) Liability for breach of the obligations arising under section 2 of the Supply of Goods and Services Act 1982 (implied terms about title etc. in certain contracts for the transfer of the property in goods) cannot be excluded or restricted by reference to any such term.

(4) Liability in respect of –
  (a) the right to transfer ownership of the goods, or give possession; or
  (b) the assurance of quiet possession to a person taking goods in pursuance of the contract,
  cannot (in a case to which subsection (3A) above does not apply) be excluded or restricted by reference to any such term except in so far as the term satisfies the requirement of reasonableness.

(4A) This section does not apply to a consumer contract (but see the provision made about such contracts in section 31 of the Consumer Rights Act 2015).

Section 7 performs the same function as s 6, but covers contracts for the hire of goods and contracts for the supply of work and materials. Again, following the CRA 2015 it no longer applies to consumer contracts. Where s 7 applies, any attempt to exclude/restrict liability for breach of an implied term as to description, quality, fitness for purpose, or compliance with sample is subject to the requirement of reasonableness. Section 7(3A) operates in the same way as s 6(1) to prevent exclusions of liability for breach of an implied term as to title arising under s 2(1) of the Supply of Goods and Services Act 1982.

7.3.3 The requirement of reasonableness

The test for reasonableness is contained in s 11 of UCTA 1977.

The 'reasonableness' test

Section 11

(1) In relation to a contract term, the requirement of reasonableness for the purposes of this Part of this Act, section 3 of the Misrepresentation Act 1967 and section 3 of the Misrepresentation Act (Northern Ireland) 1967 is that the term shall have been a fair and reasonable one to be included having regard to the circumstances which were, or ought reasonably to have been, known to or in the contemplation of the parties when the contract was made.

(2) In determining for the purposes of section 6 or 7 above whether a contract term satisfies the requirement of reasonableness, regard shall be had in particular to the matters specified in Schedule 2 to this Act; but this subsection does not prevent the court or arbitrator from holding, in accordance with any rule of law, that a term which purports to exclude or restrict any relevant liability is not a term of the contract.

(3) In relation to a notice (not being a notice having contractual effect), the requirement of reasonableness under this Act is that it should be fair and reasonable to allow reliance on it, having regard to all the circumstances obtaining when the liability arose or (but for the notice) would have arisen.

(4) Where by reference to a contract term or notice a person seeks to restrict liability to a specified sum of money, and the question arises (under this or any other Act) whether the term or notice satisfies the requirement of reasonableness, regard shall be had in particular (but without prejudice to subsection (2) above in the case of contract terms) to –
  (a) the resources which he could expect to be available to him for the purpose of meeting the liability should it arise; and
  (b) how far it was open to him to cover himself by insurance.

(5) It is for those claiming that a contract term or notice satisfies the requirement of reasonableness to show that it does.

Section 11(1) makes it clear that the point at which the reasonableness of the term is to be assessed is the date on which the contract was made. This means that, when considering the reasonableness of the term, the court should take no account of subsequent events. In particular, the court should not consider the actual breach that has occurred and for which the term is claimed to provide exclusion or limitation of liability. This can have the peculiar result of a court finding that the defendant was reasonable to exclude liability for the particular breach, but that the term used was ineffective, due to it having been drafted in unreasonably broad terms. Such an outcome is entirely consistent with the judicial policy of discouraging unnecessarily wide clauses. It is also consistent with the courts' refusal to sever or rewrite unreasonably broad exclusion clauses.

***Stewart Gill Ltd v Horatio Myer & Co Ltd* [1992] QB 600**

Facts: The plaintiffs agreed to supply, install and test an overhead conveyor system at the defendants' premises. Clause 12.4 of the contract stated: 'The customer shall not be entitled to withhold payment of any amount due to the company under the contract by reason of any payment credit set off counterclaim allegation of incorrect or defective goods or for any other reason whatsoever which the customer may allege excuses him from performing his obligations hereunder.' The defendants refused to pay alleging that the plaintiffs had breached the contract. The plaintiffs brought a claim for the outstanding payments.

Held: The Court of Appeal held that clause 12.4 was unreasonable because it could be used to prevent the defendant from setting off a payment already made and would extend to a defence based on fraud.

Stuart-Smith LJ: In my judgment it is the term as a whole that has to be reasonable and not merely some part of it. Throughout the Act the expression used is 'by reference to any contract term', the contract 'term satisfies the requirement of reasonableness': see sections 3 and 7 and in section 11(1) the reasonableness test is laid down as:

> 'In relation to a contract term, the requirement of reasonableness ... is that the term shall have been a fair and reasonable one to be included having regard to the circumstances which were, or ought reasonably to have been, known to or in the contemplation of the parties when the contract was made'.

Although the question of reasonableness is primarily one for the court when the contract term is challenged, it seems to me that the parties must also be in a position to judge this at the time the contract is made. If this is so, I find it difficult to see how such an appreciation can be made if the customer has to guess whether some, and if so which, part of the term will alone be relied upon. Section 11(2) of the Act requires the court which is determining the question of reasonableness for the purpose of sections 6 and 7 to have regard in particular to the matters specified in Schedule 2. Although Schedule 2 does not apply in the present case, the considerations there set out are usually regarded as being of general application to the question of reasonableness. Two paragraphs of these guidelines would in my judgment be unworkable unless the whole term is being considered.

Paragraph (b) provides:

> 'whether the customer received an inducement to agree to the term, or in accepting it had an opportunity of entering into a similar contract with other persons, but without having to accept a similar term' ...

If there was an inducement, it would I think be quite impossible in most cases to say that it related only to the words which the party seeking to establish reasonableness relies upon as opposed to those he wishes to delete. It is equally unreal to suppose that the customer could divine which part the vendor will ultimately seek to rely upon so as to decide whether other persons are willing to contract without the term.

Paragraph (c) provides:

> 'whether the customer knew or ought reasonably to have known of the existence and extent of the term (having regard, among other things, to any custom of the trade and any previous course of dealing between the parties)'...
>
> In my judgment the customer would be most unlikely ever to know the extent of the term if the vendor is entitled, when it is questioned as to reasonableness, to rely on only part of it.
>
> These examples in my judgment support the construction of the word term as being the whole term or clause as drafted, and not merely that part of it which may eventually be taken to be relevant to the case in point.
>
> Nor does it appear to me to be consistent with the policy and purpose of the Act to permit a contract or to impose a contractual term, which taken as a whole is completely unreasonable to put a blue pencil through the most offensive parts and say that what is left is reasonable and sufficient to exclude or restrict his liability in a manner relied upon.

The Court of Appeal was unwilling to separate out the 'unreasonable' parts of the exclusion clause from the 'reasonable' parts. It is of course open to the drafters of the contract to do this themselves. Instead of drafting the exclusion of liability as a single clause they might draft it as a number of separate subclauses. If they take this approach, the court will apply the requirement of reasonableness to each subclause individually and will not necessarily allow the unreasonableness of one clause to effect the enforceability of the others (*Watford Electronics v Sanderson CFL Ltd* [2001] 1 All ER Comm 696).

Section 11(3) states that the test of reasonableness for notices is whether it is 'fair and reasonable' to rely on the notice and the court can have regard to all the circumstances obtaining when the liability arose or (but for the notice) would have arisen.

Section 11(4) directs the court to take into account two matters when considering the reasonableness of clauses that purport to limit liability to a specific sum of money, rather than excluding it altogether. This recognises that it may be entirely reasonable for a contracting party to limit their liability, particularly when they are under-resourced or engaging in a high-risk activity.

Finally, s 11(5) places the burden of proof in relation to reasonableness on the party seeking to rely on the clause.

7.3.3.1 Guidelines in Schedule 2

As Stuart-Smith LJ noted in *Stewart Gill*, s 11(2) of the Act permits the courts to take into account the matters listed in Schedule 2 when considering the requirement of reasonableness under ss 6 and 7.

'Guidelines' for application of reasonableness test

> **Schedule 2**
>
> The matters to which regard is to be had in particular for the purposes of sections 6(1A), 7(1A) and (4), 20 and 21 are any of the following which appear to be relevant –
>
> (a) the strength of the bargaining positions of the parties relative to each other, taking into account (among other things) alternative means by which the customer's requirements could have been met;
>
> (b) whether the customer received an inducement to agree to the term, or in accepting it had an opportunity of entering into a similar contract with other persons, but without having to accept a similar term;

(c) whether the customer knew or ought reasonably to have known of the existence and extent of the term (having regard, among other things, to any custom of the trade and any previous course of dealing between the parties);
(d) where the term excludes or restricts any relevant liability if some condition is not complied with, whether it was reasonable at the time of the contract to expect that compliance with that condition would by practicable;
(e) whether the goods were manufactured, processed or adapted to the special order of the customer.

In practice, the courts have been willing to have regard to the 'guidelines' contained in Schedule 2 in cases that do not fall within the scope of ss 6 and 7 (see *Overseas Medical Supplies Ltd v Orient Transport Services Ltd* [1999] 2 Lloyd's Rep 273, discussed in detail below). The matters contained in Schedule 2 are only 'guidelines' and, therefore, there is no obligation on the court to look to them at all. Indeed, it is highly unlikely that the Court of Appeal would overturn a judge's decision on the reasonableness issue simply because one of the above guidelines had not been considered, even if the case concerned a clause covered by ss 6 or 7. Furthermore, the list of considerations is not exhaustive. The court will take into account a number of other factors that have been held to be relevant in the task of assessing reasonableness.

7.3.3.2 'Reasonableness' in the House of Lords

In this section and the next we will consider a number of cases in which the courts have sought to apply the test of reasonableness. We will see that the courts have regard to a broad range of factors. The duty of the judge is to balance these factors in a sagacious manner. In practice, the trial judge is afforded a considerable degree of latitude in undertaking this task and it will be very rare for his or her decision to be overturned by an appeal court. In this section, we will consider two decisions of the House of Lords – one applying a test of reasonableness that predated the UCTA 1977, the other dealing with the UCTA 1977 itself.

***George Mitchell (Chesterhall) Ltd v Finney Lock Seeds Ltd* [1983] 2 AC 803**

Facts: The plaintiffs were farmers in East Lothian who ordered a quantity of Finney's Late Dutch Special cabbage seed from the defendants. The seed supplied was not Finney's Late Dutch Special or any other variety of Dutch winter white cabbage, but a variety of autumn cabbage. The seed germinated and the cabbage grew but it proved to be commercially useless and had to be ploughed in. A limitation clause in the contract provided a maximum liability of no more than the price of seeds which was just over £200. The farmer claimed the loss of his profits calculated at £61,000.

Held: The House of Lords held that the limitation clause was ineffective because it failed the reasonableness test contained in s 55(4) of the Sale of Goods Act 1979 as set out in Schedule 1 of the 1979 Act, para 11 (now superseded by UCTA 1977).

Lord Bridge of Harwich: The relevant subsections of the modified section 55 provide as follows:

(1) Where a right, duty or liability would arise under a contract of sale of goods by implication of law, it may be negatived or varied by express agreement ... but the preceding provision has effect subject to the following provisions of this section ... (4) In the case of a contract of sale of goods, any term of that or any other contract exempting from all or any of the provisions of section 13, 14 or

> 15 above is void in the case of a consumer sale and is, in any other case, not enforceable to the extent that it is shown that it would not be fair or reasonable to allow reliance on the term. (5) In determining for the purposes of subsection (4) above whether or not reliance on any such term would be fair or reasonable regard shall be had to all the circumstances of the case and in particular to the following matters – (a) the strength of the bargaining positions of the seller and buyer relative to each other, taking into account, among other things, the availability of suitable alternative products and sources of supply; (b) whether the buyer received an inducement to agree to the term or in accepting it had an opportunity of buying the goods or suitable alternatives without it from any source of supply; (c) whether the buyer knew or ought reasonably to have known of the existence and extent of the term (having regard, among other things, to any custom of the trade and any previous course of dealing between the parties); (d) where the term exempts from all or any of the provisions of section 13, 14, or 15 above if some condition is not complied with, whether it was reasonable at the time of the contract to expect that compliance with that condition would be practicable; (e) whether the goods were manufactured, processed, or adapted to the special order of the buyer ...

The statutory issue ... turns on the words in subsection (4) 'to the extent that it is shown that it would not be fair or reasonable to allow reliance on' this restriction of the appellants' liabilities, having regard to the matters referred to in subsection (5).

This is the first time your Lordships' House has had to consider a modern statutory provision giving the court power to override contractual terms excluding or restricting liability, which depends on the court's view of what is 'fair and reasonable'. The particular provision of the modified section 55 of the Act of 1979 which applies in the instant case is of limited and diminishing importance. But the several provisions of the Unfair Contract Terms Act 1977 which depend on 'the requirement of reasonableness', defined in section 11 by reference to what is 'fair and reasonable', albeit in a different context, are likely to come before the courts with increasing frequency. It may, therefore, be appropriate to consider how an original decision as to what is 'fair and reasonable' made in the application of any of these provisions should be approached by an appellate court. It would not be accurate to describe such a decision as an exercise of discretion. But a decision under any of the provisions referred to will have this in common with the exercise of a discretion, that, in having regard to the various matters to which the modified section 55(5) of the Act of 1979, or section 11 of the Act of 1977 direct attention, the court must entertain a whole range of considerations, put them in the scales on one side or the other, and decide at the end of the day on which side the balance comes down. There will sometimes be room for a legitimate difference of judicial opinion as to what the answer should be, where it will be impossible to say that one view is demonstrably wrong and the other demonstrably right. It must follow, in my view, that, when asked to review such a decision on appeal, the appellate court should treat the original decision with the utmost respect and refrain from interference with it unless satisfied that it proceeded upon some erroneous principle or was plainly and obviously wrong.

Turning back to the modified section 55 of the Act of 1979, it is common ground that the onus was on the respondents to show that it would not be fair or reasonable to allow the appellants to rely on the relevant condition as limiting their liability ...

My Lords ... I turn to the application of the statutory language to the circumstances of the case. Of the particular matters to which attention is directed by paragraphs (a) to (e) of section 55(5), only those in (a) to (c) are relevant. As to paragraph (c), the respondents admittedly knew of the relevant condition (they had dealt with the appellants for many years) and, if they had read it, particularly clause 2, they would, I think, as laymen rather than lawyers, have had no difficulty in understanding what it said. This and the magnitude of the damages claimed in proportion to the price of the seeds sold are factors which weigh in the scales in the appellants' favour. The question of relative bargaining strength under paragraph (a) and of the opportunity to buy seeds without a limitation of the seedsman's liability under paragraph (b) were inter-related. The evidence was that a similar limitation of liability was universally embodied in the terms of trade between seedsmen and farmers and had been so for very many years. The limitation had never been negotiated between representative bodies but, on the other hand, had not been the subject of any protest by the National Farmers' Union. These factors, if considered in isolation, might have been equivocal. The decisive factor, however, appears from the evidence of four witnesses called for the appellants, two independent seedsmen, the chairman of the appellant company, and a director of a sister company (both being wholly owned subsidiaries of the same parent). They said that it had always been their practice, unsuccessfully attempted in the instant case, to negotiate settlements of farmers' claims for damages in excess of the price of the seeds, if they thought that the claims were 'genuine' and 'justified'. This evidence indicated a clear recognition by seedsmen in general, and the appellants in particular, that reliance on the limitation of liability imposed by the relevant condition would not be fair or reasonable.

Two further factors, if more were needed, weight the scales in favour of the respondents. The supply of autumn, instead of winter, cabbage seeds was due to the negligence of the appellants' sister company. Irrespective of its quality, the autumn variety supplied could not, according to the appellants' own evidence, be grown commercially in East Lothian. Finally, as the trial judge found, seedsmen could insure against the risk of crop failure caused by supplying the wrong variety of seeds without materially increasing the price of seeds.

My Lords, even if I felt doubts about the statutory issue, I should not, for the reasons explained earlier, think it right to interfere with the unanimous original decision of that issue by the Court of Appeal. As it is, I feel no such doubts. If I were making the original decision, I should conclude without hesitation that it would not be fair or reasonable to allow the appellants to rely on the contractual limitation of their liability.

Lord Bridge confirmed that the test of reasonableness was a balancing exercise in which the court must entertain a whole range of considerations and balance them against each other. Three factors weighed in favour of the seed sellers:

1. The clause was clear and understandable.
2. The clause was common in the trade, and had never been objected to by the National Farmers' Union.
3. The magnitude of the damages claimed in proportion to the price of the seeds sold weighed heavily in favour of the sellers.

Four considerations weighed in favour of the farmers, however:

1. The clause had been inserted by the sellers; there had been no real negotiation.
2. The loss of the crop had been caused by negligence (albeit the negligence of the sellers' sister company, rather than the sellers themselves).
3. The trial judge had found that seedsmen could insure against the risk of crop failure caused by supplying the wrong variety of seeds without significantly increasing the price of seeds.
4. There was evidence from a number of witnesses (including the chairman of the defendant company) that it was the general practice of the trade not to rely on the clause, but to use it as the basis for negotiating more substantial compensation.

For Lord Bridge, the final consideration was the most important. He considered that it was conclusive evidence that seedsmen in general and the defendants in particular did not believe that reliance on the clause would be fair and reasonable.

The House of Lords upheld the verdicts delivered at first instance and in the Court of Appeal. Lord Bridge emphasised that there was room for legitimate disagreement as to whether a clause was reasonable. For this reason, he said that the appellate courts should refrain from interference with a first instance decision 'unless satisfied that it proceeded upon some erroneous principle or was plainly and obviously wrong'.

Smith v Eric S Bush [1990] 1 AC 831

Facts: See 7.3.1.3.

Held: The House of Lords held that a clause purporting to exclude liability for the negligent performance of a survey was subject to s 2(2) of UCTA 1977. On the facts of the case the clause did not meet the requirement of reasonableness.

Lord Griffiths: [T]he question is whether the exclusion of liability contained in the disclaimer satisfies the requirement of reasonableness provided by section 2(2) of the Act of 1977. The meaning of reasonableness and the burden of proof are both dealt with in section 11(3) which provides:

> 'In relation to a notice (not being a notice having contractual effect), the requirement of reasonableness under this Act is that it should be fair and reasonable to allow reliance on it, having regard to all the circumstances obtaining when the liability arose or (but for the notice) would have arisen'.

It is clear, then, that the burden is upon the surveyor to establish that in all the circumstances it is fair and reasonable that he should be allowed to rely upon his disclaimer of liability.

I believe that it is impossible to draw up an exhaustive list of the factors that must be taken into account when a judge is faced with this very difficult decision. Nevertheless, the following matters should, in my view, always be considered.

1. Were the parties of equal bargaining power? If the court is dealing with a one-off situation between parties of equal bargaining power the requirement of reasonableness would be more easily discharged than in a case such as the present where the disclaimer is imposed upon the purchaser who has no effective power to object.
2. In the case of advice would it have been reasonably practicable to obtain the advice from an alternative source taking into account considerations of costs and time. In the present case it is urged on behalf of the surveyor that it would have been easy for the purchaser to have obtained his own report on the condition of the house, to which the purchaser replies, that he would then be required to pay twice for the same advice and that people buying at the bottom end of the market, many of whom will be young first-time buyers, are likely to be under considerable financial pressure without the money to go paying twice for the same service.
3. How difficult is the task being undertaken for which liability is being excluded. When a very difficult or dangerous undertaking is involved there may be a high risk of failure which would certainly be a pointer towards the reasonableness of excluding liability as a condition of doing the work. A valuation, on the other hand, should present no difficulty if the work is undertaken with reasonable skill and care. It is only defects which are observable by a careful visual examination that have to be taken into account and I cannot see that it places any unreasonable burden on the valuer to require him to accept responsibility for the fairly elementary degree of skill and care involved in observing, following-up and reporting on such defects. Surely it is work at the lower end of the surveyor's field of professional expertise.
4. What are the practical consequences of the decision on the question of reasonableness. This must involve the sums of money potentially at stake and the ability of the parties to bear the loss involved,

> which, in its turn, raises the question of insurance. There was once a time when it was considered improper even to mention the possible existence of insurance cover in a lawsuit. But those days are long past. Everyone knows that all prudent, professional men carry insurance, and the availability and cost of insurance must be a relevant factor when considering which of two parties should be required to bear the risk of a loss. We are dealing in this case with a loss which will be limited to the value of a modest house and against which it can be expected that the surveyor will be insured. Bearing the loss will be unlikely to cause significant hardship if it has to be borne by the surveyor but it is, on the other hand, quite possible that it will be a financial catastrophe for the purchaser who may be left with a valueless house and no money to buy another. If the law in these circumstances denies the surveyor the right to exclude his liability, it may result in a few more claims but I do not think so poorly of the surveyor's profession as to believe that the floodgates will be opened. There may be some increase in surveyors' insurance premiums which will be passed on to the public, but I cannot think that it will be anything approaching the figures involved in the difference between the Abbey National's offer of a valuation without liability and a valuation with liability discussed in the speech of my noble and learned friend, Lord Templeman. The result of denying a surveyor, in the circumstances of this case, the right to exclude liability, will result in distributing the risk of his negligence among all house purchasers through an increase in his fees to cover insurance, rather than allowing the whole of the risk to fall upon the one unfortunate purchaser.
>
> I would not, however, wish it to be thought that I would consider it unreasonable for professional men in all circumstances to seek to exclude or limit their liability for negligence. Sometimes breathtaking sums of money may turn on professional advice against which it would be impossible for the adviser to obtain adequate insurance cover and which would ruin him if he were to be held personally liable. In these circumstances it may indeed be reasonable to give the advice upon a basis of no liability or possibly of liability limited to the extent of the adviser's insurance cover.

In addition to the foregoing four factors, which will always have to be considered, there is in this case the additional feature that the surveyor is only employed in the first place because the purchaser wishes to buy the house and the purchaser in fact provides or contributes to the surveyor's fees. No one has argued that if the purchaser had employed and paid the surveyor himself, it would have been reasonable for the surveyor to exclude liability for negligence, and the present situation is not far removed from that of a direct contract between the surveyor and the purchaser. The evaluation of the foregoing matters leads me to the clear conclusion that it would not be fair and reasonable for the surveyor to be permitted to exclude liability in the circumstances of this case. I would therefore dismiss this appeal.

Once again, the availability of insurance was a significant factor for the House of Lords. The surveyor could have quite easily obtained insurance to cover his liability. This was an individual private house purchase, not a deal in relation to commercial property; and while it would have been a financial catastrophe for the purchaser to be left with a valueless house, the loss could have quite easily been absorbed by the surveyor and his insurer. Better to spread the risk through an increase in insurance premiums than to allow the whole of the risk to fall on the one unfortunate purchaser.

7.3.3.3 'Reasonableness' in the Court of Appeal

Repeatedly the Court of Appeal has emphasised its reluctance to interfere with the decision of the trial judge on the issue of reasonableness. In both *Phillips Products Ltd v Hyland* [1987] 1 WLR 659 and *St Albans City and District Council v International Computers Ltd* [1996] 4 All ER 481, the Court of Appeal refused to overturn the decision at first instance because it had not been shown to be 'plainly or obviously wrong'.

Subsequent cases have sought to give some guidance as to factors that are relevant in applying the test.

***Schenkers Ltd v Overland Shoes Ltd* [1998] 1 Lloyd's Rep 498**

Facts: The plaintiffs were the freight carriers for the defendants, who imported shoes from the Far East into the European Community. The contract stated that the plaintiffs were to reclaim the VAT payable to the Portuguese authorities and repay it to the defendants. They failed to do this and the defendants purported to set-off the sum of VAT against the money they owed to the plaintiffs. The contract between the parties contained a number of standard trading conditions of the British International Freight Association. Clause 23(A) stated: 'The Customer shall pay to the Company in cash or as otherwise agreed all sums immediately when due, without reduction or deferment on account of any claim, counterclaim or set-off.' The issue for consideration was whether clause 23(A), which prohibited set-off, satisfied the requirement of reasonableness in UCTA 1977.

Held: The Court of Appeal held that the plaintiffs had satisfied the burden on them of establishing that clause 23(A) in the circumstances satisfied the requirement of reasonableness.

Pill LJ: In my judgment, the plaintiffs have satisfied the burden upon them of establishing that cl 23(A) in the circumstances satisfies the requirement of reasonableness. The clause was in common use and well known in the trade following comprehensive discussions between reputable and representative bodies mindful of the considerations involved. It reflects a general view as to what is reasonable in the trade concerned. It was sufficiently well known that any failure by the defendant's officers, in the course of long and substantial dealings, to put their minds to the clause cannot be relied on to establish that it was unfair or unreasonable to include it in the contracts. I regard the level of disbursements as a factor which assists the plaintiffs to establish that it was fair and reasonable to include the term but not in itself a conclusive one. In a situation in which there was no significant inequality of bargaining position, the customs of the trade were an important factor. The parties were well aware of the circumstances in which business was conducted, the heads of expenditure to be incurred and the risks involved.

In present circumstances, I see little merit in the defendants' argument that the clause had not in practice been relied upon. The give and take practised by the parties in the course of substantial dealings upon the running account was admirable and conducive to a good business relationship but did not in my judgment prevent the plaintiffs, when the dispute arose, relying upon the term agreed. In *George Mitchell*, there was evidence that neither party expected the limitation of liability clause to be applied literally and a recognition that reliance on the clause was unreasonable. While there was evidence in the present case that there was no ready or frequent resort to the clause, there was no such recognition. I cannot find conduct which permits the defendants to claim that reliance on the clause would be unfair or unreasonable. For those reasons I would dismiss these appeals.

Of particular relevance to the Court of Appeal was the fact that there was equality of bargaining power and that the clause was in common use and well known in the trade. It did not matter that there was 'no ready or frequent resort to the clause', because this was due to the 'admirable give and take practised by the parties in the course of substantial dealings'. Unlike the *George Mitchell* case, it was not due to a recognition in the trade that the clause was unreasonable.

A clause contained in the British International Freight Association's standard terms also came up for consideration in *Overseas Medical Supplies Ltd v Orient Transport Services Ltd*.

***Overseas Medical Supplies Ltd v Orient Transport Services Ltd* [1999] 2 Lloyd's Rep 273**

Facts: The clause in this case stated the following: '[T]he Company's liability howsoever arising and notwithstanding that the cause of loss or damage be unexplained shall not exceed:

(i) in the case of claims for loss or damage to goods (a) the value of any goods lost or damaged or (b) a sum at the rate of two Special Drawing Rights as defined by the International Monetary Fund (hereinafter referred to as SDRs), per kilo of gross weight of any goods lost or damaged whichever shall be the least;

(ii) in the case of all other claims (a) the value of the goods the subject of the relevant transaction between the Company and its Customer or (b) a sum at the rate of two SDRs per kilo of the gross weight of the goods the subject of the said transaction, or (c) 75,000 SDRs in respect of any one transaction whichever shall be the least the value of SDRs shall be calculated as at the date when the claim is received by the Company in writing.'

The trial judge held that the clause was unreasonable.

Held: The Court of Appeal dismissed the appeal and held that the clause was unreasonable.

Potter LJ: First, so far as this Court is concerned, while the hearing of this appeal is in the form of a re-hearing and the Court is entitled to reach its own view on the evidence, its approach is constrained by a natural reluctance to disturb a first instance decision as to what is reasonable in all the circumstances of a particular case, bearing in mind that views on reasonableness may properly differ and that, in any matter where the decision depends not merely on argument but also on the effect of oral evidence, the first instance Judge has the advantage of hearing such evidence at first hand …

The treatment of various factors going to the question of reasonableness has been considered in a number of authorities from which the following observations of relevance emerge.

(1) The way in which the relevant conditions came into being and are used generally is relevant: *Singer Co (UK) Ltd v Tees and Hartlepool Port Authority* [1988] 2 Lloyd's Rep 164, at 169, applied by the Court of Appeal in *Schenkers Ltd v Overland Shoes Ltd* [1998] 1 Lloyd's Rep 498 (a case concerning an entirely different aspect of the BIFA terms).

(2) Although not specifically applicable to cases falling within s 3 of the 1977 Act, the five guidelines as to reasonableness set out in Schedule 2 are nonetheless relevant to the question of reasonableness, while bearing in mind that the Court is dealing with a commercial and not a consumer transaction. They ought therefore to be taken into account: *Stewart Gill Ltd v Horatio Myer and Co Ltd* [1992] QB 600 at p 608. Those which are relevant in this case are (a) the strength of the bargaining positions of the parties relative to each other, taking into account (among other things) alternative means by which the customer's requirements could have been met; (b) whether the customer received an inducement to agree to the term or, in accepting it, had an opportunity of entering into a similar contract with other persons, but without having to accept similar terms; (c) whether the customer knew or ought to have known of the existence and extent of the term (having regard, among other things, to any custom of the trade and any previous course of dealing between the parties).

(3) In relation to the question of equality of bargaining position, the Court will have regard not only to the question of whether the customer was obliged to use the services of the supplier but also to the question of how far it would have been practicable and convenient to go elsewhere: *Singer v Tees* at p 169 and *St Alban's City and District Council v International Computers Ltd* (1995) XXI FSR 686 at p 708.

(4) The question of reasonableness must be assessed having regard to the relevant clause viewed as a whole: it is not right to take any particular part of the clause in isolation, although it must also be viewed

against a breach of contract which is the subject matter of the present case: *AEG (UK) Ltd v Logic Resource Ltd* (Unreported save by New Law on Line, Court of Appeal, Oct 20, 1995), *per* Lord Justice Hobhouse.

(5) The reality of the consent of the customer to the supplier's clause will be a significant consideration (ibid: see also the *St Alban's City* case at pp 709–711).

(6) In cases of limitation rather than exclusion of liability, the size of the limit compared with other limits in widely used standard terms may also be relevant: *Sonicare International Ltd v East Anglia Freight Terminal Ltd* [1997] 2 Lloyd's Rep 48 at 55, per Judge Hallgarten, QC.

(7) While the availability of insurance to the supplier is relevant, it is by no means a decisive factor: see *Singer v Tees* at p 170 and *The Flamar Pride* [1990] 1 Lloyd's Rep 434, 439.

(8) The presence of a term allowing for an option to contract without the limitation clause but with a price increase in lieu is important: see *Singer v Tees* at p 170. However, as suggested in *Yates: Contracts for the Carriage of Goods* para. 7.2.25.13, if the condition works in such a way as to leave little time to put such option into effect, this may effectively eliminate the option as a factor indicating reasonableness, cf. *Phillips Products Ltd v Hyland* [1987] 1 WLR 659.

Potter LJ chose to emphasise the relevance of the bargaining position of the parties, the availability of insurance and the common use of such clauses. With respect, however, his reference to the relevance of breach in the second half of observation (4) is impossible to reconcile with the clear wording of s 11(1). As we have seen, the assessment of reasonableness is to be based on the state of knowledge of the parties at the time the contract was formed. Since the breach takes place after that point it should not be taken into account. Potter LJ's statement to the contrary, which is clearly *obiter*, should be treated with extreme caution until the House of Lords revisit the issue.

In all the cases we have looked at so far, the appeal court has refused to overturn the decision of the trial judge at first instance. This is because, as Lord Bridge indicated in *George Mitchell*, the appellate court will 'treat the original decision with the utmost respect'. The appeal court will intervene, however, if it is convinced that the judge has misdirected himself as to the proper basis for applying the reasonableness test (see *Regus (UK) Ltd v Epcot Solutions Ltd* [2008] EWCA Civ 361).

Watford Electronics Ltd v Sanderson CFL Ltd [2001] 1 All ER (Comm) 696

Facts: The defendants agreed to sell the claimants a number of computer products which turned out to be faulty. The contract contained an exclusion clause stating: 'Neither the Company nor the Customer shall be liable to the other for any claims for indirect or consequential losses whether arising from negligence or otherwise. In no event shall the Company's liability under the Contract exceed the price paid by the Customer to the Company for the Equipment connected with any claim.' The trial judge held that the clause did not satisfy the requirement of reasonableness under s 3 of the UCTA 1977.

Held: The Court of Appeal allowed the appeal.

Chadwick LJ: Where experienced businessmen representing substantial companies of equal bargaining power negotiate an agreement, they may be taken to have had regard to the matters known to them. They should, in my view be taken to be the best judge of the commercial fairness of the agreement which they have made; including the fairness of each of the terms in that agreement. They should be taken to be the best judge on the question whether the terms of the agreement are reasonable. The court should not assume that either is likely to commit his company to an agreement which he thinks is unfair, or which he thinks includes unreasonable terms. Unless satisfied that one party has, in effect, taken unfair advantage of the other – or that a term is so unreasonable that it cannot properly have been understood or considered – the court should not interfere.

> In the present case the parties did negotiate as to the price. Mr Jessa, on behalf of Watford, secured substantial concessions on price from Mr Broderick. The parties negotiated, also, as to which of them should bear the risk (or the cost of insurance against the risk) of making good the loss of profits, and other indirect or consequential loss, which Watford might suffer if the product failed to perform as intended. Mr Jessa was less successful in obtaining from Mr Broderick the concession which he wanted. The most that he could get was an undertaking that Sanderson would use its best endeavours to allocate appropriate resources to ensuring that the product performed according to specification. But, for the reasons which I have sought to explain, that was worth something to Watford; and Mr Jessa decided that he would be content with what he could get. In my view it is impossible to hold, in the circumstances of the present case, that Sanderson took unfair advantage of Watford; or that Watford, through Mr Jessa, did not properly understand and consider the effect of the term excluding indirect loss.
>
> It follows that I would hold that the term excluding indirect loss, applicable in the circumstances which I have described, was a fair and reasonable one to include in the contract.

The decision represents a 'hands-off' approach to the supervision of exclusion clauses in commercial contracts. The Court of Appeal was willing to overturn the trial judge's finding that the clause was unreasonable because the judge had failed to give due weight to the following factors:

1. There had been considerable negotiation between the parties as to which of them should bear the risk of making good the loss of profits.
2. The purchaser had successfully obtained an undertaking that the seller would use its best endeavours to allocate appropriate resources to ensuring that the product performed according to specification.
3. There was no significant difference in bargaining power between the parties.

For the Court of Appeal, the clause was reasonable because it was openly negotiated between two parties who were well capable of looking after their own interests. In high-risk contracts the parties should usually be left to allocate the risk between themselves (*Frans Maas (UK) Ltd v Samsung Electronics (UK) Ltd* [2004] 2 Lloyd's Rep 251).

This 'hands-off' approach to regulating commercial contracts was rejected by Tomlinson J on the facts of *Britvic Soft Drinks Ltd v Messer UK Ltd* [2002] 1 Lloyd's Rep 20 (affirmed [2002] EWCA Civ 548). The case concerned the exclusion of liability for CO2 not being of satisfactory quality. Tomlinson J considered the comments of Chadwick LJ in *Watford Electronics*, but concluded that on the facts of the case before him it would be 'wholly unreasonable for the supplier of a bulk commodity such as CO2 for a food application to seek to exclude liability for the commodity not being of satisfactory quality or being unfit for its purpose where that has come about as a result of a breakdown in the manufacturing process allowing the inadvertent introduction of a redundant carcinogen'.

While it is true that the court will consider each case on its merits, two final points seem apt. First, it seems that the courts are increasingly reluctant to intervene in commercial agreements on the basis of the UCTA 1977. This was recently confirmed by Tuckey LJ in *Granville Chemicals Ltd v Davis Turner & Co Ltd* [2003] 2 Lloyd's Rep 356, who concluded his judgment with these words:

> The 1977 Act obviously plays a very important role in protecting vulnerable consumers from the effects of draconian contract terms. But I am less enthusiastic about its intrusion into contracts between commercial parties of equal bargaining strength, who should generally be considered capable of being able to make contracts of their choosing and expect to be bound by their terms.

Second, in *RÖHLIG (UK) Ltd v Rock Unique Ltd* [2011] EWCA Civ 18 Moore-Bick LJ noted (at [23]):

> In principle the question must be considered separately in each case because the circumstances surrounding the contract may differ from case to case, but where a standard condition of this kind is involved I do not think that the court should be astute to draw fine distinctions between cases that in broad terms are very similar. It is important for those engaged in any commercial activity, whether as providers of goods or services or as customers, to know whether a particular clause will generally be regarded as reasonable in the context of contracts of a routine kind made between commercial parties.

7.4 Consumer Rights Act 2015

The (minimum harmonisation) European Union (EU) Directive on Unfair Terms in Consumer Contracts (Directive 93/13/EC) was, initially, transposed in the United Kingdom by the Unfair Terms in Consumer Contracts Regulations 1994 (UTCCR 1994). The UTCCR 1994 were later amended and replaced by the Unfair Terms in Consumer Contracts Regulations 1999 (UTCCR 1999), which were intended to reflect more closely the aims of the Directive. More recently the UTCCR 1999 were repealed, subject to transitional arrangements, by the Consumer Rights Act 2015 (CRA 2015) and replaced by provisions contained (largely) in Part 2 of the CRA 2015 (and, despite Brexit, it seems unlikely, given the huge amount of work which went into the Consumer Rights Act 2015, that these provisions would be repealed in the near future). A number of the provisions in Part 2 of the CRA 2015 resemble those under the UTCCR 1999 but, as is allowed in the transposition of a minimum harmonisation directive, some extensions have been enacted. The Act also took the opportunity to attempt to 'codify' an aspect of ECJ/CJEU jurisprudence (see *Pannon GSM Zrt v Erzsébet Sustikné Györfi* (C-243/08) [2009] ECR I-4713):

Section 71 Duty of court to consider fairness of term

(1) Subsection (2) applies to proceedings before a court which relate to a term of a consumer contract.

(2) The court must consider whether the term is fair even if none of the parties to the proceedings has raised that issue or indicated that it intends to raise it.

(3) But subsection (2) does not apply unless the court considers that it has before it sufficient legal and factual material to enable it to consider the fairness of the term.

7.4.1 Scope

The scope of Part 2 of the CRA 2015 is outlined in s 61:

Section 61 Contracts and notices covered by this Part

(1) This Part applies to a contract between a trader and a consumer.

(2) This does not include a contract of employment or apprenticeship.

(3) A contract to which this Part applies is referred to in this Part as a 'consumer contract'.

(4) This Part applies to a notice to the extent that it –

  (a) relates to rights or obligations as between a trader and a consumer, or

  (b) purports to exclude or restrict a trader's liability to a consumer.

(5) This does not include a notice relating to rights, obligations or liabilities as between an employer and an employee.

(6) It does not matter for the purposes of subsection (4) whether the notice is expressed to apply to a consumer, as long as it is reasonable to assume it is intended to be seen or heard by a consumer.
(7) A notice to which this Part applies is referred to in this Part as a 'consumer notice'.
(8) In this section 'notice' includes an announcement, whether or not in writing, and any other communication or purported communication.

The definition of a consumer for the purpose of Part 2 of the CRA 2015 is found in s 2(3), which states that a consumer 'means an individual acting for purposes that are wholly or mainly outside that individual's trade, business, craft or profession'. Unlike the UCTA 1977, the CRA 2015 does not apply to business-to-business (B2B) contracts, and only a natural person, not a company, can be a consumer for the purpose of Part 2 of the CRA 2015 (cf. the position under the pre-CRA 2015 version of UCTA 1977: *R & B Customs Brokers v United Dominions Trust Ltd* [1988] 1 WLR 321). In *Ashfaq v International Insurance Co of Hannover Plc* [2017] EWCA Civ 357, the Court of Appeal held that a person who, in addition to being a director of an information technology company, let out a property to students was not a consumer in respect of obtaining insurance for that property. The definition of a trader is found in s 2(2): 'a person acting for purposes relating to that person's trade, business, craft or profession, whether acting personally or through another person acting in the trader's name or on the trader's behalf.' Cf. also *Siba v Devenas (C-537/13)* [2015] Bus LR 291, *Van Gordon v Volkswagen Financial Services (UK) Ltd (t/a Audi Finance)* [2019] 4 WLUK 476 and *Pouvin and another v Électricité de France* (Case C-590/17) [2019] Bus LR 1114 (loans to employees).

The UTCCR 1999 did not apply to individually negotiated terms (see reg 5). By contrast Part 2 of the CRA 2015 applies to both individually and non-individually negotiated terms (see s 62 below). Part 2 has a wider scope than the UCTA 1977 to the extent that it applies to most types of contract term, not just, in effect, exclusion/limitation clauses. On the other hand s 73 provides that Part 2 of the CRA 2015 does not apply to terms inserted into the contract in compliance with a statutory or regulatory requirement or an international convention. In *Jones v Roundlistic Ltd* [2018] EWCA Civ 2284, the Court of Appeal held that this meant statutory or regulatory provisions which prescribed the terms and the content of those terms. Moreover, s 64 provides (partial) exemption from Part 2 to certain terms relating to the subject matter of the contract or the price:

Section 64 Exclusion from assessment of fairness

(1) A term of a consumer contract may not be assessed for fairness under section 62 to the extent that –
   (a) it specifies the main subject matter of the contract, or
   (b) the assessment is of the appropriateness of the price payable under the contract by comparison with the goods, digital content or services supplied under it.
(2) Subsection (1) excludes a term from an assessment under section 62 only if it is transparent and prominent.
(3) A term is transparent for the purposes of this Part if it is expressed in plain and intelligible language and (in the case of a written term) is legible.
(4) A term is prominent for the purposes of this section if it is brought to the consumer's attention in such a way that an average consumer would be aware of the term.
(5) In subsection (4) 'average consumer' means a consumer who is reasonably well-informed, observant and circumspect.
(6) This section does not apply to a term of a contract listed in Part 1 of Schedule 2.

We shall return to this provision, which has caused much controversy, below.

7.4.2 Control

7.4.2.1 Unfair terms

Section 62 Requirement for contract terms and notices to be fair

(1) An unfair term of a consumer contract is not binding on the consumer.

(2) An unfair consumer notice is not binding on the consumer.

(3) This does not prevent the consumer from relying on the term or notice if the consumer chooses to do so.

(4) A term is unfair if, contrary to the requirement of good faith, it causes a significant imbalance in the parties' rights and obligations under the contract to the detriment of the consumer.

(5) Whether a term is fair is to be determined –

 (a) taking into account the nature of the subject matter of the contract, and

 (b) by reference to all the circumstances existing when the term was agreed and to all of the other terms of the contract or of any other contract on which it depends.

(6) A notice is unfair if, contrary to the requirement of good faith, it causes a significant imbalance in the parties' rights and obligations to the detriment of the consumer.

(7) Whether a notice is fair is to be determined –

 (a) taking into account the nature of the subject matter of the notice, and

 (b) by reference to all the circumstances existing when the rights or obligations to which it relates arose and to the terms of any contract on which it depends.

(8) This section does not affect the operation of –

 (a) section 31 (exclusion of liability: goods contracts),

 (b) section 47 (exclusion of liability: digital content contracts),

 (c) section 57 (exclusion of liability: services contracts), or

 (d) section 65 (exclusion of negligence liability).

 ...

Section 67 Effect of an unfair term on the rest of a contract

Where a term of a consumer contract is not binding on the consumer as a result of this Part, the contract continues, so far as practicable, to have effect in every other respect.

Section 62 states that an unfair term will not be binding on the consumer, although under s 67 the contract will continue to bind the parties in so far as is practicable (see also Case C–472/11 *Banii Plus Bank Zrt v Csipai* [2013] 2 CMLR 42). The test of 'unfairness' in s 62(4) makes reference to two concepts: 'good faith' and 'significant imbalance'. While the latter concept is fairly familiar to English lawyers, the former concept has a much more European flavour and is less familiar to English lawyers. On the other hand, the CRA 2015 blacklists some terms (meaning, in effect, that they are deemed to be unfair) whilst other terms are included on an indicative list of terms which *may* be regarded as unfair (the so-called 'grey list'):

Section 63 Contract terms which may or must be regarded as unfair

(1) Part 1 of Schedule 2 contains an indicative and non-exhaustive list of terms of consumer contracts that may be regarded as unfair for the purposes of this Part.

(2) Part 1 of Schedule 2 is subject to Part 2 of that Schedule; but a term listed in Part 2 of that Schedule may nevertheless be assessed for fairness under section 62 unless section 64 or 73 applies to it.

(3) The Secretary of State may by order made by statutory instrument amend Schedule 2 so as to add, modify or remove an entry in Part 1 or Part 2 of that Schedule.
(4) An order under subsection (3) may contain transitional or transitory provision or savings.
(5) No order may be made under subsection (3) unless a draft of the statutory instrument containing it has been laid before, and approved by a resolution of, each House of Parliament.
(6) A term of a consumer contract must be regarded as unfair if it has the effect that the consumer bears the burden of proof with respect to compliance by a distance supplier or an intermediary with an obligation under any enactment or rule implementing the Distance Marketing Directive.

In addition to the type of term mentioned in s 63(6), s 62(8) identifies other terms which are, in effect, regarded as unfair. For example, s 31 provides:

31 Liability that cannot be excluded or restricted

(1) A term of a contract to supply goods is not binding on the consumer to the extent that it would exclude or restrict the trader's liability arising under any of these provisions –
  (a) section 9 (goods to be of satisfactory quality);
  (b) section 10 (goods to be fit for particular purpose);
  (c) section 11 (goods to be as described);
  (d) section 12 (other pre-contract information included in contract);
  (e) section 13 (goods to match a sample);
  (f) section 14 (goods to match a model seen or examined);
  (g) section 15 (installation as part of conformity of the goods with the contract);
  (h) section 16 (goods not conforming to contract if digital content does not conform);
  (i) section 17 (trader to have right to supply the goods etc); (j) section 28 (delivery of goods);
  (k) section 29 (passing of risk).
(2) That also means that a term of a contract to supply goods is not binding on the consumer to the extent that it would –
  (a) exclude or restrict a right or remedy in respect of a liability under a provision listed in subsection (1),
  (b) make such a right or remedy or its enforcement subject to a restrictive or onerous condition,
  (c) allow a trader to put a person at a disadvantage as a result of pursuing such a right or remedy, or
  (d) exclude or restrict rules of evidence or procedure.
(3) The reference in subsection (1) to excluding or restricting a liability also includes preventing an obligation or duty arising or limiting its extent.
(4) An agreement in writing to submit present or future differences to arbitration is not to be regarded as excluding or restricting any liability for the purposes of this section.
(5) Subsection and subsection (2) so far as it relates to liability under section 17, do not apply to a term of a contract for the hire of goods.
(6) But an express term of a contract for the hire of goods is not binding on the consumer to the extent that it would exclude or restrict a term that section 17 requires to be treated as included in the contract, unless it is inconsistent with that term (and see also section 62 (requirement for terms to be fair)).
(7) See Schedule 3 for provision about the enforcement of this section.

Section 65 Bar on exclusion or restriction of negligence liability

(1) A trader cannot by a term of a consumer contract or by a consumer notice exclude or restrict liability for death or personal injury resulting from negligence.

(2) Where a term of a consumer contract, or a consumer notice, purports to exclude or restrict a trader's liability for negligence, a person is not to be taken to have voluntarily accepted any risk merely because the person agreed to or knew about the term or notice.

(3) In this section 'personal injury' includes any disease and any impairment of physical or mental condition.

(4) In this section 'negligence' means the breach of –

(a) any obligation to take reasonable care or exercise reasonable skill in the performance of a contract where the obligation arises from an express or implied term of the contract,

(b) a common law duty to take reasonable care or exercise reasonable skill,

(c) the common duty of care imposed by the Occupiers' Liability Act 1957 or the Occupiers' Liability Act (Northern Ireland) 1957, or

(d) the duty of reasonable care imposed by section 2(1) of the Occupiers' Liability (Scotland) Act 1960.

(5) It is immaterial for the purposes of subsection (4) –

(a) whether a breach of duty or obligation was inadvertent or intentional, or

(b) whether liability for it arises directly or vicariously.

(6) This section is subject to section 66 (which makes provision about the scope of this section).

Section 66 Scope of section 65

(1) Section 65 does not apply to –

(a) any contract so far as it is a contract of insurance, including a contract to pay an annuity on human life, or

(b) any contract so far as it relates to the creation or transfer of an interest in land.

(2) Section 65 does not affect the validity of any discharge or indemnity given by a person in consideration of the receipt by that person of compensation in settlement of any claim the person has.

(3) Section 65 does not –

(a) apply to liability which is excluded or discharged as mentioned in section 4(2)(a) (exception to liability to pay damages to relatives) of the Damages (Scotland) Act 2011, or

(b) affect the operation of section 5 (discharge of liability to pay damages: exception for mesothelioma) of that Act.

(4) Section 65 does not apply to the liability of an occupier of premises to a person who obtains access to the premises for recreational purposes if –

(a) the person suffers loss or damage because of the dangerous state of the premises, and

(b) allowing the person access for those purposes is not within the purposes of the occupier's trade, business, craft or profession.

Schedule 2 contains an indicative ('grey') list of terms which *may* be regarded as unfair. That means that the terms listed are not necessarily unfair.

SCHEDULE 2 SECTION 63

CONSUMER CONTRACT TERMS WHICH MAY BE REGARDED AS UNFAIR

PART 1

LIST OFTERMS

1 A term which has the object or effect of excluding or limiting the trader's liability in the event of the death of or personal injury to the consumer resulting from an act or omission of the trader.

This does not include a term which is of no effect by virtue of section 65 (exclusion for negligence liability).

2 A term which has the object or effect of inappropriately excluding or limiting the legal rights of the consumer in relation to the trader or another party in the event of total or partial non-performance or inadequate performance by the trader of any of the contractual obligations, including the option of offsetting a debt owed to the trader against any claim which the consumer may have against the trader.

3 A term which has the object or effect of making an agreement binding on the consumer in a case where the provision of services by the trader is subject to a condition whose realisation depends on the trader's will alone.

4 A term which has the object or effect of permitting the trader to retain sums paid by the consumer where the consumer decides not to conclude or perform the contract, without providing for the consumer to receive compensation of an equivalent amount from the trader where the trader is the party cancelling the contract.

5 A term which has the object or effect of requiring that, where the consumer decides not to conclude or perform the contract, the consumer must pay the trader a disproportionately high sum in compensation or for services which have not been supplied.

6 A term which has the object or effect of requiring a consumer who fails to fulfil his obligations under the contract to pay a disproportionately high sum in compensation.

7 A term which has the object or effect of authorising the trader to dissolve the contract on a discretionary basis where the same facility is not granted to the consumer, or permitting the trader to retain the sums paid for services not yet supplied by the trader where it is the trader who dissolves the contract.

8 A term which has the object or effect of enabling the trader to terminate a contract of indeterminate duration without reasonable notice except where there are serious grounds for doing so. This is subject to paragraphs 21 (financial services) and 24 (sale of securities, foreign currency etc).

9 A term which has the object or effect of automatically extending a contract of fixed duration where the consumer does not indicate otherwise, when the deadline fixed for the consumer to express a desire not to extend the contract is unreasonably early.

10 A term which has the object or effect of irrevocably binding the consumer to terms with which the consumer has had no real opportunity of becoming acquainted before the conclusion of the contract.

11 A term which has the object or effect of enabling the trader to alter the terms of the contract unilaterally without a valid reason which is specified in the contract. This is subject to paragraphs 22 (financial services), 23 (contracts which last indefinitely) and 24 (sale of securities, foreign currency etc).

12 A term which has the object or effect of permitting the trader to determine the characteristics of the subject matter of the contract after the consumer has become bound by it. This is subject to paragraph 23 (contracts which last indefinitely).

13 A term which has the object or effect of enabling the trader to alter unilaterally without a valid reason any characteristics of the goods, digital content or services to be provided.

14 A term which has the object or effect of giving the trader the discretion to decide the price payable under the contract after the consumer has become bound by it, where no price or method of determining the price is agreed when the consumer becomes bound. This is subject to paragraphs 23 (contracts which last indefinitely), 24 (sale of securities, foreign currency etc) and 25 (price index clauses).

15 A term which has the object or effect of permitting a trader to increase the price of goods, digital content or services without giving the consumer the right to cancel the contract if the final price is too high in relation to the price agreed when the contract was concluded. This is subject to paragraphs 24 (sale of securities, foreign currency etc) and 25 (price index clauses).

16 A term which has the object or effect of giving the trader the right to determine whether the goods, digital content or services supplied are in conformity with the contract, or giving the trader the exclusive right to interpret any term of the contract.

17 A term which has the object or effect of limiting the trader's obligation to respect commitments undertaken by the trader's agents or making the trader's commitments subject to compliance with a particular formality.

18 A term which has the object or effect of obliging the consumer to fulfil all of the consumer's obligations where the trader does not perform the trader's obligations.

19 A term which has the object or effect of allowing the trader to transfer the trader's rights and obligations under the contract, where this may reduce the guarantees for the consumer, without the consumer's agreement.

20 A term which has the object or effect of excluding or hindering the consumer's right to take legal action or exercise any other legal remedy, in particular by –

(a) requiring the consumer to take disputes exclusively to arbitration not covered by legal provisions,

(b) unduly restricting the evidence available to the consumer, or

(c) imposing on the consumer a burden of proof which, according to the applicable law, should lie with another party to the contract.

PART 2

SCOPE OF PART 1

Financial services

21 Paragraph 8 (cancellation without reasonable notice) does not include a term by which a supplier of financial services reserves the right to terminate unilaterally a contract of indeterminate duration without notice where there is a valid reason, if the supplier is required to inform the consumer of the cancellation immediately.

22 Paragraph 11 (variation of contract without valid reason) does not include a term by which a supplier of financial services reserves the right to alter the rate of interest payable by or due to the consumer, or the amount of other charges for financial services without notice where there is a valid reason, if -

(a) the supplier is required to inform the consumer of the alteration at the earliest opportunity, and
(b) the consumer is free to dissolve the contract immediately.

Contracts which last indefinitely

23 Paragraphs 11 (variation of contract without valid reason), 12 (determination of characteristics of goods etc after consumer bound) and 14 (determination of price after consumer bound) do not include a term under which a trader reserves the right to alter unilaterally the conditions of a contract of indeterminate duration if –

(a) the trader is required to inform the consumer with reasonable notice, and
(b) the consumer is free to dissolve the contract.

Sale of securities, foreign currency etc

24 Paragraphs 8 (cancellation without reasonable notice), 11 (variation of contract without valid reason), 14 (determination of price after consumer bound) and 15 (increase in price) do not apply to –

(a) transactions in transferable securities, financial instruments and other products or services where the price is linked to fluctuations in a stock exchange quotation or index or a financial market rate that the trader does not control, and
(b) contracts for the purchase or sale of foreign currency, traveller's cheques or international money orders denominated in foreign currency.

Price index clauses

25 Paragraphs 14 (determination of price after consumer bound) and 15 (increase in price) do not include a term which is a price-indexation clause (where otherwise lawful), if the method by which prices vary is explicitly described.

The list is stated to be non-exhaustive (s 63(1)), which means that a clause of a type that is not featured on the list may nevertheless be found to be unfair. Many of the clauses featured are familiar to us from the discussion of the UCTA 1977 and paragraph 1(6) overlaps with the common law rules on penalties. The terms referred to in the list are stated by reference to their 'object or effect', indicating that the courts should look to the substance of the clause, not its form. This means that a term may be under suspicion, even if it does not look like a term on the list, so long as it has the same effect on consumers.

One of the first reported cases to consider the 1994 Regulations (the forerunner of the CRA 2015) concerned a term in a loan agreement issued by a bank and is detailed below.

***Director General of Fair Trading v First National Bank plc* [2002] 1 AC 481**

Facts: The defendant bank included in its loan agreement a term which stated that, should the borrower default on his repayments, interest would continue to be charged at the contractual rate until any judgment obtained by the bank was discharged. This meant that a court might order the consumer to pay off the debt by specified instalments, but the contractually agreed interest would continue to accrue while the instalments were being paid. The Director General of Fair Trading considered that the term was unfair for the purposes of reg 4 of the Unfair Terms in Consumer Contracts Regulations 1994. The trial judge held that the term was not unfair. The Court of Appeal allowed the appeal, holding that the term was unfair to the extent that it created unfair surprise and caused a significant imbalance in the rights and obligations between the parties.

Held: The House of Lords allowed the bank's appeal and held that the term was not unfair.

Lord Bingham:

10. In reliance on regulation 3(2)(b) Lord Goodhart, on behalf of the bank, submitted that no assessment might be made of the fairness of the term because it concerns the adequacy of the bank's remuneration as against the services supplied, namely the loan of money. A bank's remuneration under a credit agreement is the receipt of interest. The term, by entitling the bank to post-judgment interest, concerns the quantum and thus the adequacy of that remuneration ...

11. To this submission Mr Crow, representing the Director, gave two short answers. First, condition 8, of which the term forms part, is a default provision. Its purpose, and its only purpose, is to prescribe the consequences of a default by the borrower. It does not lay down the rate of interest which the bank is entitled to receive and the borrower bound to pay. It is an ancillary term, well outside the bounds of regulation 3(2)(b) ...

12. In agreement with the judge and the Court of Appeal, I do not accept the bank's submission on this issue. The Regulations, as Professor Sir Guenter Treitel QC has aptly observed (Treitel, *The Law of Contract*, 10th edn (1999), p 248), 'are not intended to operate as a mechanism of quality or price control' and regulation 3(2) is of 'crucial importance in recognising the parties' freedom of contract with respect to the essential features of their bargain': p 249. But there is an important 'distinction between the term or terms which express the substance of the bargain and 'incidental' (if important) terms which surround them': *Chitty on Contracts*, 28th edn (1999), vol 1, ch 15 'Unfair Terms in Consumer Contracts', p 747, para 15-025. The object of the Regulations and the Directive is to protect consumers against the inclusion of unfair and prejudicial terms in standard-form contracts into which they enter, and that object would plainly be frustrated if regulation 3(2)(b) were so broadly interpreted as to cover any terms other than those falling squarely within it. In my opinion the term, as part of a provision prescribing the consequences of default, plainly does not fall within it. It does not concern the adequacy of the interest earned by the bank as its remuneration but is designed to ensure that the bank's entitlement to interest does not come to an end on the entry of judgment. I do not think the bank's argument on merger advances its case. It appears that some judges in the past have been readier than I would be to infer that a borrower's covenant to pay interest was not intended to extend beyond the entry of judgment. But even if a borrower's obligation were ordinarily understood to extend beyond judgment even in the absence of an independent covenant, it would not alter my view of the term as an ancillary provision and not one concerned with the adequacy of the bank's remuneration as against the services supplied. It is therefore necessary to address the second question.

13. The test laid down by regulation 4(1), deriving as it does from article 3(1) of the Directive, has understandably attracted much discussion in academic and professional circles and helpful submissions were made to the House on it. It is plain from the recitals to the Directive that one of its objectives was partially to harmonise the law in this important field among all member states of the European Union. The member states have no common concept of fairness or good faith, and the Directive does not purport to state the law of any single member state. It lays down a test to be applied, whatever their pre-existing law, by all member states. If the meaning of the test were doubtful, or vulnerable to the possibility of differing interpretations in differing member states, it might be desirable or necessary to seek a ruling from the European Court of Justice on its interpretation. But the language used in expressing the test, so far as applicable in this case, is in my opinion clear and not reasonably capable of differing interpretations. A term falling within the scope of the Regulations is unfair if it causes a significant imbalance in the parties' rights and obligations under the contract to the detriment of the consumer in a manner or to an extent which is contrary to the requirement of good faith. The requirement of significant imbalance is met if a term is so weighted in favour of the supplier as to tilt the parties' rights and obligations under the contract significantly in his favour. This may be by the granting to the supplier of a beneficial option or discretion or power, or by the imposing on the consumer of a disadvantageous burden or risk or duty. The illustrative terms set out in Schedule 3 to the Regulations provide very good examples of terms which may be regarded as unfair; whether a given term is or is not to be so regarded depends on whether it causes a significant imbalance in the parties' rights and obligations under the contract. This involves looking at the contract as a whole. But the imbalance must be to the detriment of the consumer; a significant imbalance to the detriment of the supplier, assumed to be the stronger party, is not a mischief which the Regulations seek to address. The requirement of good faith in this context is one of fair and open dealing. Openness requires that the terms should be expressed fully, clearly and legibly, containing no concealed pitfalls or traps. Appropriate prominence should be given to terms which might operate disadvantageously to the customer. Fair dealing requires that a supplier should not, whether deliberately or unconsciously, take advantage of the consumer's necessity, indigence, lack of experience, unfamiliarity with the subject matter of the contract, weak bargaining position or any other factor listed in or analogous to those listed in Schedule 2 to the Regulations. Good faith in this context is not an artificial or technical concept; nor, since Lord Mansfield was its champion, is it a concept wholly unfamiliar to British lawyers. It looks to good standards of commercial morality and practice. Regulation 4(1) lays down a composite test, covering both the making and the substance of the contract, and must be applied bearing clearly in mind the objective which the Regulations are designed to promote.

... **20.** In judging the fairness of the term it is necessary to consider the position of typical parties when the contract is made. The borrower wants to borrow a sum of money, often quite a modest sum, often for purposes of improving his home. He discloses an income sufficient to finance repayment by instalments over the contract term. If he cannot do that, the bank will be unwilling to lend. The essential bargain is that the bank will make funds available to the borrower which the borrower will repay, over a period, with interest. Neither party could suppose that the bank would willingly forgo any part of its principal or interest. If the bank thought that outcome at all likely, it would not lend. If there were any room for doubt about the borrower's obligation to repay the principal in full with interest, that obligation is very clearly and unambiguously expressed in the conditions of contract. There is nothing unbalanced or detrimental to the consumer in that obligation; the absence of such a term would unbalance the contract to the detriment of the lender ...

22. Should it then be said that the provisions of the 1991 Order render the term unfair, providing as it does for a continuing obligation to pay interest after judgment notwithstanding the payment of instalments by the borrower in accordance with a court order? It is, I think, pertinent that the [Consumer Credit Act 1974], which laid down a number of stipulations with which regulated agreements must comply, did not prohibit terms providing for post-judgment interest even though it required claims to enforce regulated agreements to be brought in the county court which could not at the time award statutory interest in any circumstances. The 1974 Act was passed to protect consumers and such a prohibition would no doubt have been enacted had it been recognised as a necessary or desirable form of protection. The Crowther Committee, on whose report (Cmnd 4596, March 1971) the Act was based, did not recommend such a prohibition; indeed, it contemplated the recovery of contractual interest: see paragraphs 5.4.3, 6.6.33, 6.6.44(iv) and 6.7.16. It is also pertinent that judgments based on regulated agreements appear to have been excluded from the scope of the county court's power to award statutory interest in response to observations of Lord Donaldson of Lymington MR in *Forward Trust Ltd v Whymark* [1990] 2 QB 670, 681: but that was a case based on a flat rate agreement, in which the judgment in default would include a sum for future interest not yet accrued, in contrast with a simple rate agreement of the present kind (see [2001] 1 WLR 98, 110–111; [2000] QB 672, 679); the logic underpinning exclusion of statutory interest in the one case would not apply, at any rate with the same force, in the other. It is understandable that when a court is exercising a statutory power to order payment by instalments it should not also be empowered to order payment of statutory interest if the instalments are duly paid, but the term is directed to the recovery of contractual and not statutory interest. I do not think that the term can be stigmatised as unfair on the ground that it violates or undermines a statutory regime enacted for the protection of consumers.

23. It is of course foreseeable that a borrower, no matter how honourable and realistic his intentions when entering into a credit agreement, may fall on hard times and find himself unable to honour his obligations. The bank's standard conditions recognise that possibility by providing for the contingency of default. The 1974 Act even more fully recognises that possibility, by providing for time orders to be made and providing that when a time order is made the terms of the underlying agreement may also be amended. These provisions are clearly framed for the relief not of the borrower who, having the means to meet his contractual obligations, chooses not to do so, but for the relief of those who cannot pay or cannot pay without more time. Properly applied, these provisions enable the undeserving borrower to be distinguished from the deserving and for the contractual obligations of the deserving to be re-drawn in terms which reasonably reflect such ability, if any, as he may then have to repay within a reasonable period. Where problems arise in practice, it as to be because borrowers do not know of the effect of sections 129 and 136; neither the procedure for giving notice of default to the borrower nor the prescribed county court forms draw attention to them; and judgments will routinely be entered in the county court without the court considering whether to exercise its power under the sections.

24. I have no hesitation in accepting the proposition, inherent in the Director's submissions, that this situation is unacceptable. I have much greater difficulty in deciding whether the difficulties derive, as the Court of Appeal concluded, from the unfairness of the term or from the absence of procedural safeguards for the consumer at the stage of default. When the contract is made, default is a foreseeable contingency, not an expected outcome. It is not customary, even in consumer contracts, for notice to be given to the consumer of statutory reliefs open to him if he defaults. The 1974 Act does not require that notice of the effect of sections 129 and 136 be given. The evidence contains examples of clauses used by over 30 other lenders providing for the payment of interest after judgment, and none alerts the borrower to these potential grounds of relief. Regulation 4 is directed to the unfairness of a contract term, not the use which a supplier may make of a term which is in itself fair. It is readily understandable that a borrower may be disagreeably surprised if he finds that his contractual interest obligation continues to mount despite his duly paying the instalments ordered by the court, but it appears that the bank seeks to prevent that surprise by sending what is described in the evidence as a standard form of letter:

> 'You need only pay the amount ordered by the court under the terms of the judgment but you should be aware that under the terms of the agreement interest continues to accrue on your account. It is therefore in your interest to increase the instalment paid as soon as possible otherwise a much greater balance than the judgment debt may quickly build up'.

On balance, I do not consider that the term can properly be said to cause a significant imbalance in the parties' rights and obligations under the contract to the detriment of the consumer in a manner or to an extent which is contrary to the requirement of good faith.

25. I do not think that the issues raised in this appeal raise any question on which the House requires a ruling from the European Court of Justice to enable it to give judgment and I would not accordingly order a reference to be made.

26. For the reasons I have given, and those given by each of my noble and learned friends, I would allow the bank's appeal with costs in the House and the Court of Appeal and restore the order of the judge.

Lord Steyn:

30. My Lords, this is the first occasion on which the House has had the opportunity to examine an important branch of consumer law. It is therefore appropriate to consider the framework in which the questions before the House must be considered.

31. As between the Directive and the domestic implementing Regulations, the former is the dominant text. Fortunately, the 1994 Regulations, and even more so the Unfair Terms in Consumer Contracts Regulations 1999, appear to have implemented the Directive in domestic law in a manner which ought not to cause serious difficulty ...

33. The Directive made provision for a dual system of *ex casu* challenges and preemptive or collective challenges by appropriate bodies: see article 7. This system was domestically enacted in the 1994 Regulations, with the Director General of Fair Trading as the administering official to investigate and take action on complaints: see regulation 8. The 1999 Regulations extended the system of enforcement by including other bodies as qualified to undertake pre-emptive challenges. The system of pre-emptive challenges is a more effective way of preventing the continuing use of unfair terms and changing contracting practice than *ex casu* actions: see Susan Bright, 'Winning the battle against unfair contract terms' (2000) 20 LS 331, 333–338. It is, however, to be noted that in a pre-emptive challenge there is not a direct *lis* between the consumer and the other contracting party. The Directive and the Regulations do not always distinguish between the two situations. This point is illustrated by the emphasis in article 4.1 of the Directive and regulation 4(2) on the relevance of particular circumstances affecting a contractual relationship. The Directive and the Regulations must be made to work sensibly and effectively and this can only be done by taking into account the effects of contemplated or typical relationships between the contracting parties. Inevitably, the primary focus of such a pre-emptive challenge is on issues of substantive unfairness.

34. Under the Regulations, a term in a standard form contract that is unfair is not binding on the consumer. But certain provisions, sometimes called core terms, have been excepted from the regulatory regime. Regulation 3(2) so provides:

> 'In so far as it is in plain, intelligible language, no assessment shall be made of the fairness of any term which – (a) defines the main subject matter of the contract, or (b) concerns the adequacy of the price or remuneration, as against the goods or services sold or supplied'.

Clause 8 of the contract, the only provision in dispute, is a default provision. It prescribes remedies which only become available to the lender upon the default of the consumer. For this reason the escape route of regulation 3(2) is not available to the bank. So far as the description of terms covered by regulation 3(2) as core terms is helpful at all, I would say that clause 8 of the contract is a subsidiary term. In any event, regulation 3(2) must be given a restrictive interpretation. Unless that is done regulation 3(2) (a) will enable the main purpose of the scheme to be frustrated by endless formalistic arguments as to whether a provision is a definitional or an exclusionary provision. Similarly, regulation 3(2)(b) dealing with 'the adequacy of the price or remuneration' must be given a restrictive interpretation. After all, in a broad sense all terms of the contract are in some way related to the price or remuneration. That is not what is intended. Even price escalation clauses have been treated by the Director as subject to the fairness provision: see Susan Bright 20 LS 331, 345 and 349. It would be a gaping hole in the system if such clauses were not subject to the fairness requirement. For these further reasons I would reject the argument of the bank that regulation 3(2), and in particular 3(2)(b), take clause 8 outside the scope of the Regulations.

35. Given these conclusions the attack on the merger principle mounted by the bank was misplaced. In any event, I am not willing to uphold criticism by the bank of the well tried and tested principle of merger. I would therefore reject the bank's submissions under this heading.

36. It is now necessary to refer to the provisions which prescribe how it should be determined whether a term is unfair. Implementing article 3(1) of the Directive regulation 4(1) provides:

> "unfair term' means any term which contrary to the requirement of good faith causes a significant imbalance in the parties' rights and obligations under the contract to the detriment of the consumer'.

There are three independent requirements. But the element of detriment to the consumer may not add much. But it serves to make clear that the Directive is aimed at significant imbalance against the consumer, rather than the seller or supplier. The twin requirements of good faith and significant imbalance will in practice be determinative. Schedule 2 to the Regulations, which explains the concept of good faith, provides that regard must be had, amongst other things, to the extent to which the seller or supplier has dealt fairly and equitably with the consumer. It is an objective criterion. Good faith imports, as Lord Bingham of Cornhill has observed in his opinion, the notion of open and fair dealing: see also *Interfoto Picture Library Ltd v Stiletto Visual Programmes Ltd* [1989] QB 433. And helpfully the commentary to Lando & Beale, *Principles of European Contract Law, Parts I and II* (combined and revised 2000), p 113 prepared by the Commission of European Contract Law, explains that the purpose of the provision of good faith and fair dealing is 'to enforce community standards of decency, fairness and reasonableness in commercial transactions'; *a fortiori* that is true of consumer transactions. Schedule 3 to the Regulations (which corresponds to the annexe to the Directive) is best regarded as a check list of terms which must be regarded as potentially vulnerable. The examples given in Schedule 3 convincingly demonstrate that the argument of the bank that good faith is predominantly concerned with procedural defects in negotiating procedures cannot be sustained. Any purely procedural or even predominantly procedural interpretation of the requirement of good faith must be rejected.

37. That brings me to the element of significant imbalance. It has been pointed out by Hugh Collins that the test 'of a significant imbalance of the obligations obviously directs attention to the substantive unfairness of the contract': 'Good Faith in European Contract Law' (1994) 14 Oxford Journal of Legal Studies 229, 249. It is however, also right to say that there is a large area of overlap between the concepts of good faith and significant imbalance.

38. It is now necessary to turn to the application of these requirements to the facts of the present case. The point is a relatively narrow one. I agree that the starting point is that a lender ought to be able to recover interest at the contractual rate until the date of payment, and this applies both before and after judgment. On the other hand, counsel for the Director advanced a contrary argument. Adopting the test of asking what the position of a consumer is in the contract under consideration with or without clause 8, he said that the consumer is in a significantly worse position than he would have been if there had been no such provision. Certainly, the consumer is worse off. The difficulty facing counsel, however, is that this disadvantage to the consumer appears to be the consequence not of clause 8 but of the County Courts (Interest on Judgment Debts) Order 1991. Under this Order no statutory interest is payable on a county court judgment given in proceedings to recover money due under a regulated agreement: see article 2. Counsel said that for policy reasons it was decided that in such a case no interest may be recovered after judgment. He said that it is not open to the House to criticise directly or indirectly this legal context. In these circumstances he submitted that it is not legitimate for a court to conclude that fairness requires that a lender must be able to insist on a stipulation designed to avoid the statutory regime under the 1991 Order. Initially I was inclined to uphold this policy argument. On reflection, however, I have been persuaded that this argument cannot prevail in circumstances where the legislature has neither expressly nor by necessary implication barred a stipulation that interest may continue to accrue after judgment until payment in full.

39. For these reasons as well as the reasons given by Lord Bingham I agree that clause 8 is not unfair and I would also make the order which Lord Bingham proposes.

Lord Hope of Craighead:

40. My Lords, I have had the advantage of reading in draft the speech of my noble and learned friend, Lord Bingham of Cornhill. I agree with it, and for reasons which he has given I too would allow the appeal …

44. The primary reason which the Director has given for maintaining that the term is unfair is the uncertainty, confusion and hardship which has been shown to result from the bank's practice of claiming contractual interest from its borrowers after judgment has been given for the principal. Particular unfairness is said to arise where an order is made to pay the debt by instalments, whether under section 71 of the County Courts Act 1984 or a time order under section 129 of the 1974 Act, and where no consideration has been given to making an order under section 136 of the 1974 Act to amend the agreement so as to prevent the accrual of contractual interest on instalments which are paid when they fall due. The fact that it is commonplace for no consideration to be given to the use of section 136 when payment by instalments is being ordered is not in dispute. So it is not surprising that borrowers, on finding that they are liable for further amounts in addition to the instalments provided for in judgments obtained against them by the bank, have complained to the Director.

45. I am not persuaded that, despite these consequences, the term is unfair. The meaning to be given to the word 'unfair' in this context is laid down in regulation 4(1) of the 1994 Regulations. Guidance as to how the words used in that paragraph are to be understood is to be found in the sixteenth recital to the Directive. The recital explains what 'constitutes the requirement of good faith'. It states that an assessment of the unfair character of unfair terms must be supplemented by an overall evaluation of the different interests involved. Regulation 4(2) indicates the wide range of circumstances to be taken into account in the assessment. It provides that the assessment is to be done as at the time of the conclusion of the contract. But an appreciation of how the term will affect each party when the contract is put into effect must clearly form part of the exercise. It has been pointed out that there are considerable differences between the legal systems of the member states as to how extensive and how powerful the penetration has been of the principle of good faith and fair dealing: Lando & Beale, *Principles of European Contract Law, Parts I and II* (combined and revised, 2000), p 116. But in the present context there is no need to explore this topic in any depth. The Directive provides all the guidance that it needed as to its application.

46. Following this approach it does not seem to me that there is a significant imbalance to the detriment of the borrower in the stipulation that the interest which is payable in terms of the first part of the last sentence is to be charged after as well as before any judgment and that this obligation is not to merge in the judgment. The primary obligation in condition 4 is to pay interest on the outstanding balance due to the bank. The plain fact is that, in the event of a default by the borrower, the bank will not have recovered all of its money until the entire balance on the borrower's account has been paid. The main purpose of the last sentence is to ensure that the borrower does not enjoy the benefit of the outstanding balance after judgment without fulfilling the corresponding obligation which he has undertaken to pay interest on it as provided for in the contract. While the working out of that purpose may give rise to uncertainty in practice, the term itself does not seem to me to be unfair.

Lord Millett:

53. My Lords, I have had the advantage of reading in draft the speech of my noble and learned friend, Lord Bingham of Cornhill. I agree with it, and for the reasons he gives I too would allow the appeal. Because of the importance of the case, and because the real source of the problem remains to be tackled, I propose to add a few brief observations of my own.

54. A contractual term in a consumer contract is unfair if 'contrary to the requirement of good faith [it] causes a significant imbalance in the parties' rights and obligations under the contract to the detriment of the consumer'. There can be no one single test of this. It is obviously useful to assess the impact of an impugned term on the parties' rights and obligations by comparing the effect of the contract with the term and the effect it would have without it. But the inquiry cannot stop there. It may also be necessary to consider the effect of the inclusion of the term on the substance or core of the transaction; whether if it were drawn to his attention the consumer would be likely to be surprised by it; whether the term is a standard term, not merely in similar non-negotiable consumer contracts, but in commercial contracts freely negotiated between parties acting on level terms and at arms' length; and whether, in such cases, the party adversely affected by the inclusion of the term or his lawyer might reasonably be expected to object to its inclusion and press for its deletion. The list is not necessarily exhaustive; other approaches may sometimes be more appropriate.

55. The substance of the transaction in the present case is self-evident. It is a loan repayable by instalments with interest on the balance from time to time outstanding until the whole of the principal is repaid. The borrower would have no difficulty in understanding this. Nor would he think it unfair. If his attention were drawn to the impugned term, ie that interest should continue to be paid on the outstanding balance after as well as before judgment, he might well be surprised at the need to spell this out, but he would surely not be at all surprised by the fact. It is what he would expect. The term does not affect the substance of the transaction, which is that the borrower should continue to pay interest on the principal from time to time outstanding, nor does it impose any further or unexpected liability upon him not inherent in the basic transaction. It is included only to protect the lender from the (to modern eyes artificial) meaning placed on a covenant to pay interest by the Court of Appeal in *In re Sneyd; Exp Fewings* (1883) 25 ChD 338, where a covenant to pay interest on the balance of the principal sum from time to time remaining unpaid was construed as meaning remaining due under the covenant, so that it fell when the covenant was subsumed in the judgment.

56. The term is not only a standard term in non-negotiable loans to consumers, but in commercial loans freely negotiated between parties on equal terms and acting with professional advice. I venture to think that no lawyer advising a commercial borrower would dream of objecting to the inclusion of such a term, which merely reinforces and carries into effect what the parties themselves would regard as the essence of the transaction.

57. I am satisfied, therefore, that the term is not unfair. It does not cause an imbalance in the parties' rights and obligations; and the lender did not act in bad faith by taking advantage of the borrower's weakness of bargaining power or lack of professional advice to insist upon a term which would otherwise have been omitted.

Lord Rodger of Earlsferry:
62. My Lords, I have had the opportunity of reading the speech of my noble and learned friend, Lord Bingham in draft and, for the reasons which he gives, I too would allow the appeal.

The first issue for the House of Lords to consider was whether the term fell within the scope of the UTCCR 1994. Regulation 3(2) (a forerunner to both UTCCR 1999, reg 6(2) and CRA 2015, s 64(1)) stated:

> In so far as it is in plain, intelligible language, no assessment shall be made of the fairness of any term which –
>
> (a) defines the main subject matter of the contract, or
>
> (b) concerns the adequacy of the price or remuneration, as against the goods or services sold or supplied.

The question for the House of Lords was whether the provision as to the payment of interest following a court judgment fell under the reg 3(2) exclusions. Lord Steyn emphasised that reg 3(2) 'must be given a restrictive interpretation', otherwise the main purpose of the Regulations would be frustrated by 'endless formalistic arguments as to whether a provision is a definitional or an exclusionary provision'. Lord Bingham agreed, stating that:

> The object of the Regulations and the Directive is to protect consumers against the inclusion of unfair and prejudicial terms in standard-form contracts into which they enter, and that object would plainly be frustrated if regulation 3(2)(b) were so broadly interpreted as to cover any terms other than those falling squarely within it.

Lord Bingham noted with approval the distinction identified by *Chitty* 'between the term or terms which express the substance of the bargain and "incidental" (if important) terms which surround them'. Applying this distinction to the facts before him, Lord Bingham concluded that the term specifying the rate of interest payable after judgment was 'an ancillary provision and not one concerned with the adequacy of the bank's remuneration as against the services supplied'. For both Lord Bingham [12] and Lord Steyn [34] it was significant that the term dealt with the consequences following breach. This weighed in favour of the conclusion that the term was merely incidental or ancillary to the 'core obligation' of the contract.

The restrictive interpretation given to reg 3(2) was to be welcomed since it maintained the integrity and effectiveness of the UTCCR 1994. As Gross J explained in *Bairstow Eves v Smith* [2004] EWHC 263 (QB) (this time in relation to the reg 6(2) of the UTCCR 1999): '[R]egulation 6(2) must be given a restrictive interpretation; otherwise a coach and horses could be driven through the regulations.' Nevertheless, the House of Lords' conclusion that the term did not fall under reg 6(2) is rather more questionable. The term concerned the payment of interest. In a loan agreement, the main consideration provided by the debtor is the payment of interest. Thus, provisions as to such payment should arguably be regarded as dealing with the 'adequacy of the remuneration' received by the creditor and therefore fall under reg 6(2)(b). This is not the conclusion reached by the House of Lords, however.

Regulation 6(2) was more recently considered by the Supreme Court in *Office of Fair Trading v Abbey National plc* [2009] UKSC 6. This case concerned bank charges for unauthorised overdrafts (and similar charges). The Supreme Court held that an assessment of the fairness of such terms under the Regulations was circumscribed by reg 6(2), Lord Walker stating:

> **38.** After considering the judgments of Andrew Smith J and the Court of Appeal at length I am impressed, as no doubt all of us are, by the great care with which both courts have considered all the arguments and materials put before them. But I must respectfully say that I see force in Mr Sumption's criticisms of their approach as over-elaborate. The issue is a very important one, but it is essentially quite a short point, even when all the elements relevant to a purposive approach to construction are taken into account. I also respectfully think that the courts below, although cautioning themselves that 'core terms' is a shorthand expression for the contents of paragraphs (a) and (b) of regulation 6(2), tended to slip into treating it as an autonomous expression which itself expressed the contents of both those paragraphs.
>
> **39.** I start with the language of Article 4(2) and Regulation 6(2) (I can see no significant difference between them, although for no obvious reason Article 4(2) refers to assessing the unfair nature of a term whereas Regulation 6(2) refers to assessment of fairness of a term). Paragraphs (a) and (b) are, as I have said, concerned with the two sides of the quid pro quo inherent in any consumer contract. The main subject-matter may be goods or services. If it is goods, it may be a single item (a car or a dishwasher) or a multiplicity of items. If for instance a consumer orders a variety of goods from a mail-order catalogue – say clothing, blinds, kitchen utensils and toys – there is no possible basis on which the court can decide that some items are more essential to the contract than others. The main subject matter is simply consumer goods ordered

from a catalogue. I think that the Court of Appeal was wrong (para 55) to dismiss the difficulties raised by the banks on this point as something that the court could decide as a question of fact in the circumstances of the particular case.

40. Similarly, a supply of services may be simple (an entertainer booked to perform for an hour at a children's party) or composite (a week's stay at a five-star hotel offering a wide variety of services). Again, there is no principled basis on which the court could decide that some services are more essential to the contract than others and again the main subject matter must be described in general terms – hotel services. The services that banks offer to their current account customers are a comparable package of services. These include the collection and payment of cheques, other money transmission services, facilities for cash distribution (mainly by ATM machines either at manned branches or elsewhere) and the provision of statements in printed or electronic form.

41. When one turns to the other part of the quid pro quo of a consumer contract, the price or remuneration, the difficulty of deciding which prices are essential is just the same, and Regulation 6(2)(b) contains no indication that only an 'essential' price or remuneration is relevant. Any monetary price or remuneration payable under the contract would naturally fall within the language of paragraph (b) (I discount the absence of a reference to part of the price or remuneration for reasons already mentioned).

42. In the case of banking services supplied to a current account customer under the 'free if in credit' regime, the principal monetary consideration received by the bank consists of interest and charges on authorised and unauthorised overdrafts, and specific charges for particular non-routine services (such as expedited or foreign money transmission services). The most important element of the consideration, however, consists of the interest forgone by customers whose current accounts are in credit, since whether their credit balance is large or small, they will be receiving a relatively low rate of interest on it (sometimes a very low rate or no interest at all). The scale of this benefit is indicated by the figure for 2006 already mentioned. Mr Sumption was wary about committing himself as to whether interest foregone constituted part of the bank's price or remuneration for the purposes of Regulation 6(2)(b). Whatever view is taken as to that, it is clear that just as banking services to current account customers can aptly be described as a package, so can the consideration that moves from the customer to the bank. Interest forgone is an important part of that package for customers whose accounts are in credit, and overdraft interest and charges are the most important element for those customers who are not in credit. Lawyers are very used to speaking of a package (or bundle) of rights and obligations, and in that sense every obligation which a consumer undertakes by a consumer contract could be seen as part of the price or remuneration received by the supplier. But non-monetary obligations undertaken by a consumer contract (for instance, to take proper care of goods on hire-purchase, or to treat material supplied for a distance-learning course as available only to the customer personally) are not part of the 'price or remuneration' within the Regulation. That is the point of Lord Steyn's observation in *First National Bank*, in para 34, that 'in a broad sense all terms of the contract are in some way related to the price or remuneration'.

43. This House's decision in *First National Bank* shows that not every term that is in some way linked to monetary consideration falls within Regulation 6(2)(b). Paras (d), (e), (f) and (l) of the 'greylist' in Schedule 2 to the 1999 Regulations are an illustration of that. But the relevant term in First National Bank was a default provision. Traders ought not to be able to outflank consumers by 'drafting themselves' into a position where they can take advantage of a default provision. But *Bairstow Eves London Central Ltd v Smith* [2004] 2 EGLR 25 shows that the Court can and will be astute to prevent that. In *First National Bank* Lord Steyn indicated that what is now Regulation 6(2) should be construed restrictively, and Lord Bingham said that it should be limited to terms 'falling squarely within it'. I respectfully agree. But in my opinion the Relevant Terms and the Relevant Charges do fall squarely within Regulation 6(2)(b).

44. That conclusion is not to my mind at variance with the message to be derived from the *travaux*. It is a fairly complex message, reflecting not only a compromise between the opposing aims of consumer protection and freedom of contract, but also the contrast between consumer protection and consumer choice (the latter being more central, perhaps, to basic Community principles). This point was explored and explained in an article (not mentioned by the Court of Appeal) to which Mr Sumption referred, that is 'Good Faith in European Contract Law' by Professor Hugh Collins, (1994) 14 OJLS 229. Mr Sumption placed particular emphasis on the following passage:

> 'The history of the EC Directive on Unfair Terms in Consumer Contracts reveals the struggle between these two interpretations of the economic interests of consumers. Even at a late stage in the negotiations, the draft Directive proposed by the Commission envisaged the introduction of a general principle against substantive unfairness in consumer contracts. It invalidated terms in standard form consumer contracts which caused 'the performance of the contract to be significantly different from what the consumer could legitimately expect', or which caused 'the performance of the contract to be unduly detrimental to the consumer'. But in the battle between the advocates of consumer rights and the supporters of free competition, eventually the latter emerged victorious in the Council of Ministers. The fairness of the transaction in the sense of the price paid for the goods or services should not be subjected to review or control. This is the meaning of the obscure Article 4(2) [which is then set out]. The final reservation in this provision ['plain intelligible language'] is significant. The Directive does not require consumer contracts to be substantively fair, but it does require them to be clear. Clarity is essential for effective market competition between terms. What matters primarily for EC contract law is consumer choice, not consumer rights'.

45. The Court of Appeal took account of the travaux and of some academic writing. It recognised as an underlying value the notion that freedom of contract should prevail where there has been meaningful negotiation between supplier and consumer, so that the latter does consent to the terms of the contract. But I respectfully think the Court went too far in interpreting the language of the Directive and the 1999 Regulations in order to meet that perceived aim. The Directive and the 1999 Regulations apply only to terms which have not been individually negotiated, and the Court departed from the natural meaning of the text in order to achieve an unnecessary duplication of the exception for individually negotiated terms.

46. I would add a postscript to this part of the discussion. A variety of expressions has been used, in the courts below and in argument (and to some extent by this House in *First National Bank*), to describe those contractual terms which are subject to review in point of fairness: ancillary, subordinate, incidental, non-core, collateral. These may all be of some assistance but it is important, in considering provisions which apply across an extraordinarily wide range of consumer contracts, to treat them with caution. I venture to repeat a paragraph from an opinion of mine (in which the other members of the Appellate Committee concurred) in *College of Estate Management v Customs & Excise Commissioners* [2005] STC 1957, para 30, an appeal raising questions of Community law about whether there is a single or multiple supply, and whether it is of goods or services, for the purposes of value added tax:

> '"Ancillary" means (as Ward LJ rightly observed ([2004] STC 1471 at [39]) subservient, subordinate and ministering to something else. It was an entirely apposite term in the discussion in British Telecommunications (where the delivery of the car was subordinate to its sale) and in Card Protection Plan itself (where some peripheral parts of a package of services, and some goods of trivial value such as labels, key tabs and a medical card, were subordinate to the main package of insurance services). But there are other cases (including *Faaborg*, *Beynon* and the

> present case) in which it is inappropriate to analyse the transaction in terms of what is "principal" and "ancillary", and it is unhelpful to strain the natural meaning of "ancillary" in an attempt to do so. Food is not ancillary to restaurant services; it is of central and indispensable importance to them; nevertheless there is a single supply of services (*Faaborg*). Pharmaceuticals are not ancillary to medical care which requires the use of medication; again, they are of central and indispensable importance; nevertheless there is a single supply of services (*Beynon*)'.

Conversely, delivery of goods or peripheral extras may be disregarded as ancillary for the purposes of para (a) of Regulation 6(2), but the charges for them, if payable under the same contract, are part of the price for the purposes of para (b) ...

47. I can state my opinion much more briefly on the second main issue in the appeal, that is the application of Regulation 6(2), properly construed, to the facts. Charges for unauthorised overdrafts are monetary consideration for the package of banking services supplied to personal current account customers. They are an important part of the banks' charging structure, amounting to over 30 per cent of their revenue stream from all personal current account customers. The facts that the charges are contingent, and that the majority of customers do not incur them, are irrelevant. On the view that I take of the construction of Regulation 6(2), the fairness of the charges would be exempt from review in point of appropriateness under Regulation 6(2)(b) even if fewer customers paid them, and they formed a smaller part of the banks' revenue stream. Even if the Court of Appeal's interpretation had been correct, I do not see how it could have come to the conclusion that charges amounting to over 30 per cent of the revenue stream were (para 111) 'not part of the core or essential bargain'.

The Supreme Court decision in *Office of Fair Trading v Abbey National plc* has attracted much comment (see, for example, M Kenny, 'Orchestrating sub-prime consumer protection in retail banking: *Abbey National* in the context of Europeanised private law' (2011) 19 ERPL 43) and it is arguable that the judgment was influenced by the banking crisis (see J Devenney, 'Gordian knots in Europeanised private law: Unfair terms, bank charges and political compromises' [2011] 62 NILQ 33 at 52). Indeed, in the context of gym membership, the judgment of Kitchen J in *Office of Fair Trading v Ashbourne Management Services Ltd* [2011] EWHC 1237 (Ch) appears to have a different flavour:

> This brings me to the final part of the analysis, namely whether this assessment of fairness relates to the definition of the main subject matter of the agreements. In my judgment it does not. The assessment does not relate to the meaning or description of the length of the minimum period, the facilities to which the member gains access or the monthly subscription which he has to pay; nor does it relate to the adequacy of the price as against the facilities provided. Instead it relates to the obligation upon members to pay monthly subscriptions for the minimum period when they have overestimated the use they will make of their memberships and failed to appreciate that unforeseen circumstances may make their continued use of a gym impractical or their memberships unaffordable. Put another way, it relates to the consequences to members of early termination in light of the minimum membership period. Accordingly I believe the assessment is not precluded by regulation 6(2).

In May 2012, the Department for Business, Innovation and Skills requested the Law Commissions, particularly in the light of *OFT v Abbey National plc*, to update, in relation to consumer contracts, their 2005 Report. In July 2012 the Law Commissions published an Issues Paper (*Unfair Terms in Consumer Contracts: a new approach?*) and in March 2013 they published their advice to the Department for Business, Innovation and Skills (*Unfair Terms in Consumer Contracts: Advice to the Department for Business, Innovation and Skills*). Key recommendations were set out in the summary of the advice (pp vii–xiii):

The exemption for main subject matter and price

The current law (Part 2)

5.6 The UTD exempts certain contract terms from review, provided that they are 'in plain intelligible language'. Article 4(2) states that a fairness assessment may not relate to 'the definition of the subject matter of the contract' or 'the adequacy of the price and remuneration … as against the services or goods supplied in exchange'. These words have been copied out into the implementing regulations and are now in Regulation 6(2) of the UTCCR.

5.7 The exemption has proved particularly difficult to interpret. It has generated complex litigation, culminating in the 2009 Supreme Court decision, *Office of Fair Trading v Abbey National plc*. This was a test case against seven banks and a building society. The issue was whether charges for unauthorised overdrafts were exempt from an assessment for fairness because they were price terms.

5.8 The High Court and Court of Appeal found that the terms were not exempt, because they were not part of the essential bargain between the parties, and a typical consumer would not recognise the charges as part of the price. By contrast, the Supreme Court said that overdraft charges were exempt. It rejected the idea that price terms could be divided into those which formed the essential bargain and those which were ancillary. It said that the price should be determined 'objectively', rather than from the viewpoint of a typical consumer. The judgment has proved difficult to interpret, with regulators and businesses expressing different views.

The case for reform (Part 2)

5.9 In the Issues Paper we asked whether the law in this area was unduly uncertain. A large majority of consultees agreed that it was. Consumer groups and enforcement bodies felt that this undermined the effectiveness of the legislation:

It is virtually impossible for consumers to apply the rules confidently. [Which?]

Any law that is so complex and could lead to such great delays through judicial interpretation does not meet a fitness for purpose test for consumer protection legislation. [Trading Standards Institute]

The Supreme Court decision has led us to be very cautious in our assessment of unfair terms [Civil Aviation Authority]

5.10 Only a small minority of consultees thought that the law was certain. HSBC commented:

The Supreme Court's decision was clear that, in relation to price terms, 'any monetary price or remuneration payable under the contract' would naturally fall within the exemption.

5.11 We think that the words of the judgment may be lulling some businesses into a false sense of security. There are other ways to interpret the judgment – and it could be overturned by the Court of Justice of the European Union (CJEU). The German Federal Supreme Court takes a different view on the UTD and has reviewed ancillary bank charges for fairness.

5.12 In a world of price comparison websites, there is increasing pressure on traders to advertise low headline prices, whilst earning their profits through other charges. Given this potential undermining of competition, the law should provide effective tools to prevent abuse.

5.13 The current uncertainty has the potential to damage businesses as well as consumers. If a business uses an ancillary price term to subsidise a low headline price, the business is put at risk if the term is later found to be unfair. It faces the substantial costs of litigation; the reputational damage to its business; the cost of repaying consumers; and the demise of its business model.

5.14 We recommend that the exemption for subject matter and price should be reformed. The current law is unacceptably uncertain. It requires significant legal expertise to navigate, and even then the outcome is unpredictable. Both consumers and traders may suffer from this uncertainty.

The need to protect against small print (Part 3)

5.15 We think that the exemption should distinguish between terms which are subject to competition and those which are buried in 'small print'. Where consumers know about the terms proffered by traders, they are able to take them into account in their choices: the law should not seek to protect consumers from the consequences of their own decisions.

5.16 By contrast, consumers rarely read 'small print'. 'Small print' is a concept instantly understood by consumers in their daily lives. It is not just about font size. It is also marked by poor layout, densely phrased paragraphs and legal jargon. Often simply labelling a hyper-link as 'terms and conditions' is sufficient to ensure that most consumers do not read the document. We think that all small print terms should be assessable for fairness.

A new approach based on transparency and prominence (Part 3 and 4)

5.17 The 2005 Report proposed that the exemption should not apply to payments which are 'incidental or ancillary to the main purpose of the contract'. In Abbey National this test was considered too uncertain.

5.18 We now recommend that price or main subject matter terms should be exempt from review only if they are transparent and prominent. Both approaches distinguish between the terms which consumers take into account in their decision to buy the product and those which become lost in small print. The emphasis on prominence, however, offers a practical way of distinguishing between a headline price and other charges. It also emphasises that whether a term is exempt is within the control of the trader.

5.19 We recommend that:

(1) 'Transparent' should be defined as in plain, intelligible language; readily available; and, if in writing, legible.
(2) The test of 'prominence' should refer to the 'average consumer' test, which is widely used in European consumer law. It refers to a hypothetical consumer who is 'reasonably well informed, reasonably observant and circumspect'.

A term would be prominent if it is presented in such a way that the average consumer would be aware of the term. The more unusual or onerous the term, the more prominent it needs to be.

5.20 All terms of a contract should be transparent. As discussed below, if they are not, enforcement agencies should be able to challenge them. Clearly not all terms can be prominent. Simply because a term is not prominent does not make it unfair; nor does it raise a presumption that it is unfair. It could, however, be assessed for fairness.

Consultees' views

5.21 More than half of those responding agreed that a price term should be excluded from review, but only if it is transparent and prominent. Support came from all categories of consultee: businesses and business groups; consumer groups; public bodies; academics; and the judiciary and lawyers.

> Transparency and prominence would not only ensure fairness but also further promote competition. [Direct Line Group]
>
> Prominence of the price is key to ensure that consumers know what they are getting for their money. [MoneySavingExpert.com]

Traders can be expected to welcome the degree of control which they would have over the application of the exemption. [Malcolm Waters QC]

5.22 Only two consultees disagreed with the tests in their entirety. Several businesses had concerns, however, particularly about how they would work in practice. We think that many of these concerns can be met by guidance from regulators.

5.23 Some regulators and consumer groups argued that prominence and transparency alone may not always be sufficient. Relying on the insights of behavioural economics, they said that consumers may ignore remote or contingent charges, even if they are prominent. We note that the Directive already makes provisions for behavioural biases in the annex or 'grey list' of terms which may be regarded as unfair. We think it is helpful to clarify that grey list terms cannot fall within the exemption.

Excluded term or excluded assessment?

5.24 One particular difficulty in understanding the exemption is whether it excludes the whole term (the excluded term construction) or only an aspect of the term (the excluded assessment construction).

5.25 The case law suggests that the courts may consider some aspects of price terms, such as their timing or calculation. It is only the amount (or 'adequacy') of the price which cannot be assessed for fairness. In *Foxtons v O'Reardon*, for example, the term concerned the payment of the estate agent's commission, which was due on exchange of contracts rather than on completion of the sale. Although this was a price term, the court was able to consider the timing of the payment, as this did not involve an assessment of 'the adequacy of the price'.

5.26 In the Issues Paper we argued that it would be simpler to concentrate on the term. Following consultation we have been persuaded that this would under-implement the Directive. To ensure that the UK meets its minimum harmonisation obligation, we recommend that the legislation should follow the approach of the Directive in stating that it is only the amount of the price which is excluded from review. Other aspects of price terms, such as timing, may be assessed for fairness.

5.27 By contrast, we think that the exemption for main subject matter applies to all aspects of the term. Thus if the term specifies the main subject matter, the court may not consider its fairness at all. We considered, but rejected, the idea that a court could assess the fairness of any aspect of the main subject matter, provided that it did not consider how the main subject matter had been defined.

Suggested redraft

5.28 Although the wording will be a matter for Parliamentary Counsel, we conclude that the exemption should be redrafted along the following lines:

No assessment of fairness shall be made –

(a) of a term which specifies the main subject matter of the contract; or

(b) of the amount of the price, as against the goods or services supplied in exchange, provided that the term in question is transparent and prominent.

Guidance

5.29 It is important that the practicalities of making price charges prominent should fit in with other regulations, particularly for financial services, utilities or mobile phone contracts. We recommend that regulators should publish sector-specific guidance on the meaning of 'transparent and prominent' to assist businesses.

The grey list (part 5)

5.30 Schedule 2 of the UTCCR contains an indicative and non-exhaustive list of terms which may be regarded as unfair (the grey list). It reproduces word for word the Annex to the UTD. We recommend that the legislation should specifically state that all terms on the grey list are assessable for fairness.

5.31 Following consultation we have been persuaded that the grey list should be retained in its current form with some limited additions. We recommend three additions to the grey list. These are terms which have the object or effect of:

(1) permitting the trader to claim disproportionately high sums in compensation or for services which have not been supplied, where the consumer has attempted to cancel the contract;
(2) giving the trader discretion to decide the amount of the price after the consumer has become bound by the contract; and
(3) giving the trader discretion to decide the subject matter of the contract after the consumer has become bound by it.

Copy out and the fairness test (part 6)

5.32 In the Issues Paper we asked whether the UTCCR should be rewritten in more accessible language. We have been persuaded by the strong arguments put to us that the words of the UTD should be changed only if there is a good reason to do so. We therefore recommend that the fairness test set out in articles 3(1) and 4(1) of the UTD should be replicated in the new legislation.

The need for transparency (part 6)

5.33 Article 5 of the UTD states that written contracts 'must always be drafted in plain intelligible language'. Recital 20 expands this concept to say that 'the consumer should actually be given an opportunity to examine all the terms'. We have concluded that article 5 goes beyond the words used, and also requires that terms are legible and readily available. We therefore recommend that the legislation should require terms to be 'transparent', which incorporates all three concepts.

5.34 Article 5 does not spell out the consequences of failing to make a term transparent. We do not think that non-transparent terms are automatically unfair, though it is an important factor to consider. Under the Consumer Injunctions Directive, however, enforcement bodies must have the power to prevent their use. We recommend that the legislation should clarify that enforcement bodies may use their powers under Part 8 of the Enterprise Act 2002 against terms which are not transparent.

Of particular concern (at least pre-Brexit!) was the suggestion that the position reached in *Abbey National* failed to properly implement the Unfair Terms in Consumer Contracts Directive. As noted above, the CRA 2015, s 64 now provides:

(1) A term of a consumer contract may not be assessed for fairness under section 62 to the extent that –
  (a) it specifies the main subject matter of the contract, or
  (b) the assessment is of the appropriateness of the price payable under the contract by comparison with the goods, digital content or services supplied under it.
(2) Subsection (1) excludes a term from an assessment under section 62 only if it is transparent and prominent.

In at least two respects this provision appears to reinforce aspects of *Office of Fair Trading v Abbey National Plc*. First, s 64(1)(b) clearly inclines to Lord Walker's view that only monetary payment terms are caught by article 4(2) of the Directive. Second, s 64(2) states that '[s]ubsection (1) excludes a term from an assessment under section 62 only if it is transparent and prominent' which chimes with the analysis of *Office of Fair Trading v Foxtons* [2009] EWHC 1681 by the Supreme Court in *Office of Fair Trading v Abbey National Plc*. Yet the bigger issue is whether the controversial reading of the exclusions from the test of unfairness in article 4(2) of the Directive by the Supreme Court in *Office of Fair Trading v Abbey National Plc* should be used in relation to s 64(1)(b) of the CRA 2015.

On the one hand, the legislative history of s 64 suggests an intention that such an approach should be retained. More specifically, s 64 can be traced back to the Law Commission's advice that the issues surrounding the impact of *Office of Fair Trading v Abbey National Plc* could be dealt with by the use of transparency and prominence requirements (rather than reverting to a previous interpretation of provisions transposing article 4(2)). In *Casehub Ltd v Wolf Cola Ltd* [2017] EWHC 1169 (Ch) it was held, relying on *Office of Fair Trading v Abbey National plc*, that cancellation fees in respect of a 12-month cloud storage contract could not, as a result of s 64, be assessed for fairness if that meant assessing the appropriateness of the price in comparison with the services supplied. However, such clauses might have been challenged as unfair on other grounds.

Leaving aside the concepts of transparency and prominence (which we shall return to below), this approach creates a number of problems. Indeed, as the Law Commission recognised, it was far from clear that such an approach was in conformity with EU Law (although post-Brexit this will be less of a concern). Indeed, subsequent judgments of the CJEU cast more suspicion on the appropriateness of the approach in *Office of Fair Trading v Abbey National Plc*. For example, in *Kásler v OTP Jelzálogbank Zrt* (C-26/13) [2014] 2 All E.R. (Comm) 443 the Court of Justice of the European Union (CJEU), in the context of a consumer credit agreement, held that a term which provided the exchange rate for the repayment of a loan in a foreign currency could be assessed for unfairness:

> in so far as it contains a pecuniary obligation for the consumer to pay, in repayment instalments of the loan, the difference between the selling rate of exchange and the buying rate of exchange of the foreign currency, cannot be considered as 'remuneration', the adequacy of which as consideration for a service supplied by the lender cannot be subject of an examination as regards unfairness under Article 4(2). ([59])

Given the incomplete nature of the map left by the Supreme Court, it is not easy to compare the approach of the CJEU in *Kásler v OTP Jelzálogbank Zrt* with the approach in *Office of Fair Trading v Abbey National Plc*. Nevertheless, the approach of the CJEU did appear to be more nuanced than the rather more blunt focus on monetary terms by the Supreme Court.

Returning to our discussion of *Director General of Fair Trading v First National Bank plc*, having determined that the term was subject to review under the UTCCR 1994, their Lordships turned to consider the issue of fairness. Lord Bingham, with whom the other Law Lords agreed, noted that reg 4(1) (a forerunner of UTCCR 1999, reg 5(1) and CRA 2015, s 62(4)) identified two separate requirements: 'significant imbalance' and 'good faith'. For Lord Bingham the former requirement is predominantly concerned with the substance of the agreement. It 'involves looking at the contract as a whole' and the significant imbalance must operate 'to the detriment of the consumer'. The test of 'good faith' on the other hand, is more concerned with procedural fairness. The court must ask whether the supplier has taken advantage of the consumer's 'necessity, indigence, lack of experience, unfamiliarity with the subject matter of the contract, weak bargaining position'. All these matters relate to procedural fairness in the making of the agreement. For Lord Bingham, reg 4(1) '[laid] down a composite test, covering both the making and the substance of the contract'.

Lord Steyn took a rather different view, holding that the issue of good faith was concerned with substance as well as procedure. For his Lordship, the examples given in Schedule 3 (a forerunner of CRA 2015, Schedule 2) were conclusive evidence against the argument that good faith merely concerned procedure (at [36]). Lord Steyn's position appears to be preferable since the wording of reg 5(1) clearly envisages 'significant imbalance' as just one element in an overall test of 'good faith'. The other members of the House of Lords concurred with Lord Bingham, however, and expressed no specific view on the issue, which probably means that his analysis reflects the view of the majority. In practice, this will probably make little difference since the substantive issues will still be considered under the test of 'significant imbalance'. The Court of Appeal subsequently stated that reg 5(1) of the UTCCR 1999 sets out a composite test requiring both procedural and substantive unfairness. In *Bryen & Langley Ltd v Boston* [2005] EWCA Civ 973, Rimer LJ said (at [45]):

> [I]n assessing whether a term that has not been individually negotiated is 'unfair' for the purposes of Regulation 5(1) it is necessary to consider not merely the commercial effects of the term on the relative rights of the parties but, in particular, whether the term has been imposed on the consumer in circumstances which justify a conclusion that the supplier has fallen short of the requirements of fair dealing.

Given the uncertainty that surrounds the concept of 'unfairness', it is perhaps surprising that their Lordships declined to make a reference to the then European Court of Justice (ECJ) for a preliminary ruling on its meaning. Lord Bingham thought that such a reference was unnecessary because the language used was 'clear and not reasonably capable of differing interpretations'. This conclusion is rather doubtful, however, given the lack of consensus that exists within Member States as to the meaning of 'good faith'. Meryll Dean ('Defining unfair terms in consumer contracts – crystal ball gazing? *Director General of Fair Trading v First National Bank plc*' (2002) 65 MLR 773, 776–777) has written the following:

> [Lord Bingham's] confidence in the obvious meaning of the test and the unlikely divergence of interpretation is to be respected but, in the light of comparative research, may be somewhat misplaced. In the leading comparative analysis of the subject, Zimmerman and Whittaker studied the concept of good faith in 15 legal systems and applied it to 30 hypothetical cases. They came to the conclusion that the concept meant different things within a particular legal system as well as between legal systems. Similarly, Lando and Beale, whilst accepting that 'the principle of good faith and fair dealing is recognised or at least appears to be acted on as a guideline for contractual behaviour in all EC countries', nevertheless acknowledge the 'considerable difference between the legal systems as to how extensive and how powerful the penetration of the principle has been' ... There is no doubt that, whilst the concept may be identified as present in a variety of forms in EC legal systems, good faith means different things to different courts ... *First National Bank* was one of those situations where the House of Lords should have recognised the importance of the reference in a broader European context. As Markesinis has observed, 'the task the modern courts face is formidable; the responsibility awesome; their opportunity to harmonise legal systems indisputable'. In other words, national myopia needs to give way to a broader vision based on the Europeanisation of contract law.

Prior to Brexit it was hoped that when the issue came to be revisited by the Supreme Court it would make, if appropriate, a reference to the CJEU in order to obtain clarification of the meaning of 'good faith and fair dealing' (cf. *Office of Fair Trading v Abbey National plc* [2009] UKSC 6 and *X v Inspecteur van Rijksbelastingdienst* (C-72/14) *Van Dijk v Staatssecretaris van Financien* (C-197/14) [2016] 1 CMLR 27).

The House of Lords was unanimous in holding that the term did not contravene the Regulations. Such clauses were common in loan agreements. The obligation created by it was clear and unambiguous and involved nothing 'unbalanced or detrimental to the consumer'. Indeed, in Lord Bingham's view, 'the absence of such a term would unbalance the contract to the detriment of the lender' (at [20]). For Lord Bingham and Lord Steyn the problem lay, not in the contract term itself, but in consumers' understanding of the regulatory framework established by the Consumer Credit Act 1974 (cf. *UK Housing Alliance (North West) Ltd v Francis* [2010] EWCA Civ 117 where the protection that could be offered by a court in possession proceedings contributed to a finding that a term in a sale and leaseback arrangement was not unfair under the Regulations). In particular, there was a need to draw attention to the courts' powers under ss 129 and 136 of the 1974 Act to redraw the terms of the contract in appropriate circumstances. These provisions would allow the court to incorporate the recovery of interest into the calculation of the instalment payments for the judgment. Catherine MacMillan, 'Evolution or revolution? Unfair terms in consumer contracts' [2002] CLJ 22, 24, has provided the following helpful summary of the case:

> The decision is a welcome one. A strange aspect to this case is that while consumers could face an unpleasant state of affairs, this occurred within an existing regulatory framework. The 1974 Act arguably provides a greater degree of protection to consumers than the Directive.

In recent years, a number of other cases have considered the operation of UTCCR 1999, Reg 5(1). In *Westminster Building Co Ltd v Beckingham* [2004] EWHC 138 (TCC), the High Court upheld an adjudication clause in a contract for the renovation of a London house. Judge Thornton QC explained his decision as follows (at [31]):

> I was referred to a number of authorities of which the most helpful were *Director General of Fair Trading v First National Bank plc* [2002] 1 AC 481, HL, particularly the speech of Lord Bingham at page 494, and *Lovell Projects Ltd v Legg and Carver* [2003] BLR 452, Judge Moseley QC, particularly at paragraphs 24–31. From these authorities, I derive the following guidance as applicable to the facts of this case:
>
> 1 The terms in this case were not individually negotiated but were couched in plain and intelligible language.
> 2 The terms of the contract were decided upon by Mr Beckingham's agent, who are chartered surveyors, and Mr Beckingham had, or had available to him, competent and objective advice as to the existence and effect of the adjudication clause before he proffered and entered into the contract. Westminster did no more than accept the contract terms offered and had no reasonable need to draw to Mr Beckingham's attention the potential pitfalls to be found in the adjudication clause and in its operation during the course of the work. The clause did not, therefore contravene the requirement of good faith (see especially the speech of Lord Bingham in the *Director General of Fair Trading* case at page 494).
> 3 The clause did not, if considered at the time of making the contract, constitute a significant imbalance as to Mr Beckingham's rights …
> 4 The clause does not significantly exclude or hinder the consumer's right to take legal action or other legal remedy or restrict the evidence available to him …
>
> For all these reasons, I conclude that the adjudication clause, on the facts of this case, is not unfair and is binding on Mr Beckingham.

While the UTCCR 1999 were successfully used to challenge the validity of an adjudication clause (*Picardi v Cuniberti* [2003] BLR 487), this will be extremely difficult where the consumer has received professional advice (*Westminster Building Co Ltd v Beckingham* [2004] EWHC 138 (TCC); *Allen Wilson Shop-fitters v Buckingham* [2005] EWHC 1165 (TCC)), or where s/he has put forward the terms of the contract (*Bryen & Langley Ltd v Boston* [2005] EWCA Civ 973).

A standard form contract issued by the Royal Institute of British Architects was successfully challenged by a consumer in *Munkenbeck & Marshall v Harold*.

***Munkenbeck & Marshall v Harold* [2005] EWHC 356**

Facts: The defendant consumer engaged the claimant firm of architects to undertake architectural services. The claimant's letter of appointment stated that they were appointed on the standard terms of the Royal Institute of British Architects. The terms included the following:

> 5.13 Any sums due and remaining unpaid at the expiry of 30 days after the date of issue of an account from the Architect shall bear interest. Interest shall be payable at 8% over Bank of England base rate current at the date of issue of the account.
>
> 9.6 The Client shall indemnify the Architect in respect of his legal and other costs in any action or proceedings, together with a reasonable sum in respect of his time spent in connection with such action or proceedings or any part thereof, if:
>
> (1) the Architect obtains a judgment of the court or an Arbitrator's award in his favour for the recovery of fees and/or expenses under the Agreement; or
>
> (2) the Client fails to obtain a judgment of the court or an Arbitrator's award in the Client's favour for any claim or any part of any claim against the Architect.

In reliance on these terms, the claimant brought an action to recover unpaid fees and the costs involved in bringing the claim. The defendant challenged the terms under reg 5(1).

Held: The Court held that the terms were unfair and were not enforceable.

Judge Richard Havery QC: My conclusion on these points is this. The terms in question, 5.13 and 9.6, are unusual and onerous. They are unusual, in my judgment, notwithstanding that they form part of profession-wide standard terms. They were not drawn to the attention of Mr. Harold, who was unaware of them. There is force in the argument that clause 9.6 is there to protect the architect against unfair treatment by the client. The same may be said for the high interest rate. Those points are relevant to the question whether the requirement of good faith mentioned in regulation 5(1) has been satisfied. There is the further point that Mr. Harold was by no means without bargaining power. He negotiated a reduction in the claimant's fees from 10 per cent to 9.5 per cent of final cost. But there is an imbalance, as submitted by Mr. Roberts, and it runs to the detriment of the consumer. That imbalance is not required by the requirement to protect the position of the architect. I conclude that the terms in question are unfair in this case, and fall within regulation 5(1). By reason of regulation 8(1), they are not contractually enforceable.

It is significant to note that there was evidence of both procedural and substantive unfairness on the facts of the case. More recent case law includes *Du Plessis v Fontgary Leisure Parks Ltd* [2012] EWCA Civ 409, where the owner of a caravan park reviewed pitch fees in accordance with the relevant contract and sought to introduce a graded fees system. As a result the claimant's pitch became more expensive and the claimant argued the relevant contractual provision was 'unfair' as it created a significant imbalance in the rights and obligations of the parties. This argument was rejected by the Court of Appeal with Jackson LJ noting (at [52]): 'It should also be noted that the introduction of grading at Fontygary Leisure Park in 2008 was carried out in a fair manner. The defendant offered, at its own expense, to move caravans to less expensive pitches if any caravan owners so requested.' By contrast, in *Spreadex Ltd v Cochrane* [2012] EWHC 1290 a provision in an alleged online spread betting agreement – which provided 'You will be deemed to have authorised all trading under your account number' – was held to be 'unfair'. A had registered for online spread betting with B. C (the young son of A's girlfriend) accessed A's account and caused it to become in debit.

B argued that A was liable on the basis of the above provision. However, the court held that the relevant provision, which had no cap on liability, was contrary to 'good faith' and 'unfair'.

More recently in *Cavendish Square Holding BV v Talal El Makdessi; ParkingEye Ltd v Beavis* [2015] UKSC 67, Lord Neuberger and Lord Sumption (with whom Lord Carnwath agreed) referred to a concept of 'legitimate interest' in finding that a parking fine was not unfair (the full facts are given at 15.2.5.3):

> **104** In our opinion, the same considerations which show that the £85 charge is not a penalty, demonstrate that it is not unfair for the purpose of the Regulations.
>
> **105** The reason is that although it arguably falls within the illustrative description of potentially unfair terms at paragraph 1(e) of Schedule 2 to the Regulations, it is not within the basic test for unfairness in regulations 5(1) and 6(1). The Regulations give effect to Council Directive 93/13/EEC on unfair terms in consumer contracts, and these rather opaque provisions are lifted word for word from articles 3 and 4 of the Directive. The effect of the Regulations was considered by the House of Lords in *Director General of Fair Trading v First National Bank plc* [2001] 1 AC 481. But it is sufficient now to refer to *Aziz v Caixa d'Estalvis de Catalunya, Tarragona i Manresa (Case C-415/11)* [2013] 3 CMLR 89, which is the leading case on the topic in the Court of Justice of the European Union. *Aziz* was a reference from a Spanish court seeking guidance on the criteria for determining the fairness of three provisions in a loan agreement. They provided for (i) the acceleration of the repayment schedule in the event of the borrower's default, (ii) the charging of default interest, and (iii) the unilateral certification by the lender of the amount due for the purpose of legal proceedings. The judgment of the Court of Justice is authority for the following propositions:
>
> 1) The test of 'significant imbalance' and 'good faith' in article 3 of the Directive (regulation 5(1) of the 1999 Regulations) 'merely defines in a general way the factors that render unfair a contractual term that has not been individually negotiated' (para 67). A significant element of judgment is left to the national court, to exercise in the light of the circumstances of each case.
> 2) The question whether there is a 'significant imbalance in the parties' rights' depends mainly on whether the consumer is being deprived of an advantage which he would enjoy under national law in the absence of the contractual provision (paras 68, 75). In other words, this element of the test is concerned with provisions derogating from the legal position of the consumer under national law.
> 3) However, a provision derogating from the legal position of the consumer under national law will not necessarily be treated as unfair. The imbalance must arise 'contrary to the requirements of good faith'. That will depend on 'whether the seller or supplier, dealing fairly and equitably with the consumer, could reasonably assume that the consumer would have agreed to such a term in individual contract negotiations' (para 69).
> 4) The national court is required by article 4 of the Directive (regulation 6(1) of the 1999 Regulations) to take account of, among other things, the nature of the goods or services supplied under the contract. This includes the significance, purpose and practical effect of the term in question, and whether it is 'appropriate for securing the attainment of the objectives pursued by it in the member state concerned and does not go beyond what is necessary to achieve them' (paras 71–74). In the case of a provision whose operation is conditional upon the consumer's breach of another term of the contract, it is necessary to assess the importance of the latter term in the contractual relationship.
>
> **106** In its judgment, the Court of Justice drew heavily on the opinion of Advocate General Kokott, specifically endorsing her analysis at a number of points. That analysis, which is in the nature of things more expansive than the court's, repays careful study. In the Advocate General's view, the requirement that the 'significant imbalance' should be contrary to good faith was included in order to limit the Directive's inroads into the principle of freedom of contract. '[I]t is recognised'. she said, 'that in many cases parties

have a legitimate interest in organising their contractual relations in a manner which derogates from the [rules of national law]' (para AG73). In determining whether the seller could reasonably assume that the consumer would have agreed to the relevant term in a negotiation, it is important to consider a number of matters. These include:

> 'whether such contractual terms are common, that is to say they are used regularly in legal relations in similar contracts, or are surprising, whether there is an objective reason for the term and whether, despite the shift in the contractual balance in favour of the user of the term in relation to the substance of the term in question, the consumer is not left without protection (para AG75)'.

Advocate General Kokott returned to the question of legitimate interest when addressing default interest. She observed that a provision requiring the payment upon default of a sum exceeding the damage caused, may be justified if it serves to encourage compliance with the borrower's obligations:

> 'If default interest is intended merely as flat-rate compensation for damage caused by default, a default interest rate will be substantially excessive if it is much higher than the accepted actual damage caused by default. It is clear, however, that a high default interest rate motivates the debtor not to default on his contractual obligations and to rectify quickly any default which has already occurred. If default interest under national law is intended to encourage observance of the agreement and thus the maintenance of payment behaviour, it should be regarded as unfair only if it is much higher than is necessary to achieve that aim (para AG87)'.

Finally, the Advocate General observes that the impact of a term alleged to be unfair must be examined broadly and from both sides. Provisions favouring the lender may indirectly serve the interest of the borrower also, for example by making loans more readily available (para AG94).

107 In our opinion the term imposing the £85 charge was not unfair. The term does not exclude any right which the consumer may be said to enjoy under the general law or by statute. But it may fairly be said that in the absence of agreement on the charge, Mr Beavis would not have been liable to Parking-Eye. He would have been liable to the landowner in tort for trespass, but that liability would have been limited to the occupation value of the parking space. To that extent there was an imbalance in the parties' rights. But it did not arise 'contrary to the requirement of good faith', because ParkingEye and the landlord to whom ParkingEye was providing the service had a legitimate interest in imposing a liability on Mr Beavis in excess of the damages that would have been recoverable at common law. ParkingEye had an interest in inducing him to observe the two-hour limit in order to enable customers of the retail outlets and other members of the public to use the available parking space. To echo the observations of the Advocate General at para AG94 of her opinion, charging overstayers £85 underpinned a business model which enabled members of the public to park free of charge for two hours. This was fundamental to the contractual relationship created by Mr Beavis's acceptance of the terms of the notice, whose whole object was the efficient management of the car park. It was an interest of exactly the kind envisaged by the Advocate General at para AG87 of her opinion and by the Court of Justice at para 74 of the judgment. There is no reason to regard the amount of the charge as any higher than was necessary to achieve that objective.

108 Could ParkingEye, 'dealing fairly and equitably with the consumer ... reasonably assume that the consumer would have agreed to such a term in individual contract negotiations'? The concept of a negotiated agreement to enter a car park is somewhat artificial, but it is perfectly workable provided that one bears in mind that the test, as Advocate General Kokott pointed out in *Aziz* at para AG75, is objective. The question is not whether Mr Beavis himself would in fact have agreed to the term imposing the £85 charge in a negotiation, but whether a reasonable motorist in his position would have done so. In our view a reasonable motorist would have agreed. In the first place, motorists generally and Mr Beavis in particular did accept it. In the case of non-negotiated standard terms that would not ordinarily be entitled to much weight. But although the terms, like all standard contracts, were presented to motorists on a take it or leave it basis, they could not have been briefer, simpler or more prominently proclaimed. If you park here and stay more than two hours, you will pay £85. Motorists could hardly avoid reading the notice and were under no pressure to accept its terms.

109 Objectively, they had every reason to do so. They were being allowed two hours of free parking. In return they had to accept the risk of being charged £85 if they overstayed. Overstaying penalties are, as we have mentioned, both a normal feature of parking contracts on public and on private land, and important for the efficient management of the space in the interests of the general body of users and the neighbouring outlets which they may frequent. They are beneficial not just to ParkingEye, the landowner and the retail outlets, but to the motorists themselves, because they make parking space available to them which might otherwise be clogged up with commuters and other long-stay users. The amount of the charge was not exorbitant in comparison to the general level of penalties imposed for parking infractions. Nor is there any reason to think that it was higher than necessary to ensure considerate use by motorists of the available space. And, while we accept Mr Butcher's submission that the fact that the £85 charge is broadly comparable to charges levied by local authorities for parking in public car parks is not enough to show that it was levied in good faith, it is nonetheless a factor which assists ParkingEye in that connection. The risk of having to pay it was wholly under the motorist's own control. All that he needed was a watch. In our opinion, a hypothetical reasonable motorist would have agreed to objectively reasonable terms, and these terms are objectively reasonable.

7.4.2.2 The requirement of 'transparency'

Section 68 Requirement for transparency

(1) A trader must ensure that a written term of a consumer contract, or a consumer notice in writing, is transparent.

(2) A consumer notice is transparent for the purposes of subsection (1) if it is expressed in plain and intelligible language and it is legible.

Section 68 applies to all written terms (including terms potentially excluded from the unfairness test by s 64) and requires the trader to ensure that the terms are expressed in 'plain, intelligible language'. Section 64(3): 'A term is transparent for the purposes of this Part if it is expressed in plain and intelligible language and (in the case of a written term) is legible.' The problem with the provision is that it does not explicitly prescribe any sanction for breach and therefore its status as a requirement remains unclear. Note, however, that the Competition and Markets Authority (CMA) guidance on Part 2 of the CRA 2015 draws a link between the unfairness test and the requirement of transparency (CMA, *Unfair contract terms guidance: Guidance on the unfair terms provisions in the Consumer Rights Act 2015* (July 2015) para 2.22ff):

> In order to achieve the openness required by good faith, terms should be 'expressed fully, clearly and legibly, containing no concealed pitfalls or traps. Appropriate prominence should be given to terms which might operate disadvantageously' to the consumer. Consumers should not be assumed necessarily to be able themselves to identify (particularly in longer contracts) terms which are important, or which may operate to their disadvantage or which would be likely to surprise them, if drawn to their attention ... openness is not enough on its own, since good faith relates to the content of terms as well as the way they are expressed. Fair dealing has been authoritatively

> said to require that, in drafting and using contract terms, a trader 'should not, whether deliberately or unconsciously, take advantage' of the consumers' circumstances to their detriment ... The CMA considers the CJEU's approach demonstrates that businesses need, in formulating their contract terms, not just to resist the temptation to take advantage, but actively to take the legitimate interests of the consumer into account.

See also *Higgins & Co Lawyers Ltd v Evans* [2019] EWHC 2809. Section 69 gives statutory effect to the common law *contra proferentem* rule:

Section 69 Contract terms that may have different meanings

(1) If a term in a consumer contract, or a consumer notice, could have different meanings, the meaning that is most favourable to the consumer is to prevail.

(2) Subsection (1) does not apply to the construction of a term or a notice in proceedings on an application for an injunction or interdict under paragraph 3 of Schedule 3.

Thus if a term is ambiguous in its meaning, it will be construed in favour of the consumer. In County *Homesearch Co (Thames & Chilterns) Ltd v Cowham* [2008] 1 WLR 909 the Court of Appeal refused to apply reg 7(2), UTCCR 1999. Longmore LJ stated (at [21]):

> Mr Warwick had some difficulty in identifying the written term [Regulation 7(2) was explicitly limited to written terms] in relation to which there was a doubt about its meaning. He first identified clause 3 but, read as a whole, there is no doubt about its meaning. He then identified clause 2 but that clause specifies the agent's obligation not the client's obligation to pay. He then said that the contract as a whole did not indicate clearly enough that the implied term was not to apply. This exposed his difficulty in relying on regulation 7(2). There has to be a written term as to which there is a doubt. The fact that it may be arguable whether a term should be implied (a fact I take for granted since permission to appeal has been given) does not mean that there is a doubt about the meaning of a written term.

> More recently in *R & S Pilling (trading as Phoenix Engineering) v UK Insurance Ltd* [2019] UKSC 16 Lord Hodge (with whom Lady Hale, Lord Wilson, Lady Arden and Lord Kitchin agreed) stated:

> 51. Dealing briefly with other arguments which Phoenix has raised, I see no basis for the operation against UKI of the contra proferentem rule in this context. The necessity for corrective construction arises from the fact that the terms to meet the legal requirements, which the Chief Executive's certificate vouched, have not been expressed in the insuring clause. There is no doubt as to what those terms are as the statutory provision provides them. Nor do I derive any assistance by reference to the Unfair Terms in Consumer Contracts Regulations 1999 (SI 1999/2083) ('the 1999 Regulations'). The requirement in regulation 7 of the 1999 Regulations (now section 69 of the Consumer Rights Act 2015) that the interpretation most favourable to the consumer is to prevail where there is doubt about the meaning of a written term of a contract applies, for example, in the circumstances which I have discussed in para 48 above. But I am not persuaded that it can apply where the court, having recognised a mistake in the language used, is applying a corrective construction by reading into the clause words, which have not been expressed, to correct the mistake. It is important to recall that a corrective interpretation is available only if it is clear what a reasonable person would have understood the parties to have meant (para 46 above). Nor can the fact that UKI has amended the terms of the Policy to extend its cover since the events which gave rise to the claim in this case assist the process of construction of the terms of the Policy.

7.4.3 Enforcement

In addition to the provisions noted above (e.g., s 62 and s 71 of the CRA 2015), the CRA 2015 sets out a framework for the public enforcement of Part 2 (as did the UTCCR 1994 and UTCCR 1999): see s 70. The relevant provisions are contained in Schedule 3:

SCHEDULE 3 SECTION 70

ENFORCEMENT OF THE LAW ON UNFAIR CONTRACT TERMS AND NOTICES

Application of schedule

1. This Schedule applies to –
   (a) a term of a consumer contract,
   (b) a term proposed for use in a consumer contract,
   (c) a term which a third party recommends for use in a consumer contract, or
   (d) a consumer notice.

Consideration of complaints

2.(1) A regulator may consider a complaint about a term or notice to which this Schedule applies (a 'relevant complaint').

(2) If a regulator other than the CMA intends to consider a relevant complaint, it must notify the CMA that it intends to do so, and must then consider the complaint.

(3) If a regulator considers a relevant complaint, but decides not to make an application under paragraph 3 in relation to the complaint, it must give reasons for its decision to the person who made the complaint.

Application for injunction or interdict

3. (1) A regulator may apply for an injunction or (in Scotland) an interdict against a person if the regulator thinks that –
   (a) the person is using, or proposing or recommending the use of, a term or notice to which this Schedule applies, and
   (b) the term or notice falls within any one or more of sub-paragraphs (2), (3) or (5).

(2) A term or notice falls within this sub-paragraph if it purports to exclude or restrict liability of the kind mentioned in –
   (a) section 31 (exclusion of liability: goods contracts),
   (b) section 47 (exclusion of liability: digital content contracts),
   (c) section 57 (exclusion of liability: services contracts), or
   (d) section 65(1) (business liability for death or personal injury resulting from negligence).

(3) A term or notice falls within this sub-paragraph if it is unfair to any extent.

(4) A term within paragraph 1(1)(b) or (c) (but not within paragraph 1(1)(a)) is to be treated for the purposes of section 62(4) and (5) (assessment of fairness) as if it were a term of a contract.

(5) A term or notice falls within this sub-paragraph if it breaches section 68 (requirement for transparency).

(6) A regulator may apply for an injunction or interdict under this paragraph in relation to a term or notice whether or not it has received a relevant complaint about the term or notice.

Notification of application

4. (1) Before making an application under paragraph 3, a regulator other than the CMA must notify the CMA that it intends to do so. (2) The regulator may make the application only if –

(a) the period of 14 days beginning with the day on which the regulator notified the CMA has ended, or

(b) before the end of that period, the CMA agrees to the regulator making the application.

Determination of application

5. (1) On an application for an injunction under paragraph 3, the court may grant an injunction on such conditions, and against such of the respondents, as it thinks appropriate.

(2) On an application for an interdict under paragraph 3, the court may grant an interdict on such conditions, and against such of the defenders, as it thinks appropriate.

(3) The injunction or interdict may include provision about –

(a) a term or notice to which the application relates, or

(b) any term of a consumer contract, or any consumer notice, of a similar kind or with a similar effect.

(4) It is not a defence to an application under paragraph 3 to show that, because of a rule of law, a term to which the application relates is not, or could not be, an enforceable contract term.

(5) If a regulator other than the CMA makes the application, it must notify the CMA of –

(a) the outcome of the application, and

(b) if an injunction or interdict is granted, the conditions on which, and the persons against whom, it is granted.

Undertakings

6. (1) A regulator may accept an undertaking from a person against whom it has applied, or thinks it is entitled to apply, for an injunction or interdict under paragraph 3.

(2) The undertaking may provide that the person will comply with the conditions that are agreed between the person and the regulator about the use of terms or notices, or terms or notices of a kind, specified in the undertaking.

(3) If a regulator other than the CMA accepts an undertaking, it must notify the CMA of –

(a) the conditions on which the undertaking is accepted, and

(b) the person who gave it.

Publication, information and advice

7. (1) The CMA must arrange the publication of details of –

(a) any application it makes for an injunction or interdict under paragraph 3,

(b) any injunction or interdict under this Schedule, and

(c) any undertaking under this Schedule.

(2) The CMA must respond to a request whether a term or notice, or one of a similar kind or with a similar effect, is or has been the subject of an injunction, interdict or undertaking under this Schedule.

(3) Where the term or notice, or one of a similar kind or with a similar effect, is or has been the subject of an injunction or interdict under this Schedule, the CMA must give the person making the request a copy of the injunction or interdict.

(4) Where the term or notice, or one of a similar kind or with a similar effect, is or has been the subject of an undertaking under this Schedule, the CMA must give the person making the request –

(a) details of the undertaking, and

(b) if the person giving the undertaking has agreed to amend the term or notice, a copy of the amendments.

(5) The CMA may arrange the publication of advice and information about the provisions of this Part.

(6) In this paragraph –

(a) references to an injunction or interdict under this Schedule are to an injunction or interdict granted on an application by the CMA under paragraph 3 or notified to it under paragraph 5, and

(b) references to an undertaking are to an undertaking given to the CMA under paragraph 6 or notified to it under that paragraph.

Meaning of 'regulator'

8. (1) In this Schedule 'regulator' means –

(a) the CMA,

(b) the Department of Enterprise, Trade and Investment in Northern Ireland,

(c) a local weights and measures authority in Great Britain,

(d) the Financial Conduct Authority,

(e) the Office of Communications,

(f) the Information Commissioner,

(g) the Gas and Electricity Markets Authority,

(h) the Water Services Regulation Authority,

(i) the Office of Rail and Road,

(j) the Northern Ireland Authority for Utility Regulation, or

(k) the Consumers' Association.

(2) The Secretary of State may by order made by statutory instrument amend sub-paragraph (1) so as to add, modify or remove an entry.

(3) An order under sub-paragraph (2) may amend sub-paragraph (1) so as to add a body that is not a public authority only if the Secretary of State thinks that the body represents the interests of consumers (or consumers of a particular description).

(4) The Secretary of State must publish (and may from time to time vary) other criteria to be applied by the Secretary of State in deciding whether to add an entry to, or remove an entry from, sub-paragraph (1).

(5) An order under sub-paragraph (2) may make consequential amendments to this Schedule (including with the effect that any of its provisions apply differently, or do not apply, to a body added to sub-paragraph (1)).

(6) An order under sub-paragraph (2) may contain transitional or transitory provision or savings.

(7) No order may be made under sub-paragraph (2) unless a draft of the statutory instrument containing it has been laid before, and approved by a resolution of, each House of Parliament.

(8) In this paragraph 'public authority' has the same meaning as in section 6 of the Human Rights Act 1998.

Other definitions

9. In this Schedule – 'the CMA' means the Competition and Markets Authority; 'injunction' includes an interim injunction; 'interdict' includes an interim interdict.

The Financial Conduct Authority

10. The functions of the Financial Conduct Authority under this Schedule are to be treated as functions of the Authority under the Financial Services and Markets Act 2000.

Although *Director General of Fair Trading v First National Bank* concerned an application by the Director General for an injunction under reg 12 of the UTCCR 1994, the vast majority of cases have not reached the courts. Instead they have been resolved at a much earlier stage through negotiation between the then OFT and the businesses concerned (see Bright, 'Winning the battle against unfair terms' (2000) 20 LS 331). The public enforcement provisions in the CRA 2015 are, in fact, part of tapestry of public enforcement provisions relevant to the regulation of unfair terms. In addition to the provisions under the CRA 2015, it is possible to take public enforcement action under Part 8 of the Enterprise Act 2002 (which now provides for 'enhanced consumer measures') and under the Consumer Protection from Unfair Trading Regulations 2008.

Additional reading

Adams, J., and Brownsword, R., 'The Unfair Contract Terms Act: A Decade of Discretion' (1988) 104 LQR 94.

Beale, H., 'Unfair Contracts in Britain and Europe' (1989) 42 CLP 197.

Beale, H., 'Legislative Control of Fairness: The Directive on Unfair Terms in Consumer Contracts' in Beatson, J., and Friedmann, D (eds), *Good Faith and Fault in Contract Law* (Oxford: Clarendon, 1995).

Bradgate, R., 'Unreasonable Standard Terms' (1997) 60 MLR 582.

Collins, H., 'Good Faith in European Contract Law' (1994) 14 OJLS 229.

Devenney, J., 'Gordian Knots in Europeanised Private Law: Unfair Terms, Bank Charges and Political Compromises' (2011) 62 NILQ 33.

Devenney, J., and Kenny, M., 'Unfair Terms, Surety Transactions and European Harmonisation: A Crucible of Europeanised Private Law?' [2009] Conv 295.

MacDonald, E., 'Unifying Unfair Terms Legislation' (2004) 67 MLR 69.

Palmer, N., and Yates, D., 'The Future of the Unfair Contract Terms Act 1977' (1981) 40 CLJ 108.

Von Mehren, A., 'General Limits on the Use of Contract', Vol vii, *International Encyclopaedia of Comparative Law*, 1982, The Hague: Mohr/Nijhoff.

Yates, D., *Exclusion Clauses in Contracts*, 2nd edn (London: Sweet & Maxwell, 1982).

Chapter 8

Misrepresentation

Chapter contents

8.1 Introduction

Following the formation of an apparently valid contract, one of the parties might argue that it should not be enforced due to, for example, the conduct of the other party during negotiations or due to some fact unknown to both parties at the time of formation. In the following four chapters we will consider four categories of legal rules that govern these situations: misrepresentation (the subject of this chapter), mistake (Chapter 9), duress (Chapter 10) and undue influence (Chapter 11). The first two categories can be grouped together because misrepresentation is, effectively, the law of induced mistake and the latter two categories can be grouped together because undue influence is, in broad terms, the sister doctrine of duress.

In Chapter 6 we noted that not all statements made during the contracting process necessarily form part of any resulting contract. More specifically we noted that some pre-contractual statements are mere representations. Nevertheless, we also noted that there are remedies available in respect of some false pre-contractual representations (or actionable misrepresentations). In particular, the misrepresentee may be able to rescind the contract; and, depending on the precise circumstances, damages may also be available.

In this chapter, which is divided into six sections, we will consider important aspects of the law of misrepresentation. In Section 8.2, we will consider what constitutes an actionable misrepresentation; then we will look at the categories of misrepresentation (Section 8.3); then we will consider the remedies available for each (Section 8.4); and in Section 8.5, we will briefly examine the law on exclusion of liability for misrepresentation. Finally, we will consider the relevance on this area of law of unfair commercial practices law (Section 8.6).

Before we move on to consider what constitutes an actionable misrepresentation, three further preliminary points should be made. First, although beyond the scope of this book, it should be noted that a misrepresentation may, in some circumstances, also attract criminal liability, for example, under the Consumer Protection from Unfair Trading Regulations 2008. Initially the Consumer Protection from Unfair Trading Regulations 2008 did not provide consumers with specific rights of private redress for breach of these Regulations. However, this was, to some extent, altered by the Consumer Protection (Amendment) Regulations 2014 and so, in Section 8.6, we shall consider consumers' rights of private redress for certain misleading and aggressive practices, introduced by the Consumer Protection (Amendment) Regulations 2014. Second, s 1 of the Misrepresentation Act 1967 recognises that a pre-contractual statement may amount to both a representation *and* a term of the contract. Third, some pre-contractual statements will be neither representations nor will they form part of any resulting contract. More specifically, some pre-contractual statements will be classified as 'mere puffs'. A 'mere puff' is described by Peel and Treitel (Peel, E, *Treitel: The Law of Contract* (14th edn, London: Sweet & Maxwell, 2015), at p 407) in the following terms:

> Mere puffs are statements which are so vague that they have no effect at law or in equity. To describe land as 'fertile and improvable' is mere sales talk which affords no ground for relief. But there is a liability for more precise claims, e.g. that use of a carbolic smoke-ball will give immunity from influenza.

8.2 Actionable misrepresentations

An actionable, or operative, misrepresentation has been defined as

> a false statement of existing or past fact or law made by one party (the 'representor') before or at the time of making the contract, which is addressed to the other party (the 'representee') and which induces the other party to enter into the contract
>
> *(Beatson, J, Burrows, A, and Cartwright, J,* Anson's Law of Contract *(30th edn, Oxford: OUP, 2016), p 320).*

In this section we will consider the elements of actionable misrepresentations.

8.2.1 Statements of fact

Traditionally an actionable misrepresentation required a false statement of fact. Today, as we shall discover below, a false statement of law can also amount to an actionable misrepresentation. For present purposes it should be noted that a false statement of fact/law may be made in many ways, as was noted by Denning L.J. in the following case.

***Curtis v Chemical Cleaning & Dyeing* [1951] 1 KB 805**

Facts: Mrs Curtis took a white satin wedding dress trimmed in beads and sequins to a dry cleaner for cleaning. The shop assistant asked her to sign a 'receipt'. When she asked what the significance of the document was, the assistant replied that it excluded liability for damage by or to the beads and sequins. Mrs Curtis signed the document and left the dress with the assistant. The document actually contained a general exclusion clause, excluding all liability for damages howsoever caused. When Mrs Curtis returned for the dress, she discovered that it was badly stained. She was awarded damages by the county court judge, who held that the defendants had been guilty of negligence and were not protected by their exclusion clause because of the misrepresentation as to its character.

Held: The Court of Appeal dismissed the defendants' appeal holding that they could not rely on the general exclusion clause because of the shop assistant's misrepresentation.

Denning LJ: In my opinion, any behaviour by words or conduct is sufficient to be a misrepresentation if it is such as to mislead the other party about the existence or extent of the exemption. If the false impression is created knowingly, it is a fraudulent misrepresentation; if it is created unwittingly, it is an innocent misrepresentation; but either is sufficient to disentitle the creator of it to the benefit of the exemption.

For a discussion of formation of the contract in *Curtis*, see: *Athena Capital Fund Sicav - Fis S.C.A v Crownmark Ltd* [2019] EWHC 1952 (Comm).

8.2.1.1 Statements of intention

Statements of intention do not generally constitute an actionable misrepresentation. However, a statement of intention carries with it an implied statement of fact as to the state of mind of the representor. In other words, there is an implied statement of fact that the statement of intention is genuine at the time at which it is made. Therefore, if the statement of intention was not genuine at the time it was made, there may be an actionable misrepresentation.

***Edgington v Fitzmaurice* (1885) 24 Ch D 459**

Facts: The directors of a company issued a prospectus inviting subscriptions for debentures. The prospectus stated that it was intended to use the money obtained to make improvements in the company by altering buildings, purchasing horses and vans and developing the trade of the company. The real intention was to use the money obtained to pay off existing debts of the company.

Held: The Court of Appeal held the statement of intention was a misrepresentation of fact as to the state of mind of the directors because there had never been an intention to use the money in the manner stated.

Bowen LJ: There must be a misstatement of an existing fact: but the state of a man's mind is as much a fact as the state of his digestion. It is true that it is very difficult to prove what the state of a man's mind at a particular time is, but if it can be ascertained it is as much a fact as anything else. A misrepresentation as to the state of a man's mind is, therefore, a misstatement of fact.

On the other hand, in the absence of a contractual undertaking, there will generally be no liability if the statement of intention was genuine at the time at which it was made but it subsequently changed.

8.2.1.2 Representations of opinion

A mere statement of opinion is generally not an actionable misrepresentation. This was seen in *Bisset v Wilkinson*.

***Bisset v Wilkinson* [1927] AC 177**

Facts: Mr Wilkinson agreed to purchase certain land from Mr Bisset, on the Southern Island of New Zealand, for the purpose of sheep farming. Bisset told Wilkinson that the land would support 2,000 sheep. However, neither Bisset nor anyone else had used the land for sheep farming. Wilkinson bought the land and it failed to support 2,000 sheep. He refused to pay the outstanding balance of the purchase price and sought rescission on the ground of misrepresentation.

Held: The Judicial Committee of the Privy Council held that the statement was merely a statement of opinion which Bisset honestly held and accordingly refused to order rescission.

Lord Merrivale: In the present case ... the material facts of the transaction, the knowledge of the parties respectively, and their relative positions, the words of representation used, and the actual condition of the subject-matter spoken of, are relevant to the two inquiries necessary to be made: What was the meaning of the representation? Was it true?

In ascertaining what meaning was conveyed to the minds of the now respondents by the appellant's statement as to the two thousand sheep, the most material fact to be remembered is that, as both parties were aware, the appellant had not and, so far as appears, no other person had at any time carried on sheep-farming upon the unit of land in question. That land as a distinct holding had never constituted a sheep-farm ....

The fact that neither Bisset, nor anyone else, had ever used the land for sheep-farming was highly significant to the Privy Council. This is because a statement of opinion may be actionable if it is contradicted by other facts known to the person giving it.

***Smith v Land & House Property Corp* (1884) 28 Ch D 7**

Facts: The plaintiff put up a hotel for sale. The particulars stated that it was 'let to Mr Fleck (a most desirable tenant)', at a rental of £400 per annum, for an unexpired term of twenty-seven and a half years. Mr Fleck was a very undesirable tenant; he had not been paying his rent on time and was in arrears.

Held: The Court of Appeal held that the description of Mr Fleck as a most desirable tenant was not a mere expression of opinion, but contained an implied statement of fact that the vendors knew of no facts leading to the conclusion that he was not. The late payment of rent demonstrated that he was not a desirable tenant.

Bowen LJ: In considering whether there was a misrepresentation, I will first deal with the argument that the particulars only contain a statement of opinion about the tenant. It is material to observe that it is often fallaciously assumed that a statement of opinion cannot involve the statement of a fact. In a case where the facts are equally well known to both parties, what one of them says to the other is frequently nothing but an expression of opinion. The statement of such opinion is in a sense a statement of a fact, about the condition of the man's own mind, but only of an irrelevant fact, for it is of no consequence what the opinion is. But if the facts are not equally known to both sides, then a statement of opinion by the one who knows the facts best involves very often a statement of a material fact, for he impliedly states that he knows facts which justify his opinion. Now a landlord knows the relations between himself and his tenant, other persons either do not know them at all or do not know them equally well, and if the landlord says that he considers that the relations between himself and his tenant are satisfactory, he really avers that the facts peculiarly within his knowledge are such as to render that opinion reasonable. Now are the statements here statements which involve such a representation of material facts? They are statements on a subject as to which *prima facie* the vendors know everything and the purchasers nothing. The vendors state that the property is let to a most desirable tenant. What does that mean? I agree that it is not a guarantee that the tenant will go on paying his rent, but it is to my mind a guarantee of a different sort, and amounts at least to an assertion that nothing has occurred in the relations between the landlords and the tenant which can be considered to make the tenant an unsatisfactory one. That is an assertion of a specific fact. Was it a true assertion? Having regard to what took place between Lady Day and Midsummer [Fleck's failure to pay rent], I think that it was not.

There were two grounds for the decision in this case. The statement of opinion contained an implied statement of fact that the vendors knew of no information that would contradict the statement. On the facts of the case, the vendors knew that Mr Fleck had failed to pay his rent and this contradicted their statement of opinion. The second ground is found in Bowen L.J.'s judgment: 'If the facts are not equally known to both sides, then a statement of opinion by the one who knows the facts best involves very often a statement of a material fact.' Because the vendors, as landlord of the hotel, were in the best position to know the suitability of the tenant, their statement of opinion was treated as a statement of fact. Statements of opinion by experts are often treated as giving rise to statements of fact, because experts are in the best position to ascertain the truth of the matter.

***Esso Petroleum v Mardon* [1976] 2 All ER 5**

Facts: A representative of Esso told Mardon, a prospective tenant of a petrol filling station, that the throughput of petrol at the station was likely to reach 200,000 gallons. In giving this estimate, the representative had negligently overlooked the fact that the local planning authority had refused permission for the petrol pumps to front on to the main street. As a result of this the throughput of the station was only 78,000 gallons per year. Mardon sued Esso for negligent misrepresentation. Esso argued that their statement as to the throughput of petrol was merely a statement of opinion and therefore not actionable.

Held: The Court of Appeal held that Esso's statement as to the throughput of petrol involved a representation that reasonable care had been taken to ensure that the estimate was correct, and that this was a misrepresentation of fact.

Lord Denning MR: It seems to me that *Hedley Byrne & Co Ltd v Heller & Partners Ltd* [1964] AC 465, properly understood, covers this particular proposition: if a man, who has or professes to have special knowledge or skill, makes a representation by virtue thereof to another – be it advice, information or opinion – with the intention of inducing him to enter into a contract with him, he is under a duty to use reasonable care to see that the representation is correct, and that the advice, information or opinion is reliable. If he negligently gives unsound advice or misleading information or expresses an erroneous opinion, and thereby induces the other side to enter into a contract with him, he is liable in damages ... Applying this principle, it is plain that Esso professed to have – and did in fact have – special knowledge or skill in estimating the throughput of a filling station. They made the representation – they forecast a throughput of 200,000 gallons – intending to induce Mr Mardon to enter into a tenancy on the faith of it. They made it negligently. It was a 'fatal error' and thereby induced Mr Mardon to enter into a contract of tenancy that was disastrous to him. For this misrepresentation they are liable in damages.

8.2.1.3 Representations of law

It had previously been thought that a false statement of law was not actionable as a misrepresentation. This led to a number of contradictory decisions as the courts struggled to distinguish between representations of law and representations of fact. A couple of cases from the mid-twentieth century illustrate the point well. In *London and County Territorial & Auxiliary Forces Association v Nichols* [1949] 1 KB 35, a statement that the Rent Acts applied to a house that was known to be in the occupation of the Crown was held to be a misrepresentation of law because it involved a false proposition of law that the Rent Acts bound the Crown. However, in *Solle v Butcher* [1950] 1 KB 671, a statement that the Rent Acts did not apply to a flat because its identity had been changed by work done to it was held by the Court of Appeal to be a misrepresentation of fact.

The traditional rule that false statements of law were not actionable as misrepresentations was called into question by the decision of the House of Lords in *Kleinwort Benson Ltd v Lincoln City Council* [1999] 2 AC 349. This case overturned the well-established rule that a claimant could recover restitution of money paid under a mistake of fact, but not money paid under a mistake of law. Their Lordships did not comment on the law of misrepresentation, but having abolished the distinction between 'fact' and 'law' in the context of mistake, it is difficult to maintain the distinction in the law of misrepresentation. In *Pankhania v Hackney LBC* [2002] EWHC 2441 (Ch), the High Court expressed the view that, following *Kleinwort Benson*, misrepresentations of law were actionable. Rex Tedd QC said:

> I have concluded that the 'misrepresentation of law' rule has not survived the decision in *Kleinwort Benson Ltd v Lincoln City Council*. Its historical origin is as an off-shoot of the 'mistake of law' rule, created by analogy with it, and the two are logically inter-dependent ... The distinction between fact and law in the context of relief from misrepresentation has no more underlying principle to it than it does in the context of relief from mistake ... The survival of the 'misrepresentation of law' rule following the demise of the 'mistake of law' rule would be no more than a quixotic anachronism.

However, depending on the facts, it may be that a statement of law is only a statement of opinion: see *Bolt Burdon Solicitors v Tariq* [2016] EWHC 811 (QB).

8.2.1.4 Silence

The *general* rule is that an actionable misrepresentation cannot be made by silence.

Turner v Green [1895] 2 Ch 205

Facts: Turner and Green were engaged in a legal dispute. Turner's solicitor, Fowler, reached a settlement with Green on behalf of his client. Shortly before concluding that agreement, Fowler received a telegram informing him of certain proceedings in the action that made the settlement disadvantageous to Green. He failed to disclose this to Green. When Turner claimed specific enforcement of the agreement, Green attempted to rely upon the non-disclosure to resist the claim.

Held: The High Court held that mere non-disclosure of a material fact did not constitute a misrepresentation. Therefore rescission of the agreement was not available.

Chitty J: The distinction between suppression of a fact and mere silence is a very old one, and is to be found in a passage from Cicero (De Off lib iii c 13), which is cited by Sir Edward Fry in his book (3rd edn p 329): 'Aliud est celare, aliud tacere; neque enim id est celare quicquid reticeas'. The obligation to speak is at the root of this proposition.

In *Walters v Morgan*, where specific performance of an agreement for a lease was being sought, Campbell LC said: 'There being no fiduciary relation between vendor and purchaser in the negotiation, the purchaser is not bound to disclose any fact exclusively within his knowledge which might reasonably be expected to influence the price of the subject to be sold. Simple reticence does not amount to legal fraud, however it may be viewed by moralists. But a single word, or (I may add) a nod or a wink, or a shake of the head, or a smile from the purchaser intended to induce the vendor to believe the existence of a non-existing fact, which might influence the price of the subject to be sold, would be sufficient ground for a Court of Equity to refuse a decree for a specific performance of the agreement'. That is a correct statement of the law, and one which, it appears to me, is not to be confined to the sale of lands or goods, but is of general application, except perhaps in the case of contracts requiring *uberrima fides*, which involve a duty to make full disclosure.

It is clear that English law does not recognise a general duty to disclose material facts known to one party but not to the other. This is partly because English law does not currently impose any general duty of good faith. There are, however, a number of exceptions to this general rule.

First, a misrepresentation may arise where there has been an active attempt to conceal a defect. In *Horsfall v Thomas* (1862) 1 H & C 90, Thomas purchased a gun from Horsfall. The gun had a defect in it, which made it worthless. Horsfall attempted to conceal the defect by inserting a metal plug over the soft spot in the metal. The Court of Appeal held that the concealment could be actionable, but for other reasons, that will be considered in due course, the court held that there was no actionable misrepresentation.

Second, a partial non-disclosure may amount to an actionable misrepresentation. This arises when, for example, a party makes a statement that is literally true but is nevertheless misleading because the representor fails to disclose all the relevant information. In short, it is a half-truth.

Nottingham Patent Brick and Tile Co v Butler (1886) 16 QBD 778

Facts: Butler wished to sell a piece of land that was subject to a number of restrictive covenants, one of which precluded its use as a brickyard. The plaintiff company, which manufactured bricks, wished to purchase the land to use in its business. The company inquired of Butler's solicitor whether the land was subject to any restrictive covenants. The solicitor stated that he was not aware of any, but omitted to mention that he had not inspected the relevant documents. The company entered into a contract for the purchase of the land and paid the deposit. On discovery of the restrictive covenants they attempted to rescind the contract and recover the deposit.

Held: The Court of Appeal held there had been a misrepresentation which entitled the purchaser to rescind the contract.

Lord Esher MR: The evidence has been read to us, and I am sorry to say that I have come to the conclusion that the defendant's solicitor allowed himself to be carried away by his zeal for his client, and that he did not act with that candour to the other side with which a solicitor is bound to act under such circumstances. He allowed himself, in his zeal for his client, to make statements which were calculated to lead the other side to believe that he was stating facts within his own knowledge, and his statements in fact misled them, so that what he said amounts to a mis-statement of facts.

***Clinicare Ltd v Orchard Homes & Developments Ltd* [2004] EWHC 1694**

Facts: The claimant agreed to lease premises from the defendant. The lease imposed on the tenant a full repairing obligation. The claimant contended that it entered into the lease in reliance upon the defendant's fraudulent misrepresentation that it was unaware of the presence of dry rot and an implied negligent misrepresentation that reasonable steps had been taken to see whether dry rot existed. The defendant argued that its subsequent verbal statement about the historic existence of dry rot had corrected its initial misrepresentation.

Held: The court held that the negligent misrepresentation had not been corrected by the subsequent statement about the historic existence of dry rot.

Moses J

20. The representation that the defendant was not aware of 'woodworm, rising damp, wet or dry rot or other infestation' was plainly false .... Moreover, the representation was fraudulent in that the person who made it did so knowingly and cannot have believed in its truth. It was, at the very least, made recklessly in the sense that the person making the representation must have been careless whether it be true or false ....

22. Of equal importance is the implied representation, which the representation, that the vendor was not aware of any dry rot, carries. It is alleged that the representation amounts to a representation that Orchard had made such investigations as could reasonably be expected of them ....

25. The representation that Orchard had made such investigations as to the existence of dry rot as could reasonably be expected of it was made negligently ....

27. Orchard's first substantial defence to Clinicare's allegations relies upon Mr Eagle's oral statement to Mr Dukes that dry rot had been discovered in the staircase but that the staircase had been stripped out and replaced ....

28. [I]n my view the oral information given by Mr Eagle ... did not correct the implied representation that Orchard had made such investigations as could be reasonably be expected of them. Indeed, it tended to confirm that such investigations had been made. The oral statement of Mr Eagle carried with it the implication that the dry rot no longer existed, so far as Orchard was aware. That statement itself carried the further implication that in undertaking the replacement of the staircase Orchard had taken reasonable steps to see that replacement cured the problem of dry rot. This was wholly contradicted by the advice Orchard had been given by Armour. Orchard had chosen to ignore the advice it had been given. The implied representation contained in the oral correction that the dry rot had been cured was false, particularly when Orchard had deliberately declined to do that which it had been advised to do ....

Third, silence will be actionable as a misrepresentation if a person has made a statement that was true at the time it was made but before the contract is concluded has, to his knowledge, become false.

With v O'Flanagan [1936] Ch 575

Facts: O'Flanagan wished to sell his medical practice. In January 1934 he told With that the takings of the practice were £2,000 a year. The contract for the sale was signed in May 1934, but by that time the circumstances had changed. O'Flanagan had been unwell and, as a result of his absence, the practice had become virtually worthless. In the three weeks preceding the sale the takings of the practice averaged only £5 a week. When With took possession of the practice he discovered what had happened and brought an action for rescission of the contract.

Held: The Court of Appeal held that the change of facts should have been disclosed and that failure to do so meant that the contract could be rescinded.

Lord Wright MR: As to the law, which has been challenged, I want to say this. I take the law to be as it was stated by Fry J in *Davies v London and Provincial Marine Insurance Co* (1878) 8 Ch D 469, where it is perhaps most fully expressed. In that case certain friends of an agent had agreed to deposit a sum of money for what was alleged to have been defaults on his part. The company who had employed him were under the belief and were advised that the default of the agent constituted felony, but they were later advised that these acts did not amount to felony and they withdrew the order for his arrest, and then still later in the day the friends of the agent agreed to deposit a sum of money on the footing of what they had been told earlier in the day before the arrest had been withdrawn – these statements had not been corrected – and on that footing it was held by Fry J 'that the change of circumstances ought to have been stated to the intending sureties, and that the agreement must be rescinded and the money returned to the sureties.' ...

Very much the same was said by the same learned judge, when a Lord Justice, in *Re Scottish Petroleum Co* (1883) 23 Ch D 413 .... In these cases – I need not refer to others on this point – the position is based upon the duty to communicate the change of circumstances. The matter, however, may be put in another way though with the same effect, and that is on the ground that a representation made as a matter of inducement to enter into a contract is to be treated as a continuing representation. That view of the position was put in *Smith v Kay* (1859) 7 HL Cas 750, 769, by Lord Cranworth. He says of a representation made in negotiation some time before the date of a contract: 'It is a continuing representation. The representation does not end for ever when the representation is once made; it continues on. The pleader who drew the bill, or the young man himself, in stating his case, would say, 'Before I executed the bond I had been led to believe, and I therefore continued to believe, that it was executed pursuant to the arrangement'. The underlying principle is also stated again in a slightly different application by Lord Blackburn in *Brownlie v Campbell* (1880) 5 App Cas 925, 950. I need only quote a very short passage. Lord Blackburn says:

> 'when a statement or representation has been made in the *bona fide* belief that it is true, and the party who has made it afterwards comes to find out that it is untrue, and discovers what he should have said, he can no longer honestly keep up that silence on the subject after that has come to his knowledge, thereby allowing the other party to go on, and still more, inducing him to go on, upon a statement which was honestly made at the time when it was made, but which he has not now retracted when he has become aware that it can be no longer honestly persevered in. ...'

On these grounds, with great respect to the learned judge, I think he ought to have come to the conclusion that the plaintiffs have established their case and there ought to be a declaration rescinding the contract with the consequences which follow upon such a declaration.

There were two alternative grounds for the decision: either (1) there was a duty on O'Flanagan to notify with of the change of circumstances; or (2) the statement was a continuing representation that became untrue. On either ground, O'Flanagan was liable for misrepresentation and the contract could be rescinded.

In the above extract from his judgment in *Turner v Green*, Chitty J. referred to the fourth exception to the general rule – contracts *uberrimae fidei* (of the utmost good faith). These types of contract, which traditionally included contracts of insurance, require full disclosure of all material facts. In relation to insurance contracts, note the Consumer Insurance (Disclosure and Representations) Act 2012, s 2 which provides:

> (1) This section makes provision about disclosure and representations by a consumer to an insurer before a consumer insurance contract is entered into or varied.
> (2) It is the duty of the consumer to take reasonable care not to make a misrepresentation to the insurer.
> (3) A failure by the consumer to comply with the insurer's request to confirm or amend particulars previously given is capable of being a misrepresentation for the purposes of this Act (whether or not it could be apart from this subsection).
> (4) The duty set out in subsection (2) replaces any duty relating to disclosure or representations by a consumer to an insurer which existed in the same circumstances before this Act applied.

See also the Insurance Act 2015, s 21.

Finally, contracts entered into between persons in a fiduciary relationship may entail a duty of disclosure. Traditionally included in this category are contracts between agent and principal (*Armstrong v Jackson* [1917] 2 KB 822), solicitor and client (*Boardman v Phipps* [1967] 2 AC 46) and a company and its directors (*Regal Hastings v Gulliver* [1967] 2 AC 134, and now Companies Act 2006, Part 10).

8.2.1.5 Conduct

A misrepresentation might also stem from conduct where nothing has been said.

***Spice Girls Ltd v Aprilia World Services BV* [2002] EMLR 27**

Facts: The claimants, Spice Girls Ltd, entered into a contract with the defendants, Aprilia, for the promotion of Aprilia's new scooters – to be known as 'Spice Sonic Scooters'. The original five Spice Girls, including Geri Halliwell, participated in a commercial advertising shoot, and two days later contracted with Aprilia in relation to the use of that material. The band had known prior to the making of this agreement that Geri Halliwell intended to leave the band after the US tour in September 1998. The advertising material was due to be released after that date. Aprilia claimed that they had been induced to enter into the contract on the basis of a misrepresentation by conduct, that the Spice Girls did not know and had no reasonable grounds to believe, at or before the time of the agreement, that any of the Spice Girls had an existing declared intention to leave the group.

At first instance, Arden J found a misrepresentation by conduct. She concluded:

> Given that the benefits of the commercial shoot could not be enjoyed by Aprilia if one of the Spice Girls left the group before March 1999, participation in the shoot … carried with it a representation by conduct that the Spice Girls Ltd did not know, and had no reasonable grounds to believe, that any of the Spice Girls had an existing declared intention to leave the group before that date.

Held: The Court of Appeal dismissed the appeal and upheld the decision of Arden J. but on the basis of a broader survey of the facts.

Morritt VC: The representation for which AWS [Aprilia World Services] has contended ever since it amended its defence and counterclaim in December 1999 is that 'SGL [Spice Girls Ltd] did not know and had no reasonable grounds to believe at or before the time of entry into the agreement that any of the Spice Girls had an existing declared intention to leave the group during the minimum term of the Agreement', i.e. before March 1999. This was accepted by the judge (J1, paragraph 112) but only in respect of the commercial shoot on May 4, 1998 and 'other promotional material depicting the five Spice Girls which was intended to be used at any time during the period of the agreement'.

In our view the judge took too limited a view of the effect of the course of the negotiations as a whole and the specific documents and conduct relied on ... [A]t this stage it is sufficient to highlight the most salient facts and events.

First, shortly after the conclusion of the heads of agreement on March 4, 1998 SGL supplied the logos, images and designs depicting each of the Spice Girls which were to be used by Aprilia in the promotion of the scooters. It must have been quite obvious from all such material and the judge's finding ... that the same five girls were required for all of them. AWS was entitled to use them throughout the period of 12 months .... As we understand it such material was consistently used thereafter so as to generate a connection in the public eye between the Spice Girls and the scooters. In our view the representation contended for is necessarily implicit in that conduct from early March 1998 onwards. In, seemingly, connecting such material only to the commercial shoot on May 4, 1998, in our view, the judge seriously understated its significance.

Second, the events of March 9, 1998 were such as to bring to the attention of four of the other five directors of SGL the fact that Ms Halliwell had declared her intention to leave in September 1998. It follows that the representation implicit in the approval and use of the promotional material was false when made, or to the extent it was made before March 9, became false on March 9, 1998 ....

Third, the subsequent events merely served to affirm, not correct, the initial representation and its falsity. Thus, the photocalls in Madrid, Munich and Paris held on or between March 16 and 26 May have been unsatisfactory to Ms Fuzzi but they took place and their effect was no different to the other promotional material. There were five Spice Girls each with her 'distinct and individual image, style and personality'.

Fourth, the fax of March 30, 1998 was sent by Mr Pettett in the light of the information given to him by Ms Halliwell and the tour manager .... In our view it was an express assurance that each Spice Girl was fully committed to all the matters contained in the heads of agreement and in the draft agreement then circulating for the full term of 12 months. There is implicit in such assurance the representation for which AWS contends. That representation was false when made because of the declaration of intention made by Ms Halliwell on March 9, 1998 and never qualified or withdrawn ....

Fifth, the events of the meeting held at Wembley on April 25, 1998 demonstrated quite conclusively the falsity of all the representations previously made. Whichever formulation of the principle enunciated in *With v O'Flanagan* is adopted and whatever view is taken of the declaration made by Ms Halliwell on March 9, 1998 it is quite clear that SGL could no longer deal with AWS on the previous basis without disclosing Ms Halliwell's expressed intention .... Sixth, it is clear that far from correcting the previous misrepresentations SGL continued and affirmed them ....

Seventh, as the judge held, participation in the commercial shoot necessarily carried the same implication and was likewise false. It did nothing to correct the previous misrepresentations, indeed it gave them additional force ....

Whilst it is necessary to give each episode separate consideration it is also necessary to have regard to their cumulative effect. This is not a case of an isolated representation made at an early stage of ongoing negotiations. It is the case of a series of continuing representations made throughout the two months' negotiations leading to the Agreement. Later representations gave added force to the earlier ones; earlier representations gave focus to the later ones ....

The Court of Appeal took a broader view of the facts than Arden J. at first instance and listed seven factors that contributed to the conclusion that the Spice Girls had made a misrepresentation by conduct. As the last paragraph of the judgment makes clear, none of these factors standing alone would have been decisive, but the cumulative effect of all the factors was that there was an actionable misrepresentation. Of course, such a convoluted analysis would arguably not have been necessary if English law had recognised a general duty of good faith.

8.2.2 Misrepresentation must induce the contract

8.2.2.1 The general rule

Having established that the defendant made a potentially actionable misrepresentation, the claimant is then required to show that the misrepresentation induced the formation of the contract. Significantly, the misrepresentation does not need to be the 'sole' reason or the 'only' reason why the misrepresentee entered the contract (*Edgington v Fitzmaurice* (1885) 24 Ch D 459). In *Vald Nielsen Holding A/S v Baldorino* [2019] EWHC 1926 (Comm), at [157] Jacobs J. stated:

> it is not appropriate to try to measure the precise weight of a representation where it is one of the reasons why a representee has entered a contract. If the representation is of no real significance, then a court will decline to hold that it was one of the reasons which induced the contract. If, however, it was a matter of significance, the decision will be the other way.

JEB Fasteners Ltd v Marks, Bloom & Co [1983] 1 All ER 583

Facts: The defendants negligently prepared the accounts of a company which was taken over by the claimants. The accounts had been made available to the claimants, who had reservations about them, but they nevertheless decided to proceed with the takeover because they wished to acquire the services of two of the directors of the company. The takeover was a commercial failure. In an attempt to recover their losses, the claimants brought an action against the defendants alleging that the negligently prepared accounts had induced them into the takeover.

Held: The Court of Appeal dismissed the action on the ground that the defendants' representation did not play a 'real and substantial' part in inducing the claimants to act. They had taken over the company, not in reliance upon the accounts but because they wished to acquire the services of the two directors.

In *BV Nederlandse Industrie Van Eiprodukten v Rembrandt Enterprises, Inc.* [2019] EWCA Civ 596 Longmore L.J. stated:

> 14. It is also important to know what has to be proved by the party who has the onus of proof. Is it that the representee would/would not have acted differently but for the misrepresentation? Or is it that the representation played a part (or influenced) the decision of the representee? Or is it sufficient that the representee might/might not have acted differently?
>
> 15. It is surprising that these are still controversial questions in English law especially since the test for inducement in cases of innocent or negligent representation appears to be settled in the form that the representee has the burden of showing inducement in the sense that he has to show he would not have entered into the relevant contract had the representation not been made: see *Assicurazioni Generali SpA v Arab Insurance Group* [2003] 1 All ER (Comm) 140, *Pan Atlantic Insurance Co Ltd v Pine Top Insurance Co Ltd* [1995] 1 A.C. 501, Chitty, *Contracts*, 33rd edition, para 7-039.

Some of the controversy may be due to a failure to separate the issue of inducement from the issue of loss (for the purposes of damage): see, for example, *Marme Inversiones 2007 SL v NatWest Markets PLC, HSH Nordbank AG, Bayerische Landesbank, ING Bank NV, Caixabank SA* [2019] EWHC 366 (Comm).

Longmore L.J. continued:

> 32. In the light of these authorities it seems to me that the law at the end of the nineteenth century had assimilated the requirement of inducement in the tort of deceit and in actions for rescission for fraudulent misrepresentation and could be stated as being that the representee had to prove he had been materially 'influenced' by the representations in the sense that it was 'actively present to his mind' to use Bowen LJ's phrase; that, whereas there is a presumption that a statement, likely to induce a representee to enter into a contract, did so induce him, that is merely a presumption of fact which is to be taken into account along with all the evidence. There was no requirement as a matter of law, that the representee should state in terms that he would not have made the contract but for the misrepresentation but the absence of such a statement was part of the overall evidential picture from which the judge had to ascertain whether there was inducement or not. The fact that there were other reasons (besides the representation) for the claimant to have made the contract did not mean that he was not induced by the representation made. Insofar as *Reynell v Sprye* had said that there was no need for evidence from the claimant or that it was sufficient if the claimant 'might' have made the contract, if there had been no representation, that did not represent the law at any rate if 'might' meant something different from 'influencing' his decision in deciding whether to make the contract.
>
> ...
>
> 43. It seems to me, therefore, that overall the modern authorities do not add much to the conclusions that I drew from the Victorian authorities in para [32] above. I do not think that *Barton v Armstrong* intended to reverse the legal burden of proof but, if it did, this court must prefer the later analysis of the House of Lords and the Supreme Court that there is an evidential presumption of fact (not law) that a representee will have been induced by a fraudulent representation intended to cause him to enter the contract and that the inference will be 'very difficult to rebut' to use the words of Lord Clarke.
>
> 44. There remains the question whether, if it be the case that the burden of proof is on the representee to show that he was induced (albeit with the help of the presumption which is very difficult to rebut), it is sufficient for him to show that he might have acted differently. Both Christopher Clarke J in *Raiffeisen Zentralbank Osterreich AG v Royal Bank of Scotland Plc* [2010] EWHC 1392 (Comm) and Hamblen J in *Cassa di Risparmio della Republica di San Marino SpA v Barclays Bank Ltd* [2011] EWHC 484 (Comm) have *obiter* given some support for this being an appropriate test in cases of fraudulent misrepresentation, see paras 196–199 and 232–233 respectively.
>
> 45. I have already pointed out the ambiguity in the word 'might' which was in fact used in *Barton v Armstrong*. If it means no more than being actively present in the mind of the representee to repeat the phrase of Bowen LJ, it is perhaps a convenient shorthand. But if it means that the court cannot make up its mind on inducement and therefore decides as a matter of law to give the representee the benefit of the doubt, it is not a helpful concept because that would be contrary to the law as I conceive it to be, see para 32 above, which requires the representee to prove inducement albeit with the assistance of a presumption that 'will be very difficult to rebut'. To some extent this is a matter of terminology but terminology can be important in some cases.

8.2.2.2 Materiality

The burden of proving that the misrepresentation induced the contract rests upon the claimant. It is sometimes suggested that the claimant must also prove that the misrepresentation was 'material', that is, that it would have influenced a reasonable person in deciding whether to enter into the contract or not (although this is controversial; see Peel, E, *Treitel: The Law of Contract* (14th edn, London: Sweet & Maxwell, 2015) pp 411–413). In *Smith v Chadwick* (1884) 9 App Cas 187, 196, Lord Blackburn said:

> I think that if it is proved that the defendants with a view to induce the plaintiff to enter into a contract made a statement to the plaintiff of such a nature as would be likely to induce a person to enter into a contract, and if it is proved that the plaintiff did enter into the contract, it is a fair inference of fact that he was induced to do so by the statement.

Thus it seems that if the representation is one on which a reasonable person would have relied, this may create a rebuttable presumption that the claimant did in fact rely on the representation (*Barton v County NatWest Ltd* [1999] Lloyd's Rep Bank 408; *Dadourian Group International Inc v Simms* [2009] EWCA Civ 169). There is, however, some authority that the reverse is not necessarily true.

***Museprime Properties Ltd v Adhill Properties Ltd* (1991) 61 P & CR 111**

Facts: The defendants sold property that they owned in Finchley by auction to the plaintiffs. The auction particulars stated that the rent reviews of three leases to which the properties were subject had not been finalised. This was inaccurate but the statement was later reaffirmed by the auctioneer. The plaintiffs sought to rescind the contract for misrepresentation. The defendants argued that rescission should not be allowed because the misrepresentation was not material since no reasonable bidder would have allowed it to influence his bid.

Held: The High Court held that as long as the plaintiffs were in fact induced by the misrepresentation, which they were on the facts, that was sufficient to entitle them to rescission of the contract.

Scott J: A representation is material, in my opinion, if it is something that induces the person to whom it is made, whether solely or in conjunction with other inducements, to contract on the terms on which he does contract. I would gratefully adopt the view expressed in *Goff and Jones on the Law of Restitution*, (1986) 3rd edn, p 168 which reads:

> 'In our view any misrepresentation which induces a person to enter into a contract should be a ground for rescission of that contract. If the misrepresentation would have induced a reasonable person to enter into the contract then the court will, as we have seen, presume that the representee was so induced and the onus will be on the representor to show that the representee did not rely on the misrepresentation either wholly or in part. If, however, the misrepresentation would not have induced a reasonable person to contract, the onus will be on the representee to show that the misrepresentation induced him to act as he did. But these considerations relate to the onus of proof. To disguise them under the cloak of materiality is misleading and unnecessary'.

And, as the learned editors say a little way above that passage, the cases have tended to treat materiality as synonymous with inducement.

I respectfully agree with that view of the law and propose to apply it in this case. I do not decide as between Mr. Welch and Mr. Maunder-Taylor whether Mr. Maunder-Taylor's reliance on his ability to negotiate or succeed in obtaining on arbitration rent levels higher than those specified in the January 4, 1988, notices was reasonable or unreasonable. I will assume for present purposes that it was unreasonable, in which case the onus is on Mr. Maunder-Taylor to satisfy me that that factor did induce him, and through him Mr. Henley, and through the two of them the plaintiff company, to bid the £490,000 at the auction. Mr. Maunder-Taylor's evidence has satisfied me of that and indeed I think Mr. Primost accepted that that was the only possible conclusion from his evidence, very firmly given as it was ....

Compare, however, *Sharland v Sharland* [2015] UKSC 60 at [31]–[33] where Hale L.J. (with whom Neuberger, Clarke, Wilson, Sumption, Reed and Hodge L.JJ. agreed) appears to accept a materiality requirement in relation to misrepresentation:

> 31 Although not strictly applicable in matrimonial cases, the analogy of the remedies for misrepresentation and non-disclosure in contract may be instructive. At common law, the general effect of any misrepresentation, whether fraudulent, negligent or innocent, or of non-disclosure where there was a duty to disclose, was to render a contract voidable at the instance of a party who had thereby been induced to enter into it. This has now been modified by the Misrepresentation Act 1967, which empowers the court to impose an award of damages in lieu of rescission for negligent or innocent misrepresentation. This does not, however, apply in cases of fraudulent misrepresentation, where there is no power to impose an award of damages in lieu. The victim always has the right to rescind unless one of the general bars to rescission has arisen.
>
> 32 There is no need for us to decide in this case whether the greater flexibility which the court now has in cases of innocent or negligent misrepresentation in contract should also apply to innocent or negligent misrepresentation or non-disclosure in consent orders whether in civil or in family cases. It is clear from *Dietz* and *Livesey* that the misrepresentation or non-disclosure must be material to the decision that the court made at the time. But this is a case of fraud. It would be extraordinary if the victim of a fraudulent misrepresentation, which had led her to compromise her claim to financial remedies in a matrimonial case, were in a worse position than the victim of a fraudulent misrepresentation in an ordinary contract case, including a contract to settle a civil claim. As was held in *Smith v Kay* (1859) VII HLC 749, a party who has practised deception with a view to a particular end, which has been attained by it, cannot be allowed to deny its materiality. Furthermore, the court is in no position to protect the victim from the deception, or to conduct its statutory duties properly, because the court too has been deceived. In my view, Briggs LJ was correct in the first of the three reasons he gave for setting aside the order.
>
> 33 The only exception is where the court is satisfied that, at the time when it made the consent order, the fraud would not have influenced a reasonable person to agree to it, nor, had it known then what it knows now, would the court have made a significantly different order, whether or not the parties had agreed to it. But in my view, the burden of satisfying the court of that must lie with the perpetrator of the fraud. It was wrong in this case to place upon the victim the burden of showing that it would have made a difference.

8.2.2.3 Three key requirements of inducement

To demonstrate that the representation induced the representee to enter into the contract, the claimant must show that the representation was:

(a) known to the representee;
(b) intended to be acted on; and
(c) actually acted on.

We will examine each of these three requirements:

8.2.2.3.1 Known to representee

In *Horsfall v Thomas* (1862) 1 H & C 90, the facts of which were considered above, Thomas was unsuccessful in his claim for misrepresentation. This was because he had never inspected the gun and thus the attempted concealment did not operate upon his mind. Bramwell B said:

If the plug, which it was said was put in to conceal the defect, had never been there, his position would have been the same; for, as he did not examine the gun or form any opinion as to whether it was sound, its condition did not affect him.

8.2.2.3.2 Intended to be acted on

In addition to demonstrating that the representee knew the representation it must also, to an extent, be shown that the representation was intended to be acted upon (see also *Ludsin Overseas Ltd v Eco3 Capital Ltd* [2013] EWCA Civ 413).

***Peek v Gurney* (1873) LR 6 HL 377**

Facts: The defendants prepared a prospectus for an intended company with the aim of attracting initial investors. The prospectus contained a number of misrepresentations of fact which were known to be untrue by the defendants. Mr Peek was a subsequent purchaser of shares who relied on the prospectus in forming his decision to purchase shares from one of the original allottees. He brought an action against the defendant claiming damages for the losses which he had suffered in consequence of the purchase.

Held: The House of Lords held that Mr Peek could not recover damages because the prospectus was not intended to be acted upon by subsequent purchasers of shares.

Lord Cairns: The allotment having been completed, the prospectus, as it seems to me, had done its work; it was exhausted. The share list was full; the directors had obtained from the company the money which they desired to obtain . . . How can the directors of a company be liable, after the full original allotment of shares, for all the subsequent dealings which may take place with regard to those shares upon the Stock Exchange? If the argument of the Appellant is right, they must be liable *ad infinitum*, for I know no means of pointing out any time at which the liability would, in point of fact, cease. Not only so, but if the argument be right, they must be liable, no matter what the premium may be at which the shares may be sold. That premium may rise from time to time from circumstances altogether unconnected with the prospectus, and yet, if the argument be right, the Appellant would be entitled to call upon the directors to indemnify him up to the highest point at which the shares may be sold, for all that he may expend in buying the shares. My Lords, I ask, is there any authority for this proposition? I am aware of none.

In the case of *Peekay Intermark Ltd v Australia & New Zealand Banking Group Ltd* [2006] EWCA Civ 386, the Court of Appeal held that an investor could not claim that it was induced into an investment by a misrepresentation as to its nature when the investor had signed a document containing the final terms and conditions. Chadwick L.J. held that, in such circumstances, the investor was not entitled to rely on the earlier misrepresentation:

65. The Deputy Judge held, at paragraph 92 of his judgment, that Peekay was induced to invest 'by Mrs B's misrepresentation as to the nature of the product' . . . .

66. It is important to keep in mind that Mrs Balasubramaniam made no representation as to the actual contents of the FTCs. She had not seen those documents at the time of her telephone conversations with Mr Pawani on 1 and 2 February 1998. The effect of those conversations, as the judge found, was that Mr Pawani was given a 'rough and ready' description of the product that he would be offered. But it could not be said that Mr Pawani – an experienced investor in emerging markets – was under any misapprehension, following the telephone conversations, as to the need for a definitive and detailed description of the financial instrument to be employed (the 'product'); nor that he would have made an investment decision on behalf of Peekay if he had not received documents which he understood to contain the definitive and detailed description which he needed. And the judge made no finding to the contrary.

67. The judge found that Mr Pawani did no more than glance at the FTCs and the Risk Disclosure Statement. On the basis of that finding, the judge must be taken to have accepted that Peekay entered into the investment contract in the knowledge that the terms of that contract were to be found in those documents, but without knowing what those terms were. In holding that Peekay was induced to invest by Mrs Balasubramaniam's misrepresentation as to the nature of the product the judge inferred that Mr Pawani was entitled to, and did, assume that the terms which (as Mr Pawani knew) were to be found in the documents would not differ materially from the 'rough and ready' description which Mrs Balasubramaniam had given him a few days earlier. As he put it at paragraph 88 of his judgment: 'Mr Pawani … evidently had no prior cause to think that the FTCs would contain any nasty surprises'.

68. I am satisfied that that inference was not open to the judge. There are three reasons which lead me to that conclusion. First, given the importance which Mr Pawani professed to place on the potential for exerting influence, as an investor, on the means by which the underlying investment was liquidated or realised in the event of sovereign default in payment of the Note or of default by the counter-party to the currency hedge, it was necessary for him to give careful consideration to the FTCs. It was in those documents – and not in the 'rough and ready' description which he had been given by Mrs Balasubramaniam – that he would find the provisions that would apply in the event of default. He could not say that he was entitled to or did assume that the documents were a formality.

69. Second, it is clear that Mr Pawani, himself, regarded the documents which he had signed and returned as important. It was he who had added the words 'as per the attached document' to Mrs Balasubramaniam's draft letter of instructions ….

70. Third, Peekay could not be heard to say (through Mr Pawani) that it had thought it unnecessary to read and understand the FTCs. The Risk Disclosure Statement was a contractual document – as Mr Pawani recognised when he returned it, signed, with the letter of 7 February 1998. ANZ accepted the investment instructions in that letter on the basis of the investor's confirmation that it had read and understood the terms of the Statement. That confirmation, as it seems to me, operates as a contractual estoppel to prevent Peekay from asserting in litigation that it had not, in fact read and understood the Risk Disclosure Statement.

8.2.2.3.3 Actually acted on

Finally, it must be shown that the representee actually acted on the representation. If this cannot be established then his/her claim will fail.

***Attwood v Small* (1838) 6 Cl & Fin 232**

Facts: Attwood wished to sell a mine. He made exaggerated and untrue statements as to the mine's earning capacity. Before agreeing to purchase the mine, Small sent his own experts to assess the mine's capacity, who in error agreed with Attwood's assessment. When the true situation was discovered six months later Small claimed to rescind the contract on the grounds of misrepresentation.

Held: The House of Lords held that the action for misrepresentation failed because the purchaser had relied on his own experts rather than Attwood's misrepresentation.

While the above case shows that the representee must have actually acted upon the representation, it is clear that the representation need not have been the sole factor inducing the contract in order for it to be operative. In *Edgington v Fitzmaurice* (1885) 24 Ch D 459, the facts of which we have already considered, the plaintiff was induced to take debentures in a company partly on the basis of a misrepresentation in the company prospectus and partly because of his own mistaken belief that the debenture holders would have a charge on the company's leasehold property. The Court of Appeal held that the plaintiff was entitled to damages for fraudulent misrepresentation even though the misrepresentation was not the sole cause of his entering into the contract. Cotton L.J. said:

> It is not necessary to show that the misstatement was the sole cause of his acting as he did. If he acted on that misstatement, though he was also influenced by an erroneous supposition, the Defendants will be still liable.

Bowen L.J. agreed, stating the test to be applied thus:

> The real question is, what was the state of the Plaintiff's mind, and if his mind was disturbed by the misstatement of the Defendants, and such disturbance was in part the cause of what he did, the mere fact of his also making a mistake himself could make no difference. It resolves itself into a mere question of fact.

Similarly, in *Clinicare Ltd v Orchard Homes & Developments Ltd* [2004] EWHC 1694 (see above), the fact that the claimant had commissioned its own survey, which advised further investigation, did not bar its claim for misrepresentation. This was because the claimant's decision to enter the lease without further investigation demonstrated that the claimant had actually acted upon the defendant's negligent misrepresentation.

A misrepresentation cannot be held to have induced a contract where the representee knew that it was untrue prior to the formation of the contract (cf. *Hayward v Zurich Insurance Co Plc* [2016] UKSC 48 (suspicion that the representation was false)). The misrepresentation will still be effective, however, if there was merely an opportunity to discover the truth and that opportunity was not taken.

Redgrave v Hurd (1881) 20 Ch D 1

Facts: Mr Redgrave, a solicitor in Birmingham, placed an advertisement in the *Law Times* for the sale of his practice. Mr Hurd wished to establish himself in practice as a solicitor and had a meeting with Redgrave where he asked for details about the takings of the practice. Redgrave told him that the practice brought in £300–£400 a year. Hurd asked for information about the amount of business done for the last three years. At a subsequent meeting, Redgrave provided documents showing business of just under £200 a year. Hurd asked how the difference was made up, and Redgrave showed him a number of papers which he said related to other business not included in the summaries. These papers, which Hurd did not examine, showed only a small amount of business, and the gross returns of the business were in fact only about £200 a year. Hurd took possession of the practice, but on finding that the business was worthless, refused to complete. Redgrave brought an action for specific performance. At first instance, Fry J. held that Redgrave was entitled to specific performance because Hurd, having had the opportunity to discover the truth of Redgrave's representation, had not done so and therefore must be taken not to have relied on the representations.

Held: The Court of Appeal allowed the appeal and held that Hurd was entitled to rescind the contract. The mere opportunity to discover the truth does not preclude rescission provided that the plaintiff had relied upon the misrepresentation.

Lord Jessel MR: If a man is induced to enter into a contract by a false representation it is not a sufficient answer to him to say, 'If you had used due diligence you would have found out that the statement was untrue. You had the means afforded you of discovering its falsity, and did not choose to avail yourself of

> them'.... Nothing can be plainer, I take it, on the authorities in equity than that the effect of false representation is not got rid of on the ground that the person to whom it was made has been guilty of negligence. One of the most familiar instances in modern times is where men issue a prospectus in which they make false statements of the contracts made before the formation of a company, and then say that the contracts themselves may be inspected at the offices of the solicitors. It has always been held that those who accepted those false statements as true were not deprived of their remedy merely because they neglected to go and look at the contracts. Another instance with which we are familiar is where a vendor makes a false statement as to the contents of a lease, as, for instance, that it contains no covenant preventing the carrying on of the trade which the purchaser is known by the vendor to be desirous of carrying on upon the property. Although the lease itself might be produced at the sale, or might have been open to the inspection of the purchaser long previously to the sale, it has been repeatedly held that the vendor cannot be allowed to say, 'You were not entitled to give credit to my statement'.

Although a representee is not precluded from making a claim for misrepresentation on the grounds of his failure to take the opportunity to discover the truth, his carelessness might be taken into account when assessing damages (*Taberna Europe CDOII plc v Selskabet AF1. September 2008 In Bankruptcy (formerly known as Roskilde Bank A/S)* [2015] EWHC 871 (Comm) particularly at [181] *per* Eder J. and [2016] EWCA Civ 1262 at [52] *per* Moore-Bick L.J.). The role played by contributory negligence in the law of misrepresentation will be discussed in greater detail later in the chapter in section 8.4.2.2.2.

8.3 Categories of misrepresentation

Once it has been established that there has been an actionable misrepresentation, it is necessary to consider the state of mind of the person who made the misrepresentation. Misrepresentations broadly fall into three categories:

(a) fraudulent misrepresentations;
(b) negligent misrepresentations; and
(c) innocent misrepresentations.

It is important to ascertain which category a particular misrepresentation falls into in order to determine precisely which remedies are available. Rescission is potentially available for all three types of misrepresentation. Damages are only available as of right for negligent and fraudulent misrepresentations and the measure of damages may differ between the categories. In this section we will consider the requirements for each of the categories.

8.3.1 Fraudulent misrepresentation

Fraud was defined by Lord Herschell in *Derry v Peek*.

Derry v Peek (1889) 14 App Cas 337

Facts: A company obtained a statutory right to operate trams moved by animal power, or, with the consent of the Board of Trade, steam power. The directors assumed that the Board would give this consent as a matter of course because they had already submitted plans to the Board without any objection being made. The directors issued a prospectus containing a statement that they had the right to use steam power instead of horses. The plaintiff purchased shares in the company in reliance on this statement. The Board of Trade eventually refused their consent to the use of steam power and the company was wound up. The plaintiff brought an action against the directors for fraudulent misrepresentation.

Held: The House of Lords held that the defendants were not liable because the statement as to steam power had been made by them in the honest belief that it was true.

Lord Herschell: I think the authorities establish the following propositions: First, in order to sustain an action of deceit, there must be proof of fraud, and nothing short of that will suffice. Secondly, fraud is proved when it is shewn that a false representation has been made (1) knowingly, or (2) without belief in its truth, or (3) recklessly, careless whether it be true or false. Although I have treated the second and third as distinct cases, I think the third is but an instance of the second, for one who makes a statement under such circumstances can have no real belief in the truth of what he states. To prevent a false statement being fraudulent, there must, I think, always be an honest belief in its truth. And this probably covers the whole ground, for one who knowingly alleges that which is false, has obviously no such honest belief. Thirdly, if fraud be proved, the motive of the person guilty of it is immaterial. It matters not that there was no intention to cheat or injure the person to whom the statement was made .... In my opinion making a false statement through want of care falls far short of, and is a very different thing from, fraud, and the same may be said of a false representation honestly believed though on insufficient grounds.

Lord Herschell made a clear distinction between negligence and fraud. A false statement honestly believed does not constitute fraud (see also *Thomas Witter Ltd v TBP Industries Ltd* [1996] 2 All ER 573). The reasonableness of the representor's belief is relevant, however, in so far as it assists the court in ascertaining whether the representor really did have an honest belief in the truth of the statement. The less reasonable the belief, the less likely it is to be honest (in *Vald Nielsen Holding A/S v Baldorino* [2019] EWHC 1926 (Comm) at [148] Jacobs J. stated: 'The ingredient of dishonesty (in the above sense) must not be watered down into something akin to negligence, however gross: *The Kriti Palm*, [256]. However, the unreasonableness of the grounds of the belief, though not of itself supporting an action for deceit, will be evidence from which fraud may be inferred'). On the facts of *Derry v Peek*, the House of Lords concluded that there were reasons why the directors honestly believed that their statement was a true and fair representation of the facts.

The test for fraud is subjective. It must be shown that the representor lacked an honest belief in the truth of the statement. Consequently, the statement must be analysed from the point of view of the representor.

Akerhielm v De Mare [1959] AC 789

Facts: Mr De Mare bought shares in Dantile Ltd after Baron Akerhielm had informed him that 'about one third of the capital has already been subscribed in Denmark'. In fact some of this one third had been issued fully paid to persons resident in Kenya for services rendered in Denmark in connection with the formation of the company. The company went into insolvency and Mr De Mare brought an action for fraudulent misrepresentation, claiming that the statement indicated that the one-third of the capital had been subscribed in cash.

Held: The House of Lords held that the statement must be construed in the sense that Baron Akerhielm understood it and, on this construction, 'subscribed' did not mean subscribed in cash.

Lord Jenkins: The question is not whether the defendant in any given case honestly believed the representation to be true in the sense assigned to it by the court on an objective consideration of its truth or falsity, but whether he honestly believed the representation to be true in the sense in which he understood it albeit erroneously when it was made. This general proposition is no doubt subject to limitations. For instance, the meaning placed by the defendant on the representation made may be so far removed from the sense in which it would be understood by any reasonable person as to make it impossible to hold that the defendant honestly understood the representation to bear the meaning claimed by him and honestly believed it in that sense to be true. But that is not this case.

Finally, it has been held that the motive of the person making the representation is irrelevant to the issue of fraud. In *Polhill v Walter* (1832) 3 B & Ad 114, the representor, an agent, made a statement which he knew to be false with the sole intention of benefiting his principal. His intention was neither to benefit himself nor to injure anyone else. Notwithstanding his good motives, the representor was held liable in the tort of deceit.

8.3.2 Negligent misrepresentation

Negligent misrepresentation can be subdivided into two categories: (1) negligent misrepresentation at common law; and (2) negligent misrepresentation under statute. We will consider the reason for this subdivision when we examine negligent misrepresentation under statute.

8.3.2.1 At common law

Peel and Treitel (Peel, E, *Treitel: The Law of Contract* (14th edn, London: Sweet & Maxwell, 2015), p 422) describe common law negligent misrepresentation in the following terms:

> A misrepresentation is negligent if it is made carelessly and in breach of a duty owed by the representor to the representee to take reasonable care that the representation is accurate.

The law governing negligent misrepresentation at common law is derived from the decision of the House of Lords in *Hedley Byrne v Heller & Partners*.

Hedley Byrne v Heller & Partners [1964] AC 465

Facts: The claimants were advertising agents who booked substantial advertising space on behalf of their clients, Easipower Ltd, on terms stating that they were personally liable if Easipower defaulted. Hedley Byrne became concerned about the financial standing of Easipower and asked the defendants, who were Easipower's bankers, to give a reference on the financial standing of Easipower. The defendant replied that Easipower were 'considered good for its ordinary business transactions'. In reliance upon this reference, the claimants placed orders which, because of the subsequent default of Easipower, resulted in a loss to them of £17,000. The claimant alleged that Heller were negligent in their preparation of the reference and were therefore liable for damages.

Held: The House of Lords held that the defendant was not liable in negligence because it had included an exclusion clause stating that the reference was made 'without responsibility'. It was held, however, that in the absence of this exclusion the defendant would have been liable.

Lord Devlin: I think, therefore, that there is ample authority to justify your Lordships in saying now that the categories of special relationships which may give rise to a duty to take care in word as well as in deed are not limited to contractual relationships or to relationships of fiduciary duty, but include also relationships which in the words of Lord Shaw in *Nocton v Lord Ashburton* [1914] AC 932, 972, are 'equivalent to contract', that is, where there is an assumption of responsibility in circumstances in which, but for the absence of consideration, there would be a contract ....

I have had the advantage of reading all the opinions prepared by your Lordships and of studying the terms which your Lordships have framed by way of definition of the sort of relationship which gives rise to a responsibility towards those who act upon information or advice and so creates a duty of care towards them. I do not understand any of your Lordships to hold that it is a responsibility imposed by law upon certain types of persons or in certain sorts of situations. It is a responsibility that is voluntarily accepted or undertaken, either generally where a general relationship, such as that of solicitor and client or banker and customer, is created, or specifically in relation to a particular transaction. In the present case the appellants were not, as in *Woods v Martins Bank Ltd* [1959] 1 QB 55, the customers or potential customers of the bank. Responsibility can attach only to the single act, that is, the giving of the reference, and only if the doing of that act implied a voluntary undertaking to assume responsibility. This is a point of great importance because it is, as I understand it, the foundation for the ground on which in the end the House dismisses the appeal. I do not think it possible to formulate with exactitude all the conditions under which the law will in a specific case imply a voluntary undertaking any more than it is possible to formulate those in which the law will imply a contract ....

The case established the possibility of bringing an action in negligence for statements made without reasonable care and attention. For this to be possible, a 'duty of care' must be established between the maker of the statement and the person who has acted on it (see also *Playboy Club London Ltd v Banca Nazionale del Lavoro SpA* [2018] UKSC 43 and *Steel v NRAM Ltd (formerly NRAM plc)* [2018] UKSC 13). It is clear that the principle is not restricted to statements that induce a contract. Indeed, *Hedley Byrne* was not such a case and their Lordships did not directly consider the impact of the decision on the law relating to misrepresentation.

8.3.2.2 Under the Misrepresentation Act 1967

In addition to the common law action for negligent misstatement there is also a statutory action under s 2(1) of the Misrepresentation Act 1967. To understand why we have two separate actions we need to consider the history of the statute. Back in 1962, the Law Reform Committee issued its Tenth Report (Cmnd 1782), in which it recommended that damages should be available for negligent misrepresentation. Parliament was slow to enact implementing legislation, however, and by the time the Misrepresentation Act 1967 appeared on the statute books, the House of Lords had already decided *Hedley Byrne & Co v Heller* [1964] AC 465, and recognised the common-law action for negligent misstatement.

Misrepresentation Act 1967

Section 2

(1) Where a person has entered into a contract after a misrepresentation has been made to him by another party thereto and as a result thereof he has suffered loss, then, if the person making the misrepresentation would be liable to damages in respect thereof had the misrepresentation been made fraudulently, that person shall be so liable notwithstanding that the misrepresentation was not made fraudulently, unless he proves that he had reasonable grounds to believe and did believe up to the time the contract was made that the facts represented were true.

Section 2 of the Misrepresentation Act 1967 was amended by the Consumer Protection (Amendment) Regulations 2014 with a new s 2(4) providing:

> This section does not entitle a person to be paid damages in respect of a misrepresentation if the person has a right to redress under Part 4A of the Consumer Protection from Unfair Trading Regulations 2008 (SI 2008/1277) in respect of the conduct constituting the misrepresentation.

We shall consider the Consumer Protection (Amendment) Regulations below in Section 8.6. For present purposes, it should be noted that from a consumer's point of view this restriction may be regarded as unfortunate given, as we shall examine below, the powerful nature of the remedy under s 2(1).

The action for negligent misrepresentation under s 2(1) differs from the action at common law in at least two significant ways. First, it reverses the burden of proof. Under *Hedley Byrne v Heller* the burden is placed on the representee to establish that the representor was negligent. Under s 2(1) the representee merely has to show is that he entered into the contract in reliance upon a misrepresentation made by the other party. The burden will then shift to the representor to demonstrate that, until the time the contract was made, he had reasonable grounds to believe in the truth of the representation.

Second, unlike the common law action for negligent misstatement, section 2(1) does not require a duty of care to have existed between the representor and the representee. It merely requires proof that the misrepresentation led to the formation of a contract between the representor and the representee.

The operation of s 2(1) is illustrated by the case of Howard Marine & *Dredging Co Ltd v Ogden*.

Howard Marine & Dredging Co Ltd v Ogden [1978] QB 574

Facts: Ogden wished to hire barges from Howard Marine. During the negotiations an employee of Howard Marine, O'Loughlin, told Ogden that the carrying capacity of the barges was 1,600 tonnes. O'Loughlin based that figure on an entry in the Lloyd's Register. There was a mistake in the register, however, and the correct figure was 1,055 tonnes. The correct figure was stated in the ship's documents which were in Howard's possession. Ogden and Howard Marine concluded a contract of hire. Ogden used the barges, and the work for which they were required fell behind schedule. Ogden discovered the true carrying capacity of the barges and refused to continue paying the hire charge. Howard sued Ogden for the hire charge and Ogden counterclaimed under s 2(1) and in the tort of negligent misstatement. At first instance, the trial judge held that Howard was not liable and that Ogden was liable to pay for the hire of the barges.

Held: The Court of Appeal (Lord Denning M.R. dissenting) allowed the appeal and held that Ogden succeeded under 2(1).

Lord Denning MR

Negligent misrepresentations

Ogdens contended next that the representations by Howards, as to the carrying capacity of the barges, were made negligently, and that Howards are liable in damages for negligent misrepresentation on the principles laid down in *Hedley Byrne v Heller & Partners* [1964] AC 465.

This raises the vexed question of the scope of the doctrine of *Hedley Byrne*. It was much discussed in the Privy Council in *Mutual Life and Citizens' Assurance Co Ltd v Evatt* [1971] AC 793 and in this court in *Esso Petroleum Co Ltd v Mardon* [1976] QB 801. To my mind one of the most helpful passages is to be found in the speech of Lord Pearce in *Hedley Byrne v Heller & Partners* [1964] AC 465, 539:

> '... To import such a duty [of care] the representation must normally, I think, concern a business or professional transaction whose nature makes clear the gravity of the inquiry and the

> importance and influence attached to the answer ... A most important circumstance is the form of the inquiry and of the answer'.

To this I would add the principle stated by Lord Reid and Lord Morris of Borth-y-Gest in the Privy Council case, *Mutual Life and Citizens' Assurance Co Ltd v Evatt* [1971] AC 793, 812, which I would adopt in preference to that stated by the majority:

> '... when an inquirer consults a business man in the course of his business and makes it plain to him that he is seeking considered advice and intends to act on it in a particular way ... his action in giving such advice ... (gives rise to) ... a legal obligation to take such care as is reasonable in the whole circumstances'.

Those principles speak of the 'gravity of the inquiry' and the seeking of 'considered advice'. Those words are used so as to exclude representations made during a casual conversation in the street; or in a railway carriage; or an impromptu opinion given offhand; or 'off the cuff' on the telephone. To put it more generally, the duty is one of honesty and no more whenever the opinion, information or advice is given in circumstances in which it appears that it is unconsidered and it would not be reasonable for the recipient to act on it without taking further steps to check it ....

Applying this test, it seems to me that at these various conversations Mr O'Loughlin was under a duty to be honest, but no more. Take the first two conversations. They were on the telephone. The callers from the north wanted to know the capacity of the barges. Mr O'Loughlin answered it offhand as best he could, without looking up the file. If they had wanted considered advice, they should have written a letter and got it in writing. Take the last conversation. It was on an occasion when Mr O'Loughlin went up to the north to discuss all sorts of things. In the course of it, he was asked again the capacity of the barges. He had not got the file with him, so he answered as best he could from memory. To my mind in those circumstances it was not reasonable for Ogdens to act on his answers without checking them. They ought either to have got him to put it in writing – that would have stressed the gravity and importance of it – or they ought to have got expert advice on their own behalf – especially in a matter of such importance to them. So I agree with the judge that there was not such a situation here as to give rise to a duty of care: or to make Howards liable for negligent misrepresentation at common law.

The Misrepresentation Act 1967

Alternatively Ogdens claim damages for innocent misrepresentation under the Misrepresentation Act 1967 ....

This enactment imposes a new and serious liability on anyone who makes a representation of fact in the course of negotiations for a contract. If that representation turns out to be mistaken – then however innocent he may be – he is just as liable as if he made it fraudulently. But how different from times past! For years he was not liable in damages at all for innocent misrepresentation: see *Heilbut, Symons & Co v Buckleton* [1913] AC 30. Quite recently he was made liable if he was proved to have made it negligently: see *Esso Petroleum Co Ltd v Mardon* [1976] QB 801. But now with this Act he is made liable – unless he proves – and the burden is on him to prove – that he had reasonable ground to believe and did in fact believe that it was true.

Section 2(1) certainly applies to the representation made by Mr. O'Loughlin on July 11, 1974, when he told Ogdens that each barge could carry 1,600 tonnes. The judge found that it was a misrepresentation: that he said it with the object of getting the hire contract for Howards. They got it: and, as a result, Ogdens suffered loss. But the judge found that Mr. O'Loughlin was not negligent: and so Howards were not liable for it.

The judge's finding was criticised before us because he asked himself the question: was Mr. O'Loughlin negligent? Whereas he should have asked himself: did Mr. O'Loughlin have reasonable ground to believe that the representation was true? I think that criticism is not fair to the judge. By the word 'negligent' he was only using shorthand for the longer phrase contained in section 2(1) which he had before him. And the judge, I am sure, had the burden of proof in mind: for he had come to the conclusion that Mr. O'Loughlin was not negligent. The judge said in effect: 'I am satisfied that Mr. O'Loughlin was not negligent', and being so satisfied, the burden need not be further considered: see *Robins v National Trust Co Ltd* [1927] AC 515, 520.

It seems to me that when one examines the details, the judge's view was entirely justified. He found that Mr O'Loughlin's state of mind was this: Mr O'Loughlin had examined Lloyd's Register and had seen there that the deadweight capacity of each barge was 1,800 tonnes. That figure stuck in his mind. The judge found that 'the 1,600 tonnes was arrived at by knocking off what he considered a reasonable margin for fuel, and so on, from the 1,800 tonnes summer deadweight figure in Lloyd's Register, which was in the back of his mind'. The judge said that Mr O'Loughlin had seen at some time the German shipping documents and had seen the deadweight figure of 1,055.135 tonnes, but it did not register. All that was in his mind was the 1,800 tonnes in Lloyd's Register which was regarded in shipping circles as the Bible. That afforded reasonable ground for him to believe that the barges could each carry 1,600 tonnes payload: and that is what Mr. O'Loughlin believed.

So on this point, too, I do not think we should fault the judge. It is not right to pick his judgment to pieces by subjecting it – or the shorthand note – to literal analysis. Viewing it fairly, the judge (who had section 2(1) in front of him) must have been of opinion that the burden of proof was discharged.

Bridge LJ: I will consider first the position under the statute .... It is unfortunate that the judge never directed his mind to the question whether Mr O'Loughlin had any reasonable ground for his belief. The question he asked himself, in considering liability under the Misrepresentation Act 1967, was whether the innocent misrepresentation was negligent. He concluded that if Mr O'Loughlin had given the inaccurate information in the course of the April telephone conversations he would have been negligent to do so but that in the circumstances obtaining at the Otley interview in July there was no negligence. I take it that he meant by this that on the earlier occasions the circumstances were such that he would have been under a duty to check the accuracy of his information, but on the later occasions he was exempt from any such duty. I appreciate the basis of this distinction, but it seems to me, with respect, quite irrelevant to any question of liability under the statute. If the representee proves a misrepresentation which, if fraudulent, would have sounded in damages, the onus passes immediately to the representor to prove that he had reasonable ground to believe the facts represented. In other words the liability of the representor does not depend upon his being under a duty of care the extent of which may vary according to the circumstances in which the representation is made. In the course of negotiations leading to a contract the statute imposes an absolute obligation not to state facts which the representor cannot prove he had reasonable ground to believe.

[Bridge LJ. considered the grounds for the reasonableness of O'Loughlin's belief by reference to the transcript of the judgment at first instance.]

I am fully alive to the dangers of trial by transcript and it is to be assumed that Mr O'Loughlin was perfectly honest throughout. But the question remains whether his evidence, however benevolently viewed, is sufficient to show that he had an objectively reasonable ground to disregard the figure in the ship's documents and to prefer the Lloyd's Register figure. I think it is not. The fact that he was more interested in cubic capacity could not justify reliance on one figure of deadweight capacity in preference to another. The fact that the deadweight figure in the ship's documents was a freshwater figure was of no significance since, as he knew, the difference between freshwater and sea water deadweight capacity was minimal. Accordingly I conclude that Howards failed to prove that Mr O'Loughlin had reasonable ground to believe the truth of his misrepresentation to Mr Redpath.

Having reached a conclusion favourable to Ogdens on the issue of liability under the Misrepresentation Act 1967, I do not find it necessary to express a concluded view on the issue of negligence at common law. As at present advised I doubt if the circumstances surrounding the misrepresentation at the Otley interview were such as to impose on Howards a common law duty of care for the accuracy of the statement. If there was such a duty, I doubt if the evidence established a breach of it.

Shaw LJ: I turn next to the question of liability for negligence. I would respectfully adopt what Lord Denning MR has already said in preferring the minority opinion in *Mutual Life and Citizens' Assurance Co Ltd v Evatt* [1971] AC 793 and I would approach the problem as he has done from the standpoint of the passage he has cited from the speech of Lord Pearce in *Hedley Byrne v Heller & Partners* [1964] AC 465, 539.

Now it does seem to me that the chartering of barges for the purpose of carrying clay out to sea and there dumping it is a business transaction whose nature makes clear the importance and influence of an answer to the question: 'What is their carrying capacity in the context of the purpose of the prospective charterparties?' That the question was only asked over the telephone in April and later repeated at an interview in July does not of itself, as I see it, render the subject matter of the question less material or the impact of the answer less important. The information sought would govern the performance by Ogdens of their contract with the authority and this must have been apparent to any man of business, let alone Mr O'Loughlin. The judge so held. The information which had been asked for more than once cannot be regarded as other than important whatever the circumstances in which it was sought and given. Moreover, it was not expert advice that was sought which might honestly and reasonably have assumed different forms according to the source of it. What was asked for was a specific fact. Ogdens had not themselves any direct means of ascertaining what the fact was. Certainly they had no such ready and facile means as were available to Mr O'Loughlin. These factors in association with the relationship of the parties as owners and prospective charterers of barges to be employed for a specific purpose known to the owners did in my judgment give rise to a duty upon the owners to exercise reasonable care to be accurate in giving information of a material character which was peculiarly within their knowledge. All Mr O'Loughlin had to do was to look at documents in Howard's possession and to read them accurately. Had he done so there would have been no room for error of fact or for misconceived opinion or wrong advice. That he chose to answer an important question from mere recollection 'off the cuff' does not in my view diminish, if I may adopt the language of Lord Pearce, the 'gravity of the inquiry or the importance and influence attached to the answer'.

It is with considerable diffidence that I express this view since it is not shared by either of the other members of this court and was not held by Bristow J. Nonetheless I would venture to hold that Ogdens have a cause of action in negligence at common law. This is not, in my judgment, affected by the exception clause which does not purport to grant absolution from the consequences of negligence on the part of the owners.

There remains the issue raised by the claim under section 2(1) of the Misrepresentation Act 1967. I do not regard the telephone conversation of April and the interview of July 11, 1974, as being so casual as to give rise to no legal consequences. Certainly I find myself unable to dismiss what was said at the interview in July as inconsequential. I share the opinion expressed in this regard in the judgment of Bridge LJ which is based on the finding of the judge. I entirely agree, furthermore, with Bridge LJ's analysis of the evidence, together with the judge's findings in this regard, and I agree also with the views expressed by Bridge LJ as to the operation and effect of the relevant provisions of the Misrepresentation Act. I cannot do better than respectfully to adopt his reasoning without seeking to repeat it, and I agree with his conclusions.

The case illustrates the advantages of a claim under s 2(1). Ogden succeeded on the basis that the majority of the Court of Appeal (Shaw and Bridge L.JJ.) held that Howard had failed to demonstrate that it had reasonable grounds for belief in the truth of its statement. Crucial to this finding was the fact that Howard had the correct information in its possession at the relevant time. Lord Denning M.R. dissented, holding that it was reasonable for Howard to rely on the entry in the Lloyd's register, the mariner's 'Bible' as he put it.

Importantly, had the case been decided prior to the enactment of the Misrepresentation Act 1967 Ogden would have lost. Lord Denning M.R. and Bridge L.J. agreed that no duty of care existed between Howard Marine and Ogden. Furthermore, even if there had been a duty of care, Bridge L.J. thought that there was insufficient evidence to establish that Howard Marine had been negligent and breached that duty of care.

It is clear that in most situations a claim under s 2(1) will be more advantageous than a claim for negligent misstatement. Nevertheless, there are two reasons why a person may wish to pursue a claim in negligence at common law. First, the claimant will not have to prove the existence of a contract. This will be beneficial if the claim is against a third party, such as the claim in *Hedley Byrne* itself. It may also be beneficial when the contract has been found to be void and therefore no longer in existence. Second, a claim in negligence is not dependent upon there being a misrepresentation as defined in s 2, above.

A further problem with a claim under s 2(1) is that the section specifies that the misrepresentation must be 'made' to the other party. It has been argued that this language is inapt to cover the situation where the misrepresentation is in the form of silence. In *Banque Financière de la Cité v Westgate Insurance* [1990] 1 QB 665, Slade L.J. said:

> The expression 'misrepresentation ... made' (which is repeated in several later sections of the Act of 1967) would, in our judgment, on the ordinary meaning of words be inapt to refer to a misrepresentation which had not been made in fact but was (at most) merely deemed by the common law to have been made. If it had been the intention of the legislature that a mere failure to discharge the duty of disclosure in the case of a contract *uberrimae fidei* would fail to be treated as the 'making' of a representation within the meaning of the Act of 1967, we are of the opinion that the legislature would have said so.

8.3.3 Innocent misrepresentation

Historically, all non-fraudulent misrepresentations were known as innocent misrepresentations. Following the recognition of liability for negligent misrepresentation an innocent misrepresentation is now any misrepresentation which is neither fraudulent nor negligent. As we will see, the remedies available for an innocent misrepresentation are strictly limited. The claimant may be entitled to rescind the contract (or possibly damages in lieu of rescission) but s/he will not be entitled to claim damages in addition to rescission.

8.4 Remedies

The precise remedies available for misrepresentation differ between the three categories.

8.4.1 Rescission

All types of misrepresentation, whether fraudulent, negligent or innocent, render a contract voidable. The party misled is given the option either to have the contract set aside or, alternatively, to affirm it. If s/he elects to rescind the contract it will be set aside both retrospectively and prospectively, and the parties will be restored to their pre-contractual positions.

Prior to the Misrepresentation Act 1967, rescission was unavailable where either the misrepresentation had become a term of the contract or, in some cases, where the contract had been performed. This was changed by s 1 of the Misrepresentation Act 1967.

S 1 Removal of certain bars to rescission for innocent misrepresentation
Where a person has entered into a contract after a misrepresentation has been made to him, and:

(a) the misrepresentation has become a term of the contract; or
(b) the contract has been performed;

or both, then, if otherwise he would be entitled to rescind the contract without alleging fraud, he shall be so entitled, subject to the provisions of this Act, notwithstanding the matters mentioned in paragraphs (a) and (b) of this section.

8.4.1.1 Operation of rescission

The representee will not always require the assistance of the court in order to effect rescission. For example, if the contract remains executory, that is nothing has been done under the contract, the representee may be able to effect rescission simply by informing the other party that s/he intends to rescind. If performance has already commenced, however, the representee will often require an order of the court to ensure the co-operation of the other party.

To rescind the contract, the innocent party will normally be expected to give notice to the other party. In some situations, however, particularly where the misrepresentation was fraudulent, the innocent party may no longer be able to find the maker of the false statement. In such situations, there is authority that other reasonable steps, which clearly indicate an intention to rescind, will be sufficient.

***Car and Universal Finance Co Ltd v Caldwell* [1965] 1 QB 525**

Facts: The defendant, Mr Caldwell, sold his Jaguar car to a rogue named Mr Norris. Norris paid by cheque, and when this proved to be worthless, Caldwell sought to rescind the contract. He could not find either Norris or the car so he informed the police and the Automobile Association about the fraud and asked them to trace the car. Norris subsequently sold the car to a motor dealer who had notice of the fraud, but the car then changed hands on a number of occasions until it was eventually purchased in good faith by the plaintiff. The car was eventually seized by the police and the plaintiff sought to recover it on the ground that the contract had not been validly rescinded prior to the date that it purchased the car.

Held: The Court of Appeal held that rescission had occurred on the day that Mr Caldwell informed the police and the AA. Thus, the plaintiff had not obtained good title to the car.

Sellers LJ: This appeal raises a primary point in the law of contract. The question has arisen whether a contract which is voidable by one party can in any circumstances be terminated by that party without his rescission being communicated to the other party ....

An affirmation of a voidable contract may be established by any conduct which unequivocally manifests an intention to affirm it by the party who has the right to affirm or disaffirm. Communication of an acceptance of a contract after knowledge of a fundamental breach of it by the other party or of fraud affecting it is, of course, evidence establishing affirmation but it is not essential evidence. A party cannot reject goods sold and delivered if he uses them after knowledge of a right to reject, and the judgment cites a case where an instruction to a broker to re-sell was sufficient affirmation of the contract in question even though that conduct was not communicated. It may be said that a contract may be more readily approved and accepted than it can be terminated where a unilateral right to affirm or disaffirm arises. The disaffirmation or election to avoid a contract changes the relationship of the parties and brings their respective obligations to an end, whereas an affirmation leaves the contract effective though subject to a claim for damages for its

> breach. Where a contracting party could be communicated with, and modern facilities make communication practically world-wide and almost immediate, it would be unlikely that a party could be held to have disaffirmed a contract unless he went so far as to communicate his decision so to do. It would be what the other contracting party would normally require and unless communication were made the party's intention to rescind would not have been unequivocally or clearly demonstrated or made manifest. But in circumstances such as the present case, the other contracting party, a fraudulent rogue who would know that the vendor would want his car back as soon as he knew of the fraud, would not expect to be communicated with as a matter of right or requirement, and would deliberately, as here, do all he could to evade any such communication being made to him. In such exceptional contractual circumstances, it does not seem to me appropriate to hold that a party so acting can claim any right to have a decision to rescind communicated to him before the contract is terminated. To hold that he could would involve that the defrauding party, if skilful enough to keep out of the way, could deprive the other party to the contract of his right to rescind, a right to which he was entitled and which he would wish to exercise, as the defrauding party would well know or at least confidently suspect. The position has to be viewed, as I see it, between the two contracting parties involved in the particular contract in question. That another innocent party or parties may suffer does not in my view of the matter justify imposing on a defrauded seller an impossible task. He has to establish, clearly and unequivocally, that he terminates the contract and is no longer to be bound by it. If he cannot communicate his decision he may still satisfy a judge or jury that he had made a final and irrevocable decision and ended the contract. I am in agreement with Lord Denning MR who asked 'How is a man in the position of Caldwell ever to be able to rescind the contract when a fraudulent person absconds as Norris did here?' and answered that he can do so '... if he at once, on discovering the fraud, takes all possible steps to regain the goods even though he cannot find the rogue nor communicate with him'.
>
> **Davies LJ:** On the facts of this case Norris must be taken to have known that the defendant might, on ascertaining the fraud, wish to rescind the contract. Norris disappeared; and so did the car. The defendant could, therefore, neither communicate with Norris nor retake the car. It must, therefore, I think, be taken to be implied in the transaction between Norris and the defendant that in the event of the defendant's wishing to rescind he should be entitled to do so by the best other means possible. *Lex non cogit ad impossibilia*. It is true that it was conceivably possible that the defendant might decide not to rescind but to sue on the cheque instead; but it is most doubtful whether on the facts of this case such a possibility could have occurred to Norris as a real one. The fact that Norris knew that he was a rogue and that, therefore, the defendant was likely to be after him distinguishes this case from that of an innocent misrepresentor. It would not occur to the latter that the other party to the contract would have any right or desire to rescind, so that there would be no such implication as that which I have suggested arose in the present case.

The decision in *Caldwell* was controversial because it was effectively a decision as to which of two innocent parties should bear the loss caused by the actions of a fraudulent third party. The Court of Appeal concluded that the plaintiff should bear the loss because the defendant had taken reasonable steps to inform the fraudster of his intention to rescind. The outcome is somewhat harsh on the plaintiff who bought the car in good faith and paid in cash. Surely, in the circumstances, it would have been fairer for the loss to fall on the defendant, who had naively accepted a cheque in exchange for the car.

8.4.1.2 Bars to rescission

The law has placed a number of limitations on the right to rescind. We will consider the four main bars to rescission. If any of these bars are present the claimant will be precluded from rescinding the contract and will be left to rely on his/her remedy in damages if any.

8.4.1.2.1 Intervention of third-party rights

Caldwell provides an excellent example of the operation of this bar. On the facts of the case it was held that Caldwell had rescinded the contract prior to the purchase of the car by the plaintiff. Had he not, rescission would have been barred because of the intervention of third-party rights. This is because rescission is a restitutionary claim for which the defence of 'bona fide purchaser for value without notice' is available.

8.4.1.2.2 Counter-restitution is impossible

A party will not be permitted to rescind a contract if s/he is unable or unwilling to give back what s/he has received under the contract. The purpose of this limitation is to prevent the unjust enrichment of the party seeking to rescind. For example, suppose I purchase a car from you on the basis of a misrepresentation. Prima facie, I am entitled to rescind the contract and recover the money I have paid. But this would result in my unjust enrichment if I am unwilling to return the car because my wife still likes it. The common law took an extremely strict approach to the operation of this bar.

Clarke v Dickson (1858) EB & E 148 (HC)

Facts: The plaintiff was induced to purchase shares in a company following a misrepresentation by the defendants. Subsequently the company was registered as a company with limited liability. On discovering the misrepresentation, the plaintiff sought to rescind the contract.

Held: The court held that rescission was not available because the plaintiff could not restore the defendant to his pre-contractual position. The shares in the limited liability company were different in nature and status to the shares that existed prior to the formation of the contract.

Crompton J: When once it is settled that a contract induced by fraud is not void, but voidable at the option of the party defrauded, it seems to me to follow that, when that party exercises his option to rescind the contract, he must be in a state to rescind; that is, he must be in such a situation to be able to put the parties into their original state before the contract. Now here I will assume, what is not clear to me, that the plaintiff bought his shares from the defendants and not from the Company, and that he might at one time have been able to restore the shares to the defendants if he could, and demand the price from them. But then what did he buy? Shares in a partnership with others. He cannot return those; he has become bound to those others. Still stronger, he has changed their nature: what he now has and offers to restore are shares in a quasi corporation now in process of being wound up. That is quite enough to decide this case. The plaintiff must rescind *in toto* or not at all: he cannot both keep the shares and recover the whole price.

The facts of the case demonstrate that the bar can operate very harshly. A more flexible approach has been taken in equity.

Erlanger v New Sombrero Phosphate Co (1878) 3 App Cas 1218

Facts: The defendants, who were in a fiduciary relationship with the plaintiff, sold a phosphate mine to the plaintiff for £110,000. After working the mine for a period of time, the plaintiff sought to rescind the contract on the grounds that the defendants had breached their fiduciary duty by failing to disclose the fact that they had purchased the mine for £55,000 a few days prior to the sale. The defendants argued that rescission was unavailable because the plaintiff could not return the mine in its original condition.

Held: The House of Lords allowed the plaintiff to rescind the contract and recover the purchase price on the condition that they returned the mine and accounted for the profits they had made from working the mine.

Lord Blackburn said: [A Court of Equity] can take account of profits, and make allowance for deterioration. And I think the practice has always been for a Court of Equity to give this relief whenever, by the exercise of its powers, it can do what is *practically just*, though it cannot restore the parties precisely to the state they were in before the contract.

The key theme in Lord Blackburn's speech seems to be 'practical justice' – the court will do whatever is 'practically just'. Instead of rigidly insisting that the parties be restored to their pre-contractual positions, the court will aim to ensure that the claimant is not unjustly enriched as a result of rescission. In many cases this will be possible simply by ordering the claimant to provide a money allowance for the benefits s/he has received but cannot give back. While the courts have generally adopted a more flexible approach to the counter-restitution bar, it is important to remember that the claimant does not have a right to provide a money allowance instead of making counter-restitution (see also *Marme Inversiones 2007 SL v NatWest Markets PLC, HSH Nordbank AG, Bayerische Landesbank, ING Bank NV, Caixabank SA* [2019] EWHC 366 (Comm) at [352] where Picken J. stated:

> whereas in *Erlanger* the Court sought to achieve an outcome which returned the parties substantially to the position they had been in before the contract was entered into, the position contended for by Marme in the present case would put Marme partly in the position which it was in before the Transaction (including the Swaps) was entered into (by rescinding the Swaps) and partly in the position in which Marme would be in had the Transaction been performed (through the performance of the Senior Loan and other financing arrangements). That 'mix and match' approach is not an approach which Erlanger would justify).

The court retains the discretion to make whatever judgment it sees fit to meet the 'practical justice' of the case. In *Spence v Crawford* [1939] 3 All ER 271, Lord Wright explained the approach in the following terms:

> The court will be less ready to pull a transaction to pieces where the defendant is innocent, whereas in the case of fraud the court will exercise its jurisdiction to the full in order, if possible, to prevent the defendant from enjoying the benefits of his fraud at the expense of the innocent plaintiff.

8.4.1.2.3 Affirmation

Rescission will be barred if the person to whom the statement was made has affirmed the contract either expressly through spoken word or impliedly by conduct.

Long v Lloyd [1958] 1 WLR 753

Facts: The plaintiff purchased a lorry from the defendant, Lloyd, in reliance on the defendant's assurance that it was in 'first-class condition'. On the first journey after the sale, the dynamo broke and the plaintiff noticed a number of other serious defects including a broken oil seal and a crack in one of the wheels. The defendant offered to contribute towards the costs of the repairs. The plaintiff accepted this offer, and later sent the lorry on a journey to Middlesbrough during which it broke down. The plaintiff sought to rescind the contract on the ground of innocent misrepresentation.

Held: The Court of Appeal held that rescission was barred because the plaintiff's dispatch of the lorry to Middlesbrough amounted to an affirmation of the contract.

Pearce LJ: [T]he plaintiff, knowing all that he did about the condition and performance of the lorry, dispatched it, driven by his brother, on a business trip to Middlesbrough. That step, at all events, appears to us to have amounted, in all circumstances of the case, to a final acceptance of the lorry by the plaintiff for better or for worse, and to have conclusively extinguished any right of rescission remaining to the plaintiff after completion of the sale.

8.4.1.2.4 Lapse of time

Lapse of time may operate as evidence of affirmation, but this will rarely be so because knowledge is usually required for affirmation.

***Armstrong v Jackson* [1917] 2 KB 822**

Facts: The defendant, a stockbroker, purported to purchase specified shares for the plaintiff but instead sold the plaintiff his own shares. After a six-year delay the plaintiff discovered the fraud and sought to rescind the contract, notwithstanding that the value of the shares had considerably decreased between the date of the sale and the date of the action for rescission. The defendant claimed that rescission should be barred for delay.

Held: The High Court held that, on the facts, delay was not a bar to rescission.

McCardie J: In cases like the present the right of the party defrauded is not affected by the mere lapse of time so long as he remains in ignorance of the fraud.

It is clear that in cases of fraudulent misrepresentation, lapse of time without knowledge of the fraud will usually not constitute a bar to rescission. Exceptionally, however, in cases of innocent misrepresentation, mere lapse of time may act as a bar to rescission.

***Leaf v International Galleries* [1950] 2 KB 86**

Facts: In 1944, Mr Leaf paid £85 to International Galleries for a picture of Salisbury Cathedral. Prior to the sale, International Galleries had innocently represented to Mr Leaf that the painting was by John Constable. Five years later, in 1949, Leaf sought to re-sell the painting and discovered that it was not a Constable. He attempted to return the picture to International Galleries, but they refused to accept it, so Mr Leaf brought a claim for rescission of the contract of sale.

Held: The Court of Appeal held that rescission was barred for lapse of time.

Jenkins LJ: [C]ontracts such as this cannot be kept open and subject to the possibility of rescission indefinitely … it behoves the purchaser either to verify or, as the case may be, to disprove the representation within a reasonable time, or else stand or fall by it. If he is allowed to wait five, ten or twenty years and then reopen the bargain, there can be no finality at all. I, for my part, do not think that equity will intervene in such a case, more especially as in the present case it cannot be said that, apart from rescission, the plaintiff would have been without remedy. The county court judge was of opinion, and it seems to me that he was clearly right, that the representation that the picture was a Constable amounted to a warranty. If it amounted to a warranty, and that was broken, as on the findings of the county court judge it was, then the plaintiff had a right at law in the shape of damages for breach of warranty. That remedy he did not choose to exercise, and, although he was invited at the hearing to amend his claim so as to include a claim for breach of warranty, he declined that opportunity. That being so, it seems to me that he has no justification at all for now coming to equity five years after the event and claiming rescission. Accordingly, it seems to me that this is not a case in which the equitable remedy of rescission, assuming it to be available in the absence of fraud in respect of a completed sale of chattels, should be allowed to the plaintiff. For these reasons, I agree that the appeal fails and should be dismissed.

It seems that the justification for the lapse of time bar is the desirability of certainty and finality in contractual relationships. For Jenkins L.J., it was significant that the representation had been incorporated into the contract, giving rise to an action for damages. Given that the plaintiff was unwilling to pursue this claim, the Court of Appeal was not prepared to order rescission five years after the completion of the contract. In *Salt v Stratstone Specialist Limited* [2015] EWCA Civ 745 the Court of Appeal commented on *Leaf*:

Longmore LJ

32. The authority usually cited under this head is *Leaf v International Galleries* [1950] 2 KB 86 in which the claimant in 1944 bought a picture of Salisbury Cathedral represented to be by 'J. Constable' for £85.00. It is a somewhat curious case since one would think that a genuine Constable painting of Salisbury Cathedral, even in 1944, would be worth considerably more than £85.00, quite apart from the fact that in auctioneers' terminology 'J. Constable' is a representation very different from 'John Constable'. Be that as it may, this court did not permit rescission in 1949 partly in the light of the considerable delay between purchase and the action and partly because it held that a representor should not be in a worse position than someone who had made it a term of the contract that the picture was by Constable. If, therefore, lapse of time prevented the claimant purchaser from rejecting the picture and claiming damages for non-delivery, a representee should be in no better position. Section 35 of the Sale of Goods Act 1893 provided that the buyer was deemed to have accepted the goods 'when after a lapse of a reasonable time, he retains the goods without intimating to the seller that he has rejected them'. The Sale of Goods Act now provides (1) that a buyer is not deemed to have accepted the goods until he has had a reasonable opportunity of examining them for the purposes of ascertaining whether they are in conformity with the contract and (2) that the question that is material for the purposes of determining whether a reasonable time has elapsed (with the result that the buyer is to be deemed to have accepted the goods) includes the question whether the buyer has had such reasonable opportunity for examining the goods.

33. No point was taken at trial raising the question whether Mr Salt was, as a matter of fact, entitled to reject the car because DJ Hickman refused an application by Mr Salt to amend his pleadings to take the point. The court was thus left in ignorance whether a reasonable time had elapsed without Mr Salt having rejected the goods. For that purpose it would be relevant to inquire whether it was possible by reasonable examination of the car to tell whether it was new or not. One suspects not, since Mr Salt only became alive to the point after disclosure of documents had taken place. In any event, it would not be fair on Mr Salt to allow Stratstone now to rely on a suggestion that, because he was too late to reject the car, he was likewise too late to rescind the contract.

34. It must, moreover, be remembered that Leaf was decided well before the Misrepresentation Act was passed. It must be doubtful whether since the enactment of section 1 it is still good law that a representor should be in no worse position than if the representation had become a term of the contract, particularly if the representor takes no steps to prove that he was not negligent.

35. In all the circumstances, it does not seem to me that lapse of time on its own can be a bar to rescission in this case. As DJ Hickman pointed out, the ground on which rescission became available only became known to Mr Salt on disclosure of documents. Most of the subsequent delay has been due to the litigation process and Stratstone's wrongful refusal to take the car back and return the price.

Roth J

46. The well-known decision of this court in *Leaf v International Galleries* [1950] 2 K.B. 86, is to be read in that overall context. The facts have been summarised in the judgment of Longmore LJ. Although the only remedy sought was rescission, the assertion that the painting was by Constable was also a term of the contract and, in the leading judgment, Denning LJ held that that it was to be decided according to the principles applicable to the sale of goods. He found that the buyer had accepted the goods by reason of a lapse of time, thereby losing his right to reject. If the buyer had lost the right to reject the goods under the contract he could be no better off in seeking rescission for innocent misrepresentation.

47. Accordingly, I think the ratio of Denning LJ's judgment is that if the buyer is deemed to have accepted the goods by reason of a lapse of time, that would bar the right to rescind for an innocent misrepresentation. Although he agreed with that judgment, it is notable that Jenkins LJ stated that in 'contracts such as this' it was for the purchaser to take steps to satisfy himself as to the authenticity of the work within a reasonable time if he wished to exercise the remedy of rescission. And Lord Evershed MR emphasised the difficulty of attribution of works of art and accordingly expressed concern at the possibility of a divergent view emerging many years after purchase.

48. In the present case, as Longmore LJ points out, it is possible that Mr Salt may not have lost his contractual right to reject by lapse of time in any event: that issue was not decided since the District Judge understandably refused leave to raise that point by way of a late re-amendment of the claim. The grounds on which a right to reject goods for breach of condition is lost have been significantly qualified since Leaf was decided, by the Sale of Goods Act 1979 (as amended). But in any event, this was, on the findings of the courts below, at least a negligent misrepresentation by the employee of Stratstone. It was not suggested that Mr Salt should reasonably have discovered the true age of the car before documents revealing the position were provided on disclosure in the proceedings. In those circumstances, I think that Judge Harris was clearly correct in concluding that there was no undue delay on the part of Mr Salt.

8.4.2 Damages

In addition, or as an alternative, to rescission, the representee may also claim damages for misrepresentation. Historically, damages were generally only available in relation to fraudulent misrepresentations (under the tort of deceit). However, following *Hedley Byrne v Heller* and the enactment of the Misrepresentation Act 1967, damages have become available for negligent misrepresentation as well. In the following section we will explore the different methods of assessment of damages that the courts apply to each category of misrepresentation.

8.4.2.1 Fraudulent misrepresentation

Damages for fraudulent misrepresentation may be recovered in the tort of deceit. The Court of Appeal tackled the question of how such damages are to be calculated in *Doyle v Olby (Ironmongers) Ltd.*

Doyle v Olby (Ironmongers) Ltd [1969] 2 All ER 119

Facts: The plaintiff bought an ironmongers' business from the defendants. The defendants had made several fraudulent misrepresentations to the plaintiff concerning annual profits, sales and future competition. Specifically, the defendants told the plaintiff that most of the trade was over the counter in the ironmongers' shop. The plaintiff purchased the business subject to a covenant which stated that the defendants would not engage in a similar business within a 10-mile radius for five years. Following the purchase, the plaintiff invested £7,000 into the business. He soon discovered that the turnover had been misrepresented and, in particular, that half the trade had been obtained by the defendant's brother acting as a part-time travelling salesman. It also became apparent that a company associated to the defendants had begun canvassing the defendants' former customers in the area.

The plaintiff brought an action for fraudulent misrepresentation. At first instance, Swanwick J. found all the defendants liable for fraud and awarded the plaintiff damages of £1,500 calculated as equivalent to the cost of making good the representation or the reduction in the value of the goodwill. The plaintiff appealed against the amount of damages.

Held: The Court of Appeal allowed the appeal, holding that damages should be measured on a tort basis, not a contractual basis. The proper measure of damages was £5,500, measured by reference to all the losses directly flowing from the fraud.

Lord Denning: The judge awarded Mr. Doyle £1,500 damages. Mr. Doyle appeals against that award. He says it is far too small .... It appears ... that ... the judge accepted that the proper measure of damages was the 'cost of making good the representation', or what came to the same thing, 'the reduction in value of the goodwill' due to the misrepresentation. In so doing, he treated the representation as if it were a contractual promise, that is, as if there were a contractual term to the effect 'The trade is all over the counter. There is no need to employ a traveller'. I think it was the wrong measure. Damages for fraud and conspiracy are assessed differently from damages for breach of contract ....

The second question is what is the proper measure of damages for fraud, as distinct from damages for breach of contract? It was discussed during the argument in *Hadley v Baxendale* (1854) 9 Ex 341, and finds a place in the notes to *Smith's Leading Cases*, 13th edn (1929) at p 563, where it is suggested there is no difference. But in *McConnel v Wright* [1903] 1 Ch 546, 554, Lord Collins MR pointed out the difference. It was an action for fraudulent statements in a prospectus whereby a man was induced to take up shares. Lord Collins said of the action for fraud:

> 'It is not an action for breach of contract, and, therefore, no damages in respect of prospective gains which the person contracting was entitled by his contract to expect to come in, but it is an action of tort – it is an action for a wrong done whereby the plaintiff was tricked out of certain money in his pocket, and, therefore, prima facie, the highest limit of his damages is the whole extent of his loss, and that loss is measured by the money which was in his pocket and is now in the pocket of the company'.

But that statement was the subject of comment by Lord Atkin in *Clark v Urquhart* [1930] AC 28, 67–68. He said:

> 'I find it difficult to suppose that there is any difference in the measure of damages in an action of deceit depending upon the nature of the transaction into which the plaintiff is fraudulently induced to enter. Whether he buys shares or buys sugar, whether he subscribes for shares, or agrees to enter into a partnership, or in any other way alters his position to his detriment, in principle, the measure of damages should be the same, and whether estimated by a jury or a judge. I should have thought it would be based on the actual damage directly flowing from the

> fraudulent inducement. The formula in *McConnel v Wright* [1903] 1 Ch 546, may be correct or it may be expressed in too rigid terms'.

I think that Lord Collins did express himself in too rigid terms. He seems to have overlooked consequential damages. On principle the distinction seems to be this: in contract, the defendant has made a promise and broken it. The object of damages is to put the plaintiff in as good a position, as far as money can do it, as if the promise had been performed. In fraud, the defendant has been guilty of a deliberate wrong by inducing the plaintiff to act to his detriment. The object of damages is to compensate the plaintiff for all the loss he has suffered, so far, again, as money can do it. In contract, the damages are limited to what may reasonably be supposed to have been in the contemplation of the parties. In fraud, they are not so limited. The defendant is bound to make reparation for all the actual damages directly flowing from the fraudulent inducement. The person who has been defrauded is entitled to say:

> 'I would not have entered into this bargain at all but for your representation. Owing to your fraud, I have not only lost all the money I paid you, but, what is more, I have been put to a large amount of extra expense as well and suffered this or that extra damages'.

All such damages can be recovered, and it does not lie in the mouth of the fraudulent person to say that they could not reasonably have been foreseen. For instance, in this very case Mr. Doyle has not only lost the money which he paid for the business, which he would never have done if there had been no fraud: he put all that money in and lost it; but also he has been put to expense and loss in trying to run a business which has turned out to be a disaster for him. He is entitled to damages for all his loss, subject, of course to giving credit for any benefit that he has received. There is nothing to be taken off in mitigation: for there is nothing more that he could have done to reduce his loss. He did all that he could reasonably be expected to do.

Winn LJ: If a man in this country is made the victim of a fraudulent misrepresentation that a business in Bangkok, Hongkong, Manila or the Fiji Islands has certain equipment, certain assets, certain goodwill, certain trade contracts and profits, and is thereby induced to pay for that business, it being, of course, understood by both parties to the transaction of sale, for the procurement of which a fraudulent misrepresentation is made, that he will set out to that remote place with his family and, it may be, his household goods, at very considerable expense, and on arrival will acquire living accommodation and, perhaps, have to buy additional furniture and engage staff or servants; and if he acts upon the representations and incurs all such expenses, and the business is found to be very different from that which it was fraudulently represented to be, so that he cannot survive out in the remote place to which he has gone, and is bound to come back again, then I, speaking for myself, would not hesitate to give him all the outgoings from his pocket of the kinds which I have indicated, up to such time as he should sensibly have come home again, and had the money to come back again, less, of course, by way of set-off, any benefit which he has derived from the exploitation of such assets as he found there upon his arrival.

The Court of Appeal confirmed that damages for fraudulent misrepresentation will be measured according to the tortious measure, not the contractual measure. Damages in contract, if applied in the context of misrepresentation, would aim to put the innocent party in the position s/he would have been in had the statement been true. Damages in tort aim to put the innocent party in the position s/he would have been in had the statement not been made at all (see also *Wemyss v Karim* [2016] EWCA Civ 27 and *Morrell v Stewart* [2015] EWHC 962).

The key issue for the court was whether the plaintiff could recover damages for all his consequential losses flowing from the fraud, or whether his damages were limited by a rule of remoteness. The court insisted that the defendants were liable for all the plaintiff's losses, regardless of whether they were foreseeable. This stricter measure of damages, focusing on causation rather than remoteness, seems to be justified on the public policy ground that the courts should actively deter deliberate wrongdoing.

The effect of the rule was demonstrated in the House of Lords' decision in *Smith New Court Securities v Scrimgeour Vickers.*

Smith New Court Securities v Scrimgeour Vickers [1997] AC 254

Facts: The plaintiffs were persuaded to purchase 28 million shares in a company called Ferranti by the fraudulent misrepresentation of the defendants that there were other possible purchasers in the market. The price paid by the plaintiffs was 82.25p per share at a time when the shares were trading at 78p per share. It later transpired that Ferranti had been the victim of a major fraud (unrelated to the fraudulent misrepresentation) which caused the company's share price to plummet. The plaintiffs eventually sold the shares for between 40p and 30p per share – making a combined loss of over £11 million. The plaintiffs claimed this sum in damages from the defendants. The defendants argued that damages should be limited to the difference between the price that the plaintiffs paid (82.25p) and the price that they would have paid in the absence of the misrepresentation (78p). The Court of Appeal applied the measure contended for by the defendants.

Held: The House of Lords allowed the appeal and held that the plaintiffs were entitled to recover all the loss directly caused by the fraudulent misrepresentation, whether or not it was foreseeable.

Lord Steyn

Damages

Given the fact that the subsequent dramatic fall in the value of Ferranti shares was caused by the disclosure of an earlier fraud practised on Ferranti by a third party, the question is whether Smith is entitled to recover against Citibank the entire loss arising from the fraudulently induced transaction. Smith submits that the Court of Appeal adopted the wrong measure. Smith seeks to recover damages calculated on the basis of the price paid less the aggregate of subsequent realisations. Citibank contends that the loss attributable to the subsequent disclosure of the fraud by a third party is a misfortune risk and is irrecoverable. Citibank argues that the Court of Appeal adopted the correct measure ....

The justification for distinguishing between deceit and negligence

That brings me to the question of policy whether there is a justification for differentiating between the extent of liability for civil wrongs depending on where in the sliding scale from strict liability to intentional wrongdoing the particular civil wrong fits in. It may be said that logical symmetry and a policy of not punishing intentional wrongdoers by civil remedies favour a uniform rule. On the other hand, it is a rational and defensible strategy to impose wider liability on an intentional wrongdoer. As Hart and Honoré, *Causation in the Law*, 2nd edn (1985), p 304 observed, an innocent plaintiff may, not without reason, call on a morally reprehensible defendant to pay the whole of the loss he caused. The exclusion of heads of loss in the law of negligence, which reflects considerations of legal policy, does not necessarily avail the intentional wrongdoer. Such a policy of imposing more stringent remedies on an intentional wrongdoer serves two purposes. First it serves a deterrent purpose in discouraging fraud. Counsel for Citibank argued that the sole purpose of the law of tort generally, and the tort of deceit in particular, should be to compensate the victims of civil wrongs. That is far too narrow a view. Professor Glanville Williams identified four possible purposes of an action for damages in tort: appeasement, justice, deterrence and compensation: see 'The Aims of the Law of Tort' (1951) 4 CLP 137. He concluded, at p 172: 'Where possible the law seems to like to ride two or three horses at once; but occasionally a situation occurs where one must be selected. The tendency is then to choose the deterrent purpose for tort of intention, the compensatory purpose for other torts', and in the battle against fraud civil remedies can play a useful and beneficial role. Secondly, as between the fraudster and the innocent party, moral considerations militate in favour of requiring the fraudster to bear the risk of misfortunes directly caused by his fraud. I make no apology for referring to moral considerations. The law and morality are inextricably interwoven. To a large extent the law is simply formulated and declared morality. And, as Oliver Wendell Holmes, *The Common Law* (ed M De W Howe), p 106, observed, the very notion of deceit with its overtones of wickedness is drawn from the moral world ....

Doyle v Olby (Ironmongers) Ltd

... The logic of the decision in *Doyle v Olby (Ironmongers) Ltd*, justifies the following propositions.

(1) The plaintiff in an action for deceit is not entitled to be compensated in accordance with the contractual measure of damage, i.e. the benefit of the bargain measure. He is not entitled to be protected in respect of his positive interest in the bargain.

(2) The plaintiff in an action for deceit is, however, entitled to be compensated in respect of his negative interest. The aim is to put the plaintiff into the position he would have been in if no false representation had been made.

(3) The practical difference between the two measures was lucidly explained in a contemporary case note on *Doyle v Olby (Ironmongers) Ltd*: G H Treitel, 'Damages for Deceit' (1969) 32 MLR 556, 558–559. The author said:

> 'If the plaintiff's bargain would have been a bad one, even on the assumption that the representation was true, he will do best under the tortious measure. If, on the assumption that the representation was true, his bargain would have been a good one, he will do best under the first contractual measure (under which he may recover something even if the actual value of what he has recovered is greater than the price)'.

(4) Concentrating on the tort measure, the remoteness test whether the loss was reasonably foreseeable had been authoritatively laid down in *The Wagon Mound* in respect of the tort of negligence a few years before *Doyle v Olby (Ironmongers) Ltd* was decided ... *Doyle v Olby (Ironmongers) Ltd* settled that a wider test applies in an action for deceit.

(5) The dicta in all three judgments, as well as the actual calculation of damages in *Doyle v Olby (Ironmongers) Ltd* make clear that the victim of the fraud is entitled to compensation for all the actual loss directly flowing from the transaction induced by the wrongdoer. That includes heads of consequential loss.

(6) Significantly in the present context the rule in the previous paragraph is not tied to any process of valuation at the date of the transaction. It is squarely based on the overriding compensatory principle, widened in view of the fraud to cover all direct consequences. The legal measure is to compare the position of the plaintiff as it was before the fraudulent statement was made to him with his position as it became as a result of his reliance on the fraudulent statement ....

See also *Parabola Investments Ltd v Browallia Cal Ltd* [2010] EWCA Civ 486 and *Glossop Cartons and Print Ltd v Contact (Print and Packaging) Ltd* [2019] EWHC 2314 (Ch) at [103] where Judge Hodge QC stated:

> it should not operate to insulate the claimants from potential commercial risks which they had appreciated and had factored into their calculation of the purchase price because to do so would over-compensate the claimants for the consequences of the defendants' fraud.

Damages for fraudulent misrepresentation can also include an element of compensation for lost profits if the loss flows directly from the misrepresentation (but cf. *Mortgage Express v Countrywide Surveyors Ltd* [2016] EWHC 1830 (Ch)). In *East v Maurer* [1991] 2 All ER 733, the plaintiffs purchased a hair salon in reliance on a fraudulent misrepresentation that the seller had no intention of regularly working at another salon in the same town. The defendant did in fact open up a new salon in the town and the plaintiffs sued the defendant for their loss of profits. At first instance, the judge awarded the plaintiffs damages calculated by reference to the profit they would have made had the defendant not set up the new business. The Court of Appeal allowed the appeal, holding that the judge had wrongly applied the contract measure of damages. However, the court did take into account lost profits in its own assessment of damages. Beldam L.J. said:

> It seems to me that [the judge] should have begun by considering the kind of profit which the second defendant might have made if the representation which induced her to buy the business at Exeter Road had not been made, and that involved considering the kind of profits which *she* might have expected to make in another hairdressing business bought for a similar sum.

The measure of damages so framed looks very much like damages for breach of contract. This is not a problem, however, as Sedley L.J. explained in *Clef Aquitaine v Sovereign Chemical Industries* [2000] 3 All ER 493: '[I]t does not follow that the proper mode of ascertaining damage in certain cases of tort may not mimic reasoning more familiar in contract' (cf. also *4 Eng Ltd v Harper* [2008] EWHC 915 (noted by Mitchell [2009] LQR 12)).

Finally, following the abolition of the 'cause of action' limitation in *Kuddus v Chief Constable of Leicestershire Constabulary* [2002] 2 AC 122, exemplary damages are now potentially available for fraudulent misrepresentation (see *Parabola Investments Ltd v Browallia Cal Ltd* [2009] EWHC 1492 (Comm) at [205], *per* Flaux J.).

8.4.2.2 Negligent misstatement

Damages for negligent misrepresentation at common law are subject to the normal tort principles of remoteness.

South Australia Asset Management Corp v York Montague Ltd [1997] AC 191

Facts: The plaintiff asked the defendants to value properties on the security of which they were considering advancing money by way of mortgage. The defendants negligently overvalued the properties and in reliance on these valuations the plaintiffs loaned money which they would not otherwise have done. The borrowers defaulted on their repayments and the plaintiffs suffered significant losses as a result. The losses were magnified due to the collapse of the property market. The plaintiffs sued the defendants for negligent misstatement and sought to recover the whole of their loss on the basis that they would not have entered into the transactions at all but for the negligent valuation. The Court of Appeal allowed the plaintiffs' claim.

Held: The House of Lords allowed the appeal, holding that the plaintiffs could only recover the loss which foreseeably flowed from the negligent valuation.

Lord Hoffmann: Rules which make the wrongdoer liable for all the consequences of his wrongful conduct are exceptional and need to be justified by some special policy. Normally the law limits liability to those consequences which are attributable to that which made the act wrongful. In the case of liability in negligence for providing inaccurate information, this would mean liability for the consequences of the information being inaccurate.

For a further discussion of this case, see *Clack v Wrigleys Solicitors LLP* [2013] EWHC 413. In *Hughes-Holland v BPE Solicitors* [2017] UKSC 21 at [34]–[36], Lord Sumption (with whom Lords Neuberger, Mance, Clarke and Hodge agreed) provided some clarification of this case when stating:

> The decision in SAAMCO has often been misunderstood, not least by the writers who have criticised it. The misunderstanding arises, I think, from a tendency to overlook two fundamental features of the reasoning .... The first is that where the contribution of the defendant is to supply material which the client will take into account in making his own decision on the basis of a broader assessment of the risks, the defendant has no legal responsibility for his decision ... This is why in SAAMCO itself Lord Hoffmann had rejected the distinction made by the Court of Appeal between 'no transaction' and 'successful transaction' cases. It was 'irrelevant to the scope of the duty of care' .... The second fundamental feature of the reasoning follows from the first. It is that the principle has nothing to do with the causation of loss as that expression is usually understood in the law.

8.4.2.2.1 Misrepresentation Act 1967 s 2(1)

Section 2(1) of the Misrepresentation Act 1967 states that: 'the person making the misrepresentation [will] be liable to damages in respect thereof had the misrepresentation been made fraudulently'. In other words, a person liable under s 2(1) will be treated as if they had made the misrepresentation fraudulently. This equation with fraud raises difficult questions concerning the measure of damages. Initially, there was some suggestion that the measure should be contractual (*Watts v Spence* [1976] Ch 165), but this approach was rejected by the Court of Appeal in *Sharneyford v Edge* [1987] Ch 305, in favour of the tortious approach. The express wording of the Act seems to suggest that the fraud measure should apply and this approach received support from the Court of Appeal in the leading case on the issue.

Royscott Trust v Rogerson **[1991] 2 QB 297**

Facts: The defendant car dealer told the plaintiff finance company that a prospective hire-purchaser had paid a 20% deposit. The finance company would not have loaned as much money as it did had it known the true value of the deposit. The hire-purchaser defaulted on repayments and dishonestly sold the car. The plaintiff brought an action against the defendant for misrepresentation under s 2(1).

Held: The Court of Appeal held that the fraud measure applied and the plaintiff could recover the unpaid instalments whether or not they were foreseeable.

Balcombe LJ: The first main issue before us was: accepting that the tortious measure is the right measure, is it the measure where the tort is that of fraudulent misrepresentation, or is it the measure where the tort is negligence at common law? The difference is that in cases of fraud a plaintiff is entitled to any loss which flowed from the defendant's fraud, even if the loss could not have been foreseen: see *Doyle v Olby (Ironmongers) Ltd* [1969] 2 QB 158. In my judgment the wording of the subsection is clear: the person making the innocent misrepresentation shall be 'so liable'. i.e., liable to damages as if the representation had been made fraudulently. This was the conclusion to which Walton J came in *F & B Entertainments Ltd v Leisure Enterprises Ltd* (1976) 240 EG 455, 461. See also the decision of Sir Douglas Frank QC, sitting as a High Court judge, in *McNally v Welltrade International Ltd* [1978] IRLR 497. In each of these cases the judge held that the basis for the assessment of damages under section 2(1) of the Act of 1967 is that established in *Doyle v Olby (Ironmongers) Ltd* .... By 'so liable' I take it to mean liable as he would be if the misrepresentation had been made fraudulently.

This was also the original view of the academic writers. In an article, 'The Misrepresentation Act 1967' (1967) 30 MLR 369 by P S Atiyah and G H Treitel, the authors say, at pp 373–374:

> 'The measure of damages in the statutory action will apparently be that in an action of deceit .... But more probably the damages recoverable in the new action are the same as those recoverable in an action of deceit ...'.

Professor Treitel has since changed his view. In Treitel, *The Law of Contract*, 7th edn (1987), p 278, he says:

> 'Where the action is brought under section 2(1) of the Misrepresentation Act, one possible view is that the deceit rule will be applied by virtue of the fiction of fraud. But the preferable view is that the severity of the deceit rule can only be justified in cases of actual fraud and that remoteness under section 2(1) should depend, as in actions based on negligence, on the test of foreseeability'.

Professor Furmston in *Cheshire, Fifoot and Furmston's Law of Contract*, 11th edn (1986), p 286, says:

> '"It has been suggested" – and the reference is to the passage in Atiyah and Treitel's article cited above – 'that damages under section 2(1) should be calculated on the same principles as govern the tort of deceit. This suggestion is based on a theory that section 2(1) is based on a 'fiction of fraud'. We have already suggested that this theory is misconceived. On the other hand the action created by section 2(1) does look much more like an action in tort than one in contract and it is suggested that the rules for negligence are the natural ones to apply'.

The suggestion that the 'fiction of fraud' theory is misconceived occurs at p 271, in a passage which includes:

> 'Though it would be quixotic to defend the drafting of the section, it is suggested that there is no such 'fiction of fraud' since the section does not say that a negligent misrepresentor shall be treated for all purposes as if he were fraudulent. No doubt the wording seeks to incorporate by reference some of the rules relating to fraud but, for instance, nothing in the wording of the subsection requires the measure of damages for deceit to be applied to the statutory action'.

With all respect to the various learned authors whose works I have cited above, it seems to me that to suggest that a different measure of damage applies to an action for innocent misrepresentation under the section than that which applies to an action for fraudulent misrepresentation (deceit) at common law is to ignore the plain words of the subsection and is inconsistent with the cases to which I have referred. In my judgment, therefore, the finance company is entitled to recover from the dealer all the losses which it suffered as a result of its entering into the agreements with the dealer and the customer, even if those losses were unforeseeable, provided that they were not otherwise too remote.'

The 'fiction of fraud' interpretation of s 2(1) can lead to some startling results, particularly in light of the fact that the defendant may not even have acted negligently – remember that the burden of proof is on the defendant to prove that he had reasonable grounds for belief in the truth of his statement. Nevertheless, the Court of Appeal felt that this interpretation was the only one consistent with the plain meaning of the words used in the subsection. Richard Hooley challenged this aspect of the judgment in the following article.

Hooley, R, 'Damages and the Misrepresentation Act 1967' (1991) 107 *LQR*, pp 547, 549–551

Section 2(1) extends liability to the negligent misrepresentor without requiring his victim to establish either fraud or a duty of care. The effect of the Court of Appeal's decision is to treat the foolish but honest man as if he were dishonest. Repugnant as this may appear, if the wording of the Act is clear there is nothing for the court to do but to apply the statute: *Shepheard v Broome* [1904] AC 342, *per* Lord Lindley (at p 346). It was at all times assumed by Balcombe and Ralph Gibson LJJ that section 2(1) is so clearly worded. But is it? It is certainly arguable that the words 'that person shall be so liable', mean merely, 'that person shall be liable in damages notwithstanding that at common law damages were only available for misrepresentations proved to be fraudulent' (see Taylor (1982) 45 MLR 139 at p 141). On this interpretation the subsection establishes liability in damages but not their quantum.

There are a number of arguments to be made against this alternative interpretation of section 2(1). The first is that it leaves the door open to the argument that the appropriate measure of damages under section 2(1) is contractual. But it is submitted that so long as the courts recognise the essential nature of a mere representation as opposed to a term of the contract the tortious measure will prevail. Secondly, it ignores the fact that before the Act of 1967 common law damages were recoverable for negligent misrepresentation under *Hedley Byrne & Co Ltd v Heller & Partners Ltd* [1964] AC 465. However, when the Misrepresentation Act was passed it was generally believed that *Hedley Byrne* could not be used to impose liability for pre-contractual statements. Although this understanding was later shown to be false (*Esso Petroleum Co Ltd v Mardon* [1976] QB 801, *per* Lord Denning MR at p 820), section 2(1) was designed to establish liability in damages for negligent misrepresentation in those circumstances. Thirdly, the alternative interpretation flies in the face of the wealth of authority cited by Balcombe LJ in favour of his interpretation of section 2(1). Yet in all reported cases applying the *Doyle v Olby* measure of damages to section 2(1) there is no report of this alternative interpretation of section 2(1) being considered by the court.

Even if the arguments against this alternative interpretation prevail it is submitted that there is a strong case for Parliament to intervene and remove the reference to fraudulent misrepresentation from section 2(1). Fraudulent misrepresentation is an intentional tort where the public policy of deterring deliberate wrongdoing dictates the shift in emphasis from foreseeability to causation. No such considerations dictate that the same emphasis apply under section 2(1). On the contrary, section 2(1) has much closer links to liability under *Hedley Byrne;* and the effect of applying *Doyle v Olby* to it means that the primary basis for recovery of damages for common law negligent misstatement is foreseeability, whereas for negligent misrepresentation under the statute it is causation. It is submitted that there is no justification for this distinction.

Making liability to damages under section 2(1) the same as for fraudulent misrepresentation could have bizarre consequences. If exemplary damages are recoverable for deceit, and Peter Pain J in *Archer v Brown* [1985] QB 401 at p 423 leaves this possibility open, then are they also recoverable under section 2(1)? It is hoped not. It is also hoped that damages awarded in lieu of rescission under section 2(2) of the Misrepresentation Act 1967 continue to exclude consequential loss in the same way it is excluded from the award of an equitable indemnity on rescission. One of the main arguments for the exclusion of consequential loss from an award under section 2(2) was that by the wording of section 2(3) damages under section 2(2) are meant to be less than damages under section 2(1). If the test of remoteness under both subsections 2(1) and (2) is that of foreseeability, then it has been submitted that to make damages less under subsection (2), consequential loss is not recoverable under that subsection. If damages under section 2(1) are governed by *Doyle v Olby* and those under section 2(2) by foreseeability, then this particular argument goes out of the window (see Treitel, *Law of Contract* (7th edn) at p 279).

Hooley's criticism of the judgments in *Royscott* is compelling. In addition, it should be noted that the court's interpretation of s 2(1) was not strictly necessary to the decision in the case. This is because the act of selling on the car by the hire-purchaser was held to be a reasonably foreseeable consequence and thus damages would have been recoverable under the negligence test. The decision has also been questioned by Lord Steyn in *Smith New Court Securities v Scrimgeour Vickers* [1997] AC 254:

> The question is whether the rather loose wording of the statute compels the court to treat a person who was morally innocent as if he was guilty of fraud when it comes to the measure of damages. There has been trenchant academic criticism of the *Royscott* case: see Richard Hooley, 'Damages and the Misrepresentation Act 1967' (1991) 107 LQR 547.

His Lordship indicated that the decision in *Royscott* might be revisited, but stopped short of making any specific recommendations due to the fact that the issue was not directly before him.

Despite the doubts that have been cast on the decision in *Royscott*, it appears that it remains good law and it was applied by the High Court in *Pankhania v Hackney LBC (Damages)* [2004] EWHC 323; [2004] 1 EGLR 135. Geoffrey Vos QC said:

> Though this decision has been the subject of some academic criticism (see, for example, Lord Steyn in *Smith New Court*), and [counsel for the defendants] wished to reserve his position as to its correctness, it was accepted that it was a decision binding on me, and that I should follow it.

See also *Monde Petroleum SA v Western Zagros Ltd* [2016] EWHC 1472 (Comm).

8.4.2.2.2 Contributory negligence

Further doubt is cast on the correctness of the decision in *Royscott* by the law on contributory negligence. It is clear that, in respect of negligent misstatement, damages may be reduced on the grounds of contributory negligence, where the representee has also been at fault.

LAW REFORM (CONTRIBUTORY NEGLIGENCE) ACT 1945

Section 1

(1) Where any person suffers damage as the result partly of the fault of any other person or persons, a claim in respect of that damage shall not be defeated by reason of the fault of the person suffering the damage, but the damages recoverable in respect thereof shall be reduced to such an extent as the court thinks just and equitable having regard to the claimant's share in the responsibility of the damage.

The availability of a reduction in damages for contributory negligence was extended to misrepresentation under s 2(1) of the 1967 Act in *Gran Gelato Ltd v Richcliff (Group) Ltd* [1992] Ch 560. Sir Donald Nicholls VC said:

> ... in short, liability under the 1967 Act is essentially founded on negligence, in the sense that the defendant, the representor, did not have reasonable grounds to believe that the facts represented were true. (Of course, if he did not so believe the facts represented were true he will be liable for fraud.) This being so, it would be very odd if the defence of contributory negligence were not available to a claim under that Act. It would be very odd if contributory negligence were available as a defence to a claim for damages based on breach of duty to take care in and about the making of a particular representation, but not available to a claim for damages under the 1967 Act in respect of the same representation.

See also see *Taberna Europe CDO II Plc v Selskabet (Formerly Roskilde Bank A/S) (In Bankruptcy)* [2016] EWCA Civ 1262. This 'equation with negligence' approach is impossible to reconcile with the 'fiction of fraud' analysis applied to the law of damages under s 2(1) in *Royscott*. It has been held that a reduction for contributory negligence is not available for an action based on deceit (*Standard Chartered Bank v Pakistan National Shipping* [2003] 1 AC 959). Therefore, assuming the 'fiction of fraud' analysis is correct, a reduction should not be available under s 2(1). It is clear that the decisions in *Royscott* and *Gran Gelato* are irreconcilable, but it may be the former that was wrongly decided rather than the latter. There may also be differences in relation to limitation periods: see *Rizwan Hussain v Saleem Mukhtar* [2016] EWHC 424 (QB).

8.4.3 Damages under s 2(2) Misrepresentation Act 1967

Misrepresentation Act 1967

Section 2

(2) Where a person has entered into a contract after a misrepresentation has been made to him otherwise than fraudulently, and he would be entitled, by reason of the misrepresentation, to rescind the contract, then, if it is claimed, in any proceedings arising out of the contract, that the contract ought to be or has been rescinded, the court or arbitrator may declare the contract subsisting and award damages in lieu of rescission, if of opinion that it would be equitable to do so, having regard to the nature of the misrepresentation and the loss that would be caused by it if the contract were upheld, as well as to the loss that rescission would cause to the other party.

See also s 2(4). This section gives the court a discretion to award damages as an alternative to rescission. The exercise of the court's discretion under s 2(2) was considered by the Court of Appeal in *William Sindall plc v Cambridgeshire County Council.*

***William Sindall plc v Cambridgeshire County Council* [1994] 1 WLR 1016**

Facts: The claimants purchased a piece of land from the defendant council. The defendant innocently failed to disclose the existence of a private foul sewer running across the land, and on discovery of the sewer, the claimants sought to withdraw from the contract. This was very much in their interests because, following the sale, there had been a major property slump and the price of the land had more than halved. At first instance, a misrepresentation was found and rescission was allowed.

Held: The Court of Appeal allowed the appeal and held that there had been no misrepresentation. It was not strictly necessary to consider the operation of s 2(2) but the court did consider obiter how s 2(2) Misrepresentation Act 1967 would have been applied had an operative misrepresentation been found.

Evans LJ: Section 2(3) makes it clear that the statutory power to award damages under section 2(2) is distinct from the plaintiff's right to recover damages under section 2(1). Quoting from section 2(2) itself, such damages are awarded 'in lieu of rescission' and the court has to have regard to three factors in particular, namely, the nature of the misrepresentation, the loss that would be caused by it (sc. the misrepresentation) if the contract was upheld, and the loss that rescission would cause to the other party (sc. the non-fraudulent author of the misrepresentation). It has not been suggested that these three are the only factors which the court may take into account. The discretion is expressed in broad terms – 'if of opinion that it would be equitable to do so'. The three factors, however, in all but an exceptional case, are likely to be the ones to which most weight would be given, even if the subsection were silent in this respect ....

... [I]t would be substantially unjust, in my judgment, to deprive Cambridgeshire of the bargain which it made in 1988, albeit that the bargain was induced by a misrepresentation innocently made, but which was of little importance in relation to the contract as a whole. That misrepresentation apart, Sindall made what has proved to be so far an unfortunate bargain for them (although they remain owners of an important potential development site in what is a notoriously cyclical market). To permit them to transfer the financial consequences to Cambridgeshire, in the circumstances of this case, could properly be described as a windfall for them.

For the above reasons, and taking into account the nature of the alleged representation and the history of the matter generally, including Sindall's deliberate failure to make any serious attempt to find a solution to the difficulty which arose when the sewer was discovered, the equitable balance, in my judgment, lies in favour of upholding the contract and awarding damages in lieu of rescission in this case. If there were a live issue under section 2(2), I would award damages in lieu of rescission and order the amount of such damages to be assessed.

There remains the question of whether these damages should include the decline in the market value of the land since the contract was made. ... [I]n my judgment they should not. This conclusion may be inconsistent with the view expressed in *McGregor on Damages*, 15th edn (1988), para 1752, and in deference to the distinguished author I should explain my reasons briefly. He suggests that the measure to be adopted is:

> 'the same as the normal measure of damages in tort where the plaintiff has been induced to contract by fraudulent or negligent misrepresentation .... The overall result, therefore, is that the damages will be held to be the difference between the value transferred and the value received ... no recovery being possible for consequential losses'.

If the 'value transferred' (meaning the price paid by the plaintiff, to whom the representation was made) was the market value of the property, then there is no difference between this formula and what *McGregor* calls the contract measure, that is to say, the difference between the actual value received and the value which the property would have had, if the representation had been true: see paragraph 1718. By adopting the tort measure, therefore, as he does in paragraph 1752 in the paragraph already quoted, the author impliedly rejects the contract measure, whereas in my judgment that becomes the correct measure in circumstances where the plaintiff is entitled to an order for rescission, but rescission is refused under section 2(2) of the Act. This is because the difference in value between what the plaintiff was misled into believing that he was acquiring, and the value of what he in fact received, seems to me to be the measure of the loss caused to him by the misrepresentation in a case where he cannot rescind the contract and therefore retains the property which he received.

As *McGregor on Damages* points out, the tortious measure benefits a plaintiff who made a bad bargain, that is to say, who agreed to pay more than the market value of the property in the state in which he believed it to be, more so than the contract measure would do. Conversely, it dis-benefits one who paid less than the market value, because it disentitles him from recovering the whole of the difference which the contract measure would otherwise produce. Likewise, the right to rescind benefits a plaintiff who has paid, or agreed to pay more than, with hindsight, he should have done. The period of hindsight may be short or long; where it is long, and the value has fallen in line with the market and therefore for reasons unconnected with the misrepresentation, there is no justification, in my view, for holding that the author of the misrepresentation is liable to compensate the plaintiff for that loss, in a case where rescission is refused.

Hoffmann LJ: Under section 2(1), the measure of damages is the same as for fraudulent misrepresentation, i.e. all loss caused by the plaintiff having been induced to enter into the contract: *Cemp Properties (UK) Ltd v Dentsply Research & Development Corporation* [1991] EGLR 197. This means that the misrepresentor is invariably deprived of the benefit of the bargain (e.g. any difference between the price paid and the value of the thing sold) and may have to pay additional damages for consequential loss suffered by the representee on account of having entered into the contract. In my judgment, however, it is clear that this will not necessarily be the measure of damages under section 2(2).

First, section 2(1) provides for damages to be awarded to a person who 'has entered into a contract after a misrepresentation has been made to him by another party and as a result thereof' – sc. of having entered into the contract – 'he has suffered loss'. In contrast, section 2(2) speaks of 'the loss which would be caused by it' – sc. the misrepresentation – 'if the contract were upheld'. In my view, section 2(1) is concerned with the damage flowing from having entered into the contract, while section 2(2) is concerned with damage caused by the property not being what it was represented to be.

Secondly, section 2(3) contemplates that damages under section 2(2) may be less than damages under section 2(1) and should be taken into account when assessing damages under the latter subsection. This only makes sense if the measure of damages may be different.

> Thirdly, the Law Reform Committee report makes it clear that section 2(2) was enacted because it was thought that it might be a hardship to the representor to be deprived of the whole benefit of the bargain on account of a minor misrepresentation. It could not possibly have intended the damages in lieu to be assessed on a principle which would invariably have the same effect.
>
> The Law Reform Committee drew attention to the anomaly which already existed by which a minor misrepresentation gave rise to a right of rescission whereas a warranty in the same terms would have grounded no more than a claim for modest damages. It said that this anomaly would be exaggerated if its recommendation for abolition of the bar on rescission after completion were to be implemented. I think that section 2(2) was intended to give the court a power to eliminate this anomaly by upholding the contract and compensating the plaintiff for the loss he has suffered on account of the property not having been what it was represented to be. In other words, damages under section 2(2) should never exceed the sum which would have been awarded if the representation had been a warranty. It is not necessary for present purposes to discuss the circumstances in which they may be less.

Evans LJ suggested that there were three basic factors to which the court had regard when considering whether to exercise its discretion under s 2(2):

(1) the nature of the misrepresentation;
(2) the loss that would be caused by the misrepresentation if the contract was upheld;
(3) the loss that would be caused to the representor by rescission.

On the facts, the Court of Appeal unanimously concluded that it would have exercised its discretion to grant damages in lieu of rescission, because the misrepresentation was relatively insignificant and the loss caused to the claimants was trifling in comparison to the loss that would have been sustained by the defendant had the contract been rescinded.

On the issue of the measure of damages, Hoffmann and Evans LJJ agreed that the measure under s 2(2) should be less than the measure under s 2(1). It seems that the purpose of an award of damages under s 2(2) is to compensate the representee for the loss caused by the refusal of rescission, not the loss caused by entering into the contract in reliance on the misrepresentation.

It should also be noted that the award of damages in lieu of rescission is entirely at the discretion of the court. The representee does not have a right to recover damages under s 2(2) (see *UCB Corporate Services Ltd v Thomason* [2005] EWCA Civ 225 where no substantial damages were awarded in lieu of rescission). Moreover, it seems the court can only exercise its discretion to award damages under s 2(2) while it continues to have jurisdiction to order rescission. If the claimant has lost the right to rescission due to lapse of time or the intervention of third-party rights, damages under s 2(2) will not be available either (*Salt v Stratstone Specialist Ltd* [2015] EWCA Civ 745; *Floods of Queensferry Ltd v Shand Construction Ltd* [2000] BLR 8; *Government of Zanzibar v British Aerospace (Lancaster House) Ltd* [2000] 1 WLR 2333. But contrast *Thomas Witter Ltd v TBP Industries Ltd* [1996] 2 All ER 573).

8.4.4 Indemnity at common law

In addition to rescission, the common law also provided a remedy known as an indemnity. An indemnity is a money remedy, which can be used alongside rescission to help to put the representee back in the position s/he was in before the contract was made. Thus it is restitutionary in effect. Unlike damages, an indemnity is available for all types of misrepresentation, including innocent misrepresentations. It is a far more restricted remedy than damages and only entitles the representee to recover the cost to him/her of the obligations created by the contract with the representor. This is illustrated by the facts of *Newbigging v Adam* (1887) 34 Ch D 582, where the plaintiff was induced to enter a partnership agreement by false representations. The Court of Appeal ordered rescission; the partnership was dissolved and the plaintiff recovered the capital he had invested in the partnership. He was also granted an indemnity against the liabilities he had incurred while a partner. For the appeal to the House of Lords, see (1888) 13 App Cas 308.

8.5 Exclusion of liability for misrepresentation

Section 3 of the Misrepresentation Act 1967, as amended by s 8 of the Unfair Contract Terms Act 1977, restricts the freedom to exclude liability for misrepresentation.

MISREPRESENTATION ACT 1967

Section 3

If a contract contains a term which would exclude or restrict:

(a) any liability to which a party to a contract may be subject by reason of any misrepresentation made by him before the contract was made; or

(b) any remedy available to another party to the contract by reason of such a misrepresentation,

that term shall be of no effect except in so far as it satisfies the requirement of reasonableness as stated in section 11(1) of the Unfair Contract Terms Act 1977; and it is for those claiming that the term satisfies that requirement to show that it does.

The Consumer Rights Act 2015 inserted a new subsection into this provision:

(2) This section does not apply to a term in a consumer contract within the meaning of Part 2 of the Consumer Rights Act 2015 (but see the provision made about such contracts in section 62 of that Act).

Section 3 states that any clause which purports to exclude or restrict either liability for misrepresentation or any remedy in respect thereof will only be effective in so far as it satisfies the requirement of reasonableness under s 11 of the UCTA 1977 (see Chapter 7). In *HIH Casualty and General Insurance Ltd v Chase Manhattan Bank* [2003] UKHL 6; [2003] 2 Lloyd's Rep 61, the House of Lords confirmed that a clause purporting to exclude liability for fraudulent misrepresentation will usually be held to be unreasonable (although their Lordships did leave open the possibility of excluding such liability for a statement made by an agent, provided that sufficiently clear language was used).

In recent years there has been much debate over so-called non-reliance clauses (clauses which essentially state, for example, that a party to a contract did not rely on representations in entering into the contract). Are such clauses subject to s 3 (as an exclusion of liability) or do they simply define the obligations of the parties? Some clarity has been given to this area by the Court of Appeal decision in *First Tower Trustees Ltd, Intertrust Trustees Ltd v CDS (Superstores International) Ltd* [2018] EWCA Civ 1396. Two substantive judgments were given in this case (Lewison and Leggatt L.JJ. with Sir Colin Rimer concurring with both judgments). The Court of Appeal accepted that some clauses may *define* the parties' obligations and that such clauses would not be subject to the s 3 Misrepresentation Act 1967 (see [2018] EWCA Civ 1396 at [43] and [96]). The Court of Appeal also considered the principle of so-called 'contractual estoppel' whereby 'parties can bind themselves by contract to accept a particular state of affairs even if they know that state of affairs to be untrue' ([47] and [97]). In so doing, the following passage from the judgment of Aikens L.J. in *Springwell Navigation Corp v JP Morgan Chase Bank* [2010] EWCA Civ 1221 at [143] was approved (at [47]):

> If A and B enter into a contract then, unless there is some principle of law or statute to the contrary, they are entitled to agree what they like ... [T]here is no legal principle that states that parties cannot agree to assume that a certain state of affairs is the case at the time the contract is concluded or has been so in the past, even if that is not the case, so that the contract is made upon the basis that the present or past facts are as stated and agreed by the parties.

However, that is not the end of the matter. A valid contractual estoppel may still be subject to, for example, s 3 of the Misrepresentation Act 1967. Lewison L.J. held:

> I would hold ... that a clause which simply states (as clause 12.1 of the agreement for lease and clause 5.8 of the lease do) 'that this lease has not been entered into in reliance wholly or partly on any statement or representation made by or on behalf of the landlord' is a contract term which would have the effect of excluding liability for misrepresentation; and consequently is subject to the test of reasonableness.

Leggatt L.J. went even further (at [111]):

> For the reasons I have given, as well as those given by Lewison LJ, I would hold that *whenever* a contracting party relies on the principle of contractual estoppel to argue that, by reason of a contract term, the other party to the contract is prevented from asserting a fact which is necessary to establish liability for a pre-contractual misrepresentation, the term falls within section 3 of the Misrepresentation Act 1967. Such a term is therefore of no effect except in so far as it satisfies the requirement of reasonableness as stated in section 11 of UCTA.

8.6 Unfair commercial practices and the Consumer Protection (Amendment) Regulations 2014

The Unfair Commercial Practices Directive (2005/29/EC, OJ L149/22) was largely transposed in the U.K. by the Consumer Protection from Unfair Trading Regulations 2008 (SI 2008/1277; 'CPUTR 2008'). The CPUTR 2008, which replaced 23 earlier enactments, closely follow the wording of the Directive (see, generally, Beale, H.G, (ed), *Chitty on Contracts* (33rd edn, London: Sweet & Maxwell, 2018), para 38–145ff). A commercial practice is defined widely as

> any act, omission, course of conduct, representation or commercial communication (including advertising and marketing) by a trader, which is directly connected with the promotion, sale or supply of a product to or from consumers, whether occurring before, during or after a commercial transaction (if any) in relation to a product

and a consumer is now defined as 'an individual acting for purposes that are wholly or mainly outside that individual's business' (see reg 2). Moreover, in *R v X Ltd* [2013] EWCA Crim 818, the Court of Appeal confirmed that isolated incidents can constitute a commercial practice. Regulation 3(3)–(4) sets out when a commercial practice will be regarded as an unfair commercial practice:

(3) A commercial practice is unfair if—
(a) it contravenes the requirements of professional diligence; and
(b) it materially distorts or is likely to materially distort the economic behaviour of the average consumer with regard to the product.
(4) A commercial practice is unfair if—
(a) it is a misleading action under the provisions of regulation 5;
(b) it is a misleading omission under the provisions of regulation 6;
(c) it is aggressive under the provisions of regulation 7; or
(d) it is listed in Schedule 1.

An example of a practice listed in Schedule 1 is '[d]escribing a product as "gratis", "free", "without charge" or similar if the consumer has to pay anything other than the unavoidable cost of responding to the commercial practice and collecting or paying for delivery of the item'. In terms of sanctions/enforcement, Recital (9) of the Directive provided:

> Directive is without prejudice to individual actions brought by those who have been harmed by an unfair commercial practice. It is also without prejudice to Community and national rules on contract law, on intellectual property rights, on the health and safety aspects of products, on conditions of establishment and authorisation regimes, including those rules which, in conformity with Community law, relate to gambling activities, and to community competition rules and the national provisions implementing them ....

(Compare the recent Directive (EU) 2019/2161 of the European Parliament and of the Council of 27 November 2019 amending Council Directive 93/13/EEC and Directives 98/6/EC, 2005/29/EC and 2011/83/EU of the European Parliament and of the Council as regards the better enforcement and modernisation of Union consumer protection rules.)

The CPUTR 2008 originally relied on a dual system of enforcement consisting of (i) criminal sanctions and (ii) administrative sanctions. Initially, therefore, the CPUTR 2008 did not give consumers specific rights of private redress, a position buttressed by the original version of reg 28 which provided that '[a]n agreement shall not be void or unenforceable by reason only of a breach of these Regulations.' Instead a consumer wanting private redress from an unfair commercial practice had to fashion a remedy from pre-existing doctrines:

> The Regulations concern public enforcement rather than private redress. They do not give consumers the right to start civil actions to obtain compensation or other remedies. Instead, consumers must rely on existing private law doctrines, such as the law of misrepresentation and duress (Law Commission, *Consumer Redress for Misleading and Aggressive Practices* (Cm 8328 (2012)) viii (referring to the original Regulations)).

Yet such an exercise was not always straightforward ('[t]his is problematic: the law of misrepresentation is complex and uncertain ...': Law Commission, *Consumer Redress for Misleading and Aggressive Practices* (Cm 8328 (2012)) viii)). To some extent this was the result of the law of misrepresentation being an amalgam of (i) common law, equity and statute (e.g. Misrepresentation Act 1967) and (ii) tort and contract law (see, generally, Devenney, J, 'Re-Examining Damages for Fraudulent Misrepresentation: Towards a More Measured Response to Compensation and Deterrence', in Di Matteo, L, Rowley, K, Zhou, Q, and Santier, S, *Current Issues in Commercial Contracts: Transatlantic Perspectives* (Cambridge: Cambridge University Press, 2013) especially at pp 417–418). However, there were wider issues. First, the concept of a misleading action under the CPUTR 2008 is not necessarily the same as under the general law of misrepresentation (see, for example, *OFT v Purely Creative Ltd* [2011] EWHC 106 (Ch) where Briggs J. thought that the causation test was higher under the CPUTR 2008 than under the general law of misrepresentation and cf. *Secretary of State for Business, Innovation and Skills v PLT Anti-Marketing Ltd* [2015] EWCA Civ 76). Second, there are limited remedies for misleading omissions under the general law of misrepresentation (see, for example, *Turner v Green* [1895] 2 Ch 205). Third, there are particular limitations on the right to rescind including (i) the general unavailability of a right of partial rescission (see, generally, Poole, J, and Keyser, A, 'Justifying Partial Rescission in English Law' [2005] 121 LQR 273) and (ii) uncertainty on how long a right of rescission lasts (cf. also Law Commission, *Consumer Remedies for Faulty Goods* ((2009) Law Com 317)). Fourth, there are difficulties in the assessment of damages for misrepresentation (see Poole, J, and Devenney, J, 'Reforming Damages for Misrepresentation: The Case for Coherent Aims and Principles' [2007] *JBL* 269–305) including possibly the types of losses a consumer might be able to claim (see *Archer v Brown* [1985] QB 401). Finally, there are issues surrounding the ability and willingness of a consumer to bring an action.

Similarly, a consumer who has been subject to aggressive practices under the CPUTR 2008 might be able to fashion a private remedy from, for example, the general law of duress and/or undue influence (usually rescission). Yet these doctrines were/are not unproblematic in this context:

> ... the present private law provides only patchy and inadequate safeguards against aggressive practices. The doctrines of duress and undue influence are ill-fitted to deal with high-pressure sales techniques used to exploit consumers. Furthermore, the law of unconscionable bargains is too uncertain to deliver effective consumer protection. Finally, the Protection from Harassment Act 1997 can be useful protection against a course of conduct, but does not usually apply to one-off incidents (Law Commission, *Consumer Redress for Misleading and Aggressive Practices* (Cm 8328 (2012)) 3.51).

The foregoing resulted in calls for reform, especially against the backdrop of the strain on the public purse post the financial crisis:

> In 2009, Consumer Focus called for a private right of redress for all consumers who suffered loss through a breach of the Regulations. They pointed out that scams are all too common but relatively few prosecutions are brought. They thought that enforcement would be more effective if public authorities and consumers 'worked in tandem', using both private and public enforcement sanctions (Law Commission, *Consumer Redress for Misleading and Aggressive Practices* (Cm 8328 (2012)) viii).

The Consumer Protection (Amendment) Regulations 2014 ('CPAR 2014') inserted a new Part 4A into CPUTR 2008 giving consumers specific private rights of redress in relation to the CPUTR 2008: the remedies are the unwinding of a contract, a discount and damages. This is part of a significant overhaul of consumer law in the U.K. Consumers are given these private redress rights in relation to misleading actions and aggressive practices but not specifically misleading omissions (CPUTR 2008, reg 27B). Generally, and subject to rules on double recovery, these remedies operate in addition to existing possibilities for private redress under the general law (cf. Misrepresentation Act 1967 s 2(4)).

Unfortunately the CPAR 2014 is not a model of clarity in drafting. Regulation 27A is the gateway to the new provisions, setting out three preliminary conditions for the rights in Pt 4A to be engaged. First, there must be a particular transaction involving a consumer. The relevant transactions are set out in reg 27A(2):

> (a) the consumer enters into a contract with a trader for the sale or supply of a product by the trader (a 'business to consumer contract'),

(b) the consumer enters into a contract with a trader for the sale of goods to the trader (a 'consumer to business contract'), or
(c) the consumer makes a payment to a trader for the supply of a product (a 'consumer payment').

The second condition is that the trader (or possibly the producer) engages in a prohibited practice (viz., for these purposes, a misleading action or aggressive practice). The third condition is that the prohibited practice is a 'significant factor' in the consumer entering the contract or making the relevant payment.

The remedy of unwinding is contained in the (amended) CPUTR 2008, Regulations 27E–H, with Regulations 27E–F dealing with business to consumer contracts. The consequences of unwinding are that the contract comes to an end, the trader may have to give the consumer a refund and the goods must be made available for collection by the trader. Under reg 27E(1) unwinding is available '... if the consumer indicates to the trader that the consumer rejects the product, and does so (a) within the relevant period [90 days], and (b) at a time when the product is capable of being rejected.' Regulation 27E(8) provides:

> ... a product remains capable of being rejected only if—
>
> (a) the goods have not been fully consumed,
> (b) the service has not been fully performed,
> (c) the digital content has not been fully consumed,
> (d) the lease has not expired, or
> (e) the right has not been fully exercised ....

Significantly, a consumer is generally not required to account for use of the product:

> We believe that in most cases, requiring an allowance for use would remove the simplicity and usefulness of the remedy. Any over-compensation would be limited because the complaint must be made within three months. Given that the trader has acted in a misleading or aggressive way, this is not wholly inappropriate (Law Commission, *Consumer Redress for Misleading and Aggressive Practices* (Cm 8328 (2012)) 8.91).

In terms of the remedy of a discount, reg 27L(1) provides:

> A consumer has the right to a discount in respect of a business to consumer contract if – (a) the consumer has made one or more payments for the product to the trader or one or more payments under the contract have not been made, and (b) the consumer has not exercised the right to unwind in respect of the contract.

The (amended) CPUTR 2008 also provide a, fairly crude, sliding scale of the quantum of discounts. In terms of damages, which is of course an established remedy for misrepresentation in England and Wales, significantly, a consumer is given the right to claim damages for 'alarm, distress or physical inconvenience or discomfort' subject to a remoteness test. Unlike the other remedies, there is a due diligence defence (s 27J(5)(b): 'the trader took all reasonable precautions and exercised all due diligence to avoid the occurrence of the prohibited practice').

As a result of the CPAR 2014 the U.K. now has specific private law remedies for some unfair commercial practices. Yet these remedies, which largely operate alongside remedies under the general law, have added complexity to this area of consumer law, not least as a result of the legislative drafting. Indeed, with concerns about fragmentation in mind, there is an argument that these reforms should have been absorbed into the Consumer Rights Act 2015. Moreover, there are significant continuing issues around the ability and willingness of consumers to make full use of such remedies as well as issues of consumer education; and it is ultimately those issues which may dull the potency of these reforms.

Additional reading

Allen, D., *Misrepresentation* (London: Sweet & Maxwell, 1988).
Atiyah, P., and Treitel, G., 'Misrepresentation Act 1967' (1967) 30 *MLR* 369.
Beale, H., 'Damages in Lieu of Rescission for Misrepresentation' (1995) 111 *LQR* 60.
Beale, H., 'Points on Misrepresentation' (1995) 111 *LQR* 385.
Cartwright, J., *Misrepresentation, Mistake and Non-Disclosure* (5th edn, London: Sweet & Maxwell, 2019).
Chandler, A., and Higgins, S., 'Contributory Negligence and the Misrepresentation Act 1967, s 2(1)' [1994] *LMCLQ* 326.
Poole, J., and Devenney, J., 'Reforming Damages for Misrepresentation: The Case for Coherent Aims and Principles' (2007) *JBL* 269.
Taylor, R., 'Expectation, Reliance and Misrepresentation' (1982) 45 *MLR* 139.

Chapter 9

Mistake

Chapter contents

9.1 Introduction

In this chapter we will primarily examine the situations in which a mistake by either or both parties renders a contract void. The law of mistake is notoriously complex and brings together a number of situations that are both varied and, to some extent, lacking in conceptual unity. Professor JC Smith ('Contracts: mistake, frustration and implied terms' (1994) 110 LQR 400) famously wrote:

> One of the greatest difficulties for students of the law of contract has always, in my teaching experience, been the law relating to mistake. The brilliant analysis of the subject by Cheshire and Fifoot did an enormous amount to clarify thinking about it. But the presentation of mistake as a separate subject in a large and complex chapter through 12 editions of their admirable textbook has, I believe, unnecessarily exacerbated the inherent difficulties. The problems are generally soluble by the application of the law relating to the formation of contracts or that relating to implied terms. This is the way the late Professor Tony Thomas and I approached the problem during the gestation of Smith and Thomas and I remain convinced of its soundness.

While it is true that there is a considerable overlap between the law of mistake and other areas of the law of contract – such as offer and acceptance, misrepresentation, implied terms and frustration – there is sufficient commonality between the different types of mistake to justify their inclusion in a single chapter on 'mistake'.

The English courts have traditionally been very reluctant to allow contracts to be undermined on the ground of 'mistake'. This is unsurprising, given the general judicial desire to promote certainty in commercial transactions. It would clearly be unsatisfactory if a party to a contract was permitted to escape the transaction merely by saying, 'I'm sorry, I made a mistake'. Having said that, the courts are also, to an extent, concerned to give effect to the true intentions of the parties. For this reason, the English courts recognise the possibility of a mistake affecting the validity of a contractual obligation, but use this power to intervene with considerable caution.

9.2 Categories of mistake

Contractual mistakes can take many different forms. They may relate to the subject matter, the identity of the other party or the specific terms of the contract. The different categories of mistake were recently summarised by Lord Phillips of Matravers MR in *Great Peace Shipping Ltd v Tsavliris Salvage (International) Ltd*.

***Great Peace Shipping Ltd v Tsavliris Salvage (International) Ltd* [2003] QB 679**

Lord Phillips MR: 28. A mistake can be simply defined as an erroneous belief. Mistakes have relevance in the law of contract in a number of different circumstances. They may prevent the mutuality of agreement that is necessary for the formation of a contract. In order for two parties to conclude a contract binding in law each must agree with the other the terms of the contract. Whether two parties have entered into a contract in this way must be judged objectively, having regard to all the material facts. It may be that each party mistakenly believes that he has entered into such a contract in circumstances where an objective appraisal of the facts reveals that no agreement has been reached as to the terms of the contract. Such a case was *Raffles v Wichelhaus* (1864) 2 H & C 906 …

29. *Raffles v Wichelhaus* was a case of latent ambiguity. More commonly an objective appraisal of the negotiations between the parties may disclose that they were at cross-purposes, so that no agreement was ever reached. In such a case there will be a mutual mistake in that each party will erroneously believe that the other had agreed to his terms. This case is not concerned with the kind of mistake that prevents the formation of agreement.

30. Another type of mistake is that where the parties erroneously spell out their contract in terms which do not give effect to an antecedent agreement that they have reached. Such a mistake can result in rectification of the contract. Again, this case is not concerned with that type of mistake.

31. In the present case the parties were agreed as to the express terms of the contract. The defendants agreed that the *Great Peace* would deviate towards the *Cape Providence* and, on reaching her, escort her so as to be on hand to save the lives of her crew, should she founder. The contractual services would terminate when the salvage tug came up with the casualty. The mistake relied upon by the defendants is as to an assumption that they claim underlay the terms expressly agreed. This was that the *Great Peace* was within a few hours sailing of the *Cape Providence*. They contend that this mistake was fundamental in that it would take the *Great Peace* about 39 hours to reach a position where she could render the services which were the object of the contractual adventure.

32. Thus what we are here concerned with is an allegation of a common mistaken assumption of fact which renders the service that will be provided if the contract is performed in accordance with its terms something different from the performance that the parties contemplated. This is the type of mistake which fell to be considered in *Bell v Lever Bros Ltd* [1932] AC 161. We shall describe it as 'common mistake', although it is often alternatively described as 'mutual mistake'.

33. Mr Reeder for the defendants puts his case in two alternative ways. First he submits that performance of the contract in the circumstances as they turned out to be would have been fundamentally different from the performance contemplated by the parties, so much so that the effect of the mistake was to deprive the agreement of the consideration underlying it. Under common law, so he submits, the effect of such a mistake is to render the contract void. Mr Reeder draws a close analogy with the test to be applied when deciding whether a contract has been frustrated or whether there has been a fundamental breach. The foundation for this submission is *Bell v Lever Bros Ltd*.

34. If the facts of this case do not meet that test, Mr Reeder submits that they none the less give rise to a right of rescission in equity. He submits that such a right arises whenever the parties contract under a common mistake as to a matter that can properly be described as 'fundamental' or 'material' to the agreement in question. Here he draws an analogy with the test for rescission where one party, by innocent misrepresentation, induces the other to enter into a contract – indeed that is one situation where the parties contract under a common mistake. The foundation for this submission is *Solle v Butcher* [1950] 1 KB 671.

Great Peace Shipping is an extremely important case to which we will return in due course. For now, it will suffice to note the various categories of mistake identified by Lord Phillips MR in his judgment.

9.2.1 Common law mistake

Lord Phillips MR distinguished between two categories of common law mistake.

9.2.1.1 Mistakes that negative consent

In [28] and [29], his Lordship referred to mistakes that prevent agreement. These are mistakes in the formation of the contract which Lord Atkin referred to in *Bell v Lever Bros* [1932] AC 161 as mistakes that 'negative consent'. Within this general category, there are two situations that need to be distinguished. First, there is the situation in which the parties are at cross-purposes – neither party being aware that the other party is contracting on the basis of a different assumption about the terms of the contract. This category is often referred to as a 'mutual mistake' (see Lord Phillips at [29]), although the phrase is sometimes also, and confusingly, used to refer to another category of common-law mistake (see Lord Phillips at [32] and Beatson, J, Burrows A and Cartwright, J, *Anson's Law of Contract*, 29th edn, 2010, Oxford: OUP, p 251), which in this chapter will be labelled 'common mistake'.

The second type of situation where the mistake 'negatives consent' is where the mistake of one party is known to the other party, who may indeed have encouraged it. We will refer to this type of mistake as a 'unilateral mistake'. Here, there is a clear overlap with the law of misrepresentation. In practice, an action based on mistake might be brought where the remedies for misrepresentation would be inadequate. The classic example of such a situation is where third-party rights have intervened to bar rescission: see *Ingram v Little* [1961] 1 QB 31.

9.2.1.2 Mistakes that nullify consent

In [31] and [32], Lord Phillips MR refers to a second category of common law mistake, which he describes as 'common mistake' in preference to 'mutual mistake'. Here, the parties enter into a contract on the basis of a common assumption as to the surrounding facts, which later turns out to be false. The mistake in such situations does not preclude agreement, but instead provides the basis for undermining the contract. In the words of Lord Atkin in *Bell v Lever Bros*, the mistake 'nullifies consent'.

Professor Collins has argued (Collins, H, *The Law of Contract*, 4th edn, 2003, Cambridge: CUP, p 125) that this type of mistake is better analysed as involving an implied condition precedent that has failed:

> It is ... possible to view these authorities as merely deciding that where a contract contains an express or implied term that it will only be enforceable if a particular circumstance or state of affairs exists, the failure of the condition precedent will prevent a binding contract arising. Strictly speaking, however, on this analysis a contract has been entered into but one of its terms, which is enforceable, declares that certain events shall render the contract unenforceable and without any legal effect. There is ascription of contractual responsibility to a conditional contract, and, on failure of the condition, the contract provides that it should have no legal effect. This analysis has the potential to explain all the English cases which seem to give credence to the doctrine of mistake.

Although this theory is attractive, it was rejected by the Court of Appeal in *Great Peace Shipping* at [73] (although cf. *Graves v Graves* [2007] EWCA Civ 660).

Common mistake is closely linked to the doctrine of frustration (discussed in Chapter 12). In a sense, both concern circumstances that render the performance of the contract impossible. The difference lies in the timing of the event. In cases of common mistake, the circumstances exist at the time of formation, while in cases of frustration, the circumstances arise post-formation (see *Amalgamated Investment and Property Co Ltd v John Walker & Sons* [1977] 1 WLR 164).

9.2.2 Equitable mistake

In [34], Lord Phillips MR noted that a wider doctrine of mistake had developed in equity following the decision of the Court of Appeal in *Solle v Butcher* [1950] 1 KB 671. This enabled the court to rescind a contract in equity (equitable mistake rendered the contract voidable while common law mistake rendered the contract void), even though the facts did not meet the requirements set out by the House of Lords in *Bell v Lever Bros*. This development was radically halted by the Court of Appeal in *Great Peace Shipping*, where it was held that such a doctrine of equitable mistake was inconsistent with the law set out by the House of Lords in *Bell v Lever Bros*.

Despite this important decision, it is clear that equity still has a role to play in a number of other situations. For example, as Lord Phillips MR noted at [30], the equitable remedy of rectification is sometimes available. If an agreement has been reduced to writing and the written document contains an inaccuracy, in the form of an error or an omission, the parties may ask the court to rectify the document in order for it to conform to their oral agreement. The court also has an equitable discretion to refuse specific performance of a contract entered into under a mistake (*Malins v Freeman* (1837) 2 Keen 25). Moreover it seems there is also an equitable jurisdiction to set aside gifts made as a result of a mistake (see *Van der Merwe v Goldman* [2016] EWHC 790 (Ch) and see also *Rogge v Rogge* [2019] EWHC 1949 (Ch) on partial rescission of a gift).

9.2.3 Non est factum

The final category of mistake concerns cases where a person has signed a contract. Generally, English law holds parties to agreements that they have signed (*L'Estrange v Graucob* [1934] 2 KB 394), but there are some exceptional circumstances where the courts will accept a plea of *non est factum* – 'it is not my deed'.

9.3 Mistakes that negative consent

As noted above, there are two main types of mistake that negative consent: mutual mistake and unilateral mistake. We will consider each of these in turn.

9.3.1 Mutual mistake

The classic example of a situation that might give rise to a mutual mistake is to be found in the case of *Raffles v Wichelhaus*.

***Raffles v Wichelhaus* (1864) 2 H & C 906; 159 ER 375**

Declaration: For that it was agreed between the plaintiff and the defendants, to wit, at Liverpool, that the plaintiff should sell to the defendants, and the defendants buy of the plaintiff, certain goods, to wit, 125 bales of Surat cotton, guaranteed middling fair merchant's Dhollorah, to arrive ex 'Peerless' from Bombay; and that the cotton should be taken from the quay, and that the defendants would pay the plaintiff for the same at a certain rate, to wit, at the rate of 171/4d per pound, within a certain time then agreed upon after the arrival of the said goods in England. Averments that the said goods did arrive by the said ship from Bombay in England to wit, at Liverpool, and the plaintiff was then and there ready, and willing and offered to deliver the said goods to the defendants, & c. Breach: that the defendants refused to accept the said goods or pay the plaintiff for them.

Plea: That the said ship mentioned in the said agreement was meant and intended by the defendants to be the ship called the 'Peerless', which sailed from Bombay, to wit, in October; and that the plaintiff was not ready and willing and did not offer to deliver to the defendants any bales of cotton which arrived by the last mentioned ship, but instead thereof was only ready and willing and offered to deliver to the defendants 125 bales of Surat cotton which arrived by another and different ship, which was also called the 'Peerless', and which sailed from Bombay, to wit, in December.

Demurrer, and joinder therein
Milward, in support of the demurrer. The contract was for the sale of a number of bales of cotton of a particular description, which the plaintiff was ready to deliver. It is immaterial by what ship the cotton was to arrive, so that it was a ship called the 'Peerless'. The words 'to arrive ex 'Peerless', only mean that if the

vessel is lost on the voyage, the contract is to be at an end. [Pollock CB. It would be a question for the jury whether both parties meant the same ship called the 'Peerless'] That would be so if the contract was for the sale of a ship called the 'Peerless', but it is for the sale of cotton on board a ship of that name. [Pollock CB. The defendant only bought that cotton which was to arrive by a particular ship. It may *as* well be said, that if there is a contract for the purchase of certain goods in warehouse A, that is satisfied by the delivery of goods of the same description in warehouse B.] In that case there would be goods in both warehouses, here it does not appear that the plaintiff had any goods on board the other 'Peerless'. [Martin B. It is imposing on the defendant a contract different from that which he entered into. Pollock CB. It is like a contract for the purchase of wine coming from a particular estate in France or Spain, where there are two estates of that name.] The defendant has no right to contradict by parol evidence a written contract good upon the face of it. He does not impute misrepresentation or fraud, but only says that he fancied the ship was a different one. Intention is of no avail, unless stated at the time of the contract. [Pollock CB. One vessel sailed in October and the other in December.] The time of sailing is no part of the contract.

Mellish (Cohen with him), in support of the plea. There is nothing on the face of the contract to shew that any particular ship called the 'Peerless' was meant, but the moment it appears that two ships called the 'Peerless' were about to sail from Bombay there is a latent ambiguity, and parol evidence may be given for the purpose of shewing that the defendant meant one 'Peerless', and the plaintiff another. That being so, there was no consensus ad idem, and therefore no binding contract. He was then stopped by the Court.

Per Curiam. There must be judgment for the defendants

Judgment for the defendants.

Since the court stopped counsel's argument and provided no judgment, it is impossible to be certain of the exact basis of the decision. It may be limited to the finding that the defendants could introduce parol evidence of their intentions because of the latent ambiguity in the agreement. Later cases, however, have gone further and suggested that the court in *Raffles* accepted the argument that the latent ambiguity negatived consent. In *Smith v Hughes* (1871) LR 6 QB 597, Hannen J said:

> It is essential to the creation of a contract that both parties should agree to the same thing in the same sense. Thus, if two persons enter into an apparent contract concerning a particular person or ship, and it turns out that each of them, misled by a similarity of name, had a different person or ship in his mind, no contract would exist between them: *Raffles v Wichelhaus* 2 H & C 906; 33 LJ (Ex) 160.

More recently, in *Great Peace Shipping*, Lord Phillips MR treated *Raffles v Wichelhaus* as a case of mutual mistake where the parties were at cross-purposes.

The case is probably most famous for the debate it triggered concerning the question of whether English law adopts a subjective approach to contract formation or an objective approach. Writers, such as Pollock, argued that the court's emphasis on *consensus ad idem* showed that the law adopts a subjective approach. Other writers, such as Holmes, claimed that the case supported an objective approach. For Holmes, the case merely decided that parol evidence could be introduced. It was then left to the jury to decide, from an objective standpoint, whether the parties' intentions could be determined. Unfortunately, the case itself provides no guidance as to which of these two approaches is correct. As Professor Simpson has argued ('The Beauty of Obscurity: *Raffles v Wichelhaus and Busch* (1864)' in Leading *Cases in the Common Law*, 1995, Oxford: OUP, p 139), looking for an answer to this question in the report of *Raffles*, is like looking to see 'whether Macbeth suffered from athlete's foot' in the text of Macbeth.

Although *Raffles* is rather obscure on the point, later cases have confirmed that an objective approach will be adopted. This means that a contract will be found to exist if, from an objective standpoint, a third party would reasonably believe that the contract had been formed on particular terms (cf. *Chartbrook Ltd v Persimmon Homes Ltd* [2009] UKHL 38, discussed at 6.3.2.3ff, and *FSHC Group Holdings Ltd v GLAS Trust Corp Ltd* [2019] EWCA Civ 1361).

Frederick E Rose (London) Ltd v William H Pim Jnr & Co Ltd [1953] 2 QB 450

Facts: The plaintiffs were asked by an English firm in Egypt whether they could supply 'feveroles'. The plaintiffs did not know what these were, and they asked the defendants, who replied that they were just horsebeans. The plaintiffs entered into a contract with the defendants to purchase five hundred tons of Tunisian horsebeans. These were then supplied to the customer in Egypt, who complained that the beans were 'feves' (a larger and less valuable horsebean) instead of 'feveroles'. The customer claimed damages for breach of contract. To cover themselves against this claim, the plaintiffs started proceedings in the High Court to have the contract between themselves and the defendants rectified, so as to read 'feveroles' after the word 'horsebeans'.

Held: The Court of Appeal held that rectification was not available because the oral agreement between the parties and the written contracts were in the same terms.

Denning LJ: The parties no doubt intended that the goods should satisfy the inquiry of the Egyptian buyers, namely, 'horsebeans described in Egypt as feveroles'. They assumed that they would do so, but they made no contract to that effect. Their agreement, as outwardly expressed, both orally and in writing, was for 'horsebeans'. That is all that the defendants ever committed themselves to supply, and all they should be bound to. There was, no doubt, an erroneous assumption underlying the contract – an assumption for which it might have been set aside on the ground of misrepresentation or mistake – but that is very different from an erroneous expression of the contract, such as to give rise to rectification.

Morris LJ: It seems to me clear beyond doubt that both parties proceeded on the basis that 'feveroles' and 'horsebeans' were the same. The plaintiffs' representative expressed the matter succinctly when he said: 'I had agreed to buy because feveroles were horsebeans and horsebeans were feveroles'. In that belief the parties came to agreement, and the formal written contracts were prepared and signed. The parties had throughout a clear common intention and purpose of buying and selling horsebeans, and their written agreements faithfully embodied and exactly recorded what they had agreed. In these circumstances it seems to me that no claim for rectification can succeed.

Both parties thought that the result of what they clearly understood and clearly expressed would be that the plaintiffs as buyers would be able to satisfy the inquiry which, as the defendants knew, had been received. In that they were mistaken as a result of the advice honestly given by the defendants' market clerk. But the fact that they were under a mistaken impression as to what their agreement would achieve does not disturb the clarity and the fixity of the agreement which they in fact made. The defendants intended to offer horsebeans and the plaintiffs intended to accept horsebeans: the written agreements correctly reflected and incorporated what they had agreed.

The judge said that 'both the plaintiffs and the defendants made an oral agreement in which they intended to deal in horsebeans of the feverole type'. With respect, that was not quite the position. There was no question of contracting in reference to a 'type' of horsebeans. There was a joint understanding that they should contract in reference to 'horsebeans' simpliciter which they thought were the same as 'feveroles'. If, as now appears to be the case, they were wrong, it appears probable that they would not have acted as they did had they been enlightened. But this does not enable one party to convert the contract into something different from what it was.

On the assumption that 'feveroles' are different from 'horsebeans', it cannot be said that the parties agreed on the sale of a commodity of the separate existence of which they had no knowledge. The defendants were selling 'horsebeans', and in order to sell they would have to acquire 'horsebeans'. If 'feveroles' are different, then the defendants, and equally the plaintiffs, never even gave their minds at all to the question of a sale of some products which are different from 'horsebeans'.

Some doubt on the approach, if not the result, in *Frederick E Rose (London) Ltd v William H Pim Jnr & Co Ltd* [1953] 2 QB 450, has recently been expressed by the Court of Appeal in *FSHC Group Holdings Ltd v GLAS Trust Corp Ltd* [2019] EWCA Civ 1361, where Leggatt LJ (with whom Rose and Flaux LJJ agreed) stated:

> 63. The 'lost cause' (per Buckley LJ in *Joscelyne v Nissen* [1970] 2 QB 86, 91) of *Lovell & Christmas Ltd v Wall* was re-discovered in *Frederick E Rose (London) Ltd v William H Pim Jnr & Co Ltd* [1953] 2 QB 450. This was the 'horsebeans' case, which 'has amused generations of law students' (per Tadgell JA in *Club Cape Schanck Resort Co Ltd v Cape Country Club Pty Ltd* [2001] 3 VR 526, para 5) …
>
> 64. A passage in the judgment of Denning LJ (at 461) has since been relied on, most importantly in the *Chartbrook* case, as expounding an objective approach to rectification:
>
>> 'Rectification is concerned with contracts and documents, not with intentions. In order to get rectification it is necessary to show that the parties were in complete agreement on the terms of their contract, but by an error wrote them down wrongly; and in this regard, in order to ascertain the terms of their contract, you do not look into the inner minds of the parties – into their intentions – any more than you do in the formation of any other contract. You look at their outward acts, that is, at what they said or wrote to one another in coming to their agreement, and then compare it with the document which they have signed. If you can predicate with certainty what their contract was, and that it is, by a common mistake, wrongly expressed in the document, then you rectify the document; but nothing less will suffice'.
>
> 65. As Sir Nicholas Patten explained in the Chancery Bar Association 2013 Annual Lecture, 'Does the law need to be rectified? Chartbrook revisited', at para 12, this passage needs to be read in its historical context:
>
>> 'It was delivered some 17 years before the Court of Appeal stated unequivocally in *Joscelyne v Nissen* that the parties' pre-existing accord need not be contractual and it is little more than a statement of what many judges at that time considered the scope of rectification to be. If, as [Denning LJ] said, you can predicate with certainty what their contract was and by common mistake it was wrongly expressed in the written document, then the court can intervene to create consistency between the two. All that one is doing, indeed all that one could do in such circumstances, was to ensure that the terms of the prior contract were accurately recorded. What the parties believed those terms to mean was irrelevant. All that the court was concerned with was whether there had been a prior contract and what its terms were. That required a conventional application to the facts of the test as to whether a contract had been reached which depends upon an objective assessment of the parties' dealings and takes no account of their subjective intention or understanding of what was agreed'.
>
> 66. As Sir Nicholas Patten pointed out, this thinking comes out even more clearly in the immediately following passage of Denning LJ's judgment in *Rose v Pim* [1953] 2 QB 450 at 461-2, where he said:
>
>> 'It is not necessary that all the formalities of the contract should have been executed so as to make it enforceable at law (see *Shipley Urban District Council v Bradford Corporation*); but, formalities apart, there must have been a concluded contract. There is a passage in *Crane v Hegeman-Harris Co Inc* which suggests that a continuing common intention alone will suffice; but I am clearly of opinion that a continuing common intention is not sufficient unless it has found expression in outward agreement. There could be no certainty at all in business transactions if a party who had entered into a firm contract could afterwards turn round and claim to have it rectified on the ground that the parties intended something different. He is allowed to prove, if he can, that they agreed something different: see *Lovell & Christmas v Wall*, per Lord Cozens-Hardy MR, and per Buckley LJ, but not that they intended something different'.
>
> …

67. The question whether rectification may only be granted to bring a document into conformity with a prior concluded contract was finally resolved in the leading case of *Joscelyne v Nissen* [1970] 2 QB 86. A father entered into a written contract with his daughter by which he transferred to her his car hire business in return for her agreement to pay him a pension and discharge certain expenses. In their discussions it had been agreed between them that these expenses should include the father's gas, electricity and coal bills and the cost of home help. However, the daughter argued, and the trial judge held, that the signed contract did not on its proper interpretation, provide for payment of these expenses. The judge nevertheless rectified the written contract to provide for these expenses to be paid by the daughter, although he found that no binding contract had been concluded until the document was signed. The daughter appealed, contending that as a matter of law, the remedy of rectification was not available to the father in the absence of an antecedent concluded contract.

68. The Court of Appeal, after a full review of the authorities, rejected this contention. Russell LJ, who gave the judgment of the court, concluded that 'the law is as expounded by Simonds J in *Crane*'s case with the qualification that some outward expression of accord is required': see [1970] 2 QB 86 at 98.

69. The Court of Appeal also approved, as apt to cover the case before them, the following statement of Megaw J in *London Weekend Television Ltd v Paris and Griffith* (1969) 113 Sol J 222:

> 'Where two persons agreed expressly with one another what was the meaning of a particular phrase but did not record their definition in the contract itself, if one of the parties sought to enforce the agreement on the basis of some other meaning, he could be prevented by an action for rectification'.

Rose v Pim was explained (at 97) on the basis that:

> 'It turned out that locked separately in the breast of each party was the misapprehension that the word 'horsebeans' meant another commodity, but as we understand the case there was no communication between them to the effect that when they should speak of horsebeans that was to be their private label for the other commodity. The decision in our judgment does not assert or reinstate the view that an antecedent complete concluded contract is required for rectification: it only shows that prior accord on a term or the meaning of a phrase to be used must have been outwardly expressed or communicated between the parties'.

In so far as Denning LJ had suggested that an 'antecedent complete concluded contract' is necessary, the Court of Appeal rejected his view as inconsistent with the views of both courts in *Crane v Hegeman-Harris* and as not supported by the other judgments in *Rose v Pim*. In so far as he was speaking of 'agreement in the more general sense of an outwardly expressed accord of minds,' the Court of Appeal said that Denning LJ had done no more than accept the argument advanced by counsel for the appellant in *Rose v Pim* as to 'the true width of the views of Simonds J'. That argument was that, when Simonds J said in *Crane*'s case that it was sufficient to find a 'common continuing intention', he meant intention 'as expressed': see [1953] 2 QB 450, 457.

70. The suggestion that in *Rose v Pim* the understanding that 'horsebeans' meant 'feveroles' turned out to be 'locked separately in the breast of each party', is difficult to follow as, on the facts found in *Rose v Pim*, the plaintiffs' understanding was derived from communication with the defendants' representative. It appears that the case was indeed one in which the parties were using the word 'horsebeans' as their own private label for 'feveroles'. But as Sir Kim Lewison pointed out in the Jonathan Brock Memorial Lecture, 21 May 2008, 'If it ain't broke, don't fix it', para 50, at the time when *Rose v Pim* was decided the law had not yet clearly recognised that rectification was an available remedy where parties had deliberately chosen words but were mistaken about their meaning. That possibility, as Sir Nicholas Patten observed in the passage from his Chancery Bar Association lecture quoted earlier, was not consistent with the view that the sole function of rectification was to

ensure that the terms of the prior contract were accurately recorded. It has since, however, become well established. In *Re Butlin's Settlement Trusts* [1976] Ch 251, 260, Brightman J said that rectification is available:

> 'not only in a case where particular words have been added, omitted or wrongly written as the result of careless copying or the like. It is also available where the words of the document were purposely used but it was mistakenly considered that they bore a different meaning from their correct meaning as a matter of true construction'.

That statement of the law has been approved and applied on many occasions since, including by the House of Lords in the *Chartbrook* case, where Lord Hoffmann referred (at para 46) to the availability of rectification in such a situation as a reason why it was unnecessary to relax the rule excluding evidence of prior communications as an aid to interpreting a contract.

71. We agree with Sir Kim Lewison that the best justification for the refusal to grant the remedy of rectification in *Rose v Pim* is that the contract of which rectification was sought was part of a chain of contracts involving third parties so that, as Denning LJ observed (at 462):

> 'It would not be fair to rectify one of the contracts without rectifying all three, which is obviously impossible'.

9.3.2 Unilateral mistake

This type of mistake arises where one party is aware that the other is mistaken about an important aspect of the contract. In *Smith v Hughes* (1871) LR 6 QB 597, Cockburn CJ noted that the law of contract does not generally intervene merely because one party is more knowledgeable than the other. It is an important aspect of commercial enterprise that individuals should be free to take advantage of superior knowledge or information. To prohibit such practices would be to stultify wealth creation. However, the law does not allow a party to 'snap up' a bargain which he knew was not intended for him. In *Smith v Hughes*, Hannen J put the principle as follows: 'The promiser is not bound to fulfil a promise in a sense in which the promisee knew at the time the promiser did not intend it'. A contract was found to be void for a unilateral mistake in *Hartog v Colin & Shields*.

Hartog v Colin & Shields [1939] 3 All ER 566

Facts: The defendants agreed to sell to the plaintiff 30,000 Argentine hare skins. The price quoted by the seller was stated to be 'per pound'. This was a mistake, since the price should have been 'per piece'. The mistake meant that the skins were being offered at a price two thirds lower than would have been expected. Expert evidence was given that Argentine hare skins were generally sold at prices per piece. The plaintiff accepted the defendants' offer in the terms stated, but the defendants refused to supply on this basis, on the ground that the plaintiff was taking advantage of the defendants' mistake.

Held: The court held that the plaintiff must have realised that a mistake had been made in the offer and therefore there was no binding contract.

Singleton J: In this case, the plaintiff, a Belgian subject, claims damages against the defendants because he says they broke a contract into which they entered with him for the sale of Argentine hare skins. The defendants' answer to that claim is: 'There really was no contract, because you knew that the document which went forward to you, in the form of an offer, contained a material mistake. You realised that, and you sought to take advantage of it'.

> Counsel for the defendants took upon himself the onus of satisfying me that the plaintiff knew that there was a mistake and sought to take advantage of that mistake. In other words, realising that there was a mistake, the plaintiff did that which James LJ, in *Tamplin v James*, at p 221, described as 'snapping up the offer'. It is important, I think, to realise that in the verbal negotiations which took place in this country, and in all the discussions there had ever been, the prices of Argentine hare skins had been discussed per piece, and later, when correspondence took place, the matter was always discussed at the price per piece, and never at a price per pound. Those witnesses who were called on behalf of the plaintiff have had comparatively little experience of dealing in Argentine hare skins. Even the expert witness who was called had had very little ... Even allowing that the market was bound to fall a little, I find it difficult to believe that anyone could receive an offer for a large quantity of Argentine hares at a price so low as 3d per piece without having the gravest doubts of it.
>
> I cannot help thinking that, when this quotation in pence per pound reached Mr Hartog, the plaintiff, he must have realised ... that there was a mistake. Otherwise I cannot understand the quotation. There was an absolute difference from anything which had gone before – a difference in the manner of quotation, in that the skins are offered per pound instead of per piece ... The offer was wrongly expressed, and the defendants by their evidence, and by the correspondence, have satisfied me that the plaintiff could not reasonably have supposed that that offer contained the offerers' real intention. Indeed, I am satisfied to the contrary. That means that there must be judgment for the defendants.

The case met the two requirements set out in *Smith v Hughes*:

1 The mistake was as to a term of the contract – the price of the hare skins;
2 The plaintiff was aware that the defendants had made a mistake in regard to this term.

See also *Statoil ASA v Lewis Dreyfus Energy Sources LP* [2008] EWHC 2257 (Comm) and *UTB LLC v Sheffield United Limited* [2019] EWHC 2322 for the view that there is not a wider doctrine of equitable unilateral mistake, at least in respect of the remedy of rescission.

9.3.2.1 Unilateral mistake as to identity

Many of the cases on unilateral mistake concern the (controversial) area of mistakes as to the identity of the other contracting party. The classic scenario is where a fraudulent party (a rogue) misrepresents his or her identity in order to obtain goods on credit or in exchange for a cheque. In the majority of cases, these goods will then be sold on to an innocent third party. As a result of the misrepresentations, the contract will be voidable, but the mistaken party often will not know to rescind until after the third party has purchased the goods, by which time, of course, it will be too late. The mistaken party will therefore need to argue that the contract was void for mistake, thus meaning that no property rights passed to the rogue. Since one cannot give what one does not have (*nemo dat quod non habet*), any purported sale by the rogue to a third party will be ineffective, and the mistaken party will be able to assert his or her property rights against the third party and reclaim possession of the property.

It is generally accepted that the law in this area developed in an unsatisfactory manner. For example, it was traditionally stated that for such a mistake to be operative, and to render the contract void, it must have related to the *identity* of the other party, rather than merely to his or her *attributes*. In practice, this distinction was very difficult to apply, as Lord Denning explained in *Lewis v Averay* [1972] 1 QB 198:

> A mistake as to identity, it is said, avoids a contract: whereas a mistake as to attributes does not. But this is a distinction without a difference. A man's very name is one of his attributes. It is also a key

to his identity. If then, he gives a false name, is it a mistake as to his identity or a mistake as to his attributes? These fine distinctions do no good to the law.

The distinction between identity and attributes led to a further distinction being drawn between contracts concluded by face-to-face negotiations and contracts concluded by written correspondence. In the former situation, it is presumed that there was an intention to contract with the person present. In the latter situation, it was presumed that the true identity of the person was of fundamental importance to the contract. Some argued that this distinction was rather false. Nevertheless, it was, to an extent, recently reaffirmed by the House of Lords in Shogun Finance Ltd v Hudson [2004] 1 AC 919. We will consider that landmark decision in due course, but first we must survey the case law that preceded it.

9.3.2.1.1 Contracts concluded by written correspondence

An early example of a written contract void for mistake as to identity is to be found in the case of *Boulton v Jones*.

Boulton v Jones (1857) 2 H & N 564

Facts: The defendant sent an order for three 50 ft leather hoses to Brocklehurst, against whom he had arranged a set-off. Unknown to the defendant, Brocklehurst had just sold his business to the plaintiff who fulfilled the order. The plaintiff sent an invoice to the defendant who resisted the claim for payment on the basis that he did not intend to contract with the plaintiff.

Held: The court held that the contract was void for mistake.

Pollock CB: It is a rule of law, that if a person intends to contract with A, B cannot give himself any right under it. Here the order in writing was given to Brocklehurst.

Bramwell B: The admitted facts are, that the defendants sent to a shop an order for goods, supposing they were dealing with Brocklehurst. The plaintiff who supplied the goods, did not undeceive them. If the plaintiff were now at liberty to sue the defendants, they would be deprived of their right of set-off as against Brocklehurst. When a contract is made, in which the personality of the contracting party is or may be of importance, as a contract with a man to write a book, or the like, or where there might be a set-off, no other person can interpose and adopt the contract.

As to the difficulty that the defendants need not pay anybody, I do not see why they should, unless they have made a contract either express or implied. I decide the case on the ground that the defendants did not know that the plaintiff was the person who supplied the goods, and that allowing the plaintiff to treat the contract as made with him would be a prejudice to the defendants.

It seems that the existence of the set-off meant that the identity of the other party was of crucial importance to the defendants. The result may appear a little harsh towards the plaintiff who was not attempting to take advantage of the defendant.

A more common example of a contract void for such a mistake is to be found in *Cundy v Lindsay*.

Cundy v Lindsay (1878) 3 App Cas 459

Facts: A rogue named Blenkarn placed large orders for handkerchiefs with the plaintiffs. Blenkarn, who gave his address as 37 Wood Street, signed the order in a manner which made it look like he was 'Blenkiron & Co', a highly respectable firm which also had its business in Wood Street. The plaintiffs sent the goods on credit to 'Messrs Blenkiron & Co, 37 Wood Street'. Blenkarn never paid for the goods, and he sold them on the defendant, an innocent third party. The plaintiffs brought an action against the defendants for conversion, which required them to prove that the contract with Blenkarn was void for mistake.

Held: The House of Lords held that the contract was void for mistake as to identity.

Lord Cairns LC: My Lords, the question ... in the present case ... really becomes the very short and simple one which I am about to state. Was there any contract which, with regard to the goods in question in this case, had passed the property in the goods from the Messrs Lindsay to Alfred Blenkarn? If there was any contract passing that property, even although, as I have said, that contract might afterwards be open to a process of reduction, upon the ground of fraud, still, in the meantime, *Blenkarn* might have conveyed a good title for valuable consideration to the present Appellants.

[The jury] found that by the form of the signatures to the letters which were written by *Blenkarn*, by the mode in which his letters and his applications to the Respondents were made out, and by the way in which he left uncorrected the mode and form in which, in turn, he was addressed by the Respondents; that by all those means he led, and intended to lead, the Respondents to believe, and they did believe, that the person with whom they were communicating was not *Blenkarn*, the dishonest and irresponsible man, but was a well known and solvent house of *Blenkiron & Co.* doing business in the same street. My Lords, those things are found as matters of fact, and they are placed beyond the range of dispute and controversy in the case.

If that is so, what is the consequence? ... I ask the question, how is it possible to imagine that in that state of things any contract could have arisen between the Respondents and *Blenkarn*, the dishonest man? Of him they knew nothing, and of him they never thought. With him they never intended to deal. Their minds never, even for an instant of time rested upon him, and as between him and them there was no consensus of mind which could lead to any agreement or any contract whatever. As between him and them there was merely the one side to a contract, where, in order to produce a contract, two sides would be required. With the firm of Blenkiron & Co of course there was no contract, for as to them the matter was entirely unknown, and therefore the pretence of a contract was a failure.

The result, therefore, my Lords, is this, that your Lordships have not here to deal with one of those cases in which there is de facto a contract made which may afterwards be impeached and set aside, on the ground of fraud; but you have to deal with a case which ranges itself under a completely different chapter of law, the case namely in which the contract never comes into existence. My Lords, that being so, it is idle to talk of the property passing. The property remained, as it originally had been, the property of the Respondents, and the title which was attempted to be given to the Appellants was a title which could not be given to them.

My Lords, I therefore move your Lordships that this appeal be dismissed with costs, and the judgment of the Court of Appeal affirmed.

Lord Cairns' judgment adopted a rather subjective approach to agreement, although even from an objective point of view (in light of the fact that all of the correspondence was addressed to Blenkiron & Co), it is clear that the plaintiffs were mistaken as to the identity of whom they were dealing with.

It was significant in *Cundy v Lindsay* that the plaintiffs were able to identify the party whom they intended to contract with. If the mistaken party is unable to do this, the contract may not be void for mistake. In *King's Norton Metal Co v Edridge, Merrett & Co* (1897) 14 TLR 98, a rogue named Wallis fraudulently induced the plaintiffs to supply him with brass rivet wire on credit by pretending to be a firm called Hallam & Co. Wallis then sold the goods on to the defendants, who were innocent third parties. When the plaintiffs discovered Wallis' fraud they brought an action against the defendants in conversion. The Court of Appeal held that the action failed because the contract between Wallis and the plaintiffs was not void. The firm 'Hallam & Co' was a pure invention, created by Wallis. For this reason, it was impossible to say that the plaintiffs intended to deal with a separate entity called Hallam & Co; no such firm existed. The mistake was one as to attributes, not as to identity. The plaintiffs thought that they were dealing with a firm, when in fact they were dealing with a rogue individual.

9.3.2.1.2 Contracts concluded face to face

There were three main cases on unilateral mistake of identity in contracts concluded between parties who negotiated with one another face to face. Horridge J decided the first in the early twentieth century.

Phillips v Brooks [1919] 2 KB 243

Facts: A man called North went to a jeweller's shop and asked to see some pearls and some rings. He selected some pearls at the price of £2,550 and a ring at the price of £450. As he was writing a cheque in payment he said: 'You see who I am, I am Sir George Bullough, and he gave an address in St James's Square. After checking in a directory to confirm that Sir George lived at the address mentioned, the plaintiff allowed North to leave with the ring. The cheque was dishonoured, and North was subsequently convicted of obtaining the ring by false pretences. In the meantime, North had pledged the ring to the defendant pawnbrokers who had acted without notice. The plaintiff brought a claim for the value of the ring against the defendant.

Held: The court held that the contract was not void for mistake because the plaintiff intended to deal with the person present, even though he believed that person to be Sir George Bullough.

Horridge J: I have carefully considered the evidence of the plaintiff, and have come to the conclusion that, although he believed the person to whom he was handing the ring was Sir George Bullough, he in fact contracted to sell and deliver it to the person who came into his shop, and who was not Sir George Bullough, but a man of the name of North, who obtained the sale and delivery by means of the false pretence that he was Sir George Bullough.

The next case was rather difficult to reconcile with *Phillips v Brooks*.

Ingram v Little [1961] 1 QB 31

Facts: The plaintiffs, three elderly women, jointly owned a car which they advertised for sale. A rogue, going by the name of Hutchinson, offered to buy it for £717. When he pulled out his chequebook to pay for it, the first plaintiff told him that she would not, under any circumstances, accept a cheque, and that she was only willing to sell the car for cash. The rogue then gave them his initials, saying that he was PGM Hutchinson, who had business interests in Guildford and lived at Stanstead House, Stanstead Road, Caterham. The second plaintiff then slipped out of the room to visit the post office and consult a telephone directory which confirmed that a PGM Hutchinson lived at the address given. Having received that information, the plaintiffs decided that they would let the rogue leave with the car in exchange for the cheque. The rogue was not, however, Mr Hutchinson, and the cheque was dishonoured. In the meantime, the rogue had sold the car to the defendant, who had no notice of the fraud. The plaintiffs sought the return of the car from the defendant or, alternatively, damages for its conversion.

Held: The Court of Appeal held (Devlin LJ dissenting) that the plaintiffs had offered the car to the real PGM Hutchinson, and therefore, the rogue could not accept it. The plaintiff's unilateral mistake prevented the formation of the contract, and therefore the plaintiffs' claim in conversion succeeded.

Sellers LJ: The judge, treating the plaintiffs as the offerors and the rogue 'Hutchinson' as the offeree, found that the plaintiffs in making their offer to sell the car not for cash but for a cheque (which in the circumstances of the Bank Holiday week-end could not be banked before the following Tuesday, August 6, 1957) were under the belief that they were dealing with, and therefore making their offer to, the honest PGM Hutchinson of Caterham, whom they had reason to believe was a man of substance and standing.

'Hutchinson', the offeree, knew precisely what was in the minds of the two ladies for he had put it there and he knew that their offer was intended for PGM Hutchinson of Caterham and that they were making no offer to and had no intention to contract with him, as he was. There was no offer which he 'Hutchinson' could accept and, therefore, there was no contract.

The judge pointed out that the offer which the plaintiffs made was one which was capable of being accepted only by the honest PGM Hutchinson of Caterham and was incapable of acceptance by 'Hutchinson'. In all the circumstances of the present case I would accept the judge's findings. Indeed the conclusion so reached seems self-evident.

Is the conclusion to be held wrong in law? If it is, then, as I see it, it must be on the sole ground that as 'Hutchinson' was present, albeit making fraudulent statements to induce the plaintiffs to part with their car to him in exchange for his worthless cheque and was successful in so doing, then a bargain must have been struck with him personally, however much he deceived the plaintiffs into thinking they were dealing with someone else.

[*Phillips v Brooks*] is not an authority to establish that where an offer or acceptance is addressed to a person (although under a mistake as to his identity) who is present in person, then it must in all circumstances be treated as if actually addressed to him. I would regard the issue as a question of fact in each case depending on what was said and done and applying the elementary principles of offer and acceptance in the manner in which Slade J directed himself.

The question in each case should be solved, in my opinion, by applying the test, which Slade J applied, 'How ought the promisee to have interpreted the promise' in order to find whether a contract has been entered into.

I am in agreement with the judge when he quotes, accepts and applies the following passage from Dr. Goodhart's article ('Mistake as to identity in the Law of Contract' [1941] 57 LQR 228, 231): 'It is the interpretation of the promise which is the essential thing. This is usually based on the interpretation which a reasonable man, in the promisee's position, would place on it, but in those cases where the promisor knows that the promisee has placed a peculiar interpretation on his words, then this is the binding one. The English law is not concerned with the motives of the parties nor with the reasons which influenced their actions. For practical reasons it has limited itself to the simple questions: what did the promisor promise, and how should this be interpreted?'

Phillips v Brooks is the closest authority on which the defendant relies. Once that is distinguished on its facts, without going so far as to say it is wrong, authority leans strongly in favour of the judgment appealed from ...

The legal position is, I think, well illustrated by Dr Goodhart in the article (57 LQR 228, 241) already referred to. There is a difference between the case where A makes an offer to B in the belief that B is not B but is someone else, and the case where A makes an offer to B in the belief that B is X. In the first case B does in fact receive an offer, even though the offeror does not know that it is to B he is making it, since he believes B to be someone else. In the second case, A does not in truth make any offer to B at all; he thinks B is X, for whom alone the offer is meant. There was an offer intended for and available only to X. B cannot accept it if he knew or ought to have known that it was not addressed to him.

Pearce LJ: I agree. The question here is whether there was any contract, whether offer and acceptance met ...

The mere fact that the offeror is dealing with a person bearing an alias or false attributes does not create a mistake which will prevent the formation of a contract: *King's Norton Metal Co Ltd v Edridge, Merrett*

& Co Ltd 14 TLR 98. For in such a case there is no other identity for which the identity of the offeree is mistaken …

But where a cheat passes himself off as another identity (e.g., as someone with whom the other party is accustomed to deal), it is otherwise …

An apparent contract made orally *inter praesentes* raises particular difficulties. The offer is apparently addressed to the physical person present. Prima facie, he, by whatever name he is called, is the person to whom the offer is made. His physical presence identified by sight and hearing preponderates over vagaries of nomenclature. '*Praesentia corporis tollit errorem nominis*' said Lord Bacon (Law *Tracts* (1737), p 102). Yet clearly, though difficult, it is not impossible to rebut the prima facie presumption that the offer can be accepted by the person to whom it is physically addressed. To take two extreme instances. If a man orally commissions a portrait from some unknown artist who had deliberately passed himself off, whether by disguise or merely by verbal cosmetics, as a famous painter, the impostor could not accept the offer. For though the offer is made to him physically, it is obviously, as he knows, addressed to the famous painter. The mistake in identity on such facts is clear and the nature of the contract makes it obvious that identity was of vital importance to the offeror. At the other end of the scale, if a shopkeeper sells goods in a normal cash transaction to a man who misrepresents himself as being some well-known figure, the transaction will normally be valid. For the shopkeeper was ready to sell goods for cash to the world at large and the particular identity of the purchaser in such a contract was not of sufficient importance to override the physical presence identified by sight and hearing. Thus the nature of the proposed contract must have a strong bearing on the question of whether the intention of the offeror (as understood by his offeree) was to make his offer to some other particular identity rather than to the physical person to whom it was orally offered.

In our case, the facts lie in the debatable area between the two extremes … The man tried to make Miss Ingram take a cheque. She declined and said that the deal was off. He did not demur but set himself to reconstruct the negotiations … Thereafter, the negotiations were of a different kind from what the vendor had mistakenly believed them to be hitherto. The parties were no longer concerned with a cash sale of goods where the identity of the purchaser was prima facie unimportant. They were concerned with a credit sale in which both parties knew that the identity of the purchaser was of the utmost importance. She now realised that she was being asked to give to him possession of the car on the faith of his cheque …

It is not easy to decide whether the vendor was selling to the man in her drawing room (fraudulently misrepresented as being a man of substance with the attributes of the real Hutchinson) or to PGM Hutchinson of Stanstead House (fraudulently misrepresented as being the man in her drawing room) … The judge said: 'I have not the slightest hesitation in reaching the conclusion that the offer which the plaintiffs made to accept the cheque for £717 was one made solely to, and one which was capable of being accepted only by, the honest Hutchinson …'. In view of the experience of the judge and the care which he devoted to the present case, I should hesitate long before interfering with that finding of fact, and I would only do so if compelled by the evidence or by the view that the judge drew some erroneous inference … I am not persuaded that on the evidence he should have found otherwise.

It is argued that the judge should have come to a contrary conclusion by following *Phillips v Brooks* [1919] 2 KB 243. I do not find that case easy to evaluate, because the facts are far from clear. It appears from the report that the name of Sir George Bullough was not mentioned until after the deal had apparently been concluded and the cheque in payment of the goods had been or was being written out. Then, apparently, as a postscript or variation of the transaction, the false Sir George obtained leave to take off one of the articles without waiting for the cheque to be cleared, and the vendor thereby relinquished his lien on that article. The plaintiff in re-examination had said that he had no intention of making any contract with any other person than Sir George, but those words could hardly be true literally, since he had apparently made a contract with the man before he was told that he was Sir George.

Viscount Haldane in *Lake v Simmons* [1927] AC 487, 501 said of that case: 'Horridge J found, as a fact, that though the jeweller believed the person to whom he handed the jewel was the person he pretended to be, yet he intended to sell to the person, whoever he was, who came into the shop and paid the price, and that the misrepresentation was only as to payment.' In my view, it was a border-line case decided on its own particular facts, and is in no wise decisive of the case before us.

Devlin LJ: The point on which the present case turns is the effect of deception about the identity of a contracting party. It is a difficult point on which I have the misfortune to differ from my brethren ...

In my judgment, the court cannot arrive at a satisfactory solution in the present case except by formulating a presumption and taking it at least as a starting point. The presumption that a person is intending to contract with the person to whom he is actually addressing the words of contract seems to me to be a simple and sensible one and supported by some good authority. It is adopted in *Benjamin on Sale*, 8th edn (1950), p 102, where two decisions in the United States are referred to, *Edmunds v Merchants Despatch Co* (1883) 135 Mass 283 and *Phelps v McQuade* (1917) 220 NY 232.

The reasoning in the former case was adopted by Horridge J in *Phillips v Brooks Ltd* [1919] 2 KB 243 and the latter case is a decision of the New York Court of Appeals ...

What seems plain to me is that the presumption cannot in the present case be rebutted by piling up the evidence to show that Miss Ingram would never have contracted with H unless she had thought him to be PGM Hutchinson. That fact is conceded and, whether it is proved simpliciter or proved to the hilt, it does not go any further than to show that she was the victim of fraud. With great respect to the judge, the question that he propounded as the test is not calculated to show any more than that. He said: 'Is it to be seriously suggested that they were willing to accept the cheque of the rogue other than in the belief, created by the rogue himself, that he, the rogue, was in fact the honest PGM Hutchinson of the address in Caterham with the telephone number which they had verified?' In my judgment, there is everything to show that Miss Ingram would never have accepted H's offer if she had known the truth, but nothing to rebut the ordinary presumption that she was addressing her acceptance, in law as well as in fact, to the person to whom she was speaking. I think, therefore, that there was offer and acceptance in form.

There can be no doubt ... that the dividing line between voidness and voidability, between fundamental mistake and incidental deceit, is a very fine one. That a fine and difficult distinction has to be drawn is not necessarily any reproach to the law. But need the rights of the parties in a case like this depend on such a distinction? The great virtue of the common law is that it sets out to solve legal problems by the application to them of principles which the ordinary man is expected to recognise as sensible and just; their application in any particular case may produce what seems to him a hard result, but as principles they should be within his understanding and merit his approval. But here, contrary to its habit, the common law, instead of looking for a principle that is simple and just, rests on theoretical distinctions. Why should the question whether the defendant should or should not pay the plaintiff damages for conversion depend upon voidness or voidability, and upon inferences to be drawn from a conversation in which the defendant took no part? The true spirit of the common law is to override theoretical distinctions when they stand in the way of doing practical justice. For the doing of justice, the relevant question in this sort of case is not whether the contract was void or voidable, but which of two innocent parties shall suffer for the fraud of a third. The plain answer is that the loss should be divided between them in such proportion as is just in all the circumstances. If it be pure misfortune, the loss should be borne equally; if the fault or imprudence of either party has caused or contributed to the loss, it should be borne by that party in the whole or in the greater part. In saying this, I am suggesting nothing novel, for this sort of observation has often been made. But it is only in comparatively recent times that the idea of giving to a court power to apportion loss has found a place in our law. I have in mind particularly the Law Reform Acts of 1935, 1943 and 1945 that dealt respectively with joint tortfeasors, frustrated contracts and contributory negligence. These statutes, which I believe to have worked satisfactorily, show a modern inclination towards a decision based on a just apportionment rather than one given in black or in white according to the logic of the law. I believe it would be useful if Parliament were now to consider whether or not it is practicable by means of a similar act of law reform to provide for the victims of a fraud a better way of adjusting their mutual loss than that which has grown out of the common law.

There are two points to note here. First, it was extremely difficult to distinguish between the facts of *Ingram v Little* and those of *Phillips v Brooks*. Various attempts have been made, but none have proven convincing. Second, the real problem in cases such as these is that the court is faced with the unfortunate task of deciding which, of two innocent parties, should shoulder the burden of the rogue's fraud. Devlin LJ suggested an alternative approach to this conundrum in his dissenting judgment. We will return to this and to the difficulty of reconciling the authorities after we have considered our third case, *Lewis v Averay*.

Lewis v Averay [1972] 1 QB 198

Facts: The plaintiff put an advertisement in the newspaper offering his Austin Cooper 'S' motor car for sale. A rogue came to see the car who claimed to be Richard Greene, a well-known actor who played Robin Hood in the 'Robin Hood' series. They agreed a price of £450, and the rogue wrote out a cheque for the full amount. He wanted to take the car immediately, but the plaintiff refused. The rogue then produced a 'pass' from Pinewood Film Studios, which carried his photograph and an official stamp. On seeing the pass, the plaintiff was satisfied and let the rogue have the car in exchange for the cheque. The cheque had come from a stolen cheque book and was not honoured. By the time the plaintiff discovered the fraud, the rogue had sold the car to the defendant, who bought it in good faith. The plaintiff sued the defendant in conversion for the return of the vehicle, or its value in damages.

Held: The Court of Appeal held that the contract was voidable for fraud, but not void for mistake. The presumption that the plaintiff intended to deal with the person physically present had not been rebutted.

Lord Denning MR: The real question in the case is whether on May 8, 1969, there was a contract of sale under which the property in the car passed from Mr Lewis to the rogue. If there was such a contract, then, even though it was voidable for fraud, nevertheless Mr Averay would get a good title to the car. But if there was no contract of sale by Mr Lewis to the rogue – either because there was, on the face of it, no agreement between the parties, or because any apparent agreement was a nullity and void *ab initio* for mistake, then no property would pass from Mr Lewis to the rogue. Mr Averay would not get a good title because the rogue had no property to pass to him.

There is no doubt that Mr Lewis was mistaken as to the identity of the person who handed him the cheque ... What is the effect of this mistake? ... Who is entitled to the goods? The original seller? Or the ultimate buyer? The courts have given different answers. In *Phillips v Brooks*, the ultimate buyer was held to be entitled to the ring. In *Ingram v Little* the original seller was held to be entitled to the car. In the present case the deputy county court judge has held the original seller entitled.

It seems to me that the material facts in each case are quite indistinguishable the one from the other. In each case there was, to all outward appearance, a contract: but there was a mistake by the seller as to the identity of the buyer. This mistake was fundamental. In each case it led to the handing over of the goods. Without it the seller would not have parted with them. This case therefore raises the question: What is the effect of a mistake by one party as to the identity of the other? It has sometimes been said that if a party makes a mistake as to the identity of the person with whom he is contracting there is no contract, or, if there is a contract, it is a nullity and void, so that no property can pass under it. This has been supported by a reference to the French jurist Pothier; but I have said before, and I repeat now, his statement is no part of English law ... it is time it was dead and buried together.

For instance, in *Ingram v Little* the majority of the court suggested that the difference between *Phillips v Brooks* and *Ingram v Little* was that in *Phillips v Brooks* the contract of sale was concluded (so as to pass the property to the rogue) before the rogue made the fraudulent misrepresentation: see [1961] 1 QB 31, 51, 60: whereas in *Ingram v Little* the rogue made the fraudulent misrepresentation before the contract was concluded. My own view is that in each case the property in the goods did not pass until the seller let the rogue have the goods. Again it has been suggested that a mistake as to the identity of a person is one thing: and a mistake as to his attributes is another. A mistake as to identity, it is said, avoids a contract: whereas a mistake as to attributes does not. But this is a distinction without a difference. A man's very name is one of his attributes ...

As I listened to the argument in this case, I felt it wrong that an innocent purchaser (who knew nothing of what passed between the seller and the rogue) should have his title depend on such refinements. After all, he has acted with complete circumspection and in entire good faith: whereas it was the seller who let the rogue have the goods and thus enabled him to commit the fraud. I do not, therefore, accept the theory that a mistake as to identity renders a contract void. I think the true principle is that which underlies the decision of this court in *King's Norton Metal Co Ltd v Edridge Merrett & Co Ltd* (1897) 14 TLR 98 and of Horridge J in *Phillips v Brooks* [1919] 2 KB 243, which has stood for these last 50 years. It is this: When two parties have come to a contract – or rather what appears, on the face of it, to be a contract – the fact that one party is mistaken as to the identity of the other does not mean that there is no contract, or that the contract is a nullity and void from the beginning. It only means that the contract is voidable, that is, liable to be set aside at the instance of the mistaken person, so long as he does so before third parties have in good faith acquired rights under it.

Applied to the cases such as the present, this principle is in full accord with the presumption stated by Pearce LJ and also Devlin LJ in *Ingram v Little* [1961] 1 QB 31, 61, 66. When a dealing is had between a seller like Mr. Lewis and a person who is actually there present before him, then the presumption in law is that there is a contract, even though there is a fraudulent impersonation by the buyer representing himself as a different man than he is. There is a contract made with the very person there, who is present in person. It is liable no doubt to be avoided for fraud, but it is still a good contract under which title will pass unless and until it is avoided ...

Megaw LJ: For myself, with very great respect, I find it difficult to understand the basis, either in logic or in practical considerations, of the test laid down by the majority of the court in *Ingram v Little* [1961] 1 QB 31. That test is, I think, accurately recorded in the headnote, as follows:

> '– where a person physically present and negotiating to buy a chattel fraudulently assumed the identity of an existing third person, the test to determine to whom the offer was addressed was how ought the promisee to have interpreted the promise'.

The promisee, be it noted, is the rogue. The question of the existence of a contract and therefore the passing of property, and therefore the right of third parties, if this test is correct, is made to depend upon the view which some rogue should have formed, presumably knowing that he is a rogue, as to the state of mind of the opposite party to the negotiation, who does not know that he is dealing with a rogue.

However that may be, and assuming that the test so stated is indeed valid, in my view this appeal can be decided on a short and simple point ... The well-known textbook *Cheshire and Fifoot's on the Law of Contract* 7th edn (1969), 213 and 214, deals with the question of invalidity of a contract by virtue of unilateral mistake, and in particular unilateral mistake relating to mistaken identity. The editors describe what in their submission are certain facts that must be established in order to enable one to avoid a contract on the basis of unilateral mistake by him as to the identity of the opposite party. The first of those facts is that at the time when he made the offer he regarded the identity of the offeree as a matter of vital importance. To translate that into the facts of the present case, it must be established that at the time of offering to sell his car to the rogue, Mr Lewis regarded the identity of the rogue as a matter of vital importance. In my view, Mr Titheridge is abundantly justified, on the notes of the evidence and on the findings of the judge, in his submission that the mistake of Mr Lewis went no further than a mistake as to the attributes of the rogue. It was simply a mistake as to the creditworthiness of the man who was there present and who described himself as Mr Green ....

Lord Denning said that the material facts of *Phillips v Brooks* and *Ingram v Little* were indistinguishable from each other. Elsewhere in his judgment, he suggested that the cases were irreconcilable. Is this true? In *Ingram v Little*, Pearce LJ attempted to distinguish the facts of *Phillips v Brooks* on the ground that the contract in that case was concluded before there was any mention of 'Sir George Bullough', whereas the contract in the case before him was only concluded after the plaintiffs had verified that PGM Hutchinson did indeed live at the address they had been given. This view of *Phillips v Brooks* was first intimated by Viscount Haldane in *Lake v Simmons* [1927] AC 487. The theory is, however, difficult to reconcile with the facts of the case (see Peel, E, *Treitel: The Law of Contract*, 14th edn, 2015, London: Sweet & Maxwell, p 370).

In reality, all three cases were very similar. They involved a contract concluded by face-to-face negotiations in which the plaintiff was tricked into parting with his property by the fraudulent misrepresentation of a rogue. In all three cases, there was a prima facie presumption that the plaintiff intended to contract with the person physically present, and in each case, the plaintiff attempted to verify the identity of the rogue. Yet, for some reason, the presumption in *Ingram v Little* was held to be rebutted, while the presumption in the other two cases was not. Why? It is hard to avoid the conclusion that the decisions were motivated more by policy considerations than by principle. The court had to decide which of two innocent parties should bear the loss brought about by the fraud. In *Phillips v Brooks* and *Lewis v Averay*, as in most cases, the original owner was marginally less innocent than the third party, because he had the opportunity to uncover the fraud and stop it before it was carried out. *Ingram v Little* was a little different, however. The third-party purchaser in that case was a large car dealer, who was easily able to absorb the loss caused by the fraud, while the original owners were vulnerable old ladies who had far more limited means.

If this is correct, and the decision was best explained on policy grounds, it is to be regretted that the Court of Appeal did not unanimously adopt the approach proposed by Devlin LJ (in his dissent), which would have reached the same end (albeit through legislation) by a much more principled and consistent means. Devlin LJ expressed the view that decisions as to who should bear the loss caused by a fraud should not rest on theoretical distinctions between void and voidable contract, but instead on an assessment of the circumstances of each case: 'If it be pure misfortune, the loss should be borne equally; if the fault or imprudence of either party has caused or contributed to the loss, it should be borne by that party in the whole or in the greater part.' Devlin LJ's loss apportionment proposal was considered and rejected by the Law Reform Committee in its Twelfth Report (*Transfer of Title to Chattels*, Cmnd 2958, 1966, London: HMSO). The Committee noted that opinion was divided on the proposal, but rejected it on the ground that it was impractical and unworkable. The Committee did, however, recommend that anomalies in the law should be removed by rendering contracts entered into under a mistake as to identity voidable rather than void. Such a reform would have ensured greater protection for innocent third-party purchasers. This proposal was never implemented by Parliament, although it clearly won the approval of Lord Denning in *Lewis v Averay*.

9.3.2.1.3 The decision of the House of Lords in Shogun Finance

As the cases above show, the law governing mistake as to identity developed in an unsatisfactory manner. In Shogun Finance *Ltd v Hudson* [2002] QB 834, 842, Sedley LJ said the following:

> We have been shown the Committee's Twelfth Report on the *Transfer of Title to Chattels* (1966) (Cmnd 2958). The conclusion of its distinguished members did not chime with that of Lord Devlin (as he by then was). It was that apportionment of consequential loss was not practicable; that the loser of stolen goods should retain title unless they were bought in good faith by retail or at auction; but that a contract made under a mistake as to the buyer's identity should be voidable as against honest third parties and not void. If the last of these proposals had been adopted, it would have produced the outcome at which Lord Denning MR arrived in *Lewis v Averay* [1972] 1 QB 198. Instead, the illogical and sometimes barely perceptible distinctions made in earlier decisions, some of them representing an unarticulated judicial policy on the incidence of loss as between innocent parties, continue to represent the law.

The problems that existed in the law were twofold. First, the cases draw a controversial distinction between contracts concluded face-to-face and those concluded by written correspondence. Second, the cases dealing with face-to-face negotiations appear to contradict each other, with a mistake as to identity rendering a contract void in *Ingram v Little*, but not in *Phillips v Brooks* or *Lewis v Averay*. The House of Lords sought to resolve these problems and to clarify the law in *Shogun Finance*. The extent to which they were successful in this endeavour is open to question.

Shogun Finance Ltd v Hudson [2004] 1 AC 919

Facts: A motor dealer agreed to sell a Mitsubishi Shogun car on hire-purchase to a rogue who produced a stolen driving licence as proof of his identity (the driving licence belonged to a Mr Durlabh Patel). The dealer faxed a draft hire-purchase agreement to the claimant hire-purchase company including a copy of the stolen driving licence. The hire-purchase agreement had been signed by the rogue, forging the signature on the driving licence. The claimant checked Mr Patel's credit rating and approved the sale. The rogue then paid a deposit and was allowed to take away the car. The following day, the rogue sold the car to the defendant who purchased it in good faith. When the claimants discovered the fraud, they brought a claim against the defendant in the tort of conversion. The defendant counterclaimed that he had acquired good title to the vehicle within the meaning of section 27 of the Hire Purchase Act 1964. Ordinarily, in a hire-purchase contract, the hire-purchaser will not acquire title to the goods until after he has made all the payments. Nevertheless, s 27 provides an exception to the *nemo dat* rule that allows the rogue to give good title to an innocent third party provided that the rogue is a 'debtor' under the hire purchase agreement. Thus the case turned on the question of whether there was a valid contract between the claimant and the rogue.

The judge at first instance gave judgment for the claimant. The Court of Appeal dismissed the defendant's appeal on the ground that, since he was not the hirer named in the written hire-purchase agreement, the rogue was not the 'debtor' within the meaning of section 27 of the 1964 Act. The Court of Appeal (Sedley LJ dissenting) also rejected the claimant's alternative argument that the dealer was acting as an agent for the claimant, thereby raising the presumption that the claimants intended to deal with the rogue, as the person physically present.

Held: The House of Lords dismissed the appeal (Lords Nicholls and Millett dissenting). The title to the car had, at all material times, been in the claimant, and accordingly, the defendant could not have acquired title to it from the rogue. The rogue was not named in the agreement, nor could oral evidence be admitted to contradict the express terms of the written agreement. There was no *consensus ad idem* between the claimant and the rogue, and accordingly, the rogue had not become a 'debtor' within the meaning of s 27 of the 1964 Act.

Lord Nicholls of Birkenhead

The choice

33. In my view [*Cundy v Lindsay* (1878) 3 App Cas 459] is not reconcilable with *Phillips v Brooks* [1919] 2 KB 243 or with *Lewis v Averay* [1972] 1 QB 198 or with the starting point 'presumption' formulated by Devlin LJ in *Ingram v Little* [1961] 1 QB 31. The legal principle applicable in these cases cannot sensibly differ according to whether the transaction is negotiated face-to-face, or by letter, or by fax, or by e-mail, or over the telephone or by video link or video telephone. Typically today a purchaser pays for goods with a credit or debit card. He produces the card in person in a shop or provides details of the card over the telephone or by e-mail or by fax. When a credit or debit card is fraudulently misused in this way the essence of the transaction is the same in each case. It does not differ from one means of communication to the next. The essence of the transaction in each case is that the owner of the goods agrees to part with his goods on the basis of a fraudulent misrepresentation made by the other regarding his identity. Since the essence of the transaction is the same in each case, the law in its response should apply the same principle in each case, irrespective of the precise mode of communication of offer and acceptance.

34. Accordingly, if the law of contract is to be coherent and rescued from its present unsatisfactory and unprincipled state, the House has to make a choice: either to uphold the approach adopted in *Cundy v Lindsay* and overrule the decisions in *Phillips v Brooks* and *Lewis v Averay*, or to prefer these later decisions to *Cundy v Lindsay*.

35. I consider the latter course is the right one, for a combination of reasons. It is in line with the direction in which, under the more recent decisions, the law has now been moving for some time. It accords better with basic principle regarding the effect of fraud on the formation of a contract. It seems preferable as a matter of legal policy. As between two innocent persons the loss is more appropriately borne by the person who takes the risks inherent in parting with his goods without receiving payment. This approach fits comfortably with the intention of Parliament in enacting the limited statutory exceptions to the proprietary principle of *nemo dat quod non habet*. Thus, by section 23 of the 1979 Act Parliament protected an innocent buyer from a seller with a voidable title. The classic instance of a person with a voidable title is a person who acquired the goods by fraud: see per Bramwell LJ in *Babcock v Lawson* (1880) 5 QBD 284, 286. Further, this course is supported by writers of the distinction of Sir Jack Beatson: see *Anson's Law of Contract*, 28th edn (2002), p 332. It is consistent with the approach adopted elsewhere in the common law world, notably in the United States of America in the Uniform Commercial Code, 14th edn (1995), section 2–403. And this course makes practical sense. In a case such as the present the owner of goods has no interest in the identity of the buyer. He is interested only in creditworthiness. It is little short of absurd that a subsequent purchaser's rights depend on the precise manner in which the crook seeks to persuade the owner of his creditworthiness and permit him to take the goods away with him. This ought not to be so. The purchaser's rights should not depend upon the precise form the crook's misrepresentation takes.

36. *Cundy v Lindsay* has stood for a long time. But I see no reason to fear that adopting this conclusion will unsettle the law of contract. In practice the problems surrounding *Cundy v Lindsay* arise only when third parties' rights are in issue. To bring the law here into line with the law already existing in 'face-to-face' cases will rid the law of an anomaly. Devlin LJ's starting point presumption is a workable foundation which should apply in all cases. A person is presumed to intend to contract with the person with whom he is actually dealing, whatever be the mode of communication.

37. Although expressed by Devlin LJ as a presumption, it is not easy to think of practical circumstances where, once in point, the presumption will be displaced. The factual postulate necessary to bring the presumption into operation is that a person (O) believes that the person with whom he is dealing is the person the latter has represented himself to be. Evidence that the other's identity was of importance to O, and evidence of the steps taken to check the other's identity, will lead nowhere if the transaction proceeds on the basis of the underlying factual postulate.

The present case

38. It follows that I would allow this appeal ...

41. One further point may be noted. Some time was taken up in this case with arguments on whether the dealer was an agent for the finance company and for what purposes. This was in an endeavour to bring the case within the 'face-to-face' principle. The need for such singularly sterile arguments underlines the practical absurdity of a principle bounded in this way. The practical reality is that in the instant case the presence or absence of a representative of the finance company in the dealer's showroom made no difference to the course of events. Had an authorised representative of the finance company been present no doubt he would have inspected the driving licence himself and himself obtained the information needed by his company. As it was, a copy of the licence, together with the necessary information, were faxed to the finance company. I can see no sensible basis on which these different modes of communication should affect the outcome of this case. I would set aside the orders of the assistant recorder and the Court of Appeal, and dismiss this action. Mr Hudson acquired a good title to the car under section 27 of the 1964 Act.

Lord Hobhouse of Woodborough

44. The relevant question is ... 'Was R a debtor under the hire-purchase agreement relating to the car?' Mr Hudson contends that R was; the finance company contends that he was not. The judge and the majority of the Court of Appeal found that he was not; Sedley LJ would have held that he was.

45. What was the 'hire-purchase' agreement relied on? It was a written agreement on a standard hire-purchase printed form purporting to be signed as the 'customer' by one Durlabh Patel, the person who lived at 45 Mayflower Road, Leicester, to whom driving licence no 'PATEL506018DJ9FM' had been issued and with a date of birth 01/06/58. This was an accurate identification of the real Mr Durlabh Patel, but in no respect of R who was not the person who lived at that address, not the person to whom the driving licence had been issued and (one suspects) not a twin in age of the real Mr Patel. R forged Mr Patel's signature so as to make the signature on the hire-purchase 'agreement' appear to be the same as that on the driving licence. The parties to the written 'agreement' are Mr Patel (the 'customer'), and Shogun Finance Ltd (the creditor). There is also an offer and acceptance clause (clause 1):

> 'You [the customer named overleaf] are offering to make a legal agreement by signing this document. We [the creditor] can reject your offer, or accept it by signing it ourselves ... If we sign this document it will become legally binding at once (even before we send you a signed copy)' ...

46. The effect of this is that: (i) it re-emphasises that the customer/hirer is, and is only, the person *named* on the front of the document; (ii) it makes it clear that the agreement is the written agreement contained in the written document; (iii) the offer being accepted by the creditor is the offer contained in the document and that alone, that is to say, the offer of Mr Durlabh Patel of the address in Leicester and to whom the driving licence was issued; (iv) for a valid offer to be made, the form must have been signed by Mr Durlabh Patel; and, (v) most importantly of all, the question in issue becomes a question of the construction of this written document, not a question of factual investigation and evaluation ...

50. The [defendant's] argument also fails on another ground. There was no *consensus ad idem* between the finance company and the rogue. Leaving on one side the fact that the rogue never had any intention himself to contract with the finance company, the hire-purchase 'agreement' to which Mr Hudson pins his argument was one purportedly made by the acceptance by the finance company, by signing the creditor's box in the form, of a written offer by Mr Durlabh Patel to enter into the hire-purchase agreement. This faces Mr Hudson with a dilemma: either the contract created by that acceptance was a contract with Mr Durlabh Patel or there was no *consensus ad idem*, the rogue having no honest belief or contractual intent whatsoever and the finance company believing that it was accepting an offer by Mr Durlabh Patel. On neither alternative was there a hire-purchase agreement with the rogue. …

54. It follows that the appeal must be dismissed and the majority judgment of the Court of Appeal affirmed.

Lord Millett (dissenting)

68. [T]he real objection to the present state of the law, in my view, is that the distinction between the face-to-face contract and other contracts is unrealistic. I leave aside the criticism of the face-to-face rule made by *Corbin on Contracts*, at p 620, that it is 'somewhat fanciful to hold that B intends to sell the goods to the physical body of A in front of him, although that body is indeed part of what we call 'identity'.' My difficulty is that I cannot see that there is any difference in principle between the two situations …

69. In *Ingram v Little* [1961] 1 QB 31 Devlin LJ said, at p 66, that 'the presumption that a person is intending to contract with the person to whom he is actually addressing the words of contract seems to me to be a simple and sensible one …' I respectfully agree. But why should it be adopted only in the case of a contract entered into between persons who deal in the physical presence of each other? If the offeree's words of acceptance are taken to be addressed to the physical person standing in his presence who made the offer, what is the position where they deal with each other by telephone? Is the disembodied voice to be equated with physical presence? Is it sufficient that the parties are in the hearing of each other? Does it make a difference if the dealing is by televisual link, so that the parties are in the hearing and sight but not the presence of each other? New means of communication make the distinction untenable.

70. But in truth the distinction was always unsound. If the offeree's words of acceptance are taken to be addressed to the physical person standing in his presence who made the offer, why is the contract entered into by correspondence different? …

71. In my opinion there are only two principled solutions to the problem. The law must give preference, either to the person for whom the offer or acceptance is intended, or to the person to whom it is directed, and must do so in all cases as a matter of law. The difficulty is in deciding which solution should be adopted, for there is much to commend each of them.

72. The first solution, which gives preference to the person for whom the offer or acceptance is intended, possibly accords more closely to the existing authorities, which treat the face-to-face transaction as an exception to the general rule, and with the decision in *Cundy v Lindsay* 3 App Cas 459, the only case on the subject which has come before the House. It also accords more closely with the parties' subjective intentions, for B intends to deal with C, especially if he has checked his creditworthiness, and not with A, of whom he has never heard; while A has no intention of being bound by contract at all. From his point of view the supposed contract is merely a pretence to enable him to get hold of goods without paying for them. He does not need a contract, for he is content with possession without title. In the days when the law distinguished between trickery and deception, he would have obtained possession by a trick rather than title by false pretences.

73. The strongest argument in favour of this solution, I suppose, is that it could be said to be based on the parties' own assessment of what they mean by the counterparty's 'identity' … [A]s Treitel observes (*The Law of Contract*, 10th edn, p 277) a person may be identified by reference to any one of his attributes. He may be identified as 'the person in the room', 'the person who spoke on the telephone', 'the person who appended the illegible signature', 'the writer of the letter under reply', or 'the person who made the offer';

but he may also be identified, and sometimes more relevantly, as 'the person whose creditworthiness has been checked and found to be satisfactory'. Any of these may be the means of identifying a unique person ...

75. Given the equivocal nature of a person's 'identity', there is something to be said for selecting those aspects of the offeror's identity which are material in causing the other party to accept the offer. In the present case, for example, Mr Patel's name address and date of birth had no intrinsic relevance in themselves. The claimant would have entered into the transaction with anyone, whatever his name and address or date of birth, so long as it was satisfied that he was worthy of credit. Mr Patel's personal details were merely the information which enabled it to conduct inquiries into the credit of the person it assumed to be its customer. It makes commercial sense to treat a contract made in these circumstances as purporting to be made between the finance company and the subject of its inquiries rather than with the person who merely produced the information necessary to enable it to make them.

76. Nevertheless I have come to the conclusion that it is the second solution which ought to be adopted. All the considerations which I have mentioned, and which seem to favour the first solution, when properly analysed go to the mechanics of the deception and its materiality rather than to the identity of the offeror. They ought to come into play when consideration is given to the second question, whether the contract is voidable, rather than to the first, whether there is sufficient correlation between offer and acceptance ('*consensus ad idem*') to bring a contract into existence. Until the fraud is exposed and it is discovered that A is *not* C, the existence of a contract is not in doubt. The fraud is relevant to the question whether the contract is enforceable against B rather than its existence ...

81. ... In my opinion, once one accepts that there are two questions involved: (i) Did a contract come into existence at all? (ii) If so was the contract vitiated by fraud or mistake? There is only one principled conclusion. Whatever the medium of communication, a contract comes into existence if, on an objective appraisal of the facts, there is sufficient correlation between offer and acceptance to make it possible to say that the impostor's offer has been accepted by the person to whom it was addressed. While a person cannot intercept and accept an offer made to someone else, he should normally be treated as intending to contract with the person with whom he is dealing. Provided that the offer is made to him, then whether his acceptance of the offer is obtained by deception or mistake, and whether his mistake is as to the identity of the offeror or some material attribute of his, the transaction should result in a contract, albeit one which is voidable.

82. This rule is easy to apply and accords with principle by distinguishing between the formation of a contract as a question of fact to be determined objectively and the consequences of mistake or fraud which depend on its effect on the mind of the person affected. It avoids undesirable refinements and gives a measure of protection to innocent third parties. Of course, someone has to bear the loss where there is fraud, but it is surely fairer that the party who was actually swindled and who had an opportunity to uncover the fraud should bear the loss rather than a party who entered the picture only after the swindle had been carried out and who had none. In the present case, the claimant could easily have exposed the fraud by writing to Mr Patel, whose address it had been given, and asking him to confirm his intention to proceed with the proposed transaction. If it had been one for which statute required a cooling-off period, it no doubt it would have done ...

84. We cannot leave the law as it is. It is neither fair nor principled, and not all the authorities from which it is derived can be reconciled; some, at least, must be overruled if it is to be extricated from the present quagmire. If the law is to be rationalised and placed on a proper footing, the formulation which I have proposed has the merit of according with the recommendations made in the Twelth Report of the Law Reform Committee on the *Transfer of Title to Chattels* (Cmnd 2958) and in *Anson's Law of Contract*, 28th edn, p 332. It would also bring English law into line with the law both in the United States and in Germany ...

87. Where does this leave the authorities? Most of those which are concerned with face-to-face transactions can stand with the exception of the decision of the majority of the Court of Appeal in *Ingram v Little* [1961] 1 QB 31, which is inconsistent with *Lewis v Averay* [1972] 1 QB 198 and should be overruled. I would confirm the decision in *Phillips v Brook Ltd* [1919] 2 KB 243 ...

90. The principal obstacle which has prevented the courts from rationalising this branch of the law has been *Cundy v Lindsay* ... As an authority on the formation of contract the decision is, with respect, unconvincing. That the plaintiffs did not wish or intend to have any dealings with Blenkarn is beyond dispute; but it is far from obvious that they did not actually have such a dealing even though it was only as a result of the deception practised on them ...

93. In my view the proper conclusion on these facts is that the plaintiffs contracted with Blenkarn in the mistaken belief, induced by his fraud, that they were dealing with Blenkiron & Co, and that the resulting contract was voidable for fraud. If the plaintiffs' subjective state of mind, induced by the fraud, is put on one side, there is no justification for the question-begging assumption that the plaintiffs' letter of acceptance was directed to Blenkiron & Co and that it was the name which was right and the address which was wrong. Nor is there any justification for the suggestion that the signature was a forgery. Blenkarn, who signed the letter, did not claim that it was someone else's signature; he acknowledged and asserted that it was his own. Even those who consider that the case was rightly decided concede that the rogue could have been sued for the price of the goods: see Treitel, *The Law of Contract*, p 284. But that presupposes that there was sufficient correlation between offer and acceptance to bring a contract into existence, albeit one which was void (or voidable) at the instance of the party deceived. Yet this was the very proposition which the House rejected

...

103. [O]nce it is established that the person whose name and other personal details are stated in the contract and the person who stated them and signed the contract are not the same, the question immediately arises: which of them should be treated as the counterparty? Do the name and other details included in the contract refer to the person to whom they belong or to the impostor who included them in order to identify himself? This is not simply a question of construction. It is partly a question of fact and partly a question of law. To say, as my noble and learned friend, Lord Hobhouse of Woodborough does, that it is a question of construction which admits of only one answer, with respect simply begs the question.

104. How should the question be answered in the present case? ... If there was a contract with the rogue, it was voidable for fraud.

105. But was there such a contact at all? The contact came into being when the claimant executed its part of the agreement. The two parts corresponded in every material particular ...

106. The object of the deception was to misdirect the claimant's credit inquiries. In this it succeeded. Having satisfied itself that Mr Durlabh Patel, whom it believed to be its customer, was worthy of credit, it accepted the offer which the impostor had made, signed its part of the agreement, and authorised the dealer to deliver possession of the car to his customer as hirer under the agreement.

107. But who was his customer? It was not Mr Durlabh Patel. In my opinion it was plainly the impostor. Any other conclusion would mean that the dealer parted with the vehicle to the impostor without authority and would, presumably, be liable in conversion if the vehicle proved to be irrecoverable. This is far removed from reality. The claimant and the dealer both believed that the customer who was hiring the car and Mr Durlabh Patel were one and the same; but the claimant did not make that a condition of the dealer's authority to part with the car. From first to last it believed that the impostor who attended the dealer's showroom, gave his name as Mr Durlabh Patel, and signed the agreement in that name, was indeed Mr Durlabh Patel; in that belief it entered into a hiring agreement and authorised the dealer to deliver possession of the car to the customer who had so identified himself. In my opinion, the claimant not only took a credit risk, but also took the risk that the customer who was hiring the car was not Mr Durlabh Patel and that its credit inquiries had been fraudulently misdirected. I would hold that there was a hiring, and the impostor was the hirer.

108. This conclusion involves a departure from *Cundy v Lindsay* (1878) 3 App Cas 459, a decision of this House which has stood for more than 120 years. But its reasoning is unsound. It is vitiated by its subjective approach to the formation of contract and the necessary correlation between offer and acceptance; which may be why textbook writers treat it as an example of unilateral mistake even though this was not the basis on which it was decided. For the same reason it cannot be regarded as authoritative on the question whether a contract otherwise properly entered into is void for mistake rather than voidable. It has had an unfortunate influence on the development of the law, leading to an unprincipled distinction between face-to-face transactions and others and the indefensible conclusion that an innocent purchaser's position depends on the nature of the mistake of a third party or the precise mechanics of the fraud which had been perpetrated on him. In my view it should now be discarded and the law put on a simpler and more principled and defensible basis.

109. In my opinion only the decision in *Cundy v Lindsay* stands in the way of a rational and coherent restatement of the law. My noble and learned friend, Lord Phillips of Worth Matravers, has expressed the view that the conclusion to which Lord Nicholls and I have come conflicts not only with that case but with the approach in almost all the numerous cases which he has cited. If they had preceded *Cundy v Lindsay*, that would be a strong reason for not adopting it. But they were merely following a decision of this House by which they were bound.

Lord Phillips of Worth Matravers

119. The critical issue in this case is whether a hire-purchase agreement was ever concluded between Shogun and the rogue. If an agreement was concluded, then the rogue was the 'debtor' under section 27 of the 1964 Act and passed good title in the vehicle to Mr Hudson. If no agreement was concluded, then the rogue stole the vehicle by deception and passed no title to Mr Hudson …

Formation of contract

123. A contract is normally concluded when an offer made by one party ('the offeror') is accepted by the party to whom the offer has been made ('the offeree'). Normally the contract is only concluded when the acceptance is communicated by the offeree to the offeror. A contract will not be concluded unless the parties are agreed as to its material terms. There must be *consensus ad idem*'. Whether the parties have reached agreement on the terms is not determined by evidence of the subjective intention of each party. It is, in large measure, determined by making an objective appraisal of the exchanges between the parties. If an offeree understands an offer in accordance with its natural meaning and accepts it, the offeror cannot be heard to say that he intended the words of his offer to have a different meaning. The contract stands according to the natural meaning of the words used. There is one important exception to this principle. If the offeree knows that the offeror does not intend the terms of the offer to be those that the natural meaning of the words would suggest, he cannot, by purporting to accept the offer, bind the offeror to a contract: *Hartog v Colin & Shields* [1939] 3 All ER 566; *Smith v Hughes* (1871) LR 6 QB 597. Thus the task of ascertaining whether the parties have reached agreement as to the terms of a contract can involve quite a complex amalgam of the objective and the subjective and involve the application of a principle that bears close comparison with the doctrine of estoppel. Normally, however, the task involves no more than an objective analysis of the words used by the parties. The object of the exercise is to determine what each party *intended*, or must be deemed to have *intended*.

124. The task of ascertaining whether the parties have reached agreement as to the terms of a contract largely overlaps with the task of ascertaining what it is that the parties have agreed. The approach is the same. It requires the construction of the words used by the parties in order to deduce the *intention* of the parties – see

Chitty on Contracts, 28th edn (1999), vol 1, p 604, paras 12–042, 12–043 and the cases there cited. This is true, whether the contract is oral or in writing. The words used fall to be construed having regard to the relevant background facts and extrinsic evidence may be admitted to explain or interpret the words used. Equally, extrinsic evidence may be necessary to identify the subject matter of the contract to which the words refer.

125. Just as the parties must be shown to have agreed on the terms of the contract, so they must also be shown to have agreed the one with the other. If A makes an offer to B, but C purports to accept it, there will be no contract. Equally, if A makes an offer to B and B addresses his acceptance to C there will be no contract. Where there is an issue as to whether two persons have reached an agreement, the one with the other, the courts have tended to adopt the same approach to resolving that issue as they adopt when considering whether there has been agreement as to the terms of the contract. The court asks the question whether each *intended*, or must be deemed to have *intended*, to contract with the other. That approach gives rise to a problem where one person is mistaken as to the identity of the person with whom he is dealing, as the cases demonstrate ...

The decided cases

[His Lordship considered *Boulton v Jones* (1857) 27 LJ Ex 117; *Hardman v Booth* (1863) 1 H & C 803; *Cundy v Lindsay* (1878) 3 App Cas 459; *King's Norton Metal Co Ltd v Edridge, Merrett & Co Ltd* (1897) 14 TLR 98; *Phillips v Brooks Ltd* [1919] 2 KB 243; *Lake v Simmons* [1927] AC 487; *Ingram v Little* [1961] 1 QB 31 and *Lewis v Averay* [1972] 1 QB 198. He expressed preference for *Phillips v Brooks* over *Ingram v Little* and continued:

152. Lord Denning MR did not apply the approach of attempting to identify the intention of the plaintiff. He proceeded on the simple basis that, to all outward appearances, the plaintiff entered into an agreement with the rogue, with whom he was dealing. Both he and Phillimore LJ considered that the case was on all fours with *Phillips v Brooks* which had been rightly decided.

153. The difficulty in applying a test of *intention* to the identification of the parties to a contract arises, so it seems to me, only where the parties conduct their dealings in some form of inter-personal contact, and where one purports to have the identity of a third party. There the innocent party will have in mind, when considering with whom he is contracting, both the person with whom he is in contact and the third party whom he imagines that person to be.

154. The same problem will not normally arise where the dealings are carried out exclusively in writing. The process of construction of the written instruments, making appropriate use of extrinsic evidence, will normally enable the court to reach a firm conclusion as to the person with whom a party intends to contract. This was the position in *Boulton v Jones* 27 LJ Ex 117, *Cundy v Lindsay* 3 App Cas 459 and *King's Norton Metal Co Ltd v Edridge, Merrett & Co Ltd* 14 TLR 98. There is a substantial body of authority that demonstrates that the identity of a party to a contract in writing falls to be determined by a process of construction of the putative contract itself. I shall refer to some examples.

[His Lordship referred to a number of cases on the construction of written contracts and continued:]

161. The effect of these authorities is that a person carrying on negotiations in writing can, by describing as one of the parties to the putative agreement an individual who is unequivocally identifiable from that description, preclude any finding that the party to the putative agreement is other than the person so described. The process of construction will lead inexorably to the conclusion that the person with whom the other party intended to contract was the person thus described ...

The result in the present case

167. I have had the advantage of reading in draft the opinions of my noble and learned friends who have sat with me on this appeal. Lord Hobhouse of Woodborough and Lord Walker of Gestingthorpe have concluded that, as the contract was a written document, the identity of the hirer falls to be ascertained by construing that document. Adopting that approach, the hirer was, or more accurately purported to be, Mr Patel. As he had not authorised the conclusion of the contract, it was void.

168. Lord Nicholls of Birkenhead and Lord Millett have adopted a different approach. They point out the illogicality of applying a special approach to face-to-face dealings. What of dealings on the telephone, or by videolink? There also it could be said that each of the parties to the dealings is seeking to make a contract with the other party to the dealings. And this can even be said when the dealings are conducted by correspondence. If A writes to B making an offer and B writes back responding to that offer, B is intending to contract with the person who made that offer. If a contract is concluded in face-to-face dealings, notwithstanding that one party is masquerading as a third party, why should the result be different when the dealings are by letter?

169. Lord Nicholls of Birkenhead and Lord Millett propose an elegant solution to this illogicality. Where two individuals deal *with each other*, by whatever medium, and agree terms of a contract, then a contract will be concluded between them, notwithstanding that one has deceived the other into thinking that he has the identity of a third party. In such a situation the contract will be voidable but not void. While they accept that this approach cannot be reconciled with *Cundy v Lindsay* 3 App Cas 459, they conclude that *Cundy v Lindsay* was wrongly decided and should no longer be followed.

170. While I was strongly attracted to this solution, I have found myself unable to adopt it. *Cundy v Lindsay* exemplifies the application by English law of the same approach to identifying the parties as is applied to identifying the terms of the contract. In essence this focuses on deducing the intention of the parties from their words and conduct. Where there is some form of personal contact between individuals who are conducting negotiations, this approach gives rise to problems. In such a situation I would favour the application of a strong presumption that each intends to contract with the other, with whom he is dealing. Where, however, the dealings are exclusively conducted in writing, there is no scope or need for such a presumption. This can be illustrated by a slight adaption of the facts of the present case. Assume that the rogue had himself filled in the application form and sent it and a photocopy of Mr Patel's driving licence to Shogun. Assume further that he had been authorised to do so by Mr Patel. There can be no doubt that a contract would have been concluded between Shogun and Mr Patel. Mr Patel would have intended to contract with Shogun; Shogun would have intended to contract with Mr Patel; and this would have been demonstrated by the application form.

171. Assume now that the rogue had wrongly understood that he had been requested by Mr Patel to fill in and submit the application form on his behalf, but in fact had no authority to do so. In this situation, according to established principles of the law of agency, an apparent contract would have been concluded between Shogun and Mr Patel but, being concluded without the latter's authority, it would be a nullity. Shogun might have a claim against the rogue for breach of warranty of authority, but could not have demonstrated that a contract had been concluded with the rogue.

172. Turning to the true position – that the rogue knew he had no authority to conclude a contract in the name of Mr Patel, but fraudulently wished to induce Shogun to believe that they were entering into such a contract – I do not see by what legal principle this change in the mental attitude of the rogue could result in a binding contract being concluded with him.

173. The position is not, of course, as simple as that. Negotiations between the rogue and Shogun were not conducted exclusively by written correspondence. They were conducted with the aid of the dealer and the use of fax and telephone communications. Acceptance of the offer was conveyed by telephone via the dealer – and this might have been capable of concluding a contract, notwithstanding that clause 1 of the standard terms provided for acceptance by signature: see the discussion in *Chitty on Contracts*, 28th edn, vol 1, p 117, para 2–062. Sedley LJ considered that the dealings were analogous to face-to-face dealings and that the dealer was, in effect, the face of Shogun Finance Ltd. He considered that the face-to-face presumption should be applied.

174. The majority of the Court of Appeal considered that *Hector v Lyons* (1988) 58 P & CR 156 required them to determine the identity of the parties to the putative contract as a simple question of construction. On that basis they concluded that the putative hirer was Mr Patel and that, as the apparent contract was concluded without his authority, it was a nullity.

175. Dyson LJ considered what the result would have been had the negotiations been treated as face-to-face. He concluded [2002] QB 834, 853–854, paras 45–46 that the presumption would have been displaced by the importance that Shogun attached to the identity of the person with whom they were contracting.

176. My Lords ... Shogun's representatives were aware of the presence of the prospective hirer in the dealer's showrooms in Leicester. To an extent the dealings were interpersonal through the medium of the dealer. Should one treat them as comparable to face-to-face dealings and conclude that there was a presumption that Shogun intended to contract with the man with whom they were dealing? Should one treat the written agreement as no more than peripheral to the dealings and conclude that it does not override that presumption? I have concluded that the answer to these questions is 'no'.

177 .... Shogun put in place a system for concluding contracts that required both regulated and unregulated agreements to be entered into in writing in a form which provided essential information, including the identity of the parties to the agreement.

178. These considerations lead me to conclude that the correct approach in the present case is to treat the agreement as one concluded in writing and to approach the identification of the parties to that agreement as turning upon its construction. The particulars given in the agreement are only capable of applying to Mr Patel. It was the intention of the rogue that they should identify Mr Patel as the hirer. The hirer was so identified by Shogun. Before deciding to enter into the agreement they checked that Mr Patel existed and that he was worthy of credit. On that basis they decided to contract with him and with no one else. Mr Patel was the hirer under the agreement. As the agreement was concluded without his authority, it was a nullity. The rogue took no title under it and was in no position to convey any title to Mr Hudson.

179. For these reasons I would dismiss this appeal.

Lord Walker of Gestingthorpe

180. My Lords, I have had the advantage of reading in draft the opinion of my noble and learned friend, Lord Hobhouse of Woodborough. I agree with him that this appeal should be dismissed for the reasons given in his opinion. But because of the interest of this appeal, and the differing views among your Lordships, I wish to add some observations of my own. I begin with two general points.

181. A recurring theme in the authorities, starting with the very first sentence of the speech of Lord Cairns LC in *Cundy v Lindsay* 3 App Cas 459, 463, is the court's difficulty in deciding which of two innocent parties should bear the loss caused by the fraud of a third person (who may be beyond the reach of the law). Typically one innocent party is a seller who has parted with goods to a rogue, without obtaining payment in cash, and the other innocent party has bought the same goods from the rogue for cash. But although the court recognises both as innocent there is sometimes an inclination to regard the eventual buyer from the rogue as the more deserving of sympathy ... But your Lordships have to lay down a general rule to cover the generality of cases, and it would not be right to make any general assumption as to one innocent party being more deserving than the other. That is especially true in this case which is concerned, not with a sale but with a hire-purchase transaction, and in which the issue to be decided is (as Lord Hobhouse has pointed out) ultimately a question of statutory construction. ...

183. The other general point is that (in agreement, I think, with all your Lordships) I regard the issue in this appeal as essentially a problem about offer and acceptance; and in determining whether or not a contract has been formed by offer and acceptance, the court adopts an objective approach, and does not inquire into what either party actually intended, but into the effect, objectively assessed, of what they said or wrote ...

185. The principle to be applied in the case of face-to-face negotiations has sometimes been treated as an exception, but to my mind it is the best starting-point, as it exemplifies the simplest form of oral contract. The principle was first spelled out in England in *Phillips v Brooks Ltd* [1919] 2 KB 243, 247, following the Chief Justice of Massachusetts (Morton CJ) in *Edmunds v Merchants' Despatch Transportation* Co 135 Mass 283, 283–284:

> 'The fact that the seller was induced to sell by fraud of the buyer made the sale voidable, but not void. He could not have supposed that he was selling to any other person; his intention was to sell to the person present, and identified by sight and hearing; it does not defeat the sale because the buyer assumed a false name or practised any other deceit to induce the vendor to sell'.

The only case out of line with the principle is *Ingram v Little*. The reasoning in Devlin LJ's powerful dissenting judgment is in my view unanswerable. I consider that *Ingram v Little* was wrongly decided.

[His Lordship considered whether the principle should be viewed as a presumption or a rule of law and continued:]

187. If the principle is no more than a presumption, it is a strong presumption, and exceptions to it would be rare (in *Ingram v Little* Devlin LJ himself, at p 67, was content to leave this point open). I would hesitate to state it as an inflexible rule (apart from cases of agency) because the notion of one individual impersonating another covers a wide range of factual situations (broadly corresponding to the wide range of meaning conveyed by saying that one person knows, or knows of, another). At one end of the spectrum is the confidence trickster who falsely but convincingly asserts that he is a baronet (or a barrister, or a brain surgeon) in order to inspire confidence and obtain credit. Then there are cases like *Phillips v Brooks Ltd* and *Ingram v Little*, where the rogue falsely gives the name and address of a real person whose existence the other party can and does check (but whom the other party does not actually know by sight, or the deception would fail). The most audacious form of impersonation would be where a rogue (such as the Tichborne claimant was held to be) attempts, face-to-face, to deceive a member of the family of which he claims to be part, or someone else personally acquainted with the individual whom the rogue is impersonating. Impersonation of that sort must be very rare indeed, and probably limited to deception of those whose senses are impaired (as Isaac was when, according to chapter 27 of Genesis, Jacob successfully impersonated his elder twin brother Esau). I would not exclude the possibility that impersonation of that sort might be outside the presumption ...

188. I return to the question, which is of central importance to this appeal, whether (as Lord Nicholls and Lord Millett propose) the face-to-face principle should be applied much more generally. It may be that it should apply to an oral contract alleged to have been made on the telephone, where the parties are identified by hearing, although not by sight. An alleged oral contract made by telephone might be a case where the presumption applied, but was rebuttable. But to extend the principle to cases where the only contract was by written communication sent by post or by e-mail would be going far beyond identification by sight and hearing. Where there is an alleged contract reached by correspondence, offer and acceptance must be found, if they are to be found at all, in the terms of the documents ...

191. [Turning to the facts of the present appeal] Shogun Finance had no doubt never heard of the real Mr Patel before the day on which the written contract was signed by the rogue, forging Mr Patel's signature. But by the time it accepted the written offer it had, by efficient information technology, confirmed that Mr Patel existed and had learned a good deal of relevant information about him, including his creditworthiness. The form of contract made quite clear that Shogun Finance's intention was to accept an offer made by the real Mr Patel, and no one else. The appellant's attempt to analyse the matter as a face-to-face contract (effected through the agency of the car salesman) was accepted by Sedley LJ but in my view it must fail, for the reasons stated by Lord Hobhouse ...

We will begin by considering a point on which their Lordships seemed to be in agreement. Both the majority and the dissenters agreed that the doctrine of unilateral mistake really concerns the question of whether, from an objective standpoint, there is correspondence of the offer and the acceptance. Lord Millett summarised the approach as follows:

> Whatever the medium of communication, a contract comes into existence if, on an objective appraisal of the facts, there is sufficient correlation between offer and acceptance to make it possible to say that the impostor's offer has been accepted by the person to whom it was addressed.

However, there were important differences between the approach of the majority and the approach of the minority. Indeed even within the majority speeches there were two distinct approaches. Lord Phillips and Lord Walker upheld the traditional distinction between contracts concluded by face-to-face negotiations and contracts concluded by written correspondence. Lord Hobhouse was of the view that he did not even need to engage with this discussion. For him, the case was concerned only with the construction of a written document, which should be given certainty. Since the written contract named Mr Patel and purported to be an offer by Mr Patel, the claimant's acceptance could only relate to that offer. Parol evidence was inadmissible to contradict the terms of the written agreement. This emphasis on the written terms of the contract has since been noted by the Court of Appeal in *Dumford Trading AG v OAO Atlantrybûot* [2005] 1 Lloyd's Rep 289. Rix LJ said that Shogun Finance 'appears to emphasise the importance of construction of the written document even in matters of the identity of parties, and also to underline the danger of using extrinsic material in what is fundamentally the role of construction'.

With respect, it is submitted that Lord Hobhouse was wrong to believe that the case could be disposed of merely by reliance on the parole evidence rule. As Christopher Hare has noted ('Identity Mistakes: A Missed Opportunity' [2004] 67 MLR 993, 1006):

> Whilst commercial certainty generally demands that a written agreement should be taken at face value, the parole evidence rule is neither absolute in application nor without its critics. In particular, as Lord Nicholls suggested, the majority's application of the rule, completely ignored the fact that there had been a misrepresentation as to the identity of one of the contracting parties. It is uncontroversial that it must be possible to adduce evidence that an agreement was induced by a misrepresentation, even when that agreement has been reduced to writing.

Lord Nicholls and Lord Millett, dissenting, held that the distinction between written correspondence and face-to-face dealings was arbitrary and impossible to sustain. Lord Millett commented:

> If the offeree's words of acceptance are taken to be addressed to the physical person standing in his presence who made the offer, what is the position where they deal with each other by telephone? Is the disembodied voice to be equated with physical presence? Is it sufficient that the parties are in the hearing of each other? Does it make a difference if the dealing is by televisual link, so that the parties are in the hearing and sight but not the presence of each other? New means of communication make the distinction untenable.

Their Lordships favoured a two-step approach involving two questions: (1) did a contract come into existence at all and (2) if so, was the contract vitiated by fraud or mistake?

It can be argued that the minority's approach is to be preferred for a number of reasons. First, the distinction between written correspondence and face-to-face dealings is arguably arbitrary and unworkable. Second, the minority's approach would remove the illogical distinction between misrepresentations as to identity, which are capable of preventing a contract from being formed (if the misrepresentation is in writing), and misrepresentations as to subject-matter, which will only render a contract voidable. Finally, the minority's approach would ensure a greater level of protection for third-party purchasers. This would surely be desirable because, as Lord Nicholls observed, 'the loss is more appropriately borne by the person who takes the risks inherent in parting with his goods without receiving payment.'

It seems that the majority did not share Lord Nicholls' concern that the third party purchaser should not be burdened with the loss (see also Phang, Lee and Koh, 'Mistaken Identity in the House of Lords' (2004) 63 CLJ 24, 26). Lord Walker cautioned that, 'your Lordships have to lay down a general rule to cover the generality of cases, and it would not be right to make any general assumption as to one innocent party being more deserving than the other'. Their Lordships considered that the traditional distinction between written contracts and oral contracts was sensible and ought to be retained. Given that this decision is unlikely to be revisited in the near future, we are left with two further issues to consider. They both relate to the application of the majority's approach.

First, what forms of communication will constitute written correspondence? This is by no means an easy question to answer. The minority wrestled with the question, and even Lord Phillips devoted six paragraphs ([173]–-[178]) to considering whether the contract between Shogun and the rogue was concluded in writing. It seems that a contract concluded by fax falls within the definition of a written contract, but according to Lord Walker, a contract made by telephone does not (at [188]). What about a contract concluded by email, or text message, or over the internet or on interactive television? These are hard questions to answer, but guidance is needed if the majority's approach is to be applied to modern forms of communication.

The second point to consider is the position, post-Shogun, of contracts concluded by face-to-face negotiations. The majority held that there is a strong presumption that a contracting party intends to deal with the person who is physically present in front of him. This presumption is not easily rebutted. *Phillips v Brooks* and *Lewis v Averay* were cited with approval and *Ingram v Little* appears to have been dealt a fatal blow. Lord Millett declared that the case should be overruled (at [47]) and Lord Walker opined that it had been 'wrongly decided' (at [185]). Lord Nicholls and Lord Phillips were less forthright, but both seemed to prefer the dissenting judgment of Devlin LJ (at [22] and [145], respectively). It therefore seems that the presumption will not be rebutted merely by evidence that the mistaken party did not intend to deal with the person physically present. Something more is needed. An example given by Lord Walker is the infamous case of Arthur Orton, who impersonated Roger Tichborne in order to claim money from Roger's mother, Lady Tichborne. Such cases are, however, extremely rare.

9.4 Mistakes that nullify consent

A common mistake is a mistake that is shared by both parties to the contract. The general rule is that a contract will be void for common mistake if the mistake is 'fundamental'. The clearest example of such a mistake is where the parties make a contract about an item that has ceased to exist at the time the contract is made. For example, if A agrees to sell to B his boat, which, unknown to the parties, has been wrecked in a crash the day before the contract was made, the agreement may be void for common mistake. There is valid consent, but the consent is nullified by the pre-contractual destruction of the subject matter of the contract.

The following case is frequently cited as a classic example of a contract void for common mistake, although, as we will see, there are some doubts about the underlying basis for the decision.

Couturier v Hastie (1856) 5 HL Cas 673

Facts: The defendants agreed to sell a cargo of corn to the plaintiffs. At the time the contract was made, both parties assumed that the cargo existed. In fact, one month earlier, it had begun to deteriorate, and the captain of the ship had unloaded and sold the corn to a third party. The plaintiff repudiated the contract and the defendant brought a claim against him for the price of the goods.

Held: The House of Lords affirmed the decision of the Court of Exchequer, holding that the plaintiffs were not obliged to pay for goods because they were not in existence at the time the contract was made.

The Lord Chancellor: I have no hesitation in advising your Lordships, and at once moving that the judgment of the Court below should be affirmed. It is hardly necessary, and it has not ordinarily been usual for your Lordships to go much into the merits of a judgment which is thus unanimously affirmed by the Judges who are called in to consider it, and to assist the House in forming its judgment. But I may state shortly that the whole question turns upon the construction of the contract which was entered into between the parties ... [L]ooking to the contract itself alone, it appears to me clearly that what the parties contemplated, those who bought and those who sold, was that there was an existing something to be sold and bought, and if sold and bought, then the benefit of insurance should go with it ... The contract plainly imports that there was something which was to be sold at the time of the contract, and something to be purchased. No such thing existing, I think the Court of Exchequer Chamber has come to the only reasonable conclusion upon it, and consequently that there must be judgment given by your Lordships for the Defendants in Error.

This case has often been cited as authority that a contract entered into under a common mistake as to the existence of the subject matter is void. Indeed, this was the interpretation placed on the case by the drafters of the Sale of Goods Act (SGA) 1893. Section 6 of the 1979 Act provides the following:

> Where there is a contract for the sale of specific goods, and the goods without the knowledge of the seller have perished at the time when the contract is made, the contract is void.

However, the Lord Chancellor did not declare the contract to be void in *Couturier v Hastie*. He merely said that the plaintiffs were not liable to pay the price of the cargo. Nor did he use the word 'mistake' in his speech. It is quite possible that the case was decided on a different basis altogether – after all, his Lordship did expressly declare that 'the whole question turns upon the construction of the contract which was entered into between the parties'. Whatever the true basis for the decision in *Couturier v Hastie*, it is now clear that a contract can be void for common mistake if its subject matter has ceased to exist at the time when the contract is made.

9.4.1 Subject matter never existed

Section 6 of the SGA 1979 appears to assume that the goods did at one time exist. It therefore seems that the section will not apply in a situation where the goods *never* in fact existed.

***McRae v Commonwealth Disposals Commission* (1951) 84 CLR 377**

Facts: The Commission had invited tenders for a salvage operation in relation to an oil tanker said to be 'lying on the Jourmand Reef, which is approximately 100 miles north of Samarai'. The plaintiffs were successful in their tender, but on arrival, discovered that neither the tanker nor the reef existed. The plaintiffs sought damages for breach of contract. The Commission claimed that the contract was void for mistake.

Held: The High Court of Australia held that the Commission was in breach of its contractual warranty that there was an oil tanker at the location.

Dixon and Fullagar JJ: ... The first question to be determined is whether a contract was made between the plaintiffs and the Commission. The argument that the contract was void, or, in other words, that there was no contract, was based, as has been observed, on *Couturier v Hastie*. It is true that *Couturier v Hastie* has been commonly treated in the text-books as a case of a contract avoided by mutual mistake, and it is found cited in the company of such cases as *Gompertz v Bartlett* and *Strickland v Turner*. Section 7 of the English Sale of Goods Act 1893 is generally regarded as expressing the effect of the case. The case has not, however, been universally regarded as resting on mistake ...

In considering *Couturier v Hastie* it is necessary to remember that it was, in substance, a case in which a vendor was suing for the price of goods which he was unable to deliver ... [T]he vendor founded his claim on the provision for 'payment upon handing over shipping documents'. He was not called upon to prove a tender of the documents, because the defendant had 'repudiated' the contract, but he was able and willing to hand them over, and his argument was, in effect, that by handing them over he would be doing all that the contract required of him. The question thus raised would seem to depend entirely on the construction of the contract, and it appears really to have been so treated throughout ...

In the House of Lords ... the Lord Chancellor, in giving judgment, said: 'The whole question turns upon the meaning and construction of the contract'. A little later he said: 'What the parties contemplated ... was that there was an existing something to be sold and bought, and, if sold and bought, then the benefit of insurance should go with it'. In other words, there was not an absolute obligation to pay the price on delivery of the shipping documents (as the plaintiff contended), but an obligation to pay on delivery of those documents only if they represented at the time of the making of the contract goods in existence and capable of delivery ...

The truth is that the question whether the contract was void, or the vendor excused from performance by reason of the non-existence of the supposed subject matter, did not arise in *Couturier v Hastie*. It would have arisen if the purchaser had suffered loss through non-delivery of the corn and had sued the vendor for damages. If it had so arisen, we think that the real question would have been whether the contract was subject to an implied condition precedent that the goods were in existence. Prima facie, one would think, there would be no such implied condition precedent, the position being simply that the vendor promised that the goods were in existence ...

The position so far, then, may be summed up as follows. It was not decided in *Couturier v Hastie* that the contract in that case was void. The question whether it was void or not did not arise. If it had arisen, as in an action by the purchaser for damages, it would have turned on the ulterior question whether the contract was subject to an implied condition precedent. Whatever might then have been held on the facts of *Couturier v Hastie*, it is impossible in this case to imply any such term. The terms of the contract and the surrounding circumstances clearly exclude any such implication. The buyers relied upon, and acted upon, the assertion of the seller that there was a tanker in existence. It is not a case in which the parties can be seen to have proceeded on the basis of a common assumption of fact so as to justify the conclusion that the correctness of the assumption was intended by both parties to be a condition precedent to the creation of contractual obligations. The officers of the Commission made an assumption, but the plaintiffs did not make an assumption in the same sense. They knew nothing except what the Commission had told them. If they had been asked, they would certainly not have said: 'Of course, if there is no tanker, there is no contract'. They would have said: 'We shall have to go and take possession of the tanker. We simply accept the Commission's assurance that there is a tanker and the Commission's promise to give us that tanker'. The only proper construction of the contract is that it included a promise by the Commission that there was a tanker in the position specified. The Commission contracted that there was a tanker there ... If, on the other hand, the case of *Couturier v Hastie* and this case ought to be treated as cases raising a question of 'mistake', then the Commission cannot in this case rely on any mistake as avoiding the contract, because any mistake was induced by the serious fault of their own servants, who asserted the existence of a tanker recklessly and without any reasonable ground. There was a contract, and the Commission contracted that a tanker existed in the position specified. Since there was no such tanker, there has been a breach of contract, and the plaintiffs are entitled to damages for that breach.

Before proceeding to consider the measure of damages, one other matter should be briefly mentioned. The contract was made in Melbourne, and it would seem that its proper law is Victorian law. Section 11 of the Victorian Goods Act 1928 corresponds to s 6 of the English Sale of Goods Act 1893, and provides that 'where there is a contract for the sale of specific goods, and the goods without the knowledge of the seller have perished at the time when the contract is made the contract is void'. This has been generally supposed to represent the legislature's view of the effect of *Couturier v Hastie*. Whether it correctly represents the effect of the decision in that case or not, it seems clear that the section has no application to the facts of the present case. Here the goods never existed, and the seller ought to have known that they did not exist.

There are three points to note from the decision in *McRae*. First, the High Court of Australia did not accept that the decision in *Couturier v Hastie* was based on 'mistake'. The House of Lords merely concluded that the plaintiff was under no obligation to pay for the goods, which were not in existence at the time of the making of the contract. Second, the court held that the doctrine of mistake has no role to play where one party specifically promises that the subject matter of the contract exists. In such cases, the other party may bring a claim for breach of that promise. Third, the court held that the Victorian equivalent of s 6 of the SGA did not apply to the facts of the case before them because the goods had in fact never existed. Section 6 only has application where the goods did once exist, but have ceased to exist prior to the formation of the contract.

The second principle is important. On the facts of *McRae*, the plaintiff had undertaken an expensive salvage operation in reliance on the defendant's promise that there was an oil tanker on the Journand Reef. The defendant was in the best position to ascertain whether the tanker in fact existed, and it seems appropriate in the circumstances to hold the defendant liable for the plaintiff's reliance losses. If the contract had been held to be void for mistake, the plaintiff would not have been able to recover.

A rather vexed question exists as to whether the *McRae* principle applies when the case falls under s 6 of the SGA, that is, in situations where the goods did at one time exist, but have since ceased to exist. Section 6 states that the contract is void and the section contains no provision for the parties to agree to the contrary. Professor Atiyah ('*Couturier v Hastie* and the sale of non-existent goods' [1957] 73 LQR 340, 348–349) has suggested that s 6 is merely a rule of construction which can be overturned by a contrary intention of the parties. This approach has the merit of bringing s 6 into line with the *McRae* principle and removing the illogical distinction between cases where the goods have perished and cases where they have never existed at all. Unfortunately, the approach appears to contradict the express wording of the section. While other provisions of the Act expressly state that they are subject to the contrary intention of the parties there is no such statement in s 6.

9.4.2 Impossibility of performance

A contract may be void for common mistake if the parties believe that the contract is capable of performance when in fact it is not. Performance may be physically impossible, as in *Sheikh Bros Ltd v Ochsner* [1957] AC 136, where land was not capable of producing the quantity of sisal fibre contracted for. Alternatively, it may be legally impossible. In *Bell v Lever Bros* [1932] AC 161, 218, Lord Atkin gave the example of a contract for the sale of property which the purchaser already owns (cf. *Lictor Anstalt v Mir Steel UK Ltd* [2014] EWHC 3316 (Ch) where all parts of the agreement were [potentially] impossible). Finally, the contract may be commercially impossible if the commercial object has been defeated (*Griffith v Brymer* [1903] 19 TLR 434). In such cases, it could be said that the mistake is as to the quality of the subject matter (see Peel, E, *Treitel: The Law of Contract*, 14th edn, 2015, London: Sweet & Maxwell, p 354), which will be discussed in 9.4.3. Indeed, in *Lehman Brothers International (Europe) (In Administration) v Exotix Partners LLP* [2019] EWHC 2380 (Ch) at [194]ff, Hildyard J made a not altogether comfortable distinction between 'state of affairs cases' and 'legal impossibility' cases:

> 194. In my view, whilst recognising that there are deep waters to navigate, it is vital to distinguish cases where the mistake goes to the quality of the available or possible performance or where the subject matter simply has ceased to exist, and cases where performance in accordance with the letter of the contract always has at law been impossible. That seems to me the distinction apparent in the analysis in *The Great Peace* at [55].
>
> 195. In the one case, the essential question, which is usually at the root of any contractual dispute, is one of risk allocation: to determine where the risk of imperfect or altered performance should fall in circumstances the parties did not provide for or perhaps envisage, or in a state of affairs altered from that the parties assumed existed. In the other case, where what the contract provides for has always been impossible in law to do or be done, so that what is promised cannot be delivered, it is one of recognising that the apparent consensus has been fundamentally undermined and the consideration nullified. In the latter case, the issue is not really one governed by the principles applicable to the question as to who should bear the consequences of a common mistake. It is governed by the basic principle that (to quote Lord Atkin in *Bell v Lever Bros* at page 227, as cited by Lord Phillips MR at [60] in the *Great Peace*):
>
>> 'In these cases [referring to *Lord Kennedy v Panama, New Zealand and Australian Royal Mail Co Ltd* (1867) LR 2 QB 580 and *Smith v Hughes* (1871) LR 6 QB 597], I am inclined to think that the one party is not able to supply the very thing whether goods or services that the other party contracted to take; and therefore the contract is unenforceable by the one if executory, while if executed the other can recover back money paid on the ground of failure of consideration'.
>
> 196. Since in a case of the latter character the basis of invalidity is failure of consideration in consequence of legal impossibility, as distinct from a shared but false assumption as to a 'state of affairs', it seems to me that the elements required in order to establish common mistake as set out in the *Great Peace* at [76] are not of relevance in a 'legal impossibility' case. More particularly, it does not seem to me that, in the latter context, the Court need assess whether the mistake as to the legal quality of the subject matter is the fault of one party or the other, or whether it might have been discovered by either or both; whereas both are elements in a 'state of affairs' case: ibid in the *Great Peace*.

The distinction is not altogether comfortable as, presumably, even in a 'legal impossibility' situation one of the parties might assume the risk of that legal impossibility?

9.4.3 Common mistake as to quality

Will a contract be void for mistake if both parties are mistaken as to the quality of the subject matter? The leading House of Lords authority on the issue states that the contract will not be void unless the mistake renders the subject matter essentially different from the thing as it was believed to be.

Bell v Lever Brothers Ltd [1932] AC 161

Facts: Lever Brothers employed Bell and Snelling to serve for five years as the chairman and vice-chairman of their subsidiary company, Niger. While acting in this capacity, Bell and Snelling entered into secret speculations in cocoa, a commodity in which the Niger Company dealt. This was a breach of their employment contracts and would have justified Lever Brothers terminating their contracts without compensation. Sometime later, the Niger Company became amalgamated with another company, and the services of Bell and Snelling were no longer required. Unaware of the previous breaches of duty, Lever Brothers agreed to pay Bell and Snelling compensation of £30,000 and £20,000 respectively.

On discovering the breaches of duty, Lever Brothers sought to recover the compensation they had paid. They claimed damages and rescission of the contract on the ground of fraudulent misrepresentation and, in the alternative, brought a claim for unilateral mistake induced by fraud. At trial, the jury found that Bell and Snelling had not been fraudulent. The trial judge, however, held that the compensation agreements were void, having been made under a mutual mistake (meaning 'common mistake') as to the legal relation between the parties, each party believing, contrary to the truth, that the one was entitled to claim and the other was bound to pay compensation.

Held: The House of Lords held (Viscount Haldane and Lord Warrington of Clyffe dissenting) that the compensation agreements were not void because the mistake was as to the quality of the service contracts.

Lord Warrington of Clyffe: It is in my opinion clear that each party believed that the remunerative offices, compensation for the loss of which was the subject of the negotiations, were offices which could not be determined except by the consent of the holder thereof, and further believed that the other party was under the same belief and was treating on that footing.

The real question, therefore, is whether the erroneous assumption on the part of both parties to the agreements that the service contracts were undeterminable except by agreement was of such a fundamental character as to constitute an underlying assumption without which the parties would not have made the contract they in fact made, or whether it was only a common error as to a material element, but one not going to the root of the matter and not affecting the substance of the consideration.

With the knowledge that I am differing from the majority of your Lordships, I am unable to arrive at any conclusion except that in this case the erroneous assumption was essential to the contract which without it would not have been made.

It is true that the error was not one as to the terms of the service agreements, but it was one which, having regard to the matter on which the parties were negotiating – namely, the terms on which the service agreements were to be prematurely determined and the compensation to be paid therefor, was in my opinion as fundamental to the bargain as any error one can imagine.

The compensation agreed to be paid was in each case the amount of the full salary for the two years and a half unexpired with the addition in Mr Bell's case of £10,000 and in Mr Snelling's of £5,000. It is difficult to believe that the jury were otherwise than correct in their answer to the second branch of the group of questions numbered 5 – namely, that had Levers known of the actings of the appellants in regard to the dealings in question they would not have made the agreements now impeached or either of them ...

Lord Atkin: Mistake as to quality of the thing contracted for raises … difficult questions. In such a case a mistake will not affect assent unless it is the mistake of both parties, and is as to the existence of some quality which makes the thing without the quality essentially different from the thing as it was believed to be. Of course it may appear that the parties contracted that the article should possess the quality which one or other or both mistakenly believed it to possess. But in such a case there is a contract and the inquiry is a different one, being whether the contract as to quality amounts to a condition or a warranty, a different branch of the law. The principles to be applied are to be found in two cases which, as far as my knowledge goes, have always been treated as authoritative expositions of the law. The first is *Kennedy v Panama Royal Mail Co* LR 2 QB 580, 586.

In that case the plaintiff had applied for shares in the defendant company on the faith of a prospectus which stated falsely but innocently that the company had a binding contract with the Government of New Zealand for the carriage of mails. On discovering the true facts the plaintiff brought an action for the recovery of the sums he had paid on calls. The defendants brought a cross action for further calls … The Court came to the conclusion in that case that, though there was a misapprehension as to that which was a material part of the motive inducing the applicant to ask for the shares, it did not prevent the shares from being in substance those he applied for.

The next case is *Smith v Hughes* LR 6 QB 597, 604, 606, the well known case as to new and old oats … The Court ordered a new trial. It is not quite clear whether they considered that if the defendant's contention was correct, the parties were not *ad idem* or there was a contractual condition that the oats sold were old oats. In either case the defendant would succeed in defeating the claim.

In these cases I am inclined to think that the true analysis is that there is a contract, but that the one party is not able to supply the very thing whether goods or services that the other party contracted to take; and therefore the contract is unenforceable by the one if executory, while if executed the other can recover back money paid on the ground of failure of the consideration.

We are now in a position to apply to the facts of this case the law as to mistake so far as it has been stated … Is an agreement to terminate a broken contract different in kind from an agreement to terminate an unbroken contract, assuming that the breach has given the one party the right to declare the contract at an end? I feel the weight of the plaintiffs' contention that a contract immediately determinable is a different thing from a contract for an unexpired term, and that the difference in kind can be illustrated by the immense price of release from the longer contract as compared with the shorter … But, on the whole, I have come to the conclusion that it would be wrong to decide that an agreement to terminate a definite specified contract is void if it turns out that the agreement had already been broken and could have been terminated otherwise. The contract released is the identical contract in both cases, and the party paying for release gets exactly what he bargains for. It seems immaterial that he could have got the same result in another way, or that if he had known the true facts he would not have entered into the bargain. A buys B's horse; he thinks the horse is sound and he pays the price of a sound horse; he would certainly not have bought the horse if he had known as the fact is that the horse is unsound. If B has made no representation as to soundness and has not contracted that the horse is sound, A is bound and cannot recover back the price. A buys a picture from B; both A and B believe it to be the work of an old master, and a high price is paid. It turns out to be a modern copy. A has no remedy in the absence of representation or warranty. A agrees to take on lease or to buy from B an unfurnished dwelling-house. The house is in fact uninhabitable. A would never have entered into the bargain if he had known the fact. A has no remedy, and the position is the same whether B knew the facts or not, so long as he made no representation or gave no warranty. A buys a roadside garage business from B abutting on a public thoroughfare: unknown to A, but known to B, it has already been decided to construct a bypass road which will divert substantially the whole of the traffic from passing A's garage. Again A has no remedy. All these cases involve hardship on A and benefit B, as most people would say, unjustly. They can be supported on the ground that it is of paramount importance that contracts should be observed, and that if parties honestly comply with the essentials of the formation of contracts – i.e., agree in the same terms on the same subject-matter – they are bound, and must rely on the stipulations of the contract for protection from the effect of facts unknown to them.

This brings the discussion to the alternative mode of expressing the result of a mutual mistake. It is said that in such a case as the present there is to be implied a stipulation in the contract that a condition of its efficacy is that the facts should be as understood by both parties – namely, that the contract could not be terminated till the end of the current term ... [I]f the contract expressly or impliedly contains a term that a particular assumption is a condition of the contract, the contract is avoided if the assumption is not true. But we have not advanced far on the inquiry how to ascertain whether the contract does contain such a condition. Various words are to be found to define the state of things which make a condition. 'In the contemplation of both parties fundamental to the continued validity of the contract', 'a foundation essential to its existence', 'a fundamental reason for making it', are phrases found in the important judgment of Scrutton LJ in the present case. The first two phrases appear to me to be unexceptionable. They cover the case of a contract to serve in a particular place, the existence of which is fundamental to the service, or to procure the services of a professional vocalist, whose continued health is essential to performance. But 'a fundamental reason for making a contract' may, with respect, be misleading. The reason of one party only is presumedly not intended, but in the cases I have suggested above, of the sale of a horse or of a picture, it might be said that the fundamental reason for making the contract was the belief of both parties that the horse was sound or the picture an old master, yet in neither case would the condition as I think exist. Nothing is more dangerous than to allow oneself liberty to construct for the parties contracts which they have not in terms made by importing implications which would appear to make the contract more businesslike or more just. The implications to be made are to be no more than are 'necessary' for giving business efficacy to the transaction, and it appears to me that, both as to existing facts and future facts, a condition would not be implied unless the new state of facts makes the contract something different in kind from the contract in the original state of facts ... We therefore get a common standard for mutual mistake, and implied conditions whether as to existing or as to future facts. Does the state of the new facts destroy the identity of the subject-matter as it was in the original state of facts? To apply the principle to the infinite combinations of facts that arise in actual experience will continue to be difficult, but if this case results in establishing order into what has been a somewhat confused and difficult branch of the law it will have served a useful purpose.

Lord Atkin said that a contract will be void if the mistake is 'as to the existence of some quality which makes the thing without the quality essentially different from the thing as it was believed to be'. In most cases, this test will not be satisfied. The examples given by Lord Atkin bear this out. We do well to note the example given of a picture mistakenly believed to be the work of an old master. Such a case came before the Court of Appeal for consideration in *Leaf v International Galleries* [1950] 2 KB 86. Their lordships held that the buyer's only remedy was for innocent misrepresentation. It is also clear that it is not necessarily enough that the contract would not have been entered into if the true facts had been known: see *Triple Seven MSN 27251 Ltd v Azman Air Services Ltd* [2018] EWHC 1348 (Comm).

On the facts of *Bell v Lever Brothers*, it was held that the mistake was insufficient to render the contract void for mistake. Lever Brothers still received exactly what they had bargained for, the termination of the contracts with Bell and Snelling. It did not matter that the same result could have been achieved without having to pay compensation to the defendants. With respect, this reasoning is unconvincing. As Lord Atkin noted in his speech, Lever Brothers would not have entered into the agreement had they known of the true state of affairs. The mistake did not merely make the agreement less desirable; it made the agreement of such a nature that Lever Brothers would never have entered into it (see MacMillan, C [2003] 119 LQR 625, 658). As Lord Warrington noted in his speech, the mistake was 'as fundamental to the bargain as any error one can imagine'.

Catherine MacMillan ('How Temptation Led to Mistake: an Explanation of *Bell v Lever Bros Ltd*' [2003] 119 LQR 625) has argued that *Bell v Lever Bros* was wrongly decided, largely as a result of the subsidiary nature of the mistake claim. She concludes as follows:

> An examination of the historical surrounding to the facts behind the case of *Bell v Lever Bros* reveals that the case is not the stable bedrock necessary to support a functioning doctrine of mistake. Some of the fractures appear in the speeches of the Law Lords. One fracture is the conduct of the case by Lever Brothers in amending their pleadings to allege conduct of a near criminal nature. That they were unable to prove these new allegations did not assist their case. This pleadings point reveals yet another fracture. *Bell v Lever Brothers* was a failed case of fraudulent misrepresentation and concealment. Mistake was pleaded in the alternative and left largely unaddressed during the conduct of the trial. The result was that the evidence in the case was not what it could have been. Indeed, the case did not become a mistake case until virtually the close of the proceedings at first instance. Another fracture is that counsel themselves found the mistake cases difficult to reconcile and apply. The consideration of mistake was, thus, not entirely desirable. Yet this is a hairline fracture running along an even greater fracture – that this was a case about conduct. The lawsuit was brought because of Bell and Snelling's conduct in carrying out personal cocoa trades. Cooper, as head of Lever Brothers, believed that it was impossible for a company that permitted such conduct to function. The problem presented by the conduct was what consequences should attend upon a misdeed committed by two senior managers who had also rendered invaluable services to their employers. Upon this point, different courts reached different conclusions. The ultimate conclusion should, however, be examined in light of the difficult facts of the case.
>
> Bell and Snelling made a terrible mistake when they succumbed to temptation. There is no reason for the common law to perpetuate the legacy of this mistake by maintaining an overly rigid doctrine of contractual mistake. The application of the principles in *Bell v Lever Brothers* must be understood in light of, and limited by, the unfortunate circumstances of the case.

Despite the problems with the decision in *Bell v Lever Brothers*, it was assumed for a long time that the House of Lords had effectively closed the door on operative mistakes as to quality. Many years later, however, Steyn J confirmed that this was not the case.

Associated Japanese Bank (International) Ltd v Credit Du Nord SA [1989] 1 WLR 255

Facts: Bennett entered into a sale and lease back agreement with the plaintiff under which the plaintiff would purchase four specified packaging machines for £1 million. The defendant bank entered into a separate agreement with the plaintiff to guarantee Bennett's obligations under the leaseback agreement. Both banks believed that the machines were in existence at the time the contract was made. Bennett defaulted on the payments under the lease and the plaintiff sought to enforce the guarantee against the defendant. By this time, it had been discovered that the machines did not in fact exist.

Held: The court held that on a true construction of the guarantee agreement, there was an express condition precedent that the lease related to existing machines. Since the machines did not exist, the guarantee could not be enforced against the defendant.

Steyn J: The landmark decision is undoubtedly *Bell v Lever Brothers Ltd.* Normally a judge of first instance would simply content himself with applying the law stated by the House of Lords. There has, however, been substantial controversy about the rule established in that case ... Lord Atkin held, at p 218:

> 'a mistake will not affect assent unless it is the mistake of both parties, and is as to the existence of some quality which makes the thing without the quality essentially different from the thing as it was believed to be'.

In my view none of the other passages in Lord Atkin's speech detracts from that statement of the law ... [I]n *Solle v Butcher* [1950] 1 KB 671, 693, Denning LJ interpreted *Bell v Lever Brothers Ltd* differently. He said that a common mistake, even on a most fundamental matter, does not make the contract void at law. That was an individual opinion. Neither Bucknill LJ (who agreed in the result) nor Jenkins LJ (who dissented) even mentioned *Bell v Lever Brothers Ltd* ... With the profoundest respect to the former Master of the Rolls I am constrained to say that in my view his interpretation of *Bell v Lever Brothers Ltd* does not do justice to the speeches of the majority ... In substance the argument was that the actual decision in *Bell v Lever Brothers Ltd* contradicts the language of the speeches. If the test was not satisfied there, so the argument runs, it is difficult to see how it could ever be satisfied ... This is a point worth examining because at first glance it may seem persuasive ... Lord Atkin clearly regarded it as a hard case on the facts, but concluded 'on the whole', that the plea of common mistake must fail: see p 223. It is noteworthy that Lord Atkin commented upon the scarcity of evidence as to the subsidiaries from the boards of which the two employees resigned: see p 212. Lord Blanesburgh's speech was directed to his conclusion that the amendment ought not to be allowed. He did, however, make clear that 'The mistake must go to the whole consideration', and pointed to the advantages (other than the release from the service agreements) which Lever Brothers received: see pp 197 and 181. Lord Blanesburgh emphasised that Lever Brothers secured the future co-operation of the two employees for the carrying through of the amalgamation: see p 181. And the burden, of course, rested squarely on Lever Brothers. With due deference to the distinguished authors, who have argued that the actual decision in *Bell v Lever Brothers Ltd* contradicts the principle enunciated in the speeches, it seems to me that their analysis is altogether too simplistic, and that the actual decision was rooted in the particular facts of the case. In my judgment there is no reason to doubt the substantive reasons emerging from the speeches of the majority ...

It is clear, of course, that in this case both parties – the creditors and the guarantors – acted on the assumption that the lease related to existing machines. If they had been informed that the machines might not exist, neither the plaintiffs nor the defendants would for one moment have contemplated entering into the transaction. That by itself, I accept, is not enough to sustain the plea of common law mistake ... The real question is whether the subject matter of the guarantee (as opposed to the sale and lease) was essentially different from what it was reasonably believed to be. The real security of the guarantors was the machines. The existence of the machines, being profit-earning chattels, made it more likely that the debtor would be able to service the debt. More importantly, if the debtor defaulted, and the creditors repossessed the machines the creditors had to give credit for 97 per cent of the value of the machines. If the creditors sued the guarantors first, and the guarantors paid, the guarantors were entitled to be subrogated to the creditors' rights in respect of recovery against the debtor: see Goff and Jones, *The Law of Restitution*, 3rd edn (1986), p 533 et seq. No doubt the guarantors relied to some extent on the creditworthiness of Mr. Bennett. But I find that the prime security to which the guarantors looked was the existence of the four machines as described to both parties. For both parties the guarantee of obligations under a lease with non-existent machines was essentially different from a guarantee of a lease with four machines which both parties at the time of the contract believed to exist. The guarantee is an accessory contract. The non-existence of the subject matter of the principal contract is therefore of fundamental importance. Indeed the analogy of the classic *res extincta* cases, so much discussed in the authorities, is fairly close. In my judgment the stringent test of common law mistake is satisfied: the guarantee is void ab initio.

This was not a contract where the subject matter had ceased to exist (res *extincta*), since the machines were not the subject matter of the guarantee. Rather, the subject matter was a contract concerning the sale and leaseback of the machines, which was guaranteed by the contract between the plaintiff and the defendant. Despite this, there was a strong analogy with the *res extincta* cases, and Steyn J was satisfied that the non-existence of the machines rendered the guarantee essentially different to that which the parties thought that they had agreed to.

It is thus clear that a mistake as to the quality of the subject matter of the contract can, in exceptional cases, give rise to an operative mistake. The scarcity of cases in which such a mistake has been found, however, indicates that mistake as to quality has a very limited role to play in English law. This has been confirmed by one of the most recent decisions of the Court of Appeal on common mistake in *Great Peace Shipping Ltd v Tsavliris Salvage (International) Ltd.*

***Great Peace Shipping Ltd v Tsavliris Salvage (International) Ltd ('The Great Peace')* [2003] QB 679**

Facts: The defendants agreed to provide salvage services for a vessel, the *Cape Providence*, which had suffered serious structural damage in the South Indian Ocean. They were given the names of four vessels reported to be in the area. The nearest was said to be the *Great Peace*, a vessel owned by the claimants, and believed to be about 35 miles away from the stricken vessel. The defendants contacted the claimants and agreed to hire the *Great Peace* for a minimum of five days to escort and stand by the *Cape Providence* for the purpose of saving life. It was discovered that the vessels were in fact 410 miles apart, not 35 miles as previously understood. Once a nearer vessel was found, the claimants sought to walk away from the contract for the *Great Peace* on the ground that it was void for common mistake – both parties believing at the time of entering into the contract that the vessels were in close proximity. At first instance, Toulson J gave judgment for the claimants.

Held: The Court of Appeal dismissed the appeal, holding that the issue of whether there had been a common mistake turned on whether the mistake as to the distance between the two vessels had the effect that the service that the *Great Peace* was in a position to provide was essentially different from which the parties had agreed to. The fact that the defendants did not cancel the hire of the *Great Peace* until after another vessel had been obtained and the fact that the *Great Peace* would have arrived in time to provide several days of escort service demonstrated that performance of the contract had not been impossible. Accordingly, the contract was not void for common mistake and the defendants were liable to pay the cancellation fee.

Lord Phillips of Worth Matravers MR

50. It is generally accepted that the principles of the law of common mistake expounded by Lord Atkin in *Bell v Lever Bros Ltd* [1932] AC 161 were based on the common law ... The first step is to identify the nature of the common law doctrine of mistake that was identified, or established, by *Bell v Lever Bros Ltd.*

51. Lord Atkin and Lord Thankerton were breaking no new ground in holding void a contract where, unknown to the parties, the subject matter of the contract no longer existed at the time that the contract was concluded. The Sale of Goods Act 1893 (56 & 57 Vict c 71) was a statute which set out to codify the common law. Section 6, to which Lord Atkin referred, provided: 'When there is a contract for the sale of specific goods, and the goods without the knowledge of the seller have perished at the time when the contract is made, the contract is void'.

52. Judge Chalmers, the draftsman of the Act, commented in the first edition of his book on the Act, The Sale of Goods Act 1893 (1894), p 17: 'The rule may be based either on the ground of mutual mistake, or on the ground of impossibility of performance ...'

55. Where that which is expressly identified as the subject of a contract does not exist, the contract will necessarily be one which cannot be performed. Such a situation can readily be identified. The position is very different where there is 'a mistake as to the existence of some quality of the subject matter which makes the thing without the quality essentially different from the thing as it was believed to be'. In such a situation it may be possible to perform the letter of the contract. In support of the proposition that a contract is void in such circumstances, Lord Atkin cited two authorities, in which he said that the principles to be applied were to be found. The first was *Lord Kennedy v Panama, New Zealand and Australian Royal Mail Co Ltd* LR 2 QB 580 ...

60. The other case to which Lord Atkin referred was *Smith v Hughes* (1871) LR 6 QB:

> '597. On no view did that difficult case deal with common mistake and we are not able to see how it supported the test formulated by Lord Atkin, as set out at paragraph 47 above. Indeed, Lord Atkin himself commented [1932] AC 161, 222: 'In these cases I am inclined to think that the true analysis is that there is a contract, but that the one party is not able to supply the very thing whether goods or services that the other party contracted to take; and therefore the contract is unenforceable by the one if executory, while if executed the other can recover back money paid on the ground of failure of the consideration'.

61. We conclude that the two authorities to which Lord Atkin referred provided an insubstantial basis for his formulation of the test of common mistake in relation to the quality of the subject matter of a contract. Lord Atkin advanced an alternative basis for his test: the implication of a term of the same nature as that which was applied under the doctrine of frustration, as it was then understood. In so doing he adopted the analysis of Scrutton LJ in the Court of Appeal. It seems to us that this was a more solid jurisprudential basis for the test of common mistake that Lord Atkin was proposing. At the time of *Bell v Lever Bros Ltd* [1932] AC 161 the law of frustration and common mistake had advanced hand in hand on the foundation of a common principle. Thereafter frustration proved a more fertile ground for the development of this principle than common mistake, and consideration of the development of the law of frustration assists with the analysis of the law of common mistake …

[His Lordship then discussed various cases on frustration]

73. What do these developments in the law of frustration have to tell us about the law of common mistake? First that the theory of the implied term is as unrealistic when considering common mistake as when considering frustration. Where a fundamental assumption upon which an agreement is founded proves to be mistaken, it is not realistic to ask whether the parties impliedly agreed that in those circumstances the contract would not be binding. The avoidance of a contract on the ground of common mistake results from a rule of law under which, if it transpires that one or both of the parties have agreed to do something which it is impossible to perform, no obligation arises out of that agreement.

74. In considering whether performance of the contract is impossible, it is necessary to identify what it is that the parties agreed would be performed. This involves looking not only at the express terms, but at any implications that may arise out of the surrounding circumstances. In some cases it will be possible to identify details of the 'contractual adventure' which go beyond the terms that are expressly spelt out, in others it will not.

75. Just as the doctrine of frustration only applies if the contract contains no provision that covers the situation, the same should be true of common mistake. If, on true construction of the contract, a party warrants that the subject matter of the contract exists, or that it will be possible to perform the contract, there will be no scope to hold the contract void on the ground of common mistake.

76. [T]he following elements must be present if common mistake is to avoid a contract: (i) there must be a common assumption as to the existence of a state of affairs; (ii) there must be no warranty by either party that that state of affairs exists; (iii) the nonexistence of the state of affairs must not be attributable to the fault of either party; (iv) the non-existence of the state of affairs must render performance of the contract impossible; (v) the state of affairs may be the existence, or a vital attribute, of the consideration to be provided or circumstances which must subsist if performance of the contractual adventure is to be possible.

77. The second and third of these elements are well exemplified by the decision of the High Court of Australia in *McRae v Commonwealth Disposals Commission* (1951) 84 CLR 377 …

82. [W]hile we do not consider that the doctrine of common mistake can be satisfactorily explained by an implied term, an allegation that a contract is void for common mistake will often raise important issues of construction. Where it is possible to perform the letter of the contract, but it is alleged that there was a common mistake in relation to a fundamental assumption which renders performance of the essence of the obligation impossible, it will be necessary, by construing the contract in the light of all the material circumstances, to decide whether this is indeed the case …

84. Once the court determines that unforeseen circumstances have, indeed, resulted in the contract being impossible of performance, it is next necessary to determine whether, on true construction of the contract, one or other party has undertaken responsibility for the subsistence of the assumed state of affairs. This is another way of asking whether one or other party has undertaken the risk that it may not prove possible to perform the contract, and the answer to this question may well be the same as the answer to the question of whether the impossibility of performance is attributable to the fault of one or other of the parties.

85. Circumstances where a contract is void as a result of common mistake are likely to be less common than instances of frustration. Supervening events which defeat the contractual adventure will frequently not be the responsibility of either party. Where, however, the parties agree that something shall be done which is impossible at the time of making the agreement, it is much more likely that, on true construction of the agreement, one or other will have undertaken responsibility for the mistaken state of affairs. This may well explain why cases where contracts have been found to be void in consequence of common mistake are few and far between …

90. [In *Associated Japanese Bank (International) Ltd v Credit Du Nord SA* [1989] 1 WLR 255] Steyn J … after reviewing the authorities on common mistake … reached the following formulation of the law, at p 268:

> 'The first imperative must be that the law ought to uphold rather than destroy apparent contracts. Secondly, the common law rules as to a mistake regarding the quality of the subject matter, like the common law rules regarding commercial frustration, are designed to cope with the impact of unexpected and wholly exceptional circumstances on apparent contracts. Thirdly, such a mistake in order to attract legal consequences must substantially be shared by both parties, and must relate to facts as they existed at the time the contract was made. Fourthly, and this is the point established by *Bell v Lever Bros Ltd* [1932] AC 161, the mistake must render the subject matter of the contract essentially and radically different from the subject matter which the parties believed to exist. While the civilian distinction between the substance and attributes of the subject matter of a contract has played a role in the development of our law (and was cited in speeches in *Bell v Lever Bros Ltd*), the principle enunciated in *Bell v Lever Bros Ltd* is markedly narrower in scope than the civilian doctrine. It is therefore no longer useful to invoke the civilian distinction. The principles enunciated by Lord Atkin and Lord Thankerton represent the ratio decidendi of *Bell v Lever Bros Ltd*. Fifthly, there is a requirement which was not specifically discussed in *Bell v Lever Bros Ltd*. What happens if the party, who is seeking to rely on the mistake, had no reasonable grounds for his belief? An extreme example is that of the man who makes a contract with minimal knowledge of the facts to which the mistake relates but is content that it is a good speculative risk. In my judgment a party cannot be allowed to rely on a common mistake where the mistake consists of a belief which is entertained by him without any reasonable grounds for such belief: cf. *McRae v Commonwealth Disposals Commissions* 84 CLR 377, 408. That is not because principles such as estoppel or negligence require it, but simply because policy and good sense dictate that the positive rules regarding common mistake should be so qualified'.

91. The detailed analysis that we have carried out leads us to concur in this summary, subject to the proviso that the result in *McRae's* case can, we believe, be explained on the basis of construction, as demonstrated above. In agreeing with the analysis of Steyn J, we recognise that it is at odds with comments that Lord Denning MR made on more than one occasion about *Bell v Lever Bros Ltd* [1932] AC 161 to the effect that 'a common mistake, even on a most fundamental matter, does not make a contract void at law'...

94. Our conclusions have marched in parallel with those of Toulson J. We admire the clarity with which he has set out his conclusions, which emphasise the importance of a careful analysis of the contract and of the rights and obligations created by it as an essential precursor to consideration of the effect of an alleged mistake. We agree with him that, on the facts of the present case, the issue in relation to common mistake turns on the question of whether the mistake as to the distance apart of the two vessels had the effect that the services that the *Great Peace* was in a position to provide were something essentially different from that to which the parties had agreed. We shall defer answering that question until we have considered whether principles of equity provide a second string to the defendants' bow ...

162. We revert to the question that we left unanswered at paragraph 94. It was unquestionably a common assumption of both parties when the contract was concluded that the two vessels were in sufficiently close proximity to enable the *Great Peace* to carry out the service that she was engaged to perform. Was the distance between the two vessels so great as to confound that assumption and to render the contractual adventure impossible of performance? If so, the defendants would have an arguable case that the contract was void under the principle in *Bell v Lever Bros Ltd* [1932] AC 161.

163. Toulson J addressed this issue, at para 56:

> 'Was the *Great Peace* so far away from the *Cape Providence* at the time of the contract as to defeat the contractual purpose – or in other words to turn it into something essentially different from that for which the parties bargained? This is a question of fact and degree, but in my view the answer is No. If it had been thought really necessary, the *Cape Providence* could have altered course so that both vessels were heading toward each other. At a closing speed of 19 knots, it would have taken them about 22 hours to meet. A telling point is the reaction of the defendants on learning the true positions of the vessels. They did not want to cancel the agreement until they knew if they could find a nearer vessel to assist. Evidently the defendants did not regard the contract as devoid of purpose, or they would have cancelled at once. ...'

165 .... This reaction was a telling indication that the fact that the vessels were considerably further apart than the defendants had believed did not mean that the services that the *Great Peace* was in a position to provide were essentially different from those which the parties had envisaged when the contract was concluded. The *Great Peace* would arrive in time to provide several days of escort service. The defendants would have wished the contract to be performed but for the adventitious arrival on the scene of a vessel prepared to perform the same services. The fact that the vessels were further apart than both parties had appreciated did not mean that it was impossible to perform the contractual adventure.

166. The parties entered into a binding contract for the hire of the *Great Peace*, That contract gave the defendants an express right to cancel the contract subject to the obligation to pay the 'cancellation fee' of five days' hire. When they engaged the *Nordfarer* they cancelled the *Great Peace*. They became liable in consequence to pay the cancellation fee. There is no injustice in this result.

167. For the reasons that we have given, we would dismiss this appeal.

The Court of Appeal took the opportunity to review the whole basis for the doctrine of common mistake. In *Bell v Lever Bros*, Lord Atkin had spoken of implied terms as 'the alternative mode of expressing the result of a mutual [common] mistake' (see final paragraph of extract above). Some commentators (see Slade, 'The Myth of Mistake' [1954] 70 LQR 386; Collins, *The Law of Contract*, 4th edn, 2003, London: Lexis-Nexis, at p 125) have relied on these dicta to argue that an independent doctrine of common mistake is a 'myth'. All the cases, they argue, can be reanalysed as involving an implied condition precedent that the contract will not be enforceable unless a particular circumstance or state of affairs exists. The Court of Appeal in *Great Peace* rejected this view. Lord Phillips MR emphasised that cases of common mistake were analogous to cases of frustration (where the implied term theory has been rejected – see *Davis Contractors Ltd v Fareham UDC* [1956] 2 All ER 145). They both relate to circumstances that render the contract impossible to perform. The difference lies in the timing of the event. His lordship reasoned 'that the theory of the implied term is as unrealistic when considering common mistake as when considering frustration' (at [73]). Both doctrines, Lord Phillips insisted, rely on an independent rule of law that a contract will not be enforceable if its performance is impossible.

In [76], Lord Phillips set out the requirements for common mistake. Requirement (i) is straightforward and merely states that there must be a common assumption as to the existence of a state of affairs. Requirements (ii) and (iii) are derived from *McRae v Commonwealth Commission* (see above). The court must decide, as a question of construction, whether one of the parties has expressly or impliedly taken the risk of the assumption being mistaken. If they have, the contract will not be void for mistake. Lord Phillips noted that the circumstances where a contract will be void for common mistake are likely to be less common than instances of frustration (at [85]). This is because cases of common mistake involve events existing at the time of contracting. It is much easier to allocate the risk of one of these events than it is to allocate the risk of a subsequent event, which is far harder to predict. Lord Phillips gave no opinion as to whether requirement (ii) applies to cases falling under s 6 of the SGA 1979 (requirement (iii) is explicit in the wording of the section; and see also *National Private Air Transport Co v Kaki* [2017] EWHC 1496 (Comm), where the judge stressed that a party could not claim common mistake if there was no reasonable grounds for their mistaken belief).

The reference to 'impossibility' in requirement (iv) may be rather misleading. Although there is some support for the view that the contract will only be void if performance is literally impossible (see *Brennan v Bolt Burdon* [2005] 1 QB 303, 314, per Kay LJ; *EIC Services Ltd v Phipps* [2005] 1 WLR 1377), the statement in *Great Peace* must be read in light of the analogies that the court was drawing with the doctrine of frustration. In the law of frustration, it is only necessary to show that performance in the circumstances would be something essentially different from that to which the parties had agreed. As Chandler, Devenney and Poole have noted ('Common Mistake: Theoretical Justification and Remedial Inflexibility' [2004] JBL 34, 47), the frustration cases demonstrate that, in determining the 'impossibility' issue, the courts will be influenced by the 'justice' of the case. Such considerations seem to have influenced the mind of Lord Phillips as well, since he concluded his judgment with the words: 'There is no injustice in this result' (at [166]). Furthermore, the Court of Appeal's treatment of mistakes as to quality suggests that something less than literal impossibility is sufficient (on the difficulties of terminology in this area, see *Triple Seven MSN 27251 Ltd v Azman Air Services Ltd* [2018] EWHC 1348 (Comm) and *Swynson Ltd v Lowick Rose LLP (In Liquidation) (formerly Hurst Morrison Thomson LLP)* [2017] UKSC 32, where Lord Sumption refused to be drawn into this 'controversy'). Requirement (v) refers to a 'vital attribute', which may not have existence. This clearly extends the doctrine of common mistake beyond the *res extincta* cases. The Court of Appeal also approved of the decision in *Associated Japanese Bank*, where Steyn J recognised that there could be a common mistake as to quality if the mistake was such as to render the subject matter 'essentially and radically different' from that which the parties believed it to be. It is therefore clear that the 'impossibility' requirement does not preclude the recognition of common mistakes as to quality in exceptional cases.

Compromise agreements may cause particular difficulties as outlined by Marcus Smith J. in Elston v King [2020] EWHC 55 (Ch):

> 18. Compromise agreements – by which I mean an agreement whereby a pre-existing dispute between parties is settled by agreement – are contracts like any other. The difference between a compromise agreement and other contracts is that – unlike with other contracts – the parties reach a consensus ad idem in relation to a matter on which they disagree. The nature of that disagreement will, of course, vary from case-to-case, but oftentimes, the parties' individual expectations, and so the compromise, will be informed by their individual assessment of what a court might do were the matter to be litigated. Inevitably, this involves reaching a view not on what the facts are or what the law is, but on how the court (often a particular court) will determine certain factual and/or legal questions.
>
> 19. It is the overtness of such disagreements which as a matter of fact, if not as a matter of law, renders compromises different to other contracts. Not only is there a public interest in the finality of litigation but, more importantly for present purposes, the parties will be approaching the compromise not from a common perspective but actually from a divergent one. It is precisely this divergence which the compromise resolves, not by determining it (that is for the court, which *ex hypothesi* is not involved as an arbiter of the divergence, if there is a compromise) but by reaching an accommodation which both sides find acceptable.

The learned judge offered the following guidance on such cases:

> 21. The Court of Appeal in *Brennan v. Bolt Burdon* were plainly concerned that the effect of *Kleinwort Benson*, in holding that the law could be changed retrospectively by a later judicial declaration of the law, would be to create a form of common mistake of the most artificial sort (in that the 'mistake' only arose by way of subsequent judicial decision and did not subsist at the time of the agreement) that could create the prospect of wide-ranging attacks on contracts in general, but on compromise agreements in particular.
>
> ...
>
> 26. The difference between 'mistakes' and 'mispredictions' is one that their Lordships in *Kleinwort Benson* were well-alive to, and it is a distinction that has been considered in a number of cases concerned with unjust enrichment where the 'unjust' factor is mistake: *Marine Trade SA v. Pioneer Freight Futures*; *BP Oil International Limited v. Target Shipping Limited*; and *Jazztel plc v. Revenue and Customs Commissioners*. The first two cases were cited by the Judge; the third provides a distillation of what these cases said. At [30] in the third case, two points were made:
>
> '(i) Mistakes must be distinguished from mispredictions. A misprediction is a present belief or assumption about a future state of affairs, which is subsequently falsified; whereas a mistake involves the vitiation of the claimant's judgment at the time the enrichment is conferred. Put another way, a mistake operates only as regards the present or the past, whereas a prediction, by definition, involves the future. Whereas mistake constitutes a ground for restitution, misprediction does not. See Goff & Jones, paras 9–06–9–09; Burrows, A Restatement of the English Law of Unjust Enrichment, 1st ed (2012) ('Restatement'), pp 67–68; *Dextra Bank & Trust Co Ltd v Bank of Jamaica*, [2002] 1 All ER (Comm) 193.
>
> (ii) Mistakes can co-exist with an element of doubt. By 'doubt' is meant the claimant's conscious appreciation that the facts or law may not be as he or she believes them to be. See Goff & Jones,

paras 9–18, 9–21 and 9–24–9–25; Restatement, p 68. For example, a claimant may (wrongly) believe that he or she is legally obliged to make a payment, whilst at the same time appreciating that there is an argument that he or she is not in fact obliged to make the payment at all. Such doubts are not inconsistent with mistake, provided the doubt does not overwhelm the mistake …'

27. The difference between a mistake and misprediction – particularly where the alleged mistake co-exists with an element of doubt – can be extremely difficult and is, no doubt, very fact-sensitive. But the distinction is an important one, for it is only in cases of mistake that restitution is permitted and (although the authorities I have cited are cases in restitution) vitiation of a contract for common mistake can occur.

28. The distinction between a mistake and a misprediction is particularly acute where 'mistakes' of law are concerned. Taking the definition of mistake from the decision of the Court of Appeal in *Great Peace Shipping* as 'a common assumption as to the existence of a state of affairs' that is wrong, it is clear (as the Court of Appeal appreciated only too well in *Brennan v. Bolt Burdon*) that 'mistakes' arising by virtue of a subsequent decision of a court, reversing a decision below, can only be mistakes by virtue of the retrospective 'declaratory' theory of the common law espoused in *Kleinwort Benson*. But that does not mean to say that whenever there is a reversal of an earlier decision, there is a mistake. There will be some decisions – perhaps many – which make new law but which are susceptible of one, if not more, levels of appeal. In such a case, as Bodey J stated, the parties to a compromise cannot be unaware of the fact that the law may very well develop in a different direction to that articulated by the judge at first instance.

29. The present case is an excellent case in point. So far as I understand it, the decision in *Raithatha* was a decision on a new point, made at first instance. Although permission to appeal was given – itself revealing – the appeal was not taken forward. Two or so years later, another first instance judge reached a different conclusion in Horton, as he was perfectly entitled to do (the decision in *Raithatha* was persuasive only, and clearly did not persuade). The law is redolent with first instance decisions going in different directions, awaiting an authoritative holding of the Court of Appeal. In this case, the uncertainty did not last long: the Court of Appeal decided that *Horton* was right and *Raithatha* wrong. But, to take a hypothetical example, it is impossible to suggest that the parties entering into an income payments agreement of the sort here in issue, but after *Horton* at first instance and before the outcome in *Horton* on appeal, made a mistake. They clearly will have done no such thing, but reached an agreement based upon their assessment of which way the Court of Appeal would go in deciding between two inconsistent first instance decisions.

30. In cases where it is asserted that a compromise agreement should be set aside on grounds of this sort of mistake of law, it seems to me that the following process must be undertaken:

(1) The compromise agreement must be construed so as to understand its true meaning and effect, including as to any implied terms which may or may not exist. Naturally, that will involve examining the 'factual matrix', which in such cases will involve particular consideration of the nature of the dispute that the parties thought they were settling. To the extent that that dispute turns on points of law, it will be necessary to consider quite carefully the points at issue, including the status of any judicial decision being relied upon by the parties. To take a crude example, there is all the difference in the world between an agreement where the parties are considering a first instance decision determining a novel point of law (at one extreme) and an established rule of law, asserted and re-asserted by many courts, including the highest courts (at the other extreme).

It may be that such an assessment results in a construction of the contract where it is found that one or other party has assumed the risk of the law changing in the future, whether by way of an express or an implied term. If so, then the inquiry is at an end. The answer to the effect of a mistake will be found in the risk allocation adopted by the parties to the compromise agreement.

(2) In those cases where the contract does not provide the answer, it will be necessary to consider the nature of the change in law relied upon by the party seeking to set aside the compromise agreement, and ask 'Does this retrospective change in the law give rise to a common mistake, or did one or both of the parties simply make a misprediction about the course of future legal events?' Reverting to my crude example in the preceding sub-paragraph, a mistake will more likely arise where a well-established and unquestioned rule of law is dramatically overturned than where a single decision on a new and difficult point is overruled. The latter case, particularly if, *pace* Bodey J, the parties to a compromise should not be treated as ignorant of the fact that the common law develops (a view I entirely agree with), is a case of misprediction.

Compare also *British Red Cross v Werry* [2017] EWHC 875, where a settlement agreement in respect of a claim under the Inheritance (Provision for Family and Dependants) Act 1975 was held to be void when it was subsequently discovered that the deceased had, in fact, left a will and the partner of the deceased had been left the property in question.

9.5 Mistake in equity

From the above commentary, it is apparent that the common law rules for identifying an operative common mistake are both inflexible and restrictive. In *Solle v Butcher* [1950] 1 KB 671, Denning LJ sought to avoid the inflexibility of the traditional rules by claiming that *Bell v Lever Brothers* was only authority on the scope of the common law doctrine of mistake. He claimed that there was a much more flexible doctrine of mistake in equity, which could be applied to the facts of the case before him.

Solle v Butcher [1950] 1 KB 671

Facts: The plaintiff let a flat from the defendant at a rent of £250 per year. Both the parties believed that the flat was not subject to control under the Rent Restriction Acts, and that accordingly, £250 was a legal rent. Later, it was discovered that the flat was in fact controlled by the Rent Restriction Acts and that the maximum legal rent was £140 per year. The plaintiff brought proceedings in the country court for a declaration that the standard rent of the flat was £140 per year. The defendant claimed that the lease should be rescinded on the ground of common mistake of fact. The trial judge held that there had been no mistake of fact, though possibly there had been one of law, since both parties imagined that the Rent Restriction Acts did not apply.

Held: The Court of Appeal held (Jenkins LJ dissenting) that judgment should be given for the defendant on terms that the plaintiff must elect between rescission and paying the full rent.

Denning LJ: It is quite plain that the parties were under a mistake. They thought that the flat was not tied down to a controlled rent, whereas in fact it was. In order to see whether the lease can be avoided for this mistake it is necessary to remember that mistake is of two kinds: first, mistake which renders the contract void, that is, a nullity from the beginning, which is the kind of mistake which was dealt with by the courts of common law; and, secondly, mistake which renders the contract not void, but voidable, that is, liable to be set aside on such terms as the court thinks fit, which is the kind of mistake which was dealt with by the courts of equity. Much of the difficulty which has attended this subject has arisen because, before the fusion of law and equity, the courts of common law, in order to do justice in the case in hand, extended this doctrine of mistake beyond its proper limits and held contracts to be void which were really only voidable, a process which was capable of being attended with much injustice to third persons who had bought goods or otherwise committed themselves on the faith that there was a contract. In the well-known case of *Cundy v Lindsay*, Cundy suffered such an injustice. He bought the handkerchiefs from the rogue, Blenkarn, before the Judicature Acts came into operation. Since the fusion of law and equity, there is no reason to continue this process, and it will be found that only those contracts are now held void in which the mistake was such as to prevent the formation of any contract at all.

Let me first consider mistakes which render a contract a nullity. All previous decisions on this subject must now be read in the light of *Bell v Lever Bros Ltd*. The correct interpretation of that case, to my mind, is that, once a contract has been made, that is to say, once the parties, whatever their inmost states of mind, have to all outward appearances agreed with sufficient certainty in the same terms on the same subject matter, then the contract is good unless and until it is set aside for failure of some condition on which the existence of the contract depends, or for fraud, or on some equitable ground. Neither party can rely on his own mistake to say it was a nullity from the beginning, no matter that it was a mistake which to his mind was fundamental, and no matter that the other party knew that he was under a mistake. *A fortiori*, if the other party did not know of the mistake, but shared it. The cases where goods have perished at the time of sale, or belong to the buyer, are really contracts which are not void for mistake but are void by reason of an implied condition precedent, because the contract proceeded on the basic assumption that it was possible of performance ...

Applying these principles, it is clear that here there was a contract. The parties agreed in the same terms on the same subject-matter. It is true that the landlord was under a mistake which was to him fundamental: he would not for one moment have considered letting the flat for seven years if it meant that he could only charge 140 a year for it. He made the fundamental mistake of believing that the rent he could charge was not tied down to a controlled rent; but, whether it was his own mistake or a mistake common to both him and the tenant, it is not a ground for saying that the lease was from the beginning a nullity. Any other view would lead to remarkable results, for it would mean that, in the many cases where the parties mistakenly think a house is outside the Rent Restriction Acts when it is really within them, the tenancy would be a nullity, and the tenant would have to go; with the result that the tenants would not dare to seek to have their rents reduced to the permitted amounts lest they should be turned out.

Let me next consider mistakes which render a contract voidable, that is, liable to be set aside on some equitable ground. Whilst presupposing that a contract was good at law, or at any rate not void, the court of equity would often relieve a party from the consequences of his own mistake, so long as it could do so without injustice to third parties. The court, it was said, had power to set aside the contract whenever it was of opinion that it was unconscientious for the other party to avail himself of the legal advantage which he had obtained: *Torrance v Bolton* (1872) LR 8 Ch 118, 124, *per* James LJ.

The court had, of course, to define what it considered to be unconscientious, but in this respect equity has shown a progressive development. It is now clear that a contract will be set aside if the mistake of the one party has been induced by a material misrepresentation of the other, even though it was not fraudulent or fundamental; or if one party, knowing that the other is mistaken about the terms of an offer, or the identity of the person by whom it is made, lets him remain under his delusion and concludes a contract on the mistaken terms instead of pointing out the mistake. That is, I venture to think, the ground on which the defendant in *Smith v Hughes* would be exempted nowadays, and on which, according to the view by Blackburn J of the facts, the contract in *Lindsay v Cundy*, was voidable and not void; and on which the lease in *Sowler v Potter* [1940] 1 KB 271, was, in my opinion, voidable and not void.

A contract is also liable in equity to be set aside if the parties were under a common misapprehension either as to facts or as to their relative and respective rights, provided that the misapprehension was fundamental and that the party seeking to set it aside was not himself at fault ...

The principle so established by *Cooper v Phibbs* (1867) LR 2 HL 149 has been repeatedly acted on ...

Applying that principle to this case, the facts are that the plaintiff, the tenant, was a surveyor who was employed by the defendant, the landlord, not only to arrange finance for the purchase of the building and to negotiate with the rating authorities as to the new rateable values, but also to let the flats. He was the agent for letting, and he clearly formed the view that the building was not controlled. He told the valuation officer so. He advised the defendant what were the rents which could be charged. He read to the defendant an opinion of counsel relating to the matter, and told him that in his opinion he could charge £250 and that there was no previous control. He said that the flats came outside the Act and that the defendant was 'clear'. The defendant relied on what the plaintiff told him, and authorized the plaintiff to let at the rentals which he had suggested. The plaintiff not only let the four other flats to other people for a long period of years at the new rentals, but also took one himself for seven years at £250 a year. Now he turns round and says, quite unashamedly, that he wants to take advantage of the mistake to get the flat at £140 a year for seven years instead of the £250 a year, which is not only the rent he agreed to pay but also the fair and economic rent; and it is also the rent permitted by the Acts on compliance with the necessary formalities. If the rules of equity have become so rigid that they cannot remedy such an injustice, it is time we had a new equity, to make good the omissions of the old. But, in my view, the established rules are amply sufficient for this case ...

Cooper v Phibbs affords ample authority for saying that, by reason of the common misapprehension, this lease can be set aside on such terms as the court thinks fit ... In the ordinary way, of course, rescission is only granted when the parties can be restored to substantially the same position as that in which they were before the contract was made; but, as Lord Blackburn said in *Erlanger v New Sombrero Phosphate Co* (1878) 3 App. Cas. 1218, 1278–9: 'The practice has always been for a court of equity to give this relief whenever, by the exercise of its powers, it can do what is practically just, though it cannot restore the parties precisely to the state they were in before the contract'. That indeed was what was done in *Cooper v Phibbs*. Terms were imposed so as to do what was practically just. What terms then, should be imposed here?

If the lease were set aside without any terms being imposed, it would mean that the plaintiff, the tenant, would have to go out and would have to pay a reasonable sum for his use and occupation ... I think that this court should follow these examples and should impose terms which will enable the tenant to choose either to stay on at the proper rent or to go out.

The Court of Appeal held that there was a wider and more flexible doctrine of mistake in equity. It was wider in its scope in that it applied to mistakes that would not be operative at common law, and it was more flexible in its effect. Not only did it render the contract voidable rather than void, but it also permitted the court to order rescission on terms, as the Court of Appeal in fact did on the facts of *Solle v Butcher*.

The doctrine of equitable mistake was accepted by the High Court and the Court of Appeal in numerous subsequent cases (*Rose v Pim* [1953] 2 QB 450; *Grist v Bailey* [1967] Ch 532; *Magee v Pennine Insurance* [1969] 2 QB 507; *William Sindall Plc v Cambridgeshire CC* [1994] 1 WLR 1016; *Nutt v Read* (2000) 32 HLR 761; *Clarion Ltd v National Provident Institution* [2000] 1 WLR 1888; *West Sussex Properties Ltd v Chichester DC* [2000] NPC 74). It was never really clear, however, why the rules that apply to mistake in equity should be different to those that apply to mistake at law. Furthermore, it was difficult to reconcile *Solle v Butcher* with the decision of the House of Lords in *Bell v Lever Brothers*. If equity allows a broader range of mistakes to lead to the setting aside of a contract, why was this not even discussed in *Bell v Lever Bros*? Indeed, given that none of the usual bars to rescission applied in that case, why didn't the House of Lords set aside the contract between Bell and Lever Brothers on the ground of equitable mistake? A further problem exists as to the scope of mistake in equity. Denning LJ said that the mistake has to be 'fundamental', but this is the same terminology as the House of Lords used to describe common law mistake in *Bell v Lever Brothers*. When is a mistake fundamental enough to be operative in equity but not sufficiently fundamental to be operative at common law? There is no easy answer to this question and, as a result, the scope of equitable mistake proved impossible to determine (see *Associated Japanese Bank (International) Ltd v Credit Du Nord SA* [1989] 1 WLR 255, 268, per Steyn J; *William Sindall Plc v Cambridgeshire CC* [1994] 1 WLR 1016, 1042, per Evans LJ; *Clarion Ltd v National Provident Institution* [2000] 1 WLR 1888, 1904, per Rimer J).

In *Great Peace Shipping*, the Court of Appeal took the opportunity to review the law on equitable mistake. Lord Phillips considered the cases prior to *Bell v Lever Brothers*, focusing particularly on the decision of the House of Lords in *Cooper v Phibbs* (1867) LR 2 HL. He then considered the effect of *Bell v Lever Brothers* on mistake in equity.

***Great Peace Shipping Ltd v Tsavliris Salvage (International) Ltd ('The Great Peace')* [2003] QB 679**

Lord Phillips of Worth Matravers MR

113. In the House of Lords [1932] AC 161 the report shows that the appellants relied on both common law authorities and *Cooper v Phibbs* LR 2 HL 149 in support of the submission that a common mistake had to be as to the existence of the subject matter of the contract if it was to render it void. The respondents do not appear to have suggested that equity might provide relief where common law would not …

114. Lord Blanesburgh, when considering the pleadings, remarked [1932] AC 161, 190: 'the claim made by the heads of claim is for rescission of the agreements of settlement, relief properly consequent upon a case of voidability either for fraud or unilateral mistake induced by fraud. But if the allegation, even alternative, was that the agreements were entered into under mutual mistake of fact, then these agreements were not voidable but void ab initio, and no order on that footing is even hinted at in the relief sought' …

116. Lord Atkin, at p 218, cited *Cooper v Phibbs* LR 2 HL 149 as an example of mistake as to the subject matter of the contract: 'This is the case of *Cooper v Phibbs*, where A agreed to take a lease of a fishery from B, though contrary to the belief of both parties at the time A was tenant for life of the fishery and B appears to have had no title at all. To such a case Lord Westbury applied the principle that if parties contract under a mutual mistake and misapprehension as to their relative and respective rights the result is that the agreement is liable to be set aside as having proceeded upon a common mistake. Applied to the context the statement is only subject to the criticism that the agreement would appear to be void rather than voidable' …

118. These passages demonstrate that the House of Lords in *Bell v Lever Brothers* [1932] AC 161 considered that the intervention of equity, as demonstrated in *Cooper v Phibbs* LR 2 HL 149, took place in circumstances where the common law would have ruled the contract void for mistake. We do not find it conceivable that the House of Lords overlooked an equitable right in Lever Bros to rescind the agreement, notwithstanding that the agreement was not void for mistake at common law. The jurisprudence established no such right. Lord Atkin's test for common mistake that avoided a contract, while narrow, broadly reflected the circumstances where equity had intervened to excuse performance of a contract assumed to be binding in law.

[Having concluded that the House of Lords in *Bell v Lever Brothers* considered that the intervention of equity only took place in circumstances where the common law would have ruled the contract void for mistake, Lord Phillips moved on to consider *Solle v Butcher* and the line of cases flowing from it.]

153. A number of cases, albeit a small number, in the course of the last 50 years have purported to follow *Solle v Butcher* [1950] 1 KB 671, yet none of them defines the test of mistake that gives rise to the equitable jurisdiction to rescind in a manner that distinguishes this from the test of a mistake that renders a contract void in law, as identified in *Bell v Lever Bros Ltd* [1932] AC 161. This is, perhaps, not surprising, for Denning LJ, the author of the test in *Solle v Butcher*, set *Bell v Lever Bros Ltd* at nought. It is possible to reconcile *Solle v Butcher* and *Magee v Pennine Insurance Co Ltd* [1969] 2 QB 507 with *Bell v Lever Bros Ltd* only by postulating that there are two categories of mistake, one that renders a contract void at law and one that renders it voidable in equity. Although later cases have proceeded on this basis, it is not possible to identify that

proposition in the judgment of any of the three Lords Justices, Denning, Bucknill and Fenton Atkinson, who participated in the majority decisions in the former two cases. Nor, over 50 years, has it proved possible to define satisfactorily two different qualities of mistake, one operating in law and one in equity.

154. In *Solle v Butcher* Denning LJ identified the requirement of a common misapprehension that was 'fundamental', and that adjective has been used to describe the mistake in those cases which have followed *Solle v Butcher*. We do not find it possible to distinguish, by a process of definition, a mistake which is 'fundamental' from Lord Atkin's mistake as to quality which 'makes the thing [contracted for] essentially different from the thing [that] it was believed to be': [1932] AC 161, 218.

155. A common factor in *Solle v Butcher* and the cases which have followed it can be identified. The effect of the mistake has been to make the contract a particularly bad bargain for one of the parties. Is there a principle of equity which justifies the court in rescinding a contract where a common mistake has produced this result? ...

156. [T]he premise of equity's intrusion into the effects of the common law is that the common law rule in question is seen in the particular case to work injustice, and for some reason the common law cannot cure itself. But it is difficult to see how that can apply here. Cases of fraud and misrepresentation, and undue influence, are all catered for under other existing and uncontentious equitable rules. We are *only* concerned with the question whether relief might be given for common mistake in circumstances wider than those stipulated in *Bell v Lever Bros Ltd* [1932] AC 161. But that, surely, is a question as to where the common law should draw the line; not whether, given the common law rule, it needs to be mitigated by application of some other doctrine. The common law has drawn the line in *Bell v Lever Bros* Ltd. The effect of *Solle v Butcher* [1950] 1 KB 671 is not to supplement or mitigate the common law: it is to say that *Bell v Lever Bros Ltd* was wrongly decided.

157. Our conclusion is that it is impossible to reconcile *Solle v Butcher* with *Bell v Lever Bros* Ltd. The jurisdiction asserted in the former case has not developed. It has been a fertile source of academic debate, but in practice it has given rise to a handful of cases that have merely emphasised the confusion of this area of our jurisprudence ...

160. ... We are very conscious that we are not only scrutinising the reasoning of Lord Denning MR in *Solle v Butcher* and in *Magee v Pennine Insurance Co Ltd* [1969] 2 QB 507 but are also faced with a number of later decisions in which Lord Denning MR's approach has been approved and followed. Further, a division of this court has made it clear in *West Sussex Properties Ltd v Chichester District Council* 28 June 2000 that they felt bound by *Solle v Butcher*. However, it is to be noticed that while junior counsel in the court below in the *West Sussex Properties* case had sought to challenge the correctness of *Solle v Butcher*, in the Court of Appeal leading counsel accepted that it was good law unless and until overturned by their Lordships' House. In this case we have heard full argument, which has provided what we believe has been the first opportunity in this court for a full and mature consideration of the relation between *Bell v Lever Bros Ltd* [1932] AC 161 and *Solle v Butcher*. In the light of that consideration we can see no way that *Solle v Butcher* can stand with *Bell v Lever Bros Ltd*. In these circumstances we can see no option but so to hold.

161. We can understand why the decision in *Bell v Lever Bros Ltd* did not find favour with Lord Denning MR. An equitable jurisdiction to grant rescission on terms where a common fundamental mistake has induced a contract gives greater flexibility than a doctrine of common law which holds the contract void in such circumstances. Just as the Law Reform (Frustrated Contracts) Act 1943 was needed to temper the effect of the common law doctrine of frustration, so there is scope for legislation to give greater flexibility to our law of mistake than the common law allows.

Interestingly, on the facts of *Great Peace*, there almost certainly was not an operative mistake, either in law or in equity The *Great Peace* was only two days away from the *Cape Providence*, and it is doubtful whether such a mistake would have satisfied the test laid down by Denning LJ in *Solle v Butcher*.

On the issue of whether the Court of Appeal was correct to disapprove of *Solle*, the response has been mixed. On the one hand, it is quite clear that *Solle* is difficult to reconcile with *Bell v Lever Brothers*. It generated uncertainty in the law and was based on a questionable use of authority. On the other hand, the Court of Appeal in numerous subsequent cases followed *Solle*. It was not strictly necessary for the Court of Appeal to decide the point in *Great Peace*, and it is arguable that the issue should only have been determined by the House of Lords/Supreme Court (note, however, that subsequently, in *Pitt v Holt* [2013] UKSC 26 at [115] Lord Walker stated that the *Great Peace* had effectively overruled *Solle v Butcher*). Professor McCamus provided a scathing criticism of the decision in the following article (McCamus, JD, 'Mistaken Assumptions in Equity: Sound Doctrine or Chimera?' [2004] 40 Can Bus LJ 46, 75–76):

> [T]he decision in *The Great Peace* appears to be an unfortunate one for a variety of reasons. First, the test for operative mistake defined by the Court of Appeal in *The Great Peace* appears unduly restrictive and is likely, therefore, to lead to the manipulations characteristic of the earlier narrow versions of the test. Moreover, by failing to address the very problem identified by Denning LJ in *Solle v Butcher* – the impact of the common law void for mistake doctrine on the interests of third parties – the Court of Appeal has breathed renewed life into a doctrine that is quite unattractive from a policy perspective. Further, the attempted suppression of the equitable doctrine carries with it, at least for the purposes of English law, the suppression of the remedial flexibility afforded by that doctrine. The result is to leave mistaken assumptions doctrine in a very unsatisfactory state as, indeed, the Court of Appeal appears to concede in this case. Finally, the handling of matters of precedent and the impression the reader is given of the Court of Appeal's sense of the appropriate role of an appellate court in dealing with matters of this kind may appear troubling to some observers.

McCamus' criticisms concerning the handling of precedent and the suppression of remedial flexibility are forceful (see also *Lehman Brothers International (Europe) (In Administration) v Exotix Partners LLP* [2019] EWHC 2380 (Ch) at [19] where Hildyard J. stated: '*Great Peace* has its curiosities and is not without its critics (especially in other common law jurisdictions), although it is of course binding at this level in this jurisdiction'). We have already considered the issue of precedent above. Interestingly, the Court of Appeal itself appeared to concede the force of Denning LJ's reservations about the remedial inflexibility of the common-law doctrine (at [161]). The solution proposed by Lord Phillips was statutory reform along the lines of the Law Reform (Frustrated Contracts) Act 1943. However, as Professor Reynolds has observed (Reynolds, FMB, 'Reconsider the Contract Textbook' [2003] 199 LQR 177, 179): 'It is not clear why a statute (hardly an item of priority for law reformers) would do any better than a careful judicial interpretation of Lord Denning's doctrine, which is after all but a slight extension of lines of existing equity cases on misrepresentation and unconscionability in general'. Professor McCamus agrees ([2004] 40 Can Bus LJ 46, 81–2) stating that, 'it may be questioned whether the legislature is the ideal instrument for refashioning as subtle and complex an area of private law doctrine as the law of mistaken assumptions. It is at least a possible view of the division of responsibility between the legislature and the judiciary that the latter is, as a general matter, the appropriate instrument for the gradual refinement and modification of common law doctrine that is a hallmark of the common law system.'

9.6 *Non est factum*

In exceptional circumstances, a person who has signed a written document may be allowed a plea of *non est factum* ('it is not my deed'). A successful plea renders the contract void and unenforceable. This obviously has a significant impact on the rights of third parties, and for that reason, the courts have narrowly construed the plea. It must be shown that the person relying on the plea is permanently or temporarily unable, through no fault of his or her own, to have, without explanation, any real understanding of the document they are signing. It must also be shown that the document being signed is 'radically different' to the document which the person believed he was signing. The principles to be applied were set out by the House of Lords in *Saunders v Anglia Building Society*.

Saunders v Anglia Building Society (sub nom Gallie v Lee) [1971] AC 1004

Facts: Mrs Gallie, a widow aged 78, wished to enable her nephew to raise money on the security of her house. She knew that her nephew's business associate, Mr Lee, was to collaborate with the nephew in raising the money. Mrs Gallie was asked to sign a document assigning her interest in the house to Mr Lee. She had broken her reading glasses and so she asked Mr Lee what it was. He replied that it was a deed of gift to her nephew. She signed it, in that belief, and the nephew witnessed the signature, it being his plan for Mr Lee to raise money on the house and then repay it to him in instalments. Mr Lee subsequently mortgaged the house for £2,000 and used the money to pay off his debts. He defaulted on the mortgage instalments and the building society sought to obtain possession of the house. Mrs Gallie pleaded *non est factum* and sought a declaration that the assignment was void and that the title deeds should be delivered to her. At first instance, the judge found that the plea of *non est factum* had been established and granted the declaration requested. The Court of Appeal reversed the decision.

Held: The House of Lords dismissed the appeal. The transaction Mrs Gallie had entered into was not radically different in substance from that which she had intended.

Lord Reid: The plea of *non est factum* obviously applies when the person sought to be held liable did not in fact sign the document. But at least since the sixteenth century it has also been held to apply in certain cases so as to enable a person who in fact signed a document to say that it is not his deed. Obviously any such extension must be kept within narrow limits if it is not to shake the confidence of those who habitually and rightly rely on signatures when there is no obvious reason to doubt their validity. Originally this extension appears to have been made in favour of those who were unable to read owing to blindness or illiteracy and who therefore had to trust someone to tell them what they were signing. I think it must also apply in favour of those who are permanently or temporarily unable through no fault of their own to have without explanation any real understanding of the purport of a particular document, whether that be from defective education, illness or innate incapacity.

But that does not excuse them from taking such precautions as they reasonably can. The matter generally arises where an innocent third party has relied on a signed document in ignorance of the circumstances in which it was signed, and where he will suffer loss if the maker of the document is allowed to have it declared a nullity. So there must be a heavy burden of proof on the person who seeks to invoke this remedy. He must prove all the circumstances necessary to justify its being granted to him, and that necessarily involves his proving that he took all reasonable precautions in the circumstances. I do not say that the remedy can never be available to a man of full capacity. But that could only be in very exceptional circumstances: certainly not where his reason for not scrutinising the document before signing it was that he was too busy or too lazy. In general I do not think he can be heard to say that he signed in reliance on someone he trusted. But, particularly when he was led to believe that the document which he signed was not one which affected his legal rights, there may be cases where this plea can properly be applied in favour of a man of full capacity.

The plea cannot be available to anyone who was content to sign without taking the trouble to try to find out at least the general effect of the document. Many people do frequently sign documents put before them for signature by their solicitor or other trusted advisers without making any inquiry as to their purpose or effect. But the essence of the plea *non est factum* is that the person signing believed that the document he signed had one character or one effect whereas in fact its character or effect was quite different. He could not have such a belief unless he had taken steps or been given information which gave him some grounds for his belief. The amount of information he must have and the sufficiency of the particularity of his belief must depend on the circumstances of each case.

Further, the plea cannot be available to a person whose mistake was really a mistake as to the legal effect of the document, whether that was his own mistake or that of his adviser. That has always been the law and in this branch of the law at least I see no reason for any change ...Finally, there is the question as to what extent or in what way must there be a difference between that which in fact he signed and that which he believed he was signing. In an endeavour to keep the plea within bounds there have been many attempts to lay down a dividing line. But any dividing line suggested has been difficult to apply in practice and has sometimes led to unreasonable results. In particular I do not think that the modern division between the character and the contents of a document is at all satisfactory. Some of the older authorities suggest a more flexible test so that one can take all factors into consideration. There was a period when here, as elsewhere in the law, hard-and-fast dividing lines were sought, but I think that experience has shown that often they do not produce certainty but do produce unreasonable results.

I think that in the older authorities difference in practical result was more important than difference in legal character. If a man thinks he is signing a document which will cost him £10 and the actual document would cost him £1,000 it could not be right to deny him this remedy simply because the legal character of the two was the same. It is true that we must then deal with questions of degree, but that is a familiar task for the courts and I would not expect it to give rise to a flood of litigation.

There must, I think, be a radical difference between what he signed and what he thought he was signing – or one could use the words 'fundamental' or 'serious' or 'very substantial'. But what amounts to a radical difference will depend on all the circumstances. If he thinks he is giving property to A whereas the document gives it to B, the difference may often be of vital importance, but in the circumstances of the present case I do not think that it is. I think that it must be left to the courts to determine in each case in light of all the facts whether there was or was not a sufficiently great difference. The plea *non est factum* is in a sense illogical when applied to a case where the man in fact signed the deed. But it is none the worse for that if applied in a reasonable way.

I would dismiss this appeal.

Policy issues were very much at the fore in *Saunders*. The House of Lords had to balance the interests of Mrs Gallie against the interests of the building society that had advanced money to Mr Lee in reliance on Mrs Gallie's signature. Lord Reid opined that, in order to protect the interests of third parties, the law imposes a 'heavy burden of proof' on those seeking to rely on *non est factum*. It is now clear that the defence is not limited to the blind and illiterate. It can be invoked by anyone, although the defence will be lost if it can be shown that the claimant has been careless in signing the document (*United Dominions Trust Ltd v Western* [1976] QB 513 and *CF Asset Finance Ltd v Okonji* [2014] EWCA Civ 870). The House of Lords also rejected the traditional division between cases where the mistake was as to the 'character' of the document and cases where the mistake was as to its 'contents' (*Howatson v Webb* [1907] 1 Ch 537). Lord Reid suggested that the division had produced unreasonable results in the past. Their Lordships preferred a more flexible approach, asking whether there was a 'radical' ('fundamental', 'serious' or 'very substantial') difference between what was signed and what the claimant thought he was signing.

Additional reading

Atiyah, P.S., and Bennion, F., 'Mistake in the Construction of Contracts' (1961) 24 MLR 421.

Chandler, A., and Devenney, J., 'Mistake as to Identity and the Threads of Objectivity' (2004) 1 JOR 7.

Davies, P.S., 'Rectification versus Interpretation: The Nature and Scope of the Equitable Jurisdiction' (2016) 75 CLJ 62.

De Gregorio, M., 'Impossible Performance or Excused Performance? Common Mistake and Frustration After *Great Peace Shipping* (2005) 16 KCLJ 69.

Goodhart, A., 'Mistake as to Identify in the Law of Contract' (1941) LQR 228.

Phang, A., 'Common Mistake in English Law: The Proposed Merger of Common Law and Equity' (1989) 9 LS 291.

Simpson, A.W.B., 'Contracts for Cotton to Arrive: The Case of the Two Ships *Peerless*' (1989) 11 Cardozo L Rev 287.

Stone, J., 'The Limits of *non est factum* after *Gallie v Lee*' (1972) 88 LQR 190.

Treitel, G.H., 'Mistake in Contract' (1988) 104 LQR 501.

Chapter 10

Duress

Chapter contents

10.1 Introduction

This chapter is concerned with the law of duress, which governs situations where one party has been induced to enter into a contract as a result of illegitimate pressure of some kind. Historically, the law of duress was restricted to pressure in the form of threats of violence or some threats to goods. More recently, the courts have recognised that illegitimate pressure may include 'economic' threats (such as possibly a threat to break a contract). This has created new problems, however, due to the difficulty of ascertaining what constitutes illegitimate economic pressure. In commercial dealings, threats are often made in pre-contractual negotiations as a means of encouraging the other party to enter into the contract. For example, a party might say, 'If you do not enter into this contract we will not deal with you again in the future', or 'If you do not buy these goods from us we will not renew your credit facility next year'. These threats clearly impose pressure on the other party but it is not clear whether the pressure is illegitimate.

If it is shown that a contract has been entered into as a result of duress the contract is rendered voidable. It is often stated that there are two key elements to a duress claim. These were identified by Lord Scarman in *Universe Tankships v International Transport Workers Federation* [1983] 1 AC 366: '(1) pressure amounting to compulsion of the will of the victim; and (2) the illegitimacy of the pressure exerted'. The first element focuses on the complainant (who will be referred to as the claimant, even though s/he may on the facts of the case be the defendant): was the claimant's consent sufficiently truly given? The second element focuses on the defendant: did the defendant use illegitimate pressure to procure the contract?

The difficulty lies in establishing what constitutes a 'vitiation of consent' and what amounts to 'illegitimate pressure'. We will consider these issues in greater detail in our discussion of economic duress. However, it is also unclear whether or not exactly the same requirements apply across all of the different categories. For example, it is sometimes suggested that a more restrictive test of causation ought to apply in cases of economic duress. These issues will be considered in further detail below. First, we will consider the more straightforward categories of duress: duress of the person and duress of goods.

10.2 Duress of the person

Actual or threatened violence to the person is the most obvious form of duress. It is illustrated by the case of *Barton v Armstrong*.

Barton v Armstrong [1976] AC 104

Facts: Barton, the managing director of Landmark Corporation Ltd, executed a deed on behalf of the company agreeing to pay $320,000 to Armstrong, in order to remove him from the board of directors. Barton entered into this agreement partly for commercial reasons and partly because Armstrong had threatened to have him murdered if he did not. At first instance, the judge found that Armstrong had threatened Barton, but that the primary and predominant reason why Barton executed the deed was because of the commercial necessity of so acting. The Court of Appeal of New South Wales dismissed the appeal on the ground that Barton had failed to discharge the burden of proving that he would not have entered into the agreement but for the threats.

Held: The Privy Council, by a majority (Lord Wilberforce and Lord Simon of Glaisdale dissenting), allowed the appeal on the ground that Armstrong's threats were a reason why Barton had entered the agreement and it did not matter that Barton might have entered the agreement even if Armstrong had not made any threats. The deeds were executed under duress and were therefore void.

Lord Cross: Their Lordships turn now to consider the question of law which provoked a difference of opinion in the Court of Appeal Division. It is hardly surprising that there is no direct authority on the point, for if A threatens B with death if he does not execute some document and B, who takes A's threats seriously, executes the document it can be only in the most unusual circumstances that there can be any doubt whether the threats operated to induce him to execute the document. But this is a most unusual case and the findings of fact made below do undoubtedly raise the question whether it was necessary for Barton in order to obtain relief to establish that he would not have executed the deed in question but for the threats. In answering this question in favour of Barton, Jacobs JA relied both on a number of old common law authorities on the subject of 'duress' and also – by way of analogy – on later decisions in equity with regard to the avoidance of deeds on the ground of fraud. Their Lordships do not think that the common law authorities are of any real assistance for it seems most unlikely that the authors of the statements relied on had the sort of problem which has arisen here in mind at all. On the other hand they think that the conclusion to which Jacobs JA came was right and that it is supported by the equity decisions. The scope of common law duress was very limited and at a comparatively early date equity began to grant relief in cases where the disposition in question had been procured by the exercise of pressure which the Chancellor considered to be illegitimate – although it did not amount to common law duress. There was a parallel development in the field of dispositions induced by fraud. At common law the only remedy available to the man defrauded was an action for deceit but equity in the same period in which it was building up the doctrine of 'undue influence' came to entertain proceedings to set aside dispositions which had been obtained by fraud: see Holdsworth, *A History of English Law*, vol V (1924), pp 328–329. There is an obvious analogy between setting aside a disposition for duress or undue influence and setting it aside for fraud. In each case – to quote the words of Holmes J in *Fairbanks v Snow* (1887) 13 NE 596, 598 – 'the party has been subjected to an improper motive for action'. Again the similarity of the effect in law of metus and dolus in connection with dispositions of property is noted by Stair in his *Institutions of the Law of Scotland*, New edn. (1832), Book IV, title 40.25. Had Armstrong made a fraudulent misrepresentation to Barton for the purpose of inducing him to execute the deed of January 17, 1967, the answer to the problem which has arisen would have been clear. If it were established that Barton did not allow the representation to affect his judgment then he could not make it a ground for relief even though the representation was designed and known by Barton to be designed to affect his judgment. If on the other hand Barton relied on the misrepresentation Armstrong could not have defeated his claim to relief by showing that there were other more weighty causes which contributed to his decision to execute the deed, for in this field the court does not allow an examination into the relative importance of contributory causes. 'Once make out that there has been anything like deception, and no contract resting in any degree on that foundation can stand': *per* Lord Cranworth LJ in *Reynell v Sprye* (1852) 1 De GM & G 660, 708 – see also the other cases referred to in Cheshire and Fifoot's *Law of Contract*, 8th edn (1972), pp 250–251. Their Lordships think that the same rule should apply in cases of duress and that if Armstrong's threats were 'a' reason for Barton's executing the deed he is entitled to relief even though he might well have entered into the contract if Armstrong had uttered no threats to induce him to do so.

It remains to apply the law to the facts. What was the state of Barton's mind when he executed the deed is, of course, a question of fact and a question the answer to which depended largely on Barton's own evidence ... If Barton had to establish that he would not have made the agreement but for Armstrong's threats, then their Lordships would not dissent from the view that he had not made out his case. But no such onus lay on him. On the contrary it was for Armstrong to establish, if he could, that the threats which he was making and the unlawful pressure which he was exerting for the purpose of inducing Barton to sign the agreement and which Barton knew were being made and exerted for this purpose in fact contributed nothing to Barton's decision to sign. The judge has found that during the 10 days or so before the documents were executed Barton was in genuine fear that Armstrong was planning to have him killed if the agreement was not signed. His state of mind was described by the judge as one of 'very real mental torment' and he believed that his fears would be at end when once the documents were executed ... It is true that on the facts as their Lordships assume them to have been Armstrong's threats may have been unnecessary, but it would be unrealistic to hold that they played no part in making Barton decide to execute the documents. The proper inference to be drawn from the facts found is, their Lordships think, that though it may be that Barton would have executed the documents even if Armstrong had made no threats and exerted no unlawful pressure to induce him to do so the threats and unlawful pressure in fact contributed to his decision to sign the documents and to recommend their execution by Landmark and the other parties to them. It may be, of course, that Barton's fear of Armstrong had evaporated before he issued his writ in this action but Armstrong – understandably enough – expressly disclaimed reliance on the defence of delay on Barton's part in repudiating the deed.

In the result therefore the appeal should be allowed and a declaration made that the deeds in question were executed by Barton under duress and are void so far as concerns him. Their Lordships express no view as to what, if any, effect this may have on the rights or obligations *inter se* of the other parties to the deeds – and the order should include liberty to any of them to apply to the court of first instance for the determination of any questions which may arise between them in that regard.

Lord Wilberforce and Lord Simon of Glaisdale (dissenting): The reason why we do not agree with the majority decision is, briefly, that we regard the issues in this case as essentially issues of fact, issues moreover of a character particularly within the sphere of the trial judge bearing, as they do, upon motivation and credibility. On all important issues, clear findings have been made by Street J. and concurred in by the Court of Appeal either unanimously or by majority. Accepted rules of practice and, such rules apart, sound principle should, in our opinion, prevent a second court of appeal from reviewing them in the absence of some miscarriage of justice, or some manifest and important error of law or misdirection. In our view no such circumstance exists in this case ...

The action is one to set aside an apparently complete and valid agreement on the ground of duress. The basis of the plaintiff's claim is, thus, that though there was apparent consent there was no true consent to the agreement: that the agreement was not voluntary.

This involves consideration of what the law regards as voluntary, or its opposite; for in life, including the life of commerce and finance, many acts are done under pressure, sometimes overwhelming pressure, so that one can say that the actor had no choice but to act. Absence of choice in this sense does not negate consent in law: for this the pressure must be one of a kind which the law does not regard as legitimate. Thus, out of the various means by which consent may be obtained – advice, persuasion, influence, inducement, representation, commercial pressure – the law has come to select some which it will not accept as a reason for voluntary action: fraud, abuse of relation of confidence, undue influence, duress or coercion. In this the law, under the influence of equity, has developed from the old common law conception of duress – threat to life and limb – and it has arrived at the modern generalisation expressed by Holmes J – 'subjected to an improper motive for action': *Fairbanks v Snow*, 13 NE Reporter 596, 598.

In an action such as the present, then, the first step required of the plaintiff is to show that some illegitimate means of persuasion was used. That there were threats to Barton's life was found by the judge, though he did not accept Barton's evidence in important respects. We shall return to this point in detail later.

The next necessary step would be to establish the relationship between the illegitimate means used and the action taken. For the purposes of the present case (reserving our opinion as to cases which may arise in other contexts) we are prepared to accept, as the formula most favourable to the appellant, the test proposed by the majority, namely, that the illegitimate means used was a reason (not *the* reason, nor the *predominant* reason nor the *clinching* reason) why the complainant acted as he did. We are also prepared to accept that a decisive answer is not obtainable by asking the question whether the contract would have been made even if there had been no threats because, even if the answer to this question is affirmative, that does not prove that the contract was not made because of the threats.

Assuming therefore that what has to be decided is whether the illegitimate means used was a reason why the complainant acted as he did, it follows that his reason for acting must (unless the case is one of automatism which this is not) be a conscious reason so that the complainant can give evidence of it: 'I acted because I was forced'. If his evidence is honest and accepted, that will normally conclude the issue. If, moreover, he gives evidence, it is necessary for the court to evaluate his evidence by testing it against his credibility and his actions.

In this case Barton gave evidence – his was, for practical purposes, the only evidence supporting his case. The judge rejected it in important respects and accepted it in others. The issues as to Barton's motivations were issues purely of fact (that motivation is a question of fact hardly needs authority, but see *Cox v Smail* [1912] VLR 274 *per* Cussen J.): the findings as to motivation were largely, if not entirely, findings as to credibility. It would be difficult to find matters more peculiarly than these within the field of the trial judge who saw both contestants in the box, and who dealt carefully and at length with the credibility, or lack of credibility, of each of them ...

The judge's findings were also accepted, after careful examination by Taylor A-JA – '... the conclusion', he finds, 'that Barton entered into this agreement because he wanted to and from commercial motives only is, I think undoubtedly correct'. The appeal cannot succeed unless these most explicit findings are overturned. We consider that no basis exists for doing so.

In our opinion the case is far from being one in which a second appellate court should reverse findings made below and endorsed by a Court of Appeal. Respect for such findings – particularly where the issues depend so much upon credibility and an estimate of rival personalities – appears to us to be a central pillar of the appellate process. It is perhaps otiose, but also fair to the judges below, to say that we have no ground for thinking that the factual conclusions which they reached after so prolonged a search did not represent the truth of the situation – or at least the nearest approximation to truth that was attainable.

We would dismiss the appeal.

The Privy Council set out an extremely broad test for establishing causation in cases of duress (see also *Antonio v Antonio* [2010] EWHC 1199). In the words of Lord Cross, all Barton needed to show was that 'Armstrong's threats were "a" reason for Barton's executing the deed'. In their dissenting speech, Lord Wilberforce and Lord Simon of Glaisdale agreed with this test, noting that it was sufficient to show that the illegitimate means used 'was a reason (not *the* reason, nor the *predominant* reason nor the clinching reason) why the complainant acted as he did'. In other words it is not necessary to establish 'but for causation'. This means that a party who procures a contract by means of illegitimate pressure is not entitled to excuse his conduct by introducing evidence that the claimant had other reasons for entering into the contract.

A further point to note is that Lord Cross referred to the deeds as void, not voidable, as a consequence of the duress. With respect, it is rather difficult to know whether this is really what Lord Cross meant. Elsewhere in his speech he referred to the contract being 'set aside' as for fraud. Moreover, he recognised the potential availability of delay as a defence to repudiation of the deed, which is consistent with the view that duress renders a contract voidable. In addition, the minority appeared to take the view that the effect of duress was to render the contract voidable. Lord Wilberforce and Lord Simon of Glaisdale described the action as one to 'set aside an apparently complete and valid agreement on the ground of duress'. Nevertheless, it has sometimes been argued that Lord Cross was correct to state that the effect of duress is to render a contract void (see, for example, Lanham, D, 'Duress and void contracts' (1966) 29 MLR 615).

Such an argument rests on the assumption that there is no real consent in cases of duress. The claimant's will is 'overborne' and thus the claimant is unable to consent to entering into the contract. This view of the absence of consent in cases of duress has since been rejected (see *Universe Tankships Inc of Monrovia v International Transport Workers Federation, The Universe Sentinel* [1983] 1 AC 366;

Attorney General v R [2003] EMLR 24), and because of this the preferred view is that duress renders a contract voidable, not void (see also *Borrelli v Ting* [2010] UKPC 21 at [34], *per* Lord Saville).

10.3 Duress of goods

Historically it was believed that threats in relation to property were insufficient to constitute duress.

Skeate v Beale (1840) 11 Ad & El 983

Facts: A landlord took goods belonging to his tenant because of unpaid rent and threatened to sell them. The tenant agreed that if his landlord would withdraw a distress of £19 10 shillings in respect of rent, he would pay £3 7 shillings 6 pence at once and the remainder within one month. The tenant did not pay the remainder, claiming that he only owed £3 7 shillings 6 pence, and had entered into the agreement for the remainder in order to prevent the landlord from selling his goods. He sought to have the agreement set aside for duress.

Held: The court held that the agreement could not be set aside for duress and the tenant was required to pay the outstanding sum.

Denman CJ: We consider the law to be clear, and founded on good reason, that an agreement is not void because made under duress of goods. There is no distinction in this respect between a deed and an agreement not under seal; and, with regard to the former, the law is laid down in 2 Inst 483, and Sheppard's Touchstone, p 61, and the distinction pointed out between duress of, or menace to, the person, and duress of goods. The former is a constraining force, which not only takes away the free agency, but may leave no appeal to the law for a remedy: a man, therefore, is not bound by the agreement which he enters into under such circumstances: but the fear that goods can be taken or injured does not deprive any one of his free agency who possessed that ordinary degree of firmness that the law requires all to exert.

This perspective on duress appears rather outdated now. In particular, it seems unreasonable to expect those subject to duress of goods to appeal to the law for a remedy. In practice, it may be just as difficult to appeal to the law in cases of duress of goods as it is in cases of duress of the person. The requirement of bravery, expressed as the 'ordinary degree of firmness' by Denman CJ, is surely unreasonable in modern commercial practice. Furthermore, the decision in *Skeate v Beale* is difficult to reconcile with a line of cases, which permit the recovery of money, paid under duress of goods.

Maskell v Horner [1915] 3 KB 106

Facts: Maskell set up in business as a dealer in produce near Spitalfields Market. Horner, the owner of the market, demanded tolls from Maskell and threatened to seize his goods if he refused to pay. Maskell refused to pay and his goods were seized. He then consulted a solicitor and upon learning that other dealers outside the market paid tolls, he paid the tolls under protest for a period of 12 years. In another case, *Attorney-General v Horner (No 2)* [1913] 2 Ch 140, it was held that the tolls charged by Horner were unlawful, and Maskell sought to recover the money he had paid.

Held: The Court of Appeal held that the money could be recovered because it was paid to avoid the seizure of goods.

Lord Reading CJ: [T]he plaintiff asserts that he paid the money not voluntarily but under the pressure of actual or threatened seizure of his goods, and that he is therefore entitled to recover it as money had and received. If the facts proved support this assertion the plaintiff would, in my opinion, be entitled to succeed in this action.

If a person with knowledge of the facts pays money, which he is not in law bound to pay, and in circumstances implying that he is paying it voluntarily to close the transaction, he cannot recover it. Such a payment is in law like a gift, and the transaction cannot be reopened. If a person pays money, which he is not bound to pay, under the compulsion of urgent and pressing necessity or of seizure, actual or threatened, of his goods he can recover it as money had and received. The money is paid not under duress in the strict sense of the term, as that implies duress of person, but under the pressure of seizure or detention of goods which is analogous to that of duress. Payment under such pressure establishes that the payment is not made voluntarily to close the transaction (*per* Lord Abinger CB and *per* Parke B in *Atlee v Backhouse*). The payment is made for the purpose of averting a threatened evil and is made not with the intention of giving up a right but under immediate necessity and with the intention of preserving the right to dispute the legality of the demand (*per* Tindal CJ in *Valpy v Manley*). There are numerous instances in the books of successful claims in this form of action to recover money paid to relieve goods from seizure. Other familiar instances are cases such as *Parker v Great Western Ry Co*, where the money was paid to the railway company under protest in order to induce them to carry goods which they were refusing to carry except at rates in excess of those they were legally entitled to demand. These payments were made throughout a period of twelve months, always accompanied by the assertion that they were made under protest, and it was held that the plaintiffs were entitled to recover the excess payments as money had and received, on the ground that the payments were made under the compulsion of urgent and pressing necessity …

I come to the conclusion that the plaintiff never intended to depart, and never did depart, from the course taken by him at the commencement of the dispute. In order to preserve his right to recover, it is not, in my opinion, necessary that on every occasion there should be a refusal to pay by the plaintiff followed by seizure. It was not necessary to go through this form. The circumstances of these payments and the conduct of the plaintiff throughout the period of years satisfy me that he never made the payments voluntarily, that he never intended to give up his right to recover the sums paid, and that he only paid because he knew that a refusal to pay would be immediately followed by seizure of his goods, as in fact did happen whenever he disputed the defendant's right and refused to pay. The pressure of seizure was always present to his mind, and never ceased to operate upon it whenever demand for tolls was made. I am also satisfied that the circumstances of the payments and the conduct of the plaintiff were a sufficient indication to the defendant that the plaintiff did not intend to give up his right to recover. If any assertion or declaration of his intentions was necessary it was made to the defendant at the time and in the circumstances of the payments.

The decisions in *Skeate* and *Maskell* set up an unhappy distinction between cases in which a party *agrees* to pay a sum of money under duress of goods and cases in which a party actually *pays* a sum of money under duress of goods. In the former situation the contract remains enforceable; in the latter the complainant is entitled to recover the money paid. This distinction is unjustifiable and was rightly criticised by Professor Beatson ('Duress as a vitiating factor in contract' [1974] CLJ 97).

Indeed, the idea that duress of goods does not render a contract voidable is untenable and has been rejected in modern times.

Vantage Navigation Corporation v Suhail and Saud Bahwan Building Materials LLC, The 'Alev' [1989] 1 Lloyd's Rep 138

Facts: The plaintiffs' ship was chartered to carry a cargo of steel. The charterers were not financially sound and defaulted on their payments. Meanwhile, the property in the steel had passed from the charterers to the defendants. In negotiations, the plaintiffs told the defendants that unless they agreed to pay all outstanding sums owed by the charterers, they would not receive their cargo. The defendants agreed to this demand but later sought to have the agreement set aside for duress.

Held: The High Court held that the agreement could be avoided because it had been entered into under the illegitimate threat of economic duress and duress of goods.

Hobhouse J: The principle that agreements can be avoided if entered into under duress of goods or economic duress is now well established. See the sequence of modern authorities from *The Siboen v The Sibotre* [1976] 1 Lloyd's Rep 293 to *B & S Contracts v VG Publications* [1984] ICR 419 ...

In the present case it is clear that the agreement falls within the principles of economic duress and for that matter duress of goods. The plaintiffs did make a threat which was illegitimate, and, if it be relevant, they knew it to be illegitimate. They were under an obligation to carry the cargo to Mina Qaboos and deliver it there to the defendants. They had no right to refuse to do so or to assert any inconsistent right over the goods. They did refuse to carry the goods to Mina Qaboos and deliver them to the defendants unless the defendants met their demands. They did assert a dominion over the defendants' goods; they refused to recognize the defendants' right to have the goods. The consent of the defendants was overborne. There was a coercion of their will. They neither in law nor in fact entered into the agreement voluntarily.

... On the facts this is a clear example of the situation where the legal remedies are inadequate to meet the victim's legitimate commercial needs or to negate the compulsion operating upon him. There was no reasonable alternative open to the defendants.

The defendants have established their right to rely upon the defence of duress. The plaintiffs' claim must fail.

The judge concluded that the plaintiffs' action constituted both economic duress and duress of goods. Following the recognition of economic duress (see below), it was inevitable that duress of goods would also be recognised by the courts. The decision in *The Alev* merely confirms this.

10.4 Economic duress

Economic duress refers to illegitimate commercial pressure – for example, the threat of 'catastrophic' financial consequences. English law was slow to develop a doctrine of economic duress, largely due to the difficulty of distinguishing between legitimate and illegitimate commercial pressure. The first seeds of the doctrine were sown in the case of *D & C Builders v Rees* [1966] 2 QB 617. The plaintiff builders had undertaken work for the defendants and were owed nearly £500. The defendant knew that the plaintiffs were in financial difficulties and offered to pay them £300, telling them that they were unlikely to receive any more. The plaintiffs accepted the part-payment, but later sought to recover the balance of the debt. The Court of Appeal held that the plaintiffs could recover the balance of the debt because their consent to acceptance of part-payment was no true accord. Lord Denning MR said: 'The debtor's wife held the creditor to ransom. The creditor was in need of money to meet his own commitments and she knew it.'

The first recognition of economic duress as a basis for allowing a party to set aside a contract is probably to be found in the *obiter* comments of Kerr J in *Occidental Worldwide Investment Corp v Skibs A/S Avanti, The Siboen and The Sibotre* [1976] 1 Lloyd's Rep 293:

> [A]ssuming, as I think, that our law is open to further development in relation to contracts concluded under some form of compulsion not amounting to duress to the person, the Court must in

every case at least be satisfied that the consent of the other party was overborne by compulsion so as to deprive him of any *animus contrahendi.*

The High Court also recognised that a contract could be set aside for economic duress on the facts of North Ocean Shipping Co Ltd v Hyundai Construction Co Ltd.

***North Ocean Shipping Co Ltd v Hyundai Construction Co Ltd, The Atlantic Baron* [1979] QB 705**

Facts: The defendant shipbuilder agreed to build a tanker for the plaintiff shipowners. The contract stated a fixed price in US dollars with payment to be made in five instalments. After the plaintiffs had paid the first instalment, the dollar was devalued by 10% and the defendants threatened not to deliver the ship unless the remaining instalments were increased by 10%. The plaintiffs were advised that there was no legal ground on which the claim could be made and suggested that the matter should be referred to arbitration. The defendants declined this offer and insisted that the plaintiffs pay the increased amount. The plaintiffs were anxious that they might lose a very lucrative charter for the ship which they had arranged with Shell and so replied that although they were under no obligation to make increased payments, they would do so 'without prejudice' to their rights. The plaintiffs made the increased payments and the tanker was delivered in November 1974. In July 1975 the plaintiffs sought to recover the extra 10% they had paid. They claimed that they had delayed in their claim because they were concerned that the delivery of another ship that was being built for them might be affected.

Held: The High Court held that the defendant's threat to terminate the contract unless the plaintiffs increased their payments by 10% amounted to economic duress. The plaintiffs were not entitled to rescind the agreement, however, because they had affirmed it by making the final payments without protest and delaying their claim.

Mocatta J: I must next consider whether even if that agreement, varying the terms of the original shipbuilding contract of April 10, 1972, was made under a threat to break that original contract and the various increased instalments were made consequently under the varied agreement, the increased sums can be recovered as money had and received. [Counsel for the plaintiffs] submitted that they could be, provided they were involuntary payments and not made, albeit perhaps with some grumbling, to close the transaction.

Certainly this is the well-established position if payments are made, for example, to avoid the wrongful seizure of goods where there is no prior agreement to make such payments. The best known English case to this effect is probably *Maskell v Horner* [1915] 3 KB 106 ...

There are a number of well-known examples in the books of English cases where the payments made have been involuntary by reason of some wrongful threatened action or in-action in relation to goods and have subsequently been recovered, but where the issue has not been complicated by the payments having been made under a contract. Some of these cases have concerned threats to seize, seizure or wrongful detention of goods, *Maskell v Horner* being the best known modern example of the former two categories and *Astley v Reynolds* (1731) 2 Str 915 a good example of the latter category, where a pawnbroker refused to release plate when the plaintiff tendered the money lent and, on demand, more than the legal rate of interest, since without this the pawnbroker would not release the plaintiff's plate. The plaintiff recovered the excess, as having paid it under compulsion and it was held no answer that an alternative remedy might lie in trover.

[Counsel for the plaintiffs] referred me to other cases decided in this country bordering upon what he called economic duress as distinct from duress to goods. Thus in *Parker v Great Western Railway Co* (1844) 7 Man & G 253, approved in *Great Western Railway Co v Sutton* (1869) LR 4 HL 226, it was held that the railway was not entitled to differentiate adversely between charges on goods made against one carrier or packer using the railway and others. Excess charges payable by such persons were recovered. In advising the House of Lords in the latter case, Willes J said, at p 249:

> '... I have always understood that when a man pays more than he is bound to do by law for the performance of a duty which the law says is owed to him for nothing, or for less than he has paid, there is a compulsion or concussion in respect of which he is entitled to recover the excess by *condictio indebiti*, or action for money had and received. This is every day's practice as to excess freight'.

There has been considerable discussion in the books whether, if an agreement is made under duress of goods to pay a sum of money and there is some consideration for the agreement, the excess sum can be recovered. The authority for this suggested distinction is *Skeate v Beale* (1840) 11 Ad & El 983. It was there said by Lord Denman CJ that an agreement was not void because made under duress of goods, the distinction between that case and the cases of money paid to recover goods wrongfully seized being said to be obvious in that the agreement was not compulsorily but voluntarily entered into ... Kerr J in *Occidental Worldwide Investment Corp v Skibs A/S Avanti, The Siboen and The Sibotre* [1976] 1 Lloyd's Rep 293, 335, gave strong expression to the view that the suggested distinction based on *Skeate v Beale* would not be observed today ... I was referred to a number of cases decided overseas ... Perhaps their greatest importance, however, is the quotation in the first mentioned from the judgment of Isaacs J in *Smith v William Charlick Ltd* (1924) 34 CLR 38, 56 where he said:

> 'It is conceded that the only ground on which the promise to repay could be implied is 'compulsion. The payment is said by the respondent not to have been 'voluntary' but 'forced' from it within the contemplation of the law ... 'Compulsion' in relation to a payment of which refund is sought, and whether it is also variously called 'coercion', 'extortion', 'exaction' or 'force', includes every species of duress or conduct analogous to duress, actual or threatened, exerted by or on behalf of the payee and applied to the person or the property or any right of the person who pays ... Such compulsion is a legal wrong, and the law provides a remedy by raising a fictional promise to repay'.

These cases do not, however, expressly deal with the position arising when the threat or compulsion result in a new or varied contract. This was, or something very like it, however, the position in *Sundell's case*, 56 SR (NSW) 323 ... It would seem ... that the Australian courts would be prepared to allow the recovery of excess money paid, even under a new contract, as the result of a threat to break an earlier contract, since the threat or compulsion would be applied to the original contractual right of the party subject to the compulsion or economic duress. This also seems to be the view in the United States, where this was one of the grounds of decision in *King Construction Co v WM Smith Electric Co* (1961) 350 SW 2d 940. This view also accords with what was said in *D & C Builders v Rees* [1966] 2 QB 617, 625, *per* Lord Denning MR: 'No person can insist on a settlement procured by intimidation'. ...

Before proceeding further it may be useful to summarise the conclusions I have so far reached. First, I do not take the view that the recovery of money paid under duress other than to the person is necessarily limited to duress to goods falling within one of the categories hitherto established by the English cases. I would respectfully follow and adopt the broad statement of principle laid down by Isaacs J cited earlier and frequently quoted and applied in the Australian cases. Secondly, from this it follows that the compulsion may take the form of 'economic duress' if the necessary facts are proved. A threat to break a contract may amount to such 'economic duress'. Thirdly, if there has been such a form of duress leading to a contract for consideration, I think that contract is a voidable one which can be avoided and the excess money paid under it recovered.

I think the facts found in this case do establish that the agreement to increase the price by 10 per cent reached at the end of June 1973 was caused by what may be called 'economic duress'. The Yard were adamant in insisting on the increased price without having any legal justification for so doing and the owners realised that the Yard would not accept anything other than an unqualified agreement to the increase. The owners might have claimed damages in arbitration against the Yard with all the inherent unavoidable uncertainties of litigation, but in view of the position of the Yard *vis-à-vis* their relations with Shell it would be unreasonable to hold that this is the course they should have taken: see *Astley v Reynolds* (1731) 2 Str 915. The owners made a very reasonable offer of arbitration coupled with security for any award in the Yard's favour that might be made, but this was refused. They then made their agreement, which can truly I think be said to have been made under compulsion, by the telex of June 28 without prejudice to their rights. I do not consider the Yard's ignorance of the Shell charter material. It may well be that had they known of it they would have been even more exigent.

If I am right in the conclusion reached with some doubt earlier that there was consideration for the 10 per cent increase agreement reached at the end of June 1973, and it be right to regard this as having been reached under a kind of duress in the form of economic pressure, then what is said in *Chitty on Contracts*, 24th edn (1977), vol 1, para 442, p 207, to which both counsel referred me, is relevant, namely, that a contract entered into under duress is voidable and not void:

> '... consequently a person who has entered into a contract under duress, may either affirm or avoid such contract after the duress has ceased; and if he has so voluntarily acted under it with a full knowledge of all the circumstances he may be held bound on the ground of ratification, or if, after escaping from the duress, he takes no steps to set aside the transaction, he may be found to have affirmed it'. ...

I have already stated that no protest of any kind was made by the owners after their telex of June 28, 1973, before their claim in this arbitration on July 30, 1975, shortly after in July of that year the *Atlantic Baroness*, a sister ship of the *Atlantic Baron*, had been tendered, though, as I understand it, she was not accepted and arbitration proceedings in regard to her are in consequence taking place. There was therefore a delay between November 27, 1974, when the *Atlantic Baron* was delivered and July 30, 1975, before the owners put forward their claim.

The owners were, therefore, free from the duress on November 27, 1974, and took no action by way of protest or otherwise between their important telex of June 28, 1973, and their formal claim for the return of the excess 10 per cent paid of July 30, 1975, when they nominated their arbitrator. One cannot dismiss this delay as of no significance, though I would not consider it conclusive by itself. I do not attach any special importance to the lack of protest made at the time of the assignment, since the documents made no reference to the increased 10 per cent. However, by the time the *Atlantic Baron* was due for delivery in November 1974, market conditions had changed radically, as is found in paragraph 39 of the special case and the owners must have been aware of this. The special case finds in paragraph 40, as stated earlier, that the owners did not believe that if they made any protest in the protocol of delivery and acceptance that the Yard would have refused to deliver the vessel or the *Atlantic Baroness* and had no reason so to believe. [Counsel for the plaintiffs] naturally stressed that in the rather carefully expressed findings in paragraphs 39 to 44 of the special case, there is no finding that if at the time of the final payments the owners had withheld payment of the additional 10 per cent the Yard would not have delivered the vessel. However, after careful consideration, I have come to the conclusion that the important points here are that since there was no danger at this time in registering a protest, the final payments were made without any qualification and were followed by a delay until July 31, 1975, before the owners put forward their claim, the correct inference to draw, taking an objective view of the facts, is that the action and inaction of the owners can only be regarded as an affirmation of the variation in June 1973 of the terms of the original contract by the agreement to pay the additional 10 per cent. In reaching this conclusion I have not, of course, overlooked the findings in paragraph 45 of the special case, but I do not think that an intention on the part of the owners not to affirm the agreement for the extra payments not indicated to the Yard can avail them in the view of their overt acts.

The case is authority for the proposition that a threatened breach of contract can constitute economic duress. On the facts, the defendants' threat amounted to duress because it had no legal justification and it left the plaintiffs with no realistic alternative other than to pay the extra 10%. Mocatta J held that duress rendered the contract voidable, not void (cf. *Barton v Armstrong*). As such, the plaintiffs' right to have the contract set aside was subject to the usual bars to rescission, including delay and affirmation. On the facts, the plaintiff's delay of eight months was held to infer that the plaintiffs had affirmed the variation to the contract. This provides a stark reminder of the importance of bringing a claim as soon as practicably possible.

10.4.1 Requirements to establish a claim for economic duress

In the leading case on economic duress it was held that there are two elements that are required to establish duress.

***Universe Tankships Inc of Monrovia v International Transport Workers' Federation, The Universe Sentinel* [1983] 1 AC 366**

Facts: The plaintiffs' ship, the *Universe Sentinel*, was boycotted by the defendant union, the ITF. The plaintiffs paid $6,500 to ITF's welfare fund in order to get the ship released. They later sought to recover the money. ITF admitted economic duress but claimed that the threat had been made in furtherance of a trade dispute and so was protected by s 13 of the Trade Union Labour Relations Act 1974.

Held: The House of Lords (Lord Scarman and Lord Brandon dissenting) held that the action was not protected by the Trade Union and Labour Relations Act 1974 and therefore the money could be recovered.

Lord Diplock: My Lords, I turn to the second ground on which repayment of the $6,480 is claimed, which I will call the duress point. It is not disputed that the circumstances in which ITF demanded that the shipowners should enter into the special agreement and the typescript agreement and should pay the moneys of which the latter documents acknowledge receipt, amounted to economic duress upon the shipowners; that is to say, it is conceded that the financial consequences to the shipowners of the *Universe Sentinel* continuing to be rendered off-hire under her time charter to Texaco, while the blacking continued, were so catastrophic as to amount to a coercion of the shipowners' will which vitiated their consent to those agreements and to the payments made by them to ITF. This concession makes it unnecessary for your Lordships to use the instant appeal as the occasion for a general consideration of the developing law of economic duress as a ground for treating contracts as voidable and obtaining restitution of money paid under economic duress as money had and received to the plaintiffs' use. That economic duress may constitute a ground for such redress was recognised, albeit *obiter*, by the Privy Council in *Pao On v Lau Yiu Long* [1980] AC 614. The Board in that case referred with approval to two judgments at first instance in the commercial court which recognised that commercial pressure may constitute duress: one by Kerr J. in *Occidental Worldwide Investment Corp v Skibs A/S Avanti, The Siboen and The Sibotre*, the other by Mocatta J in *North Ocean Shipping Co Ltd v Hyundai Construction Co Ltd, The Atlantic Baron* [1979] QB 705, which traces the development of this branch of the law from its origin in the eighteenth and early nineteenth-century cases.

It is, however, in my view crucial to the decision of the instant appeal to identify the rationale of this development of the common law. It is not that the party seeking to avoid the contract which he has entered into with another party, or to recover money that he has paid to another party in response to a demand, did not know the nature or the precise terms of the contract at the time when he entered into it or did not understand the purpose for which the payment was demanded. The rationale is that his apparent consent was induced by pressure exercised upon him by that other party which the law does not regard as legitimate, with the consequence that the consent is treated in law as revocable unless approbated either expressly or by implication after the illegitimate pressure has ceased to operate on his mind. It is a rationale similar to that which underlies the avoidability of contracts entered into and the recovery of money exacted under colour of office, or under undue influence or in consequence of threats of physical duress.

Commercial pressure, in some degree, exists wherever one party to a commercial transaction is in a stronger bargaining position than the other party. It is not, however, in my view, necessary, nor would it be appropriate in the instant appeal, to enter into the general question of the kinds of circumstances, if any, in which commercial pressure, even though it amounts to a coercion of the will of a party in the weaker bargaining position, may be treated as legitimate and, accordingly, as not giving rise to any legal right of redress. In the instant appeal the economic duress complained of was exercised in the field of industrial relations to which very special considerations apply.

Lord Scarman (dissenting): It is, I think, already established law that economic pressure can in law amount to duress; and that duress, if proved, not only renders voidable a transaction into which a person has entered under its compulsion but is actionable as a tort, if it causes damage or loss: *Barton v Armstrong* [1976] AC 104 and *Pao On v Lau Yiu Long* [1980] AC 614. The authorities upon which these two cases were based reveal two elements in the wrong of duress: (1) pressure amounting to compulsion of the will of the victim; and (2) the illegitimacy of the pressure exerted. There must be pressure, the practical effect of which is compulsion or the absence of choice. Compulsion is variously described in the authorities as coercion or the vitiation of consent. The classic case of duress is, however, not the lack of will to submit but the victim's intentional submission arising from the realisation that there is no other practical choice open to him. This is the thread of principle which links the early law of duress (threat to life or limb) with later developments when the law came also to recognise as duress first the threat to property and now the threat to a man's business or trade. The development is well traced in *Goff and Jones, The Law of Restitution*, 2nd edn (1978), chapter 9.

The absence of choice can be proved in various ways, e.g. by protest, by the absence of independent advice, or by a declaration of intention to go to law to recover the money paid or the property transferred: see *Maskell v Horner* [1915] 3 KB 106. But none of these evidential matters goes to the essence of duress. The victim's silence will not assist the bully, if the lack of any practicable choice but to submit is proved. The present case is an excellent illustration. There was no protest at the time, but only a determination to do whatever was needed as rapidly as possible to release the ship. Yet nobody challenges the judge's finding that the owner acted under compulsion. He put it thus [1981] I.C.R. 129, 143:

> 'It was a matter of the most urgent commercial necessity that the plaintiffs should regain the use of their vessel. They were advised that their prospects of obtaining an injunction were minimal, the vessel would not have been released unless the payment was made, and they sought recovery of the money with sufficient speed once the duress had terminated'.

The real issue in the appeal is, therefore, as to the second element in the wrong duress: was the pressure applied by the ITF in the circumstances of this case one which the law recognises as legitimate? For, as Lord Wilberforce and Lord Simon of Glaisdale said in *Barton v Armstrong* [1976] AC 104, 121D: 'the pressure must be one of a kind which the law does not regard as legitimate'.

As the two noble and learned Lords remarked at p 121D, in life, including the life of commerce and finance, many acts are done 'under pressure, sometimes overwhelming pressure': but they are not necessarily done under duress. That depends on whether the circumstances are such that the law regards the pressure as legitimate.

In determining what is legitimate two matters may have to be considered. The first is as to the nature of the pressure. In many cases this will be decisive, though not in every case. And so the second question may have to be considered, namely, the nature of the demand which the pressure is applied to support.

The origin of the doctrine of duress in threats to life or limb, or to property, suggests strongly that the law regards the threat of unlawful action as illegitimate, whatever the demand. Duress can, of course, exist even if the threat is one of lawful action: whether it does so depends upon the nature of the demand. Blackmail is often a demand supported by a threat to do what is lawful, e.g. to report criminal conduct to the police. In many cases, therefore, 'What [one] has to justify is not the threat, but the demand . . .': see *per* Lord Atkin in *Thorne v Motor Trade Association* [1937] AC 797, 806.

The present is a case in which the nature of the demand determines whether the pressure threatened or applied, ie the blacking, was lawful or unlawful. If it was unlawful, it is conceded that the owner acted under duress and can recover. If it was lawful, it is conceded that there was no duress and the sum sought by the owner is irrecoverable. The lawfulness or otherwise of the demand depends upon whether it was an act done in contemplation or furtherance of a trade dispute. If it was, it would not be actionable in tort: section 13(1) of the Act. Although no question of tortious liability arises in this case and section 13(1) is not, therefore, directly in point, it is not possible, in my view, to say of acts which are protected by statute from suit in tort that they nevertheless can amount to duress. Parliament having enacted that such acts are not actionable in tort, it would be inconsistent with legislative policy to say that, when the remedy sought is not damages for tort but recovery of money paid, they become unlawful.

In order to determine whether the making of the demand was an act done in contemplation or furtherance of a trade dispute, it is necessary to refer to section 29 which sets out the statutory meaning of 'trade dispute'.

The issue therefore is reduced to the one question. Was the demand for contributions to the welfare fund connected with one or more of the matters specified in section 29 of the Act? It is common ground that unless the demand was connected with 'terms and conditions of employment' it was not within the section . . .

[His Lordship considered whether the demand related to the terms and conditions of employment]

I conclude that the demand for contributions related to the terms and conditions of employment on the ship, and, if it had been resisted by the owner, would have led to a trade dispute. Blacking the ship in support of the demand was, therefore, not actionable in tort. It was, accordingly, a legitimate exercise of pressure and did not constitute duress. The owner cannot recover the contributions. I would dismiss the appeal.

The minority in the House of Lords dissented on the issue of whether the ITF's conduct amounted to illegitimate pressure, but agreed that there are two requirements that must be satisfied if relief is to be available on the ground of duress:

(1) Compulsion of the will;
(2) Illegitimate pressure.

We will consider each of these requirements in turn.

10.4.1.1 Compulsion of the will

For duress to be established it must be shown that the claimant was put under pressure that amounted to a coercion of his will. In defining this requirement the courts have spoken of the pressure being such as to overbear the claimant's will so as to vitiate (cancel) his/her consent.

***Pao On v Lau Yiu Long* [1980] AC 614**

Facts: The plaintiffs agreed to sell a building under construction to the defendants. Payment for the building was to be made by an exchange of shares. To avoid depressing the market in the defendants' shares, the plaintiffs agreed to retain 60% of the shares for one year. To guarantee the plaintiffs against a fall in the share value the defendants entered a subsidiary agreement to buy back the shares at $2.5 per share after one year. The plaintiffs then realised that if the shares increased in value over $2.5 per share they would lose profit. Therefore, the plaintiffs threatened to terminate the main contract unless the subsidiary agreement was cancelled and replaced by an agreement to indemnify the plaintiffs against any reduction in the value of the shares below $2.5 per share. The defendants feared losing the building and so agreed to the plaintiffs' terms. The shares fell in value, and the plaintiffs brought a claim under the indemnity agreement to recover their loss.

Held: The Privy Council rejected the defendants' argument that the indemnity agreement should be set aside for duress because the defendant could not demonstrate that the commercial pressure had coerced their will so as to vitiate their consent.

Lord Scarman: Duress, whatever form it takes, is a coercion of the will so as to vitiate consent. Their Lordships agree with the observation of Kerr J in *Occidental Worldwide Investment Corp v Skibs A/S Avanti, The Siboen and The Sibotre* [1976] 1 Lloyd's Rep 293, 336 that in a contractual situation commercial pressure is not enough. There must be present some factor 'which could in law be regarded as a coercion of his will so as to vitiate his consent' ... In determining whether there was a coercion of will such that there was no true consent, it is material to inquire whether the person alleged to have been coerced did or did not protest; whether, at the time he was allegedly coerced into making the contract, he did or did not have an alternative course open to him such as an adequate legal remedy; whether he was independently advised; and whether after entering the contract he took steps to avoid it. All these matters are, as was recognised in *Maskell v Horner* [1915] 3 KB 106, relevant in determining whether he acted voluntarily or not.

In the present case there is unanimity amongst the judges below that there was no coercion of the first defendant's will. In the Court of Appeal the trial judge's finding (already quoted) that the first defendant considered the matter thoroughly, chose to avoid litigation, and formed the opinion that the risk in giving the guarantee was more apparent than real was upheld. In short, there was commercial pressure, but no coercion. Even if this Board was disposed, which it is not, to take a different view, it would not substitute its opinion for that of the judges below on this question of fact.

... Recently two English judges have recognised that commercial pressure may constitute duress the pressure of which can render a contract voidable: Kerr J in *Occidental Worldwide Investment Corp v Skibs A/S Avanti, The Siboen and The Sibotre* [1976] 1 Lloyd's Rep 293 and Mocatta J in *North Ocean Shipping Co Ltd v Hyundai Construction Co Ltd, The Atlantic Baron* [1979] QB 705. Both stressed that the pressure must be such that the victim's consent to the contract was not a voluntary act on his part. In their Lordships' view, there is nothing contrary to principle in recognising economic duress as a factor which may render a contract voidable, provided always that the basis of such recognition is that it must amount to a coercion of will, which vitiates consent. It must be shown that the payment made or the contract entered into was not a voluntary act.

The test prescribed by Lord Scarman requires the pressure to 'amount to a coercion of the will, which vitiates consent'. This test has caused a certain degree of controversy because it suggests that there has to be a total lack of consent (see Atiyah, 'Economic duress and the "overborne will"' (1982) 98 LQR 197; Beatson, *The Use and Abuse of Unjust Enrichment*, 1991, pp 113–117, Oxford: Clarendon). But, as Professor Enonchong has shown (Enonchong, *Duress, Undue Influence and Unconscionable Dealing*, 3rd edn, 2009, London: Sweet & Maxwell, p 11) this is to misunderstand the meaning of 'vitiation' of consent. Vitiation does not mean that the consent is negatived or destroyed; the claimant does not lose his will to act and become an automaton. Rather, his consent is tainted or 'deflected' (*Huyton SA v Peter Cremer GmbH & Co* [1999] 1 Lloyd's Rep 620, 638, *per* Mance J). The claimant is perfectly aware of what he is doing but, because of the pressure exerted on him, he feels that he has no 'real' choice. His will is 'redirected'. Lord Scarman helpfully explained the meaning of this in *Universe Tankships v ITF* (see above):

> Compulsion is variously described in the authorities as coercion or the vitiation of consent. The classic case of duress is, however, not the lack of will to submit but the victim's intentional submission arising from the realisation that there is no other practical choice open to him.

There should be 'no other practical choice open' to the claimant. Pressure will only amount to duress if it caused the victim to enter into the contract. The court must ask the question: 'Did the victim have any "practical" or "reasonable" alternative?'

B & S Contracts and Design Ltd v Victor Green Publications Ltd [1984] ICR 419

Facts: The plaintiffs agreed to erect stands for the defendants at Olympia. They planned to use employees who were to be made redundant after completion of the work. The employees refused to erect the stands unless their demand for £9,000 severance pay (to which they were not entitled) was met. The plaintiffs agreed to pay the employees £4,500 and told the defendants that they would have to terminate the contract unless the defendants agreed to pay the remaining £4,500, in addition to the contract price. If the stands were not erected the defendants faced disastrous financial consequences so they agreed to pay the employees and the contract was performed. The defendants later sought to deduct the £4,500 from the contract price and the plaintiffs sued them for breach of contract. At first instance, the trial judge dismissed the plaintiff's claim on the ground that the money had been paid under duress.

Held: The Court of Appeal dismissed the appeal.

Griffiths LJ: The facts of this case appear to me to be as follows. The plaintiffs intended to break their contract ... by allowing their workforce to walk off the job in circumstances in which they could not possibly replace it with another workforce. The defendants offered to advance the sum of £4,500 on the contract price, which would have enabled the plaintiffs to pay the men a sufficient extra sum of money to induce them to remain on the job. The plaintiffs refused this sum of money. There is no question that they refused to pay as a matter of principle. They refused to pay because they did not want to reduce the sum they would receive for the contract. They said to the defendants, 'If you will give us £4,500 we will complete the contract'. The defendants, faced with this demand, were in an impossible position. If they refused to hand over the sum of £4,500 they would not be able to erect the stands in this part of the exhibition, which would have clearly caused grave damage to their reputation and I would have thought might have exposed them to very heavy claims from the exhibitors who had leased space from them and hoped to use those stands in the ensuing exhibition. They seem to me to have been placed in the position envisaged by Lord Scarman in the Privy Council decision in *Pao On v Lau Yiu Long* [1980] AC 614, in which they were faced with no alternative course of action but to pay the sum demanded of them. It was submitted to us that there was no overt demand, but it was implicit in negotiations between the parties that the plaintiffs were putting the defendants into a corner and it was quite apparent to the defendants, by reason of the plaintiffs' conduct, that unless they handed over £4,500 the plaintiffs would walk off the job. This is, in my view, a situation in which the judge was fully entitled to find in the circumstances of this case that there was duress. As the defendants' director said, he was over a barrel, he had no alternative but to pay; he had no chance of going to any other source of labour to erect the stands ... fails.

Kerr LJ: I ... bear in mind that a threat to break a contract unless money is paid by the other party can, but by no means always will, constitute duress. It appears from the authorities that it will only constitute duress if the consequences of a refusal would be serious and immediate so that there is no reasonable

> alternative open, such as by legal redress, obtaining an injunction, etc ... [T]here was no other practical choice open to the defendants in the present case, and accordingly I agree that this is a case where money has been paid under duress, which was accordingly recoverable by the defendants provided they acted promptly as they did, and which they have recovered by deducting it from the contract price. In these circumstances the plaintiffs' claim for this additional sum must fail.

On the facts of the case it was not strictly true that the defendants had no alternative other than to pay the £4,500. They could have refused to pay and brought a claim for breach of contract. But this would not have been a 'reasonable' or 'practical' alternative because failure to erect the stands would have caused grave damage to the plaintiffs' reputation and would have exposed them to heavy claims from the exhibitors who had already agreed to lease the stands from the plaintiffs at the trade exhibition.

10.4.1.1.1 The test of causation

It was noted earlier in the chapter that the test of causation may differ depending on the type of duress under consideration. *Barton v Armstrong* confirmed that the test applicable in cases of duress of the person was that the pressure should be '*a* reason (not *the* reason, nor the *predominant* reason nor the *clinching* reason) why the complainant acted as he did'. This test set a very low threshold for causation and subsequent cases have suggested that the bar may be raised in cases of economic duress. Lord Goff made the following comments in *Dimskal Shipping Co SA v International Transport Workers Federation, The Evia Luck* [1992] 2 AC 152:

> We are here concerned with a case of economic duress. It was at one time thought that, at common law, the only form of duress which would entitle a party to avoid a contract on that ground was duress of the person. The origin for this view lay in the decision of the Court of Exchequer in *Skeate v Beale* (1840) 11 Ad & El 983. However, since the decisions of Kerr J in *Occidental Worldwide Investment Corp v Skibs A/S Avanti, The Siboen and The Sibotre* [1976] 1 Lloyd's Rep 293, of Mocatta J in *North Ocean Shipping Co Ltd v Hyundai Construction Co Ltd, The Atlantic Baron* [1979] QB 705, and of the Judicial Committee of the Privy Council in *Pao On v Lau Yiu Long* [1980] AC 614, that limitation has been discarded; and it is now accepted that economic pressure may be sufficient to amount to duress for this purpose, provided at least that the economic pressure may be characterised as illegitimate and has constituted a significant cause inducing the plaintiff to enter into the relevant contract (see *Barton v Armstrong* [1976] AC 104, 121, *per* Lord Wilberforce and Lord Simon of Glaisdale (referred to with approval in *Pao On v Lau Yiu Long* [1980] AC 614, 635, *per* Lord Scarman) and *Crescendo Management Pty Ltd v Westpac Banking Corporation* (1988) 19 NSWLR 40, 46, *per* McHugh JA).

Lord Goff inserted the word 'significant' before 'cause'. This led Mance J to conclude in *Huyton SA v Peter Cremer GmbH & Co* [1999] 1 Lloyd's Rep 620, that there is a difference between the test advocated for duress to the person in *Barton v Armstrong*, and that advocated for economic duress in *Dimskal Shipping*:

> I start with the requirement that the illegitimate pressure must, in cases of economic duress, constitute 'a significant cause' (cf. *per* Lord Goff in *The Evia Luck*, at p 120; p 165, cited above). This is contrasted in Goff and Jones on *The Law of Restitution* (4th edn) p 251, footnote 59 with the lesser requirement that it should be 'a' reason which applies in the context of duress to the person. The relevant authority in the latter context is *Barton v Armstrong* [1976] AC 104 (a case of threats to kill) ...

The use of the phrase 'a significant cause' by Lord Goff in *The Evia Luck*, supported by the weighty observation in the footnote in Goff & Jones, suggests that this relaxed view of causation in the special context of duress to the person cannot prevail in the less serious context of economic duress. The minimum basic test of subjective causation in economic duress ought, it appears to me, to be a 'but for' test. The illegitimate pressure must have been such as actually caused the making of the agreement, in the sense that it would not otherwise have been made either at all or, at least, in the terms in which it was made. In that sense, the pressure must have been decisive or clinching.

The 'significant' cause test has also been adopted in some subsequent decisions (*DSND Subsea v Petroleum Geo-Services* [2000] BLR 530; *Carillion Construction Ltd v Felix (UK) Ltd* [2001] BLR 1). It has been subjected to academic criticism, however, in terms of its basis in both authority and principle:

Enonchong, N, *Duress, Undue Influence and Unconscionable Dealing*, 3rd edn, 2019, London: Sweet & Maxwell, pp 40–41

Authority. Although Mance J's test relies of Lord Goff's statement in *Dimskal Shipping*, it is not clear that Lord Goff intended any difference between his test and that laid down in *Barton v Armstrong*. On the contrary, there is reason for suspecting that, although his language is different, Lord Goff intended no such difference. This is because the three cases cited by Lord Goff in support of his view that the pressure must be 'a significant cause' are all in line with the test in *Barton v Armstrong*. The first is *Barton* itself and Lord Goff refers specifically to the judgment of Lord Wilberforce and Lord Simon of Glaisdale and in particular to the page where they set out the test that the pressure must be 'a reason (not *the* reason, nor the *predominant* reason nor the *clinching* reason)'. Surely if Lord Goff had intended to state a different test (for economic duress) he would have said so clearly rather than rely for support on the same judgment with which he seeks to differ. The second case cited by Lord Goff is *Pao On v Lau Yiu Long* and he refers to the page where the Board expressly approved of the page where the *Barton* test is stated in the judgment of Lord Wilberforce and Lord Simon of Glaisdale in *Barton v Armstrong*. Finally, Lord Goff's reliance on the judgment of McHugh JA in *Crescendo Management Pty Ltd v Westpac Banking Corporation* shows very clearly that he did not intend to depart from the test in *Barton v Armstrong*. For McHugh JA, in a case concerned with economic duress, clearly states, in the page referred to by Lord Goff, that it is not necessary to establish that the pressure was 'the sole reason' for entering into the contract: 'It is sufficient that the illegitimate pressure was *one of the reasons* for the person entering into the agreement.' If Lord Goff intended to state a different test he may still have referred to these judgments but only to contrast them with the different test that he was enunciating. Yet he made no contrasting statement at all. It is likely that, if he intended to depart from all these cases, Lord Goff would have done so expressly with an explanation of the reasons for selecting a different test.

Moreover in *Dorimex SRL v Visage Imports Ltd*, a case of economic duress, the *Barton* test was applied at first instance where the judge held that the agreement was vitiated by economic duress because the pressure 'was one of several causes' of the agreement. On appeal the Court of Appeal did not criticise the judge.

Principle. Quite apart from authority, it is doubtful whether as a matter of principle there should be different tests of causation for different types of duress. The only reason advanced by Mance J for the view that a different test should apply in the context of economic duress is that economic pressure is less serious than death threats or other threats to the person. He stated that the *Barton* 'relaxed view of causation in the special context of duress to the person cannot prevail in the less serious context of economic duress'. It is true that threats of violence to the person are more serious than threats of economic harm. But it is not clear how it follows from this that the test for whether the threat caused a person to act in the way he did should be different. There seems no sound basis for saying that the test for causation should differ according to the type of duress, with duress to the person requiring a more relaxed test than economic duress.

> Such a view smacks of the once received notion that only a threat to the person was sufficient to amount to duress. That notion has now been discredited and abandoned. It should not be allowed to re-appear in a modified form though the idea that a different test of causation should apply in the case of economic duress so as to make it more difficult to establish economic duress than duress to the person. If it is believed that the test laid down in *Barton v Armstrong* is too relaxed and there is a need to raise the hurdle, then the question should be whether a new test is desirable. But it should be one that applies to all types of duress. Once the law has drawn the line between legitimate and illegitimate pressure, it should not discriminate further by making distinctions between different categories of illegitimate pressure when considering the question of causation. The question of causation should not be confused with the evidential question of what the coercive effect of a particular type of pressure is likely to be. It is recognised that a court is more likely to accept that a particular type of pressure caused the victim to act the way he did because the type of pressure is generally known to have such a coercive effect. For example, a court will recognise that a threat to kill the victim is likely to have a more coercive effect than a threat to refuse to repay a loan of a small amount. However, that is an evidential matter rather than a satisfactory basis for saying that the test of causation should be different according to whether the threat is to kill or to refuse to pay a small debt.

Professor Enonchong's argument from principle is compelling. The nature of the pressure is relevant to the evidential question (whether the pressure affected the claimant's will) in much the same way as the claimant's subjective circumstances are relevant, such as her age, financial position, business experience and access to legal advice (see *Daniel v Drew* [2005] EWCA Civ 507 and *Hopkins v Hopkins* [2015] EWHC 812). The causation question does not concern such matters, however, and the test to be applied should arguably be identical, regardless of the form of duress.

With respect, Professor Enonchong's criticisms on the point of authority are less convincing. Mance J's interpretation of Lord Goff in *Dimskal Shipping* was supported by a footnote in Goff & Jones, *The Law of Restitution*, 4th edn, London: Sweet & Maxwell. Lord Goff was the co-author of that work and it is to be expected that it provides the most reliable commentary on the meaning of his Lordship's speech in *Dimskal Shipping*.

10.4.1.2 Illegitimate pressure

The second element of a claim for duress is the illegitimacy of the pressure used. For some people, the word 'illegitimate' has associations with wrongdoing, but in the context of duress, illegitimacy is not necessarily synonymous with wrongdoing. Illegitimate pressure may include a threatened breach of contract (*North Ocean Shipping Co Ltd v Hyundai Construction Co Ltd, The Atlantic Baron* [1979] QB 705) and even a threatened lawful act (*CTN Cash and Carry v Gallaher* [1994] 4 All ER 714). Perhaps a useful question to ask in every situation is: Does the behaviour go beyond what a reasonable person would regard as acceptable in all the circumstances?

In *Universe Tankships Inc of Monrovia v International Transport Workers' Federation, The Universe Sentinel* [1983] 1 AC 366, the House of Lords focused its attention on whether the industrial action was unlawful under English law. Their Lordships concluded that it was and on this basis held that the contract could be set aside for duress. This approach was followed in *Dimskal Fishing v International Transport Workers' Federation, The Evia Luck* [1980] AC 614. Again, the case involved industrial action by the ITF. This time the action was lawful in Sweden where it took place, but unlawful in England. The House of Lords held (Lord Templemann dissenting) that the law to be applied in deciding the issue of legitimacy was English law and on this basis the contracts could be set aside for duress. Lord Goff made the following observations:

> If a person enters into … a contract, he has for most purposes to accept the regime of the proper law of the contract; and if under that regime a particular form of conduct constitutes duress, or for that matter undue influence, rendering the contact voidable wherever the relevant conduct occurs, he has in my opinion to accept the consequences of his conduct under that system of law. He should not assume that, simply because his conduct is lawful in the place overseas where it is performed, it cannot for that reason render English contract voidable for duress.

It is clear that a threatened breach of contract can also constitute illegitimate pressure, although it may be harder for the victim to show that the pressure amounted to a coercion of his will.

Atlas Express Ltd v Kafco (Importers and Distributors) Ltd [1989] 1 QB 833

Facts: The plaintiffs, a national road carrier, agreed with the defendants, a basket-ware importing company, to deliver their baskets to branches of Woolworths. The original contract price for delivery was £110 per trailer of baskets. After the first load had been delivered, the plaintiffs told the defendants that they would not carry any further loads unless the defendants agreed to increase the price to a minimum of £440 per trailer. The defendants relied heavily on the contract with Woolworths, and reasonably believed that it would be impossible to make alternative arrangements for carriage, so felt compelled to sign the new agreement. Later, the defendants refused to pay the increased rate and the plaintiffs brought a claim for breach of contract.

Held: The court held that the pressure exerted on the defendants amounted to economic duress. Furthermore, since the plaintiffs were already contractually bound to deliver the defendant's goods, there was no consideration for the new agreement. The defendants were not liable to pay the minimum charge of £440 per trailer.

Tucker J: The issue which I have to determine is whether the defendants are bound by the agreement signed on their behalf on 18 November 1986. The defendants contend that they are not bound, for two reasons: first because the agreement was signed under duress; second because there was no consideration for it.

The first question raises a particularly interesting point of law – whether economic duress is a concept known to English law. Economic duress must be distinguished from commercial pressure, which on any view is not sufficient to vitiate consent. The borderline between the two may in some cases be indistinct. But the authors of *Chitty on Contracts* and of *Goff and Jones, The Law of Restitution* appear to recognise that in appropriate cases economic duress may afford a defence, and in my judgment it does. It is clear to me that in a number of English cases judges have acknowledged the existence of this concept.

[The judge considered the leading cases on economic duress.]

Reverting to the case before me, I find that the defendants' apparent consent to the agreement was induced by pressure which was illegitimate and I find that it was not approbated. In my judgment that pressure can properly be described as economic duress, which is a concept recognised by English law, and which in the circumstances of the present case vitiates the defendants' apparent consent to the agreement.

In any event, I find that there was no consideration for the new agreement. The plaintiffs were already obliged to deliver the defendants' goods at the rates agreed under the terms of the original agreement. There was no consideration for the increased minimum charge of £440 per trailer.

The judge concluded that a threatened breach of contract can amount to illegitimate pressure. This finding is supported by the *dicta* of Lord Scarman in *Pao On v Lau Yiu Long*, where it was held that threatened breach of contract could, in principle, amount to economic duress. On the facts of *Pao On*, however, it was held that there was no economic duress because the threat did not amount to a coercion of the victim's will. This highlights the complex relationship between the two elements of a duress claim. In principle, the two elements are independent, but in practice the more illegitimate the pressure, the easier it may be to demonstrate coercion of the will. In *Atlas Express*, the court accepted the defendants' argument that the threatened breach of contract had coerced the defendants' will, because it left them with 'no practical alternative'. The contract with Woolworths was extremely valuable to the defendants and it could have been lost had the plaintiffs carried through their threat to cease delivering the defendants' baskets.

It is interesting to note the alternative ground relied upon by the defendants to refuse the plaintiffs' claim. The defendants argued that there was no consideration for their promise to pay £440 per trailer (see *Stilk v Myrick* (1809) 2 Camp 317; 170 ER 1168). Tucker J agreed, holding that the plaintiffs were already contractually obliged to deliver the defendants' goods and had provided no consideration for the increased charge (a similar argument was unsuccessfully made in *North Ocean Shipping Co Ltd v Hyundai Construction Co Ltd, The Atlantic Baron* [1979] QB 705). The scope for making this argument in the future is likely to be seriously diminished following the decision of the Court of Appeal in *Williams v Roffey Bros & Nicholls (Contractors) Ltd* [1991] 1 QB 1 (see Chapter 3). The recognition that the 'practical benefit' of obtaining the timely performance of an existing obligation is sufficient to form consideration for a new promise means that consideration is likely to be found in most duress situations. The claimant will probably have made the additional payment in order to avoid undesirable consequences. In most cases, it is likely that the avoidance of those consequences will be regarded as a 'practical benefit' and therefore good consideration. As a result, the doctrine of duress will become increasingly important in dealing with this type of situation (see, for example, *South Caribbean Trading Ltd v Trañgura Beheer BV* [2004] EWHC 2676 (Comm); [2005] 1 Lloyd's Rep 128).

So far, all the examples of duress that we have considered have involved conduct that is, in some respects, a breach of the law. The conduct might be a crime, a tort, or a breach of conduct. But can lawful actions constitute illegitimate pressure? Lord Scarman suggested that they could in *Universe Tankships Inc of Monrovia v International Transport Workers' Federation ('The Universe Sentinel')* [1983] 1 AC 366:

> The origin of the doctrine of duress in threats to life or limb, or to property, suggests strongly that the law regards the threat of unlawful action as illegitimate, whatever the demand. Duress can, of course, exist even if the threat is one of lawful action: whether it does so depends upon the nature of the demand. Blackmail is often a demand supported by a threat to do what is lawful, e.g. to report criminal conduct to the police. In many cases, therefore, 'What [one] has to justify is not the threat, but the demand ....': see *per* Lord Atkin in *Thorne v Motor Trade Association* [1937] AC 797, 806.

This was followed by the Court of Appeal in *CTN Cash and Carry v Gallaher*.

CTN Cash and Carry v Gallaher [1994] 4 All ER 714

Facts: The plaintiff company, which ran a cash and carry warehouse, agreed to purchase a consignment of cigarettes from the defendants. The defendants mistakenly delivered the cigarettes to the wrong warehouse. Before they could be redelivered the cigarettes were stolen. The defendants invoiced the plaintiffs for the stolen cigarettes maintaining that the cigarettes were at the plaintiffs' risk at the time they were taken. In later negotiations the defendants threatened to withdraw the plaintiffs' credit facility if it did not pay. The defendants were perfectly entitled to do this and it did not amount to an unlawful act. Eventually the plaintiffs agreed to pay for the cigarettes, but when they discovered the goods had not been at their risk they claimed repayment on the grounds that the money had been paid because of economic duress. At first instance the plaintiffs' claim was dismissed.

Held: The Court of Appeal dismissed the plaintiffs' appeal, holding that there had been no economic duress.

Steyn LJ: A ... characteristic of the case is that the defendants were in law entitled to refuse to enter into any future contracts with the plaintiffs for any reason whatever or for no reason at all. Such a decision not to deal with the plaintiffs would have been financially damaging to the defendants, but it would have been lawful. *A fortiori*, it was lawful for the defendants, for any reason or for no reason, to insist that they would no longer grant credit to the plaintiffs. The defendants' demand for payment of the invoice, coupled with the threat to withdraw credit, was neither a breach of contract nor a tort.

A .,, critically important characteristic of the case is the fact that the defendants bona fide thought that the goods were at the risk of the plaintiffs and that the plaintiffs owed the defendants the sum in question. The defendants exerted commercial pressure on the plaintiffs in order to obtain payment of a sum which they bona fide considered due to them. The defendants' motive in threatening withdrawal of credit facilities was commercial self-interest in obtaining a sum that they considered due to them ...

I ... readily accept that the fact that the defendants have used lawful means does not by itself remove the case from the scope of the doctrine of economic duress. Professor Birks, in *An Introduction to the Law of Restitution* (1989) p 177, lucidly explains:

> 'Can lawful pressures also count? This is a difficult question, because, if the answer is that they can, the only viable basis for discriminating between acceptable and unacceptable pressures is not positive law but social morality. In other words, the judges must say what pressures (though lawful outside the restitutionary context) are improper as contrary to prevailing standards. That makes the judges, not the law or the legislature, the arbiters of social evaluation. On the other hand, if the answer is that lawful pressures are always exempt, those who devise outrageous but technically lawful means of compulsion must always escape restitution until the legislature declares the abuse unlawful. It is tolerably clear that, at least where they can be confident of a general consensus in favour of their evaluation, the courts are willing to apply a standard of impropriety rather than technical unlawfulness'.

And there are a number of cases where English courts have accepted that a threat may be illegitimate when coupled with a demand for payment even if the threat is one of lawful action (see *Thorne v Motor Trade Association* [1937] 3 All ER 157 at 160–161, [1937] AC 797 at 806–807, *Mutual Finance Ltd v John Wetton & Sons Ltd* [1937] 2 All ER 657, [1937] 2 KB 389 and *Universe Tankships Inc of Monrovia v International Transport Workers' Federation* [1982] 2 All ER 67 at 76, 89, [1983] 1 AC 366 at 384, 401). On the other hand, Goff and Jones, *Law of Restitution* (3rd edn, 1986) p 240 observed that English courts have wisely not accepted any general principle that a threat not to contract with another, except on certain terms, may amount to duress.

We are being asked to extend the categories of duress of which the law will take cognisance. That is not necessarily objectionable, but it seems to me that an extension capable of covering the present case, involving 'lawful act duress' in a commercial context in pursuit of a *bona fide* claim, would be a radical one with far-reaching implications. It would introduce a substantial and undesirable element of uncertainty in the commercial bargaining process. Moreover, it will often enable *bona fide* settled accounts to be reopened when parties to commercial dealings fall out. The aim of our commercial law ought to be to encourage fair dealing between parties. But it is a mistake for the law to set its sights too highly when the critical inquiry is not whether the conduct is lawful but whether it is morally or socially unacceptable. That is the inquiry in which we are engaged. In my view there are policy considerations which militate against ruling that the defendants obtained payment of the disputed invoice by duress.

Outside the field of protected relationships, and in a purely commercial context, it might be a relatively rare case in which 'lawful act duress' can be established. And it might be particularly difficult to establish duress if the defendant bona fide considered that his demand was valid. In this complex and changing branch of the law I deliberately refrain from saying 'never'. But as the law stands, I am satisfied that the defendants' conduct in this case did not amount to duress.

It is an unattractive result, inasmuch as the defendants are allowed to retain a sum which at the trial they became aware was not in truth due to them. But in my view the law compels the result.

For these reasons, I would dismiss the appeal.

The Court of Appeal held that a refusal to contract does not constitute illegitimate pressure. Once more we are reminded that there is no duty of good faith in the negotiation of a contract. Steyn LJ did accept, however, that a threat to commit a lawful act can, in appropriate circumstances, amount to economic duress. His Lordship thought that such a concession was essential, in order to prevent 'those who devise outrageous but technically lawful means of compulsion' from escaping the doctrine of duress.

In assessing the legitimacy of the threat, the court must consider both the nature of the pressure and the nature of the demand, which the pressure is applied to support. The pressure itself might be lawful, but it will be illegitimate if it is applied for certain purposes. A bribe is a classic example of such a case. On the facts of CTN, the pressure was applied in order to obtain payment of a sum that the defendants bona fide considered due to them. Thus both the pressure and the demand were legitimate. Had the defendants not honestly believed that the goods were held at the plaintiff's risk, the outcome of the case might have been very different. The Court of Appeal's comments on this issue are, of course, *obiter* but they are supported by the views of the Privy Council (again *obiter*) in *Attorney General for England and Wales v R*.

Attorney General for England and Wales v R [2003] UKPC 22; [2003] EMLR 24

Facts: The defendant was a New Zealander and a former member of the SAS. Following the publication of a number of books concerning the activities of the Bravo Two Zero patrol in the Gulf War of 1991, the defendant and other members of his squadron were told to sign a 'confidentiality agreement', restricting their right to publish information about their experiences in the SAS. They were told that if they did not sign the agreement they would be returned to unit ('RTU'). Involuntary RTU was normally only imposed as a penalty for some disciplinary offence and involved exclusion from the social life of the regiment and the loss of its higher rates of pay. The defendant signed the agreement but six months later left the Army and returned to New Zealand. In 1998 he entered into a contract with a New Zealand publisher to publish his own account of Bravo Two Zero. The New Zealand publishers offered the UK rights to a UK publisher who sent a copy of the manuscript to the Ministry of Defence. The Attorney General then brought proceedings against the defendant in the New Zealand High Court for breach of contract. The judge held that the agreement had been obtained by duress and undue influence and was therefore unenforceable. The Court of Appeal allowed the Attorney General's appeal but refused to grant an injunction. The defendant appealed to the Privy Council.

Held: The Privy Council (Lord Scott dissenting on the issue of undue influence) dismissed the appeal.

Lord Hoffmann (delivering the judgment for the majority of the Privy Council):

15. In *Universe Tankships Inc of Monrovia v International Transport Workers Federation* [1983] 1 AC 366,400 Lord Scarman said that there were two elements in the wrong of duress. One was pressure amounting to compulsion of the will of the victim and the second was the illegitimacy of the pressure. R says that to offer him the alternative of being returned to unit, which was regarded in the SAS as a public humiliation, was compulsion of his will. It left him no practical alternative. Their Lordships are content to assume that this was the case. But, as Lord Wilberforce and Lord Simon of Glaisdale said in *Barton v Armstrong* [1976] AC 104, 121:

> 'in life ... many acts are done under pressure, sometimes overwhelming pressure, so that one can say that the actor had no choice but to act. Absence of choice in this sense does not negate consent in law: for this the pressure must be one of a kind which the law does not regard as legitimate'.

16. The legitimacy of the pressure must be examined from two aspects: first, the nature of the pressure and secondly, the nature of the demand which the pressure is applied to support: see Lord Scarman in the *Universe Tankships* case, at 401. Generally speaking, the threat of any form of unlawful action will be regarded as illegitimate. On the other hand, the fact that the threat is lawful does not necessarily make the pressure legitimate. As Lord Atkin said in *Thorne v Motor Trade Association* [1937] AC 797, 806:

> 'The ordinary blackmailer normally threatens to do what he has a perfect right to do – namely, communicate some compromising conduct to a person whose knowledge is likely to affect the person threatened ... What he has to justify is not the threat, but the demand of money'.

17. In this case, the threat was lawful. Although return to unit was not ordinarily used except on grounds of delinquency or unsuitability and was perceived by members of the SAS as a severe penalty, there is no doubt that the Crown was entitled at its discretion to transfer any member of the SAS to another unit. Furthermore, the judge found, in para [123]:

> 'The MOD could not be criticised for its motivation in introducing the contracts. They were introduced because of the concerns about the increasing number of unauthorised disclosures by former UKSF personnel and the concern that those disclosures were threatening the security of operations and personnel and were undermining the effectiveness and employability of the UKSF. Those are legitimate concerns for the MOD to have'.

18. It would follow that the MOD was reasonably entitled to regard anyone unwilling to accept the obligation of confidentiality as unsuitable for the SAS. Thus the threat was lawful and the demand supported by the threat could be justified. But the judge held that the demand was unlawful because it exceeded the powers of the Crown over a serviceman under military law. It was an attempt to restrict his freedom of expression after he had left the service and was no longer subject to military discipline.

19. The judge's reasoning was that R had signed the contract because he had been ordered to do so. The MOD could not give a serviceman an order which, as a matter of military law, he was obliged to obey after he had left the service and therefore it was an abuse of power for the MOD to try to extend the temporal reach of its orders by ordering the serviceman to sign a contract which could be enforced after he had left.

20. If R had signed the contract because as a matter of military law he had been obliged to do so, their Lordships would see much force in this reasoning. But they agree with the Court of Appeal that this was not the case. There was no order in the sense of a command which created an obligation to obey under military law. Instead, R was faced with a choice which may have constituted 'overwhelming pressure' but was not an exercise by the MOD of its legal powers over him. The legitimacy of the pressure therefore falls to be examined by normal criteria and as neither of the courts in New Zealand considered either the threat to be unlawful or the demand unreasonable, it follows that the contract was not obtained by duress.

The starting point for the Privy Council was the two elements of duress identified by Lord Scarman in *Universe Tankships v ITF*: compulsion of the will and illegitimate pressure. Their Lordships were willing to accept that there was compulsion of the soldier's will. The only alternative offered to him was that of being returned to unit, which, given the humiliation involved, was no alternative at all. Regarding the second element, Lord Hoffmann said that the legitimacy of the pressure must be examined from two perspectives:

(a) the nature of the pressure; and
(b) the nature of the demand which the pressure is applied to support.

Applying this test to the facts before them, the Privy Council took the view that the threat was in itself lawful. Although return to unit was not ordinarily used for non-disciplinary matters, there was no doubt that the Crown could at its absolute discretion transfer any member of the SAS to another unit. Furthermore, the nature of the demand in support of which the pressure was applied was also legitimate. It was entirely reasonable for the Ministry of Defence (MOD) to seek to restrict the disclosure of confidential information relating to its military operations. This case can be contrasted with *Progress Bulk Carriers Ltd v Tube City IMS LLC* [2012] EWHC 273, which involved a breach of a contract to charter a ship by the ship owners. This breach caused a delay and, ultimately, the charterers had to give their buyers a discount on the goods being shipped. The charterers considered the ship owners liable for this loss and the ship owners made a 'take it or leave it offer': essentially an offer of a substitute ship and *some* compensation in return for the charterers releasing all claims against the ship owners. The charterers reluctantly agreed (the 'settlement agreement') as they urgently had to get the goods to their buyers. Subsequently, it was argued that this settlement agreement was vitiated by duress. Cooke J agreed. Although the 'take it or leave it' offer was lawful, it amounted to illegitimate pressure given that the ship owners' earlier breach had placed the charters into a position where they had no real choice but to accept the settlement. Cooke J noted (at [44]):

> [T]he pressure created by the Owners in their demand for a waiver of rights by the Charterers has to be seen both in the light of their repudiatory breach and in the light of their subsequent conduct, including their deliberate refusal to comply with the assurances they had previously given about providing a substitute vessel and paying full compensation in respect of that breach. Their refusal to supply the substitute vessel to meet the Charterers' needs, in circumstances which they had created by their breach and their subsequent misleading activity, unless the Charterers waived their rights, could readily be found by the Arbitrators to amount to 'illegitimate pressure.

The case law remained rather unclear as to when a lawful action may constitute illegitimate pressure (cf. *Ryan v Tiuta International Ltd* [2015] BPIR 123 and *Marsden v Barclays Bank Plc* [2016] EWHC 1601). Professor Enonchong (Enonchong, *Duress, Undue Influence and Unconscionable Dealing*, 3rd edn, 2019, London: Sweet & Maxwell, p 28) had suggested that five factors emerge from the cases as being relevant:

1. whether the claimant had a reasonable alternative;
2. whether a threat of criminal proceedings was used to apply moral pressure;
3. whether the threat was made in bad faith;
4. whether the pressure was applied to support an unjustified or unreasonable demand; and
5. whether the defendant's conduct is unconscionable.

These factors are helpful for identifying the circumstances in which a threat of lawful action might be deemed to be morally or socially unacceptable and therefore illegitimate. It should be remembered, however, that the courts will exercise a great deal of caution in this area so as not to upset the expectations of commercial parties. As Steyn LJ said in *CTN Cash and Carry v Gallaher*, 'it is a mistake for the law to set its sights too highly when the critical inquiry is not whether the conduct is lawful but whether it is morally or socially unacceptable'.

Arguably more certainty has emerged recently as the result of the interplay of two cases: *Sheikh Tahnoon Bin Saeed Bin Shakhboot Al Nehayan v Ioannis Kent* [2018] EWHC 333 (Comm) and *Times Travel (UK) Ltd v Pakistan International Airlines Corp* [2019] EWCA Civ 828. In the former case the claimant had invested in the defendant's hotel business in Greece. The venture was not a success and in 2012 the claimant sought to separate his interest from the claimant's interest. To this end a framework agreement was entered into between the parties, supplemented by a promissory note on behalf of the defendant. Ultimately the defendant claimed that the framework agreement and promissory note had been procured by duress. In considering the case, Leggatt LJ made a number of comments about lawful act economic duress (at [187]–[188]):

> This is a difficult area of the law. But for my part I see no reason to doubt the correctness of the approach adopted in the Times Travel case. Whereas the distinction between lawful and unlawful behaviour may be critical in determining whether the defendant's conduct is actionable in tort, I see no reason why it should be decisive of whether the defendant can retain money or other benefits demanded from a claimant in a situation of extreme vulnerability. For this purpose it is appropriate to take account of the legitimacy of the demand and to judge the propriety of the defendant's conduct by reference *not simply to what is lawful but to basic minimum standards of acceptable behaviour.*
>
> It does seem to me, however, that the test ... could be made more precise by transposing into objective requirements the elements of the offence of blackmail. On this basis a demand coupled with a threat to commit a lawful act will be regarded as illegitimate if (a) the defendant has no reasonable grounds for making the demand and (b) the threat would not be considered by reasonable and honest people to be a proper means of reinforcing the demand. (Emphasis added.)

In other words, Leggatt LJ used an objective test. Leggatt LJ ultimately found that the framework agreement and promissory note were voidable for duress but that the defendant had chosen not to avoid the agreements. As there were also threats of violence and breach of contract, the comments of Leggatt LJ on lawful act economic duress were strictly *obiter*.

Sheikh Tahnoon Bin Saeed Bin Shakhboot Al Nehayan v Ioannis Kent [2018] EWHC 333 (Comm) was subsequently considered in *Times Travel (UK) Ltd v Pakistan International Airlines Corp* [2019] EWCA Civ 828. In that case Times Travel (UK) Ltd (TTL) was a small family-owned travel agency based in Birmingham. Its business consisted almost entirely of the sale to the Pakistani community in Birmingham of flight tickets to Pakistan. At the relevant time, Pakistan International Airlines Corp (PIAC) was the only airline offering direct flights to Pakistan from the UK. The contractual arrangements between the parties, particularly as to commission, was not straightforward (see [7]). Ultimately disputes arose between PAIC and its agents (including TTL) over commission. A trade association, APTA, was formed to represent the agents in these disputes and some of the agents brought legal action. In September 2012, PAIC lawfully gave notice to terminate all of its contracts with agents in the UK. In September 2012, PIAC also lawfully reduced TTL's ticket allocation from 300 to 60 tickets. This reduction had a major negative impact of TTL, one which could ultimately put it out of business. However, PIAC offered its agents (including TTL) a new, revised agreement. Indeed counsel for PIAC accepted that the termination notices were designed to get agents to agree to the new contracts. The new agreement changed the terms as to commission but crucially for present purposes required agents to release PIAC from claims for commission calculated on the old basis. Ultimately TTL signed this new agreement as, unless it did so, it would no longer be able to sell PIAC tickets and would almost inevitably would go out of business. Subsequently, TTL sought to avoid this agreement on the ground that it was procured by economic duress.

In the High Court ([2017] EWHC 1367), the case was heard by Warren J, who ultimately held (at [262]) that the pressure was illegitimate although his reasoning was a little unclear:

> Whether PIAC has acted in good faith or bad faith is moot. The claimants have not established that there was bad faith but nor has PIAC established good faith. It is clear to me that the whole basis on which the Notice was served and the terms of the New Agreement were formulated was to ensure that agents would lose their claims to accrued rights in a situation where some of those rights ... Whether this demonstrates bad faith is a matter on which different minds might take different views.

Moreover, he stated (at [262]) that:

> It does not, I think on any view, reflect well on PIAC that it should treat this particular agent ... in the way which it did when TT was a successful, honest and reliable agent with a substantial period of loyal service.

Returning to *Sheikh Tahnoon Bin Saeed Bin Shakhboot Al Nehayan v Ioannis Kent* [2018] EWHC 333, Leggatt LJ saw the judgment of Warren J as supporting his view that illegitimate pressure should be judged by 'basic minimum standards of acceptable behaviour' (see [187]). The judgment of Warren J was appealed to the Court of Appeal where the only live issue was whether or not the pressure used by PIAC was illegitimate. Ultimately, the Court of Appeal reversed Warren J, with David Richards LJ making the following key points: (i) Leggatt LJ's approach, that illegitimate pressure should be judged by 'basic minimum standards of acceptable behaviour', was too uncertain; (ii) the key to lawful act economic duress is good faith; (iii) good faith was to be assessed subjectively. David Richards LJ continued (at [105]):

> My conclusion on the central legal issue is that the doctrine of lawful act duress does not extend to the use of lawful pressure to achieve a result to which the person exercising pressure believes in good faith it is entitled, and that is so whether or not, objectively speaking, it has reasonable grounds for that belief.

Times Travel (UK) Ltd v Pakistan International Airlines Corp was followed in *Morley (t/a Morley Estates) v Royal Bank of Scotland Plc* [2020] EWHC 88 (Ch).

10.5 Remedies

Although there has been some disagreement in the cases (see *Barton v Armstrong*), it appears that duress renders a contract voidable, not void – in other words the victim is entitled to rescind the contract. As we have seen in the chapters on mistake (Chapter 9) and misrepresentation (Chapter 8), the right to rescission may be lost due to the existence of a bar to rescission, for example, affirmation, delay, the impossibility of counter-restitution or the intervention of third-party rights. It seems that all four of these bars apply to rescission for duress. In *North Ocean Shipping v Hyundai*, excessive delay on the part of the plaintiffs was said to bar rescission for duress. In *Halpern v Halpern* [2007] EWCA Civ 291, the Court of Appeal held that an inability to make counter-restitution would be a bar to rescission for duress. The Court did, however, note (at [74]–[75]) that counter-restitution may be possible through the payment of a monetary equivalent to restitution (citing *Erlanger v New Sombrero Phosphate Company* (1878) 3 AC 1218).

On the possibility of a private law claim under Part 4A of the Consumer Protection from Unfair Trading Regulations 2008 (as amended by the Consumer Protection (Amendment) Regulations 2014) see Section 8.6.

Additional reading

Bigwood, R., *Exploitative Contracts* (Oxford: OUP, 2003).

Birks, P., 'The Travails of Duress' [1990] LMCLQ 342.

Devenney, J., 'A Pack of Unruly Dogs: Unconscionable Bargains, Lawful Act (Economic) Duress and Clogs of the Equity of Redemption' [2002] JBL 539.

Friedman, D., 'The Objective Principle and Mistake and Involuntariness in Contract and Restitution' (2003) 119 LQR 68.

Halson, R., 'Opportunism, Economic Duress and Contractual Modifications' (1991) 107 LQR 649.

Murphy, J., 'Understanding Intimidation' (2014) 77 MLR 33.

Nolan, D., 'Economic Duress and the Availability of a Reasonable Alternative' [2000] RLR 105.

Smith, S., 'Contracting under Pressure: A Theory of Duress' [1997] CLJ 343.

Tiplady, D., 'Concepts of Duress' (1983) 99 LQR 188.

Chapter 11

Undue influence

Chapter contents

11.1 Introduction

Undue influence is, in broad terms, the equitable sister doctrine of duress. It operates to release parties from some contracts which they have entered into as a result of being 'influenced' by the other party. In the leading case of *Royal Bank of Scotland plc v Etridge (No 2)* [2002] 2 AC 773, Lord Nicholls made the following observations about undue influence:

> Undue influence is one of the grounds of relief developed by the courts of equity as a court of conscience. The objective is to ensure that the influence of one person over another is not abused. In everyday life people constantly seek to influence the decisions of others. They seek to persuade those with whom they are dealing to enter into transactions, whether great or small. The law has set limits to the means properly employable for this purpose. To this end the common law developed a principle of duress. Originally this was narrow in its scope, restricted to the more blatant forms of physical coercion, such as personal violence.
>
> Here, as elsewhere in the law, equity supplemented the common law. Equity extended the reach of the law to other unacceptable forms of persuasion. The law will investigate the manner in which the intention to enter into the transaction was secured: 'how the intention was produced', in the oft repeated words of Lord Eldon LC, from as long ago as 1807 (*Huguenin v Baseley* 14 Ves 273, 300). If the intention was produced by an unacceptable means, the law will not permit the transaction to stand. The means used is regarded as an exercise of improper or 'undue' influence, and hence unacceptable, whenever the consent thus procured ought not fairly to be treated as the expression of a person's free will. It is impossible to be more precise or definitive. The circumstances in which one person acquires influence over another, and the manner in which influence may be exercised, vary too widely to permit of any more specific criterion.

As Lord Nicholls suggests, one of the main difficulties with the doctrine of undue influence is ascertaining the limits of *legitimate* persuasion. The legitimacy of persuasion differs between contexts, so that although it may be legitimate for a sales representative to persuade me to purchase a washing machine, it may not be legitimate for my father to persuade me to sell my house to him at a discount price. The difficulty lies in ascertaining when influence becomes 'undue', so as to justify the intervention of the law. It should, however, be noted that an overborne will is not necessarily a pre-requisite of undue influence:

Hewett v First Plus Financial Group Plc [2010] EWCA Civ 312

Facts: A husband persuaded his wife to re-mortgage their home as part of a plan to refinance his debts. It later transpired that he had been having an affair at the time of the discussions about the re-mortgage. Subsequently, the mortgagee sought to repossess the property; and the wife sought to defend the action by claiming, amongst other things, that the re-mortgage was procured by undue influence, and the mortgagee had constructive notice of the undue influence.

Held: The Court of Appeal, focusing on the concealment of the husband's affair, held that the re-mortgage had been procured by undue influence.

20. As for undue influence, the Judge, Briggs J, directed himself by reference to the dictum of Ward LJ in *Daniel v Drew* [2005] EWCA Civ 507, at paragraph 36 to the effect that:

> 'The donor may be led but she must not be driven and her will must be the offspring of her own volition, not a record of someone else's'.

He concluded (as I have already described) that although Mrs Hewett faced a horrible choice, she made her own choice to participate in the re-mortgage. He found that there had been no oppression, no coercion, bullying or threats, and that Mrs Hewett had neither been frightened nor intimidated by her husband when deciding to accede to his request …

24. I have however been persuaded that Mr Hewett's concealment of his affair from his wife did amount to the exercise of undue influence against her, sufficient to vitiate the re-mortgage transaction, as between them. My reasons follow.

25. This case calls for a more detailed analysis of the law relating to undue influence than appears in the Judgment. The judge confined himself mainly to citations from *Drew v Daniel* (*supra*). That is a convenient starting point. At paragraph 33 Ward LJ cited a passage from the judgment of Lindley LJ in *Allcard v Skinner* (1887) 36 Ch Div 145 at 181–182, which included the following citation about undue influence from Lord Eldon in *Huguenin v Baseley* (1807) 14 Ves 273:

> 'Take it that she (the plaintiff) intended to give it to him (the defendant): it is by no means out of the reach of the principle. The question is, not, whether she knew, what she was doing, had done, or proposed to do, but how the intention was produced'.

It is implicit in that dictum that a finding of undue influence does not depend, as a necessary pre-requisite, upon a conclusion that the victim made no decision of her own, or that her will and intention was completely overborne. No doubt there are many examples where that is shown, but a conscious exercise of will may nonetheless be vitiated by undue influence.

26. The speech of Lord Nicholls in *Royal Bank of Scotland v Etridge* (*supra*) has come to be regarded as the most authoritative recent re-statement of the law relating to undue influence. It was, as he himself acknowledged, firmly based upon the principles to be found in *Allcard v Skinner*. At paragraphs 32 to 33, Lord Nicholls said this:

> '32. I add a cautionary note, prompted by some of the first instance judgments in the cases currently being considered by the House. It concerns the general approach to be adopted by a court when considering whether a wife's guarantee of her husband's bank overdraft was procured by her husband's undue influence. Undue influence has a connotation of impropriety. In the eye of the law, undue influence means that influence has been misused. Statements or conduct by a husband which do not pass beyond the bounds of what may be expected of a reasonable husband in the circumstances should not, without more, be castigated as undue influence. Similarly, when a husband is forecasting the future of his business, and expressing his hopes or fears, a degree of hyperbole may be only natural. Courts should not too readily treat such exaggerations as misstatements.
>
> 33. Inaccurate explanations of a proposed transaction are a different matter. So are cases where a husband, in whom a wife has reposed trust and confidence for the management of their financial affairs, prefers his interests to hers and makes a choice for both of them on that footing. Such a husband abuses the influence he has. He fails to discharge the obligation of candour and fairness he owes a wife who is looking to him to make the major financial decisions'.
>
> …

27. Lord Nicholls' analysis makes it clear that, for an obligation of candour and fairness to be owed by the husband, it is necessary to show that the wife reposes trust and confidence in him. Usually that means, trust and confidence in his conduct of the family's financial affairs. But in *Thompson v Foy* [2009] EWHC 1076 (Ch) Lewison J said this at paragraph 100:

> '100. In the light of the arguments before me, there are some additional observations I should make. First, although in *Etridge* Lord Nicholls of Birkenhead described the paradigm case of a relationship where influence is presumed as being one in which the complainant reposed trust and confidence in the other party in relation to the management of the complainant's financial affairs (§ 14), I do not consider that this description was intended to be exhaustive. To restrict the type of trust and confidence in this way would not be consistent with the authoritative exposition by Lindley LJ in *Allcard v Skinner* (1887) 36 Ch D 145 in which Lindley LJ referred to "cases in which the position of the donor to the donee has been such that it has been the duty of the donee to advise the donor, or even to manage his property for him". This very sentence was paraphrased by Lord Nicholls (§ 9). In addition, when describing the circumstances in which the burden of proof would shift (§ 21) Lord Nicholls used much more general language ... Second, the requisite trust and confidence can arise in the course of the impugned transaction itself: *Turkey v Awadh* [2005] 2 P & CR 29 (§ 11)' ...

28. In *Royal Bank of Scotland plc v Chandra & anr* [2010] EWHC 105 (Ch) David Richards J provided the following perceptive analysis of the difference between inadvertent failure to disclose and a deliberate suppression of information, in the context of a confidential husband and wife relationship:

> 'Mis-stating the position or misleading the wife is different from an inadvertent failure to disclose, a distinction familiar in the law of misrepresentation. Of course a statement which, though strictly true, is misleading without qualification will fall within these observations of Lord Nicholls. Likewise, a deliberate suppression of information because the husband knows that, if disclosed, it will deter the wife from giving the guarantee will involve an abuse by him of her confidence. It would be unconscionable and rightly categorised as unacceptable means' ...

29. Applying those principles to the present case, the first question is whether Mrs Hewett reposed a sufficient degree of trust and confidence in her husband to give rise to what Lord Nicholls described as an obligation of candour and fairness owed to her. I consider that she did, for two reasons. The first is that, as the Judge found, she regarded Mr Hewett as being in charge of the family finances, albeit not to an extent that excluded her from any participation in important decisions: see paragraph 21 of the Judgment. It would in my opinion be wrong to confine a husband's obligation of candour and fairness when proposing a risky financial transaction to his wife as confined to cases where the wife meekly follows her husband's directions without question. The purpose of an obligation of candour is that the wife should be able to make an informed decision (with or without the benefit of independent advice) properly and fairly appraised of the relevant circumstances.

30. The second reason is that the specific transaction which Mr Hewett put to his wife required her to take on trust his promise to make the instalment payments due to First Plus arising from the re-mortgage. As the Judge put it, at paragraph 22 of the Judgment, that is what Mr Hewett swore to do on their children's lives. There was therefore both a pre-existing relationship of trust and confidence, and an intensification of it derived from the very basis of the proposed transaction.

31. The second question is whether the fact that Mr Hewett was having an affair was something which his obligation of fairness and candour towards his wife required him to disclose, in connection with his request that she charge her interest in the Property as security for his debts. Mr Lightfoot for First Plus submitted that it depended upon whether that was a material fact, a question which he invited the court to decide in the negative. I consider that it was plainly a material fact calling for disclosure.

32. The horrible decision (as the Judge correctly put it) facing Mrs Hewett may be summarised as follows. Should she accede to her husband's proposal, in the hope of saving her family's home from her husband's creditors, as the basis for the continuation of a stable family life to which both she and her husband would contribute, taking the grave risk that his tendency towards financial irresponsibility would lead to the loss of both his and her beneficial interests in the Property? Or should she, by refusing his proposal, preserve her significant beneficial interest in the Property from the claims of his creditors as, in effect, a plank in the shipwreck? Central to that decision was a balancing of the reliability of her husband's promise to support the family in the future by making sure that the increased mortgage instalments were duly paid, against the risk that a failure on his part would lead to the loss not merely of his, but also of her, beneficial interest in the Property.

33. It is evident that Mrs Hewett's decision to accede to her husband's request was based upon an assumption on her part that he was as committed as she was to the marriage, to the family and to the preservation of their home life in the future. The truth was that he had already embarked upon an affair which, although by no means a certainty, carried with it the serious risk that it would lead in due course to Mr Hewett's departure from the family and withdrawal of both emotional and financial support, as eventually occurred. On that analysis of the decision facing Mrs Hewett, I consider that Mr Hewett's affair cried out for disclosure.

34. Mr Lightfoot submitted that there was no evidence at trial that, had Mrs Hewett known of her husband's affair in January 2004, she would have decided not to participate in the re-mortgage. That is in my judgment nothing to the point. It has never been part of the proof of undue influence that, but for the relevant abuse of trust, the impugned transaction would not have been entered into. The right to set aside the transaction arises not because, on a 'but for' causation analysis, it would otherwise have been avoided, but because of the equitable wrong constituted by the abuse of confidence was part of the process by which the victim's consent to it was obtained. In the present case that wrong is constituted by Mr Hewett's breach of his duty of fairness and candour to his wife, when persuading her to agree to the re-mortgage.

35. In my judgment the question whether Mr Hewett's affair was a material fact calling for disclosure is to be decided by an objective test, rather than by asking the hypothetical question whether disclosure would have made all the difference to his wife's process of decision making. The issue may be best addressed by asking whether a solicitor, consulted by Mrs Hewett for advice about the wisdom of the transaction, would have thought it relevant to know that her husband was, while asking for her unqualified trust, at the same time conducting a clandestine affair. There can in my view only be an affirmative answer to that question.

Compare *Royal Bank of Scotland Plc v Chandra* [2011] EWCA Civ 192. Note also the words of caution of Mann J in *Rosesilver Group Corp v Paton* [2015] EWHC 1758 (Ch) at [41]: 'Undue influence cases cannot be allowed to go forward on the basis of vague statements in evidence, coupled with speculative submissions on the part of counsel, especially in circumstances in which it appears to be a point added as an afterthought, and I find that the evidence as it stands does not raise an arguable case of undue influence.' An appeal in this case was dismissed: [2017] EWCA Civ 158.

11.1.1 The relationship with duress

As Lord Nicholls notes, there is some overlap between the common-law doctrine of duress and the equitable doctrine of undue influence. This was examined by Professor Enonchong in the following extract:

Enonchong, N, *Duress, Undue Influence and Unconscionable Dealing*, 3rd edn, 2019, London: Sweet & Maxwell, p 93

The objective of undue influence is similar to that of the common law doctrine of duress, namely, to draw a line between acceptable and unacceptable pressure. However, since the scope of relief on the ground of duress was originally very narrow, limited as it was to more blatant forms of physical coercion, equity supplemented the common law by means of the doctrine of undue influence. Relief was granted on the ground of undue influence in cases where equity considered the pressure to be improper or unacceptable although it did not amount to duress at common law. Like the law of duress, the law of undue influence examines the manner in which the intention to enter into a transaction was produced. If the intention was produced by an unacceptable means, the law of undue influence will not permit the transaction to stand. However, since a range of conduct that was not regarded as unacceptable at law was so regarded by equity, there was a protection gap between the two doctrines, with equity affording wider protection through undue influence than the common law could through duress. In the past this protection gap was very wide, but the greater expansion in the scope of duress in recent times has resulted in considerable overlap between the two doctrines, since both deal with overt acts of improper pressure such as unlawful threats. However, undue influence extends beyond cases involving overt act of pressure …

Unlike common law duress, it is not a requirement for undue influence that there must be pressure or threats or that the pressure must come from the defendant. Undue influence can exist in the absence of pressure or threats. This is so in cases where the relationship between two persons is such that one has acquired a degree of influence or ascendancy over the other so that the one is disposed to agree to a proposal of the ascendant party without any specific acts of persuasion.

A number of early undue influence cases concerned overt threats and pressure. In *Williams v Bayley* (1866) LR 1 HL 200, for example, a father agreed to give an equitable mortgage over his colliery in exchange for a promise by the plaintiff bankers not to prosecute his son for forging his father's signature on promissory notes. In response to this threat, the father replied, 'What be I to do? How can I help myself? You see these men will have their money'. The House of Lords held that the agreement should be set aside as being obtained by undue influence. Similarly, in *Mutual Finance Ltd v John Wetton & Sons Ltd* [1937] 2 KB 389, a guarantee was obtained from a family company under an implied, though not explicit, threat to prosecute a member of the family who was alleged to have forged the signature of the company on a previous guarantee. The guarantee was set aside as having been obtained by undue influence. Both of these cases involved pressure being placed on one party by the other in much the same way as occurs with duress. Following the expansion in the types of threats that are now treated as potentially giving rise to duress, it is possible to argue that facts such as these could now be dealt with under the doctrine of duress (although compare the observation of Porter J Mutual Finance *Ltd v John Wetton & Sons Ltd* [1937] 2 KB 389, 395 and *Al Nehayan v Kent* [2018] EWHC 333 (Comm) at [184]). Indeed, some commentators have argued that such cases should be dealt with through the doctrine of duress, leaving undue influence to deal with relationships where one party has acquired a degree of ascendancy over the other party without overt threats.

Birks, P, and Chin, NY, 'On the nature of undue influence', in Beatson, J, and Friedmann, D (eds), *Good Faith and Fault in Contract Law*, 1995, Oxford: Clarendon Press, pp 63–4

Some years ago Professor Malcolm Cope suggested that all cases of duress should be treated as undue influence. We believe the decanting should go the other way: all cases of pressure should be treated as duress. It is unfortunate if this must still be expressed as transferring them from equity to common law. It is time that in this field we overcome the old jurisdictional duality. It would be better to say simply that pressure should be litigated as pressure, or as 'duress' if that synonym is preferred. The reasons are, first, that pressure or duress is a relatively easily understood and distinct notion; secondly, that pressure had been allowed to dominate the picture and has concealed the nature of relational undue influence; and, thirdly, whatever the precise future of the requirement of manifest disadvantage in the context of undue influence, nobody has ever suggested that it has any role whatever in duress.

A consolidation of the law relating to pressure would not have been possible in earlier times because of the narrowness of the concept of operative duress. Duress to goods and other economic duress was thought not to give relief from a contract. Thanks in large measure to an influential article by Professor Beatson, that picture has been transformed. Nowadays it is clear that duress includes all illegitimate pressure and that all forms of duress can ground relief from a contract ...

It is now difficult to conceive of any pressure which will not be relieved satisfactorily, if it should be relieved at all, within the category of duress. To suggest otherwise would be to claim relief for a species of pressure which could not be characterized as illegitimate.

Although the approach of Professor Birks and Professor Chin would arguably bring more clarity and consistency to the law, it has yet to be adopted by the courts. As a result, there continues to be considerable overlap between duress and undue influence, particularly in cases concerning overt threats.

11.1.2 The meaning of 'undue'

The law will only intervene when 'influence' becomes 'undue'. But what does the word 'undue' mean? In the context of influence it has, at least, two potential meanings (fully discussed in Devenney and Chandler, 'Unconscionability and the taxonomy of undue influence' [2007] JBL 269:

1 The influence is 'undue' because it is 'illegitimate' or 'unconscionable'. This focuses on the conduct of the influencer. It is defendant-focused.
2 The influence is 'undue' because it is 'overbearing' or 'too high' and causes the influenced party to lose a certain amount of autonomy in deciding whether to enter into the contract (although compare *Hewett v First Plus Financial Group Plc* [2010] EWCA Civ 312). This focuses on the effect that the influence has on the influenced person's state of mind. It is claimant-focused.

The second meaning of 'undue' was adopted by the High Court of Australia in the case of Commercial *Bank of Australia Ltd v Amadio* (1983) 151 CLR 447. This definition of undue influence was used to distinguish the doctrine from unconscionability (discussed at the end of this chapter). Deane J put it in the following terms:

> The equitable principles relating to relief against unconscionable dealing and the principles relating to undue influence are closely related. The two doctrines are, however, distinct. Undue influence, like common law duress, looks to the quality of the consent or assent of the weaker party ...

> Unconscionable dealing looks to the conduct of the stronger party in attempting to enforce, or retain the benefit of, a dealing with a person under a special disability in circumstances where it is not consistent with equity or good conscience that he should do so.

Professor Birks and Professor Chin have argued strongly that the approach taken in *Amadio* should be followed in this country.

Birks, P, and Chin, NY, 'On the nature of undue influence', in Beatson, J, and Friedmann, D (eds), *Good Faith and Fault in Contract Law*, 1995, Oxford: Clarendon Press, p 95

> Some jurists will still be attracted by the simplicity of the defendant-sided analysis, and they will point out, correctly, that the number of cases in which there is no unconscionable behaviour will be very small. However, the rationality of the law cannot tolerate abbreviations or approximations. If there are two doctrines, there are two doctrines; and the fact that one might do perhaps ninety-five per cent of the work is no reason for pretending that the other does not exist. The correct approach will be to treat both undue influence and duress as plaintiff-sided factors which ground relief on a degree of impairment of the plaintiff's capacity to make decisions. In every case we should accept not a dogma of priority or subsidiarity, but a voluntary intellectual discipline of exhausting the plaintiff-sided analysis before proceeding to the question whether relief might be rested on unconscientious behaviour on the part of the defendant. That discipline will serve to protect all plaintiff-sided grounds for relief – spontaneous and innocently induced mistake no less than undue influence and duress, not to mention others – and will avert the unnecessary injustice which happens when plaintiffs lose cases because lawyers fail to see their winning argument.

There is some judicial support for a claimant-focused approach to undue influence (most notably in the decisions of the Court of Appeal in *Allcard v Skinner* (1887) 36 Ch D 145 and *Hammond v Osborn* [2002] EWCA Civ 885). Nevertheless, the majority of recent cases have emphasised the relevance of some form of 'wrongdoing', thus suggesting a defendant-focused approach. In *Royal Bank of Scotland v Etridge (No 2)*, their Lordships spoke of undue influence as being an 'abuse' of a position of influence. Likewise, in *R v Attorney-General for England and Wales* [2003] UKPC 22, Lord Hoffmann described undue influence as involving 'consent … obtained by unacceptable means' and 'the unfair exploitation by one party of a relationship which gives him ascendancy or influence over the other'. In National *Commercial Bank (Jamaica) Ltd v Hew* [2003] UKPC 51, Lord Millet described undue influence as involving 'abuse', 'victimisation' and 'exploitation', and in *UCB Corporate Services Ltd v Williams* [2002] EWCA Civ 555; [2003] 1 P & CR 12, Jonathan Parker LJ described the concept as involving 'improper means of persuasion'. All of these judgments suggest that the courts look to the conduct of the defendant in order to determine whether the influence exerted was 'undue'.

It is important to note that undue influence is generally concerned with procedural fairness, not substantive fairness. When considering whether undue influence has been exercised, the courts will focus on the process by which the agreement came into existence, not the agreement itself. This was explained by Lindley LJ in *Allcard v Skinner* (1887) 36 Ch D 145:

> What then is the principle? Is it that it is right and expedient to save persons from the consequence of their own folly? Or is it that it is right and expedient to save them from being victimised by other people? In my opinion the doctrine of undue influence is founded upon the second of these two principles … to protect people from being forced, tricked or misled in any way by others into parting with their property is one of the most legitimate objects of all laws. …

The law of undue influence seeks to prevent 'victimisation'; it is concerned with procedural unfairness. Was the agreement entered into as a result of the exercise of improper influence? To answer this question the court will examine both the nature of the relationship between the parties and the form of influence applied.

11.1.3 The structure of this chapter

In recent times, the House of Lords twice provided a thorough examination of the law of undue influence, that is, in 1993, in *Barclays Bank plc v O'Brien* [1994] 1 AC 180, and, in 2001, in *Royal Bank of Scotland plc v Etridge* (No 2) [2002] 2 AC 773. These two cases contain the most detailed and authoritative statements of the law in this area, and for that reason, the main focus of this chapter will be on the speeches of their Lordships in those cases, particularly in *Etridge*.

First, we will examine the traditional two categories of undue influence. Second, we will consider how the courts resolve cases in which the undue influence has been exerted by a third party and not by the defendant. Third, we will undertake a detailed analysis of the views expressed by the House of Lords in Etridge. We will then consider the remedies available for undue influence. Finally, we will consider the doctrine of unconscionability and its relationship to the law of undue influence.

11.2 Two traditional categories of undue influence

In *Barclays Bank plc v O'Brien* [1994] 1 AC 180, Lord Browne-Wilkinson divided undue influence into two categories:

> A person who has been induced to enter into a transaction by the undue influence of another ('the wrongdoer') is entitled to set that transaction aside as against the wrongdoer. Such undue influence is either actual or presumed. In *Bank of Credit and Commerce International SA v Aboody* [1990] 1 QB 923, 953, the Court of Appeal helpfully adopted the following classification.
>
> *Class 1: Actual undue influence*
>
> In these cases it is necessary for the claimant to prove affirmatively that the wrongdoer exerted undue influence on the complainant to enter into the particular transaction which is impugned.
>
> *Class 2: Presumed undue influence*
>
> In these cases the complainant only has to show, in the first instance, that there was a relationship of trust and confidence between the complainant and the wrongdoer of such a nature that it is fair to presume that the wrongdoer abused that relationship in procuring the complainant to enter into the impugned transaction. In Class 2 cases therefore there is no need to produce evidence that actual undue influence was exerted in relation to the particular transaction impugned: once a confidential relationship has been proved, the burden then shifts to the wrongdoer to prove that the complainant entered into the impugned transaction freely, for example by showing that the complainant had independent advice. Such a confidential relationship can be established in two ways, viz.,
>
> *Class 2(A)*
>
> Certain relationships (for example solicitor and client, medical advisor and patient) as a matter of law raise the presumption that undue influence has been exercised.

Class 2(B)

Even if there is no relationship falling within Class 2(A), if the complainant proves the *de facto* existence of a relationship under which the complainant generally reposed trust and confidence in the wrongdoer, the existence of such relationship raises the presumption of undue influence. In a Class 2(B) case therefore, in the absence of evidence disproving undue influence, the complainant will succeed in setting aside the impugned transaction merely by proof that the complainant reposed trust and confidence in the wrongdoer without having to prove that the wrongdoer exerted actual undue influence or otherwise abused such trust and confidence in relation to the particular transaction impugned.

While the division between actual and presumed undue influence generally remains good law, the House of Lords subsequently doubted the usefulness of the division between Class 2(A) and Class 2(B) undue influence. We will consider the reasons for this in our discussion of Etridge.

11.2.1 Actual undue influence

To make out a case for actual undue influence, it must be affirmatively proved that one party exercised undue influence over the other. The influence exercised may be much more subtle than duress and, for example, includes psychological means. There is no need to show that there was a previous history of such influence, and there is no requirement of a special relationship, although such a relationship may exist on the facts. An example of this type of undue influence is to be found on the facts of *Bank of Credit & Commerce International SA v Aboody*.

***Bank of Credit & Commerce International SA v Aboody* [1990] 1 QB 923**

Facts: The defendants were husband and wife. Mrs Aboody was 20 years younger than her husband and had married him when she was 17. She was nominally a director of her husband's business, and over a number of years, she had signed various documents relating to the business without reading them or questioning her husband about them. The documents that gave rise to the litigation were three guarantees and charges over the wife's home that were made in favour of the bank in order to support loans made to the husband's business. Mrs Aboody claimed that she had signed these agreements under the undue influence of her husband. She had taken no independent advice and her husband had deliberately concealed matters from her. The judge at first instance held that there had been actual undue influence, but refused to set aside the guarantees because it had not been proved that they were manifestly disadvantageous to the wife.

Held: The Court of Appeal dismissed the appeal. Although Mr Aboody had not acted with any improper motive, he had unduly influenced his wife. Nevertheless, the Court of Appeal refused to set aside the guarantees because it had not been shown that the transactions were to the manifest disadvantage of Mrs Aboody.

Slade LJ: Since Mrs Aboody's claim in the present case is based exclusively on undue influence, it thus becomes necessary to consider whether, contrary to the judge's view, she has shown that all or any of the six transactions were manifestly disadvantageous to her ... [O]n a fair reading of the judgment, we think it clear that the judge, while not embarking on a full scale repetition of the principal relevant factors in conducting the balancing exercise in respect of each of the six transactions, had them well in mind on each occasion. While there were substantial potential liabilities, and the risk of the loss of the family home, to be put in the balance on the debit side, there was also much to put in on the credit side. Eratex Ltd was the family business and the sole or principal means of support of Mr and Mrs Aboody. Eratex Ltd might still have collapsed with or without the facilities covered by the six transactions. But at least these facilities gave it some hope of survival. The judge found that, as at the date of the 1976 guarantee, it had 'more than an equal chance of surviving', and that, even as at December 1979, it had 'at least a reasonably good chance of surviving'. If it had survived, the potential benefits to Mrs. Aboody would have been substantial.

In the end, we can see no sufficient grounds for disagreeing with his conclusion that on balance a manifest disadvantage has not been shown by Mrs Aboody in respect of any of the six transactions.

Our conclusions on [the issue of manifest disadvantage] must lead to the dismissal of this appeal. Nevertheless, though this is not necessary for our decision, we propose to say something about the allegation of actual undue influence ...

Lindley LJ in *Allcard v Skinner* (1887) 36 ChD 145, 183, said that no court has ever attempted to define undue influence. Lord Scarman gave a warning against any attempt at comprehensive definition in *National Westminster Bank plc v Morgan* [1985] AC 686, 709. We heed this warning. Nevertheless, for the purpose of dealing with [this] issue, it is necessary briefly to consider what has to be shown if an allegation of actual undue influence is to be made out.

Leaving aside proof of manifest disadvantage, we think that a person relying on a plea of actual undue influence must show that (a) the other party to the transaction (or someone who induced the transaction for his own benefit) had the capacity to influence the complainant; (b) the influence was exercised; (c) its exercise was undue; (d) its exercise brought about the transaction ... On the evidence there appears to be no doubt that conditions (a) and (b) are satisfied. The findings of the judge show that Mrs Aboody at the invitation of her husband was habitually prepared to sign documents relating to the affairs of Eratex Ltd without considering their contents because she trusted him. They also show that he invited her to enter into the first five transactions. The present issue, therefore, resolves itself to the question whether the exercise of Mr Aboody's influence was on the facts undue ... If, contrary to our view, the five transactions were manifestly disadvantageous to Mrs Aboody, we do not see how it could be disputed that unfair advantage had been taken of her by her husband. In this context we cite a brief passage from the judge's judgment:

> 'There was more than a situation of trust; there was actual influence founded on that trust and [Mr Aboody] used it intentionally. He intended and knew that without any discussion or consideration of risk [Mrs Aboody] would sign security documents for a series of increasingly large overdrafts of the company. He never offered her any choice of her own. She was deprived altogether of the free use of any independent and informed judgment in the transaction. He never mentioned risk at all even if he thought it was a slight one. The only judgment that she could be said to have exercised was her mistaken judgment of Mr Aboody and his business capacity and probity'.

When one couples with these findings the fact that it was Mr Aboody who suggested to his wife that she should enter into the first five transactions, the unfair advantage taken of her by him became apparent. If he had positively misrepresented to her the extent of the risks involved, a plea based on misrepresentation might well have been available to her. The mere fact that in order to get his own way he chose deliberately to say nothing as to the risks, rather than to misrepresent them, would not, in our judgment, save his conduct from being unconscionable or absolve him from a charge of actual undue influence, bearing in mind that it was he who invited her to enter into them.

Slade LJ's judgment in *Aboody* provides a helpful summary of the requirements for a claim of actual undue influence. However, it must be noted that the requirement of 'manifest disadvantage' in, so-called, actual undue influence cases, was subsequently rejected by the House of Lords in *CIBC Mortgages plc v Pitt* [1994] AC 200 (overruling *Aboody* on this point). In that case, Lord Browne-Wilkinson declared:

> Actual undue influence is a species of fraud. Like any other victim of fraud, a person who has been induced by undue influence to carry out a transaction which he did not freely and knowingly enter into is entitled to have that transaction set aside as of right.

11.2.2 Presumed undue influence

To establish presumed undue influence, the influenced party must demonstrate two things:

1 A relationship of trust and confidence.
2 A transaction that 'calls for an explanation'.

Having established a presumption of undue influence, the court must then consider whether the presumption has been rebutted. We will consider each of these requirements in turn.

11.2.2.1 A relationship of trust and confidence

Traditionally, presumed undue influence was divided into two classes. The first class (class 2[A]) consisted of relationships in which the law presumed that one party had influence over the other. The class included the relationship between parent and child (*Bainbrigge v Browne* (1881) Ch D 188); guardian and ward (*Hylton v Hylton* [1754] 2 Ves Sen 547); doctor and patient (*Mitchell v Homfray* [1881] 8 QBD 587); solicitor and client (*Wright v Carter* [1903] 1 Ch 27); trustee and beneficiary (*Beningfield v Baxter* [1886] 12 App Cas 167); and spiritual adviser and follower (*Allcard v Skinner* [1887] 36 Ch D 145). Notably, it did not include the relationship between a husband and wife.

If a relationship did not fall within class 2(A), it was possible to argue that it fell within class 2(B). This class consisted of cases where one party could show, on the facts of the case, that it was a relationship in which they had reposed trust and confidence in the other. The relationship between a husband and wife could fall into this category. In *Barclays Bank v O'Brien*, Lord Browne-Wilkinson said:

> Although there is no Class 2(A) presumption of undue influence as between husband and wife, it should be emphasised that in any particular case a wife may well be able to demonstrate that de facto she did leave decisions on financial affairs to her husband thereby bringing herself within Class 2(B) i.e. that the relationship between husband and wife in the particular case was such that the wife reposed confidence and trust in her husband in relation to their financial affairs and therefore undue influence is to be presumed.

Following the decision of the House of Lords in *Etridge*, the terminology of class 2(A) and class 2(B) should no longer be used. Although relationships within class 2(A) still raise a presumption of influence, it is doubtful whether class 2(B) serves any useful purpose. We will consider these issues in greater detail when we examine the speeches in *Etridge*.

11.2.2.2 A transaction which is not readily explicable by the relationship between the parties

As we have seen, it is no longer necessary for a claimant to show that a transaction was to his 'manifest disadvantage' in order to have it set aside for *actual* undue influence. Prior to the decision of the House of Lords in *Etridge*, it was assumed that the requirement still existed in relation to cases of presumed undue influence, whether they were class 2(A) or class 2(B). In *Etridge*, however, their Lordships discarded the phrase 'manifest disadvantage' and indicated that the nature of the transaction is only of relevance to the evidential issue of whether it can be presumed that undue influence has been exerted. In other words, if the transaction is one which calls for an explanation (for example, because it benefits one party with no corresponding benefit to the other), then this will impose a burden on the dominant party to demonstrate that the transaction was not in fact obtained by the exercise of undue influence, that is by, for example, an abuse of the relationship of trust and confidence.

11.2.2.3 Rebutting the presumption of undue influence

The most common way to rebut the presumption of undue influence is to show that the vulnerable party received independent advice as to the nature and effect of the transaction (see *Hammond v Osborn* [2002] EWCA Civ 885). However, independent advice will not always be sufficient to rebut the presumption. In *Pesticcio v Niersmans* [2004] EWCA Civ 372, Mummery LJ said:

> It is the case, as held in *Inche Noriah v Omar* [1929] AC 127 at 135, that the presumption of undue influence may be rebutted by showing that the transaction was entered into 'after the nature and effect of the transaction had been fully explained to the donor by some independent qualified person'. The participation of a solicitor is not, however, a precaution which is guaranteed to work in every case. It is necessary for the court to be satisfied that the advice and explanation by, for example, a solicitor, was relevant and effective to free the donor from the impairment of the influence on his free will and to give him the necessary independence of judgment and freedom to make choices with a full appreciation of what he was doing.

Independent advice might be legal, but does not necessarily have to be so. Moreover, where the presumption of undue influence is particularly heavy, it may be necessary to show, in addition to the fact that the vulnerable party received independent advice, that he was free to act on it. In *Allcard v Skinner* (1887) 36 Ch D 145, Lindley LJ said:

> [T]he gifts made ... cannot be supported in the absence of proof that the Plaintiff could have obtained independent advice if she wished for it, and that she knew that she would have been allowed to obtain such advice if she had desired to do so. I doubt whether the gifts could have been supported if such proof had been given, unless there was also proof that she was free to act on the advice which might be given to her.

Although the usual means of rebutting the presumption of undue influence will be evidence that the vulnerable party received independent competent advice, it is possible to rebut the presumption without such evidence. In *Johnson v EBS Pensioner Trustees Ltd* (2001) 82 P & CR DG2, Patten J held that the presumption had been rebutted even though independent advice had not been provided. The complainant was an experienced businessman and Patten J held that 'he was at all relevant times fully aware of what he was entering into and more to the point did so independently of any pressure stemming from his relationship with [the other party]'. In most cases, however, it will be very difficult to rebut the presumption of undue influence without evidence of independent advice (see *Hammond v Osborn* [2002] EWCA Civ 885). See also *Hackett v Crown Prosecution Service* [2011] EWHC 1170.

11.3 Undue influence and third parties

The majority of recent cases on undue influence have been concerned with the effect, on a transaction between A and B, of undue influence by a third party (C). A classic example of this is where a wife agrees to act as surety to a bank in order to raise capital for the husband's business. If the husband has exercised undue influence over his wife, can the suretyship be set aside as against the bank? In certain situations, the courts have been prepared to intervene to find that the suretyship can be set aside due to the bank having had notice of the husband's undue influence (see generally Devenney, Fox O'Mahony and Kenny, 'Standing surety in England and Wales: the sphinx of procedural protection' [2008] LMCLQ 394).

Barclays Bank plc v O'Brien [1994] 1 AC 180

Facts: Mr and Mrs O'Brien agreed to execute a second mortgage of their matrimonial home as security for an overdraft facility extended by Barclays Bank to Mr O'Brien's company. The employee of the bank who presented the documents for the wife's signature failed to follow his manager's instructions to ensure that both defendants were fully aware of the nature of the documents and to suggest that they take legal advice if either of them were unsure about the transaction. Mrs O'Brien signed the papers without reading them in reliance on her husband's statement that the security was limited to £60,000, whereas, in fact, it was for £130,000. When the company's overdraft exceeded £154,000, the bank sought to realise the security and obtained a registrar's order for possession. The judge dismissed the wife's appeal on the grounds that Mr O'Brien was not acting on behalf of the bank and therefore they could not be held responsible for his misrepresentation. The Court of Appeal allowed Mrs O'Brien's appeal. Their Lordships found that Mrs O'Brien was an intelligent and independent-minded woman who had not been unduly influenced by Mr O'Brien. They did hold, however, that the guarantee had been entered into in reliance on an actionable misrepresentation by Mr O'Brien, and that Mrs O'Brien was entitled to special protection in equity. For this reason, the legal charge was not enforceable by the bank against Mrs O'Brien, save to the extent of the £60,000 which she had thought she was agreeing to secure.

Held: The House of Lords dismissed the bank's appeal. Although their Lordships held that there was no basis for providing special protection in equity to Mrs O'Brien, the appeal was dismissed on the grounds that the bank had constructive notice of Mr O'Brien's misrepresentation.

Lord Browne-Wilkinson

Conclusions

(**a**) **Wives.** My starting point is to clarify the basis of the law. Should wives (and perhaps others) be accorded special rights in relation to surety transactions by the recognition of a special equity applicable only to such persons engaged in such transactions? Or should they enjoy only the same protection as they would enjoy in relation to their other dealings? In my judgment, the special equity theory should be rejected. First, I can find no basis in principle for affording special protection to a limited class in relation to one type of transaction only. Second, to require the creditor to prove knowledge and understanding by the wife in all cases is to reintroduce by the back door either a presumption of undue influence of Class 2(A) (which has been decisively rejected) or the Romilly heresy (which has long been treated as bad law). Third, although Scott LJ found that there were two lines of cases one of which supported the special equity theory, on analysis although many decisions are not inconsistent with that theory the only two cases which support it are *Yerkey v Jones*, 63 CLR 649, and the decision of the Court of Appeal in the present case. Finally, it is not necessary to have recourse to a special equity theory for the proper protection of the legitimate interests of wives as I will seek to show.

In my judgment, if the doctrine of notice is properly applied, there is no need for the introduction of a special equity in these types of cases. A wife who has been induced to stand as a surety for her husband's debts by his undue influence, misrepresentation or some other legal wrong has an equity as against him to set aside that transaction. Under the ordinary principles of equity, her right to set aside that transaction will be enforceable against third parties (e.g. against a creditor) if either the husband was acting as the third party's agent or the third party had actual or constructive notice of the facts giving rise to her equity. Although there may be cases where, without artificiality, it can properly be held that the husband was acting as the agent of the creditor in procuring the wife to stand as surety, such cases will be of very rare occurrence. The key to the problem is to identify the circumstances in which the creditor will be taken to have had notice of the wife's equity to set aside the transaction.

The doctrine of notice lies at the heart of equity. Given that there are two innocent parties, each enjoying rights, the earlier right prevails against the later right if the acquirer of the later right knows of the earlier right (actual notice) or would have discovered it had he taken proper steps (constructive notice). In particular, if the party asserting that he takes free of the earlier rights of another knows of certain facts which put him on inquiry as to the possible existence of the rights of that other and he fails to make such inquiry or take such other steps as are reasonable to verify whether such earlier right does or does not exist, he will have constructive notice of the earlier right and take subject to it. Therefore where a wife has agreed to stand surety for her husband's debts as a result of undue influence or misrepresentation, the creditor will take subject to the wife's equity to set aside the transaction if the circumstances are such as to put the creditor on inquiry as to the circumstances in which she agreed to stand surety.

It is at this stage that, in my view, the 'invalidating tendency' or the law's 'tender treatment' of married women, becomes relevant ... [T]his tenderness of the law towards married women is due to the fact that, even today, many wives repose confidence and trust in their husbands in relation to their financial affairs. This tenderness of the law is reflected by the fact that voluntary dispositions by the wife in favour of her husband are more likely to be set aside than other dispositions by her: a wife is more likely to establish presumed undue influence of Class 2(B) by her husband than by others because, in practice, many wives do repose in their husbands trust and confidence in relation to their financial affairs. Moreover the informality of business dealings between spouses raises a substantial risk that the husband has not accurately stated to the wife the nature of the liability she is undertaking, i.e., he has misrepresented the position, albeit negligently.

Therefore in my judgment a creditor is put on inquiry when a wife offers to stand surety for her husband's debts by the combination of two factors: (a) the transaction is on its face not to the financial advantage of the wife; and (b) there is a substantial risk in transactions of that kind that, in procuring the wife to act as surety, the husband has committed a legal or equitable wrong that entitles the wife to set aside the transaction.

It follows that unless the creditor who is put on inquiry takes reasonable steps to satisfy himself that the wife's agreement to stand surety has been properly obtained, the creditor will have constructive notice of the wife's rights.

What, then are the reasonable steps which the creditor should take to ensure that it does not have constructive notice of the wife's rights, if any? Normally the reasonable steps necessary to avoid being fixed with constructive notice consist of making inquiry of the person who may have the earlier right (ie the wife) to see whether such right is asserted. It is plainly impossible to require of banks and other financial institutions that they should inquire of one spouse whether he or she has been unduly influenced or misled by the other. But in my judgment the creditor, in order to avoid being fixed with constructive notice, can reasonably be expected to take steps to bring home to the wife the risk she is running by standing as surety and to advise her to take independent advice. As to past transactions, it will depend on the facts of each case whether the steps taken by the creditor satisfy this test. However for the future in my judgment a creditor will have satisfied these requirements if it insists that the wife attend a private meeting (in the absence of the husband) with a representative of the creditor at which she is told of the extent of her liability as surety, warned of the risk she is running and urged to take independent legal advice. If these steps are taken in my judgment the creditor will have taken such reasonable steps as are necessary to preclude a subsequent claim that it had constructive notice of the wife's rights. I should make it clear that I have been considering the ordinary case where the creditor knows only that the wife is to stand surety for her husband's debts. I would not exclude exceptional cases where a creditor has knowledge of further facts which render the presence of undue influence not only possible but probable. In such cases, the creditor to be safe will have to insist that the wife is separately advised ...

If the law is established as I have suggested, it will hold the balance fairly between on the one hand the vulnerability of the wife who relies implicitly on her husband and, on the other hand, the practical problems of financial institutions asked to accept a secured or unsecured surety obligation from the wife for her husband's debts. In the context of suretyship, the wife will not have any right to disown her obligations just because subsequently she proves that she did not fully understand the transaction: she will, as in all other areas of her affairs, be bound by her obligations unless her husband has, by misrepresentation, undue influence or other wrong, committed an actionable wrong against her. In the normal case, a financial institution will be able to lend with confidence in reliance on the wife's surety obligation provided that it warns her (in the absence of the husband) of the amount of her potential liability and of the risk of standing surety and advises her to take independent advice ...

(**b**) **Other persons.** I have hitherto dealt only with the position where a wife stands surety for her husband's debts. But in my judgment the same principles are applicable to all other cases where there is an emotional relationship between cohabitees. The 'tenderness' shown by the law to married women is not based on the marriage ceremony but reflects the underlying risk of one cohabitee exploiting the emotional involvement and trust of the other. Now that unmarried cohabitation, whether heterosexual or homosexual, is widespread in our society, the law should recognise this. Legal wives are not the only group which are now exposed to the emotional pressure of cohabitation. Therefore if, but only if, the creditor is aware that the surety is cohabiting with the principal debtor, in my judgment the same principles should apply to them as apply to husband and wife.

In addition to the cases of cohabitees, the decision of the Court of Appeal in *Avon Finance Co Ltd v Bridger* [1985] 2 All ER 281 shows (rightly in my view) that other relationships can give rise to a similar result. In that case a son, by means of misrepresentation, persuaded his elderly parents to stand surety for his debts. The surety obligation was held to be unenforceable by the creditor *inter alia* because to the bank's knowledge the parents trusted the son in their financial dealings. In my judgment that case was rightly decided: in a case where the creditor is aware that the surety reposes trust and confidence in the principal debtor in relation to his financial affairs, the creditor is put on inquiry in just the same way as it is in relation to husband and wife.

Summary

I can therefore summarise my views as follows. Where one cohabitee has entered into an obligation to stand as surety for the debts of the other cohabitee and the creditor is aware that they are cohabitees: (1) the surety obligation will be valid and enforceable by the creditor unless the suretyship was procured by the undue influence, misrepresentation or other legal wrong of the principal debtor; (2) if there has been undue influence, misrepresentation or other legal wrong by the principal debtor, unless the creditor has taken reasonable steps to satisfy himself that the surety entered into the obligation freely and in knowledge of the true facts, the creditor will be unable to enforce the surety obligation because he will be fixed with constructive notice of the surety's right to set aside the transaction; (3) unless there are special exceptional circumstances, a creditor will have taken such reasonable steps to avoid being fixed with constructive notice if the creditor warns the surety (at a meeting not attended by the principal debtor) of the amount of her potential liability and of the risks involved and advises the surety to take independent legal advice.

I should make it clear that in referring to the husband's debts I include the debts of a company in which the husband (but not the wife) has a direct financial interest.

The decision of this case

Applying those principles to this case, to the knowledge of the bank Mr and Mrs O'Brien were man and wife. The bank took a surety obligation from Mrs O'Brien, secured on the matrimonial home, to secure the debts of a company in which Mr O'Brien was interested but in which Mrs O'Brien had no direct pecuniary interest. The bank should therefore have been put on inquiry as to the circumstances in which Mrs O'Brien had agreed to stand as surety for the debt of her husband. If the Burnham branch had properly carried out the instructions from Mr Tucker of the Woolwich branch, Mrs O'Brien would have been informed that she and the matrimonial home were potentially liable for the debts of a company which had an existing liability of £107,000 and which was to be afforded an overdraft facility of £135,000. If she had been told this, it would have counteracted Mr O'Brien's misrepresentation that the liability was limited to £60,000 and would last for only three weeks. In addition according to the side letter she would have been recommended to take independent legal advice.

Unfortunately Mr Tucker's instructions were not followed and to the knowledge of the bank (through the clerk at the Burnham branch) Mrs O'Brien signed the documents without any warning of the risks or any recommendation to take legal advice. In the circumstances the bank (having failed to take reasonable steps) is fixed with constructive notice of the wrongful misrepresentation made by Mr O'Brien to Mrs O'Brien. Mrs O'Brien is therefore entitled as against the bank to set aside the legal charge on the matrimonial home securing her husband's liability to the bank.

For these reasons I would dismiss the appeal with costs.

In the context of cohabitees, where one cohabitee agreed to stand surety for the other and the creditor was aware that the parties were cohabitees, Lord Browne-Wilkinson outlined three stages to a claim to have the transaction set aside as against the creditor:

1. The surety needed to show that the transaction was procured by a 'wrong' committed by the principal debtor. On the facts of *O'Brien*, the wrong was a misrepresentation – Mr O'Brien had told Mrs O'Brien that the security was limited to £60,000, whereas in fact it was for £130,000. It is clear that the principles expounded by Lord Browne-Wilkinson are equally applicable where the wrong committed is undue influence.
2. In the absence of actual notice, the surety needed to show that the creditor was put on inquiry. It seemed that a creditor was put on inquiry when:
   (a) the transaction was, on its face, not to the financial advantage of the surety; and
   (b) there was a substantial risk in transactions of that kind that the principal debtor committed a legal or equitable wrong that entitled the surety to set aside the transaction.
3. Once put on notice, the creditor needed to take reasonable steps to ensure that the surety's agreement to the transaction was freely given. These steps include:
   (a) warning the surety (not in the presence of the debtor) of the amount of her potential liability; and
   (b) advising the surety to take independent legal advice.

It is important to note that the basis for setting aside the transaction as against the bank in *O'Brien* was not the wrong committed by Mr O'Brien but the fact that the bank was fixed with notice of the wrong and did not take reasonable steps to ensure that Mrs O'Brien's agreement to the transaction was freely given.

Lord Browne-Wilkinson saw no reason to confine his principles to wives. He was of the view that they apply to any situation where the creditor was aware that the surety placed trust and confidence in the debtor. The only difference was that, whereas with cohabitees, the risk of undue influence or misrepresentation can be inferred from the combination of the relationship and the nature of the transaction, in other situations, it would need to be shown that the creditor had actual knowledge that the surety placed trust and confidence in the principal debtor.

The House of Lords, in *Etridge*, has now restated the law on undue influence in third-party situations. This seminal case also did much to clarify the law of undue influence as a whole.

11.4 The *Etridge* case

***Royal Bank of Scotland plc v Etridge (No 2)* [2002] 2 AC 773**

Facts: The case concerned eight conjoined appeals. Each appeal arose out of a transaction in which a wife charged her interest in her home in favour of a bank as security for her husband's indebtedness or the indebtedness of a company through which he carried on business. Seven of the appeals concerned claims by a wife that a charge which she had signed should be set aside on the ground of undue influence and the eighth concerned a claim by a wife for damages from a solicitor for negligent advice prior to signing a charge. The importance of the decision lies not so much in the specific facts of each case, but in the statements of general principle to be applied by the courts in subsequent cases.

Held: The House of Lords held that the appeals would be allowed in the second, third, fifth, seventh and eighth cases and dismissed in the first, fourth and sixth cases.

Lord Bingham of Cornhill

1. My Lords, I have had the great advantage of reading in draft the opinions prepared by each of my noble and learned friends …

3. … While the opinions of Lord Nicholls and Lord Scott show some difference of expression and approach, I do not myself discern any significant difference of legal principle applicable to these cases, and I agree with both opinions. But if I am wrong and such differences exist, it is plain that the opinion of Lord Nicholls commands the unqualified support of all members of the House.

Lord Nicholls of Birkenhead

Undue influence

6. The issues raised by these appeals make it necessary to go back to first principles. Undue influence is one of the grounds of relief developed by the courts of equity as a court of conscience. The objective is to ensure that the influence of one person over another is not abused. In everyday life people constantly seek to influence the decisions of others. They seek to persuade those with whom they are dealing to enter into transactions, whether great or small. The law has set limits to the means properly employable for this purpose. To this end the common law developed a principle of duress. Originally this was narrow in its scope, restricted to the more blatant forms of physical coercion, such as personal violence.

7. Here, as elsewhere in the law, equity supplemented the common law. Equity extended the reach of the law to other unacceptable forms of persuasion. The law will investigate the manner in which the intention to enter into the transaction was secured: 'how the intention was produced', in the oft repeated words of Lord Eldon LC, from as long ago as 1807 (*Huguenin v Baseley* 14 Ves 273, 300). If the intention was produced by an unacceptable means, the law will not permit the transaction to stand. The means used is regarded as an exercise of improper or 'undue' influence, and hence unacceptable, whenever the consent thus procured ought not fairly to be treated as the expression of a person's free will. It is impossible to be more precise or definitive. The circumstances in which one person acquires influence over another, and the manner in which influence may be exercised, vary too widely to permit of any more specific criterion.

8. Equity identified broadly two forms of unacceptable conduct. The first comprises overt acts of improper pressure or coercion such as unlawful threats. Today there is much overlap with the principle of duress as this principle has subsequently developed. The second form arises out of a relationship between two persons where one has acquired over another a measure of influence, or ascendancy, of which the ascendant person then takes unfair advantage. An example from the 19th century, when much of this law developed, is a case where an impoverished father prevailed upon his inexperienced children to charge their reversionary interests under their parents' marriage settlement with payment of his mortgage debts: see *Bainbrigge v Browne* (1881) 18 Ch D 188.

9. In cases of this latter nature the influence one person has over another provides scope for misuse without any specific overt acts of persuasion. The relationship between two individuals may be such that, without more, one of them is disposed to agree a course of action proposed by the other. Typically this occurs when one person places trust in another to look after his affairs and interests, and the latter betrays this trust by preferring his own interests. He abuses the influence he has acquired ...

10. The law has long recognised the need to prevent abuse of influence in these 'relationship' cases despite the absence of evidence of overt acts of persuasive conduct. The types of relationship, such as parent and child, in which this principle falls to be applied cannot be listed exhaustively. Relationships are infinitely various. Sir Guenter Treitel QC has rightly noted that the question is whether one party has reposed sufficient trust and confidence in the other, rather than whether the relationship between the parties belongs to a particular type: see Treitel, *The Law of Contract*, 10th edn (1999), pp 380–381. For example, the relation of banker and customer will not normally meet this criterion, but exceptionally it may: see *National Westminster Bank plc v Morgan* [1985] AC 686, 707–709.

11. Even this test is not comprehensive. The principle is not confined to cases of abuse of trust and confidence. It also includes, for instance, cases where a vulnerable person has been exploited. Indeed, there is no single touchstone for determining whether the principle is applicable. Several expressions have been used in an endeavour to encapsulate the essence: trust and confidence, reliance, dependence or vulnerability on the one hand and ascendancy, domination or control on the other. None of these descriptions is perfect. None is all embracing. Each has its proper place.

12. In *CIBC Mortgages plc v Pitt* [1994] 1 AC 200 your Lordships' House decided that in cases of undue influence disadvantage is not a necessary ingredient of the cause of action. It is not essential that the transaction should be disadvantageous to the pressurised or influenced person, either in financial terms or in any other way. However, in the nature of things, questions of undue influence will not usually arise, and the exercise of undue influence is unlikely to occur, where the transaction is innocuous. The issue is likely to arise only when, in some respect, the transaction was disadvantageous either from the outset or as matters turned out.

Burden of proof and presumptions

13. Whether a transaction was brought about by the exercise of undue influence is a question of fact. Here, as elsewhere, the general principle is that he who asserts a wrong has been committed must prove it. The burden of proving an allegation of undue influence rests upon the person who claims to have been wronged. This is the general rule. The evidence required to discharge the burden of proof depends on the nature of the alleged undue influence, the personality of the parties, their relationship, the extent to which the transaction cannot readily be accounted for by the ordinary motives of ordinary persons in that relationship, and all the circumstances of the case.

14. Proof that the complainant placed trust and confidence in the other party in relation to the management of the complainant's financial affairs, coupled with a transaction which calls for explanation, will normally be sufficient, failing satisfactory evidence to the contrary, to discharge the burden of proof. On proof of these two matters the stage is set for the court to infer that, in the absence of a satisfactory explanation, the transaction can only have been procured by undue influence. In other words, proof of these two facts is prima facie evidence that the defendant abused the influence he acquired in the parties' relationship. He preferred his own interests. He did not behave fairly to the other. So the evidential burden then shifts to him. It is for him to produce evidence to counter the inference which otherwise should be drawn.

15. *Bainbrigge v Browne* 18 Ch D 188, already mentioned, provides a good illustration of this commonplace type of forensic exercise ...

16. Generations of equity lawyers have conventionally described this situation as one in which a presumption of undue influence arises. This use of the term 'presumption' is descriptive of a shift in the evidential onus on a question of fact. When a plaintiff succeeds by this route he does so because he has succeeded in establishing a case of undue influence. The court has drawn appropriate inferences of fact upon a balanced consideration of the whole of the evidence at the end of a trial in which the burden of proof rested upon the plaintiff. The use, in the course of the trial, of the forensic tool of a shift in the evidential burden of proof should not be permitted to obscure the overall position. These cases are the equitable counterpart of common law cases where the principle of *res ipsa loquitur* is invoked. There is a rebuttable evidential presumption of undue influence.

17. The availability of this forensic tool in cases founded on abuse of influence arising from the parties' relationship has led to this type of case sometimes being labelled 'presumed undue influence'. This is by way of contrast with cases involving actual pressure or the like, which are labelled 'actual undue influence': see *Bank of Credit and Commerce International SA v Aboody* [1990] 1 QB 923, 953, and *Royal Bank of Scotland plc v Etridge (No 2)* [1998] 4 All ER 705, 711–712, paras 5–7. This usage can be a little confusing. In many cases where a plaintiff has claimed that the defendant abused the influence he acquired in a relationship of trust and confidence the plaintiff has succeeded by recourse to the rebuttable evidential presumption. But this need not be so. Such a plaintiff may succeed even where this presumption is not available to him; for instance, where the impugned transaction was not one which called for an explanation.

18. The evidential presumption discussed above is to be distinguished sharply from a different form of presumption which arises in some cases. The law has adopted a sternly protective attitude towards certain types of relationship in which one party acquires influence over another who is vulnerable and dependent and where, moreover, substantial gifts by the influenced or vulnerable person are not normally to be expected. Examples of relationships within this special class are parent and child, guardian and ward, trustee and beneficiary, solicitor and client, and medical adviser and patient. In these cases the law presumes, irrebuttably, that one party had influence over the other. The complainant need not prove he actually reposed trust and confidence in the other party. It is sufficient for him to prove the existence of the type of relationship.

19. It is now well established that husband and wife is not one of the relationships to which this latter principle applies ... Although there is no presumption, the court will nevertheless note, as a matter of fact, the opportunities for abuse which flow from a wife's confidence in her husband. The court will take this into account with all the other evidence in the case ...

Independent advice

20. Proof that the complainant received advice from a third party before entering into the impugned transaction is one of the matters a court takes into account when weighing all the evidence. The weight, or importance, to be attached to such advice depends on all the circumstances. In the normal course, advice from a solicitor or other outside adviser can be expected to bring home to a complainant a proper understanding of what he or she is about to do. But a person may understand fully the implications of a proposed transaction, for instance, a substantial gift, and yet still be acting under the undue influence of another. Proof of outside advice does not, of itself, necessarily show that the subsequent completion of the transaction was free from the exercise of undue influence. Whether it will be proper to infer that outside advice had an emancipating effect, so that the transaction was not brought about by the exercise of undue influence, is a question of fact to be decided having regard to all the evidence in the case.

Manifest disadvantage

21. As already noted, there are two prerequisites to the evidential shift in the burden of proof from the complainant to the other party. First, that the complainant reposed trust and confidence in the other party, or the other party acquired ascendancy over the complainant. Second, that the transaction is not readily explicable by the relationship of the parties.

22. Lindley LJ summarised this second prerequisite in the leading authority of *Allcard v Skinner* 36 Ch D 145, where the donor parted with almost all her property. Lindley LJ pointed out that where a gift of a small amount is made to a person standing in a confidential relationship to the donor, some proof of the exercise of the influence of the donee must be given. The mere existence of the influence is not enough. He continued, at p 185 'But if the gift is so large as not to be reasonably accounted for on the ground of friendship, relationship, charity, or other ordinary motives on which ordinary men act, the burden is upon the donee to support the gift.' …

24 …. The second prerequisite, as expressed by Lindley LJ, is good sense. It is a necessary limitation upon the width of the first prerequisite. It would be absurd for the law to presume that every gift by a child to a parent, or every transaction between a client and his solicitor or between a patient and his doctor, was brought about by undue influence unless the contrary is affirmatively proved. Such a presumption would be too far-reaching. The law would be out of touch with everyday life if the presumption were to apply to every Christmas or birthday gift by a child to a parent, or to an agreement whereby a client or patient agrees to be responsible for the reasonable fees of his legal or medical adviser. The law would be rightly open to ridicule, for transactions such as these are unexceptionable. They do not suggest that something may be amiss. So something more is needed before the law reverses the burden of proof, something which calls for an explanation. When that something more is present, the greater the disadvantage to the vulnerable person, the more cogent must be the explanation before the presumption will be regarded as rebutted.

25. This was the approach adopted by Lord Scarman in *National Westminster Bank plc v Morgan* [1985] AC 686, 703–707. He cited Lindley LJ's observations in *Allcard v Skinner* (1887) 36 Ch D 145, 185, which I have set out above … Lord Scarman concluded, at p 704: 'the Court of Appeal erred in law in holding that the presumption of undue influence can arise from the evidence of the relationship of the parties without also evidence that the transaction itself was wrongful in that it constituted *an advantage taken of the person subjected to the influence which, failing proof to the contrary, was explicable only on the basis that undue influence had been exercised to procure it*' (Emphasis added.)

26. Lord Scarman attached the label 'manifest disadvantage' to this second ingredient necessary to raise the presumption. This label has been causing difficulty. It may be apt enough when applied to straightforward transactions such as a substantial gift or a sale at an undervalue. But experience has now shown that this expression can give rise to misunderstanding. The label is being understood and applied in a way which does not accord with the meaning intended by Lord Scarman, its originator.

27. The problem has arisen in the context of wives guaranteeing payment of their husband's business debts. In recent years judge after judge has grappled with the baffling question whether a wife's guarantee of her husband's bank overdraft, together with a charge on her share of the matrimonial home, was a transaction manifestly to her disadvantage.

28. In a narrow sense, such a transaction plainly ('manifestly') is disadvantageous to the wife. She undertakes a serious financial obligation, and in return she personally receives nothing. But that would be to take an unrealistically blinkered view of such a transaction. Unlike the relationship of solicitor and client or medical adviser and patient, in the case of husband and wife there are inherent reasons why such a transaction may well be for her benefit. Ordinarily, the fortunes of husband and wife are bound up together ...

29. Which, then, is the correct approach to adopt in deciding whether a transaction is disadvantageous to the wife: the narrow approach, or the wider approach? The answer is neither. The answer lies in discarding a label which gives rise to this sort of ambiguity. The better approach is to adhere more directly to the test outlined by Lindley LJ in *Allcard v Skinner* 36 Ch D 145, and adopted by Lord Scarman in *National Westminster Bank plc v Morgan* [1985] AC 686, in the passages I have cited.

30. I return to husband and wife cases. I do not think that, in the ordinary course, a guarantee of the character I have mentioned is to be regarded as a transaction which, failing proof to the contrary, is explicable only on the basis that it has been procured by the exercise of undue influence by the husband ...

31. I have emphasised the phrase 'in the ordinary course'. There will be cases where a wife's signature of a guarantee or a charge of her share in the matrimonial home does call for explanation. Nothing I have said above is directed at such a case.

A cautionary note

32. I add a cautionary note, prompted by some of the first instance judgments in the cases currently being considered by the House. It concerns the general approach to be adopted by a court when considering whether a wife's guarantee of her husband's bank overdraft was procured by her husband's undue influence. Undue influence has a connotation of impropriety. In the eye of the law, undue influence means that influence has been misused. Statements or conduct by a husband which do not pass beyond the bounds of what may be expected of a reasonable husband in the circumstances should not, without more, be castigated as undue influence. Similarly, when a husband is forecasting the future of his business, and expressing his hopes or fears, a degree of hyperbole may be only natural. Courts should not too readily treat such exaggerations as misstatements.

33. Inaccurate explanations of a proposed transaction are a different matter. So are cases where a husband, in whom a wife has reposed trust and confidence for the management of their financial affairs, prefers his interests to hers and makes a choice for both of them on that footing. Such a husband abuses the influence he has. He fails to discharge the obligation of candour and fairness he owes a wife who is looking to him to make the major financial decisions ...

The complainant and third parties: suretyship transactions

35. If the freedom of home-owners to make economic use of their homes is not to be frustrated, a bank must be able to have confidence that a wife's signature of the necessary guarantee and charge will be as binding upon her as is the signature of anyone else on documents which he or she may sign. Otherwise banks will not be willing to lend money on the security of a jointly owned house or flat.

36. At the same time, the high degree of trust and confidence and emotional interdependence which normally characterises a marriage relationship provides scope for abuse ...

37. In *O'Brien's* case this House decided where the balance should be held between these competing interests. On the one side, there is the need to protect a wife against a husband's undue influence. On the other side, there is the need for the bank to be able to have reasonable confidence in the strength of its security. Otherwise it would not provide the required money. The problem lies in finding the course best designed to protect wives in a minority of cases without unreasonably hampering the giving and taking of security. The House produced a practical solution ... Like every compromise, the outcome falls short of achieving in full the objectives of either of the two competing interests. In particular, the steps required of banks will not guarantee that, in future, wives will not be subjected to undue influence or misled when standing as sureties. Short of prohibiting this type of suretyship transaction altogether, there is no way of achieving that result, desirable although it is ...

38. The jurisprudential route by which the House reached its conclusion in *O'Brien's* case has attracted criticism from some commentators ... In *O'Brien*, Lord Browne-Wilkinson prayed in aid the doctrine of constructive notice. In circumstances he identified, a creditor is put on inquiry. When that is so, the creditor 'will have constructive notice of the wife's rights' unless the creditor takes reasonable steps to satisfy himself that the wife's agreement to stand surety has been properly obtained: see [1994] 1 AC 180, 196.

39. Lord Browne-Wilkinson would be the first to recognise this is not a conventional use of the equitable concept of constructive notice ...

40. The traditional view of equity in this tripartite situation seems to be that a person in the position of the wife will only be relieved of her bargain if the other party to the transaction (the bank, in the present instance) was privy to the conduct which led to the wife's entry into the transaction. Knowledge is required ... The law imposes no obligation on one party to a transaction to check whether the other party's concurrence was obtained by undue influence. But *O'Brien* has introduced into the law the concept that, in certain circumstances, a party to a contract may lose the benefit of his contract, entered into in good faith, if he ought to have known that the other's concurrence had been procured by the misconduct of a third party.

41. There is a further respect in which *O'Brien* departed from conventional concepts. Traditionally, a person is deemed to have notice (that is, he has 'constructive' notice) of a prior right when he does not actually know of it but would have learned of it had he made the requisite inquiries. A purchaser will be treated as having constructive notice of all that a reasonably prudent purchaser would have discovered. In the present type of case, the steps a bank is required to take, lest it have constructive notice that the wife's concurrence was procured improperly by her husband, do not consist of making inquiries. Rather, *O'Brien* envisages that the steps taken by the bank will reduce, or even eliminate, the risk of the wife entering into the transaction under any misapprehension or as a result of undue influence by her husband. The steps are not concerned to discover whether the wife has been wronged by her husband in this way. The steps are concerned to minimise the risk that such a wrong may be committed ...

43. The route selected in *O'Brien* ought not to have an unsettling effect on established principles of contract. *O'Brien* concerned suretyship transactions. These are tripartite transactions. They involve the debtor as well as the creditor and the guarantor. The guarantor enters into the transaction at the request of the debtor. The guarantor assumes obligations. On the face of the transaction the guarantor usually receives no benefit in return, unless the guarantee is being given on a commercial basis. Leaving aside cases where the relationship between the surety and the debtor is commercial, a guarantee transaction is one-sided so far as the guarantor is concerned. The creditor knows this. Thus the decision in *O'Brien* is directed at a class of contracts which has special features of its own ...

The threshold: when the bank is put on inquiry

44. ... The House set a low level for the threshold which must be crossed before a bank is put on inquiry. For practical reasons the level is set much lower than is required to satisfy a court that, failing contrary evidence, the court may infer that the transaction was procured by undue influence. Lord Browne-Wilkinson said [1994] 1 AC 180, 196:

> 'Therefore in my judgment a creditor is put on inquiry when a wife offers to stand surety for her husband's debts by the combination of two factors: (a) the transaction is on its face not to the

financial advantage of the wife; and (b) there is a substantial risk in transactions of that kind that, in procuring the wife to act as surety, the husband has committed a legal or equitable wrong that entitles the wife to set aside the transaction'.

In my view, this passage, read in context, is to be taken to mean, quite simply, that a bank is put on inquiry whenever a wife offers to stand surety for her husband's debts …

47. The position is likewise if the husband stands surety for his wife's debts. Similarly, in the case of unmarried couples, whether heterosexual or homosexual, where the bank is aware of the relationship … Cohabitation is not essential.

48. As to the type of transactions where a bank is put on inquiry, the case where a wife becomes surety for her husband's debts is, in this context, a straightforward case. The bank is put on inquiry. On the other side of the line is the case where money is being advanced, or has been advanced, to husband and wife jointly. In such a case the bank is not put on inquiry, unless the bank is aware the loan is being made for the husband's purposes, as distinct from their joint purposes …

49. Less clear cut is the case where the wife becomes surety for the debts of a company whose shares are held by her and her husband. Her shareholding may be nominal, or she may have a minority shareholding or an equal shareholding with her husband. In my view the bank is put on inquiry in such cases, even when the wife is a director or secretary of the company. Such cases cannot be equated with joint loans …

The steps a bank should take

50. The principal area of controversy on these appeals concerns the steps a bank should take when it has been put on inquiry. In *O'Brien* [1994] 1 AC 180, 196–197 Lord Browne-Wilkinson said that a bank can reasonably be expected to take steps to bring home to the wife the risk she is running by standing as surety and to advise her to take independent advice. That test is applicable to past transactions. All the cases now before your Lordships' House fall into this category. For the future a bank satisfies these requirements if it insists that the wife attend a private meeting with a representative of the bank at which she is told of the extent of her liability as surety, warned of the risk she is running and urged to take independent legal advice. In exceptional cases the bank, to be safe, has to insist that the wife is separately advised …

53. My Lords, it is plainly neither desirable nor practicable that banks should be required to attempt to discover for themselves whether a wife's consent is being procured by the exercise of undue influence of her husband. This is not a step the banks should be expected to take. Nor, further, is it desirable or practicable that banks should be expected to insist on confirmation from a solicitor that the solicitor has satisfied himself that the wife's consent has not been procured by undue influence. As already noted, the circumstances in which banks are put on inquiry are extremely wide. They embrace every case where a wife is entering into a suretyship transaction in respect of her husband's debts. Many, if not most, wives would be understandably outraged by having to respond to the sort of questioning which would be appropriate before a responsible solicitor could give such a confirmation. In any event, solicitors are not equipped to carry out such an exercise in any really worthwhile way, and they will usually lack the necessary materials …

54. The furthest a bank can be expected to go is to take reasonable steps to satisfy itself that the wife has had brought home to her, in a meaningful way, the practical implications of the proposed transaction. This does not wholly eliminate the risk of undue influence or misrepresentation. But it does mean that a wife enters into a transaction with her eyes open so far as the basic elements of the transaction are concerned.

55. … A bank may itself provide the necessary information directly to the wife. Indeed, it is best equipped to do so. But banks are not following that course … It seems to me that, provided a suitable alternative is available, banks ought not to be compelled to take this course ... It is not unreasonable for the banks to prefer that this task should be undertaken by an independent legal adviser.

56. ... Ordinarily it will be reasonable that a bank should be able to rely upon confirmation from a solicitor, acting for the wife, that he has advised the wife appropriately.

57. The position will be otherwise if the bank knows that the solicitor has not duly advised the wife or, I would add, if the bank knows facts from which it ought to have realised that the wife has not received the appropriate advice. In such circumstances the bank will proceed at its own risk ...

The content of the legal advice

61. ... [I]n the present type of case it is not for the solicitor to veto the transaction by declining to confirm to the bank that he has explained the documents to the wife and the risks she is taking upon herself. If the solicitor considers the transaction is not in the wife's best interests, he will give reasoned advice to the wife to that effect. But at the end of the day the decision on whether to proceed is the decision of the client, not the solicitor. A wife is not to be precluded from entering into a financially unwise transaction if, for her own reasons, she wishes to do so.

62. That is the general rule. There may, of course, be exceptional circumstances where it is glaringly obvious that the wife is being grievously wronged. In such a case the solicitor should decline to act further ...

64. I turn to consider the scope of the responsibilities of a solicitor who is advising the wife ... As a first step the solicitor will need to explain to the wife the purpose for which he has become involved at all. He should explain that, should it ever become necessary, the bank will rely upon his involvement to counter any suggestion that the wife was overborne by her husband or that she did not properly understand the implications of the transaction ...

65. ... Typically, the advice a solicitor can be expected to give should cover the following matters as the core minimum. (1) He will need to explain the nature of the documents and the practical consequences these will have for the wife if she signs them. She could lose her home if her husband's business does not prosper. Her home may be her only substantial asset, as well as the family's home. She could be made bankrupt. (2) He will need to point out the seriousness of the risks involved. The wife should be told the purpose of the proposed new facility, the amount and principal terms of the new facility, and that the bank might increase the amount of the facility, or change its terms, or grant a new facility, without reference to her. She should be told the amount of her liability under her guarantee. The solicitor should discuss the wife's financial means, including her understanding of the value of the property being charged. The solicitor should discuss whether the wife or her husband has any other assets out of which repayment could be made if the husband's business should fail. These matters are relevant to the seriousness of the risks involved. (3) The solicitor will need to state clearly that the wife has a choice. The decision is hers and hers alone. Explanation of the choice facing the wife will call for some discussion of the present financial position, including the amount of the husband's present indebtedness, and the amount of his current overdraft facility. (4) The solicitor should check whether the wife wishes to proceed. She should be asked whether she is content that the solicitor should write to the bank confirming he has explained to her the nature of the documents and the practical implications they may have for her, or whether, for instance, she would prefer him to negotiate with the bank on the terms of the transaction. Matters for negotiation could include the sequence in which the various securities will be called upon or a specific or lower limit to her liabilities. The solicitor should not give any confirmation to the bank without the wife's authority.

66. The solicitor's discussion with the wife should take place at a face-to-face meeting, in the absence of the husband. It goes without saying that the solicitor's explanations should be couched in suitably non-technical language. It also goes without saying that the solicitor's task is an important one. It is not a formality.

67. The solicitor should obtain from the bank any information he needs. If the bank fails for any reason to provide information requested by the solicitor, the solicitor should decline to provide the confirmation sought by the bank.

68. As already noted, the advice which a solicitor can be expected to give must depend on the particular facts of the case. But I have set out this 'core minimum' in some detail, because the quality of the legal advice is the most disturbing feature of some of the present appeals …

Independent advice

69. I turn next to the much-vexed question whether the solicitor advising the wife must act for the wife alone …

74 … . The advantages attendant upon the employment of a solicitor acting solely for the wife do not justify the additional expense this would involve for the husband. When accepting instructions to advise the wife, the solicitor assumes responsibilities directly to her, both at law and professionally. These duties, and this is central to the reasoning on this point, are owed to the wife alone. In advising the wife the solicitor is acting for the wife alone. He is concerned only with her interests. I emphasise, therefore, that in every case the solicitor must consider carefully whether there is any conflict of duty or interest and, more widely, whether it would be in the best interests of the wife for him to accept instructions from her. If he decides to accept instructions, his assumption of legal and professional responsibilities to her ought, in the ordinary course of things, to provide sufficient assurance that he will give the requisite advice fully, carefully and conscientiously. Especially so, now that the nature of the advice called for has been clarified. If at any stage the solicitor becomes concerned that there is a real risk that other interests or duties may inhibit his advice to the wife he must cease to act for her.

Agency

75. No system ever works perfectly. There will always be cases where things go wrong, sometimes seriously wrong. The next question concerns the position when a solicitor has accepted instructions to advise a wife but he fails to do so properly …

76. Mr Sher contended that, depending on the facts, the solicitor should be regarded as the agent of the bank …

77. I cannot accept this analysis. Confirmation from the solicitor that he has advised the wife is one of the bank's preconditions for completion of the transaction. But it is central to this arrangement that in advising the wife the solicitor is acting for the wife and no one else.

78. In the ordinary case, therefore, deficiencies in the advice given are a matter between the wife and her solicitor. The bank is entitled to proceed on the assumption that a solicitor advising the wife has done his job properly …

Obtaining the solicitor's confirmation

79. I now return to the steps a bank should take when it has been put on inquiry and for its protection is looking to the fact that the wife has been advised independently by a solicitor.

(1) … Since the bank is looking for its protection to legal advice given to the wife by a solicitor who, in this respect, is acting solely for her, I consider the bank should take steps to check directly with the wife the name of the solicitor she wishes to act for her. To this end, in future the bank should

communicate directly with the wife, informing her that for its own protection it will require written confirmation from a solicitor, acting for her, to the effect that the solicitor has fully explained to her the nature of the documents and the practical implications they will have for her. She should be told that the purpose of this requirement is that thereafter she should not be able to dispute she is legally bound by the documents once she has signed them. She should be asked to nominate a solicitor whom she is willing to instruct to advise her, separately from her husband, and act for her in giving the necessary confirmation to the bank. She should be told that, if she wishes, the solicitor may be the same solicitor as is acting for her husband in the transaction. If a solicitor is already acting for the husband and the wife, she should be asked whether she would prefer that a different solicitor should act for her regarding the bank's requirement for confirmation from a solicitor. The bank should not proceed with the transaction until it has received an appropriate response directly from the wife.
(2) … [I]t should become routine practice for banks, if relying on confirmation from a solicitor for their protection, to send to the solicitor the necessary financial information. What is required must depend on the facts of the case. Ordinarily this will include information on the purpose for which the proposed new facility has been requested, the current amount of the husband's indebtedness, the amount of his current overdraft facility, and the amount and terms of any new facility. If the bank's request for security arose from a written application by the husband for a facility, a copy of the application should be sent to the solicitor. The bank will, of course, need first to obtain the consent of its customer to this circulation of confidential information. If this consent is not forthcoming the transaction will not be able to proceed.
(3) Exceptionally there may be a case where the bank believes or suspects that the wife has been misled by her husband or is not entering into the transaction of her own free will. If such a case occurs the bank must inform the wife's solicitors of the facts giving rise to its belief or suspicion.
(4) The bank should in every case obtain from the wife's solicitor a written confirmation to the effect mentioned above.

80. These steps will be applicable to future transactions. In respect of past transactions, the bank will ordinarily be regarded as having discharged its obligations if a solicitor who was acting for the wife in the transaction gave the bank confirmation to the effect that he had brought home to the wife the risks she was running by standing as surety …

A wider principle

82 …. The *O'Brien* decision cannot sensibly be regarded as confined to sexual relationships, although these are likely to be its main field of application at present. What is appropriate for sexual relationships ought, in principle, to be appropriate also for other relationships where trust and confidence are likely to exist.

83. The courts have already recognised this. Further application, or development, of the *O'Brien* principle has already taken place. In *Credit Lyonnais Bank Nederland NV v Burch* [1997] 1 All ER 144 the same principle was applied where the relationship was employer and employee …

84. The crucially important question raised by this wider application of the *O'Brien* principle concerns the circumstances which will put a bank on inquiry. A bank is put on inquiry whenever a wife stands as surety for her husband's debts. It is sufficient that the bank knows of the husband – wife relationship. That bare fact is enough … What, then, of other relationships where there is an increased risk of undue influence, such as parent and child? Is it enough that the bank knows of the relationship? … A bank should not be called upon to evaluate highly personal matters such as the degree of trust and confidence existing between the father and his daughter, with the bank put on inquiry in one case and not in another. As with wives, so with daughters, whether a bank is put on inquiry should not depend on the degree of trust and confidence the particular daughter places in her father in relation to financial matters … [K]nowledge by the bank of the relationship of father and daughter should suffice to put the bank on inquiry. When the bank knows of the relationship, it must then take reasonable steps to ensure the daughter knows what she is letting herself into …

87. [T]here is no rational cut-off point, with certain types of relationship being susceptible to the *O'Brien* principle and others not. Further, if a bank is not to be required to evaluate the extent to which its customer has influence over a proposed guarantor, the only practical way forward is to regard banks as 'put on inquiry' in every case where the relationship between the surety and the debtor is non-commercial …

88. Different considerations apply where the relationship between the debtor and guarantor is commercial, as where a guarantor is being paid a fee, or a company is guaranteeing the debts of another company in the same group. Those engaged in business can be regarded as capable of looking after themselves and understanding the risks involved in the giving of guarantees. …

Lord Clyde

91. My Lords, I have had the opportunity of reading in draft the speech of my noble and learned friend, Lord Nicholls of Birkenhead, and agree with it. I add a few observations of my own because of the importance of the appeals which we have heard.

92. I question the wisdom of the practice which has grown up, particularly since *Bank of Credit and Commerce International SA v Aboody* [1990] 1 QB 923 of attempting to make classifications of cases of undue influence. That concept is in any event not easy to define … [T]he attempt to build up classes or categories may lead to confusion. The confusion is aggravated if the names used to identify the classes do not bear their actual meaning. Thus on the face of it a division into cases of 'actual' and 'presumed' undue influence appears illogical. It appears to confuse definition and proof. There is also room for uncertainty whether the presumption is of the existence of an influence or of its quality as being undue. I would also dispute the utility of the further sophistication of subdividing 'presumed undue influence' into further categories. All these classifications to my mind add mystery rather than illumination.

Lord Hobhouse of Woodborough

Introduction

100. … To the end that lenders, those advising parties and, indeed, judges should have clear statements of the law on which to base themselves, I will state at the outset that in this speech I shall agree with my noble and learned friend Lord Nicholls and, specifically, the guidance which he gives concerning the role of the burden of proof, the duties of solicitors towards their clients (paragraphs 64–68, and paragraph 74), and the steps which a lender which has been put on inquiry should take (paragraph 79). I would stress that this guidance should not be treated as optional, to be watered down when it proves inconvenient (as may be thought to have been the fate of Lord Browne-Wilkinson's equally carefully crafted scheme). Nor should it be regarded as something which will only apply to future transactions; it has represented, and continues to represent, the reasonable response to being put on inquiry … I will, in the course of this speech and without qualifying the scope of my agreement with Lord Nicholls, mention certain points in the hope that it will add to the clarity and accuracy of the analysis. I must also express my gratitude to my noble and learned friend Lord Scott of Foscote, whose speech I have read in draft, for his summary of the facts of the eight individual cases before the House.

(1) Presumed undue influence

103. The division between presumed and actual undue influence derives from the judgments in *Allcard v Skinner*. Actual undue influence presents no relevant problem. It is an equitable wrong committed by the dominant party against the other which makes it unconscionable for the dominant party to enforce his legal rights against the other. It is typically some express conduct overbearing the other party's will …

Actual undue influence does not depend upon some preexisting relationship between the two parties though it is most commonly associated with and derives from such a relationship. He who alleges actual undue influence must prove it.

104. Presumed undue influence is different in that it necessarily involves some legally recognised relationship between the two parties. As a result of that relationship one party is treated as owing a special duty to deal fairly with the other. It is not necessary for present purposes to define the limits of the relationships which give rise to this duty. Typically they are fiduciary or closely analogous relationships. A solicitor owes a legal duty to deal fairly with his client and he must, if challenged, be prepared to show that he has done so … Such legal relationships can be described as relationships where one party is legally presumed to repose trust and confidence in the other – the other side of the coin to the duty not to abuse that confidence. But there is no presumption properly so called that the confidence has been abused. It is a matter of evidence. If all that has happened is that, say, a client has left a small bequest to his family solicitor or that a solicitor has made a reasonable charge for professional services rendered to the client, no inference of abuse or unfair dealing will arise … Thus, at the trial the judge will decide on the evidence whether he is in fact satisfied that there was no abuse of confidence. It will be appreciated that the relevance of the concept of 'manifest disadvantage' is evidential. It is relevant to the question whether there is any issue of abuse which can properly be raised … It is a fallacy to argue from the terminology normally used, 'presumed undue influence', to the position, not of presuming that one party reposed trust and confidence in the other, but of presuming that an abuse of that relationship has occurred; factual inference, yes, once the issue has been properly raised, but not a presumption.

105. The Court of Appeal in *Aboody* [1990] 1 QB 923 and Lord Browne-Wilkinson classified cases where there was a legal relationship between the parties which the law presumed to be one of trust and confidence as 'presumed undue influence: class 2(A)'. They then made the logical extrapolation that there should be a class 2(B) to cover those cases where it was proved by evidence that one party had in fact reposed trust and confidence in the other. It was then said that the same consequences flowed from this factual relationship as from the legal class 2(A) relationship …

107. In agreement with what I understand to be the view of your Lordships, I consider that the so-called class 2(B) presumption should not be adopted. It is not a useful forensic tool. The wife or other person alleging that the relevant agreement or charge is not enforceable must prove her case. She can do this by proving that she was the victim of an equitable wrong. This wrong may be an overt wrong, such as oppression; or it may be the failure to perform an equitable duty, such as a failure by one in whom trust and confidence is reposed not to abuse that trust by failing to deal fairly with her and have proper regard to her interests. Although the general burden of proof is, and remains, upon her, she can discharge that burden of proof by establishing a sufficient prima facie case to justify a decision in her favour on the balance of probabilities, the court drawing appropriate inferences from the primary facts proved. Evidentially the opposite party will then be faced with the necessity to adduce evidence sufficient to displace that conclusion. Provided it is remembered that the burden is an evidential one, the comparison with the operation of the doctrine *res ipsa loquitur* is useful.

(2) Put on inquiry

111. Before turning to discuss what are the reasonable steps to be taken by a lender who had been put on inquiry, I will pause to look at some of the practical aspects … The need to guard against lack of comprehension is important … But it is not the same as guarding against undue influence. It may be a first step but it is a fallacy to confuse the two. Comprehension is essential for any legal documents of this complexity and obscurity. But for the purpose of negativing undue influence it is necessary to be satisfied that the agreement was, also, given freely in knowledge of the true facts. It must be remembered that the equitable doctrine of undue influence has been created for the protection of those who are *sui juris* and competent to undertake legal obligations but are nevertheless vulnerable and liable to have their will unduly influenced. It is their weakness which is being protected not their inability to comprehend. I regret that I must specifically disagree with my noble and learned friend Lord Scott when (in his summary) he treats a belief on the part of a lender that the wife has understood the nature and effect of the transaction as sufficient to exonerate the lender from inquiry or as treating this as the effect of the scheme laid out by Lord Nicholls in the paragraphs to which I have referred earlier. ...

Lord Scott of Foscote

Undue influence

161 .... For my part, I doubt the utility of the Class 2B classification. Class 2A is useful in identifying particular relationships where the presumption arises. The presumption in Class 2B cases, however, is doing no more than recognising that evidence of the relationship between the dominant and subservient parties, coupled with whatever other evidence is for the time being available, may be sufficient to justify a finding of undue influence on the balance of probabilities. The onus shifts to the defendant.

Unless the defendant introduces evidence to counteract the inference of undue influence that the complainant's evidence justifies, the complainant will succeed. In my opinion, the presumption of undue influence in Class 2B cases has the same function in undue influence cases as *res ipsa loquitur* has in negligence cases. It recognises an evidential state of affairs in which the onus has shifted.

162. In the surety wife cases it should, in my opinion, be recognised that undue influence, though a possible explanation for the wife's agreement to become surety, is a relatively unlikely one. *O'Brien* itself was a misrepresentation case. Undue influence had been alleged but the undoubted pressure which the husband had brought to bear to persuade his reluctant wife to sign was not regarded by the judge or the Court of Appeal as constituting undue influence. The wife's will had not been overborne by her husband. Nor was *O'Brien* a case in which, in my opinion, there would have been at any stage in the case a presumption of undue influence.

Summary

191. My Lords I think, given the regrettable length of this opinion, I should try and summarise my views about the principles that apply and the practice that should be followed in surety wife cases.

(1) The issue as between the surety wife and the lender bank is whether the bank may rely on the apparent consent of the wife to the suretyship transaction.

If the bank knows that the surety wife's consent to the transaction has been procured by undue influence or misrepresentation, or if it has shut its eyes to the likelihood that that was so, it may not rely on her apparent consent.

(3) If the wife's consent has in fact been procured by undue influence or misrepresentation, the bank may not rely on her apparent consent unless it has good reason to believe that she understands the nature and effect of the transaction.

Unless the case has some special feature, the bank's knowledge that a solicitor is acting for the wife and has advised her about the nature and effect of the transaction will provide a good reason for the purposes of (3) above. That will also be so if the bank has a reasonable belief that a solicitor is acting for her and has so advised her. Written confirmation by a solicitor acting for the wife that he has so advised her will entitle the bank to hold that reasonable belief.

So, too, a sufficient explanation of the nature and effect of the transaction given by a senior bank official would constitute good reason for the purposes of (3) above.

(6) If there are any facts known to the bank which increase the inherent risk that the wife's consent to the transaction may have been procured by the husband's undue influence or misrepresentation, it may be necessary for the bank to be satisfied that the wife has received advice about the transaction from a solicitor independent of the husband before the bank can reasonably rely on the wife's apparent consent.

(7) If the bank has not taken reasonable steps to satisfy itself that the wife understands the nature and effect of the transaction, the wife will, subject to such matters as delay, acquiescence, change of position etc, be able to set aside the transaction if her consent was in fact procured by undue influence or misrepresentation.

(8) Subject to special instructions or special circumstances, the duty of a solicitor instructed to act for a wife proposing to stand as surety, or to give security, for her husband's debts is to try and make sure that she understands the nature and effect of the transaction.

(9) In all surety wife cases the bank should disclose to the surety wife, or to the solicitor acting for her, the amount of the existing indebtedness of the principal debtor to the bank and the amount of the proposed new loan or drawing facility.

(10) Subject to (9) above, a creditor has no greater duty of disclosure to a surety wife than to any other intending surety.

192. I am in full agreement with the analysis of the applicable principles of law and with the conclusions expressed in the opinion of my noble and learned friend, Lord Nicholls of Birkenhead. I believe the analysis I have sought to give in this opinion and my conclusions are consistent with them.

The speeches delivered in *Etridge* are of enormous significance to the law of undue influence. Not only do they provide much-needed guidance to banks and solicitors as to the procedures to be adopted in surety cases, but they also provide searching analysis of the law of undue influence in relation to two-party cases.

We will consider four separate issues. First, we will identify which of the five speeches most accurately reflects the opinion of the court. Second, we will take note of Their Lordships' observations concerning the categories of undue influence. Third, we will examine the doctrine of notice and, finally, we will consider the steps that should be taken by the bank once it has been put on inquiry.

11.4.1 The speeches

In *Etridge*, five separate speeches were delivered by the House of Lords. As is not unusual in such situations, the speeches differed in expression and approach. Lord Bingham (at [3]) sought to deal with these differences by insisting that the speeches of Lord Nicholls and Lord Scott evidenced no significant difference of legal opinion. With respect, this is somewhat doubtful. Whilst Lord Hob-house expressed his unqualified agreement with Lord Nicholls, he explicitly disagreed with Lord Scott in relation to the steps a creditor must take to avoid being fixed with notice (at [111]). This is irreconcilable with Lord Bingham's position. It is, therefore, significant that Lord Bingham concluded at [3] with these words: '[I]f I am wrong and such differences exist, it is plain that the opinion of Lord Nicholls commands the unqualified support of all members of the House.' In light of this, it is clear that, to the extent that any differences do exists, it is Lord Nicholls' speech that is to be followed.

11.4.2 The categories of undue influence

The House of Lords considered the *Aboody* classification of undue influence (Class 1, 2[A], 2[B]) and unanimously rejected it. Lord Clyde said that the division into cases of 'actual' and 'presumed' undue influence appears 'illogical', and the subdivision of presumed undue influence 'added mystery rather than illumination' (at [92]). Lord Scott agreed, expressing the view that the classification set out in Aboody had set the law on the wrong track (at [158]). In particular, Their

Lordships expressed concern about the class 2(B) presumption. Lord Nicholls emphasised the evidential nature of presumed undue influence. In a statement with which Lord Hobhouse and Lord Scott agreed, Lord Nicholls said that the term 'presumption' is merely descriptive of a shift in the evidential burden from the complainant to the alleged wrongdoer (at [16]). It is thus misleading to describe the situation as one of presumed undue influence, because undue influence is only established if the inference is incapable of being rebutted. Likewise, if the relationship falls outside of class 2(A) or class 2(B), a claim for undue influence can still succeed if the complainant is able to affirmatively prove undue influence.

In an important section of his speech (at [18]), Lord Nicholls distinguished between cases that traditionally fell within class 2(A) and those that fell within class 2(B). He said that 'the law has adopted a sternly protective attitude towards certain types of relationship' and 'in these cases the law presumes, irrebuttably, that one party had influence over the other'. It might be thought that this passage states that all relationships that previously fell within Class 2(A) (including the relationship between fiancé and fiancée (*Leeder v Stevens* [2005] EWCA Civ 50), but not the relationship between husband and wife (*Etridge* at [19], [106], and [159]–[160]) give rise to a presumption of undue influence. But this is clearly not what Lord Nicholls intended. Later, at [24], Lord Nicholls said the following: 'It would be absurd for the law to presume that every gift by a child to a parent, or every transaction between a patient and his doctor, was brought about by undue influence unless the contrary is affirmatively proved. Such a presumption is too far-reaching. The law would be out of touch with everyday life …' It is therefore clear that the irrebuttable presumption of [18] is a presumption of 'influence', not of '*undue* influence'. Certain relationships (traditionally falling within class 2[A]) automatically raise an irrebuttable presumption of influence. Other relationships (traditionally falling within class 2(B)) require additional evidence in order to raise the presumption of influence. The complainant must, for example, lead evidence that they reposed trust and confidence in the other party.

Having raised a presumption of influence, the complainant must then raise a presumption of *undue* influence. Traditionally, the concept of 'manifest disadvantage' was used for this purpose (*National Westminster Bank v Morgan* [1985] AC 686). In more recent years, however, this label has caused difficulty as, in the words of Lord Nicholls, 'judge after judge has grappled with the baffling question whether a wife's guarantee of her husband's bank overdraft, together with a charge on her share of the matrimonial home, was a transaction manifestly to her disadvantage' (at [27]). On one level, such transactions are clearly disadvantageous because the wife undertakes a serious financial obligation and receives nothing in return. On another, the transaction is often beneficial to the wife, because her financial interests are inextricably bound up with her husband's. Due to this ambiguity, Lord Nicholls recommended discarding the label 'manifest disadvantage' in favour of the approach adopted in *Allcard v Skinner* (1887) 36 Ch D 145. There, it was stated that the courts should ask whether, 'the transaction itself was wrongful in that it constituted an advantage taken of the person subjected to the influence which, failing proof to the contrary, was explicable only on the basis that undue influence had been exercised to procure it'. Stated more succinctly, the test is whether the transaction is one that 'calls for an explanation' (Lord Nicholls at [24] and Lord Scott at [155]). The Court of Appeal in *Macklin v Dowsett* [2004] EWCA Civ 904, [2004] 2 EGLR 75 has confirmed that it is no longer necessary to establish manifest disadvantage in order to raise the presumption of undue influence.

To summarise, in order to raise the presumption of undue influence, it is necessary to prove two things:

(1) A relationship of trust and confidence (cf. *Re Craig* [1971] Ch 95) – either through the automatic presumption of a former class 2(A) relationship or through evidence relating to the specific relationship; and
(2) A transaction that calls for an explanation.

Once these two elements are established, the burden of proof shifts to the alleged wrongdoer. Lord Nicholls (at [16]), Lord Hobhouse (at [107]), and Lord Scott [161] all compared this evidential presumption to the common law negligence doctrine of *res ipsa loquitur* – 'the thing speaks for itself'.

In cases like *Etridge*, where a wife stands surety for her husband's debts, it may be extremely difficult to raise the evidential presumption of undue influence. This is for two reasons. First, the relationship between a husband and wife does not fall within class 2(A). Thus, it is necessary for the wife to lead specific evidence to prove that she, for example, reposed trust and confidence in her husband. Second, in the ordinary course, a guarantee by a wife of her husband's debts is not a transaction that calls for an explanation (Lord Nicholls at [30]). It can usually be explained on the ground of their relationship and therefore does not give rise to a presumption of undue influence.

11.4.3 The doctrine of notice

Seven of the appeals in *Etridge* concerned claims by the surety against the creditor. As we noted above, the surety must prove both that the principal debtor exerted undue influence and that the creditor had notice of such influence. Lord Nicholls set a low threshold for such notice. He said that a creditor is put on inquiry whenever 'a wife offers to stand surety for her husband's debts' (at [44]). This includes situations where she stands surety for the debts of her husband's business, even when she is a shareholder or director of the company (Lord Nicholls was of the view that such factors were an unreliable guide as to who runs the business [see also *Syndicate Bank (An undertaking of the Government of India) v Kanaya W Dansingani* (2019) EWHC 3439 (Ch)]).

In addition, Lord Nicholls refused to limit the principle to married couples. Cohabitation is not necessary, and nor is a sexual relationship. Given that banks should not be called upon to evaluate highly personal matters between the parties, Lord Nicholls suggested that the only practical way forward was to regard a bank as being put on inquiry in all cases where the bank knows that 'the relationship between the surety and the debtor is non-commercial' (at [87]). This is a very expansive approach to notice that places a significant burden on banks and lending institutions. Nevertheless, it is to be welcomed since it largely removes the uncertainty that previously existed in the law and enables both the lender and the surety to know where they stand.

11.4.4 The precautions to be taken by the bank

Once put on inquiry, the bank must take a number of steps in order to protect itself. These were outlined by Lord Nicholls at [79] of his speech. Lord Hobhouse stressed that these guidelines were not to be 'watered down' or regarded as 'optional' (at [100]). In particular, the bank should communicate directly with the wife, informing her that for its own protection, it will require written confirmation from a solicitor, acting for her, to the effect that the solicitor has fully explained to her the nature of the documents and the practical implications they will have for her. The bank is under an obligation to provide the solicitor with the financial information needed to advise the wife (cf. also *North Shore Ventures Ltd v Anstead Holdings Inc* [2011] EWCA Civ 230). If the bank knows of any information that leads it to suspect that the wife is being misled by her husband, or is not entering into the transaction of her own free will, it must inform the wife's solicitors of those facts. The bank should, in every case, obtain a written confirmation from the wife's solicitor. If it does so, it will be protected. Since the solicitor is not an agent of the bank, any deficiencies in the advice given by the solicitor will not affect the validity of the charge as against the bank. The wife's only form of recourse will be to pursue an action in negligence against the solicitor.

Turning to the advice to be offered by solicitors, Lord Nicholls commented at [52] that 'the quality of the legal advice is the most disturbing feature' of some of the appeals before the House. On the much-vexed question of whether the solicitor acting for the wife must act for the wife alone,

Lord Nicholls concluded that this was unnecessary, because the benefits of such a rule were outweighed by the additional expense it would entail for the husband (at [74]). Lord Nicholls said that the solicitor should meet with the wife face-to-face and in the absence of the husband. He should explain the transaction and its implications in 'suitably non-technical language'. His advice should include the 'core minimum' set out by Lord Nicholls at [65] of his speech. The solicitor must not give any confirmation to the bank without the wife's specific authority. The purpose of these guidelines is to ensure that the wife is fully informed of the nature of the transaction she is entering into.

In his speech (at [2]), Lord Bingham succinctly summarised the main issues influencing their Lordships:

> It is important that a wife (or anyone in a like position) should not charge her interest in the matrimonial home to secure the borrowing of her husband (or anyone in a like position) without fully understanding the nature and effect of the proposed transaction and that the decision is hers, to agree or not to agree. It is important that lenders should feel able to advance money, in run- of-the-mill cases with no abnormal features, on the security of the wife's interest in the matrimonial home in reasonable confidence that, if appropriate procedures have been followed in obtaining the security, it will be enforceable if the need for enforcement arises. The law must afford both parties a measure of protection. It cannot prescribe a code which will be proof against error, misunderstanding or mishap. But it can indicate minimum requirements which, if met, will reduce the risk of error, misunderstanding or mishap to an acceptable level. The paramount need in this important field is that these minimum requirements should be clear, simple and practically operable.

It is submitted that these aims have been met by the guidelines set down in *Etridge*. The threshold for when banks will be put on notice has been lowered, thus increasing the protection afforded to sureties. At the same time, the House of Lords has provided a set of steps for avoiding liability that are clear, simple and sufficiently formulaic to keep compliance costs low. Although these steps cannot guarantee that sureties will never enter transactions under undue influence, they will certainly do much to reduce the risk of this. Furthermore, it is to be hoped that the clarity of the guidance given in Etridge will stem the flow of litigants seeking to set aside transactions on the ground of third-party undue influence.

11.5 Remedies for undue influence

In most of the cases discussed so far, the influenced party has been in the position of the defendant, seeking to use the alleged undue influence to escape from his contractual obligations. The primary remedy in such cases is rescission.

11.5.1 Rescission

The usual bars to rescission apply including: affirmation (*Mitchell v Homiray* [1881] 8 QBD 587; *Goldsworthy v Brickell* [1987] 1 Ch 378; *First National Bank v Walker* [2001] 1 FLR 505), delay (*Turner v Collins* [1871] LR 7 Ch App 329; *Allcard v Skinner* [1887] 36 Ch D 145; see also Curtis v Curtis [2011] EWCA Civ 1602); counter restitution impossible (in recent years the courts have adopted a more flexible approach to this bar, see: *O'Sullivan v Management Agency and Music Ltd* [1985] QB 428; *Hart v Burbidge* [2013] EWHC 1628 and [2014] EWCA Civ 992; and *Bainbridge v Bainbridge* [2016] EWHC 898 (Ch) [on the possibility of tracing into products exchanged for the original property]); and the intervention of third-party rights (*Cobbett v Brock* [1855] 20 Beav 524; 52 ER 706; *Bridgeman v Green* [1755] Wilm 58; 97 ER 22).

The transaction will normally be rescinded in its entirety:

TSB Bank plc v Camfield [1995] 1 All ER 951

Facts: The defendant entered into an agreement with the plaintiff bank to execute a charge over her matrimonial home in relation to her husband's debts. Her husband had innocently misrepresented that the maximum liability under this charge would be £15,000. In fact, the liability was unlimited. The bank failed to provide independent advice to the defendant in the absence of her husband, and for this reason, it was held to have had constructive notice of the husband's misrepresentation. The defendant argued that the charge should be set aside in its entirety. The plaintiff countered that the wife should remain liable for £15,000, since she had been willing to agree to a charge for this amount. At first instance, the judge entered judgment against the wife for £15,000 and made an order for possession subject to payment in full within six months.

Held: The Court of Appeal allowed the appeal holding that the charge should be set aside in its entirety as against the defendant.

Roch LJ: The judge found that had the true nature of the legal charge been made known to Mrs Camfield she would not have entered into the charge and her enjoyment of her home would never have been at risk. But for the bank's failure to take reasonable steps, Mrs Camfield would have known the true nature of the proposed legal charge and the potential risk to her interest in the family home, and she would have refused to enter into that transaction. Mrs Camfield is entitled to be placed in the position she would have been in had the misrepresentation not been made and had she been made aware of the true nature of the legal charge.

The decision in *Camield* is rather controversial. It appears to be incompatible with another line of authority stemming from *Bristol & West Building Society v Henning*, [1985] 1 WLR 778.

Ferguson, P, 'Partial rescission for misrepresentation rejected' (1995) 111 *LQR* 555, 556–558

In these cases, the claimant of a beneficial interest in a property purchased with the aid of a mortgage was held impliedly to have consented to the subordination of any beneficial interest to the rights of the mortgagee. The mortgagee's claim was, in all cases, upheld to the extent of the claimant's understanding of the amount of the proposed mortgage; and, in one case in which the mortgage advance was far beyond what the claimant believed would be raised, the mortgagee was nonetheless permitted to recover in full (see *Abbey National Building Society v Cann* [1991] 1 AC 56, 94). The contrast with *Camfield*, in which the chargee received nothing at all, is striking. Further, the evidence from which consent could be implied was, if anything, stronger in *Camfield* than in the *Henning* authorities: Mrs Camfield was given legal advice, even if she did not in fact fully understand it, and signed a document giving the chargee exactly that priority over her beneficial interest which was at issue in Henning ...

[I]n *Camfield*, there was actual consent to a charge up to £15,000, and the bank had perfectly reasonable grounds for assuming this to be the case, given Mrs Camfield's execution of the charge document after legal advice had been given to her ... Granted, Mrs Camfield would not have executed the charge had she known that it was not limited to £15,000; nonetheless, it is also true that she would have done so if it had been limited to that amount. There is actual consent to the priority of the bank's rights up to that limit, and a strong argument that she is estopped from claiming rescission, except insofar as the liability exceeded the £15,000 that she was – to the bank's knowledge – willing to risk.

The approach taken in Camfield has generated much debate (see, for example, Poole, J and Keyser, A, 'Justifying partial rescission in English law' (2005) 121 LQR 273). Nevertheless, the

Court of Appeal continues to be bound by its own decision in Camfield (see *Bank Melli Iran v Samadi-Rad* [1995] 2 FLR 367).

It is important to note that the claimant in Camfield received no benefit from the loan transaction. If she had received a benefit, the right to rescission would have been conditional upon her making counter-restitution.

Dunbar Bank plc v Nadeem [1998] 3 All ER 876

Facts: The defendant and her husband signed a joint loan facility with the claimant for the purchase of a new leasehold of the matrimonial property. At the time, the defendant's husband had been the sole lessee of the property. The loan was secured by a charge against the home. When the defendant's husband fell into arrears on the payments, the claimant brought an action for possession of the property. At first instance, the judge ordered rescission of the agreement for presumed undue influence on condition that the defendant repaid the claimant half the sum advanced to purchase the property. The defendant appealed this decision, and the claimant cross-appealed against the order to set aside the charge for presumed undue influence.

Held: The defendant's appeal was dismissed, and the claimant's cross-appeal was allowed, granting an order for possession. The Court of Appeal held that the transaction should not be set aside at all, because it was not manifestly disadvantageous to the defendant, and her husband had not taken any unfair advantage of her. If there had been undue influence, the Court of Appeal suggested (*obiter*) that the defendant could have made counter-restitution by giving up her interest in the property (which would have reverted to her husband).

Millett LJ: In the present case it is inescapable that there must have been two agreements ... By the first agreement Mrs Nadeem obtained a half interest in the equity of redemption subject to the bank's legal charge, and by the second she obtained jointly with her husband an advance of £260,000 on the terms that £210,000 would be used to buy the property which she and her husband should jointly charge in favour of the bank to secure repayment of the advance. By the second agreement she did not obtain a freestanding loan, whether of £210,000 or £105,000, which she was free to use as she thought fit. There was no possibility of her applying the advance except for the purpose of acquiring the property so that she could join in giving security to the bank for the money advanced with which to acquire it.

Accordingly, in my judgment, the extent of Mrs Nadeem's enrichment, should the legal charge be set aside, is not the money which was advanced to her and her husband jointly, but the interest in the equity of redemption which she obtained by the use of the bank's money. That is the extent of her enrichment. And it is that, in my opinion, of which she must make counter restitution.

In my judgment, however, there was no need to impose conditions on the setting aside of the legal charge in order to achieve counter restitution. On the unusual facts of the present case it would have been automatic. Mrs Nadeem cannot retain her beneficial interest in the property in priority to the bank's charge and at the same time reject the liability to repay the advance by which the property was obtained. Once the legal charge is set aside, the source of her beneficial interest in the property must be her husband. He had nothing to give her except an interest in the equity of redemption. She had no need to make counter restitution because, having set aside the legal charge, she cannot assert a beneficial interest in the property in priority to the bank's legal charge to secure repayment of the money with which the property was acquired.

In my judgment, therefore, the only effect of setting aside the legal charge would be to eliminate any personal liability on the part of Mrs Nadeem.

Rescission on terms may also be ordered where the value of the property transferred under the transaction has changed.

***Cheese v Thomas* [1994] 1 WLR 129**

Facts: The plaintiff entered into an agreement with the defendant, his great-nephew, to purchase a house for £83,000, the plaintiff contributing £43,000, and the defendant providing £40,000 by means of a building society loan. The agreement was for the plaintiff to occupy the house for the rest of his life and, thereafter, for the house to pass unencumbered to the defendant. After he had moved into the house, the plaintiff became worried that the defendant was failing to pay the mortgage instalments. He brought an action seeking to set aside the transaction for undue influence and claimed repayment of the £43,000 with interest. At first instance, the judge set aside the transaction and ordered the sale of the house. Because the housing market had slumped, the property eventually sold for £55,400. The judge ordered that the plaintiff and defendant should bear the loss on the sale of the house in the same proportions as they had contributed to the purchase price. The plaintiff appealed against this decision.

Held: The Court of Appeal dismissed the appeal holding that the court was concerned to achieve practical justice between the parties. Since the personal conduct of the defendant was not open to criticism, it was appropriate for the loss on the value of the house to be shared.

Sir Donald Nicholls VC: I approach the matter in this way. Restitution has to be made, not damages paid. Damages look at the plaintiff's loss, whereas restitution is concerned with the recovery back from the defendant of what he received under the transaction. If the transaction is set aside, the plaintiff also must return what he received. Each party must hand back what he obtained under the contract. There has to be a giving back and a taking back on both sides ... It is well established that a court of equity grants this type of relief even when it cannot restore the parties precisely to the state they were in before the contract. The court will grant relief whenever, by directing accounts and making allowances, it can do what is practically just: see *Erlanger v New Sombrero Phosphate Co* (1878) 3 App Cas 1218, 1278–1279, *per* Lord Blackburn. Here justice requires that each party should be returned as near to his original position as is now possible. Each should get back a proportionate share of the net proceeds of the house, before deducting the amount paid to the building society. Thus the £55,400 should be divided between Mr Cheese and Mr Thomas in the proportions of 43:40. Mr. Cheese should receive about £28,700 and Mr. Thomas £26,700.

A number of factors meant that it was appropriate to order rescission on terms (cf. *Smith v Cooper* [2010] EWCA Civ 722). First, the transaction was in the nature of a joint venture. Both parties had contributed to the purchase price, and both parties acquired rights under the transaction. Second, the Court of Appeal took note of the conduct of the defendant. The defendant was an 'innocent fiduciary', who had been anxious to provide his great uncle with a home. In the circumstances, it would have been unduly harsh to require the defendant to bear the full loss flowing from the slump in the property market. It should be emphasised that *Cheese v Thomas* is not an example of loss apportionment. The case involved a restitutionary claim for benefits transferred under a rescinded contract. The apportionment concerned the valuation of those benefits, not the assessment of loss.

11.5.2 Account of profits

The remedy of account of profits may also be available for undue influence, although it may be subject to a reasonable allowance for the work and skill of the person exercising the influence.

***O'Sullivan v Management Agency & Music Ltd* [1985] QB 428**

Facts: The plaintiff, a young singer, entered into a management agreement with the defendant, a highly experienced, internationally recognised manager and producer of popular music. It was subsequently held that the agreements had been obtained by undue influence. However, by the time the case came to court, all the agreements had been performed, and counter-restitution was impossible.

Held: The Court of Appeal rejected the argument that the agreements could not be set aside because counter-restitution was impossible. Instead, the court held that the agreements should be rescinded and ordered the defendants to account for their profits.

Fox LJ: It is said on behalf of the plaintiffs that, if the principle of equity is that the fiduciary must account for profits obtained through the abuse of the fiduciary relationship there is no scope for the operation of anything resembling *restitutio in integrum*. The profits must simply be given up. I think that goes too far and that the law has for long had regard to the justice of the matter. If, for example, a person is by undue influence persuaded to make a gift of a house to another and that other spent money on improving the house, I apprehend that credit could be given for the improvements ...

Accordingly, it seems to me that the principle that the court will do what is practically just as between the parties is applicable to a case of undue influence even though the parties cannot be restored to their original position. That is, in my view, applicable to the present case. The question is not whether the parties can be restored to their original position; it is what does the justice of the case require? ...

The next question is, it seems to me, the recompensing of the defendants ... Once it is accepted that the court can make an appropriate allowance to a fiduciary for his skill and labour I do not see why, in principle, it should not be able to give him some part of the profit of the venture if it was thought that justice as between the parties demanded that ... I am not satisfied that it would be proper to exclude Mr Mills and the MAM companies from all reward for their efforts. I find it impossible to believe that they did not make a significant contribution to Mr O'Sullivan's success. It would be unjust to deny them a recompense for that. I would, therefore, be prepared as was done in *Phipps v Boardman* to authorise the payment (over and above out of pocket expenses) of an allowance for the skill and labour of the first five defendants in promoting the compositions and performances and managing the business affairs of Mr. O'Sullivan ... Such an allowance could include a profit element in the way that solicitors' costs do.

11.5.3 The Consumer Protection from Unfair Trading Regulations 2008 (as Amended)

On the possibility of a private law claim under Part 4A of the Consumer Protection from Unfair Trading Regulations 2008 (as amended by the Consumer Protection (Amendment) Regulations 2014) see Section 8.6.

11.6 Unconscionability and inequality of bargaining power

It has been suggested that the approach of the courts to, for example, the issues of duress and undue influence simply reflect a general reluctance to enforce transactions that are 'unconscionable'. This type of argument was famously made by Lord Denning in *Lloyd's Bank Ltd v Bundy* [1975] QB 326.

***Lloyd's Bank Ltd v Bundy* [1975] QB 326**

The general rule

Now let me say at once that in the vast majority of cases a customer who signs a bank guarantee or a charge cannot get out of it. No bargain will be upset which is the result of the ordinary interplay of forces. There are many hard cases which are caught by this rule. Take the case of a poor man who is homeless. He agrees to pay a high rent to a landlord just to get a roof over his head. The common law will not interfere. It is left to Parliament. Next take the case of a borrower in urgent need of money. He borrows it from the bank at high interest and it is guaranteed by a friend. The guarantor gives his bond and gets nothing in return. The common law will not interfere. Parliament has intervened to prevent moneylenders charging excessive interest. But it has never interfered with banks.

Yet there are exceptions to this general rule. There are cases in our books in which the courts will set aside a contract, or a transfer of property, when the parties have not met on equal terms – when the one is so strong in bargaining power and the other so weak – that, as a matter of common fairness, it is not right that the strong should be allowed to push the weak to the wall. Hitherto those exceptional cases have been treated each as a separate category in itself. But I think the time has come when we should seek to find a principle to unite them. I put on one side contracts or transactions which are voidable for fraud or misrepresentation or mistake. All those are governed by settled principles. I go only to those where there has been inequality of bargaining power, such as to merit the intervention of the court.

The categories

The first category is that of 'duress of goods'. A typical case is when a man is in a strong bargaining position by being in possession of the goods of another by virtue of a legal right, such as by way of pawn or pledge or taken in distress. The owner is in a weak position because he is in urgent need of the goods. The stronger demands of the weaker more than is justly due: and he pays it in order to get the goods. Such a transaction is voidable. He can recover the excess: see *Astley v Reynolds* (1731) 2 Stra 915 and *Green v Duckett* (1883) 11 QBD 275. To which may be added the cases of '*colore officii*', where a man is in a strong bargaining position by virtue of his official position or public profession. He relies upon it so as to gain from the weaker – who is urgently in need – more than is justly due: see *Pigotts* case cited by Lord Kenyon CJ in *Cartwright v Rowley* (1799) 2 Esp 723, 723–724; *Parker v Bristol and Exeter Railway Co* (1851) 6 Exch 702 and *Steele v Williams* (1853) 8 Exch 625. In such cases the stronger may make his claim in good faith honestly believing that he is entitled to make his demand. He may not be guilty of any fraud or misrepresentation. The inequality of bargaining power – the strength of the one versus the urgent need of the other – renders the transaction voidable and the money paid to be recovered back: see *Maskell v Horner* [1915] 3 KB 106.

The second category is that of the 'unconscionable transaction'. A man is so placed as to be in need of special care and protection and yet his weakness is exploited by another far stronger than himself so as to get his property at a gross undervalue. The typical case is that of the 'expectant heir'. But it applies to all cases where a man comes into property, or is expected to come into it – and then being in urgent need – another gives him ready cash for it, greatly below its true worth, and so gets the property transferred to him: see *Evans v Llewellin* (1787) 1 Cox 333. Even though there be no evidence of fraud or misrepresentation, nevertheless the transaction will be set aside ... This second category is said to extend to all cases where an unfair advantage has been gained by an unconscientious use of power by a stronger party against a weaker: see the cases cited in *Halsbury's Laws of England*, 3rd edn, vol 17 (1956), p 682 and, in Canada, *Morrison v Coast Finance Ltd* (1965) 55 DLR (2d) 710 and *Knupp v Bell* (1968) 67 DLR (2d) 256.

The third category is that of 'undue influence' usually so called. These are divided into two classes as stated by Cotton LJ in *Allcard v Skinner* (1887) 36 ChD 145, 171. The first are those where the stronger has been guilty of some fraud or wrongful act – expressly so as to gain some gift or advantage from the weaker. The second are those where the stronger has not been guilty of any wrongful act, but has, through the relationship which existed between him and the weaker, gained some gift or advantage for himself. Sometimes the relationship is such as to raise a presumption of undue influence, such as parent over child, solicitor over client, doctor over patient, spiritual adviser over follower. At other times a relationship of confidence must be proved to exist ...

The fourth category is that of 'undue pressure'. The most apposite of that is *Williams v Bayley* (1866) LR 1 HL 200, where a son forged his father's name to a promissory note and, by means of it, raised money from the bank of which they were both customers. The bank said to the father, in effect: 'Take your choice – give us security for your son's debt. If you do take that on yourself, then it will all go smoothly: if you do not, we shall be bound to exercise pressure'. Thereupon the father charged his property to the bank with payment of the note. The House of Lords held that the charge was invalid because of undue pressure exerted by the bank ...

Other instances of undue pressure are where one party stipulates for an unfair advantage to which the other has no option but to submit. As where an employer – the stronger party – has employed a builder – the weaker party – to do work for him. When the builder asked for payment of sums properly due (so as to pay his workmen) the employer refused to pay unless he was given some added advantage. Stuart V-C said: 'Where an agreement, hard and inequitable in itself, has been exacted under circumstances of pressure on the part of the person who exacts it, this court will set it aside': see *Ormes v Beadel* (1860) 2 Giff 166, 174 (reversed on another ground, 2 De GF & J 333) and *D & C Builders v Rees* [1966] 2 QB 617, 625.

The fifth category is that of salvage agreements. When a vessel is in danger of sinking and seeks help, the rescuer is in a strong bargaining position. The vessel in distress is in urgent need. The parties cannot be truly said to be on equal terms. The Court of Admiralty have always recognised that fact. The 'fundamental rule' is 'if the parties have made an agreement, the court will enforce it, unless it be manifestly unfair and unjust; but if it be manifestly unfair and unjust, the court will disregard it and decree what is fair and just'. See *Akerblom v Price* (1881) 7 QBD 129, 133, *per* Brett LJ, applied in a striking case *The Port Caledonia and The Anna* [1903] P 184, when the rescuer refused to help with a rope unless he was paid £1,000.

The general principles

Gathering all together, I would suggest that through all these instances there runs a single thread. They rest on 'inequality of bargaining power'. By virtue of it, the English law gives relief to one who, without independent advice, enters into a contract upon terms which are very unfair or transfers property for a consideration which is grossly inadequate, when his bargaining power is grievously impaired by reason of his own needs or desires, or by his own ignorance or infirmity, coupled with undue influences or pressures brought to bear on him by or for the benefit of the other. When I use the word 'undue' I do not mean to suggest that the principle depends on proof of any wrongdoing. The one who stipulates for an unfair advantage may be moved solely by his own self-interest, unconscious of the distress he is bringing to the other. I have also avoided any reference to the will of the one being 'dominated' or 'overcome' by the other. One who is in extreme need may knowingly consent to a most improvident bargain, solely to relieve the straits in which he finds himself. Again, I do not mean to suggest that every transaction is saved by independent advice. But the absence of it may be fatal. With these explanations, I hope this principle will be found to reconcile the cases.

Although the label 'inequality of bargaining power' suggests procedural unfairness, it is clear that Lord Denning's principle required both procedural and substantive unfairness. In other words, there needed to be both a consideration that was grossly inadequate (substantive unfairness) and a bargaining power that has been grievously impaired (procedural unfairness). Lord Denning's principle has met with some academic support, an example of which is provided below.

Waddams, S, 'Unconscionability in contracts' (1976) 39 *MLR* 369, 390–393

Towards a general principle

The common law traditionally develops by the use of fictions. Lip service continues to be paid to an old rule, but as decisions multiply exceptions to it, it becomes an empty shell and at last can be discarded without effecting any great change in the actual practice of the courts. My argument is that this stage has now been reached in respect to a rule of unconscionability. I have attempted to show that, despite lip service to the notion of absolute freedom of contract, relief is every day given against agreements that are unfair, inequitable, unreasonable or oppressive. Unconscionability, as a word to describe such control, might not be the lexicographer's first choice, but I think it is the most acceptable general word. It has historical antecedents; it occurs consistently throughout the cases in the various branches of the law discussed; it has been accepted as a general ground of relief in modern Canadian cases, and it is recognised by statute both in Commonwealth and American jurisdictions.

An argument frequently raised against recognition of a general power of relief is that it would contribute to uncertainty. I would say that certainty, though an important value in contract law, is not an absolute one, and the cases discussed in this article show that other values cannot be suppressed. Moreover, if my argument is accepted, that is that agreements are in practice set aside quite frequently and generally, it must conduce to certainty rather than uncertainty to recognise the general principle. At present we have the worst of both worlds – what for example could be less certain than the law on exemption clauses? The effect of suppressing the true principle underlying a line of cases is to produce a rule that not only fails to relieve when relief is justified but that strikes down agreements that are perfectly fair and reasonable. Only with open recognition of the true principle can the courts begin to develop rational criteria and guidelines that will satisfactorily explain their decisions and offer a useful guide for the future. I do not underestimate the difficulty of developing such guidelines, but I do maintain that to make a start on that task would be an advance in certainty as well as in justice.

Another compelling reason for adopting a general principle of unconscionability is the need to fill the gaps between the existing islands of intervention. The clause that is not quite a penalty clause or not quite an exemption clause or just outside the provisions of the Moneylenders' Act or the Misrepresentation Act 1967 will fall under the general power to relieve and anomalous distinctions like those castigated by Lord Denning in *Bridge v Campbell Discount* will disappear.

Future development

Given the open recognition of a general principle of unconscionability one would expect the courts to develop guidelines. There is every reason to think that they would be fully equal to this task ... Clearly inequality of values exchanged cannot in itself be enough or the courts would 'throw every thing into confusion and set afloat all the contracts of mankind'. But a large inequality of exchange combined with inequality of bargaining power, the twin criteria adopted by the modem Canadian cases, goes a long way to suggest a case for relief. It is not said to be conclusive, but to cast an onus on the party seeking to uphold the transaction, an onus that might possibly be discharged on a showing that the disadvantaged party was independently advised, or that he knew of the comparative values and intended a part gift. On the other hand, not every case lends itself to analysis in terms of equality of exchange and in some cases there may be grounds for relief even when the values exchanged are approximately equal. The Supply of Goods (Implied Terms) Act 1973 offers a list of criteria to guide the courts in determining what exemption clauses are fair and reasonable. The list is not exhaustive, and, no doubt, further criteria will be judicially developed. I would readily recognise that the adoption of a principle of unconscionability is a mere beginning, but I would maintain that it is a useful beginning.

There will be a need for development of bars to relief. Execution in itself should not be a bar, but execution followed by a long delay, affirmation, and intervention of third party rights might well be held to place limits on relief. The court need not choose between an all or nothing solution, but could use the power to grant relief on conditions, as the mortgage cases grant relief to the mortgagor on payment of the mortgagee's costs. A condition of relief might appropriately be the payment of the other party's reasonable expenses incurred in reliance on the agreement, thus protecting the latter's reliance interest, but not his contractual expectation.

Contract law has been passing through a period of exceptional rigidity, but there are signs that it is capable of recovering its former flexibility, as, I think, it must if it is to meet the present needs of society.

In the above extract, Professor Waddams claims that a general doctrine of unconscionability could provide the key to understanding the pre-existing law of duress, undue influence, exemption clauses and penalty clauses. Furthermore, such a doctrine could provide the crucial basis for developing a set of criteria to determine the scope of judicial intervention in the future. However, calls for such a principle have generally not met with judicial support. In *National Westminster Bank v Morgan* [1985] AC 686, Lord Scarman expressly disapproved of Lord Denning's 'inequality of bargaining power' doctrine:

> The question which the House does have to answer is: did the court in *Lloyds Bank v Bundy* accurately state the law?
>
> Lord Denning MR believed that the doctrine of undue influence could be subsumed under a general principle that English courts will grant relief where there has been 'inequality of bargaining power' (p 339). He deliberately avoided reference to the will of one party being dominated or overcome by another. The majority of the court did not follow him; they based their decision on the orthodox view of the doctrine as expounded in *Allcard v Skinner* (1887) 36 Ch D 145. The opinion of the Master of the Rolls, therefore, was not the ground of the court's decision, which was to be found in the view of the majority, for whom Sir Eric Sachs delivered the leading judgment.
>
> Nor has counsel for the respondent sought to rely on Lord Denning MR's general principle: and, in my view, he was right not to do so. The doctrine of undue influence has been sufficiently developed not to need the support of a principle which by its formulation in the language of the law of contract is not appropriate to cover transactions of gift where there is no bargain. The fact of an unequal bargain will, of course, be a relevant feature in some cases of undue influence. But it can never become an appropriate basis of principle of an equitable doctrine which is concerned with transactions 'not to be reasonably accounted for on the ground of friendship, relationship, charity, or other ordinary motives on which ordinary men act' (Lindley LJ in *Allcard v Skinner*, at p 185), and even in the field of contract I question whether there is any need in the modern law to erect a general principle of relief against inequality of bargaining power. Parliament has undertaken the task – and it is essentially a legislative task – of enacting such restrictions upon freedom of contract as are in its judgment necessary to relieve against the mischief: for example, the hire-purchase and consumer protection legislation, of which the Supply of Goods (Implied Terms) Act 1973, Consumer Credit Act 1974, Consumer Safety Act 1978, Supply of Goods and Services Act 1982 and Insurance Companies Act 1982 are examples. I doubt whether the courts should assume the burden of formulating further restrictions.

Lord Scarman, for example, stated that the doctrine was unnecessary because Parliament had already intervened in this area to place legislative restrictions on freedom of contract. This is true, but, as Professor Waddams has noted, there are gaps in the legislative framework. Lord Scarman assumed that the courts should not fill these gaps because Parliament had already intervened. However, his Lordship could just as easily have concluded that Parliament's intervention evidenced a commitment to fairness, which should be reflected in the development of new gap-filling principles by the courts.

Typically, it has been assumed that a doctrine of unconscionability would be economically inefficient, since it inhibits freedom of contract. However, Eric Posner, a leading law and economics scholar, has forcefully made the contrary argument.

Posner, E, 'Contract law in the welfare state: a defence of the unconscionability doctrine, usury laws, and related limitations on the freedom to contract' (1995) 24 *J Legal Stud* 283, 285–287

The minimum welfare theory

I assume that the state has two commitments. First, it is committed to maintaining a free market and accordingly enforces property rights and contracts. Second, the state is committed to reducing poverty, or, more formally, to preventing all citizens from falling below a minimum welfare level. The minimum welfare level is a standard of living, not simply a net worth, and comprises the consumption of shelter, food, medical care, and other 'basic necessities'. The state maintains the minimum welfare level by transferring cash and other benefits to anyone who falls beneath it.

The simultaneous commitment to enforcement of contracts and to maintenance of a minimum welfare level raises two basic problems of concern to us here. First, it raises the problem of 'welfare opportunism'. Because loss of income or other assets entitles an individual to payment from the state, the magnitude of the loss suffered by an investor as a result of an investment failure is smaller in a welfare regime than it would be in the case of an identical investment outside of a welfare regime. The riskier the investment, the greater is the expected value of the welfare benefits and the greater is the contribution of welfare to the present value of the investment. As a result, inside a welfare regime actors make riskier investments and more often suffer failure than they would outside a welfare regime. This distortion of behaviour in the direction of risk taking, in particular, credit risk, drives up the cost of welfare.

Second, the simultaneous commitment to a free market and to poverty reduction raises the problem of 'welfare circumvention'. Some people are willing to endure a lifestyle the state considers below the minimum welfare level because they have idiosyncratic preferences – they have different views as to what count as the 'basic necessities'. Others are willing to *risk* enduring a lifestyle below the minimum welfare level for the sake of an attractive, and chancy, investment. Because we assume a free market, people in both groups would be able to exchange their right to receive welfare benefits for cash, and the cash for the idiosyncratic goods and risky investments. Although the welfare state restricts the alienation of welfare benefits – in effect, by making them illiquid, discouraging their use for idiosyncratic purposes – a person on welfare or with a low income can, in a free market, reliquidate his benefits. By borrowing against income and assets, he can use the loans to make idiosyncratic purchases of goods that are inconsistent with the minimum welfare level and to make investments that place his at risk of falling below that level.

The welfare opportunism and welfare circumvention problems are closely related. Both arise from the commitment to poverty reduction and the provision of welfare, and both result in, among other distortions, excessive risky borrowing. However, welfare opportunism is foremost a threat to the state's fisc: it increases the number of people to whom the state must pay benefits. In contrast, welfare circumvention is foremost a threat to the commitment to a minimum welfare level: it increases the number of people who fall below the minimum welfare level. Together the problems endanger any program of reducing poverty at reasonable cost.

My argument is that a partial violation of the commitment to the free market is the appropriate response to these problems. Because welfare opportunism and welfare circumvention take the form of high-risk credit activity, the state should enact laws that restrict such activity. Restrictive contract doctrines, such as usury laws, perform this function. By allowing debtors to escape from high-interest credit contracts, they force creditors to withdraw such contracts from the market, denying the debtors the opportunity to obtain high-risk credit in the first place.

So far, English law has largely shied away from any general doctrine of unconscionability. Instead, the courts have focused on specific rules that govern procedural impropriety such as duress and undue influence.

Additional reading

Atiyah, P.S., 'Contract and Fair Exchange', in Atiyah, P. (ed.), *Essays on Contract* (Oxford: Clarendon, 1986).
Bamforth, N., 'Unconscionability as a Vitiating Factor' [1995] LMCLQ 538.
Capper, D., 'Undue Influence and Unconscionability: A Rationalisation' (1998) 114 LQR 479.
Enman, S.R., 'Doctrines of Unconscionability in Canadian, English and Commonwealth Contract Law' (1987) 16 Anglo-Am LR 191.
Knowles, E., and Knowler, J., 'The Presumption of Undue Influence: Elderly Parents, Their Adult Children and Transactions between Them' (2014) 22 RLR 35.
O'Sullivan, D., 'Developing *O'Brien*' (2002) 1 18 LQR 337.
Pawlowski, M., and Brown, J., *Undue Influence and the Family Home* (London: Cavendish, 2002).
Smith, S.A., 'In Defence of Substantive Unfairness' (1996) 112 LQR 138.
Thompson, M.P., 'Wives, Sureties and Banks' [2002] Conv 174.
Wong, S., 'Revisiting *Barclays Bank v O'Brien* and Independent Legal Advice for Vulnerable Sureties' [2002] JBL 439.

Chapter 12

Frustration

Chapter contents

12.1 Introduction

In this chapter we will be considering the doctrine of frustration. This concerns the situation where, following formation of a contract, an event occurs which renders further performance impossible, illegal or radically different from that which was originally envisaged. If such an event occurs, the parties *may* be relieved from further obligations and *may* be able, for example, to recover money transferred under the contract.

There are clear links between the doctrine of frustration and the doctrine of common mistake. In a sense they both involve 'impossibility': common mistake concerning 'initial impossibility' (impossibility that arises prior to the formation of the contract) and frustration concerning 'subsequent impossibility' (impossibility that arises after formation of the contract). A significant difference between the two doctrines is that while common mistake appears to render the contract void *ab initio* (from the beginning), frustration merely discharges the parties from their future obligations.

This chapter is divided into five sections. First, we will consider the nature of the doctrine, examining the underlying basis of the doctrine of frustration. Second, we will look at the categories of event that have been recognised by the courts as possibly amounting to frustration of the contract. Third, the limitations on the doctrine will be examined. Fourth, we will consider the effects of the doctrine at common law and finally we will examine the impact of the Law Reform (Frustrated Contracts) Act 1943.

12.1.1 The nature of the doctrine

Initially, the Law of England and Wales adopted a very strict approach, insisting on the literal performance of contracts. In *Paradme v Jane* (1647) Aleyn 26, a tenant of a farm was dispossessed for two years following an invasion by Prince Rupert of Germany. The tenant claimed that he was not liable to pay rent for the two-year period. The court held in favour of the landlord: 'Now the rent is a duty created by the parties upon the reservation, and had there been a covenant to pay it, there had been no question but the lessee must have made it good, notwithstanding the interruption by enemies, for the law would not protect him beyond his own agreement ...'. The justification for refusing to discharge the parties from their obligations was that the parties could, if they wished, have included a specific term in the contract to deal with the eventuality. Such clauses (sometimes known as *force majeure* or 'hardship' clauses) are commonplace in commercial contracts and it is arguable that the *Paradine v Jane* approach is the most economically efficient since the parties are in the best position to determine the allocation of risk. Professor McKendrick ('The regulation of long term contracts in English Law', Chapter 12 in Beatson, J, and Friedmann, D (eds), *Good Faith and Fault in Contract Law* (Oxford: Clarendon Press, 1995), pp 326–327) has commented:

> [T]he diversity and sophistication of the various *force majeure* clauses which are currently in use underlines the complexity of the issues dealt with by these clauses and they are best resolved by the parties, not the courts. A *force majeure* clause can be expected to define the events which are to trigger the clause, make provision for the procedure to be followed upon the occurrence of such an event, stipulate the effect which the event is to have on the contract itself and, possibly, make provision for the adjudication of any disputes arising out of the clause .... The diversity of *force majeure* clauses suggests that it is impossible to draft a 'boiler-plate' *force majeure* clause which will be suitable for all occasions and that it would be equally impossible for the courts to provide a simple all-encompassing solution to all these problems via a wider doctrine of frustration.

Force majeure clauses are rare; however, eventually the courts recognised that the strict approach could lead to oppressive and unjust results. Blackburn J. adopted a more liberal approach in *Taylor v Caldwell*.

***Taylor v Caldwell* (1863) 3 B & S 826**

Facts: On 27 May 1861, the plaintiffs entered into a contract by which the defendants agreed to let the plaintiffs have the use of the Surrey Gardens and music hall on 17 June, 16 July, 5 August and 17 August, for the purpose of giving a series of four concerts. After the making of the agreement, but before the first day on which a concert was to be given, the music hall was destroyed by fire. The fire was not due to the fault of either party, but the damage caused was so extensive that the concerts could not go ahead as intended. The plaintiffs brought a claim against the defendants for breach of contract in failing to supply the hall.

Held: The Court of Queen's Bench held that the contract was discharged for frustration on the ground that it contained an implied condition that the parties shall be excused from performance if the subject matter of the contract is destroyed.

Blackburn J: There seems no doubt that, where there is a positive contract to do a thing not in itself unlawful, the contractor must perform it or pay damages for not doing it, although, in consequence of unforeseen accident, the performance of his contract has become unexpectedly burdensome, or even impossible .... But this rule is only applicable when the contract is positive and absolute and not subject to any condition either expressed or implied; and there are authorities which, as we think, establish the principle that where, from the nature of the contract, it appears that the parties must from the beginning have known that it could not be fulfilled unless, when the time for the fulfilment of the contract arrived, some particular specified thing continued to exist, so that when entering into the contract they must have contemplated such continued existence as the foundation of what was to be done, there, in the absence of any expressed or implied warranty that the thing shall exist, the contract is not to be construed as a positive contract, but as subject to an implied condition that the parties shall be excused in case, before breach, performance becomes impossible from the perishing of the thing without default of the contractor.

There seems little doubt that this implication tends to further the great object of making the legal construction such as to fulfil the intention of those who enter into the contract, for, in the course of affairs, men, in making such contracts, in general, would, if it were brought to their minds, say that there should be such a condition.

Accordingly, in the civil law, such an exception is implied in every obligation of the class, which they call *obligatio de certo corpore* .... Although the civil law is not of itself an authority in an English court, it affords great assistance in investigating the principles on which the law is grounded, and it seems to us that the common law authorities establish that, in such a contract, the same condition of the continued existence of the thing is implied by English law ...

It may, I think, be safely asserted to be now English law that in all contracts of loan of chattels or bailment, if the performance of the promise of the borrower or bailee to return the thing lent or borrowed becomes impossible because it has perished, this impossibility, if not arising from the fault of the bailee, or from some risk which he has taken upon himself, excuses the borrower or bailee from the performance of his promise to redeliver the chattel .... The principle seems to us to be that in contracts in which the performance depends on the continued existence of a given person or thing, a condition is implied that the impossibility of performance arising from the perishing of the person or thing shall excuse the performance. In none of these cases is the promise in words other than positive, nor is there any express stipulation that the destruction of the person or thing shall excuse the performance; that excuse is by law implied, because from the nature of the contract it is apparent that the parties contracted on the basis of the continued existence of the particular person or chattel. In the present case, looking at the whole contract, we find that the parties contracted on the basis of the continued existence of the music hall at the time when the concerts were to be given, that being essential to their performance. We think, therefore, that, the music hall having ceased to exist without fault of either party, both parties are excused, the plaintiffs from taking the gardens and paying the money, the defendants from performing their promise to give the use of the hall and gardens, and other things. The rule must be made absolute to enter the verdict for the defendants.

The first point to note is that by restricting the implied condition to 'the impossibility of performance arising from the perishing of the person or thing', Blackburn J. avoided a direct conflict with the decision in *Paradine v Jane*, since in that case the subject matter had not perished. Blackburn J. purported to recognise an exception to the general rule as stated in *Paradine v Jane*. However, as Professor Treitel (Treitel, G, *Frustration and Force Majeure*, (3rd edn, London: Sweet & Maxwell, 2014), para 2–025) has noted: 'the formulation of the exception took a form which made it possible for later judges to extend the scope of the exception, so that in the course of time what was the exception became the general rule, and conversely'. Blackburn J.'s exception was based on the view that the general rule 'is only applicable when the contract is positive and absolute and not subject to any condition either expressed or implied'. The reference to implied conditions provided the flexibility necessary for later courts to apply the exception in cases where the frustrating event was something other than the perishing of the subject matter.

The implied term approach to frustration had the merit of being consistent with the prevailing notion of freedom of contract. It based the intervention of the court not on any assumed right of the law to intervene, but on the implied intention of the parties. However, it was soon shown to be fictitious.

***Davis Contractors Ltd v Fareham UDC* [1956] AC 696**

Facts: On 9 July 1946, Davis Contractors entered into a contract to build 78 houses for Fareham UDC within eight months for £94,425. Due to unexpected circumstances, which were not the fault of either party, adequate supplies of labour were not available and the work took 22 months to complete, at a cost to Davis of £115,233. Fareham UDC paid Davis the contract price. Davis argued that the contract had been frustrated and claimed to be entitled on a *quantum meruit* to a reasonable sum for the work done (which would have exceeded the contract price).

Held: The House of Lords held that the contract had not been frustrated. The shortage of labour had rendered the contract more onerous than had been contemplated but was not sufficient to discharge the contract for frustration.

Lord Reid: Frustration has often been said to depend on adding a term to the contract by implication: for example, Lord Loreburn in *FA Tamplin Steamship Co Ltd v Anglo-Mexican Petroleum Products Co Ltd* [1916] 2 AC 397, 404 after quoting language of Lord Blackburn, said:

> 'That seems to me another way of saying that from the nature of the contract it cannot be supposed the parties, as reasonable men, intended it to be binding on them under such altered conditions. Were the altered conditions such that, had they thought of them, they would have taken their chance of them, or such that as sensible men they would have said 'if that happens, of course, it is all over between us'? What, in fact, was the true meaning of the contract? Since the parties have not provided for the contingency, ought a court to say it is obvious they would have treated the thing as at an end?'

I find great difficulty in accepting this as the correct approach because it seems to me hard to account for certain decisions of this House in this way .... I may be allowed to note an example of the artificiality of the theory of an implied term given by Lord Sands in *James Scott & Sons Ltd v Del Sel* 1922 SC 592, 597:

> 'A tiger has escaped from a travelling menagerie. The milkgirl fails to deliver the milk. Possibly the milkman may be exonerated from any breach of contract; but, even so, it would seem hardly reasonable to base that exoneration on the ground that 'tiger days excepted' must be held as if written into the milk contract'.

I think that there is much force in Lord Wright's criticism in *Denny, Mott & Dickson Ltd v James B Fraser & Co Ltd* [1944] AC 265, 275:

> 'The parties did not anticipate fully and completely, if at all, or provide for what actually happened. It is not possible, to my mind, to say that, if they had thought of it, they would have said: 'Well, if that happens, all is over between us.' On the contrary, they would almost certainly on the one side or the other have sought to introduce reservations or qualifications or compensations'.

It appears to me that frustration depends, at least in most cases, not on adding any implied term, but on the true construction of the terms which are in the contract read in light of the nature of the contract and of the relevant surrounding circumstances when the contract was made ....

Lord Radcliffe: The theory of frustration belongs to the law of contract and it is represented by a rule which the courts will apply in certain limited circumstances for the purpose of deciding that contractual obligations, *ex facie* binding, are no longer enforceable against the parties. The description of the circumstances that justify the application of the rule and, consequently, the decision whether in a particular case those circumstances exist are, I think, necessarily questions of law ....

Lord Loreburn ascribes the dissolution to an implied term of the contract that was actually made. This approach is in line with the tendency of English courts to refer all the consequences of a contract to the will of those who made it. But there is something of a logical difficulty in seeing how the parties could even impliedly have provided for something which *ex hypothesi* they neither expected nor foresaw; and the ascription of frustration to an implied term of the contract has been criticised as obscuring the true action of the court which consists in applying an objective rule of the law of contract to the contractual obligations that the parties have imposed upon themselves. So long as each theory produces the same result as the other, as normally it does, it matters little which theory is avowed (see *British Movietonews Ltd v London and District Cinemas Ltd* [1952] AC 166, 184 *per* Viscount Simon). But it may still be of some importance to recall that, if the matter is to be approached by way of implied term, the solution of any particular case is not to be found by inquiring what the parties themselves would have agreed on had they been, as they were not, forewarned. It is not merely that no one can answer that hypothetical question; it is also that the decision must be given 'irrespective of the individuals concerned, their temperaments and failings, their interest and circumstances' (*Hirji Mulji v Cheong Yue Steamship Co Ltd* [1926] AC 497). The legal effect of frustration 'does not depend on their intention or their opinions, or even knowledge, as to the event'. On the contrary, it seems that when the event occurs 'the meaning of the contract must be taken to be, not what the parties did intend (for they had neither thought nor intention regarding it), but that which the parties, as fair and reasonable men, would presumably have agreed upon if, having such possibility in view, they had made express provision as to their several rights and liabilities in the event of its occurrence' (*Dahl v Nelson* (1881) 6 App Cas 38, *per* Lord Watson).

By this time it might seem that the parties themselves have become so far disembodied spirits that their actual persons should be allowed to rest in peace. In their place there rises the figure of the fair and reasonable man and the spokesman of the fair and reasonable man, who represents after all no more than the anthropomorphic conception of justice, is and must be the court itself. So perhaps it would be simpler to say at the outset that frustration occurs whenever the law recognises that without default of either party a contractual obligation has become incapable of being performed because the circumstances in which performance is called for would render it a thing radically different from that which was undertaken by the contract. *Non haec in foedera veni.* It was not this that I promised to do.

There is, however, no uncertainty as to the materials upon which the court must proceed. 'The data for decision are, on the one hand, the terms and construction of the contract, read in the light of the then existing circumstances, and on the other hand the events which have occurred' (*Denny, Mott & Dickson Ltd v James B Fraser & Co Ltd* [1944] AC 265, 274–275 *per* Lord Wright). In the nature of things there is often no room for any elaborate inquiry. The court must act upon a general impression of what its rule requires. It is for that reason that special importance is necessarily attached to the occurrence of any unexpected event that, as it were, changes the face of things. But, even so, it is not hardship or inconvenience or material loss itself which calls the principle of frustration into play. There must be as well such a change in the significance of the obligation that the thing undertaken would, if performed, be a different thing from that contracted for.

I am bound to say that, if this is the law, the appellants' case seems to me a long way from a case of frustration. Here is a building contract entered into by a housing authority and a big firm of contractors in all the uncertainties of the post-war world. Work was begun shortly before the formal contract was executed and continued, with impediments and minor stoppages but without actual interruption, until the 78 houses contracted for had all been built. After the work had been in progress for a time the appellants raised the claim, which they repeated more than once, that they ought to be paid a larger sum for their work than the contract allowed; but the respondents refused to admit the claim and, so far as appears, no conclusive action was taken by either side which would make the conduct of one or the other a determining element in the case.

That is not in any obvious sense a frustrated contract ....

Before considering their Lordships' rejection of the implied term theory, it is important to note why the contractors' claim failed. The case is not an example of commercial impossibility at all. In fact, Davis Contractors were able to fulfil their contractual obligations at a cost of just 23 per cent over the contract price. The essence of their claim was that it had become commercially disadvantageous for them to perform the contract at the agreed price. This is not a recognised ground for discharging a contract under the law of England and Wales.

Turning to their Lordships' rejection of the implied term theory, Lord Radcliffe believed that there was 'a logical difficulty in seeing how the parties could ... impliedly have provided for something which *ex hypothesi* they neither expected nor foresaw'. This objection is perhaps overstated. *Force majeure* clauses frequently contain provisions as to the effect of unforeseen events. If this can be done by an express clause, there seems to be no reason why it cannot be done by one that is implied. Nevertheless, it is true to say that the implied term theory obscures what the courts are actually doing. As the cases reveal, the courts are really seeking to determine whether the supervening event has such an effect on the contract that it is 'unfair' to hold parties to their bargain, in the absence of fault and of any assumption of the risk by either party (cf. also *Healthcare at Home Ltd v Common Services Agency* [2014] UKSC 49 at [1]–[4] *per* Lord Reed). The theory preferred by Lords Reid and Radcliffe is based on the construction of the contract. Both of these theories were included in a list of possible bases for the doctrine of frustration provided by Lord Hailsham LC in *National Carriers v Panalpina (Northern) Ltd*.

***National Carriers v Panalpina (Northern) Ltd* [1981] AC 675**

Lord Hailsham LC: At least five theories of the basis of the doctrine of frustration have been put forward at various times, and, since the theoretical basis of the doctrine is clearly relevant to the point under discussion, I enumerate them here. The first is the 'implied term' or 'implied condition' theory on which Blackburn J. plainly relied in *Taylor v Caldwell*, as applying to the facts of the case before him. To these it is admirably suited. The weakness, it seems to me, of the implied term theory is that it raises once more the spectral figure of the officious bystander intruding on the parties at the moment of agreement ....

Counsel for the respondent sought to argue that *Taylor v Caldwell*, 3 B & S 826, could as easily have been decided on the basis of a total failure of consideration. This is the second of the five theories. But *Taylor v Caldwell* was clearly not so decided, and in any event many, if not most, cases of frustration which have followed *Taylor v Caldwell* have occurred during the currency of a contract partly executed on both sides, when no question of total failure of consideration can possibly arise.

In *Hirji Mulji v Cheong Yue Steamship Co Ltd* [1926] AC 497, 510 Lord Sumner seems to have formulated the doctrine as a '... device [sic], by which the rules as to absolute contracts are reconciled with a special exception which justice demands' and Lord Wright in *Denny, Mott & Dickson Ltd v James B Fraser & Co Ltd* [1944] AC 265, 275 seems to prefer this formulation to the implied condition view. The weakness of the formulation, however, if the implied condition theory, with which Lord Sumner coupled it, be rejected, is that, though it admirably expresses the purpose of the doctrine, it does not provide it with any theoretical basis at all.

Hirji Mulji v Cheong Yue Steamship Co Ltd is, it seems to me, really an example of the more sophisticated theory of 'frustration of the adventure' or 'foundation of the contract' formulation, said to have originated with *Jackson v Union Marine Insurance Co Ltd* (1874) LR 10 CP 125; compare also, for example, *per* Goddard J in *WJ Tatem Ltd v Gamboa* [1939] 1 KB 132, 138. This, of course, leaves open the question of what is, in any given case, the foundation of the contract or what is 'fundamental' to it, or what is the 'adventure'. Another theory, of which the parent may have been Earl Loreburn in *FA Tamplin Steamship Co Ltd v Anglo-Mexican Petroleum Products Co Ltd* [1916] 2 AC 397, is that the doctrine is based on the answer to the question: 'What in fact is the true meaning of the contract?': see p 404. This is the 'construction theory'. In *Davis Contractors Ltd v Fareham UDC* [1956] AC 696, 729 Lord Radcliffe put the matter thus, and it is the formulation I personally prefer:

> '... frustration occurs whenever the law recognises that without default of either party a contractual obligation has become incapable of being performed because the circumstances in which performance is called for would render it a thing radically different from that which was undertaken by the contract. *Non haec in foedera veni*. It was not this that I promised to do'.

Although Lord Hailsham regarded the theoretical basis of the doctrine as being 'clearly relevant to the point under discussion', several commentators have doubted its practical importance. The point is made in Beale, H (ed), *Chitty on Contracts* (33rd edn, para 23–018, London: Sweet & Maxwell, 2018):

> It is therefore difficult to discern any practical consequence which flows from the different tests .... The courts have regard to the construction of the contract, the effect of the changed circumstances on the parties' contractual obligations, the intentions of the parties (objectively construed) and

> the demands of justice in deciding whether or not a contract has been frustrated. No one factor is conclusive: the court will balance these different factors in determining whether a contract has been frustrated.

Professor Treitel agrees. He notes that in *Davis Contractors*, Lord Reid stated that the parties' intentions were relevant to the implied term theory, but not to the construction theory. Professor Treitel (Treitel, G, *Frustration and Force Majeure* (3rd edn, London: Sweet & Maxwell, 2014), para 16–017) doubts whether this is true:

> [I]n construing the contract, the court does not wholly disregard the intention of the parties. The court may not indeed have to ask: what would the parties have said, had they thought of the frustrating event? But it does have to ask: in what circumstances did the parties intend the contract to operate? In answering this question, the court will no doubt apply an objective test and may refuse to admit evidence of the parties' 'subjective intent'; but it is only after the question has been answered that the intention of the parties becomes irrelevant: that is, it is not necessary to go on and ask whether they would (if they had considered the event) have agreed to discharge, or to some other compromise solution. But this question does not arise under the 'implied term' theory either, as frustration at common law always results in total discharge of the contract.

In *Great Peace Shipping Ltd v Tsavliris Salvage (International) Ltd* [2003] QB 679 Lord Phillips M.R. regarded the doctrine of frustration as a 'rule of law'. See also *Gold Group Properties Ltd v BDW Trading Ltd* [2010] EWHC 323. The doctrine of frustration was more recently considered in *Canary Wharf (BP4) T1 Ltd v European Medicines Agency* [2019] EWHC 335 (Ch). That case involved a 25-year lease of premises by the European Medicines Agency (E.M.A.) in Canary Wharf, London. In 2017, following a referendum in the U.K., the U.K. gave the E.U. notice of its intention to withdraw from the E.U. In 2018, EU Regulation 2018/1718 made provision for the relocation of the E.M.A. to Amsterdam. As a result the E.M.A. wrote to its landlord stating: 'Having considered the position under English law, we have decided to inform you that if and when Brexit occurs, we will be treating that event as a frustration of the Lease.' It became clear that the actual withdrawal (which had not at that time happened) was the basis of the frustration claim (see [13]). Nevertheless, the parties sought clarification of the legal position prior to the potentially frustrating act. One difficulty was that the shape/form of any Brexit was far from clear at that point. Therefore Marcus Smith J. had to consider various scenarios (and also had to tackle some tricky conflict of laws issues). The learned judge stated: 'I accept – as anyone would – that the withdrawal of the United Kingdom from the European Union is a seismic event, and I have found that it is not one that was in the contemplation of either party at the time the Agreements were concluded' (at [241]). Ultimately, however, he concluded that this particular contract has not been frustrated. We shall consider the learned judge's reasons at various points in this chapter. For present purposes, it is important to note his view of the basis of the doctrine of frustration (at [27]):

> ... certainly since *Panalpina*, the prevailing wisdom is that the ... approach that I have described best encapsulates the essence of the doctrine of frustration. Whether a contract is frustrated depends upon a consideration of the nature of the bargain of the parties when considered in the light of the supervening event said to frustrate that bargain. Only if the supervening event renders the performance of the bargain 'radically different', when compared to the considerations in play at the conclusion of the contract, will the contract be frustrated.

On the practical differences between the different theories of frustration, Marcus Smith J. noted (at [26]):

> ... there may be little difference in outcome between the construction of the contract theory and the 'performance is radically different' test. But there is, in my judgment, a very material difference

in how these two theories work in their application. Under the former, the true construction of the contract resolves all; the latter theory recognises the importance of the true construction of the contract, but also recognises that even construction has its limits when faced with extreme and unforeseeable supervening events.

12.2 Frustrating events

It is impossible to formulate an exhaustive list of possible frustrating events. The following are given as examples of events which have been recognised by the courts as capable of amounting to frustrating events.

12.2.1 Impossibility

Impossibility of performance is the most obvious ground of frustration and it may arise for a number of reasons.

12.2.1.1 Destruction of the subject matter

In *Taylor v Caldwell*, the performance of the contract was rendered impossible by the destruction of the subject matter. The case is actually an example of partial impossibility because the contract related to the use of the hall and the gardens, but it was only the hall that was destroyed by the fire. Nevertheless, the use of the hall was deemed to be a fundamental element of the contract (the hall being required for the giving of concerts) and its destruction was sufficient to frustrate it.

Furthermore, it may not be necessary to show a complete destruction of the subject matter as long as the nature of the thing has been materially altered. In *Asfar v Blundell* [1896] 1 QB 123, a cargo of dates was being carried on a barge that sunk in the Thames. The dates were recovered and, although they were still of value for the purpose of distillation into spirit, they had become contaminated with sewage and were in such a condition of fermentation that they were no longer merchantable as dates. Lord Esher MR said:

> The nature of a thing is not necessarily altered because the thing itself has been damaged; wheat or rice may be damaged, but may still remain the things dealt with as wheat or rice in business. But if the nature of the thing is altered, and it becomes for business purposes something else, so that it is not dealt with by business people as the thing which it originally was, the question for determination is whether the thing insured, the original article of commerce, has become a total loss. If it is so changed in its nature by the perils of the sea as to become an unmerchantable thing, which no buyer would buy and no honest seller would sell, then there is a total loss. That test was applied in the present case by the learned judge in the Court below, who decided as a fact that the dates had been so deteriorated that they had become something which was not merchantable as dates. If that was so, there was a total loss of the dates.

See also *Bunge SA v Kyla Shipping Co Ltd* [2012] EWHC 3522 and [2013] EWCA Civ 734. It should also be noted that s 7 of the Sale of Goods Act 1979 provides:

> Where there is an agreement to sell specific goods and subsequently the goods, without any fault on the part of the seller or buyer, perish before the risk passes to the buyer, the agreement is avoided.

It will be noted that s 7 of the Sale of Goods Act 1979 applies to contracts concerning 'specific goods' which are defined by s 61 of the Sale of Goods Act 1979 as 'goods identified and agreed on at the time a contract of sale is made'. Contracts for the sale of 'specific goods' should be contrasted with contracts for the sale of 'unascertained goods'. Professor Bradgate (Bradgate, R, *Commercial Law* (3rd edn, London: Butterworths, 2000), p 235) outlines the distinction between 'specific' and 'unascertained' goods:

> a contract to sell a particular second hand car is a contract to sell specific goods. 'Unascertained goods' are not defined by the Act, but it is clear that any goods which are not specific are unascertained. Thus wherever goods are sold purely by a generic description, they are unascertained: for instance, a contract to sell '1,000 gallons of oil' or 'a new Ford Focus' would be a contract to sell unascertained goods.

Can a contract for the sale of unascertained goods be frustrated at common law? The case of *CTI Group Inc v Transclear SA* [2008] EWCA Civ 856 is particularly instructive. Moore-Bick L.J. stated (at [23]):

> These authorities, in particular *Société Co-operative Suisse des Céréales et Matières Fourragères v La Plata Cereal Company S.A.* and *Lewis Emanuel & Son Ltd v Sammut*, make it clear that the principles of frustration are capable of applying to a contract for the sale by description of unascertained goods of a specified origin, a conclusion that is also supported by the observations of Russell J in *In re Badische Co Ltd* [1921] 2 Ch 331 at pages 381–383, another case on which Mr. Nolan relied. However, they also make it clear that, in the absence of some exceptional supervening event, such a contract will not be frustrated simply by a failure on the part of the ultimate supplier to make goods available for delivery. The reason for that is not far to seek: it is implicit in a contract of this kind that the seller will either supply the goods himself or (more likely) will make arrangements, directly or indirectly, for the goods to be supplied by others. In other words, he undertakes a personal obligation to procure the delivery of contractual goods and thereby takes the risk of his supplier's failure to perform. That obligation will be discharged by frustration if a supervening event not contemplated by the contract renders that performance impossible or fundamentally different from what was originally envisaged, but most events which result in the failure of a supplier to provide the goods will not fall into that category. A few, however, such as a prohibition of export rendering the shipment of the goods unlawful, usually will. It is not surprising, therefore, that the authorities support Mr Kenny's submission that the contract will not be frustrated if, although delivery remains physically and legally possible, the seller's supplier chooses (for whatever reason) not to make the goods available.

12.2.1.2 Death or incapacity

A contract for personal services may be frustrated on the death of either party (*Cutter v Powell* (1795) 6 TR 320). The same principle may apply where either party is permanently incapacitated from performing the contract. In *Condor v Barron Knights* [1966] 1 WLR 87, a 17-year-old drummer collapsed and was admitted to a psychiatric hospital. Medical opinion was that he would only be fit to work four nights a week. The band had engagements for seven nights a week and so the defendants decided to dismiss him. The court held it was, in a business sense, impossible for the drummer to perform the contract and for that reason the contract was discharged for frustration. See also *Atwal v Rochester* [2010] EWHC 2338, where a building contract was held to be frustrated when the sole trader, who was to carry out the building work, had a heart attack. H.H.J. Kirkham stated (at [30]–[31]):

> There is no authority directly on this point. I have referred already to the decisions in *Notcutt* and *Condor*. In both of those cases the individuals in question had been taken ill and in both cases were unlikely to be able to continue to work. In each of those cases the court concluded that the contract

had been discharged by frustration. This case, however, unlike those cases, is not concerned with a master/servant or employer/employee relationship.

In my judgment this was a personal contract. Mr and Mrs Atwal chose to contract with Mr Rochester as a sole trader. They chose him personally because he was known to the family and had built up a personal relationship of trust. They chose him because his price was very substantially below the market price. With Mr Rochester, Mr and Mrs Atwal were getting almost twice as much work for the price as they would have done had they engaged other contractors. It must have been clear that Mr and Mrs Atwal were entirely dependent upon Mr Rochester's continuing in his role for the job to be completed. There was no one else to whom he could entrust the work if he was unable, himself, to continue to work.

More recently in *Blankley v Central Manchester and Manchester Children's University Hospitals NHS Trust* [2015] EWCA Civ 18 (a case involving a conditional fee agreement (CFA) between a solicitor and a client, where the client subsequently lost capacity), Richards L.J. at [36]–[39] stated:

36. There is much to be said in favour of a fresh examination or reconsideration of the principle in *Yonge v Toynbee* and related authorities in this area. It is potentially unfair and unsatisfactory for a client's supervening incapacity to have the effect of terminating automatically the solicitor's authority to act on the client's behalf in the litigation, exposing the solicitor to the risk of liability to other parties for breach of warranty of authority in respect of steps taken in the litigation even when the solicitor is not aware of the incapacity, and depriving him of authority to take any steps to protect the client's position when he does become aware of it – to the extent that it is said that he acts without authority, albeit apparently in accordance with good practice, in applying to the court for the appointment of a deputy and/or litigation friend. One might at least expect the principle to be qualified so that (i) the solicitor retains authority to act so long as he is unaware of the incapacity and (ii) he retains authority to take necessary steps in consequence of the incapacity, including an application to the court for the appointment of a deputy and/or litigation friend, when he does become aware of it. It might also be preferable to talk in terms of 'suspension' rather than 'termination' of authority, on the basis that the solicitor's authority is restored if the client regains capacity or a litigation friend is appointed to continue the litigation on the client's behalf.

37. The present appeal, however, does not require us to re-examine the principle in *Yonge v Toynbee* or to grasp the 'hot potato' left on one side by the Supreme Court in *Dunhill v Burgin*. The issue in the appeal is a much narrower one and can be resolved on the assumption that the principle in *Yonge v Toynbee* is good law. The defendant's essential case is that the claimant's supervening incapacity caused the CFA to be terminated by reason of frustration because the claimant could not give instructions to the solicitor and the contract therefore became incapable of performance. The judge rejected that case. If he was correct to do so, as in my view he was, it is unnecessary to address any underlying issues concerning the principle in *Yonge v Toynbee*.

38. The defendant's case that the CFA was frustrated depends on the proposition that the obligation to give instructions was personal to the claimant and could not be discharged by the giving of instructions by a receiver/deputy acting on her behalf. Whilst a solicitor's retainer is in one sense a personal contract, I very much doubt whether it requires instructions to be given by the client personally even in the general run of cases. It must be commonplace for instructions to be given through an agent, such as an accountant or managing agent or a spouse. But whatever the general position, the parties must have contemplated in the particular circumstances of this case that the claimant might suffer from a further period of incapacity in which she would be unable to give instructions personally but they could be given by a litigation friend or a receiver/deputy or on her behalf. I accept Mr Spearman's submissions on that point (see paragraph 31 above). The fact that supervening incapacity prevented the claimant from giving instructions personally did not render the contract of retainer impossible of performance; it simply gave rise to a short period of delay pending appointment of a receiver/deputy who could continue the conduct of the proceedings on the claimant's behalf and give instructions to the solicitors for that purpose.

39. I also accept Mr Spearman's submission (paragraph 32 above) that if the claimant was under an obligation to give instructions personally and was unable to comply with that obligation by reason of her supervening incapacity, the situation was covered by the express terms of the CFA, which entitled the solicitors in that event to end the contract and to require payment of their basic charges and disbursements. The unattractiveness of such a result is a further indication that it cannot have been the intention of the parties that the claimant had to give instructions personally; but if that was their intention, and the situation arose in which the claimant was unable to give such instructions, the contract catered expressly for the consequences and it cannot possibly be said that this was a fundamentally different situation from anything contemplated by the contract.

More recently in *Canary Wharf (BP4) T1 Ltd v European Medicines Agency* [2019] EWHC 335 (Ch) (facts given above in Section 12.1.1), Marcus Smith J. held that the contract had not been frustrated by subsequent illegality as: (i) the E.M.A. would continue to have capacity to use and/or dispose of the premises post-Brexit; and (ii) even if the E.M.A. did not have this capacity, the frustration was self-induced (on which see Section 12.3.1).

12.2.1.3 Unavailability or delay

A contract may be frustrated if the subject matter is temporarily unavailable. The court may have to determine whether the contractual performance when resumed will be fundamentally different to what the parties had agreed to.

***Jackson v Union Marine Insurance Company Ltd* (1874) LR 10 CP 125**

Facts: The plaintiff shipowner entered into a charterparty by which the ship was to 'proceed with all possible dispatch from Liverpool to Newport, and there load a cargo of iron rails for San Francisco'. The ship set sail from Liverpool on 2 January 1872 but ran aground on the following day in Carnarvon Bay. The repairs took eight months to complete. In the meantime, on 15 February, the charterers repudiated the charter and chartered another ship to carry the rails. The shipowner brought an action on his insurance policy. In order to make a claim it was necessary for him to show that he could not have brought a claim against the charterers for failing to load. A jury found that the time necessary for repairs was so long as to make it unreasonable for the charterers to supply the agreed cargo at the end of August and so long as to put an end, in a commercial sense, to the commercial speculation entered upon by the shipowner and the charterers.

Held: The Exchequer Chamber affirmed the decision of the court below, holding that the contract was frustrated and the charterers were not under an obligation to load. Accordingly, the shipowner was entitled to make a claim under his insurance policy.

Bramwell B: I understand that the jury have found that the voyage the parties contemplated had become impossible; that a voyage undertaken after the ship was sufficiently repaired would have been a different voyage, not, indeed, different as to the ports of loading and discharge, but different as a different adventure – a voyage for which at the time of the charter the plaintiff had not in intention engaged the ship, nor the charterers the cargo; a voyage as different as though it had been described as intended to be a spring voyage, while the one after the repair would be an autumn voyage ....

The question turns on the construction and effect of the charter. By it the vessel is to sail to Newport with all possible dispatch, perils of the seas excepted. It is said this constitutes the only agreement as to time, and, provided all possible dispatch is used, it matters not when she arrives at Newport. I am of a different opinion. If this charterparty be read as a charter for a definite voyage or adventure, then it follows that there is *necessarily* an implied condition that the ship shall arrive at Newport in time for it. Thus, if a ship was chartered to go from Newport to St Michael's in terms in time for the fruit season, and take coals out and bring fruit home, it would follow ... that, if she did not get to Newport in time to get to St Michael's for the fruit season, the charterer would not be bound to load at Newport, though she had used all possible dispatch to get there, and though there was an exception of perils of the seas.

The court concluded that performance after the delay would have been a different voyage altogether, and of no use to the charterer. It is, however, useful to contrast this case with *Edwinton Commercial Corp v Tsavliris Russ*.

***Edwinton Commercial Corp v Tsavliris Russ (Worldwide Salvage & Towage) Ltd* [2007] EWCA Civ 547**

Facts: The charterer of a vessel, which was used in a salvage operation, claimed that the charter had been frustrated following, in the late stages of the charter, the unlawful detention of the vessel by port authorities in Karachi.

Held: The contract was not frustrated.

Rix LJ

110. In the course of the parties' submissions we heard much to the effect that such and such a factor 'excluded' or 'precluded' the doctrine of frustration, or made it 'inapplicable'; or, on the other side, that such and such a factor was critical or at least amounted to a prima facie rule. I am not much attracted by that approach, for I do not believe that it is supported by a fair reading of the authorities as a whole. Of course, the doctrine needs an overall test, such as that provided by Lord Radcliffe, if it is not to descend into a morass of quasi-discretionary decisions. Moreover, in any particular case, it may be possible to detect one, or perhaps more, particular factors which have driven the result there. However, the cases demonstrate to my mind that their circumstances can be so various as to defy rule making.

111. In my judgment, the application of the doctrine of frustration requires a multifactorial approach. Among the factors which have to be considered are the terms of the contract itself, its matrix or context, the parties' knowledge, expectations, assumptions and contemplations, in particular as to risk, as at the time of contract, at any rate so far as these can be ascribed mutually and objectively, and then the nature of the supervening event, and the parties' reasonable and objectively ascertainable calculations as to the possibilities of future performance in the new circumstances. Since the subject matter of the doctrine of frustration is contract, and contracts are about the allocation of risk, and since the allocation and assumption of risk is not simply a matter of express or implied provision but may also depend on less easily defined matters such as 'the contemplation of the parties', the application of the doctrine can often be a difficult one. In such circumstances, the test of 'radically different' is important: it tells us that the doctrine is not to be lightly invoked; that mere incidence of expense or delay or onerousness is not sufficient; and that there has to be, as it were, a break in identity between the contract as provided for and contemplated and its performance in the new circumstances.

112. What the 'radically different' test, however, does not in itself tell us is that the doctrine is one of justice, as has been repeatedly affirmed on the highest authority. Ultimately the application of the test cannot safely be performed without the consequences of the decision, one way or the other, being measured against the demands of justice. Part of that calculation is the consideration that the frustration of a contract may well mean that the contractual allocation of risk is reversed. A time charter is a good example. Under such a charter, the risk of delay, subject to express provision for the cessation of hire under an off-hire clause, is absolutely on the charterer. If, however, a charter is frustrated by delay, then the risk of delay is wholly reversed: the delay now falls on the owner. If the provisions of a contract in their literal sense are to make way for the absolving effect of frustration, then that must, in my judgment, be in the interests of justice and not against those interests. Since the purpose of the doctrine is to do justice, then its application cannot be divorced from considerations of justice. Those considerations are among the most important of the factors which a tribunal has to bear in mind.

113. Mr Hamblen submitted that whereas the demands of justice play an underlying role, they should not be overstated .... I respectfully agree ....

114. Mr Hamblen further cited two authorities. In *Notcutt v Universal Equipment Co (London) Ltd* [1986] 1 WLR 641, this court had to consider a contract of employment which the trial judge had found to have been frustrated by the permanent incapacity of an employee. The narrow issue was whether the contract should have come to an end by frustration (without notice) or whether the proper way of ending it was by the employer giving notice, during which period there would have been a statutory requirement of sick pay. The appeal was dismissed. There was a submission, based upon some of the dicta cited above, that an additional condition for the incidence of frustration was that the survival of the contract should be unjust. In his judgment (with which the only other member of the court, Sheldon J) agreed, Dillon LJ said (at 647):

> 'I do not for my part see that these references to justice or injustice introduce any further factor. If the unexpected event produces an ultimate situation which, as a matter of construction, is not within the scope of the contract or would render performance impossible or something radically different from that which was undertaken by the contract, then it is unjust that the contracting party should be held to be still bound by the contract in those altered circumstances. I approach the facts of this case on the footing that the test to be satisfied is that explained by Lord Reid and Lord Radcliffe in the passages set out above'

115. In a case in which the contract was overcome by permanent disability and the court considered that it would be unjust for the contract to survive in such circumstances, I see no difficulty with these observations.

116. In *Eridania SpA v Rudolf Oetker (The 'Fjord Wind')* [1999] 1 Lloyd's Rep 307 at 328/9 Moore-Bick J said, with reference to Bingham LJ's reference to the demands of justice in *The Super Servant Two* [see below], that –

> 'his intention was clearly to describe the considerations which had given rise to the development of the doctrine rather than to suggest that the Court is entitled to adopt a more liberal approach than would be indicated by Lord Radcliffe's speech. I am unable, therefore, to accept Mr Gee's submission that in this case I ought to have regard to some wider considerations of justice and fairness than the earlier authorities would otherwise suggest'.

117. I turn then to the facts of this case. I agree with Mr Hamblen that the critical question was whether, as of 13 October, (or 17 October, and for present purposes I am content to adopt either date), the delay which had already occurred and prospective further delay would have led the parties at that time to have reasonably concluded that the charter was frustrated. No later date of frustration was relied upon. For these purposes, since on the facts a delay of some 5 weeks had already occurred and the prospective delay involved in a revised strategy involving litigating in the Pakistani courts would involve a further 4 to 6 weeks at least, the first question to consider is whether Mr Hamblen is right in his submission that the Bailhache J test of comparing the probable length of the delay with the unexpired duration of the charter is the critical or main and in any event overbearing test to apply (see *Anglo-Northern*, *Bank Line*, *Tatem v Gamboa*).

118. In my judgment it is not. It may be an important consideration, but it is, on our facts, only the starting point. In the first place, the development of the law shows that such a single-factored approach is too blunt an instrument. As stated above, a finding of frustration of a charter of no longer than a year, based on requisition during the First World War, against the view that requisition meant 'goodbye to them', was in any event close to inevitable. Secondly, requisition, like seizure in *Tatem v Gamboa*, could not be rectified; whereas in our case, the consequences of the detention by the port authorities remained very much a matter for enquiry, negotiation, diplomacy, and, whatever the ordering of the tactics, legal pressure. Thirdly, where, as in our case, the supervening event comes at the very end of a charter, with redelivery as essentially the only remaining obligation, the effect of the detention on the performance of the charter is purely a question of the financial consequences of the delay, which will fall on one party or the other, depending on whether the charter binds or does not bind. It is not like the different situation where the supervening event either postpones or, which may be even worse, interrupts the heart of the adventure itself: as, for instance, in *Tatem v Gamboa* or *The Fjord Wind*. In our case, the purpose for which the *Sea Angel* had been chartered, namely the lightening of the casualty, had been performed.

119. Fourthly, in general terms the contractual risk of such delay caused by detention by government authorities was firmly on the charterers, Tsavliris. I will develop this below: but in essence it follows from their obligation to pay hire, subject to the off-hire clause, until redelivery. And even the off-hire clause itself expressly provided for 'detention by the authorities at home or abroad' but not in terms which were relied on as covering the particular event here. Fifthly, as was even common ground, the risk of detention by the littoral authorities arising out of a salvage situation where there was a concern about pollution was, at any rate in general terms, foreseeable. This remained the case even if, as Mr Hamblen submitted, the particular form in which that risk showed itself in this case was unforeseeable, or only weakly foreseeable, or was even unprecedented. Sixthly, that general risk was foreseeable by the salvage industry as a whole, and was provided for by the terms of that industry: see SCOPIC and Brice's commentary on it. Indeed, in my view the particular risk which occurred was within the provisions of SCOPIC. As such, those matters were part of the matrix itself of the charter under enquiry. In this connection, I bear in mind that Global were not themselves part of the salvage industry: but they chartered the vessel to well-known international salvors, to perform salvage services directly to a casualty, at a high price which reflected the emergencies and risks of such services: and therefore the foreseeable risks of the salvage context, and the incidence of those risks subject to SCOPIC, are properly part of the matrix of the charter. In justice, they bear particularly on Tsavliris, the salvors, themselves.

120. Seventhly, it is now common ground, on the particular facts of this case, that, short as the charter was, a mere 20 days, and shorter still as the unexpired period of the charter was, a mere 3 days, there was no frustration until the strategy of commercial negotiation had initially failed (by 13 or 17 October), some five weeks after the detention began. So, in any event, this is not a case like *Anglo-Northern* and *Tatem v Gamboa*, where the charters were frustrated then and there by the supervening event. Ours is one of those 'wait and see' situations discussed in other authorities. In such situations, it is a matter for assessment, on all the circumstances of the case, whether by a particular date the tribunal of fact, putting itself in the position of the parties, and viewing the matter in the role of reasonable and well-informed men, concludes that those parties would, or properly speaking should, have formed the view that, in all fairness and consistently with the demands of justice, their contract, as something whose performance in the new circumstances, past and prospective, had become 'radically different', had ceased to bind.

121. For these reasons, some of which have been sufficiently grounded above, and others of which I shall elaborate below, it seems to me that the primary point on which Tsavliris have founded their claim to frustration fails. I turn to discuss particular aspects of these reasons.

12.2.1.4 Government intervention

A contract may be frustrated by government intervention. For example, if, following a declaration of war, one of the parties to the contract has become an enemy alien, then the contract will be frustrated (*Fibrosa Spolka Ackyjna v Fairbairn Lawson Combe Barbour Ltd* [1943] AC 32). Similarly, if property is requisitioned by the government, this may have the effect of frustrating the contract if the intervention radically alters the nature of the contract.

***FA Tamplin Steamship Company Ltd v Anglo-Mexican Petroleum Products Co Ltd* [1916] 2 AC 397**

Facts: The defendants chartered a tank steamship for a period of five years to be used for the carriage of oil. The charterparty contained the usual exceptions, including arrests and restraints of princes, rulers and peoples. The charterers also were permitted to sublet the ship to the Admiralty or other service. Following the outbreak of the war, when the charterparty still had three years to run, the ship was requisitioned by the Admiralty for use as a transport for troops. The owners claimed that the charterparty had been discharged by the requisition. The charterers, who wished to continue with the contract, claimed that the government's intervention was not sufficient to frustrate the contract.

Held: The House of Lords held (Viscount Haldane and Lord Atkinson dissenting), that the contract had not been frustrated.

Earl Loreburn: Taking into account … all that has happened, I cannot infer that the interruption either has been or will be in this case such as makes it unreasonable to require the parties to go on. There may be many months during which this ship will be available for commercial purposes before the five years have expired. It might be a valuable right for the charterer during those months to have the use of this ship at the stipulated freight. Why should he be deprived of it? No one can say that he will or that he will not regain the use of the ship, for it depends upon contingencies which are incalculable. The owner will continue to receive the freight he bargained for so long as the contract entitles him to it, and if, during the time for which the charterer is entitled to the use of the ship, the owner received from the Government any sums of money for the use of her, he will be accountable to the charterer …. Loss may arise to someone whether it be decided that these people are or that they are not still bound by the charterparty. But the test for answering that question is not the loss that either may sustain. It is this: Ought we to imply a condition in the contract that an interruption such as this shall excuse the parties from further performance of it? I think not. I think they took their chance of lesser interruptions, and the condition I should imply goes no further than that they should be excused if substantially the whole contract became impossible of performance, or in other words impracticable, by some cause for which neither was responsible. Accordingly I am of opinion that this charterparty did not come to an end when the steamer was requisitioned and that the requisition did not suspend it or affect the rights of the owners or charterers under it, and that the appeal fails.

It will be noted that Earl Loreburn relied on the 'implied term' approach to frustration. There is no reason to believe, however, that a different outcome would have been reached had, for example, a 'construction' approach been applied. The contract was not deemed to have been frustrated because it was still likely that the ship would have been available for commercial purposes prior to the expiry of the contract. The owners had failed to demonstrate that 'substantially the whole contract' had become 'impossible of performance'. The contract will not be frustrated merely because government intervention has made the contract more difficult or costly to perform.

***Tsakiroglou & Co Ltd v Noble Thorl GmbH* [1962] AC 93**

Facts: The appellants agreed to sell Sudanese groundnuts to the respondents for shipment from Port Sudan to Hamburg. Both parties expected that the shipment would be made via the Suez Canal but there was no express term in the written contract to this effect. On 2 November 1956 the Suez Canal was closed, and the only alternative route available to the appellants was to ship the goods round the Cape of Good Hope. This would have taken twice as long and doubled the cost of carriage. The appellants failed to ship the goods and the respondents sued for non-performance.

Held: The House of Lords refused to imply a term into the contract that the goods should be shipped via the Suez Canal and held that the contract had not been frustrated. Although the alternative route via the Cape of Hope involved a change in the method of performance, it did not amount to a fundamental change from that which had been agreed.

Viscount Simmonds: I come then to the main issue and, as usual, I find two questions interlocked: (1) What does the contract mean? In other words, is there an implied term that the goods shall be carried by a particular route? (2) Is the contract frustrated?

It is convenient to examine the first question first, though the answer may be inconclusive. For it appears to me that it does not automatically follow that, because one term of a contract, for example, that the goods shall be carried by a particular route, becomes impossible of performance, the whole contract is thereby abrogated. Nor does it follow, because as a matter of construction a term cannot be implied, that the contract may not be frustrated by events. In the instant case, for example, the impossibility of the route via Suez, if that were assumed to be the implied contractual obligation, would not necessarily spell the frustration of the contract.

It is put in the forefront of the appellants' case that the contract was a contract for the shipment of goods via Suez. This contention can only prevail if a term is implied, for the contract does not say so. To say that that is nevertheless its meaning is to say in other words that the term must be implied. For this I see no ground …

I turn now to what was the main argument for the appellants: that the contract was frustrated by the closure of the Canal from November 2, 1956, till April 1957. Were it not for the decision of McNair J in *Green's case* [1959] 1 QB 131, I should not have thought this contention arguable and I must say with the greatest respect to that learned judge that I cannot think he has given full weight to the decisions old and new of this House upon the doctrine of frustration …. [H]e concluded that the continued availability of the Suez route was a fundamental assumption at the time when the contract was made and that to impose upon the sellers the obligation to ship by an emergency route via the Cape would be to impose upon them a fundamentally different obligation which neither party could at the time when the contract was performed have dreamed that the sellers would be required to perform. Your Lordships will observe how similar this line of argument is to that which supports the implication of a term that the route should be via Suez and no other. I can see no justification for it. We are concerned with a CIF contract for the sale of goods, not a contract of affreightment, though part of the sellers' obligation will be to procure a contract of affreightment. There is no evidence that the buyers attached any importance to the route. They were content that the nuts should be shipped at any date in November or December. There was no evidence, and I suppose could not be, that the nuts would deteriorate as the result of a longer voyage and a double crossing of the Equator, nor any evidence that the market was seasonable. In a word, there was no evidence that the buyers cared by what route or, within reasonable limits, when the nuts arrived. What, then, of the sellers? I recall the well-known passage in the speech of Lord Atkinson in *Johnson v Taylor Bros & Co Ltd* [1920] AC 144, 155, where he states the obligations of the vendor of goods under a CIF contract, and ask which of these obligations is (to use McNair J's word) 'fundamentally' altered by a change of route. Clearly the contract of affreightment will be different and so may be the terms of insurance. In both these respects the sellers may be put to greater cost: their profit may be reduced or even disappear. But it hardly needs reasserting that an increase of expense is not a ground of frustration: see *Larrinaga Co Ltd v Société Franco-Américaine des Phosphates de Medulla, Paris* (1922) 38 TLR 739; 28 Com Cas 160, CA.

Nothing else remains to justify the view that the nature of the contract was 'fundamentally' altered .... I venture to say what I have said myself before and others more authoritatively have said before me: that the doctrine of frustration must be applied within very narrow limits. In my opinion this case falls far short of satisfying the necessary conditions.

The mere fact that the method of performance had become impossible was insufficient to frustrate the contract. It was necessary to show that the nature of the contract had been 'fundamentally altered' by the closure of the Suez Canal, and the appellants had failed to demonstrate this.

The government intervention need not relate to international matters. In *Gamerco SA v ICM/Fair Warning (Agency) Ltd* [1995] 1 WLR 1226, the Spanish government's decision to close a stadium due to structural defects was held to frustrate a contract to hold a rock concert there. Garland J. concluded:

I am in no doubt whatsoever that this contract was frustrated when, due to the discovery of high alumina cement in the construction of the stadium, its use was banned pending further investigations and the permit for its use was revoked.

12.2.2 Supervening illegality

Here we are concerned with contracts that are legal when formed, but have become illegal due to a supervening prohibition.

***Denny, Mott & Dickson Ltd v James B Fraser & Company Ltd* [1944] AC 265**

Facts: In 1929, the respondents and appellants entered into an agreement under which the respondents leased the appellants a timber yard (with an option to purchase it) and agreed to purchase all their supplies of timber from the appellants. In 1939, further transactions in timber were made illegal by virtue of the Control of Timber (No 4) Order 1939. The appellants continued to occupy the timber yard and in July 1941 sent a letter to the respondents purporting to terminate the agreement and stating their intention to exercise the option to purchase the timber yard.

Held: The House of Lords held that the agreement was a single contract which had been discharged due to frustration of its main object. The respondents were therefore unable to exercise the option to purchase the timber yard.

In the following section we will examine a number of limitations on the doctrine of frustration. In particular, we will see that there may be no frustration if the parties foresaw the event or assumed the risk of it occurring. Neither of these limitations applies when the contract is frustrated by supervening illegality (*Ertel Bieber and Co v Rio Tinto Co Ltd* [1918] AC 260). This is because, in such cases, the public interest in seeing the law observed may trump the importance of achieving a fair distribution of losses between the parties (see Peel, E, *Treitel: The Law of Contract* (14th edn, London: Sweet & Maxwell, 2015), p 1058).

12.2.3 Frustration of purpose

As we have seen, it is very rare for the courts to hold that a contract has been frustrated by an event that merely renders its performance more difficult or expensive than anticipated (*Davis Contractors Ltd v Fareham UDC* [1956] AC 696; *Tsakiroglou & Co Ltd v Noble Thorl GmbH* [1962] AC 93). The courts will not permit the doctrine to be used as a means of escape for a party that has simply entered into a bad bargain. Similarly, the courts are reluctant to hold that a contract has been discharged merely because its purpose has been frustrated (compare also *Flying Music Co Ltd v Theater Entertainment SA* [2017] EWHC 3192 (QB) where a contract for theatre performances was not frustrated by civil unrest in Greece, as the civil unrest was present at the time the contract was signed and had not got worse). This is illustrated by the cases of *Krell v Henry* and *Herne Bay Steam Boat Co v Hutton*.

Krell v Henry [1903] 2 KB 740

Facts: The defendant had agreed to hire from the plaintiff some rooms at 56A Pall Mall to watch the coronation procession of King Edward VII on 26 and 27 June 1902. He paid £25 as a deposit and was to pay the balance of £50 on 24 June. The King became seriously ill and the coronation processions were postponed. The defendant refused to pay the balance and the plaintiff brought a claim for the outstanding balance. The defendant counter-claimed to recover the £25 deposit he had paid. At first instance, Darling J. held that there was an implied term in the contract that the procession should take place. Accordingly, he gave judgment for the defendant on both the claim and the counter-claim.

Held: The Court of Appeal dismissed the appeal, holding that the contract had been frustrated.

Vaughan Williams LJ: The real question in this case is the extent of the application in English law of the principle of the Roman law which has been adopted and acted on in many English decisions, and notably in the case of *Taylor v Caldwell* (1863) 3 B & S 826 ....

English law applies the principle not only to cases where the performance of the contract becomes impossible by the cessation of existence of the thing which is the subject-matter of the contract, but also to cases where the event which renders the contract incapable of performance is the cessation or non-existence of an express condition or state of things, going to the root of the contract, and essential to its performance. It is said, on the one side, that the specified thing, state of things, or condition the continued existence of which is necessary for the fulfilment of the contract, so that the parties entering into the contract must have contemplated the continued existence of that thing, condition, or state of things as the foundation of what was to be done under the contract, is limited to things which are either the subject-matter of the contract or a condition or state of things, present or anticipated, which is expressly mentioned in the contract. But, on the other side, it is said that the condition or state of things need not be expressly specified, but that it is sufficient if that condition or state of things clearly appears by extrinsic evidence to have been assumed by the parties to be the foundation or basis of the contract, and the event which causes the impossibility is of such a character that it cannot reasonably be supposed to have been in the contemplation of the contracting parties when the contract was made. In such a case the contracting parties will not be held bound by the general words which, though large enough to include, were not used with reference to a possibility of a particular event rendering performance of the contract impossible. I do not think that the principle of the civil law as introduced into the English law is limited to cases in which the event causing the impossibility of performance is the destruction or non-existence of some thing which is the subject-matter of the contract or of some condition or state of things expressly specified as a condition of it. I think that you first have to ascertain, not necessarily from the terms of the contract, but, if required, from necessary inferences, drawn from surrounding circumstances recognised by both contracting parties, what is the substance of the contract, and then to ask the question whether that substantial contract needs for its foundation the assumption of the existence of a particular state of things. If it does, this will limit the operation of the general words, and in such case, if the contract becomes impossible of performance by reason of the non-existence of the state of things assumed by both contracting parties as the foundation of the contract, there will be no breach of the contract thus limited. Now what are the facts of the present case? The contract is contained in two letters of June 20 which passed between the defendant and the plaintiff's agent, Mr Cecil Bisgood. These letters do not mention the coronation, but speak merely of the taking of Mr Krell's chambers, or, rather, of the use of them, in the daytime of June 26 and 27, for the sum of £75, £25 then paid, balance £50 to be paid on the 24th. But the affidavits, which by agreement between the parties are to be taken as stating the facts of the case, shew that the plaintiff exhibited on his premises, third floor, 56A, Pall Mall, an announcement to the effect that windows to view the Royal coronation procession were to be let, and that the defendant was induced by that announcement to apply to the housekeeper on the premises, who said that the owner was willing to let the suite of rooms for the purpose of seeing the Royal procession for both days, but not nights, of June 26 and 27. In my judgment the use of the rooms was let and taken for the purpose of seeing the Royal procession. It was not a demise of the rooms, or even an agreement to let and take the rooms. It is a licence to use rooms for a particular purpose and none other. And in my judgment the taking place of those processions on the days proclaimed along the proclaimed route, which passed 56A, Pall Mall, was regarded by both contracting parties as the foundation of the contract; and I think that it cannot reasonably be supposed to have been in the contemplation of the contracting parties, when the contract was made, that the coronation would not be held on the proclaimed days, or the processions not take place on those days along the proclaimed route; and I think that the words imposing on the defendant the obligation to accept and pay for the use of the rooms for the named days, although general and unconditional, were not used with reference to the possibility of the particular contingency which afterwards occurred. It was suggested in the course of the argument that if the occurrence, on the proclaimed days, of the coronation and the procession in this case were the foundation of the contract, and if the general words are thereby limited or qualified, so that in the event of the non-occurrence of the coronation and procession along the proclaimed route they would discharge both parties from further performance of the contract, it would follow that if a cabman was engaged to take someone to Epsom on Derby Day at a suitable enhanced price for such a journey, say £10, both parties to the contract would be discharged in the contingency of the race at Epsom for some reason becoming impossible; but I do not think this follows, for I do not think that in the cab case the happening of the race would be the foundation of the contract. No doubt the purpose of the engager would be to go to see the Derby, and the price would be proportionately high; but the cab had no special qualifications for the purpose which led to the selection of the cab for this particular occasion. Any other cab would have done as well. Moreover, I think that, under the cab contract, the hirer, even if the race went off, could have said, 'Drive me to Epsom; I will pay you the agreed sum; you have nothing to do with the purpose for which I hired the cab,' and that if the cabman refused he would have been guilty of a breach of contract, there being nothing to qualify his promise to drive the hirer to Epsom on a particular day. Whereas in the case of the coronation, there is not merely the purpose of the hirer to see the coronation procession, but it is the coronation procession and the relative position of the rooms which is the basis of the contract as much for the lessor as the hirer; and I think that if the King, before the coronation day and after the contract, had died, the hirer could not have insisted on having the rooms on the days named. It could not in the cab case be reasonably said that seeing the Derby race was the foundation of the contract, as it was of the licence in this case. Whereas in the present case, where the rooms were offered and taken, by reason of their peculiar suitability from the position of the rooms for a view of the coronation procession, surely the view of the coronation procession was the foundation of the contract, which is a very different thing from the purpose of the man who engaged the cab – namely, to see the race – being held to be the foundation of the contract. Each case must be judged by its own circumstances. In each case one must ask oneself, first, what, having regard to all the circumstances, was the foundation of the contract? Secondly, was the performance of the contract prevented? Thirdly, was the event which prevented the performance of the contract of such a character that it cannot reasonably be said to have been in the contemplation of the parties at the date of the contract? If all these questions are answered in the affirmative (as I think they should be in this case), I think both parties are discharged from further performance of the contract. I think that the coronation procession was the foundation of this contract, and that the non-happening of it prevented the performance of the contract; and, secondly, I think that the non-happening of the procession, to use the words of Sir James Hannen in *Baily v De Crespigny* (1869) LR 4 QB 180, was an event 'of such a character that it cannot reasonably be supposed to have been in the contemplation of the contracting parties when the contract was made, and that they are not to be held bound by general words which, though large enough to include, were not used with reference to the possibility of the particular contingency which afterwards happened' ....

In the present case the condition which fails and prevents the achievement of that which was, in the contemplation of both parties, the foundation of the contract, is not expressly mentioned either as a condition of the contract or the purpose of it; but I think for the reasons which I have given that the principle of *Taylor v Caldwell* ought to be applied.

[Romer and Stirling JJ delivered concurring judgments.]

***Herne Bay Steam Boat Company v Hutton* [1903] 2 KB 683**

Facts: Mr Hutton agreed to hire the steamship *Cynthia* from Herne Bay for 28 and 29 June 'for the purpose of viewing the naval review and for a day's cruise round the fleet'. The hire charge was £250 and Mr Hutton paid a deposit of £50. On 25 June the review was officially cancelled because of the King's illness, but the fleet remained in place. Mr Hutton sought to repudiate the contract. Herne Bay brought a claim for the balance owing minus the profit they had made from using the *Cynthia* for their own purposes on 28 and 29 June. Mr Hutton counter-claimed for the return of his £50 deposit. At first instance, Grantham J. held that neither Herne Bay nor Mr Hutton could recover.

Held: The Court of Appeal allowed the appeal, holding that the contract had not been frustrated and accordingly the plaintiffs were entitled to recover damages for breach of contract.

Vaughan Williams LJ: Mr Hutton, in hiring this vessel, had two objects in view: first, of taking people to see the naval review, and, secondly, of taking them round the fleet. Those, no doubt, were the purposes of Mr Hutton, but it does not seem to me that because, as it is said, those purposes became impossible, it would be a very legitimate inference that the happening of the naval review was contemplated by both parties as the basis and foundation of this contract, so as to bring the case within the doctrine of *Taylor v Caldwell* (1863) 3 B & S 826.

On the contrary, when the contract is properly regarded, I think the purpose of Mr Hutton, whether of seeing the naval review or of going round the fleet with a party of paying guests, does not lay the foundation of the contract within the authorities.

Having expressed that view, I do not know that there is any advantage to be gained by going on in any way to define what are the circumstances which might or might not constitute the happening of a particular contingency as the foundation of a contract. I will content myself with saying this, that I see nothing that makes this contract differ from a case where, for instance, a person has engaged a brake to take himself and a party to Epsom to see the races there, but for some reason or other, such as the spread of an infectious disease, the races are postponed. In such a case it could not be said that he could be relieved of his bargain. So in the present case it is sufficient to say that the happening of the naval review was not the foundation of the contract.

Romer LJ: In my opinion, as my Lord has said, it is a contract for the hiring of a ship by the defendant for a certain voyage, though having, no doubt, a special object, namely, to see the naval review and the fleet; but it appears to me that the object was a matter with which the defendant, as hirer of the ship, was alone concerned, and not the plaintiffs, the owners of the ship.

The case cannot, in my opinion, be distinguished in principle from many common cases in which, on the hiring of a ship, you find the objects of the hiring stated. Very often you find the details of the voyage stated with particularity, and also the nature and details of the cargo to be carried. If the voyage is intended to be one of pleasure, the object in view may also be stated, which is a matter that concerns the passengers. But this statement of the objects of the hirer of the ship would not, in my opinion, justify him in saying that the owner of the ship had those objects just as much in view as the hirer himself. The owner would say, 'I have an interest in the ship as a passenger or cargo carrying machine, and I enter into the contract simply in that capacity; it is for the hirer to concern himself about the objects'.

The view I have expressed with regard to the general effect of the contract before us is borne out by the following considerations. The ship (as a ship) had nothing particular to do with the review or the fleet except as a convenient carrier of passengers to see it: any other ship suitable for carrying passengers would have done equally as well. Just as in the case of the hire of a cab or other vehicle, although the object of the hirer might be stated, that statement would not make the object any the less a matter for the hirer alone, and would not directly affect the person who was letting out the vehicle for hire. In the present case I may point out that it cannot be said that by reason of the failure to hold the naval review there was a total failure of consideration. That cannot be so. Nor is there anything like a total destruction of the subject-matter of the contract. Nor can we, in my opinion, imply in this contract any condition in favour of the defendant which would enable him to escape liability. A condition ought only to be implied in order to carry out the presumed intention of the parties, and I cannot ascertain any such presumed intention here. It follows that, in my opinion, so far as the plaintiffs are concerned, the objects of the passengers on this voyage with regard to sight-seeing do not form the subject-matter or essence of this contract ....

Stirling LJ: It is said that, by reason of the reference in the contract to the 'naval review', the existence of the review formed the basis of the contract, and that as the review failed to take place the parties became discharged from the further performance of the contract, in accordance with the doctrine of *Taylor v Caldwell*. I am unable to arrive at that conclusion. It seems to me that the reference in the contract to the naval review is easily explained; it was inserted in order to define more exactly the nature of the voyage, and I am unable to treat it as being such a reference as to constitute the naval review the foundation of the contract so as to entitle either party to the benefit of the doctrine in *Taylor v Caldwell*. I come to this conclusion the more readily because the object of the voyage is not limited to the naval review, but also extends to a cruise round the fleet. The fleet was there, and passengers might have been found willing to go round it. It is true that in the event which happened the object of the voyage became limited, but, in my opinion, that was the risk of the defendant whose venture the taking the passengers was.

Much ink has been spilt on identifying the distinction between *Krell* and *Hutton*. Both cases were decided at the same time by the same panel of judges, yet they appear to be hard to reconcile. Why was a contract to let a room for the viewing of the coronation frustrated by the cancellation of the coronation, while a contract to hire a boat from which to watch the naval review was not? A number of answers have been suggested:

1. The purpose in *Krell* (watching the coronation) was wholly frustrated by the postponement of the coronation, whereas the purpose in *Hutton* was only partially frustrated. As Stirling L.J. noted, the object of the voyage was not limited to the naval review, but also extended to a cruise round the fleet. The fleet was still in place, and so the tour could go still ahead. Professor Treitel (Treitel, G, *Frustration and Force Majeure* (3rd edn, London: Sweet & Maxwell, 2014), pp 201–204, para 7–014) has commented:

> [This] reflects a recurrent feature of the cases on frustration of purpose, which shows that the approach of the law to partial frustration of purpose differs from that which it adopts to partial impossibility. In cases of partial impossibility, a contract can be discharged if its *main* purpose can no longer be achieved; but in cases of frustration of purpose the courts have applied the more rigorous test of asking whether *any* part of the contractual purpose (other than a part which was wholly trivial) could still be achieved: if so, they have refused to apply the doctrine of discharge.

2. The 'common purpose' of both parties in *Krell* was for the rooms to be used for the viewing of the procession and this purpose was frustrated when the coronation was postponed. There was no such common purpose in Hutton. Romer L.J. considered that, '[the] statement of the objects of the hirer of the ship would not … justify him in saying that the owner of the ship had those objects just as much in view as the hirer himself.' This meant that, although the postponement had frustrated Hutton's purpose in entering into the contract, it had not frustrated Herne Bay's purpose, which was presumably to provide a tour of the fleet. Professor Treitel (at para 7–014) has written:

   > This emphasis on the requirement that the purpose of *both* parties must be frustrated is found also in other English and American cases. It means that the supervening event must prevent one party from supplying, and the other from obtaining, what the former had contracted to provide and the latter to acquire under the contract.

   This also explains why the contract was not frustrated in Vaughan L.J.'s example of the taxi cab hired to go to Epsom on Derby Day. Although it was the hirer's purpose to view the Derby, this was not the taxi owner's purpose.
3. Professor Brownsword ('Towards a rational law of contract', in Willhelmson, T (ed), *Perspectives on Critical Contract Law* (Aldershot: Dartmouth, 1993), pp 246–247) has suggested that the true distinction lies in the fact Hutton was engaged in a commercial enterprise (he intended to sell tickets for the trip on the *Cynthia* at a profit), whereas Henry was in effect a 'consumer', whose only interest was in getting a good view of the procession. The Court of Appeal in *Hutton* was unwilling to allow the doctrine of frustration to be used as a means of escaping from a bad commercial bargain.
4. A further explanation of the decision in *Krell* was provided by Posner CJ in *Northern Indiana Public Service Co v Carbon County Coal Co* 799 F 2d 265 (1986). He noted that, 'Krell could always relet the room, at the premium rental, for the coronation's new date'. However, as Professor Treitel has observed (at para 7–011), this argument overlooks the fact that the procession that eventually took place in October took a different route from the one that was planned for June. Furthermore, it fails to take into account the expenditure that Mr Krell had wasted on making preparations for the June procession.

Krell v Henry was recently considered in *Canary Wharf (BP4) T1 Ltd v European Medicines Agency* [2019] EWHC 335 (Ch), with Marcus Smith J. noting:

> What the parties were buying and selling [in *Krell*] was, quite literally, a room with a view. Their common purpose was just that: whilst the parties surely would have been in opposition in bargaining on price, the thing that they were bargaining about was predicated on the procession taking place. Matters would have been very different had the room been a hotel room charging a higher rate because of the higher demand for rooms on that particular day due to the Coronation …. I have held that it is possible – notwithstanding the true construction of a contract – for that contract nevertheless to be discharged if the common purpose of the bargain (which I have found to be

something *beyond* the true construction of the contract) is frustrated. In this case, I find no common purpose beyond the purpose to be derived from a construction of the Lease. This is not a case like *Krell v Henry* where the parties had a common purpose going beyond their agreement, which was thwarted ([37], [244] emphasis added).

12.3 Limitations on the doctrine

We now move on to consider three specific limitations on the doctrine of frustration.

12.3.1 Self-induced frustration

The event that renders performance of the contract 'radically different' from that which was envisaged must not be attributable to the fault of the party seeking to rely on it. As Lord Sumner said in *Bank Line Ltd v Arthur Capel & Co* [1919] AC 435, 452:

> [I]t is now well settled that the principle of frustration of an adventure assumes that the frustration arises without blame or fault on either side. Reliance cannot be placed on a self-induced frustration; indeed, such conduct might give the other party the option to treat the contract as repudiated.

If a party wishes to argue that a frustrating event is self-induced by the other party they must prove it on the balance of probabilities (*Joseph Constantine Steamship Line Ltd v Imperial Smelting Corpn Ltd* [1942] AC 154). The limitation on self-induced frustration is relatively straightforward but, in practice, it is often difficult to apply.

***Maritime National Fish Ltd v Ocean Trawlers Ltd* [1935] AC 524**

Facts: The appellants chartered a steam trawler, the *St Cuthbert*, from the respondents. It was fitted with an 'otter trawl', which it was an offence to use without a licence from the Minister of Fisheries. In March 1933 the appellants applied for licences for the five trawlers which they were operating. The Minister said that he would only grant three licences and asked the appellants to name the three trawlers in respect of which the licences would apply. The three trawler names given by the appellants did not include the *St Cuthbert*. The appellants thereupon claimed that the charterparty had been frustrated by the Minister's refusal to issue a licence. The respondents brought a claim for the hire due under the charter. The trial judge, Doull J., gave judgment for the appellants. This decision was reversed by the Supreme Court of Nova Scotia.

Held: The Privy Council dismissed the appeal. The contract had not been frustrated because the appellants' own election had prevented the respondents' trawler from being used as an otter trawl.

Lord Wright (delivering the opinion of the Privy Council): It is clear that the appellants were free to select any three of the five trawlers they were operating and could, had they willed, have selected the *St Cuthbert* as one, in which event a licence would have been granted to her. It is immaterial to speculate why they preferred to put forward for licences the three trawlers which they actually selected. Nor is it material, as between the appellants and the respondents, that the appellants were operating other trawlers to three of which they gave the preference. What matters is that they could have got a licence for the *St Cuthbert* if they had so minded. If the case be figured as one in which the *St Cuthbert* was removed from the category of privileged trawlers, it was by the appellants' hand that she was so removed, because it was their hand that guided the hand of the Minister in placing the licences where he did and thereby excluding the *St Cuthbert*. The essence of 'frustration' is that it should not be due to the act or election of the party ....

If it be assumed that the performance of the contract was dependent on a licence being granted, it was that election which prevented performance, and on that assumption it was the appellants' own default which frustrated the adventure: the appellants cannot rely on their own default to excuse them from liability under the contract ...

[T]heir Lordships are of opinion that the loss of the *St Cuthbert's* licence can correctly be described, quoad the appellants, as 'a self-induced frustration' .... On this ground ... their Lordships are of opinion that the appeal should be dismissed with costs.

Few would argue with the decision in *Maritime National Fish Ltd*. The appellants had a choice as to the allocation of the licences and decided to allocate them to their own trawlers rather than to the *St Cuthbert*. The issue would have been much more difficult had all the trawlers been chartered to the appellants, so that they had to decide which of the five chartered ships should be denied a licence. An analogous situation arose in *The Super Servant Two*.

J Lauritzen AS v Wijsmuller BV (The Super Servant Two) **[1990] 1 Lloyd's Rep 1**

Facts: The defendants, Wijsmuller, agreed to carry Lauritzen's drilling rig (the *Dan King*) from a shipyard in Japan to a delivery location off the coast of the Netherlands. The rig was to be delivered on a date between 20 June 1981 and 20 August 1981, using either the *Super Servant One* or the *Super Servant Two*. The contract contained a *force majeure* clause which provided the following:

> 17. *Cancellation*
>
> **17.1** Wijsmuller has the right to cancel its performance under this Contract whether the loading has been completed or not, in the event of force majeure, Acts of God, perils or danger and accidents of the sea, acts of war, warlike-operations, acts of public enemies, restraint of princes, rulers or people or seizure under legal process, quarantine restrictions, civil commotions, blockade, strikes, lockout, closure of the Suez or Panama Canal, congestion of harbours or any other circumstances whatsoever, causing extra-ordinary periods of delay and similar events and/or circumstances, abnormal increases in prices and wages, scarcity of fuel and similar events, which reasonably may impede, prevent or delay the performance of this contract.

The defendants had intended to use *Super Servant Two* for the *Dan King* contract and had entered into other contracts which they intended to perform using *Super Servant One*. On 29 January 1981, *Super Servant Two* sank. The defendants informed the plaintiffs that they could no longer carry out the *Dan King* contract, claiming that they were permitted to cancel the contract under cl 17 and that, in any event, the contract had been frustrated by the sinking of *Super Servant Two*.

Held: The Court of Appeal held that the contract could only be cancelled under cl 17 if the loss of *Super Servant Two* had not been due to the negligence of the defendants. The doctrine of frustration did not operate on the facts of the case because the defendants could have fulfilled their contractual obligations by using *Super Servant One*. Additionally, the defendants would be precluded from relying on the doctrine of frustration if it could be shown that the loss of *Super Servant Two* had been caused by their own negligence.

Bingham LJ: Certain propositions, established by the highest authority, are not open to question:

1. The doctrine of frustration was evolved to mitigate the rigour of the common law's insistence on literal performance of absolute promises .... The object of the doctrine was to give effect to the demands of justice, to achieve a just and reasonable result, to do what is reasonable and fair, as an expedient to escape from injustice where such would result from enforcement of a contract in its literal terms after a significant change in circumstances ....
2. Since the effect of frustration is to kill the contract and discharge the parties from further liability under it, the doctrine is not to be lightly invoked, must be kept within very narrow limits and ought not to be extended ....
3. Frustration brings the contract to an end forthwith, without more and automatically ....
4. The essence of frustration is that it should not be due to the act or election of the party seeking to rely on it .... A frustrating event must be some outside event or extraneous change of situation. ...
5. A frustrating event must take place without blame or fault on the side of the party seeking to rely on it ....

Question 2(a)

Mr Clarke for Wijsmuller submitted that the extraneous supervening event necessary to found a plea of frustration occurred when *Super Servant Two* sank on Jan 29, 1981. The *Dan King* contract was not, however, thereupon frustrated but remained alive until Wijsmuller decided a fortnight later that that contract could not be, or would not be, performed. There was, he submitted, factually, no break in the chain of causation between the supervening event and the non-performance of the contract. He acknowledged that *Maritime National Fish Ltd* contained observations on their face inimical to his argument, but distinguished that as a decision on causation confined to its own peculiar facts and laying down no general rule. For authoritative support Mr Clarke relied on cases dealing with the application of *force majeure* clauses in commodity contracts, and in particular on an unreported judgment of Mr Justice Robert Goff, as he then was, adopted with approval by the Court of Appeal in *Bremer Handelsgesellschaft mbH v Continental Grain Co* [1983] 1 Lloyd's Rep 269 at p 292:

> '... the question resolves itself into a question of causation; in my judgment, at least in a case in which a seller can (as in the present case) claim the protection of a clause which protects him where fulfilment is hindered by the excepted peril, subsequent delivery of his available stock to other customers will not be regarded as an independent cause of shortage, provided that in making such delivery the seller acted reasonably in all the circumstances of the case ...'

A similar approach was reflected in other cases: see, for example, *Intertradex SA v Lesieur – Tourteaux SARL* [1977] 2 Lloyd's Rep 146 at p 115, *per* Mr Justice Donaldson as he then was; [1978] 2 Lloyd's Rep 509 at p 513, *per* Lord Denning, MR. Reliance was also placed on passages in *The Law of Contract* (7th edn) by Professor Treitel, which the Judge quoted in his judgment at p 152. Thus, Mr Clarke urged, this was a case in which Wijsmuller could not perform all their contracts once *Super Servant Two* was lost; they acted reasonably (as we must assume) in treating the *Dan King* contract as one they could not perform; so the sinking had the direct result of making that contract impossible to perform.

Mr Legh-Jones answered that since the contract provided for the carriage to be performed by one or other vessel the loss of one did not render performance radically different, still less impossible. That apart, Wijsmuller's argument fell foul of the principles summarised above since (among other things) the frustration they sought to establish did not bring the contract to an end forthwith, without more and automatically and was not independent of the act or election of Wijsmuller. The *force majeure* cases were good law so far as they went, but it was one thing to construe and apply a consensual *force majeure* clause, another to determine whether the facts were such that the law should hold the contract to be discharged.

The doctrine of frustration depends on a comparison between circumstances as they are or are assumed to be when a contract is made and circumstances as they are when a contract is, or would be, due to be performed. It is trite law that disappointed expectations do not of themselves give rise to frustrated contracts. To frustrate, an event must significantly change –

> '... the nature (not merely the expense or onerousness) of the outstanding contractual rights and/or obligations from what the parties could reasonably have contemplated at the time of [the contract's] execution ... [*National Carriers Ltd*, at p 700, *per* Lord Simon of Glaisdale]'.

Had the *Dan King* contract provided for carriage by *Super Servant Two* with no alternative, and that vessel had been lost before the time for performance, then assuming no negligence by Wijsmuller (as for purposes of this question we must), I feel sure the contract would have been frustrated. The doctrine must avail a party who contracts to perform a contract of carriage with a vessel which, through no fault of his, no longer exists. But that is not this case. The *Dan King* contract did provide an alternative. When that contract was made, one of the contracts eventually performed by *Super Servant One* during the period of contractual carriage of *Dan King* had been made, the other had not, at any rate finally. Wijsmuller have not alleged that when the *Dan King* contract was made either vessel was earmarked for its performance. That, no doubt, is why an option was contracted for. Had it been foreseen when the *Dan King* contract was made that *Super Servant Two* would be unavailable for performance, whether because she had been deliberately sold or accidentally sunk, Lauritzen at least would have thought it no matter since the carriage could be performed with the other. I accordingly accept Mr Legh-Jones' submission that the present case does not fall within the very limited class of cases in which the law will relieve one party from an absolute promise he has chosen to make.

But I also accept Mr Legh-Jones' submission that Wijsmuller's argument is subject to other fatal flaws. If, as was argued, the contract was frustrated when Wijsmuller made or communicated their decision on Feb 16, it deprives language of all meaning to describe the contract as coming to an end automatically. It was, indeed, because the contract did not come to an end automatically on Jan. 29, that Wijsmuller needed a fortnight to review their schedules and their commercial options. I cannot, furthermore, reconcile Wijsmuller's argument with the reasoning or the decision in *Maritime National Fish Ltd*. In that case the Privy Council declined to speculate why the charterers selected three of the five vessels to be licensed but, as I understand the case, regarded the interposition of human choice after the allegedly frustrating event as fatal to the plea of frustration. If Wijsmuller are entitled to succeed here, I cannot see why the charterers lost there. The cases on frustrating delay do not, I think, help Wijsmuller since it is actual and prospective delay (whether or not recognized as frustrating by a party at the time) which frustrates the contract, not a party's election or decision to treat the delay as frustrating.

I have no doubt that *force majeure* clauses are, where their terms permit, to be construed and applied as in the commodity cases on which Wijsmuller relied, but it is in my view inconsistent with the doctrine of frustration as previously understood on high authority that its application should depend on any decision, however reasonable and commercial, of the party seeking to rely on it.

I reach the same conclusion as the Judge for the reasons which he lucidly and persuasively gave.

Question 2(b)

The issue between the parties was short and fundamental: what is meant by saying that a frustrating event, to be relied on, must occur without the fault or default, or without blame attaching to, the party relying on it?

Mr Clarke's answer was that a party was precluded from relying on an event only when he had acted deliberately or in breach of an actionable duty in causing it. Those conditions were not met here since it was not alleged Wijsmuller sank *Super Servant Two* deliberately and at the material time Wijsmuller owed Lauritzen no duty of care if (as I have held) cl 15 did not apply when the vessel sank. Mr Clarke relied on tentative doubts expressed in *Joseph Constantine Steamship Ltd*, whether mere negligence would render an event 'self-induced' and on a statement of Lord Diplock in *Cheall v Association of Professional Executive and Clerical Computer Staff* [1983] 2 AC 180 at pp 188–189 ...

Wijsmuller's test would, in my judgment, confine the law in a legalistic strait-jacket and distract attention from the real question, which is whether the frustrating event relied upon is truly an outside event or extraneous change of situation or whether it is an event which the party seeking to rely on it had the means and opportunity to prevent but nevertheless caused or permitted to come about. A fine test of legal duty is inappropriate; what is needed is a pragmatic judgment whether a party seeking to rely on an event as discharging him from a contractual promise was himself responsible for the occurrence of that event.

Lauritzen have pleaded in some detail the grounds on which they say that *Super Servant Two* was lost as a result of the carelessness of Wijsmuller, their servants or agents. If those allegations are made good to any significant extent Wijsmuller would (even if my answer to Question 2(a) is wrong) be precluded from relying on their plea of frustration.

I would answer this question also as the Judge did and would therefore dismiss the appeal.

Dillon LJ: Issues 2(a) and (b) are concerned with frustration. Was the contract frustrated by the sinking of *Super Servant Two* or by that event coupled with the subsequent election by the defendants to use *Super Servant One* on other voyages and not for carrying the *Dan King*? ...

It is the view of Professor Treitel, expressed both in his own book on the *Law of Contract* – see the 7th edn at pp 674–675 and 700–701 – and in the current editions of well-known textbooks of which he is editor or an editor, that where a party has entered into a number of contracts with other parties and an uncontemplated supervening event has the result that he is deprived of the means of satisfying all those contracts, he can, provided he acts 'reasonably' in making his election, elect to use such means as remains available to him to perform some of the contracts, and claim that the others, which he does not perform, have been frustrated by the supervening event. The reasoning depends on the proposition that if it is known to those concerned that the party will have entered into commitments with others and if he acts 'reasonably' in his allocation of his remaining means to his commitments, the chain of causation between the uncontemplated supervening event and the non-performance of those of his contracts which will not have been performed will not have been broken by the election to apply his remaining means in a 'reasonable' way. Similar reasoning was, as my Lord has pointed out, used by Mr Justice Robert Goff in relation to an exceptions clause in the unreported case of *Westfalische Central-Genossenschaft GmbH v Seabright Chemicals Ltd.*

Such an approach is however inconsistent to my mind with the view expressed by Lord Wright in that passage in *Maritime National Fish* ... where he said: 'It is immaterial to speculate why they preferred to put forward for licences the three trawlers which they actually selected.' It is also, as my Lord has pointed out, inconsistent with the long accepted view that frustration brings the contract to an end forthwith, without more ado, automatically. Plainly the sinking of *Super Servant Two* did not do that, since even after that sinking the defendants could have used *Super Servant One* to perform the contract.

We in this Court should apply *Maritime National Fish* and the other authorities to which my Lord has referred. Accordingly I agree with my Lord and the learned Judge that issues 2(a) and (b) should be answered in the negative.

The first point to note is that a party will only be entitled to rely on the doctrine of frustration if s/he can show that the frustrating event took place 'without blame or fault' on his/her part. For this reason, the Court of Appeal held that the defendants would be precluded from relying on the doctrine of frustration if it could be shown that *Super Servant Two* had been lost as a result of their own negligence.

Second, Bingham L.J. held that the mere existence of a choice for one of the parties was sufficient to preclude reliance on the doctrine of frustration. He relied on the decision of the Privy Council in *Maritime National Fish Ltd*, and distinguished the authorities relied on by the defendants on the ground that they concerned the construction of *force majeure* clauses rather than the operation of frustration. The decision in *Super Servant Two* has been strongly criticised by Professor Treitel (Treitel, G, *Frustration and Force Majeure* (3rd edn, London: Sweet & Maxwell, 2014), para 14–024):

> Three lines of reasoning are given in the judgments but it is submitted with great respect that none of them is wholly convincing. First, it was said that the *Maritime National Fish* case had established that a party could not rely on frustration where his failure or inability was due to his 'election'; and that the court in *The Super Servant Two* should follow the decision. It is, however, submitted that the two cases are readily distinguishable: in the *Maritime National Fish* case it was possible for the charterer to perform *all* the contracts which he had made with the owners of the other trawlers, even though only three licences had been allocated to him; while in *The Super Servant Two* it was no longer possible, after the loss of the ship, for the carrier to perform all the contracts which he had made to carry drilling rigs during the period in question. Secondly, it was said that, if the carrier were given a choice which of the contracts he would perform, frustration of the other or others could come about only as a result of the exercise of that choice, and such a position would be inconsistent with the rule that frustration occurs automatically, *without* any election by either party. Again, it is submitted that this line of reasoning is not conclusive since the rule that frustration operates automatically is subject to qualification precisely in cases of allegedly self-induced frustration .... Moreover, the element of 'election' could be eliminated if the question, which of the contracts was to be discharged, were left to be determined, not by the free choice of the promisor, but by a rule of law, e.g. by a rule to the effect that the various contracts should for this purpose rank in the order in which they were made. It may, from this point of view, be relevant that, in *The Super Servant Two*, some of the contracts which the carrier chose to perform (by the use of his other ship during the relevant period) had not been made 'at any rate finally' until *after* the contract with the claimant .... The third reason given for the decision is that: 'It is within the promisor's own control how many contracts he enters into and the risk should be his'. But this reasoning seems to undermine the whole basis of the doctrine of frustration: it has just as much force where the promisor enters into a single contract as it has where he enters into two or more, with different contracting parties. This, indeed, is the fundamental objection to the reasoning of *The Super Servant Two*, and it is submitted that the rationale of the doctrine should lead to discharge of some of the contracts where the supervening event which makes it impossible to perform them all occurs without the fault of the party claiming discharge. Consistency with the reasoning of the *Maritime National Fish* case could be preserved by holding that *which* contracts were to be discharged should depend, not on the free election of the party who can no longer perform them all, but on a rule of law. On this view, the actual decision in *The Super Servant Two* could be justified by reference to the order in which the various contracts with the carrier were made.

Professor Treitel's criticisms are compelling. In practice, however, the effects of the rule are often mitigated by the inclusion of a specific clause in the contract to deal with the situation if it arises. Indeed, in *The Super Servant Two*, the Court of Appeal held that the defendants were entitled to rely on cl 17 of the contract (a *force majeure* clause), provided that the sinking of the vessel was not caused by their own negligence, even though the contract was not held to have been frustrated under the common law. This brings us on to our second limitation – events foreseen and provided for in the contract.

12.3.2 Events foreseen and provided for

If the contract itself makes provision for the supervening event, then the doctrine of frustration will generally have no role to play. It is a question of construction whether the terms of the contract are apt to cover the situation that has arisen. Historically, the courts have narrowly construed *force majeure* clauses. In *Jackson v Union Marine Insurance Co Ltd* (1874) LR 10 CP 125 (the facts of which we have already considered in Section 12.2.1.3), the charter stated that the ship should 'proceed with all possible dispatch (dangers and accidents of navigation excepted)'. It was held by the Exchequer Chamber that the exception in the contract absolved the shipowner of liability in the event of delay, but did not give him the right to bring an action if the delay was bad enough to frustrate the contract. Bramwell B said:

> Now, what is the effect of the exception of perils of the seas, and of delay being caused there by? ... I think this: they excuse the shipowner, but give him no right. The charterer has no cause of action, but is released from the charter. When I say *he* is, I think *both* are. The condition precedent has not been performed, but by default of neither .... The exception is an excuse for him who is to do the act, and operates to save him from an action and make his non-performance not a breach of contract, but does not operate to take away the right the other party would have had, if the non-performance had been a breach of contract, to retire from the engagement: and, if one party may, so may the other.

Similarly, the House of Lords adopted a narrow construction of words defining an event in:

Metropolitan Water Board v Dick Kerr [1918] AC 119

Facts: In 1914, the defendants agreed to construct a reservoir for the plaintiff water board. The work was to be completed within six years, subject to a proviso (condition 32) that

> if by reason of ... any difficulties, impediments, obstructions, oppositions, doubts, disputes, or differences, whatsoever and howsoever occasioned, the contractor shall, in the opinion of the engineer (whose decision shall be final), have been unduly delayed or impeded in the completion of this contract, it shall be lawful for the engineer, if he shall so think fit, to grant ... such extension of time either prospectively or retrospectively ... as to him may seem reasonable.

In 1916, the Ministry of Munitions ordered the contractors to cease work on the contract pursuant to their powers under the Defence of the Realm Acts and Regulations. The defendants claimed that the contract had been frustrated. The plaintiffs argued that the contract had not been frustrated on the ground that the event was provided for by the terms of the contract.

Held: The House of Lords held that the provision was only intended to deal with temporary delays and did not apply to the prohibition of the Ministry. Accordingly, the contract was discharged for frustration.

Lord Finlay LC: It is admitted that the prosecution of the works became illegal in consequence of the action of the Minister of Munitions. It became illegal on February 21, 1916, and remains illegal at the present time. This is not a case of a short and temporary stoppage, but of a prohibition in consequence of war, which has already been in force for the greater part of two years, and will, according to all appearances, last as long as the war itself, as it was the result of the necessity of preventing the diversion to civil purposes of labour and material required for purposes immediately connected with the war. Condition 32 provides for cases in which the contractor has, in the opinion of the engineer, been unduly delayed or impeded in the completion of his contract by any of the causes therein enumerated or by any other causes, so that an extension of time was reasonable. Condition 32 does not cover the case in which the interruption is of such a character and duration that it vitally and fundamentally changes the conditions of the contract, and could not possibly have been in the contemplation of the parties to the contract when it was made.

Traditionally it was clear that parties needed to be very specific if they intended a clause to deal with an event that would otherwise amount to frustration. In modern times, however, the courts have shown an increased willingness to interpret *force majeure* clauses within their factual matrix, giving effect to the purposes that such clauses are intended to fulfil.

12.3.3 Events foreseen and not provided for

It is sometimes stated that the doctrine of frustration does not apply to events which were foreseen, but not provided for. However, in *The Eugenia* [1964] 2 QB 226 at 239, Lord Denning MR boldly, and not without controversy, challenged this view:

> It has frequently been said that the doctrine of frustration only applies when the new situation is 'unforeseen' or 'unexpected' or 'uncontemplated', as if that were an essential feature. But it is not so. The only thing that is essential is that the parties should have made no provision for it in their contract. The only relevance of it being 'unforeseen' is this: If the parties did not foresee anything of the kind happening, you can readily infer they have made no provision for it: whereas, if they did foresee it, you would expect them to make provision for it. But cases have occurred where the parties have foreseen the danger ahead, and yet made no provision for it in the contract. Such was the case in the Spanish Civil War when a ship was let on charter to the republican government. The purpose was to evacuate refugees. The parties foresaw that she might be seized by the nationalists. But they made no provision for it in their contract. Yet, when she was seized, the contract was frustrated, see *W. J. Tatem Ltd v Gamboa* .... So here the parties foresaw that the canal might become impassable: it was the very thing they feared. But they made no provision for it. So there is room for the doctrine to apply if it be a proper case for it.

More recently in *Edwinton Commercial Corp v Tsavliris Russ (Worldwide Salvage & Towage) Ltd* [2007] EWCA Civ 547 (discussed above) Rix L.J. stated (at [127]):

> In a sense, most events are to a greater or lesser degree foreseeable. That does not mean that they cannot lead to frustration. Even events which are not merely foreseen but made the subject of express contractual provision may lead to frustration: as occurs when an event such as a strike, or a restraint of princes, lasts for so long as to go beyond the risk assumed under the contract and to render performance radically different from that contracted for. However, as *Treitel* shows through his analysis of the cases, and as *Chitty* summarises, the less that an event, in its type and its impact, is foreseeable, the more likely it is to be a factor which, depending on other factors in the case, may lead on to frustration.

It was even more recently considered in *Canary Wharf (BP4) T1 Ltd v European Medicines Agency* [2019] EWHC 335 (Ch). Marcus Smith J. noted (at [211]):

> The foreseeability of the frustrating event is relevant only insofar as it informs the parties' knowledge, expectations, assumptions and contemplations, in particular as to risk. If a future event is sufficiently foreseeable that it should have informed the manner in which the parties framed their agreement (particularly so far as the risk allocation provisions were concerned), then (to put it no higher than this) a court will be inclined to consider that the parties will have framed their agreement taking this factor into account. Foreseeability is, thus, no more than a factor to be taken into account.

12.4 Effects of frustration: common law

The effects of a frustrating event are governed by the common law and the provisions of the Law Reform (Frustrated Contracts) Act (LR(FC)A) 1943. In this section we will examine the common law rules; in the next section we will consider the main provisions of the LR(FC)A 1943 and how these impact on the common law rules. We will see that the objectives of the doctrine of frustration become important in this context. The common law historically adopted the view that the aim of the doctrine of frustration was to relieve the parties from the burden of having to perform obligations that had subsequently become impossible. This objective is arguably achieved by the automatic termination of the contract and a limited right to restitutionary relief. A wider role for the doctrine has been envisaged by Parliament. The LR(FC)A 1943 arguably enables the courts to apportion the losses resulting from the frustrating event by means of a more flexible form of restitutionary relief.

12.4.1 Automatic discharge

If a contract is frustrated it is automatically discharged at common law.

***Hirji Mulji v Cheong Yue Steamship Co Ltd* [1926] AC 497**

Facts: In November 1916, the respondents entered into a charterparty under which they agreed to place their ship, the *Singaporean*, at the disposal of the appellants on 1 March 1917 for ten months. Shortly afterwards, the ship was requisitioned by the Government. The respondents thought that the ship would soon be released and asked the appellants whether they would still be willing to take up the charter when this happened. The appellants said that they would. In fact, the ship was not released until February 1919 and the appellants refused to take delivery of her at that time. The respondents argued that the appellants had affirmed the contract after the frustrating event and were therefore bound to take delivery of the ship.

Held: The Privy Council held that the contract had been automatically discharged by the frustrating event. Accordingly, affirmation of the contract was not possible.

Lord Sumner (delivering the opinion of the Privy Council): Throughout the line of cases, now a long one, in which it has been held that certain events frustrate the commercial adventure contemplated by the parties when they made the contract, there runs an almost continuous series of expressions to the effect that such a frustration brings the contract to an end forthwith, without more and automatically ... Whatever the consequences of the frustration may be upon the conduct of the parties, its legal effect does not depend on their intention or their opinions, or even knowledge, as to the event, which has brought this about, but on its occurrence in such circumstances as show it to be inconsistent with further prosecution of the adventure. Sometimes the event is such as to speak for itself, like the outbreak of war on August 4, 1914, in *Horlock v Beal*: see per Lord Wrenbury [1916] 1 AC 486, 528. Sometimes the frustration is evident, when the gravity and the circumstances of the breakdown can be known, as in *Bensaude*'s case [1897] AC 609; sometimes, as in the case of requisition, when it can be known that in all reasonable probability the delay will be prolonged and a fortiori when it has continued so long as to defeat the adventure. Frustration is then complete. It operates automatically: *Larrinaga & Co's* case (1922) 27 Com Cas 160. What the parties say and do is only evidence, and not necessarily weighty evidence, of the view to be taken of the event by informed and experienced minds.

12.4.2 Prospective operation of discharge

Frustration discharges the contract prospectively (on the relevance of the subsequent actions of the parties see *Armchair Answercall Ltd v People in Mind Ltd* [2016] EWCA Civ 1039 at [51].). This means that the parties are excused from their future obligations but not from the obligations that existed prior to the time of the frustrating event. This can lead to one party being unjustly enriched at the expense of the other. For example, suppose that I agree to provide you with a room from which to view the coronation of the new King of England. Under the agreement you are required to pay me in full, 10 days prior to the coronation. Tragically, the new King dies two days before his coronation and the contract is frustrated. I am no longer bound to provide you with the room, since the frustrating event has automatically discharged my future obligations. You, however, are unable to recover the money you paid in advance, since the obligation to pay the money arose prior to the frustrating event.

The traditional common law position was that money paid prior to the frustrating event could not be recovered and money payable prior to discharge remained due (*Chandler v Webster* [1904] 1 KB 493). This rule was based on the mistaken assumption that a restitutionary claim for total failure of consideration could only be made if the underlying contract had been rescinded *ab initio* (from the beginning – as in cases of common mistake). In other words, total failure of consideration requires a total failure of the contractual promise, that is, the contractual consideration. This view was rejected by the House of Lords in *Fibrosa Spolka Akcyjna v Fairbairn Lawson Combe Barbour Ltd* [1943] AC 32. Viscount Simon LC distinguished consideration in the formation of a contract from restitutionary failure of consideration:

> In English law, an enforceable contract may be formed by an exchange of a promise for a promise, or by the exchange of a promise for an act ... and thus, in the law relating to the formation of a contract, the promise to do a thing may often be the consideration, but when one is considering the law of failure of consideration and of the quasi-contractual right to recover money on that ground, it is, generally speaking, not the promise which is referred to as the performance of the promise. The money was paid to secure performance and, if performance fails, the inducement which brought about the payment is not fulfilled.

Failure of consideration thus means failure of performance, not failure of the promise. Accordingly, a party can recover money paid under the frustrated contract as long as s/he has received no part of the performance which s/he bargained for in exchange for the payment.

However, the 'total failure' requirement represents a significant limitation. If the other party has provided any part of the bargained-for performance, no matter how small, recovery will not be possible. In *Whincup v Hughes* (1871) LR 6 CP 78, a father paid a premium of £25 to have his son apprenticed to a watchmaker for six years. The watchmaker died after one year, frustrating the contract. It was held that the father could not recover the premium in respect of the remaining five years because the consideration for the payment had only partially failed. A second limitation on the operation of restitution in this context at common law is that it does not take into account any expenditure that may have been incurred by the recipient in relation to the contract. This means that a recipient will be left out of pocket if s/he has spent some or all of the prepayment on materials necessary for performance. The common law may also fail to provide assistance to a party who has supplied services prior to the frustration of the contract, as seen in *Appleby v Myers*.

Appleby v Myers (1867) LR 2 CP 651

Facts: The plaintiffs contracted to erect and maintain certain machinery at the defendant's factory for a period of two years. Payment was to be made on completion of the work. After some of the work had been completed, the factory and all the machinery in it were destroyed by fire.

Held: The Exchequer Chamber held that the contract was frustrated and both parties were discharged from future performance. The plaintiffs were not entitled to be paid in respect of any of the work that had been completed because the obligation to pay had not arisen at the time the contract was frustrated.

Blackburn J: Had the accidental fire left the defendant's premises untouched, and only injured a part of the work which the plaintiffs had already done, we apprehend that it is clear the plaintiffs under such a contract as the present must have done that part over again, in order to fulfil their contract to complete the whole and 'put it to work for the sums above named respectively'. As it is, they are, according to the principle laid down in *Taylor v Caldwell*, excused from completing the work; but they are not therefore entitled to any compensation for what they have done, but which has, without any fault of the defendant, perished. The case is in principle like that of a shipowner who has been excused from the performance of his contract to carry goods to their destination, because his ship has been disabled by one of the excepted perils, but who is not therefore entitled to any payment on account of the part-performance of the voyage, unless there is something to justify the conclusion that there has been a fresh contract to pay freight pro rata.

The LR(FC)A 1943 was enacted to address some of these inadequacies in the common law.

12.5 Effects of frustration: Law Reform (Frustrated Contracts) Act 1943

The provisions of the LR(FC)A 1943 are set out in full below:

S 1 Adjustment of rights and liabilities of parties to frustrated contracts

(1) Where a contract governed by English law has become impossible of performance or been otherwise frustrated, and the parties thereto have for that reason been discharged from the further performance of the contract, the following provisions of this section shall, subject to the provisions of section two of this Act, have effect in relation thereto.

(2) All sums paid or payable to any party in pursuance of the contract before the time when the parties were so discharged (in this Act referred to as 'the time of discharge') shall, in the case of sums so paid, be recoverable from him as money received by him for the use of the party by whom the sums were paid, and, in the case of sums so payable, cease to be so payable:

Provided that, if the party to whom the sums were so paid or payable incurred expenses before the time of discharge in, or for the purpose of, the performance of the contract, the court may, if it considers it just to do so having regard to all the circumstances of the case, allow him to retain or, as the case may be, recover the whole or any part of the sums so paid or payable, not being an amount in excess of the expenses so incurred.

(3) Where any party to the contract has, by reason of anything done by any other party thereto in, or for the purpose of, the performance of the contract, obtained a valuable benefit (other than a payment of money to which the last foregoing subsection applies) before the time of discharge, there shall be recoverable from him by the said other party such sum (if any), not exceeding the value of the said benefit to the party obtaining it, as the court considers just, having regard to all the circumstances of the case and, in particular,—

(a) the amount of any expenses incurred before the time of discharge by the benefited party in, or for the purpose of, the performance of the contract, including any sums paid or payable by him to any other party in pursuance of the contract and retained or recoverable by that party under the last foregoing subsection, and

(b) the effect, in relation to the said benefit, of the circumstances giving rise to the frustration of the contract.

(4) In estimating, for the purposes of the foregoing provisions of this section, the amount of any expenses incurred by any party to the contract, the court may, without prejudice to the generality of the said provisions, include such sum as appears to be reasonable in respect of overhead expenses and in respect of any work or services performed personally by the said party.

(5) In considering whether any sum ought to be recovered or retained under the foregoing provisions of this section by any party to the contract, the court shall not take into account any sums which have, by reason of the circumstances giving rise to the frustration of the contract, become payable to that party under any contract of insurance unless there was an obligation to insure imposed by an express term of the frustrated contract or by or under any enactment.

(6) Where any person has assumed obligations under the contract in consideration of the conferring of a benefit by any other party to the contract upon any other person, whether a party to the contract or not, the court may, if in all the circumstances of the case it considers it just to do so, treat for the purposes of subsection (3) of this section any benefit so conferred as a benefit obtained by the person who has assumed the obligations as aforesaid.

S 2 Provision as to application of this act

(1) This Act shall apply to contracts, whether made before or after the commencement of this Act, as respects which the time of discharge is on or after the first day of July, nineteen hundred and forty-three, but not to contracts as respects which the time of discharge is before the said date.

(2) This Act shall apply to contracts to which the Crown is a party in like manner as to contracts between subjects.

(3) Where any contract to which this Act applies contains any provision which, upon the true construction of the contract, is intended to have effect in the event of circumstances arising which operate, or would but for the said provision operate, to frustrate the contract, or is intended to have effect whether such circumstances arise or not, the court shall give effect to the said provision and shall only give effect to the foregoing section of this Act to such extent, if any, as appears to the court to be consistent with the said provision.

(4) Where it appears to the court that a part of any contract to which this Act applies can properly be severed from the remainder of the contract, being a part wholly performed before the time of discharge, or so performed except for the payment in respect of that part of the contract of sums which are or can be ascertained under the contract, the court shall treat that part of the contract as if it were a separate contract and had not been frustrated and shall treat the foregoing section of this Act as only applicable to the remainder of that contract.

(5) This Act shall not apply—

(a) to any charterparty, except a time charterparty or a charterparty by way of demise, or to any contract (other than a charterparty) for the carriage of goods by sea; or

(b) to any contract of insurance, save as is provided by subsection (5) of the foregoing section; or

(c) to any contract to which [section 7 of the Sale of Goods Act 1979] (which avoids contracts for the sale of specific goods which perish before the risk has passed to the buyer) applies, or to any other contract for the sale, or for the sale and delivery, of specific goods, where the contract is frustrated by reason of the fact that the goods have perished.

12.5.1 The scope of the act

Section 2 sets out some important limitations on the scope of the Act. Section 2(3) makes it clear that the parties can agree to exclude the provisions of the LR(FC)A 1943. If the parties chose to do this, such exclusion will not be subject to the UCTA 1977, since s 29(1)(a) of the 1977 Act states that the Act does not affect any contractual provision that 'is authorised … by the express terms

… of an enactment'. The exclusion may, however, be affected by the UTCCR 1999 if it is contained in a standard form consumer contract. In practice, the fact that s 2(3) expressly authorises the parties to exclude the LR(FC)A 1943, is likely to support the conclusion that the term is not 'unfair'.

Section 2(4) provides that if parts of the contract that have been wholly performed can properly be severed from the remainder of the contract, they are to be treated as a separate contract, which has not been frustrated. The remainder of the contract will be subject to s 1 of the LR(FC) A 1943.

Section 2(5) contains a list of contracts that are excluded from the scope of the Act. This includes particular charterparties and contracts of insurance. It also includes contracts falling within s 7 of the Sale of Goods Act 1979. Professor Glanville Williams has argued convincingly that there is no justification for this latter exclusion (see *Law Reform (Frustrated Contracts) Act 1943* (London: Stevens, 1944)).

12.5.2 The key provisions of the act

There are two key provisions in the LR(FC)A 1943. The first, s 1(2), deals with money paid or owing under the contract prior to the frustrating event; and the second, s 1(3), deals with the situation where a party has obtained a non-money benefit before the time of discharge. The leading case on the operation of these provisions is *BP Exploration Co (Libya) Ltd v Hunt (No 2)*.

***BP Exploration Co (Libya) Ltd v Hunt (No 2)* [1979] 1 WLR 783**

Facts: The defendant, Mr Hunt, was the owner of an oil concession in Libya. He entered into a 'farm-in' agreement with the plaintiff oil company under which they would explore, develop and operate the oil concession and also make 'farm-in' contributions to the defendant in cash and oil. In return, the plaintiff would receive a half share of the concession. Furthermore, if oil was found, the plaintiff would be entitled to repayment of its expenditure (both the 'farm-in' contributions and a half share of the expenditure on exploration and development) out of the defendant's share of the oil. Large quantities of oil were discovered and the field came on stream in 1967. In 1971, following a revolution in Libya, the plaintiff's interest in the oil field was expropriated by the Libyan government. The defendant continued to export oil from the field until 11 June 1973, when his interest was expropriated. By this time, the plaintiff had already received approximately one-third of the 50 million barrels of 'reimbursement oil' to which it was entitled. It also received some compensation from the Libyan government in relation to the facilities left at the field. The plaintiff claimed that the contract had been frustrated by the expropriation of its interest in the oil field and sought an award of a just sum under s 1(3) of the LR(FC)A 1943.

Held: Goff J. held that the contract was frustrated and awarded the plaintiff a just sum under s 1(3) of the LR(FC)A 1943.

Goff J

(1) *The principle of recovery*

(a) The principle, which is common to both section 1(2) and (3), and indeed is the fundamental principle underlying the Act itself, is prevention of the unjust enrichment of either party to the contract at the other's expense. It was submitted by [counsel for the plaintiff] that the principle common to both subsections was one of restitution for net benefits received, the net benefit being the benefit less an appropriate deduction for expenses incurred by the defendant. This is broadly correct so far as section 1(2) is concerned; but under section 1(3) the net benefit of the defendant simply provides an upper limit to the award – it does not measure the amount of the award to be made to the plaintiff. This is because in section 1(3) a distinction is drawn between the plaintiff's performance under the contract, and the benefit which the defendant has obtained by reason of that performance – a distinction about which I shall have more to say later in this judgment: and the net benefit obtained by the defendant from the plaintiff's performance may be more than a just sum payable in respect of such performance, in which event a sum equal to the defendant's net benefit would not be an appropriate sum to award to the plaintiff. I therefore consider it better to state the principle underlying the Act as being the principle of unjust enrichment, which underlies the right of recovery in very many cases in English law, and indeed is the basic principle of the English law of restitution, of which the Act forms part.

(b) Although section 1(2) and (3) is concerned with restitution in respect of different types of benefit, it is right to construe the two subsections as flowing from the same basic principle and therefore, so far as their different subject matters permit, to achieve consistency between them. Even so, it is always necessary to bear in mind the difference between awards of restitution in respect of money payments and awards where the benefit conferred by the plaintiff does not consist of a payment of money. Money has the peculiar character of a universal medium of exchange. By its receipt, the recipient is inevitably benefited; and (subject to problems arising from such matters as inflation, change of position and the time value of money) the loss suffered by the plaintiff is generally equal to the defendant's gain, so that no difficulty arises concerning the amount to be repaid. The same cannot be said of other benefits, such as goods or services. By their nature, services cannot be restored; nor in many cases can goods be restored, for example where they have been consumed or transferred to another. Furthermore the identity and value of the resulting benefit to the recipient may be debatable. From the very nature of things, therefore, the problem of restitution in respect of such benefits is more complex than in cases where the benefit takes the form of a money payment; and the solution of the problem has been made no easier by the form in which the legislature has chosen to draft section 1(3) of the Act.

(c) The Act is not designed to do certain things: (i) It is not designed to apportion the loss between the parties. There is no general power under either section 1(2) or section 1(3) to make any allowance for expenses incurred by the plaintiff (except, under the proviso to section 1(2), to enable him to enforce *pro tanto* payment of a sum payable but unpaid before frustration); and expenses incurred by the defendant are only relevant in so far as they go to reduce the net benefit obtained by him and thereby limit any award to the plaintiff. (ii) It is not concerned to put the parties in the position in which they would have been if the contract had been performed. (iii) It is not concerned to restore the parties to the position they were in before the contract was made. A remedy designed to prevent unjust enrichment may not achieve that result; for expenditure may be incurred by either party under the contract which confers no benefit on the other, and in respect of which no remedy is available under the Act.

(d) An award under the Act may have the effect of rescuing the plaintiff from an unprofitable bargain. This may certainly be true under section 1(2), if the plaintiff has paid the price in advance for an expected return which, if furnished, would have proved unprofitable; if the contract is frustrated before any part of that expected return is received, and before any expenditure is incurred by the defendant, the plaintiff is entitled to the return of the price he has paid, irrespective of the consideration he would have recovered had the contract been performed. Consistently with section 1(2), there is nothing in section 1(3) which necessarily limits an award to the contract consideration. But the contract consideration may nevertheless be highly relevant to the assessment of the just sum to be awarded under section 1(3); this is a matter to which I will revert later in this judgment.

(2) Claims under section 1(2)

Where an award is made under section 1(2), it is, generally speaking, simply an award for the repayment of money which has been paid to the defendant in pursuance of the contract, subject to an allowance in respect of expenses incurred by the defendant. It is not necessary that the consideration for the payment should have wholly failed: claims under section 1(2) are not limited to cases of total failure of consideration, and cases of partial failure of consideration can be catered for by a cross-claim by the defendant under section 1(2) or section 1(3) or both. There is no discretion in the court in respect of a claim under section 1(2), except in respect of the allowance for expenses; subject to such an allowance (and, of course, a cross-claim) the plaintiff is entitled to repayment of the money he has paid. The allowance for expenses is probably best rationalised as a statutory recognition of the defence of change of position. True, the expenses need not have been incurred by reason of the plaintiff's payment; but they must have been incurred in, or for the purpose of, the performance of the contract under which the plaintiff's payment has been made, and for that reason it is just that they should be brought into account. No provision is made in the subsection for any increase in the sum recoverable by the plaintiff, or in the amount of expenses to be allowed to the defendant, to allow for the time value of money. The money may have been paid, or the expenses incurred, many years before the date of frustration; but the cause of action accrues on that date, and the sum recoverable under the Act as at that date can be no greater than the sum actually paid, though the defendant may have had the use of the money over many years, and indeed may have profited from its use. Of course, the question whether the court may award interest from the date of the accrual of the cause of action is an entirely different matter, to which I shall refer later in this judgment.

(3) *Claims under section 1(3)*

(a) *General.* In contract, where an award is made under section 1(3), the process is more complicated. First, it has to be shown that the defendant has, by reason of something done by the plaintiff in, or for the purpose of, the performance of the contract, obtained a valuable benefit (other than a payment of money) before the time of discharge. That benefit has to be identified, and valued, and such value forms the upper limit of the award. Secondly, the court may award to the plaintiff such sum, not greater than the value of such benefit, as it considers just having regard to all the circumstances of the case, including in particular the matters specified in section 1(3)(a) and (b). In the case of an award under section 1(3) there are, therefore, two distinct stages – the identification and valuation of the benefit, and the award of the just sum. The amount to be awarded is the just sum, unless the defendant's benefit is less, in which event the award will be limited to the amount of that benefit. The distinction between the identification and valuation of the defendant's benefit, and the assessment of the just sum, is the most controversial part of the Act. It represents the solution adopted by the legislature of the problem of restitution in cases where the benefit does not consist of a payment of money, but the solution so adopted has been criticised by some commentators as productive of injustice, and it certainly gives rise to considerable problems, to which I shall refer in due course.

(b) *Identification of the defendant's benefit.* In the course of the argument before me, there was much dispute whether, in the case of services, the benefit should be identified as the services themselves, or as the end product of the services. One example canvassed (because it bore some relationship to the facts of the present case) was the example of prospecting for minerals. If minerals are discovered, should the benefit be regarded (as counsel for the defendant contended) simply as the services of prospecting, or (as counsel for the plaintiff contended) as the minerals themselves being the end product of the successful exercise? Now, I am satisfied that it was the intention of the legislature, to be derived from section 1(3) as a matter of construction, that the benefit should in an appropriate case be identified as the end product of the services. This appears, in my judgment, not only from the fact that section 1(3) distinguishes between the plaintiff's performance and the defendant's benefit, but also from section 1(3)(b) which clearly relates to the product of the plaintiff's performance. Let me take the example of a building contract. Suppose that a contract for work on a building is frustrated by a fire which destroys the building and which, therefore, also destroys a substantial amount of work already done by the plaintiff. Although it might be thought just to award the plaintiff a sum assessed on a *quantum meruit* basis, probably a rateable part of the contract price, in respect of the work he has done, the effect of section 1(3)(b) will be to reduce the award to nil, because of the effect, in relation to the defendant's benefit, of the circumstances giving rise to the frustration of the contract. It is quite plain that, in section 1(3)(b), the word 'benefit' is intended to refer, in the example I have given, to the actual improvement to the building, because that is what will be affected by the frustrating event; the subsection therefore contemplates that, in such a case, the benefit is the end product of the plaintiff's services, not the services themselves. This will not be so in every case, since in some cases the services will have no end product; for example, where the services consist of doing such work as surveying, or transporting goods. In each case, it is necessary to ask the question: what benefit has the defendant obtained by reason of the plaintiff's contractual performance? But it must not be forgotten that in section 1(3) the relevance of the value of the benefit is to fix a ceiling to the award. If, for example, in a building contract, the building is only partially completed, the value of the partially completed building (i.e. the product of the services) will fix a ceiling for the award; the stage of the work may be such that the uncompleted building may be worth less than the value of the work and materials that have gone into it, particularly as completion by another builder may cost more than completion by the original builder would have cost. In other cases, however, the actual benefit to the defendant may be considerably more than the appropriate or just sum to be awarded to the plaintiff, in which event the value of the benefit will not in fact determine the quantum of the award. I should add, however, that, in a case of prospecting, it would usually be wrong to identify the discovered mineral as the benefit. In such a case there is always (whether the prospecting is successful or not) the benefit of the prospecting itself, i.e. of knowing whether or not the land contains any deposit of the relevant minerals; if the prospecting is successful, the benefit may include also the enhanced value of the land by reason of the discovery; if the prospector's contractual task goes beyond discovery and includes development and production, the benefit will include the further enhancement of the land by reason of the installation of the facilities, and also the benefit of in part transforming a valuable mineral deposit into a marketable commodity.

I add by way of footnote that all these difficulties would have been avoided if the legislature had thought it right to treat the services themselves as the benefit. In the opinion of many commentators, it would be more just to do so; after all, the services in question have been requested by the defendant, who normally takes the risk that they may prove worthless, from whatever cause. In the example I have given of the building destroyed by fire, there is much to be said for the view that the builder should be paid for the work he has done, unless he has (for example, by agreeing to insure the works) taken upon himself the risk of destruction by fire. But my task is to construe the Act as it stands. On the true construction of the Act, it is in my judgment clear that the defendant's benefit must, in an appropriate case, be identified as the end product of the plaintiff's services, despite the difficulties which this construction creates, difficulties which are met again when one comes to value the benefit ....

(d) *Valuing the benefit*. Since the benefit may be identified with the product of the plaintiff's performance, great problems arise in the valuation of the benefit. First, how does one solve the problem which arises from the fact that a small service may confer an enormous benefit, and conversely, a very substantial service may confer only a very small benefit? The answer presumably is that at the stage of valuation of the benefit (as opposed to assessment of the just sum) the task of the court is simply to assess the value of the benefit to the defendant. For example, if a prospector after some very simple prospecting discovers a large and unexpected deposit of a valuable mineral, the benefit to the defendant (namely, the enhancement in the value of the land) may be enormous; it must be valued as such, always bearing in mind that the assessment of a just sum may very well lead to a much smaller amount being awarded to the plaintiff. But conversely, the plaintiff may have undertaken building work for a substantial sum which is, objectively speaking, of little or no value – for example, he may commence the redecoration, to the defendant's execrable taste, of rooms which are in good decorative order. If the contract is frustrated before the work is complete, and the work is unaffected by the frustrating event, it can be argued that the defendant has obtained no benefit, because the defendant's property has been reduced in value by the plaintiff's work; but the partial work must be treated as a benefit to the defendant, since he requested it, and valued as such. Secondly, at what point in time is the benefit to be valued? If there is a lapse of time between the date of the receipt of the benefit, and the date of frustration, there may in the meanwhile be a substantial variation in the value of the benefit. If the benefit had simply been identified as the services rendered, this problem would not arise; the court would simply award a reasonable remuneration for the services rendered at the time when they were rendered, the defendant taking the risk of any subsequent depreciation and the benefit of any subsequent appreciation in value. But that is not what the Act provides: section

1(3)(b) makes it plain that the plaintiff is to take the risk of depreciation or destruction by the frustrating event. If the effect of the frustrating event upon the value of the benefit is to be measured, it must surely be measured upon the benefit as at the date of frustration. For example, let it be supposed that a builder does work which doubles in value by the date of frustration, and is then so severely damaged by fire that the contract is frustrated; the valuation of the residue must surely be made on the basis of the value as at the date of frustration ....

Other problems can arise from the valuation of the defendant's benefit as the end product; I shall come to these later in the consideration of the facts of the present case. But there is a further problem which I should refer to, before leaving this topic. Section 1(3)(a) requires the court to have regard to the amount of any expenditure incurred before the time of discharge by the benefited party in, or for the purpose of, the performance of the contract. The question arises – should this matter be taken into account at the stage of valuation of the benefit, or of assessment of the just sum? Take a simple example. Suppose that the defendant's benefit is valued at £150, and that a just sum is assessed at £100, but that there remain to be taken into account defendant's expenses of £75: is the award to be £75 or £25? The clue to this problem lies, in my judgment, in the fact that the allowance for expenses is a statutory recognition of the defence of change of position. Only to the extent that the position of the defendant has so changed that it would be unjust to award restitution, should the court make an allowance for expenses. Suppose that the plaintiff does work for the defendant which produces no valuable end product, or a benefit no greater in value than the just sum to be awarded in respect of the work; there is then no reason why the whole of the relevant expenses should not be set off against the just sum. But suppose that the defendant has reaped a large benefit from the plaintiff's work, far greater in value than the just sum to be awarded for the work. In such circumstances it would be quite wrong to set off the whole of the defendant's expenses against the just sum. The question whether the defendant has suffered a change of position has to be judged in the light of all the circumstances of the case. Accordingly, on the Act as it stands, under section 1(3) the proper course is to deduct the expenses from the value of the benefit, with the effect that only in so far as they reduce the value of the benefit below the amount of the just sum which would otherwise be awarded will they have any practical bearing on the award ....

(e) *Assessment of the just sum.* The principle underlying the Act is prevention of the unjust enrichment of the defendant at the plaintiff's expense. Where, as in cases under section 1(2), the benefit conferred on the defendant consists of payment of a sum of money, the plaintiff's expense and the defendant's enrichment are generally equal; and, subject to other relevant factors, the award of restitution will consist simply of an order for repayment of a like sum of money. But where the benefit does not consist of money, then the defendant's enrichment will rarely be equal to the plaintiff's expense. In such cases, where (as in the case of a benefit conferred under a contract thereafter frustrated) the benefit has been requested by the defendant, the basic measure of recovery in restitution is the reasonable value of the plaintiff's performance – in a case of services, a *quantum meruit* or reasonable remuneration, and in a case of goods, a *quantum valebat* or reasonable price. Such cases are to be contrasted with cases where such a benefit has not been requested by the defendant. In the latter class of case, recovery is rare in restitution; but if the sole basis of recovery was that the defendant had been incontrovertibly benefited, it might be legitimate to limit recovery to the defendant's actual benefit – a limit which has (perhaps inappropriately) been imported by the legislature into section 1(3) of the Act. However, under section 1(3) as it stands, if the defendant's actual benefit is less than the just or reasonable sum which would otherwise be awarded to the plaintiff, the award must be reduced to a sum equal to the amount of the defendant's benefit.

A crucial question, upon which the Act is surprisingly silent, is this: what bearing do the terms of the contract, under which the plaintiff has acted, have upon the assessment of the just sum? First, the terms upon which the work was done may serve to indicate the full scope of the work done, and so be relevant to the sum awarded in respect of such work. For example, if I do work under a contract under which I am to receive a substantial prize if successful, and nothing if I fail, and the contract is frustrated before the

> work is complete but not before a substantial benefit has been obtained by the defendant, the element of risk taken by the plaintiff may be held to have the effect of enhancing the amount of any sum to be awarded. Secondly, the contract consideration is always relevant as providing some evidence of what will be a reasonable sum to be awarded in respect of the plaintiff's work. Thus if a prospector, employed for a fee, discovers a gold mine before the contract under which he is employed is frustrated (for example, by illegality or by his illness or disablement) at a time when his work was incomplete, the court may think it just to make an award in the nature of a reasonable fee for what he has done (though of course the benefit obtained by the defendant will be far greater), and a rateable part of the contract fee may provide useful evidence of the level of sum to be awarded. If, however, the contract had provided that he was to receive a stake in the concession, then the just sum might be enhanced on the basis that, in all the circumstances, a reasonable sum should take account of such a factor: *cf. Way v Latilla* [1937] 3 All ER 759. Thirdly, however, the contract consideration, or a rateable part of it, may provide a limit to the sum to be awarded. To take a fairly extreme example, a poor householder or a small businessman may obtain a contract for building work to be done to his premises at considerably less than the market price, on the basis that he cannot afford to pay more. In such a case, the court may consider it just to limit the award to a rateable part of the contract price, on the ground that it was the understanding of the parties that in no circumstances (including the circumstances of the contract being frustrated) should the plaintiff recover more than the contract price or a rateable part of it. Such a limit may properly be said to arise by virtue of the operation of section 2(3) of the Act. But it must not be forgotten that, unlike money, services can never be restored, nor usually can goods, since they are likely to have been either consumed or disposed of, or to have depreciated in value; and since, *ex hypothesi*, the defendant will only have been prepared to contract for the goods or services on the basis that he paid no more than the contract consideration, it may be unjust to compel him, by an award under the Act, to pay more than that consideration, or a rateable part of it, in respect of the services or goods he has received. It is unnecessary for me to decide whether this will always be so; but it is likely that in most cases this will impose an important limit upon the sum to be awarded – indeed it may well be the most relevant limit to an award under section 1(3) of the Act. The legal basis of the limit may be section 2(3) of the Act; but even if that subsection is inapplicable, it is open to the court, in an appropriate case, to give effect to such a limit in assessing the just sum to be awarded under section 1(3), because in many cases it would be unjust to impose upon the defendant an obligation to make restitution under the subsection at higher than the contract rate.

Applying this approach to the facts of the case, Goff J. found that the valuable benefit obtained by the defendant, following frustration of the contract, consisted of the value of the oil he had actually obtained from the oilfield, plus the compensation received from the Libyan government. This produced a 'valuable benefit' of $85 million. In assessing the 'just sum', Goff J. took into account the expenses incurred by the plaintiff and the 'farm-in' contributions received by the defendant, and then deducted from this figure the value of the reimbursement oil received by the plaintiff. This produced a total of $35 million, which, being less than the 'valuable benefit', was awarded in full.

For our purposes, we do not need to focus on the complex facts of the case. Instead we will direct our attention to the comments made by Goff J. about the key provisions of the Act.

12.5.2.1 The underlying purpose of the LR(FC)A 1943

Goff J. considered that the purpose underlying the LR(FC)A 1943 was the prevention of unjust enrichment. The Court of Appeal generally affirmed his decision (as did the House of Lords), although Lawton L.J. noted:

> Mr Rokison, on behalf of the plaintiffs, accepted that there could be more than one way of assessing a just sum. He pointed out that there was nothing in the Act to indicate that its purpose was to enable the judge to apportion losses or profits, or to put the parties in the positions which they would have been in if the contract had been fully performed or if it had never been made. This we accept. He submitted that the concept behind the Act was to prevent unjust enrichment. This is what the judge had thought. We get no help from the use of words which are not in the statute.

It has been suggested that the assessment of a 'just sum' under s 1(3) exposes the fact that the LR(FC)A 1943 is really just a mechanism for loss apportionment. Haycroft and Waksman ('Frustration and Restitution' [1984] *JBL* 207, 225) have written:

> Unjust enrichment cannot be regarded as the basis of the Act; to suggest otherwise simply ignores its wording and the conceptual distortion which follows from such an idea can be seen to lead to great practical difficulties.
>
> All that can be ventured about the real basis of the Act is that it is designed to provide a flexible machinery for the adjustment of loss.
>
> The inclusion of the word 'just' merely sets a general standard for the exercise of the court's discretion as can be found in many other statutes, and should not be seen as an invocation of the principle of unjust enrichment.

On the other hand, although the LR(FC)A 1943 does confer some discretion on the court, it is not clear that this amounts to 'a flexible machinery for the adjustment of loss'. The first step for the court is to identify the benefit that the defendant has obtained at the claimant's expense. This figure operates as a ceiling for the claim and arguably ensures that recovery is limited to the amount by which the defendant has been unjustly enriched at the claimant's expense. It is only at this stage that the judicial discretion comes into play. This discretion allows the courts to reduce recovery to take into account the losses sustained by the defendant, but it does not allow for the apportionment of losses which are not matched by a corresponding enrichment. Thus the discretion to adjust recovery is only a very narrow discretion and it arguably operates within the general framework of recovery for unjust enrichment.

12.5.2.2 Operation of section 1(2): restitution of money

As Goff J. notes, a major change brought about by s 1(2) of the LR(FC)A 1943 is that money paid under a frustrated contract is recoverable, even where there is not a total failure of consideration. This is a significant improvement on the common law position.

Section 1(2) also introduces a proviso that permits the court to set off against the advance payment any expenses that may have been incurred by the defendant prior to the frustrating event. Goff J. suggested that this proviso is 'best rationalised as a statutory recognition of the defence of change of position'. This would mean that the defendant is permitted, as of right, to set off expenses incurred in 'the performance of the contract under which the plaintiff's payment has been made'. A different view was, however, taken by Garland J. in *Gamerco SA v ICM/Fair Warming (Agency) Ltd* [1995] 1 WLR 1226. The case concerned a contract to promote a Guns N' Roses concert, which was frustrated by the Spanish government's decision to close the stadium in which the concert was due to take place. The plaintiff had paid the defendant $412,500 prior to the frustrating event and sought to recover this amount under s 1(2). The defendants had incurred expenditure of approximately $50,000 and argued that they should be allowed to retain this amount. Garland J. held that, taking into account the plaintiff's loss (approximately $450,000), justice would be done by allowing the plaintiffs to recover the advance payment in full without any deduction for the defendant's expenses. He concluded his judgment as follows:

The approach to the proviso

The following have to be established: (1) that the defendants incurred expenses paid or payable (2) before the discharge of the contract on 2 July (3) in performance of the contract (which is not applicable) or (4) for the purposes of the performance of the contract, and (5) that it is just in all the circumstances to allow them to retain the whole or any part of the sums so paid or payable.

The onus of establishing these matters must lie on the defendant. It is, in the broad sense, his case to be made out and I am assisted by the Victorian case of *Lobb v Vasey Housing Auxiliary (War Widows Guild)* [1963] VR 239 under the corresponding Victorian Act of 1959, which is in very similar terms to the Act of 1943.

I have already dealt with (1), (2) and (4) so far as the evidence allows. I turn to (5) .... Various views have been advanced as to how the court should exercise its discretion and these can be categorised as follows.

(1) *Total retention.* This view was advanced by the Law Revision Committee in 1939 (Cmd. 6009) on the questionable ground 'that it is reasonable to assume that in stipulating for prepayment the payee intended to protect himself from loss under the contract'. As the editor of *Chitty on Contracts*, 27th edn. (1994), vol. 1, p 1141, para. 23–060, note 51 (Mr E G McKendrick) comments: 'He probably intends to protect himself against the possibility of the other party's insolvency or default in payment'. To this, one can add: 'and secure his own cash flow'.

In *BP Exploration Co (Libya) Ltd v Hunt (No 2)* [1979] 1 WLR 783, Robert Goff J considered the principle of recovery under subsections (2) and (3). He said: ...

> 'There is no discretion in the court in respect of a claim under section 1(2), except in respect of the allowance for expenses; subject to such an allowance ... the plaintiff is entitled to repayment of the money he has paid. The allowance for expenses is probably best rationalised as a statutory recognition of the defence of change of position. True, the expenses need not have been incurred by reason of the plaintiff's payments; but they must have been incurred in, or for the purpose of, the performance of the contract under which the plaintiff's payment has been made, and for that reason it is just that they should be brought into account'.

I do not derive any specific assistance from the *BP Exploration Co* case. There was no question of any change of position as a result of the plaintiffs' advance payment.

(2) *Equal division.* This was discussed by Professor Treitel in *Frustration and Force Majeure*, pp 555–556, paras 15–059 and 15–060. There is some attraction in splitting the loss, but what if the losses are very unequal? Professor Treitel considers statutory provisions in Canada and Australia but makes the point that unequal division is unnecessarily rigid and was rejected by the Law Revision Committee in the 1939 report to which reference has already been made. The parties may, he suggests, have had an unequal means of providing against the loss by insurers, but he appears to overlook subsection (5). It may well be that one party's expenses are entirely thrown away while the other is left with some realisable or otherwise usable benefit or advantage. Their losses may, as in the present case, be very unequal. Professor Treitel therefore favours the third view.

(3) *Broad discretion.* It is self-evident that any rigid rule is liable to produce injustice. The words 'if it considers it just to do so having regard to all the circumstances of the case' clearly confer a very broad discretion. Obviously the court must not take into account anything which is not 'a circumstance of the case' or fail to take into account anything that is and then exercise its discretion rationally. I see no indication in the Act, the authorities or the relevant literature that the court is obliged to incline towards either total retention or equal division. Its task is to do justice in a situation which the parties had neither contemplated nor provided for, and to mitigate the possible harshness of allowing all loss to lie where it has fallen.

I have not found my task easy. As I have made clear, I would have welcomed assistance on the true measure of the defendants' loss and the proper treatment of overhead and non-specific expenditure.

> Because the defendants have plainly suffered some loss, I have made a robust assumption. In all the circumstances, and having particular regard to the plaintiffs' loss, I consider that justice is done by making no deduction under the proviso.

Carter and Tolhurst ('Gigs n' restitution – frustration and the statutory adjustment of payments and expenses' (1996) 10 *JCL* 264) have criticised the approach adopted by Garland J. in *Gamerco*. They note that the judge gave no reason for his rejection of the 'change of position' rationalisation and question why he neglected to consider the position at common law. They conclude as follows:

> [W]hether or not one accepts change of position as the rationalisation, it ought at least to have been clear that the Band was entitled to something, because the circumstances activated the defence. In this regard it may be important that the proviso requires an award of 'the whole or ... part of the sums so paid or payable, not being an amount in excess of the expenses ... incurred. Arguably, there was no discretion to award a nil sum. In other words, the discretion was to award a sum which was just in the circumstances. But even if that is not the correct interpretation, it can at least be said that once the Band proved some expenses, Garland J ought to have awarded something unless it was unjust to do so. Clearly, there was nothing in the evidence to indicate that a zero sum was a just sum.

It is, perhaps, regrettable that Garland J. refused to identify any principles upon which the discretion exercisable under s 1(2) is to be based. We are left with a discretion that is both ill-defined and difficult to apply. All we can really say is what the discretion is not. First, attractive though the theory may be, the proviso cannot be rationalised as a form of change of position defence. This is because the proviso allows the courts to take into account 'all the circumstances of the case', including the claimant's loss (*Gamerco*). Such considerations are irrelevant to change of position, which focuses solely on the loss sustained by the defendant. Second, however, the proviso cannot be rationalised as a full-blown mechanism for loss apportionment either. This is because recovery is only possible where the claimant was obliged to pay money prior to the frustrating event, and recovery is limited to the value of the advance payment. In truth, what we have in s 1(2) is a severely restricted mechanism for loss apportionment, arbitrarily limited by the value of the defendant's enrichment.

12.5.2.3 Operation of section 1(3): restitution of non-money benefits

Goff J. indicated that there are three stages to the operation of s 1(3). First, it has to be shown that the defendant has obtained a 'valuable benefit' from the claimant prior to the time of discharge. Second, the benefit must be valued (see, generally, *Benedetti v Sawiris* [2013] UKSC 50). Third, the court must determine what would be a 'just sum' to award to the claimant, having regard to all the circumstances of the case, including in particular the matters specified in s 1(3)(a) and (b).

In relation to the valuing of the benefit, Goff J. noted that s 1(3)(b) of the Act requires the court to take into account 'the effect, in relation to the said benefit, of the circumstances giving rise to the frustration of the contract'. This led him to the conclusion that the benefit is to be identified as the end product of the claimant's services rather than the services themselves. If this is correct, then *Appleby v Myers* would be decided in the same way today. It will be remembered that in *Appleby v Myers* the plaintiff provided valuable machinery to the defendant, which was subsequently destroyed by fire. According to Goff J.'s interpretation of s 1(3)(b) this would mean that the 'valuable benefit' received by the defendant was nil, and since the 'just sum' cannot exceed the 'valuable benefit', the 'just sum' must also be nil. There are reasons to believe that Goff J.'s approach to the interpretation of s 1(3) is incorrect.

Burrows, A, *The Law of Restitution*, 3rd edn, 2011, Oxford: OUP, p 370

With great respect, it is possible that Robert Goff J took a false step regarding there being a crucial difference, so far as restitution is concerned, between the end product of contracted-for services and the services (or performance of the services) themselves. *Even if there is an end product produced by the services the defendant's benefit comprises his saving of expense in paying for the services producing that end product.* And the crucial line between when services constitute mere reliance loss to the performer and when they become objectively beneficial to the other party (and hence, subject to subjective devaluation, potentially fall within the law on unjust enrichment) is, it is submitted, when the other party receives the services. Where the purpose of the services is to produce an end product (e.g., building work) it is true that one regards the owner as receiving the services at the time when it receives part of the end product (e.g., when the first part of the building is erected). But the same notion of receipt explains why a theatregoer is only objectively benefited when the play begins or why a home owner who engages a gardener to mow the lawn is only objectively benefited when the gardener starts to cut the lawn. On an unjust enrichment interpretation of s 1(3) the important distinction is therefore between services that are not received and services that are received and not between services and the end product of those services.

Once one excises the distinction between end product and services the acute problems encountered by Robert Goff J in interpreting s 1(3) disappear. For example, there is now no problem of a small service producing very substantial end products and vice versa; there is no need to carve out inconsistent 'exceptions' where there is no end product or an end product of no objective value; there is no reason to confine a true unjust enrichment analysis to the assessment of the just sum; and, while the same conclusion may be reached by applying 'change of position' reasoning, s 1 (3) (b) does not have to be interpreted as meaning that no valuable benefit was obtained where a building under construction is destroyed by fire.

Peel, E, *Treitel on the Law of Contract*, 14th edn, 2015, London: Sweet & Maxwell, p 1091

[A]n alternative interpretation of s 1(3) is to be preferred. This would make the destruction of the benefit relevant, not to the identification of the benefit, but to the assessment of the just sum. Two points seem to support such an interpretation. First, s 1(3) applies where a valuable benefit has been obtained *before* the time of discharge: thus to identify the benefit in a case like *Appleby v Myers* the court must look at the facts as they were before, and not after, the fire. The partly completed installation would at least prima facie be a benefit, since completion of the installation would be likely to cost less after part of the work had been done. Secondly, there is the structure of the subsection. This begins by setting out the circumstances in which the court has power to make an award (i.e. when a valuable benefit has been obtained) and then provides guidelines for the exercise of that power. The guideline contained in s 1(3) (b) is introduced by the words 'such sum as the court thinks just having regard to ...'; and these words seem to link the guideline to the *exercise* rather than to the *existence* of the court's discretion. This interpretation cannot cause any injustice, for if the court thinks that very little or nothing should be awarded it can exercise its discretion to that effect; and for this purpose the court can take the destruction of the benefit into account so as to split the loss in such proportions as the court thinks just. But if such destruction necessarily led to the conclusion that no valuable benefit had been obtained before frustration, the court would have no discretion to award anything at all. It would be a pity if this useful discretion were restricted in a way that is neither clearly required by the words of the subsection nor necessary to promote justice.

It is submitted that the criticisms of Professor Burrows and Professor Treitel are compelling. Although the destruction of the end product is relevant to the assessment of the just sum under s 1(3), it should not be taken into account at the earlier stage of assessing the benefit received by the defendant. The view expressed by Goff J. that s 1(3)(a) is a statutory recognition of the change of position defence should also be rejected. This is clearly too narrow a view of the provision, given that s 1(3)(a) and (b) clearly allow the courts, within limits, to apportion the losses between the parties.

12.5.3 Criticisms of the Law Reform (Frustrated Contracts) Act 1943

The LR(FC)A 1943 has been criticised on a number of grounds. Professor McKendrick ('The consequences of frustration – the Law Reform (Frustrated Contracts) Act 1943' in *Force Majeure and Frustration of Contract* (2nd edn, London: Lloyd's of London Press, 1995), p 243) writes:

> It is now clear that the Law Reform (Frustrated Contracts) Act 1943 suffers from a number of deficiencies and that the Law Reform Commission of British Columbia was right to conclude that the Act 'was not well thought out or well drafted'.

Criticisms of the LR(FC)A 1943 generally proceed on two fronts. First, it is argued that the LR(FC) A 1943 Act leaves too much discretion to the trial judge. Professor McKendrick (above at p 238) writes:

> Lawton LJ [in *BP v Hunt*] concluded that '[w]hat is just is what the trial judge thinks is just' and he held that an appellate court is not entitled to interfere with the assessment of the just sum by the trial judge 'unless it is so plainly wrong that it cannot be just'. This leaves the issue virtually to the untrammelled discretion of the trial judge and it is regrettable that the Court of Appeal did not establish guidelines to assist trial judges in the exercise of their discretion and to ensure a measure of consistency in decided cases and out of court settlement.

McKendrick's criticisms are, perhaps, overstated. If the parties desire certainty, then this can be achieved by incorporating a *force majeure* clause into the contract. Indeed, this is what many commercial contractors choose to do. The rules on frustration often only come into play when something unforeseen has occurred. It is pointless suggesting that contractual planning can be made more efficient in this area by the adoption of fixed guidelines, given that frustration often involves events that the parties have not planned for. The problem is arguably not that the LR(FC)A 1943 confers too much discretion on the courts, but that it limits that discretion in arbitrary ways.

This leads us onto our second ground for criticising the Act, which is that it is hopelessly muddled. Graham Virgo (*The Principles of the Law of Restitution* (3rd edn, Oxford: OUP, 2015), pp 365–366) writes:

> Subsections 1(2) and 1(3) of the 1943 Act are somewhat schizophrenic provisions, embodying as they do both principles of restitution founded on the reversal of the defendant's unjust enrichment and the allocation of losses between the parties. But this attempt to allocate losses is half-hearted.

Professor Campbell (*Remedies in Contract and Tort* (2nd edn, Cambridge: CUP, 2002), p 248) agrees, arguing that the proviso under s 1(2) is a 'curious hybrid unknown to reliance or restitution' with 'no sound foundation in either principle'. Would it be better then to replace the LR(FC)A 1943 with a new scheme, which allows for the full apportionment of losses between the parties? Stewart and Carter think not.

Stewart, A, and Carter, JW, 'Frustrated contracts and statutory adjustment: the case for a reappraisal' (1992) *CLJ* 66, 109–110

[I]t is our view that the philosophy of loss apportionment should be rejected. We have already questioned the assumptions underlying the notion that post-frustration losses should be shared. For all the incursions of equity in Australia, the common law of contract in that country, as much as in Britain, is still marked by a refusal to view ordinary commercial transactions as joint ventures. Unconscionable conduct is increasingly attracting liability, but the point has not yet been reached where contractors are expected to take positive steps to conserve the welfare of their partners. And even if this admittedly harsh and individualist stance were to be rejected, the case for apportionment would still lack substance. If one looks past the slogans, it is hard to find convincing reasons, economic or otherwise, for compelling one party to act as the other's insurer.

Moreover, even if a favourable view were taken of the principle of loss apportionment, successfully putting it into practice appears to be another matter altogether. The three statutory models [in South Australia, New South Wales and British Columbia] amply demonstrate what we consider the impracticability of finding a workable formula which adequately separates out those losses to be attributed to the frustrated contract from those which are referable to the parties' general business activities, or which fairly and predictably identifies the losses of one which can reasonably be foisted on the other. Nor does there appear to be an acceptable way of respecting the strength or weakness of the original bargain. Only the British Columbian Act adopts a workable approach; but that is achieved by excluding all anticipatory or overhead expenses from the equation, a restrictive approach which becomes so arbitrary in its application as to make a mockery of the apportionment principle and which is as biased in its own way to recipients as the New South Wales and South Australian schemes are to performers.

Professor Burrows (*The Law of Restitution* (3rd edn, London: Butterworths, 2011), p 366) argues that loss splitting 'contradicts the basic individualistic tradition of contract law whereby contracting parties are viewed as pursuing their own self-interest and taking their own risk'. It will also lead to uncertainty, Professor Burrows contends, not least because it will require the courts to take into account the relative fault of the parties (see, generally, Mitchell, C, Mitchell, P and Waterson, S, *Goff and Jones: The Law of Unjust Enrichment* (9th edn, London: Sweet & Maxwell, 2016), Ch. 20).

Other commentators argue that we should adopt a scheme of full apportionment of losses.

McKendrick, E, 'Frustration, restitution and loss apportionment', in Burrows, A (ed), *Essays on the Law of Restitution*, 1991, Oxford: Clarendon Press, pp 168–169

[T]here are arguments in favour of apportioning the loss between the parties. The first is that apportionment of loss is 'economically sounder' because 'each of the two parties may be able to bear half the loss without serious consequences when the whole loss might come close to ruining him'. The second argument is that a failure to take explicit account of the reliance interest may lead to the adoption of an unnatural definition of benefit. Restitution lawyers have been warned about adopting an 'over-inclusive concept of enrichment' and of 'marginalising' the 'principle of injurious reliance'. The classic example of this process is, of course, the British Columbian Frustrated Contracts Act which ... defines a benefit as 'something done in the fulfilment of contractual obligations whether or not the person for whose benefit it was done received the benefit. To force losses incurred into the language of benefit distorts the concept of benefit and hinders the development of a principle of injurious reliance in English law.

The final argument is that the situation with which frustrated contracts legislation is concerned 'is the familiar one in which one of two parties has to suffer loss for which neither is responsible' and that in the 'normal case' the just course 'would be to order the retention or repayment of half the loss incurred'. The 'justice' involved in being required to share in the losses of the other party may not be readily apparent. But, while it may be true to say that contracting parties enter into contracts to serve their own interests, it should not be assumed that upholding the pursuit of self-interest is the basis of the doctrine of frustration .... It must ... be remembered that the frustrating event which has occurred is one which neither party has foreseen and neither party has assumed the risk of its occurrence. Moreover, neither party has been at fault. Justice and reasonableness surely demand that such expenditure be brought into account so that, on the frustration of a contract, the position is reached whereby both parties are discharged from their obligations to perform in the future (the expectation interest of neither party being protected), benefits conferred must be paid for (thus protecting the restitution interest), and losses suffered as a result of wasted expenditure be apportioned between the parties (thus taking account of the reliance interest).

On balance, it might be argued that a scheme that allows for the full apportionment of losses is preferable. The arguments levelled against such an approach largely ignore the fact that we are dealing with events that are unforeseen and not provided for by the contract. In such a context, arguments based on the need for certainty and the individualistic tradition of contract law seems to carry less weight.

Should we therefore expect to see a change in the law? The answer is probably no. In the 50 years since the Act was passed, there have been few decisions interpreting the Act. This suggests that its provisions do not present any real problems for the commercial community. Professor Campbell (*Remedies in Contract and Tort* (2nd edn, Cambridge: CUP, 2002), p 253) explains why:

> Competent commercial parties, faced with the absurdity of the law of ... frustration, have included modification provisions in contracts of sufficient value and complexity to make this worthwhile. These clauses provide for non-binding alternative dispute resolution or arbitration (including arbitration *ex aequo et bono*), which gives the parties far more flexibility to apportion loss than any conceivable restitutionary recasting of the frustration rules might do.

It therefore seems that reform is unlikely for the simple reason that the law of frustration is of little practical importance in the commercial world.

Additional reading

Devenney, J.P., and Quick, O., 'Frustrating Performance: Contracts and Clinical Competence in the New NHS' (2006) 8 *Medical Law International* 79.

Law Reform Committee of British Columbia, 'Report on the Need for Frustrated Contracts Legislation in British Columbia' (Project No 8).

Lookofsy, J., 'Impediments and Hardship in International Sales: A Commentary on Catherine Kessedjian's "Competing Approaches to Force Majeure and Hardship"' (2005) 25 *International Review of Law and Economics* 434.

MacMillan, C., 'English Contract Law and the Great War: The Development of a Doctrine of Frustration' (2014) 2 *CLH* 278.

Posner, R.A., and Rosenfield, A.M., 'Impossibility and Related Doctrines in Contract Law: An Economic Analysis' (1977) 6 *JLS* 83.

Schanze, E., 'Failure of Long-Term Contracts and the Duty to Re-negotiate', in Rose, F. (ed.), *Failure of Contracts* (Oxford: Hart Publishing, 1997).

Smith, J.C., 'Contracts: Mistake, Frustration and Implied Terms' (1994) 110 *LQR* 400.

Weiss, P.D., 'Apportioning Loss After Discharge of a Burdensome Contract: A Statutory Solution' (1960) 69 *YLJ* 1054.

Chapter 13

Illegality

Chapter contents

13.1 Introduction

An agreement which possesses all of the requisite elements of a binding contract may nevertheless be wholly or partly unenforceable due to the contravention of a legal rule or a principle of public policy (in this chapter, such unenforceable agreements will be described as 'illegal contracts' whether or not such agreements also result in criminal liability). These rules or policies may be derived from statute or from the common law. In some cases, the contract will be illegal in its formation, such as a contract to commit a crime. In others, questions of illegality will only arise in the performance of an otherwise valid contract. For example, in a contract for the carriage of goods, the vehicle that is used to transport the goods may be driven recklessly, but what effect, if any, does this have on the contract? In this chapter, we will examine the concept of illegality and public policy in Contract Law. We will consider the underlying basis of the doctrine of illegality, the categories of illegality and the effects of illegality on the enforcement of the relevant contract.

13.2 Policy arguments

The courts do not always explain the reasons why they intervene to render particular agreements unenforceable on the grounds of illegality and/or public policy and, as we shall see below, declaring some agreements unenforceable is not without controversy, particularly in the light of changing social norms. A good starting point is the oft-quoted speech of Lord Mansfield in *Holman v Johnson* (1775) 1 Cowp 341:

> No court will lend its aid to a man who founds his cause of action upon an immoral or illegal act. If from the plaintiff's own stating or otherwise, the cause of action appears to arise *ex turpi causa* (i.e. out of an evil cause), or the transgression of a positive law of this country, there the courts says he has no right to be assisted.

In general terms, the courts intervene because it would be contrary to public policy for a court to assist a party that is seeking to rely on 'illegality'. The court has an interest in protecting its own integrity, and for this reason, the judge himself can introduce the issue of illegality, even if it has not been pleaded by the parties (*North Western Salt v Electrolytic Alkali Co* [1914] AC 461). See also *Singularis Holdings Ltd (In Official Liquidation) (A Company Incorporated in the Cayman Islands) v Daiwa Capital Markets Europe Ltd* [2019] UKSC 50 at [21], where Lady Hale (with whom Lord Reed, Lord Lloyd-Jones, Lord Sales and Lord Thomas agreed) stated:

> I should, however, record my reservations about the view expressed by the Court of Appeal as to the role of an appellate court in relation to the illegality defence: that 'an appellate court should only interfere if the first instance judge has proceeded on an erroneous legal basis, taken into account matters that were legally irrelevant, or failed to take into account matters that were legally relevant' (para 65). Daiwa point out that applying the defence is 'not akin to the exercise of discretion' (citing Lord Neuberger in *Patel v Mirza*, at para 175) and an appellate court is as well placed to evaluate the arguments as is the trial judge. It is not necessary to resolve this in order to resolve this appeal and there are cases concerning the illegality defence pending in the Supreme Court where it should not be assumed that this Court will endorse the approach of the Court of Appeal.

A number of commentators have attempted to explore more fully the policies underlying this area of the law. We start with the fifth edition of Professor Atiyah's *An Introduction to the Law of Contract* (cf. the 6th edition, edited by Professor S. Smith, *Atiyah's Introduction to the Law of Contract*, 6th edn, 2006, OUP, Oxford, Chapter 8).

Atiyah, PS, *An Introduction to the Law of Contract*, 5th edn, 1995, Oxford: Clarendon Press, pp 342–344

The policy considerations involved here appear to include at least the following factors, though not all will be involved in every case. First, there is the desirability of deterring parties from criminal or anti-social conduct, and the associated (though different) object of punishing them if they commit such conduct. Normally it is the criminal law that performs these functions, but there may be forms of anti-social conduct which are not criminal, and yet which it may be desirable to deter (eg prostitution), and there may also be advantages in using contract law as an additional deterrent over and above that provided by the criminal law ...

A second policy consideration which is undoubtedly involved in some cases is the undesirability of jeopardizing the dignity of the courts. Respect for the law and Courts of Justice is an important aspect of judicial policy, and this respect could be gravely impaired if courts were required to adjudicate on certain types of illegal transaction ...

A third possible policy consideration may in some cases be the desirability of bringing an illegal or undesirable state of affairs to an end. If, for instance, a woman takes a lease of a flat and then uses it for prostitution, it may be desirable that the landlord should be able to evict her by legal process, in order to terminate this state of affairs.

It will be seen that some of these factors may well conflict in any given case. For example, if a landlord knowingly lets premises to a prostitute and then seeks to evict her for non-payment of rent, the first and third policy considerations would conflict ... But apart from conflicts of this nature in the relevant policy considerations, there is often likely to be conflict between the considerations suggesting that illegal contracts should not be enforced, and the general desirability of upholding contracts ... [T]here is an acute conflict between the desire to do justice between the individual parties and the more general considerations ... concerning the undesirability of enforcing illegal contracts. In this situation the traditional result has been to ignore the injustice which may be done in the individual case in the belief that this is outweighed by the public interest in refusing redress in such cases. But in recent years there has been a perceptible trend in the reverse direction ...

Enonchong, N, *Illegal Transactions*, 1998, London: LLP, pp 15–17

The overall object of the defence of illegality and the forfeiture rule is the protection of the public through deterrence from crime and other illegal conduct. Thus in *Amicable Insurance Society v Bolland assignees* of a forger failed to recover the proceeds of a life insurance policy on the death of the forger at the hands of justice by reason of his forgery. The Lord Chancellor said that if such a contract were enforceable it would 'take away one of those restraints operating on the minds of men against the commission of crimes' ... If indeed the policy behind the principle is deterrence then it may be argued that for the deterrent effect to have force there must be a clear rule which is applied strictly by the courts and is known, at least by lawyers who advise members of the public.

Some have expressed doubts about the deterrent effect of the illegality defence and the forfeiture rule. In *Tinsley v Milligan*, for example, Lord Lowry made it clear that he was 'not impressed' by the argument that a defence of illegality which precludes a transferor from recovering property transferred for an illegal purpose acts as a deterrent to persons in the transferor's position. One reason advanced for this view is that such persons may not be aware of the rule and are unlikely to consult a reputable solicitor. Other judges have advanced essentially the same argument. But the argument is surprising. And it is the more startling when it is put forward in a case, such as *Tribe v Tribe*, where the parties' scheme to break the law had been carefully contrived after obtaining professional advice from accountants and lawyers ...

> In any event, if deterrence is not the policy objective of the broad principles there is another policy on which they have been put. This has been identified as a policy which seeks to protect the integrity of the judicial system from the disrepute which would attach to it if the courts were seen to be encouraging conduct which they ought to denounce ... [I]t has been argued [that] it would reflect adversely on the judicial system if the public were to perceive a fundamental inconsistency in the law, as would be the case if a civil remedy were provided to a plaintiff on the basis of his conduct which is criminal.

Professor Atiyah and Professor Enonchong note two main reasons for refusing to enforce illegal contracts:

1 Deterrence of wrongdoing.
2 Protection of the integrity of the civil justice system.

The illegality doctrine in Contract Law was explored recently, in detail, by the Supreme Court in *Patel v Mirza* [2016] UKSC 42. The case was heard by nine Justices and Lord Toulson (with whom Lady Hale, Lord Kerr, Lord Wilson and Lord Hodge agreed) stated:

> **22.** From its study of the case law and academic writing, the Commission identified the principal policy rationales for the illegality doctrine as 1) furthering the purpose of the rule infringed by the claimant's behaviour, 2) consistency, 3) prevention of profit from the claimant's wrongdoing, 4) deterrence and 5) maintaining the integrity of the legal system. It observed that these rationales were not mutually exclusive but overlapped to a greater or lesser degree. A sixth possible rationale, punishment, was controversial. The large majority of consultees considered that punishment was a matter for the criminal courts (to which one might add regulators) and should not be invoked in determining parties' civil disputes. (LCCP 189, paras 2.5–2.31.)
>
> **23.** The conclusion that the illegality defence presented serious problems represented the overwhelming view of academic commentators and consultees generally. The Commission analysed the problems under four heads – complexity, uncertainty, arbitrariness and lack of transparency. It did not suggest that the problems resulted generally in unsatisfactory outcomes, but it was critical of the way in which they were reached. It said that, on the whole, the case law illustrated the judges threading a path through the various rules and exceptions in order to reach outcomes which for the most part would be regarded as fair between the parties involved, although there were instances of results which the Commission considered to be unduly harsh, for example in unlawful employment cases. Generally, the courts managed to avoid unnecessarily harsh decisions either by creating exceptions to the general rules or by straining the application of the relevant rules on the particular facts so as to meet the justice of the case. Seldom was there an open discussion in the judgments of the considerations which led the court to its decision. (LCCP 189, paras 3.50–3.60.) ...
>
> **120.** The essential rationale of the illegality doctrine is that it would be contrary to the public interest to enforce a claim if to do so would be harmful to the integrity of the legal system (or, possibly, certain aspects of public morality, the boundaries of which have never been made entirely clear and which do not arise for consideration in this case). In assessing whether the public interest would be harmed in that way, it is necessary a) to consider the underlying purpose of the prohibition which has been transgressed and whether that purpose will be enhanced by denial of the claim, b) to consider any other relevant public policy on which the denial of the claim may have an impact and c) to consider whether denial of the claim would be a proportionate response to the illegality, bearing in mind that punishment is a matter for the

criminal courts. Within that framework, various factors may be relevant, but it would be a mistake to suggest that the court is free to decide a case in an undisciplined way. The public interest is best served by a principled and transparent assessment of the considerations identified, rather by than the application of a formal approach capable of producing results which may appear arbitrary, unjust or disproportionate.

121. A claimant, such as Mr Patel, who satisfies the ordinary requirements of a claim for unjust enrichment, should not be debarred from enforcing his claim by reason only of the fact that the money which he seeks to recover was paid for an unlawful purpose. There may be rare cases where for some particular reason the enforcement of such a claim might be regarded as undermining the integrity of the justice system, but there are no such circumstances in this case. I would dismiss the appeal.

As Lord Toulson hints at [121], at times, the policy against enforcing illegal contracts has come into conflict with the desirability of preventing the defendant from being unjustly enriched at the claimant's expense. If restitution of benefits conferred under an illegal contract is not allowed, the defendant may be left with a substantial and undeserved windfall. The problems associated with a strict application of the policy against illegal contracts were recognised by Bingham LJ in *Saunders v Edwards* [1987] 2 All ER 651:

> Where issues of illegality are raised, the courts have to steer a middle course between two unacceptable positions. On the one hand it is unacceptable that any court of law should aid or lend its authority to a party seeking to pursue or enforce an object or agreement which the law prohibits. On the other hand, it is unacceptable that the court should, on the first indication of unlawfulness affecting any aspect of a transaction, draw up its skirts and refuse all assistance to the plaintiff, no matter how serious his loss or how disproportionate his loss to the unlawfulness of his conduct.

The balance to be struck between these two competing policies will be considered in greater detail when we examine the effect of illegality later in this chapter. However, at this stage, it is important to consider how the courts approach questions of illegality in Contract Law. In recent times, the illegality doctrine in Contract Law has been considered on a number of occasions by the Supreme Court, including: *Allen v Hounga* [2014] UKSC 47; *Les Laboratoires Servier v Apotex Inc* [2014] UKSC 55; *Bilta (UK) Ltd (In Liquidation) v Nazir* [2015] UKSC 23; and *Patel v Mirza* [2016] UKSC 42. After *Allen v Hounga* [2014] UKSC 47 and *Les Laboratoires Servier v Apotex Inc* [2014] UKSC 55, Buckley noted some differences of approach within the Supreme Court:

Buckley, RA, 'Illegality in the Supreme Court' (2015) 131 *LQR* 341, 341–343

The concept of illegality, when deployed to resist the enforcement of a civil obligation, has an extraordinary propensity to cause confusion and to generate judicial opinions of striking diversity. If any doubts still exist as to the validity of this proposition they will surely now be dispelled by the Supreme Court. Two differently constituted divisions of that court have recently handed down, within four months of each other, leading judgments which embody radically different (and potentially conflicting) approaches to the subject ...

In *Hounga v Allen* Lord Wilson referred to the much criticised decision of the House of Lords in *Tinsley v Milligan* [1994] 1 A.C. 340; [1993] 3 All E.R. 65, with its emphatic rejection of 'affronting the public conscience' as the criterion for applying the illegality defence. It will be recalled that in that case, which involved criminal deception as to the ownership of a house in order to claim welfare benefits, the majority avoided the operation of the illegality doctrine by holding that the claimant did not need to 'rely' on

> the deception in order to obtain her contribution to the purchase-money when the house was eventually sold. Lord Wilson went on to observe (following Lord Phillips in *Stone & Rolls Ltd v Moore Stephens* [2009] UKHL 39; [2009] A.C. 1391 at [25]) that it was necessary to 'soften' the 'reliance test', favoured by the majority in Tinsley, by considering the 'underlying policy'. Lord Wilson then considered the various attempts which have been made in illegality cases to conceptualise the relationship between the wrongdoing and the claim, using the language of 'inextricable link' (see, e.g. *Cross v Kirby, The Times*, April 5, 2000; [2000] CA Transcript No. 321) or 'causation' (see per Lord Hoffmann in *Gray v Thames Trains Ltd* [2009] UKHL 33; [2009] A.C. 1339 at [54]). *While apparently* expressing a tentative preference for the former over the latter, and expressing his own view that the 'inextricable link' requirement was not satisfied in *Hounga v Allen* itself, Lord Wilson nevertheless frankly conceded that both approaches involved an ineradicable degree of subjectivity in their application (see at [40]). Returning to the underlying policy issues in the case Lord Wilson said (referring to the well-known judgment of McLachlin J in the Canadian case of *Hall v Herbert* [1993] 2 S.C.R. 159; [1993] 101 D.L.R. [4th] 129) that 'concern to preserve the integrity of the legal system is a helpful rationale of the aspect of policy which founds the defence' (at [43]). His Lordship then considered various possible policy factors in the case itself including profit from wrongdoing, evasion of the criminal law, and encouraging entry into unlawful employment contracts. In view of the nature of the claim, which was for compensation under a statutory tort as distinct from contractual enforcement of the employment contract itself, all these factors could confidently be discounted and the case resolved in the claimant's favour …
>
> The pragmatism reflected in the judgments in *Hounga v Allen* is in sharp contrast with the approach adopted by Lord Sumption when delivering the leading judgment in *Les Laboratoires Servier v Apotex*. Illegality cases were to be resolved by the application of rules of law; any approach which required consideration of policy issues would render the law too unpredictable (see [2015] 1 A.C. 430 at [9] et seq.). The 'law' had been authoritatively laid down by the House of Lords in *Tinsley v Milligan* and it was the duty of lower courts to follow it even if its application might appear harsh in the particular circumstances, otherwise the law would dissolve into uncertainty. With respect, this argument is unconvincing. The 'reliance' test favoured by the majority in *Tinsley v Milligan* is itself far from 'certain' in its application, and potentially arbitrary in its operation (if the purchasers of the house in that case had been married the presumption of advancement could have led to the case being decided the other way for reasons wholly unrelated to the underlying issue of illegality). Legal certainty requires rather more than ex cathedra assertions of authority at the expense of the merits. In addition to the operation of precedent it requires intellectual coherence and some degree of consistency with intuitive notions of justice. Anything less invites judicial evasion of apparently inflexible 'rules' by the invocation of technicalities unrelated to the issues of substance. The illegality defence is particularly prone to this phenomenon, as *Tinsley v Milligan* itself illustrates. It is with this in mind that the Law Commission has recently urged the courts to undertake more explicit analyses of the relevant policy factors in illegality cases (see The Illegality Defence (HMSO, 2010), Law Com. No.320), a welcome approach apparently seen in action by the Supreme Court itself in *Hounga v Allen*.

These differences in approach were acknowledged by the Supreme Court in *Patel v Mirza* [2016] UKSC 42 with, for example, Lord Toulson (at [81]) stating:

> After *Les Laboratoires Servier v Apotex Inc* came *Bilta (UK) Ltd v Nazir (No 2)* [2016] AC 1. There was a sharp division of opinion about the proper approach to the defence illegality between, on the one hand, a strictly rule-based approach and, on the other hand, a more flexible approach by which the court would look at the policies underlying the doctrine and decide whether they militated in favour of the defence, taking into account a range of potentially relevant factors. The majority did not consider it necessary to resolve the difference in that case, since it did not affect the result, but Lord Neuberger said at para 15 that it needed to be addressed as soon as appropriately possible.

Similarly, Lord Sumption (at [226]) stated:

> The present appeal exposes, not for the first time, a long-standing schism between those judges and writers who regard the law of illegality as calling for the application of clear rules, and those who would wish address the equities of each case as it arises. There are recent statements of this court in support of both points of view: see *Les Laboratoires Servier v Apotex Inc* [2015] AC 340 and *Hounga v Allen* [2014] 1 WLR 2889, paras 44–45. It also raises one of the most basic problems of a system of judge-made customary law such as the common law. The common law is not an uninhabited island on which judges are at liberty to plant whatever suits their personal tastes. It is a body of instincts and principles which, barring some radical change in the values of our society, is developed organically, building on what was there before. It has a greater inherent flexibility and capacity to develop independently of legislation than codified systems do. But there is a price to be paid for this advantage in terms of certainty and accessibility to those who are not professional lawyers. The equities of a particular case are important. But there are pragmatic limits to what law can achieve without becoming arbitrary, incoherent and unpredictable even to the best advised citizen, and without inviting unforeseen and undesirable collateral consequences.

As is apparent in the extract from Lord Toulson's judgment on p 574, the majority of the Supreme Court adopted the wider, underlying policy approach, with Lord Toulson stating:

82. In his *Restatement of the English Law of Contract* (Oxford University Press, 2016), pp 221–222, Professor Andrew Burrows explained the difficulty of attempting to state the law in relation to illegality:

> 'Leaving aside the law on what one can loosely label 'statutory illegality' [cases where a statute makes a contract or a contract term unenforceable by either or one party] the law on the effect of illegality in contract (which one may loosely refer to as 'the common law of illegality') is in a state of flux ...
>
> Traditionally, two Latin maxims have often been referred to without greatly illuminating the legal position: *ex turpi causa non oritur actio* ('no action arises from a disgraceful cause') and *in pari delicto potior est conditio defendentis* ('where both parties are equally in the wrong the position of the defendant is the stronger'). As previously understood, illegality in the law of contract – as developed from those Latin maxims – was governed by a series of rules which tended to distinguish, for example, between illegality in formation and illegality in performance. Unfortunately, commentators and courts have found it very difficult to state those rules with confidence and precision. Hence the textbook treatments not only differ from each other but are characterised by long-winded attempts to explain the law. Sharp propositions when offered by the courts or the books have to be qualified by reference to cases or hypothetical examples that do not fit those rules; and convincing justifications of those rules have proved elusive. More recently, therefore, and in line with a similar trend in respect of illegality as a defence in tort, some courts have favoured greater flexibility culminating in a 'range of factors' approach aimed at achieving a proportionate response to contractual illegality in preference to the traditional rule-based approach'.

83. Since the law was at a crossroads, Professor Burrows set out alternative possible formulations of a 'rule-based approach' and a 'range of factors approach'.

84. One possible version of a rule-based approach, at p 224, which *Tinsley v Milligan* and *Les Laboratoires Servier v Apotex Inc* could be interpreted as supporting, would be a single master rule based on reliance:

'If the formation, purpose or performance of a contract involves conduct that is illegal (such as a crime) or contrary to public policy (such as a restraint of trade), a party cannot enforce the contract if it has to rely on that conduct to establish its claim'.

85. An alternative rule-based formulation, at p 225, saw the reliance rule as only one of a number of rules and essentially confined to the creation of property rights. On this approach a formulation of the rules might be:

'Rule 1. A contract which has as its purpose, or is intended to be performed in a manner that involves, conduct that is illegal (such as a crime) or contrary to public policy (such as a restraint of trade) is unenforceable (a) by either party if both parties knew of that purpose or intention; or (b) by one party if only that party knew of that purpose or intention.

Rule 2. If rule 1 is inapplicable because it is only the performance of a contract that involves conduct that is illegal or contrary to public policy, the contract is unenforceable by the party who performed in that objectionable way but is enforceable by the other party unless that party knew of, and participated in, that objectionable performance.

Rule 3. Proprietary rights created by a contract that involves conduct that is illegal or contrary to public policy will not be recognised unless the claimant can establish the proprietary rights without reliance on that conduct'.

86. Professor Burrows identified six criticisms of those rules and, more generally, of a 'rule-based' approach to illegality.

87. First, the difficulty with the *Tinsley v Milligan* reliance rule, whether as a master rule or as a rule restricted to cases involving the assertion of proprietary rights, was that it could produce different results according to procedural technicality which had nothing to do with the underlying policies. The decision of the Court of Appeal in *Collier v Collier* [2002] EWCA 1095; [2002] BPIR 1057 provides a good illustration. A father granted a lease of property to his daughter to hold on trust for him in order to deceive creditors. His claim to beneficial title was rejected on the ground of illegality, because it was held that he needed to rely on the illegal purpose in order to rebut the presumption of illegality which arose in favour of the daughter. Mance LJ considered at paras 105–106 what appeared to be the distinction introduced by *Tinsley v Milligan* between a beneficial interest which could be established by 'some objectively provable and apparently neutral fact' and a beneficial interest arising only from an agreement made for an unlawful purpose. He described the effect as 'little more than cosmetic' where the court was perfectly well aware of the close involvement of both parties in the illegality. Tempted as he was to adopt a severely limited view of the meaning of reliance (encouraged by the judgment of Dawson J in *Nelson v Nelson*), he rightly did not consider that it was open to the Court of Appeal on the authorities to do so. He expressed strong sympathy with the criticisms of the law expressed by the Law Commission, and he concluded at para 113 that he had no liking for the result which the court was compelled to reach.

88. Second, the difficulties with rule 1 were illustrated by the *ParkingEye* case. The illegality in that case went to the contract as formed, because from the outset it was intended to send out to customers a form of letter of demand which contained some deliberate inaccuracies. The rule as stated did not permit differentiation between minor and serious illegality or between peripheral and central illegality. To have deprived ParkingEye of what would otherwise have been a contractual entitlement to damages of £350,000 would have been disproportionate. Moreover, as Sir Robin Jacob pointed out in that case, at paras 33–34, there was something odd about a rule which differentiated according to whether the intention was formed before or after the contract was made.

89. Third, as with the criticism of rule 1, the reference in rule 2 to performance that involved illegal conduct drew no distinction between serious criminality and relatively minor breach of a statutory regulation.

90. Fourth, although a purported advantage of firm rules is greater certainty, the cases do not always fit the rules because courts have often sought ways around them when they do not like the consequence. The flexible approach would not only produce more acceptable results, but would in practice be no less certain than the rule-based approach.

91. Fifth, although Lord Mansfield made it clear in *Holman v Johnson* that the illegality defence operates as a rule of public policy and is not designed to achieve justice between the parties, that does not mean that any result, however arbitrary, is acceptable. The law should strive for the most desirable policy outcome, and it may be that it is best achieved by taking into account a range of factors.

92. Sixth, although it may be argued that if there are deficiencies in the traditional rules, the way forward is to refine the rules to remove the deficiencies by appropriate exceptions, that task is one which has never been satisfactorily accomplished. The reason is that there are so many variables, for example, in seriousness of the illegality, the knowledge and intentions of the parties, the centrality of the illegality, the effect of denying the defence and the sanctions which the law already imposes. To reach the best result in terms of policy, the judges need to have the flexibility to consider and weigh a range of factors in the light of the facts of the particular case before them.

93. If a 'range of factors' approach were preferred, Professor Burrows suggested, at pp 229–230, that a possible formulation would read as follows:

> 'If the formation, purpose or performance of a contract involves conduct that is illegal (such as a crime) or contrary to public policy (such as a restraint of trade), the contract is unenforceable by one or either party if to deny enforcement would be an appropriate response to that conduct, taking into account where relevant –
>
> (a) how seriously illegal or contrary to public policy the conduct was;
> (b) whether the party seeking enforcement knew of, or intended, the conduct;
> (c) how central to the contract or its performance the conduct was;
> (d) how serious a sanction the denial of enforcement is for the party seeking enforcement;
> (e) whether denying enforcement will further the purpose of the rule which the conduct has infringed;
> (f) whether denying enforcement will act as a deterrent to conduct that is illegal or contrary to public policy;
> (g) whether denying enforcement will ensure that the party seeking enforcement does not profit from the conduct;
> (h) whether denying enforcement will avoid inconsistency in the law thereby maintaining the integrity of the legal system'.

Professor Burrows noted that the final factor is capable of a wider or narrower approach, depending on what one understands by inconsistency.

94. The reference to what is an 'appropriate response' brings to the surface the moral dimension underlying the doctrine of illegality, which inevitably influences the minds of judges and peeps out in their judgments from time to time. *Tinsley v Milligan* caused disquiet to Lord Goff and others precisely because its reasoning jarred with their sense of what was just and appropriate.

The way forward

95. In *Yarmouth v France* (1887) 19 QBD 647, 653, Lord Esher MR said:

> 'I detest the attempt to fetter the law by maxims. They are almost invariably misleading: they are for the most part so large and general in their language that they always include something which really is not intended to be included in them'.

In *Lissenden v CA v Bosch Ltd* [1940] AC 412,435, Lord Wright quoted Lord Esher's words and added:

> 'Indeed these general formulae are found in experience often to distract the court's mind from the actual exigencies of the case, and to induce the court to quote them as offering a ready made solution'.

96. The maxims *ex turpi causa* and *in pari delicto* are no exception. It is interesting that, according to Professor JK Grodecki, Lord Mansfield himself was 'conscious that if the brocard *in pari delicto* was to be a beneficial rule of jurisprudence it should not be allowed to become rigid and inflexible': *In pari delicto potior est conditio defendentis* (1955) 71 LQR 254, 258. Professor Grodecki gave examples including *Smith v Bromley* (1760) 2 Doug KB 696n; 99 ER 441 and *Walker v Chapman* (1773) Lofft 342, 98 ER 684.

97. In *Smith v Bromley* (the earliest case in which the maxim in pari delicto appears to have been used) Lord Mansfield granted recovery to the plaintiff of money paid by the plaintiff to procure her brother's discharge from bankruptcy, which was an illegal consideration. As he explained, Lord Mansfield, at p 698, regarded it as in the public interest that the plaintiff should be repaid notwithstanding the illegal purpose of the payment:

> 'Upon the whole, I am persuaded it is necessary, for the better support and maintenance of the law, to allow this action; for no man will venture to take, if he knows he is liable to refund'.

98. In *Walker v Chapman* the defendant, who was a page to the King, offered to take a bribe of £50 from the plaintiff in return for securing him a place in the Customs. The bribe was paid but the plaintiff did not obtain the appointment and so he sued for the return of his money. It was argued for the defendant that no action would lie, the plaintiff being party to an iniquitous contract, and that the law would not suffer a party to 'draw justice from a foul fountain'. Lord Mansfield rejected the defence, distinguishing between a claim to overturn an illegal contract and a claim to obtain benefit from it. Later judges have taken a different and stricter approach.

99. Looking behind the maxims, there are two broad discernible policy reasons for the common law doctrine of illegality as a defence to a civil claim. One is that a person should not be allowed to profit from his own wrongdoing. The other, linked, consideration is that the law should be coherent and not self-defeating, condoning illegality by giving with the left hand what it takes with the right hand.

100. Lord Goff observed in the *Spycatcher* case, *Attorney General v Guardian Newspapers Ltd (No 2)* [1990] 1 AC 109, 286, that the 'statement that a man shall not be allowed to profit from his own wrong is in very general terms, and does not of itself provide any sure guidance to the solution of a problem in any particular case. In *Hall v Hebert* [1993] 2 SCR 159 McLachlin J favoured giving a narrow meaning to profit but, more fundamentally, she expressed the view (at 175–176) that, as a rationale, the statement that a plaintiff will not be allowed to profit from his or her own wrongdoing does not fully explain why particular claims have been rejected, and that it may have the undesirable effect of tempting judges to focus on whether the plaintiff is 'getting something' out of the wrongdoing, rather than on the question whether allowing recovery for something which was illegal would produce inconsistency and disharmony in the law, and so cause damage to the integrity of the legal system.

101. That is a valuable insight, with which I agree. I agree also with Professor Burrows' observation that this expression leaves open what is meant by inconsistency (or disharmony) in a particular case, but I do not see this as a weakness. It is not a matter which can be determined mechanistically. So how is the court to determine the matter if not by some mechanistic process? In answer to that question I would say that one cannot judge whether allowing a claim which is in some way tainted by illegality would be contrary to the public interest, because it would be harmful to the integrity of the legal system, without a) considering the underlying purpose of the prohibition which has been transgressed, b) considering conversely any other relevant public policies which may be rendered ineffective or less effective by denial of the claim, and c) keeping in mind the possibility of overkill unless the law is applied with a due sense of proportionality. We are, after all, in the area of public policy. That trio of necessary considerations can be found in the case law.

102. The relevance of taking into account the purpose of the relevant prohibition is self-evident. The importance of taking account of the relevant statutory context is illustrated by *Hardy v Motor Insurers' Bureau* [1964] 2 QB 745. The Road Traffic Act 1960 required a motorist to be insured against the risk of causing death or personal injury through the use of a vehicle on a road, but a line of authorities established that a contract to indemnify a person against the consequences of a deliberate criminal act is unenforceable. The plaintiff, a security officer at a factory, was injured when he was trying to question the driver of a van, who drove off at speed and dragged him along the road. The driver was convicted of unlawfully causing grievous bodily harm. The driver being uninsured, the plaintiff sued the defendant under an agreement between the defendant and the Minister of Transport, by which the defendant agreed to satisfy any judgment against a motorist for a liability required to be covered under a motor insurance policy. The defendant relied on the maxim *ex turpi causa*, arguing that a contract purporting to insure the driver against his own deliberate criminal conduct would have been unlawful. The defence was rejected. Diplock LJ said at p 767:

> 'The rule of law on which the major premise is based – *ex turpi causa non oritur actio* – is concerned not specifically with the lawfulness of contracts but generally with the enforcement of rights by the courts, whether or not such rights arise under contract. All that the rule means is that the courts will not enforce a right which would otherwise be enforceable if the right arises out of an act committed by the person asserting the right (or by someone who is regarded in law as his successor) which is regarded by the court as sufficiently anti-social to justify the court's refusing to enforce that right'.

He observed that the purpose of the relevant statutory provision was the protection of persons who suffered injury on the road by the wrongful acts of motorists. This purpose would have been defeated if the common law doctrine of illegality had been applied so as to bar the plaintiff's claim.

103. *Hounga v Allen* and *R (Best) v Chief Land Registrar* are illustrations of cases in which there were countervailing public interest considerations, which needed to be balanced.

104. As to the dangers of overkill, Lord Wright gave a salutary warning in *Vita Food Products Inc v Unus Shipping Co Ltd* [1939] AC 277, 293:

> 'Nor must it be forgotten that the rule by which contracts not expressly forbidden by statute or declared to be void are in proper cases nullified for disobedience to a statute is a rule of public policy only, and public policy understood in a wider sense may at times be better served by refusing to nullify a bargain save on serious and sufficient grounds'.

105. To similar effect Devlin J questioned 'whether public policy is well served by driving from the seat of judgment everyone who has been guilty of a minor transgression' in *St John Shipping Corpn v Joseph Rank Ltd* [1957] 1 QB 267, 288–289.

106. In *Saunders v Edwards* [1987] 1 WLR 1116, 1134, Bingham LJ said:

> 'Where issues of illegality are raised, the courts have (as it seems to me) to steer a middle course between two unacceptable positions. On the one hand it is unacceptable that any court of law should aid or lend its authority to a party seeking to pursue or enforce an object or agreement which the law prohibits. On the other hand, it is unacceptable that the court should, on the first

indication of unlawfulness affecting any aspect of a transaction, draw up its skirts and refuse all assistance to the plaintiff, no matter how serious his loss nor how disproportionate his loss to the unlawfulness of his conduct'.

107. In considering whether it would be disproportionate to refuse relief to which the claimant would otherwise be entitled, as a matter of public policy, various factors may be relevant. Professor Burrows' list is helpful but I would not attempt to lay down a prescriptive or definitive list because of the infinite possible variety of cases. Potentially relevant factors include the seriousness of the conduct, its centrality to the contract, whether it was intentional and whether there was marked disparity in the parties' respective culpability.

108. The integrity and harmony of the law permit – and I would say require – such flexibility. Part of the harmony of the law is its division of responsibility between the criminal and civil courts and tribunals. Punishment for wrongdoing is the responsibility of the criminal courts and, in some instances, statutory regulators. It should also be noted that under the Proceeds of Crime Act 2002 the state has wide powers to confiscate proceeds of crime, whether on a conviction or without a conviction. Punishment is not generally the function of the civil courts, which are concerned with determining private rights and obligations. The broad principle is not in doubt that the public interest requires that the civil courts should not undermine the effectiveness of the criminal law; but nor should they impose what would amount in substance to an additional penalty disproportionate to the nature and seriousness of any wrongdoing. *ParkingEye* is a good example of a case where denial of claim would have been disproportionate. The claimant did not set out to break the law. If it had realised that the letters which it was proposing to send were legally objectionable, the text would have been changed. The illegality did not affect the main performance of the contract. Denial of the claim would have given the defendant a very substantial unjust reward. Respect for the integrity of the justice system is not enhanced if it appears to produce results which are arbitrary, unjust or disproportionate.

109. The courts must obviously abide by the terms of any statute, but I conclude that it is right for a court which is considering the application of the common law doctrine of illegality to have regard to the policy factors involved and to the nature and circumstances of the illegal conduct in determining whether the public interest in preserving the integrity of the justice system should result in denial of the relief claimed. I put it in that way rather than whether the contract should be regarded as tainted by illegality, because the question is whether the relief claimed should be granted.

Some might argue that Lord Toulson's approach introduces more uncertainty into this area of law (cf. Lord Sumption at [263]). On the other hand, it might be argued that, overall, it more accurately represents the approach taken by the courts (cf. also *Ritz Hotel Casino Ltd v Daher* [2014] EWHC 2847 (QB)). See also *Iranian Offshore Engineering and Construction Company v Dean Investment Holdings SA (formerly known as Dean International Trading S.A.)* [2019] EWHC 472 (Comm) and *Okedina v Chilake* [2019] IRLR 905 at [62], where Underhill LJ stated:

> In his judgment in *Patel v Mirza* Lord Toulson was attempting to identity the broad principles underlying the illegality rule. His judgment does not require a reconsideration of how the rule has been applied in the previous case-law except where such an application is inconsistent with those principles. In the case of a contract of employment which has been illegally performed, there is nothing in *Patel v Mirza* inconsistent with the well-established approach in Hall as regards 'third category' cases. As Mr Reade puts it, Hall is how *Patel v Mirza* plays out in that particular type of case. Accordingly, the ET was quite right to treat its findings about the claimant's 'knowledge plus participation' as conclusive and the EAT was right to endorse that approach.

Note also *Vald. Nielsen Holding A/S, Newwatch Limited v Baldorino* [2019] EWHC 1926 (Comm) at [715], where Jacobs J stated:

> I was not persuaded that the proportionality exercise contemplated by the Supreme Court in *Patel v Mirza* contemplated an examination of a party's behaviour within the context of the litigation.

On some of the limits to *Patel v Mirza*, see *Rashid v Nasrullah* [2018] EWCA Civ 2685 and *RBRG Trading (UK) Ltd v Sinocore International Co Ltd* [2018] EWCA Civ 838.

13.3 Categories of illegality

Categorising illegal contracts (in the wider sense mentioned above) is a notoriously difficult task, and there is no perfect classification. For the sake of simplicity, we will consider illegal contracts under two main headings: statutory illegality and common-law illegality. Our focus in this section is on the circumstances where a contract may be held to be illegal, rather than on the consequences of that illegality (which will be dealt with in 13.4), although there is inevitably some overlap.

13.3.1 Statutory illegality

Statute may render a contract 'illegal' either in its formation or in its performance. The contract may be declared void, unenforceable or illegal. On the question of statutory interpretation see *Okedina v Chilake* [2019] IRLR 905, where Underhill LJ stated:

> 12. The essential starting-point is to recognise that there are two distinct bases on which a claim under, or arising out of, a contract may be defeated on the ground of illegality. These are nowadays generally referred to as 'statutory' and 'common law' illegality. Put very briefly:
>
> (1) Statutory illegality applies where a legislative provision either (a) prohibits the making of a contract so that it is unenforceable by either party or (b) provides that it, or some particular term, is unenforceable by one or other party. The underlying principle is straightforward: if the legislation itself has provided that the contract is unenforceable, in full or in the relevant respect, the court is bound to respect that provision. That being the rationale, the knowledge or culpability of the party who is prevented from recovering is irrelevant: it is a simple matter of obeying the statute.
>
> (2) Common law illegality arises where the formation, purpose or performance of the contract involves conduct that is illegal or contrary to public policy and where to deny enforcement to one or other party is an appropriate response to that conduct. The nature of the rule has long been controversial, but the controversy has been resolved by the decision of the Supreme Court in *Patel v Mirza* [2016] UKSC 42, [2017] AC 467. The majority of the Court adopted an approach based on an assessment of what the public interest requires in a particular case, having regard to a range of factors. At para. 101 of his judgment Lord Toulson, with whom the majority agreed, said:
>
> > 'One cannot judge whether allowing a claim which is in some way tainted by illegality would be contrary to the public interest, because it would be harmful to the integrity of the legal system, without (a) considering the underlying purpose of the prohibition which has been transgressed, (b) considering conversely any other relevant public policies which may be rendered ineffective or less effective by denial of

the claim, and (c) keeping in mind the possibility of overkill unless the law is applied with a due sense of proportionality'.

Patel v Mirza is not directly concerned with statutory illegality, though there are references to it in Lord Toulson's judgment – particularly at para. 40 and the beginning of para. 109 (pp. 484–5 and 501 G–H).

The formulations in the first sentences of (1) and (2) above are gratefully adopted (with slight editing) from section 44 of Professor *Burrows' Restatement of the English Law of Contract*.

13. Traditionally employment lawyers have tended to refer to the judgment of Peter Gibson LJ in *Hall v Woolston Hall Leisure Ltd* [2001] ICR 99 as the authoritative statement of the distinction between the two kinds of illegality (see paras. 30–31 (p. 108 E-H)), with statutory illegality being referred to as the second category of illegality and common law illegality as the third 1. Peter Gibson LJ identifies the touchstone for the availability of a defence in 'third category' cases as being that the employee has knowingly participated in the illegal performance of the contract – so-called 'knowledge plus participation' (para. 31, quoting Scarman LJ in *Ashmore, Benson, Pease & Co Ltd v. A V Dawson Ltd* [1973] 1 WLR 828).

...

44. The starting-point must be the fact that we are not here concerned with a statutory provision, like that in *Mahmoud and Ispahani*, which says in terms that neither party may do the thing which is the subject-matter of the contract – in that case, buy/sell; in this case, employ/be employed. Neither section 15 nor section 21 of the 1996 Act says that no person shall be a party to a contract of employment where the employee does not have the appropriate immigration status, or that such a contract should be unenforceable by either party. They fall short of saying so in two respects. First, they do no more than provide for a penalty in the event of such employment. Second, they impose the penalty only on the employer. The authorities cited above make it clear that in such a case the legislature is not necessarily to be taken to have intended to prohibit the contract in the sense with which we are concerned: see in particular the passage from the judgment of Kerr LJ in *Phoenix* quoted at para. 22.
45. Although that starting-point is accepted by Ms Prince, its importance must not be overlooked. It is a healthy principle that Courts should be slow to give a statute an effect that is not expressly stated. Parliament should say what it means.
46. The question thus is whether an intention can be implied into section 15 and/or 21 that a contract of employment where the employee does not have the appropriate immigration status should be unenforceable by either party. In answering that question it is necessary, as Kerr LJ puts it under head (ii) in the passage cited from *Phoenix*, to have regard to 'considerations of public policy in the light of the mischief which the statute is designed to prevent, its language, scope and purpose, the consequences for the innocent party, and any other relevant considerations'. The test is of course one of necessity.

13.3.1.1 Contracts illegal in their formation

Until recently, s 18 of the Gaming Act 1845 provided the following:

All contracts or agreements, whether by parole or in writing, by way of gaming or wagering, shall be null and void; and no suit shall be brought or maintained in any court of law and equity for recovering any sum of money or valuable thing alleged to be won upon any wager, or which shall have been deposited in the hands of any person to abide the event on which any wager shall have been made: Provided always, that this enactment shall not be deemed to apply to any subscription or contribution, or agreement to subscribe or contribute, for or towards any plate, prize, or sum of money to be awarded to the winner or winners of any lawful game, sport, pastime, or exercise.

The Act made gaming and wagering contracts void and unenforceable. It did not make them illegal. This meant that people were still free to enter into gambling agreements, they simply could not enforce them in the courts. However, s 334 of the Gambling Act 2005, which came into effect on 1 September 2007, repealed s 18 of the Gaming Act 1845. Gambling contracts entered into after this date are legally enforceable.

A statute may establish a licensing system that expressly prohibits contracts made in violation of the system.

***Re Mahmoud and Ispahani* [1921] 2 KB 716**

Facts: At the time of the case, contracts for the sale of linseed oil were governed by the regulations contained in the Seeds, Oils and Fats Order, 1919. These provided that 'a person shall not either on his own behalf or on behalf of any other person buy or sell or otherwise deal in' linseed oil 'except under and in accordance with the terms of a licence issued by or under the authority of the Food Controller'. The plaintiff seller, who had a licence, asked the defendant whether he had a licence. The defendant replied that he did even though he did not. When the plaintiff attempted to deliver the oil, the defendant refused to take delivery on the ground that the contract was illegal, as he did not possess a licence under the Order. The plaintiff brought a claim for damages for non-acceptance.

Held: The Court of Appeal held that, as the defendant had no licence, the contract of sale was prohibited, and no claim could be made under the contract.

Atkin LJ: When the Court has to deal with the question whether a particular contract or class of contract is prohibited by statute, it may find an express prohibition in the statute, or it may have to infer the prohibition from the fact that the statute imposes a penalty upon the person entering into that class of contract. In the latter case one has to examine very carefully the precise terms of the statute imposing the penalty upon the individual. One may find that the statute imposes a penalty upon an individual, and yet does not prohibit the contract if it is made with a party who is innocent of the offence which is created by the statute. I prefer not to deal with the question of contracts forbidden by the common law as being contrary to public policy, because, despite the great authority of Parke B. (*Cope v Rowlands*, 2 M & W 157), I think a question might be raised whether or not it is right to say that those contracts are prohibited by the common law. The right view may be that the common law refuses to enforce them. I think a different set of circumstances may arise in respect of such contracts as those, but here it appears to me to be plain that this particular contract was expressly prohibited by the terms of the Order which imposes the necessity of a compliance with the licence. With great respect to the learned judge, I think the underlying fallacy in his judgment is that he has not directed his attention to the terms of the licence or to the terms of the Order which says that no sale shall be made unless it complies with the terms of the licence. When one looks at the licence one finds an express prohibition against the plaintiff selling to the defendant as the latter had not a licence. I do not think it is necessary to pursue the matter any further so far as the statutory prohibition is concerned.

It might be thought that this decision was somewhat harsh; the claimant was innocent after all, and he had proceeded with the transaction in reliance on the defendant's misrepresentation that he possessed the necessary licence. Nevertheless, the Court of Appeal held that the policy underlying the regulation in question was to prevent the trade of linseed oil other than between those who held licences. The innocence of the seller was irrelevant in the pursuit of this particular policy. Cf. also *RTA (Business Consultants) Ltd v Bracewell* [2015] EWHC 630 (QB). It should also be noted that a contract that is in some way prohibited by subordinate legislation may also be regarded as an 'illegal' contract.

***Mohamed v Alaga & Co (a firm)* [2000] 1 WLR 1815**

Facts: The plaintiff, a leading member of the Somali community in the UK, claimed that the defendant solicitor had agreed to pay him 50 per cent of the relevant legal aid fees in return for introducing Somali asylum seekers and assisting in the preparation and presentation of their claims. The defendant accepted that the plaintiff had been engaged to work as an interpreter and translator, but denied the existence of the agreement as alleged. In any event, he claimed that a contract made in the terms alleged would be unenforceable, due to it being contrary to rules 3 and 7 of the Solicitor's Practice Rules 1990, made under s 31 of the Solicitors Act 1974. Lightman J held that since the agreement was in breach of the Solicitors' Rules, it was void and unenforceable, even though the plaintiff was unaware of the Rules. The judge also refused to allow the plaintiff's claim for a *quantum meruit* in relation to the work he had done.

Held: The Court of Appeal held that the contract was void and unenforceable for illegality but upheld the plaintiff's claim for a *quantum meruit* on the ground that the parties were not equally to blame.

Lord Bingham CJ: The first issue on this appeal concerns the plaintiff's right under the contract which is assumed to have been made to recover 50 per cent of the legal aid fees received by the solicitors. [Counsel for the plaintiff], in a well-constructed argument, advanced a series of propositions which I hope may be fairly summarised as involving five main planks.

(1) In the absence of any statutory or other legal restriction everyone is free to make any contract they like and such contracts are enforceable.
(2) While the Solicitors Act confers power on the Law Society to make rules to regulate the conduct of solicitors, the Law Society has no power to regulate the conduct of the public at large who are not solicitors.
(3) Thus, while the Law Society may lawfully forbid solicitors to make fee-sharing agreements, it has no power to forbid anyone else, nor to ordain that such agreements shall be unenforceable save by solicitors.
(4) In the absence of an effective legal prohibition a non-solicitor party who makes a fee-sharing agreement with a solicitor is entitled to enforce it.
(5) It would be repugnant if the party prohibited from making such an agreement (the solicitor) were free to take the benefits accruing to him under the agreement, but were then entitled to plead the illegality of the agreement when called upon to pay the consideration due to the other contracting party, particularly when (as assumed here) that party is ignorant of the prohibition binding on the solicitor.

While recognising that that argument is by no means without force, I would not for my part accept it. I reject it for these reasons:

(1) Section 31 confers power on the Law Society to make, with the concurrence of the Master of the Rolls, subordinate legislation governing the professional practice and conduct of solicitors.
(2) When making such subordinate legislation the Law Society is acting in the public interest and not (should there be any conflict) in the narrower interests of the solicitor's profession: see *Swain v The Law Society* [1983] 1 AC 598. The concurrence of the Master of the Rolls is required as a guarantee that the interests of the public are fully safeguarded.
(3) By rule 3 of the Practice Rules, and by the Referral Code, solicitors are permitted to accept referrals and introductions only provided that introducers are not rewarded by commission or otherwise.
(4) By rule 7 solicitors are prohibited from sharing fees or agreeing to do so.
(5) Thus there is a prohibition on the making by solicitors of agreements of the kind assumed to have been made in this case.

> (6) Although it is true that the prohibition is only imposed in terms on solicitors, and they alone are liable to imposition of a professional penalty for breach, a contract requires the concurrence of at least two parties and the effect of the prohibition, if observed, is to outlaw the making of such agreements.
> (7) There are substantial reasons why, in the public interest, such agreements should be outlawed, some of those reasons being described by Lightman J.
> (8) It follows that it would defeat the public interest, which rule 7 in particular exists to promote, if a non-solicitor party to a fee-sharing agreement could enlist the aid of the court to enforce against a solicitor an agreement which the solicitor is prohibited from making.
> (9) If the court were to allow its process to be used to enforce agreements of this kind, the risk would inevitably arise that such agreements would abound, out with the knowledge of the Law Society, to the detriment of the public ...
>
> It seems to me that that passage is unhelpful to the plaintiff. This is in my judgment plainly a case in which the relevant legislation (rule 7) prohibits not only the act but the contract to perform it also. Despite [Counsel for the plaintiff's] argument, I have little hesitation in agreeing with Lightman J on this first point.

The Court of Appeal concluded that the public interest, which rule 7 existed to promote, would be defeated if a non-solicitor could enlist the aid of the court to enforce an agreement which the solicitor was prohibited from making. In particular, Lord Bingham was concerned that, were the court to enforce the contract, such agreements would abound outside the knowledge of the Law Society. The case was followed one year later by the Court of Appeal in *Awwad v Geraghty & Co* [2000] QB 570 (although cf. *FPH Law v Brown (t/a Integrum Law)* [2016] EWHC 1681 (QB), affirmed on appeal [2018] EWCA Civ 1629). It was also approved by the Supreme Court in *Patel v Mirza* [2016] UKSC 42. More recently, in *Okedina v Chilake* [2019] IRLR 905 at [53], Underhill LJ stated: 'As for *Mohamed v Alaga & Co* [2000] 1 WLR 1815, I do not believe that Lord Bingham CJ's "point (6)" can be treated as enunciating a universal proposition that, because a contract requires the concurrence of at least two parties, any prohibition on one party entering the contract necessarily renders it unenforceable by the other. That would be wholly contrary to the authorities reviewed above, which require a case-by-case assessment of the public interest. It is clear that his proposition was directed to a contract of the kind in question, and that indeed appears from the following points (7)–(9) which directly address the public interest in that case.' Later in this chapter, we will return to *Mohammed v Alaga* to consider the claim for a *quantum meruit*, a claim that succeeded in the Court of Appeal.

13.3.1.2 Contracts illegal in their performance

In some cases, the contract may be legal in its formation, but performed in a manner that contravenes statute (see, for example, *Anderson Ltd v Daniel* [1924] 1 KB 138, where a statutory requirement relating to invoices was not complied with).

It is sometimes difficult for the courts to determine the precise effect of the statute on the contract concerned, as demonstrated in *St John Shipping Corp v Joseph Rank Ltd*.

***St John Shipping Corp v Joseph Rank Ltd* [1957] 1 QB 267**

Facts: The defendants chartered a ship from the plaintiffs to carry grain from the USA to the UK. The ship was overloaded in contravention of s 44 of the Merchant Shipping (Safety and Load Line Conventions) Act 1932. When the ship arrived in the UK, the master was prosecuted and fined £1,200. The defendants paid for part of the freight, but withheld a sum equivalent to the value of the freight earned by overloading. The plaintiffs brought a claim for the balance of the freight owed. The defendants contended that the plaintiffs were not entitled to recover any part of the sum because they had performed the contract in an illegal manner.

Held: The court held that the plaintiffs could recover the balance of the freight due. The contravention of a statute in the performance of a contract does not render the contract illegal unless the contract, as performed, was one that the statute meant to prohibit. The Merchant Shipping (Safety and Load Line Conventions) Act 1932 did not prohibit the contract of carriage which was made in contravention of its provisions.

Devlin J: There are two general principles. The first is that a contract which is entered into with the object of committing an illegal act is unenforceable. The application of this principle depends upon proof of the intent, at the time the contract was made, to break the law; if the intent is mutual the contract is not enforceable at all, and, if unilateral, it is unenforceable at the suit of the party who is proved to have it. This principle is not involved here. Whether or not the overloading was deliberate when it was done, there is no proof that it was contemplated when the contract of carriage was made. The second principle is that the court will not enforce a contract which is expressly or impliedly prohibited by statute. If the contract is of this class it does not matter what the intent of the parties is; if the statute prohibits the contract, it is unenforceable whether the parties meant to break the law or not. A significant distinction between the two classes is this. In the former class you have only to look and see what acts the statute prohibits; it does not matter whether or not it prohibits a contract; if a contract is deliberately made to do a prohibited act, that contract will be unenforceable. In the latter class, you have to consider not what acts the statute prohibits, but what contracts it prohibits; but you are not concerned at all with the intent of the parties; if the parties enter into a prohibited contract, that contract is unenforceable …

Two questions are involved. The first – and the one which hitherto has usually settled the matter – is: does the statute mean to prohibit contracts at all? But if this be answered in the affirmative, then one must ask: does this contract belong to the class which the statute intends to prohibit? For example, a person is forbidden by statute from using an unlicensed vehicle on the highway. If one asks oneself whether there is in such an enactment an implied prohibition of all contracts for the use of unlicensed vehicles, the answer may well be that there is, and that contracts of hire would be unenforceable. But if one asks oneself whether there is an implied prohibition of contracts for the carriage of goods by unlicensed vehicles or for the repairing of unlicensed vehicles or for the garaging of unlicensed vehicles, the answer may well be different. The answer might be that collateral contracts of this sort are not within the ambit of the statute.

The relevant section of the Act of 1932, section 44, provides that the ship 'shall not be so loaded as to submerge' the appropriate loadline. It may be that a contract for the loading of the ship which necessarily has this effect would be unenforceable. It might be, for example, that the contract for bunkering at Port Everglades which had the effect of submerging the loadline, if governed by English law, would have been unenforceable. But an implied prohibition of contracts of loading does not necessarily extend to contracts for the carriage of goods by improperly loaded vessels. Of course, if the parties knowingly agree to ship goods by an overloaded vessel, such a contract would be illegal; but its illegality does not depend on whether it is impliedly prohibited by the statute, since it falls within the first of the two general heads of illegality I noted above where there is an intent to break the law. The way to test the question whether a particular class of contract is prohibited by the statute is to test it in relation to a contract made in ignorance of its effect.

In my judgment, contracts for the carriage of goods are not within the ambit of this statute at all. A court should not hold that any contract or class of contracts is prohibited by statute unless there is a clear implication, or 'necessary inference', as Parke B put it, that the statute so intended. If a contract has as its whole object the doing of the very act which the statute prohibits, it can be argued that you can hardly make sense of a statute which forbids an act and yet permits to be made a contract to do it; that is a clear implication. But unless you get a clear implication of that sort, I think that a court ought to be very slow to hold that a statute intends to interfere with the rights and remedies given by the ordinary law of contract. Caution in this respect is, I think, especially necessary in these times when so much of commercial life is governed by regulations of one sort or another, which may easily be broken without wicked intent. Persons who deliberately set out to break the law cannot expect to be aided in a court of justice, but it is a different matter when the law is unwittingly broken. To nullify a bargain in such circumstances frequently means that in a case – perhaps of such triviality that no authority would have felt it worth while to prosecute – a seller, because he cannot enforce his civil rights, may forfeit a sum vastly in excess of any penalty that a criminal court would impose; and the sum forfeited will not go into the public purse but into the pockets of someone who is lucky enough to pick up the windfall or astute enough to have contrived to get it. It is questionable how far this contributes to public morality. In *Vita Food Products Inc v Unus Shipping Co* [1939] AC 277 Lord Wright said: 'Nor must it be forgotten that the rule by which contracts not expressly forbidden by statute or declared to be void are in proper cases nullified for disobedience to a statute is a rule of public policy only, and public policy understood in a wider sense may at times be better served by refusing to nullify a bargain save on serious and sufficient grounds'. It may be questionable also whether public policy is well served by driving from the seat of judgment everyone who has been guilty of a minor transgression. Commercial men who have unwittingly offended against one of a multiplicity of regulations may nevertheless feel that they have not thereby forfeited all right to justice, and may go elsewhere for it if courts of law will not give it to them. In the last resort they will, if necessary, set up their own machinery for dealing with their own disputes in the way that those whom the law puts beyond the pale, such as gamblers, have done. I have said enough, and perhaps more than enough, to show how important it is that the courts should be slow to imply the statutory prohibition of contracts, and should do so only when the implication is quite clear. I have felt justified in saying as much because, to any judge who sits in what is called the Commercial Court, it must be a matter of special concern. This court was instituted more than half a century ago so that it might solve the disputes of commercial men in a way which they understood and appreciated, and it is a particular misfortune for it if it has to deny that service to any except those who are clearly undeserving of it.

The Act of 1932 imposes a penalty which is itself designed to deprive the offender of the benefits of his crime. It would be a curious thing if the operation could be performed twice – once by the criminal law and then again by the civil. It would be curious, too, if in a case in which the magistrates had thought fit to impose only a nominal fine, their decision could, in effect, be overridden in a civil action. But the question whether the rule applies to statutory offences is an important one which I do not wish to decide in the present case ...

The rights which cannot be enforced must be those 'directly resulting' from the crime. That means, I think, that for a right to money or to property to be unenforceable the property or money must be identifiable as something to which, but for the crime, the plaintiff would have had no right or title. That cannot be said in this case. The amount of the profit which the plaintiffs made from the crime, that is to say, the amount of freight which, but for the overloading, they could not have earned on this voyage, was, as I have said, £2,295. The quantity of cargo consigned to the defendants was approximately 35 per cent of the whole and, therefore, even if it were permissible to treat the benefit as being divisible pro rata over the whole of the cargo, the amount embodied in the claim against the defendants would not be more than 35 per cent of £2,300. That would not justify the withholding of £2,000 ... But in truth there is no warrant for any particular form of division. The fact is that in this type of case no claim or part of a claim for freight can be clearly identified as being the excess illegally earned.

Devlin J said that it was necessary to ask two questions:

1 Does the statute prohibit contracts at all?
2 Does this contract belong to the class that the statute is intended to prohibit?

The 1932 Act provided a specific penalty for non-compliance in the form of a criminal fine. Devlin J was concerned that the civil courts should not inflict double punishment by refusing to enforce the contract as well (see also *Hughes v Asset Managers plc* [1995] 3 All ER 669). The judge also emphasised that the knowledge of the parties was crucial. Had the facts been different, and the plaintiff been aware that the goods were to be shipped on an overloaded vessel, it seems he would have declared the contract to be unenforceable (although see *ParkingEye Ltd v Somerfield Stores Ltd* [2012] EWCA Civ 1338, particularly at [30]–[31] and [64]–[80]). Devlin J was also keen to draw attention to the fact that commercial illegality covers a broad spectrum of wrongdoing. He warned that the commercial courts should be reluctant to nullify a bargain when the illegality consists of a mere triviality, especially when such judicial action is likely to result in a windfall accruing to one of the parties. The conflict between these two contrasting policy objectives was noted in the introduction to this chapter. In the final paragraph of his judgment, Devlin J provided a helpful summary of the test to be applied in cases of statutory illegality. He said that 'the rights which cannot be enforced must be those "directly resulting" from the crime'. It is not sufficient that the contract merely relates to the illegal conduct. The contract itself must be 'directly resulting' from the illegal conduct. On the facts of *St John Shipping*, it could not be said that the carriage of goods contract was directly resulting from the breach of the 1932 Act.

Archbolds (Freightage) Ltd v S Spanglett Ltd [1961] 1 QB 374

Facts: The defendant furniture manufacturers owned a number of vans with 'C' licences, enabling them, under the Road and Rail Traffic Act 1933, to carry their own goods, but not the goods of others. The plaintiffs, believing that the defendants possessed 'A' licences, arranged for the defendants to carry 200 cases of whisky from Leeds to London. The whisky was stolen on the journey due to the negligence of the defendants' driver. The defendants argued that they were not liable, because the contract was illegal. At first instance, Slade J held for the plaintiffs.

Held: The Court of Appeal dismissed the appeal. There was no evidence that the plaintiffs knew, or should have known, that the defendants' van did not have an 'A' licence, and that being so, the contract was not prohibited either expressly or impliedly by the statute. Nor was the contract illegal on the ground of public policy.

Pearce LJ: If a contract is expressly or by necessary implication forbidden by statute, or if it is *ex facie* illegal, or if both parties know that though *ex facie* legal it can only be performed by illegality or is intended to be performed illegally, the law will not help the plaintiffs in any way that is a direct or indirect enforcement of rights under the contract and for this purpose both parties are presumed to know the law.

The first question, therefore, is whether this contract of carriage was forbidden by statute. The two cases on which the defendants mainly rely are *In re an Arbitration between Mahmoud and Isphani* [1921] 2 KB 716 and *J Dennis & Co Ltd v Munn* [1949] 2 KB 327. In both those cases the plaintiffs were unable to enforce their rights under contracts forbidden by statute ... In neither case could the plaintiff bring his contract within the exception that alone would have made its subject-matter lawful, namely, by showing the existence of a licence. Therefore, the core of both contracts was the mischief expressly forbidden by the statutory order and the statutory regulation respectively.

In *Mahmoud's* case the object of the order was to prevent (except under licence) a person buying and a person selling, and both parties were liable to penalties. A contract of sale between those persons was therefore expressly forbidden. In *Dennis's* case the object of the regulation was to prevent (except under licence) owners from performing building operations, and builders from carrying out the work for them. Both parties were liable to penalties and a contract between these persons for carrying out an unlawful operation would be forbidden by implication.

The case before us is somewhat different. The carriage of the plaintiffs' whisky was not as such prohibited; the statute merely regulated the means by which carriers should carry goods. Therefore this contract was not expressly forbidden by the statute.

Was it then forbidden by implication? The Road and Rail Traffic Act, 1933, section 1, says: 'no person shall use a goods vehicle on a road for the carriage of goods ... except under licence', and provides that such use shall be an offence. Did the statute thereby intend to forbid by implication all contracts whose performance must on all the facts (whether known or not) result in a contravention of that section?

The plaintiffs' part of the contract could not constitute an illegal use of the vehicle by them since they were not 'using' the vehicle. If they were aware of the true facts they would, of course, be guilty of aiding and abetting the defendants, but if they acted in good faith they would not be guilty of any offence under the statute ...

The object of the Road and Rail Traffic Act, 1933, was not (in this connection) to interfere with the owner of goods or his facilities for transport, but to control those who provided the transport, with a view to promoting its efficiency. Transport of goods was not made illegal but the various licence holders were prohibited from encroaching on one another's territory, the intention of the Act being to provide an orderly and comprehensive service. Penalties were provided for those licence holders who went outside the bounds of their allotted spheres. These penalties apply to those using the vehicle but not to the goods owner. Though the latter could be convicted of aiding and abetting any breach, the restrictions were not aimed at him. Thus a contract of carriage was, in the sense used by Devlin J, 'collateral', and it was not impliedly forbidden by the statute.

This view is supported by common sense and convenience. If the other view were held it would have far-reaching effects. For instance, if a carrier induces me (who is, in fact, ignorant of any illegality) to entrust goods to him and negligently destroys them, he would only have to show that (though unknown to me) his licence had expired, or did not properly cover the transportation, or that he was uninsured, and I should then be without a remedy against him. Or, again, if I ride in a taxicab and the driver leaves me stranded in some deserted spot, he would only have to show that he was (though unknown to me) unlicensed or uninsured, and I should be without remedy. This appears to me an undesirable extension of the implications of a statute ...

It is for the defendants to show that contracts by the owner for the carriage of goods are within the ambit of the implied prohibition of the Road and Rail Traffic Act, 1933. In my judgment they have not done so.

The next question is whether this contract though not forbidden by statute was *ex facie* illegal. Must any reasonable person on hearing the terms of the contract (which presumed knowledge of the law) realise that it was illegal? There is nothing illegal in its terms. Further knowledge, namely, knowledge of the fact that Randall's van was not properly licensed, would show that it could only be performed by contravention of the statute, but that does not make the contract *ex facie* illegal.

However, if both parties had that knowledge the contract would be unenforceable as being a contract which to their knowledge could not be carried out without a violation of the law: see *per* Lord Blackburn in *Waugh v Morris* (1873) LR 8 QB 202, 208. But where one party is ignorant of the fact that will make the performance illegal, is it established that the innocent party cannot obtain relief against the guilty party? The case has been argued with skill and care on both sides, and yet no case has been cited to us establishing the proposition that where a contract is on the face of it legal and is not forbidden by statute, but must in fact produce illegality by reason of a circumstance known to one party only, it should be held illegal so as to debar the innocent party from relief. In the absence of such a case I do not feel compelled to so unsatisfactory a conclusion, which would injure the innocent, benefit the guilty, and put a premium on deceit.

Such a conclusion (in cases like this where a contract is not forbidden by statute) can only derive from public policy ... No question of moral turpitude arises here. The alleged illegality is, so far as the plaintiffs were concerned, the permitting of their goods to be carried by the wrong carrier, namely, a carrier who unknown to them was not allowed by his licence to carry that particular class of goods. The plaintiffs were never in delicto since they did not know the vital fact that would make the performance of the contract illegal.

In my view, therefore, public policy does not constrain us to refuse our aid to the plaintiffs and they are therefore entitled to succeed. I would dismiss the appeal.

The argument of the defendants was quite outrageous. They were using their own illegal performance as a defence to a claim by the innocent plaintiffs. This was an example of illegality being used as a technical defence to wrongdoing. The argument was given short shrift by the Court of Appeal. Since the contract could have been performed in a legal manner, the illegal performance could not be used as a defence. The statute neither expressly nor impliedly prohibited contracts of carriage. It seems the situation would have been different, however, had the plaintiffs known that the defendants did not hold an 'A' licence. In such a situation, Pearce LJ stated that the law would have been unwilling to help the plaintiffs. This is not always the case, however, as was shown by the decision in *Ailion v Spiekermann* [1976] Ch 158. The case concerned a contract for the assignment of a lease with a premium. Such contracts were illegal under s 86(1) of the Rent Act 1968, and both parties were aware of this. Nevertheless, the court held that the premium requirement could be severed, and the remainder of the agreement enforced by the court. We will return to consider severance later in the chapter, when we examine the effects of illegality.

The difficulties in distinguishing cases in this area provided some of the background for the Supreme Court in *Patel v Mirza* [2016] UKSC 42 to move to a wider, underlying policy approach, with Lord Toulson stating:

6. As to illegality in the manner of performance of a contract, Mance LJ observed in *Hall v Woolston Hall Leisure Ltd* [2001] 1 WLR 225, 246, that the conceptual basis on which a contract not illegal nor prohibited at the time of its formation may become unenforceable due to the manner of its performance is open to debate. In *Anderson Ltd v Daniel* [1924] 1 KB 138 a claim for the price of goods was held to be unenforceable because the seller had failed to give the buyer an invoice containing details which the seller was required to give him by statute. In the *St John Shipping* case Devlin J rejected the interpretation that the claim in *Anderson Ltd v Daniel* failed because in the course of performing a legal contract the plaintiff had done something illegal. The correct interpretation, he said, was that 'the way in which the contract was performed turned it into the sort of contract that was prohibited by the statute': [1957] 1 QB 267, 284. In the *St John Shipping* case the claim was for freight under a charter party. In the course of taking on bunkers the vessel was overloaded and the master thereby committed an offence, for which he was prosecuted and fined £1,200. The extra freight earned by the overloading was £2,295 and to that extent the ship owners stood to profit from their wrong. The cargo owners refused to pay that part of the freight. Devlin J rejected their defence. He held that since the goods had been delivered safely, the ship owners had proved all that they needed. He was not prepared to construe the statute as having the effect of making the contract prohibited. If it had been otherwise, the ship owners would not have been entitled to any freight and would therefore have suffered an additional penalty, much greater than that provided for by Parliament, for conduct which might have been unintentional.

7. In *Ashmore, Benson, Pease and Co Ltd v Dawson* [1973] 1 WLR 828 the Court of Appeal adopted a different approach. Manufacturers of heavy engineering equipment entered into a contract of carriage with road hauliers. There was nothing illegal in the formation of the contract, but the hauliers overloaded the vehicles which were to transport the load, in breach of road traffic regulations, and one of the lorries toppled over during the journey as a result of the driver's negligence. The manufacturers' transport manager was present when the goods were loaded and was aware of the overloading. A claim by the manufacturers for the cost of repair of the damaged load was rejected on grounds of illegality. The Court of Appeal did not perform the same analysis as had Devlin J in the *St John Shipping* case. They held simply that the manufacturers participated in the illegal performance of the contract and were therefore barred from suing on it.

8. These and other cases led the Law Commission to describe the effect that unlawful performance has on the parties' contractual rights as very unclear. (Consultative Report on the Illegality Defence, LCCP 189 [2009], para 3.27.)

There is authority that the courts may apply a test of remoteness when considering whether illegal performance renders a contract illegal. Such a test was applied by Field J in *21st Century Logistic Solutions Ltd (In Liquidation) v Madysen Ltd* (2004) 2 Lloyd's Rep 92. The claimants, 21st Century, commenced proceedings against the defendants for the price of 7,200 computers sold and delivered. The defendants denied liability on the ground that the claimants' operations sought to defraud Her Majesty's Customs and Excise. The claimants purchased the CPUs VAT-free from suppliers in Luxembourg and sold them on to businesses in the UK with a VAT element included in the price. Field J held that the contract was lawful and enforceable, because there was insufficient proximity between the claimants' fraudulent intention and the contract. He said:

> In my opinion 21stC's fraudulent intention is too remote from the contract for it to be held that the contract is unenforceable on grounds of illegality. The VAT element in the price paid for a supply is not held on trust by the supplier for HMCE. A taxable supplier's only material obligations under the VAT legislation are to account for VAT at the end of each accounting period and to keep proper records. The use of the VAT element of sale proceeds on some purpose other than payment of VAT due to HMCE is therefore not unlawful. It follows that the fraud on HMCE intended by 21stC would only have been finally committed when 21stC failed to account to HMCE at the end of the relevant accounting period. The contract between 21stC and Madysen was a straightforward agreement for the sale of goods. In and of itself it was a lawful contract. It provided the opportunity for Darren King to profit from the intended fraud but that was all: the crucial act that had to be performed to work the fraud was a failure to account to HMCE.

In summary, when considering whether a contract is unenforceable for statutory illegality, the court will ask itself two questions. First, does the statute prohibit contracts? The remedies provided by the statute will often prove determinative on this issue. Second, is this particular contract illegal? Here, the court will consider the knowledge of the parties, the relative fault of the parties and the proximity of the illegality to the contract. These considerations will often overlap with the more general issue of the effect of illegality, which will be considered in greater detail below.

13.3.2 Common law illegality

Broadly speaking, common law illegality is based on considerations of public policy. If a court decides that a contract is 'contrary to public policy', it can declare it to be illegal and wholly or partly unenforceable.

13.3.2.1 Public policy

Public policy as a ground for invalidating an agreement is a powerful weapon in the hands of the judiciary, and for this reason, the courts have traditionally emphasised the need to keep it on a tight reign. In *Richardson v Mellish* (1824) 2 Bing 229, Burrough J said that 'public policy is a very unruly horse, and once you get astride it you never know where it will carry you'. Other judges have adopted a more flexible attitude. In *Enderby Town FC Ltd v The Football Association* [1971] Ch 591, Lord Denning drew on Burrough J's metaphor and said: 'I disagree. With a good man in the saddle, the unruly horse can be kept in control. It can jump over obstacles. It can leap the fences put up by fictions and come down on the side of justice.'

It has been said that the categories of common-law public policy are closed so that the courts will not apply the concept to a type of contract to which it has not been applied in the past. In *Printing and Numerical Registering Company v Sampson* (1875) LR 19 Eq 462, Jessel MR said:

> It must not be forgotten that you are not to extend arbitrarily those rules which say that a given contract is void as being against public policy, because if there is one thing which more than another public policy requires it is that men of full age and competent understanding shall have the utmost liberty of contracting, and that their contracts when entered into freely and voluntarily shall be held sacred and shall be enforced by Courts of justice. Therefore, you have this paramount public policy to consider – that you are not lightly to interfere with this freedom of contract. Now, there is no doubt public policy may say that a contract to commit a crime, or a contract to give a reward to another to commit a crime, is necessarily void. The decisions have gone further, and contracts to commit an immoral offence, or to give money or reward to another to commit an immoral offence, or to induce another to do something against the general rules of morality, though far more indefinite than the previous class, have always been held to be void. I should be sorry to extend the doctrine much further. I do not say there are no other cases to which it does apply; but I should be sorry to extend it much further.

In *Janson v Drieiontein Consolidated Mines Ltd* [1902] AC 484, Lord Halsbury LC went even further:

> In treating of various branches of the law learned persons have analysed the sources of the law, and have sometimes expressed their opinion that such and such a provision is bad because it is contrary to public policy; but I deny that any Court can invent a new head of public policy; so a contract for marriage brokerage, the creation of a perpetuity, a contract in restraint of trade, a gaming or wagering contract, or, what is relevant here, the assisting of the King's enemies, are all undoubtedly unlawful things; and you may say that it is because they are contrary to public policy they are unlawful; but it is because these things have been either enacted or assumed to be by the common law unlawful, and not because a judge or Court have a right to declare that such and such things are in his or their view contrary to public policy.

It is arguably true that restricting the scope of common law illegality promotes certainty and keeps judicial discretion within reasonable bounds. However, Lord Halsbury's claim that the categories of common-law illegality are now closed is somewhat doubtful. Indeed, in *Fender v St John Mildmay* [1938] AC 1, Lord Atkin explicitly disapproved of this part of Lord Halsbury's speech:

> In [*Janson v Driefontein*] Lord Halsbury indeed appeared to decide that the categories of public policy are closed, and that the principle could not be invoked anew unless the case could be brought within some principle of public policy already recognized by the law. I do not find, however, that this view received the express assent of the other members of the House; and it seems to me, with respect, too rigid.

In practice, there may be little difference between creating a new category of public policy and expanding a pre-existing category to incorporate a new situation. For this reason, to some extent, it does not really matter whether we speak of the categories being closed or open; either way, the courts will intervene where necessary in the interests of public policy. Moreover, the recognition that a category of public policy may be closed by the courts as a result of changes in society's values (contrast *Cowan v Milbourn* (1867) LR 2 Exch 230 and *Bowman v Secular Society* [1917] AC 406) strongly suggests that new categories might also be opened up as a result of changes in social attitudes and advances in technology. See also *XX v Whittington Hospital NHS Trust* [2018] EWCA Civ 2832 McCombe LJ stated:

> 64. Thus, 'public policy' in our law is well-recognised to be variable and is not ossified for all time, once identified in any particular context.

This was in the content of surrogacy arrangements, where McCombe also stated:

> 50. It is argued for Ms X that public policy is notoriously not immutable. It has been recognised in other fields that the common law has to reflect changes in attitude over time. The change in the law as to marital rape is cited as an example: R v R [1992] 1 AC 599.
> 51. In the present field, it is submitted further that social conditions have moved. Within the immediate confines of surrogacy legislation, whereas the 'parental order' jurisdiction was only available to married couples at the time of Briody: see section 30(1) (2) of the HFEA 1990, it is now open to civil partners and those living in an 'enduring family relationship'. In 2016, the High Court declared that the exclusion of single persons from the jurisdiction under section 54 of the HFEA 2008 was incompatible with anti-discrimination provisions of article 14 of the Human Rights Convention, taken in conjunction with article 8: see *In re Z (A Child) (Surrogate Father: Parental Order) (No 2)* [2017] Fam 25 (Sir James Munby P). As a result, the incompatibility was removed by the introduction of a new section 54A into the HFEA 2008, to permit parental orders to be made in favour of a single applicant.

13.3.2.2 Categories

The courts have developed a number of well-established categories of public policy. We will consider some of these in turn.

13.3.2.2.1 Contracts to commit a criminal offence

The expression 'contract killer' is an oxymoron, because contracts to commit a crime are generally unenforceable. In *Bigos v Bousted* [1951] 1 All ER 92, the High Court refused to enforce a contract for the supply of foreign currency because it constituted an offence under s 1(1) of the Exchange Control Act 1947.

13.3.2.2.2 Contracts to commit a tort

An agreement to commit a civil wrong may be wholly or partly unenforceable, certainly if there is a deliberate intention to commit the civil wrong. In *Allen v Rescous* (1675) 2 Lev 174; 83 ER 505, the defendant agreed to pay the plaintiff a sum of money in return for his promise to beat another person 'out of a close'. The Court held that the 'consideration and whole contract' was 'illegal and void'. A contract for the publication of a libel is also illegal and unenforceable. In *Clay v Yates* (1856) 1 H & N 73 (1856), the plaintiff agreed to publish a book written by the defendant. On delivery of the manuscript, the plaintiff discovered that the dedication in the book was libellous. He refused to publish that part of the book, and the defendant refused to pay him for any of the work he had done. Martin B held that although the contract was illegal, the defendant was liable 'to pay the plaintiff for that part which he has performed'.

13.3.2.2.3 Contracts to defraud the revenue

A contract that is designed to defraud the revenue is 'illegal'.

***Alexander v Rayson* [1936] 1 KB 169**

Facts: In 1929, the plaintiff agreed to let a flat in Piccadilly to the defendant at a rent of £1,200 per year. The agreement was effected by two documents. The first was a lease for £450 per year together with the benefits of certain services rendered by the plaintiff, and the second was a service agreement providing for the plaintiff to render services which were practically the same as those to be provided under the lease, in consideration of an extra £750 per year. The defendant refused to pay an instalment due under the agreement, and when the plaintiff sought to recover, the defendant argued that the contract was void for illegality and that its enforcement would be contrary to public policy. The purpose of the two agreements was that only the lease would be disclosed to the Westminster City Council, so that the rateable value of the flat would be reduced.

Held: The Court of Appeal held that the plaintiff could not enforce either the lease or the service agreement since he intended to use the agreements for an illegal purpose.

Judgment of the Court (Greer, Romer and Scott LJJ): It is settled law that an agreement to do an act that is illegal or immoral or contrary to public policy, or to do any act for a consideration that is illegal, immoral or contrary to public policy, is unlawful and therefore void. But it often happens that an agreement which in itself is not unlawful is made with the intention of one or both parties to make use of the subject matter for an unlawful purpose, that is to say a purpose that is illegal, immoral or contrary to public policy. The most common instance of this is an agreement for the sale or letting of an object, where the agreement is unobjectionable on the face of it, but where the intention of both or one of the parties is that the object shall be used by the purchaser or hirer for an unlawful purpose. In such a case any party to the agreement who had the unlawful intention is precluded from suing upon it. *Ex turpi causa non oritur actio.* The action does not lie because the Court will not lend its help to such a plaintiff.

13.3.2.2.4 Contracts to indemnify

It is generally illegal to indemnify against criminal liability. There is an exception, however, where the criminal offence is one of strict liability and the court is satisfied that the defendant is morally innocent.

***Osman v J Ralph Moss Ltd* [1970] 1 Lloyd's Rep 313**

Facts: The plaintiff was of Turkish origin and struggled to read and understand English. The defendant brokers negligently failed to inform the plaintiff that his motor insurance policy had expired due to the collapse of the insurance company. The plaintiff was involved in a motor accident and fined £25 by Beacontree Magistrates. He sought to recover this sum from the defendants in an action for negligence.

Held: The Court of Appeal held that the plaintiff could recover the amount of the fine from the defendants in damages.

Sachs LJ: Having examined the authorities as to cases where the person fined was under an absolute liability, it appears that such fine can be recovered in circumstances such as the present as damages unless it is shown that there was on the part of the person fined a degree of *mens rea* or of culpable negligence in the matter which resulted in the fine. The onus in cases such as the present is on the defendants, who were the true cause of the sequence of events leading to the fine, to show that there are circumstances which make that fine irrecoverable as damages by the plaintiff.

A contract to indemnify against civil liability will be legal and enforceable unless the wrong consists of deliberate and intentional conduct. See also *Mulcaire v News Group Newspapers Ltd* [2011] EWHC 3469, where, after a criminal action, joint tortfeasors entered into an indemnity contract under which one agreed to indemnify the other in respect of the costs etc. arising from a resulting civil action. Sir Andrew Morritt was of the opinion that such a contract of indemnity, entered into after a criminal action in respect of civil liability resulting from that criminal action, did not necessarily contravene public policy.

***Geismar v Sun Alliance & London Insurance Ltd* [1978] QB 383**

Facts: The plaintiff had imported various items of jewellery into the United Kingdom without having declared them for the payment of customs and excise duty. He had thus committed an offence in relation to the non-payment of duty, and the jewellery was liable to forfeiture at any time. The jewellery was subsequently stolen from the plaintiff's home, and he brought a claim against the defendant insurers under his building and contents policy. The defendants refused to pay out on the claim on the grounds of public policy.

Held: The Court of Appeal held that the plaintiff could not recover under the policy for the uncustomed jewellery, because this would allow him to recover in respect of items that might have been confiscated at any time. Permitting the plaintiff to benefit in such a way would have been contrary to public policy.

Talbot J: The plaintiff is seeking the assistance of the court to enforce contracts of insurance so that he may be indemnified against loss of articles which he deliberately and intentionally imported into this country in breach of the Customs and Excise Act 1952.

I am not concerned with cases of unintentional importation or of innocent possession of uncustomed goods. I would think that different considerations would apply in those cases. But where there is a deliberate breach of the law I do not think the court ought to assist the plaintiff to derive a profit from it, even though it is sought indirectly through an indemnity under an insurance policy.

The operation of public policy in this area is particularly well illustrated by *Gardner v Moore* [1984] AC 548, where the first defendant deliberately drove his car into the plaintiff following an altercation. This amounted to an offence of wounding with intent to cause grievous bodily harm under s 18 of the Offences against the Person Act 1861, for which the defendant was sentenced to three years' imprisonment. The defendant was uninsured at the time of the incident, and therefore the plaintiff joined the Motor Insurers' Bureau (MIB) as second defendants. The question was whether it would be contrary to public policy to allow the MIB to indemnify the driver. Lord Hailsham LC (with whom the other Law Lords agreed) concluded that it would not:

The MIB agreements impose on the appellants an obligation to underwrite this liability so far as regards uninsured or untraceable tortfeasors. The two agreements were intended precisely to protect the innocent third party either because the insurer did not choose or was not able to discharge his liability under section 149 of the Road Traffic Act 1972, or where the wrongdoer was not covered by a relevant policy of insurance at all (which is the present appeal) or was untraceable. To invoke, as the MIB now do, the well-known doctrine of public policy that a man may not profit by the consequences of his own wrongdoing seems to me to stand the principle of public policy on its head. There are no socially desirable consequences flowing from its application in the sense contended for by the appellants. On the contrary, all the pointers in sections 143 and 145 read alone, or in sections 143 and 145 as read in conjunction with sections 148 and 149, seem to me to point exactly in the opposite direction. The construction of the MIB agreement contended for by the appellants is contrary to the grammatical sense of the agreement, read, as it must be read, in the context of the statute, and the construction of the statute contended for by the appellants is contrary both to its manifest grammatical meaning and to the policy illustrated by its more mature articulation.

13.3.2.2.5 Contracts prejudicial to the administration of justice

A contract that is prejudicial to the administration of justice is contrary to public policy and therefore void. Examples of such contracts include (at least some) agreements to withhold information about wrongdoing and agreements to oust the jurisdiction of the courts. An example of the former is seen in *Initial Services Ltd v Putterill*.

Initial Services Ltd v Putterill [1968] 1 QB 396

Facts: The defendant was employed as the sales manager of the plaintiff launderers. He resigned his position and took with him a number of documents belonging to the plaintiff. He disclosed these documents to reporters from the Daily Mail, who published articles alleging the existence of a liaison system between laundries by which they artificially inflated their prices. The plaintiff claimed damages against the defendant for breach of an implied term to the effect that he would not disclose to strangers confidential information obtained by him in the course of or as a result of his employment. The defendant claimed that there was an exception to this implied term if the employer's misconduct was of such a nature that it was in the public interest to disclose it. He alleged this to be the case on the facts because the plaintiff's conduct was contrary to section 6 of the Restrictive Trade Practices Act 1956, and should have been registered under section 9 of that Act and referred to the Monopolies Commission. Cusack J refused to strike out the defence and the plaintiffs appealed.

Held: The Court of Appeal dismissed the appeal. A term purporting to prevent an employee from disclosing misconduct which ought in the public interest to be disclosed to an appropriate person is illegal and unenforceable. It was arguable that the information disclosed by the defendant fell within this category, and therefore there was no ground for striking out the defendant's defence.

Lord Denning MR: In support of the appeal, Mr Michael Kerr said that in the employment of every servant there is implied an obligation that he will not, before or after his service, disclose information or documents which he has received in confidence. Now I quite agree that there is such an obligation. It is imposed by law. But it is subject to exceptions. Take a simple instance. Suppose a master tells his servant: 'I am going to falsify these sale notes and deceive the customers. You are not to say anything about it to anyone'. If the master thereafter falsifies the sale notes, the servant is entitled to say: 'I am not going to stay any longer in the service of a man who does such a thing. I will leave him and report it to the customers'. It was so held in *Gartside v Outram* (1856) 26 L J Ch 113.

Mr Michael Kerr suggested that this exception was confined to cases where the master has been 'guilty of a crime or fraud'. But I do not think that it is so limited. It extends to any misconduct of such a nature that it ought in the public interest to be disclosed to others. Wood, VC put it in a vivid phrase: 'There is no confidence as to the disclosure of iniquity'.

In *Weld-Blundell v Stephens* [1919] 1 KB 520, Bankes LJ rather suggested that the exception is limited to the proposed or contemplated commission of a crime or a civil wrong. But I should have thought that was too limited. The exception should extend to crimes, frauds and misdeeds, both those actually committed as well as those in contemplation, provided always – and this is essential – that the disclosure is justified in the public interest. The reason is because 'no private obligations can dispense with that universal one which lies on every member of the society to discover every design which may be formed, contrary to the laws of the society, to destroy the public welfare' (see *Annesley v Anglesea (Earl)* (1743) LR 5 QB 317n; 17 State Tr 1139).

The disclosure must, I should think, be to one who has a proper interest to receive the information. Thus it would be proper to disclose a crime to the police; or a breach of the Restrictive Trade Practices Act to the registrar. There may be cases where the misdeed is of such a character that the public interest may demand, or at least excuse, publication on a broader field, even to the press.

Let me apply these principles to the particular facts of this case, because we are only concerned to see whether the defence of Mr Putterill is arguable or not. Firstly, as to the Restrictive Trade Practices Act. If the allegations of the defence are correct, there was an agreement or arrangement between these laundry firms which should have been registered. If it had been registered, particulars of it would have been entered in the register. Once on the register, any individual on paying the requisite amount, I think one shilling, could have obtained full particulars of that agreement or arrangement. Now I ask myself: Is this laundry company entitled to say that that information is confidential, seeing that they ought to have supplied it themselves to the registrar, and it would then have been made public? There is an argument at least that such information was not within the realm of confidence to which the master could hold his servant ... I am not prepared to say that this defence is unfounded. I think this matter should go for trial. I would dismiss the appeal.

Agreements that purport to oust the jurisdiction of the court are also contrary to public policy, as illustrated by the case of *Baker v Jones*.

Baker v Jones [1954] 1 WLR 1005

Facts: The rules of the British Amateur Weightlifters' Association vested the government of the association in a central council consisting of the officers and a number of the members of the association. The rules stated that the council was to be the sole interpreter of the rules of the association, and was to act on behalf of the association regarding any matter not dealt with by the rules. In all circumstances, the decision of the council was to be final.

Held: The High Court held that the rules were void to the extent that they purported to give the council the power to make final decisions on questions of law.

Lynskey J: Although parties to a contract may, in general, make any contract they like, there are certain limitations imposed by public policy, and one of those limitations may be that the parties cannot, by contract, oust the ordinary courts from their jurisdiction (*Scott v Avery* (1856) 5 HLC 811). The parties can, of course, make a tribunal or council the final arbiter on questions of fact. They can leave questions of law to the decision of a tribunal, but they cannot make it the final arbiter on questions of law. They cannot prevent its decisions being examined by the courts. As Denning LJ said in *Lee v Showmen's Guild of Great Britain* [1952] 2 QB 329, 342:

> 'If parties should seek, by agreement, to take the law out of the hands of the courts and put it into the hands of a private tribunal, without any recourse at all to the courts in case of error of law, then the agreement is to that extent contrary to public policy and void'.

With this statement of the law I respectfully agree. The interpretation of the rules is a question of law which the courts will examine. In my view, therefore, the provision in the BAWLA rules, making the central council the sole interpreter of the rules and their decision in all cases final, is contrary to public policy and void.

There are a number of qualifications to the general rule against agreements purporting to oust the jurisdiction of the courts. First, the parties may insert a clause into the contract stating that any dispute between the parties is to be resolved by referral to arbitration. In *Scott v Avery* (1855) 5 HLC 811, the House of Lords upheld a clause stating that the award of an arbitrator was to be a condition precedent to the accrual of a cause of action. It was said that such a clause did not oust the jurisdiction of the court, but merely meant that the cause of action was not complete until the arbitration award was made. Under the Arbitration Act 1996, there is a limited right of appeal to the court on a point of law, but only with the agreement of the other side, or the leave of the court itself.

ARBITRATION ACT 1996

Appeal on point of law

Section 69

(1) Unless otherwise agreed by the parties, a party to arbitral proceedings may (upon notice to the other parties and to the tribunal) appeal to the court on a question of law arising out of an award made in the proceedings.
An agreement to dispense with reasons for the tribunal's award shall be considered an agreement to exclude the court's jurisdiction under this section.

(2) An appeal shall not be brought under this section except –
    (a) with the agreement of all the other parties to the proceedings, or
    (b) with the leave of the court.

The right to appeal is also subject to the restrictions in section 70(2) and (3).

(3) Leave to appeal shall be given only if the court is satisfied –
    (a) that the determination of the question will substantially affect the rights of one or more of the parties,
    (b) that the question is one which the tribunal was asked to determine,
    (c) that, on the basis of the findings of fact in the award –
        (i) the decision of the tribunal on the question is obviously wrong, or
        (ii) the question is one of general public importance and the decision of the tribunal is at least open to serious doubt, and
    (d) that, despite the agreement of the parties to resolve the matter by arbitration, it is just and proper in all the circumstances for the court to determine the question.

A second qualification to the general rule against contracts purporting to oust the jurisdiction of the courts concerns maintenance agreements. In *Hyman v Hyman* [1929] AC 601, a husband, as part of a separation agreement, promised to pay his wife a lump sum of £2,200 and a weekly allowance of £20 in return for her promise not to apply to the court for maintenance. The House of Lords held that the agreement was contrary to public policy, and therefore did not prevent the wife from applying to the court for maintenance. Lord Atkin said:

> In my view no agreement between the spouses can prevent the Court from considering the question whether in the circumstances of the particular case it shall think fit to order the husband to make some reasonable payment to the wife, 'having regard to her fortune, if any, to the ability of her husband and to the conduct of the parties. The wife's right to future maintenance is a matter of public concern, which she cannot barter away.

Although such agreements are void to the extent that the wife is free to apply to the court for maintenance, they are valid and enforceable in respect of the husband's promise to pay. This is confirmed by s 34 of the Matrimonial Causes Act 1973, which states:

> (1) If a maintenance agreement includes a provision purporting to restrict any right to apply to a court for an order containing financial arrangements, then –
> (a) that provision shall be void; but
> (b) any other financial arrangements contained in the agreement shall not thereby be rendered void or unenforceable and shall, unless they are void or unenforceable for any other reason ... be binding on the parties to the agreement.

13.3.2.2.6 Contracts prejudicial to the institution of marriage and family life

Traditionally, the courts considered it to be in the interests of society to preserve the status of marriage. For this reason, agreements that were regarded as threatening to the institution of marriage were likely to be unenforceable.

Brodie v Brodie [1917] P 271

Facts: Mr Brodie agreed to marry the woman who was carrying his child on condition that a written agreement to separate was drawn up prior to the marriage. The effect of this agreement was to preclude the woman from bringing legal proceedings against Mr Brodie.

Held: The Court held that the agreement was contrary to public policy and therefore could not be enforced. The woman was entitled to petition the court for restitution of conjugal rights.

Horridge J: I find as a fact that ... the two documents formed part of an agreement entered into before marriage for future separation. Such an agreement is void and against public policy: see *Cocksedge v Cocksedge* (1844) 14 Sim 244, the judgment of Rigby LJ in *Marlborough v Marlborough* [1901] 1 Ch 165, 171, and the judgment of Kennedy LJ in *Wilson v Carnley* [1908] 1 KB 729, 743. I therefore hold the plea of the respondent is no answer to the petition.

The rule set out in *Brodie v Brodie* did not apply to an agreement made in anticipation of an immediate separation. It was not contrary to public policy for separating parties to make agreements as to the distribution of their joint property or the maintenance of one of the parties. Nor did the rule affect agreements between spouses who have been separated and have subsequently been reconciled, since it was presumed that the making of such an agreement was likely to aid the reconciliation (*Harrison v Harrison* [1910] 1 KB 35). However, in *Radmacher v Granatino* [2010] UKSC 42, Lord Phillips stated:

> 52. We wholeheartedly endorse the conclusion of the Board in paras 38 and 39 that the old rule that agreements providing for future separation are contrary to public policy is obsolete and should be swept away, for the reasons given by the Board. But for reasons that we shall explain, this should not be restricted to post-nuptial agreements. If parties who have made such an agreement, whether ante-nuptial or post-nuptial, then decide to live apart, we can see no reason why they should not be entitled to enforce their agreement. This right will, however, prove nugatory if one or other objects to the terms of the agreement, for this is likely to result in the party who objects initiating proceedings for divorce or judicial separation and, arguing in ancillary relief proceedings that he or she should not be held to the terms of the agreement.

In that case, the Supreme Court stated that when a court was considering ancillary relief after the breakdown of a marriage, weight (possibly even decisive weight) could be given to any ante-nuptial agreement. (It should also be noted that the Law Commission has considered marital property agreements: see Cooke [2012] Fam Law 323.)

Agreements that aim to restrict or limit the freedom of a person to marry are generally 'illegal' (*Lowe v Peers* [1768] 4 Burr 2225). Likewise, contracts for the brokerage of marriage are traditionally regarded as contrary to public policy.

***Hermann v Charlesworth* [1905] 2 KB 123**

Facts: The plaintiff, Miss Hermann, entered into an agreement with the defendant under which she would be required to pay him £250 if he introduced her to a gentleman whom she later married. She paid a deposit of £52 which, after several unsuccessful introductions, she sought to recover. The county court judge held that the agreement was illegal. However, since the parties were not in *pari delicto*, the defendant being the more culpable as having instigated the agreement, the plaintiff was entitled to recover the deposit. The Divisional Court reversed the decision of the county court judge on the ground that the contract was not one of marriage brokerage.

Held: The Court of Appeal allowed the appeal, holding that the contract was one of marriage brokerage and the plaintiff was entitled to recover her £52 deposit.

Collins MR: The Divisional Court came to the conclusion that the particular arrangement in this case to procure introductions with a view to marriage, giving the lady a choice among the persons introduced to her, was not within the mischief attributed to marriage brokage contracts. As I understand, they took the view that a marriage brokage contract was confined to the case of a contract to procure marriage with one particular person. Going back to the principle on which this branch of the law as to such contracts rests, I am unable to find any ground for that distinction. It seems to me that the principle is as much violated in the class of cases to which the present one belongs as in cases where the contract relates to bringing about a marriage with a particular individual.

It is unlikely that this case would be decided in the same way today, given the popularity of 'dating' and 'introduction' agencies. Perhaps this is one example of the way in which public policy evolves in line with changing attitudes in society.

13.3.2.2.7 Contracts promoting sexual immorality

Contracts promoting sexual immorality are deemed to be contrary to public policy. The conduct concerned need not constitute a criminal offence, and the courts will generally refuse to enforce any contract that directly or indirectly promotes sexual immorality (the meaning of which may, of course, change over time).

Pearce v Brooks (1865–1866) LR 1 Ex 213

Facts: The plaintiff coach-builders supplied the defendant with an ornamental brougham (a type of carriage), which was to be paid for by instalments. After one instalment had been paid, the brougham was returned in a damaged condition. The plaintiff brought a claim to recover the 15 guineas that was owed for early return of the brougham. At trial, the jury found that the plaintiff knew that the defendant was a prostitute, and supplied the brougham in the knowledge that it was to be used by her to attract men.

Held: The Court of Exchequer held that the contract was illegal, and that the plaintiff could not recover the unpaid instalment from the defendant.

Pollock CB: ... I have always considered it as settled law, that any person who contributes to the performance of an illegal act by supplying a thing with the knowledge that it is going to be used for that purpose, cannot recover the price of the thing so supplied. If, to create that incapacity, it was ever considered necessary that the price should be bargained or expected to be paid out of the fruits of the illegal act (which I do not stop to examine), that proposition had been overruled by the cases I have referred to, and has now ceased to be law. Nor can any distinction be made between an illegal and an immoral purpose; the rule which is applicable to the matter is, *Ex turpi causa non oritur actio*, and whether it is an immoral or an illegal purpose in which the plaintiff has participated, it comes equally within the terms of that maxim, and the effect is the same; no cause of action can arise out of either the one or the other.

Pigott B: ... If a woman, who is known to be a prostitute, wants an ornamental brougham, there can be very little doubt for what purpose she requires it ... It cannot be necessary that the plaintiffs should look to the proceeds of the immoral act for payment; the law would indeed be blind if it supported a contract where the parties were silent as to the mode of payment, and refused to support a similar contract in the rare case where the parties were imprudent enough to express it. The plaintiffs knew the woman's mode of life, and where the means of payment would come from, and to require the proposed addition to the rule would be to make it futile.

Bramwell B: I am of the same opinion. There is no doubt that the woman was a prostitute; no doubt to my mind that the plaintiffs knew it; there was cogent evidence of the fact, and the jury have so found. The only fact really in dispute is for what purpose was the brougham hired, and if for an immoral purpose, did the plaintiffs know it? At the trial I doubted whether there was evidence of this, but, for the reasons I have already stated, I think the jury were entitled to infer, as they did, that it was hired for the purpose of display, that is, for the purpose of enabling the defendant to pursue her calling, and that the plaintiffs knew it. That being made out, my difficulty was, whether, though the defendant hired the brougham for that purpose, it could be said that the plaintiffs let it for the same purpose. In one sense, it was not for the same purpose. If a man were to ask for duelling pistols, and to say: 'I think I shall fight a duel to-morrow', might not the seller answer: 'I do not want to know your purpose; I have nothing to do with it; that is your business: mine is to sell the pistols, and I look only to the profit of trade'. No doubt the act would be immoral, but I have felt a doubt whether it would be illegal; and I should still feel it, but that the authority of *Cannan v Bryce* 3 B & A 179 and *M'Kinnell v Robinson* 3 M & W 434 concludes the matter. In the latter case the plea does not say that the money was lent on the terms that the borrower should game with it; but only that it was borrowed by the defendant, and lent by the plaintiff 'for the purpose of the defendant's illegally playing and gaming therewith'. The case was argued by Mr Justice Crompton against the plea, and by Mr Justice Wightman in support of it; and the considered judgment of the Court was delivered by Lord Abinger, who says (p 441):

> 'As the plea states that the money for which the action is brought was lent for the purpose of illegally playing and gaming therewith, at the illegal game of "Hazard", this money cannot be recovered back, on the principle, not for the first time laid down, but fully settled in the case of

> *Cannan v Bryce*. This principle is that the repayment of money, lent for the express purpose of accomplishing an illegal object, cannot be enforced'.

This Court, then, following *Cannan v Bryce*, decided that it need not be part of the bargain that the subject of the contract should be used unlawfully, but that it is enough if it is handed over for the purpose that the borrower shall so apply it. We are, then, concluded by authority on the point; and, as I have no doubt that the finding of the jury was right, the rule must be discharged.

It was crucial to the decision in *Pearce v Brooks* that both parties knew that the brougham was to be used for the purposes of prostitution. Had this not been known to the plaintiff, it is highly likely that recovery would have been allowed. Indeed, in *Appleton v Campbell* (1826) 2 C & P 347; 172 ER 157 – a case concerning the recovery of board and lodging for a room rented to a prostitute – the court held that the plaintiff would only be denied recovery if he knew that the defendant intended to use the room to entertain her clients. There are thus two factors that are necessary for the contract to be unenforceable. First, it must be shown that the plaintiff knew that the other party was a prostitute; and second, it must be shown that the plaintiff knew that what was supplied under the contract was to be used for the purposes of prostitution. Cf. *Patel v Mirza* [2016] UKSC 42 (below).

13.3.2.2.8 Contract prejudicial to the interests of state

Contracts that are prejudicial to the interests of state are unenforceable on the ground of common law illegality. One obvious example of such a contract is a trading agreement between a British citizen and a foreign enemy in time of war (*Potts v Bell* [1800] 8 Term R 548). This category of common law illegality has now been recognised by Parliament in the Trading with the Enemy Act 1939.

13.3.2.2.9 Contracts promoting corruption in public life

The final category of common law illegality concerns contracts that tend to promote corruption in public life. It is contrary to public policy to sell public offices and honours.

Parkinson v College of Ambulance Ltd [1925] 2 KB 1

Facts: Mr Harrison, the secretary of the College of Ambulance, fraudulently represented to Mr Parkinson that he would receive a knighthood if he made a large donation to the charity. Mr Parkinson, relying upon that representation, made a donation of £3,000. When he failed to receive the knighthood, Parkinson brought an action against the College and Mr Harrison to recover the money he had paid as money had and received or as damages for deceit or breach of contract.

Held: It was held that a contract for the purchase of a title was contrary to public policy. Since Mr Parkinson knew that he was entering into an illegal contract, he could not recover the money he had paid to the charity.

Lush J: The contract, in my opinion, is one that could not be sanctioned or recognized in a Court of justice. Such a contract as that which the plaintiff and Harrison made is, in my judgment, an illegal and improper contract to enter into. I do not, of course, say that it involves the same degree of moral turpitude that an actually immoral contract involves; still less a contract to commit a crime … The money paid by the plaintiff was not paid as the price or 'wages' of immorality. It was not paid as a bribe to Harrison. It was paid to a public charity, a meritorious service in itself. But the contract which was entered into is not a contract which one can describe as innocent in itself …

> Now the first question to consider is this. The contract being against public policy, and being of the character that I have described, can the plaintiff still rely upon the fraud of Harrison and recover damages against him; and can he, as against the college, recover the £3,000 which the college has received through that fraud, as money had and received to his use? ... [T]he plaintiff knew that he was entering into an illegal and improper contract. He was not deceived as to the legality of the contract he was making. How then can he say that he is excused? How can he say that he has suffered a loss through being defrauded into making a contract which he knew he ought never to have made? The answer is that he ought not to have made it. Where he was deceived was that he thought he would make a profit, derive a benefit from his unlawful act. He cannot be heard to say that. He has himself to blame for the loss that he has incurred. It is no excuse to say that Harrison was more blameworthy than he, which is all that he really can say. That being the position, the plaintiff is in this difficulty. He cannot recover damages either against Harrison or the college, because he is disclosing or setting up a contract which is unlawful, and which he had no right to make. For the same reason he cannot recover the £3,000 from the college as money had and received.

The conclusion on available remedies, however, now needs to be read in the light of *Patel v Mirza* [2016] UKSC 42, where Lord Toulson stated:

> **117.** In support of his argument that this purpose was sufficient to disentitle Mr Patel from obtaining the return of his money, Mr Collings relied on cases such as *Parkinson v College of Ambulance Ltd* [1925] 2 KB 1. In that case the plaintiff made a donation to a charity to secure a knighthood. When the honour failed to materialise he sued for the return of his money. The claim was rejected.
>
> **118.** Bribes of all kinds are odious and corrupting, but it does not follow that it is in the public interest to prevent their repayment. There are two sides to the equation. If today it transpired that a bribe had been paid to a political party, a charity or a holder of public office, it might be regarded it as more repugnant to the public interest that the recipient should keep it than that it should be returned. We are not directly concerned with such a case but I refer to it because of the reliance placed on that line of authorities.

Cf. *National Iranian Oil Co v Crescent Petroleum Co International Ltd* [2016] EWHC 510 (Comm). Lord Neuberger went further and stated (at [150]):

> I agree with the view that the decision in Parkinson represented 'a new and regrettable extension of the scope of the maxim' of ex turpi causa (to quote from Professor Grodecki's article [1955] 71 LQR 254, 263), and I consider that it should be overruled.

13.4 The effect of illegality

Our starting point is that the courts traditionally adopted a strict approach to the effect of illegality, refusing to enforce illegal contracts. Moreover, until the Supreme Court decision in *Patel v Mirza* [2016] UKSC 42, it seemed the courts would also, generally, refuse to order restitution of benefits conferred under such contracts. Lord Mansfield explained the principle in *Holman v Johnson* (1775) 1 Cowp 341:

> The objection, that a contract is immoral or illegal as between plaintiff and defendant sounds at all times very ill in the mouth of the defendant. It is not for his sake, however, that the objection is ever

> allowed; but it is founded in general principles of policy, which the defendant has the advantage of, contrary to the real justice, as between him and the plaintiff, by accident, if I may so say. The principle of public policy is this; *ex dolo malo non oritur actio*. No court will lend its aid to a man who founds his cause of action upon an immoral or an illegal act. If, from the plaintiff's own stating or otherwise, the cause of action appears to arise *ex turpi causa*, or the transgression of a positive law of this country, there the Court says he has no right to be assisted. It is upon that ground the Court goes; not for the sake of the defendant, but because they will not lend their aid to such a plaintiff. So if the plaintiff and defendant were to change sides, and the defendant was to bring his action against the plaintiff, the latter would then have the advantage of it; for where both are equally in fault, *potior est conditio defendentis*.

Lord Mansfield pronounced two Latin maxims that were applicable to illegal contracts:

1 *ex dolo malo non oritur actio* – no right of action can have its origin in fraud;
2 *in pari delicto potior est conditio defendentis* – where the parties are equally at fault, the court will favour the defendant.

However, in *Patel v Mirza* [2016] UKSC 42, Lord Toulson stated:

> 121. A claimant, such as Mr Patel, who satisfies the ordinary requirements of a claim for unjust enrichment, should not be debarred from enforcing his claim by reason only of the fact that the money which he seeks to recover was paid for an unlawful purpose. There may be rare cases where for some particular reason the enforcement of such a claim might be regarded as undermining the integrity of the justice system, but there are no such circumstances in this case. I would dismiss the appeal.

See also *Baxter v Todd* [2019] EWHC 1959, where Deputy Master Bowles stated:

> 109. Even if it can, it seems to me that it would only be in an extreme and obvious case that the denial by the court of enforcement of legal, or equitable, rights, where those rights relate to some misconduct in respect of an application for social housing, would be an appropriate means of protecting the process.
>
> 110. I have no doubt that experienced housing authorities already have stringent processes in place to ensure that the process of provision is not abused and it seems to me that the intervention of the civil court, by way of a refusal of relief to an otherwise entitled litigant, in effect pour encourager les autres, is not, in any usual case, including the present case, one which is appropriate, or necessary, to prevent harm to the social housing process. Rather, it seems to me, in this context, also, that, from the perspective of the overall perception of the legal system and the legal process and the integrity of that process, the refusal to enforce rights, where rights exist, is more likely to be of harm than if the courts lean in favour of the enforcement of rights which have, otherwise, been made out.

13.4.1 Exceptions to the strict rules

Indeed, these maxims were by no means universally applied, not least because the seriousness and public policy of the illegality varies. Thus, in *Achbolds (Freightage) Ltd v S Spanglett Ltd* [1961] 1 QB 374, the Court of Appeal enforced a contract in favour of an innocent plaintiff who was unaware of the fact that the defendant intended to perform the contract in an illegal manner. In *21st Century Logistic Solutions Ltd (In Liquidation) v Madysen Ltd* (2004) 2 Lloyd's Rep 92, Field J enforced a contract in favour of a plaintiff who had participated in a VAT fraud on the basis that the illegality was 'too remote' from the contract to prevent its enforcement. It also appears that a contract will be enforced if the illegality is 'one-way', and the innocent party is ignorant of the facts that constitute the illegality. In *Bloxsome v Williams* (1824) 3 B & C 232, the plaintiff agreed to purchase a horse from the defendant for 39 guineas, subject to a warranty that the horse was not more than seven years old and sound. Unknown to the plaintiff, the defendant exercised trade as a horse dealer and for that reason the sale, which took place on a Sunday, was illegal under s 2 of the Sunday Observance Act 1677. The horse proved to be unsound and was, in fact, more than 17 years old. The defendant claimed that the plaintiff was barred from bringing a claim for breach of warranty, because the contract was void for illegality. Bayley J rejected this argument:

> [T]he defendant was the person offending within the meaning of the statute by exercising his ordinary calling on the Sunday. He might be thereby deprived of any right to sue upon a contract so illegally made, and upon the same principle any other person knowingly aiding him in the breach of the law, by becoming a party to such a contract, with the knowledge that it was illegal, could not sue upon it. But in this case the fact that the defendant was a dealer in horses was not known to the plaintiff or his son, he therefore has not knowingly concurred in aiding the defendant to offend the law, and that being so, it is not competent to the defendant to set up his own breach of the law as an answer to this action.

Bloxsome v Williams should be distinguished from *Re Mahmoud and Ispahani* (see above), where the statute had the effect of making the contract unlawful, per se. This meant that the intentions of the parties were irrelevant, and the plaintiff was denied recovery even though he had been unaware of the fact that the defendant did not possess a linseed oil licence. The harsh results of this rule might be relieved if the claimant is able to establish a claim on some alternative ground independent of the illegal contract. We will consider this in further detail below.

The difficulties in distinguishing cases in this area provided some of the background for the Supreme Court in *Patel v Mirza* [2016] UKSC 42 to move to a wider, underlying policy approach, with Lord Toulson stating:

> **3.** Take the law of contract. A contract may be prohibited by a statute; or it may be entered into for an illegal or immoral purpose, which may be that of one or both parties; or performance according to its terms may involve the commission of an offence; or it may be intended by one or both parties to be performed in a way which will involve the commission of an offence; or an unlawful act may be committed in the course of its performance. The application of the doctrine of illegality to each of these different situations has caused a good deal of uncertainty, complexity and sometimes inconsistency.
> **4.** *Holman v Johnson* involved a claim for the price of goods which the plaintiff sold to the defendant in Dunkirk, knowing that the defendant's purpose was to smuggle the goods into England. The plaintiff was met with a defence of illegality. The defence failed. Lord Mansfield held that knowledge on the part of the plaintiff that the defendant intended to smuggle the goods did not affect the plaintiff's entitlement to recover the price of the goods, since he was not himself involved in the smuggling. By contrast, in *Pearce v Brooks* (1866) LR 1 Ex 213 a claim by a coachbuilder against a prostitute for the hire of what was described in the law report as an 'ornamental brougham' was held to be unenforceable for illegality after the jury found that the defendant hired it for the purpose of prostitution and that the plaintiff knew that this was her purpose. It would seem that the difference between *Holman v Johnson* and *Pearce v Brooks* had to do

with the type of goods supplied, because in both cases the plaintiff knew that the defendant was entering into the contract for an illegal or immoral purpose. In *JM Allan (Merchandising) Ltd v Cloke* [1963] 2 QB 340, 348, Lord Denning MR endeavoured to rationalise the authorities by saying that 'active participation debars, but knowledge by itself does not'. However, the Law Commission commented in its discussion of the subject in its Consultation Paper on *Illegal Transactions: the Effect of Illegality on Contracts and Trusts*, LCCP 154 (1999) that the case law lacks clear guidance on what amounts to 'participation' in this context.

13.4.1.1 Parties not equally to blame

Prior to the decision of the Supreme Court in *Patel v Mirza* [2016] UKSC 42, it seemed that one possible exception to supposed rule against restitution in this context was that a claimant might be entitled to recover money paid under an illegal contract where the parties are not equally to blame. Such a situation might have, for example, arisen if the policy behind the rule rendering the contract illegal concerned the protection of a class of people of whom the claimant was a member. In such situations, it seemed sensible to allow the 'victim' to recover money paid under the contract.

***Kiriri Cotton Co Ltd v Dewani* [1960] AC 192**

Facts: The defendant let a flat to the plaintiff in Kampala, Uganda. The lease was for a period of seven years, and in consideration of a premium and a rent. Charging a premium was illegal under section 3 (2) of the Uganda Rent Restriction Ordinance 1949, although neither party knew this at the time. When the plaintiff discovered that the charging of a premium was illegal, he sought to recover the money paid. The High Court of Uganda gave judgment for the plaintiff, and this decision was affirmed by the Court of Appeal for Eastern Africa. The defendant appealed to the Privy Council.

Held: The Privy Council dismissed the appeal. The duty of observing the law was firmly placed on the landlord for the protection of the tenant. Because of this, the parties were not *in pari delicto*, and the plaintiff could recover the premium.

Lord Denning: [I]f as between the two of them the duty of observing the law is placed on the shoulders of the one rather than the other – it being imposed on him specially for the protection of the other then they are not in *pari delicto* and the money can be recovered back ... In applying these principles to the present case, the most important thing to observe is that the Rent Restriction Ordinance was intended to protect tenants from being exploited by landlords in days of housing shortage ... This is apparent from the fact that the penalty is imposed only on the landlord or his agent and not upon the tenant ... It may be that the tenant who pays money is an accomplice or an aider and abettor (see *Johnson v Youden* [1950] 1 KB 544 and section 3 of the Rent Restriction (Amendment) Ordinance, 1954), but he can hardly be said to be *in pari delicto* with the landlord. The duty of observing the law is firmly placed by the Ordinance on the shoulders of the landlord for the protection of the tenant: and if the law is broken, the landlord must take the primary responsibility. Whether it be a rich tenant who pays a premium as a bribe in order to 'jump the queue', or a poor tenant who is at his wit's end to find accommodation, neither is so much to blame as the landlord who is using his property rights so as to exploit those in need of a roof over their heads.

Seeing then that the parties are not *in pari delicto*, the tenant is entitled to recover the premium by the common law: and it is not necessary to find a remedy given by the Ordinance, either expressly or by implication.

Similarly, a claimant might also have been entitled to recover money paid or property transferred under an illegal contract if he entered into the contract as a result of the other party's fraudulent misrepresentation. In *Hughes v Liverpool Victoria Legal Friendly Society* [1916] 2 KB 482, the plaintiff took up five life insurance policies on the lives of persons in which she had no insurable interest. The defendants had fraudulently told her that the policies were valid and enforceable. When the plaintiff discovered that the policies were illegal and void, she sought to recover the premiums she had paid. The Court of Appeal held that she was entitled to recover, because the parties were not *in pari delicto*. Bankes LJ said:

> Given fraud, the authorities seem to me to be all one way, namely, that an innocent plaintiff is entitled to say that he is not *in pari delicto* with the defendants whose agents by a false and fraudulent representation induced him to believe that the transaction was an innocent one, and one which was enforceable in law. On these grounds, in my opinion, the appellant is entitled to succeed.

It is clear that, had the misrepresentation not been fraudulent, the plaintiff would have been denied recovery (*Harse v Pearl Life Assurance Co* [1904] 1 KB 558).

Likewise, if the claimant was in a weak bargaining position, so that there was virtually no choice as to whether to enter into the contract, he may also have been entitled to restitution.

Atkinson v Denby (1862) 7 H & N 934; 158 ER 749

Facts: The plaintiff, who was in financial difficulty, offered his creditors a composition agreement of five shillings in the pound. The defendant, who was one of the plaintiff's creditors, refused to accept the agreement unless the plaintiff paid him £50, so gaining an advantage over the other creditors. The plaintiff paid, but later brought an action to recover the £50.

Held: The Exchequer Chamber held that although the agreement was an illegal contract, the oppression meant that the parties did not stand *in pari delicto*, and the plaintiff was entitled to recover the £50 in an action for money had and received.

Cockburn CJ: Where a debtor offers his creditors a composition, whereby they are all to receive the same proportionate amount in respect of their debts, it is contrary to the policy of the law to allow him to purchase the consent of one creditor by payment of his debt in full. It is said that both parties are *in pari delicto*. It is true that both are *in delicto*, because the act is a fraud upon the other creditors, but it is not *par delictum*, because the one has the power to dictate, the other no alternative but to submit.

Restitution may also have been available under an illegal contract if the claimant was unaware of the facts constituting the illegality. In *Oom v Bruce* (1810) 12 East 225, the plaintiffs entered into a contract of insurance with the defendants in respect of goods to be transported from St Petersburg to London on board the ship 'Elbe'. Unknown to the plaintiffs, hostilities broke out between Great Britain and Russia on the day before the contract was concluded. This meant that the contract was void and unenforceable. The plaintiffs sought to recover the premiums they had paid under the illegal contract. Lord Ellenborough CJ said:

> [T]he plaintiffs had no knowledge of the commencement of hostilities by Russia, when they effected this insurance; and, therefore, no fault is imputable to them for entering into the contract; and there is no reason why they should not recover back the premiums which they have paid for an insurance from which, without any fault imputable to themselves, they could never have derived any benefit.

Finally, it was sometimes possible to recover a *quantum meruit* for work done under an illegal contract where the parties were not equally to blame. For example, in *Mohamed v Alaga* [2000] 1 WLR 1815 (the facts of which we have already considered above), the Court of Appeal held that although the contract was void for illegality, the plaintiff could recover a *quantum meruit* for the work he had done in introducing Somali asylum seekers to the defendants. Lord Bingham MR explained the award as follows:

> [T]he plaintiff is not seeking to recover any part of the consideration payable under the unlawful contract, but simply a reasonable reward for professional services rendered. I accept that as an accurate description of what on this limited basis the plaintiff is, in truth, seeking. It is furthermore in my judgment relevant that the parties are not in a situation in which their blameworthiness is equal. The defendant is a solicitor's firm and bound by the rules. It should reasonably be assumed to know what the rules are and to comply with them. If, in truth, it made the agreement as alleged, then it would seem very probable that it acted in knowing disregard of professional rules binding upon it. By contrast the plaintiff, on the assumption made (which I have no difficulty in accepting), was ignorant that there was any reason why the defendant should not make the agreement which he says was made. In other commercial fields, after all, such agreements are common.

As noted above, following *Mirza* [2016] UKSC 42, the supposed rule against restitution in this context has been displaced. However, that does not mean that the above cases are now irrelevant (see above at p 579ff). For example Lord Toulson stated:

> **67.** The Court of Appeal supported and followed the approach of the Law Commission in *Les Laboratoires Servier v Apotex Inc* [2012] EWCA Civ 593, [2013] Bus LR 80 and *ParkingEye Ltd v Somerfield Stores Ltd* [2013] QB 840. In the latter case *ParkingEye* contracted to provide a system of automated monitoring of car parking at Somerfield's supermarkets. The system recorded vehicle registration numbers and customers would be charged for staying beyond a set period. The contract was to be for an initial term of 15 months and ParkingEye's remuneration was to come from the charges levied over that period. Overstayers were to be sent letters of demand in a standard form agreed between the parties in advance of the conclusion of the contract. If the first demand did not result in payment, it was to be followed by a series of further demands in stronger terms. The third pro forma letter was deceptive because it falsely represented that ParkingEye had the authority and intention to issue proceedings against the customer if payment was not made within a stipulated period. Six months into the contract Somerfield repudiated it for reasons unconnected with the letters of demand. By that time the monitoring system had been installed at 17 of its stores. ParkingEye's claim for damages was met with a defence which included a plea of illegality based on the intended use of deception in the performance of the contract.
>
> **68.** The trial judge rejected the defence and awarded ParkingEye damages of £350,000 for loss of profits caused by Somerfield's repudiatory breach. The Court of Appeal upheld his decision. The legally objectionable letter was only a small part of the intended performance of the contract and was not essential to it. The judge had found that ParkingEye did not appreciate that the letter would be legally objectionable when the parties agreed on its form, and that, if someone had pointed the matter out, the letter would have been changed. When its objectionable nature occurred to Somerfield, the proper and reasonable course would have been for Somerfield to raise the matter with ParkingEye and continue to honour the contract, so long as ParkingEye made the necessary alteration and performed the contract in a lawful manner, as it would have done. The court held that denial of ParkingEye's claim was not justified by the policies underlying the doctrine of illegality and would have led to a disproportionate result.

69. In that case I said at paras 52–53:

> 'Rather than having over-complex rules which are indiscriminate in theory but less so in practice, it is better and more honest that the court should look openly at the underlying policy factors and reach a balanced judgment in each case for reasons articulated by it.

53. This is not to suggest that a list of policy factors should become a complete substitute for the rules about illegality in the law of contract which the courts have developed, but rather that those rules are to be developed and applied with the degree of flexibility necessary to give proper effect to the underlying policy factors'.

70. On the relevance of ParkingEye's state of mind, I referred at para 66 to *Waugh v Morris* (1873) LR 8 QB 202. The case arose from a charter party under which a cargo of hay was to be shipped from Trouville to London. On arrival in London the master learned that a few months before the conclusion of the contract an order had been published under the Contagious Diseases (Animals) Act 1869 making it illegal to land hay brought from France. The master refrained from landing the cargo and, after some delay, the charterer transhipped and exported it. Meanwhile the contractual laydays had expired and the owner claimed for detention. The charterer resisted the claim on the ground that the contract was void for illegality, because its purpose was the delivery of the consignment to London, which was prohibited by law. The defence was rejected.

71. Giving the judgment of the court, Blackburn J said that all that the owner had bargained for was that on the ship's arrival in London the freight should be paid and the cargo unloaded. He contemplated that it would be landed and thought that this would be legal; but if he had thought of the possibility of the landing being prohibited, he would probably and rightly have expected that the charterer would not violate the law. Blackburn J said at 208:

> 'We quite agree, that, where a contract is to do a thing which cannot be performed without a violation of the law it is void, whether the parties knew the law or not. But we think, that in order to avoid a contract which can be legally performed, on the ground that there was an intention to perform it in an illegal manner, it is necessary to show that there was the wicked intention to break the law; and, if this be so, the knowledge of what the law is becomes of great importance'.

72. Since the decisions of the Court of Appeal in *Les Laboratoires Servier v Apotex Inc* and the *ParkingEye* case, there have been three decisions by the Supreme Court involving the doctrine of illegality. The first was *Hounga v Allen* [2014] 1 WLR 2889, a case with features similar to *Nizamuddowlah v Bengal Cabaret Inc*. Miss Hounga was a 14-year old Nigerian. Mr and Mrs Allen offered to employ her as a home help in the UK in return for schooling and £50 per month. With their help she entered the UK on false identity documents and obtained a six months' visitor's visa. The plan was masterminded by Mrs Allen's brother who lived in Lagos. He drafted an affidavit for Miss Hounga to swear, giving her surname as that of Mrs Allen's mother and a false date of birth. The affidavit led to the issue of a passport in that name. Mrs Allen's family then arranged for Miss Hounga to be taken to the British High Commission in Lagos, where she produced a document purporting to be an invitation from Mrs Allen's mother pretending to invite her granddaughter to visit her in the United Kingdom. The High Commission was duped into issuing her with entry clearance. Mrs Allen's brother then bought a ticket for Miss Hounga to travel to England. On arrival at Heathrow Miss Hounga confirmed to an immigration officer that the purpose of her visit was to stay with her grandmother. Subsequently a psychologist reported that Miss Hounga, who was illiterate, had low cognitive functioning, a learning disability and a developmental age much lower than her chronological age. Nevertheless she knew that she had entered the UK on false pretences, that it was illegal for her to remain beyond six months and that it was illegal for her to take employment in the UK.

73. After her arrival Miss Hounga lived at the Allens' home, looking after their children and doing housework. She was not enrolled in a school or paid any wages. She was told by Mrs Allen that if she were found by the police she would be sent to prison. This caused her extreme concern. Mrs Allen also subjected her to serious physical abuse. After 18 months an incident occurred in which Mrs Allen beat Miss Hounga, threw her out of the house and poured water over her. Miss Hounga slept that night in the Allens' garden in wet clothes. Next day they refused to let her back in, and she made her way to a supermarket car park, where she was found and taken to the social services department of the local authority.

74. Miss Hounga brought claims against the Allens in the employment tribunal for unfair dismissal, breach of contract and unpaid wages. They were dismissed on the ground that her contract of employment was unlawful. She appealed unsuccessfully to the appeal tribunal and she did not seek to appeal further. Neither the Court of Appeal nor the Supreme Court therefore had occasion to consider whether she was entitled to be paid for the services which she rendered on a quantum meruit (by analogy with cases such as *Mohamed v Alaga & Co* and *Nizamuddowlah v Bengal Cabaret Inc* et al).

75. Miss Hounga also claimed to have been the victim of the statutory tort of unlawful discrimination under the Race Relations Act 1976, section 4(2)(c), in relation to her dismissal. The tribunal found that she had been dismissed because of her vulnerability consequent upon her immigration status. She was therefore the victim of unlawful discrimination and she was awarded compensation for her resulting injury to feelings. The tribunal's order was set aside by the Court of Appeal, which held that the claim was tainted by the illegal nature of her employment and that for the court to uphold it would be to condone the illegality, but it was restored by the Supreme Court. The leading judgment was given by Lord Wilson, with whom Lady Hale and Lord Kerr agreed.

76. Lord Wilson did not consider that the solution of the case lay either in asking whether Miss Allen needed to rely on an illegal contract or in asking whether there was an inextricable link between the illegality to which she was a party and her claim. At the heart of the judgment Lord Wilson set out his approach in para 42:

> 'The defence of illegality rests on the foundation of public policy. "The principle of public policy is this …" said Lord Mansfield by way of preface to his classic exposition of the defence in *Holman v Johnson* (1775) 1 Cowp 341, 343. "Rules which rest on the foundation of public policy, not being rules which belong to the fixed or customary law, are capable, on proper occasion, of expansion or modification": *Maxim Nordenfelt Guns and Ammunition Co v Nordenfelt* [1893] 1 Ch 630, 661 (Bowen LJ). So it is necessary, first, to ask 'What is the aspect of public policy which founds the defence?' and, second, to ask "But is there another aspect of public policy to which the application of the defence would run counter?"'

77. On the first question, drawing on the judgment of McLachlin J in *Hall v Hebert*, Lord Wilson addressed the policy consideration of preserving the integrity of the legal system and not allowing persons to profit from their illegal conduct. He concluded that an award of compensation for damage to Miss Hounga's feelings was not a form of profit from her employment; it did not permit evasion of a penalty prescribed by the criminal law; and it did not compromise the integrity of the legal system. Conversely, he said that application of the defence could encourage those in the situation of Mrs Allen to believe that they could discriminate against people like Miss Hounga with impunity and could thereby compromise the integrity of the legal system. On the second question, Lord Wilson said that the Court of Appeal's decision ran strikingly counter to the public policy against forms of people trafficking and in favour of the protection of its victims. Weighing the policy considerations, he concluded that insofar as any public policy existed in favour of applying the illegality defence, it should give way to the public policy to which its application would be an affront.

78. *Hounga v Allen* was a case in tort, but Lord Wilson's approach to the illegality defence was applied by the Court of Appeal in *R (Best) v Chief Land Registrar* [2016] QB 23, where the issue was whether a claim to be registered under the Land Registration Act 2002 ('LRA') as the proprietor of a residential building by adverse possession was barred by illegality. The circumstances were that part of the relevant period of possession involved the commission of trespass which constituted a criminal offence under section 144 of the Legal Aid, Sentencing and Punishment of Offenders Act 2012 ('LASPOA').

79. Sales LJ (with whom McCombe LJ agreed) expressed the view, at para 51, that the best guidance on the relevant analytical framework was to be found in Lord Wilson's judgment (from which he quoted para 42 and the passage which followed it). Applying that guidance, he examined the public policy considerations underlying the provisions of the LRA governing acquisition of title to land and the public policy considerations underlying section 144 of LASPOA. He concluded that the mischief at which section 144 was aimed was far removed from the intended operation of the law of adverse possession and that public policy did not preclude the claim for registration.

80. After *Hounga v Allen* came the decision of the Supreme *Court in Les Laboratoires Servier v Apotex Inc* [2015] AC 430. The issue of illegality arose in the context of a claim to enforce a cross-undertaking in damages given as a condition of an interlocutory injunction in proceedings which ultimately failed. The claim was therefore akin to a claim in contract. The facts were somewhat complicated but do not matter for present purposes. The court held unanimously that the Court of Appeal had reached the right result, but the majority of this court expressed the view, at para 21, that the Court of Appeal's decision could not possibly be justified by the considerations put forward by that court, which had in broad terms followed the approach commended by the Law Commission. I expressed a different view, at para 62, observing that the Court of Appeal had adopted a similar approach to that taken by this court in *Hounga v Allen*.

13.4.1.2 Claim not based on the illegal contract

Prior to the decision of the Supreme Court in *Patel v Mirza* [2016] UKSC 42, it seemed that another possible exception to the supposed rule against restitution in this context was that a claimant might be able to recover property transferred under an illegal contract if he was able to assert his claim without reliance on the illegality. He might have done this in a number of ways.

13.4.1.2.1 Legal title

First, the claimant may have been able to assert a claim based on retention of legal title. This might have been possible under, for example, a contract of bailment or lease.

***Bowmakers Ltd v Barnet Instruments Ltd* [1945] KB 65**

Facts: The defendants entered into three hire purchase agreements with the plaintiffs for the acquisition of machine tools. These agreements were illegal under a government order which required those disposing of machine tools to obtain a licence from the Minister of Supply. The plaintiffs had not obtained such a licence. The defendants sold the machines which were the subject of two of the agreements, but kept the others. They refused to return them to the plaintiffs, or to pay the hire. The plaintiffs brought a claim for conversion.

Held: The Court of Appeal held that the plaintiffs could establish their rights over the machine tools without the need to rely on the illegal contracts. The defendants' rights as bailees came to an end with their actions, and so, the plaintiffs could assert their basic right of ownership.

Du Parcq LJ: The question, then, is whether in the circumstances the plaintiffs are without a remedy. So far as their claim in conversion is concerned, they are not relying on the hiring agreements at all. On the contrary, they are willing to admit for this purpose that they cannot rely on them. They simply say that the machines were their property, and this, we think, cannot be denied. We understood Mr Gallop to concede that the property had passed from Smith to the plaintiffs, and still remained in the plaintiffs at the date of the conversion …

Why then should not the plaintiffs have what is their own? No question of the defendants' rights arises. They do not, and cannot, pretend to have had any legal right to possession of the goods at the date of the conversion. Their counsel has to rely, not on any alleged right of theirs, but on the requirements of public policy. He was entitled, and bound, to do so, although, as Lord Mansfield long ago observed, 'The objection, that a contract is immoral or illegal as between plaintiff and defendant, sounds at all times very ill in the mouth of the defendant'. 'No court', Lord Mansfield added, 'will lend its aid to a man who founds his cause of action upon an immoral or an illegal act': *Holman v Johnson* (1775) 1 Cowp 341, 343 … Prima facie, a man is entitled to his own property, and it is not a general principle of our law (as was suggested) that when one man's goods have got into another's possession in consequence of some unlawful dealings between them, the true owner can never be allowed to recover those goods by an action. The necessity of such a principle to the interests and advancement of public policy is certainly not obvious. The suggestion that it exists is not, in our opinion, supported by authority. It would, indeed, be astonishing if (to take one instance) a person in the position of the defendant in *Pearce v Brooks* (1866) LR 1 Ex 213, supposing that she had converted the plaintiff's brougham to her own use, were to be permitted, in the supposed interests of public policy, to keep it or the proceeds of its sale for her own benefit …

In our opinion, a man's right to possess his own chattels will as a general rule be enforced against one who, without any claim of right, is detaining them, or has converted them to his own use, even though it may appear either from the pleadings, or in the course of the trial, that the chattels in question came into the defendant's possession by reason of an illegal contract between himself and the plaintiff, provided that the plaintiff does not seek, and is not forced, either to found his claim on the illegal contract or to plead its illegality in order to support his claim.

Mr Gallop sought to derive assistance from the decision of the Court of Queen's Bench in *Taylor v Chester* (1869) LR 4 QB 309. The decision there was, however, entirely consonant with the view which we have expressed. It differed from the present case in one essential respect, since in that case the defendant had prima facie a right to possession of the half-note which the plaintiff claimed. She was holding it as a pledge to secure the payment of money which remained due. The plaintiff could only defeat her plea by showing that the money due had been lent for an immoral purpose, and this could not avail him since he was *in pari delicto* with her …

Du Parcq LJ's reference to *Taylor v Chester* (1869) LR 4 QB 309 served to illustrate how difficult it could be to establish a proprietary right without reference to the illegal contract. Taylor deposited half a £50 bank note with Chester by way of pledge to guarantee payment for a night of debauchery at Chester's brothel. Taylor sought to recover the half-note, but failed on the ground that he could not establish his proprietary right without reference to the illegal contract.

Some commentators have suggested that similar problems arise on the facts of Bowmakers. While the bailee's right to possession was clearly brought to an end in relation to the first and third agreements following the resale of the machine tools, the same cannot be said for the defendants' right to possession under the second agreement. Here, the machine tools had not been resold; the defendant had merely refused to pay the hire charge on them. It was therefore impossible for the plaintiff to establish his proprietary right to the tools without reference to the illegal contract.

Hamson, CJ, 'Illegal Contracts and Limited Interests' (1949) 10 *CLJ* 249, 258–259

The question in *Bowmakers' Case* is: 'when can a bailor recover from the bailee under an illegal bailment the chattel bailed or its value?' The simplest answer would no doubt have been to treat an illegal bailment as a bailment at will and to permit the bailor always to recover the chattel upon mere demand. This answer has, however, been rejected in *Taylor v Chester*, despite Herschell's argument; and the court in *Bowmakers' Case* accepts that decision as correct. The bailee accordingly still acquires, by virtue of the illegal bailment, some interest or property in the chattel other than one defeasible merely on demand. In *Bowmakers' Case*, however, the court goes on to hold that the bailor can recover the chattel bailed under an illegal hire purchase contract even though the only wrongful act by the bailee, in one of the instances, was his mere continuance in possession after demand made for the return of the chattel upon his failure to pay some instalments of the hire reserved by the bailment. Those instalments could not, by reason of the illegality, be recovered directly by action against the bailee. The difficulty is that the court, while declaring, as indeed it was bound to, that 'no claim founded on an illegal contract will be enforced' and that 'no technical meaning must be ascribed to the words "founded on an illegal contract"', nevertheless appears to come very close, under cover of an action in tort, to enforcing the terms of the illegal bailment against the defendants.

It is suggested that, despite the court's laudable desire to avoid technicalities, the question who is to keep a chattel which has been subject of an illegal contract will continue to be decided with the aid of very abstruse technicalities, that the established principle that delivery or conveyance under an illegal contract effects a valid transfer of property or of an interest in property is itself no mean technicality and forms the basis of rules which are therefore likely to have a technical bias; and that in *Bowmakers' Case* perhaps the court applied the technicalities with less consideration than they merited, and with results which both to the technician and to the layman are somewhat startling.

13.4.1.2.2 Equitable title

The decision in *Bowmakers' Case* was certainly controversial in relation to its application to the facts of the second agreement. Nevertheless, its central premise was followed and applied by the House of Lords in relation to a claim based upon equitable title. In *Tinsley v Milligan* [1994] 1 AC 340, the House of Lords (by a bare majority) held that an equitable interest by way of resulting trust could be enforced by the defendant because it was possible to establish the equitable interest without reference to the illegal purpose. Lord Browne-Wilkinson said:

> Neither at law nor in equity will the court enforce an illegal contract which has been partially, but not fully, performed. However, it does not follow that all acts done under a partially performed contract are of no effect. In particular it is now clearly established that at law (as opposed to in equity), property in goods or land can pass under, or pursuant to, such a contract. If so, the rights of the owner of the legal title thereby acquired will be enforced, provided that the plaintiff can establish such title without pleading or leading evidence of the illegality. It is said that the property lies where it falls, even though legal title to the property was acquired as a result of the property passing under the illegal contract itself …
>
> The position at law is well illustrated by the decision in *Bowmakers v Barnet Instruments* [1945] KB 65 … In my judgment to draw such distinctions between property rights enforceable at law and those which require the intervention of equity would be surprising. More than 100 years has elapsed since the administration of law and equity became fused. The reality of the matter is that, in 1993, English law has one single law of property made up of legal and equitable interests. Although for historical reasons legal estates and equitable estates have differing incidents,

> the person owning either type of estate has a right of property, a right *in rem* not merely a right *in personam*. If the law is that a party is entitled to enforce a property right acquired under an illegal transaction, in my judgment the same rule ought to apply to any property right so acquired, whether such right is legal or equitable …
>
> A party to an illegality can recover by virtue of a legal or equitable property interest if, but only if, he can establish his title without relying on his own illegality. As applied in the present case, that principle would operate as follows. Miss Milligan established a resulting trust by showing that she had contributed to the purchase price of the house and that there was common understanding between her and Miss Tinsley that they owned the house equally. She had no need to allege or prove *why* the house was conveyed into the name of Miss Tinsley alone, since that fact was irrelevant to her claim: it was enough to show that the house was in fact vested in Miss Tinsley alone. The illegality only emerged at all because Miss Tinsley sought to raise it. Having proved these facts, Miss Milligan had raised a presumption of resulting trust. There was no evidence to rebut that presumption. Therefore Miss Milligan should succeed.

The opposite presumption, the presumption of advancement, was to be abolished by s 199 of the Equality Act 2010, but this section has not yet been brought into force. In any event, *Tinsley v Milligan* was overruled by the Supreme Court in *Patel v Mirza* [2016] UKSC 42, with Lord Toulson stating:

110. I agree with the criticisms made in *Nelson v Nelson* and by academic commentators of the reliance rule as laid down in *Bowmakers* and *Tinsley v Milligan*, and I would hold that it should no longer be followed. Unless a statute provides otherwise (expressly or by necessary implication), property can pass under a transaction which is illegal as a contract: *Singh v Ali* [1960] AC 167, 176, and *Sharma v Simposh Ltd* [2013] Ch 23, paras 27–44. There may be circumstances in which a court will refuse to lend its assistance to an owner to enforce his title as, for example, where to do so would be to assist the claimant in a drug trafficking operation, but the outcome should not depend on a procedural question.

111. In *Bowmakers* [1945] 1 KB 65 the claim was for conversion of goods which had been obtained by the plaintiffs and supplied to the defendant under transactions which were assumed to be tainted by illegality. The Court of Appeal rightly said, at p 71, that 'a man's right to possess his own chattels will as a general rule be enforced against one who, without any claim of right, is detaining them or has converted them to his own use, even though it may appear either from the pleadings, or in the course of the trial, that the chattels in question came into the defendant's possession by reason of an illegal contract between himself and the plaintiff', but it added the qualifying words 'provided that the plaintiff does not seek, and is not forced, either to found his claim on the illegal contract or to plead its illegality in order to support his claim'. The objections to the proviso have already been identified. It makes the question whether the court will refuse its assistance to the claimant to enforce his title to his property depend on a procedural question and it has led to uncertain case law about what constitutes reliance. The court ended its judgment, at p 72, by saying:

> 'We are satisfied that no rule of law, and no considerations of public policy, compel the court to dismiss the plaintiffs' claim in the case before us, and to do so would be, in our opinion, a manifest injustice'.

That conclusion, rather than the answer to a procedural question, should have been the end of the illegality defence, since it is based on public policy.

112. In *Tinsley v Milligan*, even if Miss Milligan had not owned up and come to terms with the DSS, it would have been disproportionate to have prevented her from enforcing her equitable interest in the property and conversely to have left Miss Tinsley unjustly enriched.

113. Critics of the 'range of factors' approach say that it would create unacceptable uncertainty. I would make three points in reply. First, one of the principal criticisms of the law has been its uncertainty and unpredictability. Doctrinally it is riven with uncertainties: see, for example, paras 4–8 above. There is also uncertainty how a court will in practice steer its way in order to reach what appears to be a just and reasonable result. Second, I am not aware of evidence that uncertainty has been a source of serious problems in those jurisdictions which have taken a relatively flexible approach. Third, there are areas in which certainty is particularly important. Ordinary citizens and businesses enter into all sorts of everyday lawful activities which are governed by well understood rules of law. Lord Mansfield said in *Vallejo v Wheeler* (1774) 1 Cowp 143, 153:

> 'In all mercantile transactions the great object should be certainty: and therefore, it is of more consequence that a rule should be certain, than whether the rule is established one way or the other. Because speculators in trade then know what ground to go upon'.

The same considerations do not apply in the same way to people contemplating unlawful activity. When he came to decide cases involving illegality, Lord Mansfield acted in accordance with his judgment about where the public interest lay: see paras 96–98.

114. In *Tinsley v Milligan* Lord Goff considered that if the law was to move in a more flexible direction, to which he was not opposed in principle, there should be a full investigation by the Law Commission (which has happened) and that any reform should be through legislation. Realistically, the prospect of legislation can be ignored. The government declined to take forward the Commission's bill on trusts because it was not seen to be 'a pressing priority for government' (a phrase familiar to the Commission), and there is no reason for optimism that it would take a different view if presented with a wider bill. In *Clayton v The Queen* (2006) 231 ALR 500, para 119, Kirby J said that waiting for a modern Parliament to grapple with issues of law reform is like 'waiting for the Greek Kalends. It will not happen' and that 'Eventually courts must accept this and shoulder their own responsibility for the state of the common law'. The responsibility of the courts for dealing with defects in the common law was recently emphasised by this court in *R v Jogee* [2016] 2 WLR 681, para 85, and *Knauer v Ministry of Justice* [2016] 2 WLR 672, para 26. In each of those cases the court decided that it should depart from previous decisions of the House of Lords. That is never a step taken lightly. In departing from *Tinsley v Milligan* it is material that it has been widely criticised; that people cannot be said to have entered into lawful transactions in reliance on the law as then stated; and, most fundamentally, that the criticisms are well founded.

115. In the present case I would endorse the approach and conclusion of Gloster LJ. She correctly asked herself whether the policy underlying the rule which made the contract between Mr Patel and Mr Mirza illegal would be stultified if Mr Patel's claim in unjust enrichment were allowed. After examining the policy underlying the statutory provisions about insider dealing, she concluded that there was no logical basis why considerations of public policy should require Mr Patel to forfeit the moneys which he paid into Mr Mirza's account, and which were never used for the purpose for which they were paid. She said that such a result would not be a just and proportionate response to the illegality. I agree. It seems likely that Lord Mansfield would also have agreed: see *Walker v Chapman*. Mr Patel is seeking to unwind the arrangement, not to profit from it.

13.4.1.2.3 Tort

Another, possible, exception to the supposed rule against restitution in this context was that a claimant may have been able to make a claim in the law of tort if he was able to assert his right without reliance on the illegal contract. This has, of course, been potentially widened by the decision of the Supreme Court in *Patel v Mirza* [2016] UKSC 42.

Saunders v Edwards [1987] 1 WLR 1116

Facts: The plaintiffs agreed to purchase a London flat from the defendant for £45,000 in reliance on the defendant's fraudulent misrepresentation that the flat included a roof top terrace. During the pre-contract negotiations, the parties agreed to apportion the purchase price between the chattels and the flat. A value of £5,000 was placed on the chattels, even though they were worth much less than that. This was done in order to save £300 on stamp duty. When the plaintiffs discovered that they had no right to use the roof terrace, they brought an action for fraudulent misrepresentation. The defendant contended that the plaintiffs were barred from bringing such a claim because the contract was tainted by illegality.

Held: The Court of Appeal held that, although the plaintiffs' performance of the contract may have been tainted by illegality, they could still bring a claim for fraudulent misrepresentation, since they did not need to rely on the illegal contract.

Bingham LJ: Even if it be assumed that these plaintiffs deliberately inflated the value of the fixtures and fittings and reduced the value of the flat so as unlawfully to avoid payment of stamp duty properly payable, I do not think that the plaintiffs' claim can be said to arise from that unlawfulness. The action arises from the first defendant's fraud, not theirs. The loss which they have suffered as a result of the first defendant's fraudulent misrepresentation was neither greater nor smaller than it would have been however the purchase price had been apportioned. Their claim is a very simple one. They overpaid because they were deceived. Public policy does not in my view require that the defendant should be left to enjoy the fruits of his deceit simply because the plaintiffs in their turn deceived the Inland Revenue (if they did).

13.4.1.2.4 A collateral contract

A final, further possible exception to the supposed rule against restitution in this context was that a court might allow the claimant to assert a 'collateral contract'. This contract had to be, it seemed, independent of the original transaction, otherwise it would also be tainted with illegality. In *Fisher v Bridges* (1854) 3 E & B 642, the plaintiff agreed to convey land to the defendant for a purpose known to be illegal (the land was to be sold by way of lottery). The defendant still owed money under the transaction and so executed a deed, promising to pay the plaintiff the outstanding sum. The Court of Exchequer held that this deed was unenforceable, because it was tainted by the illegality of the original transaction. *Fisher v Bridges* can be contrasted with the facts of *Strongman v Sincock*, where the Court of Appeal held that the collateral agreement was genuinely independent of the original transaction.

Strongman (1945) Ltd v Sincock [1955] 2 QB 525

Facts: The defendant architect employed the plaintiff builders to convert some of his old buildings into modern homes. He promised orally that he would obtain all the licences necessary under regulation 56A of the Defence (General) Regulations 1939. The defendant did obtain a licence, but it only covered one third of the cost of the works. The defendant paid one third of the contract price for the work performed, but refused to pay the remainder. The plaintiffs brought a claim for the outstanding sum. The defendant resisted the claim, insisting that the sum could not be recovered, since the underlying contract was illegal.

Held: The Court of Appeal held that, although the main contract was illegal, the plaintiff's assurance that he would obtain the necessary licences amounted to a collateral contract, which was not tainted by illegality. Since the defendants had not been morally to blame for the failure to obtain the necessary licences, they could bring a claim under the collateral agreement.

Denning LJ: Let me say first that the builders cannot sue here on the contract to do the work, which was done in 1948 and 1949. At that time it was unlawful under defence Regulation 56A for the work to be done without a proper licence. Licences were only in force to the amount of £2,150. When work was done to the value of over £6,000 the builders and the architect were all guilty of an offence for which they might have been prosecuted. Under many decisions in this court it has been held that a builder doing work without a licence cannot recover under the contract.

The builders seek to overcome this objection by saying that there was a warranty, or (putting it more accurately) a promise by the architect that he would get supplementary licences, or that if he failed to get them he would stop the work. The builders say that on the faith of that promise they did the work, and as the promise was broken they can recover damages in respect of it.

The first question raised before us was whether there was such a promise, or warranty, as it was called. On this point the finding of the official referee was this: 'I am satisfied that when the plaintiffs agreed to do work for the defendant he assured them that he would get all licences which were necessary, and that if the work exceeded the amounts of the original licences he would apply for supplementary licences. I am also satisfied that he said that if he failed to get a supplementary licence he would instruct them to stop work. Consequently I regard the plea of warranty as being well founded'. ...

The second question is whether the builders can recover in law on this collateral promise. The promise itself was not illegal, but it is said that damages cannot be recovered for the breach of it. It is said that, if damages could be recovered, it would be an easy way of getting round the law about illegality. This does not alarm me at all. It is, of course, a settled principle that a man cannot recover for the consequences of his own unlawful act, but this has always been confined to cases where the doer of the act knows it to be unlawful or is himself in some way morally culpable. It does not apply when he is an entirely innocent party ... I think the law is that, although a man may have been guilty of an offence which is absolutely prohibited so that he is answerable in a criminal court, nevertheless if he has been led to commit that offence by the representation or by the promise of another, then in those circumstances he can recover damages for fraud if there is fraud, or for breach of promise or warranty if he prove such to have been given, provided always that he himself has not been guilty of culpable negligence on his part disabling him from that remedy.

[Counsel for the defendant] referred us to the observations of this court in *In re Mahmoud & Ispahani* [1921] 2 KB 716. On a consideration of that case it seems to me that the court only decided that no action lay upon the contract for the purchase of goods. They did not decide whether there was an action for fraud or breach of promise or warranty: and I do not think that their observations were intended to express any view on the matter.

The third question is whether the plaintiffs were guilty of negligence. I can well see that if there was culpable negligence on the part of the person seeking damages, he might not be entitled to recover ... It was contended before us by [counsel for the defendant] that on the facts of this case there must have been negligence and that in point of law the official referee ought to have found it. I think not. The official referee found: 'I do not consider that the plaintiffs in the present case have done an immoral act, nor were they negligent in not insisting on the production of supplementary licences. They had done a great deal of other work for the defendant without any question being raised with regard to the sufficiency of the licences'.

As I said at the beginning of this case, it comes very ill from the mouth of the defendant to raise this point as against the plaintiffs. His attitude was well shown by an observation which he made to the solicitor, Mr. Ratcliffe. He said: 'If the Nicholls can be bluffed they deserve to lose their money'. In other words, he was saying: 'If they were fools enough to trust in me, they ought to lose their money'. That is a very wrong attitude for a professional man, an architect, to take up. It shows quite clearly that on his own admission he has misled them and now seeks to turn it to his own advantage. In my judgment, his objection fails. On the findings of the official referee, the plaintiffs were entirely innocent people who were led into this unfortunate illegality by the representation of the architect, amounting to a collateral contract, that he would get the licences. That contract not having been fulfilled, I see no objection in point of law to the plaintiffs recovering the damages, and I think that the appeal should be dismissed.

Although the Court of Appeal arguably reached an instinctively just result, the decision in the case raised a number of difficulties. First, what was the consideration for the architect's promise under the collateral contract? Presumably, it was the fulfilment of the building obligation, but the builders were already obliged to do this under the main contract (*Stilk v Myrick* [1809] 2 Camp 317). The builders could argue, of course, that the main agreement was void for illegality, and therefore they were under no obligation to do the work, but this still leaves us with the problem that it is very odd to speak of a 'collateral contract' when there was no main contract to which it was 'collateral'.

Second, the decision was difficult to reconcile with the outcome in *Re Mahmoud & Ispahani* [1921] 2 KB 716. Denning LJ sought to distinguish *Re Mahmoud* on the ground that the court in that case had not been asked to consider whether there had been a breach of a collateral warranty. Does that mean that recovery would have been possible had the plaintiff argued for the existence of a collateral warranty? Professors Peel and Treitel (Peel, E, *Treitel: The Law of Contract*, 14th edn, 2015, London: Sweet & Maxwell, p 608) have argued that this should not follow:

> [T]o allow the innocent party to sue on a 'collateral warranty' in a case like *Re Mahmoud and Ispahani* would be quite inconsistent with the rationale of the rule denying him a remedy on the contract. It would be mere sophistry to say: we will protect the public interest by denying a remedy on the contract, but we will also protect the innocent claimant by giving him as good a remedy on a collateral warranty. This remedy should be granted only where it will provide no incentive to do the illegal act and where the innocent party was not careless.

The collateral contract is a powerful weapon in the hands of the courts. In *Strongman v Sincock*, Birkett LJ expressed his view that 'it is a very good thing that in almost every case where a litigant comes without merit the court does its very best to see that justice is done'. The collateral contract can be a judicial device for ensuring that justice is done. As such, its scope and application will be strictly limited (although cf. the need to use it in this context following *Patel v Mirza* [2016] UKSC 42).

13.4.1.3 Illegal purpose not yet carried out

Prior to the decision of the Supreme Court in *Patel v Mirza* [2016] UKSC 42, it seemed that a claimant may have been able to recover money paid or goods transferred under an illegal contract if he was able to show that he had withdrawn from the contract before it had been substantially performed. This is sometimes referred to as the *locus poenitentiae* ('the space for repentance'). There were, it seemed, two traditional requirements; the withdrawal must be:

(a) on time; and
(b) on a voluntary basis.

13.4.1.3.1 On time

Withdrawal must have been made before the illegal purpose is carried out.

***Taylor v Bowers* (1876) 1 QBD 291**

Facts: The plaintiff was in dire financial circumstance. In order to defraud his creditors, he made a fictitious assignment of his stock to a friend. Meetings of the creditors had already taken place, but no compromise had been reached. In the meantime, the friend had mortgaged the stock to the defendant, who was aware of the fictitious assignment. The plaintiff sought to recover the stock from the defendant.

Held: The Court of Appeal held that, because the fraudulent purpose had not been carried out, the plaintiff was not relying on the illegal transaction and was therefore entitled to recover his goods.

Mellish LJ: If money is paid or goods delivered for an illegal purpose, the person who had so paid the money or delivered the goods may recover them back before the illegal purpose is carried out; but if he waits till the illegal purpose is carried out, or if he seeks to enforce the illegal transaction, in neither case can he maintain an action; the law will not allow that to be done. In the present action the facts come within the first alternative; and I am of opinion that the Queen's Bench Division has properly held, that the plaintiff does not require the aid of the illegal transaction, but is really bringing the action to set it aside.

The case was followed by the Court of Appeal in *Tribe v Tribe* [1996] Ch 107, where the plaintiff transferred shares to his son in order to keep them out of the hands of his landlords, who were expected to be seeking substantial contributions towards the cost of repairs on property rented by the father. In the event, the repairs were not required, and the plaintiff sought to recover the shares from his son. The Court of Appeal, following *Taylor v Bowers* and *Tinsley v Milligan*, allowed the father to recover the shares. Millett LJ said: 'The transferor can lead evidence of the illegal purpose whenever it is necessary for him to do so provided that he has withdrawn from the transaction before the illegal purpose has been *wholly or partly* carried into effect'. When the illegal purpose had been substantially carried into effect, recovery would not be allowed.

Kearley v Thomson (1890) 24 QBD 742

Facts: The defendant firm of solicitors was acting on behalf of a credit or against a bankrupt named Clarke. The plaintiff, a friend of Clarke's, agreed to pay the defendants their costs, in return for which they would neither appear at the public examination of Clarke, nor oppose his order for discharge. The defendants, on receiving the promised payment, did not appear at Clarke's examination, in accordance with their illegal agreement. The plaintiff subsequently changed his mind and sought to recover the money he had paid prior to the application for Clarke's discharge.

Held: The Court of Appeal held that the illegal purpose of the agreement concerned interference with the course of justice. Since this purpose had been substantially achieved, the withdrawal came too late.

Fry LJ: What is the condition of things if the illegal purpose has been carried into effect in a material part, but remains unperformed in another material part? As I have already pointed out in the present case, the contract was that the defendants should not appear at the public examination of the bankrupt or at the application for an order of discharge. It was performed as regards the first; but the other application has not yet been made. Can it be contended that, if the illegal contract has been partly carried into effect and partly remains unperformed, the money can still be recovered? In my judgment it cannot be so contended with success ... I hold, therefore, that where there has been a partial carrying into effect of an illegal purpose in a substantial manner, it is impossible though there remains something not performed, that the money paid under that illegal contract can be recovered back.

13.4.1.3.2 On a voluntary basis

For a long time, it seemed that the second requirement for a valid withdrawal was that it must have been voluntary. If the purpose of the contract was simply frustrated by the intervention of the police or a third party, or by the other party's breach of contract, recovery would not be allowed (cf. *Patel v Mirza* [2014] EWCA Civ 1947 [below]).

Bigos v Bousted [1951] 1 All ER 92

Facts: The plaintiff, in contravention of s 1 of the Exchange Control Act 1947, agreed to supply the defendant with the equivalent of £150 in Italian currency. As security for his promise, the defendant deposited with the plaintiff a share certificate for 140 shares in a company. The plaintiff failed to supply the Italian currency, and the defendant's wife and daughter had to return to England sooner than they would have returned had they received the money. The defendant sought to recover the share certificate, arguing that although the contract was an illegal one, it was still executory, and therefore he was entitled to withdraw from it and obtain restitution.

Held: The court held that the reason that the illegal transaction was not carried out was due to the plaintiff's dishonesty, not to any repentance on the part of the defendant. Therefore, the defendant was not entitled to recover the share certificate.

Pritchard J: I confess that there was a time when I thought it would be right to apply to the facts of this case the reasoning of the decision in *Taylor v Bowers*, but, having considered all the authorities, I do not take that view. I think that what is to be extracted from the authorities may be stated as follows. I think that they show, first, that there is a distinction between what may, for convenience, be called the repentance cases, on the one hand, and the frustration cases, on the other hand. If a particular case may be held to fall within the category of repentance cases, I think the law is that the court will help a person who repents, provided his repentance comes before the illegal purpose has been substantially performed. If I were able, in this case, to take the view that the defendant had brought himself within that sphere of the authorities, it might well be that I would have been able to help him by saying that his repentance had come before the illegal purpose had been substantially performed, but I do not take that view. I think, however, that this case falls within the category of cases which I call the frustration case ...

On the return of the defendant's wife and daughter from Italy the whole project fell to the ground. There was no repentance which caused the contract not to be carried out. The defendant desired that it should be carried out until the plaintiff failed to do so, and, when she failed, the defendant's wife and daughter had to return to England because, as the result of the plaintiff's failure, they could no longer afford to stay in Italy. By the plaintiff's failure the whole venture was frustrated, and, in those circumstances, I do not think that the reason for this illegal contract not having come to fruition was the repentance of the defendant. The reason was that the whole object of the contract was frustrated by the failure on the part of the plaintiff to provide the lira which she had contracted to provide in Italy.

The Court of Appeal in *Patel v Mirza* [2014] EWCA Civ 1947 discussed *Bigos v Bousted* in detail with Rimer LJ stating:

44. The question for us, however, is whether it makes any difference if the claimant's withdrawal from the illegal agreement is not because of a change of mind that he no longer wishes to participate in it; but because the agreement is no longer capable of being performed at all. I have not found the answer to that easy, and my mind has wavered on it since we reserved judgment; and that we have taken rather longer to deliver our judgments than might ordinarily have been expected is at least in part explained by the fact that we considered it necessary to go back to counsel for assistance on certain questions. If *Bigos* was rightly decided, it seems to me to be an authority that comes closest to supporting the judge's decision in this case.

45. I have, however, decided that the point to which I have just referred makes no difference. That is, I consider that it is equally open to Mr Patel to rely on the wholly unperformed illegal agreement and be entitled to recover his money. It appears clear that the Court of Appeal in *Tribe* did not regard *Bigos* as establishing a principle that stood in the way of the plaintiff's claim in the case before it. In particular, I would regard as unattractive a distinction between cases (a) where the withdrawal is from an illegal agreement that is no longer needed for the purpose for which it was designed, and (b) where the withdrawal is from an illegal agreement that cannot be or is anyway not going to be performed. The drawing of any such distinction would, I consider, depend on holding that 'genuine repentance' on the part of the withdrawer is required. But I would take my lead from Millett LJ in *Tribe* and hold, in respectful agreement with him, that such repentance is not required. I consider that if, as in *Tribe*, voluntary withdrawal from an illegal agreement when it had ceased to be needed is sufficient to entitle the claimant to recover, it would be an odd distinction if a claimant were nevertheless not entitled to recover by relying on an illegal agreement that neither was performed nor could be performed. To recognise such a distinction would, I consider, require proof of a true sense of penitence, something that was not required or expected of the successful claimant in *Tribe*. Whether that was a correct course for this court to adopt might be a matter upon which some would have a different view. It appears to me, however, that the essence of what can be derived from Tribe is that, so long as the illegal agreement has not been carried into effect to any extent, the claimant can rely on it and recover. That is this case.

The majority of the Supreme Court in the same case side-stepped the issue by stating:

116. It is not necessary to discuss the question of *locus poenitentiae* which troubled the courts below, as it has troubled other courts, because it assumed importance only because of a wrong approach to the issue whether Mr Patel was prima facie entitled to the recovery of his money. In place of the basic rule and limited exceptions to which I referred at para 44 above, I would hold that a person who satisfies the ordinary requirements of a claim in unjust enrichment will not prima facie be debarred from recovering money paid or property transferred by reason of the fact that the consideration which has failed was an unlawful consideration. I do not exclude the possibility that there may be particular reason for the court to refuse its assistance to the claimant, applying the kind of exercise which Gloster LJ applied in this case, just as there may be a particular reason for the court to refuse to assist an owner to enforce his title to property, but such cases are likely to be rare. (At para 110 I gave the example of a drug trafficker.) In *Tappenden v Randall* (1801) 2 Bos & Pul 467, 471, 126 ER 1388, 1390, a case of a successful claim for the repayment of money paid for an unenforceable consideration which failed, Heath J said obiter that there might be 'cases where the contract may be of a nature too grossly immoral for the court to enter into any discussion of it: as where one man has paid money by way of hire to another to murder a third person'. The case was mentioned by the Law Commission (LCCP 189, para 4.53), but there is a dearth of later case law on the point. This is hardly surprising because a person who takes out a contract on the life of a third person is not likely to advertise his guilt by suing. But as a matter of legal analysis it is sufficient for present purposes to identify the framework within which such an issue may be decided. No particular reason has been advanced in this case to justify Mr Mirza's retention of the monies beyond the fact that it was paid to him for the unlawful purpose of placing an insider bet.

Presumably the issue of *locus poenitentiae* is not completely irrelevant to the underlying policy approach adopted by the majority in that case.

13.4.2 Severance

In some cases, the illegality only taints part of the agreement. In such situations, the courts have the jurisdiction to sever the illegal part as long as the remainder of the agreement is left substantially intact (*Henry Pigot's Case* (1572–1616) 11 Co Rep 26; 77 ER 1177). If the entire contract is tainted by the illegality, severance will not be possible. In *Napier v National Business Agency* [1951] 2 All ER 264, the plaintiff was employed to act as the defendant's secretary and accountant at a salary of £13 a week together with £6 a week for expenses. Both parties knew that the plaintiff's expenses would never reach £6 a week, but this provision was included in order to defraud the Inland Revenue. Following his summary dismissal, the plaintiff brought a claim for payment in lieu of notice. The Court of Appeal denied the claim on the basis that the whole agreement was tainted by illegality. Sir Raymond Evershed MR said:

> [T]he further point arises whether the terms of the agreement relating to the two branches of the plaintiff's reward can be severed, ie, whether the plaintiff can reject the tainted part of the contract relating to the £6 a week for expenses, and sue only, as he has done, in respect of the £13 a week for remuneration simply so called. I think the answer to that point is in the negative. The contract is, to my mind, not severable. It cannot properly be treated as consisting of two separate and distinct bargains, and, therefore, although it is true that the plaintiff sues only in respect of £13 a week, he is really seeking to enforce a contract which is tainted to the extent I have mentioned. It being so tainted, I think that the court will not enforce it at his suit.

By contrast, in *Carney v Herbert* [1985] AC 301, severance was permitted. The case concerned a contract for the sale of shares by instalments. The sellers asked for security for the payment of these instalments, but the security given was illegal under s 67 of the Companies Act 1961. The Privy Council held that the illegal security could be severed from the contract for the purchase of shares. The defendant therefore remained liable to pay the purchase price of the shares. Lord Brightman concluded:

> The plaintiffs wanted only the purchase money. It made no difference to the plaintiffs, or to the nature of the transaction, what security was provided so long as it was satisfactory security. The mortgage did not go to the heart of the transaction, and its elimination would leave unchanged the subject matter of the contract and the primary obligations of the vendors and the purchaser. The debenture is therefore capable of being severed from the remainder of the transaction and its illegality does not taint the whole contract. There is no public policy objection to the enforcement of the contract from which the debenture has been divorced.

The possibility of severance most commonly arises in cases concerning contracts in restraint of trade, which are beyond the scope of this chapter. Interestingly, it seems that, until recently, a more restrictive approach to severance was taken, to some extent, in the context of restraint of trade. This was considered recently by the Supreme Court in *Egon Zehnder Ltd v Tillman* [2019] UKSC 32 with Lord Wilson JSC (with whom Baroness Hale PSC, Lord Kerr, Lord Briggs and Lady Arden JJSC agreed) stating:

> **54.** Where part of a contract is unenforceable, the enforceability of the remainder represents an issue which arises far more widely than in contracts of employment. In *Carney v Herbert* [1985] AC 301 the problem was that the security for payment of the price, for which a contract for the sale of shares had provided, was not only a guarantee but also mortgages which were statutorily illegal. The Privy Council indorsed a decision of the Supreme Court of New South Wales that the provision for mortgages could be severed and removed from the contract, with the result that the guarantee should be enforced. Lord Brightman, who delivered the

judgment of the Board, observed at p 309 that tests for determining severability in certain types of case were not always applied satisfactorily in others. But then, with hesitation, he suggested at p 317:

> 'that, as a general rule, where parties enter into a lawful contract ... and there is an ancillary provision which is illegal but exists for the exclusive benefit of the plaintiff, the court may and probably will, if the justice of the case so requires, and there is no public policy objection, permit the plaintiff ... to enforce the contract without the illegal provision'.

55. It is clear that considerations of public policy drove the evolution of the doctrine under common law that post-employment restraints of trade were, unless reasonable, void: see paras 23 to 25 above. It is less clear that, until the early years of the last century, considerations of public policy also drove a more restrictive approach to severance in post-employment restraints of trade than was adopted in other areas. Take, for example, *Chesman v Nainby* (1726) 2 Ld Raym 1456. Miss Nainby traded as a draper from her home in Drury Lane. Prior to her marriage Mrs Chesman became apprenticed to Miss Nainby. Mrs Chesman entered into a bond that, after leaving Miss Nainby's service, she would not trade as a draper, nor assist anyone else to do so, within half a mile of Miss Nainby's home in Drury Lane or of 'any other house that [Miss Nainby] shall think proper to remove to' and that, in the event of breach, she would pay Miss Nainby £100. After leaving Miss Nainby's service Mrs Chesman assisted her husband to trade as a draper elsewhere up Drury Lane. It was held in the Court of Common Pleas, and upheld on appeal first by the Court of King's Bench and then by the House of Lords itself in accordance with the opinion of its judicial members, that Mrs Chesman owed Miss Nainby £100. Applying the recent decision in Mitchel v Reynolds addressed in para 25 above, the court accepted that it was unreasonable to seek to restrict Mrs Chesman from trading, or continuing to trade, within half a mile of any other house to which Miss Nainby might at any stage move, even 'in the remotest part of the kingdom'. Nevertheless at p 1459 it upheld Miss Nainby's submission

> 'that if a bond is given, with condition to do several things, and some are agreeable to law, and some against the common law; the bond shall be good as to the doing the things agreeable to law, and only void as to those that are against the law'

56. Early in the last century, however, a much more restrictive view was suddenly taken of the availability of severance in post-employment covenants. The reasons of public policy which drove a conclusion that, unless reasonable, they were void were adopted and expanded to suggest a further conclusion that, where parts of them were unreasonable, not even the reasonable parts should usually be enforced.

...

83. Nevertheless both of the requirements which were shoe-horned into the law by the *Attwood* case were, as we have seen, to prove both instantly controversial and ultimately unsatisfactory. An inquiry whether the covenant proposed to be severed was indeed one covenant or whether in effect it was more than one covenant proved to be of elusive application, largely dependent on the eye of the beholder. Why was the list of prohibited trades in the *Attwood* case one covenant but the list of prohibited areas in each of the *Putsman* and *Scorer* cases in effect more than one covenant? And, being a question noted in para 78(e) above, why should an unreasonable restraint of insignificant proportions fail to qualify for severance just because of its place in a single covenant? The second requirement - of triviality or technicality - reflected an attempt to sideline application of the entire severance principle to post-employment restraints. It is far from clear that, even in 1913 and 1920, public policy demanded it; and in 1972 in the T Lucas case, it was rightly criticised in the strongest possible terms, following which it fell away.

84. It therefore becomes appropriate to analyse the effect of each of the three criteria indorsed in the *Beckett* case.

85. The first is that 'the unenforceable provision is capable of being removed without the necessity of adding to or modifying the wording of what remains'. This is the so-called 'blue pencil' test. Unfortunately it can work capriciously and, if the aspiration of our judgments today had been to discern in the common law a principle which can always be applied so as to produce a sensible outcome, we would have laboured in vain. In his judgment in the Divisional Court in the *Attwood* case, cited in para 61 above, Bailhache J said at p 155:

> '... the courts will sever in a proper case where the severance can be performed by a blue pencil but not otherwise. To give an illustration, a covenant 'not to carry on business in Birmingham or within 100 miles' may be severed so as to reduce the area to Birmingham, but a covenant 'not to carry on business within 100 miles of Birmingham' will not be severed so as to read 'will not carry on business in Birmingham'. The distinction seems artificial, but is I think settled'.

The distinction is indeed settled. It is inherent in the word 'severance' itself, which means cutting things up and does not extend to adding things in. The 'blue pencil' criterion is a significant brake on application of the principle; and, although it can work arbitrarily, it is in my view an appropriate brake on the ability of employers to secure severance of an unreasonable restraint customarily devised by themselves. Were it ever to be thought appropriate to confer on the court a power to rewrite a restraint so as to make it reasonable, it would surely have to be achieved by legislation along the lines of that in New Zealand which has been noticed in para 79 above.

86. The second criterion is that 'the remaining terms continue to be supported by adequate consideration'. It goes without saying that an employer who sues on a covenant made otherwise than under seal must show that he provided consideration for it. But why is it said to be a prerequisite of his ability to sever? The answer is surely to be found in the unusual circumstances of the *Sadler* and *Marshall* cases, which generated the criteria adopted in the *Beckett* case. In those two cases it was the claimant employee who secured severance of unreasonable obligations cast by the contract upon himself. In that situation the court needed to satisfy itself (and in each case it did so) that, were his unreasonable obligation to be removed, there would nevertheless remain consideration passing from him under the contract such as would support the obligation which he was seeking to enforce. In the usual post-employment situation, however, the need to do so does not arise. A claimant employer who asks the court to sever and remove part of a covenant made by the defendant employee is in no way proposing to diminish the consideration passing from himself under the contract such as is necessary to support the obligation which he seeks to enforce. In the usual situation the second requirement can be ignored.

87. The third criterion is that 'the removal of the unenforceable provision does not so change the character of the contract that it becomes 'not the sort of contract that the parties entered into at all'. This is the crucial criterion and I find it impossible to equate it with the Attwood requirement, as suggested by the Court of Appeal. In my view this third criterion was rightly imported into the general jurisprudence by the *Beckett* case and has rightly been applied by our courts ever since then, otherwise than in the decision under appeal. But I suggest, with respect, that the criterion would better be expressed as being whether removal of the provision would not generate any major change in the overall effect of all the post-employment restraints in the contract. It is for the employer to establish that its removal would not do so. The focus is on the legal effect of the restraints, which will remain constant, not on their perhaps changing significance for the parties and in particular for the employee.

13.5 Proposals for reform

In 1999, the Law Commission put out a consultation paper (Consultation Paper No 154, *Illegal Transactions: The Effect of Illegality on Contracts and Trusts*, 1999) criticising the current law in the following terms (at para 2.2):

> The rules relating to when illegality is a defence to the enforcement of contractual obligations are numerous and complex. It is difficult to extract the various principles applied by the courts and some of the decisions are hard to reconcile.

The Commission's provisional proposal was that the current rules on illegality should be replaced by a structured discretion. This is summarised in paras 1.18–1.21 of the Consultation Paper:

> 1.18 Our broad provisional proposal is that the present technical and complex rules governing the effect of illegality in relation to contracts and trusts should be replaced by a discretion. Under that discretion the court could decide whether or not to enforce an illegal transaction, to recognise that property rights have been transferred or created by it, or to allow benefits conferred under it to be recovered. We do not, however, recommend that the court should have an open-ended discretion to produce whatever it considers to be the 'just' solution. That is, we provisionally propose that, generally, illegality should continue to be used only as a defence to what would otherwise be a standard claim for a contractual or restitutionary remedy or for the recognition of legal or equitable property rights. We discuss one possible exception to this general rule (withdrawal during the *locus poenitentiae*), where illegality may act as a cause of action.
>
> 1.19 We also provisionally recommend that the proposed discretion should be structured, in order to provide greater certainty and guidance. We therefore provisionally propose that, in exercising its discretion, a court should consider: (i) the seriousness of the illegality involved; (ii) the knowledge and intention of the party seeking to enforce the illegal transaction, seeking the recognition of legal or equitable rights under it, or seeking to recover benefits conferred under it; (iii) whether refusing to allow standard rights and remedies would deter illegality; (iv) whether refusing to allow standard rights and remedies would further the purpose of the rule which renders the transaction illegal; and (v) whether refusing to allow standard rights and remedies would be proportionate to the illegality involved.
>
> 1.20 Where, however, a statute has expressly provided what should be the effect of the involvement of illegality on a transaction, we provisionally recommend that our proposed discretion should not apply. That is, we do not suggest that the courts should be able to use the discretion to override the express provisions of a statute.
>
> 1.21 We consider that these provisional proposals would have two major advantages over the present law. First, a court would be able to reach its decision on the facts of a particular case using open and explicit reasoning, giving full effect to the relevance of the illegality on the transaction. Secondly, we believe that the provisional proposals would be likely to result in illegality being used less frequently to deny a plaintiff his or her usual rights or remedies. That is, under the discretion, illegality would only act as a defence where there is a clear and justifiable public interest that it should do so.

One of the main criticisms levelled at the proposed 'structured discretion' was that it would produce uncertainty and unpredictability in commercial transactions. These concerns may have been somewhat overstated, however, as Professor Buckley has shown.

Buckley, RA, 'Illegal transactions: chaos or discretion?' (2000) 20 *LS* 155, 179–180

> The difficulties surrounding the definition of an illegal transaction, and the consequent problem of ensuring that the *scope* of any proposed reform is clear and unambiguous, might be prayed in aid by those who fear that a regime based upon statutory discretion might have a wider impact than intended and infect commercial law with destabilising uncertainty. More specifically, opponents of reform might object that rescuing parties to illegal transactions from the consequences of their activities could paradoxically give

preferential treatment to such parties as contrasted with those whose contracts fail for other reasons. The importance of ensuring that property rights remain clear, and that the policies underlying findings of illegality are not disregarded or compromised, might also be advanced as reasons for proceeding with caution. But these arguments represent a challenge to get the proposals right rather than overwhelming arguments against reform. The high degree of uncertainty which already characterises this area is apt to impose disproportionate penalties upon parties to commercial transactions. And the confused doctrines of 'reliance' and *locus poenitentiae* cause confusion in relation to the enforceability of property rights. Overall, the existing law in England relating to illegality in contract is in a chaotic state; leading the House of Lords in *Tinsley v Milligan* to call for an examination by the Law Commission. In all the Commonwealth countries – now including England – in which reform has been considered, an approach centred upon the conferring of an overt judicial discretion has been perceived to be the only route forward. Judicial attempts to compress the infinite variety of situations, with all their complexity and differing degrees of gravity, into fixed rules have merely resulted in artificial technicalities and in arbitrariness.

However, in March 2010, the Law Commission published a report (Law Com No 320, *The Illegality Defence*) where a much more limited reform was proposed:

1.4 We have reached the conclusion that it is not possible to lay down strict rules about when the illegality defence should apply. Instead, the courts should consider the policy rationales that underlie the defence and apply them to the facts of the case. On the one hand, the courts should attempt to do justice between the parties, enforcing the rights set down by law. On the other hand, the courts must not permit a claimant to profit from a wrong. They should deter illegal conduct and not allow the legal system to be abused by criminals.

Our review

1.5 This final report concludes a long-running review of the illegality defence, which has considered how the defence applies to the law of contract, unjust enrichment, tort and trusts.

1.6 In our 2009 consultative report we argued that in most areas of law, the courts could make the law clearer, more certain and less arbitrary simply by explaining the policy reasons that underlie their decisions. In contract, tort and unjust enrichment cases, we thought that the courts were usually applying the illegality doctrine in a fair way to reach the right policy outcome. We said that it was open to the courts to develop the law by explaining their reasoning in policy terms.

1.7 In the area of trusts, however, we thought there was a need for legislative reform. We provisionally recommended that the courts should be given a statutory discretion to decide the effect of illegality on trusts in at least some cases.

1.8 Our final recommendations follow the provisional recommendations in our 2009 consultative report. The recent case law shows that the courts have become more open in explaining the policy reasons behind the illegality defence. Therefore, in most areas of law, we think that the illegality defence should be left to developments in the common law.

1.9 However, for trusts law we think that there is a need for a short, targeted Bill. This report therefore includes a draft Bill to be laid before Parliament.

1.10 Given the width of the subject, we have kept this final report fairly short. Those looking for a full account of the law should read our 2009 consultative report. Those interested in the social effects of our draft Bill should turn to the impact assessment at the back of this report.

Developments in contract and tort law

1.11 Since January 2009, the House of Lords has heard two cases involving the illegality defence. As we explain in Part 3, they show that the law is developing in the way we hoped.

1.12 The first, *Gray v Thames Trains*, looked at the illegality defence in tort. The judges rejected the mechanical use of a formal test, such as whether a party must 'rely' on the illegality. As Lord Hoffmann explained, the illegality defence is based upon a group of policy reasons, which vary in different situations. In each case, the policy reasons must be considered against the facts of the case to reach a fair outcome.

1.13 The second case, *Stone & Rolls v Moore Stephens*, concerned the illegality defence in both tort and contract. Again, Lord Phillips stressed that it is necessary to look at the policy underlying the illegality defence.

1.14 Two subsequent High Court decisions, *Nayyar v Denton Wilde Sapte* and *K/S Lincoln v CB Richard Ellis Hotels Ltd*, have applied this reasoning. They seem to indicate that incremental change is taking place, as we hoped.

The illegality defence in trusts

Background

1.15 Calls for law reform arose out of the 1994 House of Lords decision, *Tinsley v Milligan*. Here a lesbian couple bought a house together using joint money. However, they registered it in the name of only one of them so that the other could claim social security benefits to which she was not entitled.

1.16 When the couple fell out, the registered owner (Ms Tinsley) sought to evict her former partner (Ms Milligan) from the house. Ms Milligan counterclaimed, on the basis that she had contributed half of the purchase money, and was therefore entitled to half the house. In legal terms, she argued that she was entitled to a beneficial interest under a 'resulting trust'. Ms Tinsley countered that Ms Milligan was not entitled to ask the court to help her enforce the trust because she had behaved illegally.

1.17 The House of Lords held that the so-called 'reliance principle' applied: Ms Milligan won, because she could prove her interest in the property without needing to 'rely' on her illegal conduct. The outcome of the case depended on the legal starting point or 'presumption' applied by trust law. In this case, once Ms Milligan had shown that she contributed towards the purchase price, the law 'presumed' a resulting trust.

1.18 However, if the relationship had been different, the courts may have been forced to reach the opposite conclusion. For example, if a father had given money to a daughter, the 'presumption of advancement' would apply. This archaic and discriminatory 19th century rule presumes that if a man gives money to his fiancée, wife or children, he intends to make a gift. The 'reliance principle' means that a father could not rely on evidence of his true intention to keep ownership of the property where this was based on an illegal motive. However, a mother in the same circumstances would be given her property back.

Problems with the law

1.19 In *Tinsley v Milligan*, the court was clearly reluctant to deprive Ms Milligan of her interest. As Lord Goff pointed out, it seemed harsh to deprive her of her life savings for a relatively minor fraud. Equally, it seemed wrong to give an unjustified windfall to Ms Tinsley who was implicated in the same fraud. Thus in standard cases, the courts tend to ignore the effect of any illegality.

1.20 However, two criticisms are made of this:

(1) In some cases the courts may be required to enforce the trusts, despite very serious illegality.

(2) In a few arbitrary cases, the claimant trying to enforce a beneficial interest will lose, even though the illegality is minor. The result depends not on the merits of the case, but on obscure legal presumptions, which are often outdated and may be discriminatory. Under human rights law, if people are to be deprived of valuable property rights, the law should be clear, proportionate, and justifiable.

1.21 There are other uncertainties. For example, in some cases, claimants are allowed their money back if they withdraw from the trust arrangement before the illegal purpose has been carried out. However, the scope of this is unclear.

Abolishing the presumption of advancement

1.22 In 2006, we considered whether the law could be made fairer simply by abolishing the presumption of advancement. However, we concluded that this would not solve all the problems.

1.23 In 2007, a House of Lords decision, *Stack v Dowden*, introduced further uncertainty into the law. The case appears to overturn the presumption that property is held on trust in the proportions to which the parties contributed towards the purchase money. Instead, in cases involving a family home, the starting point is that the property is owned by the registered owner. The non-owner is therefore required to produce evidence that the parties intended this to be different, so as to prove a 'constructive trust'.

1.24 It is difficult to tell what effect this will have where cohabitants have placed the property in one of their names for an illegal purpose. It seems that the claimant may lead some evidence of a common intention to own property jointly, but not the most direct evidence, if this is associated with the illegality. As a result, the law is uncertain and complex, and is likely to lead to arbitrary results. Some claimants will win and some will lose, depending on how far any given conversation or action reveals the illegal intention of the parties.

The social context of trust disputes

1.25 In *Tinsley v Milligan*, the issue arose in the context of the breakdown of a cohabiting relationship. Cohabitants are the group most likely to be affected by our recommendations.

1.26 In the case of married couples or civil partners, the court has a general discretion to transfer property as it thinks is fair. It does not have this discretion for cohabitants. Instead, unmarried couples are forced to rely on the complexities of trust law. In our impact assessment, we estimate that around 450,000 couples in England and Wales buy property together but place the property into the sole name of one partner. In the event of the dispute, it is then up to the party who is not the registered owner to argue that they have a beneficial interest. This may be on the basis of their contribution to the purchase price (a resulting trust) or a common intention to own the property together (a constructive trust).

1.27 However, disputes over trusts of this sort also arise in other contexts, whenever family members, friends or business partners own property together.

1.28 There is wide potential for constructive or resulting trusts to raise issues of illegality, although the actual number of cases taken to court each year is low. The parties may attempt to hide assets from creditors, or potential creditors, or from an ex-spouse. People may also use trust arrangements to evade tax or to claim state benefits to which they are not entitled.

Our recommendations

1.29 This report includes a seven-clause draft Bill to reform the law on illegality in trusts. This is a limited, targeted reform. The Bill would apply where a trust has been created or continued to conceal the beneficiary's interest for a criminal purpose. These are the circumstances in which it is easiest to abuse the trust mechanism.

1.30 We recommend that in most cases a beneficiary would be able to rely on their normal legal rights. However, in 'exceptional circumstances' the court would have a discretion to deny the beneficiary their normal right to enforce the trust.

1.31 The draft Bill sets out a list of factors that the courts may take into account, including the conduct of the parties; the value of the interest at stake; whether refusing the claim would act as a deterrent; and the interests of third parties.

1.32 Where the court decides that the beneficiary should not receive the property, the court will then have to decide to whom the interest belongs. In a simple case, involving a claimant beneficial owner and a defendant legal owner, we recommend that the beneficial interest should be transferred to the legal owner. In more complex cases we recommend that the court should be given a power to decide whether the property should belong to the trustee, the settlor or another beneficiary under the trust.

1.33 It is important that the draft Bill should not prejudice the powers of the State to confiscate the proceeds of crime. The draft Bill therefore includes a small amendment to the Proceeds of Crime Act 2002. This is designed to ensure that even if the court exercises its discretion to allow a trustee or other party to keep the property, the property can still be recovered by the State. (Summary, 1.4–1.33.)

These proposals are now rather overshadowed by the decision of the Supreme Court in *Patel v Mirza* [2016] UKSC 42.

Additional reading

Buckley, R., 'Illegality in Contract and Conceptual Reasoning' (1983) 12 Anglo-American Law Review 280.
Cohen, N., 'The Quiet Revolution in the Enforcement of Illegal Contracts' [1994] LMCLQ 163.
Coote, B., 'Another Look at *Bowmakers v Barnet Instruments*' (1972) 35 MLR 38.
Enonchong, N., 'Title Claims and Illegal Transactions' (1995) 111 LQR 135.
Furmston, M., 'The Analysis of Illegal Contracts' (1966) 16 U of Tor LJ 267.
Grodecki, J.K., 'In *pari delicto* potior est conditio defendentis' (1955) 71 LQR 254.
McLauchlan, D.W., 'Contract and Commercial Law Reform in New Zealand' (1984–1985) 11 NZULR 36.
Stewart, A., 'Contractual Illegality and the Recognition of Proprietary Interests' (1986) 1 JCL 134.
Stowe, H., 'The "Unruly Horse" Has Bolted: *Tinsley v Milligan*' (1994) 57 MLR 441.

Chapter 14

Discharge by performance or breach

Chapter contents

14.1 Introduction

In this chapter, we are concerned with the ways in which a contract may be discharged, thus freeing the parties from their obligations under it. There are four main ways in which a contract may be discharged:

1 **Discharge by agreement.** The parties may expressly agree to extinguish continuing obligations under the contract. If the contract is still executory on both sides, this will be unproblematic, because each party will be agreeing to release their rights under the contract in exchange for the other party's agreement to do the same. The situation is much more difficult, however, where the executory obligations are all on one side, as, for instance, where a window cleaner has cleaned the windows of a house as agreed but the owner has not yet paid the price. If the parties agree to discharge the contract, it seems the window cleaner will receive nothing of value in exchange for his agreement to release his rights under the contract. This issue has already been dealt with in Chapter 3, in connection with the doctrine of consideration and the equitable concept of promissory estoppel, and there is no need to discuss it further here.
2 **Discharge by frustration.** As we saw in Chapter 12, the occurrence of a frustrating event will automatically discharge the contract and free the parties from their continuing obligations under it.
3 **Discharge by performance.** If the parties have done all that they are bound to do under a contract, it will be discharged by performance.
4 **Discharge by breach.** A breach of contract may (depending on, for example, the nature of the term breached) entitle the 'innocent party' to terminate the contract.

The focus in this chapter is on discharge by performance or breach. Some textbooks treat these topics separately, but as Professor Furmston (*Cheshire, Fifoot and Furmston's Law of Contract*, 17th edn, 2017, Oxford: OUP, p 660) notes, there are good reasons to consider the topics together:

> It is easy to see that if one party completely and perfectly performs what he has promised to do, his obligations are at an end. However, important and difficult questions arise as to the effect of something less than perfect performance. From the viewpoint of the performer, this is a problem in performance but to the other party it will appear as a problem in breach, since usually a less than perfect performance will be a breach.

14.2 Discharge by performance

The most important questions we need to ask are: what constitutes satisfactory performance? Must performance conform precisely to what is stipulated in the contract? If there is some minor defect in performance, does this entitle the other party to withhold its own performance of the contract?

14.2.1 Performance must be precise and exact

The general rule is that performance must be precise and exact. If there is even a slight deviation from the terms of the contract, the innocent party may be entitled to claim that the contract has not been performed; and, on this ground, claim damages and possibly termination of the contract. The strict application of this rule can be seen in the following two cases, both of which were decided under s 13 of the then Sale of Goods Act 1893.

***Re Moore & Co Ltd and Laundauer & Co* [1921] 2 KB 519**

Facts: The defendants agreed to buy 3,000 tins of Australian canned fruit from the plaintiffs. The goods were stated as being in cases containing 30 tins each, payment to be per dozen tins. When the goods were delivered, a substantial part of the consignment was packaged in cases of 24 tins. The buyers refused to take delivery, and the dispute was referred to arbitration. The arbitrator held that there was no difference in the market value of the goods, and therefore, the delivery of the consignment was a good delivery.

Held: The Court of Appeal held that the contract was for a sale of goods by description, and that as the goods contracted for had been mixed with goods of another description, the defendants were entitled under s 30(3) of the Sale of Goods Act 1893 to reject the whole consignment.

Bankes LJ: If it is true to say, as I think it is, that this is a sale of goods by description, and the statement in the contract that the goods are packed thirty tins in a case is part of the description, there is, under s 13 of the Sale of Goods Act, 1893, an implied condition that the goods shall correspond with the description. The goods tendered did not as to about one-half correspond with that description. The effect of that is stated in s 30, sub-s 3, which provides that 'where the seller delivers to the buyer the goods he contracted to sell mixed with goods of a different description not included in the contract, the buyer may accept the goods which are in accordance with the contract and reject the rest, or he may reject the whole'.

That was the buyers' position as defined by the Act, and they rejected the whole. The question of law, as stated by the umpire, admits, as it seems to me, of only one answer – namely, that the buyers were entitled to reject the whole.

***Arcos Ltd v EA Ronaasen & Son* [1933] AC 470**

Facts: The English buyers had ordered a quantity of staves of Russian redwood and whitewood for use in the making of cement barrels. The contract description allowed some variation in the length and in the breadth of the staves, but stipulated that they should be inch thick. Most of the staves delivered were 9/16 inch thick. They were still perfectly usable for making barrels. Six months after delivery, in a falling market, the buyers sought to reject the goods on the grounds that they did not conform to the contract description.

Held: The House of Lords affirmed the decision of the Court of Appeal, holding that the buyers were entitled to demand goods matching the description in the contract and were therefore not bound to accept the consignment.

Lord Atkin: It was contended that in all commercial contracts the question was whether there was a 'substantial' compliance with the contract: there always must be some margin: and it is for the tribunal of fact to determine whether the margin is exceeded or not. I cannot agree. If the written contract specifies conditions of weight, measurement and the like, those conditions must be complied with. A ton does not mean about a ton, or a yard about a yard. Still less when you descend to minute measurements does 1/2 inch mean about 1/2 inch. If the seller wants a margin he must and in my experience does stipulate for it. Of course by recognized trade usage particular figures may be given a different meaning, as in a baker's dozen; or there may be even incorporated a definite margin more or less: but there is no evidence or finding of such a usage in the present case.

No doubt there may be microscopic deviations which business men and therefore lawyers will ignore. And in this respect it is necessary to remember that description and quantity are not necessarily the same: and that the legal rights in respect of them are regulated by different sections of the code, description by s 13, quantity by s 30. It will be found that most of the cases that admit any deviation from the contract are cases where there has been an excess or deficiency in quantity which the Court has considered negligible. But apart from this consideration the right view is that the conditions of the contract must be strictly performed. If a condition is not performed the buyer has a right to reject. I do not myself think that there is any difference between business men and lawyers on this matter. No doubt, in business, men often find it unnecessary or inexpedient to insist on their strict legal rights. In a normal market if they get something substantially like the specified goods they may take them with or without grumbling and a claim for an allowance. But in a falling market I find that buyers are often as eager to insist on their legal rights as courts of law are ready to maintain them. No doubt at all times sellers are prepared to take a liberal view as to the rigidity of their own obligations, and possibly buyers who in turn are sellers may also dislike too much precision. But buyers are not, as far as my experience goes, inclined to think that the rights defined in the code are in excess of business needs.

It may be desirable to add that the result in this case is in no way affected by the umpire's finding that the goods were fit for the particular purpose for which they were required. The implied condition under s 14, sub-s 1, unless of course the contract provides otherwise, is additional to the condition under s 13. A man may require goods for a particular purpose and make it known to the seller so as to secure the implied condition of fitness for that purpose: but there is no reason why he should not abandon that purpose if he pleases, and apply the goods to any purpose for which the description makes them suitable. If they do not correspond with the description there seems no business or legal reason why he should not reject them if he finds it convenient so to do.

It seems that only if the deviation in performance is 'microscopic' will the contract nevertheless be taken to have been performed. Section 13 of the Sale of Goods Act 1893 is now contained in s 13 of the Sale of Goods Act (SGA) 1979 (which was discussed, along with recent significant reforms, in Chapter 6). In recent years, the courts have taken a more flexible approach to the requirement that goods must meet their description (although it is not yet clear what approach the courts will adopt under s 11 of the Consumer Rights Act 2015). In *Reardon Smith Line Ltd v Hansen-Tangen* [1976] 1 WLR 989, the House of Lords refused to accept that, by analogy with s 13 of the SGA 1979, delivery of a tanker could be rejected on the ground that it was constructed at a different yard to that stipulated in the contract. Lord Wilberforce said:

> I am not prepared to accept that authorities as to, 'description' in sale of goods cases are to be extended, or applied, to such a contract as we have here. Some of these cases either in themselves (Re *Moore & Co and Laundauer & Co* [1921] 2 KB 519) or as they have been interpreted (eg *Behn v Burness* [1863] 3 B & S 751) I find to be excessively technical and due for fresh examination in this House. Even if a strict and technical view must be taken as regards the description of unascertained future goods (e.g., commodities) as to which each detail of the description must be assumed to be vital, it may be, and in my opinion is, right to treat other contracts of sale of goods in a similar manner to other contracts generally so as to ask whether a particular item in a description constitutes a substantial ingredient of the 'identity' of the thing sold, and only if it does to treat it as a condition (see *Couchman v Hill* [1947] KB 554, 559, *per* Scott LJ).

It should also be noted that s 13 of the SGA 1979 has also been mitigated to some extent by s 15A(1), which (as amended by the Consumer Rights Act 2015) provides:

Where in the case of a contract of sale –

(a) the buyer would, apart from this subsection, have the right to reject goods by reason of a breach on the part of the seller of a term implied by section 13, 14 or 15 above, but
(b) the breach is so slight that it would be unreasonable for him to reject them, the breach is not to be treated as a breach of condition but may be treated as a breach of warranty.

Section 15A places a significant restriction on a buyer's right to 'insist on their strict legal rights' (per Lord Wilberforce in *Arcos*). It is subject to a number of limitations, however, which significantly restrict its scope. First, the breach must only be slight. Second, it must be unreasonable for the buyer to reject the goods. Third, it does not apply to consumer buyers.

14.2.2 Partial performance

It follows from the rule that performance must be precise and exact, that a party who only partially performs a contract will often not be entitled to payment.

***Cutter v Powell* (1795) 6 Term Rep 320; [1775–1802] All ER Rep 159**

Facts: The defendant agreed to pay Mr Cutter 30 guineas in return for him serving as second mate on a voyage from Jamaica to Liverpool. The ship 'Governor Party' set sail from Kingston on 2nd August 1793 and arrived at Liverpool on 9th October 1793. Mr Cutter died on 20 September, 19 days prior to the ship's arrival at Liverpool. Mr Cutter's widow brought an action to recover a proportion of the contract price.

Held: The Court held that Mr Cutter had undertaken an entire obligation and completion of the voyage was a condition precedent for payment. Since Mr Cutter had not completed the voyage, his widow was not entitled to recover the contract price.

Lord Kenyon CJ: [I]t seems to me at present that the decision of this case may proceed on the particular words of this contract and the precise facts here stated, without touching marine contracts in general. That where the parties have come to an express contract none can be implied has prevailed so long as to be reduced to an axiom in the law. Here the defendant expressly promised to pay the intestate thirty guineas, provided he proceeded, continued and did his duty as second mate in the ship from Jamaica to Liverpool; and the accompanying circumstances disclosed in the case are that the common rate of wages is four pounds per month, when the party is paid in proportion to the time he serves: and that this voyage is generally performed in two months. Therefore if there had been no contract between these parties, all that the intestate could have recovered on a *quantum meruit* for the voyage would have been eight pounds; whereas here the defendant contracted to pay thirty guineas provided the mate continued to do his duty as mate during the whole voyage, in which case the latter would have received nearly four times as much as if he were paid for the number of months he served. He stipulated to receive the larger sum if the whole duty were performed, and nothing unless the whole of that duty were performed: it was a kind of insurance. On this particular contract my opinion is formed at present; at the same time I must say that if we were assured the notes are in universal use, and that the commercial world have received and acted upon them in a different sense, I should give up my own opinion.

Ashurst J: We cannot collect that there is any custom prevailing among merchants on these contracts; and therefore we have nothing to guide us but the terms of the contract itself. This is a written contract, and it speaks for itself. And as it is entire, and as the defendant's promise depends on a condition precedent to be performed by the other party, the condition must be performed before the other party is entitled to receive any thing under it. It has been argued however that the plaintiff may now recover on a *quantum meruit* but she has no right to desert the agreement; for wherever there is an express contract the parties must be guided by it; and one party cannot relinquish or abide by it as it may suit his advantage. Here the intestate was by the terms of his contract to perform a given duty before he could call upon the defendant to pay him any thing; it was a condition precedent, without performing which the defendant is not liable. And that seems to me to conclude the question: the intestate did not perform the contract on his part; he was not indeed to blame for not doing it; but still as this was a condition precedent, and as he did not perform it, his representative is not entitled to recover.

The contract was interpreted as being an 'entire contract'. Cutter was only entitled to payment upon completion of the voyage. The court justified this result on the ground that the promised payment was vastly in excess of the market rate for such a voyage. The court viewed the contract as being something of a gamble; Cutter agreeing to take the chance of a larger sum at the end of the voyage, rather than accepting a smaller wage payable on a weekly basis. This reasoning has been doubted by Professor Dockray ('*Cutter v Powell*: a trip outside the text' (2001) 117 LQR 664, 673), who has pointed out that the court overlooked the fact that Cutter's special skill as a carpenter would have been of special value to Powell:

> Thomas Cutter had a special value to Powell as a second mate since as well as being a seaman, he was also a shipwright, a necessary skill in wooden ships on long voyages and especially valued in slave ships, in which the carpenter was responsible amongst other things for the secure construction of the 'rooms' below the main deck in which slaves were confined, and for the barricade on deck that was usually erected to guard against a revolt. The normal rate of pay for the carpenter on a Liverpool slave ship in 1792 was up to £10 a month for a round trip. This and the evidence of rates on pay in Jamaica after February 1793 make the offer of 30 guineas for 10 weeks work, in war-time, on an old ship not sailing in convoy, appear less extraordinary that it seemed to the court.

Whether or not the court was correct to construe the agreement as an 'entire contract', the case has subsequently been taken to lay down a general rule that nothing is payable under an 'entire contract' until the contract has been performed in full.

14.2.2.1 Severable obligations

The rule in *Cutter v Powell* will only apply if the contract is 'entire'. If it is severable or divisible, the party in breach may be able to recover payment for each part of the performance provided. Most contracts of employment will be treated as severable, and the employee will be entitled to recover payment for the period actually served. Indeed, had the contract in *Cutter v Powell* specified a certain rate per week, rather than a lump sum on completion, it is highly likely that Cutter's widow would have been able to recover. In *Taylor v Laird* (1856) 1 H & N 266 25 LJ Ex 329, the plaintiff was employed to command a steamer 'for an exploring and trading voyage up the river Niger and its tributaries … at the rate of £50 per month commencing from 1st December 1857'. The vessel proceeded up the Niger under the command of the plaintiff until it reached Dagbo, at which point the plaintiff refused to proceed and abandoned the command. It was held that this was not an entire contract for the whole voyage. The contract expressly provided for payment each month, and the plaintiff was entitled to claim for the months served. Pollock CB said:

> We are of opinion that the plaintiff is entitled to a verdict for £500 on the first count, on the ground that the contract between the parties was for a monthly payment, that eight of those months had

elapsed and only seven been paid for … 'per month' means 'each month' or 'monthly', and gives a cause of action as each month accrues, which, once vested, is not subsequently lost or divested by the plaintiff's desertion or abandonment of his contract. The words are plain; and no mercantile man would doubt what was meant. But further, if this meaning is not given, the result would be, that had the plaintiff died or the voyage failed at the last moment, nothing would be payable by the defendant, because, according to his contention, the performance of the entire work contracted for was a condition precedent to the right to receive anything. This cannot have been intended.

Statute now provides that salaries may be treated as 'accruing from day to day'.

APPORTIONMENT ACT 1870

S 2 Rents to accrue from day to day and be apportionable in respect of time
All rents, annuities, dividends, and other periodical payments in the nature of income (whether reserved or made payable under an instrument in writing or otherwise) shall, like interest on money lent, be considered as accruing from day to day, and shall be apportionable in respect of time accordingly.

S 5 Interpretation of terms
In the construction of this Act –

… The word 'annuities' includes salaries and pensions.

As a result of these provisions, a person who leaves a contract of employment may be entitled to be paid *pro rata* for the work s/he has completed.

Building contracts will often be construed as entire if they provide for payment in full on completion of the work. It is possible, however, for such contracts to contain concurrent, but independent, obligations. In *Bolton v Mahadeva* [1972] 1 WLR 1009, the plaintiff had agreed to install a central heating system and to supply a bathroom suite. The central heating system turned out to be defective, and the defendant was not required to pay for this part of the contract. He was, however, obliged to pay for the supply of the bathroom suite, which was held to be a severable obligation.

14.2.2.2 Substantial performance

The doctrine of substantial performance provides a controversial exception to the rule that an entire contract must be performed in full. If a contract has been substantially performed, the promisee will not be discharged from the obligation to pay, but will be entitled to a set-off, or a counterclaim, for damages in respect of any loss caused by the partial failure to perform.

***H Dakin & Co Ltd v Lee* [1916] 1 KB 566**

Facts: The plaintiff builders agreed to perform certain repairs on the defendant's house at a cost of £264. The defendant refused to pay for the work on the ground that it had not been completed to specification in three important respects: (1) the concrete underpinning was only half the contract depth; (2) the columns to support a bay window were of 4 inch diameter solid iron, instead of the specified 5 inch diameter hollow iron; and (3) the joists over the bay window were not cleated at angles and not bolted to caps and to each other. The official referee held that the plaintiffs had not performed their contract, and were therefore not entitled to recover any part of the contract price or any sum in respect of the work completed.

Held: The Court of Appeal allowed the appeal, holding that there was a distinction between failing to perform and performing badly. The plaintiffs were entitled to recover the contract price with a set-off for the loss caused by the breach.

Pickford LJ: We have been told that if we affirm this judgment we shall be upsetting all the cases which have ever been decided in regard to contracts made for payment of a lump sum. To my mind our decision does not interfere with any one of them. Certainly I have not the slightest wish to differ from the view that if a man agrees to do a certain amount of work for a lump sum and only does part of it he cannot sue for the lump sum; but I cannot accept the proposition that if a man agrees to do a certain amount of work for a lump sum every breach which he makes of that contract by doing his work badly, or by omitting some small portion of it, is an abandonment of his contract, or is only a performance of part of his contract, so that he cannot be paid his lump sum. It seems to me that there would be a performance of the contract, although some part of it was done badly, and that seems to me to be the position here.

Dakin v Lee was followed by the Court of Appeal in *Hoenig v Isaacs* [1952] 2 All ER 176. Here, the plaintiff, an interior decorator, agreed to decorate and furnish the defendant's flat at a cost of £750. The defendant refused to pay the balance of the contract price on the ground that there were a number of defects in the furniture supplied, which would cost £55 to repair. The Court of Appeal held that there had been substantial performance of the contract, and that the plaintiff could recover the contract price, subject to a set-off for the cost of making good the defects. Romer LJ said:

> [W]hen a man fully performs his contract in the sense that he supplies all that he agreed to supply but what he supplies is subject to defects of so minor a character that he can be said to have substantially performed his promise, it is, in my judgment, far more equitable to apply the *H Dakin & Co Ltd v Lee* principle than to deprive him wholly of his contractual rights and relegate him to such remedy (if any) as he may have on a *quantum meruit*, nor, in my judgment, are we compelled to a contrary view (having regard to the nature and terms of the agreement and the official referee's finding) by any of the cases in the books.

It has been argued (Peel, E, *Treitel: The Law of Contract*, 14th edn, 2015, London: Sweet & Maxwell, p 922) that *Hoenig v Isaacs* was not decided on the ground that the plaintiff had substantially performed an 'entire contract'. He claims that such an explanation of the case is based on the error that *contracts*, as opposed to particular obligations, can be entire. According to Peel and Treitel, the plaintiff in *Hoenig v Isaacs* (and by implication, *Dakin v Lee*) undertook two independent and severable obligations: an obligation as to the quantity of the work and an obligation as to its quality. The former obligation was entire; the latter was not. Since it was only the latter obligation that was breached, the fact that the obligation was substantially performed was sufficient to preclude discharge. This analysis is appealing, but it sits uneasily with Pickford LJ's judgment in *Dakin v Lee*, where his lordship recognised that there may still be 'substantial performance' of the contract, even when the contractor has breached the contract by 'omitting some small portion of it'. See also *William Clark Partnership Limited v Dock St PCT Limited* [2015] EWHC 2923 (TCC).

It is clear that the doctrine of 'substantial performance' only has a limited role to play in mitigating the harshness of the 'entire contract' rule, since it is often difficult to establish that the contract has been substantially performed.

Bolton v Mahadeva [1972] 1 WLR 1009

Facts: The plaintiff agreed to install a central heating system in the defendant's house for a lump sum of £560. The system gave off insufficient and uneven heat, and also caused fumes in one of the rooms. The defendant refused to pay for the work. At first instance, the judge held that the plaintiff was entitled to recover the contract price (less the cost of rectifying the defects) since he had substantially performed the contract.

Held: The Court of Appeal allowed the appeal. The plaintiff was not entitled to recover, as there had been no substantial performance.

Cairns LJ: In considering whether there was substantial performance I am of opinion that it is relevant to take into account both the nature of the defects and the proportion between the cost of rectifying them and the contract price. It would be wrong to say that the contractor is only entitled to payment if the defects are so trifling as to be covered by the *de minimis* rule.

The main matters that were complained of in this case were that when the heating system was put on, fumes were given out which made some of the living rooms (to put it at the lowest) extremely uncomfortable and inconvenient to use; secondly, that by reason of there being insufficient radiators and insufficient insulation, the heating obtained by the central heating system was far below what it should have been ...

Now, certainly it appears to me that the nature and amount of the defects in this case were far different from those which the court had to consider in *H Dakin & Co Ltd v Lee* [1916] 1 KB 566 and *Hoenig v Isaacs* [1952] 2 All ER 176. For my part, I find it impossible to say that the judge was right in reaching the conclusion that in those circumstances the contract had been substantially performed. The contract was a contract to install a central heating system. If a central heating system when installed is such that it does not heat the house adequately and is such, further, that fumes are given out, so as to make living rooms uncomfortable, and if the putting right of those defects is not something which can be done by some slight amendment of the system, then I think that the contract is not substantially performed.

Sachs LJ: When ... one looks at the aggregate of the number of defects that [the trial judge] held to have been established, at the importance of some of those defects, and at the way in which some of them prevented the installation being one that did what was intended, I find myself, like Cairns LJ, quite unable to agree that there was a substantial performance by the plaintiff of this lump sum contract. It is not merely that so very much of the work was shoddy, but it is the general ineffectiveness of it for its primary purpose that leads me to that conclusion.

It is interesting to note that the defect in *Bolton v Mahadeva* was a defect as to the quality of the plaintiff's work, not as to its quantity. The plaintiff had fitted a complete central heating system, but it was so defective that it failed to fulfil its 'primary purpose'. It is thus clear that a serious defect as to quality may be construed as constituting only partial performance of an entire contract.

The doctrine of substantial performance is rarely used in practice (for a well-known example of its use, see *Williams v Roffey Bros & Nicholls (Contractors) Ltd* [1991] 1 QB 1). This is probably because the doctrine is difficult to reconcile with the general rule that nothing is payable under an 'entire' contract until it has been fully performed. As Beatson, Burrows and Cartwright (*Anson's Law of Contract*, 30th edn, 2016, Oxford OUP, at p 480) note, the doctrine of substantial performance effectively sets aside the contractual allocation of risks. For this reason, it might be suggested that the doctrine should either be restricted or abolished. In its place, the courts might develop the rules allowing for restitution under contracts discharged for breach. It is to these rules that we now turn.

14.2.2.3 Restitution of benefits in kind

Can a party who renders incomplete performance under an entire contract claim restitution for the value of their partial performance? It seems that, in certain circumstances, s/he may do so, as long as the non-breaching party voluntarily accepted the benefits conferred.

Christy v Row (1808) 1 Taunt 300; 127 ER 849

Facts: The case concerned a contract of carriage in relation to seven keels of coal from Shields to Hamburg. The ship was prevented by restraints of princes from reaching Hamburg. At the defendant's request, the plaintiff delivered the cargo to Gluckstadt.

Held: The court held that the plaintiff was entitled to recover freight at the contract rate of £20 per keel.

Mansfield CJ: The master then having delivered, and the consignees having accepted, this part of the cargo, is the master to receive nothing for carrying it? I can find no justice in that: it might as well be contended that if goods are sent to Exeter, and the consignee meets, and takes them at Honiton, the waggon must proceed empty to Exeter, or the carrier be entitled to nothing. But it is said, that the true meaning of the agreement and the bill of lading, taken together, is, not that the Defendant should be liable, but that the freight should be taken by Ross and Schleiden. What then is the meaning of the agreement, by which the freighter positively undertakes that the freight shall be paid for, after the rate of £20 per keel, and that, by a good bill? To say that the Defendant is not liable, would be wholly to do away this contract. I therefore think that the Plaintiff is entitled to recover £140 given him for the freight of the seven keels.

This case did not concern a breach of contract, since the parties had included an exclusion clause in the contract for 'restraints of princes and rulers'. Nevertheless, the case did establish the important principle that a person who voluntarily accepts partial or defective performance of a contract may be required to make some payment for it (cf. *Diamandis v Wills* [2015] EWHC 312 (Ch), where no claim was possible as the situation was still governed by the original contract). The plaintiff in *Christy v Row* recovered the full freight, but later cases have established that the claimant is only entitled to freight *pro rata* for the proportion of the voyage actually completed. Mansfield CJ said that liability was based on a fresh agreement involving an implied promise to pay for the benefits received. This implied contract analysis of restitutionary liability has since been rejected by the courts in favour of an analysis based on unjust enrichment.

Restitution will generally (see J Beatson, A Burrows and J Cartwright, *Anson's Law of Contract*, 30th edn, 2016, Oxford: OUP, p 482) not be available for partial performance if the party not in breach has no option other than to accept the performance, as seen in *Sumpter v Hedges*.

Sumpter v Hedges [1898] 1 QB 673

Facts: The plaintiff, a builder, agreed to build two houses and stables on the defendant's land for £565. The plaintiff did work to the value of £333, but then abandoned the contract because he had no money left. The defendant finished the building work himself using materials that the plaintiff had left behind at the premises. The plaintiff brought a claim for the value of the materials and the value of the work he had done. At first instance, the judge allowed the claim for the value of the materials, but refused to award a *quantum meruit* in respect of the work which the plaintiff had done on the buildings.

Held: The Court of Appeal dismissed the appeal and refused to award the plaintiff a *quantum meruit* for the work he had done.

Collins LJ: I think the case is really concluded by the finding of the learned judge to the effect that the plaintiff had abandoned the contract. If the plaintiff had merely broken his contract in some way so as not to give the defendant the right to treat him as having abandoned the contract, and the defendant had then proceeded to finish the work himself, the plaintiff might perhaps have been entitled to sue on a *quantum meruit* on the ground that the defendant had taken the benefit of the work done. But that is not the present case. There are cases in which, though the plaintiff has abandoned the performance of a contract, it is possible for him to raise the inference of a new contract to pay for the work done on a *quantum meruit* from the defendant's having taken the benefit of that work, but, in order that that may be done, the circumstances must be such as to give an option to the defendant to take or not to take the benefit of the work done. It is only where the circumstances are such as to give that option that there is any evidence on which to ground the inference of a new contract. Where, as in the case of work done on land, the circumstances are such as to give the defendant no option whether he will take the benefit of the work or not, then one must look to other facts than the mere taking the benefit of the work in order to ground the inference of a new contract. In this case I see no other facts on which such an inference can be founded. The mere fact that a defendant is in possession of what he cannot help keeping, or even has done work upon it, affords no ground for such an inference. He is not bound to keep unfinished a building which in an incomplete state would be a nuisance on his land. I am therefore of opinion that the plaintiff was not entitled to recover for the work which he had done.

The result in *Sumpter v Hedges* appears to be rather unfair. The defendant had clearly been benefited by the plaintiff's work, having received a considerable part of what he had bargained for. Indeed, the consequence of denying restitution was that the buildings were constructed at a price considerably less than the defendant had contracted for.

14.2.3 Time of performance

Once the contractually stipulated time for performance has passed, the party who has unjustifiably failed to perform will usually be liable to pay damages for breach. In addition, the innocent party may be entitled to terminate the contract for breach if it is held that 'time was of the essence' of the contract.

The common law took the view that, unless the parties had expressed a contrary intention, time was of the essence of the contract (*Parkin v Thorold* [1852] 16 Beav 59; 51 ER 698). Equity took the opposite view, holding that time was not of the essence of the contract unless the parties had specifically made it so. This meant that, where it could do so without injustice, equity decreed specific performance, notwithstanding the failure of the plaintiff to meet the contractually stipulated time for completion (*Stickney v Keeble* [1915] AC 386). The administration of equity and the common law was fused by the Judicature Acts 1873 and 1875, and the supremacy of equity was confirmed by s 25(11) of the 1873 Act, which provided:

> Generally in all matters not herein-before particularly mentioned, in which there is any conflict or variance between the rules of equity and the rules of the common law with reference to the same matter, the rules of equity shall prevail.

Section 41 of the Law of Property Act 1925 provides:

s 41 Stipulations not of the essence of a contract
Stipulations in a contract, as to time or otherwise, which according to rules of equity are not deemed to be or to have become of the essence of the contract, are also construed and have effect at law in accordance with the same rules.

Section 10 of the SGA 1979 also confirms that time is not of the essence of a contract of sale unless the parties expressly provide otherwise:

s 10 Stipulations about time

(1) Unless a different intention appears from the terms of the contract, stipulations as to time of payment are not of the essence of a contract of sale.

(2) Whether any other stipulation as to time is or is not of the essence of the contract depends on the terms of the contract.

(3) In a contract of sale 'month' *prima facie* means calendar month.

Note also s 28 of the Consumer Rights Act 2015, particularly s 28(6):

(1) This section applies to any sales contract.

(2) Unless the trader and the consumer have agreed otherwise, the contract is to be treated as including a term that the trader must deliver the goods to the consumer.

(3) Unless there is an agreed time or period, the contract is to be treated as including a term that the trader must deliver the goods –
(a) without undue delay, and
(b) in any event, not more than 30 days after the day on which the contract is entered into.

(4) In this section –
- (a) an 'agreed' time or period means a time or period agreed by the trader and the consumer for delivery of the goods;
- (b) if there is an obligation to deliver the goods at the time the contract is entered into, that time counts as the 'agreed' time.

(5) Subsections (6) and (7) apply if the trader does not deliver the goods in accordance with subsection (3) or at the agreed time or within the agreed period.

(6) If the circumstances are that –
- (a) the trader has refused to deliver the goods,
- (b) delivery of the goods at the agreed time or within the agreed period is essential taking into account all the relevant circumstances at the time the contract was entered into, or
- (c) the consumer told the trader before the contract was entered into that delivery in accordance with subsection (3), or at the agreed time or within the agreed period, was essential, then the consumer may treat the contract as at an end.

(7) In any other circumstances, the consumer may specify a period that is appropriate in the circumstances and require the trader to deliver the goods before the end of that period.

(8) If the consumer specifies a period under subsection (7) but the goods are not delivered within that period, then the consumer may treat the contract as at an end.

(9) If the consumer treats the contract as at an end under subsection (6) or (8), the trader must without undue delay reimburse all payments made under the contract.

(10) If subsection (6) or (8) applies but the consumer does not treat the contract as at an end –
- (a) that does not prevent the consumer from cancelling the order for any of the goods or rejecting goods that have been delivered, and
- (b) the trader must without undue delay reimburse all payments made under the contract in respect of any goods for which the consumer cancels the order or which the consumer rejects ...

Section 41 of the Law of Property Act 1925 was considered in the following case:

***United Scientific Holdings Ltd v Burnley Borough Council* [1978] AC 904**

Facts: The appellants had leased premises to the respondents for 99 years at a rent of £1,000 per year from 31 August 1962. The lease contained a rent review clause which provided that during the year preceding the second and subsequent 10-year periods of the lease, the appellants could take steps to activate the machinery for a rent review if they wished to raise the rent. The appellants took no steps to implement the rent review until 12 October 1972. The respondents argued that time was of the essence, and that since the appellants had not acted in time, they were debarred from raising the rent for the following ten years. At first instance, the judge held that time was of the essence. This decision was upheld by the Court of Appeal.

Held: The House of Lords allowed the appeal, holding that there was nothing in the lease to displace the presumption that time was not of the essence of the contract.

Lord Simon of Glaisdale: My Lords, I have had the privilege of reading in draft the speech delivered by my noble and learned friend on the Woolsack. I agree with his arguments culminating in the propositions that, in general, in modern English law time is prima facie not of the essence of a contract, and that there is nothing in the two leases the subject of the instant appeals which rebuts that presumption so as to make the stipulations as to time essential to the operation of their rent review clauses.

The respective outlooks of the old common law and equity on contractual stipulations as to time diverged owing to their different historical developments ... [B]y 1873 the two systems [of law and equity] had evolved into a situation whereby in the courts of common law stipulations as to time were prima facie regarded as of the essence of a contract, while in the Court of Chancery stipulations as to time were prima facie regarded as not essential ... No doubt further evolution would have taken place in each system, and they would probably have further converged. But before any such further development could take place, both systems had to be brought together (also with those applied in Doctors' Commons) in a single code to be administered in one Supreme Court of Judicature. This involved determining which system should prevail in those respects where they were at variance. Those that were in legislative contemplation were resolved in section 25 (1) to (10) of the Supreme Court of Judicature Act 1873. But it was envisaged (correctly as it proved) that there might be other respects not within the immediate contemplation of Parliament where the rules of common law and equity diverged. So subsection (11) provided:

> 'Generally in all matters not hereinbefore particularly mentioned, in which there is any conflict or variance between the rules of equity and the rules of the common law with reference to the same matter, the rules of equity shall prevail'.

One of the contemplated differences between the rules of common law and equity was with regard to contractual stipulations as to time. That difference was resolved in favour of equity by section 25(7), replaced by section 41 of the consolidating Law of Property Act 1925, which is the provision that falls for construction in the instant appeals ...

This can only be interpreted by bearing in mind that the object of section 25 of the Supreme Court of Judicature Act 1873 was to reconcile the differences between common law and equity so that the two systems (together with the admiralty, testamentary and matrimonial) could form a single coherent code. This merely reinforces the plain and ordinary sense of the words. I cannot read section 41 of the Law of Property Act as meaning other than that, whenever contractual stipulations as to time fall for consideration in any court, they shall not be construed as essential, except where equity would before 1875 have so construed them – ie, only when the strict observance of the stipulated time for performance was a matter of express agreement or of necessary implication.

In my view the modern law in the case of contracts of all types is correctly summarised in *Halsbury's Laws of England*, 4th edn, vol 9, para 481, p 338:

> 'Time will not be considered to be of the essence unless: (1) the parties expressly stipulate that conditions as to time must be strictly complied with; or (2) the nature of the subject matter of the contract or the surrounding circumstances show that time should be considered to be of the essence;' …

Lord Fraser of Tullybelton: I consider that section 41 should now be taken to mean what it appears to say and that the law is correctly summarised in the following passage from *Halsbury's Laws of England*, 4th edn, vol 9, para 481:

> 'The modern law, in the case of contracts of all types, may be summarised as follows. Time will not be considered to be of the essence unless: (1) the parties expressly stipulate that conditions as to time must be strictly complied with; or (2) the nature of the subject matter of the contract or the surrounding circumstances show that time should be considered to be of the essence; or (3) a party who has been subject to unreasonable delay gives notice to the party in default making time of the essence' …

Clearly neither the first nor the third of these exceptions is applicable to either of the instant appeals. The question is whether the nature of the subject matter or the surrounding circumstances of rent review clauses as a class show that all or any stipulations as to time in such clauses normally fall within the second exception … It was argued on behalf of the respondents … that tenants would be seriously prejudiced if the new rent were not ascertained before the review date because they would not know the amount of their liability for the future. This argument carried considerable weight with the Court of Appeal in the *Burnley* case. But I think, with respect, that the prejudice likely to be caused to the tenant by the rent not being ascertained until after the review date has been exaggerated and that the likely prejudice to the landlord has been understated. In time of inflation it is to be expected that the landlord will call for a review on every occasion where he is entitled to do so, especially if (as in both the instant appeals) a review cannot lead to the rent being reduced below the level that would prevail if there were no review. So far as the tenant is concerned, he will of course want to know the amount of his liability but he will normally be able with the aid of skilled advice to arrive at a reasonably close estimate of the current market rent. So far as the landlord is concerned, he may be very seriously prejudiced by delay in ascertaining the reviewed rent if, as is usual, it is higher than the former rent, because he will be unable to collect the reviewed rent until it has been ascertained, and any delay will keep him out of his money representing the difference between it and the former rent. Conversely the tenant will have the use of the money until the reviewed rent has been ascertained …

As the substance of a review clause is, in my opinion, to provide machinery for ascertaining the market rent from time to time, at the intervals agreed in the interests of both parties, rather than to confer a benefit on the landlord, it seems to me that stipulations as to time ought not to be strictly enforced unless there is something in a particular clause to indicate that time is of the essence in that case …

I am of the opinion that the equitable rule against treating time as of the essence of a contract is applicable to rent review clauses unless there is some special reason for excluding its application to a particular clause. The rule would of course be excluded if the review clause expressly stated that time was to be of the essence. It would also be excluded if the context clearly indicated that that was the intention of the parties – as for instance where the tenant had a right to break the lease by notice given by a specified date which was later than the last date for serving the landlord's trigger notice. The tenant's notice to terminate the contract would be one where the time limit was mandatory, and the necessary implication is that the time limit for giving the landlords notice of review must also be mandatory …

The House of Lords refused to be bound by the common law and equitable rules prior to 1873 and preferred to look at the nature of the contract itself. Three of the Law Lords (Viscount

Dilhourne, Lord Simon and Lord Fraser) approved of the statement of the law given in *Halsbury's Laws of England*, which stated that time is not presumed to be of the essence of the contract. All three Law Lords also agreed that the presumption could be rebutted if: (1) the parties expressly stipulate that conditions as to time must be strictly complied with; or (2) the nature of the subject matter of the contract or the surrounding circumstances show that time should be considered to be of the essence. The first category is unproblematic. The second has been the cause of some debate. It has been suggested that commercial contracts should be regarded as always falling within its scope. In *Bunge Corporation v Tradax Export SA* [1981] 1 WLR 711, Lord Wilberforce said:

> I do not doubt that, in suitable cases, the courts should not be reluctant, if the intentions of the parties as shown by the contract so indicate, to hold that an obligation has the force of a condition, and that indeed they should usually do so in the case of time clauses in mercantile contracts ... [T]he statement of the law in *Halsbury's Laws of England*, 4th edn, vol. 9 (1974), paras 481–482, including the footnotes to paragraph 482 (generally approved in the House in the United Scientific Holdings case), appears to me to be correct, in particular in asserting (1) that the court will require precise compliance with stipulations as to time wherever the circumstances of the case indicate that this would fulfil the intention of the parties, and (2) that broadly speaking time will be considered of the essence in 'mercantile' contracts.

This statement is problematic for two reasons. First, it suggests a different *prima facie* rule. The starkness of this contradiction is increased, given that Lord Wilberforce expressly approved of the statement in *Halsbury* in the very same sentence. Second, Lord Wilberforce's statement is irreconcilable with the position adopted by Lord Diplock in *United Scientific Holdings*:

> I do not think that the question of principle ... can be solved by classifying the contract of tenancy as being of a commercial character. In some stipulations in commercial contracts as to the time when something must be done by one of the parties or some event must occur, time is of the essence; in others it is not. In commercial contracts for the sale of goods prima facie a stipulated time of delivery is of the essence, but prima facie a stipulated time of payment is not (Sale of Goods Act 1893, section 10 (1)) ...

Lord Wilberforce dismissed *United Scientific Holdings* as 'a case on which I do not need to comment on this occasion' (at p 716). In light of the apparent conflict between the two decisions, it is regrettable that Lord Wilberforce did not seek to elaborate further. It is probably best to view the issue as being determined on the basis of the commercial context of the contract in question, rather than of the basis of any specific presumption (see Peel, E, *Treitel: The Law of Contract*, 14th edn, 2015, London: Sweet & Maxwell, p 1026, but compare *Kuwait Rocks Co v AMN Bulkcarriers Inc* [2013] EWHC 865 at [110] [time generally of the essence in mercantile contracts], a case explicitly not followed in *Spar Shipping AS v Grand China Logistics Holding (Group) Co Ltd* [2015] EWHC 718 [Comm] and then overruled on this point by the Court of Appeal in *Spar Shipping*: [2016] EWCA Civ 982). See also *ARK Shipping Company LLC v Silverburn Shipping (IoM) Ltd* [2019] EWCA Civ 1161.

Lord Fraser also approved of the third limb of the paragraph from *Halsbury*, which stated that the presumption will not operate if '(3) a party who has been subject to unreasonable delay gives notice to the party in default making time of the essence' (compare *Behzadi v Shaftsbury Hotels Ltd* [1992] Ch 1). Normally, if time is not of the essence, late performance will only be a ground for termination if it causes a 'frustrating delay', that is, the delay deprives the party not in default of substantially the whole benefit of the contract (*Universal Cargo Carriers Corpn v Citati* [1957] 2 QB 401). If the delay does not amount to a 'frustrating delay', the party not in default can either wait until the delay becomes a 'frustrating delay', or he can give notice to the other, making time of the essence. If he does this, it will only be necessary for him to give a reasonable time for further performance rather than waiting the longer period necessary for a 'frustrating delay'. More recently, in *Urban I (Blonk Street) Ltd v Ayres* [2013] EWCA Civ 816 at [42]-[44] the Chancellor (Sir Terence Etherton) stated (in the context of a sale of land):

> **42** The Judge was in a most difficult situation. This field of law is complex. The case law has developed in significant respects over time and is not always consistent. Observations by Lewison LJ and Rix LJ in the recent case of *Samarenko* show how, even today, aspects of the law relating to time provisions in contracts for the sale of land and the relevance of notices to complete can be puzzling and that there is still room for clarification of the law.
>
> **43** As I have said, one of the reasons for the complexity and some obscurity in this area of the law is that it has steadily developed over the past 300 years. That development has not, however, always taken place in a clear and consistent way and has often been bedevilled by a lack of understanding of the different strands of equity and common law, particularly as they existed before the coming into force in 1875 of the Supreme Court of Judicature Act 1873 ('the 1873 Act'). The important cases are too numerous to set out here. It is sufficient to say that, aside from section 25 of the 1873 Act and section 41 of the Law of Property Act 1925, important milestones have included the decision or observations in *Pordage v Cole* (1669) 1 Wms. Saund. 319; *Boone v Eyre* (1789) 126 E.R 148; *Seton v Slade* (1802) 7 Ves. Jun. 265; *Davidson v Gwynne* (1810) 12 East 381; *Martindale v Smith* (1841) 1 Q.B. 389; *Parkin v Thorold* (1852) 16 Beav 59; *Stickney v Keeble* [1915] AC 386; *Hong Kong Fir Shipping Co Limited v Kawasaki Kisen Kaisha Ltd* [1962] 2 QB 26; *United Scientific Holdings Limited v Burnley BC* [1978] AC 904; *Raineri v Miles* [1981] AC 1050; *Behzadi v Shaftesbury Hotels Ltd* [1992] Ch. 1.
>
> **44** This is not the place to examine those cases and the developing jurisprudence in detail. I consider that the following principles under the current law, which are relevant to the present case, can be extracted from them.
>
> (1) It is necessary to distinguish between three types of contractual time provision. They are those which are conditions in the technical sense that any breach of them, however slight, is a repudiatory breach of contract which entitles the other party to terminate the contract immediately; those which are warranties in the technical sense that any breach of them, however serious, will only ever entitle the other party to damages and not to terminate the contract; and those which are so-called innominate terms, breach of which will only be a repudiation of the contract entitling the other party to terminate the contract if the breach deprives him or her of substantially the whole benefit which it was intended they should obtain from the contract or, in simpler language, which goes to the root of the contract: *Hong Kong Fir Shipping Co Ltd* at 69 to 70. It is a matter to be determined on ordinary principles of contractual interpretation into which of those categories the term falls.
>
> (2) Where a contract for the sale of land does not contain any specified date for completion, and subject to any contractual indication to the contrary, it is implied that completion will be within a reasonable time. There is no breach of contract until that that time has arrived: *Behzadi* at 12G–13A and 23E.
>
> (3) The moment that the contractual date for completion has passed the contract-breaker who has delayed completing is liable in damages: *Raineri*.
>
> (4) Where the contractual date for completion has passed the contract-breaker is still entitled to specific performance of the contract unless it would be inequitable to grant that relief: *Stickney* at 416, *Seton v Slade*.
>
> (5) It would be inequitable for there to be a grant of specific performance to the contract-breaker if the parties have expressly stated in the contract that the contract can be terminated forthwith upon breach of the time provision or if it is to be implied from all the circumstances that they so intended: *Parkin v Thorold* at 66. Accordingly, if, on the proper interpretation of the contract, the time provision is a condition in the technical sense I have mentioned, it is difficult to imagine that the court would

grant the contract breaker specific performance. I respectfully agree, in this regard, with the doubt expressed by Rix LJ in Samarenko at [64] as to whether equity, as a distinct species of legal principles, now has anything to add in the context of contractual terms of fundamental importance.

(6) Service of a valid written notice to complete after the contractual completion date has passed has the effect of bringing to an end the possibility of equity's intervention by the grant of specific performance to the contract-breaker. A valid notice is one which calls on the contract-breaker to perform within a reasonable period, specifying exactly what it is that party must do and what consequences will follow (that is to say, exercise of the right to terminate if he or she fails to do so): *Re Olympia & York Canary Wharf Limited (No.2)* [1993] BCC 159 at 169 C to F citing *Behzadi* at 12B to E. Statements in many of the cases and some textbooks that the service of a notice to complete makes time of the essence in equity are incorrect. Absent any relevant express provisions in the contract (as are to be found in the Standard Conditions, for example), it is contrary to all principle for one party to be able unilaterally to transform one type of contractual provision (namely, an innominate term or a warranty in the strict sense) into something different (a condition in the strict sense). Equity's role, in this context, always has been to relieve a contract-breaker against the strict legal rights of the other party, not to enhance them: *Parkin v Thorold* at 71, *Behzadi* at 12 and 24.

(7) Accordingly, absent any relevant express terms in the contract, where a completion notice has been served and expired following breach of a time provision which is an innominate term the question whether the other party can terminate the contract depends upon that party's ordinary legal rights. This depends upon two matters which, again, have often been confused in the case law. Firstly, the contract-breaker will have repudiated the contract, entitling the other party to terminate it, if and when the delay has been such as in all the circumstances to deprive the other party of substantially the whole benefit it was intended he or she should obtain from the contract, that is to say it has gone to the root of the contract. The delay may or may not have reached that point at the time that the notice to complete has expired: comp. *Peregrine Systems Ltd v Steria Ltd* [2005] EWCA Civ 239 at [15]. Secondly, the contract-breaker will have repudiated the contract, or as it is sometimes put, renounced the contract, entitling the other party to terminate it, if the contract-breaker has demonstrated an intention never to carry out the contract or, at any event, only to do so in a manner substantially inconsistent with his or her contractual obligations such as to deprive the other party of substantially the whole benefit which it was intended they should receive under the contract: *Federal Commerce & Navigation Co Ltd v Molena Alpha Inc (The Nanfri)* [1979] AC 757 at 778–779 (Lord Wilberforce citing passages from several other cases). The failure to comply with the notice to complete may be some evidence of that, but an intention to renounce must be determined in the light of the evidence as a whole: *Eminence Property Developments Ltd v Heaney* [2010] EWCA Civ 1168 at [61] to [64]. I agree with Lewison LJ's further thoughts on this aspect when, in *Samarenko* at [42], he resiled from his earlier position in *Multi-Veste 226 BV v NI Summer Row Unitholder BV* [2011] EWHC 2026 (Ch) at 201.

(8) Where, in the case of a time provision which is an innominate term, a completion notice has not been served on the contract-breaker, an award of specific performance will be available to the contract-breaker until such time as the grant of that remedy would be inequitable. It is difficult to see in principle why that would be any different to the time when the breach due to the delay is such as to go to the root of the contract.

14.3 Discharge by breach

A number of consequences may flow from a breach of contract. Every breach gives rise to a claim for damages; some will entitle the innocent party to seek an order of specific performance, and some will give rise to a right to terminate the contract. It is those breaches that give rise to a right to terminate that we are concerned with in this chapter, since on termination, the parties will be discharged from their future obligations. The innocent party will also be entitled to claim damages for losses sustained as a result of the breach of contract.

14.3.1 Effect of repudiatory breach

A breach of contract that gives rise to a right to terminate the contract is called a 'repudiatory breach'. At various times, it has been suggested that a repudiatory breach will bring a contract to an end automatically, irrespective of the wishes of the parties. For example, in *Harbutts Plasticine v Wayne Tank and Pump* [1970] 1 QB 447 Lord Denning MR said:

> In considering the consequences of a fundamental breach, it is necessary to draw a distinction between a fundamental breach which still leaves the contract open to be performed, and a fundamental breach which itself brings the contract to an end.
>
> (i) *The first group*
> In cases where the contract is still open to be performed, the effect of a fundamental breach is this: it gives the innocent party, when he gets to know of it, an option either to *affirm* the contract or to disaffirm it. If he elects to *affirm* it, then it remains in being *for the future* on both sides. Each has a right to sue for damages for *past or future* breaches. If he elects to disaffirm it (namely, accepts the fundamental breach as determining the contract), then it is at an end from that moment. It does not continue into the future. All that is left is the right to sue for past breaches or for the fundamental breach, but there is no right to sue for *future* breaches.
>
> (ii) *The second group*
> In cases where the fundamental breach itself brings the contract to an end, there is no room for any option in the innocent party. The present case is typical of this group. The fire was so disastrous that it destroyed the mill itself. If the fire had been accidental, it would certainly have meant that the contract was frustrated and brought to an end by a supervening event; just as in the leading case in 1863 when the Surrey Music Hall was burnt down: see *Taylor v Caldwell* (1863) 3 B & S 826. At the time of the fire at this mill, the cause of it was not known. It might have been no one's fault. In that case the contract would plainly have been frustrated. It would have been automatically at an end, so far as the future was concerned, with no option on either side. Does it make any difference because, after many years, the cause of the fire has been found? It has been found to be the fault of the defendants. I cannot think that this makes any difference. The contract came to an end when the mill was burnt down. It came to an end by a frustrating event, without either side having an election to continue it. It is not to be revived simply because it has been found to be the fault of one of the parties. All that happens is that the innocent party can sue the guilty party for the breach.
>
> All that I have said thus far is so obvious that it needs no authority.

The view that a repudiatory breach automatically brings a contract to an end was rejected by the House of Lords in *Photo Production Ltd v Securicor Transport Ltd* [1980] AC 827 (see also *Geys v Société Générale, London Branch* [2012] UKSC 63). It is now clear that the effect of a repudiatory breach is to give the innocent party a choice whether to terminate the contract or to allow it to continue. The right to terminate is a self-help remedy. It does not require the intervention of the courts, although the courts may exercise a supervisory jurisdiction (see Harris, D, Campbell, D and Halson, R, *Remedies in Contract and Tort*, 2nd edn, 2002, Cambridge: CUP, p 56).

The courts sometimes refer to termination for repudiatory breach as rescission, but rescission in this context is quite different to rescission for misrepresentation or undue influence. First, there will always be a right to claim damages for repudiatory breach, whereas in cases of innocent misrepresentation, rescission alone may be the remedy. Second, termination for repudiatory breach only discharges future obligations. It does not operate retrospectively, whereas rescission for misrepresentation requires the whole transaction to be undone. Lord Wilberforce explained the difference in *Johnson v Agnew* [1980] AC 367:

> [I]t is important to dissipate a fertile source of confusion and to make clear that although the vendor is sometimes referred to ... as 'rescinding' the contract, this so-called 'rescission' is quite different from rescission ab initio, such as may arise for example in cases of mistake, fraud or lack of consent. In those cases, the contract is treated in law as never having come into existence ... In the case of an accepted repudiatory breach the contract has come into existence but has been put an end to or discharged. Whatever contrary indications may be disinterred from old authorities, it is now quite clear, under the general law of contract, that acceptance of a repudiatory breach does not bring about 'rescission *ab initio*'. I need only quote one passage to establish these propositions. In *Heyman v Darwins Ltd* [1942] AC 356 Lord Porter said, at p 399:
>
>> 'To say that the contract is rescinded or has come to an end or has ceased to exist may in individual cases convey the truth with sufficient accuracy, but the fuller expression that the injured party is thereby absolved from future performance of his obligations under the contract is a more exact description of the position. Strictly speaking, to say that on acceptance of the renunciation of a contract the contract is rescinded is incorrect. In such a case the injured party may accept the renunciation as a breach going to the root of the whole of the consideration. By that acceptance he is discharged from further performance and may bring an action for damages, but the contract itself is not rescinded'.

14.3.2 Nature of repudiatory breach

What types of breach of contract entitle the innocent party to treat the contract as repudiated and, therefore, to terminate it? There are a number of different ways to approach this issue:

1 It could be left to the parties to determine what types of breach give rise to a right to terminate the contract. The problem with this approach is that, for example, often the parties do not make express provision for the consequences of breach.
2 The law could establish a set of rules which categorise terms according to what consequences will flow from their breach. The focus is on the nature of the term broken rather than on the breach itself. The problem with this approach is that, as noted below, it lacks flexibility and can lead to injustice.
3 The issue could be left to the sole discretion of the courts to be determined in light of all the circumstances of the case, including the consequences of the actual breach. The problem with this approach is that it may undermine certainty and make it very difficult for the parties to predict what consequences will flow from a breach of contract.

Historically, English law has emphasised the need for certainty and classified terms as either 'conditions' of 'warranties'. However, the courts have also acknowledged the need for flexibility and recognised the existence of intermediate or innominate terms, where the right to terminate depends on the seriousness of the breach. This section is divided into three parts. First, we will consider the traditional distinction between conditions and warranties. Second, we will trace the development of intermediate terms and finally, we will consider the role played by the parties in the categorisation of terms.

14.3.2.1 Conditions and warranties

Contract terms are traditionally labelled as being either conditions or warranties. This distinction was explained by Fletcher Moulton LJ in *Wallis, Son & Wells v Pratt and Haynes* [1910] 2 KB 1003:

> A party to a contract who has performed, or is ready and willing to perform, his obligations under that contract is entitled to the performance by the other contracting party of all the obligations which rest upon him. But from a very early period of our law it has been recognised that such obligations are not all of equal importance. There are some which go so directly to the substance of the contract or, in other words, are so essential to its very nature that their non-performance may fairly be considered by the other party as a substantial failure to perform the contract at all. On the other hand there are other obligations which, though they must be performed, are not so vital that a failure to perform them goes to the substance of the contract. Both classes are equally obligations under the contract, and the breach of any one of them entitles the other party to damages. But in the case of the former class he has the alternative of treating the contract as being completely broken by the nonperformance and (if he takes the proper steps) he can refuse to perform any of the obligations resting upon himself and sue the other party for a total failure to perform the contract. Although the decisions are fairly consistent in recognising this distinction between the two classes of obligations under a contract there has not been a similar consistency in the nomenclature applied to them. I do not, however, propose to discuss this matter, because later usage has consecrated the term 'condition' to describe an obligation of the former class and 'warranty' to describe an obligation of the latter class. I do not think that the choice of terms is happy, especially so far as regards the word 'condition', for it is a word which is used in many other connections and has considerable variety of meaning. But its use with regard to the obligations under a contract is well known and recognised, and no confusion need arise if proper regard be had to the context.
>
> This usage has been followed in the codification of the law of the contract of sale in the Sale of Goods Act ...

As Fletcher Moulton LJ notes, the drafters of the Sale of Goods Act also adopted the terminology.

SALE OF GOODS ACT 1979

> **s 11 When condition to be treated as warranty**
>
> (3) Whether a stipulation in a contract of sale is a condition, the breach of which may give rise to a right to treat the contract as repudiated, or a warranty, the breach of which may give rise to a claim for damages but not to a right to reject the goods and treat the contract as repudiated, depends in each case on the construction of the contract; and a stipulation may be a condition, though called a warranty in the contract.

The Act uses the terminology of condition and warranty to distinguish between repudiatory and other breaches (compare the Consumer Rights Act 2015, discussed above in Section 6.3.3, which does not use such terminology but explicitly sets out the remedies, or at least some of the remedies, for breach of particular statutory terms). If the term is a condition, the breach will be repudiatory, but if the term is a warranty, the breach will only give rise to a claim for damages.

At this point, it is important to note (as Fletcher Moulton LJ recognised) that the words 'condition' and 'warranty' are likely to cause confusion because they have a number of different meanings in other contexts:

Treitel, G, '"Conditions" and "Conditions Precedent"' (1990) 106 *LQR* 185

One of the most notorious sources of difficulty in the law of contract is the variety of senses in which it uses the expression 'condition'. One source of confusion is the use of the expression 'condition precedent' in both a contingent and a promissory sense; and the present writer would with respect agree with the view of Sir Robin Cooke P in the recent New Zealand case of *Robertson Enterprises Ltd v Cope* (April 6, 1989), that failure to distinguish between these two senses can lead to arguments which are 'unnecessarily complicated'. One might even regret the fact that the common law uses the expression 'condition' in a promissory sense at all; but the usage is deeply embedded in the relevant legislation and case-law. Even the concept of promissory condition is used in two senses, and it is with these senses that this note is concerned. The first relates to the order of performance, while the second relates to the conformity of the performance rendered with that promised. Where a promise relates to the time of performance, it is easy to lose sight of the distinction between these two senses, but the distinction exists even in such cases, for promises may be performed at the wrong time but in the right order. One way of reducing the difficulty is to use 'condition' with different points of contrast for the two purposes just described: that is, to contrast 'conditions precedent' with 'concurrent condition' and 'independent covenant' when discussing the order of performance (e.g. Sale of Goods Act 1979, s 28; *The Odenfeld* [1978] 2 Lloyd's Rep. 357), while contrasting 'condition' with 'warranty' (and, more recently, with 'intermediate term') when discussing problems of conformity (eg Sale of Goods Act 1979, ss 11–15). Historically, this approach gives rise to problems since references to 'condition precedent' were formerly common in discussions of the condition-warranty distinction (eg in *Bentsen v Taylor Sons & Co* [1983] 2 QB 274 at p 281). But in modern discussions of this distinction, such references have become relatively less common, and they are misleading in that 'condition precedent' (when used in relation to the order of performance) refers to an event (i.e. the performance of one party's obligation) while 'condition' (when used in relation to the conformity of performance) refers to a term of the contract (or to the content of one party's obligation).

Conditions (relating to a term of the contract) must be distinguished from conditions precedent (relating to the order of performance of the contract). The word 'warranty' can also give rise to confusion, because it is sometimes used in other contexts to refer to a 'promise' or a 'guarantee'. Care is needed, therefore, to ensure that the meaning of these words is clear when they are being used to discuss contractual terms.

A term may be classified as a condition for one of three reasons:

1 Statute provides so – see ss 13–15 SGA 1979.
2 The contract expressly states that it is – see below.
3 The court construes it as a condition.

The main factor that the courts will consider in determining whether the term should be construed as a condition will be its importance to the contract as a whole. In *L Schuler AG v Wickman Machine Tool Sales Ltd* [1974] AC 235, Lord Reid said:

> [A] condition ... is a term the breach of which by one party gives to the other an option either to terminate the contract or to let the contract proceed and, if he so desires, sue for damages for the breach. Sometimes a breach of a term gives that option to the aggrieved party because it is of a fundamental character going to the root of the contract, sometimes it gives that option because the parties have chosen to stipulate that it shall have that effect.

The traditional approach of the courts is well illustrated by contrasting the following two cases from the late nineteenth century.

Bettini v Gye (1875–1876) 1 QBD 183

Facts: The plaintiff singer, Mr Bettini, agreed to fill the part of prime tenor assoluto for the defendant's opera. Paragraph 7 of the contract stated: 'Mr Bettini agrees to be in London without fail at least six days before the commencement of his engagement, for the purpose of rehearsals'. Due to temporary illness, the plaintiff arrived four days late for rehearsals. The defendant purported to terminate the contract for breach of clause 7.

Held: The Divisional Court held that the term was not a condition, because it did not go to the root of the contract.

Blackburn J: The question raised by the demurrer is, not whether the plaintiff has any excuse for failing to fulfil this part of his contract, which may prevent his being liable in damages for not doing so, but whether his failure to do so justified the defendant in refusing to proceed with the engagement, and fulfil his, the defendant's part. And the answer to that question depends on whether this part of the contract is a condition precedent to the defendant's liability, or only an independent agreement, a breach of which will not justify a repudiation of the contract, but will only be a cause of action for compensation in damages ...

We think the answer to this question depends on the true construction of the contract taken as a whole.

Parties may think some matter, apparently of very little importance, essential; and if they sufficiently express an intention to make the literal fulfilment of such a thing a condition precedent, it will be one; or they may think that the performance of some matter, apparently of essential importance and prima facie a condition precedent, is not really vital, and may be compensated for in damages, and if they sufficiently expressed such an intention, it will not be a condition precedent.

In this case, if to the 7th paragraph of the agreement there had been added words to this effect: 'And if Mr Bettini is not there at the stipulated time Mr Gye may refuse to proceed further with the agreement'; or if, on the other hand, it had been said, 'And if not there, Mr Gye may postpone the commencement of Mr Bettini's engagement for as many days as Mr Bettini makes default, and he shall forfeit twice his salary for that time', there could have been no question raised in the case. But there is no such declaration of the intention of the parties either way. And in the absence of such an express declaration, we think that we are to look to the whole contract, and applying the rule stated by Parke, B., to be acknowledged, see whether the particular stipulation goes to the root of the matter, so that a failure to perform it would render the performance of the rest of the contract by the plaintiff a thing different in substance from what the defendant has stipulated for; or whether it merely partially affects it and may be compensated for in damages. Accordingly, as it is one or the other, we think it must be taken to be or not to be intended to be a condition precedent.

If the plaintiff's engagement had been only to sing in operas at the theatre, it might very well be that previous attendance at rehearsals with the actors in company with whom he was to perform was essential. And if the engagement had been only for a few performances, or for a short time, it would afford a strong argument that attendance for the purpose of rehearsals during the six days immediately before the commencement of the engagement was a vital part of the agreement. But we find, on looking to the agreement, that the plaintiff was to sing in theatres, halls, and drawing-rooms, both public and private, from the 30th of March to the 13th of July, 1875, and that he was to sing in concerts as well as in operas, and was not to sing anywhere out of the theatre in Great Britain or Ireland from the 1st of January to the 31st of December, 1875, without the written permission of the defendant, except at a distance of more than fifty miles from London.

The plaintiff, therefore, has, in consequence of this agreement, been deprived of the power of earning anything in London from the 1st of January to the 30th of March; and though the defendant has, perhaps, not received any benefit from this, so as to preclude him from any longer treating as a condition precedent what had originally been one, we think this at least affords a strong argument for saying that subsequent stipulations are not intended to be conditions precedent, unless the nature of the thing strongly shews they must be so.

And, as far as we can see, the failure to attend at rehearsals during the six days immediately before the 30th of March could only affect the theatrical performances and, perhaps, the singing in duets or concerted pieces during the first week or fortnight of this engagement, which is to sing in theatres, halls, and drawing-rooms, and concerts for fifteen weeks.

We think, therefore, that it does not go to the root of the matter so as to require us to consider it a condition precedent.

Poussard v Spiers and Pond (1875–1876) 1 QBD 410

Facts: The plaintiff singer agreed to play the part of Friquette in Lecocq's opera 'Les Pres Saint Gervais', commencing on or about the 14th November. The first performance was announced for 28th November, and no objection was raised by the plaintiff as to this delay. She attended several rehearsals, but was then taken ill. As a result of her illness, the plaintiff missed the remaining rehearsals and the first four performances of the opera. By the time the plaintiff was well enough to return, the defendant had found a replacement for her, and he purported to treat her failure to appear as a repudiatory breach.

Held: The Divisional Court held that the plaintiff's failure to perform on the opening and early performances went to the root of the contract and was a breach of condition.

Blackburn J: We think that the question, whether the failure of a skilled and capable artiste to perform in a new piece through serious illness is so important as to go to the root of the consideration, must to some extent depend on the evidence; and is a mixed question of law and fact. Theoretically, the facts should be left to and found separately by the jury, it being for the judge or the Court to say whether they, being so found, shew a breach of a condition precedent or not. But this course is often (if not generally) impracticable; and if we can see that the proper facts have been found, we should act on these without regard to the form of the questions.

Now, in the present case, we must consider what were the courses open to the defendants under the circumstances. They might, it was said on the argument before us (though not on the trial), have postponed the bringing out of the piece till the recovery of Madame Poussard, and if her illness had been a temporary hoarseness incapacitating her from singing on the Saturday, but sure to be removed by the Monday, that might have been a proper course to pursue. But the illness here was a serious one, of uncertain duration, and if the plaintiff had at the trial suggested that this was the proper course, it would, no doubt, have been shewn that it would have been a ruinous course; and that it would have been much better to have abandoned the piece altogether than to have postponed it from day to day for an uncertain time, during which the theatre would have been a heavy loss.

The remaining alternatives were to employ a temporary substitute until such time as the plaintiff's wife should recover; and if a temporary substitute capable of performing the part adequately could have been obtained upon such a precarious engagement on any reasonable terms, that would have been a right course to pursue; but if no substitute capable of performing the part adequately could be obtained, except on the terms that she should be permanently engaged at higher pay than the plaintiff's wife, in our opinion it follows, as a matter of law, that the failure on the plaintiff's part went to the root of the matter and discharged the defendants.

The failure of Madame Poussard to meet the obligation to be present at the opening performances of the opera was treated as much more serious than Mr Bettini's failure to meet the obligation to be present for the rehearsals. Breach of the former term went to the root of the contract, whereas breach of the latter term did not.

The categorisation of terms as either conditions or warranties is arguably a rather cumbersome procedure for determining the availability of remedies. It implies that the actual consequence of a particular breach is not a relevant factor. If a term is categorised as a 'condition', any breach of it will potentially give rise to a right to terminate the contract, no matter how trivial the breach or how easily it can be remedied. Similarly, a breach of warranty will only ever give rise to a claim for damages. The innocent party will not be entitled to terminate the contract, no matter how serious the breach or how great the loss caused. This approach has the merit of certainty, in that it enables the parties to accurately predict whether a particular breach will give rise to a right to terminate the contract. But it is also inflexible, perhaps giving rise to anomalous and unjust results.

14.3.2.2 Intermediate terms

The perceived inflexibility of the traditional categorisation led the Court of Appeal to recognise an intermediate category in 1962 in the case of *Hong Kong Fir Shipping Co Ltd v Kawasaki Kisen Kaisha Ltd*.

***Hong Kong Fir Shipping Co Ltd v Kawasaki Kisen Kaisha Ltd* [1962] 2 QB 26**

Facts: The defendant chartered a ship from the plaintiff on a 24-month time charter. The charterparty stated that the ship was 'in every way fitted for ordinary cargo service', and Clause 3 provided that the owners should 'maintain her in a thoroughly efficient state in hull and machinery during service'. The ship was delivered to the defendant on 13 February 1957, and on that date, set sail from Liverpool to Newport News, Virginia, to load a cargo of coal for carriage to Osaka. At the date of delivery, the ship was unseaworthy, because she had old engines. Her age was such that she needed to be maintained by an experienced, competent, careful and adequate team of engine room staff. There were insufficient numbers of staff and the chief engineer was inefficient and an alcoholic. As a result, repairs had to be carried out on the way to Osaka. In June 1957, following a fall in freight rates since the date of the charter, the defendant terminated the charterparty. The plaintiff brought a claim for damages for wrongful repudiation. At first instance, Salmon J found for the plaintiffs.

Held: The Court of Appeal dismissed the appeal, holding that the breach of contract was not sufficiently serious to entitle the defendants to terminate the contract.

Sellers LJ: In my judgment authority over many decades and reason support the conclusion in this case that there was no breach of a condition which entitled the charterers to accept it as a repudiation and to withdraw from the charter. It was not contended that the maintenance clause is so fundamental a matter as to amount to a condition of the contract. It is a warranty which sounds in damages.

Upjohn LJ: Why is this apparently basic and underlying condition of seaworthiness not, in fact, treated as a condition? It is for the simple reason that the seaworthiness clause is breached by the slightest failure to be fitted 'in every way' for service. Thus, to take examples from the judgments in some of the cases ... if a nail is missing from one of the timbers of a wooden vessel or if proper medical supplies or two anchors are not on board at the time of sailing, the owners are in breach of the seaworthiness stipulation. It is contrary to common sense to suppose that in such circumstances the parties contemplated that the charterer should at once be entitled to treat the contract as at an end for such trifling breaches ...

It is open to the parties to a contract to make it clear either expressly or by necessary implication that a particular stipulation is to be regarded as a condition which goes to the root of the contract, so that it is clear that the parties contemplate that any breach of it entitles the other party at once to treat the contract as at an end. That matter has to be determined as a question of the proper interpretation of the contract ... Where, however, upon the true construction of the contract, the parties have not made a particular stipulation a condition, it would in my judgment be unsound and misleading to conclude that, being a warranty, damages is necessarily a sufficient remedy.

In my judgment the remedies open to the innocent party for breach of a stipulation which is not a condition strictly so called, depend entirely upon the nature of the breach and its foreseeable consequences. Breaches of stipulation fall, naturally, into two classes. First there is the case where the owner by his conduct indicates that he considers himself no longer bound to perform his part of the contract; in that case, of course, the charterer may accept the repudiation and treat the contract as at an end. The second class of case is, of course, the more usual one and that is where, due to misfortune such as the perils of the sea, engine failures, incompetence of the crew and so on, the owner is unable to perform a particular stipulation precisely in accordance with the terms of the contract try he never so hard to remedy it. In that case the question to be answered is, does the breach of the stipulation go so much to the root of the contract that it makes further commercial performance of the contract impossible, or in other words is the whole contract frustrated? If yea, the innocent party may treat the contract as at an end. If nay, his claim sounds in damages only.

If I have correctly stated the principles, then as the stipulation as to the seaworthiness is not a condition in the strict sense the question to be answered is, did the initial unseaworthiness as found by the judge, and from which there has been no appeal, go so much to the root of the contract that the charterers were then and there entitled to treat the charterparty as at an end? The only unseaworthiness alleged, serious though it was, was the insufficiency and incompetence of the crew, but that surely cannot be treated as going to the root of the contract for the parties must have contemplated that in such an event the crew could be changed and augmented. In my judgment, on this part of his case Mr. Roskill necessarily fails.

Diplock LJ: Every synallagmatic contract contains in it the seeds of the problem: in what event will a party be relieved of his undertaking to do that which he has agreed to do but has not yet done? The contract may itself expressly define some of these events, as in the cancellation clause in a charterparty; but, human prescience being limited, it seldom does so exhaustively and often fails to do so at all. In some classes of contracts such as sale of goods, marine insurance, contracts of affreightment evidenced by bills of lading and those between parties to bills of exchange, Parliament has defined by statute some of the events not provided for expressly in individual contracts of that class; but where an event occurs the occurrence of which neither the parties nor Parliament have expressly stated will discharge one of the parties from further performance of his undertakings, it is for the court to determine whether the event has this effect or not.

The test whether an event has this effect or not has been stated in a number of metaphors all of which I think amount to the same thing: does the occurrence of the event deprive the party who has further undertakings still to perform of substantially the whole benefit which it was the intention of the parties as expressed in the contract that he should obtain as the consideration for performing those undertakings?

This test is applicable whether or not the event occurs as a result of the default of one of the parties to the contract, but the consequences of the event are different in the two cases. Where the event occurs as a result of the default of one party, the party in default cannot rely upon it as relieving himself of the performance of any further undertakings on his part, and the innocent party, although entitled to, need not treat the event as relieving him of the further performance of his own undertakings. This is only a specific application of the fundamental legal and moral rule that a man should not be allowed to take advantage of his own wrong. Where the event occurs as a result of the default of neither party, each is relieved of the further performance of his own undertakings, and their rights in respect of undertakings previously performed are now regulated by the Law Reform (Frustrated Contracts) Act, 1943.

This branch of the common law has reached its present stage by the normal process of historical growth, and the fallacy in [counsel for the defendant's] contention that a different test is applicable when the event occurs as a result of the default of one party from that applicable in cases of frustration where the event occurs as a result of the default of neither party lies, in my view, from a failure to view the cases in their historical context. The problem: in what event will a party to a contract be relieved of his undertaking to do that which he has agreed to do but has not yet done? has exercised the English courts for centuries ...

Once it is appreciated that it is the event and not the fact that the event is a result of a breach of contract which relieves the party not in default of further performance of his obligations, two consequences follow: (1) The test whether the event relied upon has this consequence is the same whether the event is the result of the other party's breach of contract or not, as Devlin J pointed out in *Universal Cargo Carriers Corporation v Citati* [1957] 2 QB 401, 434; (2) The question whether an event which is the result of the other party's breach of contract has this consequence cannot be answered by treating all contractual undertakings as falling into one of two separate categories: 'conditions' the breach of which gives rise to an event which relieves the party not in default of further performance of his obligations, and 'warranties' the breach of which does not give rise to such an event.

Lawyers tend to speak of this classification as if it were comprehensive, partly for the historical reasons which I have already mentioned and partly because Parliament itself adopted it in the Sale of Goods Act, 1893, as respects a number of implied terms in contracts for the sale of goods and has in that Act used the expressions 'condition' and 'warranty' in that meaning. But it is by no means true of contractual undertakings in general at common law.

No doubt there are many simple contractual undertakings, sometimes express but more often because of their very simplicity ('It goes without saying') to be implied, of which it can be predicated that every breach of such an undertaking must give rise to an event which will deprive the party not in default of substantially the whole benefit which it was intended that he should obtain from the contract. And such a stipulation, unless the parties have agreed that breach of it shall not entitle the non-defaulting party to treat the contract as repudiated, is a 'condition'. So too there may be other simple contractual undertakings of which it can be predicated that no breach can give rise to an event which will deprive the party not in default of substantially the whole benefit which it was intended that he should obtain from the contract; and such a stipulation, unless the parties have agreed that breach of it shall entitle the non-defaulting party to treat the contract as repudiated, is a 'warranty'.

There are, however, many contractual undertakings of a more complex character which cannot be categorised as being 'conditions' or 'warranties', if the late nineteenth-century meaning adopted in the Sale of Goods Act, 1893, and used by Bowen LJ in *Bentsen v Taylor, Sons & Co* [1893] 2 QB 274, 280; 9 TLR 552, CA, be given to those terms. Of such undertakings all that can be predicated is that some breaches will and others will not give rise to an event which will deprive the party not in default of substantially the whole benefit which it was intended that he should obtain from the contract; and the legal consequences of a breach of such an undertaking, unless provided for expressly in the contract, depend upon the nature of the event to which the breach gives rise and do not follow automatically from a prior classification of the undertaking as a 'condition' or a 'warranty'. For instance, to take Bramwell B's example in *Jackson v Union Marine Insurance Co Ltd* itself, breach of an undertaking by a shipowner to sail with all possible dispatch to a named port does not necessarily relieve the charterer of further performance of his obligation under the charterparty, but if the breach is so prolonged that the contemplated voyage is frustrated it does have this effect.

As my brethren have already pointed out, the shipowners' undertaking to tender a seaworthy ship has, as a result of numerous decisions as to what can amount to 'unseaworthiness', become one of the most complex of contractual undertakings. It embraces obligations with respect to every part of the hull and machinery, stores and equipment and the crew itself. It can be broken by the presence of trivial defects easily and rapidly remediable as well as by defects which must inevitably result in a total loss of the vessel.

Consequently the problem in this case is, in my view, neither solved nor soluble by debating whether the shipowner's express or implied undertaking to tender a seaworthy ship is a 'condition' or a 'warranty'. It is like so many other contractual terms an undertaking one breach of which may give rise to an event which relieves the charterer of further performance of his undertakings if he so elects and another breach of which may not give rise to such an event but entitle him only to monetary compensation in the form of damages. It is, with all deference to [counsel for the defendant's] skilful argument, by no means surprising that among the many hundreds of previous cases about the shipowner's undertaking to deliver a seaworthy ship there is none where it was found profitable to discuss in the judgments the question whether that undertaking is a 'condition' or a 'warranty'; for the true answer, as I have already indicated, is that it is neither, but one of that large class of contractual undertakings one breach of which may have the same effect as that ascribed to a breach of 'condition' under the Sale of Goods Act, 1893, and a different breach of which may have only the same effect as that ascribed to a breach of 'warranty' under that Act ...

What the judge had to do in the present case, as in any other case where one party to a contract relies upon a breach by the other party as giving him a right to elect to rescind the contract, and the contract itself makes no express provision as to this, was to look at the events which had occurred as a result of the breach at the time at which the charterers purported to rescind the charterparty and to decide whether the occurrence of those events deprived the charterers of substantially the whole benefit which it was the intention of the parties as expressed in the charterparty that the charterers should obtain from the further performance of their own contractual undertakings ...

The question which the judge had to ask himself was, as he rightly decided, whether or not at the date when the charterers purported to rescind the contract, namely, June 6, 1957, or when the shipowners purported to accept such rescission, namely, August 8, 1957, the delay which had already occurred as a result of the incompetence of the engine-room staff, and the delay which was likely to occur in repairing the engines of the vessel and the conduct of the shipowners by that date in taking steps to remedy these two matters, were, when taken together, such as to deprive the charterers of substantially the whole benefit which it was the intention of the parties they should obtain from further use of the vessel under the charterparty.

In my view, in his judgment – on which I would not seek to improve – the judge took into account and gave due weight to all the relevant considerations and arrived at the right answer for the right reasons.

The term in question was the undertaking as to the 'seaworthiness' of the ship. This proved to be problematic, because the term could be breached in a number of different ways. For example, the failure to supply the correct number of anchors at the time of sailing could render the ship 'unseaworthy', just as much as a major defect in the hull. Their lordships adopted three different approaches to this problem:

1 Sellers LJ adopted the most straightforward approach. He classified the term as a warranty and held that its breach only entitled the defendant to damages.
2 Diplock LJ adopted a more innovative approach. He refused to classify the term as either a condition or a warranty. Instead, he classified it as an intermediate term, holding that the remedial consequences of its breach depended on the effect of the actual breach that had occurred (the third approach outlined at the start of this section). If the breach was so serious as to deprive the innocent party of substantially the whole of the performance to which he was entitled, it would be treated as repudiatory, in the same way as if it was a breach of a condition; if it was less serious, it would give rise only to a remedy in damages, like a warranty.

3 Upjohn LJ adopted a third approach. He said that the crucial question to ask was whether the term was a condition. If it was, it automatically gave rise to a right to terminate the contract. If it was not, it did not inevitably follow that the defendant's only remedy was in damages. Instead, the court would examine the effects of the breach and determine whether the defendant ought to be entitled to terminate the contract. Lord Denning restated this approach in *Cehave NV v Bremer Handelgesellschaft mbH. (The Hansa Nord)* [1976] QB 44, 66.

The remedial flexibility provided by the latter two approaches is noteworthy. Essentially, Diplock LJ's test provides for three categories of term – conditions, warranties and intermediate terms – while Upjohn LJ's test provides for just two: conditions and intermediate terms. Upjohn LJ's test has the merit of avoiding the difficulty of distinguishing between warranties and intermediate terms.

Reynolds, FMB, 'Discharge of contract by breach' (1981) 97 *LQR* 541, 548

The word 'warranty', with its different usages in different parts of the law (eg insurance) and in ordinary speech (the manufacturer's warranty) is productive of confusion. Its prominence seems connected with the old idea that in a sale, the warranty was separate from the sale, and actionable by a separate action: but warranty in the general context of breach of contract seems to mean a little more than a contractual promise other than the central obligation of the contract, and not always even that. It is submitted that the use of the term could well be abandoned, with the simple result that the *Hong Kong Fir* test applies to all promises which are not conditions. If this is too difficult to achieve, the use of the term warranty should be retained for all contractual promises other than conditions, without any implication that there are terms *no* breach of which can ever entitle to discharge. Either route would make the phrase 'innominate' or 'intermediate term' superfluous. The existence of *three* categories is surely unnecessary.

Yet, it is Diplock LJ's approach that has found favour with the courts and the commentators.

Peel, E, *Treitel on the Law of Contract*, 14th edn, 2015, London: Sweet & Maxwell, pp 987–988

The general view is that there are three classes of contractual terms: conditions, the breach of which at common law gives rise to a right to terminate; warranties, the breach of which gives rise only to a right to damages; and intermediate terms, the breach of which gives rise to a right to terminate if it is sufficiently serious, but otherwise sounds only in damages. There is, however, support for the alternative view that there are only two categories: conditions and other terms. This view is based on the argument that the injured party may be entitled to terminate even for a breach of warranty, if the effect of the breach is sufficiently serious. There is considerable force in this argument and if it is correct a warranty may be said to resemble an intermediate term, in that the availability of termination as a remedy for breach of either type of term depends on the seriousness of the breach. Nevertheless, the weight of authority supports the continued existence of the threefold division of contractual terms. It is respectfully submitted that this is the preferable view since the distinction between warranties and intermediate terms remains for practical purposes an important one. Even if, in extreme cases, termination is available for breach of warranty, there is at least a *prima facie* rule that the normal remedy for such a breach is by way of damages. In relation to intermediate terms, there is no such *prima facie* rule; so that (to put the matter at its lowest) there is a greater likelihood that termination will be available for breach of an intermediate term than for breach of warranty.

A further point to note from the case is that Diplock LJ appeared to suggest that a term would only be classified as a condition if every breach of it would 'deprive the party not in default of substantially the whole benefit which it was intended that he should obtain from the contract'.

This suggestion was based on a rather questionable analogy with the law of frustration, and it has since been rejected by the House of Lords in *Bunge Corporation v Tradax Export SA* [1981] 1 WLR 711. Indeed the judgment of Diplock LJ was subjected to detailed analysis by Lewison LJ in *Ampurius Nu Homes Holdings Ltd v Telford Homes (Creekside) Ltd* [2013] EWCA Civ 577 at [38]–[53]:

38 *Hongkong Fir Shipping Co Ltd v Kawasaki Kisen Kaisha Ltd* is a seminal case which bears on a number of points raised in this appeal. I must therefore deal with it in some detail. The charterparty in that case was a time charter of 24 months. The vessel was delivered to the charterers on February 13, 1957, and on that day sailed from Liverpool to Virginia, to pick up a cargo of coal and carry it to Osaka. The vessel's machinery was in reasonably good condition at Liverpool but because of its age needed to be maintained by an experienced, competent, careful and adequate engine room staff. But the chief engineer was an inefficient alcoholic, and the engine room complement was insufficient. So there were many serious breakdowns in the machinery en route. On the voyage from Liverpool to Osaka she was at sea eight and a half weeks, off hire for about five weeks and had about £21,400 spent on her for repairs. She reached Osaka on May 25 when a further period of about 15 weeks and an expenditure of £37,500 were required to make her ready for sea. In June, 1957, the charterers purported to terminate the charter. The grounds on which they claimed to be entitled to do so were (1) a breach of the obligation under clause 1 of the charterparty to deliver a seaworthy vessel; (2) a breach of the obligation under clause 3 of the charterparty to maintain the vessel properly; and (3) a breach of the obligation to deliver a vessel capable of making about 12½ knots in good weather and smooth water. This last breach was not proved on the evidence. In addition the charterers argued that they were entitled to terminate the charter because of the failure of the owners to remedy the breaches (a) within a reasonable time, or (b) on the ground that the breaches were such that the delay involved in remedying them frustrated the commercial purpose of the charter. I have set this out at some length because it shows that what the case was about was the impact of actual (accrued) breaches and not merely threatened or anticipatory breaches. Salmon J held that the breaches were not sufficiently serious as to amount to a repudiation; and this court dismissed an appeal against his decision.

39 The first question that Diplock LJ posed in *Hongkong Fir Shipping Co Ltd v Kawasaki Kisen Kaisha Ltd* was how to decide whether the occurrence of an event discharged the parties to a contract from further performance of their obligations, where the contract itself was silent. The answer he gave at the outset of his judgment was:

> 'The test whether an event has this effect or not has been stated in a number of metaphors all of which I think amount to the same thing: does the occurrence of the event deprive the party who has further undertakings still to perform of substantially the whole benefit which it was the intention of the parties as expressed in the contract that he should obtain as the consideration for performing those undertakings?
>
> This test is applicable whether or not the event occurs as a result of the default of one of the parties to the contract, but the consequences of the event are different in the two cases. Where the event occurs as a result of the default of one party, the party in default cannot rely upon it as relieving himself of the performance of any further undertakings on his part, and the innocent party, although entitled to, need not treat the event as relieving him of the further performance of his own undertakings'.

40 Later he continued:

> 'Once it is appreciated that it is the event and not the fact that the event is a result of a breach of contract which relieves the party not in default of further performance of his obligations, two consequences follow. (1) The test whether the event relied upon has this consequence is the same whether the event is the result of the other party's breach of contract or not, as

> Devlin J. pointed out in *Universal Cargo Carriers Corporation v Citati*. (2) The question whether an event which is the result of the other party's breach of contract has this consequence cannot be answered by treating all contractual undertakings as falling into one of two separate categories: 'conditions' the breach of which gives rise to an event which relieves the party not in default of further performance of his obligations, and 'warranties' the breach of which does not give rise to such an event'.

41 In *Hongkong Fir* Upjohn LJ also took the view that the effect of the breach had to amount to frustration of the contract. He said:

> 'In my judgment the remedies open to the innocent party for breach of a stipulation which is not a condition strictly so called, depend entirely upon the nature of the breach and its foreseeable consequences. Breaches of stipulation fall, naturally, into two classes. First there is the case where the owner by his conduct indicates that he considers himself no longer bound to perform his part of the contract; in that case, of course, the charterer may accept the repudiation and treat the contract as at an end. The second class of case is, of course, the more usual one and that is where, due to misfortune such as the perils of the sea, engine failures, incompetence of the crew and so on, the owner is unable to perform a particular stipulation precisely in accordance with the terms of the contract try he never so hard to remedy it. In that case the question to be answered is, does the breach of the stipulation go so much to the root of the contract that it makes further commercial performance of the contract impossible, or in other words is the whole contract frustrated? If yea, the innocent party may treat the contract as at an end. If nay, his claim sounds in damages only'.

42 In *Hongkong Fir* Diplock LJ addressed the question: at what time should the seriousness and character of the breach be evaluated? He said:

> 'What the judge had to do in the present case, as in any other case where one party to a contract relies upon a breach by the other party as giving him a right to elect to rescind the contract, and the contract itself makes no express provision as to this, was to look at the events which had occurred as a result of the breach at the time at which the charterers purported to rescind the charterparty and to decide whether the occurrence of those events deprived the charterers of substantially the whole benefit which it was the intention of the parties as expressed in the charterparty that the charterers should obtain from the further performance of their own contractual undertakings'.

43 Thus, turning to the facts, Diplock LJ said:

> 'The question which the judge had to ask himself was, as he rightly decided, whether or not at the date when the charterers purported to rescind the contract, namely, June 6, 1957, or when the shipowners purported to accept such rescission, namely, August 8, 1957, the delay which had already occurred as a result of the incompetence of the engine-room staff, and the delay which was likely to occur in repairing the engines of the vessel and the conduct of the shipowners by that date in taking steps to remedy these two matters, were, when taken together, such as to deprive the charterers of substantially the whole benefit which it was the intention of the parties they should obtain from further use of the vessel under the charterparty'.

44 There are three points which emerge from this. First, the task of the court is to look at the position as at the date of purported termination of the contract even in a case of actual rather than anticipatory breach. Second, in looking at the position at that date, the court must take into account any steps taken by the guilty party to remedy accrued breaches of contract. Third, the court must also take account of likely future events, judged by reference to objective facts as at the date of purported termination.

45 As the judge pointed out in our case Diplock LJ also referred to *Jackson v Union Marine Insurance Co Ltd* (1874–1875) LR 10 CP 125, upon which the judge himself placed some reliance. Diplock LJ treated that case as authority for the proposition that delay will justify termination of a contract 'if the breach is so prolonged that the contemplated voyage is frustrated.' This was also the conclusion of Devlin J in *Universal Cargo Carriers Corporation v Citati* [1957] 2 QB 401 which was clearly approved in *Hongkong Fir*.

46 In *Universal Cargo Carriers Corporation v Citati* Devlin J said:

> 'But a party to a contract may not purchase indefinite delay by paying damages and a charterer may not keep a ship indefinitely on demurrage. When the delay becomes so prolonged that the breach assumes a character so grave as to go to the root of the contract, the aggrieved party is entitled to rescind. What is the yardstick by which this length of delay is to be measured? Those considered in the arbitration can now be reduced to two: first, the conception of a reasonable time, and secondly, such delay as would frustrate the charterparty. The arbitrator, it is clear, preferred the first. But in my opinion the second has been settled as the correct one by a long line of authorities.'

47 The test favoured by Diplock LJ was applied by this court in *Shawton Engineering Ltd v DGP International Ltd* [2005] EWCA Civ 1359; [2006] BLR 1. That was a case of a contract for the design and manufacture of a number of packages for a handling plant for nuclear waste. The contractor was behind schedule in completing the work. May LJ said at [32]:

> 'Shawton could only in law legitimately determine the contracts for delay if either:
>
> (a) they gave reasonable notice making time of the essence; or
> (b) DGP's failure to complete within a reasonable time was a fundamental breach such that the gravity of the breach had the effect of depriving Shawton of substantially the whole benefit which it was the intention of the parties that they should obtain from the contracts.
>
> Where time is not of the essence and where the party said to be in breach by delay is nevertheless making an effort to perform the contract, it is intrinsically difficult for the other party to establish a fundamental breach in this sense.'

48 These authorities adopt as the relevant test whether the breach has deprived the injured party of 'substantially the whole benefit' of the contract; which is the same test as that applicable to frustration. This sets the bar high. Other cases adopt a view that is more favourable to the injured party. Thus in *Decro-Wall International SA v Practitioners in Marketing Ltd* [1971] 1 WLR 361, the defendant distributors of the plaintiff's goods were slow in meeting bills of exchange. But their ability to meet the bills eventually, albeit late, was not in doubt. This court held that they had not repudiated the contract. Salmon LJ said that if the contract did not spell out the consequences of breach 'the courts must look at the practical results of the breach in order to decide whether or not it does go to the root of the contract.' Sachs LJ said that 'to constitute repudiation a breach of contract must go to the root of that contract.' Buckley LJ said:

> 'To constitute repudiation, the threatened breach must be such as to deprive the injured party of a substantial part of the benefit to which he is entitled under the contract. The measure of the necessary degree of substantiality has been expressed in a variety of ways in the cases. It has been said that the breach must be of an essential term, or of a fundamental term of the contract, or that it must go to the root of the contract.'

49 On the face of it therefore there is a tension between the test of deprivation of 'substantially the whole benefit' (Diplock LJ) and 'a substantial part of the benefit' (Buckley LJ). In *Federal Commerce & Navigation Co Ltd v Molena Alpha Inc (The Nanfri)* [1979] AC 757 Lord Wilberforce quoted a number of different formulations of the test (including those of Diplock LJ and Buckley LJ) and said:

> 'The difference in expression between these two last formulations does not, in my opinion, reflect a divergence of principle, but arises from and is related to the particular contract under consideration: they represent, in other words, applications to different contracts, of the common principle that, to amount to repudiation a breach must go to the root of the contract'.

50 The trouble with expressing important propositions of English law in metaphorical terms is that it is difficult to be sure what they mean. As the High Court of Australia majority judgment pointed out in *Koompahtoo Local Aboriginal Land Council v Sanpine Pty Ltd* [2007] HCA 61 (2007) 82 AJLR 345 at [54] to describe a breach as 'going to the root of the contract' is:

> '... a conclusory description that takes account of the nature of the contract and the relationship it creates, the nature of the term, the kind and degree of the breach, and the consequences of the breach for the other party'.

51 Whatever test one adopts, it seems to me that the starting point must be to consider what benefit the injured party was intended to obtain from performance of the contract. In our case, the benefit that Ampurius was intended to obtain from performance of the contract was, first and foremost, a leasehold interest of 999 years duration in four blocks. In other words, what Ampurius bargained for was the right to possession of those units for 999 years, and the right for a like period to exploitation of the rents and profits to be derived from them. It was to take the blocks in pairs, with a gap of seven months between each handover (although acknowledging that the seven month gap was dependent on meeting dates described as 'Target Dates'). The first pair of blocks was to be handed over just over twenty one months after the contract was signed. I do not think that the judge gave adequate weight to the ultimate objective of the contract, viz. the grant to Ampurius of 999 year leases. He concentrated on the expected effects on the marketing period. This, in my judgment, permeates his consideration of what practical effect the breaches of contract had.

52 The next thing to consider is the effect of the breach on the injured party. What financial loss has it caused? How much of the intended benefit under the contract has the injured party already received? Can the injured party be adequately compensated by an award of damages? Is the breach likely to be repeated? Will the guilty party resume compliance with his obligations? Has the breach fundamentally changed the value of future performance of the guilty party's outstanding obligations?

53 I agree with the judge that if Ampurius were only ever to be able to acquire interests in two out of the four blocks, then it would have been deprived of the benefit of a substantial part of the contract. That is because it would not have acquired two out of the four promised 999 year leases. But that is not this case.

The decision in *Hong Kong Fir* has been highly influential, giving the courts the remedial flexibility that they had long craved for. It has even been adopted in relation to sale of goods contracts.

***Cehave NV v Bremer Handelgesellschaft mbH. (The Hansa Nord)* [1976] QB 44, 66**

Facts: The German sellers agreed to sell, to the Dutch buyers, 12,000 tons of US citrus pulp pellets for use as animal feed. The contract was made on the Grain and Feed Association (GAFTA) terms. Clause 7 provided 'shipment to be made in good condition'. The buyers paid the price of £100,000 and received the shipping documents, but when the goods arrived at Rotterdam, it was discovered that part of the shipment had been damaged by overheating. The buyers rejected the whole shipment, and when the sellers refused to refund the purchase price, the buyers applied to the Rotterdam county court to obtain an order for the shipment to be sold. The shipment was sold on 2 June to an importer who, on the same day, resold the whole cargo to the buyers for the same sum of £30,000. The buyers then used the entire cargo for their original purpose, making animal feed. Mocatta J held in the buyer's favour. Terms under the Sale of Goods Act must be either conditions or warranties, and since breach of the 'shipped in good condition' term might have serious consequences, it had to be a condition. The sellers appealed.

Held: The Court of Appeal allowed the appeal. The 'shipped in good condition' term was an intermediate term. Since the whole cargo was eventually used for its intended purpose as animal feed, the breach did not go to the root of the contract and the buyers, though entitled to damages, were not entitled to reject.

Lord Denning MR: 'Shipped in good condition'. Was this a condition strictly so called, so that *any* breach of it entitled the buyer to reject the goods? Or was it an intermediate stipulation, so that the buyer cannot reject unless the breach is so serious as to go to the root of the contract? If there was any previous authority holding it to be a *condition* strictly so called, we should abide by it, just as we did with the clause 'expected ready to load': see *Finnish Government (Ministry of Food) v H Ford & C Ltd* (1921) 6 Ll L Rep 188 ... But, there is no such authority with the clause 'shipped in good condition'. I regard this clause as comparable to a clause as to quality, such as 'fair average quality'. If a small portion of the goods sold was a little below that standard, it would be met by commercial men by an allowance off the price. The buyer would have no right to reject the whole lot unless the divergence was serious and substantial: see *Biggin & Co Ltd v Permanite Ltd* [1951] 1 KB 422, 439, *per* Devlin J and *Christopher Hill Ltd v Ashington Piggeries Ltd* [1972] AC 441, 511, *per* Lord Diplock. ...

In my opinion, therefore, the term 'shipped in good condition' was not a condition strictly so called: nor was it a warranty strictly so called. It was one of those intermediate stipulations which gives no right to reject unless the breach goes to the root of the contract.

On the facts stated by the board of appeal, I do not think the buyer was entitled to reject these instalments of the contract. The board only said that 'not all the goods in hold no. 1 were shipped in good condition'. That does not say how many were bad. In any case, their condition cannot have been very bad, seeing that all of them were in fact used for the intended purpose. The breach did not go to the root of the contract. The buyer is entitled to damages, but not to rejection.

Merchantable

The board of appeal made this finding: 'The goods in hold 1 were 'merchantable' on arrival at Rotterdam in a commercial sense, though at a lower price than would be paid for sound goods; we find and hold, however, that they were not 'of merchantable quality' within the meaning of the phrase when used in the Sale of Goods Act 1893'.

The board of appeal were not lawyers: but they had a legal adviser and I am afraid that in reaching that finding they were not advised correctly. The statute uses the words 'merchantable quality' in a commercial sense. The board should, therefore, have applied it in the commercial sense. They should not have been persuaded to give it some other 'statutory sense'.

Now we were taken through many of the definitions which have been given by judges of 'merchantable quality' ... For myself, I think the definition in the latest statute is the best that has yet been devised. It is contained in section 7(2) of the Supply of Goods (Implied Terms) Act 1973. The statute itself only applies to contracts made after May 18, 1973. But the definition seems to me appropriate for contracts made before it. It runs as follows:

> 'Goods of any kind are of merchantable quality within the meaning of this Act if they are as fit for the purpose or purposes for which goods of that kind are commonly bought as it is reasonable to expect having regard to any description applied to them, the price (if relevant) and all other relevant circumstances; and any reference in this Act to unmerchantable goods shall be construed accordingly'.

In applying that definition, it is as well to remember that, by the statute, we are dealing with an implied *condition*, strictly so called, and not a warranty. For any breach of it, therefore, the buyer is entitled to *reject* the goods: or, alternatively, if he chooses to accept them or has accepted them, he has a remedy in damages. In these circumstances, I should have thought a fair way of testing merchantability would be to ask a commercial man: was the breach such that the buyer should be able to reject the goods? In answering that question the commercial man would have regard to the various matters mentioned in the new statutory definition ... If there was a clause, express or implied, which would give the buyer an allowance off the price for the particular shortcomings, such that a commercial man would say: 'The buyer is entitled to a price allowance but not to reject them' – again the goods would be of merchantable quality. The buyer would be entitled to an allowance or damages in lieu, but not entitled to reject the lot.

Our present case comes within that last illustration. These citrus pulp pellets were bought for cattle food. That was the purpose for which such pellets are commonly bought. They were as fit for that purpose as it was reasonable to expect. That is shown by the fact that they were actually used for that purpose. Some of them arrived damaged, but not to such an extent that the buyer was entitled to reject the cargo in both holds or either of them. That damage was such as to entitle the buyer to an allowance off the price for breach of the clause 'shipped in good condition': but not such as to entitle him to reject the lot on the ground that it was not of 'merchantable quality' ... Having found that in a commercial sense the goods were merchantable, there was no breach of section 14(2).

Roskill LJ: In my view, a court should not be over ready, unless required by statute or authority so to do, to construe a term in a contract as a 'condition' any breach of which gives rise to a right to reject rather than as a term any breach of which sounds in damages – I deliberately avoid the use of the word 'warranty' at this juncture. In principle contracts are made to be performed and not to be avoided according to the whims of market fluctuation and where there is a free choice between two possible constructions I think the court should tend to prefer that construction which will ensure performance and not encourage avoidance of contractual obligations ...

In principle it is not easy to see why the law relating to contracts for the sale of goods should be different from the law relating to the performance of other contractual obligations, whether charterparties or other types of contract. Sale of goods law is but one branch of the general law of contract. It is desirable that the same legal principles should apply to the law of contract as a whole and that different legal principles should not apply to different branches of that law.

Ormrod LJ: If one asks oneself the question in the form, 'Did the parties intend that the buyer should be entitled to reject the goods if they were not shipped in good condition?' the answer must be that it depends on the nature and effects of the breach. This is directly in line with Diplock LJ's approach in the *Hongkong Fir Shipping Co* case [1962] 2 QB 26, 69–70, not surprisingly, since there can be very little difference in principle between whether the ship is seaworthy and whether goods are in good condition. There is obviously a strong case for applying the general principle of the *Hongkong Fir Shipping Co* case to contracts for the sale of goods. The question remains, however ... whether it is open to the court to do so. The parties themselves, of course, can do it by express agreement as, indeed, they have done in the present case in relation to quality ... If it can be done expressly, it can be done by implication, unless it is in some way prohibited. [Counsel for the buyers] argues that section 11(1)(b) compels the court to choose between condition and warranty. I do not think that the subsection was intended to have any prohibitory effect. It is essentially a definition section, defining 'condition' and 'warranty' in terms of remedies. Nor is the classification absolutely rigid, for it provides that a buyer may treat a condition as a warranty if he wishes, by accepting the goods. It does not, however, envisage the possibility that a breach of warranty might go to the root of the contract, and so, in certain circumstances, entitle the buyer to treat the contract as repudiated. But the law has developed since the Act was passed. It is now accepted as a general principle since the *Hongkong Fir Shipping Co* case [1962] 2 QB 26, that it is the events resulting from the breach, rather than the breach itself, which may destroy the consideration for the buyer's promise and so enable him to treat the contract as repudiated.

The problem is how to integrate this principle with section 11(1)(b). In practice it may not arise very often ... The difficulty only arises if the court had already categorised the stipulation as a warranty. The present case provides an example. If the relevant part of clause 7 is construed as a warranty in this case, and later, another dispute occurs in relation to another contract in the same form, between the same parties, for the sale of similar goods, in which the breach of clause 7 has produced much more serious consequences for the buyer, is the court bound by its decision in this case to hold that the buyer is precluded from rejecting the goods under the later contract because, as a matter of construction, it has already categorised the stipulation as a warranty? ... If the answer is in the affirmative section 11(1)(b) has, by implication, excluded one of the general common law rules of contract. It was clearly not intended to have this effect and I agree with Lord Denning MR, for the reasons that he has given in his judgment, that the Act should not, if it can be avoided, be construed in this way. Section 61(2) seems to provide an answer. If this view is correct it is bound to have important repercussions on the way in which courts in future will approach the construction of stipulations in contracts for the sale of goods. It will no longer be necessary to place so much emphasis on the potential effects of a breach on the buyer, and to feel obliged, as Mocatta J did in this case, to construe a stipulation as a condition because in other cases or in other circumstances the buyer ought to be entitled to reject. Consequently, the court will be freer to regard stipulations, as a matter of construction, as warranties, if what might be called the 'back-up' rule of the common law is available to protect buyers who ought to be able to reject in proper circumstances. I doubt whether, strictly speaking, this involves the creation of a third category of stipulations; rather, it recognises another ground for holding that a buyer is entitled to reject, namely, that, de facto, the consideration for his promise has been wholly destroyed.

The result may be summarised in this way. When a breach of contract has taken place the question arises: 'Is the party who is not in breach entitled in law to treat the contract as repudiated or, in the case of a buyer, to reject the goods?' The answer depends on the answers to a series of other questions. Adopting Upjohn LJ's judgment in the *Hongkong Fir Shipping Co* case [1962] 2 QB 26, 64, the first question is: 'Does the contract expressly provide that in the event of the breach of the term in question the other party is entitled to terminate the contract or reject the goods?' If the answer is No, the next question is: 'Does the contract when correctly construed so provide?' The relevant term, for example, may be described as a 'condition'. The question then arises whether this word is used as a code word for the phrase 'shall be entitled to repudiate the contract or reject the goods', or in some other sense, as in *Wickman Machine Tool Sales Ltd v L Schuler AG* [1972] 1 WLR 840. The next question is whether the breach of the relevant term creates a right to repudiate or reject. This may arise either from statute or as a result of judicial decision on particular contractual terms. For example, if the requirements of section 14(1) or (2) of the Sale of Goods Act 1893 are fulfilled, the buyer will be entitled to reject the goods, as a result of this section, read with section 11(2). In fact, in all those sections of the Sale of Goods Act 1893 which create implied conditions the word 'condition' is, by definition a code word for 'breach of this term will entitle the buyer to reject the goods', subject to any other relevant provision of the Act.

In other cases, the courts have decided that breach of some specific terms, such as, for example, an 'expected ready to load' stipulation, will ipso facto give rise to a right in the other party to repudiate the contract: *The Mihalis Angelos* [1971] 1 QB 164, 194, *per* Lord Denning MR. In these two classes of case the consequences of the breach are irrelevant or, more accurately, are assumed to go to the root of the contract, and to justify repudiation. There remains the non-specific class where the events produced by the breach are such that it is reasonable to describe the breach as going to the root of the contract and so justifying repudiation.

If this approach is permissible in the present case I would unhesitatingly hold that the stipulation in clause 7 that the goods were to be shipped in good condition was not a condition, and that on the facts of this case the breach did not go to the root of the contract, and that, consequently, the buyers were not entitled to reject the goods.

There are two important points to note here. First, the Court of Appeal unanimously rejected the argument that the sellers had breached s 14(2) of the SGA 1893 by supplying goods that were not of 'merchantable quality'. This was uncontroversial, given that the goods were still fit for their original purpose, and were in fact used for that purpose by the buyers. Of more interest to us are the comments made by Lord Denning about how the issue of merchantability should be determined. He suggested that 'in these circumstances … a fair way of testing merchantability would be to ask a commercial man: was the breach such that the buyer should be able to reject the goods?' In other words, was the effect of the breach such that the conduct amounted to a breach of an implied *condition*? By this ingenious method, Lord Denning imported the *Hong Kong Fir* approach into the analysis of statutorily implied conditions though the back door. While ingenious, this analysis is extremely dubious, and it was not supported by either of the other members of the Court of Appeal. In any event, the case has probably now been superseded by the more specific statutory definitions of quality to be found in the SGA 1979.

The second point to note is that the court unanimously agreed that the *Hong Kong Fir* approach should apply to an express term in a sale of goods contract. The term in question, cl 7 (which provided that the goods should be 'shipped in good condition') was held to be an intermediate term and not a condition. Since the goods were still fit for their original purpose, the breach was of insufficient seriousness to justify termination. Mr Weir (Weir, T, 'Contract – the buyer's right to reject defective goods' [1976] CLJ 33) has criticised this decision, complaining that it 'rewards incompetence'. He notes that the seller had made a very good bargain; the market for pellets having fallen rapidly after the contract was made. By refusing to let the buyer terminate the contract, the Court of Appeal effectively forced the buyer to pay not only the true value of the spoilt cargo, but the seller's profit as well. Weir criticises the result and summarises the unhappy state of the law in the following way: 'The guilty party is to get all that he bargained for unless the innocent party gets no part of what he bargained for'.

Mr Weir's criticisms carry some force, but it should not be forgotten that the buyer was attempting to escape from a bad bargain. Cehave had received the goods they had bargained for (albeit in a slightly different condition), but wished to withdraw from the transaction in order to pursue a better bargain elsewhere. The Court of Appeal's decision prevented them from doing this (see Brownsword, R, '*Retrieving reasons, retrieving rationality? A new look at the right to withdraw for breach of contract*' (1992) 5 JCL 83). Unfortunately, it also left us with a degree of uncertainty in the law. Whereas in the past, commercial lawyers had often been able to accurately predict when a breach of contract would give rise to a right to terminate a contract, the approach taken by the Court of Appeal in *The Hansa Nord* suggested that this would no longer always be possible. On the other hand, there has been some evidence of a different approach being adopted in relation to some common clauses in commercial contracts. The seeds for such an approach were sown by the Court of Appeal in *The Mihalis Angelos*.

***Maredelanto Compania Naviera SA v Bergbau-Handel GmbH (The Mihalis Angelos)* [1971] 1 QB 164**

Facts: A ship was chartered to transport a cargo of minerals from Haiphong. The charterparty contained a clause to the effect that the ship was 'expected ready to load under this charter about 1 July 1965'. The charterers were unable to get the cargo to the port in time and purported to cancel the charter on 17 July. The owners brought an action for wrongful repudiation. The charterers argued that they were entitled to terminate the contract on 17 July, following the owner's breach of the readiness to load clause.

Held: The Court of Appeal held that the readiness to load clause was a condition, breach of which entitled the charterers to terminate the contract.

Megaw LJ: In my judgment, such a term in a charterparty ought to be regarded as being a condition of the contract, in the old sense of the word 'condition': that is, that when it has been broken, the other party can, if he wishes, by intimation to the party in breach, elect to be released from performance of his further obligations under the contract; and he can validly do so without having to establish that on the facts of the particular case the breach has produced serious consequences which can be treated as 'going to the root of the contract' or as being 'fundamental', or whatever other metaphor may be thought appropriate for a frustration case ... One of the essential elements of law is some measure of uniformity. One of the important elements of the law is predictability. At any rate in commercial law, there are obvious and substantial advantages in having, where possible, a firm and definite rule for a particular class of legal relationship: for example, as here, the legal categorisation of a particular, definable type of contractual clause in common use. It is surely much better, both for shipowners and charterers (and, incidentally, for their advisers), when a contractual obligation of this nature is under consideration, and still more when they are faced with the necessity for an urgent decision as to the effects of a suspected breach of it, to be able to say categorically: 'If a breach is proved, then the charterer can put an end to the contract', rather than that they should be left to ponder whether or not the courts would be likely, in the particular case, when the evidence has been heard, to decide that in the particular circumstances the breach was or was not such as 'to go to the root of the contract'. Where justice does not require greater flexibility, there is everything to be said for, and nothing against, a degree of rigidity in legal principle.

As we have seen earlier in the chapter, a similar approach was taken to a time clause in a mercantile contract in *Bunge Corporation v Tradax Export SA* [1981] 1 WLR 711. Lord Wilberforce said that to treat time clauses in mercantile contracts as intermediate terms would be 'commercially most undesirable':

It would expose the parties, after a breach of one, two, three, seven and other numbers of days to an argument whether this delay would have left time for the seller to provide the goods. It would make it, at the time, at least difficult, and sometimes impossible, for the supplier to know whether he could do so. It would fatally remove from a vital provision in the contract that certainty which is the most indispensable quality of mercantile contracts, and lead to a large increase in arbitrations. It would confine the seller – perhaps after arbitration and reference through the courts – to a remedy in damages which might be extremely difficult to quantify. These are all serious objections in practice. But I am clear that the submission is unacceptable in law. The judgment of Diplock LJ does not give any support and ought not to give any encouragement to any such proposition; for beyond doubt it recognises that it is open to the parties to agree that, as regards a particular obligation, any breach shall entitle the party not in default to treat the contract as repudiated ... It remains true, as Lord Roskill has pointed out in *Cehave NV v Bremer Handelgesellschaft mbH. (The Hansa Nord)* [1976] QB 44, 66, that the courts should not be too ready to interpret contractual clauses as conditions. And I have myself commended, and continue to commend, the greater flexibility in the law

> of contracts to which Hongkong Fir points the way (*Reardon Smith Line Ltd v Yngvar Hansen-Tangen (trading as HE Hansen-Tangen)* [1976] 1 WLR 989, 998). But I do not doubt that, in suitable cases, the courts should not be reluctant, if the intentions of the parties as shown by the contract so indicate, to hold that an obligation has the force of a condition, and that indeed they should usually do so in the case of time clauses in mercantile contracts.

Applying this approach to the facts of the case, the House of Lords held that a four-day delay in giving notice of the ship's readiness to load was a breach of condition, entitling the sellers to terminate the contract. The same approach was applied by the Privy Council in *Union Eagle Ltd v Golden Achievement Ltd* [1997] AC 514, again in relation to a time clause. More recently, the approach has been applied to a clause guaranteeing the acquisition of approval of a vessel within a specified period of time: *BS & N Ltd v Micado Shipping Ltd (Malta) (The Seaflower)* [2001] 1 Lloyd's Rep 341.

This line of cases may give the impression that a term will be held to be a condition whenever the demands of commerce require it. The reality, however, is much more complex. When the parties fail to stipulate whether a term is a condition, warranty or intermediate term, the court must engage in a delicate interpretative exercise to determine the true nature of the term. Inevitably, judicial differences will mean that different results will be reached by different judges (see *Universal Bulk Carriers Pte Ltd v Andre et Cie SA* [2001] 2 Lloyd's Rep 65, where a time clause in a charterparty was held not to be a condition, and *Spar Shipping AS v Grand China Logistics Holding (Group) Co Ltd* [2015] EWHC 718 (Comm) and [2016] EWCA Civ 982, where payment of hire under particular charterparties (NYPE 1993) was held not to be a condition). More recently, in *Ark Shipping Co LLC v Silverburn Shipping (IoM) Ltd (The Arctic)* [2019] EWCA Civ 1161, the Court of Appeal, in the context of a charter party, held that, unless it is clear that a term is intended to be a condition (or indeed a warranty), it would be treated as an innominate term if the consequences of breach could be trivial or very serious. Accordingly, this area of the law continues to be shrouded in uncertainty.

14.3.2.3 Categorisation by the parties

The parties are, of course, free to stipulate the nature of the terms in the contract itself. For example, the contract may expressly provide that some of the terms are conditions, while the rest are warranties. The use of such labels will not, however, be conclusive, as *L Schuler AG v Wickman Machine Tools Sales Ltd* shows.

***L Schuler AG v Wickman Machine Tools Sales Ltd* [1974] AC 235**

Facts: Wickman was appointed as the sole UK distributor of Schuler's panel presses. Clause 7(b) of the contract provided that, 'It shall be [a] condition of this agreement that [Wickman] shall send its representatives to visit' the six largest United Kingdom motor manufacturers 'at least once in every week' to solicit orders for panel presses. Wickman's representatives failed to make a number of these weekly visits, and Schuler terminated the agreement under clause 11(a)(i). That clause provided that either party could terminate the agreement if the other committed a material breach of its obligations and failed to remedy it within 60 days of being required to do so. Wickman brought a claim for wrongful termination.

Held: The House of Lords (Lord Wilberforce dissenting) held that the word 'condition' in clause 7(b) did not make the clause a condition in the sense that a single breach of it, however trivial, would entitle the innocent party to terminate the whole contract.

Lord Reid: In the ordinary use of the English language 'condition' has many meanings, some of which have nothing to do with agreements. In connection with an agreement it may mean a pre-condition: something which must happen or be done before the agreement can take effect. Or it may mean some state of affairs which must continue to exist if the agreement is to remain in force. The legal meaning on which Schuler relies is, I think, one which would not occur to a layman; a condition in that sense is not something which has an automatic effect. It is a term the breach of which by one party gives to the other an option either to terminate the contract or to let the contract proceed and, if he so desires, sue for damages for the breach.

Sometimes a breach of a term gives that option to the aggrieved party because it is of a fundamental character going to the root of the contract, sometimes it gives that option because the parties have chosen to stipulate that it shall have that effect. Blackburn J said in *Bettini v Gye* (1876) 1 QBD 183, 187: 'Parties may think some matter, apparently of very little importance, essential; and if they sufficiently express an intention to make the literal fulfilment of such a thing a condition precedent, it will be one; ...'

In the present case it is not contended that Wickman's failures to make visits amounted in themselves to fundamental breaches. What is contended is that the terms of clause 7 'sufficiently express an intention' to make any breach, however small, of the obligation to make visits a condition so that any breach shall entitle Schuler to rescind the whole contract if they so desire.

Schuler maintains that the use of the word 'condition' is in itself enough to establish this intention. No doubt some words used by lawyers do have a rigid inflexible meaning. But we must remember that we are seeking to discover intention as disclosed by the contract as a whole. Use of the word 'condition' is an indication – even a strong indication – of such an intention but it is by no means conclusive.

The fact that a particular construction leads to a very unreasonable result must be a relevant consideration. The more unreasonable the result the more unlikely it is that the parties can have intended it, and if they do intend it the more necessary it is that they shall make that intention abundantly clear.

Clause 7(b) requires that over a long period each of the six firms shall be visited every week by one or other of two named representatives. It makes no provision for Wickman being entitled to substitute others even on the death or retirement of one of the named representatives. Even if one could imply some right to do this, it makes no provision for both representatives being ill during a particular week. And it makes no provision for the possibility that one or other of the firms may tell Wickman that they cannot receive Wickman's representative during a particular week. So if the parties gave any thought to the matter at all they must have realised the probability that in a few cases out of the 1,400 required visits a visit as stipulated would be impossible. But if Schuler's contention is right, failure to make even one visit entitles them to terminate the contract however blameless Wickman might be.

This is so unreasonable that it must make me search for some other possible meaning of the contract. If none can be found then Wickman must suffer the consequences. But only if that is the only possible interpretation.

If I have to construe clause 7 standing by itself then I do find difficulty in reaching any other interpretation. But if clause 7 must be read with clause 11 the difficulty disappears. The word 'condition' would make any breach of clause 7(b), however excusable, a material breach. That would then entitle Schuler to give notice under clause 11(a)(i) requiring the breach to be remedied. There would be no point in giving such a notice if Wickman were clearly not in fault but if it were given Wickman would have no difficulty in showing that the breach had been remedied. If Wickman were at fault then on receiving such a notice they would have to amend their system so that they could show that the breach had been remedied. If they did not do that within the period of the notice then Schuler would be entitled to rescind.

In my view, that is a possible and reasonable construction of the contract and I would therefore adopt it. The contract is so obscure that I can have no confidence that this is its true meaning but for the reasons which I have given I think that it is the preferable construction. It follows that Schuler was not entitled to rescind the contract as it purported to do. So I would dismiss this appeal.

Lord Wilberforce: Does clause 7(b) amount to a 'condition' or a 'term'? (To call it an important or material term adds, with all respect, nothing but some intellectual assuagement.) My Lords, I am clear in my own mind that it is a condition, but your Lordships take the contrary view. On a matter of construction of a particular document, to develop the reasons for a minority opinion serves no purpose. I am all the more happy to refrain from so doing because the judgments of Mocatta J, Stephenson LJ, and indeed of Edmund Davies LJ, on construction, give me complete satisfaction and I could in any case add little of value to their reasons. I would only add that, for my part, to call the clause arbitrary, capricious or fantastic, or to introduce as a test of its validity the ubiquitous reasonable man (I do not know whether he is English or German) is to assume, contrary to the evidence, that both parties to this contract adopted a standard of easygoing tolerance rather than one of aggressive, insistent punctuality and efficiency. This is not an assumption I am prepared to make, nor do I think myself entitled to impose the former standard upon the parties if their words indicate, as they plainly do, the latter. I note finally, that the result of treating the clause, so careful and specific in its requirements, as a term is, in effect, to deprive the appellants of any remedy in respect of admitted and by no means minimal breaches. The arbitrator's finding that these breaches were not 'material' was not, in my opinion, justified in law in the face of the parties' own characterisation of them in their document: indeed the fact that he was able to do so, and so leave the appellants without remedy, argues strongly that the legal basis of his finding – that clause 7(b) was merely a term – is unsound. I would allow this appeal.

In total there were 20 clauses in the contract. Only cl 7(b) was referred to as a 'condition', which would seem to indicate that the parties intended that any breach of it would be repudiatory. This was not, however, the interpretation adopted by the majority. Lord Reid's view was that such an interpretation was so unreasonable that some other possible meaning had to be found. The other meaning advanced by his Lordship was to treat the clause as merely indicative of the type of 'material breach' that would trigger the operation of cl 11. This meaning, it is submitted, is even less satisfactory than the meaning advanced by Schuler. Clause 11 provided for termination in the event of a 'material breach' not being 'remedied' within 60 days of notice being given. In what sense could Wickman's failure to make regular weekly visits have been remedied? It was not possible for Wickman to go back in time and make the missed visits. The answer adopted by Lord Reid was that Wickman could have remedied the breach by amending its internal systems so as to ensure that the breach did not recur. But this interpretation of the word 'remedy' is surely rather generous towards Wickman.

It is hard to escape the conclusion that the majority were guilty of rewriting the parties' agreement. Judicial intervention on this scale is rather worrying. Even more concerning is the fact that the approach seems to have been repeated several years later by the Court of Appeal. This time the parties expressly stipulated the circumstances in which the right to terminate for breach would arise.

***Rice v Great Yarmouth Borough Council* [2001] 3 LGLR 4**

Facts: The claimant contracted with the defendant council to provide leisure management and grounds maintenance services for a period of four years. Clause 23.2.1 of the contract provided: 'If the contractor commits a breach of any of its obligations under the Contract; ... the Council may, without prejudice to any accrued rights or remedies under the Contract, terminate the Contractor's employment under the Contract by notice in writing having immediate effect.' Clause 27 also entitled the defendant to serve 'default notices' on the claimant specifying breaches and the time permitted for rectification. Approximately three months after the contract had commenced, the defendant started to serve default notices on the claimant. Several months later, the defendant informed the claimant that they were terminating the contract under clause 23. The claimant sought to recover damages for wrongful repudiation. At first instance, the judge held that clause 23 should not be interpreted literally, and that there should only be a right to terminate the contract where the breach was serious enough to be repudiatory. The defendant appealed.

Held: The Court of Appeal dismissed the appeal, holding that the clause should be interpreted in a common sense way so as to limit the defendant's right to terminate to situations where the claimant's breach had been repudiatory.

Hale LJ: The council argued first that clause 23.2.1 should be applied literally so as to give them the right to terminate the contract for the breach of any of the obligations contained in it, other than the trivial. The judge was referred to a number of well-known authorities. On the one hand, 'it is open to the parties to agree that, as regards a particular obligation, any breach shall entitle the party not in default to treat the contract as repudiated': see *Bunge Corporation v Tradax Export SA* [1981] 1 WLR 711, *per* Lord Wilberforce at 715E. On the other hand, '... if detailed semantic and syntactical analysis of words in a commercial contract is going to lead to a conclusion that flouts business commonsense, it must yield to business commonsense': see *Antaios Compania SA v Sakeb Rederierna* [1985] AC 191, *per* Lord Diplock at p 201D. The judge pointed out that none of these authorities '... dealt with commercial circumstances having many parallels to those of a local authority and a contractor who is contractually required for a period of years to provide a wide variety of services on a repetitive basis'.

He continued: 'There has long been a tension in the world of contract between an attachment to literal meaning that makes for certainty with all in black and white and the parties knowing exactly where they are and little room for the relative unpredictability of judicial intervention, and a desire to avoid consequences seen as unfair or seen as offending commercial commonsense'. As to which line of authority should apply, he concluded: 'In the context of a contract intended to last for four years, involving substantial investment or at least substantial undertaking of financial obligations by one party and involving a myriad of obligations of differing importance and varying frequency, I have no hesitation in holding that the common sense interpretation should be imposed upon the strict words of the contract and that a repudiatory breach or an accumulation of breaches that as a whole can properly be described as repudiatory are a precondition to termination pursuant to clause 23.2.1'.

Another point in favour of a commercial, common sense interpretation was '... that ephemeral breaches, even where substantial and not trivial, are subject to substantial contractual disciplines, default notices, deductions, performance by others at the contractor's expense and so on'. ...

In my view the judge was entirely right to reach the conclusion he did on this aspect of the case and for the reasons he gave.

The council argued that, in any event, the totality of breaches found by the judge were sufficient to justify it in terminating the contract ... In my view, the judge was right to ask himself whether the cumulative breaches were such as to justify an inference that the contractor would continue to deliver a substandard performance. However, I would agree with [counsel for the defendant] that the inference should be that the council would thereby be deprived of a substantial part of the totality of that which it had contracted for that year, subject to the additional possibility that some aspects of the contract were so important that the parties are to be taken to have intended that depriving the council of that part of the contract would be sufficient in itself. That is not what the judge found in this case.

Once it is accepted that the proven breaches are relevant to show what will happen in the future, it is clear that the judge was entitled to take both the drought and the knock on effect of the council's own behaviour in relation to the summer bedding into account. He examined the facts of this case in great detail over a trial lasting some 13 days. He was well placed to evaluate the true importance of the proven breaches in the context of the contracts as a whole and all the circumstances of the case. He had a judgment to make. If anything, the test which he applied was somewhat more favourable to the council than the test which, in my judgment, he should have applied. He was undoubtedly entitled to reach the conclusion that he did.

I would dismiss this appeal.

(May and Peter Gibson LJJ concurred.)

The Court of Appeal refused to accept the literal meaning of cl 23.2.1. Instead, in agreement with the trial judge, their lordships insisted that a common-sense interpretation ought to be imposed upon the strict words of the contract. That meaning, according to their Lordships, was that termination under cl 23 could only operate where there was a repudiatory breach or an accumulation of breaches that could be said to be repudiatory (see also *Spar Shipping AS v Grand China Logistics Holding (Group) Co Ltd* [2015] EWHC 718 (Comm), affirmed [2016] EWCA Civ). Such an interpretation arguably, however, renders the clause utterly meaningless. The defendant council already had a right to terminate the contract on the occurrence of a repudiatory breach under the general law. Why would the defendant insert a clause into the contract if its only effect was to restate rights that already existed under the general law? The answer, of course, is that they would not.

The decision in *Rice* is cause for concern. It means that the parties must be absolutely explicit if they wish to provide for termination of the contract on the occurrence of a breach that is not a repudiatory breach at common law. Fortunately, the instrumental approach adopted by the courts in *Schuler* and *Rice* does not seem to be commonplace. Elsewhere, the courts have emphasised the need to give effect to the parties' express categorisation of terms. In *Awilco A/S v Fulvia SpA di Navigazione (The Chikuma)* [1981] 1 WLR 314, for example, Lord Bridge emphasised the need to maintain commercial certainty by giving effect to the plain meaning of the terms of the contract:

> The ideal at which the courts should aim, in construing such clauses, is to produce a result, such that in any given situation both parties seeking legal advice as to their rights and obligations can expect the same clear and confident answer from their advisers and neither will be tempted to embark on long and expensive litigation in the belief that victory depends on winning the sympathy of the court. This ideal may never be fully attainable, but we shall certainly never even approximate to it unless we strive to follow clear and consistent principles and steadfastly refuse to be blown off course by the supposed merits of individual cases.

14.3.3 Anticipatory breach

An anticipatory breach occurs where, before the time for performance, one party, for example, informs the other that they intend to break the contract or otherwise renounces the contract. Indeed, the renunciation may be through an accumulation of breaches (see *Force India Formula One Team Ltd v Etihad Airways PJSC* [2010] EWCA Civ 1051). In *Geden Operations Ltd v Dry Bulk Handy Holdings Inc, M/V Bulk Uruguay'* [2014] EWHC 885 (Comm) at [15] Popplewell J stated:

> Anticipatory breach is the name given to conduct of one party to a contract before the time for performance of his obligations has arrived which is sufficient to entitle the other contracting party to treat himself as discharged from further performance. It may consist of one or both of two kinds of conduct. The first, renunciation, comprises words or conduct which evince an intention by the contracting party no longer to be bound by his contractual obligations. The second, self-induced impossibility, comprises conduct by the contracting party which puts it out of his power to perform his contractual obligations. In each case the anticipatory breach must be repudiatory in character. That is to say that the breach of contractual obligations, which the party's conduct anticipates that he cannot or will not perform, must be of the same character as would entitle the other party to treat himself as discharged from future performance if it occurred after the time for performance had arisen. So the anticipated breach must be breach of a condition, or breach of an innominate term which goes to the root of the contract or deprives the innocent party of substantially the whole benefit of the contract.

The rule in English law is that an anticipatory breach gives rise to an immediate right to treat the contract as repudiated and to bring a claim for damages.

Höchster v De La Tour (1853) 2 El & Bl 678; 118 ER 922

Facts: On 12 April 1852, the defendant engaged the plaintiff to work as his courier for three months beginning on 1 June 1852. On 11 May, the defendant wrote to the plaintiff to inform him that his services were no longer required. On 22 May, the plaintiff commenced an action for breach of contract, and the defendant responded that there could be no breach of contract before 1 June.

Held: The Court held that the plaintiff could commence an action on 22 May and did not have to wait until 1 June.

Lord Campbell CJ: The defendant's counsel very powerfully contended that, if the plaintiff was not contented to dissolve the contract and to abandon all remedy upon it, he was bound to remain ready and willing to perform it till the day when the actual employment as courier in the service of the defendant was to begin, and that there could be no breach of the agreement, before that day, to give a right to action. But it cannot be laid down as a universal rule that, where by agreement an act is to be done on a future day, no action can be brought for breach of agreement till the day for doing the act has arrived. If a man promises to marry a woman on a future day and before that day marries another woman, he is instantly liable to an action for breach of promise of marriage: *Short v Stone*. If a man contracts to execute a lease on and from a future day for a certain term, and, before that day, executes a lease to another for the same term, he may be immediately sued for breaking the contract: *Ford v Tiley* ([1827] 6 B & C 325). So, if a man contracts to sell and deliver specific goods on a future day, and before that day he sells and delivers them to another, he is immediately liable to an action at the suit of the person with whom he first contracted to sell and deliver them: *Bowdell v Parsons* ([1808] 10 East 359). One reason alleged in support of such an action is that the defendant has, before that day, rendered it impossible for the plaintiff to perform the contract at the day, but this does not necessarily follow, for, prior to the day fixed for doing the act, the first wife may have died, a surrender of the lease executed might be obtained, and the defendant might have re-purchased the goods as to be in a situation to sell and deliver them to the plaintiff. Another reason may be that where there is a contract to do an act on a future day there is a relation constituted between the parties in the meantime by the contract, and that they impliedly promise that in the meantime neither will do any thing to the prejudice of the other inconsistent with that relation. As an example, a man and woman engaged to marry are affianced to one another during the period between the time of the engagement and the celebration of the marriage.

In the present case, of traveller and courier, from the day of hiring till the day when the employment was to begin, the parties were engaged to each other, and it seems to be a beach of an implied contract if either of them renounces the engagement ... If the plaintiff has no remedy for breach of contract unless he treats the contract as in force, and acts upon it down to June 1, 1852, it follows that, till then, he must enter into no employment which will interfere with his promise 'to start with the defendant on such travels on the day and year', and that he must then be properly equipped in all respects as a courier for three months' tour on the continent of Europe.

But it is surely much more rational, and more for the benefit of both parties, that, after the renunciation of the agreement by the defendant, the plaintiff should be at liberty to consider himself absolved from any future performance of it, retaining his right to sue for any damage he has suffered from breach of it. Thus, instead of remaining idle and laying out money in preparations which must be useless, he is at liberty to seek service under another employer, which would go to mitigation of the damages to which he would otherwise be entitled for a breach of contract. It seems strange that the defendant, after renouncing the contract, and absolutely declaring that he will never act under it, should be permitted to object that faith is given to his assertion, and that an opportunity is not left to him of changing his mind. If the plaintiff is barred of any remedy by entering into an engagement inconsistent with starting as a courier with the defendant on June 1, he is prejudiced by putting faith in the defendant's assertion, and it would be more consonant with principle, if the defendant were precluded from saying that he had not broken the contract when he declared that he entirely renounced it ...

If it should be held that, upon a contract to do an act on a future day, a renunciation of the contract by one party dispenses with a condition to be performed in the meantime by the other, there seems no reason for requiring the other to wait till the day arrives before seeking his remedy by action, and the only ground on which the condition can be dispensed with seems to be that the renunciation may be treated as a breach of the contract. Upon the whole, we think that the declaration in this case is sufficient ... [W]e must give judgment for the plaintiff.

The reason for allowing an action on an anticipatory breach was explained by Lord Cockburn CJ in *Frost v Knight* (1872) LR 7 Exch 111. The case concerned a situation very similar to one of the examples given by Lord Campbell CJ in *Hochster*. The defendant promised to marry the plaintiff as soon as his father died (the defendant's father did not approve of the plaintiff). During the father's lifetime, the defendant broke off the engagement. The plaintiff sued for breach of the promise, even though the father was still alive. In explaining why the plaintiff's claim succeeded, Lord Cockburn CJ said:

> It is true ... that there can be no actual breach of a contract by reason of nonperformance so long as the time for performance has not yet arrived. But, on the other hand, there is – and the decision in *Hochster v De la Tour* proceeds on that assumption – a breach of the contract when the promisor repudiates it and declares he will no longer be bound by it. The promisee has an inchoate right to the performance of the bargain, which becomes complete when the time for performance has arrived. In the mean time he has a right to have the contract kept open as a subsisting and effective contract. Its unimpaired and unimpeached efficacy may be essential to his interests. His rights acquired under it may be dealt with by him in various ways for his benefit and advantage. Of all such advantage the repudiation of the contract by the other party, and the announcement that it never will be fulfilled, must of course deprive him. It is therefore quite right to hold that such an announcement amounts to a violation of the contract *in omnibus*, and that upon it the promisee, if so minded, may at once treat it as a breach of the entire contract, and bring his action accordingly.

The innocent party does not, of course, have to accept the anticipatory breach as repudiating the contract. As we will see in the following section, the innocent party may elect to affirm the contract and wait for the time for performance. It has even been held that the innocent party can generally affirm the contract, even if this will lead to a significant increase in his loss (*White and Carter (Councils) Ltd v McGregor* [1962] AC 413).

If the innocent party accepts the anticipatory breach and terminates the contract, it is immediately entitled to sue for damages. These damages will be limited to the extent of the innocent party's actual loss from the breach. This was recently considered in *Golden Strait Corpn v Nippon Yusen Kubishika Kaisha*.

Golden Strait Corpn v Nippon Yusen Kubishika Kaisha ('The Golden Victory')
[2006] 1 WLR 533 (CA); [2007] UKHL 12 (HL)

Facts: In 1998, the defendant agreed to charter a ship from the claimant on a seven-year charterparty. Clause 33 of the charterparty provided that each party had a right to cancel the charter in the event of war between any two of a number of countries including the United States, the United Kingdom and Iraq. On 14 December 2001, the defendant committed an anticipatory breach by purporting to redeliver the vessel to the claimant. The anticipatory breach was accepted by Golden Strait three days later, and the charterparty was therefore terminated by the claimant on 17 December 2001, approximately four years before the date on which the charterparty would have expired. In March 2003, the United States and the United Kingdom went to war against Iraq. In September 2003, the claimant brought an action against the defendant claiming damages for the charterer's repudiation. The defendant did not dispute its liability, but did dispute the claimant's assessment of damages, which was calculated by reference to the remaining four years under the charterparty, rather than the 14-month period between the acceptance of the breach and the outbreak of war. Both the arbitrator and Langley J, at first instance, ruled in favour of the defendant, holding that the war had placed a limit on the damages recoverable.

Held: The Court of Appeal ([2006] I WLR 533) dismissed the claimant's appeal, holding that damages were to be calculated having regard to the fact that the defendant would have cancelled the charter under the war clause.

Lord Mance (in the Court of Appeal):

23. ... As the judge observed, this charter always had inherent in it the uncertainty involved in the War Clause. In many circumstances, this uncertainty could be disregarded – e.g. if damages were being assessed after the end of the original charter period and no relevant war had occurred, or if damages were being assessed during the original charter period on the basis that there was no significant prospect of any such war. In other circumstances, if damages were being assessed during the original charter period, account might have to be taken of the contingency (to use Lord Denning's word) or chance (to use Waller LJ's) that a war might occur, and consideration would then also have to be given to whether or not charterers would in that event probably cancel.

24. Certainty, finality and ease of settlement are all of course important general considerations. But the element of uncertainty, resulting from the War Clause, meant that the owners were never entitled to absolute confidence that the charter would run for its full 7 year period. They never had an asset which they could bank or sell on that basis. There is no reason why the transmutation of their claims to performance of the charter into claims for damages for non-performance of the charter should improve their position in this respect.

25. Further, as Mr Young submitted, the assessment of damages often depends on, or is informed by, subsequent events, and the claim for loss on the spot market from 17th December 2001 until 1st April 2002, the claim based on a substitute rate as from 1st April 2002 and the claim for loss of a profit share – which as I have said would surely depend on looking at actual market rates over the balance of the original charter – are all instances applicable in this case. The additional need to take into account the now known fact of the Second Gulf War is simply another instance.

26. In any event, I consider that this is a situation where any considerations of the type mentioned in the first sentence of paragraph 24 above would have, so far as necessary, to yield to the greater importance of achieving an assessment of damages and compensation which more accurately reflects the actual loss which the owners can, at whatever is the date of assessment, now be seen to have suffered as a result of the charterers' repudiation.

The claimant in *The Golden Victory* argued that damages ought to be calculated at or very shortly after the date of breach, and that subsequent events (such as the outbreak of the Gulf War triggering the war clause) were irrelevant to the calculation of damages unless those subsequent events could be said to have been inevitable at the date of the breach. The argument was founded on the view that the acceptance of the anticipatory breach 'crystallised' the amount of damages recoverable. Such a rule, it was argued, was essential in order to maintain business certainty. The Court of Appeal rejected this line of argument. While recognising that certainty, finality and ease of settlement were important considerations in the assessment of damages for repudiatory breach, Lord Mance noted that uncertainty was already written into the charterparty. The war clause meant that Golden Strait was never entitled to absolute confidence that the charter would run for its full seven-year period. Furthermore, in his Lordship's view, considerations of certainty needed 'to yield to the greater importance of achieving an assessment of damages and compensation that more accurately reflects the actual loss which the owners can, at whatever is the date of assessment, now be seen to have suffered as a result of the charterers' repudiation'. The Court of Appeal's decision was subsequently affirmed by the House of Lords (Lord Bingham and Lord Walker dissenting): [2007] UKHL 12. Lord Scott stated:

34. The assessment at the date of breach rule is particularly apt to cater for cases where a contract for the sale of goods in respect of which there is a market has been repudiated. The loss caused by the breach to the seller or the buyer, as the case may be, can be measured by the difference between the contract price and the market price at the time of the breach. The seller can re-sell his goods in the market. The buyer can buy substitute goods in the market. Thereby the loss caused by the breach can be fixed. But even here some period must usually be allowed to enable the necessary arrangements for the substitute sale or purchase to be made (see e.g. *Kaines v Österreichische* [1993] 2 Lloyd's Rep 1). The relevant market price for the purpose of assessing the quantum of the recoverable loss will be the market price at the expiration of that period.

35. In cases, however, where the contract for sale of goods is not simply a contract for a one-off sale, but is a contract for the supply of goods over some specified period, the application of the general rule may not be in the least apt. Take the case of a three year contract for the supply of goods and a repudiatory breach of the contract at the end of the first year. The breach is accepted and damages are claimed but before the assessment of the damages an event occurs that, if it had occurred while the contract was still on foot, would have been a frustrating event terminating the contract, e.g. legislation prohibiting any sale of the goods. The contractual benefit of which the victim of the breach of contract had been deprived by the breach would not have extended beyond the date of the frustrating event. So on what principled basis could the victim claim compensation attributable to a loss of contractual benefit after that date? Any rule that required damages attributable to that period to be paid would be inconsistent with the overriding compensatory principle on which awards of contractual damages ought to be based.

36. The same would, in my opinion, be true of any anticipatory breach the acceptance of which had terminated an executory contract. The contractual benefit for the loss of which the victim of the breach can seek compensation cannot escape the uncertainties of the future. If, at the time the assessment of damages takes place, there were nothing to suggest that the expected benefit of the executory contract would not, if the contract had remained on foot, have duly accrued, then the quantum of damages would be unaffected by uncertainties that would be no more than conceptual. If there were a real possibility that an event would happen terminating the contract, or in some way reducing the contractual benefit to which the damages claimant would, if the contract had remained on foot, have become entitled, then the quantum of damages might need, in order to reflect the extent of the chance that that possibility might materialize, to be reduced proportionately. The lodestar is that the damages should represent the value of the contractual benefits of which the claimant had been deprived by the breach of contract, no less but also no more. But if a terminating event had happened, speculation would not be needed, an estimate of the extent of the chance of such a happening would no longer be necessary and, in relation to the period during which the contract would have remained executory had it not been for the terminating event, it would be apparent that the earlier anticipatory breach of contract had deprived the victim of the breach of nothing. In the *Bwllfa* case [1903] AC 426, Lord Halsbury at 429 rejected the proposition that 'because you could not arrive at the true sum when the notice was given, you should shut your eyes to the true sum now you do know it, because you could not have guessed it then' and Lord Robertson said at 432, that 'estimate and conjecture are superseded by facts as the proper media concludendi' and, at 433, that 'as in this instance facts are available, they are not to be shut out'. Their Lordships were not dealing with a contractual, or tortious, damages issue but with the quantum of compensation to be paid under the Waterworks Clauses Act 1847. Their approach, however, is to my mind as apt for our purposes on this appeal as to theirs on that appeal.

37. My noble and learned friend Lord Bingham, in what has been rightly described as a strong dissent, has referred (in para 9) to the overriding compensatory principle that the injured party is entitled to such damages as will put him in the same financial position as if the contract had been performed. On the facts of the present case, however, the contract contained clause 33 and would not have required any performance by the Charterers after March 2003. It should follow that, in principle, the owners, the injured party, are not entitled to any damages in respect of the period thereafter. As at the date of the Owners' acceptance of the Charterers' repudiation of the charterparty, the proposition that what at that date the Owners had lost was a charterparty with slightly less than four years to run requires qualification. The charterparty contained clause 33. The Owners had lost a charterparty which contained a provision that would enable the Charterers to terminate the charterparty if a certain event happened. The event did happen. It happened before the damages had been assessed. It was accepted in argument before your Lordships that the Owners' charterparty rights would not, in practice, have been marketable for a capital sum. The contractual benefit of the charterparty to the Owners, the benefit of which they were deprived by the repudiatory breach, was the right to receive the hire rate during the currency of the charterparty. The termination of the charterparty under clause 33 would necessarily have brought to an end that right.

38 .The arguments of the Owners offend the compensatory principle. They are seeking compensation exceeding the value of the contractual benefits of which they were deprived. Their case requires the assessor to speculate about what might happen over the period 17 December 2001 to 6 December 2005 regarding the occurrence of a clause 33 event and to shut his eyes to the actual happening of a clause 33 event in March 2003. The argued justification for thus offending the compensatory principle is that priority should be given to the so-called principle of certainty. My Lords there is, in my opinion, no such principle. Certainty is a desideratum and a very important one, particularly in commercial contracts. But it is not a principle and must give way to principle. Otherwise incoherence of principle is the likely result. The achievement of certainty in relation to commercial contracts depends, I would suggest, on firm and settled principles of the law of contract rather than on the tailoring of principle in order to frustrate tactics of delay to which many litigants in many areas of litigation are wont to resort. Be that as it may, the compensatory principle that must underlie awards of contractual damages is, in my opinion, clear and requires the appeal in the case to be dismissed. I wish also to express my agreement with the reasons given by my noble and learned friends Lord Carswell and Lord Brown of Eaton-under-Heywood for coming to the same conclusion.

It is thus clear that subsequent events can be taken into account in the assessment of damages for an anticipatory breach in order to ensure that the claimant is not overcompensated for its loss. However, in *Bunge SA v Nidera BV (formerly Nidera Handelscompagnie BV)* [2013] 1 CLC 325 at [54]–[55] Hamblen J raised issues about the scope of the decision in *The Golden Victory*:

54 ... I would not accept that it is settled law that the *Golden Victory* approach applies to a one-off sale of goods contract such as this. The majority in *The Golden Victory* recognised that they were departing from the general rule that damages in respect of a marketable commodity fall to be assessed by reference to the available market price at the date of breach, but considered that the compensatory principle justified them so doing in the circumstances. However, The *Golden Victory* concerned a period contract and the departure from the general rule was only adopted in relation to the period element of the damages claim, not the applicable hire rate. Further, as the Board observed, Lord Scott at para. 34 recognised that the assessment at the date of breach rule 'is particularly apt' in sale of goods cases, as is reflected in the Sale of Goods Act. At para. 35 he drew a distinction between a one-off sale and 'a contract for the supply of goods over some specified period'. It is also to be noted that *Benjamin* treats *The Golden Victory* as being relevant to sale of goods cases because its 'reasoning could apply to long term contracts for the sale of goods' (para. 19–170).

55 Although there are passages in the majority judgments in *The Golden Victory* which are put in very general terms, I would for my part regard it as very much an open question whether The Golden Victory approach would apply in a one-off sale of goods contract where there is an available market and damages fall to be assessed in accordance with the Sale of Goods Act. There is in such a case no difficulty about valuing what has been lost. The innocent party is compensated for the value of what he has lost at the time he loses it. Having had a mitigation opportunity which can be valued without difficulty by reference to the market there is no need or warrant to consider subsequent events. Fixing the damages by reference to market value promotes certainty and predictability, and helps inform the innocent party's decision whether or not to terminate. However, the matter was not fully argued and since it is not necessary to decide it on this appeal I do not propose to do so.

The case involved a contract for the sale of Russian milling wheat which was, prior to the shipping period and in breach of contract, cancelled. It transpired that the contract could, subsequently, have been legitimately cancelled, within the shipping period and under the terms of the contact, following a Russian embargo on the export of wheat. To what extent, if at all, could the subsequent ability to legitimately cancel the contract be taken into account in calculating damages? This required a consideration of *The Golden Victory* and the Supreme Court in *Bunge SA v Nidera BV (formerly Nidera Handelscompagnie BV)* [2015] UKSC 43 clarified the scope of the decision in *The Golden Victory*. Lord Sumption (with whom Lord Neuberger, Lord Mance, Lord Clarke and Lord Toulson agreed) stated:

16 ... That situation gives rise to two potential questions which are not always sufficiently distinguished in the case-law. The first question is: assuming that there is an available market, as at what date is the market price to be determined for the purpose of assessing damages? It is clear that once that date is determined, any subsequent change in the market price is irrelevant. Most of the case-law on the measure of damages for the repudiation of a contract of sale arises out of disputes about the relevant market price, and this is what judges speaking of the breach-date rule are usually referring to. The second question is: in what if any circumstances will it be relevant to take account of contingencies (other than a change in the market price) if subsequent events show that they would have reduced the value of performance, perhaps to nothing, even without the defaulter's renunciation? This may happen, for example, if the injured party would have been unable to perform it when the time for performance arrived, or if the defaulter would have been relieved of the obligation to perform by frustration or under the express terms.

17 The answer to the first question, although like section 51(3) it is only a prima facie answer, is that where there is an available market for the goods, the market price is determined as at the contractual date of delivery, unless the buyer should have mitigated by going into the market and entering into a substitute contract at some earlier stage: *Garnac Grain Co Ine v HMFFauré & Fairclough Ltd* [1968] AC 1130, 1168; *Tai Hing Cotton Mill Ltd v Kamsing Knitting Factory* [1979] AC 91, 102. Normally, however, the injured party will be required to mitigate his loss by going into the market for a substitute contract as soon as is reasonable after the original contract was terminated. Damages will then be assessed by reference to the price which he obtained. If he chooses not to do so, damages will generally be assessed by reference to the market price at the time when he should have done: *Koch Marine Ine v d'Amica Societa di Navigazione (The Elena D'Amico)* [1980] 1 Lloyd's 75, 87, 89. The result is that in practice where there is a renunciation and an available market, the relevant market price for the purposes of assessing damages will generally be determined not by the prima facie measure but by the principles of mitigation.

18 The answer to the second question was given initially by the Court of Appeal in *Maredelanto Compania Naviera SA v Bergbau-Handel GmbH (The Mihalis Angelos)* [1971] 1 QB 164 and then by the House of Lords in *Golden Strait Corpn v Nippon Yusen Kubishika Kaisha (The Golden Victory)* [2007] 2 AC 353.

19 In the first of these cases the Court of Appeal held that on the assumption that the voyage charterers of *The Mihalis Angelos* had repudiated the contract they were nevertheless not liable for substantial damages. This was because if the contract had continued they would have terminated it lawfully for breach of a condition as to the time of the vessel's arrival at the port of delivery. Lord Denning and Edmund Davies LJ put the matter entirely generally. In Lord Denning's words (at p 196), 'You must take into account all contingencies which might have reduced or extinguished the loss'. But difficulty arose from the suggestion of Megaw LJ (at pp 209–210) that the result turned on the fact that the vessel was 'predestined' to arrive late at the port of delivery.

20 The subsequent decision in *The Golden Victory* disposed of the argument, based on Megaw LJ's dictum, that a subsequent event which would have reduced or extinguished the loss had to be inevitable, viewed at the time when the repudiation was accepted. The facts were that a seven-year time charter had been brought to an end by the charterer's repudiation in the course of performance some four years before its contractual terms but only fourteen months before it would have been cancelled in any event under a war clause. At the time when the charterers' repudiation was accepted, war was far from inevitable. It was found to be no more than a possibility. The question was how long it should be assumed, in those circumstances, that the charterparty would have lasted if it had not been wrongfully terminated. The House held by a majority that the overriding principle (or 'lodestar') was the compensatory principle. Irrespective of the date as at which the market price was ascertained, it was necessary to take account of contingencies known at the date of the arbitrator's assessment to have occurred, if their effect was that the contract would have been lawfully terminated at or before its contractual term. It followed that damages were to be assessed on the assumption that the charter would have lasted for another 14 months.

21 The reasoning has to some extent been obscured by the focus on the implications of the so-called 'breach-date rule' and on the competing demands of certainty and compensation. The real difference between the majority and the minority turned on the question what was being valued for the purpose assessing damages. The majority were valuing the chartered service that would actually have been performed if the charterparty had not been wrongfully brought to a premature end. On that footing, the notional substitute contract, whenever it was made and at whatever market rate, would have made no difference because it would have been subject to the same war clause as the original contract: see Lord Scott of Foscote at para 37, and Lord Brown of Eaton-under-Heywood at paras 76–78 and 82. The minority on the other hand considered that one should value not the chartered service which would actually have been performed, but the charterparty itself, assessed at the time that it was terminated, by reference to the terms of a notional substitute concluded as soon as possible after the termination of the original. That would vary, not according to the actual outcome, but according to the outcomes which were perceived as possible or probable at the time that the notional substitute contract was made. The possibility or probability of war would then be factored into the price agreed in the substitute contract: see Lord Bingham of Cornhill at paras 22 and Lord Walker of Gestingthorpe at paras 45–46. I think that the majority's view on this point was correct. Sections 50 and 51 of the Sale of Goods Act, like the corresponding principles of the common law, are concerned with the price of the goods or services which would have been delivered under the contract. They are not concerned with the value of the contract as an article of commerce in itself. As Lord Brown observed at paras 82–83, even if the charterparty rights could have been sold for a capital sum, this was not a proper basis for assessing loss, and an assessment which proceeded as if it were would 'extend the effect of the available market rule well beyond its proper scope'.

22 The leading speech for the majority, which was delivered by Lord Scott of Foscote, contains dicta which have sometimes been taken to suggest a distinction between a contract for a one-off sale and a contract for the supply of goods or services over a period of time: see paras 34–35. These dicta influenced both the Appeal Board and Hamblen J in the present case. But I do not think that Lord Scott was suggesting that the underlying principle was any different in the case of a one-off sale. Where the only question is the relevant date for taking the market price, the financial consequences of the breach may be said to 'crystallise' at that date. But where, after that date, some supervening event occurs which shows that that neither the original contract (had it continued) nor the notional substitute contract at the market price would ever have been performed, the concept of 'crystallising' the assessment of damages at that price is unhelpful. The occurrence of the supervening event would have reduced the value of performance, possibly to nothing, even if the contract had not been wrongfully terminated and whatever the relevant market price. The nature of that problem does not differ according to whether the contract provides for a single act of performance or several successive ones. Nor, as it seems to me, is there any principled reason why the majority's solution should be any different in the two cases. If a distinction were to be made between them, it is difficult to see how *The Mihalis Angelos*, which concerned a contract for a single voyage, could have been decided as it was. As Lord Scott observed in *The Golden Victory* at para 36, the compensatory principle would be equally offended by disregarding subsequent events serving to reduce or eliminate the loss under 'any anticipatory breach the acceptance of which had terminated an executory contract'. The most that can be said about one-off contracts of sale is that the facts may be different. In particular, if the injured party goes into the market and enters into a substitute contract by way of mitigation, it will not necessarily be subject to the same contingencies as the original contract.

23 The principle upheld in *The Golden Victory* has come in for a certain amount of academic criticism and judicial doubt. To my mind both the criticism and the doubt are unjustified. The most comprehensive and influential critic has been Professor Treitel. His views were set out in their fullest form in a case note on the decision of the Court of Appeal, which had reached the same conclusion as the majority of the Appellate Committee: see 'Assessment of Damages for Wrongful Repudiation', (2007) 123 LQR 9. Professor Treitel's case note was cited to the Appellate Committee but evidently did not move them. His main criticisms were, first, that the decision failed to distinguish between the different supervening events (successful mitigation by the defaulting party, inability of the innocent party to perform, cancellation under an express provision) which may serve to reduce or extinguish the loss; secondly, that it took no account of the collateral motives that might have moved the party who had repudiated the contract to cancel it lawfully at a later stage if it had continued; and, thirdly, that it attached insufficient weight to the commercial value of certainty. I am no more convinced by these criticisms than the Appellate Committee was in *The Golden Victory*. The principle which the Committee applied was neither new nor heterodox. There is no principled reason why, in order to determine the value of the contractual performance which has been lost by the repudiation, one should not consider what would have happened if the repudiation had not occurred. On the contrary, this seems to be fundamental to any assessment of damages designed to compensate the injured party for the consequences of the breach. If the contract had not been repudiated, it would have been lawfully cancellable. If it was lawfully cancellable, the charterer would have been entitled to avail himself of that right regardless of his motive. The only question is whether he would in fact have done so, a question which in practice would probably have been determined by his financial interest. Commercial certainty is undoubtedly important, although its significance will inevitably vary from one contract to another. But it can rarely be thought to justify an award of substantial damages to someone who has not suffered any. As Lord Mance pointed out in the Court of Appeal in *The Golden Victory* [2006] 1 WLR 533, para 24, the degree of uncertainty involved in that case was no greater than the uncertainty inherent in the contract itself. The parties' obligations were always defeasible in the uncertain event of war, just as their obligations under the contract presently in issue were always defeasible in the uncertain event of an export embargo.

Accordingly, only nominal damages were awarded. See also *Hooper v Oates* [2013] EWCA Civ 91. More recently, *Classic Maritime Inc v Limbungan Makmur SDN BHD, Lion Diversified Holdings BHD* [2019] EWCA Civ 1102 Males LJ stated:

80. Both *The Golden Victory* and *Bunge v Nidera* were concerned with the assessment of damages for an anticipatory breach by renunciation which required the court to value the innocent party's right to future performance, in the former case the right to performance of what was in effect an instalment contract with monthly hire payments and in the latter case the right to performance of a single supply of goods. In both cases the compensatory principle operated to reduce or extinguish the innocent party's claim for damages. That was because the value of the performance to which that party was entitled was adversely affected by events which occurred after the acceptance of the repudiation. However, the fundamental principle is clear.

81. The present case is not concerned with an anticipatory breach, but with actual breaches as a result of the charterer's failure to supply cargoes for each of the five shipments in issue. It is common ground that, subject only to clause 32, the charterer's obligation to supply cargoes was an absolute obligation (see *The Nikmary* [2003] EWCA Civ 1715, [2004] 1 Lloyd's Rep 55). Thus the performance to which the shipowner was entitled, once it was determined that clause 32 did not provide the charterer with a defence, was the supply of cargoes. The value of that performance was the freights which the shipowner would have earned if the cargoes had been supplied less the cost of earning them. In principle, therefore, the comparison which application of the compensatory principle required was between (1) the freights which the shipowner would have earned less the cost of earning them and (2) the actual position in which the shipowner found itself as a result of the breach. It is now agreed that this comparison would result in a damages award of over US$19 million.

82. The comparison which the judge carried out was different. It was between the shipowner's position if the charterer had been ready and willing to perform and the shipowner's actual position. The judge said at [146] that undertaking this comparison did not involve 'an impermissible sleight of hand' but I do not agree. The character's obligation was not to be ready and willing to supply a cargo in each case, but actually to supply one. The charterer was not in breach because it was unwilling to perform, but because it failed to do so, even if the reason why it failed to do so was because it was unwilling.

83. In the case of an anticipatory breach (i.e. a renunciation in advance of the time for performance), a party repudiates a contract if it demonstrates an unwillingness to perform, in which case (as in *The Golden Victory* and *Bunge v Nidera*) it may be necessary to consider whether, if it had not demonstrated that unwillingness, it would nevertheless have been excused from performance by later events. If so, that will affect the value of the rights which the innocent party has lost. But that is not so in the case of an actual breach, as in the present case. In the present case, where there is an absolute obligation to supply a cargo, whether the charterer was ready and willing to supply is neither here nor there. Nor is it relevant whether performance is impossible as (in the absence of a defence such as frustration or illegality) impossibility is not a defence: *Taylor v Caldwell* (1863) 3 B&S 826 at page 833. The simple fact is that the charterer failed to do what it had promised to do and is thereby in breach.

84. Although the judge described his approach as an application of the compensatory principle which was realistic because it took account of the reason why the charterer was in breach of its duty to supply the cargoes, this was in my judgment an irrelevant consideration in the assessment of damages. There is no case, or at any rate none which was cited to us, in which the reason why a party is in breach of contract has been held to justify, let alone require, a different approach to the compensatory principle.

14.3.4 The right of election

On the occurrence of an anticipatory breach, the innocent party must elect either to terminate the contract and claim for damages, or to affirm the contract, notwithstanding the breach. The general rule is that the innocent party must communicate its decision to the other party. This is not, however, always necessary.

***Vitol SA v Norelf Ltd (The 'Santa Clara')* [1996] AC 800**

Facts: On 11 February 1991, Vitol agreed to purchase, from Norelf, a cargo of propane. On 8 March, while the ship was still loading, Vitol sent a telex to Norelf purporting to repudiate the contract. It was subsequently accepted that this communication amounted to an anticipatory breach. Neither party took any further step to perform the contract. On 15 March, following a slump in the market for propane, Norelf resold the cargo at a significantly reduced price. Norelf brought a claim for the difference between the contract price and the price they received for the cargo. The arbitrator found for Norelf, holding that its failure to take any further step to perform the contract constituted sufficient communication of acceptance of Vitol's anticipatory breach. Phillips J upheld the arbitrator's decision. The Court of Appeal, however, reversed the decision, holding that Norelf's failure to perform did not constitute a clear and unequivocal acceptance of the Vitol's anticipatory breach. This was because silence and inaction is as much consistent with affirmation of the contract as it is with the acceptance of a repudiation. Norelf appealed to the House of Lords.

Held: The House of Lords allowed the appeal.

Lord Steyn: I would accept as established law the following propositions. (1) Where a party has repudiated a contract the aggrieved party has an election to accept the repudiation or to affirm the contract: *Fercometal SARL v Mediterranean Shipping Co SA* [1989] AC 788. (2) An act of acceptance of a repudiation requires no particular form: a communication does not have to be couched in the language of acceptance. It is sufficient that the communication or conduct clearly and unequivocally conveys to the repudiating party that that aggrieved party is treating the contract as at an end. (3) It is rightly conceded by counsel for the buyers that the aggrieved party need not personally, or by an agent, notify the repudiating party of his election to treat the contract as at an end. It is sufficient that the fact of the election comes to the repudiating party's attention, e.g. notification by an unauthorised broker or other intermediary may be sufficient: *Wood Factory Pty Ltd v Kiritos Pty Ltd* (1985) 2 NSWLR 105, 146, *per* McHugh JA; *Majik Markets Pty Ltd v S & M Motor Repairs Pty Ltd (No 1)* (1987) 10 NSWLR 49, 54, *per* Young J; *Carter and Harland, Contract Law in Australia*, 3rd edn (1996), pp 689–691, para 1970.

The arbitrator did not put forward any heterodox general theory of the law of repudiation. On the contrary he expressly stated that unless the repudiation was accepted by the sellers and the acceptance was communicated to the buyers the election was of no effect. It is plain that the arbitrator directed himself correctly in accordance with the governing general principle. The criticism of the arbitrator's reasoning centres on his conclusion that 'the failure of [the sellers] to take any further step to perform the contract

> which was apparent to [the buyers] constituted sufficient communication of acceptance'. By that statement the arbitrator was simply recording a finding that the buyers knew that the sellers were treating the contract as at an end. That interpretation is reinforced by the paragraph in his award read as a whole. The only question is whether the relevant holding of the arbitrator was wrong in law.
>
> It is now possible to turn directly to the first issue posed, namely whether non-performance of an obligation is ever as a matter of law capable of constituting an act of acceptance. On this aspect I found the judgment of Phillips J entirely convincing. One cannot generalise on the point. It all depends on the particular contractual relationship and the particular circumstances of the case. But, like Phillips J, I am satisfied that a failure to perform may sometimes signify to a repudiating party an election by the aggrieved party to treat the contract as at an end. Postulate the case where an employer at the end of a day tells a contractor that he, the employer, is repudiating the contract and that the contractor need not return the next day. The contractor does not return the next day or at all. It seems to me that the contractor's failure to return may, in the absence of any other explanation, convey a decision to treat the contract as at an end. Another example may be an overseas sale providing for shipment on a named ship in a given month. The seller is obliged to obtain an export licence. The buyer repudiates the contract before loading starts. To the knowledge of the buyer the seller does not apply for an export licence with the result that the transaction cannot proceed. In such circumstances it may well be that an ordinary businessman, circumstanced as the parties were, would conclude that the seller was treating the contract as at an end. Taking the present case as illustrative, it is important to bear in mind that the tender of a bill of lading is the pre-condition to payment of the price. Why should an arbitrator not be able to infer that when, in the days and weeks following loading and the sailing of the vessel, the seller failed to tender a bill of lading to the buyer he clearly conveyed to a trader that he was treating the contract as at an end? ... Turning to the observation of Nourse LJ [1996] QB 108, 116–117, that a failure to perform a contractual obligation is necessarily and always equivocal I respectfully disagree.
>
> Sometimes in the practical world of businessmen an omission to act may be as pregnant with meaning as a positive declaration. While the analogy of offer and acceptance is imperfect, it is not without significance that while the general principle is that there can be no acceptance of an offer by silence, our law does in exceptional cases recognise acceptance of an offer by silence. Thus in *Rust v Abbey Life Assurance Co Ltd* [1979] 2 Lloyd's Rep 334 the Court of Appeal held that a failure by a proposed insured to reject a proffered insurance policy for seven months justified on its own an inference of acceptance: see also *Treitel, The Law of Contract*, 9th edn (1995), pp 30–32. Similarly, in the different field of repudiation, a failure to perform may sometimes be given a colour by special circumstances and may only be explicable to a reasonable person in the position of the repudiating party as an election to accept the repudiation.
>
> My Lords, I would answer the question posed by this case in the same way as Phillips J. did. In truth the arbitrator inferred an election, and communication of it, from the tenor of the rejection telex and the failure, inter alia, to tender the bill of lading. That was an issue of fact within the exclusive jurisdiction of the arbitrator.
>
> For these reasons I would allow the appeal of the sellers.

It is always safer, however, for the innocent party to communicate their intention to terminate in clear and unequivocal terms. This avoids the danger of the acceptance not being effective and the innocent party taking action, which itself constitutes a repudiatory breach of obligations under the contract. The right to terminate the contract may be lost through lapse of time if 'thereby there [i]s prejudice to the defendant' (*Alen v Robles* [1969] 1 WLR 1193, 1196, *per* Fenton Atkinson LJ). The innocent party is, of course, entitled to wait for performance of the contract, but if s/he does so, s/ he runs the risk of losing his/her right to terminate (cf. *Tele2 International Card Co SA v Post Office Ltd* [2009] EWCA Civ 9). This was explained by Rix LJ in *Stocznia Gdanska SA v Latvian Shipping Co* [2002] 2 Lloyd's Rep 436, 452:

> [T]here is of course a middle ground between acceptance of repudiation and affirmation of the contract, and that is the period when the innocent party is making up his mind what to do. If he does nothing for too long, there may come a time when the law will treat him as having affirmed. If he maintains the contract in being for the moment, while reserving his right to treat it as repudiated if his contract partner persists in his repudiation, then he has not yet elected. As long as the contract remains alive, the innocent party runs the risk that a merely anticipatory repudiatory breach, a thing 'writ in water' until acceptance can be overtaken by another event which prejudices the innocent party's rights under the contract – such as frustration or even his own breach. He also runs the risk, if that is the right word, that the party in repudiation will resume performance of the contract and thus end any continuing right in the innocent party to elect to accept the former repudiation as terminating the contract.

Subsequently, in *White Rosebay Shipping SA v Hong Kong Chain Glory Shipping Ltd* [2013] EWHC 1355, Teare J stated (at [22]):

> Mr. Gunning said that Rix LJ made no mention of the innocent party having 'a reasonable period' in which to decide whether to accept a renunciation and that all that Rix LJ was saying was that if the innocent party 'does nothing for too long' the innocent party may be treated as having affirmed and that the circumstances Rix LJ had in mind were that another event may prejudice the innocent party's rights (such as frustration or the innocent party's own breach) or the party in repudiation may resume performance. It is true that Rix LJ pointed out that the innocent party ran the risk that an unaccepted renunciation, being a thing 'writ in water' until acceptance, could be overtaken by other events such as those mentioned. But the effect of what Rix LJ said before pointing that out was that the innocent party had a reasonable period of time in which to make his mind up what to do. This is how his observation is understood in Chitty on Contracts Vol.1 at paragraph 24–002.

14.3.3.1 Risks of acceptance

When a party treats an action by the other party as repudiatory, that party runs the risk of committing a repudiatory breach themselves if the court determines that the other party's actions did not constitute a repudiation of the contract. We have seen plenty of examples of this. In *Hong Kong Fir Shipping* [1962] 2 QB 26, the defendant was liable for wrongful repudiation because the failure of the plaintiff to provide a seaworthy ship did not constitute a repudiatory breach of the contract. Similarly, in *The Hansa Nord* [1976] QB 44, the pellets provided by the German sellers were not sufficiently damaged to provide a ground for the Dutch buyers' repudiation of the contract. Accordingly, the buyers were liable for wrongful repudiation. In *Federal Commerce and Navigation Ltd v Molena Alpha Inc (The'Nanfri')* [1979] AC 757, the charterers under three six-year charterparties deducted various amounts from the hire they paid to the owners. The owners objected to this, and by a telex on 4 October 1977, informed the charterers that the masters of all three ships were being instructed 'to withdraw all direct or implied authority to the charterer or its agents to sign bills of lading'. The House of Lords held that this amounted to a repudiatory breach by the owners, entitling the charterers to terminate the charterparties.

14.3.3.2 Risks of affirmation

Once the innocent party has elected to affirm the contract, their decision is final and irrevocable. The only exception to this rule is if the party in default continues with their non-performance or commits a fresh repudiatory breach, giving rise to a new right to terminate the contract (*Johnson v Agnew* [1980] AC 367). The irrevocability of the election to affirm means that it carries risks as well. For example, having affirmed the contract, the innocent party is not entitled to rely on the breach to justify their own subsequent failure to fulfil their contractual obligations (*Fercometal Sarl v Mediterranean Shipping Co SA* [1989] AC 788). Similarly, following an affirmation of the contract, the innocent party loses the right to bring an action if, prior to the time for performance, the contract is discharged for frustration.

Avery v Bowden (1855) 5 E & B 714

Facts: The defendant chartered a ship from the plaintiff to load a cargo at Odessa. The contract stated that the cargo was to be loaded within 45 days. Before that time had elapsed, an agent for the defendant informed the master of the ship that the cargo would not be available in time. The master elected to affirm the contract and remained at port in Odessa. Before the 45-day period had elapsed, war broke out between England and Russia. This constituted a frustration of the contract because it was no longer legally impossible to load the cargo at an enemy port. The plaintiff brought a claim for damages.

Held: The Court held that the plaintiff could not recover damages for breach of contract. The anticipatory breach had been affirmed by the master of the defendant's ship. The contract was then frustrated, discharging the defendant's future obligations.

Lord Campbell CJ: The war having dissolved the contract on the 1st of April, when the defendant was prevented from loading the ship without trading with the Queen's enemies, it was incumbent upon the plaintiff to prove that the cause of action on which he sues had previously accrued to him. But we think that, giving credit to what his witnesses swore, no previous cause of action is proved ...

It thus appears that the captain of The 'Lebanon', who represented the plaintiff down to the 16th day of April, and long after the declaration of war was known at Odessa, continuously insisted on the performance of the charter party by the defendant, and remained at Odessa demanding a cargo. Was there any evidence that, on or before the 1st of April, a cause of action had accrued to the plaintiff for breach of the charter party? We think not. According to our decision in *Hochster v De La Tour* (2 E & B 678), to which we adhere, if the defendant, within the running days and before the declaration of war, had positively informed the captain of The Lebanon that no cargo had been provided or would be provided for him at Odessa, and that there was no use in his remaining there any longer, the captain might have treated this as a breach and renunciation of the contract; and thereupon, sailing away from Odessa, he might have loaded a cargo at a friendly port from another person; whereupon the plaintiff would have had a right to maintain an action on the charter party to recover damages equal to the loss he had sustained from the breach of contract on the part of the defendant. The language used by the defendant's agent before the declaration of war can hardly be considered as amounting to a renunciation of the contract: but, if it had been much stronger, we conceive that it could not be considered as constituting a cause of action after the captain still continued to insist upon having a cargo in fulfilment of the charter party.

Judgment for the defendant.

Additional reading

Bojczuk, W., 'When is a Condition not a Condition?' [1987] JBL 353.

Carter, J.W., and Tolhurst, G., 'Contract Damages Following Discharge for Repudiation – Revisiting Later Events' (2016) 132 LQR 1.

Corbin, A., 'Conditions in the Law of Contract' (1919) 28 Yale L J 739.
Girvin, S.D., 'Time Charter Overlap: Determining Legitimacy and the Operation of Repudiatory Breach of Contract' [1995] JBL 200.
Goh, Y., and Man, Y., 'Rationalising Anticipatory Breach in Executed Contracts' (2016) 75 CLJ 18.
Liu, Q., 'Accepted Anticipatory Breach: Duty of Mitigation and Damages Assessment' [2006] LMCLQ 17.
Opeskin, B., 'Damages for Breach of Contract Terminated under Express Terms' (1990) 106 LQR 293.
Smith, J.C., 'Anticipatory Breach of Contract', in Lomnicka, E., and Morse, C.J.G. (eds), *Contemporary Issues in Commercial Law; Essays in Honour of A G Guest* (London: Sweet & Maxwell, 1994).
Stannard, J.E., 'In the Contractual Last Chance Saloon: Notices Making Time of the Essence' (2004) 120 LQR 137.
Treitel, G.H., 'Affirmation after Repudiatory Breach' (1998) 114 LQR 22.
Treitel, G.H., 'Assessment of Damages for Wrongful Repudiation' (2007) 123 LQR 9.

Chapter 15

Remedies

Chapter contents

15.1 Introduction

In this chapter we shall be considering remedies for breach of contract. In recent years there has been considerable debate about the meaning of the word 'remedy'. Professor Birks famously argued that the word 'remedy' should be jettisoned from our legal dictionary because of its inherent 'instability' and its tendency to 'impede' the development of a classification of responses to private law actions (see, particularly, Birks, P., 'Rights, wrongs and remedies' (2000) 20 OJLS 1, 3–4). This drastic course of action is probably not necessary. For example, Rafal Zakrzewski has provided us with a stable core meaning of remedy in his work *Remedies Reclassified*, 2005, Oxford: OUP. He suggests that we should 'use the term "remedy" only in the sense of the rights arising from certain court orders or pronouncements'.

We will consider the two main remedies for breach of contract in this chapter – the award of damages and, more briefly, the order of specific relief. Following a breach of contract, the courts generally aim to award a remedy that puts the claimant 'in a situation as beneficial to him as if the agreement were specifically performed' (*Harnett v Yielding* (1805) 2 Sch & Lef 549, 553). Usually an award of compensatory damages will be sufficient to achieve this purpose because the claimant, for example, can use the damages to purchase substitute performance from an alternative source. In some situations, however, substitute performance will be unavailable or will be insufficient to protect the claimant's interest in performance of the contract. In such cases, the courts may turn to alternative remedies, such as gain-based damages or specific relief (indeed, under the Consumer Rights Act 2015 a consumer may be able to choose remedies such as repair or replacement when a trader delivers goods which do not conform with the contract (see s 23) or the remedy of repeat performance where a trader performs a service which does not conform with the contract (see s 55)). We will see that the principle underlying the availability of each of these remedies is the protection of the parties' bargained-for interest in performance.

We will begin by considering the remedy of damages, and will then examine specific relief.

15.2 Damages

Damages will be available as of right, following every breach of contract. Several legal commentators have suggested that the sole purpose of damages is compensation for loss. Our starting point is that damages for breach of contract are compensatory in nature. This principle was recently underlined by the Supreme Court in *Morris-Garner v One Step (Support) Ltd* [2018] UKSC 20, although the Supreme Court did note that the law is tolerant of some imprecision where the loss cannot be precisely measured (see also *Aarons v Brocket Hall (Jersey) Ltd* [2018] EWHC 222 (QB) on the general non-availability of exemplary damages). However, this general principle must now be read in the light of, for example, the decision of the House of Lords in *Attorney General v Blake* [2001] 1 AC 268.

15.2.1 Compensatory damages: the different measures

The purpose of compensatory damages is to compensate the claimant for the loss he has suffered as a result of the breach of contract. In a two-part article in the *Yale Law Journal* entitled 'The reliance interest in contract damages', Fuller and Perdue famously expounded the three different measures of compensatory damages, which they labelled the reliance, expectation and restitution interests (but cf. Campbell, D., 'Better than Fuller: a two interest model of remedies for breach of contract' (2015) 78 MLR 296). The article was significant both for the terminology it used and for its elevation of the reliance interest above the expectation interest.

Fuller, L, and Purdue Jr, W, 'The reliance interest in contract damages' (1936) 46 *YLJ* 52, 52–62

The proposition that legal rules can be understood only with reference to the purposes they serve would today scarcely be regarded as an exciting truth. The notion that law exists as a means to an end has been commonplace for at least half a century. There is, however, no justification for assuming, because this attitude has now achieved respectability, and even triteness, that it enjoys a pervasive application in practice. Certainly there are even today few legal treatises of which it may be said that the author has throughout clearly defined the purposes which his definitions and distinctions serve …

In no field is this more true than in that of damages. In the assessment of damages the law tends to be conceived, not as a purposive ordering of human affairs, but as a kind of juristic mensuration. The language of the decisions sounds in terms not of command but of discovery.

… For example, one frequently finds the 'normal' rule of contract damages (which awards to the promisee the value of the expectancy, 'the lost profit') treated as a mere corollary of a more fundamental principle, that the purpose of granting damages is to make 'compensation' for injury. Yet in this case we 'compensate' the plaintiff by giving him something he never had. This seems on the face of things a queer kind of 'compensation. We can, to be sure, make the term 'compensation' seem appropriate by saying that the defendant's breach 'deprived' the plaintiff of the expectancy. But this is in essence only a metaphorical statement of the effect of the legal rule. In actuality the loss which the plaintiff suffers (deprivation of the expectancy) is not a datum of nature but the reflection of a normative order. It appears as a 'loss' only by reference to an unstated *ought*. Consequently, when the law gauges damages by the value of the promised performance it is not merely measuring a quantum, but is seeking an end, however vaguely conceived this end may be.

It is for this reason that it is impossible to separate the law of contract damages from the larger body of motives and policies which constitutes the general law of contracts. It is, unfortunately for the simplicity of our subject, impossible to assume that the purposive and policy-directed element of contract law has been exhausted in the rules which define contract and breach. If this were possible the law of contract damages would indeed be simple, and we would have but one measure of recovery for all contracts. Of course this is not the case …

The purposes pursued in awarding contract damages

It is convenient to distinguish three principal purposes which may be pursued in awarding contract damages. These purposes, and the situations in which they become appropriate, may be stated briefly as follows:

Firstly, the plaintiff has in reliance on the promise of the defendant conferred some value on the defendant. The defendant fails to perform his promise. The court may force the defendant to disgorge the value he received from the plaintiff. The object here may be termed the prevention of gain by the defaulting promisor at the expense of the promisee; more briefly, the prevention of unjust enrichment. The interest protected may be called the *restitution interest* …

Secondly, the plaintiff has in reliance on the promise of the defendant changed his position. For example, the buyer under a contract for the sale of land has incurred expense in the investigation of the seller's title, or has neglected the opportunity to enter other contracts. We may award damages to the plaintiff for the purpose of undoing the harm which his reliance on the defendant's promise has caused him. Our object is to put him in as good a position as he was in before the promise was made. The interest protected in this case may be called the *reliance interest*.

Thirdly, without insisting on reliance by the promisee or enrichment of the promisor, we may seek to give the promisee the value of the expectancy which the promise created. We may in a suit for specific performance actually compel the defendant to render the promised performance to the plaintiff, or, in a suit for damages, we may make the defendant pay the money value of this performance. Here our object is to put the plaintiff in as good a position as he would have occupied had the defendant performed his promise. The interest protected in this case we may call the *expectation interest*.

It will be observed that what we have called the restitution interest unites two elements: (1) reliance by the promisee, (2) a resultant gain to the promisor. It may for some purposes be necessary to separate these elements. In some cases a defaulting promisor may after his breach be left with an unjust gain which was not taken from the promisee (a third party furnished the consideration), or which was not the result of reliance by the promisee (the promisor violated a promise not to appropriate the promisee's goods). Even in those cases where the promisor's gain results from the promisee's reliance it may happen that damages will be assessed somewhat differently, depending on whether we take the promisor's gain or the promisee's loss as the standard of measurement. Generally, however, in the cases we shall be discussing, gain by the promisor will be accompanied by a corresponding and, so far as its legal measurement is concerned, identical loss to the promisee, so that for our purposes the most workable classification is one which presupposes in the restitution interest a correlation of promisor's gain and promisee's loss. If, as we shall assume, the gain involved in the restitution interest results from and is identical with the plaintiff's loss through reliance, then the restitution interest is merely a special case of the reliance interest; all of the cases coming under the restitution interest will be covered by the reliance interest, and the reliance interest will be broader than the restitution interest only to the extent that it includes cases where the plaintiff has relied on the defendant's promise without enriching the defendant ...

It is obvious that the three 'interests' we have distinguished do not present equal claims to judicial intervention. It may be assumed that ordinary standards of justice would regard the need for judicial intervention as decreasing in the order in which we have listed the three interests. The 'restitution interest', involving a combination of unjust impoverishment with unjust gain, presents the strongest case for relief. If, following Aristotle, we regard the purpose of justice as the maintenance of an equilibrium of goods among members of society, the restitution interest presents twice as strong a claim to judicial intervention as the reliance interest, since if A not only causes B to lose one unit but appropriates that unit to himself, the resulting discrepancy between A and B is not one unit but two.

On the other hand, the promisee who has actually relied on the promise, even though he may not thereby have enriched the promisor, certainly presents a more pressing case for relief than the promisee who merely demands satisfaction for his disappointment in not getting what was promised him. In passing from compensation for change of position to compensation for loss of expectancy we pass, to use Aristotle's terms again, from the realm of corrective justice to that of distributive justice. The law no longer seeks merely to heal a disturbed status quo, but to bring into being a new situation. It ceases to act defensively or restoratively, and assumes a more active role. With the transition, the justification for legal relief loses its self-evident quality. It is as a matter of fact no easy thing to explain why the normal rule of contract recovery should be that which measures damages by the value of the promised performance. Since this 'normal rule' throws its shadow across our whole subject it will be necessary to examine the possible reasons for its existence. It may be said parenthetically that the discussion which follows, though directed primarily to the normal measure of recovery where damages are sought, also has relevance to the more general question, why should a promise which has not been relied on ever be enforced at all, whether by a decree of specific performance or by an award of damages? ...

Why should the law ever protect the expectation interest?

Perhaps the most obvious answer to this question is one which we may label 'psychological'. This answer would run something as follows: The breach of a promise arouses in the promisee a sense of injury. This feeling is not confined to cases where the promisee has relied on the promise. Whether or not he has actually changed his position because of the promise, the promisee has formed an attitude of expectancy such that a breach of the promise causes him to feel that he has been 'deprived' of something which was 'his'. Since this sentiment is a relatively uniform one, the law has no occasion to go back on it. It accepts it as a datum and builds its rule about it.

The difficulty with this explanation is that the law does in fact go back on the sense of injury which the breach of a promise engenders. No legal system attempts to invest with juristic sanction all promises.

Some rule or combination of rules effects a sifting out for enforcement of those promises deemed important enough to society to justify the law's concern with them. Whatever the principles which control this sifting out process may be, they are not convertible into terms of the degree of resentment which the breach of a particular kind of promise arouses. Therefore, though it may be assumed that the impulse to assuage disappointment is one shared by those who make and influence the law, this impulse can hardly be regarded as the key which solves the whole problem of the protection accorded by the law to the expectation interest.

A second possible explanation for the rule protecting the expectancy may be found in the much-discussed 'will theory' of contract law. This theory views the contracting parties as exercising, so to speak, a legislative power, so that the legal enforcement of a contract becomes merely an implementing by the state of a kind of private law already established by the parties ... It is not necessary to discuss here the contribution which the will theory is capable of making to a philosophy of contract law. Certainly some borrowings from the theory are discernible in most attempts to rationalize the bases of contract liability. It is enough to note here that while the will theory undoubtedly has some bearing on the problem of contract damages, it cannot be regarded as dictating in all cases a recovery of the expectancy. If a contract represents a kind of private law, it is a law which usually says nothing at all about what shall be done when it is violated. A contract is in this respect like an imperfect statute which provides no penalties, and which leaves it to the courts to find a way to effectuate its purposes. There would, therefore, be no necessary contradiction between the will theory and a rule which limited damages to the reliance interest. Under such a rule the penalty for violating the norm established by the contract would simply consist in being compelled to compensate the other party for detrimental reliance ...

A third and more promising solution of our difficulty lies in an economic or institutional approach. The essence of a credit economy lies in the fact that it tends to eliminate the distinction between present and future (promised) goods. Expectations of future values become, for purposes of trade, present values. In a society in which credit has become a significant and pervasive institution, it is inevitable that the expectancy created by an enforceable promise should be regarded as a kind of property, and breach of the promise as an injury to that property. In such a society the breach of a promise works an 'actual' diminution of the promisee's assets ...

The most obvious objection which can be made to the economic or institutional explanation is that it involves a *petitio principii*. A promise has present value, why? Because the law enforces it. 'The expectancy, regarded as a present value, is not the cause of legal intervention but the consequence of it. This objection may be reinforced by a reference to legal history. Promises were enforced long before there was anything corresponding to a general system of 'credit', and recovery was from the beginning measured by the value of the promised performance, the 'agreed price'. It may therefore be argued that the 'credit system' when it finally emerged was itself in large part built on the foundations of a juristic development which preceded it.

The view just suggested asserts the primacy of law over economics; it sees law not as the creature but as the creator of social institutions. The shift of emphasis thus implied suggests the possibility of a fourth explanation for the law's protection of the unrelied-on expectancy, which we may call *juristic*. This explanation would seek a justification for the normal rule of recovery in some policy consciously pursued by courts and other lawmakers. It would assume that courts have protected the expectation interest because they have considered it wise to do so, not through a blind acquiescence in habitual ways of thinking and feeling, or through an equally blind deference to the individual will. Approaching the problem from this point of view, we are forced to find not a mere explanation for the rule in the form of some sentimental, volitional, or institutional datum, but articulate reasons for its existence.

What reasons can be advanced? In the first place, even if our interest were confined to protecting promisees against an out-of-pocket loss, it would still be possible to justify the rule granting the value of the expectancy, both as a cure for, and as a prophylaxis against, losses of this sort.

It is a cure for these losses in the sense that it offers the measure of recovery most likely to reimburse the plaintiff for the (often very numerous and very difficult to prove) individual acts and forbearances which make up his total reliance on the contract. If we take into account 'gains prevented' by reliance, that is, losses involved in foregoing the opportunity to enter other contracts, the notion that the rule protecting the expectancy is adopted as the most effective means of compensating for detrimental reliance seems not at all far-fetched. Physicians with an extensive practice often charge their patients the full office call fee for broken appointments. Such a charge looks on the face of things like a claim to the promised fee; it seems to be based on the 'expectation interest'. Yet the physician making the charge will quite justifiably regard it as compensation for the loss of the opportunity to gain a similar fee from a different patient. This foregoing of other opportunities is involved to some extent in entering most contracts, and the impossibility of subjecting this type of reliance to any kind of measurement may justify a categorical rule granting the value of the expectancy as the most effective way of compensating for such losses.

The rule that the plaintiff must after the defendant's breach take steps to mitigate damages tends to corroborate the suspicion that there lies hidden behind the protection of the expectancy a concern to compensate the plaintiff for the loss of the opportunity to enter other contracts. Where after the defendant's breach the opportunity remains open to the plaintiff to sell his services or goods elsewhere, or to fill his needs from another source, he is bound to embrace that opportunity. Viewed in this way the rule of 'avoidable harms' is a qualification on the protection accorded the expectancy, since it means that the plaintiff, in those cases where it is applied, is protected only to the extent that he has in reliance on the contract foregone other equally advantageous opportunities for accomplishing the same end.

But, as we have suggested, the rule measuring damages by the expectancy may also be regarded as a prophylaxis against the losses resulting from detrimental reliance. Whatever tends to discourage breach of contract tends to prevent the losses occasioned through reliance. Since the expectation interest furnishes a more easily administered measure of recovery than the reliance interest, it will in practice offer a more effective sanction against contract breach. It is therefore possible to view the rule measuring damages by the expectancy in a quasi-criminal aspect, its purpose being not so much to compensate the promisee as to penalize breach of promise by the promisor. The rule enforcing the unrelied-on promise finds the same justification, on this theory, as an ordinance which fines a man for driving through a stop-light when no other vehicle is in sight.

In seeking justification for the rule granting the value of the expectancy there is no need, however, to restrict ourselves by the assumption, hitherto made, that the rule can only be intended to cure or prevent the losses caused by reliance. A justification can be developed from a less negative point of view. It may be said that there is not only a policy in favor of preventing and undoing the harms resulting from reliance, but also a policy in favor of promoting and facilitating reliance on business agreements. As in the case of the stop-light ordinance we are interested not only in preventing collisions but in speeding traffic. Agreements can accomplish little, either for their makers or for society, unless they are made the basis for action. When business agreements are not only made but are also acted on, the division of labor is facilitated, goods find their way to the places where they are most needed, and economic activity is generally stimulated. These advantages would be threatened by any rule which limited legal protection to the reliance interest. Such a rule would in practice tend to discourage reliance. The difficulties in proving reliance and subjecting it to pecuniary measurement are such that the business man knowing, or sensing, that these obstacles stood in the way of judicial relief would hesitate to rely on a promise in any case where the legal sanction was of significance to him. To encourage reliance we must therefore dispense with its proof. For this reason it has been found wise to make recovery on a promise independent of reliance, both in the sense that in some cases the promise is enforced though not relied on (as in the bilateral business agreement) and in the sense that recovery is not limited to the detriment incurred in reliance.

The juristic explanation in its final form is then twofold. It rests the protection accorded the expectancy on (1) the need for curing and preventing the harms occasioned by reliance, and (2) the need for facilitating reliance on business agreements.

Fuller and Perdue challenged the traditional assumption that expectation damages are the primary measure of relief. The authors adopt a corrective justice approach to contract damages and argue that the need for judicial intervention is much stronger where the promisee has changed his position in reliance on the promise. Thus, the restitution and reliance interests are much more worthy of judicial protection than the expectation interest.

Ultimately Fuller and Perdue stop short of arguing for the abolition of expectation damages. Their real thesis is that the theoretical justification for such damages is not rooted in a commitment to protecting the expectations created by a binding promise. Rather, expectation damages serve two functions that both relate to the reliance interest: (1) they provide a cure for reliance losses where the promisee has foregone the opportunity to enter into other contracts; (2) they act as a prophylaxis (a deterrent) against reliance losses.

Fuller and Perdue's thesis has been developed by other authors, most notably Professor Atiyah, who has used it to challenge the court's willingness to enforce purely executory contracts.

Atiyah, P, 'Contracts, promises and the law of obligations', in Atiyah, P, *Essays on Contract*, 1986, Oxford: Clarendon Press, pp 39–40

Virtually all discussion of the source of contractual and promissory obligation, in law and in morality, has failed to draw the all important distinction between promises and contracts which rest purely on intention, and promises and contracts which depend partly on action. Surely, nobody can doubt that morally speaking promises are more strongly binding where payment has already been received, or where there is a clear and significant act in reliance which would worsen the position of the promisee if the promise were not performed ... [I]t may be suggested that promises themselves are frequently of an evidentiary character. The purpose of a promise, far from being, as is so often assumed, to create some wholly independent source of an obligation, is frequently to bolster up an already existing duty. Promises help to clarify, to quantify, to give precision to moral obligations, many of which already exist or would arise anyhow from the performance of acts which are contemplated or invited by the promise. The promise which is given without any independent reason for it is a peculiarity, just as the wholly executory contract is a legal peculiarity. Is it pure coincidence that the phrase, a 'gratuitous promise', means both a promise without payment and a promise without reason? Could it then be that the refusal of English law to recognise the binding force of executory gratuitous promises is not the peculiarity, the idiosyncrasy it has so long been thought to be? Might it not be that the real oddity lies in the belief that a bare promise creates a moral obligation and should create a legal obligation, without any inquiry into the reason for which the promise was given, or the effect that the promise has had?

These arguments, of course, require much greater development than they can be given here; but enough has been said to show that, if they stand up to further examination, they should suffice to dethrone the executory contract from the central place which it occupies in contract theory. The consequences of this would be to require some drastic redrawing of the lines of the conceptual structure of contractual and promissory obligation. In the first place, the distinction between contract and restitution would surely come crashing to the ground ...

This passage forms part of a larger thesis, which challenges the traditional distinction between voluntarily assumed obligations (in the law of contract) and legally imposed obligations (in the law of tort). Professor Atiyah suggests that the law of obligations could be recast around the notions of benefit and reliance. This thesis has failed to win the support of the academy or the judiciary and it has been subjected to sustained criticism by Professor Burrows in 'Contract, tort and restitution – a satisfactory distinction or not' (1983) 99 LQR 217, and Professor Birks in 'Restitution and the freedom of contract' [1983] CLP 141. More recently, Professor Friedman ('The performance interest in contract damages' (1995) 11 LQR 628) has forcefully challenged Fuller and Purdue's analysis of the primacy of the reliance interest.

As Friedman notes, the terminology used by Fuller and Perdue has had a much greater impact on the development of the law than the substantive content of their thesis. The courts regularly reason in terms of the 'expectation', 'reliance' and 'restitution' interests of a contract, but far from relegating the 'expectation' interest to only peripheral significance, the major trend in modern contract law has been 'the strengthening of the protection afforded to the performance interest'. We will see this as we examine the different remedial responses to a breach of contract. First, we will consider the three different measures of compensatory damages, and notice how the protection of the performance interest of the contract has been clearly evident in recent decisions.

15.2.1.1 The expectation measure

Damages measured on the expectation basis aim to put the claimant in the position s/he would have been in had the contract been performed. Parke B classically expounded this measure in *Robinson v Harman* (1848) 1 Ex 850, 855:

> The rule of the common law is, that where a party sustains a loss by reason of a breach of contract, he is, so far as money can do it, to be placed in the same situation, with respect to damages, as if the contract had been performed.

This statement expresses a clear commitment to protection of the expectation interest of a contract. The claimant is entitled to receive through an award of damages the benefits that s/he would have received had the contract been successfully completed. In addition, the claimant will also be entitled to recover any consequential losses flowing from the breach.

Calculation of the expectation interest is simply a matter of looking at where the claimant would have ended up if the contract had been performed according to its terms. Problems do arise, however, when the profit, if any, that would have been made from the completed contract is uncertain.

Chaplin v Hicks [1911] 2 KB 786

Facts: The plaintiff, an actress, entered a competition organised by the defendant, a well-known actor and theatre manager. The prize was a three-year term of employment at the defendant's theatre. The plaintiff was successful at the first stage of the competition, being selected by readers of a newspaper as one of 50 out of 6,000 entrants to proceed to the second stage of the competition. The second stage involved an interview with the defendant, who would then select the 12 who would receive the promised engagements. The plaintiff was deprived of the opportunity to attend the interview due to a breach of contract by the defendant. She brought an action against the defendant, claiming damages for the loss of a chance of winning the competition. The jury found in favour of the plaintiff and assessed the damages at £100. The defendant appealed.

Held: The Court of Appeal dismissed the appeal and upheld the award at first instance.

Vaughan Williams LJ: I am of opinion that this appeal should be dismissed ... It was said that the plaintiff's chance of winning a prize turned on such a number of contingencies that it was impossible for any one, even after arriving at the conclusion that the plaintiff had lost her opportunity by the breach, to say that there was any assessable value of that loss. It is said that in a case which involves so many contingencies it is impossible to say what was the plaintiff's pecuniary loss. I am unable to agree with that contention. I agree that the presence of all the contingencies upon which the gaining of the prize might depend makes the calculation not only difficult but incapable of being carried out with certainty or precision. The proposition is that, whenever the contingencies on which the result depends are numerous and difficult to deal with, it is impossible to recover any damages for the loss of the chance or opportunity of winning the prize ... I do not agree with the contention that, if certainty is impossible of attainment, the damages for a breach of contract are unassessable. I agree, however, that damages might be so unassessable that the doctrine of averages would be inapplicable because the necessary figures for working upon would not be forthcoming; there are several decisions, which I need not deal with, to that effect. I only wish to deny with emphasis that, because precision cannot be arrived at, the jury has no function in the assessment of damages ...

[F]rom first to last there were, as there are now, many cases in which it was difficult to apply definite rules. In the case of a breach of a contract for the delivery of goods the damages are usually supplied by the fact of there being a market in which similar goods can be immediately bought, and the difference between the contract price and the price given for the substituted goods in the open market is the measure of damages; that rule has been always recognized. Sometimes, however, there is no market for the particular class of goods; but no one has ever suggested that, because there is no market, there are no damages. In such a case the jury must do the best they can, and it may be that the amount of their verdict will really be a matter of guesswork. But the fact that damages cannot be assessed with certainty does not relieve the wrongdoer of the necessity of paying damages for his breach of contract. I do not wish to lay down any such rule as that a judge can in every case leave it to the jury to assess damages for a breach of contract. There are cases, no doubt, where the loss is so dependent on the mere unrestricted volition of another that it is impossible to say that there is any assessable loss resulting from the breach. In the present case there is no such difficulty ... The jury came to the conclusion that the taking away from the plaintiff of the opportunity of competition, as one of a body of fifty, when twelve prizes were to be distributed, deprived the plaintiff of something which had a monetary value. I think that they were right and that this appeal fails.

The case shows that the courts are committed to overcoming assessment difficulties wherever possible. It is interesting to note that the award of damages may have had the effect of putting Ms Chaplin in a better position than she would have been in had the contract not been broken. This is because it is quite possible that she would not have been selected, even if she had been able to attend the audition. The award may be explained on the ground that it contained a punitive element. This is certainly hinted at in Vaughan Williams LJ's statement: 'the fact that damages cannot be assessed with certainty does not relieve the wrong-doer of the necessity of paying damages for his breach of contract.' In other words, the damages were awarded to mark the court's disapproval of the defendant's conduct. Cf. *Chweidan v Mishcon de Reya* [2014] EWHC 2685.

Damages measured on the expectation measure aim to put the claimant in a position as beneficial to him or her as if the contract had been performed. In recent times, there has been some discussion about how to measure the claimant's expectation interest. There are two principal methods of calculation:

1. **Diminution of value.** This is the difference in value between the performance for which the claimant contracted and the performance which s/he received. This measure essentially protects the claimant's economic interest in performance.
2. **Cost of cure.** This measure enables the claimant to obtain performance itself rather than the economic value of performance. In a real sense it is a form of substitute specific relief (see Smith, S, 'Substitute Specific Relief', in Rickett, C, *Justifying Remedies in the Law of Obligations*, 2008, Oxford: Hart).

Sometimes the difference in value between these two measures is insignificant. However, in some cases the difference can be very substantial indeed, and the parties may devote a considerable amount of legal argument as to which method of calculation ought to be used.

***Tito v Waddell (No 2)* [1977] Ch 106**

Facts: The case concerned phosphate mining operations on Ocean Island in the South Pacific. The defendant, British Phosphate Commissioners, had promised to replant the island with 'coconuts and other food-bearing trees' once it had completed its mining operations. The company failed to do this and the islanders claimed the cost of cure calculated at 73,140 Australian dollars per acre.

Held: Megarry VC refused to award damages measured on the 'cost of cure' basis because, by the time of the action, all the islanders had resettled 1,500 miles away on an island called Rabi. His Lordship awarded damages measured on the 'diminution in value' basis at a mere A$75 per acre.

Megarry VC: [I]t is clear that in some cases of a contract to do work to the plaintiff's land the measure of damages for breach is the reduction in value of the plaintiff's interest in the land, and in other cases it is the cost of doing the work. But which? I have been unable to find any clear statement of principle in the cases or books put before me, or in other sources that I consulted.

In the absence of any clear authority on the matter before me, I think I must consider it as a matter of principle. I do this in relation to the breach of a contract to do work on the land of another, whether to build, repair, replant or anything else: and I put it very broadly. First, it is fundamental to all questions of damages that they are to compensate the plaintiff for his loss or injury by putting him as nearly as possible in the same position as he would have been in had he not suffered the wrong ... Second, if the plaintiff has suffered monetary loss, as by a reduction in the value of his property by reason of the wrong, that is plainly a loss that he is entitled to be recouped ... Third, if the plaintiff can establish that his loss consists of or includes the cost of doing work which in breach of contract the defendant has failed to do, then he can recover as damages a sum equivalent to that cost. It is for the plaintiff to establish this: the essential question is what his loss is.

In the present case, the loss caused to the plaintiffs by the British Phosphate Commissioners' failure to replant is the diminution in the value of their land resulting from that failure, or, if it is established that the land would be replanted, the cost of replanting ... Have the plaintiffs shown that the cost of replanting represents the loss to them caused by the failure to perform the replanting obligation? Only one answer to that question seems possible, and that is No. The plaintiffs own small scattered plots of land; there is nothing to establish that the owners of neighbouring plots of land, who are not parties to these proceedings, would procure the replanting of their plots rather than keep any damages for themselves or other purposes; the Banabans are now well established in Rabi, over 1,500 miles away; and there they have an island over 10 times the size and unaffected by mining, as contrasted with the much smaller Ocean Island with some five-sixths of it mined.

Tito v Waddell demonstrates that the courts' commitment to protecting the claimants' performance interest is not absolute. It was crucial to Megarry VC that the plaintiffs had no intention of using the damages to effect the cure, that is to replant Ocean Island. It is somewhat surprising that the claimants' intention was so crucial to the decision, given that the courts normally refuse to take into account the use to which a claimant puts an award of damages. Nevertheless, this approach and the general reluctance to awarding 'cost of cure' damages where it would be out of all proportion to the benefit thereby obtained was followed by the House of Lords in *Ruxley Electronics & Construction Ltd v Forsyth*.

***Ruxley Electronics & Construction Ltd v Forsyth* [1996] AC 344**

Facts: Forsyth agreed to build a swimming pool in Ruxley's garden. The contract specified that the pool would have a diving area seven feet, six inches deep. When constructed, the diving area was only six feet deep. This was still a safe depth for diving and one which did not affect the value of the pool. Forsyth was not happy, however, and he brought an action for breach of contract claiming the cost of having the pool demolished and rebuilt (the cost of cure), a sum of £21,560.

At first instance the judge rejected the claim for 'cost of cure' damages on the ground that it was an unreasonable claim in the circumstances, but awarded Forsyth 'loss of amenity damages' of £2,500. This award was reversed by the Court of Appeal which held that damages should be awarded at the amount required to place Forsyth in the same position as he would have been in had the contract been performed, which in the circumstances was the cost of rebuilding the pool. Ruxley appealed to the House of Lords.

Held: The House of Lords allowed the appeal, holding that the cost of cure of rebuilding the pool was out of all proportion to any benefit that would be obtained. Ruxley did not challenge the first instance award of £2,500 in loss of amenity damages, and so this award was reinstated.

Lord Jauncey: Damages are designed to compensate for an established loss and not to provide a gratuitous benefit to the aggrieved party from which it follows that the reasonableness of an award of damages is to be linked directly to the loss sustained. If it is unreasonable in a particular case to award the cost of reinstatement it must be because the loss sustained does not extend to the need to reinstate ...

I take the example suggested during argument by my noble and learned friend, Lord Bridge of Harwich. A man contracts for the building of a house and specifies that one of the lower courses of brick should be blue. The builder uses yellow brick instead. In all other respects the house conforms to the contractual specification. To replace the yellow bricks with blue would involve extensive demolition and reconstruction at a very large cost. It would clearly be unreasonable to award to the owner the cost of reconstructing because his loss was not the necessary cost of reconstruction of his house, which was entirely adequate for its design purpose, but merely the lack of aesthetic pleasure which he might have derived from the sight of blue bricks. Thus in the present appeal the respondent has acquired a perfectly serviceable swimming pool, albeit one lacking the specified depth. His loss is thus not the lack of a useable pool with consequent need to construct a new one. Indeed were he to receive the cost of building a new one and retain the existing one he would have recovered not compensation for loss but a very substantial gratuitous benefit, something which damages are not intended to provide.

My Lords, the trial judge found that it would be unreasonable to incur the cost of demolishing the existing pool and building a new and deeper one. In so doing he implicitly recognised that the respondent's loss did not extend to the cost of reinstatement. He was, in my view, entirely justified in reaching that conclusion. It therefore follows that the appeal must be allowed.

It only remains to mention two further matters. The appellant argued that the cost of re-instatement should only be allowed as damages where there was shown to be an intention on the part of the aggrieved party to carry out the work. Having already decided that the appeal should be allowed I no longer find it necessary to reach a conclusion on this matter. However I should emphasise that in the normal case the court has no concern with the use to which a plaintiff puts an award of damages for a loss which has been established. Thus irreparable damage to an article as a result of a breach of contract will entitle the owner to recover the value of the article irrespective of whether he intends to replace it with a similar one or to spend the money on something else. Intention, or lack of it, to reinstate can have relevance only to reasonableness and hence to the extent of the loss which has been sustained. Once that loss has been established intention as to the subsequent use of the damages ceases to be relevant.

The second matter relates to the award of £2,500 for loss of amenity made by the trial judge. The respondent argued that he erred in law in making such award. However as the appellant did not challenge it, I find it unnecessary to express any opinion on the matter.

Lord Mustill: I add some observations of my own on the award by the trial judge of damages in a sum intermediate between, on the one hand, the full cost of reinstatement, and on the other the amount by which the malperformance has diminished the market value of the property on which the work was done: in this particular case, nil. This is a question of everyday practical importance to householders who have engaged contractors to carry out small building works, and then find (as often happens) that performance has fallen short of what was promised. I think it proper to enter on the question here, although there is no appeal against the award, because the possibility of such a recovery in a suitable case sheds light on the employer's claim that reinstatement is the only proper measure of damage.

The proposition that these two measures of damage represent the only permissible bases of recovery lie at the heart of the employer's case. From this he reasons that there is a presumption in favour of the cost of restitution, since this is the only way in which he can be given what the contractor had promised to provide. Finally, he contends that there is nothing in the facts of the present case to rebut this presumption.

The attraction of this argument is its avoidance of the conclusion that, in a case such as the present, unless the employer can prove that the defects have depreciated the market value of the property the householder can recover nothing at all. This conclusion would be unacceptable to the average householder, and it is unacceptable to me. It is a common feature of small building works performed on residential property that the cost of the work is not fully reflected by an increase in the market value of the house, and that comparatively minor deviations from specification or sound workmanship may have no direct financial effect at all. Yet the householder must surely be entitled to say that he chose to obtain from the builder a promise to produce a particular result because he wanted to make his house more comfortable, more convenient and more conformable to his own particular tastes; not because he had in mind that the work might increase the amount which he would receive if, contrary to expectation, he thought it expedient in the future to exchange his home for cash. To say that in order to escape unscathed the builder has only to show that to the mind of the average onlooker, or the average potential buyer, the results which he has produced seem just as good as those which he had promised would make a part of the promise illusory, and unbalance the bargain. In the valuable analysis contained in *Radford v De Froberville* [1977] 1 WLR 1262, Oliver J emphasised, at p 1270, that it was for the plaintiff to judge what performance he required in exchange for the price. The court should honour that choice. *Pacta sunt servanda.* If the appellant's argument leads to the conclusion that in all cases like the present the employer is entitled to no more than nominal damages, the average householder would say that there must be something wrong with the law.

In my opinion there would indeed be something wrong if, on the hypothesis that cost of reinstatement and the depreciation in value were the only available measures of recovery, the rejection of the former necessarily entailed the adoption of the latter; and the court might be driven to opt for the cost of reinstatement, absurd as the consequence might often be, simply to escape from the conclusion that the promisor can please himself whether or not to comply with the wishes of the promise which, as embodied in the contract, formed part of the consideration for the price. Having taken on the job the contractor is morally as well as legally obliged to give the employer what he stipulated to obtain, and this obligation ought not to be devalued. In my opinion however the hypothesis is not correct. There are not two alternative measures of damage, at opposite poles, but only one; namely, the loss truly suffered by the promisee. In some cases the loss cannot be fairly measured except by reference to the full cost of repairing the deficiency in performance. In others, and in particular those where the contract is designed to fulfil a purely commercial purpose, the loss will very often consist only of the monetary detriment brought about by the breach of contract. But these remedies are not exhaustive, for the law must cater for those occasions where the value of the promise to the promisee exceeds the financial enhancement of his position which full performance will secure. This excess, often referred to in the literature as the 'consumer surplus' (see for example the valuable discussion by Harris, Ogus and Philips (1979) 95 LQR 581) is usually incapable of precise valuation in terms of money, exactly because it represents a personal, subjective and non-monetary gain. Nevertheless where it exists the law should recognise it and compensate the promisee if the misperformance takes it away. The lurid bathroom tiles, or the grotesque folly instanced in argument by my noble and learned friend, Lord Keith of Kinkel, may be so discordant with general taste that in purely economic terms the builder may be said to do the employer a favour by failing to install them. But this is too narrow and materialistic a view of the transaction. Neither the contractor nor the court has the right to substitute for the employer's individual expectation of performance a criterion derived from what ordinary people would regard as sensible. As my Lords have shown, the test of reasonableness plays a central part in determining the basis of recovery, and will indeed be decisive in a case such as the present when the cost of reinstatement would be wholly disproportionate to the non-monetary loss suffered by the employer. But it would be equally unreasonable to deny all recovery for such a loss. The amount may be small, and since it cannot be quantified directly there may be room for difference of opinion about what it should be. But in several fields the judges are well accustomed to putting figures to intangibles, and I see no reason why the imprecision of the exercise should be a barrier, if that is what fairness demands.

My Lords, once this is recognised the puzzling and paradoxical feature of this case, that it seems to involve a contest of absurdities, simply falls away. There is no need to remedy the injustice of awarding too little, by unjustly awarding far too much. The judgment of the trial judge acknowledges that the employer has suffered a true loss and expresses it in terms of money. Since there is no longer any issue about the amount of the award, as distinct from the principle, I would simply restore his judgment by allowing the appeal.

Lord Lloyd:

Reasonableness

The starting point is *Robinson v Harman* 1 Exch 850, where Parke B said:

> 'The rule of the common law is, that where a party sustains a loss by reason of a breach of contract, he is, so far as money can do it, to be placed in the same situation, with respect to damages, as if the contract had been performed'.

This does not mean that in every case of breach of contract the plaintiff can obtain the monetary equivalent of specific performance. It is first necessary to ascertain the loss the plaintiff has in fact suffered by reason of the breach ... In building cases, the pecuniary loss is almost always measured in one of two ways; either the difference in value of the work done or the cost of reinstatement. Where the cost of reinstatement is less than the difference in value, the measure of damages will invariably be the cost of reinstatement. By claiming the difference in value the plaintiff would be failing to take reasonable steps to mitigate his loss. In many ordinary cases, too, where reinstatement presents no special problem, the cost of reinstatement will be the obvious measure of damages, even where there is little or no difference in value, or where the difference in value is hard to assess. This is why it is often said that the cost of reinstatement is the ordinary measure of damages for defective performance under a building contract.

But it is not the only measure of damages ... If the court takes the view that it would be unreasonable for the plaintiff to insist on reinstatement, as where, for example, the expense of the work involved would be out of all proportion to the benefit to be obtained, then the plaintiff will be confined to the difference in value. If the judge had assessed the difference in value in the present case at, say, £5,000, I have little doubt that the Court of Appeal would have taken that figure rather than £21,560. The difficulty arises because the judge has, in the light of the expert evidence, assessed the difference in value as nil. But that cannot make reasonable what he has found to be unreasonable.

So I cannot accept that reasonableness is confined to the doctrine of mitigation. It has a wider impact ... How then does [counsel for the defendant] seek to support the majority judgment? It can only be, I think, by attacking the judge's finding of fact that the cost of rebuilding the pool would have been out of all proportion to the benefit to be obtained. [Counsel for the defendant] argues that this was not an ordinary commercial contract but a contract for a personal preference ... I am far from saying that personal preferences are irrelevant when choosing the appropriate measure of damages ('predilections' was the word used by Ackner LJ in *GW Atkins Ltd v Scott* 7 Const LJ 215, 221, adopting the language of Oliver J in *Radford v De Froberville* [1977] 1 WLR 1262). But such cases should not be elevated into a separate category with special rules. If, to take an example mentioned in the course of argument, a landowner wishes to build a folly in his grounds, it is no answer to a claim for defective workmanship that many people might regard the presence of a well built folly as reducing the value of the estate. The eccentric landowner is entitled to his whim, provided the cost of reinstatement is not unreasonable. But the difficulty of that line of argument in the present case is that the judge, as is clear from his judgment, took Mr. Forsyth's personal preferences and predilections into account. Nevertheless, he found as a fact that the cost of reinstatement was unreasonable in the circumstances. The Court of Appeal ought not to have disturbed that finding …

Intention

I fully accept that the courts are not normally concerned with what a plaintiff does with his damages. But it does not follow that intention is not relevant to reasonableness, at least in those cases where the plaintiff does not intend to reinstate. Suppose in the present case Mr Forsyth had died, and the action had been continued by his executors. Is it to be supposed that they would be able to recover the cost of reinstatement, even though they intended to put the property on the market without delay?

There is, as Staughton LJ observed, a good deal of authority to the effect that intention may be relevant to a claim for damages based on cost of reinstatement. The clearest decisions on the point are those of Sir Robert Megarry V-C in *Tito v Waddell (No 2)* [1977] Ch 106, and Oliver J in *Radford v De Froberville* [1977] 1 WLR 1262 … In the present case the judge found as a fact that Mr Forsyth's stated intention of rebuilding the pool would not persist for long after the litigation had been concluded. In these circumstances it would be 'mere pretence' to say that the cost of rebuilding the pool is the loss which he has in fact suffered.

Loss of amenity

I turn last to the head of damages under which the judge awarded £2,500 …

Addis v Gramophone Co Ltd [1909] AC 488 established the general rule that in claims for breach of contract, the plaintiff cannot recover damages for his injured feelings. But the rule, like most rules, is subject to exceptions. One of the well established exceptions is when the object of the contract is to afford pleasure, as, for example, where the plaintiff has booked a holiday with a tour operator. If the tour operator is in breach of contract by failing to provide what the contract called for, the plaintiff may recover damages for his disappointment: see *Jarvis v Swan Tours Ltd* [1973] QB 233 and *Jackson v Horizon Holidays Ltd* [1975] 1 WLR 1468.

This was, as I understand it, the principle which Judge Diamond applied in the present case. He took the view that the contract was one 'for the provision of a pleasurable amenity. In the event, Mr. Forsyth's pleasure was not so great as it would have been if the swimming pool had been 7 feet 6 inches deep. This was a view which the judge was entitled to take. If it involves a further inroad on the rule in *Addis v Gramophone Co Ltd* [1909] AC 488, then so be it. But I prefer to regard it as a logical application or adaptation of the existing exception to a new situation. I should, however, add this note of warning. Mr Forsyth was, I think, lucky to have obtained so large an award for his disappointed expectations. But as there was no criticism from any quarter as to the quantum of the award as distinct from the underlying principle, it would not be right for your Lordships to interfere with the judge's figure. That leaves one last question for consideration. I have expressed agreement with the judge's approach to damages based on loss of amenity on the facts of the present case. But in most cases such an approach would not be available. What is then to be the position where, in the case of a new house, the building does not conform in some minor respect to the contract, as, for example, where there is a difference in level between two rooms, necessitating a step. Suppose there is no measurable difference in value of the complete house, and the cost of reinstatement would be prohibitive. Is there any reason why the court should not award by way of damages for breach of contract some modest sum, not based on difference in value, but solely to compensate the buyer for his disappointed expectations? Is the law of damages so inflexible, as I asked earlier, that it cannot find some middle ground in such a case? I do not give a final answer to that question in the present case. But it may be that it would have afforded an alternative ground for justifying the judge's award of damages and if the judge had wanted a precedent, he could have found it in Sir David Cairns's judgment in *GW Atkins Ltd v Scott* 7 Const LJ 215, where, it will be remembered, the Court of Appeal upheld the judge's award of £250 for defective tiling. Sir David Cairns said, at p 221:

> 'There are many circumstances where a judge has nothing but his common sense to guide him in fixing the quantum of damages, for instance, for pain and suffering, for loss of pleasurable activities or for inconvenience of one kind or another'.

If it is accepted that the award of £2,500 should be upheld, then that at once disposes of [counsel for the defendant's] argument that Mr Forsyth is entitled to the cost of reinstatement, because he must be entitled to something. But even if he were entitled to nothing for loss of amenity, or for difference in value, it would not follow as [counsel for the defendant] argued that he was entitled to the cost of reinstatement. There is no escape from the judge's finding of fact that to insist on the cost of reinstatement in the circumstances of the present case was unreasonable.

I would therefore allow the appeal and restore the judgment of Judge Diamond.

In *Ruxley*, their Lordships were faced with a dilemma. Should they award damages on the diminution of value basis, which would be nominal on the ground that Mr Forsyth's economic expectations had not been affected? Or should they award cost of cure damages to protect Mr Forsyth's expectation of performance, even though this would result in a windfall for Mr Forsyth because, despite his protestations to the contrary, he was unlikely to use the money to rebuild the pool?

On the facts of *Ruxley*, a unanimous House of Lords held that it would be unreasonable to award the cost of rebuilding the swimming pool. Two reasons were given for this. First, the cost of rebuilding the pool would have been out of all proportion to the benefit to be obtained by Mr Forsyth. He had a perfectly safe and useable swimming pool. As Lord Jauncey put it, 'were he to receive the cost of building a new one and retain the existing one he would have recovered not compensation for loss but a very substantial gratuitous benefit, something which damages are not intended to provide'. Their Lordships were not only concerned with the risk of over-compensating Mr Forsyth, but also with the danger of causing unnecessary hardship to Ruxley.

Second, the House of Lords found that cost of cure damages would be unreasonable because Forsyth had no real intention of effecting the cure. Both Lords Jauncey and Lloyd noted that the courts are usually unconcerned about how the plaintiff uses an award of damages once loss has been established. Intention was relevant, however, to the issue of whether a cost of cure award would be reasonable. A claimant's intention to cure a particular breach is crucial evidence of the extent of his non-pecuniary loss flowing from the breach. The fact that Mr Forsyth's stated intention of rebuilding the pool was unlikely to persist for long after the litigation meant that 'it would be "mere pretence" to say that the cost of rebuilding the pool is the loss which he has in fact suffered' (*per* Lord Lloyd).

The House of Lords rejected the 'cost of cure' measure for overcompensating Forsyth, but also rejected the 'diminution of value' measure for under-compensating him. Their Lordships preferred to reinstate the award made by the judge at first instance of £2,500 in 'loss of amenity' damages (on the possibility of claiming 'loss of amenity' damages with other heads of damages see *Harrison v Shepherd Homes Ltd* [2011] EWHC 1811 at [264]). But what is the precise nature of this award? There are two possibilities. First, it could be based on the concept of the 'consumer surplus' as suggested by Lord Mustill. Such an award compensates the claimant for loss of his non-pecuniary interest in performance, that is, something he had contracted for which went beyond the market value of performance. Second, the award could be an example of damages awarded to compensate Forsyth for Ruxley's failure to provide him with the pleasure that he had contracted to receive (see *Jarvis v Swan Tours Ltd* [1973] QB 233), as suggested by Lord Lloyd. Some subsequent cases (such as *Alfred McAlpine Construction Ltd v Panatown Ltd* [2001] 1 AC 518, 588, *per* Lord Millett; *Farley v Skinner* [2002] 2 AC 732, 767, *per* Lord Scott) have suggested that the award was of the former type although this is not always clear. For example, in *Newman v Framewood Manor Management Co Ltd* [2012] EWCA Civ 159, where a sauna was provided instead of a jacuzzi, Lady Justice Arden stated (at [48]–[54]):

> **48** In my judgment, the judge was correct not to award specific performance. The jacuzzi had been replaced by the sauna at considerable cost. Moreover, the cost of the installing of a new jacuzzi was estimated at £20,000. To incur this cost would be excessive and disproportionate when compared with the loss of amenity. This result would be similar to that in *Ruxley Electronics and Construction Ltd v Forsyth* [1996] AC 344, where the House of Lords refused to award substantial damages for the installation of a swimming pool to a depth of six foot rather than the intended seven foot six inches for which the parties had contracted, and instead approved the award of damages for loss of amenity.
>
> **49** As to damages for loss of amenity, in my judgment the judge was wrong not to make an award. The judge's holding that the sauna was a sufficient replacement for the jacuzzi was made in the context of whether there was any financial loss due to a diminution in the value of the leasehold interest of Mrs Newman. There was indeed no evidence that the value of her lease was likely to be affected by the question whether she had the right to use a sauna or a jacuzzi. In any event, such a right would be a comparatively small aspect of the rights conferred by the lease.
>
> **50** As I read the judge's judgment, the judge expressed no conclusion on the claim for damages for loss of amenity. There was, however, evidence from Mrs Newman in support of her claim that she liked to use it when her grandchildren came to stay. It is correct that Mrs Newman did not go on to say that she did not, therefore, regard the sauna as a replacement. Mr Jones submits that her claim for damages for loss of amenity must therefore fail. However, in my judgment, the sauna and jacuzzi are so different that, unless there is some evidence that a person deprived of a jacuzzi accepted a sauna as a substitute, acceptance of the substitute should not be inferred. Accordingly, if it was the Company's case that she was adequately compensated by the provision of the sauna and that this offset her loss, that should have been put to her in cross-examination. That did not occur.
>
> **51** In any event, the question of what her personal preferences were is not conclusive, any more than it was a question whether a majority of leaseholders at Framewood Manor were prepared to approve the change. The question, in my judgment, was also whether a reasonable person with knowledge of the circumstances in which people acquired leasehold interests in this sort of development would say that it was not a substitute for a jacuzzi.
>
> **52** In my judgment, a reasonable person would reach this conclusion. A sauna and a jacuzzi do not serve the same function. A sauna uses steam to induce perspiration in an enclosed space. A jacuzzi, on the other hand, uses warm aerated water and is fitted with a whirlpool, and is usually situated near a swimming pool. A jacuzzi would be much more useful as a facility to enjoy safely with one's young children or grandchildren than a sauna. Both would require adult supervision but a child would clearly have to be older to use a sauna for any length of time than he or she would have to be to use a jacuzzi. The development at Framewood Manor was after all for private residential use by individuals and families. It was reasonable to expect that a resident might wish to entertain young children.

53 In those circumstances, I would substitute for the relevant part of the judge's order an award of damages to cover loss of amenity since the jacuzzi was removed. Sums awarded for loss of amenity are for reasons of policy generally low. The jacuzzi was decommissioned in July 2008, leaving a period of nearly 2% years down to trial. In my judgment, a award of £1,000 would cover the loss of amenity to trial.

54 Clearly the loss of amenity would continue into the future. I would therefore award a further modest sum to cover this, namely £2,500.

In addition, it is also clear that the award of £2,500 was at the upper end of the permissible scale, but due to the fact that Ruxley did not contest the award, the House of Lords was happy to uphold it. The last issue for us to consider is whether the damages awarded in *Ruxley* provided adequate protection to Mr Forsyth's performance interest. Opinion is divided on the issue. It is clear that the award provided better protection than diminution of value damages would have. However, the award failed to provide Forsyth with the means of obtaining substitute performance. It was insufficient to pay for another builder to come to his house and construct a pool seven feet, six inches deep. Did this mean that the court was unwilling to protect Forsyth's interest in performance? It is submitted that the answer to this question should be no. Cost of cure damages are a form of monetised specific performance. Their aim is to allow the claimant to cure the breach. If the claimant has no intention of doing this, the rationale for the award disappears. This is why cost of cure damages were refused on the facts of *Ruxley*. The award would not have accurately represented the value of the bargained-for performance.

The extent to which the law provides protection to the claimant's interest in performance is also very much at issue in cases concerning loss of performance to a third party. To illustrate, if I contract with you to retile the roof of my mother's house and you fail to perform, do I have a claim against you for damages even though your breach had caused me no financial loss? If the answer to that question is no, does that mean that you can wilfully refuse to perform in the full knowledge that you will not be required to pay more than nominal damages. These issues arose for consideration in *Alfred McAlpine Constructions Ltd v Panatown Ltd*. The issues at stake in the case were very complex and the law report very long. The claim for damages was made on two grounds. For reasons of simplicity, we will only consider one ground here (the other ground is considered in Chapter 5): what the House of Lords described as the 'broad ground'.

Alfred McAlpine Constructions Ltd v Panatown Ltd [2001] 1 AC 518

Facts: McAlpine entered into a contract with Panatown to design and build an office block and multi-storey car park on a site in Cambridge. Panatown alleged that the building was seriously defective and might even have to be demolished, thus raising the possibility of a £40 million claim arising from breach of a £10 million contract. However, at no stage had Panatown owned the construction site, which at all times belonged to their associated company Unex Investment Properties Ltd ('UIPL'). The reason for this arrangement was that it (legitimately) avoided the payment of VAT. On the day the construction contract was signed, McAlpine entered into a separate Duty of Care Deed (the 'DCD') with UIPL under which McAlpine accepted limited liability for negligence.

Panatown claimed damages for breach of contract on two grounds. The 'broad ground' was a claim for the loss that they, as promisee, had sustained as a result of McAlpine's failure to perform the contract. In other words, they claimed damages for loss of performance of the contract, even though that loss of performance had not caused them any financial loss. The Court of Appeal held that Panatown was entitled to recover substantial damages.

Held: The House of Lords allowed the appeal. In relation to the broad ground, four Law Lords, Lords Goff, Millett, Jauncey and Browne-Wilkinson, acknowledged that, in principle, there was a claim for loss of performance even if that loss of performance had caused no financial loss to the claimant. However, two of those Law Lords, Lords Jauncey and Browne-Wilkinson, were of the view that Panatown's claim on this ground was excluded by the existence of the DCD with UIPL. Lord Clyde denied the existence of a claim for loss of performance altogether.

Lord Clyde: I turn accordingly to what was referred to in the argument as the broader ground ... What it proposes is that the innocent party to the contract should recover damages for himself as a compensation for what is seen to be his own loss ... This approach however seems to me to have been developed into two formulations.

The first formulation, and the seeds of the second, are found in the speech of Lord Griffiths in the *St Martins case* [1994] 1 AC 85, 96. At the outset his Lordship expressed the opinion that the Corporation, faced with a breach by McAlpine of their contractual duty to perform the contract with sound materials and with all reasonable skill and care, would be entitled to recover from McAlpine the cost of remedying the defect in the work as the normal measure of damages. He then dealt with two possible objections. First, it should not matter that the work was not being done on property owned by Corporation. Where a husband instructs repairs to the roof of the matrimonial home it cannot be said that he has not suffered damage because he did not own the property. He suffers the damage measured by the cost of a proper completion of the repair:

> 'In cases such as the present the person who places the contract has suffered financial loss because he has to spend money to give him the benefit of the bargain which the defendant had promised but failed to deliver. (See p 97.)'

The second objection, that the Corporation had in fact been reimbursed for the cost of the repairs was answered by the consideration that the person who actually pays for the repairs is of no concern to the party who broke the contract. But Lord Griffiths added, at p 97:

> 'The court will of course wish to be satisfied that the repairs have been or are likely to be carried out but if they are carried out the cost of doing them must fall upon the defendant who broke his contract'.

In the first formulation this approach can be seen as identifying a loss upon the innocent party who requires to instruct the remedial work. That loss is, or may be, measured by the cost of the repair. The essential for this formulation appears to be that the repair work is to be, or at least is likely to be, carried out. This consideration does not appear to be simply relevant to the reasonableness of allowing the damages to be measured by the cost of repair. It is an essential condition for the application of the approach, so as to establish a loss on the part of the plaintiff. Thus far the approach appears to be consistent with principle, and in particular with the principle of privity. It can cover the case where A contracts with B to pay a sum of money to C and B fails to do so. The loss to A is in the necessity to find other funds to pay to C and provided that he is going to pay C, or indeed has done so, he should be able to recover the sum by way of damages for breach of contract from B. If it was evident that A had no intention to pay C, having perhaps changed his mind, then he would not be able to recover the amount from B because he would have sustained no loss, and his damages would at best be nominal.

But there can also be found in Lord Griffiths's speech the idea that the loss is not just constituted by the failure in performance but indeed consists in that failure. This is the 'second formulation'. In relation to the suggestion that the husband who instructs repair work to the roof of his wife's house and has to pay for another builder to make good the faulty repair work has sustained no damage Lord Griffiths observed, at p 97:

> 'Such a result would in my view be absurd and the answer is that the husband has suffered loss because he did not receive the bargain for which he had contracted with the first builder and the measure of damages is the cost of securing the performance of that bargain by completing the roof repairs properly by the second builder'.

That is to say that the fact that the innocent party did not receive the bargain for which he contracted is itself a loss. As Steyn LJ put it in *Darlington Borough Council v Wiltshier Northern Ltd* [1995] 1 WLR 68, 80: 'He suffers a loss of bargain or of expectation interest'. ...

I find some difficulty in adopting the second formulation as a sound way forward ... The loss of an expectation which is here referred to seems to me to be coming very close to a way of describing a breach of contract. A breach of contract may cause a loss, but is not in itself a loss in any meaningful sense. When one refers to a loss in the context of a breach of contract, one is in my view referring to the incidence of some personal or patrimonial damage. A loss of expectation might be a loss in the proper sense if damages were awarded for the distress or inconvenience caused by the disappointment. Professor Coote ('Contract Damages, *Ruxley* and the Performance Interest' [1997] CLJ 537) draws a distinction between benefits in law, that is bargained-for contractual rights, and benefits in fact, that is the enjoyment of the fruits of performance. Certainly the former may constitute an asset with a commercial value. But while frustration may destroy the rights altogether so that the contract is no longer enforceable, a failure in the obligation to perform does not destroy the asset. On the contrary it remains as the necessary legal basis for a remedy. A failure in performance of a contractual obligation does not entail a loss of the bargained-for contractual rights. Those rights remain so as to enable performance of the contract to be enforced, as by an order for specific performance. If one party to a contract repudiates it and that repudiation is accepted, then, to quote Lord Porter in *Heyman v Darwins Ltd* [1942] AC 356, 399, 'By that acceptance he is discharged from further performance and may bring an action for damages, but the contract itself is not rescinded'. The primary obligations under the contract may come to an end, but secondary obligations then arise, among them being the obligation to compensate the innocent party. The original rights may not then be enforced. But a consequential right arises in the innocent party to obtain a remedy from the party who repudiated the contract for his failure in performance.

Lord Goff: I wish to state that I find persuasive the reasoning and conclusion expressed by Lord Griffiths in his opinion in the *St Martins case* [1994] 1 AC 85, that the employer under a building contract may in principle recover substantial damages from the building contractor, because he has not received the performance which he was entitled to receive from the contractor under the contract, notwithstanding that the property in the building site was vested in a third party. The example given by Lord Griffiths of a husband contracting for repairs to the matrimonial home which is owned by his wife is most telling. It is not difficult to imagine other examples, not only within the family, but also, for example, where work is done for charitable purposes – as where a wealthy man who lives in a village decides to carry out at his own expense major repairs to, or renovation or even reconstruction of, the village hall, and himself enters into a contract with a local builder to carry out the work to the existing building which belongs to another, for example to trustees, or to the parish council. Nobody in such circumstances would imagine that there could be any legal obstacle in the way of the charitable donor enforcing the contract against the builder by recovering damages from him if he failed to perform his obligations under the building contract, for example because his work failed to comply with the contract specification ...

I do not regard Lord Griffiths's broader ground as a departure from existing authority, but as a reaffirmation of existing legal principle. Indeed, I know of no authority which stands in its way. On the contrary, there have been statements in the cases which provide support for his view. Thus in *Darlington Borough Council v Wiltshier Northern Ltd* [1995] 1 WLR 68, 80, Steyn LJ described Lord Griffiths's broader ground as based on classic contractual theory, a statement with which I respectfully agree. Moreover, Lord Griffiths's reasoning was foreshadowed in the opinions of members of the Appellate Committee in *Woodar Investment Development Ltd v Wimpey Construction UK Ltd* [1980] 1 WLR 277; see especially the opinion of

Lord Keith of Kinkel, at pp 297–298, and in addition the more tentative statements of Lord Salmon, at p 291, and Lord Scarman, at pp 300–301 … Even if it is not thought, as I think, that the solution which I prefer is in accordance with existing principle, nevertheless it is surely within the scope of the type of development of the common law which, especially in the law of obligations, is habitually undertaken by appellate judges as part of their ordinary judicial function …

The present case provides, in my opinion, a classic example of a case which falls properly within the judicial province. I, for my part, have therefore no doubt that it is desirable, indeed essential, that the problem in the present case should be the subject of judicial solution by providing proper recognition of the plaintiff's interest in the performance of the contractual obligations which are owed to him …

The DCD

I now turn to the second issue in the case, which relates to the possible impact of the DCD on Panatown's remedy against McAlpine in damages.

It was the submission of McAlpine that the existence of the building owner's remedy under the DCD had the effect of precluding Panatown from recovering damages from McAlpine under the building contract …

This reasoning has, however, no application to Lord Griffiths' broader ground, under which the employer is seeking to recover damages for his own account in respect of his own loss, ie the damage to his interest in the performance of the building contract to which he, as employer, is party and under which he has contracted to pay for the building. The mere fact that the building contractor, McAlpine, has entered into a separate contract in different terms with another party with regard to possible defects in the building which is the subject of the building contract cannot of itself detract from its obligations to the employer under the building contract itself.

For the reasons I have given, I would dismiss McAlpine's appeal from the decision of the Court of Appeal, and I would order that McAlpine pay the costs of the appeal to your Lordships' House.

Lord Jauncey: Since writing this speech, I have had the advantage of reading in draft the speech of my noble and learned friend, Lord Goff of Chieveley. I respectfully agree with his rejection of the proposition that the employer under a building contract is unable to recover substantial damages for breach of the contract if the work in question is to be performed on land or buildings which are not his property. In such a case the employer's right to substantial damages will, in my view, depend upon whether he has made good or intends to make good the effects of the breach … This produces a sensible result and avoids the recovery of an 'un-covenanted' profit by an employer who does not intend to take steps to remedy the breach.

However, there is a further matter to be considered in this case, namely the DCD in favour of UIPL. This, in my view, is equally relevant to the broader as to the narrow ground. The former as does the latter seeks to find a rational way of avoiding the 'black hole'. What is the justification for allowing A to recover from B as his own a loss which is truly that of C when C has his own remedy against B? I would submit none … I therefore consider that Panatown is not entitled to recover under Mr Friedman's broader ground not only because they have suffered no financial loss but also because UIPL have a direct right of action against McAlpine under the DCD.

Lord Browne-Wilkinson: I will assume that the broader ground is sound in law and that in the ordinary case where the third party (C) has no direct cause of action against the building contractor (B) A can recover damages from B on the broader ground. Even on that assumption, in my judgment Panatown has no right to substantial damages in this case because UIPL (the owner of the land) has a direct cause of action under the DCD.

The essential feature of the broader ground is that the contracting party A, although not himself suffering the physical or pecuniary damage sustained by the third party C, has suffered his own damage being the loss of his performance interest, ie the failure to provide C with the benefit that B had contracted for C to receive. In my judgment it follows that the critical factor is to determine what interest A had in the provision of the service for the third party C. If, as in the present case, the whole contractual scheme was designed, inter alia, to give UPIL and its successors a legal remedy against McAlpine for failure to perform the building contract with due care, I cannot see that Panatown has suffered any damage to its performance interests: subject to any defence based on limitation of actions, the physical and pecuniary damage suffered by UPIL can be redressed by UPIL exercising its own cause of action against McAlpine. It is not clear to me why this has not occurred in the present case: but, subject to questions of limitation which were not explored, there is no reason even now why UPIL should not be bringing the proceedings against McAlpine. The fact that the DCD may have been primarily directed to ensuring that UPIL's successors in title should enjoy a remedy in tort against McAlpine is nothing to the point: the contractual provisions were directed to ensuring that UPIL and its successors in title did have the legal right to sue McAlpine direct. So long as UPIL enjoys this right Panatown has suffered no failure to satisfy its performance interest ...

For these reasons I would allow the appeal.

Lord Millett: To my mind the most significant feature of the academic literature is that no one has suggested that the adoption of the broad ground would have any adverse consequences on commercial arrangements. Nor, despite every incentive to do so, has McAlpine been able to suggest a situation in which it would cause difficulties or defeat the commercial expectations of the parties. In my view it would help to rationalise the law and provide a sound basis for decisions like *Ruxley Electronics and Construction Ltd v Forsyth* [1996] AC 344 and *Jackson v Horizon Holidays* [1975] 1 WLR 1468. If it is adopted, it will be for future consideration whether it would provide the better solution in cases such as *St Martins* also.

In the *Ruxley* case your Lordships' House refused to allow the full costs of reinstatement on the well-recognised ground that reinstatement would be an unreasonable course to take. But it was not constrained to withhold substantial damages on the ground that the value of the property was unaffected by the breach. It expressly rejected the view that these were the only two possible measures of damage in a building case. It awarded an intermediate sum for 'loss of amenity'. The evidence, however, showed that, viewed objectively, there was no loss of amenity either. The amenity in question was entirely subjective to the plaintiff; and its loss could equally well, and perhaps more accurately, be described as defeated expectation ...

It must be wrong to adopt a Procrustean approach which leaves parties without a remedy for breach of contract because their arrangements do not fit neatly into some precast contractual formula. When such arrangements have been freely entered into and are of an everyday character or are commercially advantageous to the parties, it is surely time to re-examine the position.

This is the product of the narrow accountants' balance sheet quantification of loss which measures the loss suffered by the promisee by the diminution in his overall financial position resulting from the breach. One of the consequences of this approach is to produce an artificial distinction between a contract for the supply of goods to a third party and a contract for the supply of services to a third party. A man who buys a car for his wife is entitled to substantial damages if an inferior car is supplied, on the assumption (not necessarily true) that the property in the car is intended to vest momentarily in him before being transferred to his wife, whereas a man who orders his wife's car to be repaired is entitled to nominal damages only if the work is imperfectly carried out. This is surely indefensible; the reality of the matter is that in both cases the man is willing to undertake a contractual liability in order to be able to provide a benefit to his wife.

The idea that a contracting party is entitled to damages measured by the value of his own defeated interest in having the contract performed was not new in 1994. A strong case for its adoption in the case of consumer contracts was made in an important article 'Contract Remedies and the Consumer Surplus' (1979) 95 LQR 581, in which the authors explained that this would make a significant difference only in a minority of cases ...

[His Lordship discussed the decisions in *Woodar Investment Development Ltd v Wimpey Construction UK Ltd* [1980] 1 WLR 277 and *Radford v De Froberville* [1977] 1 WLR 1262.]

The seed was planted more than 20 years ago. It has been long in germination, but it has been watered and nurtured by favourable judicial and academic commentators in the meantime. I think the time has come to give it the imprimatur of your Lordships' House. I am not impressed by the argument that such a radical change, with the attendant risk of opening the floodgates to capricious and complex claims to damages in unforeseen situations of every kind, should be left to Parliament. In the first place, I do not think that it is a radical change. I respectfully agree with Steyn LJ in *Darlington Borough Council v Wiltshier Northern Ltd* [1995] 1 WLR 68, that it is based on orthodox contractual principles. And in the second place, the development of the remedial response to civil wrongs and the appropriate measure of damages are matters which have traditionally been the province of the judiciary. For the present I would restrict the broad ground to building contracts and other contracts for the supply of work and materials where the claim is in respect of defective or incomplete work or delay in completing it. I would not exclude the claim for damages for delay, since the performance interest extends to having the work done timeously as well as properly. There is no difficulty in quantifying the loss due to delay, at least in the family or group context. In the case of building contracts the broad ground is in line with the principle that the prima facie measure of damages is the cost of repair rather than the reduction in the market value of the property or any loss of amenity, even where the cost of repair is substantially greater, subject only to the qualification that the carrying out of the repairs must be a reasonable course to adopt …

Does the existence of the DCD bar recovery?

I am unable to accept McAlpine's submission that the parties were well aware of the problem caused by the fact that Panatown was not the owner of the site, and that the DCD was intended to cater for this. It is much more likely that the parties, being businessmen and more sensible than lawyers, assumed that it made no difference which company in the group owned the land. If the present problem had been foreseen, Panatown would surely have insisted on taking the benefit of an unqualified warranty such as was proposed to be given to a future tenant. It would make no commercial sense for a future tenant to have a more effective remedy than either the building employer or the building owner.

I agree with the Court of Appeal that the existence of the DCD does not demonstrate an intention that any damages caused by defective or incomplete performance of McAlpine's obligations under the building contract should be recoverable by UIPL under the DCD and not by Panatown under the building contract. I do not, however, agree with their formulation of the question: whether the parties contemplated that the DCD would 'replace' the more detailed provisions of the building contract. It is not correct to ask whether Panatown would have had a claim under the building contract if there had been no DCD and then ask whether the parties intended to replace that claim by a claim by UIPL under the DCD. If it be relevant to impute intention to the parties, the correct approach is to examine the whole complex of contracts and ask whether they contemplated that the building contract could be enforced by Panatown.

But the broad ground does not rest on imputed intention … [It] is based on ordinary contractual principles. It has nothing to do with the privity rule. The plaintiff is a contracting party who recovers for his own loss, not that of a third party. Whatever arrangements the third party may have entered into, these do not concern the plaintiff and cannot deprive him of his contractual rights …

The real significance of the DCD is different. By giving the third party a cause of action, it raises the spectre of double recovery. Even though the plaintiff recovers for his own loss, this obviously reflects the loss sustained by the third party. The case is, therefore, an example, not unknown in other contexts, where breach of a single obligation creates a liability to two different parties. Since performance of the primary obligation to do the work would have discharged the liability to both parties, so must performance of the secondary obligation to pay damages. Payment of damages to either must *pro tanto* discharge the liability to both. The problem, in my view, is not one of double recovery, but of ensuring that the damages are paid to the right party.

There can be no complaint by the building employer if the damages are recovered by the building owner, since he was the intended beneficiary of the arrangements in the first place. The building employer's performance interest will be satisfied by carrying out the remedial work or by providing the building owner with the means to pay for it to be done. This provides the key to the proper approach in the converse case like the present where the action is brought by the building employer despite the existence of a cause of action in the building owner. Since the building employer's expectation loss reflects and cannot exceed the loss suffered by the building owner, and would be satisfied by any award of damages to the latter, his claim should normally be subordinated to any claim made by the building owner. While, therefore, I do not accept that Panatown's claim to substantial damages is excluded by the existence of the DCD, I think that an action like the present should normally be stayed in order to allow the building owner to bring his own proceedings. The court will need to be satisfied that the building owner is not proposing to make his own claim and is content to allow his claim to be discharged by payment to the building employer before allowing the building employer's action to proceed.

In the present case UIPL is fully aware of the present proceedings and supports Panatown's claim to substantial damages. It has no wish to be forced to invoke its own subsidiary and inferior remedy under the DCD. There is no need to join it in the proceedings or require it to enter into a formal waiver of its claim under the DCD. Any claim it may have under the DCD will be satisfied by the payment of damages to Panatown.

I would dismiss the appeal.

Ultimately, the issue that decided the case was the existence of the DCD. The majority of their Lordships (Lords Goff and Millett dissenting) held that because UIPL had a claim against McAlpine under the DCD there was no 'legal black hole'. It is respectfully submitted that this conclusion is wrong. The DCD conferred significantly fewer rights on UIPL than the main contract conferred on Panatown. The purpose of the DCD was to provide the means for future purchasers of the land to sue McAlpine for negligent building defects. The main contract conferred more substantial rights on Panatown including strict liability for the building work and an arbitration clause. By deciding that the DCD superseded the main contract, the majority of the House of Lords effectively cast these additional rights into the legal 'black hole'. Even more worrying was that their Lordships allowed the performance interest of a non-party, UIPL, to trump the performance interest of an actual party, Panatown, who had provided the consideration for the promise from McAlpine.

The most interesting feature of the case was the sharp disagreement between their Lordships on the status of the 'broad ground' – the claim that Panatown were entitled to compensation for loss of their performance interest. Lord Clyde was clearly of the view that no such claim existed: 'A breach of contract may cause a loss, but is not in itself a loss in any meaningful sense.' Lords Goff and Millett disagreed, the latter referring to Lord Clyde's approach as being founded on a 'narrow accountants' balance sheet quantification of loss'. It appears that Lord Jauncey sided with Lord Clyde. Thus it was left to Lord Browne-Wilkinson to decide the issue. Ultimately he decided that the claim should fail because of the existence of the DCD, which meant that his comments on the broad ground were strictly *obiter*. However, his Lordship did say that he would 'assume that the broader ground was sound in law'. This is extremely significant. Effectively it meant that the majority of the House of Lords were of the view that a promisee's interest in performance ought to be protected even if he had suffered no pecuniary loss.

McKendrick, E, 'The common law at work: the saga of *Alfred McAlpine Construction Ltd v Panatown Ltd*' (2003) *OUCLJ* 145, 167–168

[T]he central question of principle that is, in my view posed by the fact pattern in *Panatown* [is]: what rights are conferred on a promisee by an enforceable promise? ...

In many ways, it is surprising that, at this stage in the development of our law of contract, such a fundamental question remains without a definitive answer. Yet the cases do not speak with one voice. It is probably fair to say that the courts have traditionally awarded damages to claimants in order to compensate them for the financial losses they have suffered as a result of the breach. In many ways this is not surprising. Many, if not most, contracting parties enter into a contract in order to make a profit and the law reflects that reality in the approach which it adopts in the assessment of damages payable in the event of a breach. But not all contracting parties enter into contracts with a view to making money. This is particularly true in the case of consumers. The consumer who orders a new bathroom suite does not enter into the contract in order to make a profit but to obtain a particular suite of his or her choice. Local authorities who enter into contracts for the provision of services or amenities for residents do not do so with a view to enhancing their own financial position but rather to provide a service for their constituents. Similarly, Panatown did not enter into a contract with McAlpine in order to make a profit itself but rather to benefit the corporate group as a whole. Against this background, it is suggested that the conception of loss adopted by the law of contract should extend beyond physical damage and financial loss in order to reflect the fact that, increasingly, we enter into contracts with a view other than to make money. Thus we enter into contract in pursuit of our leisure interests or to obtain services which promote the quality of our lives but do not directly enhance our financial position. These are interests which our society values and they should be reflected in the law of contract ... There is more to life than money and there is more to the law of contract than the protection of financial interests. This should be reflected in the conception of loss adopted by the law of contract and in the rules applicable to the assessment of damages.

Professor McKendrick's views are intriguing. Fuller and Perdue's legacy arguably left us with an unduly economic driven conception of the law of contract. Instead of speaking of a promisee's interest in 'performance', we have been encouraged to refer to the promisee's 'expectation' interest. This conceals the fact that the parties' real expectation is an expectation of performance, not merely the economic value of performance.

Whether this will be fully recognised in the future is still a matter of doubt. Although Lord Millett argued that the damages awarded in *Ruxley* were really awarded on this basis, this is somewhat doubtful. Furthermore, the speeches in *Panatown* were inconclusive because of their *obiter* nature (and this aspect of *Panatown* had received a mixed reception in the courts: cf. *DRC Distribution Ltd v Ulva Ltd* [2007] EWHC 1716 at [69]–[79], and *Giedo van der Garde BV v Force India Formula One Team Ltd* [2010] EWHC 2373 at [484]). More recently, however, the broad ground gained some support in *Lowick Rose LLP (in liquidation) v Swynson Ltd* [2017] UKSC 32 at [17] from Lord Sumption (cf. Lord Mance at [53]).

15.2.1.2 The reliance measure

Where it proves difficult for the claimant to calculate the profits that would have been made had the contract not been broken, s/he may instead seek recovery of the expenditure that s/he incurred in anticipation of the contract. This measure is referred to as the 'reliance measure'. The result of this type of award is that the claimant is essentially put back into the position /she was in prior to the contract being made. Reliance damages are backwards looking and to this extent they are like damages in the law of tort. The Court of Appeal awarded reliance damages in *Anglia Television Ltd v Reed*.

***Anglia Television Ltd v Reed* [1972] 1 QB 60**

Facts: Robert Reed was an actor who was under a contract to play a leading role in a film for television entitled 'The Man in the Wood'. The film was about an American man married to an English woman who had an adventure in an English wood! At a late stage Reed withdrew from the film and the project was unable to go ahead. Anglia Television sued Reed for breach of contract. Due to the uncertainties of the entertainment industry, Anglia Television were unable to accurately estimate the profits they would have made from the film. Therefore, Anglia sought to recover the expenses they had incurred in setting up the film. At first instance, the Master awarded Anglia Television damages of £2,750, a sum that included expenditure incurred by Anglia Television prior to the contract with Reed.

Held: The Court of Appeal dismissed the appeal.

Lord Denning MR: It seems to me that a plaintiff in such a case as this has an election: he can either claim for loss of profits; or for his wasted expenditure. But he must elect between them. He cannot claim both. If he has not suffered any loss of profits – or if he cannot prove what his profits would have been – he can claim in the alternative the expenditure which has been thrown away, that is, wasted, by reason of the breach ...

If the plaintiff claims the wasted expenditure, he is not limited to the expenditure incurred *after* the contract was concluded. He can claim also the expenditure incurred *before* the contract, provided that it was such as would reasonably be in the contemplation of the parties as likely to be wasted if the contract was broken. Applying that principle here, it is plain that, when Mr. Reed entered into this contract, he must have known perfectly well that much expenditure had already been incurred on director's fees and the like. He must have contemplated – or, at any rate, it is reasonably to be imputed to him – that if he broke his contract, all that expenditure would be wasted, whether or not it was incurred before or after the contract. He must pay damages for all the expenditure so wasted and thrown away. This view is supported by the recent decision of Brightman J in *Lloyd v Stanbury* [1971] 1 WLR 535. There was a contract for the sale of land. In anticipation of the contract – and before it was concluded – the purchaser went to much expense in moving a caravan to the site and in getting his furniture there. The seller afterwards entered into a contract to sell the land to the purchaser, but afterwards broke his contract. The land had not increased in value, so the purchaser could not claim for any loss of profit. But Brightman J. held, at p 547, that he could recover the cost of moving the caravan and furniture, because it was 'within the contemplation of the parties when the contract was signed'. That decision is in accord with the correct principle, namely, that wasted expenditure can be recovered when it is wasted by reason of the defendant's breach of contract. It is true that, if the defendant had never entered into the contract, he would not be liable, and the expenditure would have been incurred by the plaintiff without redress; but, the defendant having made his contract and broken it, it does not lie in his mouth to say he is not liable, when it was because of his breach that the expenditure has been wasted.

The decision in *Reed* was controversial because the Court of Appeal allowed Anglia to recover damages in respect of pre-contractual expenditure. Lord Denning justified this on the ground that, at the time the contract was entered into, Reed must have been aware of the expenditure that had already taken place. Professor Anthony Ogus has doubted that this is a sound basis for allowing recovery of pre-contractual expenditure under the heading of reliance losses.

Ogus, A, 'Damages for pre-contract expenditure' (1972) 35 *MLR* 423, 424

The measure of damages so envisaged would not put the plaintiffs in the position they would have been in if the contract had not been made, for the expenses would still have been incurred. The expenses were incurred not in reliance on the defendant's promise to perform – they were incurred merely in the hope that agreement with the defendant would be secured. There was indeed no causal connection between the loss (the wasted expenses) and either the making of the contract or its breach. In the United States of America these theoretical objections have proved decisive: all attempts to recover pre-contract expenditure (where there was no special agreement binding the defaulting party to pay) have failed.

Now it may be conceded that dogmatically to insist that there may be recovery of expenditure incurred only from the moment that the contract was complete may lead to artificial results. If the parties have clearly reached agreement on the substance of the contract and all that remains is for their legal advisers to draft and execute the contract, it would be unfair to the plaintiff to disallow a claim for expenses incurred at this stage. On the other hand, the doctrine of *restitutio in integrum* which lies at the heart of the reliance interest award surely dictates that while a contract is still being negotiated a party who incurs expenditure does so at his own risk. Perhaps the best solution would be for the reliance interest award to comprise those expenses incurred as from the time when there was substantial agreement between the parties.

Professor Ogus seems to be correct, assuming that the damages awarded in the case were really awarded to compensate for reliance losses. However, it is quite possible that the award could be re-characterised as an award of expectation damages, in which case the decision is more readily explicable. This will be considered in further detail below. The decision as to whether to seek expectation or reliance damages will normally lie with the claimant, as Lord Denning confirmed in *Anglia Television v Reed*. In some circumstances, however, the court may decide that reliance is the appropriate measure.

McRae v Commonwealth Disposals Commission (1951) 84 CLR 377

Facts: The defendants invited tenders for the purchase of a shipwrecked oil tanker stated to be lying on Journand Reef in the Pacific. McRae made an offer, which was accepted. They were unable to locate Journand Reef on a map and, on inquiry, were supplied by the defendants with the latitude and longitude at which the tanker was alleged to be lying. At considerable expense, McRae fitted out a salvage expedition. When they arrived at the stated site they found that the tanker was not there and proved that it did not exist and never had existed.

Held: The High Court of Australia held that McRae was entitled to recover from the defendant damages for breach of contract. The amount McRae was entitled to recover as damages was the agreed purchase price of the shipwreck together with the expenditure wasted in reliance on the promise that there was an oil tanker at the locality given. The court refused to award damages measured on the expectation basis because the lost profits were too speculative.

Dixon and Fullagar JJ: [I]f we approach this case as an ordinary case of wrongful non-delivery of goods sold, and attempt to apply the ordinary rules for arriving at the sum to be awarded as damages, we seem to find ourselves at once in insuperable difficulties. There was obviously no market into which the buyers could go to mitigate their loss, and the rule normally applied would require us to arrive at the value of the goods to the buyer at the place where they ought to have been delivered and at the time when they ought to have been delivered. But it is quite impossible to place any value on what the Commission purported to sell ...

It was strongly argued for the plaintiffs that mere difficulty in estimating damages did not relieve a tribunal from the responsibility of assessing them as best it could. This is undoubtedly true. In the well-known case of *Chaplin v Hicks* [1911] 2 KB 786 Vaughan Williams LJ said: 'The fact that damages cannot be assessed with certainty does not relieve the wrongdoer of the necessity of paying damages for his breach of contract'

... The present case seems to be more like *Sapwell v Bass* (1910) 2 KB 486 than *Chaplin v Hicks* ... It does not seem possible to say that 'any assessable loss has resulted from' non-delivery as such ... Here we seem to have something which cannot be assessed. If there were nothing more in this case than a promise to deliver a stranded tanker and a failure to deliver a stranded tanker, the plaintiffs would, of course, be entitled to recover the price paid by them, but beyond that, in our opinion, only nominal damages.

There is, however, more in this case than that, and the truth is that to regard this case as a simple case of breach of contract by non-delivery of goods would be to take an unreal and misleading view of it. The practical substance of the case lies in these three factors – (1) the Commission promised that there was a tanker at or near to the specified place; (2) in reliance on that promise the plaintiffs expended considerable sums, of money; (3) there was in fact no tanker at or anywhere near to the specified place. In the waste of their considerable expenditure seems to lie the real and understandable grievance of the plaintiffs.

The decision in *McRae* demonstrates that the court itself might refuse to award damages measured on the expectation basis where it is difficult to prove loss. In other situations, the court might refuse to award reliance damages. The most common situation in which reliance damages are refused is when they would enable a claimant to escape from a bad bargain.

***C & P Haulage v Middleton* [1983] 1 WLR 1461**

Facts: Middleton permitted C & P Haulage to use their premises for a car repair business. The licence expressly provided for the use to be reviewed every six months and for any fixtures put in by the defendant to be left on the premises following termination of the licence. Despite this clause, C & P Haulage undertook extensive building works on the premises. Several weeks before the end of the six-month period, Middleton summarily ejected C & P haulage from its premises. The owner of C & P Haulage was forced to run the business out of the garage at his home. C & P Haulage claimed damages calculated by reference to its expenditure on improving Middleton's premises.

Held: The Court of Appeal rejected C & P Haulage's claim on the ground that the cost of the improvements would have been lost in any event when the licence was lawfully terminated after six months.

Ackner LJ: It is not the function of the courts where there is a breach of contract knowingly, as this would be the case, to put a plaintiff in a better financial position than if the contract had been properly performed. In this case the plaintiff would indeed be in a better position because, as I have already indicated, had the contract been lawfully determined as it could have been in the middle of December, there would have been no question of his recovering these expenses.

Fox LJ: The present case seems to me to be quite different both from *Anglia Television Ltd v Reed* [1972] 1 QB 60 and from *Lloyd v Stanbury* [1971] 1 WLR 535 in that while it is true that the expenditure could in a sense be said to be wasted in consequence of the breach of contract, it was equally likely to be wasted if there had been no breach, because the plaintiffs wanted to get the defendant out and could terminate the licence at quite short notice. A high risk of waste was from the very first inherent in the nature of the contract itself, breach or no breach. The reality of the matter is that the waste resulted from what was, on the defendant's side, a very unsatisfactory and dangerous bargain.

C & P Haulage were unable to recover their reliance losses because they would have incurred the loss in any event when the licence was lawfully terminated after six months. The loss flowed from C & P Haulage's poor judgment in entering into a bad bargain, not from Middleton's breach of contract. Allowing recovery in such circumstances would have enabled C & P Haulage to avoid the contractual allocation of risk.

It is arguable that the burden of proving that the bargain was not 'bad' should ordinarily fall on the claimant (*Dataliner Ltd v Vehicle Builders & Repairers Association*, (1995) *The Independent*, 30 August). However, certainly if the nature of the breach is such that it is impossible for the claimant to do so, the burden of proof shifts to the defendant (*CCC Films (London) Ltd v Impact Quadrant Films Ltd* [1985] QB 16 and cf. *Omak Maritime Ltd v Mamola Challenger Shipping Co* [2010] EWHC 2026 (Comm)). This is arguably only fair because it was the defendant's breach that occasioned the need to assess damages. However, more recent authority suggests that the burden of proof is generally on the defendant (see, for example, *Grange v Quinn* [2013] EWCA Civ 24 and *Thai Airways International Public Company Ltd v KI Holdings Co Ltd* [2015] EWHC 1250 (Comm)). In any case, it will often be a difficult burden to discharge.

It is often assumed that a claimant cannot recover both reliance damages and expectation damages. The remedies are said to be alternative, not cumulative. Thus Beatson, Burrows and Cartwright write: 'A claimant who recovers for the loss of a bargain cannot, as a general rule, combine a claim for reliance loss with one for loss of expectation so as to recover twice in respect of the same loss' (*Anson's Law of Contract*, 30th edn, 2016, Oxford: OUP, p 573). The case usually cited for this proposition is *Cullinane v British Rema Manufacturing Co Ltd*.

Cullinane v British Rema Manufacturing Co Ltd [1954] 1 QB 292

Facts: The claimant purchased a clay pulverizing machine from the defendants who warranted that the plant would be able to process the plaintiff's clay at the rate of six tons per hour. When it failed to do so the claimant sought damages under two heads:

(1) the expenditure incurred on installing the machine, with interest, making allowance for the unpaid balance of the purchase price and the residual value of the machine at the time of the claim.

(2) the loss of profit for the three years up to the hearing of the case, deducting from this sum interest on capital, depreciation, maintenance and other expenses.

The official referee awarded £7,370 damages for capital thrown away, plus interest and £8,913 loss of profit.

Held: The majority of the Court of Appeal (Morris LJ dissenting) allowed the appeal, holding that the damages awarded were excessive and should be reduced. The claimant could not recover both his capital loss and his loss of gross profits because this would result in double recovery. He must elect between the two claims.

The decision in *Cullinane* has been subjected to searching academic criticism.

Harris, D, Campbell, D, and Halson, R, _Remedies in Contract and Tort_, 2nd edn, 2002, Cambridge: CUP, p 131

It is submitted that the position taken by the majority in this case is confused: their concern to avoid double recovery led them to overlook the fact that a *net* loss of profit can be calculated in such a way as to avoid overlapping with the wasted capital expenditure. They were correct in holding that *gross* profit expected to be earned by the machine during its useful life would include the expected return of the capital expenditure by C. But, as Morris LJ pointed out in his dissent, C was not claiming his expected profits, but his net profit calculated after a deduction of depreciation, which represented the return to him of the capital element; therefore his claim for his net capital outlay did not overlap with his claim for loss of net profits. It is submitted that the view of Morris LJ is to be preferred, and that a split claim should be permitted so long as the calculations show that no overlapping occurs in the different heads of claim.

It is submitted that the criticisms of Harris, Campbell and Halson are correct. Indeed, their position is supported by the more recent case of *Naughton v O'Callaghan* [1990] 3 All ER 94, where the claimant was permitted to recover both his net loss of profit and the expenses he had incurred in reliance on the contract. Finally, it was noted above that, in the cases in which the courts have purported to award reliance damages, the damages could be re-characterised as examples of expectation damages. This re-characterisation helps to explain the decision in *Anglia Television v Reed* and provides a more convincing rationale for the bad bargain rule in *C & P Haulage v Middleton*.

15.2.1.3 The restitution measure

Fuller and Perdue describe the restitution interest in the following terms: 'the plaintiff has in reliance on the promise of the defendant conferred some value on the defendant. The defendant fails to perform his promise. The court may force the defendant to disgorge the value he received from the plaintiff.' The authors note that the object of restitutionary damages is the prevention of unjust enrichment. In the contractual context, an actionable unjust enrichment may occur in a number of different situations.

The particular example that Fuller and Perdue give is a claim for restitution, based on a total failure of consideration following a repudiatory breach. If such a breach is accepted, and the claimant agrees to return any benefits received, then s/he will be entitled to claim restitution of any goods or money which have been transferred to the defendant. The claim is based on unjust enrichment by subtraction, not on the wrong of breach of contract. This is important because it enables a claimant, following a breach of contract, to claim both restitution for unjust enrichment and compensatory damages for the breach of contract. This is precisely what occurred on the facts of *Millar's Machinery Co Ltd v David Way & Son* (1935) 40 Com Cas 204. The case concerned a contract for the sale of a machine, which was defective on delivery and rejected by the purchaser. The disappointed purchaser was able to recover the price paid (restitution for unjust enrichment), the installation costs (reliance damages) and the profits he had lost from use of the machine (expectation damages).

15.2.2 Compensatory damages for non-pecuniary losses

An award of compensatory damages, whether calculated by reference to the expectation measure or the reliance measure, is primarily concerned with economic loss of one kind or another, and as such is pecuniary. In some situations, however, non-pecuniary losses will be caused by a breach of contract. For example, if I purchase a defective car, which catches fire and causes serious injury to me, there is no reason why I should not be able to recover damages for the pain and suffering caused to me.

***Grant v Australian Knitting Mills Ltd* [1936] AC 85**

Facts: The claimant, Grant, bought a pair of underpants manufactured by the defendants. After wearing the underpants, Grant contracted dermatitis. The dermatitis got so bad that Grant was confined to bed for 17 weeks and the attendant physician believed for some time that he was going to die. Grant claimed that the dermatitis had been caused by the presence of free sulphites in the cuffs and ankle ends of the underpants and sued the defendant for breach of an implied warranty in the contract of sale. At first instance, the judge awarded Grant A$2,450 in damages in respect of the physical injury caused by the breach of contract.

Held: The House of Lords dismissed the defendant's appeal and upheld the first instance award.

It is clear that compensatory damages can be recovered in respect of personal injury caused by a breach of contract. It is less clear, however, whether damages can be recovered in relation to mental distress, anguish or annoyance caused by a breach of contract (as opposed to psychiatric injury, on which see *Yapp v Foreign and Commonwealth Office* [2014] EWCA Civ 1512). The courts have generally been wary of awarding damages in such circumstances, due, for example, to concerns about opening the floodgates to claims (see *Less v Hussain* [2012] EWHC 3513).

15.2.2.1 The traditional rule

The traditional rule was that a person had no right to compensation for the upset caused by a breach of contract.

***Addis v Gramophone Co Ltd* [1909] AC 488**

Facts: Addis was employed as the manager of Gramophone's business in Calcutta at a salary together with commission on trade done. His contract entitled him to six months' notice. The defendants gave him notice and immediately replaced him with another employee. This action deprived the plaintiff of his right to act as manager during the notice period, and thus deprived him of the commission he would have earned. The plaintiff sued for breach of contract.

Held: The House of Lords held that, although the plaintiff could recover a sum representing his salary for the period of notice and the commission he would have earned during that period, he could not recover damages to compensate him for the harsh manner in which he was dismissed.

Lord Loreburn LC: I cannot agree that the manner of dismissal affects these damages. Such considerations have never been allowed to influence damages in this kind of case ... If there be a dismissal without notice the employer must pay an indemnity; but that indemnity cannot include compensation either for the injured feelings of the servant, or for the loss he may sustain from the fact that his having been dismissed of itself makes it more difficult for him to obtain fresh employment.

Addis was followed in a more recent dismissal case.

***Bliss v South East Thames RHA* [1985] IRLR 308**

Facts: Bliss was a consultant orthopaedic surgeon. His relationship with one of his colleagues deteriorated and as a result the health authority required the surgeon to undergo a psychiatric examination. He refused and was suspended. Bliss sued the health authority for breach of contract and, at first instance, was awarded £2,000 for mental distress.

Held: The Court of Appeal allowed the Health Authority's appeal, holding that it was bound by *Addis v Gramophone*, and that damages could not be awarded for mental distress in an action for wrongful dismissal.

The decisions in *Addis* and *Bliss* must now be considered in light of the speeches delivered by the House of Lords in *Malik v BCCI* [1998] AC 20. The facts of that case were given in Chapter 6. The House of Lords held that where the employer had breached an implied term of trust and confidence in an employment contract damages might, in some circumstances, be recovered for the difficulty in obtaining future employment (see also *Edwards v Chesterfield Royal Hospital NHS Foundation Trust* [2011] UKSC 58). In *Oraki v Bramston* [2015] EWHC 2046 Proudman J considered, without fully deciding, whether a claimant could bring a claim for mental distress against their trustee in bankruptcy. On appeal ([2017] EWCA Civ 403) David Richards LJ stated at [222]: 'The judge also held that, even if a bankrupt can bring a personal claim against his or her trustee, damages for mental distress are not recoverable. While I am inclined to think that may be right, I do not propose to express a concluded view on it.'

15.2.2.2 Exceptions to the traditional rule

A number of exceptions have developed over the years since *Addis*. It has been held that damages for distress and disappointment can be recovered where the purpose of the contract is the provision of pleasure and enjoyment.

***Jarvis v Swan Tours Ltd* [1973] QB 233**

Facts: James Jarvis, a solicitor, paid £63.45 for a 15-day Christmas winter sports holiday with Swan Tours. Swan Tours' brochures promised a 'house-party' with a variety of activities, entertainment (including a yodelling evening) and food and drink. The holiday was a great disappointment and the provisions fell far short of the brochure descriptions. There were only 13 people at the hotel in the first week and Jarvis was on his own in the second week. The county court judge found that for the first week he got a holiday which was to some extent inferior and, for the second week, a holiday which was very largely inferior to what he had been led to expect and awarded him £31.72 damages. Jarvis appealed against the amount of damages.

Held: The Court of Appeal allowed the appeal, holding that Jarvis was entitled to be compensated for his disappointment and distress at the loss of the entertainment and facilities for enjoyment which he had been promised in the defendants' brochure. The court held that his damages should be increased to £125.

Lord Denning MR: In a proper case damages for mental distress can be recovered in contract, just as damages for shock can be recovered in tort. One such case is a contract for a holiday, or any other contract to provide entertainment and enjoyment. If the contracting party breaks his contract, damages can be given for the disappointment, the distress, the upset and frustration caused by the breach. I know that it is difficult to assess in terms of money, but it is no more difficult than the assessment which the courts have to make every day in personal injury cases for loss of amenities.

It seems, however, that this exception did not generally extend to commercial contracts.

***Hayes v James and Charles Dodd (a firm)* [1990] 2 All ER 815**

Facts: Hayes ran a motor repair business. He instructed a solicitor to represent him in the purchase of a new workshop. The solicitors gave Hayes an assurance that a right of way existed in relation to access to the property which Hayes was interested in purchasing. This turned out to be untrue, and Hayes's business failed. He sued the solicitors for breach of contract. At first instance, the judge awarded damages on the basis of capital expenditure thrown away, plus expenses (including interest) and damages for anguish and vexation.

Held: The Court of Appeal allowed the appeal in part, holding that the damages for anguish and vexation were not recoverable, as they arose out of a purely commercial contract.

Staughton LJ: [D]amages for mental distress in contract are, as a matter of policy, limited to certain classes of case. I would broadly follow the classification of Dillon LJ in *Bliss v South East Thames RHA*: '... where the contract which has been broken was itself a contract to provide peace of mind or freedom from distress'. It may be that the class is somewhat larger than that. But it should not, in my judgment, include any case where the object of the contract was not comfort or pleasure, or the relief of discomfort, but simply carrying on a commercial activity with a view to profit.

The general rule and its exceptions were restated by Bingham LJ in *Watts v Morrow* [1991] 1 WLR 1421:

> A contract-breaker is not in general liable for any distress, frustration, anxiety, displeasure, vexation, tension or aggravation which his breach of contract may cause to the innocent party. This rule is not, I think, founded on the assumption that such reactions are not foreseeable, which they surely are or may be, but on considerations of policy.
>
> But the rule is not absolute. Where the very object of a contract is to provide pleasure, relaxation, peace of mind or freedom from molestation, damages will be awarded if the fruit of the contract is not provided or if the contrary result is procured instead ... In cases not falling within this exceptional category, damages are in my view recoverable for *physical inconvenience* and discomfort caused by the breach and mental suffering directly related to that inconvenience and discomfort.

Bingham LJ's summary of the law permitted recovery of damages for non-pecuniary loss in two categories of case:

1 Cases where the 'very object' of the contract is the provision of pleasure, relaxation, peace of mind or freedom from molestation, for example, contracts for a holiday (*Jarvis v Swan Tours* [1973] QB 233), a holiday rental car (*Jackson v Chrysler Acceptances Ltd* [1978] RTR 474), wedding photographs (*Diesen v Sampson* [1971] SLT (Sh Ct) 49), or burial rights (*Reed v Madon* [1989] Ch 408).
2 Cases where the breach of contract has caused 'physical inconvenience and discomfort'.

For some time, *Watts* was the leading case on recovery for non-pecuniary loss in Contract Law. It has now been superseded by the decision of the House of Lords in *Farley v Skinner*.

Farley v Skinner [2002] 2 AC 732

Facts: Mr Farley employed Mr Skinner to survey a house that he was considering purchasing as a country residence. The house was situated close to Gatwick Airport so Farley asked Skinner to investigate, in addition to the usual matters, whether the property would be affected by aircraft noise, telling him that he did not want to be on a flight path. Skinner reported: 'You have also asked whether we felt the property might be affected by aircraft noise, but we were not conscious of this during the time of our inspection, and think it unlikely that the property will suffer greatly from such noise, although some planes will inevitably cross the area, depending on the direction of the wind and the positioning of the flight paths.' After moving in, Farley discovered that the house was close to a navigation beacon which is used by aircraft waiting to land at Gatwick and, as a result, the property was substantially affected by noise. Farley brought an action for damages, alleging that Skinner had been negligent in carrying out his obligations under the contract. At first instance, the judge held that Skinner was liable for breach of contract. The judge found that the value of the house was not affected by the breach, but awarded Farley damages of £10,000 for the distress and inconvenience caused to him by the aircraft noise. The Court of Appeal reversed this award of non-pecuniary damages on the ground that, applying the *Watts v Morrow* tests, Farley had not experienced any physical discomfort and inconvenience as a result of the breach of contract, and that the object of the contract was not the provision of pleasure or peace of mind.

Held: The House of Lords allowed Farley's appeal and restored the judgment at first instance. Damages for non-pecuniary loss were available under both of Bingham LJ's categories from *Watts v Morrow*.

Lord Steyn:

The very object of the contract: the framework

... An important development for this branch of the law was *Ruxley Electronics & Construction Ltd v Forsyth* [1996] AC 344 ... [Lord Steyn set out the facts and continued] Lord Mustill and Lord Lloyd of Berwick justified the award in carefully reasoned judgments which carried the approval of four of the Law Lords. It is sufficient for present purposes to mention that for Lord Mustill, at p 360, the principle of *pacta sunt servanda* would be eroded if the law did not take account of the fact that the consumer often demands specifications which, although not of economic value, have value to him. This is sometimes called the 'consumer surplus': see Harris, Ogus and Phillips, 'Contract Remedies and the Consumer Surplus' (1979) 95 LQR 581. Lord Mustill rejected the idea that 'the promisor can please himself whether or not to comply with the wishes of the promise which, as embodied in the contract, formed part of the consideration for the price'. Lords Keith of Kinkel and Bridge of Harwich agreed with Lord Mustill's judgment and with Lord Lloyd of Berwick's similar reasoning. Labels sometimes obscure rather than illuminate. I do not therefore set much store by the description 'consumer surplus'. But the controlling principles stated by Lord Mustill and Lord Lloyd are important. It is difficult to reconcile this decision of the House with the decision of the Court of Appeal [2000] Lloyd's Rep PN 516 in the present case. I will in due course return to the way in which the majority attempted to distinguish *Ruxley Electronics & Construction Ltd v Forsyth* [1996] AC 344. At this stage, however, I draw attention to the fact that the majority in the Court of Appeal, at p 521, regarded the relevant observations of Lord Mustill and Lord Lloyd as *obiter dicta*. I am satisfied that the principles enunciated in Ruxley's case in support of the award of £2,500 for a breach of respect of the provision of a pleasurable amenity have been authoritatively established.

The very object of the contract: the arguments against the plaintiff's claim

Counsel for the surveyor advanced three separate arguments each of which he said was sufficient to defeat the plaintiff's claim. First, he submitted that even if a major or important part of the contract was to give pleasure, relaxation and peace of mind, that was not enough. It is an indispensable requirement that the object of the entire contract must be of this type. Secondly, he submitted that the exceptional category does not extend to a breach of a contractual duty of care, even if imposed to secure pleasure, relaxation and peace of mind. It only covers cases where the promisor guarantees achievement of such an object. Thirdly, he submitted that by not moving out of Riverside House the plaintiff forfeited any right to recover non-pecuniary damages.

The first argument fastened onto a narrow reading of the words 'the very object of [the] contract' as employed by Bingham LJ in *Watts v Morrow* [1991] 1 WLR 1421, 1445. Cases where a major or important part of the contract was to secure pleasure, relaxation and peace of mind were not under consideration in *Watts v Morrow*. It is difficult to see what the principled justification for such a limitation might be ... Counsel was, however, assisted by the decision of the Court of Appeal in *Knott v Bolton* (1995) 11 Const LJ 375, which in the present case the Court of Appeal treated as binding on it. In *Knott v Bolton* an architect was asked to design a wide staircase for a gallery and impressive entrance hall. He failed to do so. The plaintiff spent money in improving the staircase to some extent and he recovered the cost of the changes. The plaintiff also claimed damages for disappointment and distress at the lack of an impressive staircase. In agreement with the trial judge the Court of Appeal disallowed this part of his claim. Reliance was placed on the dicta of Bingham LJ in *Watts v Morrow* [1991] 1 WLR 1421, 1445.

Interpreting the *dicta* of Bingham LJ in *Watts v Morrow* narrowly the Court of Appeal in *Knott v Bolton* ruled that the central object of the contract was to design a house, not to provide pleasure to the occupiers of the house. It is important, however, to note that *Knott v Bolton* was decided a few months before the decision of the House in *Ruxley Electronics & Construction Ltd v Forsyth* [1996] AC 344. In any event, the technicality of the reasoning in *Knott v Bolton*, and therefore in the Court of Appeal judgments in the present case, is apparent. It is obvious, and conceded, that if an architect is employed only to design a staircase, or a surveyor is employed only to investigate aircraft noise, the breach of such a distinct obligation may result in an award of non-pecuniary damages. Logically the same must be the case if the architect or surveyor, apart from entering into a general retainer, concludes a separate contract, separately remunerated, in respect of the design of a staircase or the investigation of aircraft noise. If this is so the distinction drawn in *Knott v Bolton* and in the present case is a matter of form and not substance …

There is no reason in principle or policy why the scope of recovery in the exceptional category should depend on the object of the contract as ascertained from all its constituent parts. It is sufficient if a major or important object of the contract is to give pleasure, relaxation or peace of mind …

That brings me to the second issue, namely whether the plaintiff's claim is barred by reason of the fact that the surveyor undertook an obligation to exercise reasonable care and did not guarantee the achievement of a result. This was the basis upon which Hale LJ after the first hearing in the Court of Appeal thought that the claim should be disallowed. This reasoning was adopted by the second Court of Appeal and formed an essential part of the reasoning of the majority. This was the basis on which they distinguished *Ruxley Electronics & Construction Ltd v Forsyth* [1996] AC 344. Against the broad sweep of differently framed contractual undertakings, and the central purpose of contract law in promoting the observance of contractual promises, I am satisfied that this distinction ought not to prevail. It is certainly not rooted in precedent … I fully accept, of course, that contractual guarantees of performance and promises to exercise reasonable care are fundamentally different. The former may sometimes give greater protection than the latter. Proving breach of an obligation of reasonable care may be more difficult than proving breach of a guarantee. On the other hand, a party may in practice be willing to settle for the relative reassurance offered by the obligation of reasonable care undertaken by a professional man. But why should this difference between an absolute and relative contractual promise require a distinction in respect of the recovery of non-pecuniary damages? Take the example of a travel agent who is consulted by a couple who are looking for a golfing holiday in France. Why should it make a difference in respect of the recoverability of non-pecuniary damages for a spoiled holiday whether the travel agent gives a guarantee that there is a golf course very near the hotel, represents that to be the case, or negligently advises that all hotels of the particular chain of hotels are situated next to golf courses? If the nearest golf course is in fact 50 miles away a breach may be established. It may spoil the holiday of the couple. It is difficult to see why in principle only those plaintiffs who negotiate guarantees may recover non-pecuniary damages for a breach of contract. It is a singularly unattractive result that a professional man, who undertakes a specific obligation to exercise reasonable care to investigate a matter judged and communicated to be important by his customer, can in Lord Mustill's words in *Ruxley Electronics & Construction Ltd v Forsyth* [1996] AC 344, 360 'please himself whether or not to comply with the wishes of the promise which, as embodied in the contract, formed part of the consideration for the price'. If that were the law it would be seriously deficient. I am satisfied that it is not the law. In my view the distinction drawn by Hale LJ and by the majority in the Court of Appeal between contractual guarantees and obligations of reasonable care is unsound …

Quantum

In the surveyor's written case it was submitted that the award of £10,000 was excessive. It was certainly high. Given that the plaintiff is stuck indefinitely with a position which he sought to avoid by the terms of his contract with the surveyor I am not prepared to interfere with the judge's evaluation on the special facts of the case. On the other hand, I have to say that the size of the award appears to be at the very top end of what could possibly be regarded as appropriate damages. Like Bingham LJ in *Watts v Morrow* [1991] 1 WLR 1421, 1445h I consider that awards in this area should be restrained and modest. It is important that logical and beneficial developments in this corner of the law should not contribute to the creation of a society bent on litigation.

Lord Clyde: The judge found that the plaintiff was not a man of excessive susceptibility and he refers to the inconvenience he was suffering as 'real discomfort'. I do not consider it appropriate to explore the detail of the inconvenience as being 'physical', either because it impacts upon his eardrums, or because it has some geographical element, such as the relative locations of the aircraft and the property, or the obviously greater audibility of their movements when the plaintiff is seeking to enjoy the amenity of the terrace and the gardens than when he is inside the house. In my view the real discomfort which the judge found to exist constituted an inconvenience to the plaintiff which is not a mere matter of disappointment or sentiment. It is unnecessary that the noise should be so great as to make it impossible for the plaintiff to sit at all on his terrace. Plainly it significantly interferes with his enjoyment of the property and in my view that inconvenience is something for which damages can and should be awarded.

... In my view the appeal can be allowed on the foregoing basis.

But it is possible to approach the case as one of the exceptional kind in which the claim would be for damages for disappointment. If that approach was adopted so as to seek damages for disappointment, I consider that it should also succeed.

It should be observed at the outset that damages should not be awarded, unless perhaps nominally, for the fact of a breach of contract as distinct from the consequences of the breach. That was a point which I sought to stress in *Alfred McAlpine Constructions v Panatown Ltd* [2001] 1 AC 518. For an award to be made a loss or injury has to be identified which is a consequence of the breach but not too remote from it, and which somehow or other can be expressed and quantified in terms of a sum of money. So disappointment merely at the fact that the contract has been breached is not a proper ground for an award. The mere fact of the loss of a bargain should not be the subject of compensation. But that is not the kind of claim which the plaintiff is making here. What he is seeking is damages for the inconvenience of the noise, the invasion of the peace and quiet which he expected the property to possess and the diminution in his use and enjoyment of the property on account of the aircraft noise.

The critical factor on this approach, as it seems to me, is that the plaintiff made the specific request of the defendant to discover whether the property might be affected by aircraft noise. It is suggested that because this point was wrapped up together with a number of other matters in the instructions given by the plaintiff it cannot be regarded as constituting the 'very object' of the contract. But that approach seems to me simply to be playing with words. What is referred to as a breach of contract is often a breach of a particular provision in a contract. The effect of that breach may affect the continued existence of the other terms of the contract, so as to bring the whole to an end. But the point which is the focus of concern is a particular provision in the whole agreement. I can see no reason for distinguishing the present case from a situation where the plaintiff had instructed the defendant simply to advise on the matter of aircraft noise, having already obtained a survey report covering all the other matters ...

The request for the report on aircraft noise was additional to the usual matters expected of a surveyor in the survey of a property and could properly have attracted an extra fee if he had spent extra time researching that issue. It is the specific provision relating to the peacefulness of the property in respect of aircraft noise which makes the present case out of the ordinary. The criterion is not some general characteristic of the contract, as, for example, that it is or is not a 'commercial' contract. The critical factor is the object of the particular agreement.

The present case can in my view qualify as one of the exceptional cases where a contract for peace or pleasure has been made and breached, thereby entitling the injured party to claim damages for the disappointment occasioned by the breach.

Lord Hutton: I ... consider that there is no valid distinction between a case where a party promises to achieve a result and a case where a party is under a contractual obligation to take reasonable care to achieve a result. Suppose a case where a householder's enjoyment of his garden is spoilt by an unpleasant smell from a septic tank at the bottom of the garden and he employs a company to clean out the tank. If the contract constituted a promise by the company to clean out the tank and it failed to do so, with the result that the smell continued, I think that in accordance with the principle stated by Lord Mustill in *Ruxley v Forsyth* [1996] AC 344, 360–361 the householder would be entitled to recover a modest sum of damages for the annoyance caused by the continuation of the smell. But if the contract provided that the company would exercise reasonable care and skill to clean out the tank and due to its negligence the tank was not cleaned out, I consider that the householder would also be entitled to damages ...

It will be for the courts, in the differing circumstances of individual cases, to apply the principles stated in your Lordships' speeches in this case, and the matter is not one where any precise test or verbal formula can be applied, but … I consider that as a general approach it would be appropriate to treat as cases falling within the exception and calling for an award of damages those where: (1) the matter in respect of which the individual claimant seeks damages is of importance to him, and (2) the individual claimant has made clear to the other party that the matter is of importance to him, and (3) the action to be taken in relation to the matter is made a specific term of the contract. If these three conditions are satisfied, as they are in the present case, then I consider that the claim for damages should not be rejected on the ground that the fulfilment of that obligation is not the principal object of the contract or on the ground that the other party does not receive special and specific remuneration in respect of the performance of that obligation …

Physical inconvenience and discomfort

… The aircraft noise was something which affected the plaintiff through his hearing and can be regarded as having a physical effect upon him, and on the evidence which was before him I consider that it was open to the judge to find that the plaintiff suffered physical inconvenience and discomfort.

I agree with Judge and Clarke LJJ that on first impression the award of £10,000 damages appears to be a very high one, but I also agree with them that this is a very unusual case where the inconvenience and discomfort caused to the plaintiff will continue, and on further consideration I do not consider that it would be right for an appellate court to set aside the award as being excessive. Therefore I would allow the appeal and restore the order of the judge.

Lord Scott: Ruxley's case establishes, in my opinion, that if a party's contractual performance has failed to provide to the other contracting party something to which that other was, under the contract, entitled, and which, if provided, would have been of value to that party, then, if there is no other way of compensating the injured party, the injured party should be compensated in damages to the extent of that value. Quantification of that value will in many cases be difficult and may often seem arbitrary. In Ruxley's case the value placed on the amenity value of which the pool owner had been deprived was £2,500. By that award, the pool owner was placed, so far as money could do it, in the position he would have been in if the diving area of the pool had been constructed to the specified depth.

In Ruxley's case the breach of contract by the builders had not caused any consequential loss to the pool owner. He had simply been deprived of the benefit of a pool built to the depth specified in the contract. It was not a case where the recovery of damages for consequential loss consisting of vexation, anxiety or other species of mental distress had to be considered.

In *Watts v Morrow* [1991] 1 WLR 1421, however, that matter did have to be considered. As in the present case, the litigation in *Watts v Morrow* resulted from a surveyor's report. The report had negligently failed to disclose a number of defects in the property. The clients, who had purchased the property in reliance on the report, remedied the defects and sued for damages. The judge awarded them the costs of the repairs and also general damages of £4,000 each for 'distress and inconvenience' (p 1424). As to the cost of repairs, the Court of Appeal substituted an award of damages based on the difference between the value of the property as the surveyor's report had represented it to be and the value as it actually was. Nothing, for present purposes, turns on that. As to the damages for 'distress and inconvenience' the Court of Appeal upheld the award in principle but held that the damages should be limited to a modest sum for the physical discomfort endured and reduced the award to £750 for each plaintiff. Bingham LJ, at p 1445, in an important passage, set out the principles to be applied where contractual damages for distress and inconvenience are claimed:

> 'A contract-breaker is not in general liable for any distress, frustration, anxiety, displeasure, vexation, tension or aggravation which his breach of contract may cause to the innocent party. This

rule is not, I think, founded on the assumption that such reactions are not foreseeable, which they surely are or may be, but on considerations of policy.

But the rule is not absolute. Where the very object of a contract is to provide pleasure, relaxation, peace of mind or freedom from molestation, damages will be awarded if the fruit of the contract is not provided or if the contrary result is procured instead. If the law did not cater for this exceptional category of case it would be defective. A contract to survey the condition of a house for a prospective purchaser does not, however, fall within this exceptional category.

In cases not falling within this exceptional category, damages are in my view recoverable for physical inconvenience and discomfort caused by the breach and mental suffering directly related to that inconvenience and discomfort'.

In the passage I have cited, Bingham LJ was dealing with claims for consequential damage consisting of the intangible mental states and sensory experiences to which he refers. Save for the matters referred to in the first paragraph, all of which reflect or are brought about by the injured party's disappointment at the contract breaker's failure to carry out his contractual obligations, and recovery for which, if there is nothing more, is ruled out on policy grounds, Bingham LJ's approach is, in my view, wholly consistent with established principles for the recovery of contractual damages.

There are, however, two qualifications that I would respectfully make to the proposition in the final paragraph of the cited passage that damages 'for physical inconvenience and discomfort caused by the breach' are recoverable.

First, there will, in many cases, be an additional remoteness hurdle for the injured party to clear. Consequential damage, including damage consisting of inconvenience or discomfort, must, in order to be recoverable, be such as, at the time of the contract, was reasonably foreseeable as liable to result from the breach: see *McGregor on Damages*, 16th edn, pp 159–160, para 250.

Second, the adjective 'physical', in the phrase 'physical inconvenience and discomfort', requires, I think, some explanation or definition. The distinction between the 'physical' and the 'non-physical' is not always clear and may depend on the context. Is being awoken at night by aircraft noise 'physical'? If it is, is being unable to sleep because of worry and anxiety 'physical'? What about a reduction in light caused by the erection of a building under a planning permission that an errant surveyor ought to have warned his purchaser-client about but had failed to do so? In my opinion, the critical distinction to be drawn is not a distinction between the different types of inconvenience or discomfort of which complaint may be made but a distinction based on the cause of the inconvenience or discomfort. If the cause is no more than disappointment that the contractual obligation has been broken, damages are not recoverable even if the disappointment has led to a complete mental breakdown. But, if the cause of the inconvenience or discomfort is a sensory (sight, touch, hearing, smell etc) experience, damages can, subject to the remoteness rules, be recovered.

In summary, the principle expressed in *Ruxley Electronics and Construction Ltd v Forsyth* [1996] AC 344 should be used to provide damages for deprivation of a contractual benefit where it is apparent that the injured party has been deprived of something of value but the ordinary means of measuring the recoverable damages are inapplicable. The principle expressed in *Watts v Morrow* [1991] 1 WLR 1421 should be used to determine whether and when contractual damages for inconvenience or discomfort can be recovered . . .

It is time for me to turn to the present case and apply the principles expressed in *Ruxley Electronics and Construction Ltd v Forsyth* [1996] AC 344 and *Watts v Morrow* [1991] 1 WLR 1421. In my judgment, Mr Farley is entitled to be compensated for the 'real discomfort' that the judge found he suffered. He is so entitled on either of two alternative bases.

First, he was deprived of the contractual benefit to which he was entitled. He was entitled to information about the aircraft noise from Gatwick-bound aircraft that Mr Skinner, through negligence, had failed to supply him with. If Mr Farley had, in the event, decided not to purchase Riverside House, the value to him of the contractual benefit of which he had been deprived would have been nil. But he did buy the property. And he took his decision to do so without the advantage of being able to take into account the information to which he was contractually entitled. If he had had that information he would not have bought. So the information clearly would have had a value to him. Prima facie, in my opinion, he is entitled to be compensated accordingly.

In these circumstances, it seems to me, it is open to the court to adopt a *Ruxley Electronics and Construction Ltd v Forsyth* [1996] AC 344 approach and place a value on the contractual benefit of which Mr Farley has been deprived. In deciding on the amount, the discomfort experienced by Mr Farley can, in my view, properly be taken into account. If he had had the aircraft noise information he would not have bought Riverside House and would not have had that discomfort.

Alternatively, Mr Farley can, in my opinion, claim compensation for the discomfort as consequential loss. Had it not been for the breach of contract, he would not have suffered the discomfort. It was caused by the breach of contract in a *causa sine qua non* sense. Was the discomfort a consequence that should reasonably have been contemplated by the parties at the time of contract as liable to result from the breach? In my opinion, it was. It was obviously within the reasonable contemplation of the parties that, deprived of the information about aircraft noise that he ought to have had, Mr Farley would make a decision to purchase that he would not otherwise have made. Having purchased, he would, having become aware of the noise, either sell in which case at least the expenses of the resale would have been recoverable as damages or he would keep the property and put up with the noise. In the latter event, it was within the reasonable contemplation of the parties that he would experience discomfort from the noise of the aircraft. And the discomfort was 'physical' in the sense that Bingham LJ in *Watts v Morrow* [1991] 1 WLR 1421, 1445 had in mind. In my opinion, the application of *Watts v Morrow* principles entitles Mr Farley to damages for discomfort caused by the aircraft noise.

I would add that if there had been an appreciable reduction in the market value of the property caused by the aircraft noise, Mr Farley could not have recovered both that difference in value and damages for discomfort. To allow both would allow double recovery for the same item.

A number of observations can be made:

15.2.2.2.1 The very object of the contract category

First, it is clear that Bingham LJ's first category from *Watts v Morrow* should not be too narrowly confined (cf. also *Glen Haysman v Mrs Rogers Films Ltd* [2008] EWHC 2494 (QB) and *Herrmann v Withers LLP* [2012] EWHC 1492). The contract does not have to be solely concerned with the provision of pleasure. According to Lord Steyn, 'it is sufficient if a major or important object of the contract is to give pleasure, relaxation or peace of mind'. This is entirely sensible and avoids the injustice of cases like *Knott v Bolton* (1995) 11 Const LJ 375, where the claimants were denied a remedy for an architect's breach in designing their house because the contract also had an economic purpose. As Lord Clyde noted, it would be ludicrous to distinguish between the facts of *Farley* and a situation where the plaintiff had instructed the defendant simply to advise on the matter of aircraft noise, having already obtained a survey report covering all the other matters.

Lord Hutton attempted to provide specific guidance as to when the provision of pleasure would be a sufficiently major and important object of the contract. He set out three requirements: '(1) the matter in respect of which the individual claimant seeks damages is of importance to him, and (2) the individual claimant has made clear to the other party that the matter is of importance to him, and (3) the action to be taken in relation to the matter is made a specific term of the contract.' Lord Scott appeared to go even further. Relying on *Ruxley* he concluded that, 'if a party's contractual performance has failed to provide to the other contracting party something to which that other was, under the contract, entitled, and which, if provided, would have been of value to that party, then, if there is no other way of compensating the injured party, the injured party should be compensated in damages to the extent of that value.' The question for Lord Scott is therefore simply whether there is an obligation of the relevant type in the contract. It does not have to be a major part of the contract. At the heart of Lord Scott's analysis is a commitment to protecting the performance interest of the contract (but see Lord Clyde's restatement of the position he adopted in *Alfred McAlpine*). However, in *Harrison v Shepherd Homes Ltd* [2011] EWHC 1811, a case involving the purchase of houses on a new development, Ramsey J stated:

> In relation to the first head of loss I consider that SHL are correct. This is a case of a sales contract for the purchase of a house. As Lord Scott said in *Farley v Skinner* it is sufficient if a major or important object of the contract is to give pleasure, relaxation or peace of mind. There is no express term to that effect and I do not consider that one should be implied. Whilst the fulfilment of the obligation to provide a properly designed and constructed property and to remedy any defects may give 'pleasure, relaxation, peace of mind' that is not the object. I do not consider that a major or important object was to avoid the worry arising from defects in the property or the failure to make good those defects. In those circumstances I do not consider that there is any room for an award of that type of damages. This is not a contract of the exceptional type mentioned by Lord Bingham in *Watts v Morrow*.

On the difficulties of classifying this type of loss see *Moorjani v Durban Estates Ltd* [2015] EWCA Civ 1252.

Their Lordships also emphasised that non-pecuniary damages could be recovered for breach of negative obligations as well as breach of positive obligations. Lord Hutton gave the following example:

> Suppose a case where a householder's enjoyment of his garden is spoilt by an unpleasant smell from a septic tank at the bottom of the garden and he employs a company to clean out the tank. If the contract constituted a promise by the company to clean out the tank and it failed to do so, with the result that the smell continued, I think that ... the householder would be entitled to recover a modest sum of damages for the annoyance caused by the continuation of the smell. But if the contract provided that the company would exercise reasonable care and skill to clean out the tank and due to its negligence the tank was not cleaned out, I consider that the householder would also be entitled to damages.

The obligation breached in *Farley* was a negative obligation. Skinner did not undertake to guarantee that the property was unaffected by aircraft noise, but to exercise reasonable care in checking whether the house was so affected. This did not make any difference, however, and Farley was entitled to recover damages for his non-pecuniary loss flowing from Skinner's breach of a negative obligation.

15.2.2.2.2 Physical inconvenience and discomfort

Their Lordships were also of the view that Mr Farley could have recovered damages for his non-pecuniary loss under Bingham LJ's second category – non-pecuniary loss flowing out of physical inconvenience and discomfort. In fact this was Lord Clyde's primary ground for his decision. The Court of Appeal had held that Mr Farley could not recover under this category because the aircraft noise did not constitute 'physical inconvenience'. The House of Lords disagreed. Their Lordships opined that the distinction between physical and non-physical was unhelpful. Lord Scott asked:

'Is being awoken at night by aircraft noise "physical"? If it is, is being unable to sleep because of worry and anxiety "physical"? What about a reduction in light caused by the erection of a building under a planning permission that an errant surveyor ought to have warned his purchaser-client about, but had failed to do so?'

For Lord Clyde the true distinction exists between real discomfort for which non-pecuniary damages are recoverable and mere disappointment for which they are not. On the facts, the aircraft noise constituted real discomfort and inconvenience to Mr Farley, which went beyond mere disappointment or sentiment. Lord Scott came to a similar conclusion, but for him, the crucial fact was that the inconvenience of the aircraft noise was a sensory experience. He said: 'If the cause is no more than disappointment that the contractual obligation has been broken, damages are not recoverable even if the disappointment has led to a complete mental breakdown. But, if the cause of the inconvenience or discomfort is a sensory (sight, touch, hearing, smell, etc.) experience, damages can, subject to the remoteness rules, be recovered.' Of the two definitions, Lord Scott's is probably the most workable.

15.2.2.2.3 Quantum

On the issue of quantification, their Lordships were of the view that the judge's award of £10,000 was at the top end of the scale (see *Milner v Carnival Plc* [2010] EWCA Civ 389). However, they were not prepared to deem it excessive because of the continuing impact of the discomfort and inconvenience. Lord Steyn noted that awards of non-pecuniary damages should be restrained and modest in order to prevent the creation of a 'society bent on litigation', but he declined to give any specific guidance on how judges should approach the issue of quantification in the future. One limiting factor that was introduced, however, was Lord Scott's insistence that a claimant could not recover damages for both discomfort and diminution of value. In his view, to allow both would allow double recovery for the same loss.

The principles set out in *Farley v Skinner* were further applied in *Hamilton-Jones v David & Snape (a firm)*.

Hamilton-Jones v David & Snape (a firm) [2004] 1 WLR 924

Facts: The claimant approached the defendant solicitors after the breakdown of her marriage. She was extremely concerned that her husband would attempt to abduct her children and take them back to his native country, Tunisia. The defendant obtained 'residence' and 'prohibited steps' orders for the claimant and notified the passport agency, asking it not to issue passports in respect of her children. The passport agency confirmed that the children's names would remain on its register for a year. After a year the registration lapsed. The claimant's husband succeeded in becoming a British citizen and had the children's names added to the passport. He used this passport to remove the children from the UK. The claimant sued the defendant for breach of contract and claimed damages for the mental distress sustained as a result of the breach.

Held: The High Court held that the claimant was entitled to recover damages of £20,000 in respect of the distress which she had suffered.

Neuberger J: I return ... to what I regard as the centrally relevant, and difficult, question, namely, whether it can fairly be said that the contract between the claimant and the defendants in the present case can be said to have had as its object the provision of 'pleasure, relaxation, peace of mind or freedom from molestation', or something akin thereto. There is obviously room for argument, whether one judges the matter from the perception of the claimant or of the defendants, as to the primary purpose of the claimant's instruction to the defendants from February 1994 until July 1996. For a relatively altruistic parent, the claimant's primary concern could be said to have been the children; a more selfish parent would have had her own interests in the forefront. However, on any view, it appears to me that both the claimant and the defendants would have had in mind that a significant reason for the claimant instructing the defendants was with a view to ensuring, so far as possible, that the claimant retained custody of her children for her own pleasure and peace of mind. It would, I think, be a relatively unusual parent who, in the position of the claimant in the present case, would not have had, and would not be perceived by her solicitors to have had, her own peace of mind and pleasure in the company of her children as an important factor. In these circumstances, subject to any further argument which the defendants might raise, I consider that the principles as developed in *Watts v Morrow* [1991] 1 WLR 1421 and in *Farley v Skinner* [2002] 2 AC 732 indicate that the claimant should be entitled to recover damages for mental distress ...

The measure of damages to be awarded to the claimant for mental distress raises a very difficult problem, albeit that it is the sort of problem with which the court is not infrequently faced. As was said by Mummery LJ in *Vento v Constable of West Yorkshire Police* [2003] ICR 318, 331, para 50, 'translating hurt feelings into hard currency is bound to be an artificial exercise'. In that case, the Court of Appeal said, at p 335, para 65, that general damages for injured feelings where 'there had been a lengthy campaign of discriminatory harassment on the ground of sex or race' should normally be between £15,000 and £25,000 ...'

[Neuberger J outlined the details of the case and continued:]

'Describing the grief, anxiety and hurt she must have suffered, and the mitigating factors, does not make it any easier to translate her mental distress into monetary consideration. I have not been referred to any authority which gives convincingly helpful guidance as to the right figure. In my view, bearing in mind the serious distress which, as I find, was caused to the claimant, both by the initial shock of the twins being kidnapped by Mr Bougossa and taken to Tunisia, and by the continuing loss of having the company of, and the ability to bring up, the twins, albeit subject to the mitigating factors I have mentioned, I think that the correct measure of damages is £20,000.

The fairly substantial award suggests that the courts may be willing to move beyond the cautious approach to quantification advocated by the House of Lords in *Farley v Skinner*. Of course, the award in *Hamilton-Jones* may be explicable on the exceptional facts of the case. Nevertheless, if such large sums continue to be awarded and the courts embrace the expansive definition of the categories advocated by Lord Scott in *Farley*, the floodgates for claims may open. More and more, the courts will need to rely on the rules limiting recovery of damages, which will be discussed in the following section.

15.2.3 Limitations on the recovery of damages

We have already considered some restrictions on the type and measure of loss that can be claimed in an action for breach of contract. In addition, there are a number of rules that limit the claimant's ability to obtain full protection of his performance interest. These rules mean that the claimant can only recover for losses which are in broad terms: (i) causally linked to the breach of contract; (ii) reasonably foreseeable; and (iii) unavoidable. We will consider each of these limitations in turn.

15.2.3.1 Causation

A claimant must demonstrate that her/his loss has been caused by the breach of contract. S/he cannot recover damages for loss caused by a supervening event and in some circumstances her/his award may be reduced if it is proven that her/his own negligence contributed to the loss.

15.2.3.1.1 Supervening events

The claimant must prove that the breach of contract was the 'dominant' or 'effective' cause of the loss. The courts often need to resort to common sense principles in ascertaining whether the breach was the cause of the loss. In *Galoo Ltd v Bright Grahame Murray* [1994] 1 WLR 1360, 1374–1375, Glidewell LJ said:

> If a breach of contract by a defendant is to be held to entitle the plaintiff to claim damages, it must first be held to have been an 'effective' or 'dominant' cause of his loss. The test in *Quinn v Burch Bros (Builders) Ltd* [1966] 2 QB 370, that it is necessary to distinguish between a breach of contract which causes a loss to the plaintiff and one which merely gives the opportunity for him to sustain the loss, is helpful but still leaves the question to be answered 'How does the court decide whether the breach of duty was the cause of the loss or merely the occasion for the loss?' ... The answer in the end is 'By the application of the court's common sense'.

15.2.3.2 Contributory negligence

Since 1945, it has sometimes been possible for the courts to reduce the amount of damages recoverable in tort on the ground that the claimant's own negligence contributed to his loss.

LAW REFORM (CONTRIBUTORY NEGLIGENCE) ACT 1945

Section 1. Apportionment of liability in case of contributory negligence

(1) Where any person suffers damage as the result partly of his own fault and partly of the fault of any other person or persons, a claim in respect of that damage shall not be defeated by reason of the fault of the person suffering the damage, but the damages recoverable in respect thereof shall be reduced to such extent as the court thinks just and equitable having regard to the claimant's share in the responsibility for the damage ...

Section 4. Interpretation

The following expressions have the meanings hereby respectively assigned to them, that is to say –

> 'fault' means negligence, breach of statutory duty or other act or omission which gives rise to a liability in tort or would, apart from this Act, give rise to the defence of contributory negligence.

The current law on contributory negligence in contract was stated by Hobhouse J and the Court of Appeal in *Forsikringsaktieselskapet Vesta v Butcher* [1986] 2 All ER 488 and [1988] 3 WLR 565 (affirmed on other grounds: [1989] AC 852). The courts distinguished three different types of situation:

(1) Where the defendant's liability arises from some contractual provision which does not depend on negligence on the part of the defendant.
(2) Where the defendant's liability arises from a contractual obligation which is expressed in terms of taking care (or its equivalent) but does not correspond to a common law duty to take care which would exist in the given case independently of contract.
(3) Where the defendant's liability in contract is the same as his liability in the tort of negligence independent of the existence of any contract.

In *Vesta* it was held that the Act applies to the third situation and, accordingly, damages can be reduced for contributory negligence where the contractual duty of care co-exists with the tortious duty of care (affirmed by the House of Lords in *Platform Home Loans Ltd v Oyston Shipways* [2000] 2 AC 190). The Act does not apply in the first category, however.

Barclays Bank plc v Fairclough Building Ltd [1995] QB 214

Facts: Fairclough agreed to carry out work for Barclays Bank at Millbrook Industrial Estate, Wythenshawe. The work included the cleaning of roofs made of corrugated asbestos sheets. Fairclough failed to take any of the recommended precautions when using the high pressure hose method of cleaning the asbestos roofs, with the result that the premises became contaminated by asbestos and required extensive remedial works. Barclays brought an action to recover the costs of the works, claiming that Fairclough had breached two of the main obligations under the contract. Fairclough accepted liability but contended that Barclays Bank had been contributorily negligent, in that it had failed to supervise the work through its architectural services department. Barclays Bank countered that its claim lay only in contract and thus the defence of contributory negligence was not available. At first instance, the judge held that the breach of contract was co-existent with a breach of a duty of care in tort. As such, the defence of contributory negligence was available and damages could be reduced by 40 per cent.

Held: The Court of Appeal allowed the appeal holding that, where the defendant had breached a strict contractual obligation, damages could not be reduced on the grounds of contributory negligence.

Beldam LJ: [The courts have classified] contractual duties under three headings: (i) where a party's liability arises from breach of a contractual provision which does not depend on a failure to take reasonable care; (ii) where the liability arises from an express contractual obligation to take care which does not correspond to any duty which would exist independently of the contract; (iii) where the liability for breach of contract is the same as, and coextensive with, a liability in tort independently of the existence of a contract. This analysis was adopted by Hobhouse J in *Forsikringsaktieselskapet Vesta v Butcher* [1986] 2 All ER 488 and by the Court of Appeal in the same case [1989] AC 852, 860, 862, 866–867. The judgments in the Court of Appeal in that case assert that in category (iii) cases the Court of Appeal is bound by the decision in *Sayers v Harlow Urban District Council* [1958] 1 WLR 623 to admit the availability of the defence.

... [I]n category (i) cases there is no decision in which contributory negligence has been held to be a partial defence. There are powerful dicta to the effect that it cannot be: see the judgment of the court in *Tennant Radiant Heat Ltd v Warrington Development Corporation* [1988] 1 EGLR 41, in *Bank of Nova Scotia v Hellenic Mutual War Risks Association (Bermuda) Ltd* [1990] 1 QB 818, 904, and the observations of Nolan LJ in *Schering Agrochemicals Ltd v Resibel NV SA* (unreported), 26 November 1992; Court of Appeal (Civil Division) Transcript No 1298 of 1992, noted in (1993) 109 LQR 175, 177 ...

I have already stated my conclusion that in the present case the defendant was in breach of two conditions which required strict performance and did not depend on a mere failure to take reasonable care ... In my judgment ... in the present state of the law contributory negligence is not a defence to a claim for damages founded on breach of a strict contractual obligation. I do not believe the wording of the Law Reform (Contributory Negligence) Act 1945 can reasonably sustain an argument to the contrary. Even if it did, in the present case the nature of the contract and the obligation undertaken by the skilled contractor did not impose on the plaintiff any duty in its own interest to prevent the defendant from committing the breaches of contract. To hold otherwise would, I consider, be equivalent to implying into the contract an obligation on the part of the plaintiff inconsistent with the express terms agreed by the parties. The contract clearly laid down the extent of the obligations of the plaintiff as architect and of the defendant. It was the defendant who was to provide appropriate supervision on site, not the architect.

Simon Brown LJ: The very imposition of a strict liability on the defendant is to my mind inconsistent with an apportionment of the loss. And not least because of the absurdities that the contrary approach carries in its wake. Assume a defendant, clearly liable under a strict contractual duty. Is his position to be improved by demonstrating that besides breaching that duty he was in addition negligent? Take this very case. Is this contract really to be construed so that the defendant is advantaged by an assertion of its own liability in nuisance or trespass as well as in contract? Are we to have trials at which the defendant calls an expert to implicate him in tortious liability, whilst the plaintiff's expert seeks paradoxically to exonerate him? The answer to all these questions is surely 'No'. Whatever arguments exist for apportionment in other categories of case – and these are persuasively deployed in the 1993 Law Commission Report (Law Com. No 219) – to my mind there are none in the present type of case and I for my part would construe the contract accordingly.

It is unclear whether the defence of contributory negligence is also unavailable for a claim in category (2) – cases where the contractual liability is based on 'negligence', but there is no concurrent duty in tort. The Law Commission, however, has recommended that contributory negligence should be available in category (2) cases by analogy to category (3) cases.

Law Commission, *Contributory Negligence as a Defence in Contract*, Law Com No 219 (1993)

Liability for breach of a contractual duty of reasonable care

4.7 Where the plaintiff has suffered damage partly as the result of his own failure to take reasonable care for the protection of himself or his interests and partly as the result of the defendant's breach of a contractual duty to take reasonable care or exercise reasonable skill, we believe that it is correct in principle for his damages to be apportioned. As we stated in the consultation paper, there is a clear similarity in substance between an action for breach of a contractual duty of care and an action for a breach of a tortious duty of reasonable care. Whether a duty of reasonable care is classified as tortious or contractual does not affect the content of that duty, and it is not, in our view, desirable that the availability of apportionment should depend upon how the duty is classified. Furthermore, where the defendant undertakes only a contractual duty of reasonable care, he has not (in contrast to the case where he has accepted a strict contractual obligation) guaranteed to produce a particular outcome. Thus it is unfair to assume that he has undertaken to compensate the plaintiff even where the plaintiff has contributed to his own loss ... [T]he rules on causation, remoteness and mitigation do not provide an adequate substitute for apportionment and can be unfair to either defendant or plaintiff. This is because they either produce 'all or nothing' results, or do not have the flexibility of apportionment on the basis of what the court thinks just and equitable, given the agreed allocation of risks.

The decision in *Fairclough* can lead to some surprising results. It may be in a defendant's interest to argue that he is concurrently liable in tort as well as in contract so that he can take advantage of the 1945 Act to reduce his liability. Likewise, it may be in a claimant's interest to deny that he has a claim in tort so that he can recover full damages from the defendant in a claim for breach of contract (see *Barclays Bank plc v Fairclough Building Ltd (No 2)* [1995] IRLR 605). This bizarre state of affairs is difficult to justify. Two solutions present themselves. Either contributory negligence should be allowed as a defence to all claims for breach of contract (see Burrows, 'Contributory Negligence' in Contract: Ammunition for the Law Commission' (1993) 109 LQR 175) or it should be denied any role in the law of contract. Either solution is better than the present state of affairs.

15.2.3.3 Remoteness

The rule of remoteness prevents losses extending too far, thereby placing unreasonable burdens on the defendant. An example of such a burden was given by Willes J in *British Columbia & Vancouver Island Spar, Lumber and Saw Mill Co v Nettleship* (1868) 3 LR CP 499, 508: 'where a man going to be married to an heiress, his horse having cast a shoe on the journey, employed a blacksmith to replace it, who did the work so unskilfully that the horse was lamed, and, the ride not arriving in time, the lady married another; and the blacksmith was held liable for the loss of the marriage.'

Francis Dawson has argued that the remoteness rule determines 'the extent of the secondary obligation undertaken by the promisor. It does so by assessing the extent of the liability to which the promisor may be presumed to have assented when undertaking his primary obligation' (Dawson, F, 'Reflections on Certain Aspects of the Law of Damages for Breach of Contract' (1995) 9 JCL 125, 125).

The seminal case on remoteness in the law of contract is *Hadley v Baxendale* (although compare *Transfield Shipping Inc v Mercator Shipping Inc* [2008] UKHL 48 which will be considered below).

Hadley v Baxendale (1854) 9 Exch 341; 156 ER 145

Facts: The plaintiff, the owner of a flour mill, contracted with the defendant, a common carrier, for the transport of a broken crank shaft from the plaintiff's mill to an engineer, who was going to use the broken shaft as a pattern by which to make a new shaft. In breach of contract, the defendant delayed in delivering the crank shaft to the engineer. As a result, the plaintiffs did not receive the new shaft until five days after the date agreed with the carrier. The plaintiff claimed damages for the loss of profit for the five days that the mill was shut as a consequence of the defendant's breach of contract.

Held: The Exchequer Court held that the loss of profits could not be recovered because the loss was too remote.

Alderson B: Now we think the proper rule in such a case as the present is this: Where two parties have made a contract which one of them has broken, the damages which the other party ought to receive in respect of such breach of contract should be such as may fairly and reasonably be considered either arising naturally, i.e., according to the usual course of things, from such breach of contract itself, or such as may reasonably be supposed to have been in the contemplation of both parties, at the time they made the contract, as the probable result of the breach of it. Now, if the special circumstances under which the contract was actually made were communicated by the plaintiffs to the defendants, and thus known to both parties, the damages resulting from the breach of such a contract, which they would reasonably contemplate, would be the amount of injury which would ordinarily follow from a breach of contract under these special circumstances so known and communicated. But, on the other hand, if these special circumstances were wholly unknown to the party breaking the contract, he, at the most, could only be supposed to have had in his contemplation the amount of injury which would arise generally, and in the great multitude of cases not affected by any special circumstances, from such a breach of contract. For, had the special circumstances been known, the parties might have specially provided for the breach of contract by special terms as to the damages in that case; and of this advantage it would be very unjust to deprive them ... Now, in the present case, if we are to apply the principles above laid down, we find that the only circumstances here communicated by the plaintiffs to the defendants at the time the contract was made, were, that the article to be carried was the broken shaft of a mill, and that the plaintiffs were the millers of that mill. But how do these circumstances shew reasonably that the profits of the mill must be stopped by an unreasonable delay in the delivery of the broken shaft by the carrier to the third person? Suppose the plaintiffs had another shaft in their possession put up or putting up at the time, and that they only wished to send back the broken shaft to the engineer who made it; it is clear that this would be quite consistent with the above circumstances, and yet the unreasonable delay in the delivery would have no effect upon the intermediate profits of the mill. Or, again, suppose that, at the time of the delivery to the carrier, the machinery of the mill had been in other respects defective, then, also, the same results would follow. Here it is true that the shaft was actually sent back to serve as a model for a new one, and that the want of a new one was the only cause of the stoppage of the mill, and that the loss of profits really arose from not sending down the new shaft in proper time, and that this arose from the delay in delivering the broken one to serve as a model. But it is obvious that, in the great multitude of cases of millers sending off broken shafts to third persons by a carrier under ordinary circumstances, such consequences would not, in all probability, have occurred; and these special circumstances were here never communicated by the plaintiffs to the defendants. It follows, therefore, that the loss of profits here cannot reasonably be considered such a consequence of the breach of contract as could have been fairly and reasonably contemplated by both the parties when they made this contract. For such loss would neither have flowed naturally from the breach of this contract in the great multitude of such cases occurring under ordinary circumstances, nor were the special circumstances, which, perhaps, would have made it a reasonable and natural consequence of such breach of contract, communicated to or known by the defendants.

There are two aspects of the *Hadley v Baxendale* test that should be noted. First, it is clear that the focus of the test is on the knowledge of the parties at the time the contract is made. The reason for this is that, if the parties are aware of the risk, they can make changes to the terms of the contract to allocate the risk. In the example given above by Willes J, had the blacksmith been aware of the marriage he could have decided to: (a) charge a higher price; (b) incorporate a limitation or exclusion clause; (c) take out insurance to cover the risk; (d) refuse to enter the contract at all. There is some uncertainty about the type of knowledge that is required to hold the defendant liable for the losses sustained. It seems that 'knowledge' means more than mere 'awareness'. The relevant information must be communicated to the defendant in a context where it is clear that the defendant is expected to assume the risk. Thus in *Kemp v Intasun Holidays* [1987] BTLC 353, communication of the claimant's medical condition at the time a holiday was booked was insufficient to make the defendant liable for losses resulting from it. If communication takes place as part of pre-contractual negotiations, however, it will normally be assumed that the defendant has accepted liability (see *Simpson v London and North Western Railway Co* (1876) 1 QBD 274). Professor Danzig has noted the inflexibility of the notice requirement and its inappropriateness in the modern industrial world.

Danzig, R, '*Hadley v Baxendale*: a study in the industrialization of the law' (1975) 4 *JLS* 249, 279–280

Whether viewed as a simple 'notice' or a more exacting 'contemplation' requirement, however, this portion of the rule in *Hadley v Baxendale* runs counter to the tide of an industrializing economy. It was already somewhat out of date when expressed in the Exchequer opinion. For in *Hadley v Baxendale*, the court spoke as though entrepreneurs were universally flexible enough and enterprises small enough for individuals to be able to serve 'notice' over the counter of specialized needs calling for unusual arrangements. But in mass-transition situations a seller cannot plausibly engage in an individualized 'contemplation' of the consequences of breach and a subsequent tailoring of a transaction. In the course of his conversion of a family business into a modern industrial enterprise, Baxendale made Pickfords itself into an operation where the contemplation branch of the rule in *Hadley v Baxendale* was no longer viable. Even in the 1820s the Pickfords' operations were 'highly complex' ...

By 1865 the business ... was 'an enormous mercantile establishment with a huge staff of busy clerks, messengers and porters ... It is divided into innumerable departments, the employees in each of which find it as much as they can comfortably do to master its details without troubling themselves about any other.

A century later most enterprises fragment and standardize operations in just this way. This development – and the law's recognition of it – makes it self-evidently impossible to serve legally cognizable notice on, for example, an airline that a scheduled flight is of special importance or on the telephone company that uninterrupted service is particularly vital at a particular point in a firm's business cycle.

The second important aspect of the test in *Hadley v Baxendale* is that it appears to have two parts:

1 losses that may fairly and reasonably be considered to arise *naturally* from the breach;
2 losses that may reasonably be supposed to have been in the *contemplation* of both parties, at the time they made the contract.

Later decisions (*Victoria Laundry (Windsor) Ltd v Newman Industries* [1949] 2 KB 528; *Koufos v C Czarnikow Ltd, The Heron II* [1969] 1 AC 350) have treated these two parts as aspects of the same general principle. In the recent case of *Jackson v Royal Bank of Scotland* [2005] 1 WLR 377, 390–391, Lord Walker said:

> In my opinion the familiar passage from the judgment of Alderson B ... cannot be construed and applied as if it were a statutory text, nor are its two limbs mutually exclusive. The first limb ... tends to beg the question, since it makes the damages recoverable under the first limb depend on how the breach of contract is characterised. If for instance (by reference to the facts of *Hadley v Baxendale* itself) the breach is described simply as a carrier's failure to convey goods from Gloucester and deliver them to Greenwich within two days as promised, it is a matter of speculation what damages would arise naturally and in the ordinary course. If on the other hand the breach is described as a delay in delivering to the manufacturer at Greenwich a broken crankshaft to serve as a model for a new crankshaft urgently required for the only steam engine at a busy flour mill at Gloucester (which was standing idle until the new crankshaft arrived) then loss of business profits is seen to be an entirely natural consequence. The appropriate characterisation of the breach depends on the terms of the contract, its business context, and the reasonable contemplation of the parties (although Baron Alderson used the latter expression in relation to the second limb).

Both limbs of the test are concerned with the same question: Did the defendant know, or ought s/he reasonably to have known, that such a loss was likely to result from the breach of contract? The first limb deals with normal types of loss, which the reasonable defendant is deemed to know about because they arise naturally from a breach of contract. The second limb deals with the more unusual types of loss, which the defendant will only be liable for if s/he had sufficient actual knowledge of the risk. The application of this two-limbed test can be seen in *Victoria Laundry (Windsor) v Newman Industries*.

Victoria Laundry (Windsor) v Newman Industries [1949] 2 KB 528

Facts: The plaintiffs, launderers and dyers, entered into a contract with the defendants for the purchase of a large boiler. At the time the contract was concluded, the boiler was installed at the defendants' premises. The defendants hired a third party to dismantle the boiler. During the dismantling, the boiler rolled over and sustained serious damage. This meant that delivery of the boiler was delayed by five months. The defendants were aware of the nature of the plaintiffs' business, and had been informed by a letter from the plaintiffs that they intended to put the boiler in use in the shortest possible space of time. In an action for breach of contract, the plaintiffs claimed damages for the loss of profits they had sustained as a result of the delay.

Held: The Court of Appeal held that the plaintiffs were entitled to recover damages for lost profits at a level reasonably to be anticipated from a business of its kind. However, the plaintiffs could not recover damages for lost profits on some particularly lucrative dyeing contracts with the Ministry of Defence, of which the defendants were unaware.

Asquith LJ: What propositions applicable to the present case emerge from the authorities as a whole ...? We think they include the following:

(1) It is well settled that the governing purpose of damages is to put the party whose rights have been violated in the same position, so far as money can do so, as if his rights had been observed: *Sally Wertheim v Chicoutimi Pulp Company* [1911] AC 301. This purpose, if relentlessly pursued, would provide him with a complete indemnity for all loss de facto resulting from a particular breach, however improbable, however unpredictable. This, in contract at least, is recognised as too harsh a rule. Hence,

(2) In cases of breach of contract the aggrieved party is only entitled to recover such part of the loss actually resulting as was at the time of the contract reasonably foreseeable as liable to result from the breach.

(3) What was at that time reasonably so foreseeable depends on the knowledge then possessed by the parties or, at all events, by the party who later commits the breach.

(4) For this purpose, knowledge 'possessed' is of two kinds; one imputed, the other actual. Everyone, as a reasonable person, is taken to know the 'ordinary course of things' and consequently what loss is liable to result from a breach of contract in that ordinary course. This is the subject matter of the 'first rule' in *Hadley v Baxendale* 9 Exch. 341. But to this knowledge, which a contract-breaker is assumed to possess whether he actually possesses it or not, there may have to be added in a particular case knowledge which he actually possesses, of special circumstances outside the 'ordinary course of things', of such a kind that a breach in those special circumstances would be liable to cause more loss. Such a case attracts the operation of the 'second rule' so as to make additional loss also recoverable.

(5) In order to make the contract-breaker liable under either rule it is not necessary that he should actually have asked himself what loss is liable to result from a breach. As has often been pointed out, parties at the time of contracting contemplate not the breach of the contract, but its performance. It suffices that, if he had considered the question, he would as a reasonable man have concluded that the loss in question was liable to result (see certain observations of Lord du Parcq in the recent case of *A/B Karlshamns Oliefabriker v Monarch Steamship Company Limited* [1949] AC 196).

(6) Nor, finally, to make a particular loss recoverable, need it be proved that upon a given state of knowledge the defendant could, as a reasonable man, foresee that a breach must necessarily result in that loss. It is enough if he could foresee it was likely so to result. It is indeed enough, to borrow from the language of Lord du Parcq in the same case, at page 158, if the loss (or some factor without which it would not have occurred) is a 'serious possibility' or a 'real danger'. For short, we have used the word 'liable' to result. Possibly the colloquialism 'on the cards' indicates the shade of meaning with some approach to accuracy.

If these, indeed, are the principles applicable, what is the effect of their application to the facts of this case? ... No commercial concern commonly purchases for the purposes of its business a very large and expensive structure like this – a boiler 19 feet high and costing over £2,000 – with any other motive, and no supplier, let alone an engineering company, which has promised delivery of such an article by a particular date, with knowledge that it was to be put into use immediately on delivery, can reasonably contend that it could not foresee that loss of business (in the sense indicated above) would be liable to result to the purchaser from a long delay in the delivery thereof. The suggestion that, for all the supplier knew, the boiler might have been needed simply as a 'standby', to be used in a possibly distant future, is gratuitous and was plainly negatived by the terms of the letter of April 26, 1946.'

[In respect of losses flowing from the contract with the Ministry of Defence he continued:]

'Here, no doubt, the learned judge had in mind the particularly lucrative dyeing contracts to which the plaintiffs looked forward and which they mention in para 10 of the statement of claim. We agree that in order that the plaintiffs should recover specifically and as such the profits expected on these contracts, the defendants would have had to know, at the time of their agreement with the plaintiffs, of the prospect and terms of such contracts. We also agree that they did not in fact know these things. It does not, however, follow that the plaintiffs are precluded from recovering some general (and perhaps conjectural) sum for loss of business in respect of dyeing contracts to be reasonably expected, any more than in respect of laundering contracts to be reasonably expected.

The plaintiffs' claim did not succeed in relation to the loss of profits on the contracts with the Ministry of Defence because the defendant did not have actual knowledge of these contracts. The Court of Appeal drew a distinction between ordinary business profits and exceptional profits. This is arguably a distinction of degree rather than kind, and in the following case the Court of Appeal held that only the type of loss (and not the extent of the loss) needed to be foreseeable.

***Parsons (Livestock) Ltd v Uttley Ingham & Co Ltd* [1978] QB 791**

Facts: The plaintiffs ordered a bulk food storage hopper from the defendants. They informed the defendants that they intended to use the hopper to store pignuts for feeding their top grade pigherd. When they installed the hopper, the defendants failed to notice that the ventilator at the top of the hopper was closed. As a result, the pignuts dispensed by the hopper were mouldy and a large number of pigs contracted E. coli. The plaintiffs brought an action for breach of contract claiming substantial damages including loss of profit. The defendants denied that they were liable for the loss of profits on the ground that the loss was too remote a consequence of the breach of contract.

Held: The Court of Appeal held that the defendants were liable for the loss of profits because some harm to the pigs was within the reasonable contemplation of the parties as something which would result from supplying a hopper that was unfit for the purpose of storing food for pigs.

Scarman LJ: The judge put it this way:

> 'The natural result of feeding toxic food to animals is damage to their health and may be death, which is what occurred, albeit from a hitherto unknown disease and to particularly susceptible animals. There was therefore no need to invoke the question of reasonable contemplation in order to make the defendant liable'.

The judge in this critical passage is contrasting a natural result, i.e. one which people placed as these parties were would consider as a serious possibility, with a special, specific result, i.e. E. coli disease, which, as he later found, the parties could not at the time of contract reasonably have contemplated as a consequence. He distinguished between 'presumed contemplation' based on a special knowledge from ordinary understanding based upon general knowledge and concludes that the case falls within the latter category. He does so because he has held that the assumption, or hypothesis, to be made is that the parties had in mind at the time of contract not a breach of warranty limited to the delivery of mouldy nuts but a warranty as to the fitness of the hopper for its purpose. The assumption is of the parties asking themselves not what is likely to happen if the nuts are mouldy but what is likely to happen to the pigs if the hopper is unfit for storing nuts suitable to be fed to them. While, on his finding, nobody at the time of contract could have expected E. coli to ensue from eating mouldy nuts, he is clearly – and, as a matter of common sense, rightly – saying that people would contemplate, upon the second assumption, the serious possibility of injury and even death among the pigs.

And so the question becomes: was he right to make the assumption he did? In my judgment, he was: see *Grant v Australian Knitting Mills Ltd* [1936] AC 85, and particularly the well-known passage in the speech of Lord Wright at pp 97–100.

I would agree with *McGregor on Damages*, 13th edn (1972), pp 131–132 that:

> '... in contract as in tort, it should suffice that, if physical injury or damage is within the contemplation of the parties, recovery is not to be limited because the degree of physical injury or damage could not have been anticipated'.

This is so, in my judgment, not because there is, or ought to be, a specific rule of law governing cases of physical injury but because it would be absurd to regulate damages in such cases upon the necessity of supposing the parties had a prophetic foresight as to the exact nature of the injury that does in fact arise. It is enough if upon the hypothesis predicated physical injury must have been a serious possibility. Though in loss of market or loss of profit cases the factual analysis will be very different from cases of physical injury, the same principles, in my judgment, apply. Given the situation of the parties at the time of contract, was the loss of profit, or market, a serious possibility, something that would have been in their minds had they contemplated breach?

By permitting the courts to draw the line between type of loss and extent of loss, the law has imported a significant degree of judicial discretion into the rule of remoteness. But is it really possible to maintain that illness and death are the same type of loss while ordinary loss of profits and exceptional loss of profits are not? The House of Lords confirmed the latter distinction in the case of *Balfour Beatty Construction (Scotland) Ltd v Scottish Power plc* [1994] SLT 807 (but compare also *Transfield Shipping Inc v Mercator Shipping Inc* [2008] UKHL 48, discussed below). The defendants agreed to supply electricity to the plaintiffs who were the main construction company working on the Edinburgh bypass. The supply of electricity failed while the plaintiff was in the middle of the construction of an aqueduct. This work required a 'continuous pour' of concrete and, as a result of the failure, the work which had been done was worthless and had to be demolished. The House of Lords refused to award damages for the full losses suffered by the plaintiff because there was no evidence that the defendants were aware of the need for a continuous pour. Nor was it possible to presume that the defendants were aware of the plaintiffs' business activities.

Ultimately, the judicial discretion inherent in the distinction between type of loss and extent of loss enables the courts to allocate the responsibility for the consequences of breach in a way that corresponds to the implied assumption of responsibility between the parties. This is arguably desirable. Had *Balfour Beatty* been decided the other way, Scottish Power would have been forced to recoup the cost of meeting the damages claim by raising prices for consumers. Arguably this would have been unfair on society as a whole. Balfour Beatty had voluntarily engaged in a high-risk construction project that required a constant supply of electricity. They had failed to inform Scottish Power of this exceptional use and had not negotiated express terms as to the allocation of risk. In such circumstances, it is surely fair to presume that Balfour Beatty had accepted the risk and assumed responsibility for any exceptional loss flowing from the breach of contract by Scottish Power.

It is necessary to consider the degree of risk that must be proven in order to recover damages for breach of contract. In the law of tort, the test is one of 'reasonable foreseeability'. In the law of contract, the test appears to be stricter.

Koufos v C Czarnikow Ltd, The Heron II [1969] 1 AC 350

Facts: The plaintiff chartered a ship to carry a cargo of sugar from Constanza to Basrah. In breach of contract, the ship deviated from its route and reached Basrah nine days late. The sugar was sold immediately but the market price for sugar had fallen significantly. The plaintiff sought to recover the difference in price as damages. The defendant argued that they were unaware of the charters' intention to sell the sugar.

Held: The House of Lords held that the defendants were liable for the loss.

Lord Reid: I am satisfied that the court did not intend that every type of damage which was reasonably foreseeable by the parties when the contract was made should either be considered as arising naturally, i.e., in the usual course of things, or be supposed to have been in the contemplation of the parties. Indeed the decision makes it clear that a type of damage which was plainly foreseeable as a real possibility but which would only occur in a small minority of cases cannot be regarded as arising in the usual course of things or be supposed to have been in the contemplation of the parties: the parties are not supposed to contemplate as grounds for the recovery of damage any type of loss or damage which on the knowledge available to the defendant would appear to him as only likely to occur in a small minority of cases. In cases like *Hadley v Baxendale* (1854) 9 Exch 341, or the present case it is not enough that in fact the plaintiff's loss was directly caused by the defendant's breach of contract. It clearly was so caused in both. The crucial question is whether, on the information available to the defendant when the contract was made, he should, or the reasonable man in his position would, have realised that such loss was sufficiently likely to result from the breach of contract to make it proper to hold that the loss flowed naturally from the breach or that loss of that kind should have been within his contemplation.

The modern rule of tort is quite different and it imposes a much wider liability. The defendant will be liable for any type of damage which is reasonably foreseeable as liable to happen even in the most unusual case, unless the risk is so small that a reasonable man would in the whole circumstances feel justified in neglecting it and there is good reason for the difference. In contract, if one party wishes to protect himself against a risk which to the other party would appear unusual, he can direct the other party's attention to it before the contract is made, and I need not stop to consider in what circumstances the other party will then be held to have accepted responsibility in that event. But in tort there is no opportunity for the injured party to protect himself in that way, and the tortfeasor cannot reasonably complain if he has to pay for some very unusual but nevertheless foreseeable damage which results from his wrongdoing. I have no doubt that today a tortfeasor would be held liable for a type of damage as unlikely as was the stoppage of Hadley's Mill for lack of a crankshaft: to anyone with the knowledge the carrier had that may have seemed unlikely but the chance of it happening would have been seen to be far from negligible. But it does not at all follow that *Hadley v Baxendale* 9 Exch. 341 would today be differently decided.

Lord Morris: [Referring to *R & H Hall Ltd v W H Pim (Junior) & Co Ltd* 33 Com Cas 324 he continued] Though that case was one in which the parties had made express provisions in regard to sub-sales with the result that they must have 'recognised' that a purchaser might have to pay damages to his sub-purchaser if the vendor failed to deliver, the expressions used in the speeches illustrate that damages could be recoverable in respect of a loss which might occur or which the parties could contemplate as not unlikely to occur. The present case is one in which no special information was given to the carrier as to what the respondents intended to do with the goods after they arrived at Basrah. In those circumstances in deciding what damages would fairly and reasonably be regarded as arising if the delivery of the goods was delayed I think that the reasonable contemplation of a reasonable ship owner at the time of the making of the charterparty must be considered. I think that such a ship owner must reasonably have contemplated that if he delivered the sugar at Basrah some nine or ten days later than he could and should have delivered it then a loss by reason of a fall in the market price of sugar at Basrah was one that was liable to result or at least was not unlikely to result.

Lord Pearce: In 1948 in *Monarch Steamship Co Ltd v Karlshamns Oljefabriker (A/B)* [1949] AC 196, a case of damages for delay in carriage by sea, Lord du Parcq used the words 'at least a serious possibility' and 'a real danger which must be taken into account'. Lord Uthwatt spoke of 'the chance of war, not as a possibility of academic interest ... but as furnishing matter which commercially ought to be taken into account' and Lord Morton of Henryton spoke of 'a grave risk'.

Accordingly in my opinion the expressions used in the *Victoria Laundry* case were right. I do not however accept the colloquialism 'on the cards' as being a useful test because I am not sure just what nuance it has either in my own personal vocabulary or in that of others. I suspect that it owes its attraction, like many other colloquialisms, to the fact that one may utter it without having the trouble of really thinking out with precision what one means oneself or what others will understand by it, a spurious attraction which in general makes colloquialism unsuitable for definition, though it is often useful as shorthand for a collection of definable ideas. It was in this latter convenient sense that the judgment uses the ambiguous words 'liable to result'. They were not intended as a further or different test from 'serious possibility' or 'real danger'.

Lord Upjohn: It is clear that on the one hand the test of foreseeability as laid down in the case of tort is not the test for breach of contract; nor on the other hand must the loser establish that the loss was a near certainty or an odds-on probability. I am content to adopt as the test a 'real danger' or a 'serious possibility'. There may be a shade of difference between these two phrases but the assessment of damages is not an exact science and what to one judge or jury will appear a real danger may appear to another judge or jury to be a serious possibility ...

Applying this test to the facts of this case ... the *Heron II* took very nearly 50 per cent more than the reasonably predicted time and for no other reason than her owner's breaches of contract. It is perfectly true that at the time of the contract nothing was said as to the purpose for which the charterer wanted the sugar delivered at Basrah; he might have wanted to do so to stock up his supply of sugar or to carry out a contract already entered into which had nothing to do with the market at Basrah; or he might sell it during the voyage, but all that is pure speculation. It seems to me that on the facts of this case the parties must be assumed to have contemplated that there would be a punctual delivery to the port of discharge and that port having a market in sugar there was a real danger that as a result of a delay in breach of contract the charterer would miss the market and would suffer loss accordingly. It being established that the goods were in fact destined for the market the ship owner is liable for that loss.

It is somewhat difficult to ascertain the precise test to be used in future cases. Lord Reid spoke in terms of the loss being 'sufficiently likely to result' from the breach of contract. Lord Morris used the phrases 'not unlikely to occur' and 'liable to result'. Lords Pearce and Upjohn preferred the words 'a real danger' or 'a serious possibility'. However, the Law Lords did agree that a higher degree of likelihood of the loss occurring was required in contract than in the law of tort.

The relevant remoteness rules in the Law of Contract were recently examined by the House of Lords in *Transfield Shipping Inc of Panama v Mercator Shipping Inc of Monrovia* ('*The Achilleas*').

***Transfield Shipping Inc of Panama v Mercator Shipping Inc of Monrovia* (*'The Achilleas'*) [2008] UKHL 48**

Facts: A ship was chartered at a rate of $16,750 per day. It was due to be redelivered by 2 May 2004. The owners, therefore, chartered the ship to a third party from 8 May 2004 at a rate of $39,500 per day. Subsequently it became clear that the ship would not be redelivered in time for the 8 May charter. As a result, and in order to stop the 8 May charter from being cancelled, the owners negotiated a later start date for that charter in return for a revised charter rate of $31,500 per day. Thereafter the owners claimed damages for the late redelivery of the ship. The key issue was whether the damages should be assessed by reference to the profit lost through the renegotiation of the 8 May charter ($8,000 for 191 days which amounted, after some adjustments, to $1,364,584.37); or by reference to the difference between the original charter rate of $16,750 per day and the market rate for the period by which the ship was delayed (this amounted to $158,301.17). At both first instance and in the Court of Appeal it was held that the loss of $1,364,584.37 was not too remote. The case was then appealed to the House of Lords.

Held: The profit lost as a result of the renegotiation was too remote.

Lord Hoffmann: My Lords,

1. The *Achilleas* is a single-decker bulk carrier of some 69,000 dwt built in 1994. By a time charter dated 22 January 2003 the owners let her to the charterers for about five to seven months at a daily hire rate of US$13,500. By an addendum dated 12 September 2003 the parties fixed the vessel for a further five to seven months at a daily rate of US$16,750. The latest date for redelivery was 2 May 2004.

2. By April 2004, market rates had more than doubled compared with the previous September. On 20 April 2004 the charterers gave notice of redelivery between 30 April and 2 May 2004. On the following day, the owners fixed the vessel for a new four to six month hire to another charterer, following on from the current charter, at a daily rate of US$39,500. The latest date for delivery to the new charterers, after which they were entitled to cancel, was 8 May 2004.

3. With less than a fortnight of the charter to run, the charterers fixed the vessel under a subcharter to carry coals from Quingdao in China across the Yellow Sea to discharge at two Japanese ports, Tobata and Oita. If this voyage could not reasonably have been expected to allow redelivery by 2 May 2004, the owners could probably have refused to perform it: see *Torvald Klaveness A/S v Arni Maritime Corpn (The Gregos)* [1995] 1 Lloyd's Rep 1. But they made no objection. The vessel completed loading at Quingdao on 24 April. It discharged at Tobata, went on to Oita, but was unfortunately delayed there and not redelivered to the owners until 11 May.

4. By 5 May it had become clear to everyone that the vessel would not be available to the new charterers before the cancelling date of 8 May. By that time, rates had fallen again. In return for an extension of the cancellation date to 11 May, the owners agreed to reduce the rate of hire for the new fixture to $31,500 a day.

5. The owners claimed damages for the loss of the difference between the original rate and the reduced rate over the period of the fixture. At US$8,000 a day, that came to US$1,364,584.37. The charterers said that the owners were not entitled to damages calculated by reference to their dealings with the new charterers and that they were entitled only to the difference between the market rate and the charter rate for the nine days during which they were deprived of the use of the ship. That came to $158,301.17.

6. The arbitrators, by a majority, found for the owners. They said that the loss on the new fixture fell within the first rule in *Hadley v Baxendale* (1854) 9 Exch 341, 354 as arising 'naturally, ie according to the usual course of things, from such breach of contract itself'. It fell within that rule because it was damage 'of a kind which the [charterer], when he made the contract, ought to have realised was not unlikely to result from a breach of contract [by delay in redelivery]': see Lord Reid in *C Czarnikow Ltd v Koufos (The Heron II)* [1969] 1 AC 350, 382–383. The dissenting arbitrator did not deny that a charterer would have known that the owners would very likely enter into a following fixture during the course of the charter and that late delivery might cause them to lose it. But he said that a reasonable man in the position of the charterers would not have understood that he was assuming liability for the risk of the type of loss in question. The general understanding in the shipping market was that liability was restricted to the difference between the market rate and the charter rate for the overrun period and 'any departure from this rule [is] likely to give rise to a real risk of serious commercial uncertainty which the industry as a whole would regard as undesirable'.

7. The majority arbitrators, in their turn, did not deny that the general understanding in the industry was that liability was so limited. They said (at para 17):

> 'The charterers submitted that if they had asked their lawyers or their Club what damages they would be liable for if the vessel was redelivered late, the answer would have been that they would be liable for the difference between the market rate and the charter rate for the period of the late delivery. We agree that lawyers would have given such an answer'.

8. But the majority said that this was irrelevant. A broker 'in a commercial situation' would have said that the 'not unlikely' results arising from late delivery would include missing dates for a subsequent fixture, a dry docking or the sale of the vessel. Therefore, as a matter of law, damages for loss of these types was recoverable. The understanding of shipping lawyers was wrong.

9. On appeal from the arbitrators, Christopher Clarke J [2007] 1 Lloyd's Rep 19 and the Court of Appeal (Ward, Tuckey and Rix LJJ) [2007] 2 Lloyd's Rep 555 upheld the majority decision. The case therefore raises a fundamental point of principle in the law of contractual damages: is the rule that a party may recover losses which were foreseeable ('not unlikely') an external rule of law, imposed upon the parties to every contract in default of express provision to the contrary, or is it a prima facie assumption about what the parties may be taken to have intended, no doubt applicable in the great majority of cases but capable of rebuttal in cases in which the context, surrounding circumstances or general understanding in the relevant market shows that a party would not reasonably have been regarded as assuming responsibility for such losses?

10. Before I come to this point of principle, I should say something about the authorities upon which the understanding of shipping lawyers was based. There is no case in which the question now in issue has been raised. But that in itself may be significant. This cannot have been the first time that freight rates have been volatile. There must have been previous cases in which late redelivery caused the loss of a profitable following fixture. But there is no reported case in which such a claim has been made. Instead, there has been a uniform series of dicta over many years in which judges have said or assumed that the damages for late delivery are the difference between the charter rate and the market rate: see for examples Lord Denning MR in *Alma Shipping Corpn of Monrovia v Mantovani (The Dione)* [1975] 1 Lloyd's Rep 115, 117–118; Lord Denning MR in *Arta Shipping Co Ltd v Thai Europe Tapioca Service Ltd (The Johnny)* [1977] 2 Lloyd's Rep 1, 2; Bingham LJ in *Hyundai Merchant Marine Co Ltd v Gesuri Chartering Co Ltd (The Peonia)* [1991] 1 Lloyd's Rep 100, 118. Textbooks have said the same: see Scrutton on *Charterparties* 20th edn (1996), pp 348–349; Wilford and others *Time Charters* 5th edn (2003), at para 4.20. Nowhere is there a suggestion of even a theoretical possibility of damages for the loss of a following fixture.

11. The question of principle has been extensively discussed in the literature. Recent articles by Adam Kramer ('An Agreement-Centred Approach to Remoteness and Contract Damages' in Cohen and McKendrick (eds), *Comparative Remedies for Breach of Contract* (2004) pp 249–286), Andrew Tettenborn ('*Hadley v Baxendale* Foreseeability: A principle beyond its sell-by date' (2007) 23 Journal of Contract Law 120–147) and Andrew Robertson ('The basis of the remoteness rule in contract' (2008) 28 Legal Studies 172–196) are particularly illuminating. They show that there is a good deal of support in the authorities and academic writings for the proposition that the extent of a party's liability for damages is founded upon the interpretation of the particular contract; not upon the interpretation of any particular language in the contract, but (as in the case of an implied term) upon the interpretation of the contract as a whole, construed in its commercial setting. Professor Robertson considers this approach somewhat artificial, since there is seldom any helpful evidence about the extent of the risks the particular parties would have thought they were accepting. I agree that cases of departure from the ordinary foreseeability rule based on individual circumstances will be unusual, but limitations on the extent of liability in particular types of contract arising out of general expectations in certain markets, such as banking and shipping, are likely to be more common. There is, I think, an analogy with the distinction which Lord Cross of Chelsea drew in *Liverpool City Council v Irwin* [1977] AC 239, 257–258 between terms implied into all contracts of a certain type and the implication of a term into a particular contract.

12. It seems to me logical to found liability for damages upon the intention of the parties (objectively ascertained) because all contractual liability is voluntarily undertaken. It must be in principle wrong to hold someone liable for risks for which the people entering into such a contract in their particular market, would not reasonably be considered to have undertaken.

13. The view which the parties take of the responsibilities and risks they are undertaking will determine the other terms of the contract and in particular the price to be paid. Anyone asked to assume a large and unpredictable risk will require some premium in exchange. A rule of law which imposes liability upon a party for a risk which he reasonably thought was excluded gives the other party something for nothing. And as Willes J said in *British Columbia Saw Mill Co Ltd v Nettleship* (1868) LR 3 CP 499, 508:

> 'I am disposed to take the narrow view, that one of two contracting parties ought not to be allowed to obtain an advantage which he has not paid for'.

14. In their submissions to the House, the owners said that the 'starting point' was that damages were designed to put the innocent party, so far as it is possible, in the position as if the contract had been performed: see *Robinson v Harman* (1848) 1 Exch 850, 855. However, in *Banque Bruxelles Lambert SA v Eagle Star Insurance Co Ltd (sub nom South Australia Asset Management Corpn v York Montague Ltd)* [1997] AC 191, 211, I said (with the concurrence of the other members of the House):

> 'I think that this was the wrong place to begin. Before one can consider the principle on which one should calculate the damages to which a plaintiff is entitled as compensation for loss, it is necessary to decide for what kind of loss he is entitled to compensation. A correct description of the loss for which the valuer is liable must precede any consideration of the measure of damages'.

15. In other words, one must first decide whether the loss for which compensation is sought is of a 'kind' or 'type' for which the contract-breaker ought fairly to be taken to have accepted responsibility. In the *South Australia* case the question was whether a valuer, who had (in breach of an implied term to exercise reasonable care and skill) negligently advised his client bank that property which it proposed to take as security for a loan was worth a good deal more than its actual market value, should be liable not only for losses attributable to the deficient security but also for further losses attributable to a fall in the property market. The House decided that he should not be liable for this kind of loss:

> 'In the case of an implied contractual duty, the nature and extent of the liability is defined by the term which the law implies. As in the case of any implied term, the process is one of construction of the agreement as a whole in its commercial setting. The contractual duty to provide a valuation and the known purpose of that valuation compel the conclusion that the contract includes a duty of care. The scope of the duty, in the sense of the consequences for which the valuer is responsible, is that which the law regards as best giving effect to the express obligations assumed by the valuer: neither cutting them down so that the lender obtains less than he was reasonably entitled to expect, nor extending them so as to impose on the valuer a liability greater than he could reasonably have thought he was undertaking'. (p 212)

16. What is true of an implied contractual duty (to take reasonable care in the valuation) is equally true of an express contractual duty (to redeliver the ship on the appointed day). In both cases, the consequences for which the contracting party will be liable are those which 'the law regards as best giving effect to the express obligations assumed' and '[not] extending them so as to impose on the [contracting party] a liability greater than he could reasonably have thought he was undertaking'.

17. The effect of the *South Australia* case was to exclude from liability the damages attributable to a fall in the property market notwithstanding that those losses were foreseeable in the sense of being 'not unlikely' (property values go down as well as up) and had been caused by the negligent valuation in the sense that, but for the valuation, the bank would not have lent at all and there was no evidence to show that it would have lost its money in some other way. It was excluded on the ground that it was outside the scope of the liability which the parties would reasonably have considered that the valuer was undertaking.

18. That seems to me in accordance with the careful way in which Robert Goff J stated the principle in *Satef-Huttenes Albertus SpA v Paloma Tercera Shipping Co SA (The Pegase)* [1981] Lloyd's Rep 175, 183, where the emphasis is upon what a reasonable person would have considered to be the extent of his responsibility:

> 'The test appears to be: have the facts in question come to the defendant's knowledge in such circumstances that a reasonable person in the shoes of the defendant would, if he had considered the matter at the time of making the contract, have contemplated that, in the event of a breach by him, such facts were to be taken into account when considering his responsibility for loss suffered by the plaintiff as a result of such breach'.

19. A similar approach was taken by the Court of Appeal in *Mulvenna v Royal Bank of Scotland plc* [2003] EWCA Civ 1112, mentioned by Professor Robertson in the article to which I have referred. This was an application to strike out a claim for damages for the loss of profits which the claimant said he would have made if the bank had complied with its agreement to provide him with funds for a property development. The Court of Appeal held that even on the assumption that the bank knew of the purpose for which the funds were required and that it was foreseeable that he would suffer loss of profit if he did not receive them, the damages were not recoverable. Sir Anthony Evans said:

> 'The authorities to which we were referred ... demonstrate that the concept of reasonable foreseeability is not a complete guide to the circumstances in which damages are recoverable as a matter of law. Even if the loss was reasonably foreseeable as a consequence of the breach of duty in question (or of contract, for the same principles apply), it may nevertheless be regarded as 'too remote a consequence' or as not a consequence at all, and the damages claim is disallowed. In effect, the chain of consequences is cut off as a matter of law, either because it is regarded as unreasonable to impose liability for that consequence of the breach (The *Pegase* [1981] 1 Lloyd's Rep 175 Robert Goff J), or because the scope of the duty is limited so as to exclude it (*Banque Bruxelles SA v Eagle Star* [1997] AC 191), or because as a matter of commonsense the breach cannot be said to have caused the loss, although it may have provided the opportunity for it to occur ...'

20. By way of explanation for why in such a case liability for lost profits is excluded, Professor Robertson (at p 183) offers what seem to me to be some plausible reasons:

> 'It may be considered unjust that the bank should be held liable for the loss of profits simply because the bank knew of the proposed development at the time the re-financing agreement was made. The imposition of such a burden on the bank may be considered unjust because it is inconsistent with commercial practice for a bank to accept such a risk in a transaction of this type, or because the quantum of the liability is disproportionate to the scale of the transaction or the benefit the bank stood to receive'.

21. It is generally accepted that a contracting party will be liable for damages for losses which are unforeseeably large, if loss of that type or kind fell within one or other of the rules in *Hadley v Baxendale*: see, for example, Staughton J in *Transworld Oil Ltd v North Bay Shipping Corpn (The Rio Claro)* [1987] Lloyd's Rep 173, 175 and *Jackson v Royal Bank of Scotland plc* [2005] 1 WLR 377. That is generally an inclusive principle: if losses of that type are foreseeable, damages will include compensation for those losses, however large. But the *South Australia* and *Mulvenna* cases show that it may also be an exclusive principle and that a party may not be liable for foreseeable losses because they are not of the type or kind for which he can be treated as having assumed responsibility.

22. What is the basis for deciding whether loss is of the same type or a different type? It is not a question of Platonist metaphysics. The distinction must rest upon some principle of the law of contract. In my opinion, the only rational basis for the distinction is that it reflects what would have been reasonable and have been regarded by the contracting party as significant for the purposes of the risk he was undertaking. In *Victoria Laundry (Windsor) Ltd v Newman Industries Ltd* [1949] 2 KB 528, where the plaintiffs claimed for loss of the profits from their laundry business because of late delivery of a boiler, the Court of Appeal did not regard 'loss of profits from the laundry business' as a single type of loss. They distinguished (at p 543) losses from 'particularly lucrative dyeing contracts' as a different type of loss which would only be recoverable if the defendant had sufficient knowledge of them to make it reasonable to attribute to him acceptance of liability for such losses. The vendor of the boilers would have regarded the profits on these contracts as a different and higher form of risk than the general risk of loss of profits by the laundry.

23. If, therefore, one considers what these parties, contracting against the background of market expectations found by the arbitrators, would reasonably have considered the extent of the liability they were undertaking, I think it is clear that they would have considered losses arising from the loss of the following fixture a type or kind of loss for which the charterer was not assuming responsibility. Such a risk would be completely unquantifiable, because although the parties would regard it as likely that the owners would at some time during the currency of the charter enter into a forward fixture, they would have no idea when that would be done or what its length or other terms would be. If it was clear to the owners that the last voyage was bound to overrun and put the following fixture at risk, it was open to them to refuse to undertake it. What this shows is that the purpose of the provision for timely redelivery in the charterparty is to enable the ship to be at the full disposal of the owner from the redelivery date. If the charterer's orders will defeat this right, the owner may reject them. If the orders are accepted and the last voyage overruns, the owner is entitled to be paid for the overrun at the market rate. All this will be known to both parties. It does not require any knowledge of the owner's arrangements for the next charter. That is regarded by the market as being, as the saying goes, *res inter alios acta*.

24. The findings of the majority arbitrators shows that they considered their decision to be contrary to what would have been the expectations of the parties, but dictated by the rules in *Hadley v Baxendale* as explained in *The Heron II* [1969] 1 AC 350. But in my opinion these rules are not so inflexible; they are intended to give effect to the presumed intentions of the parties and not to contradict them.

25. The owners submit that the question of whether the damage is too remote is a question of fact on which the arbitrators have found in their favour. It is true that the question of whether the damage was foreseeable is a question of fact: see *Monarch Steamship Co Ltd v Karlshamns Oljefabriker (A/B)* [1949] AC 196. But the question of whether a given type of loss is one for which a party assumed contractual responsibility involves the interpretation of the contract as a whole against its commercial background, and this, like all questions of interpretation, is a question of law.

26. The owners say that the parties are entirely at liberty to insert an express term excluding consequential loss if they want to do so. Some standard forms of charter do. I suppose it can be said of many disputes over interpretation, especially over implied terms, that the parties could have used express words or at any rate expressed themselves more clearly than they have done. But, as I have indicated, the implication of a term as a matter of construction of the contract as a whole in its commercial context and the implication of the limits of damages liability seem to me to involve the application of essentially the same techniques of interpretation. In both cases, the court is engaged in construing the agreement to reflect the liabilities which the parties may reasonably be expected to have assumed and paid for. It cannot decline this task on the ground that the parties could have spared it the trouble by using clearer language. In my opinion, the findings of the arbitrators and the commercial background to the agreement are sufficient to make it clear that the charterer cannot reasonably be regarded as having assumed the risk of the owner's loss of profit on the following charter. I would therefore allow the appeal.

Lord Hope:

28. The majority arbitrators based their approach on their understanding of the test of remoteness as explained in *The Heron II* [1969] 1 AC 350, and in particular by Lord Reid at pp 382–383, as being to ask whether the loss in question was:

> 'of a kind which the defendant, when he made the contract, ought to have realised was not unlikely to result from [the] breach'.

This had the result, as they put it, that the parties' knowledge of the markets within which they operated at the date of the addendum which extended the original charter period was more than sufficient for the loss claimed to be within their contemplation. Counsel for the charterers had agreed in exchanges with members of the tribunal that the 'not unlikely' results arising from the late delivery of the vessel would include missing dates for a subsequent fixture. The majority then asked themselves what was within the contemplation of the parties as a not unlikely result of a breach which resulted in missing such a date, bearing in mind that it was agreed that the market rates for tonnage go up and down, sometimes quite rapidly. They answered this question in the owners' favour. On the facts, they said, the need to adjust the relevant dates for the subsequent employment of the vessel through the revised terms agreed with the new charterers was within the contemplation of the parties as a not unlikely result of the breach. It might be that the precise amount of the loss could be seriously affected by market factors such as a sharp drop of the rate for the particular type of vessel during the relevant period. But the type of loss was readily identifiable.

29. The minority arbitrator pointed out that this would be to impose on the charterers a completely unquantifiable risk in what is a relatively common situation – late delivery under a time charter – given the exigencies of the shipping industry. If the test was what a reasonable man in the position of the charterers would have understood at the time of entering into the charter, it was impossible to conclude that they would or should have understood that they were assuming responsibility for the risk of loss of a particular follow-on fixture concluded by the owners. They had no knowledge of or control over the duration of any follow-on fixture which the owners might conclude. The fundamental problem that he had with the owners' argument was that if damages of this type were recoverable without particular knowledge sufficient to justify an assumption of risk it was difficult to see where a line was to be drawn, and there was a real risk of serious commercial uncertainty which the industry as a whole would regard as undesirable.

30. Both approaches share a common, and as it seems to me an entirely orthodox, starting point. They ask what should fairly and reasonably be regarded as having been in the contemplation of the parties at the time when the contract was entered into. The refinement that, on the facts of this case, the relevant date was the date of the addendum is not of any practical significance. Both parties were experienced in the market within which they were operating. Late delivery under a time charter is a relatively common situation, and it is not difficult to conclude that the parties must have had in contemplation when they entered into the contract that this might occur. Nor it is difficult to conclude – indeed this was conceded by counsel for the charterers – that in a market where owners expect to keep their assets in continuous employment dates late delivery will result in missing the date for a subsequent fixture. The critical question however is whether the parties must be assumed to have contracted with each other on the basis that the charterers were assuming responsibility for the consequences of that event. It is at this point that the two approaches part company.

31. Assumption of responsibility, which forms the basis of the law of remoteness of damage in contract, is determined by more than what at the time of the contract was reasonably foreseeable. It is important to bear in mind that, as Lord Reid pointed out in *The Heron II* [1969] 1 AC 350, 385, the rule that applies in tort is quite different and imposes a much wider liability than that which applies in contract. The defendant in tort will be liable for any type of loss and damage which is reasonably foreseeable as likely to result from the act or omission for which he is held liable. Reasonable foreseeability is the criterion by which the extent of that liability is to be judged, and it may result in his having to pay for something that, although reasonably foreseeable, was very unusual, not likely to occur and much greater in amount than he could have anticipated. In contract it is different and, said Lord Reid, at p 386, there is good reason for the difference:

> 'In contract, if one party wishes to protect himself against a risk which to the other party would appear unusual, he can direct the other party's attention to it before the contract is made, and I need not stop to consider in what circumstances the other party will then be held to have accepted responsibility in that event'.

32. The point that Lord Reid was making here was that the more unusual the consequence, the more likely it is that provision will be made for it in the contract if it is to result in liability. Account may be taken of it in the rates that are provided for in the contract. Or terms may be written into the contract to provide for the extent, if any, of the liability. That is the way that commercial contracts are entered into. As Blackburn J said in *Cory v Thames Ironworks Co* (1868) LR 3 QB 181, 190–191, if the damage were exceptional and unnatural it would be hard on a party to be made liable for it because, had he known what the consequences would be, he would probably have stipulated for more time or made greater exertions if he had known the extreme mischief that would follow from the non-fulfilment of his contract. The fact that the loss was foreseeable – the kind of result that the parties would have had in mind, as the majority arbitrators put it – is not the test. Greater precision is needed than that. The question is whether the loss was a type of loss for which the party can reasonably be assumed to have assumed responsibility.

33. How then is this question to be addressed? The statement of principle by Robert Goff J in *The Pegase* [1981] 1 Lloyd's Rep 175, 183 asks whether, if he had considered the matter, at the time of making the contract, the defendant would have contemplated that, in the event of a breach by him, the facts in question would be taken into account in considering his responsibility for loss suffered as a result of the breach. This depends on the degree of relevant knowledge held by him at the time of entering into the contract. Alderson B in *Hadley v Baxendale* (1854) 9 Exch 341, 354–355, distinguished between special circumstances that were wholly unknown to the party breaking the contract and the amount of injury which would arise generally and in the great multitude of cases not affected by any special circumstances. Losses in the latter category are losses which the parties may be taken to have in contemplation and to make provision for, in one way or another, in their contract. Losses in the former are losses which the party in breach was unable to contemplate when considering the terms on which he could agree to enter into the contract. These statements direct attention to the extent of the charterer's knowledge of the facts that are in question in this case.

34. In this case it was within the parties' contemplation that an injury which would arise generally from late delivery would be loss of use at the market rate, as compared with the charter rate, during the relevant period. This something that everybody who deals in the market knows about and can be expected to take into account. But the charterers could not be expected to know how, if – as was not unlikely – there was a subsequent fixture, the owners would deal with any new charterers. This was something over which they had no control and, at the time of entering into the contract, was completely unpredictable. Nothing was known at that time about the terms on which any subsequent fixture might be entered into – how short or long the period would be, for example, or what was to happen should the previous charter overrun and the owner be unable to meet the new commencement date. It is true that neither party had any control over the state of the market. But in the ordinary course of things rates in the market will fluctuate. So it can be presumed that the party in breach has assumed responsibility for any loss caused by delay which can be measured by comparing the charter rate with the market rate during that period. There can be no such presumption where the loss claimed is not the product of the market itself, which can be contemplated, but results from arrangements entered into between the owners and the new charterers, which cannot.

35. In the Court of Appeal [2007] 2 Lloyd's Rep 555, para 117 Rix LJ observed that the doctrine of remoteness is ultimately designed to reflect the public policy of the law. Developing this theme, he said in para 119 that it would be undesirable and uncommercial for damages for late delivery to be limited to the period of the overrun unless the owners could show that they had given their charterers special information of their follow-on fixture. It was undesirable, he said because this would put the owners too much at the mercy of their charterers at time of raised market rates. That seems to me, with respect, to overstate the position. The owners too are in the market and can at least expect to be compensated at market rates for the period of any delay. But he also said that it was uncommercial, because a new fixture would in all probability not be fixed until at or about the time of the redelivery. So the demand would be for information that the owner could not provide when entering into the contract.

36. In my opinion the commercial considerations point the other way. This was the crucial point in the case which led the minority arbitrator to dissent from the majority. As he pointed out, a party cannot be expected to assume responsibility for something that he cannot control and, because he does not know anything about it, cannot quantify. It is not enough for him to know in general and on open-ended terms that there is likely to be a follow-on fixture. This was the error which lies at the heart of the decision of the majority. What he needs is some information that will enable him to assess the extent of any liability. The policy of the law is that effect should be given to the presumed intention of the parties. That is why the damages that are recoverable for breach of contract are limited to what happens in ordinary circumstances – in the great multitude of cases, as Alderson B put it in *Hadley v Baxendale* – where an assumption of responsibility can be presumed, or what arises from special circumstances known to or communicated to the party who is in breach at the time of entering into the contract which because he knew about he can be expected to provide for. This is a principle of general application. We are dealing in this case with a highly specialised area of commercial law. But the principle by which the issue must be resolved is that which applies in the law of contract generally.

37. For these reasons, which owe much to my noble and learned friends' careful review of the authorities, I too would allow the appeal.

Lord Rodger:

47. Today, as for more than 150 years, the starting-point for determining the measure of damages for breach of contract is the judgment of Alderson B in *Hadley v Baxendale* (1854) 9 Exch 341. The story is well known. The plaintiff owners of a flour mill in Gloucester arranged for the defendant common carriers (the firm of Pickfords) to take their broken mill shaft to a firm in Greenwich which was to use it as a pattern to produce a new shaft. Unknown to the defendants – as the court held – the plaintiffs had no other shaft and so could not operate their mill until they got the new one. In breach of contract, the defendants delayed in transporting the broken shaft. The plaintiffs sued the defendants for the profits which they lost from being unable to operate their mill during the period of delay. The Court of Exchequer held that they could not recover the loss of profits ...

51. In *Victoria Laundry (Windsor) Ltd v Newman Industries Ltd* [1949] 2 KB 528, 539–540, Asquith LJ explained that 'Everyone, as a reasonable person, is taken to know the 'ordinary course of things' and consequently what loss is liable to result from a breach of contract in that ordinary course'. He went on to say that, for loss to be recoverable, the defendant did not need to foresee that a breach must necessarily result in that loss: 'It is in enough if he could foresee it was likely so to result. It is indeed enough, to borrow from the language of Lord du Parcq in the [*Monarch Steamship*] case, at p 158, if the loss (or some factor without which it would not have occurred) is a 'serious possibility' or a 'real danger'. For short, we have used the words 'liable to result'.

52. As Lord Reid pointed out in *The Heron II* [1969] 1 AC 350, 389E–G, by referring to foreseeability, Asquith LJ cannot have been intending to assimilate the measure of damages in contract and tort. Moreover, there might appear to be a certain tension between the idea that, to be recoverable, a loss must be something which would result from the breach in the ordinary course and the idea that it is enough that the loss is just something which is liable to result. Lord Reid therefore surmised that Asquith LJ might have meant that the loss was foreseeable as a likely result. That appears to be an appropriate way of reconciling the two aspects of Asquith LJ's opinion. In any event, amidst a cascade of different expressions, it is important not to lose sight of the basic point that, in the absence of special knowledge, a party entering into a contract can only be supposed to contemplate the losses which are *likely* to result from the breach in question – in other words, those losses which will generally happen in the ordinary course of things if the breach occurs. Those are the losses for which the party in breach is held responsible – the stated rationale being that, other losses not having been in contemplation, the parties had no opportunity to provide for them.

53. In the present case, the arbitrators found that – as conceded by counsel then acting for the charterers – missing a date for a subsequent fixture was a 'not unlikely' result of the late redelivery of a vessel. That concession has been criticised elsewhere, but the House must proceed on the basis that, when they entered into the addendum, the parties could reasonably have contemplated that it was not unlikely that the owners would miss a date for a subsequent fixture if the Achilleas were redelivered late. The majority of the arbitrators also found that, at the time of contracting, the parties, who were both engaged in the business of shipping, would have known that market rates for tonnage go up and down, sometimes quite rapidly. Nevertheless, as Rix LJ himself pointed out [2007] 2 Lloyd's Rep 555, 577, para 120 – when seeking to combat any criticism that the Court of Appeal's decision would throw the situation in general into confusion because late redelivery and changing market conditions are common occurrences – 'It requires extremely volatile market conditions to create the situation which occurred here'. In other words, the extent of the relevant rise and fall in the market within a short time was actually unusual. The owners' loss stemmed from that unusual occurrence.

54. The obligation of the charterers was to redeliver the vessel to the owners by midnight on 2 May. Therefore, the charterers are taken to have had in contemplation, at the time when they entered into the addendum, the loss which would generally happen in the ordinary course of things if the vessel were delivered some nine days late so that the owners missed the cancelling date for a follow-on fixture. Obviously, that would include loss suffered as a result of the owners not having been paid under the contract for the charterers' use of the vessel for the period after midnight on 2 May. So, as both sides agree, the owners had to be compensated for that loss by the payment of damages. But the parties would also have contemplated that, if the owners lost a fixture, they would then be in a position to enter the market for a substitute fixture. Of course, in some cases, the available market rate would be lower and, in some cases, higher, than the rate under the lost fixture. But the parties would reasonably contemplate that, for the most part, the availability of the market would protect the owners if they lost a fixture. That I understand to be the thinking which lies behind the dicta to the effect that the appropriate measure of damages for late redelivery of a vessel is the difference between the charter rate and the market rate if the market rate is higher than the charter rate for the period between the final terminal date and redelivery: *Hyundai Merchant Marine Co Ltd v Gesuri Chartering Co Ltd (The Peonia)* [1991] 1 Lloyd's Rep 100, 108. In that passage Bingham LJ was adopting the approach which had been indicated in earlier authorities: *Alma Shipping Corpn of Monrovia v*

Mantovani (The Dione) [1975] 1 Lloyd's Rep 115, 117–118, *per* Lord Denning MR, and *Arta Shipping Co Ltd v Thai Europe Tapioca Service Ltd (The Johnny)* [1977] 2 Lloyd's Rep 1, 2, *per* Lord Denning MR.

55. More particularly, this understanding of the general position lies behind the observations of Lord Mustill in *Torvald Klaveness A/S v Arni Maritime Corpn (The Gregos)* [1995] 1 Lloyd's Rep 1. In that case, when the charterers insisted on proceeding with a voyage which had become illegitimate by the time it was due to commence, the owners refused. The owners began to negotiate a replacement fixture with a concern named Navios, involving a higher rate of freight plus a bonus. In the event, the parties to the original charterparty reached a without prejudice agreement under which the owners would perform the voyage and, if in subsequent proceedings it were held that they had been justified in refusing to perform it, they would be entitled to a sum reflecting the difference between the chartered rate of hire and the more advantageous terms of the proposed substitute fixture with Navios ...

56. In these circumstances the House did not need to deal with the measure of damages in a case of late redelivery. Nevertheless, Lord Mustill said that the obligation of the charterers was to redeliver the vessel on or before the final date or to pay damages for breach of contract. He added [1995] 1 Lloyd's Rep 1, 5, 'On damages, see ... *The Peonia* ...' – so endorsing, *en passant*, what Bingham LJ had said in that case.

57. In the Court of Appeal in *The Gregos* Hirst LJ had drawn attention to what he described as 'the charterers' windfall damages' under the without prejudice agreement by comparison with the damages which would have been awarded simply in respect of a few days' late re-delivery: [1993] 2 Lloyd's Rep 335, 348. Lord Mustill said this [1995] 1 Lloyd's Rep 1, 10:

> 'At first sight, this apparently anomalous result is a good reason for questioning whether the claim for repudiation was soundly based. On closer examination, however, the anomaly consists, not so much in the size of the damages, but in the fact that damages were awarded at all. Imagine that the without prejudice agreement had not been made, and that the owners, having treated the charter as wrongfully repudiated, had accepted a substitute fixture with Navios. If one then asked what loss had the repudiation caused the owners to suffer, the answer would be – None. On the contrary, the charterers' wrongful act would have enabled the owners to make a profit. Even if they had not accepted the substitute employment they might very well have suffered no loss, since they would have been in the favourable position of having their ship free in the right place at the right time to take a spot fixture on a rising market. In neither event would the owners ordinarily recover any damages for the wrongful repudiation'.

The implication from this passage is that, ordinarily, the appropriate measure of damages will be that set out by Bingham LJ in *The Peonia*, since owners will be able to obtain substitute employment for their vessel.

58. I would enter two caveats. First, it may be that, at least in some cases, when concluding a charterparty, a charterer could reasonably contemplate that late delivery of a vessel of that particular type, in a certain area of the world, at a certain season of the year would mean that the market for its services would be poor. In these circumstances, the owners might have a claim for some general sum for loss of business, somewhat along the line of the damages for the loss of business envisaged by the Court of Appeal in *Victoria Laundry (Windsor) Ltd v Newman Industries Ltd* [1949] 2 KB 528, 542–543. Because of the agreement on figures, the matter was not explored in this case and I express no view on it. But, even if some such loss of business could have been reasonably contemplated, as *Victoria Laundry* shows, this would not mean that the owners' particular loss of profit as a result of the re-negotiation of the Cargill fixture should be recoverable. To hold otherwise would risk undermining the first limb of *Hadley v Baxendale*, which limits the charterers' liability to 'the amount of injury' that would arise 'ordinarily' or 'generally'.

59. Secondly, the position on damages might also be different, if, for example – when a charterparty was entered into – the owners drew the charterers' attention to the existence of a forward charter of many months' duration for which the vessel had to be delivered on a particular date. The charterers would know that a failure to redeliver the vessel in time to allow the owners to deliver it under that charter would be liable to result in the loss of that fixture. Then the second rule or limb in *Hadley v Baxendale* might well come into play. But the point does not arise in this case.

60. Returning to the present case, I am satisfied that, when they entered into the addendum in September 2003, neither party would reasonably have contemplated that an overrun of nine days would 'in the ordinary course of things' cause the owners the kind of loss for which they claim damages. That loss was not the 'ordinary consequence' of a breach of that kind. It occurred in this case only because of the extremely volatile market conditions which produced both the owners' initial (particularly lucrative) transaction, with a third party, and the subsequent pressure on the owners to accept a lower rate for that fixture. Back in September 2003, this loss could not have been reasonably foreseen as being likely to arise out of the delay in question. It was, accordingly, too remote to give rise to a claim for damages for breach of contract.

61. Rix LJ objects, [2007] 2 Lloyd's Rep 555, 577, para 119, that such an approach is uncommercial because to demand that, before the charterers are held liable, they would need to know more than they already do in the ordinary course of events, is to demand something that cannot be provided. But that is simply to criticise the long-standing rule of the English law of contract under which a party is not liable for this kind of loss, precisely because it arises out of unusual circumstances which are not – indeed, cannot be – within the contemplation of the parties when they enter into the contract. In any event, it would not, in my view, make good commercial sense to hold a charterer liable for such a potentially extensive loss which neither party could quantify at the time of contracting.

62. Rix LJ also describes the charterers as 'happily [draining] the last drop and more of profit at a time of raised market rates': [2007] 2 Lloyd's Rep 555, 577, para 119. But, in reality, at the outset the sub-contract and the final voyage amounted to nothing more than a legitimate use of the vessel which the charterers had hired until 2 May and for which they were paying the owners the agreed daily rate. The delay which led to the breach of contract was caused by supervening circumstances over which the charterers had no control. The charterers' legitimate actions under their contract provide no commercial or legal justification for fixing them with liability for the owners' loss of profit, due to the effects of an 'extremely volatile market' in relation to an arrangement with a third party about which the charterers knew nothing.

63. I have not found it necessary to explore the issues concerning *South Australia Asset Management Corpn v York Montague Ltd* [1997] AC 191 and assumption of responsibility, which my noble and learned friend, Lord Hoffmann, has raised. Nevertheless, I am otherwise in substantial agreement with his reasons as well as with those to be given by Lord Walker of Gestingthorpe. I would allow the appeal.

Lord Walker:
87. For these reasons, and for the further reasons given by my noble and learned friend Lord Hoffmann, Lord Hope and Lord Rodger, whose opinions I have had the advantage of reading in draft, I would allow this appeal.

Baroness Hale:
93. My Lords, I hope that I have understood this correctly, for it seems to me that it adds an interesting but novel dimension to the way in which the question of remoteness of damage in contract is to be answered, a dimension which does not clearly emerge from the classic authorities. There is scarcely a hint of it in *The Heron II*, apart perhaps from Lord Reid's reference, at p 385, to the loss being 'sufficiently likely to result from the breach of contract *to make it proper* to hold that the loss flowed naturally from the breach or that loss of that kind should have been within his contemplation' (emphasis supplied). In general, *The Heron II*

points the other way, as it emphasises that there are no special rules applying to charterparties and that the law of remoteness in contract is not the same as the law of remoteness in tort. There is more than a hint of it in the judgment of Waller LJ in *Mulvenna v Royal Bank of Scotland plc* [2003] EWCA Civ 1112, but in the context of the 'second limb' of *Hadley v Baxendale* where knowledge of an unusual risk is posited. To incorporate it generally would be to introduce into ordinary contractual liability the principle adopted in the context of liability for professional negligence in *South Australia Asset Management Corpn v York Montague Ltd* [1997] AC 191, 211. In an examination, this might well make the difference between a congratulatory and an ordinary first class answer to the question. But despite the excellence of counsels' arguments it was not explored before us, although it is explored in academic textbooks and other writings, including those cited by Lord Hoffmann in paragraph 11 of his opinion. I note, however, that the most recent of these, Professor Robertson's article on 'The basis of the remoteness rule in contract' (2008) 28 Legal Studies 172 argues strongly to the contrary. I am not immediately attracted to the idea of introducing into the law of contract the concept of the scope of duty which has perforce had to be developed in the law of negligence. The rule in *Hadley v Baxendale* asks what the parties must be taken to have had in their contemplation, rather than what they actually had in their contemplation, but the criterion by which this is judged is a factual one. Questions of assumption of risk depend upon a wider range of factors and value judgments. This type of reasoning is, as Lord Steyn put it in *Aneco Reinsurance Underwriting Ltd v Johnson & Higgins Ltd* [2002] 1 Lloyd's Rep 157, para 186, a '*deus ex machina*'. Although its result in this case may be to bring about certainty and clarity in this particular market, such an imposed limit on liability could easily be at the expense of justice in some future case. It could also introduce much room for argument in other contractual contexts. Therefore, if this appeal is to be allowed, as to which I continue to have doubts, I would prefer it to be allowed on the narrower ground identified by Lord Rodger, leaving the wider ground to be fully explored in another case and another context.

One of the notable features of *The Achilleas* is the different approaches of their Lordships. More specifically, Lord Rodger and Baroness Hale adopted quite an orthodox analysis. For example, at [60] Lord Rodger stated that the loss was too remote, given that it 'could not have been reasonably foreseen'. By contrast Lord Hoffmann and Lord Hope essentially felt that the loss was too remote as there had been no assumption of responsibility.

Peel, E, 'Remoteness re-visited' (2009) 125 *LQR* 6, 7–12

According to Lord Rodger of Earlsferry (with whom Baroness Hale agreed): 'this loss could not have been reasonably foreseen as being likely to arise out of the delay in question. It was accordingly too remote to give rise to a claim for damages for breach of contract' (at [60]). The difficulty with this seemingly entirely orthodox approach is that it depends on what one regards as 'the loss' which must reasonably have been foreseen. For Lord Rodger, it was not so much the lost fixture which had to have been contemplated, but the financial consequences of that loss which had occurred in this case 'only because of the extremely volatile market conditions which produced both the owners' initial (particularly lucrative) transaction … and the subsequent pressure on the owners to accept a lower rate for that fixture' (at [60]).

…

An alternative and more radical approach to remoteness was taken by Lord Hoffmann and Lord Hope of Craighead. Although he gave a substantive speech of his own, one trusts that Lord Hope will not be offended if, because of the confines of this note, that approach is conveyed by reference to what was said by Lord Hoffmann. In his opinion the case raised a fundamental point of principle:

> 'Is the rule that a party may recover losses which were foreseeable ("not unlikely") an external rule of law, imposed upon the parties to every contract in default of express provision to the contrary, or is it a prima facie assumption about what the parties may be taken to have

> intended, no doubt applicable in the great majority of cases but capable of rebuttal in cases in which the context, surrounding circumstances or general understanding in the relevant market shows that a party would not reasonably have been regarded as assuming responsibility for such losses (at [9])'.

For Lord Hoffmann (and Lord Hope), it is the latter. While stressing that departure from the ordinary foreseeability rule will be unusual, he nonetheless was of the view that it is the idea that the parties have assumed responsibility for the losses flowing from their breach which provides the intellectual underpinning of the rule of remoteness.

As he had done in the earlier case of *South Australia Asset Management Corp v York Montague Ltd* [1997] AC 191 HL, Lord Hoffmann stressed that the question with which the courts are really concerned is the scope of the duty undertaken by the defendant, ie one must decide 'whether the loss for which compensation is sought is of a "kind" or "type" for which the contract-breaker ought fairly to be taken to have accepted responsibility' (at [15]). For him, it is in the context of assuming responsibility or accepting risk that the distinction between different types of loss makes most sense: 'it reflects what would reasonably have been regarded by the contracting party as significant for the purposes of the risk he was undertaking' (at [22]). This explains why the additional profits in the *Victoria Laundry* case were too remote: 'The vendor of the boilers would have regarded the profits on these contracts as a different and higher form of risk than the general risk of loss of profits by the laundry' (at [22]). In *The Achilleas* therefore the damages claimed were too remote because, although a lost fixture was foreseen as not unlikely, the presumption that the losses flowing from it could be recovered was rebutted by the particular context of the market in which they occurred:

> 'If ... one considers what these parties, contracting against the background of market expectations found by the arbitrators, would reasonably have considered the extent of the liability they were undertaking, I think it is clear that they would have considered losses arising from the loss of the following fixture a type or kind of loss for which the charterer was not assuming responsibility (at [23])'.

Lord Hoffmann presents a compelling analysis and one in which he considers it 'logical to found liability for damages upon the intention of the parties (objectively ascertained) because all contractual liability is voluntarily undertaken' (at [12]). But his approach is more than just a logical extension of the rule of remoteness as previously understood and, again with respect, it may be one of doubtful utility.

It has certainly been recognised before that, in some cases, 'something more' than the reasonable contemplation of a type of loss may be necessary before the loss can be regarded as not too remote and the 'something more' has sometimes been articulated in terms of the acceptance of risk (see, e.g. Christopher Clarke J (at [65]) and Rix LJ (at [115]) in the present case). But dicta to this effect have always been concerned with losses falling within the 'second limb' of the rule of remoteness, ie losses due to special circumstances of which the defendant would be unaware unless they were communicated to him. There are some tried and trusted hypothetical examples which are used to illustrate the point: the taxi-driver who, before he accepts the fare, is informed about the crucial meeting to which he must get his passenger; or the petrol station owner who, before he fills the customer's tank, is told of the crucial flight which his customer is about to catch to clinch a business deal. If the taxi driver, in breach of contract, fails to get his passenger to the meeting on time, or the petrol station owner fills the tank with the wrong sort of petrol and causes his customer to miss the flight, are they to be held liable for the lost business opportunity? Almost certainly not, but that answer cannot be reached by saying the lost opportunity was not reasonably contemplated at the time of the contract. One explanation is to say that neither the driver nor the station owner 'accepted the risk' of such loss and once one begins to think in such terms, it may seem a logical extension to ask the same question in all cases, including those like *The Achilleas* in which the losses in question fell within the first limb. But this is still a big step (too big for Baroness Hale (at [93])) and, arguably, a false one.

The language of 'accepting risk' is not entirely apt since it can convey the idea that liability for the losses which flow from one party's breach is simply a question of discerning the intention of the parties, but that is a view which has hitherto been rejected (see, e.g. *The Heron II* at 422, *per* Lord Upjohn). It is preferable to say of examples such as the taxi driver and the petrol station owner that it is not 'reasonable' to impose liability (The *Heron II* at 422), or that it is not 'proper' to do so (The *Heron II* at 385, *per* Lord Reid), for, contrary to Lord Hoffmann, it is respectfully submitted that the rule of remoteness is an external rule of law. It is not, however, a completely inflexible rule. Without suggesting that the circumstances in which it might be appropriate to depart from the test of reasonable contemplation of the type of loss are closed (see, e.g. *Restatement of Contracts (2d)*, s 351(3), comment *f* (1981)), one explanation for the likely result in the hypothetical examples considered above is that the defendant was given no reasonable opportunity to limit his liability. If it assists to think of cases concerned with 'second limb' losses in terms of implied undertakings, in the past such references seem to have been to an undertaking implied *in law* (*Robophone Facilities Ltd v Blank* [1966] 1 WLR 1428, CA at 1448). When Lord Hoffmann suggests therefore that in *all* cases it is simply a question of discerning the intention of the parties, of looking for a term implied *in fact* (though see his reference to *Liverpool City Council v Irwin* [1977] AC 239, HL (at [11])), this is more than a logical extension of what has gone before.

What he therefore advocates is a new approach to remoteness, but as noted above, it has been rejected before and one suspects that this is because of doubts as to its utility. The task of discerning the intention of the parties through the interpretation of the contract as a whole would often be an artificial one since there may be little or no evidence about the extent of the risks the parties would have thought they were accepting (see Robertson (2008) 28 LS 172, cited by Lord Hoffmann at [11]). There is also the risk of uncertainty and *The Achilleas* might be thought to provide a case in point. The principal reason for Lord Hoffmann's conclusion that the charterers had not assumed responsibility for a lost fixture was 'market expectation', but this was an expectation not based on any firm decision in law and the owners clearly did not regard it as so well embedded that, when a lost fixture did convert into a financial loss, they should not claim for it. It may be questioned whether market expectation was sufficient to overturn the particularly strong prima facie assumption that losses which fall within the first limb of the rule of remoteness should be recoverable. Another possible indication of the scope of one party's duty is the price charged for its performance. One implication of Lord Hoffmann's approach is that built into the market rate for charters is a limit on liability to the overrun period measure; if that were to be removed, rates would have to be renegotiated, presumably downwards to reflect the increased risk for charterers. Given the decision of the House of Lords, one will never know if that would have been the case but it is equally likely that, had the decision of the Court of Appeal been upheld, it would still have been impossible to tell, such are the many variables that determine charter rates and make the chartering market such a volatile one. A full-scale economic analysis may be the last thing Lord Hoffmann was suggesting for cases on remoteness, but that may be what is invited once one accepts that even losses falling within the first limb can be regarded as too remote if the evidence can be found to argue that the defendant had not assumed responsibility for them. There is, at the very least, the risk of considerable uncertainty here which could be avoided. The better answer, it is submitted, is to do what Lord Hoffmann seeks to reject and apply the default rule of liability for reasonably contemplated types of loss unless the parties have stipulated for an express provision to the contrary (see Rix LJ at [120]), or there is a proper basis for such an implied term (which seems very unlikely), at least in cases where they have had a reasonable opportunity to do so (cf. the hypothetical examples considered above).

It may well be that the decision in *The Achilleas* does not have a profound effect in practice. Certainly, whether or not it is the orthodox default rule or the intention-based rule which prevails, contract draftsmen will continue to try and insert clauses which either make known the prospect of loss on behalf of potential claimants, or seek to exclude it on behalf of potential defendants. As Lord Hoffmann stressed, departure from the ordinary foreseeability rule will be rare.

So what impact has *The Achilleas* had on the remoteness rules in this area of law? In *ASM Shipping Ltd of India v TTMI Ltd of England* [2009] 1 Lloyd's Rep 293, Flaux J considered that *The Achilleas* did not fundamentally alter the relevant remoteness rules in contract law. Cf. *Saipol SA v Inerco Trade SA* [2014] EWHC 2211. Subsequently in *Supershield Ltd v Siemens Building Technologies FE Ltd* [2010] EWCA Civ 7 at [43], Toulson LJ stated:

> *Hadley v Baxendale* remains a standard rule but it has been rationalised on the basis that it reflects the expectation to be imputed to the parties in the ordinary case, ie that a contract breaker should ordinarily be liable to the other party for damage resulting from his breach if, but only if, at the time of making the contract a reasonable person in his shoes would have had damage of that kind in mind as not unlikely to result from a breach. However, *South Australia* and *Transfield Shipping* are authority that there may be cases where the court, on examining the contract and the commercial background, decides that the standard approach would not reflect the expectation or intention reasonably to be imputed to the parties. In those two instances the effect was exclusionary; the contract breaker was held not to be liable for loss which resulted from its breach although some loss of the kind was not unlikely. But logically the same principle may have an inclusionary effect. If, on the proper analysis of the contract against its commercial background, the loss was within the scope of the duty, it cannot be regarded as too remote, even if it would not have occurred in ordinary circumstances.

More recently, in *John Grimes Partnership Ltd v Gubbins* [2013] EWCA Civ 37 Sir David Keene (at [17]–[24]) linked the remoteness rules to implied terms:

> **17** The expression 'remoteness of damage' is concerned, as is well-known, with the principles applied by the law to determine which types of losses suffered by a contracting party may be compensated for in damages when those losses may be said to have been caused by a breach of contract by the other party. As a result of applying such a legal test, some types of loss caused by the breach may be regarded as too remote for the contract-breaker to be held liable, despite there being a causal link between the breach and those losses. The classic exposition of the legal test in *Hadley v Baxendale* (*ante*) has been considered and re-formulated in a number of cases since the mid-nineteenth century and it is unnecessary to trace the development of the test, at any rate until one comes to the House of Lords decision in *The Heron II* (*ante*), some forty years ago. Their Lordships in that latter case expressed the test in a number of different ways, but all of them focused on what the defendant at the time of making the contract ought reasonably to have contemplated would result from the breach of the contract. The degree of likelihood of a particular kind of consequence of breach required in order for there to be liability was described in various ways. Lord Reid's formulation was that a type of loss was not too remote if the defendant at time of contract ought to have realised that it was 'not unlikely' to result from the breach (page 388 E–F), and Lord Morris of Borth-y-Gest agreed. Lord Pearce and Lord Upjohn put it in terms that a reasonable person would have appreciated that there was a 'serious possibility' or 'a real danger'. Thus, if the type or kind of loss was, at the time of contract, reasonably foreseeable by the defendant as not unlikely to result from his breach (had he contemplated a breach), then such a type or kind of loss is not too remote. What was known to the defendant at the time of contract will clearly be relevant to what was reasonably foreseeable.
>
> **18** This approach has been applied in a very large number of cases since *The Heron II*: see, for example, *H Parsons (Livestock) Ltd v Uttley Ingham and Co Ltd* [1978] QB 791. Given the reliance placed by the present appellant on *The Achilleas*, and particularly on the speech of Lord Hoffmann, it is necessary to ask whether and, if so, in what way, the long-established approach to remoteness has been modified by that more recent decision.

19 The essence of *The Achilleas* was an emphasis upon the presumed intention of the parties at the time of contract. The House of Lords was dealing with a charterparty case where the arbitrators had expressly found there to be a 'general understanding in the shipping market ... that liability [in the event of late redelivery of the ship] was restricted to the difference between the market rate and the charter rate for the overrun period': paragraph 6. In other words, there was that general expectation that a charterer who returned a vessel late was liable in damages only for the period of late delivery and not for losses incurred through the owners losing a follow-on charter. This was the factual context for Lord Hoffmann's statement at paragraph 15 that a court:

> 'must first decide whether the loss for which compensation is sought is of a "kind" or "type" for which the contract-breaker ought fairly to be taken to have accepted responsibility'.

As he said:

> 'It must in principle be wrong to hold someone liable for risks for which the people entering into such a contract *in their particular market* would not reasonably be considered to have undertaken: paragraph 12 (emphasis added)'.

20 Lord Hoffmann went on to say that:

> 'the question of whether a given type of loss is one for which a party assumed contractual responsibility involves the interpretation of the contract as a whole against its commercial background, and this, like all questions of interpretation, is a question of law'.

It seems to me quite clear that Lord Hoffmann was not seeking to depart wholesale from the 'reasonably foreseeable' test of remoteness, but rather to stress that what was reasonably foreseeable might sometime not prevail as the test if there were particular circumstances demonstrating that the parties could not have contracted on the basis that the defendant was to bear the liability of a particular kind of loss, even though reasonably foreseeable as a 'not unlikely' consequence of breach. Thus at paragraph 11 he said:

> '**11.** I agree that cases of departure from the ordinary foreseeability rule based on individual circumstances will be unusual, but limitations on the extent of liability in particular types of contract arising out of general expectations in certain markets, such as banking and shipping, are likely to be more common'.

21 Not all the members of the House in *The Achilleas* gave judgment in quite the same terms as Lord Hoffmann, but it is unnecessary to take time on a detailed analysis of the other speeches, since the decision has been carefully considered by this court in a decision binding upon us, *Supershield Ltd v Siemens Building Technologies FE Ltd* (*ante*). That case arose out of a contract for the installation of a sprinkler system in an office building. The supply of water came from a tank, where a float was supposed to cut off the inflow of water to the tank when enough had entered. A connection to the float failed, leading to flooding. There was a bund and a drainage system intended to cope with such an accidental overflow, but the drains had become blocked. Both the trial judge and the Court of Appeal held that, despite the blocked drains, the failure of the float connection was nonetheless an effective cause of the flood. So causation was established.

22 But it was contended by the appellant that the loss was too remote, because in the normal or usual course of things, the bund and drains system would have dealt with the problem. Toulson L.J., with whom the other two members of the court agreed, referred to *Hadley v Baxendale*, *The Heron II*, the *SAAMCO* case (*ante*) and *The Achilleas*. He then at paragraph 43 stated:

> '*Hadley v Baxendale* remains a standard rule but it has been rationalised on the basis that it reflects the expectation to be imputed to the parties in the ordinary case, i.e. that a contract

breaker should ordinarily be liable to the other party for damage resulting from his breach if, but only if, at the time of making the contract a reasonable person in his shoes would have had damage of that kind in mind as not unlikely to result from a breach. However, South Australia and Transfield Shipping are authority that there may be cases where the court, on examining the contract and the commercial background, decides that the standard approach would not reflect the expectation or intention reasonably to be imputed to the parties'.

The appeal failed.

23 That passage from paragraph 43 of *Supershield* was cited and followed by my Lord, Tomlinson J., as he then was, in *Pindell Ltdv Air Asia Berhad* (2011) 2 All ER (Comm) 396. The Judge there said that, like a number of other judges (who he listed), he did not consider that the decision in *The Achilleas* had effected a major change in the approach to the recoverability of damages for breach of contract, and he set out the passage from *Supershield* quoted above.

24 I too agree with the summary of the law provided by Toulson L.J. in *Supershield*, although I would put it in slightly different language. It seems to me to be right to bear in mind, as Lord Hoffmann emphasised in *The Achilleas*, that one is dealing with the law of contract, where the situation is governed by what has been agreed between the parties. If there is no express term dealing with what types of losses a party is accepting potential liability for if he breaks the contract, then the law in effect implies a term to determine the answer. Normally, there is an implied term accepting responsibility for the types of losses which can reasonably be foreseen at the time of contract to be not unlikely to result if the contract is broken. But if there is evidence in a particular case that the nature of the contract and the commercial background, or indeed other relevant special circumstances, render that implied assumption of responsibility inappropriate for a type of loss, then the contract-breaker escapes liability. Such was the case in *The Achilleas*.

15.2.3.4 Mitigation

Following a breach of contract, a claimant is not entitled to sit back and watch his losses accumulate. He is, in a sense, under an obligation to take reasonable steps to 'mitigate' his loss. The principle of mitigation is described by Professor Bridge in the following extract.

Bridge, M, 'Mitigation of damages in contract and the meaning of avoidable loss' (1989) 105 *LQR* 398, 398–399

The principle of mitigation breaks down into three basic rules. First, a party injured upon the occurrence of a breach of contract may not hold the contract-breaker responsible in respect of losses which he could reasonably have avoided. Secondly, expenses reasonably incurred in avoiding or minimising a loss resulting from breach of contract may be charged to the contract-breaker. Thirdly, regardless of whether an injured party in the circumstances had to mitigate, any action he does take after the breach of contract, which in fact avoids or minimises the loss, will serve correspondingly to diminish the contract-breaker's liability in damages ...

[A] few preliminary observations have to be made. First of all, it is quite inaccurate to speak of the plaintiff having a 'duty' to mitigate, for it is not met by any corresponding right of the defendant that mitigation take place. Rather, the principle of mitigation operates *pro tanto* as a conditional bar to the recovery of damages. Since, however, the language of duty is so well entrenched and difficult to substitute, it will be used throughout this article.

Secondly, the burden of proof that mitigation should have taken place rests on the defendant, though the plaintiff has to show that loss incurred was in fact caused by the defendant's breach of contract. Since the rule is commonly explained in the language of factual causation, a degree of tension plainly exists between these two propositions. This tension, however, may be abated in practice by the use of tactical or evidentiary presumptions. As the plaintiff points to the apparent link between his loss and the defendant's breach, the defendant is driven to show why the loss should more properly be attributed to the plaintiff's failure to mitigate.

The final preliminary observation is that the plaintiff who ought to mitigate will not be held to an extraordinary standard of behaviour. The extent to which there should have been mitigation is a question of fact and the plaintiff must take steps consistent with the demands of reasonable and prudent action. The plaintiff will not have to embark upon a difficult and hazardous course of action, nor to act in such a way as to impair his commercial reputation. Subjective circumstances are taken into account to the extent of relieving an impecunious plaintiff from incurring expenditure, provided such impecuniosity does not betoken a reprehensible abdication of commercial responsibility on entering into the contractual adventure.

The obligation to mitigate was laid down by the House of Lords in *British Westinghouse Electric and Manufacturing Co v Underground Electric Railways Co of London* [1912] AC 673. Viscount Haldane explained that the obligation:

> imposes on a plaintiff the duty of taking all reasonable steps to mitigate the loss consequent on the breach, and debars him from claiming any part of the damage which is due to his neglect to take such steps. In the words of James LJ in *Dunkirk Colliery Co v Lever* (1878) 9 Ch D 20, at p 25, 'The person who has broken the contract is not to be exposed to additional cost by reason of the plaintiffs not doing what they ought to have done as reasonable men, and the plaintiffs not being under any obligation to do anything otherwise than in the ordinary course of business'.
>
> As James LJ indicates, this second principle does not impose on the plaintiff an obligation to take any step which a reasonable and prudent man would not ordinarily take in the course of his business. But when in the course of his business he has taken action arising out of the transaction, which action has diminished his loss, the effect in actual diminution of the loss he has suffered may be taken into account even though there was no duty on him to act.

The principle of mitigation has both a positive and a negative limb:

(1) If the claimant effectively takes steps to mitigate his loss, s/he will only be entitled to recover her/his actual losses (cf. *Dalwood Marine Co v Nordana Line SA* [2009] EWHC 3394 (Comm)). S/he will not be permitted to recover the hypothetical sum that s/he would have obtained had s/he failed to take steps to mitigate his loss, even though those steps might have gone beyond what could reasonably have been expected. For example, if a seller fails to deliver on a contract for the sale of 100 widgets and the buyer manages to find an alternative widget supplier on eBay who will sell at the same price, the buyer will only be entitled to nominal damages. The burden of proof is on the defendant to show that the claimant's loss was fully or partially mitigated (see *Thai Airways International Public Co Ltd v KI Holdings Co Ltd* [2015] EWHC 1250 (Comm)). In *Fulton Shipping Inc of Panama v Globalia Business Travel SAU* [2017] UKSC 43 the owners of a ship claimed damages from the charterers of the ship who had repudiated the contract. The owners had terminated the contract and sold the ship for $23.7 million before the world financial crisis. At the time of the trial the ship would only have been worth $7 million. The charterers claimed that the shipowners should give them credit for the difference between the price of the ship sold and the price it would have sold for in 2009 (approximately

$17 million). Popplewell J disagreed on the ground that the charterers' breach had not caused this benefit – it merely provided the shipowners with an opportunity to sale the ship. The Court of Appeal disagreed and reversed the decision of Popplewell J. In so doing it was influenced by the fact that the principles of mitigation might sometimes require a shipowner to sell a ship and, if so, relevant benefits (such as the additional amount received on an earlier sale) so received would need to be taken into account. On a further appeal to the Supreme Court, Lord Clarke (with whom Lord Neuberger, Lord Mance, Lord Sumption, and Lord Hodge agreed) allowed the appeal, preferring the view of Popplewell J:

> That difference or loss was, in my opinion, not on the face of it caused by the repudiation of the charterparty. The repudiation resulted in a prospective loss of income for a period of about two years. Yet, there was nothing about the premature termination of the charterparty which made it necessary to sell the vessel, either at all or at any particular time. Indeed, it could have been sold during the term of the charterparty. If the owners decide to sell the vessel, whether before or after termination of the charterparty, they are making a commercial decision at their own risk about the disposal of an interest in the vessel which was no part of the subject matter of the charterparty and had nothing to do with the charterers. ([32]).

Subsequently in *Quinn Infrastructure Services Ltd v Stephen Sullivan* [2019] EWHC 2863 (Comm), HHJ Pelling QC stated:

> 93. If and to the extent the formulation adopted by Lord Clarke in *Fulton Shipping Inc v Globalia Business Travel SAU* [2017] UKSC 43 [2017] 1 WLR 2581 at [16] is different from that adopted in *Swynson Limited v Lowick Rose LLP* (ibid.) it makes no difference to the outcome. Here the benefit (being the payment from BT to the claimant) was caused by the claim for payment by the third defendant which payments were made by BT to the claimant in accordance with the agreement between the claimant and BT whereby BT agreed to reimburse the claimant in respect of its actual costs of developing Auto Allocator.
>
> 94. There is an apparent conflict of view between that expressed by implication in [16] the judgment of Lord Clarke on the one hand and those in *Swynson Limited v Lowick Rose LLP* (*ibid.*) on the other concerning the continuing role that justice, reasonableness and public policy has to play in this area of the law. On that issue, I respectfully prefer the view of Lord Sumption that those concepts were '... the basis on which the law has arrived at the relevant principles ...' and are not '... a licence for discarding those principles and deciding each case on what may be regarded as its broader commercial merits' and those of Lord Neuberger at [98] that that justice, reasonableness and public policy '... should not be treated by judges as a green light for doing whatever seems fair on the facts of a particular case ...'. I have arrived at that conclusion because whilst Lord Clarke appears to approve the summary of principles formulated by the first instance judge quoted at [16], he does not apply the principle identified in sub-paragraph (11) of the first instance judge's summary when arriving at his disposal conclusions at [29] to [37]. It is noteworthy that Lords Neuberger and Sumption each sat in both cases and obviously did not consider there was any conflict between what was decided in *Fulton Shipping Inc v Globalia Business Travel SAU* (*ibid.*) and what they decided in *Swynson Limited v Lowick Rose LLP* (*ibid.*).

Compare also *Assetco Plc v Grant Thornton UK LLP* [2019] EWHC 150 (Comm) at [1062].

(2) The claimant is required to act and must take reasonable steps to minimise his loss (see *SC Confectia SA v Miss Mania Wholesale Ltd* [2014] EWCA Civ 1484). S/he will be debarred from recovering damages in respect of loss attributable to his failure to mitigate.

As Professor Bridge notes, mitigation is not a duty in the legal sense because the defendant cannot sue the claimant for failure to mitigate. However, the fact that the claimant is barred from recovering damages in respect of losses attributable to his failure to mitigate gives the claimant a substantial incentive to mitigate his losses. In practice, the doctrine of mitigation amounts to a significant qualification of the law's commitment to protection of the claimant's interest in performance.

Sometimes mitigation may require the claimant to go to significant lengths to reduce his losses (although generally the duty is not high: *Lombard North Central plc v Automobile World (UK) Ltd* [2010] EWCA Civ 20 at [72], *per* Rix LJ). It may even require him to accept an offer of alternative performance from the party in breach (see *Manton Hire and Sales Ltd v Ash Manor Cheese Co Ltd* [2013] EWCA Civ 548 where the offer was unclear).

Payzu Ltd v Saunders [1919] 2 KB 581

Facts: The plaintiff entered into a contract with the defendant for the sale of a quantity of silk, to be delivered in instalments. The contract provided for payment within one month of delivery of each instalment. The plaintiff failed to make punctual payment for the first instalment. The defendant, in breach of contract, refused to deliver any further instalments unless the plaintiff agreed to pay in cash with each order. The plaintiff refused to accept this offer, and, the market price of the goods having risen, brought an action against the defendant for breach of contract, claiming as damages the difference between the market price and the contract price.

Held: The Court of Appeal held that the defendant was liable for damages but that the plaintiff should have mitigated its loss by accepting the defendant's offer. As a result the plaintiff was only entitled to damages for such loss as it would have suffered if it had accepted that offer.

Scrutton LJ: The plaintiff must take 'all reasonable steps to mitigate the loss consequent on the breach', and this principle 'debars him from claiming any part of the damage which is due to his neglect to take such steps': *British Westinghouse Electric and Manufacturing Co v Underground Electric Railways Co of London* [1912] AC 673, *per* Lord Haldane LC. [Counsel for the plaintiff] has contended that in considering what steps should be taken to mitigate the damage all contractual relations with the party in default must be excluded. That is contrary to my experience. In certain cases of personal service it may be unreasonable to expect a plaintiff to consider an offer from the other party who has grossly injured him; but in commercial contracts it is generally reasonable to accept an offer from the party in default.

The decision in *Payzu* has been criticised by Professor Bridge.

Bridge, M, 'Mitigation of damages in contract and the meaning of avoidable loss' (1989) 105 _LQR_ 398, 413–414

The decision in *Payzu* seems thoroughly sensible and pragmatical. Indeed, it appears not to have troubled or even intrigued commentators. Yet, it is worth examining in some detail the trial judge's assertion that 'extraordinary results would follow if the plaintiffs were entitled to reject the defendant's offer and incur a substantial measure of loss which would have been avoided by their acceptance of the offer.

The contract concerned raw silk fabric used in the manufacture of formal ladies' attire. On the basis of the meagre information contained in the report, there was evidently an available market in which the value of the commodity could be measured from time to time. It is not possible, however, to quantify the volume of trading. On the plaintiff's own evidence, the market was rising and there was a shortage of crêpe de chine. Putting aside the small difficulty of the date of reference to the market, the following problem presents itself. Any loss suffered by the plaintiff in not taking the goods at the below-market price offered by the defendant was exactly matched by the defendant's gain when, liberated by the plaintiff's refusal to take up the goods, she was enabled to dispose of those same goods at the higher market rate. Another way of putting the matter is to say that the defendant was enriched by the plaintiff's failure to mitigate. She was permitted to recover the market rise she had lost after contracting at the lower rate, a rise moreover that she would still have lost had the plaintiff accepted her offer of mitigation. This must be wrong. The doctrine of mitigation should not be applied where it serves only to reverse the roles of contract-breaker and injured party. There was nothing in the case to show a loss of trading volume when the defendant declined to take the goods and, furthermore, it is most unlikely that such a loss could have occurred, given the rising value of crêpe de chine and the shortage of available stocks on the market at the relevant time. If the rules of mitigation exist to prevent an unfair imposition of loss on the defendant, it is impossible to see such a policy at work in the present case, which appears rather to punish the plaintiff for its tactical mistake in not accepting the defendant's offer.

Mitigation presents a number of problems in the context of anticipatory breach. Normally a claimant has the option either to terminate the contract or to affirm it. Is the claimant entitled to affirm the contract even though this will lead to a significant increase in his or her loss if the defendant fails to perform?

White and Carter (Councils) Ltd v McGregor [1962] AC 413

Facts: The defendants contracted to purchase advertising space on litter bins belonging to the plaintiffs. This contract was wrongfully cancelled by the defendants. The plaintiffs refused to accept the anticipatory breach and they went ahead with the production and display of the advertisements over the full three-year term of the contract. The defendants refused to pay any sums due under the contract and the plaintiffs sued for the whole amount.

Held: The House of Lords held, by a majority of 3:2, that there is no obligation on the plaintiffs in such a situation to mitigate their losses. The plaintiffs were not obliged to accept the repudiation and claim damages for the full sum due under the contract.

Lord Reid: The general rule cannot be in doubt. It was settled in Scotland at least as early as 1848 and it has been authoritatively stated time and again in both Scotland and England. If one party to a contract repudiates it in the sense of making it clear to the other party that he refuses or will refuse to carry out his part of the contract, the other party, the innocent party, has an option. He may accept that repudiation and sue for damages for breach of contract, whether or not the time for performance has come; or he may if he chooses disregard or refuse to accept it and then the contract remains in full effect ...

I need not refer to the numerous authorities. They are not disputed by the respondent but he points out that in all of them the party who refused to accept the repudiation had no active duties under the contract. The innocent party's option is generally said to be to *wait* until the date of performance and then to claim damages estimated as at that date. There is no case in which it is said that he may, in face of the repudiation, go on and incur useless expense in performing the contract and then claim the contract price. The option, it is argued, is merely as to the date as at which damages are to be assessed.

Developing this argument, the respondent points out that in most cases the innocent party cannot complete the contract himself without the other party doing, allowing or accepting something, and that it is purely fortuitous that the appellants can do so in this case. In most cases by refusing co-operation the party in breach can compel the innocent party to restrict his claim to damages. Then it was said that, even where the innocent party can complete the contract without such co-operation, it is against the public interest that he should be allowed to do so. An example was developed in argument. A company might engage an expert to go abroad and prepare an elaborate report and then repudiate the contract before anything was done. To allow such an expert then to waste thousands of pounds in preparing the report cannot be right if a much smaller sum of damages would give him full compensation for his loss. It would merely enable the expert to extort a settlement giving him far more than reasonable compensation.

The respondent founds on the decision of the First Division in *Langford & Co Ltd v Dutch*. There an advertising contractor agreed to exhibit a film for a year. Four days after this agreement was made the advertiser repudiated it but, as in the present case, the contractor refused to accept the repudiation and proceeded to exhibit the film and sue for the contract price. The Sheriff-Substitute dismissed the action as irrelevant and his decision was affirmed on appeal. In the course of a short opinion Lord President Cooper said: 'It appears to me that, apart from wholly exceptional circumstances of which there is no trace in the averments on this record, the law of Scotland does not afford to a person in the position of the pursuers the remedy which is here sought. The pursuers could not force the defender to accept a year's advertisement which she did not want, though they could of course claim damages for her breach of contract. On the averments the only reasonable and proper course, which the pursuers should have adopted, would have been to treat the defender as having repudiated the contract and as being on that account liable in damages, the measure of which we are, of course, not in a position to discuss'.

The Lord President cited no authority and I am in doubt as to what principle he had in mind ...

We must now decide whether that case was rightly decided. In my judgment it was not. It could only be supported on one or other of two grounds. It might be said that, because in most cases the circumstances are such that an innocent party is unable to complete the contract and earn the contract price without the assent or cooperation of the other party, therefore in cases where he can do so he should not be allowed to do so. I can see no justification for that.

The other ground would be that there is some general equitable principle or element of public policy which requires this limitation of the contractual rights of the innocent party. It may well be that, if it can be shown that a person has no legitimate interest, financial or otherwise, in performing the contract rather than claiming damages, he ought not to be allowed to saddle the other party with an additional burden with no benefit to himself. If a party has no interest to enforce a stipulation, he cannot in general enforce it: so it might be said that, if a party has no interest to insist on a particular remedy, he ought not to be allowed to insist on it. And, just as a party is not allowed to enforce a penalty, so he ought not to be allowed to penalise the other party by taking one course when another is equally advantageous to him. If I may revert to the example which I gave of a company engaging an expert to prepare an elaborate report and then repudiating before anything was done, it might be that the company could show that the expert had no substantial or legitimate interest in carrying out the work rather than accepting damages: I would think that the *de minimis* principle would apply in determining whether his interest was substantial, and that he might have a legitimate interest other than an immediate financial interest. But if the expert had no such interest then that might be regarded as a proper case for the exercise of the general equitable jurisdiction of the court. But that is not this case. Here the respondent did not set out to prove that the appellants had no legitimate interest in completing the contract and claiming the contract price rather than claiming damages; there is nothing in the findings of fact to support such a case, and it seems improbable that any such case could have been proved. It is, in my judgment, impossible to say that the appellants should be deprived of their right to claim the contract price merely because the benefit to them, as against claiming damages and re-letting their advertising space, might be small in comparison with the loss to the respondent: that is the most that could be said in favour of the respondent. Parliament has on many occasions relieved parties from certain kinds of improvident or oppressive contracts, but the common law can only do that in very limited circumstances. Accordingly, I am unable to avoid the conclusion that this appeal must be allowed and the case remitted so that decree can be pronounced as craved in the initial writ.

Lord Morton of Henryton [dissenting]: It is well established that repudiation by one party does not put an end to a contract. The other party can say 'I hold you to your contract, which still remains in force'. What then is his remedy if the repudiating party persists in his repudiation and refuses to carry out his part of the contract? The contract has been broken. The innocent party is entitled to be compensated by damages for any loss which he has suffered by reason of the breach, and in a limited class of cases the court will decree specific implement. The law of Scotland provides no other remedy for a breach of contract and there is no reported case which decides that the innocent party may act as the appellants have acted. The present case is one in which specific implement could not be decreed, since the only obligation of the respondent under the contract was to pay a sum of money for services to be rendered by the appellants. Yet the appellants are claiming a kind of inverted specific implement of the contract. They first insist on performing their part of the contract, against the will of the other party, and then claim that he must perform his part and pay the contract price for unwanted services. In my opinion, my Lords, the appellants' only remedy was damages, and they were bound to take steps to minimise their loss, according to a well-established rule of law. Far from doing this, having incurred no expense at the date of the repudiation, they made no attempt to procure another advertiser, but deliberately went on to incur expense and perform unwanted services with the intention of creating a money debt which did not exist at the date of the repudiation.

Lord Hodson: It is settled as a fundamental rule of the law of contract that repudiation by one of the parties to a contract does not itself discharge it. See Viscount Simon's speech in *Heyman v Darwins Ltd* [1942] AC 356, 361, citing with approval the following sentence from a judgment of Scrutton LJ in *Golding v London and Edinburgh Insurance Co Ltd* (1932) 43 Lloyd's Law Rep 487, 488: 'I have never been able to understand what effect the repudiation of one party has unless the other party accepts the repudiation'.

In *Howard v Pickford Tool Co Ltd* [1951] 1 KB 417, 421, Asquith LJ said: 'An unaccepted repudiation is a thing writ in water and of no value to anybody: it confers no legal rights of any sort or kind'. These are English cases but that the law of Scotland is the same is, I think, clear from the authorities, of which I need only refer to one, namely, *Howie v Anderson* 10 D 355, where language to the same effect is to be found in the opinions of the Lord President and Lord Moncrieff.

It follows that, if, as here, there was no acceptance, the contract remains alive for the benefit of both parties and the party who has repudiated can change his mind but it does not follow that the party at the receiving end of the proffered repudiation is bound to accept it before the time for performance and is left to his remedy in damages for breach.

[Counsel for the respondent] did not seek to dispute the general proposition of law to which I have referred but sought to argue that if at the date of performance by the innocent party the guilty party maintains his refusal to accept performance and the innocent party does not accept the repudiation, although the contract still survives, it does not survive so far as the right of the innocent party to perform it is concerned but survives only for the purpose of enforcing remedies open to him by way of damages or specific implement. This produces an impossible result; if the innocent party is deprived of some of his rights it involves putting an end to the contract except in cases, unlike this, where, in the exercise of the court's discretion, the remedy of specific implement is available.

The true position is that the contract survives and does so not only where specific implement is available. When the assistance of the court is not required the innocent party can choose whether he will accept repudiation and sue for damages for anticipatory breach or await the date of performance by the guilty party. Then, if there is failure in performance, his rights are preserved.

It may be unfortunate that the appellants have saddled themselves with an unwanted contract causing an apparent waste of time and money. No doubt this aspect impressed the Court of Session but there is no equity which can assist the respondent. It is trite that equity will not rewrite an improvident contract where there is no disability on either side. There is no duty laid upon a party to a subsisting contract to vary it at the behest of the other party so as to deprive himself of the benefit given to him by the contract. To hold otherwise would be to introduce a novel equitable doctrine that a party was not to be held to his contract unless the court in a given instance thought it reasonable so to do. In this case it would make an action for debt a claim for a discretionary remedy. This would introduce an uncertainty into the field of contract which appears to be unsupported by authority either in English or Scottish law save for the one case upon which the Court of Session founded its opinion and which must, in my judgment, be taken to have been wrongly decided.

The decision in *White & Carter* has been criticised for encouraging wasteful performance and causing undue hardship to the contract breaker (see Furmston, M, 'The Case of the Insistent Performer' (1962) 25 MLR 364; Goodhart, W, 'Measure of Damages when a Contract is Repudiated' (1962) 78 LQR 263). Lord Reid's speech did admit of two restrictions on the innocent party's right to affirm a contract following an anticipatory breach:

1 **Need for co-operation.** This is a practical limitation on the right to affirm. In most cases, the innocent party will be forced to repudiate the contract because he will not be able to complete his own performance without the co-operation of the defendant. In *Ministry of Sound (Ireland) Ltd v World Online Ltd* [2003] 2 All ER (Comm) 823, Nicholas Strauss QC explained this limitation in the following terms: 'In essence, the principle is that the breach of contract does not convert a dependent obligation into an independent one; if the right to the payment claimed is dependent upon the performance of contractual obligations, the prevention of performance by the other party's breach of contract does not alter the position.' See also *Geys v Société Générale, London Branch* [2012] UKSC 63.
2 **Legitimate interest.** This is a legal limitation on the right to affirm. The innocent party cannot affirm the contract unless he can prove that he has a legitimate interest, financial or otherwise, in performing the contract. As Lord Reid noted, the defendants in *White & Carter* did not attempt to do this, but that is fairly unsurprising given that they were not aware of the need to do so until Lord Reid told them! In *Ocean Marine Navigation Ltd v Koch Carbon Inc ('The Dynamic')* [2003] 2 Lloyd's Rep 693, 698, Simon J summarised the law on the legitimate interest requirement as follows: '(i) The burden is on the *contract-breaker* to show that the innocent party has no legitimate interest in performing the contract rather than claiming damages. (ii) This burden is not discharged merely by showing that the benefit to the other party is small in comparison to the loss to the contract breaker. (iii) The exception to the general rule applies only in extreme cases: where damages would be an adequate remedy and where an election to keep the contract alive would be unreasonable.'

Lord Reid did not specify what might constitute a legitimate interest, but subsequent cases have provided some guidance on the issue. In *Gator Shipping Corp v Trans-Asiatic Oil Ltd SA ('The Odenfeld')* [1978] 2 Lloyd's Rep 357, Kerr J held that the owners of a ship under a time charter had a legitimate interest in continuing with the contract because it would have been difficult to find other employment for the ship and damages would have been difficult to quantify.

In other cases, the courts have been more receptive to the argument that the contract should be terminated because the innocent party has no legitimate interest in performance. For example, in *Attica Sea Carriers Corp v Ferrostaal Poseidon Bulk Reederei GmbH ('The Puerto Buitrago')* [1976] 1 Lloyd's Rep 250, a charterer attempted to return a ship early and unrepaired in breach of the terms of the contract. This was because the repairs would have cost £2 million when the value of the ship fully repaired was only £1 million. The ship owner refused to accept the return of the ship, insisting that the charterers were liable to continue to pay the charter hire until the ship was repaired. The Court of Appeal rejected this argument for a number of reasons, including the fact that the shipowners had no legitimate interest in continuing the charter. A similar outcome was reached in *Clea Shipping Corp v Bulk Oil International Ltd* ('*The Alaskan Trader*') [1984] 1 All ER 129. The plaintiff charterers attempted to return a ship one year into a two-year charterparty, due to the ship having developed a serious engine defect that would have required extensive repairs over a period of several months. The owners proceeded to repair the ship and kept it fully manned and ready for the plaintiff's use for the remaining nine months of the charterparty. The arbitrator, Lloyd J, held that the owners did not have a legitimate interest in continuing with the charterparty. Furthermore, even though it might have been difficult to rehire the ship, Lloyd J was of the opinion that damages would not have been too difficult to assess. More recently, in *MSC Mediterranean Shipping Co SA v Cottonex Anstalt* [2015] EWHC 283 (Comm) Leggatt J linked this principle to a concept of good faith:

> 97. The principle can be seen in a wider context. There is increasing recognition in the common law world of the need for good faith in contractual dealings. Further impetus has been given to this development by the unanimous judgment of the Supreme Court of Canada in *Bhasin v Hrynew*, 2014 SCC 71, given on 13 November 2014, holding that good faith contractual performance is a general organizing principle of the common law of contract which underpins and informs more specific rules and doctrines. One such more specific rule which is now firmly established in English law is that, in the absence of very clear language to the contrary, a contractual discretion must be exercised in good faith for the purpose for which it was conferred, and must not be exercised arbitrarily, capriciously or unreasonably (in the sense of irrationally): see e.g. *Abu Dhabi National Tanker Co v Product Star Shipping Ltd (The 'Product Star') (No 2)* [1993] 1 Lloyd's Rep 397, 404; *Paragon Finance Plc v Nash* [2002] 1 WLR 685, paras 39–41; *Socimer International Bank Ltd v Standard Bank London Ltd* [2008] 1 Lloyd's Rep 558, 575–577; *British Telecommunications Plc v Telefónica O2 UK Ltd* [2014] UKSC 42, para 37. The cases in this line of authority have all been concerned with the exercise of discretionary powers conferred by the express terms of the contract, whereas the choice whether or not to terminate the contract in response to a repudiatory breach is one which arises by operation of law. However, I cannot see why this should make any difference in principle. In each case one party to the contract has a decision to make on a matter which affects the interests of the other party to the contract whose interests are not the same. The same reason exists in each case to imply some constraint on the decision-maker's freedom to act purely in its own self-interest. The essential concern, as Rix LJ observed in the *Socimer* case at para 66, is that the decision-maker's power should not be abused.
>
> 98. I would accordingly regard the line of authority dealing with the exercise of an option to terminate the contract and the line of authority dealing with the exercise of a contractual discretion as concerned with materially identical questions and as establishing essentially the same test.

In that case, Leggatt J held that the carriers had no legitimate interest in continuing (rather than terminating and claiming damages) with a contract which required the shippers to pay demurrage for a delay in returning containers which had been used to ship goods:

> In these circumstances I conclude that the Carrier had no legitimate interest in keeping the contracts of carriage in force after that date in order to continue claiming demurrage. Its election to do so, and to go on doing so ever since, can in my view properly be described as wholly unreasonable. It is wholly unreasonable because the Carrier has not been keeping the contracts alive in order to invoke the demurrage clause for a proper purpose but in order, in effect, to seek to generate an unending stream of free income. ([121])

There was no evidence to show that the carriers were suffering any financial loss as a result of the delay in returning the containers; yet the relevant clause potentially allowed them charge demurrage indefinitely (unless, as Leggatt J thought, the relevant clause was, if unfettered, penal in nature). On appeal ([2016] EWCA Civ 789) Moore-Bick LJ appeared in agreement on the no legitimate interest point (see [43]) but held, on the facts, that it did not arise as the purpose of the adventure had been commercially frustrated. Moore-Bick LJ had less sympathy with the attempt by Leggatt J to link legitimate interest to a concept of good faith (see [45]) and to the clause being penal in nature (see [46]).

15.2.4 Gain-based damages?

Historically, it has been assumed that damages for breach of contract are always compensatory – assessed by reference to the claimant's loss. Gain-based damages – measured by reference to the defendant's gain – were not thought to be available. In more recent years, however, the courts have come to recognise that gain-based damages have a role to play in the protection of the claimant's performance interest.

There are four distinct parts to this section. The first part considers the historical development of gain-based damages, the second part examines the landmark case of *A-G v Blake*, the third considers how the *A-G v Blake* test has been applied in later cases, and the fourth traces the development of a separate measure of damages (so called 'negotiating damages') which until recently became, to some extent, intertwined with the remedy awarded in *A-G v Blake*.

15.2.4.1 The history of gain-based damages for breach of contract

As recently as 1993, the Court of Appeal insisted that gain-based damages were unavailable for breach of contract.

***Surrey County Council v Bredero Homes Ltd* [1993] 1 WLR 1361**

Facts: The plaintiff council sold a piece of land to Bredero Homes at a price of £1.5 million. Bredero covenanted to develop the land in accordance with a scheme to which the council had agreed. However, in breach of covenant, Bredero built five extra homes on the site. The plaintiff sued Bredero for breach of covenant. The judge found Bredero liable for breach of contract but awarded merely nominal damages because the council had suffered no pecuniary loss. The plaintiff appealed, claiming that it was entitled to damages measured by reference to the profit acquired by Bredero as a result of its breach.

Held: The Court of Appeal dismissed the appeal, holding that since damages for breach of contract were awarded as compensation for loss, the damages awarded to the plaintiff had to be merely nominal.

Dillon LJ: The plaintiffs have suffered no damage. Therefore on basic principles, as damages are awarded to compensate loss, the damages must be merely nominal.

Steyn LJ: The introduction of restitutionary remedies to deprive cynical contract breakers of the fruits of their breaches of contract will lead to greater uncertainty in the assessment of damages in commercial and consumer disputes. It is of paramount importance that the way in which disputes are likely to be resolved by the courts must be readily predictable. Given the premise that the aggrieved party has suffered no loss, is such a dramatic extension of restitutionary remedies justified in order to confer a windfall in each case on the aggrieved party? I think not. In any event such a widespread availability of restitutionary remedies will have a tendency to discourage economic activity in relevant situations ... In a range of cases such liability would fall on underwriters who have insured relevant liability risks. Inevitably underwriters would have to be compensated for the new species of potential claims. Insurance premiums would have to go up. That, too, is a consequence which mitigates against the proposed extension. The recognition of the proposed extension will in my view not serve the public interest. It is sound policy to guard against extending the protection of the law of obligations too widely. For these substantive and policy reasons I regard it as undesirable that the range of restitutionary remedies should be extended in the way in which we have been invited to do so.

The Court of Appeal rejected Surrey County Council's claim on the grounds that an award of gain-based damages lacked historical precedent and was likely to lead to commercial uncertainty. There may be some weight in the latter objection, but the former was, arguably, not strictly true. There was at least one case where it could be *argued* that gain-based damages had been awarded for breach of contract; a case that would later be referred to as a 'solitary beacon, showing that in contract as well as tort damages are not always narrowly confined to recoupment of financial loss' (*A-G v Blake* [2001] 1 AC 268, 283 *per* Lord Nicholls).

***Wrotham Park Estate Co Ltd v Parkside Homes Ltd* [1974] 1 WLR 798**

Facts: The defendant, Parkside Homes, erected homes on their land in breach of a covenant with Wrotham Park. The homes did not affect the value of Wrotham Park's land and thus compensatory damages would have been merely nominal. Wrotham Park sought a mandatory injunction requiring the demolition of the homes.

Held: Brightman J refused to grant a mandatory injunction on the grounds that it would have constituted an unpardonable waste of much needed houses. He awarded damages in lieu of an injunction calculated at five per cent of Parkside's anticipated profit.

Brightman J: In the present case I am faced with the problem of what damages ought to be awarded to the plaintiffs in the place of mandatory injunctions which would have restored the plaintiffs' rights. If the plaintiffs are merely given a nominal sum, or no sum, in substitution for injunctions, it seems to me that justice will manifestly not have been done.

As I have said, the general rule would be to measure damages by reference to that sum which would place the plaintiffs in the same position as if the covenant had not been broken. Parkside and the individual purchasers could have avoided breaking the covenant in two ways. One course would have been not to develop the allotment site. The other course would have been for Parkside to have sought from the plaintiffs a relaxation of the covenant. On the facts of this particular case the plaintiffs, rightly conscious of their obligations towards existing residents, would clearly not have granted any relaxation, but for present purposes I must assume that it could have been induced to do so. In my judgment a just substitute for a mandatory injunction would be such a sum of money as might reasonably have been demanded by the plaintiffs from Parkside as a quid pro quo for relaxing the covenant ...

I think that damages must be assessed in such a case on a basis which is fair and, in all the circumstances, in my judgment a sum equal to five per cent of Parkside's anticipated profit is the most that is fair. I accordingly award the sum of £2,500 in substitution for mandatory injunctions.

15.2.4.2 The landmark case

The apparent conflict between *Wrotham Park* and *Bredero Homes* was considered in the landmark case of *A-G v Blake*.

Attorney General v Blake [2001] 1 AC 268

Facts: Blake was a Soviet informant who was working as a member of the British Secret Intelligence Service. On discovery of his treason he was tried and imprisoned in the UK but in 1966 he escaped custody and fled to Moscow. Whilst in Moscow, he wrote his autobiography outlining details of his work with the British Secret Services. This book was published in 1990 and Blake was set to receive significant royalties from the book. At the time that Blake joined the secret service he had signed a lifelong contract stating that he would never disclose anything about his work, either in the press or in book form. The publication of his autobiography clearly breached this undertaking. The Attorney General brought an action against Blake to recover the profits that Blake had made as a result of his breach of contract.

Held: The House of Lords (Lord Hobhouse dissenting) upheld the Crown's claim for gain-based damages.

Lord Nicholls of Birkenhead:

Breach of contract

I turn to consider the remedies available for breaches of contract. The basic remedy is an award of damages. In the much quoted words of Baron Parke, the rule of the common law is that where a party sustains a loss by reason of a breach of contract, he is, so far as money can do it, to be placed in the same position as if the contract had been performed: *Robinson v Harman* (1848) 1 Exch 850, 855. Leaving aside the anomalous exception of punitive damages, damages are compensatory. That is axiomatic. It is equally well established that an award of damages, assessed by reference to financial loss, is not always 'adequate' as a remedy for a breach of contract. The law recognises that a party to a contract may have an interest in performance which is not readily measurable in terms of money. On breach the innocent party suffers a loss. He fails to obtain the benefit promised by the other party to the contract. To him the loss may be as important as financially measurable loss, or more so. An award of damages, assessed by reference to financial loss, will not recompense him properly. For him a financially assessed measure of damages is inadequate.

The classic example of this type of case, as every law student knows, is a contract for the sale of land. The buyer of a house may be attracted by features which have little or no impact on the value of the house. An award of damages, based on strictly financial criteria, would fail to recompense a disappointed buyer for this head of loss. The primary response of the law to this type of case is to ensure, if possible, that the contract is performed in accordance with its terms. The court may make orders compelling the party who has committed a breach of contract, or is threatening to do so, to carry out his contractual obligations. To this end the court has wide powers to grant injunctive relief. The court will, for instance, readily make orders for the specific performance of contracts for the sale of land, and sometimes it will do so in respect of contracts for the sale of goods ...

All this is trite law. In practice, these specific remedies go a long way towards providing suitable protection for innocent parties who will suffer loss from breaches of contract which are not adequately remediable by an award of damages. But these remedies are not always available. For instance, confidential information may be published in breach of a non-disclosure agreement before the innocent party has time to apply to the court for urgent relief. Then the breach is irreversible. Further, these specific remedies are discretionary. Contractual obligations vary infinitely. So do the circumstances in which breaches occur, and the circumstances in which remedies are sought. The court may, for instance, decline to grant specific relief on the ground that this would be oppressive.

An instance of this nature occurred in *Wrotham Park v Parkside Homes* [1974] 1 WLR 798. For social and economic reasons the court refused to make a mandatory order for the demolition of houses built on land burdened with a restrictive covenant. Instead, Brightman J made an award of damages under the jurisdiction which originated with Lord Cairns's Act. The existence of the new houses did not diminish the value of the benefited land by one farthing. The judge considered that if the plaintiffs were given a nominal sum, or no sum, justice would manifestly not have been done. He assessed the damages at 5%

of the developer's anticipated profit, this being the amount of money which could reasonably have been demanded for a relaxation of the covenant ...

I turn to the decision of the Court of Appeal in *Surrey County Council v Bredero Homes* [1993] 1 WLR 1361 ... This is a difficult decision. It has attracted criticism from academic commentators and also in judgments of Sir Thomas Bingham MR and Millett LJ in *Jaggard v Sawyer* [1995] 1 WLR 269. I need not pursue the detailed criticisms. In the *Bredero* case Dillon LJ himself noted, at p 1364, that had the covenant been worded differently, there could have been provision for payment of an increased price if a further planning permission were forthcoming. That would have been enforceable. But, according to the *Bredero* decision, a covenant not to erect any further houses without permission, intended to achieve the same result, may be breached with impunity. That would be a sorry reflection on the law. Suffice to say, in so far as the *Bredero* decision is inconsistent with the approach adopted in the *Wrotham Park* case, the latter approach is to be preferred.

The *Wrotham Park* case, therefore, still shines, rather as a solitary beacon, showing that in contract as well as tort damages are not always narrowly confined to recoupment of financial loss. In a suitable case damages for breach of contract may be measured by the benefit gained by the wrongdoer from the breach. The defendant must make a reasonable payment in respect of the benefit he has gained. In the present case the Crown seeks to go further. The claim is for all the profits of Blake's book which the publisher has not yet paid him. This raises the question whether an account of profits can ever be given as a remedy for breach of contract. The researches of counsel have been unable to discover any case where the court has made such an order on a claim for breach of contract ...

There is a light sprinkling of cases where courts have made orders having the same effect as an order for an account of profits, but the courts seem always to have attached a different label. A person who, in breach of contract, sells land twice over must surrender his profits on the second sale to the original buyer. Since courts regularly make orders for the specific performance of contracts for the sale of land, a seller of land is, to an extent, regarded as holding the land on trust for the buyer: *Lake v Bayliss* [1974] 1 WLR 1073. In *Reid-Newfoundland Co v Anglo-American Telegraph Co Ltd* [1912] AC 555 a railway company agreed not to transmit any commercial messages over a particular telegraph wire except for the benefit and account of the telegraph company. The Privy Council held that the railway company was liable to account as a trustee for the profits it wrongfully made from its use of the wire for commercial purposes. In *British Motor Trade Association v Gilbert* [1951] 2 All ER 641 the plaintiff suffered no financial loss but the award of damages for breach of contract effectively stripped the wrongdoer of the profit he had made from his wrongful venture into the black market for new cars.

These cases illustrate that circumstances do arise when the just response to a breach of contract is that the wrongdoer should not be permitted to retain any profit from the breach. In these cases the courts have reached the desired result by straining existing concepts. Professor Peter Birks has deplored the 'failure of jurisprudence when the law is forced into this kind of abusive instrumentalism'; see 'Profits of Breach of Contract' (1993) 109 LQR 518, 520 ...

My conclusion is that there seems to be no reason, in principle, why the court must in all circumstances rule out an account of profits as a remedy for breach of contract. I prefer to avoid the unhappy expression 'restitutionary damages'. Remedies are the law's response to a wrong (or, more precisely, to a cause of action). When, exceptionally, a just response to a breach of contract so requires, the court should be able to grant the discretionary remedy of requiring a defendant to account to the plaintiff for the benefits he has received from his breach of contract. In the same way as a plaintiff's interest in performance of a contract may render it just and equitable for the court to make an order for specific performance or grant an injunction, so the plaintiff's interest in performance may make it just and equitable that the defendant should retain no benefit from his breach of contract.

The state of the authorities encourages me to reach this conclusion, rather than the reverse. The law recognises that damages are not always a sufficient remedy for breach of contract. This is the foundation of the court's jurisdiction to grant the remedies of specific performance and injunction.

Even when awarding damages, the law does not adhere slavishly to the concept of compensation for financially measurable loss. When the circumstances require, damages are measured by reference to the benefit obtained by the wrongdoer. This applies to interference with property rights. Recently, the like approach has been adopted to breach of contract. Further, in certain circumstances an account of profits is ordered in preference to an award of damages. Sometimes the injured party is given the choice: either compensatory damages or an account of the wrongdoer's profits. Breach of confidence is an instance of this. If confidential information is wrongfully divulged in breach of a non-disclosure agreement, it would be nothing short of sophistry to say that an account of profits may be ordered in respect of the equitable wrong but not in respect of the breach of contract which governs the relationship between the parties. With the established authorities going thus far, I consider it would be only a modest step for the law to recognise openly that, exceptionally, an account of profits may be the most appropriate remedy for breach of contract. It is not as though this step would contradict some recognised principle applied consistently throughout the law to the grant or withholding of the remedy of an account of profits. No such principle is discernible.

The main argument against the availability of an account of profits as a remedy for breach of contract is that the circumstances where this remedy may be granted will be uncertain. This will have an unsettling effect on commercial contracts where certainty is important. I do not think these fears are well founded. I see no reason why, in practice, the availability of the remedy of an account of profits need disturb settled expectations in the commercial or consumer world. An account of profits will be appropriate only in exceptional circumstances. Normally the remedies of damages, specific performance and injunction, coupled with the characterisation of some contractual obligations as fiduciary, will provide an adequate response to a breach of contract. It will be only in exceptional cases, where those remedies are inadequate, that any question of accounting for profits will arise. No fixed rules can be prescribed. The court will have regard to all the circumstances, including the subject matter of the contract, the purpose of the contractual provision which has been breached, the circumstances in which the breach occurred, the consequences of the breach and the circumstances in which relief is being sought. A useful general guide, although not exhaustive, is whether the plaintiff had a legitimate interest in preventing the defendant's profit-making activity and, hence, in depriving him of his profit.

It would be difficult, and unwise, to attempt to be more specific. In the Court of Appeal [1998] Ch 439 Lord Woolf MR suggested there are at least two situations in which justice requires the award of restitutionary damages where compensatory damages would be inadequate: see p 458. Lord Woolf MR was not there addressing the question of when an account of profits, in the conventional sense, should be available. But I should add that, so far as an account of profits is concerned, the suggested categorisation would not assist. The first suggested category was the case of 'skimped' performance, where the defendant fails to provide the full extent of services he has contracted to provide. He should be liable to pay back the amount of expenditure he saved by the breach. This is a much discussed problem. But a part refund of the price agreed for services would not fall within the scope of an account of profits as ordinarily understood. Nor does an account of profits seem to be needed in this context. The resolution of the problem of cases of skimped performance, where the plaintiff does not get what was agreed, may best be found elsewhere. If a shopkeeper supplies inferior and cheaper goods than those ordered and paid for, he has to refund the difference in price. That would be the outcome of a claim for damages for breach of contract. That would be so, irrespective of whether the goods in fact served the intended purpose. There must be scope for a similar approach, without any straining of principle, in cases where the defendant provided inferior and cheaper services than those contracted for.

The second suggested category was where the defendant has obtained his profit by doing the very thing he contracted not to do. This category is defined too widely to assist. The category is apt to embrace all express negative obligations. But something more is required than mere breach of such an obligation before an account of profits will be the appropriate remedy.

Lord Woolf MR [1998] Ch 439, 457, 458, also suggested three facts which should not be a sufficient ground for departing from the normal basis on which damages are awarded: the fact that the breach was cynical and deliberate; the fact that the breach enabled the defendant to enter into a more profitable contract elsewhere; and the fact that by entering into a new and more profitable contract the defendant put it out of his power to perform his contract with the plaintiff. I agree that none of these facts would be, by itself, a good reason for ordering an account of profits.

The present case

The present case is exceptional. The context is employment as a member of the security and intelligence services. Secret information is the lifeblood of these services. In the 1950s Blake deliberately committed repeated breaches of his undertaking not to divulge official information gained as a result of his employment. He caused untold and immeasurable damage to the public interest he had committed himself to serve. When he joined the Secret Intelligence Service Blake expressly agreed in writing that he would not disclose official information, during or after his service, in book form or otherwise. He was employed on that basis. That was the basis on which he acquired official information. The Crown had and has a legitimate interest in preventing Blake profiting from the disclosure of official information, whether classified or not, while a member of the service and thereafter. Neither he, nor any other member of the service, should have a financial incentive to break his undertaking. It is of paramount importance that members of the service should have complete confidence in all their dealings with each other, and that those recruited as informers should have the like confidence. Undermining the willingness of prospective informers to co-operate with the services, or undermining the morale and trust between members of the services when engaged on secret and dangerous operations, would jeopardise the effectiveness of the service. An absolute rule against disclosure, visible to all, makes good sense.

In considering what would be a just response to a breach of Blake's undertaking the court has to take these considerations into account. The undertaking, if not a fiduciary obligation, was closely akin to a fiduciary obligation, where an account of profits is a standard remedy in the event of breach. Had the information which Blake has now disclosed still been confidential, an account of profits would have been ordered, almost as a matter of course. In the special circumstances of the intelligence services, the same conclusion should follow even though the information is no longer confidential. That would be a just response to the breach. I am reinforced in this view by noting that most of the profits from the book derive indirectly from the extremely serious and damaging breaches of the same undertaking committed by Blake in the 1950s. As already mentioned, but for his notoriety as an infamous spy his autobiography would not have commanded royalties of the magnitude Jonathan Cape agreed to pay.

Lord Steyn: In the Court of Appeal in *Surrey County Council v Bredero Homes Ltd* [1993] 1 WLR 1361, I discussed some of the difficulties inherent in creating a general remedy for the recovery of restitutionary damages for breach of contract. On that occasion I remarked that it is not traditional to describe a claim for restitution following a breach of contract as damages. The terminology is however less important than the substance: under consideration are claims for the disgorgement of profits against a contract breaker. There has been a substantial academic debate on the merits of the actual decision in the *Bredero* case. Since this issue has not been directly debated in the present case I propose to express no view on it. But it is right to acknowledge that the academic comment has been critical of the decision in the *Bredero* case I would, however, respectfully offer a comment on the valuable academic debate. On the one hand, there is no or virtually no support for a general action for disgorgement of profits made by a contract breaker by reason of his breach. On the other hand, there is significantly absent from the post-Bredero academic comment a reasoned statement of the particular circumstances when such a remedy should be available. That is not surprising because it is a notoriously difficult subject. But the Court of Appeal has been bold. It is said that the remedy should be available in two situations, *viz* (1) in cases of 'skimped' performance (where the 'gain' would take the form of expense saved) and (2) 'where the defendant has obtained his profit by doing the very thing which he contracted not to do'. The second would cover the present case. But it potentially has wide application. Sir Guenter Treitel QC in *The Law of Contract*, 10th edn (1999), pp 868–869, has questioned the soundness of the observations of the Court of Appeal: see also the valuable comment by Janet O'Sullivan, 'Reflections on the role of restitutionary damages to protect contractual expectations' (to be published) and Hanoch Dagan, 'Restitutionary Damages for Breach of Contract: An Exercise in Private Law Theory' [2000] 1 Theoretical Inquiries in Law 115. I am not at present willing to endorse the broad observations of the Court of Appeal. Exceptions to the general principle that there is no remedy for disgorgement of profits against a contract breaker are best hammered out on the anvil of concrete cases.

Lord Hobhouse: My Lords, when he opened this appeal, Mr Clayton, to whose pro bono services on behalf of the appellant George Blake I, too, would wish to pay tribute, warned your Lordships against being drawn into making bad law in order to enable an intuitively just decision to be given against a traitor.

Your Lordships have concluded that this claim should be allowed. I cannot join your Lordships in that conclusion. I have two primary difficulties. The first is the facts of the present case. The speech of my noble and learned friend explores what is the 'just response' to the defendant's conduct. The 'just response' visualised in the present case is, however it is formulated, that Blake should be punished and deprived of any fruits of conduct connected with his former criminal and reprehensible conduct. The Crown have made no secret of this. It is not a commercial claim in support of any commercial interest. It is a claim relating to past criminal conduct. The way it was put by the Court of Appeal [1998] Ch 439, 464 was:

> 'The ordinary member of the public would be shocked if the position was that the courts were powerless to prevent [Blake] profiting from his criminal conduct'.

The answer given by my noble and learned friend does not reflect the essentially punitive nature of the claim and seeks to apply principles of law which are only appropriate where commercial or proprietary interests are involved. Blake has made a financial gain but he has not done so at the expense of the Crown or making use of any property of or commercial interest of the Crown either in law or equity.

My second difficulty is that the reasoning of my noble and learned friend depends upon the conclusion that there is some gap in the existing state of the law which requires to be filled by a new remedy. He accepts that the term 'restitutionary damages' is unsatisfactory but, with respect, does not fully examine why this is so, drawing the necessary conclusions.

In his speech, Lord Nicholls acknowledged that a common fear associated with the availability of gain-based damages was that their availability would be uncertain and would lead to commercial instability. His Lordship dismissed such fears as being unfounded, but a closer examination of his speech reveals much fuel for such fears.

Lord Nicholls began his exposition of the test to be applied by declaring that no fixed rules could be prescribed. Such a statement necessarily strikes fear into all those pursuing clarity and certainty in the commercial law. His Lordship continued by recommending that the courts should have regard 'to all the circumstances, including the subject matter of the contract, the purpose of the contractual provision which has been breached, the circumstances in which the breach occurred, the consequences of the breach and the circumstances in which relief is being sought'. This statement tells us little, if anything, about how the courts should go about deciding whether to award gain-based damages. It merely declares that the award of such damages is at the discretion of the court (see also *Walsh v Shanahan* [2013] EWCA Civ 411). This is hardly conducive to certain and consistent court practice.

Fortunately, Lord Nicholls did provide what he referred to as a 'useful guide' for the courts. Gain-based damages should be available whenever compensatory damages are inadequate and the 'plaintiff has a legitimate interest in preventing the defendant's profit-making activity'. The problem with this test is that it is ambiguous in the extreme. When does a plaintiff have a legitimate interest in preventing the defendant's profit-making activity? Or perhaps, it is more appropriate to ask: When does a plaintiff *not* have a legitimate interest in preventing the defendant's profit-making activity? Surely the innocent party in every case of breach of contract has some legitimate interest in preventing the defendant from profiting by his breach.

Lord Nicholls did provide some guidance as to what amounts to a 'legitimate interest' by reference to the facts of *Blake* itself. He said, 'the Crown had and has a legitimate interest in preventing Blake profiting from the disclosure of official information, whether classified or not, while a member of the service and thereafter'. While it is undoubtedly true that the Crown had a legitimate interest in preventing Blake's profit-making breach while he was a member of the secret service, it is far less obvious that such an interest subsisted Blake's treachery and escape to the Soviet Union. Why did such a legitimate interest still exist? Blake was no longer in the employment of the Secret Service and the information was no longer confidential since it had been published in a national newspaper. What 'legitimate interest' remained except the interest that the contract should be performed according to its terms? If this were sufficient, then gain-based damages would be available for every breach of contract whenever the contract breaker makes a profit and alternative remedies are inadequate. This may of course be a welcome outcome for some, but it certainly was not Lord Nicholls's intention, since earlier in his speech he insisted that gain-based damages should only be 'exceptionally' available. Thus Lord Nicholls's 'useful general guide' must be narrower in application than it at first appears. But how much narrower? Ultimately, this is a question that can only be answered by later courts as they seek to interpret and apply Lord Nicholls's criteria. As Lord Steyn said in *Blake*:

> Exceptions to the general principle that there is no remedy for disgorgement of profits [gain-based damages] against a contract breaker are best hammered out on the anvil of concrete cases.

The 'anvil of concrete cases' that have applied *Blake* are considered in the next part of this section. Before moving on to consider those, it is important to note the warning issued by Lord Hobhouse in his dissent. He cautioned his fellow Law Lords, 'against being drawn into making bad law in order to enable an intuitively just decision to be given against a traitor'. It is arguable that this is precisely what the majority did in formulating the vague and unworkable 'legitimate interest' test. Professor Steve Hedley has suggested that the facts of *Blake* were so exceptional that it is of little value as a precedent.

Hedley, S, '"Very much the wrong people": the House of Lords and publication of spy memoirs' (2000) *Web JCLI*

> The reasoning of their lordships ... cannot, I think, be severed from its Cold War roots, and is of little value as a precedent, except of course in relation to the publication of spy memoirs. The hope that their lordships might make a serious contribution to the difficult problems of restitution was not an unreasonable one ... But in the event, that hope has been dashed. Despite a veneer of restitutionary reasoning, the case quickly departs from the doctrinal and commercial concerns that would have to be at the forefront of any real solution to those problems. It is to be hoped that the Lords will someday soon return to them, undistracted by past battles, and alert to the real dangers we confront.

Undoubtedly, Professor Hedley's criticisms of the case are well founded since the 'legitimate interest' test is riddled with problems. Later cases, however, have relied on *Blake* as a precedent (contrary to Hedley's assertions) and refined Lord Nicholls's criteria into an arguably workable test (and in *Morris-Garner v One Step (Support) Ltd* [2018] UKSC 20 Lord Reed stressed at [82] that the correctness of the *Blake* decision was not in question in that appeal).

15.2.4.3 Application of Lord Nicholls's 'useful guide'

The first case to follow and apply the decision in *Blake* was *Esso Petroleum Co Ltd v Niad Ltd*.

Esso Petroleum Co Ltd v Niad Ltd [2001] EWHC Ch 458

Facts: The case concerned the operation of a petrol marketing scheme called 'Pricewatch'. Petrol dealers agreed to report competitors' prices and to abide by prices set daily by Esso in return for financial support from Esso to assist them to do this. Niad broke the agreement by failing to maintain prices as agreed on four occasions. Esso sued Niad for breach of contract. Since Esso was unable to establish the loss it had sustained it claimed gain-based damages for the breach of contract.

Held: Morritt VC held that Niad was liable and Esso was entitled to either an account of profits or a restitutionary remedy, requiring Niad to pay to Esso the amount by which the actual prices charged to customers had exceeded the recommended prices.

Morritt VC: If [a claim for expectation damages] is pursued Esso will have to establish that it has lost sales of motor fuels by reason of the failure of Niad to charge at or below the Pricewatch recommended price. This may not be easy. In any event the amount is unlikely to be commensurate with the amount of additional price support derived by Niad from Pricewatch which it should have passed on to its customers.

For this reason Esso seeks an account of the profits derived by Niad from its breaches of contract. It relies on the recent decision of the House of Lords in *AG v Blake* [2001] 1 AC 268. But this too is unlikely to yield by way of recompense the amount of additional price support obtained by Niad from Pricewatch which it did not pass on. No doubt it is for this reason that Esso also seeks a restitutionary remedy whereby it recovers the amount by which the charges made at the Leyburn Service Station exceeded the recommended prices on the basis of unjust enrichment. It is accepted that these remedies are alternative not cumulative; but Esso contends that it is entitled to the judgment of the court on which of them is available before electing which to pursue …

In my judgment the remedy of an account of profits should be available for breaches of contract such as these. First, damages is an inadequate remedy. It is almost impossible to attribute lost sales to a breach by one out of several hundred dealers who operated Pricewatch. Second, the obligation to implement and maintain the recommended pump prices was fundamental to Pricewatch. Failure to observe it gives the lie to the advertising campaign by which it was publicised and therefore undermines the effectiveness of Pricewatch in achieving the benefits intended for both Esso and all its dealers within Pricewatch. Third, complaint was made of Niad on four occasions. On all of them Niad appeared to comply without demur. It now appears that the breaches of its obligation were much more extensive than Esso at first thought. Fourth, Esso undoubtedly has a legitimate interest in preventing Niad from profiting from its breach of obligation.

I turn then to the restitutionary remedy. It is undoubted that Niad obtained a benefit, in the form of the price support, to which it was only entitled if it complied with its obligation to implement and maintain the recommended pump prices to be supported. In these circumstances it can hardly be denied that Niad was enriched to the extent that it charged pump prices in excess of the recommended prices. The enrichment was unjust because it was obtained in breach of contract. It was obtained at the expense of Esso because Esso was providing price support for a lower price than that charged by Niad. I can see no reason why this remedy should be unavailable to Esso if it wishes to pursue it. Indeed it appears to me to be the most appropriate remedy in that it matches most closely the reality of the case, namely that Niad took an extra benefit to which it was not entitled. It is just that it should be made to restore it to its effective source.

The decision in *Niad* was significant because it demonstrated that gain-based damages are available outside of the exceptional circumstances of *Blake* (see *Luxe Holding Ltd v Midland Resources Holding Ltd* [2010] EWHC 1908). Indeed, despite the warnings of Lord Hobhouse and Professor Hedley, gain-based damages were awarded for breach of a commercial contract.

Morritt VC acknowledged at the outset that gain-based damages remain an exceptional remedy. Nevertheless, he thought that they were appropriate on the facts of the case for four reasons: (i) compensatory damages were an inadequate remedy; (ii) the obligation to implement and maintain the recommended pump prices was fundamental to the contract; (iii) complaint was made of the defendant on four occasions and the defendant gave the appearance of complying with Esso's request; and (iv) Esso had a legitimate interest in preventing the defendant from profiting from its breach of obligation.

At first sight, Morritt VC appeared to be applying more stringent criteria than those set out by Lord Nicholls in *Blake*. However, on a closer examination it can be seen that the Vice Chancellor's four reasons were really just an elaboration of Lord Nicholls's two criteria: (1) compensatory damages must be inadequate; (2) the claimant must have a legitimate interest in preventing the defendant's profit-making breach. Reasons (i) and (iii) concerned the inadequacy of damages requirement. Compensatory damages were inadequate because of the difficulty of determining loss and the fact that the breach was calculated, extensive and deliberate. Reasons (ii) and (iv) concerned the legitimate interest requirement. This is obvious in relation to reason (iv) since it really just restates Lord Nicholls's test. Reason (ii) provides a more stringent requirement for establishing a legitimate interest. It requires the claimant to prove that the breach went to the root of the contract and gave lie to its integrity. Thus the judgment delivered in *Niad* goes some way to clarifying and developing the 'legitimate interest' test established in *Blake*.

The final point to note about the case is that Morritt VC arguably identified two alternative gain-based remedies: an account of profits and a restitutionary remedy.

15.2.4.4 Two measures of gain-based damages?

The Court of Appeal also made a distinction between different remedies in *Experience Hendrix LLC v PPX Enterprises Inc.*

Experience Hendrix LLC v PPX Enterprises Inc, Edward Chalpin
[2003] EWCA Civ 323; [2003] EMLR 25

Facts: The claimant was the estate of Jimi Hendrix, the rock legend of the 1960s, who died in 1970 from a drug overdose. The respondents, PPX Enterprises Inc were Jimi Hendrix's former recording company. In 1967, PPX brought proceedings against Jimi Hendrix for alleged breaches of a recording contract that required Hendrix to record exclusively for PPX. These proceedings were eventually settled in 1973, three years after Hendrix's death, and the contract of settlement was incorporated into an order of the court. Since 1973, however, PPX had exploited various master recordings in breach of the settlement agreement. Experience Hendrix brought an action for breach of the settlement agreement. At first instance, Buckley J granted an injunction to restrain PPX from future unauthorised use of the master recordings, but held that Experience Hendrix was only entitled to nominal damages in respect of the past breaches. The claimant appealed.

Held: The Court of Appeal allowed the appeal and awarded damages measured on the *Wrotham Park* basis. The Court declined to award a full account of profits because the facts of *Hendrix* were not sufficiently exceptional to justify such an order.

Mance LJ: I turn to apply these principles to the present facts. As in *Blake*, we are concerned with a breach of a negative obligation, and PPX did do the very thing it had contracted not to do ... On the other hand, there are also obvious distinctions from *Blake's* case. First, we are not concerned with a subject anything like as special or sensitive as national security. The State's special interest in preventing a spy benefiting by breaches of his contractual duty of secrecy, and so removing at least part of the financial attraction of such breaches, has no parallel in this case. Second, the notoriety which accounted for the magnitude of Blake's royalty earning capacity derived from his prior breaches of secrecy, and that too has no present parallel. Third, there is no direct analogy between PPX's position and that of a fiduciary.

The case of *Niad* presents a similar feature to the present, in so far as damages may be said to be an inadequate remedy, because of the practical impossibility in each case of demonstrating the effect of a defendant's undoubted breaches on the appellant's general programme of promoting their product. But, despite [counsel for the appellants'] evidence, it is not shown that the present defendant's breaches went to the root of the appellant's programme or gave the lie to its integrity. Nor is the present a case where the defendant can be said to have profited directly, by receipt under the agreement which it broke of monies that it ought in fairness to restore ...

I consider that any reasonable observer of the situation would conclude that, as a matter of practical justice, PPX should make (at the least) reasonable payment for its use of masters in breach of the settlement agreement ... It would in these circumstances be anomalous and unjust, if PPX could, by simply breaching the agreement, avoid paying royalties or any sum, when they have to pay royalties in respect of Schedule A masters and they would have expected that, even if consent to the extension or renewal of existing licences of non-Schedule A masters was forthcoming at all, it would only be on terms as to payment of further royalties ...

However, I do not regard this case as exceptional to the point where the Court should order a full account of all profits which have been or may be made by PPX by its breaches. I have already drawn attention to significant features of *Blake* which have no counterpart in this case ... Here, the breaches, though deliberate, took place in a commercial context. PPX, though knowingly and deliberately breaching its contract, acted as it did in the course of a business, to which it no doubt gave some expenditure of time and effort and probably the use of connections and some skill (although how much is evidently in issue, and is not a matter on which we can at this stage reach any view). An account of profits would involve a detailed assessment of such matters, which, as is very clear from *Blake*, should not lightly be ordered.

For the past, in the absence of any proven loss, I would confine any financial remedy to an order that PPX pay a reasonable sum for its use of material in breach of the settlement agreement. That sum can properly be described as being 'such sum as might reasonably have been demanded' by Jimi Hendrix's estate 'as a quid pro quo for agreeing to permit the two licences into which PPX entered in breach of the settlement agreement', which was the approach adopted by Brightman J in *Wrotham Park* ... This involves an element of artificiality, if, as in *Wrotham Park*, no permission would ever have been given on any terms. And, where no injunction is possible, even the value of a bargaining opportunity depends on the value which the court puts on the right infringed (cf. paragraph 19 above, citing Lord Nicholls in *Blake*). That said, the approach adopted by Brightman J has the merit of directing the court's attention to the commercial value of the right infringed and of enabling it to assess the sum payable by reference to the fees that might in other contexts be demanded and paid between willing parties. It points in the present case towards orders that PPX pay over, by way of damages, a proportion of each of the advances received to date and (subject to deduction of such proportion) an appropriate royalty rate on retail selling prices. I would therefore allow the appeal against the judge's decision on the first point and declare accordingly.

The decision of the Court of Appeal in this case was significant, not least because it distinguished between two different measures of damages, which some argued were both gain-based.

Cunnington, R, 'Rock, restitution and disgorgement' (2004) *JO & R* 46, 47–50

In *Hendrix* the Court of Appeal was of the view that there are essentially two different types of gain-based damages, measured on two different bases. Such a distinction had already been drawn by Morritt VC two years earlier in the case of *Esso Petroleum v Niad* ...

The *Blake* measure

In *Blake*, the Crown's claim was 'for all the profits of Blake's book which the publisher had not yet paid him. Commentators have drawn a distinction between gain-based awards that require a defendant to 'give up' a gain and gain-based awards that require a defendant to 'give back' a gain. The measure of damages awarded in *Blake* was of the former category. Blake was required to give a full account of his gross profit without any allowance being made for the time, effort and skill which he put into writing the book.

Blake was not compelled to 'give back' the profits to the Crown, he was compelled to 'give up' or disgorge the profits. It was unnecessary for the Crown to show that the profits received by Blake had been derived directly from the Crown. Indeed, the Attorney General would still have been entitled to claim an account of profits even if Blake had been able to demonstrate that all of his profits had been generated by his own work and skill. In the words of Dr Edelman: 'Whether a transfer of value occurs or not is irrelevant.'

The *Blake* measure is a blunt tool which requires the defendant to give up all of the profits he has made from the breach. This was affirmed by Mance LJ in *Hendrix*, who said that to apply the *Blake* measure would be to 'order a full account of all profits which have been made or may be made by PPX by its breaches.' The *Blake* measure of damages is calculated by reference to the actual profit accruing to the defendant from the wrong. Whether the profits are derived from the claimant or not is irrelevant. There need be no transfer of value and there need be no loss sustained by the claimant.

The *Wrotham Park* measure

The measure of damages applied by the House of Lords in *Blake* was very different to the measure applied in the cases relied upon by the Crown ... The primary authority for the Crown was *Wrotham Park Estate Ltd v Parkside Homes Ltd* ... It is clear that the damages awarded in *Wrotham Park* were not compensatory in the ordinary sense ... Nor were they an account of profits. Lord Nicholls has suggested, extra-judicially, that the *Wrotham Park* case is an example of partial disgorgement of profits ... These comments have been used to support the thesis that gain-based damages for breach of contract are awarded, 'on a "sliding scale" extending from various levels of partial disgorgement (hypothetical release damages) to total disgorgement (account of profits).' It is respectfully submitted that there is no such sliding scale. Lord Nicholls was mistaken in his comments because the damages awarded in *Wrotham Park* were calculated by reference to Parkside's *anticipated* profit, not by reference to Parkside's *actual* profit. The *Wrotham Park* damages were not a partial account of profits. They had nothing to do with Parkside's actual profits. They were calculated by reference to, 'such sum as might reasonably have been demanded by the plaintiffs from Parkside as a *quid pro quo* for relaxing the covenant. Brightman J held such a sum was roughly equivalent to five per cent of their *anticipated* profit.

The *Blake* measure of damages is a real assessment of the actual profits received by the defendant as a consequence of his breach. The *Wrotham Park* measure is a judicial assessment of the objective value received by the defendant as a consequence of his breach. Dr Edelman has described the *Wrotham Park* measure of damages as, 'a monetary award which reverses a transfer of value. It is an award which gives back value transferred from a claimant to a defendant as a result of a defendant's wrong and is almost always measured by the objective gain received by the defendant.' This understanding of the *Wrotham Park* measure of damages is affirmed by the decision of the Court of Appeal in *Hendrix*. Mance LJ said that, if the measure was to be applied to the facts of *Hendrix*, the court would award damages equivalent to what would be a 'reasonable payment for the use of masters in breach of the settlement agreement'. This is a judicially determined value placed on the objective benefit transferred from Experience Hendrix to PPX. It is not tied to the actual profit made by the defendant. This was confirmed by Mance LJ who said: 'In such a context it is natural to pay regard to any profit made by the wrongdoer (although a wrongdoer surely cannot always rely on avoiding having to make reasonable recompense by showing that despite his wrong he failed, perhaps simply due to his own incompetence, to make any profit).' Thus the *Wrotham Park* measure of damages is different to the *Blake* measure; it is a judicially assessed measure that can exceed the *Blake* measure where the defendant, by his own incompetence, has failed to make any profit.

The next important issue to address is the juridical basis of the *Wrotham Park* measure of damages. Were they restitutionary, i.e. gain-based, or were they compensatory? ... [I]n his dissenting speech in *Blake* Lord Hobhouse described *Wrotham Park* as a case decided on compensatory principles – the claimant's loss being, 'the sum which he could have extracted from the defendant as the price of his consent to the development'. In *Hendrix*, Mance LJ noted Lord Hobhouse's comments and said: 'Whether the adoption of a standard measure of damages represents a departure from a compensatory approach depends upon what one understands by compensation and whether the term is only apt in circumstances where an injured party's financial position, viewed subjectively, is being precisely restored.'

Pey-Woan Lee has argued that this statement in *Hendrix* supports the view that the damages awarded in *Wrotham Park* were compensatory damages for a lost opportunity to bargain. It is respectfully submitted that such an analysis of *Wrotham Park* is fallacious.

The 'Damages for Lost Opportunity to Bargain' thesis was originally articulated by Sharpe and Waddams in their seminal 1982 article of the same name. They contended that, in circumstances where the defendant has profited from his violation of the claimant's property right, damages can be awarded based upon the defendant's gain to compensate the claimant for his lost opportunity to bargain.

A number of commentators have rightly rejected this approach as being fictitious. The main objection to the approach is that gain-based damages have been awarded in cases where either: (a) the claimant would never have agreed to release the defendant from his obligations; or (b) there never had been an opportunity to bargain release from the defendant's obligations. Indeed, both these objections arise on the facts of *Wrotham Park* itself. Brightman J made it clear that the claimants 'rightly conscious of their obligations towards existing residents', would clearly not have granted any relaxation of the restrictive covenant. Furthermore, there was never an opportunity to bargain release with the second defendants who were the purchasers of the properties from Parkside Homes. They did not purchase the properties until after the building work was complete. By this time the covenant was unenforceable because a mandatory injunction would, in the words of Brightman J, constitute 'an unpardonable waste of much needed houses'. Therefore, there was no historical point at which the claimant would have been able to enforce the covenant against the second defendants. The damages awarded against the second defendants cannot be considered to be compensation for a lost opportunity to bargain since no such opportunity ever existed with the second defendants.

Fortunately it seems that, contrary to Lee's assertions, the Court of Appeal in *Hendrix* did not adopt the Lost Opportunity to Bargain theory to explain the *Wrotham Park* measure of damages. Peter Gibson LJ referred to the theory as wholly fictional in the context of cases where the claimant would never have agreed to release the defendant from his obligations. Mance LJ also noted the artificiality of the approach, and described the award as 'the value which the court puts on the right infringed. This value is not compensatory and it is not based on the actual profit made by the defendant. It is a judicially determined assessment of the objective value received by the defendant as a consequence of his breach – it is restitutionary.

Cunnington argued that the Court of Appeal identified two different measures of gain-based damages:

1 **The *Blake* measure** – requiring the defendant to 'give up' his actual gain – a real assessment of the actual profits received by the defendant as a consequence of the breach of contract.
2 **The *Wrotham Park* measure** – requiring the defendant to 'give back' a particular gain – a judicial assessment of the objective value received by the defendant, at the expense of the claimant, as a consequence of the breach of contract (on the difficulties in assessing such a sum see *CF Partners (UK) LLP v Barclays Bank plc* [2014] EWHC 3049 (Ch)).

The difficulty for such an overall argument is that recent cases tend to regard *Wrotham Park* damages (and sometimes even *Blake*-type damages) as compensatory in nature (cf. Cunnington, 'Changing Conceptions of Compensation' (2007) 66 CLJ 557). For example, in *WWF – World Wide Fund for Nature v World Wrestling Federation Entertainment Inc* [2007] EWCA Civ 286 at [59] Chadwick LJ stated:

> When the court makes an award of damages on the *Wrotham Park* basis it does so because it is satisfied that that is a just response to circumstances in which the compensation which is the claimant's due cannot be measured (or cannot be measured solely) by reference to identifiable financial loss. Lord Nicholls' analysis in *Attorney General v Blake* demonstrates that there are exceptional cases in which the just response to circumstances in which the compensation which is the claimant's due cannot be measured by reference to identifiable financial loss is an order which deprives the wrongdoer of all the fruits of his wrong. The circumstances in which an award of damages on the *Wrotham Park* basis may be an appropriate response, and those in which the appropriate response is an account of profits, may differ in degree. But the underlying feature, in both cases, is that the court recognises the need to compensate the claimant in circumstances where he cannot demonstrate identifiable financial loss. To label an award of damages on the *Wrotham Park* basis as a 'compensatory' remedy and an order for an account of profits as a 'gains-based' remedy does not assist an understanding of the principles on which the court acts. The two remedies should, I think, each be seen as a flexible response to the need to compensate the claimant for the wrong which has been done to him.

(See also, for example, *Pell Frischmann Engineering Ltd v Bow Valley Iran Ltd* [2009] UKPC 45 at [48], *per* Lord Walker, and *Giedo van der Garde BV v Force India Formula One Team Ltd* [2010] EWHC 2373 (QB).) Cf. *Arroyo v Equion Energia Ltd (formerly BP Exploration Co (Colombia) Ltd)* [2013] EWHC 3150 (TCC) at [66] on the possibility of combining awards. This issue now appears to be settled following *Morris-Garner v One Step (Support) Ltd* [2018] UKSC 20 where the Supreme Court regarded the damages in *Wrotham Park* as compensatory in nature. Any suggestion that the award in *Blake* was compensatory in nature has also been dispelled by *Morris-Garner v One Step (Support) Ltd* [2018] UKSC 20 where Lord Reed (with whom Lady Hale, Lord Wilson and Lord Carnwath agreed) was of the opinion that the award in *Blake* was not compensatory in nature.

Returning to our discussion of *Hendrix*, *Blake* damages were not awarded. The reason for this is unclear. Mance LJ identified and applied the criteria expounded by Lord Nicholls in *Blake*:

1 Compensatory damages were inadequate 'because of the practical impossibility in each case of demonstrating the effect of a defendant's undoubted breaches on the appellant's general programme of promoting their product.' Compare *BritNed Development Ltd v ABB AB, ABB Ltd* [2019] EWCA Civ 1840 where the Court of Appeal held that difficulty in assessing damages is not in itself enough to open the possibility of *Blake*-style damages.
2 Experience Hendrix had a legitimate *interest* in preventing the PPX's profit-making activity, which was evidenced by the availability of an injunction to prevent PPX from breaching the settlement agreement again in the future.

Despite the fact that these two criteria were fulfilled, Mance LJ refused to award the *Blake* measure on the ground that two further criteria (taken from the judgment in *Niad*) had not been fulfilled:

1 PPX's breach had not gone to the root of the contract and given lie to its integrity.
2 The profits received by PPX were not derived directly from the breach of contract.

With respect, these two conclusions are open to debate. First, it is surely arguable that PPX's breaches did go to the root of the settlement agreement. The purpose of the agreement was to prevent PPX exploiting Hendrix's songs without fair compensation. This purpose was achieved by providing that only some of the songs could be exploited. PPX violated the very basis of this agreement by licensing many of the songs that they were not entitled to exploit. Thus it appears that Experience Hendrix did have a legitimate interest in preventing PPX's profit-making breach. The breach went to the very root of the contract and 'gave lie to its integrity'. Second, it is difficult to understand why Mance LJ concluded that the profits received by PPX were not derived directly from the breach of contract. The use of the masters' recordings was the breach of the settlement agreement of 1973. Therefore, the profits derived from the use of the masters' recordings were directly derived from the breach of contract.

Although the Court of Appeal refused to award *Blake* damages the court did award damages measured on the *Wrotham Park* basis. It seems that the crucial fact influencing this decision was the inadequacy of traditional compensatory damages. As Mance LJ observed in relation to the facts of *Hendrix*: 'any reasonable observer of the situation would conclude that, as a matter of practical justice, PPX should make (at the least) reasonable payment for its use of masters in breach of the settlement agreement'. *Hendrix* was considered, in the context of a confidentiality agreement, in *Vercoe v Rutland Fund Management Ltd* [2010] EWHC 424 (Ch), where Sales J stated:

> **339.** In my view, Lord Nicholls' speech in *Blake* has opened the way to a more principled examination of the circumstances in which an account of profits will be ordered by the courts and where it will not. His reasoning at p 285C–E, comparing remedies available in contract and for breach of confidence in relation to the same underlying facts, flows in both directions. It both opens up the possibility of an award of an account of profits in relation to breach of contract relating to confidential information and also opens up the possibility for a more principled debate about when an account of profits should be refused in relation to a breach of confidence, and a damages award (typically assessed by reference to a notional reasonable price to buy release from the claimant's rights, similar to the award made in *Wrotham Park* and *Seager v Copydex*) made instead. Both in cases of breach of contract and in cases of breach of confidence, the question (at a high level of generality) is, what is the just response to the wrong in question (cf. Lord Nicholls at p 284H, set out above)? In both cases, to adapt Lord Nicholls' formulation at p 285A, the test is whether the claimant's interest in performance of the obligation in question (whether regarded as an equitable obligation or a contractual obligation) makes it just and equitable that the defendant should retain no benefit from his breach of that obligation. Again, I think that there is a broad parallel with the way in which the courts will, as in *Ruxley Electronics and Construction Ltd v Forsyth* [1996] AC 344, control the amount of damages to be awarded in a contract case by reference to the strength of the claimant's interest in performance of a contractual obligation, judged on an objective basis and weighing that against countervailing legitimate interests of the defendant, to ensure that the remedy awarded is not oppressive and is properly proportionate to the wrong done to the claimant.
>
> **340.** Although in a certain sense the courts' decisions about these matters might be described as discretionary, in truth I think the courts are now seeking to articulate underlying principles which will govern the choices to be made as to the remedy or remedies available in any given case. In some situations, where the rights of the claimant are of a particularly powerful kind and his interest in full performance is recognised

as being particularly strong, there may well be a tendency to recognise that the claimant should be entitled to a choice of remedy (both as between damages and an account of profits, and also possibly as between different bases of calculation of damages, such as by reference to loss actually suffered or by reference to a notional reasonable agreement to buy release from his rights). There are indications in the authorities that this may more readily be found to be appropriate in cases involving infringement of property rights (see, for an historic example, *Siddell v Vickers*, and also *Blake* at 278D–280F and *Devenish Nutrition Ltd v Sanofi-Aventis SA* [2008] EWCA Civ 1086; [2009] Ch 390, at [75] and [155], cf. [144]). This may reflect the particular importance usually attached to property rights and the extent of protection they are to be afforded in law – although one might think that in relation to ordinary rights in relation to property of a kind which is regularly bought and sold in a market, damages assessed by reference to a notional buy-out fee may often represent an appropriate and fair remedy, and it is possible that the law may develop in that way. By contrast, it may be more appropriate to award an account of profits where the right in question is of a kind where it would never be reasonable to expect that it could be bought out for some reasonable fee, so that it is accordingly deserving of a particularly high level of protection (such as the promise to keep state secrets which was in issue in *Blake*, which was classified as an exceptional case meriting such an award, and rights to protection under established fiduciary relationships, where trust between the parties rather than a purely commercial relationship is regarded as central to the obligations in question).

341. Cases will frequently arise where a significant choice falls to be made between damages calculated by reference to a notional reasonable buy out fee and an account of profits. Then in my judgment, in the light of *Blake*, where one is not dealing with infringement of a right which is clearly proprietary in nature (such as intellectual property in the form of a patent, as in *Siddell v Vickers*) and there is nothing exceptional to indicate that the defendant should never have been entitled to adopt a commercial approach in deciding how to behave in relation to that right, the appropriate remedy is likely to be an award of damages assessed by reference to a reasonable buy out fee rather than an account of profits. The law will control the choice between these remedies, having regard to the need to strike a fair balance between the interests of the parties at the remedial stage, rather than leaving it to the discretion of the claimant. The significance of *Seager v Copydex* is that it shows that, even in relation to confidential information closely akin to a patent (such as a secret manufacturing design or process), the law will not necessarily afford protection to the claimant extending to an account of profits. Still more strongly will that be the case as one moves further away from confidential information in a form resembling classic intellectual property rights towards forms of obligation in respect of confidential information more akin to purely personal obligations in contract and tort.

342. This approach is, I think, supported by the judgments in the Court of Appeal in *Experience Hendrix*. In that case the defendant licensed masters of recordings of certain music in breach of its agreement with the claimant that they should not be licensed, and thereby made a profit. The claimant's claim for an account of profits arising from the breach of the agreement was dismissed, even though the breach was deliberate, because the case was not exceptional (there was no special interest of the claimant in having its rights protected, unlike in *Blake*) but rather arose in a commercial context, and the defendant was not in the position of a fiduciary or any position analogous to that. The claimant was instead awarded a payment equivalent to the reasonable notional royalties which would have been paid by the defendant to buy release from its obligations so as to be able to license the masters as it did: see in particular [37] and [43]–[45] (Mance LJ) and [55] (Peter Gibson LJ).

343. The approach which I adopt also, in my view, produces a coherent picture regarding the extent of protection afforded by the law, moving from lesser protection in relation to an ordinary commercial context to greater protection where there is a fiduciary relationship, rather than too readily equiparating the two. In a commercial context, as reflected in *Experience Hendrix*, a degree of self-seeking and ruthless behaviour is expected and accepted to a degree. In a fiduciary relationship, by contrast, self-seeking behaviour is required to be reined in on the grounds that special obligations of trust have been assumed by the fiduciary to the other party. It seems natural that the law governing the extent of the remedies available in these different contexts should reflect the strength of the interest which the law recognises in each case as deserving protection and the increased importance of deterring abusive behaviour in a fiduciary relationship. As observed by James Edelman (*Gain-Based Damages: Contract, Tort, Equity and Intellectual Property* at 214), it is not obvious why the remedies for breach of confidence should necessarily be the same as for breach of fiduciary duty, so as to allow an account of profits; nor is it obvious why they should be more than the remedy available for, say, the tort of deceit.

344. The law relating to breach of confidence covers a very wide range of different factual situations, and it is unsurprising that the strength of the arguments in favour of any particular remedy or set of remedies in respect of a particular breach of confidence varies across that range. Sometimes the nature of the obligation of confidence may be closely similar to a fiduciary obligation (as in the special context of obligations imposed on officers of the Secret Intelligence Service in *Blake*), in which case it may be appropriate for remedies to be available similar to those in respect of a breach of fiduciary duty; sometimes the nature of the obligation may be closely similar to the obligations which protect forms of intellectual property (as in *Corsets Silhouette* and *Seager v Copydex*), in which case it may be appropriate for remedies to be fashioned equivalent to those available in that context; sometimes (as observed by Lord Nicholls in *Blake*) the obligation may spring from a contract, or arise in circumstances closely similar to a contractual relationship, in which case the appropriate remedy (in the absence of exceptional circumstances) is likely to be similar to those available for breach of contract; in yet other cases, e.g. where the law of confidence is used to address use of private information obtained by a stranger, a relevant analogy may be drawn from the law of tort.

345. In the present case, I consider that an award of an account of the profits made by the defendants would not be an appropriate remedy in relation to the claimants' breach of confidence claim. For reasons given below, there was no fiduciary relationship between RFML and the claimants. Nor did the claimants provide RFML with information about a secret design or process analogous to other forms of intellectual property. The relationship between them was founded upon a contractual relationship, in which each side bargained at arm's length to define the obligations to be accepted by RFML in respect of the business idea or opportunity which Mr Vercoe and Mr Pratt had identified. The negative covenant given by RFML as to use of the confidential information was broadly equivalent to the restrictive covenant in *Wrotham Park*, and a remedy fashioned by reference to the same kind of notional reasonable transaction to buy release from the claimant's rights as was considered in that case seems eminently suitable in this case. There are the same sufficient means of determining the notional fair or reasonable price appropriate for this case as there were in that case.

See also *Jones v Ricoh UK Ltd* [2010] EWHC 1743 (Ch). Damages on the *Wrotham Park* basis were recently considered by the Supreme Court in *Morris-Garner v One Step (Support) Ltd* [2018] UKSC 20. The claimant was a company which provided care for vulnerable adults and children and the defendants were a former director/shareholder of the company and a former manager of the company. The defendants were bound, for a period of time, by certain covenants not to: compete with the claimant company; solicit the claimant company's clients; nor use the claimant company's confidential information. Ultimately the claimant company alleged these covenants had been breached. The judge found that there had been some breaches of the covenants and, therefore, the issue became the measure of damages. Moreover the judge held that, as the loss was difficult to assess, the claimant could, if it wished, instead claim hypothetical release damages. The Court of Appeal rejected the appeal but subsequently the Supreme Court allowed an appeal.

Lord Reed (with whom Lady Hale, Lord Wilson and Lord Carnwath agreed) was of the opinion that the award in *Wrotham Park* was compensatory in nature ([95]). That award was made in lieu of an injunction (as permitted under Lord Cairns' Act) and, as such, one 'possible method of quantifying damages under this head is on the basis of the economic value of the right which the court has declined to enforce, and which it has consequently rendered worthless' ([95]). In valuing such a right a court might use 'the amount which the claimant might reasonably have demanded as a *quid pro quo* for the relaxation of the obligation in question' (so-called 'negotiating damages') ([95]). Moreover, Lord Reed recognised that negotiating damages might also be awarded at common law in appropriate circumstances. In particular, such damages might be awarded where the breach of contract results in the 'loss of a valuable asset created or protected by the right which was infringed' ([95]). Examples might include the breach of a restrictive covenant over land, the breach of an intellectual property agreement or the breach of a confidentiality agreement ([92]). In such cases, the imaginary negotiation is merely a tool for determining the value of the relevant asset ([91]). Crucially, Lord Reed was of the opinion that not all contract rights were to be considered as an asset in this sense ([93]) although it is, perhaps, not clear how the distinction will be made. Moreover, Lord Reed disagreed with some of the wider statements in *Hendrix* that negotiating damages could be used more widely to achieve 'practical justice'. Nevertheless Lord Reed agreed with the decision in the case on the basis, essentially, that it involved the breach of an intellectual property agreement ([89]).

More recently in *Priyanka Shipping Ltd v Glory Bulk Carriers Pte Ltd* [2019] EWHC 2804 (Comm), David Edwards QC (sitting as a Judge of the High Court) held that 'negotiating damages' were not available where the purchaser of a ship used the ship in breach of a provision as to the permitted use of the ship:

> 189.The critical question in this case is whether the Seller can bring itself within [95(10)] of Lord Reed JSC's judgment in *One Step* and say that this is a case where negotiating damages can be awarded, namely where:
>
> > '... the loss suffered by the claimant is appropriately measured by reference to the economic value of the right which has been breached, considered as an asset'.
>
> 190.It is plain from the remainder of the paragraph, however, that such an approach is not available in the case of a breach of any contractual right, but only where:
>
> > '... the breach of contract results in the loss of a valuable asset created or protected by the right which was infringed'.
>
> The paragraph implicitly regards the relevant asset not as the contractual right itself but as something else, a valuable asset 'created or protected by the right'. The rationale, as the paragraph goes on to say, is that the claimant has been deprived of an asset – the defendant has taken something for which the claimant was entitled to require payment.
>
> 191.The explanation as to what Lord Reed JSC meant in this paragraph, and the distinction that he had in mind, is to be found in [92] and [93], which themselves reflect observations made earlier in his judgment to which I have already drawn attention.
>
> 192.The opening sentence of [93] makes clear that negotiating damages do not constitute the measure of a claimant's loss in the case of every breach of a contractual obligation. In [92] and [93] Lord Reed JSC explained, however, that they may be available:
>
> > '92. [...] where the breach of contract results in the loss of a valuable asset created or protected by the right which was infringed, as for example in cases concerned with the breach of a restrictive covenant over land, an intellectual property agreement or a confidentiality agreement'.

'93. [...] [in the case of] some contractual rights, such as a right to control the use of land, intellectual property or confidential information'.

193.The present case is not one which is concerned with breach of a restrictive covenant over land or of a contractual right to control the use of land, or with breach of an intellectual property agreement or a confidentiality agreement. It is not, therefore, concerned with breaches of any of specific types of agreement or covenant that Lord Reed JSC mentioned.

194.Mr Hill, QC, however, rightly points out that in [92] Lord Reed JSC referred to these types of cases simply as examples. His submission, set out in paragraph 110 of his skeleton argument, was that, although not one of these specific types, clause 19 of the MOA could be regarded as analogous to a restrictive covenant on the sale of land, such as that in issue in *Wrotham Park*, to the collateral agreement preventing the development of land in *Lane v O'Brien Homes* [2004] EWHC 303 (QB) (Lane) on which Mr Hill, QC also relied, or to the restriction on exploitation in the settlement agreement in *Experience Hendrix*.

195.I do not agree. Although it is plainly right that Lord Reed JSC only gave examples, what this and earlier passages in his judgment show is that what he had in mind were situations where there was some asset or property (or something analogous to it such as confidential information, arguably not property in the strict sense of the term) distinct from the contractual right itself.

i) A restrictive covenant will run with the land, and as Lord Reed JSC explained is enforceable by the beneficiary in equity against future owners;
ii) In the case of a breach of an intellectual property agreement or a confidence agreement, there is intellectual property or information which the terms of agreement exist to protect.

196.That is not the position here. As I indicated in paragraph 163 above, once the Vessel was sold and delivered to the Buyer, the Seller had no proprietary or financial interest in her. The Buyer's use of the Vessel for trading, though in breach of clause 19, did not involve the Buyer taking or using something in which the Seller had an interest, a valuable asset, for which the Seller was entitled to require payment.

197.Mr Hill, QC said at paragraph 112 of his skeleton argument that, by breaching clause 19 of the MOA, the Buyer had:

'... unilaterally taken from Sellers the right to trade the Vessel'.

That, however, is incorrect: once the Seller had sold and delivered the Vessel to the Buyer, it had no right to trade the Vessel itself.

198.Mr Hill, QC's reliance on Wrotham Park, Lane and Experience Hendrix is, in my judgment, similarly misplaced:

iii) *Wrotham Park* concerned a restrictive covenant over land; the beneficiary had, through the covenant, an interest in and a right to control the land; cases involving restrictive covenants were one of the specific examples that Lord Reed JSC gave;
iv) Lane did not involve a restrictive covenant as such, but a collateral agreement between the seller and the buyer of the land intended to limit the land's future development. As apparent from paragraphs 11 and 21 of the judgment, however, counsel conceded that the fact that there was a collateral contract and not a restrictive covenant made no difference and that a Wrotham Park award could be made. Given the concession, the case provides little assistance;
v) *Experience Hendrix* is not an easy case – that much is plain from Lord Reed JSC's judgment. It is, perhaps, best regarded as at or near the limit of the circumstances in which an award of negotiating damages will be appropriate. As Lord Reed, however, observed, the decision can be justified on an orthodox basis given the circumstances of the settlement described in

paragraph 184 above, the impact of the proceedings, if they had continued, on the defendant's ability to exploit the masters in which it held the copyright, and the aim of the relevant provision which was seemingly in part to protect the value of Jimi Hendrix's own property.

199.In my judgment, the nature of the Seller's clause 19 right is, in fact, more analogous to the non-compete obligation in *One Step*, which Lord Reed JSC made clear at [93] and [99] he did not consider fell within the category of cases where negotiating damages were available as a measure of the Seller's loss. My conclusion is that the present case is not a case where negotiating damages are available.

200.In circumstances where the Seller's only pleaded claim for damages, both at common law for breach of contract and under section 50 of the Senior Courts Act 1981 , is for negotiating damages, and where I have decided that damages assessed on such a basis are not available, the result is that, for the breaches of clause 19 in respect of the First Fixture and the Second Fixture, the Seller is entitled only to nominal damages.

In terms of calculating 'the notional fair or reasonable price' in *32Red Plc v WHG (International) Ltd* [2013] EWHC 815, an intellectual property case, Newey J stated (at [22]–[33]):

22 As already mentioned, 32Red's claim is based on what has been termed the 'user principle'. Nicholls LJ coined the term in *Stoke-on-Trent City Council v W & J Wass Ltd* [1988] 1 WLR 1406 (at 1416) to refer to the principle that a person who has wrongfully used another's property can be liable to pay, as damages, a reasonable sum for such use.

23 This principle is well-established in relation to patent infringement. In *General Tire & Rubber Co v Firestone Tyre & Rubber Co Ltd* [1975] 1 WLR 819, Lord Wilberforce explained (at 824–825) that damages for patent infringement are assessed in three main ways. In the first place, if the claimant exploits the invention by manufacturing and selling goods at a profit, and the effect of the infringement has been to divert sales to the defendant, the 'measure of damages will . . . normally be the profit which would have been realised by the owner of the patent if the sales had been made by him'. Secondly, if the claimant exploits his patent by granting licences in return for royalty payments, 'the measure of damages [the defendant] must pay will be the sums which he would have paid by way of royalty if, instead of acting illegally, he had acted legally'. Thirdly, where it is not possible to prove either that there is a normal rate of profit or a normal royalty, damages fall to be assessed by considering what price could reasonably have been charged for permission to carry out the infringing acts. This last method of assessing damages can be seen as an application of the user principle (see *Stoke-on-Trent City Council v W & J Wass Ltd*, at 1416–1417, and *Force India Formula One Team Ltd v 1 Malaysia Racing Team Sdn Bhd* [2012] EWHC 616 (Ch), [2012] RPC 29 at paragraph 376).

24 On occasions, the Courts adopt essentially the same approach when assessing contractual damages. As Lord Nicholls of Birkenhead explained in *Attorney General v Blake* [2001] 1 AC 268 (at 283–284), in contract as well as tort damages will in a suitable case:

> 'be measured by the benefit gained by the wrongdoer from the breach. The defendant must make a reasonable payment in respect of the benefit he has gained'.

25 In *Force India*, Arnold J extracted from the authorities the following principles for the assessment of such damages (see paragraph 386):

(i) The overriding principle is that the damages are compensatory: see *Attorney-General v Blake* at 298 (Lord Hobhouse of Woodborough, dissenting but not on this point), *Hendrix v PPX* at [26] (Mance LJ, as he then was) and *WWF v World Wrestling* at [56] (Chadwick LJ).

(ii) The primary basis for the assessment is to consider what sum would have [been] arrived at in negotiations between the parties, had each been making reasonable use of their respective bargaining positions, bearing in mind the information available to the parties and the commercial context at the time that notional negotiation should have taken place: see *PPX v Hendrix* at [45], *WWF v World Wrestling* at [55], *Lunn v Liverpool* at [25] and *Pell v Bow* at [48]–[49], [51] (Lord Walker of Gestingthorpe).

(iii) The fact that one or both parties would not in practice have agreed to make a deal is irrelevant: see *Pell v Bow* at [49].

(iv) As a general rule, the assessment is to be made as at the date of the breach: see *Lunn Poly* at [29] and *Pell v Bow* at [50].

(v) Where there has been nothing like an actual negotiation between the parties, it is reasonable for the court to look at the eventual outcome and to consider whether or not that is a useful guide to what the parties would have thought at the time of their hypothetical bargain: see *Pell v Bow* at [51].

(vi) The court can take into account other relevant factors, and in particular delay on the part of the claimant in asserting its rights: see *Pell v Bow* at [54].

26 With regard to point (v), the authority cited is *Pell Frischmann Engineering Ltd v Bow Valley Iran Ltd* [2009] UKPC 45, [2011] 1 WLR 2370. In that case, the Privy Council endorsed (in paragraph 50) a passage from Neuberger LJ's judgment in *Lunn Poly Ltd v Liverpool & Lancashire Properties Ltd* [2006] EWCA Civ 430, [2006] 2 EGLR 29 reading as follows:

> 'Given that negotiating damages under [Lord Cairns'] Act are meant to be compensatory, and are normally to be assessed or valued at the date of breach, principle and consistency indicate that post-valuation events are normally irrelevant; but, given the quasi-equitable nature of such damages, the judge may, where there are good reasons, direct a departure from the norm either by selecting a different valuation date or by directing that a specific post-valuation date event be taken into account'.

27 The defendants' pleaded case was that user principle damages are not available in the present case. By the time of the hearing, however, they had accepted that such damages can potentially be appropriate for trade mark infringement. The parties now differ as to how much should be awarded rather than whether there should be any award at all.

Specific issues

28 Two questions call for particular consideration in the present case:

(i) How far are the specific characteristics and circumstances of the parties important to the assessment of user principle damages?

(ii) How far is it appropriate to have regard to alternative courses of action which would have been available to the parties at the date of the hypothetical negotiation?

The significance of the parties' characteristics and circumstances

29 There are plainly limits to the extent to which the Courts will have regard to the parties' actual attributes when assessing user principle damages. The parties are taken to have been willing to make a deal even if one or both of them would not in reality have been prepared to do so. It is also assumed that the parties would have acted reasonably regardless of whether that would in fact have been the case.

30 *Irvine v Talksport Ltd* [2003] EWCA Civ 423, [2003] FSR 35 indicates that a defendant's financial circumstances are not material as such, either. The case involved the assessment of damages for passing off. At first instance, the judge had concluded that the defendant's financial position was irrelevant because there was 'no question of a reasonable endorsement fee being assessed on the basis that the defendant had no money and therefore could not pay' (see paragraph 74). On appeal, Jonathan Parker LJ (with whom Schiemann and Brooke LJJ agreed) said that the judge had been right on this point (see paragraph 106).

31 Particular character traits of the parties also fall to be disregarded. In *Stadium Capital Holdings (No.2) Ltd v St Marylebone Property Co plc* [2011] EWHC 2856 (Ch), [2012] 1 P&CR 7, where damages for trespass had to be assessed in respect of an advertising hoarding which projected into the claimant's airspace, Vos J said (in paragraph 71):

> 'The personal characteristics of the parties, as opposed to the objective factors with which they were faced, are to be ignored'.

On this basis, he could not 'assume that a reasonable hypothetical site owner has either the easygoing characteristics of [former owners of the site] any more than the exceptionally aggressive approach of [the claimant]' (paragraph 71).

32 Matters such as those mentioned in the last two paragraphs are evidently not considered to provide any guidance as to what a right is worth. In contrast, the Courts do, as it seems to me, have regard to the circumstances in which the individual parties were placed at the time of the hypothetical negotiation. It is implicit in the passage from Vos J's judgment in the *Stadium Capital Holdings* case that he considered that 'the objective factors with which [the parties] were faced' are relevant. Earlier cases point in the same direction. For example, in *Wrotham Park Estate Co Ltd v Parkside Homes Ltd* [1974] 1 WLR 798, where houses had been built in breach of a restrictive covenant, damages were calculated, not in the abstract, but by reference to the profit that the defendant would have expected to make from its development. In *Sinclair v Gavaghan* [2007] EWHC 2256 (Ch), where the defendants had trespassed on a piece of land referred to as 'the Red Triangle' when gaining access to a plot beyond ('the Yellow Land') which they were developing, Patten J similarly took account of circumstances particular to the defendants: he had regard both (a) to the significance of the trespass in the context of the defendants' development of the Yellow Land and (b) to the fact that they owned neighbouring land ('No. 21'). In *Field Common Ltd v Elmbridge BC* [2009] 1 P&CR 1, Warren J said (in paragraph 78) that the hypothetical negotiation is 'designed to establish the value of the wrongful use to the defendant and not some objective figure as between hypothetical persons negotiating for a hypothetical licence' and that the negotiation 'would be one between the actual parties, albeit that they are to be treated as parties willing to deal with each other with a view to reaching a reasonable result'.

33 The same point can be seen in an intellectual property context in the *General Tire* case. Lord Wilberforce said this (at 833):

> 'My Lords, this passage is, in my opinion, unsupportable in law or in fact. In law it rests upon the hypothesis that what has to be considered, in measuring the loss a patentee sustains through an infringement, is some bargain struck between some abstract licensor and some abstract licensee uncontaminated by the qualities of the actual actors. But this is not so. The 'willing licensor' and 'willing licensee' to which reference is often made (and I do not object to it so long as we do not import analogies from other fields) is always the actual licensor and the actual licensee who, one assumes, are each willing to negotiate with the other – they bargain as they are, with their strengths and weaknesses, in the market as it exists. It is one thing (and legitimate) to say of a

particular bargain that it was not comparable or made in comparable circumstances with the bargain which the court is endeavouring to assume, so as, for example, to reject as comparable a bargain made in settlement of litigation. It is quite another thing to reject matters (other than any doubt as to the validity of the patent itself) of which either side, or both sides, would necessarily and relevantly take account when seeking agreement'.

The 'actual licensor' and 'actual licensee' are thus assumed to bargain 'as they are, with their strengths and weaknesses.

15.2.5 Liquidated damages and penalty clauses

15.2.5.1 Background

The parties to a contract may specifically agree on the compensation to be paid in the event of a breach. Such a term is referred to as a liquidated damages clause because it liquidates the sum payable on the occurrence of a breach. As a general rule, the courts are inclined to uphold liquidated damages clauses because, for example, they enable the parties to allocate between themselves the extent of the risks assumed (on issues of interpretation which may arise, see *Triple Point Technology Inc v PTT Public Co Ltd* [2019] EWCA Civ 230).

Harris, D, Campbell, D and Halson, R, *Remedies in Contract and Tort*, 2nd edn, 2002, London: Butterworths, pp 139–142

In comparison with unliquidated damages assessed under the ordinary rules (causation, remoteness, mitigation, etc) an agreed provision has the following advantages:

(1) Reduction in post-breach transaction costs. This is the orthodox argument: C can avoid the cost and difficulty of proving the actual loss which he suffers; he 'derives an advantage from having the figure fixed and so being assured of payment without the expense and difficulty of proof. The more difficult the proof, the more likely it is that an agreed sum will be enforced; and the higher the probability of enforcement, the greater the incentive on D to settle C's claim out of court. Although there will be a saving in post-breach transaction costs in these relatively rare situations of breach, this saving may be outweighed by certain pre-breach costs. Most obviously these include the extra costs of negotiating the agreed damages clause ...

(2) Avoiding the risk of under-compensation. At the time of contracting, the promisee C may fear that a damages award assessed under the ordinary principles would be inadequate compensation. Consequential or indirect losses may not be covered, nor may loss of reputation or idiosyncratic losses. An agreed damages clause may be the best way of dealing with the unusual risks – better even than C's informing D of the risks in the hope that damages would be awarded under the second rule in *Hadley v Baxendale* ...

(3) An assurance of reliability. If D the promissor is able to accept an obvious disincentive to breach he can give C an assurance that his promise to perform can be relied upon ...

(4) Limitation of liability. An agreed damages clause may perform the same function as an exemption clause: an agreed sum may place a *ceiling* on the financial risk which D is willing to accept ... These clauses may often be designed as the basis for insurance arrangements to be made by the parties. C may obtain insurance against the risk of loss beyond the agreed ceiling, but D may not be able to obtain insurance against a potentially unlimited risk, or against the consequences of his own failure to perform, and he may be unwilling to accept an uninsurable responsibility for unpredictable loss.

(5) Flexibility. The final advantage is the ability to combine the relevant factors. An agreed damages clause permits the parties to take account of all the factors in any combination. The agreed sum will be a 'trade-off' of the various factors in the foregoing list of advantages, plus any other factors, so as to produce the correct 'mix' of factors to suit the particular case. Among the other factors will be:
   (a) The different attitudes of the parties to the risk of the particular breach occurring …
   (b) The extent of insurance protection desired by C. If C obtains the consent of D to an enforceable agreed damages clause, he has purchased a form of lump-sum insurance against the consequences of non-performance …
   (c) C may wish (to the extent permitted by the 'genuine pre-estimate' test) to give D the desired level of incentive actually to perform.

In view of the advantages of agreed damages clauses, it is not surprising that generally economic analysis supports their enforcement (except in cases of initial 'unfairness or other bargaining abnormalities').

15.2.5.2 A genuine pre-estimate of loss likely to be caused by the breach?

As Harris *et al* note, liquidated damages clauses are generally enforced by the courts because they promote economic efficiency and facilitate freedom of contract. The traditional restriction placed on such clauses was that they had to represent a 'genuine' or '*bona fide*' pre-estimate of the actual loss likely to be caused by the breach. If not, such clauses would have been classified as an unenforceable penalty and damages would have been awarded on the usual principles for assessing damages for breach of contract (for potential criminal liability in relation to the use of penalty clauses see *R v Whatcott* [2019] EWCA Crim 1889). This rule was famously discussed in *Dunlop Pneumatic Tyre Co Ltd v New Garage and Motor Co Ltd*.

***Dunlop Pneumatic Tyre Co Ltd v New Garage and Motor Co Ltd* [1915] AC 79**

Facts: A contract was agreed for the supply of car tyres and inner tubes to the respondents who would in turn sell the goods on to their customers. The contract contained a clause stating that a sum of £5 would be payable 'by way of liquidated damages and not as a penalty' if the respondents sold the tyres at a price lower than the list price. The respondents committed a breach of contract by selling the tyres to Motorists Mutual Co-operative Society at a price less than the current list price. The appellants brought an action for payment of the agreed sum. At first instance, the judge held that the clause was a valid liquidated damages clause but on appeal this decision was overturned and the clause was held to be an unenforceable penalty clause.

Held: The House of Lords allowed the appeal and held that the clause was not a penalty clause with the result that the appellants were entitled to enforce the clause.

Lord Dunedin: I shall content myself with stating succinctly the various propositions which I think are deducible from the decisions which rank as authoritative:

1. Though the parties to a contract who use the words 'penalty' or 'liquidated damages' may *prima facie* be supposed to mean what they say, yet the expression used is not conclusive. The Court must find out whether the payment stipulated is in truth a penalty or liquidated damages. This doctrine may be said to be found *passim* in nearly every case.

2. The essence of a penalty is a payment of money stipulated as *in terrorem* of the offending party; the essence of liquidated damages is a genuine covenanted pre-estimate of damage (*Clydebank Engineering and Shipbuilding Co v Don Jose Ramos Yzquierdo y Castaneda*).
3. The question whether a sum stipulated is penalty or liquidated damages is a question of construction to be decided upon the terms and inherent circumstances of each particular contract, judged of as at the time of the making of the contract, not as at the time of the breach (*Public Works Commissioner v Hills* and *Webster v Bosanquet*).
4. To assist this task of construction various tests have been suggested, which if applicable to the case under consideration may prove helpful, or even conclusive. Such are:
   (a) It will be held to be penalty if the sum stipulated for is extravagant and unconscionable in amount in comparison with the greatest loss that could conceivably be proved to have followed from the breach. (Illustration given by Lord Halsbury in *Clydebank Case*.)
   (b) It will be held to be a penalty if the breach consists only in not paying a sum of money, and the sum stipulated is a sum greater than the sum which ought to have been paid (*Kemble v Farren*). This, though one of the most ancient instances, is truly a corollary to the last test. Whether it had its historical origin in the doctrine of the common law that when A promised to pay B a sum of money on a certain day and did not do so, B could only recover the sum with, in certain cases, interest, but could never recover further damages for non-timeous payment, or whether it was a survival of the time when equity reformed unconscionable bargains merely because they were unconscionable – a subject which much exercised Jessel MR in *Wallis v Smith* – is probably more interesting than material.
   (c) There is a presumption (but no more) that it is penalty when 'a single lump sum is made payable by way of compensation, on the occurrence of one or more or all of several events, some of which may occasion serious and others but trifling damage' (Lord Watson in *Lord Elphinstone v Monkland Iron and Coal Co*).

   On the other hand:

   (d) It is no obstacle to the sum stipulated being a genuine pre-estimate of damage, that the consequences of the breach are such as to make precise pre-estimation almost an impossibility. On the contrary, that is just the situation when it is probable that pre-estimated damage was the true bargain between the parties (*Clydebank Case*, Lord Halsbury; *Webster v Bosanquet Lord Mersey*).

Turning now to the facts of the case, it is evident that the damage apprehended by the appellants owing to the breaking of the agreement was an indirect and not a direct damage. So long as they got their price from the respondents for each article sold, it could not matter to them directly what the respondents did with it. Indirectly it did. Accordingly, the agreement is headed 'Price Maintenance Agreement', and the way in which the appellants would be damaged if prices were cut is clearly explained in evidence by Mr Baisley, and no successful attempt is made to controvert that evidence. But though damage as a whole from such a practice would be certain, yet damage from any one sale would be impossible to forecast. It is just, therefore, one of those cases where it seems quite reasonable for parties to contract that they should estimate that damage at a certain figure, and provided that figure is not extravagant there would seem no reason to suspect that it is not truly a bargain to assess damages, but rather a penalty to be held *in terrorem*.

The argument of the respondents ... overpressed, in my judgment, the *dictum* of Lord Watson in *Lord Elphinstone's Case*, reading it as if he had said that the matter was conclusive, instead of saying, as he did, that it raised a presumption ...

I have considerable doubt whether the stipulated payment here can fairly be said to deal with breaches, 'some of which' – I am quoting Lord Watson's words – 'may occasion serious and others but trifling damage'. As a mere matter of construction, I doubt whether clause 5 applies to anything but sales below price. But I will assume that it does. None the less the mischief, as I have already pointed out, is an indirect mischief, and I see no data on which, as a matter of construction, I could settle in my own mind that the indirect damage from selling a cover would differ in magnitude from the indirect damage from selling a tube; or that the indirect damage from a cutting-price sale would differ from the indirect damage from supply at a full price to a hostile, because prohibited, agent. You cannot weigh such things in a chemical balance. The character of the agricultural land which was ruined by slag heaps in *Elphinstone's Case* was not all the same, but no objection was raised by Lord Watson to applying an overhead rate per acre, the sum not being in itself unconscionable.

I think *Elphinstone's Case*, or rather the dicta in it, do go this length, that if there are various breaches to which one indiscriminate sum to be paid in breach is applied, then the strength of the chain must be taken at its weakest link. If you can clearly see that the loss on one particular breach could never amount to the stipulated sum, then you may come to the conclusion that the sum is penalty. But further than this it does not go; so, for the reasons already stated, I do not think the present case forms an instance of what I have just expressed.

The House of Lords held that the parties' own statement as to the nature of the clause was not conclusive of the issue. The court still had to determine whether the clause was a 'genuine pre-estimate of damage' or an 'extravagant and unconscionable' sum in comparison with the loss likely to be sustained following a breach. The situation in *Dunlop* was complicated, due to the fact that the liquidated sum was payable on the occurrence of a range of events each of which could have led to a range of different losses. The argument was that this universal application of the clause showed that it was not a genuine pre-estimate of loss. Their Lordships rejected this argument. The losses flowing from each event were indirect and difficult to predict ('you cannot weigh such things in a chemical balance'). Because of this, it was acceptable to use a liquidated damages clause to 'average' the likely losses resulting from a range of breaches.

The House of Lords also emphasised that the time for assessing the clause was the time of the contract, not the time of breach. Similarly, on the facts, in *Taiwan Scot Co Ltd v The Masters Golf Company Ltd* [2009] EWCA Civ 685 the Court of Appeal felt that a 15 per cent interest rate was not penal in character, Longmore LJ stating (at [17]):

> With respect to the judge, it was either a penalty or it was not. One forgets, in these recessionary days, that interest rates were considerably higher in 2001 than they are now. It does not seem to me that a contractual rate of 15% was in any way exorbitant in July 2001. It was a rate agreed by two commercial concerns in the economic circumstances of the time and it should not lightly be set aside. In this respect, I disagree with the judge. For my part, I would award interest at the rate of 15% on the sum of US$160,000 from 3 August 2001 up to the date of the inadequate payment on 8 January 2002 and at the same rate on the balance which the judge correctly held due, until the date of judgment. Thereafter, of course, the judgment sum will carry interest at the judgment rate.

Nevertheless, it was clear that what happened subsequently could provide helpful evidence of what loss might reasonably have been expected at the time the contract was entered into.

Philips Hong Kong Ltd v Attorney General of Hong Kong (1993) 61 BLR 41

Facts: The plaintiffs agreed to design, supply, test and install a computerised supervisory system for the approach roads and twin tube tunnels which were to be constructed under Smuggler's Ridge and Needle Hill Mountains in Hong Kong. The contract stipulated liquidated damages that would be payable if the plaintiff failed to meet 'Key Dates' by which certain items had to be completed so as to enable other contractors to continue with their work unimpeded. The contract also contained a separate liquidated damages clause for failure to complete the whole project on time. Philips successfully claimed that the clauses were unenforceable as penalties. The Court of Appeal of Hong Kong reversed this decision and Philips appealed to the Privy Council.

Held: The Privy Council dismissed the appeal.

Lord Woolf: [T]he court should not adopt an approach to provisions as to liquidated damages which could, as indicated earlier, defeat their purpose.

Except possibly in the case of situations where one of the parties to the contract is able to dominate the other as to the choice of the terms of a contract, it will normally be insufficient to establish that a provision is objectionably penal to identify situations where the application of the provision could result in a larger sum being recovered by the injured party than his actual loss. Even in such situations so long as the sum payable in the event of non-compliance with the contract is not extravagant, having regard to the range of losses that it could reasonably be anticipated it would have to cover at the time the contract was made, it can still be a genuine pre-estimate of the loss that would be suffered and so a perfectly valid liquidated damage provision. The use in argument of unlikely illustrations should therefore not assist a party to defeat a provision as to liquidated damages …

A difficulty can arise where the range of possible loss is broad. Where it should be obvious that, in relation to part of the range, the liquidated damages are totally out of proportion to certain of the losses which may be incurred, the failure to make special provision for those losses may result in the 'liquidated damages' not being recoverable … However the court has to be careful not to set too stringent a standard and bear in mind that what the parties have agreed should normally be upheld. Any other approach will lead to undesirable uncertainty especially in commercial contracts.

In seeking to establish that the sum described in the Philips contract as liquidated damages was in fact a penalty, Philips has to surmount the strong inference to the contrary resulting from its agreement to make the payments as liquidated damages and the fact that it is not suggested in these proceedings that the sum claimed is excessive in relation to the actual loss suffered by the Government. The fact that the issue has to be determined objectively, judged at the date the contract was made, does not mean what actually happens subsequently is irrelevant. On the contrary, it can provide valuable evidence as to what could reasonably be expected to be the loss at the time the contract was made. Likewise the fact that two parties who should be well capable of protecting their respective commercial interests agreed the allegedly penal provision suggests that the formula for calculating liquidated damages is unlikely to be oppressive.

The Privy Council adopted a flexible (and some might say unpredictable) approach to assessing liquidated damages clauses. The court considered all of the circumstances of the case. On the facts of *Philips*, their Lordships were clearly influenced by the fact that this was a commercial contract, entered into by two parties who were well capable of protecting their respective commercial interests (cf. *Lansat Shipping Co Ltd v Glencore Grain BV* [2009] EWCA Civ 855). To establish that the clause was a penalty, the plaintiffs would have had to have shown that the stipulated sum was extravagant and out of all proportion to the loss likely to be sustained. It was not enough merely to show that the clause could result in a larger sum being recovered than the loss actually suffered by the defendant. The court was unimpressed by such hypothetical illustrations. It was, however, willing to consider subsequent events as evidence of what could reasonably be expected to be the loss at the time the contract was agreed.

The distinction between liquidated damages and penalties was subsequently considered by the High Court in *Alfred McAlpine Capital Projects Ltd v Tilebox Ltd.*

***Alfred McAlpine Capital Projects Ltd v Tilebox Ltd* [2005] EWHC 281 (TCC)**

Facts: Tilebox, a property developer, entered into a building contract with McAlpine. The contract contained a clause which provided that £45,000 per week would be payable if completion of the project was delayed. In fact, completion was delayed by many months and McAlpine claimed that the clause was a penalty and therefore invalid.

Held: It was held that the clause was a valid liquidated damages clause.

Jackson J: Let me … make four general observations, which are pertinent to the issues in the present case.

1. There seem to be two strands in the authorities. In some cases judges consider whether there is an unconscionable or extravagant disproportion between the damages stipulated in the contract and the true amount of damages likely to be suffered. In other cases the courts consider whether the level of damages stipulated was reasonable. Mr Darling submits, and I accept, that these two strands can be reconciled. In my view, a pre-estimate of damages does not have to be right in order to be reasonable. There must be a substantial discrepancy between the level of damages stipulated in the contract and the level of damages which is likely to be suffered before it can be said that the agreed pre-estimate is unreasonable.
2. Although many authorities use or echo the phrase 'genuine pre-estimate', the test does not turn upon the genuineness or honesty of the party or parties who made the pre-estimate. The test is primarily an objective one, even though the court has some regard to the thought processes of the parties at the time of contracting.
3. Because the rule about penalties is an anomaly within the law of contract, the courts are predisposed, where possible, to uphold contractual terms which fix the level of damages for breach. This predisposition is even stronger in the case of commercial contracts freely entered into between parties of comparable bargaining power.
4. Looking at the bundle of authorities provided in this case, I note only four cases where the relevant clause has been struck down as a penalty. These are *Commissioner of Public Works v Hills* [1906] AC 368, *Bridge v Campbell Discount Co Ltd* [1962] AC 600, *Workers Trust and Merchant Bank Ltd v Dojap Investments Ltd* [1993] AC 573, and *Ariston SRL v Charly Records* (Court of Appeal 13th March 1990). In each of these four cases there was, in fact, a very wide gulf between (a) the level of damages likely to be suffered, and (b) the level of damages stipulated in the contract.

Once again the court emphasised that it was committed to upholding liquidated damages clauses, especially when the clause was agreed at arm's length between commercial parties. Jackson J held that the sum of £45,000 was 'at or slightly above the top of the range of possible weekly losses', but that the difference was not nearly wide enough to make the clause a penalty. A substantial disparity would have been required.

Yet there were also indications from the Court of Appeal that a broader approach needs to be taken to the question of whether the clause amounts to a genuine pre-estimate of loss.

***Murray v Leisureplay* [2005] EWCA Civ 963; [2005] IRLR 946**

Facts: The appellant, Mr Murray, set up Murray Financial Corporation (later to become Leisureplay plc) in June 1988. He was appointed Chief Executive Director of the company on a service agreement which contained a 'golden parachute' clause (clause 17). This stated that Mr Murray was entitled to the payment of a year's gross salary in the event of his employment being terminated without one year's notice. On

7 May 2003, Mr Murray received a letter from Leisureplay purporting to terminate his employment with effect from 30 June 2003. The letter did not contain an offer of payment in accordance with the terms of the agreement. Mr Murray brought a claim for liquidated damages under the 'golden parachute' clause. At first instance, Bunton J held that the clause was unenforceable as a penalty. It exceeded the amount available under the common law, and was not a genuine pre-estimate of loss. Mr Murray appealed this decision.

Held: The Court of Appeal allowed Murray's appeal, holding that the clause was a genuine pre-estimate of loss.

Arden LJ:

54. ... [I]n my judgment, the following (with the explanation given below) constitutes a practical step by step guide as to the questions which the court should ask in a case like this:

i) To what breaches of contract does the contractual damages provision apply?

ii) What amount is payable on breach under that clause in the parties' agreement?

iii) What amount would be payable if a claim for damages for breach of contract was brought under common law?

iv) What were the parties' reasons for agreeing for the relevant clause?

v) Has the party who seeks to establish that the clause is a penalty shown that the amount payable under the clause was imposed *in terrorem*, or that it does not constitute a genuine pre-estimate of loss for the purposes of the *Dunlop* case, and, if he has shown the latter, is there some other reason which justifies the discrepancy between i) and ii) above? ...

69. The burden of showing that a clause for the payment of damages on breach is a penalty clause is on the party who seeks to escape liability under it, not on the party who seeks to enforce it ...

70. The judge considered that the deciding issue was the absence of an allowance for the failure to mitigate. Any allowance, however, which the parties could have made would of necessity have been rough and ready. The judge was also concerned by the lack of any evidence as to any independent review of the clause by the other directors. As against that, however, there was no concealment of the terms from the board, who did indeed approve them and MFC was advised by solicitors. Furthermore, and perhaps of more significance for the type of review that the court makes on a penalty issue, the term agreed was not out of line with market expectations. Particulars of the directors' service agreements had been included in the pathfinder prospectus issued by MFC's financial advisers, Peel Hunt. The particulars related to Mr Murray's agreement before the reduction of the period under clause 17 to one year, with three years only if there was an agreement to acquire (for example) an insurance company. The reaction of at least one investor was that the provision for three years was excessive. No objection was taken to the provisions disclosed for other directors, providing for one year's gross salary alone. The clause in the agreement was then amended, and the offering of shares and admission to trading on the Alternative Investment Market, was successfully achieved. The inference to be drawn from this sequence of events in my judgment is that the clause as finally agreed did not cut across market expectations ...

71. The next point is that the agreement contains some fierce restrictions on competition. During the period of the agreement, Mr Murray was only due to work for MFC for three days a week. Nonetheless, as clause 12 of the agreement set out above shows, Mr Murray could not after termination of his agreement engage for one year in any business which competed with MFC. The type of business was restricted to the business of acquiring building societies and other financial institutions etc 'being activities of a kind with which [Mr Murray] was concerned to a material extent during the period of one year prior to termination of his contract' ... [T]he restrictions which Mr Murray undertook to observe on termination of his contract were important and significant. He had set out to make his name in business through the acquisition of building societies and so the restriction could result in his not being able to pursue his business plans during the year following termination, leading to diminished earnings after that year was up. If MFC wanted a restriction of this kind, it would not be unreasonable for Mr Murray to demand some recompense …

74. There are other relevant points. Clause 17 gave MFC the advantage that if it wanted to dismiss Mr Murray it could effect a clean break and know the measure of its financial exposure without what might well be damaging publicity and lengthy litigation. If MFC wanted to terminate the agreement, it would no doubt be because Mr Murray's continued connection with MFC was damaging to MFC. In those circumstances as a commercial matter it might well want to end the relationship swiftly and without the glare of publicity. Damages for breach of an employment contract can be difficult to determine in advance because of the difficulty of knowing what alternative employment might be available. The negotiation of clause 17 achieves the further advantage of avoiding spending management time and money on lawyers' fees to work such damages out …

76. In the circumstances, I have come to a different conclusion from the judge. On the facts of this case, it is not shown that the parties could not reasonably have come to the view that clause 17 was a genuine pre-estimate of damage or that it was not otherwise justifiable. MFC was of course the contract-breaker. In the considerations referred to above, I have taken into account the disadvantages to it of wrongful termination without a pre-determined damages clause. I do not consider that the court is precluded from taking such matters into account. To do so is consistent with freedom of contract, which the doctrine of penalties has so far as possible to respect. Such considerations may help explain why a party may wish to take on an obligation which (without that explanation) might be considered to be sufficiently onerous to be a penalty within paragraph a) of Lord Dunedin's guidance. Such considerations may indeed be best described as justification for the clause said to be a penalty, rather than elements of a genuine pre-estimate of the damage. In my formulation of the steps above, I do not intend to exclude such considerations or the possibility that a clause could be justified on this sort of ground alone.

Clarke LJ:

105. I have had the benefit of reading the judgments of Arden LJ and Buxton LJJ in draft. I agree with them that the appeal on the penalty issue should be allowed. In so far as there is a difference of approach between them, I prefer the broader approach of Buxton LJ.

Buxton LJ:

113. The approach that should be applied at trial would be in more general terms than that suggested by my Lady … that always requires a comparison between the liquidated and the common law damages to see if the comparison discloses a discrepancy; and then requires that discrepancy to be justified as a genuine pre-estimate of damages, or by some other form of justification.

114. I venture to disagree with that approach because it introduces a rigid and inflexible element into what should be a broad and general question. It is also inconsistent with warnings by judges of high authority that, at least in connexion with commercial contracts, great caution should be exercised before striking down a clause as penal; and with the tests that they have postulated to that end. My Lady has cited in her paragraph 66 the observations of Diplock LJ in *Robophone v Blank* [1966] 1 WLR 1428 at p 1447. I would add the well-known passage of Lord Woolf in *Philips Hong Kong v A-G of Hong Kong* (1993) 61 BLR 49 at pp 58–59:

> 'Except possibly in the case of situations where one of the parties to the contract is able to dominate the other as to the choice of the terms of a contract, it will normally be insufficient to establish that a provision is objectionably penal to identify situations where the application of

> the provision could result in a larger sum being recovered by the injured party than his actual loss. Even in such situations so long as the sum payable in the event of non-compliance with the contract is not extravagant, having regard to the range of losses that it could reasonably be anticipated it would have to cover at the time the contract was made, it can still be a genuine pre-estimate of the loss that would be suffered and so a perfectly valid liquidated damages provision'.

And exclusive concentration on the factual difference between the liquidated and the contractual damages overlooks a principal test formulated by Lord Dunedin to identify a penalty, [1915] AC at p 87, that:

> 'It will be held to be a penalty if the sum stipulated for is extravagant and unconscionable in amount in comparison with the greatest loss that could conceivably be proved to have followed from the breach'.

115. Neither the literal wording of that test nor the spirit of it applies here. Mr Murray's terms were generous, but they were not unconscionable. As to the absence of any requirement of mitigation in clause 17.1, to which as we have seen the judge attached determinative importance, two comments have to be made. First, it must have been difficult to say with confidence at the time of entering into the contract what might happen to Mr Murray were he to be dismissed: provisions protecting an employee in the case of wrongful termination may take the form that they do because such an event can damage his future employability, at least in the short term. Second, in order to meet this criticism a pre-estimate of damages clause would have to be drafted to encompass not only the fact of mitigation in terms of income from other sources but also the duty to seek such mitigation. Such a clause would directly invite disputes about the reasonableness of Mr Murray's behaviour after termination, of the kind that clauses stipulating the amount of compensation are precisely designed to avoid ...

116. It is therefore necessary to stand back and look at the reality of this agreement. Although I agree that evidence about it is sparse, I am prepared to take judicial notice of the fact that an entrepreneurial company such as MFC, promoting a product conceived by one man, will often place a high value upon retaining the services, and the loyalty and attention, of that one man as its chief executive: to the extent of including in his 'package' generous reassurance against the eventuality of dismissal. That such reassurance exceeds the likely amount of contractual damages on dismissal does not render the terms penal unless the party seeking to avoid the terms can demonstrate that they meet the test of extravagance posited by Lord Dunedin and by Lord Woolf. I regard that as a comparatively broad and simple question, that will not normally call for detailed analysis of the contractual background. Applying that test, which I accept differs from that adopted by my Lady, I would accordingly allow the appeal on the penalty issue.

The majority in the Court of Appeal (Buxton and Clarke LJJ) rejected Arden LJ's step-by-step analysis. In their view, her emphasis on the comparison between the liquidated sum and the amount payable as common law damages introduced a 'rigid and inflexible element into what should be a broad and general question' (at [114]). They preferred the test set out by Lord Dunedin in Dunlop: 'It will be held to be a penalty if the sum stipulated for is extravagant and unconscionable in amount in comparison with the greatest loss that could conceivably be proved to have followed from the breach.'

The decision in *Murray* is of particular interest because of the emphasis placed by their Lordships on various contextual factors, most notably the intentions of the parties. Arden LJ thought that the discrepancy between the amount payable under the clause and the amount payable in a claim for damages was justifiable on the ground that the clause was part of an agreement that placed onerous restrictions on Mr Murray and enabled Leisureplay to dismiss him without the damaging publicity and cost of lengthy litigation (at [71] and [74]). Buxton LJ also alluded to contextual factors including the benefit of such clauses to companies seeking to attract key employees (at [116]). This is all in stark contrast to the traditional mechanical flavour of the *Dunlop Pneumatic Tyre* test (cf. also *Azimut-Benetti SPA v Healy* [2010] EWHC 2234 (Comm)).

15.2.5.3 Recasting the penalty rule

In *Makdessi v Cavendish Square Holdings BV* and *ParkingEye Ltd v Beavis* [2015] UKSC 67 the Supreme Court considered, in detail, the operation of the penalty rule, the first time the Supreme Court (or House of Lords) had done so for a century (see [1] *per* Lord Neuberger and Lord Sumption). In so doing, the Supreme Court resisted calls for both the abolition and extension of the penalty rule in relation to contracts.

***Makdessi v Cavendish Square Holdings BV; ParkingEye Ltd v Beavis* [2015] UKSC 67**

Facts: There were two conjoined appeals. The first case (*Makdessi*) concerned a share purchase contract in respect of a marketing company between commercial parties. Under the agreement the seller agreed not to compete with the marketing company. The contract provided that if the non-competition stipulation was breached (a) no further instalments would be payable under the contract (clause 5.1) and (b) the buyer would have an option to buy the seller's remaining shares at a reduced price (as it would disregard goodwill, clause 5.6). The seller breached the non-competition stipulation and the buyer sought to exercise clauses 5.1 and 5.6. The seller claimed that these clauses were unenforceable on the ground that they were penalty clauses. This claim was rejected at first instance but accepted by the Court of Appeal. The second case (*ParkingEye*) involved a car park where parking was free for the first two hours but, if that period was exceeded, a fee of £85 was payable. The defendant parked his car for almost three hours and subsequently refused to pay the £85 fee on the ground that it was a penalty clause. At first instance and in the Court of Appeal the defendant's argument failed.

Held: The law relating to penalty clauses needed to be recast. More specifically a penalty clause is a secondary obligation which bears no proportion to the legitimate interest, if any, which the innocent party has in the enforcement of the primary obligation(s). Applying this to the facts of *Makdessi* the Supreme Court held that relevant clauses were not penal. The buyer had a legitimate interest in the compliance with non-competition stipulations which were crucial to the health of the company. Moreover both parties were experienced commercial parties with the benefit of legal advice. As regards *ParkingEye* the Supreme Court also held that the fee was not penal in nature. Although it did not represent the loss which the claimant would suffer as a result of the defendant staying beyond two hours, the claimant had a legitimate interest in the efficient functioning of the car park and was comparable to charges in the locality.

Lord Neuberger and Lord Sumption (with whom Lord Carnwath agreed):

In what circumstances is the penalty rule engaged?

12 In England, it has always been considered that a provision could not be a penalty unless it provided an exorbitant alternative to common law damages. This meant that it had to be a provision operating upon a breach of contract. In *Moss Empires Ltd v Olympia (Liverpool) Ltd* [1939] AC 544, this was taken for granted by Lord Atkin (p 551) and Lord Porter (p 558). As a matter of authority the question is settled in England by the decision of the House of Lords in *Export Credits Guarantee Department v Universal Oil Products Co* [1983] 1 WLR 399 ('ECGD'). Lord Roskill, with whom the rest of the committee agreed, said at p 403:

> '[P]erhaps the main purpose, of the law relating to penalty clauses is to prevent a plaintiff recovering a sum of money in respect of a breach of contract committed by a defendant which bears little or no relationship to the loss actually suffered by the plaintiff as a result of the breach by the defendant. But it is not and never has been for the courts to relieve a party from the

consequences of what may in the event prove to be an onerous or possibly even a commercially imprudent bargain'.

As Lord Hodge points out in his judgment, the Scottish authorities are to the same effect.

13 This principle is worth restating at the outset of any analysis of the penalty rule, because it explains much about the way in which it has developed. There is a fundamental difference between a jurisdiction to review the fairness of a contractual obligation and a jurisdiction to regulate the remedy for its breach. Leaving aside challenges going to the reality of consent, such as those based on fraud, duress or undue influence, the courts do not review the fairness of men's bargains either at law or in equity. The penalty rule regulates only the remedies available for breach of a party's primary obligations, not the primary obligations themselves. This was not a new concept in 1983, when ECGD was decided. It had been the foundation of the equitable jurisdiction, which depended on the treatment of penal defeasible bonds as secondary obligations or, as Lord Thurlow LC put it in 1783 in *Sloman* as 'collateral' or 'accessional' to the primary obligation. And it provided the whole basis of the classic distinction made at law between a penalty and a genuine pre-estimate of loss, the former being essentially a way of punishing the contract-breaker rather than compensating the innocent party for his breach. We shall return to that distinction below.

14 This means that in some cases the application of the penalty rule may depend on how the relevant obligation is framed in the instrument, ie whether as a conditional primary obligation or a secondary obligation providing a contractual alternative to damages at law. Thus, where a contract contains an obligation on one party to perform an act, and also provides that, if he does not perform it, he will pay the other party a specified sum of money, the obligation to pay the specified sum is a secondary obligation which is capable of being a penalty; but if the contract does not impose (expressly or impliedly) an obligation to perform the act, but simply provides that, if one party does not perform, he will pay the other party a specified sum, the obligation to pay the specified sum is a conditional primary obligation and cannot be a penalty.

15 However, the capricious consequences of this state of affairs are mitigated by the fact that, as the equitable jurisdiction shows, the classification of terms for the purpose of the penalty rule depends on the substance of the term and not on its form or on the label which the parties have chosen to attach to it. As Lord Radcliffe said in *Campbell Discount Co Ltd v Bridge* [1962] AC 600, 622, '[t]he intention of the parties themselves', by which he clearly meant the intention as expressed in the agreement, 'is never conclusive and may be overruled or ignored if the court considers that even its clear expression does not represent 'the real nature of the transaction' or what 'in truth' it is taken to be' (and cf. per Lord Templeman in *Street v Mountford* [1985] AC 809, 819). This aspect of the equitable jurisdiction was inherited by the courts of common law, and has been firmly established since the earliest common law cases.

16 Payment of a sum of money is the classic obligation under a penalty clause and, in almost every reported case involving a damages clause, the provision stipulates for the payment of money. However, it seems to us that there is no reason why an obligation to transfer assets (either for nothing or at an undervalue) should not be capable of constituting a penalty. While the penalty rule may be somewhat artificial, it would heighten its artificiality to no evident purpose if it were otherwise. Similarly, the fact that a sum is paid over by one party to the other party as a deposit, in the sense of some sort of surety for the first party's contractual performance, does not prevent the sum being a penalty, if the second party in due course forfeits the deposit in accordance with the contractual terms, following the first party's breach of contract – see the Privy Council decisions in *Public Works Comr v Hills* [1906] AC 368, 375–376, and *Workers Trust & Merchant Bank Ltd v Dojap Investments Ltd* [1993] AC 573. By contrast, in *Else* (1982) at p 146, Hoffmann LJ, citing *Stockloser v Johnson* [1954] 1 QB 476 in support, said that, unlike a case where 'money has been deposited as security for due performance of [a] party's obligation', 'retention of instalments which have been paid under contract so as to become the absolute property of the vendor does not fall within the penalty rule', although, he added that it was 'subject ... to the jurisdiction for relief against forfeiture'.

17 The relationship between penalty clauses and forfeiture clauses is not entirely easy. Given that they had the same origin in equity, but that the law on penalties was then developed through common law while the law on forfeitures was not, this is unsurprising. Some things appear to be clear. Where a proprietary interest or a 'proprietary or possessory right' (such as a patent or a lease) is granted or transferred subject to revocation or determination on breach, the clause providing for determination or revocation is a forfeiture and cannot be a penalty, and, while it is enforceable, relief from forfeiture may be granted: see *BICC plc v Burndy Corpn* [1985] Ch 232, 246–247 and 252 (Dillon LJ) and *The 'Scaptrade'*, pp 701–703, (Lord Diplock). But this does not mean that relief from forfeiture is unavailable in cases not involving land – see *Cukurova Finance International Ltd v Alfa Telecom Turkey Ltd (No 2)* [2013] UKPC 2, [2015] 2 WLR 875, especially at paras 92–97, and the cases cited there.

18 What is less clear is whether a provision is capable of being both a penalty clause and a forfeiture clause. It is inappropriate to consider that issue in any detail in this judgment, as we have heard very little argument on forfeitures – unsurprisingly because in neither appeal has it been alleged that any provision in issue is a forfeiture from which relief could be granted. But it is right to mention the possibility that, in some circumstances, a provision could, at least potentially, be a penalty clause as well as a forfeiture clause. We see the force of the arguments to that effect advanced by Lord Mance and Lord Hodge in their judgments.

What makes a contractual provision penal?

19 As we have already observed, until relatively recently this question was answered almost entirely by reference to straightforward liquidated damages clauses. It was in that context that the House of Lords sought to restate the law in two seminal decisions at the beginning of the 20th century, *Clydebank* in 1904 and *Dunlop* in 1915.

20 *Clydebank* was a Scottish appeal about a shipbuilding contract with a provision (described as a 'penalty') for the payment of £500 per week for delayed delivery. The provision was held to be a valid liquidated damages clause, not a penalty. Lord Halsbury (p 10) said that the distinction between the two depended on:

> 'whether it is, what I think gave the jurisdiction to the courts in both countries to interfere at all in an agreement between the parties, unconscionable and extravagant, and one which no court ought to allow to be enforced'

Lord Halsbury declined to lay down any 'abstract rule' for determining what was unconscionable or extravagant, saying only that it must depend on 'the nature of the transaction – the thing to be done, the loss likely to accrue to the person who is endeavouring to enforce the performance of the contract, and so forth'. Lord Halsbury's formulation has proved influential, and the two other members of the Appellate Committee both delivered concurring judgments agreeing with it. It is, however, worth drawing attention to an observation of Lord Robertson (pp 19–20) which points to the principle underlying the contrasting expressions 'liquidated damages' and 'penalty':

> 'Now, all such agreements, whether the thing be called penalty or be called liquidate damage, are in intention and effect what Professor Bell calls 'instruments of restraint', and in that sense penal. But the clear presence of this does not in the least degree invalidate the stipulation. The question remains, had the respondents no interest to protect by that clause, or was that interest palpably incommensurate with the sums agreed on? It seems to me that to put this question, in the present instance, is to answer it'.

21 *Dunlop* arose out of a contract for the supply of tyres, covers and tubes by a manufacturer to a garage. The contract contained a number of terms designed to protect the manufacturer's brand, including prohibitions on tampering with the marks, restrictions on the unauthorised export or exhibition of the goods, and on resales to unapproved persons. There was also a resale price maintenance clause, which would now be unlawful but was a legitimate restriction of competition according to the notions prevailing in 1914. It was this clause which the purchaser had broken. The contract provided for the payment of £5 for every tyre, cover or tube sold in breach of any provision of the agreement. Once again, the provision was held to be a valid liquidated damages clause. In his speech, Lord Dunedin formulated four tests 'which, if applicable to the case under consideration, may prove helpful, or even conclusive' (p 87). They were (a) that the provision would be penal if 'the sum stipulated for is extravagant and unconscionable in amount in comparison with the greatest loss that could conceivably be proved to have followed from the breach'; (b) that the provision would be penal if the breach consisted only in the non-payment of money and it provided for the payment of a larger sum; (c) that there was 'a presumption (but no more)' that it would be penal if it was payable in a number of events of varying gravity; and (d) that it would not be treated as penal by reason only of the impossibility of precisely pre-estimating the true loss.

22 Lord Dunedin's speech in *Dunlop* achieved the status of a quasi-statutory code in the subsequent case law. Some of the many decisions on the validity of damages clauses are little more than a detailed exegesis or application of his four tests with a view to discovering whether the clause in issue can be brought within one or more of them. In our view, this is unfortunate. In the first place, Lord Dunedin proposed his four tests not as rules but only as considerations which might prove helpful or even conclusive 'if applicable to the case under consideration'. He did not suggest that they were applicable to every case in which the law of penalties was engaged. Second, as Lord Dunedin himself acknowledged, the essential question was whether the clause impugned was 'unconscionable' or 'extravagant'. The four tests are a useful tool for deciding whether these expressions can properly be applied to simple damages clauses in standard contracts. But they are not easily applied to more complex cases. To deal with those, it is necessary to consider the rationale of the penalty rule at a more fundamental level. What is it that makes a provision for the consequences of breach 'unconscionable'? And by comparison with what is a penalty clause said to be 'extravagant'? Third, none of the other three Law Lords expressly agreed with Lord Dunedin's reasoning, and the four tests do not all feature in any of their speeches. Indeed, it appears that, in his analysis at pp 101–102, Lord Parmoor may have taken a more restrictive view of what constituted a penalty than did Lord Dunedin. More generally, the other members of the Appellate Committee gave their own reasons for concurring in the result, and they also repay consideration. For present purposes, the most instructive is that of Lord Atkinson, who approached the matter on an altogether broader basis.

23 Lord Atkinson pointed (pp 90–91) to the critical importance to *Dunlop* of the protection of their brand, reputation and goodwill, and their authorised distribution network. Against this background, he observed (pp 91–92):

> 'It has been urged that as the sum of £5 becomes payable on the sale of even one tube at a shilling less than the listed price, and as it was impossible that the appellant company should lose that sum on such a transaction, the sum fixed must be a penalty. In the sense of direct and immediate loss the appellants lose nothing by such a sale. It is the agent or dealer who loses by selling at a price less than that at which he buys, but the appellants have to look at their trade in globo, and to prevent the setting up, in reference to all their goods anywhere and everywhere, a system of injurious undercutting. The object of the appellants in making this agreement, if the substance and reality of the thing and the real nature of the transaction be looked at, would appear to be a single one, namely, to prevent the disorganization of their trading system and the consequent injury to their trade in many directions. The means of effecting this is by keeping up their price to the public to the level of their price list, this last

> being secured by contracting that a sum of £5 shall be paid for every one of the three classes of articles named sold or offered for sale at prices below those named on the list. The very fact that this sum is to be paid if a tyre cover or tube be merely offered for sale, though not sold, shows that it was the consequential injury to their trade due to undercutting that they had in view. They had an obvious interest to prevent this undercutting, and on the evidence it would appear to me impossible to say that that interest was incommensurate with the sum agreed to be paid'.

Lord Atkinson went on to draw an analogy, which has particular resonance in the Cavendish appeal, with a clause dealing with damages for breach of a restrictive covenant on the canvassing of business by a former employee. In this context, he said (pp 92–93):

> 'It is, I think, quite misleading to concentrate one's attention upon the particular act or acts by which, in such cases as this, the rivalry in trade is set up, and the repute acquired by the former employee that he works cheaper and charges less than his old master, and to lose sight of the risk to the latter that old customers, once tempted to leave him, may never return to deal with him, or that business that might otherwise have come to him may be captured by his rival. The consequential injuries to the trader's business arising from each breach by the employee of his covenant cannot be measured by the direct loss in a monetary point of view on the particular transaction constituting the breach'.

Lord Atkinson was making substantially the same point as Lord Robertson had made in *Clydebank*. The question was: what was the nature and extent of the innocent party's interest in the performance of the relevant obligation. That interest was not necessarily limited to the mere recovery of compensation for the breach. Lord Atkinson considered that the underlying purpose of the resale price maintenance clause gave Dunlop a wider interest in enforcing the damages clause than pecuniary compensation. £5 per item was not incommensurate with that interest even if it was incommensurate with the loss occasioned by the wrongful sale of a single item.

24 Although the other members of the Appellate Committee did not express themselves in the same terms as Lord Atkinson, their approach was entirely consistent with his. Lord Parker at p 97 said that 'whether the sum agreed to be paid on the breach is really a penalty must depend on the circumstances of each particular case', and at p 99, echoing Lord Atkinson's fuller treatment of the point, as just set out, he described the damage which would result from any breach as '[consisting] in the disturbance or derangement of the system of distribution by means of which [Dunlop's] goods reach the ultimate consumer'. In their speeches, Lord Dunedin (p 87), Lord Parker (p 98) and Lord Parmoor (p 103) ultimately were content to rest their decision that the £5 was not a penalty on the ground that an exact pre-estimate of loss was impossible, whereas, in the passages quoted above, Lord Atkinson analysed why that was so. It seems clear that the actual result of the case was strongly influenced by Lord Atkinson's reasoning. The clause was upheld although, on the face of it, it failed all but the last of Lord Dunedin's tests. The £5 per item applied to breaches of very variable significance and it was impossible to relate the loss attributable to the sale of that item. It was justifiable only by reference to the wider interests identified by Lord Atkinson.

25 The great majority of cases decided in England since Dunlop have concerned more or less standard damages clauses in consumer contracts, and Lord Dunedin's four tests have proved perfectly adequate for dealing with those. More recently, however, the courts have returned to the possibility of a broader test in less straightforward cases, in the context of the supposed 'commercial justification' for clauses which might otherwise be regarded as penal. An early example is the decision of the House of Lords in *The 'Scaptrade'*, where at p 702, Lord Diplock, with whom the rest of the Appellate Committee agreed, observed that a right to withdraw a time-chartered vessel for non-payment of advance hire was not a penalty because its commercial purpose was to create a fund from which the cost of providing the chartered service could be funded.

26 In *Lordsvale Finance plc v Bank of Zambia* [1996] QB 752, Colman J was concerned with a common form provision in a syndicated loan agreement for interest to be payable at a higher rate during any period when the borrower was in default. There was authority that such provisions were penal: *Lady Holles v Wyse* (1693) 2 Vern 289; *Strode v Parker* (1694) 2 Vern 316, *Wallingford v Mutual Society* (1880) 5 App Cas 685, 702 (Lord Hatherley). But Colman J held that the clause was valid because its predominant purpose was not to deter default but to reflect the greater credit risk associated with a borrower in default. At pp 763–764, he observed that a provision for the payment of money upon breach could not be categorised as a penalty simply because it was not a genuine pre-estimate of damages, saying that there would seem to be:

> 'no reason in principle why a contractual provision the effect of which was to increase the consideration payable under an executory contract upon the happening of a default should be struck down as a penalty if the increase could in the circumstances be explained as commercially justifiable, provided always that its dominant purpose was not to deter the other party from breach'.

27 Colman J's approach was approved by Mance LJ, delivering the leading judgment in the Court of Appeal in *Cine Bes Filmcilik ve Yapimcilik v United International Pictures* [2004] 1 CLC 401, para 13. A similar view was taken by Arden LJ in *Murray v Leisureplay plc* [2005] IRLR 946, para 54, where she posed the question:

> 'Has the party who seeks to establish that the clause is a penalty shown that the amount payable under the clause was imposed *in terrorem*, or that it does not constitute a genuine pre-estimate of loss for the purposes of the Dunlop case, and, *if he has shown the latter, is there some other reason which justifies the discrepancy between [the amount payable under the clause and the amount payable by way of damages in common law]?*' (emphasis added).

She considered that the clause in question had advantages for both sides, and pointed out that no evidence had been adduced to show that the clause lacked commercial justification: see paras 70–76. But Buxton LJ put the matter on a wider basis for which Clarke LJ (para 105) expressed a preference. He referred to the speech of Lord Atkinson in Dunlop and suggested that the ratio of the actual decision in that case had been that 'an explanation of the clause in commercial rather than deterrent terms was available'. All three members of the court endorsed the approach of Colman J in *Lordsvale* and Mance LJ in *Cine Bes*.

28 Colman J in *Lordsvale* and Arden LJ in *Murray* were inclined to rationalise the introduction of commercial justification as part of the test, by treating it as evidence that the impugned clause was not intended to deter. Later decisions in which a commercial rationale has been held inconsistent with the application of the penalty rule, have tended to follow that approach: see, for example, *Euro London Appointments Ltd v Claessens International Ltd* [2006] 2 Lloyd's Rep 436, *General Trading Company (Holdings) Ltd v Richmond Corpn Ltd* [2008] 2 Lloyd's Rep 475. It had the advantage of enabling them to reconcile the concept of commercial justification with Lord Dunedin's four tests. But we have some misgivings about it. The assumption that a provision cannot have a deterrent purpose if there is a commercial justification, seems to us to be questionable. By the same token, we agree with Lord Radcliffe's observations in *Campbell Discount* at p 622, where he said:

> '... I do not myself think that it helps to identify a penalty, to describe it as in the nature of a threat 'to be enforced in terrorem' (to use Lord Halsbury's phrase in *Elphinstone v Monkland Iron & Coal Co Ltd* (1886) 11 App Cas 332, 348). I do not find that that description adds anything of substance to the idea conveyed by the word 'penalty' itself, and it obscures the fact that

> penalties may quite readily be undertaken by parties who are not in the least terrorised by the prospect of having to pay them and yet are, as I understand it, entitled to claim the protection of the court when they are called upon to make good their promises'.

Moreover, the penal character of a clause depends on its purpose, which is ordinarily an inference from its effect. As we have already explained, this is a question of construction, to which evidence of the commercial background is of course relevant in the ordinary way. But, for the same reason, the answer cannot depend on evidence of actual intention: see *Chartbrook Ltd v Persimmon Homes Ltd* [2009] AC 1101, paras 28–47 (Lord Hoffmann). However, while we have misgivings about some aspects of their reasoning, these aspects are peripheral to the essential point which Colman J and Buxton LJ were making, and we consider that their emphasis on justification provides a valuable insight into the real basis of the penalty rule. It is the same insight as that of Lord Robertson in Clydebank and Lord Atkinson in *Dunlop*. A damages clause may properly be justified by some other consideration than the desire to recover compensation for a breach. This must depend on whether the innocent party has a legitimate interest in performance extending beyond the prospect of pecuniary compensation flowing directly from the breach in question.

29 The availability of remedies for a breach of duty is not simply a question of providing a financial substitute for performance. It engages broader social and economic considerations, one of which is that the law will not generally make a remedy available to a party, the adverse impact of which on the defaulter significantly exceeds any legitimate interest of the innocent party. In the famous case of *White & Carter (Councils) Ltd v McGregor* [1962] AC 413, Lord Reid observed, at p 431:

> 'It may well be that, if it can be shown that a person has no legitimate interest, financial or otherwise, in performing the contract rather than claiming damages, he ought not to be allowed to saddle the other party with an additional burden with no benefit to himself. If a party has no interest to enforce a stipulation, he cannot in general enforce it: so it might be said that, if a party has no interest to insist on a particular remedy, he ought not to be allowed to insist on it. And, just as a party is not allowed to enforce a penalty, so he ought not to be allowed to penalise the other party by taking one course when another is equally advantageous to him ... Here the respondent did not set out to prove that the appellants had no legitimate interest in completing the contract and claiming the contract price rather than claiming damages ... Parliament has on many occasions relieved parties from certain kinds of improvident or oppressive contracts, but the common law can only do that in very limited circumstances'.

In *White & Carter* the innocent party was entitled to ignore the repudiation of the contract-breaker and proceed to perform, claiming his remuneration in debt rather than limiting himself to damages, notwithstanding that this course might be a great deal more expensive for the contract-breaker. This, according to Lord Reid (p 431), was because the contract-breaker 'did not set out to prove that the appellants had no legitimate interest in completing the contract and claiming the contract price rather than claiming damages'.

30 More generally, the attitude of the courts, reflecting that of the Court of Chancery, is that specific performance of contractual obligations should ordinarily be refused where damages would be an adequate remedy. This is because the minimum condition for an order of specific performance is that the innocent party should have a legitimate interest extending beyond pecuniary compensation for the breach. The paradigm case is the purchase of land or certain chattels such as ships, which the law recognises as unique. Because of their uniqueness the purchaser's interest extends beyond the mere award of damages as a substitute for performance. As Lord Hoffmann put it in addressing a very similar issue 'the purpose of the law of contract is not to punish wrongdoing but to satisfy the expectations of the party entitled to performance': *Co-operative Insurance Society Ltd v Argyll Stores (Holdings) Ltd* [1998] AC 1, 15.

31 In our opinion, the law relating to penalties has become the prisoner of artificial categorisation, itself the result of unsatisfactory distinctions: between a penalty and genuine pre-estimate of loss, and between a genuine pre-estimate of loss and a deterrent. These distinctions originate in an over-literal reading of Lord Dunedin's four tests and a tendency to treat them *as almost immutable rules of general application which exhaust the field*. In *Legione v Hateley* (1983) 152 CLR 406, 445, Mason and Deane JJ defined a penalty as follows:

> 'A penalty, as its name suggests, is in the nature of a punishment for non-observance of a contractual stipulation; it consists of the imposition of an additional or different liability upon breach of the contractual stipulation ...'

All definition is treacherous as applied to such a protean concept. This one can fairly be said to be too wide in the sense that it appears to be apt to cover many provisions which would not be penalties (for example most, if not all, forfeiture clauses). However, in so far as it refers to 'punishment' and 'an additional or different liability' as opposed to '*in terrorem*' and 'genuine pre-estimate of loss', this definition seems to us to get closer to the concept of a penalty than any other definition we have seen. The real question when a contractual provision is challenged as a penalty is whether it is penal, not whether it is a pre-estimate of loss. These are not natural opposites or mutually exclusive categories. A damages clause may be neither or both. The fact that the clause is not a pre-estimate of loss does not therefore, at any rate without more, mean that it is penal. To describe it as a deterrent (or, to use the Latin equivalent, *in terrorem*) does not add anything. A deterrent provision in a contract is simply one species of provision designed to influence the conduct of the party potentially affected. It is no different in this respect from a contractual inducement. Neither is it inherently penal or contrary to the policy of the law. The question whether it is enforceable should depend on whether the means by which the contracting party's conduct is to be influenced are 'unconscionable' or (which will usually amount to the same thing) 'extravagant' by reference to some norm.

32 The true test is whether the impugned provision is a secondary obligation which imposes a detriment on the contract-breaker out of all proportion to any legitimate interest of the innocent party in the enforcement of the primary obligation. The innocent party can have no proper interest in simply punishing the defaulter. His interest is in performance or in some appropriate alternative to performance. In the case of a straightforward damages clause, that interest will rarely extend beyond compensation for the breach, and we therefore expect that Lord Dunedin's four tests would usually be perfectly adequate to determine its validity. But compensation is not necessarily the only legitimate interest that the innocent party may have in the performance of the defaulter's primary obligations. This was recognised in the early days of the penalty rule, when it was still the creature of equity, and is reflected in Lord Macclesfield's observation in *Peachy* (quoted in para 5 above) about the application of the penalty rule to provisions which were 'never intended by way of compensation, for which equity would not relieve. It was reflected in the result in *Dunlop*. And it is recognised in the more recent decisions about commercial justification. And, as Lord Hodge shows, it is the principle underlying the Scottish authorities.

33 The penalty rule is an interference with freedom of contract. It undermines the certainty which parties are entitled to expect of the law. Diplock LJ was neither the first nor the last to observe that 'The court should not be astute to descry a 'penalty clause': *Robophone* at p 1447. As Lord Woolf said, speaking for the Privy Council in *Philips Hong Kong Ltd v Attorney General of Hong Kong* (1993) 61 BLR 41, 59, 'the court has to be careful not to set too stringent a standard and bear in mind that what the parties have agreed should normally be upheld'. not least because '[a]ny other approach will lead to undesirable uncertainty especially in commercial contracts'.

34 Although the penalty rule originates in the concern of the courts to prevent exploitation in an age when credit was scarce and borrowers were particularly vulnerable, the modern rule is substantive, not procedural. It does not normally depend for its operation on a finding that advantage was taken of one party. As Lord Wright MR observed in *Imperial Tobacco Company of Great Britain and Ireland v Parslay* [1936] 2 All ER 515, 523:

> 'A millionaire may enter into a contract in which he is to pay liquidated damages, or a poor man may enter into a similar contract with a millionaire, but in each case the question is exactly the same, namely, whether the sum stipulated as damages for the breach was exorbitant or extravagant . . .'

35 But for all that, the circumstances in which the contract was made are not entirely irrelevant. In a negotiated contract between properly advised parties of comparable bargaining power, the strong initial presumption must be that the parties themselves are the best judges of what is legitimate in a provision dealing with the consequences of breach. In that connection, it is worth noting that in *Philips Hong Kong* at pp 57–59, Lord Woolf specifically referred to the possibility of taking into account the fact that 'one of the parties to the contract is able to dominate the other as to the choice of the terms of a contract' when deciding whether a damages clause was a penalty. In doing so, he reflected the view expressed by Mason and Wilson JJ in *AMEV-UDC* at p 194 that the courts were thereby able to 'strike a balance between the competing interests of freedom of contract and protection of weak contracting parties' (citing Atiyah, *The Rise and Fall of Freedom of Contract* (1979), Chapter 22). However, Lord Woolf was rightly at pains to point out that this did not mean that the courts could thereby adopt 'some broader discretionary approach'. The notion that the bargaining position of the parties may be relevant is also supported by Lord Browne-Wilkinson giving the judgment of the Privy Council in *Workers Bank*. At p 580, he rejected the notion that 'the test of reasonableness [could] depend upon the practice of one class of vendor, which exercises considerable financial muscle' as it would allow such people 'to evade the law against penalties by adopting practices of their own'. In his judgment, he decided that, in contracts for sale of land, a clause providing for a forfeitable deposit of 10% of the purchase price was valid, although it was an anomalous exception to the penalty rule. However, he held that the clause providing for a forfeitable 25% deposit in that case was invalid because 'in Jamaica, the customary deposit has been 10%' and '[a] vendor who seeks to obtain a larger amount by way of forfeitable deposit must show special circumstances which justify such a deposit', which the appellant vendor in that case failed to do.

Lord Mance:

> '152 In my opinion, the development of the law indicated by the authorities discussed in paras 145 to 151 above is a sound one. It is most easily explained on the basis that the dichotomy between the compensatory and the penal is not exclusive. There may be interests beyond the compensatory which justify the imposition on a party in breach of an additional financial burden. The maintenance of a system of trade, which only functions if all trading partners adhere to it (*Dunlop*), may itself be viewed in this light; so can terms of settlement which provide on default for payment of costs which a party was prepared to forego if the settlement was honoured (*Cine Bes*); likewise, also the revision of financial terms to match circumstances disclosed or brought about by a breach (*Lordsvale* and other cases). What is necessary in each case is to consider, first, whether any (and if so what) legitimate business interest is served and protected by the clause, and, second, whether, assuming such an interest to exist, the provision made for the interest is nevertheless in the circumstances extravagant, exorbitant or unconscionable. In judging what is extravagant, exorbitant or unconscionable, I consider (despite contrary expressions of view) that the extent to which the parties were negotiating at arm's length on the basis of legal advice and had every opportunity to appreciate what they were agreeing must at least be a relevant factor.'

Lord Hodge:

> '255 I therefore conclude that the correct test for a penalty is whether the sum or remedy stipulated as a consequence of a breach of contract is exorbitant or unconscionable when regard is had to the innocent party's interest in the performance of the contract. Where the test is to be applied to a clause fixing the level of damages to be paid on breach, an extravagant disproportion between the stipulated sum and the highest level of damages that could possibly arise from the breach would amount to a penalty and thus be unenforceable. In other circumstances the contractual provision that applies on breach is measured against the interest of the innocent party which is protected by the contract and the court asks whether the remedy is exorbitant or unconscionable.'

Lord Toulson (dissenting in part):

> '293 On the essential nature of a penalty clause, I would highlight and endorse Lord Hodge's succinct statement at para 255 that 'the correct test for a penalty is whether the sum or remedy stipulated as a consequence of a breach of contract is exorbitant or unconscionable when regard is had to the innocent party's interest in the performance of the contract'. Parties and courts should focus on that test, bearing in mind a) that it is impossible to lay down abstract rules about what may or may not be 'extravagant or unconscionable', because it depends on the particular facts and circumstances established in the individual case (as Lord Halsbury said in the *Clydebank* case, [1905] AC 6, 10, and Lord Parmoor said in the *Dunlop* case, [1915] AC 79, 101), and b) that 'exorbitant or unconscionable' are strong words. I agree with Lord Mance (para 152) that the word 'unconscionable' in this context means much the same as 'extravagant'.

The Supreme Court in *Makdessi v Cavendish Square Holdings BV* and *ParkingEye Ltd v Beavis* reinforced a distinction between primary obligations (to which the penalty rule does not apply) and secondary obligations (to which the penalty rule does apply). See also *In re B (Children) (Removal from Jurisdiction: Enforcement of Contact Order)* [2015] EWCA Civ 1302 at [65] per MacFarlane LJ and cf. *Longulf Trading (UK) Limited v Niyazi Onen Gida San AS* [2019] EWHC 1573 (Comm) at [39]. Yet the distinction is not always straightforward as is illustrated by its application to the *Makdessi* case where the Supreme Court was clearly uneasy on whether clause 5.1 was a primary or secondary obligation:

> On the jurisdiction issue as applied to the facts in *Cavendish*, Lords Neuberger and Sumption, with whom Lord Carnwath agreed, held that despite the fact that it was activated by a breach, cl.5.1 was a substantive price adjustment clause. The clause did not involve a breach qua breach, and did not contain a secondary obligation; rather, 'in reality' the clause was one whereby the value of the primary obligation to pay the purchase price was reduced if an event took place, and that event just happened to be Mr Makdessi's failure to observe the restrictive covenants (at [74]). Lords Hodge, Clarke and Toulson recognised the 'strong argument' that cl.5.1 contained a substantive primary obligation, but preferred to keep an 'open mind' and alternatively analysed the clause as involving a secondary obligation (at [270], [291] and [292]). Lord Mance did not expressly engage with the issue. Accordingly, there was no clear majority on the proper classification of cl.5.1. Conversely, a majority interpreted cl.5.6 as containing a secondary obligation (at [183], [280], [291] and [292]; cf. [83]). Consequently, the clause was clearly reviewable. (Conte, C, 'The penalty rule revisited' (2016) 132 LQR 382, 384).

Similarly the anchoring of the test for a penalty clause to the vague concept of the legitimate interest of the innocent party may fuel further litigation:

> Respectful of the tradition of blatantly interfering with freedom of contract, it falls to the court to determine the legitimacy of the promisee's interest in performance, and the 'proportionality' of the means agreed for enforcing it. That Lord Reid's notorious qualification to *White & Carter (Councils) Ltd v McGregor* [1962] A.C. 413, 431, was cited (at [29]) as authority for this 'legitimate interest' inquiry provides but scant comfort. Even Homer sometimes nods and J.W. Carter points out that Lord Reid's dicta were tentative and 'uncharacteristically vague': (2012) 128 L.Q.R. 490, 491. We are further told (at [32]): 'The innocent party can have no proper interest in simply punishing the defaulter' – i.e. the aim must be to secure performance and not in inflicting punishment per se. But, even if we grant that regulation of contractual sado-masochism is a proper goal of public policy (*sed quaere*), is it a real problem? Rather (as Tony Weir observed about the 'disinterested malevolence' required in the tort of lawful means conspiracy), a contractual clause inserted purely to mete out punishment for punishment's sake must be *rara avis* indeed (cf. *Economic Torts* (Oxford 1997), 73). (Morgan, J, 'The penalty clause doctrine: unlovable but untouchable' (2016) 75 LQR 11, 12).

More recently in *CFL Finance Ltd v Jonathan Bass* [2019] EWHC 1839, Judge Briggs stated:

> '48. There is little guidance on what may constitute a legitimate interest, save that there can be no legitimate interest in punishing the defaulting party. The high interest rates that were imposed as a condition for lending to Lanza with very high defaulting rates were in keeping with (i) the nature of the lending that was urgent and very short term and (ii) the nature of the lender which was known as a lender of last resort. Such a lender is only approached in circumstances where the lending is for short term and a borrower is unable to obtain finance elsewhere. I infer that MG was unable to obtain finance for Lanza from other sources. The failure of MG to respond positively in repaying the debt due under his guarantee and submitting to the Tomlin Order as a result of a threat to issue an application for summary judgment many years later may go some way to legitimizing CFL's particular concern or interest in MG's performance. Although not expressly stated by MG, the argument must be that CFL had no such legitimate interest and therefore the high interest rates found in the secondary obligation contained in Clause 5 of the Contract were intended to punish MG. By accelerating payment and requiring compound interest, Clause 5 went beyond mere compensation for breach of operative clause 2 of the Contract. The full background and legitimacy issue has not been covered by the evidence, but in my judgment find that the observation made by Lord Hodge JSC in *Makdessi* [266] pushes the penalty argument below the threshold test of a serious and genuine dispute. This is because 'the extent of the disproportion is likely to depend on the bargaining power of the parties and their access to legal advice … the greater the equality of bargaining power, the greater the access to legal advice, the less likely it is that the clause will be held to be a penalty': Goode on Commercial Law 3.136. As I have mentioned Mr Kirk did not advance the penalty argument in oral submissions but has cited *Makdessi* to advance his case. There has been no submission that there was inequality of bargaining power. MG must accept that he had access to legal advice and was advised by skilled lawyers. In my judgment these factors lead me to conclude that it is not genuinely arguable that there is any disproportion between the parties, or that the Contract was not entered into with eyes wide open and on careful legal advice.
> 49. In reaching my conclusion I have in mind that 'the power to strike down a penalty clause is a blatant interference with freedom of contract and is designed for the sole purpose of providing relief against oppression for the party having to pay the stipulated sum. It has no place where there is no oppression': *Elsey v J.G. Collins Insurance Agencies Ltd* (1978) 83 D.L.R. (3rd) 1, 15. There is no obvious oppression where parties freely enter into a contract at arms-length following litigation and where the challenging party had the benefit of legal advice. This is sufficient to put pay to the argument insofar as it was advanced, but there is an additional reason why I find in favour of CFL on this issue.'

15.3 Specific relief

As noted at the beginning of this chapter, an award of damages is usually sufficient to put the claimant 'in a situation as beneficial to him as if the agreement were specifically performed' (*Harnett* v *Yielding* (1805) 2 Sch & Lef 549, 553). However, in certain situations damages will be inadequate for this purpose and the courts will need to consider whether an order of specific relief ought to be made.

In this section we will be examining two different forms of specific relief: specific performance and injunctions. An order of specific performance compels the defendant to perform his positive contractual obligations. An injunction restrains the defendant from acting in breach of his negative obligations. The sanction for failure to comply with either is that the person concerned will be in contempt of court and will face either a fine or possibly even imprisonment. Other forms of specific relief may also be available. For example, under s 19 of the Consumer Rights Act 2015 a consumer might have a right of repair or replacement in relation to defective goods, or under s 54 a consumer may have the right to request repeat performance in relation to services.

15.3.1 Specific performance

Specific performance has its roots in the courts' equitable jurisdiction to grant remedies to supplement the common law. As a result, the remedy is awarded at the discretion of the court and will only be available instead of damages when the court 'can by that means do more and complete justice' (*Wilson v Northampton and Banbury Junction Rwy Co* (1874) 9 Ch App 279, 284, *per* Lord Selbourne). The discretionary element in specific performance inevitably means that its availability is subject to a degree of uncertainty. Over the years, however, the courts have developed a number of rules about its use, and these mean that in most cases it will be fairly easy to predict whether or not an order is likely to be granted.

15.3.1.1 Adequacy of damages

The first rule is that specific performance will only be available in situations where compensatory damages are inadequate to do justice between the parties. This adequacy-of-damages test is, in various forms, long established and controversial. Professor Dawson once described it as, 'an unnecessary and irksome restriction of specific performance', which is applied in an 'arbitrary and irrational' way (Dawson, J., 'Specific Performance in France and Germany' (1959) 57 Mich LR 495, 532). This criticism may be true, but the test is generally considered to perform an invaluable role in restraining the use of coercive remedies that carry the threat of contempt proceedings. Moreover, in *Evans Marshall & Co Ltd v Bertola SA and Another* [1973] 1 WLR 349 at 379 Sachs LJ stated: 'The standard question in relation to the grant of an injunction, "Are damages an adequate remedy?", might perhaps, in the light of the authorities of recent years, be rewritten: "Is it just, in all the circumstances, that a plaintiff should be confined to his remedy in damages?"' Over the years, the courts have established a number of well-recognised situations in which damages are generally deemed to be inadequate.

15.3.1.1.1 No market substitute

If no market substitute for performance is available, damages may be deemed to be inadequate. This is the reason why contracts concerning land are specifically enforceable. The courts assume that land is unique and that no market substitute is available (*Adderley v Dixon* (1824) 1 Sim & St 607, 610, *per* Leach VC). On this basis, specific performance is available in respect of contracts for the sale of land, for the grant of an interest in land and even for the grant of a licence to occupy land (*Verroll v Great Yarmouth Borough Council* [1981] QB 202).

Contracts for the sale of goods are generally not specifically enforceable because damages can be used to purchase substitute performance (cf. Sale of Goods Act 1979, s 52, as amended by the Consumer Rights Act 2015). There are two situations, however, where specific performance may be available. First, where the subject matter of the contract is unique – such as a rare book, a sculpture or a painting – substitute performance will be *prima facie* unavailable, and the court may be willing to order specific performance. In *Falcke v Gray* (1859) 4 Drew 651, this was the ground for ordering specific performance of a contract for the sale of two oriental jars. In the words of Kindersley VC, the jars were of such 'unusual beauty, rarity and distinction' that damages would provide an inadequate remedy for nonperformance since substitutes were not available.

Second, specific performance may be ordered of contracts for the sale of non-unique goods if circumstances exist that mean that substitutes are practically unavailable.

Sky Petroleum Ltd v VIP Petroleum Ltd [1974] 1 WLR 576

Facts: The plaintiffs entered into a contract with the defendants for the supply of petrol and diesel for a period of 10 years. At a time when the supply of petrol was restricted and the plaintiffs had no prospect of finding an alternative source of supply, the defendants purported to terminate the contract. The plaintiffs sought an injunction to restrain the defendants from withholding supplies.

Held: Goulding J granted the injunction even though he acknowledged that it amounted to specific performance of a contract to buy and sell personal property.

Goulding J: Now I come to the most serious hurdle in the way of the plaintiffs which is the well known doctrine that the court refuses specific performance of a contract to sell and purchase chattels not specific or ascertained ... [T]he *ratio* behind the rule is, as I believe, that under the ordinary contract for the sale of non-specific goods, damages are a sufficient remedy. That, to my mind, is lacking in the circumstances of the present case. The evidence suggests, and indeed it is common knowledge that the petroleum market is in an unusual state in which a would-be buyer cannot go out into the market and contract with another seller, possibly at some sacrifice as to price. Here, the defendants appear for practical purposes to be the plaintiffs' sole means of keeping their business going, and I am prepared so far to depart from the general rule as to try to preserve the position under the contract until a later date. I therefore propose to grant an injunction.

15.3.1.1.2 Only nominal damages available

Another situation in which damages may be inadequate is where damages are merely nominal because the claimant has suffered no pecuniary loss.

Beswick v Beswick [1968] AC 58

Facts: Mr Beswick made a contract with his nephew whereby the nephew promised to make payments to Mr Beswick's widow during his lifetime in return for Mr Beswick's promise to transfer his business to the nephew. When Mr Beswick died, the nephew refused to pay and Mrs Beswick brought an action for breach of contract in her capacity as Mr Beswick's personal representative. The nephew argued that, since Mr Beswick had died, his estate had suffered no loss as a result of the breach of contract, and thus nominal damages were adequate.

Held: The House of Lords rejected the nephew's argument and ordered specific performance of the agreement.

Lord Pearce: It is argued that the estate can only recover nominal damages and that no other remedy is open, either to the estate or to the personal plaintiff. Such a result would be wholly repugnant to justice and commonsense and if the argument were right it would show a very serious defect in the law.

In the first place, I do not accept the view that damages must be nominal ... It is not necessary, however, to consider the amount of damages more closely since this is a case in which, as the Court of Appeal rightly decided, the more appropriate remedy is that of specific performance.

The administratrix is entitled, if she so prefers, to enforce the agreement rather than accept its repudiation, and specific performance is more convenient than an action for arrears of payment followed by separate actions as each sum falls due. Moreover, damages for breach would be a less appropriate remedy since the parties to the agreement were intending an annuity for a widow; and a lump sum of damages does not accord with this. If (contrary to my view) the argument that a derisory sum of damages is all that can be obtained be right, the remedy of damages in this case is manifestly useless.

The present case presents all the features which led the equity courts to apply their remedy of specific performance. The contract was for the sale of a business. The defendant could on his part clearly have obtained specific performance of it if Beswick senior or his administratrix had defaulted. Mutuality is a ground in favour of specific performance. Moreover, the defendant on his side has received the whole benefit of the contract and it is a matter of conscience for the court to see that he now performs his part of it.

Lord Hodson: [I]t is said nominal damages are adequate and the remedy of specific performance ought not to be granted. That is, with all respect, wholly to misunderstand that principle. Equity will grant specific performance when damages are inadequate to meet the justice of the case.

But in any event quantum of damages seldom affects the right to specific performance. If X contracts with Y to buy Blackacre or a rare chattel for a fancy price because the property or chattel has caught his fancy he is entitled to enforce his bargain and it matters not that he could not prove any damage.

In this case the court ought to grant a specific performance order all the more because damages *are* nominal. C has received all the property; justice demands that he pay the price and this can only be done in the circumstances by equitable relief.

A number of comments can be made about this decision. First, it will not always be the case that specific performance will be ordered whenever compensatory damages are merely nominal. If that were so, specific performance would be available in all cases where the contract has been breached and substitute performance is available at a lower price than the contractually agreed one. The claimant must demonstrate that s/he has a non-pecuniary interest in performance, which would not be protected by an award of nominal damages. In *Beswick*, the uncle had a non-pecuniary interest in seeing his wife provided for after his death. Such an interest would not have received adequate protection from an award of nominal damages.

Second, Lord Pearce indicated in his speech that the inadequacy of compensatory damages is not a 'necessary' requirement of a claim for specific performance. Instead, he emphasised that specific performance will be awarded whenever it is deemed to be the most 'appropriate' remedy. Jones and Goodhart (Jones, G and Goodhart, W, *Specific Performance*, 2nd edn, 1996, London: Butterworths, p 37) have written:

> The alternative test, 'which is the more effective remedy in serving the ends of justice?', has the merit of greater clarity and directs the court to the real question which should be answered. It may encourage the courts to grant specific performance more freely. It is unlikely, however, that there will be a significant extension of equitable jurisdiction for the simple reason that most innocent

> parties will still be anxious immediately to mitigate their loss and will therefore sue for damages. Moreover, in most cases damages will remain the most effective remedy in serving the ends of justice.

The shift from language of 'inadequacy' to that of 'appropriateness' or 'effectiveness' does not mean that the inadequacy of damages is no longer important; it is simply no longer decisive. Whether the shift is merely one of terminology instead of substance remains to be seen.

15.3.1.2 Factors affecting the availability of specific performance

Once the claimant has demonstrated that compensatory damages would be inadequate the court has jurisdiction to order specific performance, but it may, of course, refuse to make such an order on discretionary grounds. The rest of this section looks at these grounds.

15.3.1.2.1 The need for constant supervision

Specific performance will not be ordered if it is likely to require constant supervision by the court. In *Ryan v Mutual Tontine Westminster Chambers Association* [1893] 1 Ch 116, the Court of Appeal refused to order specific performance of a covenant to provide a porter for the tenants of a block of residential flats. The reason given by Lord Esher MR was that such an order 'would require constant superintendence by the Court, which the Court in such cases has always declined to give'. The constant supervision restriction must now be understood in the light of the House of Lords' decision in *Co-operative Insurance Society Ltd v Argyll Stores (Holdings) Ltd*.

***Co-operative Insurance Society Ltd v Argyll Stores (Holdings) Ltd* [1998] AC 1**

Facts: Argyll leased a unit for use as a supermarket in a new shopping centre owned by Co-operative Insurance Society. The lease contained the following covenant: 'To keep the demised premises open for retail trade during the usual hours of business in the locality and the display windows properly dressed in a suitable manner in keeping with a good class parade of shops.' Competition in the supermarket business was fierce and Argyll decided to scale down its operations. The supermarket in Co-operative's shopping centre had made a loss of £70,000 in the previous year, so Argyll announced its intention to close the store. Co-operative Insurance sought specific performance of the covenant in the lease. At first instance the trial judge refused specific performance. The Court of Appeal reversed this decision.

Held: The House of Lords allowed Argyll's appeal and held that it was not normally appropriate to give an order of specific performance requiring someone to carry on a business.

Lord Hoffmann: The most frequent reason given in the cases for declining to order someone to carry on a business is that it would require constant supervision by the court ... There has, I think, been some misunderstanding about what is meant by continued superintendence. It may at first sight suggest that the judge (or some other officer of the court) would literally have to supervise the execution of the order. In *CH Giles & Co Ltd v Morris* [1972] 1 WLR 307, 318 Megarry J said that 'difficulties of constant superintendence' were a 'narrow consideration' because:

> 'there is normally no question of the court having to send its officers to supervise the performance of the order ... Performance ... is normally secured by the realisation of the person enjoined that he is liable to be punished for contempt if evidence of his disobedience to the order is put before the court ...'

This is, of course, true but does not really meet the point. The judges who have said that the need for constant supervision was an objection to such orders were no doubt well aware that supervision would in practice take the form of rulings by the court, on applications made by the parties, as to whether there had been a breach of the order. It is the possibility of the court having to give an indefinite series of such rulings in order to ensure the execution of the order which has been regarded as undesirable.

Why should this be so? A principal reason is that, as Megarry J pointed out in the passage to which I have referred, the only means available to the court to enforce its order is the quasi-criminal procedure of punishment for contempt. This is a powerful weapon; so powerful, in fact, as often to be unsuitable as an instrument for adjudicating upon the disputes which may arise over whether a business is being run in accordance with the terms of the court's order. The heavy-handed nature of the enforcement mechanism is a consideration which may go to the exercise of the court's discretion in other cases as well, but its use to compel the running of a business is perhaps the paradigm case of its disadvantages and it is in this context that I shall discuss them.

The prospect of committal or even a fine, with the damage to commercial reputation which will be caused by a finding of contempt of court, is likely to have at least two undesirable consequences. First, the defendant, who *ex hypothesi* did not think that it was in his economic interest to run the business at all, now has to make decisions under a sword of Damocles which may descend if the way the business is run does not conform to the terms of the order. This is, as one might say, no way to run a business ...

Secondly, the seriousness of a finding of contempt for the defendant means that any application to enforce the order is likely to be a heavy and expensive piece of litigation. The possibility of repeated applications over a period of time means that, in comparison with a once-and-for-all inquiry as to damages, the enforcement of the remedy is likely to be expensive in terms of cost to the parties and the resources of the judicial system.

This is a convenient point at which to distinguish between orders which require a defendant to carry on an activity, such as running a business over a more or less extended period of time, and orders which require him to achieve a result. The possibility of repeated applications for rulings on compliance with the order which arises in the former case does not exist to anything like the same extent in the latter. Even if the achievement of the result is a complicated matter which will take some time, the court, if called upon to rule, only has to examine the finished work and say whether it complies with the order ...

This distinction between orders to carry on activities and orders to achieve results explains why the courts have in appropriate circumstances ordered specific performance of building contracts and repairing covenants: see *Wolverhampton Corporation v Emmons* [1901] 1 KB 515 (building contract) and *Jeune v Queens Cross Properties* [1974] Ch 97 (repairing covenant).

Lord Hoffmann attempted to explain the rationale behind the constant supervision restriction (see also *Alia Finance Holdings AD v Quarzwerke GmbH* [2015] EWHC 243 (Ch)). It did not envisage that the court would literally have to supervise the execution of the order. Rather, it was concerned to prevent the possibility of the court being required to give an indefinite series of rulings over a period of time to ensure compliance with the order. This would be an utterly inappropriate way to run a business, not least because such rulings would be backed up with the heavy-handed remedy of contempt of court, thus draining the resources of the judicial system. A one-off award of damages would be much more satisfactory.

Lord Hoffmann also took the opportunity to distinguish between orders that require a defendant to carry on an activity – such as running a business – and orders that require a defendant to achieve a result. The potential for repeated orders on compliance in the former category of case does not exist to anything like the same extent in the latter. This distinction helps to explain the decision in *Wolverhampton Corp v Emmons* [1901] 1 KB 515, where the Court of Appeal ordered specific performance of a contract for the construction of eight new houses. AL Smith MR said that the building plans 'define the work to be done sufficiently to enable the Court to make an order for specific performance'.

15.3.1.2.2 Personal services

It is a well-established rule that equity generally will not enforce a contract for personal service at the suit of either party. This is for both moral and practical reasons. First, forcing a defendant to work for the claimant by fear of imprisonment would constitute a serious infringement of his or her personal liberty. Second, it would be undesirable for the state to enforce the continuance of a 'personal relationship' between two unwilling parties.

In more recent times the traditional rule against the enforcement of contracts for personal service has been questioned (although statute has also intervened). This is due to the fact that the modern relationship of employer and employee is much less personal than the traditional relationship of master and servant, which subsisted at the time that the general rule was recognised. Where it can be established that mutual trust and respect remains between the parties, specific performance may be available. In *Hill v CA Parsons & Co Ltd* [1972] 1 Ch 305, for example, an order was made because the dismissal had resulted from union pressure, rather than a dispute between the employer and employee. Cf. *Ashworth v Royal National Theatre* [2014] EWHC 1176.

15.3.1.2.3 The need for mutuality

It is sometimes stated that a court will not order specific performance in favour of a claimant unless it could also have ordered specific performance in favour of the defendant. The leading case on the mutuality rule is *Price v Strange*.

***Price v Strange* [1978] Ch 337**

Facts: The defendant granted the plaintiff a continuation of the underlease of a maisonette in return for an increase in rent and an agreement to carry out certain works of repair. When the plaintiff had completed half the work the defendant refused to allow him to continue and purported to terminate the agreement. The plaintiff brought an action for specific performance of the agreement. The judge dismissed the action on the grounds that the plaintiff's obligations to carry out the repairs would not have been specifically enforceable, so that there was a lack of mutuality.

Held: The Court of Appeal allowed the appeal. The date for assessing mutuality was the time of trial and by this time all the repairs had been carried out and there was no risk of the defendant being required to grant the underlease whilst not being able to enforce the obligation to carry out the repairs.

Goff LJ: The true principle is that one judges the defence of want of mutuality on the facts and circumstances as they exist at the hearing, albeit in the light of the whole conduct of the parties in relation to the subject matter, and in the absence of any other disqualifying circumstances the court will grant specific performance if it can be done without injustice or unfairness to the defendant.

Buckley LJ: The time at which the mutual availability of specific performance and its importance must be considered is, in my opinion, the time of judgment, and the principle to be applied can I think be stated simply as follows: the court will not compel a defendant to perform his obligations specifically if it cannot at the same time ensure that any unperformed obligations of the plaintiff will be specifically performed, unless, perhaps, damages would be an adequate remedy to the defendant for any default on the plaintiff's part.

The decision in *Price v Strange* confirms that the time of trial is the correct point at which to assess mutuality. Furthermore, the Court of Appeal advocated a more flexible approach to the mutuality requirement, confirming that lack of mutuality is not an absolute bar to an order of specific performance. This was followed in the more recent case of *Rainbow Estates Ltd v Tokenhold Ltd* [1999] Ch 64, 69, where Lawrence Collins QC said:

> [A]s regards the requirement of mutuality, it is now clear that it does not follow from the fact that specific performance is not available to one party that it is not available to the other: want of mutuality is a discretionary, and not an absolute, bar to specific performance. The court will grant specific performance if it can be done without injustice or unfairness to the defendant: *Price v Strange* [1978] Ch 337, 357, *per* Goff LJ.

15.3.1.2.4 Hardship to the defendant

Specific performance may be refused on the ground that the order will cause severe hardship to the defendant. In *Denne v Light* (1857) 8 DM & G 774, the court refused to grant specific performance of a contract for the sale of land. This was because it would have left the buyer with a plot wholly surrounded by land owned by others, all of whom were unwilling to grant him a right of way. Severe hardship may be a ground for refusing specific performance even when the hardship does not arise directly from the contract.

Patel v Ali [1984] Ch 283

Facts: The defendant, Mrs Ali, and a Mr Ahmed agreed to sell Mrs Ali's home to Mr and Mrs Patel. Contracts were exchanged in July 1979 but completion of the sale was delayed for various reasons. In 1980, it was discovered that the defendant had bone cancer in her right thigh and she became heavily dependent on her neighbours for support and care. This support network would have been lost if she had been forced to move house and it would have been very expensive for her to pay for alternative help. The plaintiffs eventually sought specific performance of the contract for sale.

Held: Goulding J refused to order specific performance on the grounds that it would cause undue hardship to the defendant. The plaintiffs were left to their remedy in damages.

Goulding J: Another limitation suggested by [counsel for the plaintiffs] was that, in the reported cases, as he said, hardship successfully relied on has always related to the subject matter of the contract and has not been just a personal hardship of the defendant. Certainly, mere pecuniary difficulties, whether of purchaser or of vendor, afford no excuse from performance of a contract. In a wider sense than that, I do not think the suggested universal proposition can be sustained ...

The important and true principle, in my view, is that only in extraordinary and persuasive circumstances can hardship supply an excuse for resisting performance of a contract for the sale of immovable property. A person of full capacity who sells or buys a house takes the risk of hardship to himself and his dependents, whether arising from existing facts or unexpectedly supervening in the interval before completion. This is where, to my mind, great importance attaches to the immense delay in the present case, not attributable to the defendant's conduct. Even after issue of the writ, she could not complete, if she had wanted to, without the concurrence of the absent Mr. Ahmed. Thus, in a sense, she can say she is being asked to do what she never bargained for, namely to complete the sale after more than four years, after all the unforeseeable changes that such a period entails.

Goulding J made clear that the defence of severe hardship is only available in 'extraordinary and persuasive circumstances'. Mere pecuniary difficulties are not sufficient. Hardship must be combined with some additional factor. On the facts of *Patel v Ali* the plaintiff's delay in seeking specific performance provided that additional factor.

15.3.1.2.5 Conduct of the claimant

Specific performance is an equitable remedy and as such the claimant is required to come to the court with 'clean hands'. Specific performance will be refused if the contract has been procured by means that are unfair, even if those means do not amount to grounds that will void the contract. In *Mountford v Scott* [1975] Ch 258, the plaintiff was denied specific performance on the grounds that he had taken advantage of the illiteracy of a defendant who had not been independently advised. Similarly, in *Walters v Morgan* (1861) 3 DF & J 718, the court refused to order specific performance of a lease over land because the seller had been 'surprised and was induced to sign the agreement in ignorance of the value of his property.'

15.3.2 Injunctions

An injunction restrains the defendant from acting in breach of his negative contractual obligations.

There are several different types of injunction that the court can order. Injunctions can be either mandatory or prohibitory. Prohibitory injunctions apply to future breaches and order a person to refrain from, or to discontinue from, a breach. Mandatory injunctions are ordered against past breaches and require the defendant to undo his wrong. For example, if a person plans to build a house on his land in breach of a restrictive covenant, a prohibitory injunction can be requested to prevent him from proceeding with this course of action. If, however, the house has already been completed the claimant can obtain a mandatory injunction for the demolition of the house.

Additional reading

Burrows, A., 'Limitations on Compensation', in Burrows, A., and Peel, E. (eds), *Commercial Remedies: Current Issues and Problems* (Oxford: OUP, 2003).

Cartwright, J., 'Remoteness of Damage in Contract and Tort: A Reconsideration' [1996] CLJ 488.

Chandler, A., and Devenney, J., 'Breach of Contract and the Expectation Deficit: Inconvenience and Disappointment' (2007) 27 LS 126.

Coote, B., 'The Performance Interest, *Panatown*, and the Problem of Loss' (2001) 1 17 LQR 81.

Cunnington, R., 'A Lost Opportunity to Clarify' (2007) 123 LQR 48.

Davies, P., 'Being Specific about Specific Performance' [2018] Conv 324.

Edelman, J., *Gain-Based Damages* (Oxford: Hart, 2002).

Goetz, R., and Scott, R., 'Liquidated Damages, Penalties and the Just Compensation Principle' (1977) 77 Col LR 554.

Harris, D., 'Specific Performance – A Regular Remedy for Consumers' (2003) 1 19 LQR 541.

Kramer, A., 'An Agreement-Centred Approach to Remoteness and Contract Damages', in Cohen, N., and McKendrick, E. (eds), *Comparative Remedies for Breach of Contract* (Oxford: Hart, 2004).

McKendrick, E., and Graham, M., 'The Sky's the Limit: Contractual Damages for Non-pecuniary Loss' [2002] LMCLQ 161.

Index

For Product Safety Concerns and Information please contact our EU
representative GPSR@taylorandfrancis.com
Taylor & Francis Verlag GmbH, Kaufingerstraße 24, 80331 München, Germany

www.ingramcontent.com/pod-product-compliance
Ingram Content Group UK Ltd.
Pitfield, Milton Keynes, MK11 3LW, UK
UKHW052054230926
475702UK00031B/2804

* 9 7 8 0 3 6 7 2 2 2 9 5 6 *